BRAZIL

MICHAEL SOMMERS

D0966872

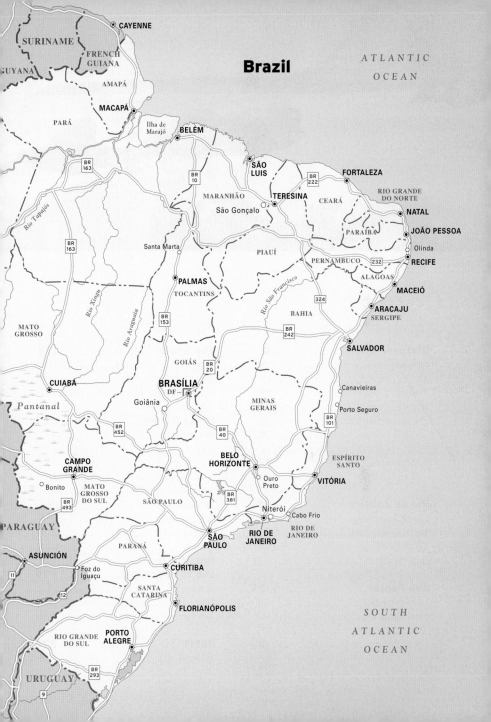

Contents

DISCOVER
Brazil

It's not surprising that at the turn of the last century, Brazil was sometimes referred to as "the Brazils"—after all, how could "Brazil" in its singular form possibly contain the vastly diverse worlds that coexist in South America's largest nation?

Most people hear Brazil and imagine themselves stretched out on a sugary beach lapped by warm turquoise waters, sipping lime caipirinhas. Indeed, Brazil's continent-size coastline is sheer bliss for surfers and divers, dog paddlers and sun worshippers. Yet it's also home to the desertlike Sertão, lush coastal mountain-scapes, the dense Amazon rain forest, and the Pantanal, a wetland ecosystem teeming with giant otters, jaguars, and a symphony of bird calls.

Brazil has something for all travelers. If you want to kick back and zone out, its casual vibe and mesmerizing scenery will have you in a state of Zen. But if you're in search of challenges and thrills, the endless opportunities range from hang gliding over Rio's Guanabara Bay and rafting beneath Iguaçu Falls to dune-buggying across the beaches of Ceará and swimming with pink river dolphins in the Rio Negro.

Brazil is lulling, but it's also intense. Its landscapes are invariably dramatic, often secluded, and mind-numbingly beautiful. Its cities thrum with overlapping rhythms

---

Clockwise from top left: Jardim Botânico, Curitiba; hibiscus; traditional lacework, Maceió; typical Northeastern *jangada;* Chapada Diamantina, Bahia; Palácio da Alvorada, Brasília.

and unexpected contrasts. Cutting-edge cultural centers sit next to 18th-century baroque churches. Surfer boys in flip-flops parade their dripping boards past gleaming skyscrapers. And when it's time to eat, drink, and be merry, there are *boteco*s (bars) that host samba jams and serve *feijoada*, the succulent national stew of beans and salted meat, as well as sophisticated clubs that throb to *tecno bossa* and restaurants where your mango might be topped by seared foie gras.

As varied as their country are Brazilians themselves—a mixture of indigenous, African, and European peoples, all of whom have left profound marks on Brazil's unique culture. Despite difficult economic and social circumstances, you'll find Brazilians to be warm, good-humored, and champions at the art of enjoying themselves. Carnaval is merely one example of the many celebrations that allow Brazilians to let loose with contagious *alegria* (joyfulness). No matter which of the many "Brazils" you visit, you won't leave without some of it rubbing off on you.

Clockwise from top left: São Paulo's skyline at night; Chapada dos Veadeiros; Instituto Moreira Salles, Rio de Janeiro; torch lily.

Planning Your Trip

Where to Go

Rio de Janeiro

Squeezed between lush mountains and the Atlantic Ocean, Rio de Janeiro is one of the world's most visually stunning cities. Historically and culturally rich, its iconic sights include **Pão de Açúcar, Corcovado,** and the beaches of **Copacabana** and **Ipanema.** Its compelling architecture and **terrific museums** are complemented by a relaxing vibe and **pulsing nightlife.** The small state of Rio de Janeiro has numerous getaways from the urban bustle, ranging from cool **mountain retreats** and virgin **Atlantic rain forests** to beautiful **sandy beaches.**

São Paulo

The city of São Paulo, Brazil's economic and cultural powerhouse, is often overlooked by foreign tourists, but this megametropolis offers a wealth of artistic, gastronomic, **nightlife**, and **shopping** options. Its electric hustle can be felt on the main drag of **Avenida Paulista,** but urban oases, such as **Parque do Ibirapuera,** also abound. The interior of São Paulo state possesses **Alpine-style resorts** and **unspoiled swaths of forest.** The **Litoral Norte** features a string of trendy beach resort towns whose sugary sands are framed by mountains.

The South

Known as O Sul (The South), the trio of narrow states running south from São Paulo is very different from the rest of Brazil. The area was settled largely by 19th-century immigrants from Germany, Poland, Ukraine, and Italy, and European influence remains strong. Striking

Cristo Redentor, Corcovado, Rio de Janeiro

The Northeast Coast

Pernambuco and Alagoas

Bahia

The Amazon

Brasília, Goiás, and the Pantanal

Minas Gerais

São Paulo

Rio de Janeiro

The South

© AVALON TRAVEL

architecture. Brasília is the gateway to the state of Goiás, which features **colonial towns** and the savanna-like **Cerrado** riddled with **waterfalls.** Farther west, **Mato Grosso** and **Mato Grosso do Sul** constitute a vast Wild West region with a frontier feel. Both states share the **Pantanal,** the world's largest wetlands, which teems with **wildlife.**

Bahia

Salvador was Brazil's first capital, a legacy that has left it with a captivating historical center and one of Brazil's most potent traditional cultures. A strong **African influence** colors everything from religious celebrations and *festas* to music, dance, and cuisine. Bahia boasts Brazil's longest coastline and some of its most captivating **tropical beaches.** Inland, the **Chapada Diamantina** is a lush oasis of mountains and waterfalls, speckled with colonial diamond-mining towns.

natural attractions include the windswept beaches of **Santa Catarina,** the rugged **Serra Gaúcha mountain range** of **Rio Grande do Sul,** and the jaw-dropping, body-drenching spectacle of **Iguaçu Falls.**

Minas Gerais

Despite important mining and metal industries and the sophisticated capital, **Belo Horizonte,** this inland state has a rural character enhanced by its craggy mountains, robust **cuisine,** and bracing *cachaças.* Minas Gerais is also steeped in **history**: You'll find extravagant baroque churches lined with pure gold along with 17th-century colonial mining towns such as **Ouro Preto, Mariana, São João del Rei, Tiradentes,** and **Diamantina.** Collectively known as the *cidades históricas,* each one has its own flavor, but all showcase splendid Brazilian colonial architecture.

Brasília, Goiás, and the Pantanal

Brazil's space-age capital, Brasília, sits in a flat plateau region known as the Planalto. The city symbolically marks the heart of Brazil and offers a unique mélange of **utopian modernist**

Pernambuco and Alagoas

Pernambuco's coastal capital, **Recife,** is steeped in a vibrant local culture, while **Olinda** is one of Brazil's most seductive colonial towns, with baroque churches perched on palmy hills and a thriving artists' scene. Inland, the rich culture of the **Sertão** offers a feast of *forró,* sun-dried beef, and artisanal traditions. Heading south, the coast is lined with drop-dead **gorgeous beaches.** The snorkeling is superb along the coast of **Alagoas,** a tiny state to the south, anchored by its laid-back capital, **Maceió.**

The Northeast Coast

The beachscapes in this region, which extend uninterrupted from **Rio Grande do Norte** across the state of **Ceará** and into **Maranhão,** vary from Saharan dunes navigable by buggy, sand board, or dromedary to **sweeping white** beaches backed by crumbling red cliffs. The bustling and touristy capital cities of **Natal** and **Fortaleza** offer access to rustic resorts, such as the famously secluded **Jericoacoara.** Maranhão provides a transition between the arid Northeast and the lush, wet Amazon. Its island capital of **São Luís** possesses an atmospheric colonial center.

The Amazon

The vast forested region bisected by the Amazon River and its thousands of tributaries is referred to as O Norte (The North). Its two largest states, **Amazonas** and **Pará,** are sparsely populated, and the river continues to be the major source of life and transportation. The **rain forest** is best explored from trips out of Amazonas's buzzing capital, **Manaus,** and the town of **Santarém,** where you can also bask on white-sand river beaches. At the Amazon's mouth is the alluring colonial city of **Belém** and the Switzerland-size **Ilha de Marajó.**

When to Go

Most of Brazil boasts a **tropical climate,** which means that you'll encounter warm temperatures year-round, particularly in the Northeast and the Amazon. Bahia, Alagoas, and Pernambuco each have **rainy seasons (May-August). Wet seasons (May-December)** in the Amazon and Pantanal last for six months. The South is the only region that has a real **"winter,"** which you'd probably rather avoid unless you're in the mood for fondue and fireplaces. **Summers** can be sweltering, particularly in Rio and São Paulo. Ultimately, the best times to visit the Southeast and South are **March-June** and **September-November.**

The other main consideration is **high season** versus **off-season.** During the summer,

sunset in Bonito

Cheap Tricks

Foreign travelers are surprised by the inflated costs that have made Brazil an increasingly costly destination. Here are a few tips to help you enjoy Brazil without breaking the bank:

- **Avoid summer** (Dec.-Jan. and July) and travel in the off-season for discounts.

- Hit the beaches, mountains, and rural getaways **during the week** to beat weekend crowds and high accommodation prices.

- Consider a stay in one of Brazil's alluring new generation of **hostels**; almost all have inexpensive private rooms.

- Domestic airfares are a real deal (and cheaper than long-distance buses) if you **book in advance.**

- **Eat cheap.** Healthy and authentic fare can be had at banquet-like per-kilo restaurants. *Bares de suco* (juice bars) serve vitamin-packed smoothies and healthy sandwiches. At *botecos* (local bars), feast on affordable *petiscos* (appetizers) or full portions of *comida caseira* (home cooking).

- Many public and private **cultural centers** host high-quality art exhibits, dance and theatrical performances, and musical shows for free or next to no charge. In particular, look for those operated by SESC, Banco do Brasil, Caixa Federal, and Oi.

Brazilians take long holiday weekends and inevitably head to the closest beach. The biggest exodus takes place from **late December through Carnaval,** and there's another in **July.** During these times, all beaches, mountain resorts, and eco-destinations fill up. Accommodation prices can rise by up to 50 percent, and plane tickets need to be purchased in advance. Summer means heat, crowds, and higher prices, but it's also when Brazil kicks into high gear with intense party scenes and multiple *festas*. If you prefer tranquility and like your beaches and mountains remote and secluded, plan your trip to coincide with off-season. You'll discover Brazilians in a less revved-up state, and in otherwise touristy areas, the diminished hustle and hassle can be very welcome.

Before You Go

Passports and Visas

If your country requires Brazilians to have **travel visas,** you will have to get a one from the nearest Brazilian consulate before entering Brazil. Currently, citizens of Canada, the United States, and Australia require visas. Citizens of the United Kingdom, other European Union countries, and New Zealand don't need visas, but do need a **passport** that is valid for six months and need a return ticket. On arrival, you'll be given a 90-day tourist visa.

Vaccinations

The one vaccination that is required for Brazil is **yellow fever,** which is absolutely essential for visiting the Amazon region. Be sure to bring an International Certificate of Vaccination yellow booklet, since Brazilian authorities will

Praia de Tabuba, Barra de Santo Antônio

sometimes ask for proof of vaccination for travelers going to and from the Amazon.

Transportation

The two main gateways are **Rio de Janeiro's Tom Jobim Airport** and **São Paulo's Guarulhos Airport.** If you're planning to travel to far-flung destinations within Brazil, consider buying a **Brazil Airpass,** sold by both TAM and GOL airlines; these can only be purchased abroad along with your international ticket.

Flying is an ideal way to get from one region to another, but with the exception of the Amazon, you can also get anywhere by bus. Due to lack of passable roads, the Amazon is a region where flying is a must (unless you want to spend days on a boat). There are many regional *aerotaxis,* but it's safest to stick to the main domestic operators.

For shorter **bus trips,** an advance ticket isn't necessary, but for interstate travel (especially during high-season or holiday periods), purchase your ticket beforehand. Major companies sell tickets via travel agents and online; often your best (and only) option is to purchase them at the *rodoviária* (bus station).

To visit natural attractions around big cities and to go beach hopping, having a **rental car** gives you more freedom to hit off-the-beaten-track places. If you rent a car, avoid driving at night. An international driver's license is more widely recognized than a foreign license, but the latter is valid for up to six months.

The Best of Brazil

Three weeks is the bare minimum required to get a quick sampling of some of Brazil's noteworthy attractions, landscapes, and culture. Considering the country's sheer size and diversity, and the distances and travel time involved, this itinerary is very selective (and depends upon lots of air travel). Don't have three weeks at your disposal? Then choose, mix, or match from each of these weeklong itineraries built around a certain region.

Rio de Janeiro and Minas Gerais
DAY 1
RIO

Land in **Rio de Janeiro** (most flights from North America arrive in the morning) and go straight to your hotel. Lather up with sunscreen and recover from the long flight with some refreshing coconut water and a nap on **Copacabana** or **Ipanema** beach. Take refuge from the noonday sun at one of the healthy per-kilo restaurants in Ipanema or Leblon, and do some boutique browsing. In the late afternoon, take a taxi to **Pão de Açúcar** and ride the cable car to the top for a view of **Baía de Guanabara** as the city lights come on. After dinner, go bar- or club-hopping in the **Zona Sul.**

DAY 2
RIO

Head to the **Centro** to visit museums and historic sights. The **Museu Histórico Nacional** condenses 500 fascinating years of Brazilian history and culture into a couple of engaging hours punctuated with bright indigenous headdresses and gold imperial thrones. Other architectural highlights include the **Igreja da Ordem Terceira de São Francisco da Penitência, Confeitaria Colombo, Paço Imperial,** and **Centro Cultural Banco do Brasil.** Have a late lunch in Centro, then take quick cab ride up to **Santa Teresa** to wander the cobblestoned streets

cable car, Pão de Açúcar, in Rio de Janeiro

Arcos da Lapa, Rio de Janeiro

and check out the **Museu Chácara do Céu.** Linger in a traditional *botequim* (neighborhood bar) for happy hour and dine at one of the romantic eateries. Head to nearby **Lapa** to experience its famous **bohemian nightlife** against an aural backdrop of live **samba.**

DAY 3
PLANE FROM RIO TO BELO
HORIZONTE: 1 HOUR

Spend the morning exploring Rio's natural attributes. Languorous souls can amble around the imperial palm-shaded lanes of the **Jardim Botânico** and then head to nearby **Parque Lage** for lunch. Those seeking a greater physical challenge should schedule in advance to **hang glide** off **Pedra Bonita,** scale the scenic sides of **Pão de Açúcar,** or go **hiking** through the rain forest of **Parque Nacional da Tijuca.** In the afternoon, check out of your hotel and head to the airport to catch a flight to **Belo Horizonte.** Spend your evening in "BH," savoring *petiscos*, artisanal beer, and cachaças at one of the city's countless *botecos* in bohemian neighborhoods such as **Santo Antônio** and **São Pedro.**

DAY 4
BUS FROM BELO HORIZONTE
TO INHOTIM: 2 HOURS

Catch the 8:15am bus for the fantastic **Instituto de Arte Contemporânea Inhotim** (open Tues.-Sun.) and spend the day exploring Brazil's largest collection of contemporary art amidst the country's largest botanical garden. At 4:30pm (5pm weekends), break the spell by taking the bus back to Belo Horizonte.

DAYS 5-6
BUS FROM BELO HORIZONTE
TO OURO PRETO: 2 HOURS

In the morning, catch a bus to the most resplendent of Minas Gerais's historic gold-mining cities: **Ouro Preto.** Check into a centuries-old *pousada*, fortify yourself with traditional Mineiro fare at the lavish buffet served at **Chafariz,** then tackle the town's steep cobblestoned hills and baroque churches. You'll overdose on cherubs and

Ouro Preto, Minas Gerais

gold leaf long before you see all 27 of Ouro Preto's churches. Not to be missed are the **Igreja Matriz de Nossa Senhora do Pilar** and the **Igreja de São Francisco de Assis.** If you can, make it the **Museu do Oratório.** In the evenings, sample artisanal *cachaças* at lively bars.

DAY 7
BUS FROM OURO PRETO TO BELO HORIZONTE: 2 HOURS

Wake up early for the morning bus to **Belo Horizonte.** If going home, fly back to Rio. Or add another week by hopping a plane to **Foz do Iguaçu** via São Paulo.

Iguaçu Falls and the Pantanal
DAYS 8-9
PLANE FROM BELO HORIZONTE TO FOZ DO IGUAÇU: 4.5 HOURS

If you have some bucks to burn in Foz, check into the landmark **Hotel das Cataratas,** located within the **Parque Nacional do Iguaçu.** Spend the next two days visiting the Brazilian and Argentinean sides of the magnificent **Iguaçu**

Falls; you'll need one day for each to fit in adventures such as **boat trips** beneath the falls, **whitewater rafting** down the Rio Iguaçu, and **hikes** through the lush rain forest.

DAY 10
PLANE FROM FOZ DO IGUAÇU TO CUIABÁ: 6.5-8 HOURS

Fly into **Cuiabá** via São Paulo. The capital of **Mato Grosso,** this Wild West city is a gateway for discovering the **Pantanal** wetlands, which are full of exotic flora and fauna. After dining at a local *peixaria,* where you can sample the typical dishes made from the region's river fish, turn in early.

DAYS 11-13
DRIVE FROM CUIABÁ TO TRANSPANTANEIRA HIGHWAY: 2.5-5 HOURS

Rise at dawn and join your guided, all-inclusive ecotour into the Pantanal, whose only link to civilization is the Transpantaneira Highway (1.5 hours south of Cuiabá). Spend the next

Iguaçu Falls, Parque Nacional do Iguaçu

Best Beaches

BEST URBAN BEACHES

· **Copacabana** and **Ipanema** in Rio de Janeiro (pages 48 and 49)

· **Porto da Barra** in Salvador in Bahia (page 349)

· **Praia de Ponta Verde** in Maceió (page 447)

· **Ponta Negra** in Natal (page 467)

· **Praia do Futuro** in Fortaleza (page 483)

BEST ISLAND PARADISES

· **Ilha Grande** in Rio de Janeiro (page 100)

· **Ilhabela** in São Paulo (page 164)

· **Ilha de Boipeba** in Bahia (page 386)

· **Fernando de Noronha** in Pernambuco (page 439)

· **Ilha de Marajó** in Pará (page 535)

BEST PARTY BEACHES

· **Búzios** in Rio de Janeiro (page 95)

· **Maresias** in São Paulo (page 162)

· **Praia da Joaquina** in Santa Catarina (page 203)

· **Morro de São Paulo** in Bahia (page 384)

· **Praia da Pipa** in Rio Grande do Norte (page 476)

HIPPEST BEACHES

· **Praia do Rosa** in Santa Catarina (page 214)

· **Trancoso** in Bahia (page 401)

· **Jericoacoara** in Ceará (page 494)

BEST TOTAL GETAWAYS

· **Lagoinha do Leste** in Santa Catarina (page 203)

· **Caraíva** in Bahia (page 405)

· **Praia dos Carneiros** in Pernambuco (page 437)

· **São Miguel dos Milagres** in Alagoas (page 456)

· **Lençóis Maranhenses** in Maranhão (page 508)

· **Alter do Chão** in Pará (page 542)

Igreja de Nosso Senhor do Bonfim, Salvador

three days **horseback riding, canoeing, and hiking** through unspoiled landscapes in search of giant otters, elusive jaguars, and brilliant-colored macaws. Spend your nights at traditional cattle ranches, known as *fazenda lodges.*

DAY 14
DRIVE FROM TRANSPANTANEIRA HIGHWAY TO CUIABÁ: 2.5-5 HOURS
Return from your *fazenda* lodge to Cuiabá. If you're going home, take a flight back to Rio; otherwise hop a plane to **Salvador,** the historic coastal capital of **Bahia,** via Brasília.

Salvador and Bahia
DAY 15
PLANE FROM CUIABÁ TO SALVADOR: 5.5-7.5 HOURS
In Salvador, check into a hotel in the beach neighborhood of **Barra** or the colonial districts of **Pelourinho** or **Santo Antônio.** Spend the day wandering through the steep cobblestoned streets of the Pelourinho, or "Pelô." Among this historic neighborhood's exceptional treasures are the baroque **Igreja e Convento de São Francisco** and the **Museu Afro-Brasileiro,** which offers a good overview of Bahia's Candomblé religion. In the evening, check with the municipal tourist office to see if there are any Candomblé *festas* being held at traditional *terreiros.* Otherwise, head to picturesque **Santo Antônio.** Some of the historic houses are occupied by terraced bars overlooking the **Baía de Todos os Santos.** Indulge in icy beers and an *escondidinho* while watching the sun set.

DAY 16
SALVADOR
Spend the morning visiting sights in the **Cidade Baixa** (Lower City) such as the hilltop **Igreja de Nosso Senhor do Bonfim,** the chaotic and colorful **Feira de São Joaquim,** and the **Museu de Arte Moderna,** located in a colonial sugar cane estate overlooking the sea. From here, it's a close bus or cab ride to **Porto da Barra,** a beach in the Barra neighborhood. After sunset, take a bus, car, or taxi along the coast to **Rio Vermelho** to feast on *acarajés* and discover the city's bohemian *bairro* (neighborhood).

DAYS 17-20
DRIVE FROM SALVADOR TO
LINHA VERDE: 1.5-2 HOURS
FAST LAUNCH FROM SALVADOR TO
MORRO DE SÃO PAULO: 2.5 HOURS
Treat yourself to several days of relaxation on a
beautiful Bahian beach and make the most of
your time by selecting one relatively close. The
easiest getaway is north along the Linha Verde.
Shack up in **Praia do Forte** (somewhat chic and
touristy) or **Imbassaí** (tranquil with a cosmo-
politan edge).

FAST LAUNCH FROM MORRO
TO BOIPEBA: 1 HOUR
Alternatively, you can hop a fast launch from the
Cidade Baixa to **Morro de São Paulo** (party
central) or to **Ilha de Boipeba** (gorgeously secluded, but getting here is a little trickier and can
take longer); both lie south of Salvador.

On the morning of your last day, drive back to
Salvador in time for your afternoon flight to Rio
and your connecting flight home.

The Best of São Paulo and Rio de Janeiro

Brazil's two "marvelous cities," Rio and São
Paulo, are only 5-6 hours apart by bus or car. To
get from one metropolis to the other, there are
two possibilities: an inland route that meanders
through the lush mountains of the Serra do Mar,
and a coastal route of stunning mainland and
island beaches and trendy resort towns. Rent a
car and do them both! The distances are manageable, roads are well-maintained, and a round-trip
gives you the best of both worlds in two weeks or
less. Driving also allows you to visit attractions
off the beaten track.

São Paulo's Centro by night

São Paulo

DAY 1

Most international flights land in **São Paulo,** and "Sampa" is a good place to begin. Check into your hotel then head for lunch in Centro or Jardins. Spend the afternoon poking around **Centro's** mishmash of architecture and monuments. Stroll around **Jardins,** checking out boutiques as the light fades. Jardins is a fine place for cocktails in a fashionable bar, such as **Skye,** with its fabulous city views, followed by dinner at **D.O.M.** for celebrated contemporary Brazilian cuisine. Or spend the evening eating, drinking, and dancing the night away in the bars and clubs of hip **Baixo Augusta.**

DAY 2

Take half a day to visit either the **Museu de Arte de São Paulo** and **Avenida Paulista;** the **Museu Afro Brasil** and **Museu de Arte Moderna** at **Parque do Ibirapuera;** or the **Pinacoteca do Estado** and **Museu da Língua Portuguesa** at the **Estação da Luz.** You can also combine destinations and make a full day of it. Otherwise, take time to browse through hip **Vila Madalena,** a fun place to dine, drink, and hear live music.

EXTEND YOUR STAY

Take a tasting tour of the **Mercado Municipal.** Visit the interactive and entertaining temple to *futebol* that is the **Museu do Futebol** and then take your stoked testosterone to a **soccer match** at one of Sampa's stadiums. Immerse yourself in music at the **Sala São Paulo** or the **Auditório Ibirapuera.** Get a heavy dose of culture (visual and musical) at the myriad **SESC** cultural centers throughout town.

DAYS 3-4

DRIVE FROM SÃO PAULO TO
BANANAL: 3.5-4 HOURS

Pick up a rental car in the morning and drive from São Paulo to **Bananal.** On the way, stop for breakfast and walk around the pretty colonial town of **São José do Barreiro.** Arrive in Bananal in time for a late lunch, then spend the afternoon leisurely exploring the town. Spend the night in town or at a *pousada* in a converted plantation manor nearby. The next morning, visit a coffee plantation, such as **Fazenda dos Coqueiros,** before heading to the **Recanto da Cachoeira,** where you can while away the rest of the day doused by cascades.

Rio de Janeiro

DAY 5

DRIVE FROM BANANAL TO
RIO DE JANEIRO: 3-3.5 HOURS

Get up early and head to **Rio de Janeiro.** Check into a hotel and then go for lunch in the **Zona Sul.** Hit the beaches of **Copacabana** and **Ipanema** for some fun in the sun, then have dinner in a restaurant in Ipanema or Leblon, followed by a *chope* (draft beer) at a *botequim* (neighborhood-style bar).

DAY 6

Explore the historical sights of **Centro,** which include **Cinelândia, Paço Imperial,** and the **Igreja do Mosteiro de São Bento.** Among the many museums and cultural centers, standouts include the **Museu de Arte do Rio,** located in the historic port district, and the **Centro Cultural Banco do Brasil.** After lunch in Centro at the **Brasserie Rosário,** take a quick bus or cab ride to atmospheric **Santa Teresa,** where you can visit the **Museu Chácara do Céu.** In the evening, put on your dancing shoes and visit the lively bars and dance halls of bohemian **Lapa.**

DAY 7

Avoid the crowds and take advantage of the morning light by heading out early to **Cosme Velho** for a ride up to **Corcovado** on the first *bonde* at 8:30am. Drop by the **Museu Internacional de Arte Naïf do Brasil** and then walk down toward Botafogo to visit the **Casa Daros** museum of contemporary Latin American art. You're only a tunnel away from Copacabana—and a cheap and fabulous lunch at **Bar do David,** located

Brazilians' fame for merrymaking is not an exaggeration. Carnaval is a spectacular example, but the year is filled with fantastic events.

Carnaval drummers

- **Réveillon:** Fireworks, cheap champagne, and revelers clad in white wade into the sea with flowers for the Afro-Brazilian sea goddess, Iemanjá. The biggest bash is in Rio (Jan. 1).

- **Lavagem do Bonfim:** Bahianas lead a procession through Salvador's Cidade Baixa for the ritual washing of the steps of the Igreja do Bonfim with perfume (second Thurs. in Jan.).

- **Carnaval:** Five days of throbbing music and unbridled hedonism. The biggest festivities are in Rio de Janeiro, Salvador, Recife, and Olinda (Feb.-Mar.).

- **Cavalhadas:** A haunting re-creation of a medieval battle between Christians and Moors is dramatized in the colonial town of Pirenópolis in Goiás (May).

- **Parada de Orgulho GLBT:** Avenida Paulista shuts down for São Paulo's exuberant Gay Pride Parade (May).

- **Festas Juninas:** In the northeastern Sertão, June is devoted to bonfires, *forró* dancing, drinking fruit liqueurs, and eating delicacies made from corn in celebration of Santo Antônio, São João, and São Pedro. One of the biggest events is the Festa de São João in Caruaru, Pernambuco (mid-late June).

- **Bumba-Meu-Boi:** In São Luís, Maranhão, splendid costumes, pounding drums, and whirling dancers characterize this popular *festa* (end of June).

- **Círio de Nazaré:** The highlight of the Amazon's most important religious festival is the procession of Pará's patron saint, Nossa Senhora de Nazaré, through the streets of Belém (second weekend of Oct.).

in the Chapéu Mangueira *favela*. Work off all that *feijoada* by walking along the crescent of Copacabana beach to Ipanema. Watch the sun set in the company of a caipirinha before heading to one of the gourmet eateries in neighboring Leblon, such as **Zuka** or **CT Boucherie.** Follow this with al fresco drinks at one of the breezy kiosks around the Lagoa Rodrigo de Freitas.

EXTEND YOUR STAY
Spend a few hours strolling beneath the imperial palms at the **Jardim Botânico.** Take a half-day jungle hike through the **Parque Nacional da Tijuca** or soar through the air on a hang glider from the **Pedra Bonita.** Ascend the landmark hump of **Pão de Açúcar** by cable car or with climbing equipment. Bike around the shore of the **Lagoa Rodrigo de Freitas** (or pedal in a swan boat across its surface), then flake out in one of the surrounding kiosk restaurant-bars. For a glimpse into vibrant hillside life and culture, take a *favela* tour.

DAY 8
DRIVE FROM RIO DE JANEIRO TO ANGRA DOS REIS: 3-3.5 HOURS
BOAT FROM ANGRA TO ILHA GRANDE: 45-90 MIN.

Pick up a rental car and head down the **Costa Verde** to **Angra dos Reis.** Stash your car in the parking lot near the ferry and then take the boat across to **Ilha Grande.** After checking into a *pousada* in or around **Vila Abraão,** have lunch and explore the pretty village. If time permits, take a boat trip to one of the island's most splendid beaches, **Saco do Céu.**

DAY 9
ILHA GRANDE

Get up early to take a full-day boat excursion to the island's most secluded and stunning beaches. You'll visit around eight of them, with stops for swimming and snorkeling. Back in Vila Abraão, satisfy your hunger by devouring fresh seafood. Hike (or take a taxi-boat) to **Praia Lopes Mendes,** considered the island's most spectacular beach, and swim, snorkel, and soak in the sun all day. If you're feeling more botanically inclined, take a **trekking tour** through the jungle.

DAY 10
BOAT FROM ILHA GRANDE TO ANGRA DOS REIS: 45-90 MIN.
DRIVE FROM ANGRA TO PARATY: 1 HOUR

Return to Angra dos Reis and drive south to **Paraty,** where you'll spend the night at one of many centuries-old *pousadas* sprinkled throughout the historic center. For lunch, **Banana da Terra** is a fine place to sample local fare. In the afternoon, head to the nearby beach of **Paraty-Mirim.** For a festive evening, dine at **Casa do Fogo,** where the majority of dishes are lit on fire.

DAY 11
PARATY

Spend the day exploring the beaches around Paraty. At the nearby beach of **Trindade,** 30 minutes away, lie out in the sun or hike through the Atlantic rain forest to more deserted beaches,

Leblon beach, Rio de Janeiro

Ilha Grande, Rio de Janeiro

Lagoa Rodrigo de Freitas, Rio de Janeiro

such as **Praia Cachadaço,** which is good for snorkeling. Both **Paraty Tours** and **Paraty Explorer** offer half-day diving, kayaking, and schooner tours as well as treks into the surrounding Atlantic rain forest and to Brazil's only fjord; **Saco do Mamanguá.** At the end of the day, return to Paraty.

DAY 12
DRIVE FROM PARATY TO
UBATUBA: 1 HOUR

Leave Paraty early, heading south. Stop for a swim at a deserted beach, such as **Praia do Prumirim** or **Praia de Puruba.** Stop for lunch in **Ubatuba** to feast on regional seafood dishes at **Peixe com Banana** and then continue south to **Praia do Lázaro.** Check into a *pousada* and then walk to the adjacent beach of **Domingas Dias** for a dip and some sun.

DAY 13
DRIVE FROM UBATUBA TO
SÃO SEBASTIÃO: 90 MIN.

Drive south past São Sebastião and stop at **Toque-Toque** for a quick dip. Continue south to the beaches of **Camburi** and **Camburizinho** (30 min.), where you can lunch at one of many fine restaurants. After dessert and coffee, soak up your final rays of sun. Depending on what time your flight leaves the next day, stay overnight in Camburi or Camburizinho or return to São Paulo (2.5 hours) and spend the night in the city.

DAY 14
DRIVE FROM SÃO SEBASTIÃO TO
SÃO PAULO: 2.5-3 HOURS

If you spent the night on the coast, return to **São Paulo** in time to hand in your car and catch your flight. If you spent the night in São Paulo, you could visit a museum or go shopping in **Jardins** and have a leisurely farewell lunch at **Tordesilhas** before heading to the airport.

Two Weeks Along the Amazon

Spend 14 days exploring the world's largest, most diverse, and most mysterious rain forest. For a base, use the jungle capital of Manaus, located at the point at which the Rio Solimões and Rio Negro meet to begin the Rio Amazonas, or Belém, a striking colonial city with rich culinary and cultural traditions. Midway between the cities is Santarém, a lazy river outpost that offers an authentic taste of life along the Amazon as well as the pristine white-sand river beaches of Alter do Chão.

Day 1
MANAUS
Arrive in **Manaus.** If you're flying directly via Miami, you'll arrive in the morning and check into a hotel. If you're flying via São Paulo, you'll arrive late in the afternoon. The two major sights you'll want to see are the sumptuous **Teatro Amazonas** and the spectacle of the Rio Negro merging with the Rio Solimões to form the mighty Amazon, known as the **Meeting of the Waters.** Extra time can be spent exploring the market and a museum or two near **Centro.** Sample local river fish and *caboclinho* sandwiches. In the evening, catch a performance at the Teatro or soak up local atmosphere in one of Centro's classic *botecos*.

Days 2-4
TAXI OR SPEEDBOAT FROM MANAUS TO NOVO AIRÃO: 2-3.5 HOURS
Leave Manaus and head up the Rio Negro to Novo Airão, point of departure for trips among the 400 islands of the **Arquipélago de Anavilhanas,** the second-largest freshwater archipelago in the world, and the **Parque Nacional do Jaú,** the largest forest reserve in the Americas. Stay in

Meeting of the Waters near Manaus

Novo Airão and take an ecotour into the rain forest, or check into the all-inclusive **Anavilhanas Jungle Lodge.** A minimum of two nights at a jungle lodge in the heart of the forest is an ideal Amazonian baptism. Meals, guided excursions, and most activities, such as piranha fishing and swimming with river dolphins, are included.

Day 5
PLANE FROM MANAUS TO SANTARÉM: 1 HOUR

Return to Manaus and fly to **Santarém** on the shores of **Rio Tapajós.** Check into a *pousada* and wander around this riverside town watching boats come and go, and dine at **Trapiche Bistro Orla,** a funky bistro that prepares local fish with contemporary twists.

Day 6
TAXI/BUS FROM SANTARÉM TO ALTER DO CHÃO: 30 MIN.-1 HOUR

Take an early bus to **Alter do Chão,** known as "the Caribbean of the Amazon" because of its pristine river beaches. Check into a *pousada* and then spend the day sunning on the beach and taking **canoe trips** along the river. Make sure you're at **Ponta do Cururu** in late afternoon to watch pink river dolphins frolic in the setting sun.

Days 7-8
ALTER DO CHÃO

Book a full-day excursion to the **Floresta Nacional do Tapajós,** where you can hike or canoe through the rain forest and observe rubber tappers at work. Spend a night in the home of one of the members of the local indigenous communities for an unforgettable experience. The next day, consider a full-day outing to the **Canal do Jari,** where the Tapajós and Amazon Rivers meet amid a flurry of wildlife activity.

Days 9-10
PLANE FROM SANTARÉM TO BELÉM: 1 HOUR

Return to Santarém and fly into **Belém.** Spend the morning wandering through the exotic wares at the **Mercado Ver-o-Peso.** Then explore the compact colonial district of **Cidade Velha,**

Alter do Chão

Be an Ecotourist

Brazil's rich, abundant biomes are constantly under siege. Many conservation projects try to study and preserve these rich ecosystems and their unique inhabitants and the following accept foreign volunteers.

PRESERVING MATA ATLÂNTICA, RIO DE JANEIRO STATE

Reserva Ecológica de Guapiaçu (www.regua.co.uk) is a nature reserve two hours from Rio that welcomes volunteers (1-3 months). Responsibilities include managing an eco-lodge, teaching English, marking jungle trails, planting trees, caring for rare nursery specimens, and working as an assistant bird or nature guide.

PRESERVING CERRADO, MATO GROSSO DO SUL STATE

Kaya (www.kayavolunteer.com) and **Blue Lizard Adventures** (www.bluelizardadventures.com) seek volunteers (2-12 weeks) to work with local farmers promoting sustainable ranch activities and to study the behavior of key wildlife species. Both are based in the southern Pantanal region, three hours from Campo Grande.

jaguar cubs

PRESERVING RIVER OTTERS, SANTA CATARINA STATE

Volunteers (1 day-13 weeks) can help the **Ekko Brasil Institute** (www.ekkobrasil.org.br) study and preserve the almost extinct neotropical river otter. Research, field work, environmental education, and caring for otters in captivity take place on Santa Catarina island, near Florianópolis.

PRESERVING JAGUARS, PARANÁ STATE

Located on a forested nature refuge 45 minutes from Curitiba, the **Jaguar Conservationist Reserve** (http://brazilianexperience.com.br) is a breeding ground for jaguars. Volunteers feed animals, assist vets, and plant native trees and plants. Cuddling baby jaguars is a major bonus. Accommodations are with local families in a nearby village.

where you can poke into churches and rubber barons' palaces.

Head to **Parque Mangal das Garças** to check out exotic birds and butterflies. Visit the **Centro Cultural São José Liberto** to see (and purchase) precious gemstones. In the evening, feast on Amazonian cuisine at one of Belém's fine restaurants, such as **Lá em Casa,** located at the **Estação das Docas.** The bars at these renovated docks are also a good place to have a nightcap and listen to some live music.

Day 11
BELÉM

Book a boat trip with **Amazon Star Turismo** along the **Ilha do Papagaio** to watch the

the harbor in Belém

island's parrots wake up. Return to Belém and visit the glorious **Basílica de Nossa Senhora de Nazaré**, then the **Museu Paraense Emílio Goeldi** to explore its vast, pioneering collection of Amazonian flora and fauna. If you missed the early-morning boat trip, take a **sunset cruise** along the **Rio Guamá.** Don't leave town without having savored an exotic fruit ice cream at **Cairu.**

Days 12-14

FERRY FROM BELÉM TO ILHA DE MARAJÓ: 3 HOURS

Take a boat to **Ilha de Marajó** and check into a *fazenda* lodge on a working water buffalo farm. For the next two days, canoe through mangroves, sprawl on deserted beaches, and visit the towns of **Soure** and **Salvaterra.** Try buffalo steaks, as well as cheese and desserts made with buffalo milk. On the last day, return to Belém and catch a flight to São Paulo or Manaus.

Rio de Janeiro

Highlights

★ **Corcovado:** Crowned by the all-embracing statue of Christ the Redeemer, "Hunchback" mountain was recently voted one of the Seven Modern Wonders of the World (page 46).

★ **Pão de Açúcar:** One of Rio's most instantly recognizable icons, this monumental chunk of sugar loaf-shaped granite rises out of the Baía de Guanabara (page 47).

★ **Copacabana Beach:** Urban beaches don't get any more dazzling than this gorgeous arc of sugary fine sand that is a microcosm unto itself (page 48).

★ **Ipanema and Leblon:** More than just fabulous beaches, these two adjacent neighborhoods are the eternal epitome of Carioca cool, with shady streets, bars, boutiques, restaurants, and a bossa nova vibe (page 49).

★ **Carnaval:** Samba the day and night away for five days at Rio's spectacularly hedonistic *festa* to end all *festas* (page 55).

★ **Floresta da Tijuca:** Brazil's largest urban park, Floresta da Tijuca is a lush green oasis of native Atlantic forest that is perfect for a refreshing getaway (page 68).

★ **Museu Imperial:** The former summer residence of Dom Pedro II, located in Petrópolis, offers a glimpse into the life of an emperor in the tropics (page 87).

★ **Búzios:** Brazil's version of Saint-Tropez is a tropical chic playground with sophisticated amenities, a celebrated nightlife, and beaches for every taste under the sun (page 95).

★ **Ilha Grande:** The largest of the many islands in the Bay of Angra dos Reis, Ilha Grande is an island paradise that captures the essence and ethos of "back to nature" (page 100).

★ **Paraty:** One of the most charming and best-preserved Portuguese colonial towns in Brazil is surrounded by breathtaking mountains and idyllic beaches (page 103).

E ven if you've never been, it's easy to hear "Rio" and automatically conjure up its postcard sights: the *Christ the Redeemer* statue atop lush Corcovado, the sweeping white crescent of Copacabana beach, and Pão de Açúcar.

When you do finally arrive, it's a shock—these landmarks are even more impressive in real life. After all, this is the city that Cariocas (residents of Rio) refer to proudly as the *Cidade Maravilhosa* (Marvelous City).

Like many a modern tourist, Brazil's imperial family enjoyed Rio to the hilt, but when they couldn't stand the heat, they literally took to the hills. Emperor Pedro II went so far as to build an ornate pink summer palace (now a fascinating museum) in the mountains. Only an hour from Rio—but usually 5-10 degrees cooler—Petrópolis, Teresópolis, and other neighboring towns continue to offer refuge to vacationers who can take advantage of sophisticated amenities surrounded by majestic scenery. When nature beckons, the national parks of Serra dos Órgãos and Itatiaia are close by with their orchid-laced hiking trails winding through native Atlantic forest.

Natural attractions are also in abundance along the coasts of Rio de Janeiro state. East of the city are the upscale resort towns of Cabo Frio and Búzios, which offer beautiful sandy beaches with calm pools for snorkeling and big waves for surfers. Búzios is particularly charming, with cobblestoned streets and shades of Saint-Tropez. Those in search of more tranquil options can head south along the Costa Verde (Green Coast), named for the verdant mountains that provide a striking backdrop to the unspoiled beaches. Highlights along this coast include the island paradise of Ilha Grande and the beautifully preserved colonial town of Paraty.

PLANNING YOUR TIME

One week will give you time to explore museums and historic sights, shop, and lounge on the city's famous beaches as well as take a day trip or two to the surrounding beaches or mountains of Rio de Janeiro state. Despite the great variety of its attractions, Rio de Janeiro

Previous: Ipanema beach; the waterfront of Ipanema and Copacabana Beach. **Above:** Pão de Açúcar

Rio de Janeiro City

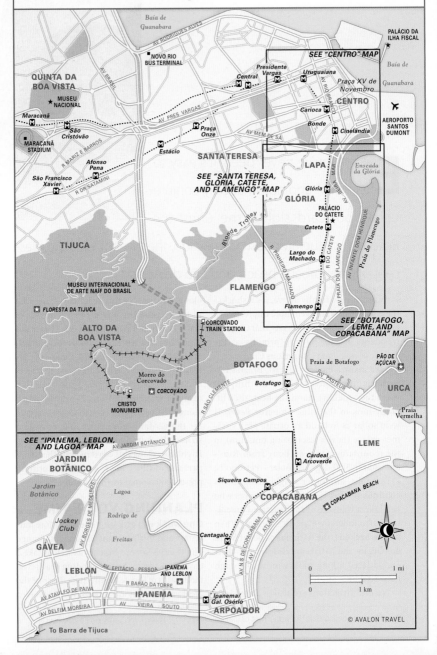

Baía de Guanabara

PALÁCIO DA ILHA FISCAL

AV RODRIGUES ALVES

SEE "CENTRO" MAP

Baía de Guanabara

NOVO RIO BUS TERMINAL

AV BRASIL

QUINTA DA BOA VISTA

MUSEU NACIONAL

Maracanã

São Cristóvão

MARACANÃ STADIUM

R MARIZ E BARROS

Afonso Pena

São Francisco Xavier

R DR SATAMINI

AV PRES VARGAS

Presidente Vargas

Central

Praça Onze

AV MEM DE SÁ

Estácio

Praça XV de Novembro

Uruguaiana

AV RIO BRANCO

CENTRO

Carioca

Bonde

Cinelândia

AEROPORTO SANTOS DUMONT

SANTA TERESA

LAPA

Enseada da Glória

SEE "SANTA TERESA, GLÓRIA, CATETE, AND FLAMENGO" MAP

Glória

GLÓRIA

Blonde Trolley

PALÁCIO DO CATETE

Catete

AV BEIRA MAR

Praia do Flamengo

AV INFANTE DOM HENRIQUE

TIJUCA

MUSEU INTERNACIONAL DE ARTE NAÏF DO BRASIL

FLORESTA DA TIJUCA

R PINHEIRO MACHADO

Largo do Machado

R DO CATETE

AV PRAIA DO FLAMENGO

FLAMENGO

Flamengo

ALTO DA BOA VISTA

CORCOVADO TRAIN STATION

SEE "BOTAFOGO, LEME, AND COPACABANA" MAP

Morro do Corcovado

CORCOVADO

CRISTO MONUMENT

R SÃO CLEMENTE

BOTAFOGO

Botafogo

Praia de Botafogo

AV PASTEUR

PÃO DE AÇÚCAR

URCA

Praia Vermelha

SEE "IPANEMA, LEBLON, AND LAGOA" MAP

AV JARDIM BOTÂNICO

JARDIM BOTÂNICO

Jardim Botânico

Lagoa

Rodrigo de Freitas

AV BORGES DE MEDEIROS

Jockey Club

GÁVEA

LEBLON

AV EPITÁCIO PESSOA

IPANEMA AND LEBLON

R BARÃO DA TORRE

AV ATAULFO DE PAIVA

AV DELFIM MOREIRA

IPANEMA

AV VIEIRA SOUTO

Cardeal Arcoverde

Siqueira Campos

COPACABANA

COPACABANA BEACH

COPACABANA BEACH

AV N S DE COPACABANA

AV ATLÂNTICA

Cantagalo

Ipanema/ Gal. Osório

ARPOADOR

LEME

0   1 mi

0   1 km

© AVALON TRAVEL

To Barra de Tijuca

state is compact, and most sights are only two or three hours away. While some of these destinations (such as Petrópolis and Teresópolis) can be visited as day trips from Rio, it would be a crime to rush when faced with such intense natural beauty and relaxing environs. Two or three days reserved for the mountains surrounding Petrópolis and Itatiaia and another couple (at least) for the beautiful beaches of Búzios and Arraial do Cabo (north of Rio) or Ilha Grande and Paraty (south of Rio) will give you adequate time to unwind and explore.

There are several factors to consider when planning a trip. In **summer** (Dec.-early Mar.), Rio sizzles—both figuratively (festivities and nightlife are at their zenith) and literally (with temperatures hovering around 40°C/104°F

and lots of sticky humidity). Make sure you have an air-conditioned hotel, or head for the much cooler hills. Another option is to visit in **winter** (June-Sept.), when the sun is less intense and the beaches won't be quite so crowded (at least during the week). Nights are comfortably cool (15-20°C/60-70°F). The cold fronts that come up from Argentina, bringing cool winds and rain that can last for two or three days, are the only thing to watch out for. Rio enjoys a considerable amount of precipitation throughout the year; December to March, rains are particularly frequent. To take part in either of Rio's most famous and fabulous festivities—Réveillon (New Year's Eve) and Carnaval—prepare to have deep pockets and to make flight and hotel bookings months in advance.

Rio de Janeiro City

Rio's setting is incomparable: This tropical metropolis of 8 million is both urban and urbane, yet every street seems to end in an explosion of towering green or a soothing slice of blue. The 500-year-old city is also hardly lacking in impressive architecture. Its downtown is a treasure trove of baroque churches, imperial palaces (many converted into cultural centers), and monumental buildings and squares. History of a more recent variety is present in the Zona Sul neighborhoods of Copacabana, Ipanema, and Leblon; all three are famed for the stunning white-sand beaches that serve as playgrounds for Cariocas and tourists from all walks of life. It was here that bossa nova was born and the bikini made its mark. Despite all the beautiful people, Zona Sul retains a relaxed casualness that is typical of Rio. Sip a fresh tropical nectar at a juice bar or enjoy an icy beer at one of many rustic bars known as *botequins,* and watch as barefoot surfer boys and bikini girls in Havaianas stroll through the streets.

While daytime in Rio is languid, nighttime sizzles with possibilities. For dinner, choose

from a profusion of world-class restaurants. Then either chill at a swanky Zona Sul lounge, dance, drink, and flirt at a nightclub, or join the pulsating throngs in the historic *bairros* of Lapa, Saúde, and Gamboa, who flock to listen to live *chorinho, forró,* and, of course, samba.

Speaking of samba, it's impossible to mention Rio without alluding to the world-famous extravaganza known as Carnaval. It doesn't matter whether you take in the parades at the Sambódromo, dance through the streets with a traditional neighborhood *bloco* (Carnaval group), or merely make it to one of the *escola de samba* (samba school) rehearsals held throughout the year. The Carnaval spirit is highly contagious. Like Rio itself, it will leave you wanting more.

ORIENTATION

What's left of Rio's colonial past and most of its churches and museums are concentrated in its old downtown core, known as **Centro**. However, beaches, shopping, restaurants, nightlife, and most hotels—as well as access to the Floresta da Tijuca—are in the more upscale **Zona Sul** neighborhoods. The area north of Centro is known as the **Zona Norte.** This vast urban zone is home to Rio's lower-class neighborhoods and encompasses the Rodoviária Novo Rio (bus station), Aeroporto Internacional Tom Jobim (Galeão), and Maracanã soccer stadium.

Despite Rio's sprawl, getting around the Centro and Zona Sul neighborhoods is fairly easy. An excellent Metrô service links Zona Norte, Centro, Flamengo, Botafogo, Copacabana, and Ipanema, and an efficiently integrated Metrô-express and standard bus service allows you to easily access other neighborhoods, including Cosme Velho, Leblon, Gávea, Jardim Botânico, São Conrado, and Barra. Walking is a wonderful way to explore the city. During the day, it's quite safe to stroll around (with the exception of Centro on weekends). At night more care should be taken, although most Zona Sul neighborhoods are quite bright and busy until at least 10pm.

SIGHTS
Centro

Centro refers to Rio's historic downtown commercial district, where cobblestoned alleys, grand baroque churches, turn-of-the-20th-century architecture, and the ubiquitous high-rises and urban chaos of a 21st-century megalopolis make up a fascinating patchwork. As an antidote to the upscale beach culture of Zona Sul, pockets of the Centro are quite interesting, particularly if you want to get a sense of Rio's rich past.

Despite the traffic, navigating the area is quite easy on foot. Centro is also well served by buses from both the Zona Sul and Zona Norte (take anything marked Centro, Praça XV, or Praça Mauá) and by Metrô (the most convenient stations are Cinelândia, Carioca, Uruguaiana, Presidente Vargas, and Praça Onze). During the day and into the early evening Centro is usually jam-packed, but at night and on weekends the area is a ghost town and quite unsafe to stroll around. If taking in an exhibition or performance during these times, it's best to take a taxi.

Centro

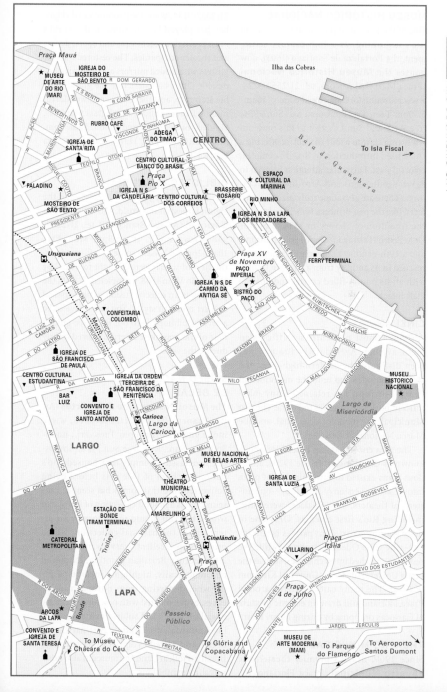

Praça Mauá

★ MUSEU DE ARTE DO RIO (MAR)

IGREJA DO MOSTEIRO DE SÃO BENTO

R DOM GERARDO

R S BENTO

R CONS SARAIVA

BECO DE BRAGANÇA

R ACRE

R BENEDITINOS

AV RIO

R MAIRINK VEIGA

RUBRO CAFÉ

VISCONDE

INHAÚMA

ADEGA DO TIMÃO

R VISC ITABORAÍ

CENTRO

Ilha das Cobras

IGREJA DE SANTA RITA

R TEÓFILO OTONI

MIGUEL COUTO

R BRANCO

CENTRO CULTURAL BANCO DO BRASIL

Praça Pio X

Baía de Guanabara

To Isla Fiscal →

▼ PALADINO

MOSTEIRO DE SÃO BENTO

AV PRESIDENTE VARGAS

ALFÂNDEGA

IGREJA N S DA CANDELÁRIA

CENTRO CULTURAL DOS CORREIOS

▼ BRASSERIE ROSÁRIO

ESPAÇO CULTURAL DA MARINHA

RIO MINHO

IGREJA N S DA LAPA DOS MERCADORES

R DA

MIGUEL COUTO

AIRES

R DO ROSÁRIO

DE TEIO MARÇO

R DO

AV PRESIDENTE

R CAIS PHAROUX

FERRY TERMINAL

Ⓜ Uruguaiana

DE BUENOS

R DO OUVIDOR

DA QUITANDA

R DO CARMO

Praça XV de Novembro

PAÇO IMPERIAL

AV MERCADO

KUBITSCHEK

R LUIZ DE CAMÕES

URUGUAIANA

Metrô

CONFEITARIA COLOMBO

GONÇALVES DIAS

R SETE DE SETEMBRO

R DA ASSEMBLEIA

R SÃO JOSÉ

IGREJA N S DE CARMO DA ANTIGA SÉ

BISTRÔ DO PAÇO

AV ALFREDO

AGACHE

R DO TEATRO

IGREJA DE SÃO FRANCISCO DE PAULA

RODRIGO

R ERASMO BRAGA

R SÃO JOSÉ

R MISERICÓRDIA

CENTRO CULTURAL ESTUDANTINA

DA CARIOCA

IGREJA DA ORDEM TERCEIRA DE SÃO FRANCISCO DA PENITÊNCIA

AV NILO PEÇANHA

R MAL AGUINALDO

LD DE MISERICÓRDIA

MUSEU HISTORICO NACIONAL

BAR LUIZ

CONVENTO E IGREJA DE SANTO ANTÔNIO

R BITENCOURT

Ⓜ Carioca

Largo da Carioca

R 13 DE MAIO

BARROSO

ALM

DEBRET

R DE STA LUZIA

Largo da Misericórdia

LARGO

AV REPÚBLICA

R EVARISTO DA VEIGA

R HEITOR DE MELO

MUSEU NACIONAL DE BELAS ARTES

PORTO ALEGRE

AV PRESIDENTE ANTONIO CARLOS

MARECHAL CAMARA

DO CHILE

R MÉXICO

ARAÚJO

GRAÇA

R ARANHA

IGREJA DE SANTA LUZIA

AV CHURCHILL

THÉATRO MUNICIPAL

BIBLIOTECA NACIONAL ★

AV FRANKLIN ROOSEVELT

ESTAÇÃO DE BONDE (TRAM TERMINAL)

AMARELINHO

EÇO SERRADOR

R ÁLVARO ALVIM

SENADOR DANTAS

Cinelândia

R BRANCO

DE STA

Ⓜ

Metrô

VILLARINO ▼

Praça Itália

TREVO DOS ESTUDANTES

Trolley

CATEDRAL METROPOLITANA

Praça Floriano

AV PRESIDENT WILSON

DE FONTOURA

Praça 4 de Julho

HENRIQUE

R DOS ARCOS

R MURTINHO NOBRE

Bonde

DO PASSEIO

Passeio Público

R JOÃO NEVES DE

AV INFANTE DOM

R JARDEL JERCULIS

ARCOS DA LAPA ★

LAPA

TEIXEIRA

CONVENTO E IGREJA DE SANTA TERESA

To Museu Chácara do Céu

DE FREITAS

To Glória and Copacabana

MUSEU DE ARTE MODERNA (MAM) ★

To Parque do Flamengo

To Aeroporto Santos Dumont →

MUSEU HISTÓRICO NACIONAL

One of the few surviving constructions from Rio's beginnings as a 16th-century settlement, the Fortaleza de Santiago (1603), now houses the **Museu Histórico Nacional** (Praça Marechal Âncora, tel. 21/2550-9224, www.museuhistoriconacional.com.br, 10am-5:30pm Tues.-Fri., 2pm-6pm Sat.-Sun., R$6, free Wed. and Sun.). A visit to this museum is a fitting start to a tour of Centro, offering a condensed introduction to Brazil's complex, colorful past. Particular attention is given to Brazil's indigenous and Afro-Brazilian cultures. There are also some truly precious artifacts, like the pen Princesa Isabel used to sign the Abolition of Slavery in 1888, Emperor Dom Pedro II's dragon-capped golden throne, and a 19th-century homeopathic pharmacy, rescued in its entirety from a street in Centro with all its potion-filled crystal and opaline vials intact.

CINELÂNDIA

Although most of Centro's traffic-laden main avenue, Avenida Rio Branco, has been disfigured by modern high-rises, the stretch that opens up onto the monumental **Praça Floriano** has retained many magnificent buildings, among them the Theatro Municipal, the Biblioteca Nacional, and the Museu Nacional de Belas Artes.

The area encompassing Praça Floriano is known as **Cinelândia**. In the 1920s, ambitious plans existed to turn this elegant plaza into a Carioca version of Broadway—only instead of theaters, movie palaces were built, including Rio's first cinemas. Only one of these glamorous art deco palaces is still intact—the Cine Odeon Petrobras—while the rest were snatched up by churches, such as the Igreja Universal de Deus (Universal Kingdom of God). The many cafés scattered around Praça Floriano still draw an eclectic mixture of Cariocas dropping by during happy hour.

THEATRO MUNICIPAL

Since 1909, Brazil's premier theater, the **Theatro Municipal** (Praça Floriano, tel. 21/2332-9134, www.theatromunicipal.rj.gov. br), has played host to some of the world's most prestigious orchestras and opera, dance, and theater companies. The restored interior glitters with gilded mirrors and crystal chandeliers. Onyx banisters line the grand marble staircase, and there are some wonderful mosaic frescoes and stained-glass windows. Guided tours are offered (noon, 2pm, 3pm, and 4pm Tues.-Fri., 11am, noon, and 1pm Sat., R$10).

BIBLIOTECA NACIONAL

The largest library in Latin America and the eighth largest in the world, Rio's **Biblioteca Nacional** (Av. Rio Branco 219, tel. 21/2220-9484, www.bn.br, 10am-5pm Mon.-Fri., 10am-2pm Sat.) boasts some 13 million tomes, the first of which were brought to Brazil by Dom João VI in 1808. Completed in 1910, the building is an eclectic fusion of neoclassical and art nouveau styles. You don't have to be a serious bibliophile to opt for a free guided tour of the grandiose interior, offered hourly during the week.

MUSEU NACIONAL DE BELAS ARTES

The **Museu Nacional de Belas Artes** (Av. Rio Branco 199, tel. 21/2240-0068, www. mnba.gov.br, 10am-6pm Tues.-Fri., noon-5pm Sat.-Sun., R$8, free Sun.) is an imposing neoclassical temple that housed Rio's national school of fine arts before being converted into this somewhat somber museum. It has a modest collection of European works, but you should really focus your attention on the national collection, which provides an excellent overview of 19th- and 20th-century Brazilian painting. Displayed chronologically, highlights include painters who, departing from European influences, experimented with new and distinctly Brazilian styles and subject matter, including Anita Malfatti, Cândido Portinari, Lasar Segall, and Alfredo Volpi. A gallery displays Brazilian folk art, and the museum also hosts traveling exhibitions.

Following Avenida Rio Branco north brings you to **Largo** and **Rua da Carioca,** a bustling area filled vendors and a maze of cobblestoned streets. You will immediately be impressed by the monumental hillside complex of the Igreja de São Francisco da Penitência and the Convento de Santo Antônio.

CONVENTO DE SANTO ANTÔNIO

Built in the early 1600s to house Franciscan monks, the **Convento de Santo Antônio** (Largo da Carioca, tel. 21/2262-0129, 8am-6pm Mon.-Fri., 8am-11am Sat.) is one of Rio's oldest surviving buildings. Although most of the church was been modified, you can admire some baroque works and a finely wrought sacristy panel of blue-and-white Portuguese azulejos (ceramic tiles) illustrating the life of Santo Antônio.

IGREJA DE SÃO FRANCISCO DA PENITÊNCIA

The interior of the **Igreja de São Francisco da Penitência** (Largo da Carioca, tel. 21/2262-0197, 9am-4pm Tues.-Fri., R$2), one of Rio's most sumptuous baroque jewels, may blind you by the sheer amount of pure gold on display—400 kilograms (880 pounds), to be precise. While the church took 115 years to build (construction began in 1657), the final 30 years were almost exclusively dedicated to covering the beautifully sculpted cedar altars and naves in gold.

REAL GABINETE PORTUGUÊS DE LEITURA

Stylized sailors' knots, seashells, and Moorish motifs mark the facade of the **Real Gabinete Português de Leitura** (Rua Luís de Camões 30, tel. 21/2221-3138, www.realgabinete.com. br, 9am-6pm Mon.-Fri., free). Inside is a large library of works in the Portuguese language and a stunning reading room with mile-high ceilings, jacaranda tables, and seemingly endless polished wood bookshelves. To get here from the Largo da Carioca, walk down Rua da Carioca to Praça Tiradentes, then take a right on Avenida Passos.

PRAÇA XV

Historically, Praça XV comprised the symbolic heart of Centro. Its full name, **Praça XV de Novembro,** refers to November 15, 1899, the day when Brazil's first president, Manuel Deodoro de Fonseca, declared Brazil a republic. Many significant historical events have taken place here—among them the crowning of Brazil's two emperors, Pedro I and Pedro II, and the abolition of slavery in 1888.

PAÇO IMPERIAL

Praça XV once served as a large public patio to the stately **Paço (Palácio) Imperial** (Praça XV de Novembro 48, tel. 21/2215-2622, www. pacoimperial.com.br, 11am-7pm Tues.-Sun., free). Built in 1743, the palace was a residence for Portugal's colonial governors; it then housed the Portuguese court when Dom João VI fled Napoleon's forces in 1808. Today, it contains temporary exhibits of contemporary art. Overlooking the internal courtyard is a lovely café and restaurant, the Bistrô do Paço, as well as Arlequim, an excellent book and music store that often hosts pocket shows.

Directly across Praça XV from the Paço Imperial, an impressive arch leads down the **Beco de Telles,** a cobblestoned alley lined with elegant 19th-century buildings. Wander down this street and the equally narrow and atmospheric Travessa do Comércio, Rua Visconde de Itaboraí, and Rua Ouvidor to get a sense of what Rio was like in the 18th and 19th centuries.

IGREJA NOSSA SENHORA DE CARMO DA ANTIGA SÉ

The **Igreja Nossa Senhora de Carmo da Antiga Sé** (Rua Sete de Setembro 14, tel. 21/2242-7766, 7am-4pm Mon.-Fri., free) sits across from Praça XV. Constructed in 1761, it served as Rio's principal cathedral until 1980. Many of the city's major religious commemorations—including Emperor Pedro I's coronation and the baptism and marriage of Emperor Pedro II—were celebrated here. Serious history buffs should check out the sound-and-light show (1:30pm Tues.-Fri., noon and 1pm Sat., 12:30 and 1pm Sun., R$8), in which a holographic priest recounts the church's history. A small **museum** (10am-3:30pm Tues.-Fri., 11am-2pm Sat.-Sun., R$5) displays vestiges of the original 16th-century chapel along with a crypt containing the remains of Brazil's "discoverer," Pedro Álvares Cabral.

ESPAÇO CULTURAL DA MARINHA AND THE ILHA FISCAL

Along the waterfront, the **Espaço Cultural da Marinha** (Av. Alfred Agache, near Praça XV, tel. 21/2233-9165, www.mar.mil.br, noon-5pm Tues.-Sun., free) features a small collection of antique maps, navigating equipment, and buried treasure rescued from sunken ships in the Baía de Guanabara, offering an engaging glimpse of Brazil's maritime history. Kids will have fun clambering about on the World War II-era torpedo destroyer and a cool 1970s submarine, both moored outside the main building.

From here, you can take a guided trip by boat or minibus across the bay to the **Ilha Fiscal,** the site of a neo-Gothic castle that once housed a customs collection center. The extravagant construction resembles something out of a fairy tale: It was here that the last legendary royal ball of the Brazilian empire was held—one week before the declaration of Brazil as a republic. Boat trips depart at 12:30pm, 2pm, and 3:30pm Thurs.-Sun. Tours (R$20) last 1.5 hours.

IGREJA NOSSA SENHORA DA CANDELÁRIA

You can't miss the monumental **Igreja Nossa Senhora da Candelária** (Praça Pio X, tel. 21/2233-2324, 7:30am-4pm Mon.-Fri., 8am-noon Sat., 9am-1pm Sun., free). Begun in 1775, the present church took more than 100 years to complete, which accounts for its mixture of baroque and Renaissance elements. Ceiling panels recount the legend of the original 16th-century chapel's construction by a shipwrecked captain whose life was miraculously saved.

IGREJA DO MOSTEIRO DE SÃO BENTO

Located north of Praça Mauá, the **Igreja do Mosteiro de São Bento** (Rua Dom Geraldo 68, tel. 21/2206-8100, 7am-6pm daily) is Rio's most magnificent example of baroque architecture. Instead of being blindingly ostentatious, the lavish gold interior has a warm and burnished hue, the result of soft lighting used to preserve the precious artwork (which includes some exceptionally fine sculpted saints and painted panels). On Sunday morning you can take part in the 10am mass, in which the Benedictine monks chant Gregorian hymns accompanied by an organ (arrive early if you want a seat.). Access to the monastery is via an elevator located at Rua Dom Geraldo 40.

MUSEU DE ARTE DO RIO

The **Museu de Arte do Rio** (Praça Mauá 5, tel. 21/2203-1235, www.museudeartedorio.org.br, 10am-5pm Tues.-Sun., R$8, free Tues.) is one of the more promising symbols of the transformation and revitalization of Rio's historic port district. A futuristic roof of curvaceous concrete and a suspended walkway unite two completely antithetical buildings: the 19th-century eclectic-style Palacete Dom João VI and a 1950s modernist-style bus terminal. Within the former are four floors devoted to permanent and temporary exhibits focusing on art related to Rio. Windows offer ample opportunities for sea-gazing; hence the aptness of the museum's acronym, MAR (ocean).

Zona Norte

When traveling from the Tom Jobim international airport to Centro or Zona Sul, you'll get your first sight of Rio's sprawling Zona Norte district. The area is largely residential, with working-class and poor neighborhoods alongside vast *favelas*. Poverty and drug-related violence make large pockets extremely unsafe. The exception is the Quinta da Boa Vista (fairly close to Centro and easily accessible by Metrô), a vast park with some sights, among them the Museu Nacional. If you have

Port Revival

Rio's Port Zone stretches north from Praça Mauá, encompassing the *bairros* of Saúde and Gamboa. Occupation of these *bairros* dates back to early colonial days, when aristocrats built villas along the hillsides overlooking the beach-fringed Baía da Guanabara. In the late 1700s, the beaches vanished, as did the well-to-do residents, when the Cais de Valongo replaced Praça XV as the city's disembarkation point for the more than 1 million African slaves who would arrive in Rio over the next century. Those that survived the voyage (on average less than half) were taken to *casas de engorda* ("fattening houses") to gain weight before being sold at the Mercado Valongo, which during the 19th century was the largest slave market in the world.

While waiting to be hauled off to gold mines and coffee plantations, slaves congregated in the square known as Largo de São Francisco da Prainha, where they chanted and beat rhythms on improvised drums—resulting in the birth of Rio's samba. Numerous elements of African culture persevered, earning the port zone the nickname "Little Africa." Following the abolition of slavery, many free slaves from Bahia migrated to the area and began settling on the hillside known as Morro da Providência. Considered Rio's first *favela*, this community still retains its strong Afro-Brazilian roots.

The Port Zone had been neglected until, spurred on by the 2014 World Cup and 2016 Olympics, the area was earmarked for a major overhaul. Baptized Porto Maravilha, the massive revitalization project plans to improve existing communities and create new ones by investing in residential, commercial, and cultural spaces, such as the **Museu de Arte do Rio** and the completed **Museu de Amanhã** (Museum of Tomorrow).

There's also been a movement to highlight the area's past as a cradle of Afro-Brazilian culture. Saúde and Gamboa have become hot spots to hear traditional samba, particularly in the picturesque square known as Pedra do Sal, where *samba de rodas* erupt every Monday and Friday night. A **Historical and Archaeological Circuit Celebrating African Heritage** (http://portomaravilha. com.br/circuito) allows visitors to investigate historically important sites.

some extra time to kill, you can combine its attractions into a day trip.

QUINTA DA BOA VISTA AND MUSEU NACIONAL

A former sugar plantation, the **Quinta da Boa Vista** (Av. Pedro II between Rua Almirante Baltazar and Rua Dom Meinrado, São Cristóvão, 9am-4:30pm Tues.-Sun.) was where Brazil's imperial family took up residence between 1822 and 1889. The expansive grounds feature tree-lined walkways, flower gardens, lakes, and even a zoo.

The emperors lived in the stately neoclassical Palácio de São Cristóvão, now home to the **Museu Nacional** (tel. 21/2562-6901, www. museunacional.ufrj.br, 10am-4pm Tues.-Sun., R$3). Brazil's oldest scientific museum houses an enormous, somewhat dusty collection started by Dom João VI. The archaeological section focuses on prehistoric Latin American peoples, while the ethnological collection has

some artifacts related to Brazil's indigenous cultures. Among the highlights is the Bendigo Meteorite, which landed in the state of Bahia in 1888 and is the heaviest metallic mass ever known to have crashed through the planet's atmosphere. To get to the Quinta da Boa Vista, take the Metrô to São Cristóvão.

FEIRA DE SÃO CRISTÓVÃO

Near the Quinta da Boa Vista is the traditional **Feira de São Cristóvão** (Pavilhão de São Cristóvão, São Cristóvão, tel. 21/2580-5335, www.feiradesaocristovao.org.br, 10am-6pm Tues.-Thurs., 10am-10pm Fri.-Sun., R$3). Also known as the Centro Luiz Gonzaga de Tradições Nordestinas, this massive outdoor market has 700 *barracas* (stalls), where vendors hawk products ranging from handwoven hammocks from Ceará and leather hats and sandals from the sunbaked Sertão to jars of herb-infused *cachaças* from Bahia. Tuesday-Thursday you'll find lots of places for typical lunches. The good times don't really roll, however, until the weekends, when the *barracas* stay open around the clock and *nordestino* expats and fun-loving Cariocas congregate to listen to performances of *forró* and *repentistas* (musical preachers) as well as samba and *música popular Brasileiro* (MPB). To get to the *feira*, take any bus marked São Cristóvão leaving from the Zona Sul. By night, take a taxi.

Lapa

One of Rio's most traditional and notorious neighborhoods, Lapa has had many incarnations. It was originally a beach known as the "Spanish Sands" before being paved over and made into a rather posh 19th-century residential neighborhood. The **Passeio Público** (Rua do Passeio Público, Lapa, 7:30am-9pm daily) evokes what Lapa must have been like when it was still a swank *bairro* where well-to-do families strolled beneath the shady trees of this elegant park.

By the turn of the 20th century, Lapa's fortunes had declined. Until the late 1990s, the neighborhood was very down and out. Then, unexpectedly, a renaissance began to take hold of Lapa, which became famous for its intensely vibrant nightlife, where Cariocas from all walks of life congregate to eat, drink, and dance the night away. Lapa is still somewhat seedy around the edges—take cabs at night. It's still a wonderfully atmospheric slice of old Rio that shouldn't be missed.

ARCOS DA LAPA

Lapa's most iconic landmark is the **Arcos da Lapa** (much of it passes above Largo da Lapa). Originally known as the Aqueduto da Carioca, this distinctly Roman 42-arch aqueduct was built in 1750 to supply fresh water from the Rio da Carioca to the residents of Centro.

CATEDRAL METROPOLITANA

Close to the Arcos de Lapa, the **Catedral Metropolitana** (Av. República de Chile 245, tel. 21/2240-2669, 7am-6pm daily, free) is a cone-shaped modernist cathedral built between 1964 and 1979. The spacious interior is coupled with a pared-down minimalism conducive to contemplation. Visit on a sunny day and be bewitched by the colorful patterns refracted through the four immense stained-glass windows. A small **Museu de Arte Sacra** (R$2) includes objects such as the baptismal fonts used to christen the emperors' offspring and the gold roses Princesa Isabel received from Pope Leo XII after abolishing slavery.

Santa Teresa

In the 19th century, wealthy Cariocas built gracious villas along Santa Teresa's narrow winding streets, with terraces and balconies overlooking the blue waters of the Baía de Guanabara. The views are still alluring—as is the neighborhood, which is why after a long period of decline many artists began to move in during the 1960s and '70s, snatching up the dilapidated villas for a song and transforming them into ateliers and galleries. A second revitalization began to take place in 2005, resulting in the trickling in of boutique hotels and fashionable bistros as well as improved security (surrounded by *favelas*, Santa Teresa has traditionally had a somewhat questionable reputation).

Santa Teresa has gradually evolved into a vibrant community, and many small-scale artistic and musical events take place in "Santa" on a regular basis. Among the most popular is **Portas Abertas** (www.chavemestra.com.br), during which resident artists literally "open doors" to their homes and studios—usually during a weekend in mid-August—so you can view their work (and their often fantastic living spaces).

Until *bonde* (trolley) service resumes, get here via minibus (from Largo da Carioca in Centro) or by taxi, but be forewarned that some cabbies refuse to tackle the steep slopes due to the difficulty of getting a return fare. On foot, the quickest, least-exhausting climbs are via the Escadaria Selarón in Lapa and Rua Cândido Mendes (near the Glória Metrô station) in Glória.

MUSEU CHÁCARA DO CÉU

The **Museu Chácara do Céu** (Rua Murtinho Nobre 93, tel. 21/3970-1126, www.museuscastromaya.com.br, noon-5pm Wed.-Mon., R$2, free Wed.) is among Rio's loveliest museums. Surrounded by a hilltop garden, the museum is located in a modernist house built in 1957 by Raimundo Castro Maia, a wealthy business magnate whose impressive private collection includes the works of some fine Brazilian masters, such as Alberto da Veiga Guignard, Emiliano Di Cavalcanti, and Cândido Portinari.

Adjacent to the museum is the **Parque das Ruínas** (Rua Murtinho Nobre 169, tel. 21/2215-0621, 8am-8pm Tues.-Sun.), a small but leafy park built around the atmospheric ruins of a palace that belonged to Laurinda Santos Lobo, a wealthy Carioca who was a generous patron of the arts during the early 1900s. Today, its renovated remains house a cultural center that features art exhibits. A small café offers magnificent views.

Glória and Catete

In the mid-19th century, the neighborhoods of Glória and Catete lured Rio's burgeoning upper-middle class, and they remained fashionable addresses until the mid-20th century. Since then, the area has lost some of its luster; however, Catete in particular is quite lively, with lots of local bars and restaurants.

IGREJA NOSSA SENHORA DA GLÓRIA DO OUTEIRO

The *bairro* Glória is named after the dazzling white **Igreja Nossa Senhora da Glória do Outeiro** (Praça Nossa Senhora da Glória, Glória, tel. 21/2557-4600, www.outeirodagloria.org.br, 9am-noon and 1pm-5pm Mon.-Fri., 9am-noon Sat.-Sun., free). This early baroque church, built between 1714 and 1739, is one of the most stunning in Rio and a personal favorite of the Brazilian royal family; many princes and princesses have been baptized here. Visiting involves a steep climb up the Ladeira da Glória or a less-exhausting ride up the restored 1940s funicular (accessed at Rua do Russell 300). If the church is closed, ask for the keys at the **Museu da Imperial Irmandade de Nossa Senhora da Glória** (in the annex of the church on Praça Nossa Senhora da Glória, 9am-5pm Mon.-Fri., 9am-1pm Sat.-Sun., R$2), a small museum with religious art, ex-votos, and some personal belongings of the Empress Teresa Cristina.

bucolic Santa Teresa

Favelas

The first *favelas* ("slums") in Rio de Janeiro developed in the late 1890s. The federal government had offered land to demobilized soldiers from northeastern Brazil so that they could settle on Rio's vacant slopes. When the government went back on its word, the soldiers occupied the promised land and baptized it Morro da Favela (*favela* is a tough, thorny plant native to the semiarid Northeast). Subsequent *favelados* were freed slaves who immigrated to Rio in search of work and settled on the hillsides. As Rio grew, so did its *favelas*. Today, Rio has more than 600 *favelas*, home to 20-25 percent of the city's population. Unfortunately, they are growing at a much faster rate than the rest of the city.

Rio's *favelas* are notorious for their proximity to Rio's upscale neighborhoods and the drug cartels that control many of them. The drug lords maintain order and security in return for residents' loyalty. Consequences include drug use, drug dealing, and violent shoot-outs between drug lords and the police. While some *favelas* are desolate places where families live in minuscule shacks, others have developed into organized communities that engage in grassroots activism. Residents may have low-paying jobs in surrounding neighborhoods, access to day care, medical clinics, and local businesses, and live in concrete or cinder-block houses with fridges, stoves, TVs, and Wi-Fi.

Over the last two decades, projects such as Favela Bairro have helped integrate these communities into the city's urban fabric. *Favelas* are now included on city maps, and *favelados* are being given legal titles to their property. Rio's government has also installed permanent police units (UPPs) in many of Rio's more centrally located *favelas*.

Favela tours are available with guides such as English-speaking Marcelo Armstrong, who has been operating **Favela Tour** (tel. 21/3322-2727, www.favelatour.com.br) for more than 20 years. He leads groups on three-hour walking tours of the *favelas* of Rocinha and Vila Canoas; part of the tour fee is donated to community projects. Personalized tours are available with **Favela Adventure** (tel. 21/8221-5572, http://favelatour.org), founded by Rocinha native DJ Zezinho. During a customized tour (4-6 hours), visitors are adopted by English-speaking residents as they visit capoeira classes, samba *festas*, and local eateries.

PALÁCIO AND PARQUE DO CATETE

When Brazil was declared a republic, the **Palácio do Catete,** the former mansion of a German baron, became the official residence of Brazil's presidents. It remained so until 1960, when president No. 18, Juscelino Kubitschek, moved the capital to Brasília. Kubitschek was also responsible for transforming his opulent former digs into the **Museu da República** (Rua do Catete 153, Catete, tel. 21/3235-2650, www.museudarepublica.org.br, 10am-4:30pm Tues.-Fri., 11am-5:30pm Sat.-Sun., R$6, free Wed. and Sun.). The highlight is the apartment where President Getúlio Vargas lived—and died. Seemingly frozen in time from the day he shot himself in 1954, it features the smoking revolver along with his bloodied pajamas with the fatal bullet hole. The palace itself, with its stained-glass windows, shiny parquet floors, and lavish marble fixtures, is quite grand.

It is surrounded by the **Parque do Catete** (9am-6pm daily), a green oasis decked out with imperial palms, fish ponds, and serpentine paths. The grounds include an exhibition space, a theater, a small cinema, and a café. Adjacent to the *palácio* is the small **Museu de Folclore Edison Carneiro** (Rua do Catete 179-181, Catete, tel. 21/2285-0441, www.cnfcp.gov.br, 9am-5pm Tues.-Fri., 3pm-6pm Sat.-Sun., free), which has a collection of Brazilian folk art.

Flamengo and Laranjeiras

Stretching along the Baía de Guanabara from Centro to the tunnel that leads to Copacabana is the sprawling *bairro* of Flamengo. In the 19th and early 20th centuries, it was one of Rio's poshest residential neighborhoods. To this day, gracious belle epoque mansions and art deco apartment buildings still line its wide avenues and tree-lined side streets.

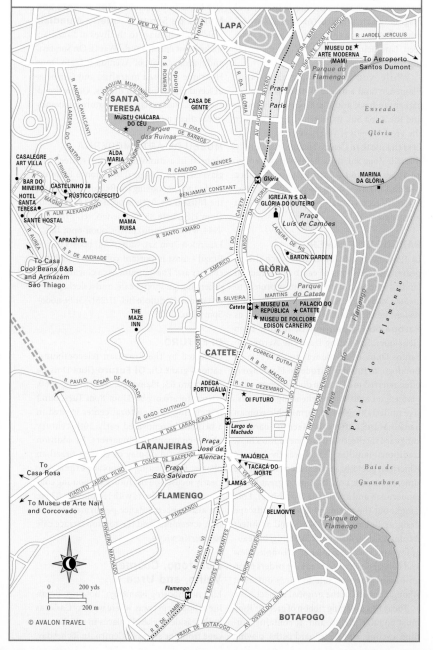

Santa Teresa, Glória, Catete, and Flamengo

AV MEM DA SÁ

Trolley

LAPA

R JARDEL JERCULIS

R S ROMERO

R DA GLÓRIA

Blonde

R JOAQUIM MURTINHO

AV INFANTE DOM HENRIQUE

AV BEIRA MAR

MUSEU DE
ARTE MODERNA ★
(MAM)

To Aeroporto
Santos Dumont

Parque do
Flamengo

SANTA
TERESA

CASA DE
GENTE

Praça
Paris

Enseada
da
Glória

R ANDRÉ CAVALCANTI

MUSEU CHÁCARA
DO CÉU ★

R DIAS
DE BARROS

Parque
das Ruínas

LADEIRA DO CASTRO

R TRIUNFO

ALDA
MARIA

R ALM ALEXANDRINO

R CÂNDIDO

MENDES

MARINA
DA GLÓRIA

CASALEGRE
ART VILLA

Gloria

BAR DO
MINEIRO

MAGNO

CASTELINHO 38

R BENJAMIM CONSTANT

AV AUGUSTO SEVERO

R DA GLÓRIA

IGREJA N S DA
GLÓRIA DO OUTEIRO

HOTEL
SANTA
TERESA

RÚSTICO/CAFECITO

R ALM ALEXANDRINO

Praça
Luís de Camões

SANTÉ HOSTAL

R AUREA

MAMA
RUISA

R SANTO AMARO

LARGO DA GLÓRIA

Ladeira de NS

APRAZÍVEL

R F DE ANDRADE

BARON GARDEN

To Casa
Cool Beans B&B
and Armazém
São Thiago

R P AMÉRICO

GLÓRIA

Parque
do Catete

Flamengo

Praia
do
Flamengo

R BENTO

R SILVEIRA

MARTINS

Catete

MUSEU DA ★
REPÚBLICA

PALACIO DO
★ CATETE

THE
MAZE
INN

★ MUSEU DE FOLCLORE
EDISON CARNEIRO

LISBOA

R F VIANA

R PAULO CÉSAR DE ANDRADE

CATETE

R CORREIA DUTRA

R B DE MACEDO

R GAGO COUTINHO

ADEGA
PORTUGÁLIA

R 2 DE DEZEMBRO

OI FUTURO

AV INFANTE DOM HENRIQUE

Parque do Flamengo

PRAIA DO FLAMENGO

R DAS LARANJEIRAS

Largo do
Machado

Praça
José de
Alencar

LARANJEIRAS

To
Casa Rosa

R CONDE DE BAEPENDI

MAJÓRICA

Praça
São Salvador

TACACÁ DO
NORTE

R VERGUEIRO

Baía de
Guanabara

LAMAS

To Museu de Arte Naïf
and Corcovado

VIADUTO JARDEL FILHO

FLAMENGO

R PAISSANDU

BELMONTE

Parque do
Flamengo

RUA PINHEIRO MACHADO

R PAULO VI

0   200 yds

0   200 m

Flamengo

R MARQUES DE ABRANTES

R SENHOR VERGUEIRO

© AVALON TRAVEL

R B DE ITAMBI

PRAIA DE BOTAFOGO

AV OSWALDO CRUZ

BOTAFOGO

Squeezed between Flamengo, Catete, and Cosme Velho is the equally lovely *bairro* of Laranjeiras, whose name attests to its rural origins, when orchards of "orange trees" reigned. Although there are few sights to be seen, Laranjeiras is one of Rio's most charming neighborhoods.

While you'll glimpse snatches of Flamengo (and adjacent Botafogo) as you're careening back and forth between Centro and the Zona Sul, its worthwhile to wander the area's streets if you have time to spare. Less chaotic than Centro and far less touristy than the Zona Sul, these neighborhoods offer an appealing and colorful slice of Carioca life, and the area shelters one of Rio's most extensive recreational spaces, the Parque do Flamengo.

PARQUE DO FLAMENGO

In 1960, much of Flamengo's beach disappeared beneath tons of earth. This radical landfill was part of an ambitious project to create a vast public park on prime oceanfront real estate that would come to be known as **Parque do Flamengo** (Av. Infante Dom Henrique). Extending from the Aeroporto Santos Dumont all the way to the Praia de Botafogo, to this day Parque do Flamengo is often referred to as Aterro do Flamengo—the Flamengo Landfill. Spearheading this massive undertaking was a formidable woman named Maria Carlota de Macedo Soares. A vanguard intellectual from one of Rio's most traditional families, "Lota" was the lover of American poet Elizabeth Bishop (who, at the time, lived with Lota in Rio). A great fan of modernism and a self-taught architect, Lota sought out the talents of leading landscape designer Roberto Burle Marx and architect Affonso Eduardo Reidy. Battling bureaucracy and machismo—her all-male crew and colleagues balked at taking orders from a woman—she was able to carry out most (though not all) of the original project.

Today this sweeping ribbon of green is Rio's most popular playground. It contains running, cycling, and skateboard paths, playing fields, a children's park, a puppet theater, and an area reserved for model planes. It is also home to the somber **Monumento aos Mortos de Segunda Guerra Mundial,** which pays homage to the lives of Brazilian soldiers lost during World War II. On Sundays and holidays, part of Avenida Infante Dom Henrique is closed to traffic, and Cariocas descend on the park in droves. On weekend evenings, outdoor concerts feature top names in Brazilian music.

MUSEU DE ARTE MODERNA

Housed in a stunning modernist steel and glass creation, designed by Affonso Eduardo Reidy and overlooking the Baía de Guanabara, the **Museu de Arte Moderna** (Av. Infante Dom Henrique 85, Flamengo, tel. 21/2240-4944, www.mamrio.com.br, noon-6pm Tues.-Fri., noon-7pm Sat.-Sun., R$8) boasts one of Brazil's most important collections of 20th-century art. The museum has a cinema, an excellent design shop, a café, and a sleek, pricey restaurant, **Laguiole** (tel. 21/2517-3129, noon-5pm Mon.-Fri.).

OI FUTURO

Operated by the Brazilian telecommunications giant Oi, **Oi Futuro** (Rua Dois de Dezembro 63, Flamengo, tel. 21/3131-3060, www.oifuturo.org.br, 11am-8pm Tues.-Sun.) is a cutting-edge cultural center located in a brilliantly renovated early 20th-century phone company headquarters. In addition to a delightful display of vintage Brazilian phones, Oi's rotating temporary exhibits are clearly focused on the future, combining contemporary visual arts with technology. There are also concerts, dance performances, and film screenings, and the rooftop terrace café has terrific views.

Botafogo, Cosme Velho, and Urca

Like neighboring Flamengo, Botafogo began life as bucolic getaway where wealthy Cariocas built seaside weekend palaces in which to escape from the stress of Centro. In its heyday, the white crescent beach of Botafogo was the equivalent of Ipanema today. Although it remains lovely from an aesthetic viewpoint (and serves as a very scenic soccer field), the pollution here means nobody would dream of bathing in its waters these days. The neighborhood has suffered from an onslaught of verticalization via modern high-rises and shopping centers. However, its tranquil, leafy side streets are stuffed with cinemas, bookstores, and restaurants that are prized by Cariocas and largely ignored by tourists.

To the north of Botafogo, Cosme Velho is a pretty residential neighborhood that winds its way up the hills toward Corcovado. At the Estação Cosme Velho, hordes of tourists line up to catch the mini-train that whisks them up the mountain to the outstretched arms of *Cristo Redentor.*

Squeezed onto a promontory facing Botafogo, the tiny residential neighborhood of Urca has resisted much of the urban mayhem characteristic of Rio's other beachside *bairros.* It is a lovely place to stroll around, take in some alluring views, and watch local fisherman cast their lines off into the Baía de Guanabara.

MUSEU DO ÍNDIO

Occupying a handsome 19th-century mansion in Botafogo, the **Museu do Índio** (Rua das Palmeiras 55, Botofago, tel. 21/3214-8700, www.museudoindio.org.br, 9am-5:30pm Tues.-Fri., 1pm-5pm Sat.-Sun., R$3, free Sun.) was founded in 1953 by noted Brazilian anthropologist Darcy Ribeiro. Linked to FUNAI—Brazil's national foundation of indigenous affairs—it possesses an important collection of artifacts reflecting Brazil's diverse native peoples. Among the objects on display are hunting and cooking implements, traditional costumes—including headdresses fashioned out of the Technicolor plumage of Amazonian parrots and toucans—musical instruments, and religious talismans. The museum shop sells an attractive (and decently priced) array of authentic handicrafts.

MORRO DONA MARTA

Rising up from Rua São Clemente, Dona Marta was one of Rio's most infamously dangerous *favelas* before becoming the first to receive a UPP (Police Pacification Unit) in 2008. Shortly thereafter, residents were happy to receive a *plano inclinado* elevator to whisk them up the *morro* to their homes (instead of the 788 precarious stairs cut into the vertiginously steep hillside). Today, visitors can also take the free elevator, which makes five stops on its way to the top. At Estação 3, visit Praça Cantão, where dozens of homes have been painted in juicy fruit hues by Dutch artists Dre Urhann and Jeroen Koolhaas. At the summit, the Mirante Dona Marta offers stunning city and bay views, while the statue of *Cristo Redentor* looms overhead. A short walk through narrow streets leads to the Espaço Michael Jackson, where a lifelike bronze statue and mosaic mural by artist Romero Britto commemorates the spot where MJ filmed the Spike Lee-directed video to his song "They Don't Care About Us."

Free maps are available at the Rio Top Tour kiosk near the entrance to the elevator. If you don't speak Portuguese, take one of themed tours with local resident Thiago Firminio, who runs **Favela Santa Marta Tour** (tel. 21/9177-9459, www.favelasantamartatour.blogspot.com.br, 2 hours, R$50).

CASA DAROS

Rio scored a coup when it was chosen to house the first Latin American outpost by the Swiss Daros Foundation, whose Zurich headquarters consolidates one of the most renowned collections of Latin American art on the planet. **Casa Daros** (Rua General Severiano 159, Botafogo, tel. 21/2275-0246, www.casa-daros.net, noon-8pm Wed.-Sat., noon-6pm Sun., R$12, free Wed.) plays host to temporary exhibits as well as a permanent collection of 117 works by contemporary artists. The Casa alone is worth a visit; the landmark neoclassical house dates to 1866 and originally functioned as an orphanage. The imposing building was designed by Francisco

Joaquim de Bethancourt da Silva, who is also responsible for the Centro Cultural Banco do Brasil. There is a boutique and the wonderful café-restaurant, **Mira!,** where you can enjoy a meal al fresco beneath a row of elegant imperial palms.

★ CORCOVADO

One of Rio's most instantly recognizable and oft-visited icons, "Hunchback" (the English translation lacks the lyrical sonority of its Portuguese name) Corcovado mountain rises straight up from the center of Rio to a lofty 700 meters (2,300 feet). Equally iconic is the 30-meter (100-foot) art deco statue *Cristo Redentor* (Christ the Redeemer), his outstretched arms enveloping the surrounding city, which crowns Corcovado's sheer granite face. The statue, a gift from France to commemorate 100 years of Brazilian independence in 1921, didn't actually make it up to the top of the mountain until 1931. Since then, however, it has become a true beacon, visible from almost anywhere in the city. It is particularly striking at night when, due to a powerful illumination system, the *Cristo* glows like an otherworldly angel against the darkened sky.

The most scenic way to get to the top of Corcovado is by taking the 19th-century cogwheel train from the **Estação de Ferro do Corcovado** (Rua Cosme Velho 530, Cosme Velho, www.corcovado.com.br, tel. 21/2558-1329, departures every 30 minutes 8:30am-7pm daily, R$46 round-trip), which was inaugurated in 1884 by Dom Pedro II. The crazily steep ride takes 17 minutes—with a stop at Paineiras station—and treats you to stunning views, especially if you're at the back or on the right side of the train. At the top, reach the *Cristo* by walking up a flight of 220 steep steps or taking an escalator or panoramic elevator. From Paineiras station, where there's a parking lot for cars, you can hop a van (make sure it's registered with IBAMA, the parks organization)—round-trip fares cost R$21 (Mon.-Fri.) and R$31 (Sat.-Sun.). It's best to beat the crowds by heading up early on a weekday morning, when you'll have the added privilege of seeing Rio bathed in golden light—be sure to choose a clear day for your visit.

MUSEU INTERNACIONAL DE ARTE NAÏF DO BRASIL

The **Museu Internacional de Arte Naïf do Brasil** (Rua Cosme Velho 561, Cosme Velho, tel. 21/2205-8612, 10am-6pm Tues.-Fri., 10am-5pm Sat.-Sun., R$12) lays claim to having the world's largest collection of *arte naïf,* or naive art. The delightfully expressive and colorful paintings in this colonial mansion portray many elements of popular Brazilian culture, including *futebol,* Carnaval, and scenes from daily life. Although most of the exhibited works, spanning five centuries, are by self-taught Brazilian artists, there are international works from more than 100 countries. A small boutique sells *naïf* art from contemporary artists, and there's also an organic café.

A little farther uphill from the museum, on the opposite side of the street, is the **Largo de**

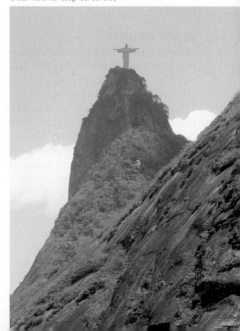

Cristo Redentor atop Corcovado

Pão de Açúcar

and small shops. The second stop is at the actual 396-meter (1,300-foot) summit of Pão de Açúcar, where you can toast the view with champagne or a beer.

The cars depart for the top every 20 minutes from **Praia Vermelha** (Av. Pasteur 520, Urca, tel. 21/2546-8400, www.bondinho. com.br, 8am-9pm daily, ticket booths close at 7:45pm, R$53 round-trip). Be sure the day is a clear one, but to avoid long lines, steer clear of weekends, holidays, and peak hours (10am-3pm). If you're in a romantic frame of mind—or would like to be—make the trip in the late afternoon. The sunset and twilight, with the lights of Rio glittering in the dusk against the mountain silhouettes, are truly bewitching.

Adventurous types can hike the steep but short trails from Praça General Tibúrcio up to Morro da Urca (and continue by cable car at a reduced rate) or scale Morro Pão de Açúcar in the company of a climbing outfit. The 2.4-km (1.5-mi) Pista Claudio Coutinho is an easier, paved trail that winds its way along the sea-lapped base of both *morros*.

Boticário (Rua Cosme Velho 822). Named after the imperial family's *boticário* (apothecary), who was a resident, this enchanting 19th-century square resembles a period film set, with colorfully painted villas offset by tropical foliage.

★ PÃO DE AÇÚCAR

The monumental chunk of granite guarding the entrance to the Baía de Guanabara is known as **Pão de Açúcar**. Rio's original Tupi inhabitants referred to it as *pau-nh-acugua* (high, pointed, mountain). When the Portuguese arrived on the scene, both the Tupi term and the mountain reminded them of a *pão de açúcar* (sugar loaf), a conical mound of sugar made by pouring liquid cane juice into a rounded mold. The name stuck.

Reach the summit by taking a glass-sided **cable car** up the mountain—an unforgettably scenic journey offering panoramic views of Rio and the Baía de Guanabara. The first stop is at **Morro da Urca,** a 210-meter (690-foot) mountain, where there is a restaurant

Copacabana and Leme

Although its glamour days are long gone, Copacabana still manages to live up to its legend as the world's most famous strip of white sand. Originally a tiny fishing village, with the construction of the luxurious Copacabana Palace hotel in 1923, the wealthy and fabulous came flocking. A slew of streamlined art deco apartment buildings soon rose up along the beachfront's Avenida Atlântica. Before long, "Copa" was not just *the* place to live but *the* place to party. Tycoons, movie stars, royalty, and the international jet set transformed its sweeping carpet of sand into their personal playground.

While many of Rio's rich and fashionable have since moved on to the more chic neighborhoods of Ipanema and Leblon, Copa has become—for better or for worse—one of Rio's most eclectic, vibrant, and democratic neighborhoods, a place where street kids and millionaires, models and muscle men, doormen and nannies from the Northeast of

Beach Dos and Don'ts

Cariocas have developed a very sophisticated *cultura de praia* with habits and codes worth taking note of if you want to blend in.

- **Don't** wear a bathing suit from home; purchase one on location. Rio's cutting-edge bikini and *sunga* (the male version of a bikini) styles are light-years ahead of the rest of the world, and prices are generally affordable.

- **Do** wear flip-flops (Havaianas are the coolest) to and from the beach and **don't** wear shoes.

- **Don't** take any valuables to the beach and don't leave possessions unguarded. Take a beach bag instead of a purse and ask a respectable-looking neighbor to keep an eye on your stuff while you take a dip.

- **Don't** bring a towel to the beach. *Cangas* are lighter, de rigueur, and are sold all over the beaches. For more comfort, rent a chair.

- **Don't** schlep food or drinks to the beach. Rio's beaches are well-serviced with food and drink vendors.

- **Don't** go swimming if a red flag is flying; Rio's beaches have strong currents in places. Only go in the water where locals are already swimming.

- **Don't** get a sunburn. Not only will you suffer on your vacation, but the red lobster look will brand you a foolish gringo.

If you're female:

- **Do** know that Cariocas are not shy about revealing a lot of flesh. However…

- **Don't** take your top off. Topless sunbathing is a no-no and Cariocas are very proud of their tan lines.

- **Do** cover up (lightly) with a lightweight top and microshorts or skirts when walking to/from the beach.

If you're male:

- **Don't** don a Speedo-style bathing suit. Stylish *sungas* are modeled on men's full briefs.

- **Do** know that surfing shorts are for surfing or wearing over your bathing suit, *not* for lounging around on the sand or swimming.

- **Do** flaunt your bare chest to/from the beach, but otherwise wear a T-shirt.

Brazil, and American tourists from the deepest Midwest all rub shoulders. During the day senior citizens swarm the beaches and the dozens of bakeries along the main drag of Avenida Nossa Senhora de Copacabana, but by night the stretch of Avenida Atlântica toward Ipanema is a hot spot for prostitutes and for the (many foreign) johns who travel to Copa in search of more piquant forms of R&R. Inland from the ocean, unpretentious neighborhood restaurants, *botecos*, and street markets coexist alongside 24-hour gyms and juice bars. Copa may be a little seedy in places, but it is also fun—and whatever you may think of the *bairro*, there is no denying the allure of its beach.

★ COPACABANA BEACH

Urban beaches don't get any more dazzling than this 4.5-kilometer (2.8-mi) strip that stretches in a gorgeous arc from Pão de Açúcar to the Forte de Copacabana. The sand is sugary fine and white, and a striking contrast to the blue of the open Atlantic and the hypnotically wavy, white-and-black mosaic promenade that separates it from busy Avenida Atlântica. From dawn to dusk there is always something happening on Copa's beach—whether it's a sunrise yoga class for seniors, a *Vogue* photo shoot, or an early evening volleyball practice for preteen girls. You can get a tan or a tattoo, drink a caipirinha at a fancy *barraca* or an icy *água de coco* sold by one of many hundreds of *ambulantes,* who hawk everything from strangely addictive bags of Globo *biscoitos* to transistor radios. Of course, in a pinch, you can go swimming—the chilly temperatures coupled with an undercurrent demand caution—but you can also do so much more.

Like the neighborhood itself, Copacabana beach is stratified, with different points occupied by different "tribes." The 1-kilometer (0.6-mi) stretch closest to the Túnel Novo that leads to Botafogo—between Morro do Leme and Avenida Princesa Isabel—is known as **Praia do Leme** (the small, attractive residential *bairro* behind it is also known as Leme). Leme's warm waters are popular with families and older residents, while its swells lure surfers. A short path around the base of Pedra do Leme offers great views, or head to the nearby army base and follow a 20-minute paved trail that winds through a hummingbird-filled Atlantic forest to the summit, which is guarded by the whitewashed 18th-century **Forte Duque de Caxias** (Praça Almirante Júlio de Noronha, Leme, tel. 21/3223-5076, www.cep.ensino.eb.br, 9:30am-4:30pm Tues.-Sun., R$4).

The stretch of Copacabana in front of the Copacabana Palace is a gay haunt, while the patch near Rua Santa Clara is popular with fans of *futebol* and *futevolei* (a Brazilian version of volleyball). Closer to Ipanema, Postos 5 and 6 (posto refers to the beacon-like lifeguard posts) draw an eclectic mix of seniors and *favela* kids. At the very end, in front of the Forte de Copacabana, is one of the oldest and most traditional fishermen's colonies in Rio.

★ Ipanema and Leblon

The most coveted—and expensive—slice of beachfront property in Rio de Janeiro is the area from which the first chords of "A Garota de Ipanema" ("The Girl from Ipanema") were set down by two poets. The year was 1962, and Tom Jobim and Vinicius de Moraes were at their favorite neighborhood bar when an enticingly bronzed young Carioca sashayed by on her way to the beach, inspiring the languorously cool bossa nova jewel.

Copacabana beach

Botafogo, Leme, and Copacabana

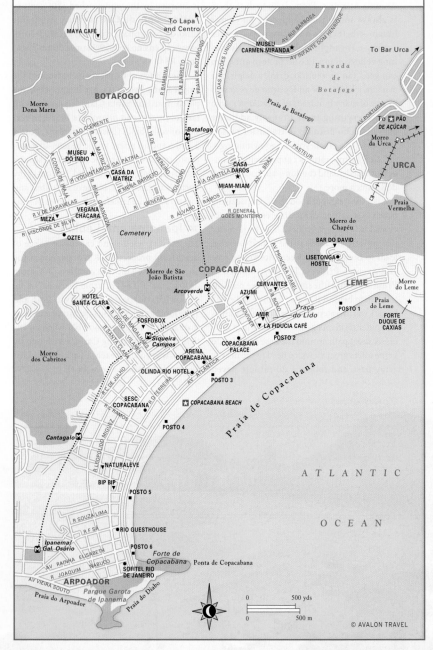

To Lapa and Centro

MAYA CAFÉ

MUSEU CARMEN MIRANDA

To Bar Urca

AV RUI BARBOSA

AV INFANTE DOM HENRIQUE

Enseada de Botafogo

R BAMBINA

R M BARRETO

PRAIA DE BOTAFOGO

AV DAS NAÇÕES UNIDAS

BOTAFOGO

Morro Dona Marta

R SÃO CLEMENTE

R DA MATRIZ

R 18 DE FEVEREIRO

R REAL GRANDEZA

Botafogo

Praia de Botafogo

AV PORTUGAL

To PÃO DE AÇÚCAR

Morro da Urca

MUSEU DO ÍNDIO

R CONDE DE IRAJÁ

R VOLUNTÁRIOS DA PÁTRIA

CASA DA MATRIZ

R MENA BARRETO

HOLIDO PIO

R A QUINTELA

CASA DAROS

AV N BRAZ

AV PASTEUR

URCA

Praia Vermelha

R GENERAL RAMOS

MIAM-MIAM

R V DE CARAVELAS

VEGANA CHÁCARA

R GENERAL

R ÁLVARO RAMOS

R GENERAL GOES MONTEIRO

Morro do Chapéu

MEZA

R VISCONDE DE SILVA

OZTEL

Cemetery

Morro de São João Batista

COPACABANA

BAR DO DAVID

LISETONGA HOSTEL

AV PRINCESA ISABEL

CERVANTES

Arcoverde

AZUMI

R BOJCO

LEME

Morro do Leme

HOTEL SANTA CLARA

R DÉCIO VILARES

FOSFOBOX

R DUVIVIER

AMIR

LA FIDUCIA CAFÉ

Praça do Lido

POSTO 1

Praia do Leme

FORTE DUQUE DE CAXIAS

Morro dos Cabritos

R SANTA CLARA

Siqueira Campos

ARENA COPACABANA

COPACABANA PALACE

POSTO 2

R C DE JULHO

OLINDA RIO HOTEL

AV ATLÂNTICA

POSTO 3

Praia de Copacabana

R C RAMOS

R D O FERREIRA

SESC COPACABANA

COPACABANA BEACH

Cantagalo

POSTO 4

R LEOPOLDO MIGUEZ

NATURALEVE

BIP BIP

POSTO 5

ATLANTIC

OCEAN

R SOUZA LIMA

R F SÁ

RIO GUESTHOUSE

Ipanema/ Gal. Osório

POSTO 6

Forte de Copacabana

Ponta de Copacabana

AV RAINHA ELISABETH

R JOAQUIM NABUCO

SOFITEL RIO DE JANEIRO

AV VIEIRA SOUTO

ARPOADOR

Parque Garota de Ipanema

Praia do Arpoador

Praia do Diabo

0   500 yds
0   500 m

© AVALON TRAVEL

Ipanema beach

the heads of "Two Brothers." During the week, the beaches are tranquil, but when the weekend rolls around, the sand is a sea of bikinied and *sunga*-ed bodies, engaging in activities as varied as playing *futevolei* and smoking illicit joints. On Sundays, the main oceanfront drags of Avenida Viera Souto (Ipanema) and Avenida Delfim Moreira (Leblon) are closed to traffic, and the whole area becomes a massive outdoor recreational scene.

Like Copa, Ipanema and Leblon are divided into tribal territories. With its big waves, **Praia do Arpoador** (the edge of Ipanema closest to Copa) is a mecca for surfers. The area around **Posto 8** (off Rua Farme de Amoedo) is a magnet for gay men to show off their *sungas,* while **Posto 9** (the area off of Rua Vinicius de Moraes) has long been the territory of artists and intellectuals who would rather flaunt their leftist viewpoints. **Posto 10** is pretty much a family affair, where young couples congregate with their tots to take advantage of the playground and diaper-changing facilities.

Lagoa

When strolling along the shady streets of Ipanema and Leblon, you'll see a vast lagoon ringed by luxury villas and apartment buildings set against the backdrop of mountains, including Corcovado. The **Lagoa Rodrigo de Freitas**—or simply Lagoa—is a saltwater lagoon of posh private clubs, skating parks, tennis courts, and a heliport where already svelte Cariocas power-walk, jog, and cycle until they break a sweat. The less athletically inclined prefer to sip an *água de coco* or a caipirinha at one of the many kiosks around the lagoon; all serve food and drinks. In the evening, live music is often played at the kiosks (the best are near the Parque dos Patins and the Corte do Cangalo).

On the north side of the Lagoa, the lower reaches of **Parque da Catacumba** (Av. Epitácio Pessoa 300, Lagoa, tel. 21/2247-9949, 8am-5pm, Tues.-Sun.) consist of winding paths through jungly gardens, a vivid backdrop for 31 sculptures created by Brazilian

Since then, Ipanema has been a magnet for a cosmopolitan mix of artists, musicians, and leftist intellectuals, along with a rich and trendy crowd who consistently fall prey to its tree-lined streets, fashionable bars and boutiques, and magnificent white sands. Ipanema retains a more bohemian edge than neighboring Leblon, which is slightly more sedate and residential (and richer), but no less appealing. Both, however, carry off the impressive feat of being both incredibly chic and disarmingly casual. To wit: The sight of tattooed surfer boys carrying their boards past the discreetly jeweled millionaires ensconced at the terraces of five-star restaurants is extremely common.

Ipanema and Leblon are essentially one long and captivating beach divided by the narrow Jardim de Alah canal. Straighter and narrower than Copacabana, this beach is no less scenic—Ipanema begins at the **Pedra do Arpoador,** a dramatic rock jutting into the sea, and Leblon ends at the twin-headed **Morro de Dois Irmãos,** a fantastically shaped mountain that really does conjure up

Ipanema, Leblon, and Lagoa

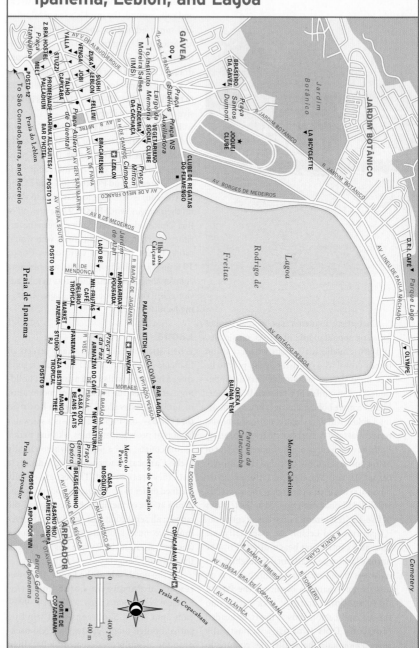

GÁVEA

AV. PDE. L. FRANCA

AV. V DE ALBUQUERQUE

To Instituto
Moreira Salles
(IMS)

BRASEIRO
DA GÁVEA

Praça
Santos
Dumont

JOQUEI
CLUBE

Jardim
Botânico

JARDIM BOTÂNICO

LA BICYCLETTE

R. JARDIM BOTÂNICO

R. JARDIM BOTÂNICO

Z. BRA HOSTEL
YALLA
VENGAI
ZUKA
JOBI
STUZZI
CAPIXABA
SUSHI
LEBLON
FELLINI
ACADEMIA
DA CACHAÇA

Praça NS
SOAL CLUBE

Largo da
VEGETARIANO

Praça
Sibélius Auxiliadora

Praça
Atiel JOQUEI
CLUBE

Ataulpha
MELT
PALLADIUM
PROMENADE: MARINA ALLSUITES/
POSTO 12
BAR D'HOTEL
BRACARENSE
LEBLON

R. N DE CAMPOS

Milton
Campos

Praça
Atahyr

Jardim
de Alah

AV. DE MELO FRANCO

CLUBE DE REGATAS
DO FLAMENGO

AV. BORGES DE MEDEIROS

Lagoa
Rodrigo de
Freitas

Praça
de Quental

AV. DE PAIVA

AV. V. DE NÓTRE

AV. V. DE MEDEIROS

Ilha dos
Caiçaras

POSTO 11

POSTO 10

AV. VIEIRA SOUTO

R. DE
MENDONÇA

LADO BÉ

To São Conrado, Barra, and Recreio

Praia do Leblon

Praia de Ipanema

R. BARÃO DE JAGUARIPE

MARGARIDA'S
POUSADA

MIL-FRUTAS
CAFÉ
DELIRIO
TROPICAL
MARKET
IPANEMA

R. VISC.

R. BARÃO DA TORRE

PALAPHITA KITCH
CICLOVIA
BAR LAGOA

da Paz

Praça NS

AV. EPITÁCIO PESSOA

IPANEMA

MORAES

Lagoa
Rodrigo de
Freitas

STUDIO
TROPICAL
RJ

ZAZA BISTRO
TROPICAL

IPANEMA INN

MANGO
TREE

ARMAZÉM DO CAFÉ
DE PIRAJÁ

NEW NATURAL

CASA COOL
BEANS FLATS

BRASILERINHO
Osório

Praça
General

OKEKA
BAIANA TEM

Morro do
Pavão

Morro do
Cangagão

D.R.I. CAFÉ

AV. LINEIRO DE PAULA MACHADO

Parque Lage

OLYMPE

Lagoa

Parque da
Catacumba

Morro dos Cabritos

AV. H. DOOSWORTH

POSTO 9

CASA
MOSQUITO

AVENIDA E.D.A. BELGICA

POSTO 6-8

BARRETO-LONDRA

R. FRANCISCO SÁ

R. GENERAL
R. R. BARÃO DA TORRE

FASANO RIO/
ÁRPOADOR INN

R. OTAVIANO

ÁRPOADOR

Parque Garota
de Ipanema

FORTE DE
COPACABANA

Parque
de Ipanema

Praia do Arpoador

COPACABANA BEACH

AV. NOSSA SRA DE COPACABANA

R. BARATA RIBEIRO

R. SANTA CLARA

R. TONELERO

AV. ATLÂNTICA

Praia de Copacabana

Cemetery

0   400 yds.

0   400 m

and international artists. A steep but easy 20-minute trail leads through replanted Atlantic rain forest to lookout points that offer sublime views of the entire Zona Sul. The park's name stems from the belief that the site originally sheltered "catacombs" for Rio's original Tamoio inhabitants.

Jardim Botânico

On the far side of the Lagoa (across from Ipanema) is the lush upscale neighborhood of Jardim Botânico. Some of the city's chicest restaurants and bars are tucked away here.

A 138-hectare (340-acre) urban oasis, the **Jardim Botânico** itself (Rua Jardim Botânico 1008, tel. 21/3874-1808, www.jbrj.gov.br, 8am-5pm daily, R$7) offers an unparalleled mix of native Atlantic forest, lagoons covered with giant lily pads, and more than 8,000 plant species. Many of them—pineapples, cinnamon, and tea among them—were introduced here prior to their cultivation in the rest of Brazil. Highlights include the scent garden, the cactus garden, and the fabulous *orquidário*, featuring more than 1,000 species of wild orchids. Kids (and adults) with a fondness for the mildly gruesome will enjoy the carnivorous plant collection.

Adjacent to the Jardim Botânico is the **Parque Lage** (Rua Jardim Botânico 414, tel. 21/3257-1800, 8am-5pm daily, free), designed by 19th-century English landscaper John Tyndale. Its winding paths snake around small ponds, grottos, an aquarium, and through the lush tropical landscape that covers the lower slopes of Corcovado (a steep trail winds up through the **Parque Nacional da Tijuca**). In the midst of the greenery is the early 20th-century mansion of a wealthy industrialist who built the stately abode for his opera singer wife. The internal courtyard is home to **D.R.I. Café** (Rua Jardim Botânico 414, tel. 21/2226-8125, www.driculinaria. com.br, 9am-5pm daily), a beguiling spot for coffee. The palace houses the Escola de Artes Visuais, an art school where temporary exhibits are often held.

Gávea

Less hip and happening than Ipanema and neighboring Leblon, Gávea is still an attractive neighborhood with lots of leafy streets, easy access to the Lagoa, and a lively bar scene.

JOQUEI CLUBE

You've likely never seen a racetrack with such stupendous surroundings (the *Cristo Redentor* hovers directly above the bleachers). Built in 1926, Rio's Joquei Clube, also known as the **Hipódromo da Gávea** (Praça Santos Dumont 131, tel. 21/3534-9000, www. jcb.com.br) was featured in a scene in the 1946 Hitchcock film *Notorious,* during which Cary Grant and Ingrid Bergman take some time out from espionage and romance to bet on the horses. Even if you don't want to gamble (race times are 6:15pm Mon., 5pm Fri., 2:45pm Sat.-Sun.), the club is a fun place to grab a drink (no shorts allowed) or to indulge in a relaxing massage or treatment at **Nirvana** (tel. 21/2187-0100, www.enirvana.com.br), an airy spa that offers yoga and Pilates.

INSTITUTO MOREIRA SALLES

Located halfway up a steep hill full of striking villas, the **Instituto Moreira Salles** (IMS; Rua Marquês de São Vicente 476, tel. 21/3284-7400, www.ims.com.br, 11am-8pm Tues.-Sun., free) is one of the city's loveliest cultural centers. One of Rio's most prominent families, the Moreira Salles (owners of Unibanco, a major bank) commissioned architect Olavo Redig de Campos to build this house in 1951, and the result is Brazilian modernism at its most streamlined and alluring. The equally enticing gardens were landscaped by Roberto Burle Marx. The Moreira Salles family has always had a strong commitment to the arts (Walter Salles Jr., director of the films *Central Station* and *The Motorcycle Diaries*, is a member of the clan), and part of their important collection of historical photographs, many depicting 19th- and 20th-century Rio de Janeiro, can be viewed, along with temporary exhibitions. There is also a cinema, boutique, and a café that serves a lavish afternoon tea and breakfasts on weekends.

São Conrado, Barra, and Recreio

Rio's coastal road, Avenida Niemeyer, goes through a long tunnel that burrows beneath the Morro de Dois Irmãos, whose slopes are home to one of Rio's largest *favelas,* Vidigal. While their beaches are attractive, the neighborhoods here lack the history and charm of the Zona Sul, and none were laid out with pedestrians in mind—cars rule, but the coastline is also well served by buses from the Zona Sul, with destinations marked Barra and Recreio.

São Conrado is a small neighborhood full of luxury high-rise condominiums and a fancy shopping mall. In a startling contrast, these posh edifices gaze directly onto Rio's biggest and most notorious *favela:* **Rocinha,** home to more than 200,000 residents, whose brick and cement dwellings cover the otherwise rain forest-carpeted Morro de Dois Irmãos. Although Rio is all about glaring contradictions and brutal extremes, nowhere else is the divide between rich and poor so prominently, fascinatingly, and perversely apparent. São Conrado's main draw is the small and spectacular **Praia do Pepino** (Cucumber Beach), where hang gliders burn off their adrenaline after taking off from the neighboring peaks of Pedra da Gávea and Pedra Bonita.

Another long tunnel brings you to the developed, suburban, Miami-like *bairro* of **Barra da Tijuca,** known simply as Barra. Two decades ago, this 16-kilometer (10-mi) stretch of coastline was little more than a long, wild sweep of white sand with a few *barracas.* Barra's saving grace is its beach, which remains amazingly unspoiled, particularly during the week. The trendiest strip, at the beginning of the Barra between Postos 1 and 2, is known as **Praia do Pepê** (access from Av. do Pepê). Although the surf is rough, you can swim here.

Barra da Tijuca turns into the 11-kilometer (7-mi) long beach known as **Recreio dos Bandeirantes,** whose rough waves are a magnet for Rio's surfing crowd. Particularly attractive is the small and secluded **Prainha** beach, at the end of Recreio. The spectacular waves and presence of several renowned surfing academies make it a mecca for surfers. Even more deserted is **Grumari,** whose reddish sands are framed by spectacular mountains covered in lush native Atlantic forest. Both Prainha and Grumari are located in protected nature reserves. Despite the fact they can't be reached by bus, they can fill up on the weekends with Cariocas seeking a quick back-to-nature fix. Near Grumari, **Praia de Abricó** is Rio's only nude beach.

MUSEU CASA DO PONTAL

Inland from the far end of Recreio dos Bandeirantes is the **Museu Casa do Pontal** (Estrada do Pontal 3295, tel. 21/2490-3278, www.popular.art.br/museucasadopontal, 9:30am-5pm Tues.-Sun., R$10). Back in the late 1940s, French designer and art collector Jacques Van de Beuque began traveling throughout Brazil (especially the Northeast), where he discovered a fantastically rich artisanal tradition that nobody—not even Brazilians—was aware of. To preserve and promote these works, he built a vast house surrounded by tranquil gardens. Today, it shelters the largest collection of Brazilian folk art in the country, with more than 5,000 works ranging from wonderful clay figures of popular Northeast folk heroes to the extravagant costumes worn by celebrants of traditional Bumba-Meu-Boi *festas.* To get here by bus from the Zona Sul, take any bus going to Barra da Tijuca and get off at Barra Shopping to transfer to the 703 or S-20 bus going to Recreio, which will let you off in front of the museum's entrance. Although it takes well over an hour to get here, the final destination is worth it.

SÍTIO ROBERTO BURLE MARX

The idyllic **Sítio Roberto Burle Marx** (Estrada Roberto Burle Marx 2019, tel. 21/2410-1412, www.sitioburlemarx.blogspot. com, tours by appointment only 9:30am and

1:30pm Tues.-Sun., R$10) is another attraction worth the time and effort to get to. Between 1949 and 1994, this bucolic country estate was the primary residence of renowned landscape architect Roberto Burle Marx, whose most famous projects in Rio include the Parque do Flamengo and Copacabana's iconic black-and-white mosaic "wave" promenade. The colonial house (originally part of a coffee plantation) and adjoining atelier have been transformed into a museum where you can admire the artist's works, possessions, and rich collection of Brazilian folk art. The surrounding nursery and gardens—featuring more than 3,500 plant species collected from Brazil and around the world—were designed with great flair. Indeed, it was said about Marx—who was also a painter—that he used plants as other artists used paint. If you don't have a car, take the bus marked Marambaia-Passeio (No. 387) that passes through the Zona Sul.

ENTERTAINMENT AND EVENTS

Rio boasts a dynamic arts scene. For information (in Portuguese), check out the arts sections of the two daily papers, *Jornal do Brasil* and *O Globo,* or purchase *Veja Rio,* which comes with *Veja* magazine and offers comprehensive listings of everything going on in the city. For upcoming events in English as well as Portuguese, visit www.rioguiaoficial.com.br. *Time Out*'s online English guide to Rio (www.timeout.com.br/rio-de-janeiro/en) is another great source, as is the weekly newspaper *The Rio Times* (www.riotimesonline.com).

★ Carnaval

Why is it that whenever people hear the word *Carnaval,* Rio de Janeiro automatically springs to mind? Rio isn't the only city to host this bacchanalian celebration, but its signature parades, balls, and *escolas de sambas* combined with nonstop merrymaking have made it the most spectacular of Brazil's Carnavals. To experience Rio's hedonistic five-day *festa* in all its butt-swaying, ear-blasting, eye-popping, mind-blowing glory,

make sure to book your accommodations *far* in advance.

DESFILES DAS ESCOLAS

The **Desfiles das Escolas de Samba** is the most famous Carnaval event. It consists of the *desfiles* (parades) of the top *escolas de samba* (known as the Grupo Especial, or Special Group). These take place in a massive concrete stadium called the **Sambódromo** (Rua Marquês de Sapucaí, Praça Onze, Cidade Nova). Designed by Oscar Niemeyer, it can seat 78,000 people. *Desfiles* are held on the Sunday and Monday nights of Carnaval and involve 12 *escolas de samba* that compete against each other.

Each night, six *escolas* have 80 minutes to strut their stuff for a table of judges, who award points for various aspects of their performances, among them choreography, costumes, floats, decorations, *samba de enredo* (theme song), and percussion. Every year, the *escolas* invest incredible amounts of money, time, hard work, and talent in an attempt to outdo one another and be crowned champion. If you miss the competition itself, on the following Saturday you can catch the top schools performing in the championship parade, which also takes place at the Sambódromo. Tickets to this "best of" compilation event are much cheaper than those for the *desfiles.*

Getting cheap **tickets** to the Sambódromo is a tricky affair. Most are purchased long before the event itself—they usually go on sale in January—within minutes of going on sale. Savvy scalpers and travel agents often snatch up the best seats. Two good sources of information are **Rio Services Carnival** (www.rio-carnival.net), which sells tickets online via PayPal, and **Riotur** (www.rioguiaoficial.com.br), the municipal tourist secretariat. The latter sells expensive tickets (R$990-1,600) in private boxes for tourists, which are much more comfortable than the regular concrete bleachers. Tickets for other sections range R$130-600. Try to sit in the central sections (Sections 5, 7, and 9), which offer the best views and the most animation. You can also

Off-Season Carnaval Activities

If you can't get to Rio for Carnaval, you can still experience an authentic slice of the action by taking part in the *ensaios* (rehearsals) every weekend by Rio's various *escolas de samba*. Get a behind-the-scenes glimpse at the makings of a successful *desfile* (parade) and soak up some authentic neighborhood atmosphere, all while listening to terrific samba. Since most schools are in the Zona Norte, sometimes close to *favelas*, take a tour or taxi. The Mangueira and Salgueiro samba schools are the most popular for tourists and are also closest to the Centro.

- **Beija Flor** (Prainha Wallace Paes Leme 1025, Nilópolis, tel. 21/2791-2866, www.beija-flor.com.br)

- **Grande Rio** (Rua Almirante Barroso 5-6, Duque de Caixias, tel. 21/2671-3585, www.academicos-dogranderio.com.br)

- **Império Serrano** (Av. Ministro Edgar Romero 114, Madureira, tel. 21/2489-8722, www.imperi-oserrano.com)

- **Mangueira** (Rua Visconde de Niterói 1072, Mangueira, tel. 21/3872-6878, www.mangueira.com.br)

- **Portela** (Rua Clara Nunes 81, Madureira, tel. 21/2489-6440, www.gresportela.com.br)

- **Salgueiro** (Rua Silva Teles 104, Andaraí, tel. 21/2238-9226, www.salgueiro.com.br)

- **Unidos da Tijuca** (Clube dos Portuários, Rua Francisco Bicalho 47, Cidade Nova, tel. 21/2263-9679, www.unidosdatijuca.com.br)

As Carnaval approaches, the *escolas de samba* hold dress rehearsals at the Sambódromo, which are open to the public. You can also catch them at the **Cidade do Samba** (Rua Rivadávia Correia 60, Gamboa, tel. 24/2213-2503, www.cidadedosambarj.globo.com, 10am-5pm Tues.-Sat., R$5), a vast complex created out of Rio's abandoned dockside warehouses. Here the *Grupo Especial escolas* have ample space to store materials, sew costumes, build allegorical floats, and display their talents to the public (usually Thurs. nights, when a combined show and buffet costs a whopping R$190). Make sure you take a taxi here.

For more information about *escolas de samba* and *ensaios*, contact the **Liga das Escolas de Samba** (tel. 21/3213-5151, www.liesa.globo.com).

purchase tickets online (make sure the agency is reputable) or in person at Rio travel agencies, which usually charge a commission. If you find yourself without tickets at the last minute, head straight for the Sambódromo and look around for scalpers; they'll be looking around for you. If you're willing to miss the first couple of schools and arrive fashionably late (like most Cariocas), you can usually get some good bargains—make sure you get a plastic card with a magnetic strip, accompanied by a paper ticket with a seat and the *correct* date.

Although you can get to the Sambódromo by bus, these are usually packed, rowdy, and full of pickpockets. You're better off taking a taxi or the Metrô (which runs 24 hours during Carnaval) to Praça Onze (if you're seated in an even-numbered sector) or Central (for an odd-numbered sector).

STREET CARNAVAL

More than 300 neighborhood and resident association *blocos* and *bandas* traditionally take to the streets and let loose in an explosion of music and merrymaking that many swear is way more fun than sitting around in the Sambódromo. Although the costumes of the *blocos* aren't as ornate as those of the *escolas de samba*, some are highly inventive and downright hilarious. Many men—both gay and straight—dress in drag. To join in the fun, all you have to do is appear at a *bloco*'s headquarters on the day and time of its parades (Riotur provides this info). Check to see if you're expected to don the *bloco*'s traditional colors or to purchase a T-shirt (sold on the spot). Festivities usually kick off in the afternoon and last far into the night; for times and dates, pick up a free *Carnaval de Rua* guide published by Riotur or check out their site for online schedules.

BLOCOS AND BANDAS

Centro is home to some of the city's most traditional *blocos*. Among the most popular are **Bafo de Onça, Bloco Cacique de Ramos,** and **Cordão do Bola Preta,** whose followers sport lots of *bolas pretas* (black polka dots). Santa Teresa features the **Carmelitas de Santa Teresa,** Glória has the **Banda da Glória,** and Botafogo boasts several lively traditional *blocos*, among them **Barbas, Bloco de Segunda,** and **Dois Pra Lá, Dois Prá Cá.** Copa's most famous *bloco* is **Bip Bip,** many of whose members are professional musicians, while bohemian Ipanema has some of the most wildly alternative groups, among them **Banda Ipanema, Símpatia É Quase Amor,** and the **Banda Carmen Miranda,** in which men of all sexual orientations don platform shoes and tutti-frutti turbans to pay their respects to the Brazilian Bombshell.

Other outdoor shows and festivities fill the city. Thousands flock to the municipal bash held outside the Sambódromo at **Terreirão do Samba,** as well as the popular **Baile da Cinelândia** and the alternative **Rio Folia,** held beneath the Arcos da Lapa.

CARNAVAL BALLS

The extravagant Carnaval balls of yesteryear are alive and well at Rio's clubs and hotels. Live samba bands supply the rhythms, and costumes—many of them quite spectacular—are de rigueur. Despite air-conditioning, the atmosphere is guaranteed to get hot and steamy as the night wears on. The most famous and fabulous event (costumes or formal wear required) is the **Magic Ball** held at the Copacabana Palace (Av. Atlântica 1702, Copacabana, tel. 21/2445-8790) on Saturday night, which attracts an international throng of rich and gorgeous people for whom R$2,000 (for standing room) is chump change. Tickets to most other balls, however, are in a much more affordable range (R$40-160). The gay-friendly thematic bashes held at Cinelândia's **Scala** club (Av Treze de Maio 23, Centro, tel. 21/2239-4448, www.scalario.com.br) every night during Carnaval are some of the wildest and most spectacular, culminating on the last night with the immensely popular **Gala Gay.** Many other clubs also organize *bailes* in which gay men go all out in terms of cross-dressing. Since the one thing Cariocas don't take lightly is Carnaval, no matter where you go, you'll be expected to show up in a seriously extravagant costume.

Réveillon

Ringing in the New Year on **Copacabana Beach** ranks among the most magical and mystical New Year experiences. As night falls, millions of people clad in white congregate on the sands of Copacabana. The white symbolizes the purity of the new year and is also the color associated with Iemanjá, a popular Afro-Brazilian religious deity (*orixá*) whose title is Queen of the Seas. Revelers arrive at the beach bearing her favorite gifts: roses, perfumes, jewelry, and champagne. At the stroke of midnight, they wade into the ocean and toss their offerings into the dark Atlantic. If Iemanjá accepts their gifts, they are ensured a happy year. If the waves sweep them back to shore, better luck next time.

Midnight also signals the start of a gigantic fireworks display and a series of open-air live music shows. Then it's dancing and drinking the night away under the stars until morning, when everyone rings in the first day of the year (and rinses off the night's excesses) with a dip in the ocean.

Performing Arts

Rio's most prestigious performing arts space is the **Theatro Municipal** (Praça Floriano,

Centro, tel. 21/2332-9134, www.theatromunicipal.rj.gov.br), which hosts the biggest national and international names in music, dance, opera, and theater. It also has its own renowned symphony orchestra, opera company, and ballet troupe.

Located inside the grandiose neoclassical former headquarters of the Banco do Brasil, the **Centro Cultural Banco do Brasil** (CCBB; Rua 1 de Março 66, Centro, tel. 21/3808-2000, 9am-9pm Tues.-Sun., www.culturabancodobrasil.com.br/portal) offers a consistently excellent selection of some of Rio's—and Brazil's—finest contemporary theater, dance, film, and music. Many events are free. Banco do Brasil is a major patron of the arts, and the CCBB's magnificent interior welcomes most major national and international art exhibits as well as musical and theatrical performances that travel to and throughout Brazil. With a bookstore and café, it is also a favorite meeting point for Cariocas.

The **Espaço Cultural dos Correios** (Rua Visconde de Itaboraí 20, Centro, tel. 21/2253-1580, www.correios.com.br, noon-7pm Tues.-Sun.) has a great café that overlooks the adjacent Praça dos Correios, where live musical performances frequently take place. On the same street, the **Casa França-Brasil** (Rua Visconde de Itaboraí 78, Centro, tel. 21/2332-5120, www.fcfb.rj.gov.br, 10am-8pm Tues.-Sun.) hosts temporary art exhibits.

One of Rio's oldest and most distinguished theaters, **Teatro João Caetano** (Praça Tiradentes, Centro, tel. 21/2332-9166) features a diverse range of musical and dance as well as theatrical performances. **Fundição Progresso** (Rua dos Arcos 24, Lapa, tel. 21/2220-5070, www.fundicaoprogresso.com.br) is a cleverly renovated historic foundry that operates as a multifaceted performance space. On any given day, you might hear legendary *sambistas,* internationally acclaimed indie rockers, or the Petrobras Symphony Orchestra. It's home to the Intrépida Troupe, a performance group whose works fuse theater, dance, and circus.

The concrete behemoth known as the

Cidade das Artes (Av. das Américas 5300, Barra da Tijuca, tel. 21/3325-0102, www.cidadedasartes.org) is responsible for bringing a much-needed shot of high culture to the Zona Ouest. Designed by French architect Christian de Portzarparc, it is the largest cultural center in Latin America, possessing state-of-the-art concert spaces, theaters, and cinemas.

Concert Halls

Rio's biggest concert hall is the gigantic, state-of-the-art **Citibank Hall** (Av. Ayrton Senna 3000, Shopping Via Parque, Barra da Tijuca, tel. 11/4003-5588, www.citibankhall.com.br), where major national and international musical, theatrical, and dance events take place. Located beneath the Arcos de Lapa, **Circo Voador** (Rua dos Arcos, Lapa, tel. 21/2533-0354, www.circovoador.com.br) has been one of the city's vanguard outdoor musical venues since the 1980s. The "Flying Circus" continues to host big national stars as well as alternative local bands and theatrical groups. Adjacent to the Museu de Arte Moderno, **Viva Rio** (Av. Infante Dom Henrique 85, Parque do Flamengo, tel. 21/2272-2900, www.vivario.com.br) boasts a humungous concert hall where a diverse sampling of homegrown and imported musical talents are savored against the backdrop of Guanabara Bay. The Carmen-inspired **Miranda** (Av. Borges de Medeiros 1424, Lagoa, tel. 21/2239-0305, www.mirandabrasil.com.br), located in the Lagoon entertainment complex, is a swanky and vaguely retro supper club hosting a diverse range of Brazilian musical and performing artists.

Cinema

Rio is one of Latin America's most important film markets, and you can see everything from Hollywood blockbusters to national, European, independent, and art films. One of the city's biggest cinephile hangouts is the **Espaço Itaú de Cinema** (Praia de Botafogo 316, Botafogo, tel. 21/2559-8750, www.itaucinemas.com.br), with six state-of-the-art screens, a cool bar, and a great bookstore. Nearby are the **Estação Rio**

(Rua Voluntários da Pátria 35, Botafogo, tel. 21/2266-9955) and the **Estação Botafogo** (Rua Voluntários da Pátria 88, Botafogo, tel. 21/2226-1988), which show a mixture of national and international films.

Although Rio was once home to an impressive number of glamorous movie palaces, there are now just two survivors that still screen films. The **Cine Odeon Petrobras** (Praça Mahatma Gandhi 5, Centro, tel. 21/2240-1093, www.grupoestacao.com.br) is a handsomely restored art deco gem in Cinelândia that often hosts star-studded premieres, and the **Roxy** (Av. Nossa Senhora de Copacabana 945-A, Copacabana, tel. 21/2461-2461, www.kinoplex.com.br) is an art deco theater inaugurated in 1938 that has it all: a sweeping staircase, plush lobby, and three large-screen theaters. Far more modern, the **Cinépolis Lagoon** (Av. Borges de Medeiros 1424, Lagoa, tel. 21/3029-2544, www.cinepolis.com.br) is a multiplex whose terrace bar offers incomparable views of the Lagoa and Corcovado.

In late September-early October, it's worth checking out the **Festival do Rio** (www.festivaldorio.com.br), an outstanding international film festival.

NIGHTLIFE

As laid-back and relaxing as Rio can be by day, at night it becomes a buzzing hive of activity. Rio is one of the most musical cities you'll ever encounter, and there is no shortage of bars, clubs, dance halls, and open air venues featuring live performances of Brazil's myriad musical styles. Since Cariocas rarely listen to music without succumbing to the urge to move their bodies, most of these places feature dancing as well. For those who prefer a more globalized beat, the city has its share of nightclubs and discos, although in terms of contemporary sounds, São Paulo has the advantage. Although most of Centro shuts down after happy hour, the more traditional bohemian *bairros* of Santa Teresa and Lapa, and more recently the old port zone *bairros* of Saúde and Gamboa, have been reclaimed by new bohos

who flock to hear samba, *chorinho, forró,* and other homegrown melodies. The swankier watering holes and night spots of the Zona Sul offer more internationally urban brands of fun, albeit with a decidedly bossa nova twist.

Centro

Centro doesn't have much nightlife to speak of. However, amid its narrow old streets are some of the city's oldest and most atmospheric *botequins,* which fill up when happy hour rolls around. Accompanying the ongoing revitalization of the port zone, the adjacent neighborhoods of Saúde and Gamboa, which have long been a hotbed of Afro-Brazilian culture, are earning accolades as the next Lapa.

BARS
Adega do Timão (Rua Visconde de Itaboaraí 10, tel. 21/2516-91255, noon-midnight Tues.-Sun.) is a charming little bar decorated with nautical gear and a fancy crystal chandelier thrown in for good measure. Its proximity to the Centro Cultural Banco do Brasil and Espaço Cultura dos Correios has made it an obligatory beer stop for the culture crowd.

Bar Luiz (Rua da Carioca 39, tel. 21/2262-6900, www.barluiz.com.br, 11am-8pm Mon., 11am-10pm Tues.-Fri., 11am-6pm Sat.) is a classic Carioca *botequim* with a German accent—and menu, including a famous potato salad as well as various sausages and schnitzels.

Amarelinho (Praça Floriano 55-B, Cinelândia, tel. 21/2240-8434, www.amarelinhodacinelandia.com.br, 11am-2am daily) is Cinelândia's most famous yellow-tiled outdoor bar for people-watching and monument-gazing. Close by, **Villarino** (Av. Calógeras 6, Loja B, tel. 21/2240-9634, www.villarino.com.br, noon-10pm Mon.-Fri.) was a favorite haunt of a midcentury bohemian crowd that included Tom Jobim and Vinicius de Moraes, who used it as their private clubhouse. Today the retro *uisqueria* (whiskey bar) with its scarlet banquettes attracts a suit-and-tie crowd who alternate whiskey shots with bites of prosciutto and brie sandwiches.

Gay Rio

While Rio's vibe is quite gay friendly, few specifically gay venues exist. GLS (a Brazilian slang term for *gay, lesbica, e simpatisante;* i.e., gay friendly) spaces rule, with gays, lesbians, and heteros mixing socially. For more info about Rio's gay scene, visit www.riogaylife.com.

CENTRO
Cine Ideal (Rua da Carioca 62, tel. 21/2221-1984, http://cineideal.com.br, 11:30pm-close Fri.-Sat., cover R$25-30) is a disco with bars and a rooftop lounge.

PORT ZONE
The Week (Rua Sacadura Cabral 150, Saúde, tel. 21/2253-1020, www.week.com.br, midnight-close Sat., cover R$40-60) is a more massive and upscale São Paulo import.

LAPA
Buraco da Lacraia (Rua André Cavalcanti 58, tel. 21/2221-1984, http://buracodalacraia.com.br, 11pm-close Fri.-Sat., cover R$30-40) showcases drag shows, videoke contests, snooker, and electronic games. The beer is fantastically cheap.

IPANEMA
The high-profile strip of Ipanema beach stretching from Posto 8 to Posto 9 (nicknamed "Farme Gay") is home to beach *barracas* flying rainbow flags and the toned outlines of well-oiled "Barbies" (as muscle men are called). The street perpendicular to the beach, **Rua Farme de Amoedo** also attracts a gay crowd.

Tô'Nem Aí (Rua Farme de Amoedo 87-A, tel. 21/2247-8403, www.tounemai.com.br, noon-3am daily) is a laid-back bar that draws a mixed crowd and offers great views of the action.

Galeria Café (Rua Teixeira de Melo 31, tel. 21/2523-8250, www.galeriacafe.com.br, 10:30pm-close Wed.-Sat., noon-8pm Sun., cover R$28-38), one street over, is a hip, hybrid space sheltering a café and art gallery. At night, it holds sizzling *festas* that reel in a trendy crowd.

COPACABANA
The gay crowd has conquered a prize strip of beach, on the doorstep of the Copacabana Palace, baptized "Praia da Bolsa" (Handbag Beach).

The **Rainbow** (noon-close daily) kiosk is a haven for Rio's transgendered community, who often perform in between caipis and pizza slices.

Le Boy (Rua Raul Pompéia 102, tel. 21/2513-4993, www.leboy.com.br, 11pm-close Tues.-Sun., cover R$15-25) is Rio's classic and notorious temple of gaydom. This enormous club offers go-go boys, a *quarto escuro* (dark room), and Tuesday's Strip Nights.

La Cueva (Rua Miguel Lemos 51, tel. 21/2267-1367, www.boatelacueva.com.br, 11pm-close, R$20) means "The Cave," which describes this dim, yet friendly basement lair where the entrance fee earns you two drinks.

LIVE MUSIC
Trapiche Gamboa (Rua Sacadura Cabral 155, Saúde, tel. 21/2516-0868, www.trapiche-gamboa.com, 6:30pm-close Tues.-Fri., 8pm-close Sat., cover R$12-20) was a pioneer when it opened in 2004. Occupying a handsomely restored 19th-century warehouse, it still offers some of the best live samba performances in town. Nearby, "Pedra do Sal" is the name of the gigantic chunk of granite anchoring the historic **Largo João da Baiana** (Rua Argemiro Bulcão, Gamboa, 7:30pm-close Mon., Wed., and Fri.), site of a former slave market as well as the believed birthplace of Carioca samba. It's a picturesque place to hear the vibrant *rodas de samba* pounded out by master sambistas.

Gafieiras were originally ballrooms where Rio's working classes danced the night away. They sprang up in Centro during the 1920s; by 1930, there were more than 450. Sadly, the sole survivor still hosting ballroom dancing is **Centro Cultural Estudantina Musical** (Praça Tiradentes 79, tel. 21/2232-1149, www.estudantinamusical.com.br, 7pm-1am Wed., 8pm-1am Fri., 10pm-2am Sat., cover R$15-20), whose decor conjures up its 1928 beginnings. Apart from orchestras playing traditional ballroom ditties (usually Sat.), you'll hear live bands playing samba, *choro,* and jazz. The mixed crowd includes people of all ages.

Lapa

Lapa is the city's undisputed hot spot to listen and dance to live music. Starting Thursday, its many bars, clubs, and narrow streets (particularly Rua Joaquim Silva) pulse with a variety of rhythms, revelers from every Carioca *bairro,* and tourists eager to samba. Although not quite as edgy as it used to be, Lapa still rules Rio's musical roost.

BARS

Like Centro, Lapa has some wonderful old *botequins.* **Bar Brasil** (Av. Mem de Sá 90, tel. 21/2509-5943, noon-midnight Mon.-Fri., 11:30am-6pm Sat.) is a neighborhood institution, serving German food such as *eisbein, kassler,* and sauerkraut—perfect between sips of frothy beer. The canvases on the walls are by Chilean artist Jorge Selarón, who is responsible for the mosaic-covered staircase that leads up to Santa Teresa. **Barzinho** (Rua do Lavradio 170, Lapa, tel. 21/2221-4709, www.barzinho, 6pm-2am Tues.-Wed., 6pm-3am Thurs., 6pm-4am Fri.-Sat.) opened in late 2013. This dimly lit hipster haunt provides an alternative to Lapa's trademark samba-inflected grittiness with bright neon colors and pulsing DJ-spun electronica. Events range from pop-up theater to performance art, while classic bar grub gets a sophisticated lease on life.

LIVE MUSIC AND NIGHTCLUBS

In Lapa's streets and renovated old buildings you'll encounter an astonishing diversity of music, and new bars and clubs are opening all the time. The majority are on Rua do Lavradio and Rua Mem de Sá. For listings and schedules, check out www.lanalapa.com.br.

One of the city's most enchanting bars, **Rio Scenarium** (Rua do Lavradio 20, tel. 21/3147-9000, www.rioscenarium.com.br, 6:30pm-2:30am Tues-Sat., cover R$20-35) is perpetually packed. If it has lost some of its cachet (lots of gringos trying to samba), it has retained its unique charm. Located on Lapa's antiques row, Rio Scenarium's three floors are full of antiques, which are rented out to film and TV productions—you can sit, sprawl, and lounge on certain pieces while others are merely eye candy. On most nights, top names in samba, *choro,* and *forró* perform. Arrive early (before 8pm) or reserve a table.

Carioca da Gema (Rua Mem de Sá 79, tel. 21/2221-0043, www.barcariocadagema. com.br, 6pm-close Mon.-Fri., 8pm-close Sat., cover R$25-30) is a classic spot to listen to top-quality samba and *choro* performed by big names and rising stars. The ambiance is warm and rustic, and there is a copious menu. **Clube dos Democráticos** (Rua do Riachuelo 91-93, Lapa, tel. 21/2252-4611, www.clubedosdemocraticos.com.br, 6pm-close Wed.-Sat., 8pm-close Sun., cover R$15-35) has been around since 1867. Members were a forward-thinking republican and abolitionist bunch whose bashes were legendary well into the 1940s. Today, dance soirees are held regularly in the vast ballroom. Music ranges from samba to *choro,* and the crowd is young.

In Carioca-ese, "40°" refers to the temperature (in Celsius) that descends on the city in the heat of summer. The name is apt: **Lapa 40°** (Rua Riachuelo 97, Lapa, tel. 21/3970-1329, www.lapa40graus.com.br, 6pm-4am daily, cover R$15-35) is one of Lapa's perennial hot spots. More than a bar or nightclub, it is a four-floor entertainment complex outfitted with a bar, a ballroom, and a stage for live shows as well as a *tabacaria* (for smoking cigars), a *uisqueiria* (for doing whiskey shots), and dart boards. Oh, and if you get bored, there is an entire floor outfitted with 30 pool and billiard tables.

Santa Teresa

BARS

The unpretentious bars of "Santa" lure an alternative crowd charmed by the laid-back vibe of this boho *bairro*. Inspired by the typically rustic bars of Minas Gerais, **Bar do Mineiro** (Rua Paschoal Carlos Magno 99, tel. 21/2221-9227, 11am-1am Tues.-Sat., 11am-midnight Sun.) is a charmingly old-fashioned *botequim* accessorized with black-and-white photos and miniature wooden *bondes*.

Opened in 1919, **Armazém São Thiago** (Rua Áurea 26, tel. 21/2232-0822, www.armazemsaothiago.com.br, noon-midnight Mon.-Sat., noon-10pm Sun.), also known as Bar do Gomes, was once a general store that sold *secos e molhados* (dry goods and spirits). The *molhados* persevered, and today the dark wood shelves and cabinets are stacked sky-high with bottles and cases of wine and *cachaça*. A wooden fridge, marble-topped tables, art deco fixtures, and jocular waiters round out the retro pleasures. The clientele is made up of spirited locals.

Flamengo and Laranjeiras

Flamengo and Laranjeiras are home to some of the city's most traditional watering holes, where you can eat and drink well while soaking up authentic Carioca atmosphere.

BARS

A Flamengo favorite, **Belmonte** (Praia do Flamengo 300, tel. 21/2552-3349, 9am-4am daily) gets so busy in the late afternoons that customers stand and balance their cups on shiny metal barrels of beer. Although other locations have opened throughout the city, this original bar, opened in 1952, is the most atmospheric.

LIVE MUSIC

Casa Rosa (Rua Alice 550, Laranjeiras, tel. 21/2557-2562, www.casarosa.com.br, 11pm-close Fri.-Sat., 5pm-close Sun., cover R$10-30) is quite literally pink (a shocking one at that), but from the turn of the 20th century to the late 1980s its chromatic association was red: It was the town's most famous bordello, frequented by Laranjeiras's resident politicians, magnates, and military officers. Now one of Rio's coolest cultural centers, on weekends it rocks with live music and dance *festas* such as Friday's Baile Alice and Sunday's famous Feijoada do Projeto Raiz.

Botafogo, Cosme Velho, and Urca

BARS

Bar Urca (Rua Cândido Gaffré 205, Urca, tel. 21/2295-8744, www.barurca.com.br, 7am-11pm Mon.-Sat., 9am-9pm Sun.) is among the most scenic *botequins* in Rio, with a bewitching view over the Baía de Guanabara. The upstairs dining room functions as a restaurant whose menu emphasizes fish and seafood dishes, but you can also savor *petiscos* such as grilled sardines while soaking up the sun out on the seawall (many locals bring their own beach chairs). Amidst Botafogo's blossoming alternative bar scene, **Comuna** (Rua Sorocaba 585, Botafogo, tel. 21/3253-8797, http://comuna.cc, 6pm-2am Tues.-Thurs., 6pm-4am Fri.-Sat., 6pm-midnight Sun.) is one of the coolest. The brainchild of four university pals, this hybrid cultural space is an unpretentious and friendly place to tap into Rio's creative pulse.

NIGHTCLUBS

A pioneer of Rio's alternative music and party scene, **Casa da Matriz** (Rua Henrique Novaes 107, Botofago, tel. 21/2266-1014, http://beta.matrizonline.com.br/casadamatriz, 9pm-midnight Tues., 8pm-5am Wed., 11pm-6am Thurs.-Sat., cover R$15-30) hosts some of the most happening dance parties in town, courtesy of a roster of house DJs. Wander around the historic house (decked out so it feels like a bonafide house party), where you can play arcade games or flake out on a sofa. Arrive and leave early to avoid crazy long lines.

Copacabana and Leme

Copa throbs at night, but more as a result of red-light district action on Avenida Atlântica and the oceanfront restaurants and bars crammed with international tourists. Nonetheless, there are a few exceptional enclaves as well as the *quiosques* (kiosks) that strategically line the beach itself.

BARS

Cervantes (Av. Prado Junior 335, Copacabana, tel. 21/2275-6147, www.restaurantecervantes.com.br, noon-4am Sun. and Tues.-Thurs., noon-6am Fri.-Sat.) is one of Copa's favorite *botequins,* especially after a night of carousing. The house specialties are the impossibly thick sandwiches—most feature *abacaxi,* a native species of pineapple.

Bip Bip (Rua Almirante Gonçalves 50, Copacabana, Loja D, tel. 21/2267-9696, 7pm-1am daily) is a tiny hole-in-the-wall *botequim* with two saving graces: its location on a quiet Copa street, which allows tables and chairs to be arranged outside, and terrific musical jams by top Carioca samba, *choro,* and bossa nova performers. Utterly unpretentious, "Bip" is a welcome antidote to Copa's touristy oceanfront bars.

NIGHTCLUBS

Fosfobox (Rua Siqueira Campos 143, 22-A, Copacabana, tel. 21/2548-7498, www.fosfobox.com.br, 11pm-close Tues.-Sun., R$20-50) is one of the Zona Sul's only underground basement clubs. Depending on your spatial sensibilities, "Fosfo" is either intimate or claustrophobic, but the upstairs Fosfobar is definitely conducive to mellowing out. Spun by top national DJs, the soundtrack ranges from rock to funk to techno. The scene is Copa cool with a gritty, industrial edge.

Ipanema and Leblon

Both Ipanema and Leblon possess a vibrant nightlife that runs the gamut from laid-back, beloved sidewalk *botequins* to stylish bars, lounges, and a few nightclubs that attract an eternally fashionable crowd.

BARS

Jobi (Rua Ataulfo de Paiva 1166-B, Leblon, tel. 21/2274-0547, 10am-4am Sun.-Thurs., 10am-6am Fri.-Sat.) is a classic Leblon address, long frequented by artists, journalists, and intellectuals. It's perennially chosen as one of the city's top bars due to the quality of its *chope* and flavorful *petiscos.* Arrive early if you want a table.

Close by, **Bracarense** (Rua José Linhares 85, Leblon, tel. 21/2294-3549, 7am-midnight Mon.-Sat., 9am-10pm Sun.) is quite tiny, but the surrounding sidewalk at this laid-back neighborhood bar overflows with tables and stools. The *petiscos* here are justly celebrated.

If you're feeling beer-weary, head to the **Academia da Cachaça** (Rua Conde da Bernadote 26, Leblon, tel. 21/2529-2680, www.academiadacachaca.com.br, noon-2:30am daily) to savor one of the city's most famous caipirinhas. Lured by the hundreds of bottles of Brazil's national liquor on display (and available for purchase), you might also want to sample some of the finer *pingas* on the menu.

If you can't afford to splurge on a room at the Philippe Starck-designed Hotel Fasano, the next best thing is a cocktail in its supremely sophisticated lounge, **Barreto-Londra** (Av. Vieira Souto 80, Ipanema, tel. 21/3202-4000, www.hotelfasano.com.br, 8pm-1am Mon.-Wed., 8pm-4am Thurs.-Sat.), one of *the* places to see and be seen in the Zona Sul (reservations recommended). Trendiness aside, the warm brick walls, inviting leather sofas, elegant service, and a mean apple martini will have you mellow in no time.

LIVE MUSIC

Studio RJ (Av. Vieira Souto 110, Ipanema, tel. 21/2523-1204, www.studiorj.org, 9pm-close Tues.-Sat., 7pm-close Sun., cover R$25-50) offers a compelling mélange of homegrown and imported bands and DJs.

Tuesday night's Jazzmania has a loyal following. Rivaling the superb acoustics are dreamy views of Ipanema beach.

NIGHTCLUBS

Melt (Rua Rita Ludolf 47, Leblon, www.melt-bar.com.br, tel. 21/2249-9309, 10pm-4am Tues.-Sat., cover R$30-50) is utterly Leblon: sleek, chic, and globalized, just like the toned and tanned crowd that works up a glow on the dance floor. The musical selection—ranging from samba rock to hip-hop—is courtesy of a handful of rotating DJs. Creative dishes are served in the candlelit downstairs lounge.

Lagoa and Jardim Botânico
QUIOSQUES

With its stunning views of Corcovado and many *quiosques* (kiosks), Lagoa has become quite a scene. One of the most imaginative is **Palaphita Kitch** (Av. Epitácio Pessoa, Kiosk 20, Parque do Cantagalo, Lagoa, tel. 21/2227-0837, www.palaphitakitch.com.br, 6pm-1am Sun.-Thurs., 6pm-3am Fri.-Sat.), where Zona Sul cool meets the Amazon rain forest with lounge furniture made from reforested wood; at night, the place is lit by torches. For a taste of Bahia, head to **OkeKa Baiana Tem** (Kiosk 14, Epitácio Pessoa, Lagoa, tel. 21/8297-9766, www.okekabaianatem.com.br, 5pm-midnight Tues.-Fri., 2pm-midnight Sat., 8:30am-midnight Sun.). Amidst Catholic-Candomblé iconography, try tasty, if pricey, *acarajés* (crunchy black-eyed pea fritters) and *moquecas* (fish or seafood stews).

BARS

Overlooking the Lagoa, **Bar Lagoa** (Av. Epitácio Pessoa 1674, Lagoa, tel. 21/2523-1135, 6pm-2am Mon.-Fri., noon-2am Sat.-Sun.) is a beloved *botequim* whose art deco interior hasn't changed much since the 1930s. It was originally named Bar Berlin; the owner strategically changed its name during World War II, but the kitchen continues to serve hearty yet simple German fare.

Worthwhile for vittles and views is **Lagoon** (Av. Borges de Medeiros 1424, Lagoa, www.lagoon.com.br, noon-2am, daily), a glistening entertainment complex that's home to cinemas and a musical supper club.

Gávea

The area known as Baixa Gávea has been a nocturnal hot spot for years, luring young Zona Sulistas to the lively bars fanning out from Praça Santos Dumont.

BARS

Braseiro da Gávea (Praça Santos Dumont 116, Gávea, tel. 21/2239-7494, noon-1am Sun.-Thurs., noon-3am Fri.-Sat.) is one of the most traditional *botequins* in the area. It serves up a delicious charcoal-grilled *picanha* (rump-steak) chicken with fries to satiate late-night hunger pangs.

NIGHTCLUBS

00 (Av. Padre Leonel França 240, Gávea, tel. 21/2540-8041, www.00site.com.br, 10pm-5am Tues.-Sat., 5pm-2am Sun., cover R$20-50), or "Zero Zero" (as it is pronounced) is located inside Rio's planetarium, and the likes of Mick Jagger and Javier Bardem have been cropping up amid the usual bevy of wealthy young Zona Sulistas and TV celebs—but it isn't star-gazing that makes this one of Rio's top nightspots. The stylish space is the real attraction: Merging outdoor gardens and an Asian fusion restaurant with an indoor lounge and dance floor, 00 oozes glammy sophistication. To keep clients on their well-pedicured toes, the tunes are eclectic and vary from house to '80s and '90s memorabilia, with guest DJs taking charge of frequent *festas*.

SHOPPING

The best things to buy in Rio (as opposed to elsewhere) are Brazilian beach fashions and surf wear, antiques, CDs, DVDs, and vinyl by classic and contemporary musicians, along with traditional percussion instruments. Precious and semiprecious stones are a classic purchase. You can also find traditional arts and crafts from all over the country.

Shopping Malls

Rio's *shoppings* are more than just malls: They are microcosms where Cariocas can shop till they drop, as well as wander, gossip, flirt, read, eat, check out a movie or play, and even go skating. Depending on the neighborhood, the clientele, shops, and ambiance vary widely. Hours of operation are always 10am-10pm Monday-Saturday, 3pm-9pm Sunday.

Shopping Rio Sul (Rua Lauro Müller 116, Botafogo, tel. 21/2122-8070, www.riosul. com.br) is one of the oldest and most popular *shoppings*. Its convenient location in Botafogo, close to the tunnel entrance to Copacabana, means that every single bus under the sun passes by.

The title for the chicest *shopping* in town goes to the **São Conrado Fashion Mall** (Estrada da Gávea 899, São Conrado, tel. 21/2111-4444, www.scfashionmall.com.br), a small but sleek mall with tropical foliage and skylights. The boutiques are all *feshun* (Carioca-speak for "fashion"), meaning tasteful and pricey.

Giving São Conrado a serious run for its *reais* is **Shopping Leblon** (Av. Afrânio Melo Franco 290, Leblon, tel. 21/2430-5122, www. shoppingleblon.com.br). Befitting its Leblon address, it is a beautiful place for beautiful people, with 200 stylish stores, cinemas, and a cultural center; a food court boasts stunning views of Lagoa Rodrigo de Freitas and Corcovado.

Located in a suburban neighborhood, **Barra Shopping** (Av. das Américas 4666, Barra da Tijuca, tel. 21/4003-4131, www.barrashopping.com.br) is the most massive of Rio's malls, with more than 500 stores.

Antiques

As the former imperial and republican capital of Brazil, Rio offers hidden treasures—if you have the patience to find them. **Shopping dos Antiquários** (Rua Siqueira Campos 143, Copacabana, tel. 21/2255-3461, 10am-7pm Mon.-Sat.) is a slightly beat-up, weirdly futuristic shopping center—Rio's first—dating from the 1960s. Its more than 70 antiques stores specialize in everything from colonial furniture, baroque sacred art, and antique dolls to art deco dishware and Bakelite jewelry.

Rio's other antiques mecca is Lapa's **Rua do Lavradio.** Alongside classic antiques stores and secondhand shops are boutiques specializing in early to mid-20th-century Brazilian designs and furnishings such as **Ateliê e Movelaria Belmonte** (Rua do Lavradio 34, Lapa, tel. 21/2507-6873, www. ateliebelmonte.com.br, 9am-6pm Mon.-Fri., 11am-2pm Sat.) and **Mercado Moderno** (Rua do Lavradio 130, Lapa, tel. 21/2508-6083, 9am-6pm Mon.-Fri., 9am-3pm Sat.). On the first Saturday afternoon of every month, the local merchants' association organizes the **Feira do Rio Antigo,** in which all the stores on Rua Lavradio join together with other antiques dealers for an open-air market.

Arts and Crafts

Neither Rio nor the surrounding state has much to boast of in terms of folk art or traditional crafts. However, if you won't be traveling to other parts of Brazil, there are a few recommended boutiques where you can pick up some authentic *artesanato*. The snug interior of **La Vereda** (Rua Almirante Alexandrino 428, Santa Teresa, tel. 21/2507-0317, www.lavereda.com.br, 10am-8pm daily) showcases a well-chosen collection of traditional art and handicrafts from all over Brazil as well as contemporary works by Santa's many neighborhood artists. **Brasil & Cia** (Rua Maria Quitéria 27, Ipanema, tel. 21/2267-4603, www.brasilecia.com.br, 10am-7pm Mon.-Fri., 10am-4pm Sat.) works with a hand-picked group of talented artists from all over the country who create decorative objects that, while steeped in regional traditions, also bear the individual mark of their creators. The owner of **Pé de Boi** (Rua Ipiranga 55, Laranjeiras, tel. 21/2285-4395, www.pedeboi. com.br, 9am-7pm Mon.-Fri., 9am-1pm Sat.) has an encyclopedic knowledge of Brazilian folk art; most of the vivid sculptures, toys, and decorative objects on display in this gallery space have been culled from the Northeast, Amazon, and Minas Gerais.

Books and Music

Livrarias aren't just for reading or browsing, but for seeing and being seen. They fill up on weekends and at night with real and pretend intellectuals who spill into the delightful cafés and bistros that coexist with stacks of books and magazines. Events include author readings and live performances of jazz, samba, *chorinho,* and bossa nova—enhancing the romance factor. The best *livrarias* are in Ipanema and Leblon.

The main branch of **Livraria da Travessa** (Rua Visconde de Pirajá 572, Ipanema, tel. 21/3205-9002, www.travessa.com.br, 9am-midnight Mon.-Sat., 11am-midnight Sun.) has an extensive collection of books about Rio (some in English) as well as lots of CDs and DVDs. Its sleek mezzanine bistro, **Bazaar,** has delicious things to nibble on. You'll find other branches in Centro and Barra. Cozy **Livraria Argumento** (Rua Dias Ferreira 417, Leblon, tel. 21/2239-5294, www.livraria-argumento.com.br, 9am-midnight Mon.-Sat., 11am-midnight Sun.) is like a second home to many Leblon residents.

Many *livrarias* have good, if rapidly shrinking, CD and DVD sections devoted to Brazilian music. Inside the Paço Imperial, **Arlequim** (Praça XV de Novembro 48, Centro, tel. 21/2533-4359, www.arlequim.com.br) is a welcoming store with a rich selection of Brazilian music available in CD, DVD, and Blu-ray. They also stage live musical performances.

Biscoito Fino (www.biscoitofino.com.br) is an indie record label whose mission is to produce intelligent and innovative MPB (*biscoito fino,* or fine cookie, is a Brazilian expression meaning high quality). Biscoito Fino embraces promising vanguard artists as well as consecrated legends who are weary of corporate labels, and is also involved in uncovering lost relics from Brazil's musical past (including some amazing *choro* recordings). It also launched Biscoitinho, specializing in

popular Brazilian music for children. You can also find Biscoito Fino kiosks in Shopping Rio Sul and Shopping da Gávea.

Maracatu Brasil (Rua Ipiranga 49, Laranjeiras, tel. 21/2557-4754, www.maracatubrasil.com.br, noon-8pm Mon.-Fri.) combines a music school and recording studio with a great array of new and used traditional, handcrafted, and modern Brazilian percussion instruments that can be rented as well as purchased. When you drop in, check to see who's performing in the small courtyard out back; talented percussionists often give happy-hour shows. And if you're interested in learning to play drums in a samba *bloco,* sign up for lessons taught by top-notch musicians.

Cachaça and Cigars

A beloved relic of Copa's heyday, **Charutaria Lollô** (Av. Nossa Senhora de Copacabana 683, Copacabana tel. 21/2235-0625, 7am-11pm daily) has been the place to go for a smoke and a *cafezinho* since it first opened in 1952. Savor both on the spot, or do like Tom Jobim, who strolled by every Sunday to buy a box of his favorite cigars, and make your purchases to go. **Garapa Doida** (Rua Carlos Góis 234, Loja F, Leblon, tel. 21/2274-8186, 11am-8pm Mon.-Fri., 11am-5pm Sat.) reunites more than 150 brands of *pinga* from all over Brazil; all have been certified by government institutions and approved by connoisseurs (clients are also encouraged to sample the wares). Among the rarest is Senador, from Minas Gerais, which is aged for 18 years in barrels made of native *garapa* wood.

Clothing and Accessories

Ipanema's tree-lined streets are stuffed with boutiques selling the latest creations from Brazilian and Carioca designers. The largest concentration of stores can be found on Rua Barão da Torre, Rua Gárcia d'Avila, Rua Anibal de Mendonça, and Rua Visconde de Pirajá, where many *galerias* (similar to micro-malls) offer hidden treasures.

Rio fashion is all about beachwear. Men can indulge in surf wear and some summery casual wear (jeans and T-shirts), but otherwise Carioca designers cater more to women, with clingy, sexy lines and designs in bright colors with interesting details. **Blue Man** (www.blueman.com.br), **Lenny** (www.lenny.com.br), **Bum Bum** (www.bumbum.com.br), **Salinas** (www.salinascompras.com.br), and **Rosa Chá** (www.rosacha.com.br) are all Carioca labels whose eternally fashionable *sungas* and bikinis are sold at their various brand-name boutiques around town as well as at *shoppings* such as Rio Sul, Leblon, and São Conrado Fashion Mall.

Women will also find lots of great shoes—the higher-heeled, the better—while both sexes will delight in the variety of funky flip-flops available. For an amazing selection of Havaianas, head to **Havaianas** (Rua Farme de Amoedo 76, Ipanema, tel. 21/2267-7395, http://br.havaianas.com, 9am-7pm Mon.-Fri., 10am-7pm Sat., 10am-6pm Sun.), where you can slip into flip-flops ranging from basic to customized. Aside from this Ipanema outpost, you'll find more than 40 stores throughout the city.

If you're young and male, you'll make out better at **Galeria River** (Rua Francisco Otaviano 67, Arpoador, tel. 21/2247-8387, www.galeriariver.com.br, 9am-8pm Mon.-Sat.), an alternative enclave whose tiny but well-stocked stores are devoted entirely to the art, lifestyle, and fashion of surf. This is a great place to get a surfer haircut, a tattoo or three, or to energize yourself with a super-healthy *vitamina,* full of fruit juices and medicinal herbs.

For an urban style with latent beach possibilities, check out streetwear brands with a distinctly Carioca flavor, such as **Totem** (Rua Visconde de Pirajá 500, Ipanema, tel. 21/2540-9977 www.totempraia.com.br) and **Osklen** (Rua Maria Quiteria 86, Ipanema, tel. 21/2227-2911, www.osklen.com).

Gilson Martins (Rua Visconde de Pirajá 462, Ipanema, tel. 21/2227-6178, www.gilsonmartins.com.br) designs ingenious Carioca bags in comic-book colors that are as sculptural as they are functional.

Jewelry

Rio's equivalent of Tiffany's is **H. Stern** (Rua Visconde de Pirajá 490, Ipanema, tel. 21/2274-3447, www.hstern.com.br, 10am-7pm Mon.-Fri., 10am-2pm Sat.). Its PR team sends flyers to basically every hotel in Rio offering to pick you up, take you to the Ipanema headquarters for a tour of their ateliers, and bring you back home again (hopefully with a small bag full of pricey rocks). Specialists in Brazil's precious and semiprecious stones, the jewelers here create innovative contemporary designs as well as more classic, conservative bling.

Antonio Bernardo (Rua Gárcia d'Avila 121, Ipanema, tel. 21/2512-7204, www.antoniobernardo.com.br, 10am-8pm Mon.-Fri., 10am-4pm Sat.) is a goldsmith, artist, and orchid lover (he adopted the Jardim Botânico's *orquidário*) who designs beautifully wrought contemporary jewelry. For something a little more eco-chic, consider a bio-bijou fashioned by Amazonas-born **Maria Oiticica** (http://loja.mariaoiticica.com.br). You'll find a boutique in Shopping Leblon.

Markets

Rio has some lively outdoor markets, most held on weekends. The most famous is Ipanema's **Feira Hippie** (Praça General Osório, Ipanema, 9am-6pm Sun.). It features a crowded but lively jumble-sale atmosphere that attracts an awful lot of tourists (and pickpockets) and is somewhat overrated. If you are in Centro between 9am and 5pm on a Saturday, you might enjoy browsing through the cornucopia of antiques and bric-a-brac on display at Praça XV's **Feira de Antiguidades.** On Sunday, the same goods migrate to Gávea's Praça Santos Dumont.

For more contemporary wares, head to **Babilônia Feira Hype,** which takes place on alternate weekends at the Lagoa's Clube Monte Líbano (Av. Borge de Medeiros 701, Leblon, www.babiloniafeirahype.com.br, 2pm-10pm every second Sat.-Sun., R$10). This fashion-forward market has an assortment of clothing, jewelry, and design pieces by up-and-coming Rio designers as well as outdoor eateries.

SPORTS AND RECREATION

Blessed with so many natural attractions, it is unsurprising that Cariocas are a pretty sporty bunch. Beach activities—everything from walking, jogging, and yoga to surfing, soccer, and volleyball—are very popular, as are radical sports, especially those that take advantage of the city's mountain peaks. The exuberantly green Floresta da Tijuca offers an oasis for athletes who want to commune with nature.

★ Floresta da Tijuca

Although the dense tropical forest that covers Rio's mountains possesses a primeval quality, the truth is that by the 19th century, the original Atlantic forest that had existed for thousands of years had been almost completely cleared to make way for sugar and coffee plantations. The deforestation was so dire that by the mid-1800s, Rio was facing an ecological disaster that menaced the city's water supply. Fortunately, inspired Emperor Dom Pedro II had a green conscience. In 1861, he ordered that 3,300 hectares be replanted with native foliage—the first example of government-mandated reforestation in Brazil's history. Over time, the forest returned to its original state, and today this urban rain forest boasts an astounding variety of exotic trees and animals ranging from jewel-colored hummingbirds to monkeys, squirrels, and armadillos.

Within the Floresta lies the largest urban park in Brazil, the **Parque Nacional da Tijuca** (tel. 21/2492-2252, www.parquedatijuca.com.br, 8am-5pm daily). Divided into four sectors, the most-visited is Serra da Carioca, which also has the best infrastructure. Better for walking and climbing are Pedras da Gávea e Bonita and Floresta da Tijuca. Floresta da Tijuca is home to the main visitor center, **Praça Afonso Viseu** (Estrada da Cascatinha 850, Tijuca), where you can buy maps and get guide recommendations. To get here, take the Metrô to Saens Pena, then hop on a bus to Barra da Tijuca, stopping at the main Alto da Boa Vista entrance. Near the entrance are three restaurants and a café. A second visitor center is at **Parque Lage** (Rua Jardim Botânico 414, Jardim Botânico), in Serra da Carioca.

The park has more than 100 walking trails—many quite easy—along with waterfalls, grottoes, and lookout points that offer stunning views of the city. The most spectacular are the **Mesa do Imperador** (Emperor's Table)—where Dom Pedro II liked to picnic with members of his court—and the **Vista Chinesa.** Although trails are well marked, explore the park in the company of a local or an organized group to avoid getting lost (or robbed). Customized tours in English are available; recommended outfits include **Rio Hiking** (tel. 21/2552-9204, www.riohiking.com.br) or **Jungle Me** (tel. 21/4105-7533, www.jungleme.com.br, R$150-200 pp).

Not far from the Tijuca entrance (accessible by foot, bus, or car), the **Museu do Açude** (Estrada do Açude 764, Alto da Boa Vista, tel. 21/3433-4990, www.museuscastromaya.com.br, 11am-5pm Wed.-Mon., R$2, free Thurs.) exhibits the art collection of wealthy industrialist Raymundo Ottoni de Castro Maya. The main treat, however, is the permanent installation space, which includes giant works by some of Brazil's most important contemporary artists.

Boating

Get out on the blue waters of the Baía da Guanabara. **Saveiro's Tour** (Av. Infante Dom Henrique, Marina da Glória, Glória, tel. 21/2225-6064, www.saveiros.com.br) rents out all types of seaworthy vessels as well as water skis. Those interested in a mini-cruise can charter a posh yacht that will take you up and down the coast to destinations such as Búzios, Ilha Grande, Angra dos Reis, and Paraty. A two-hour tour around the Baía da Guanabara costs R$50 pp.

Cycling

Rio has more than 300 kilometers (186 mi) of bike paths. Those in search of a languorous outing can take to the paths that line the

Copacabana beach

beaches (stretching from Flamengo to Leblon and then along Barra) and ring the Lagoa Rodrigo de Freitas. Hard-core jocks can take on the steep trails leading into the Floresta da Tijuca. You can rent bikes in many places along the Zona Sul beaches and around the Lagoa. A particularly wide range of models are available at **Bike & Lazer** (Rua Visconde de Pirajá 135-B, Ipanema, tel. 21/2267-7778, www.bikelazer.com.br, R$15 per hour), which has a second location in Laranjeiras near Largo do Machado (Rua das Laranjeiras 58, tel. 21/2285-7941). Kiosks surrounding Lagoa de Freitas also rent bikes (R$10 per hour).

Hiking and Climbing

Friendly, English-speaking mother-and-son team Denise Werneck and Gabriel operate **Rio Hiking** (tel. 21/2552-9204, www.riohiking.com.br). Expeditions in and around the city and surrounding state range from walks in the park to Iron Man-level challenges as well as biking, diving, and kayaking. **Jungle Me** (tel. 21/4105-7533, www.jungleme.com.

br) specializes in nature hiking. Top tours include hikes in Floresta da Tijuca and along the unique and little-explored Zona Oueste beaches. Full-day tours cost around R$140-180 pp.

Companhia da Escalada (tel. 21/2567-7105, www.companhiadaescalada.com.br, R$100-160 pp) and **Climb in Rio** (tel. 21/2245-1108, www.climbinrio.com) organize rock-climbing classes and excursions for beginners and experts as well as multiday adventures to peaks throughout Rio state, such as the Serra dos Orgãos and Itatiaia. Half-day climbs average around R$220 pp.

Hang Gliding

The popularity of hang gliding in Rio is second only to surfing. A classic (and breathtaking) trip is to jump off Pedra Bonita (in the Parque Nacional da Tijuca) and glide down to the Praia do Pepino in São Conrado. Both **Just Fly** (tel. 21/2268-0565, http://justflyinrio.blogspot.com) and **Super Fly** (tel. 21/3322-2286, www.riosuperfly.com.br) charge around R$250 for the 15-minute thrill, including transportation to and from your hotel. Flights may be cancelled if weather conditions are less than ideal; schedule an early take-off for more leeway.

Surfing

To facilitate getting around town, the city ingeniously operates a special **Surf Bus** (tel. 21/8515-2289 or 21/9799-5039, www.surf-bus.com.br) equipped to deal with boards and dripping bodies. Leaving from Largo do Machado in Botafogo, it travels all the way down the coast from Copacabana to Prainha, departing at 7am, 10am, 1pm, and 4pm. Despite the fact that it's equipped with air-conditioning, a minibar, and a 29-inch TV that screens surfing DVDs, the cost is only R$5.

If you want to hone your technique, **Escola de Surf Rico de Souza** (Av. Lúcio Costa 3300, Barra, tel. 21/8777-7775, http://ricosurf.globo.com) offers daily surfing lessons at its headquarters (in front of Posto 4) and at Prainha (Praia da Macumba) as well as equipment rental. Private lessons for both cost R$100 per hour; group lessons are considerably cheaper. To buy or rent surf equipment, check out the stores at **Galeria River** (Rua Francisco Otaviano 67, www.galeriariver.com.br).

Soccer

Brazil's favorite sport is also Rio's, and you'll see everyone from women to *favela* kids to beer-bellied seniors shooting and scoring, particularly on the beaches. To see the real deal, head to the largest *futebol* stadium in the world: **Maracanã** (Rua Professor Eurico Rabelo, Maracanã, tel. 0800-062-7222, www. maracana.com, R$30-60). Built in 1950 to host the World Cup and majorly revamped for the 2014 Cup, the stadium seats close to 80,000 people. Even if soccer leaves you cold, it's worth taking in a game for the sheer theatrics of the crowd, who toot whistles, beat drums, unfurl gigantic banners, and wield smoke bombs in team colors. When things aren't going well, fans shed tears, implore saints, and hurl death threats. When victory rears its head, it's more like a collective mini-Carnaval.

Rio's four biggest and most traditional teams are Flamengo, Fluminense, Botafogo, and Vasco da Gama. Each has its die-hard followers, but the most toxic rivalry of all is the legendary Flamengo-Fluminense ("Fla-Flu") match-up. Games are played throughout the week (usually Wed.-Thurs. nights and weekend afternoons). Avoid rabid fans on the bus by taking the Metrô or a taxi. **Be a Local** (tel. 21/9643-0366, http://bealocal.com) can score tickets and provide both local chaperones and gringo cohorts. During the day, Maracanã is open for 50-minute guided tours (9am-5pm daily, 8am-11am game days, R$10).

ACCOMMODATIONS

Hotels in Rio feel entitled to charge a lot for the (undisputed) pleasure of staying in the *Cidade Maravilhosa*, and you'll find scads of hotels catering to international visitors near the beaches of Copacabana, Ipanema, and Leblon. Copacabana has the most options, but many that line the beachfront of Avenida Atlântica are overpriced chains that (aside from high-end luxury hotels) offer fairly standard guest rooms in various states of decay. An increasing number have received well-overdue renovations, and a few classic hotels from Copa's 1950s heyday have been treated to makeovers.

Ipanema's accommodations veer between luxury beachfront and mediocre two-stars charging four-star prices. This has begun to shift thanks to some conscientious upgrading as well as the opening of several appealing B&Bs. The opening of atmospheric and affordable guesthouses, as well as boutique hotels in historic houses, is a welcome trend in other traditional residential *bairros* such as Botafogo, Gávea, Santa Teresa (especially), and even Leblon.

To meet the demands of the 2014 World Cup and 2016 Summer Olympics, Rio's hotel sector should have undertaken a major expansion spree. Apart from uninspiring chain hotels in Barra, it didn't. As a result, extremely high occupation rates are driving up prices. Rio's high season now lasts all year—except for New Year's and Carnaval, when rates skyrocket and advance reservations are essential.

Centro and Lapa

Centro and Lapa appeal more to business travelers than to sun worshippers who might find it frustrating to be so far from the glittering sands of Copacabana and Ipanema. Both are well served by Metrô and bus, so you can get anywhere you want fast, and prices are less expensive than in Zona Sul. On the downside, neither neighborhood is very safe (particularly Centro, which is deserted at night and on weekends), so be prepared to spend a lot on cab fare.

R$50-200

Hotel Belas Artes (Av. Visconde do Rio Branco 52, Centro, tel. 21/2252-6336, www. hotelbelasartes.com.br, R$140-180 d), in a handsome historic building in the heart of Centro, is a well-regarded hotel that offers simply furnished but spotless guest rooms with high ceilings and wooden floors—all for an unbeatable price. Expect some street noise.

R$200-400

The formerly down-and-out **Arcos Rio Palace** (Av. Mem de Sá 117, Lapa, tel. 21/2242-8116, www.arcosriopalacehotel.com.br, R$290 d) is now a safe, spotless, and comfortable hotel. Amenities include a swimming pool, sauna, fitness room, and friendly service. The real bonus is direct access to Lapa's vibrant nightlife (and noise); request a room on a top floor.

Santa Teresa

Bucolic and bohemian "Santa" provides a wonderful antidote to the Zona Sul beach scene, where visionary entrepreneurs are taking advantage of the abundance of atmospheric belle epoque villas and going the restoration route.

R$50-200

Possibly Rio's best hostel, **Santê Hostel** (Rua Felício dos Santos 62, tel. 21/8883-0164, www.hostelworld.com, R$180 d, R$32-37pp) offers a few communal and double rooms in a private family home full of creature comforts and whimsical details. Charming family members and staff take guests under their collective wing, and gigantic old windows, hardwood floors, a gorgeous tiled communal kitchen, and even a purring cat add value to an already great bargain.

Staying at eco-conscious, French-owned **Casa da Gente** (Rua Gonçalves Fontes 33, tel. 21/2232-2634, www.casadagente.com, R$175-265 d) is like crashing at the *casa* of your coolest aunt. You're handed a key and then have full run of the crazily vertical, four-story house with its art-infested nooks and crannies, communal kitchen, and surreal lawn-covered terrace overlooking Lapa (from which you're only steps away; be prepared for drifting ambient noise).

R$200-400

Casalegre Art Vila (Rua Monte Alegre 316, tel. 21/98670-6158, www.casalegre.com.br, R$200-290 d) channels Santa's artistic-boho vibe. Eight eccentric rooms in this delightfully rambling colonial mansion are full of art, antiques, and ambiance; some rooms have kitchenettes, where guests stay for weeks or even months at reduced rates. The casa doubles as a gallery space, and a courtyard café encourages mingling.

As laid-back, good-humored, and flawlessly efficient as its American expat owners, ★ **Casa Cool Beans B&B** (Rua Laurindo Santos Lobo 136, tel. 21/2262-0552, www.casacoolbeans.com, R$260-340 d) has 10 spacious rooms and chalets located near neighborhood hotspot Bar do Gomes. Perks range from giant plush towels to maple syrup with your breakfast pancakes, along with lush gardens and a pool. **Castelinho 38** (Rua Triunfo 38, tel. 21/2252-2549, www.castelinho38.com, R$250-340 d) occupies a delightfully Hollywoodesque castle built in the 1860s, complete with turrets and towers. Each of the 10 lovely guest rooms is named after a fruit tree or tropical plant. Wood floors, lofty ceilings, and lots of light reign, as does a hippie vibe: A "Well-Being" space allows guests to indulge in yoga, Pilates, and "sacred dances."

Experience life with the locals by staying as a guest in a private home. ★ **Cama e Café** (Rua Paschoal Carlos Magno 90, tel. 21/2225-4366, www.camaecafe.com.br, R$150-300) is a bed-and-breakfast network that links travelers and (often very interesting) residents. In Santa Teresa, you can choose from dozens of offerings based on factors such as cost, comfort, and common interests. Many of the hosts are artists and liberal professionals with at least a smattering of English and an impressive knowledge of the city.

R$400-600

The French owner of **Mama Ruisa** (Rua Santa Cristina 132, tel. 21/2242-1281, www.mamaruisa.com, R$500-650 d) ceaselessly combed antiques stores with the goal of creating an elegant and retro ambiance for this gleaming mansion's seven guest rooms, then added landscaped gardens punctuated by an inviting blue pool. The fabulous city views glimpsed through the trees are the only indication you're in Rio. Spa services (manicures, pedicures, massages) and chauffeured city tours are available.

OVER R$600

A former 200-year-old coffee plantation mansion, luxurious **Hotel Santa Teresa** (Rua Almirante Alexandrino 660, tel. 21/3382-0200, www.santa-teresa-hotel.com, R$850-1,700 d) was transformed into a swanky hotel in the 1920s. Today, the French-owned and -operated hotel is Rio's only member of the Relais & Châteaux hotel group. Seductive trappings include an infinity pool, lush gardens, a spa, and the romantic Bar dos Descasados. The restaurant, **Térèze**, racks up accolades for its inventive "New World" cuisine.

Glória and Catete

Lively and convenient Glória and Catete are somewhat frayed around the edges, but offer some very good deals if you're not too picky.

R$50-200

One of Glória's few accommodations options, the **Baron Garden** (Rua Barão de Guaratiba 195, Glória, tel. 21/2245-2749, www.barongarden.com, R$150-180 d, R$70 pp) is set at the top of a steep hill and offers 16 beds, including private doubles and an eight-bed dorm. While the trappings are hardly luxe, the house has plenty of character, and the arduous climb is compensated by the stunning views. Friendly owners cultivate a homey vibe conducive to rustling up meals in the gleaming kitchen or chilling out by the pool.

You've never seen an English B&B like the one built by former British war correspondent Bob Nadkarni. ★ **The Maze Inn** (Rua Tavares Bastos 414, Casa 66, Catete, tel. 21/2558-5547, http://jazzrio.com, R$150-180 d) features a labyrinth-like ensemble of curving concrete buildings adorned with Gaudí-esque mosaics and Nadkarni's artwork, all set amidst mountains as well as the surrounding *favela* of Tavares Bastos (though in terms of safety, the only shooting you'll encounter is TV and movie crews). The small suites are light on furnishings but heavy on atmosphere; there are also housekeeping units with living rooms and kitchens. You'll have difficulty tearing yourself away from the rooftop terrace, where Pão de Açúcar seems close enough to touch. Even if you don't check in, it's worth checking out the monthly Friday night jazz performances, which have become a cult event. Transportation up the hill is provided by frequent VW vans (R$3) and moto-taxis (R$4).

Botafogo, Cosme Velho, and Urca
R$50-200

Oztel (Rua Pinheiro Guimarães 91, Botafogo, tel. 21/3042-1853, www.oztel.com.br, R$120-150 d, R$49-57 pp) has a laid-back vibe that dovetails perfectly with its location on a tranquil residential street whose cool factor has intensified with the opening of the owners' nearby bar, **Meza.** Collective hostel rooms are airy and spotless, but the style quotient kicks in with the whimsically decorated, very affordable private rooms and extends to a lounge and hang-out area, where pop-up events are held. A young staff of hipsters (without the attitude) generously dole out insider travel tips.

R$200-400

Halfway up a winding (but easily walkable) road to Corcovado and camouflaged by a patch of Tijuca Forest, **O Veleiro** (Rua Mundo Novo 1440, Botafogo, tel. 21/2554-8980, www.oveleiro.com.br, R$240-280 d) is one of Rio's first and most restive B&Bs. Smoothly administered by a Canadian-Carioca couple as amiable as they are efficient, the historic house has three guest rooms, appealing living areas, a pool, and lush gardens that merge with the surrounding jungle. Monkeys, toucans, and hummingbirds bestow a delicious sense of being away from it all.

Copacabana and Leme
R$50-200

If you're young in age or spirit, but low on bucks, ★ **Lisetonga Hostel** (Laderia Ary Barroso, Casa 15, Leme, tel. 21/2541-0393, www.lisetongahostel.com, R$90 d, R$40-60 pp) is ideal. Occupying a castlelike villa a short but steep climb from Leme's beach, Lisetonga provides bunks and a warm communal ambience. Travelers can discover the city together with the help of the personable staff, then regroup around the bar in time for happy hour. Winding staircases, hammock-strewn courtyards, and a colorful kitchen have induced many to temporarily move in; reservations are advised.

R$200-400

It's five blocks from the beach, but those in search of a little piece of mind and a great deal will find **Hotel Santa Clara** (Rua Décio Villares 316, Copacabana, tel. 21/2256-2650, www.hotelsantaclara.com.br, R$210-240 d) in a location nicely removed from Copa's bustle (but adjacent to the Metrô). Try for guest rooms facing the front, particularly on the top floor, which are the brightest and breeziest.

On the same street, **SESC Copacabana** (Rua Domingos Ferreira 160, Copacabana, tel. 21/2548-1088, www.sescrio.org.br, R$360-430 d) is not only a great deal for Copa, but you get to stay in an architectural landmark designed by Oscar Niemeyer. Guest rooms are coolly minimalist, and those above the 10th floor offer terrific views of Corcovado.

R$400-600

Inaugurated in 1949, when Copa's glamour was peaking, the classy art deco facade of the **Olinda Rio Hotel** (Av. Atlântica 2230, Copacabana, tel. 21/2159-9000, www.olindariohotel.com, R$370-480 d) is a welcome contrast amidst a sea of high-rises. Step inside and the flashback continues: awash in Italian marble, Persian carpets, and crystal chandeliers,

the lobby oozes grandeur. Splurge for the oceanfront rooms with balconies.

Rio's only beachfront B&B (and a penthouse no less!), ★ **Rio Guesthouse** (Rua Francisco Sá 5, Copacabana, tel. 21/2521-8586, www.rioguesthouse.com.br, R$360-530 d) consists of a handful of comfortable, color-coded rooms and Art Deco salons with glass walls and terraces that gape upon Copacabana's hypnotic crescent. Hostess Marta is like the Carioca mom you wish you always had.

OVER R$600

One of the most legendary hotels in the world and a national landmark, the refurbished ★ **Copacabana Palace** (Av. Atlântica 1702, Copacabana, tel. 21/2548-7070, www.copacabanapalace.com, R$1,490-2,100 d) is as famous as the beach it sits on. When this dazzling white hotel was constructed in 1923, Copacabana was little more than an unspoiled strip of sand surrounded by mountains. A decade later, the Palace played a prominent role in the RKO classic *Flying Down to Rio,* the first film to pair Fred Astaire and Ginger Rogers. Since then, the Palace has continued to attract a cavalcade of international stars, jet-setters, heads of state, and royalty without losing a shred of its elegance. When not holed up in the luxury of their poshly furnished rooms, these privileged guests can often be spotted lounging around the Olympic-size pool, getting pampered in the spa, playing a few sets on the rooftop tennis court, or dining in one of the two highly reputed restaurants, Cipriani and Pérgula. The extravagant cost is worth every penny.

The Palace's most serious rival is the **Sofitel Rio de Janeiro** (Av. Atlântica 4240, Copacabana, tel. 21/2525-1232, www.sofitel.com, R$750-1,250 d). What this ultramodern, somewhat overpriced hotel lacks in charm and pedigree, it tries to make up for with a dazzling array of enticing extras. The swanky guest rooms are outfitted with plasma TVs, immense beds, and balconies overlooking the entire length of Copacabana beach. Two strategically positioned rooftop pools allow you to catch both morning and afternoon rays. Other bonuses include **Le Pré Catalan,** considered one of Rio's top French restaurants, and a location on the frontier between Copa and Ipanema.

One of Avenue Atlântica's best values, the **Arena Copacabana** (Av. Atlântica 2064, Copacabana, tel. 21/3034-1501, http://arena-hotel.com.br, R$560-880 d) is a polished affair; contemporary rooms are tricked out with the latest modern conveniences (though Wi-Fi is *not* free). The more expensive ones have sea views, but all can indulge in the rooftop pool along with a sauna and fitness room.

Ipanema and Leblon
R$50-200

One Ipanema's best hostels, **The Mango Tree** (Rua Prudente de Moraes 594, Ipanema, tel. 21/2287-9255, www.mangotreehostel.com, R$170-240 d, R$60 pp) offers clean but basic accommodations in a restored 1930s villa only a block from Posto 9, Ipanema's hippest patch of sand. Small size combined with a "no noise after 10pm" rule dissuades late-night party animals, but plenty of socializing goes on in the common spaces, which include a deck hung with hammocks, a barbecue pit, and a garden with the mascot *mangueira* (mango tree).

Z.Bra Hostel (Av. Gal. San Martin 1212, Leblon, tel. 21/3596-2386, www.zbrahostel. com, R$140-175 d, R$55-60 pp) is a block from the beach (parasols are available), in the heart of the action. Rooms are small but stylishly efficient, and a loungey hang-out space sports delightfully mashed-up furnishings and a pre-party atmosphere nourished by the hostel bar. The gregarious staff can organize outings far beyond Leblon's borders.

R$200-400

One of Ipanema's only *pousadas,* **Margarida's Pousada** (Rua Barão da Torre 600, Ipanema tel. 21/2238-1840, www. margaridaspousada.com, R$270) is a three-story building whose basic yet homey rooms (for 2-4 people) are well cared for by kind,

no-nonsense owner Margarida. A big bonus is the coveted location midway between Ipanema beach and the Lagoa.

R$400-600

One of Ipanema's best value hotels, **Ipanema Inn** (Rua Maria Quitéria 27, Ipanema, tel. 21/2523-6093, http://ipanemainn.com.br, R$390-510 d) has a terrific location only half a block from the beach, yet that half-block makes a world of difference in terms of price. Quarters are tight, but the spotless guest rooms are modern and service is good. If you plan to spend most of your time on the beach, this is a convenient choice.

The **Arpoador Inn** (Rua Francisco Otaviano 177, Ipanema, tel. 21/2523-0060, http://arpoadorinn.com.br, R$390-610 d) is not only the most affordable beachfront hotel in Ipanema but is within spitting distance of Copacabana, and looks right onto the surfer's mecca of Praia do Arpoador. Rooms themselves are functional but not overly attractive—if you want a sea view, you'll have to pay a lot extra for it.

Brought to you by the same American duo who created Santa Teresa's Casa Cool Beans B&B, ★ **Casa Cool Beans Flats** (Rua Vinícius de Moraes 72, Ipanema, tel. 21/8204-1458, http://flats.casacoolbeans. com, R$350-670) is a revolutionary concept for Rio that straddles an *apart-hotel* with a B&B. Occupying the four floors of an atmospheric 1940s building, studio and one-bedroom suites are sunny, glossy, and modern. Amenities include daily housekeeping, breakfast vouchers for a local café, and the advice of co-owner David.

OVER R$600

The brainchild of two French expats, ★ **Casa Mosquito** (Rua San Roman 222, Ipanema, tel. 21/3586-5042, http://casamosquito.com, R$670-1,200 d) is an exquisite boutique-style guesthouse. Hidden on a steep street that climbs from Metrô Ipanema up to Morro do Pavão, views include both the *favela* and the beach. Inspired by iconic Brazilian personalities, decorated with Gallic panache, and dotted with patios, the rooms are split between a 1940s building and newer annex. Gourmet meals feature daily produce (breakfast not included).

A favorite of business execs, the **Promenade Palladium** (Av. General Artigas 200, Leblon, tel. 21/3171-7400, www. hotel-promenade-palladium.com, R$620-840 d) is comfortable if bland, with a prime Leblon location.

The Fasano family—which owns some of São Paulo's most celebrated high-class hotels and restaurants—procured Philippe Starck to oversee the design of the **Fasano Rio Hotel** (Av. Vieira Souto 80, Ipanema, tel. 21/3202-4000, www.fasano.com.br, R$1,560-2,100 d). With a team of Brazilian artists, the French design guru sought to conjure up the spell of 1950s Rio with a contemporary twist. The sea is prominently on display from the fabulous rooftop pool, fitness center, and spa as well as the sumptuous guest rooms—in the deluxe apartments, you can even see the ocean while taking a shower. Both the elegant **Al Mare** restaurant and the clubby **Baretto-Londra** bar are fervent fashionista hot spots.

Ruling the luxury roost of Leblon is Rio's "other" boutique hotel: the **Marina All-Suites** (Av. Delfim Moreira 696, Leblon, tel. 21/2172-1100, www.marinaallsuites.com.br, R$870-1,270 d). The 39 suites range from sizable to massive, and the beautiful decor is as personalized as the pampering you'll receive from the staff. The result is top-of-the-line comfort that is both refined and homelike, which explains the faithfulness of a classy celeb clientele (Gisele prefers the Diamante suite). Other model types can be seen hanging around the penthouse pool, taking in a film at the in-house movie theater, or downing caipirinhas at the enchanting **Bar d'Hotel.**

FOOD

Rio has an impressive restaurant scene featuring the best of so-called *alta* and *baixa culinária* (high and low cuisine). *Alta* cuisine has really taken off in Rio since the 1990s. The neighborhoods of Ipanema, Leblon, Jardim Botânico, and, to a lesser extent, Centro have seen a rise in stylish eateries owned and operated by some of the country's vanguard chefs. Meanwhile, many traditional neighborhood *churrascarias* and *botequins* offer up tasty *comida caseira* (home cooking) ranging from hearty *caldos* (soups), robust sandwiches, and barbecued chicken and beef to the classic Saturday *feijoada.*

Although carnivores fare well in Rio, seafood lovers will be equally spoiled. In keeping with Cariocas' fame as a body-conscious bunch, there are also numerous vegetarian, organic, and all-around healthy eateries—many of them self-service per-kilo buffets where diners can control their weight down to the last gram—particularly in the Zona Sul, where juice bars serve up dozens of varieties of fresh fruit juices, vitamin drinks, and healthy *sanduiches naturais.*

In recent times, a new crop of charming cafés has sprung up, many of them located in the city's cultural centers, cinemas, and *livrarias* (bookstores), where the desserts tend to be quite fabulous. As you'll witness everywhere from the street *barracas* in Lapa to the *padarias* (bakeries) in Copa, Cariocas have a pronounced sweet tooth, and satisfying sugar cravings is absurdly easy.

Although Rio's top restaurants are not cheap, it's definitely worth your while to splurge once or twice (also know that many offer more reasonably priced weekday *menus executivos* for lunch). You can then atone for your sins by seeking out more reasonably priced culinary experiences at the city's beach *barracas,* bars, bakeries, and bookstores.

Centro

You'll find a wide range of eating options in Rio's commercial hub, from speedy self-service buffets and bars serving *prato feitos,* or "PFs"—simple home-cooked specials of the day, usually consisting of the basic meat, beans, and rice triumvirate—to contemporary bistros, many located near the area's museums and cultural centers.

Botequins

Rio is legendary for its *botequins*, informal bars that function as neighborhood headquarters for residents from all walks of life. Whether considered *pé sujo* ("dirty foot," mildly mangy holes-in-the-wall) or *pé limpo* ("clean foot," somewhat more refined and upscale), the simple *botequim* is a democratic enclave where Cariocas get together to talk about *futebol*, politics, or their sex lives for hours at a time.

The drink of choice is an ice-cold *chope* (draft) served in traditional glasses that come in three sizes: the *tulipa* ("tulip"), the *garotinho* ("little boy"), and the rarely seen, mug-size *caldeireta* (Cariocas subscribe to the belief that the larger the glass, the warmer and more undrinkable the beer gets). There are always plenty of mouthwatering *petiscos* (bar snacks); the most common are *bolinhos de bacalhau* (deep-fried codfish balls), *carne seca desfiada* (shredded sun-dried beef), and velvety thick *caldo de feijão* (black bean broth), traditionally served with chopped cilantro, *torresmos* (pork rinds), lime, and *pimenta* (hot pepper).

CAFÉS AND SNACKS

★ **Confeitaria Colombo** (Rua Gonçalves Dias 32, tel. 21/2505-1500, www.confeitaria-colombo.com.br, 9am-8pm Mon.-Fri., 9am-5pm Sat.) is an exceptionally elegant belle epoque café, one of the few vestiges of how grand life must have been if you were an aristocrat in turn-of-the-20th-century Rio. More than a century later, Colombo is still a Rio institution: While working Cariocas cluster around the bar chasing pastries with *cafezinhos,* slack-jawed tourists can take *chá da tarde* (high tea) in the salon or indulge in the Saturday afternoon *feijoada,* accompanied by live samba and choro.

Ideally located in the foyer of the Centro do Comércio do Café (the 100-year-old regulating body of Brazil's prize crop), **Rubro Café** (Rua da Quitanda 191, tel. 21/2223-2265, www.rubrocafe.com.br, 7am-6pm Mon.-Fri.) is where the people who really *know* about coffee go to get their caffeine fix. More than 20 gourmet coffee drinks are served in this airy, modern space, as well as breakfast fare, sandwiches, salads, and desserts.

BISTROS AND LIGHT FARE

Looking out onto a whitewashed courtyard inside the Paço Imperial, **Bistrô do Paço** (Praça XV 48, tel. 21/2262-3613, www.bistro.com.br, 11:30am-7:30pm Mon.-Fri., noon-7pm Sat.-Sun., R$20-35) offers a tranquil oasis from the surrounding noise and traffic of Centro. Lunch is a rapid but tasteful affair with delicious salads, sandwiches, and daily specials.

Brasserie Rosário (Rua do Rosário 34, tel. 21/2518-3533, www.brasserierosario.com.br, 11am-9pm Mon.-Fri., 11am-6pm Sat., R$20-40) is a gourmet café, delicatessen, bakery, wine cellar, and bistro all rolled into one attractive, high-ceilinged, stone-walled building that once housed the Imperial Treasury. Happy-hour jazz and samba sessions at 6pm have a loyal following.

LOCAL COMFORT FOOD

With wooden shelves crammed to the ceiling with glittery bottles, **Paladino** (Rua Uruguaiana 224, tel. 21/2263-2094, 7am-8:30pm Mon.-Fri., 8am-noon Sat., R$15-25) is a quintessential Carioc *boteco* that's been around for more than a century. It's beloved by downtown workers for its cheap, home-cooked lunch specials, particularly omelets stuffed with *bacalhau* and shrimp.

SEAFOOD

Rio's oldest restaurant, **Rio Minho** (Rua do Ouvidor 10, tel. 21/2509-2338, 11am-3pm Mon.-Fri., R$40-55) hasn't changed much since it first opened its doors in 1884. The small traditional eatery is famed for its *sopa Leão Veloso,* a heady bouillabaisse-like stew of shrimp and fish heads flavored with leeks and cilantro. Owner Ramon Dominguez also owns Anexo next door, which serves smaller (and cheaper) portions.

Lapa

Lapa really comes into its own at night, which is also when you're more likely to find more appetizing sustenance. Bars are much more prevalent than restaurants, and they all serve *petiscos*. For a full-fledged meal, your best bet is to seek out traditional *botequins*. A good option is **Nova Capela** (Av. Mem de Sá 96, tel. 21/2252-6228, 11am-4am daily, R$20-35), the only one of Lapa's old-time *botequins* that stays open into the wee hours. Over the years it has become the classic pit stop after sambaing the night away at Lapa's neighboring clubs and dance halls.

Santa Teresa

Santa's ongoing metamorphosis into an alternative arts *bairro* has spilled over into its restaurant scene, as local entrepreneurs, artists, and an increasing number of European expats are transforming century-old mini-palaces into gourmet eateries with bewitching views. Local residents often head to a handful of charming, decades-old *botecos* that continue to serve up *petiscos* and *comida caseira* at much more affordable prices.

CAFÉS AND SNACKS

From her home, **Alda Maria** (Rua Almirante Alexandrino 116, tel. 21/2232-1320, www.aldadocesportugueses.com.br, 2pm-7pm Tues.-Sun.) sells Portuguese sweets and pastries that she makes using recipes passed down by her grandmother. Cholesterol-phobics beware: Invented centuries ago in Portuguese convents, most of the pastries rely heavily on eggs (Alda Maria claims she cracks more than 800 a week).

At **Cafecito** (Rua Paschoal Carlos Magno 121, tel. 21/2221-9439, www.cafecito.com.br, 9am-10pm Sun.-Tues. and Thurs., 9am-11pm Fri.-Sat., R$15-35), one of Santa's inexplicably few cafes, the terrace—festooned with orchids and the occasional monkey—is a languorous place to relax. Options include

gourmet sandwiches, tapa-ish portions, and craft beers.

BRAZILIAN

Romantic and aptly named ★ **Rústico** (Rua Paschoal Carlos Magno 121, tel. 21/2221-9439, 1pm-10pm Sun.-Tues. and Thurs., 1pm-1am Fri.-Sat., R$25-45) is just up the stone steps from Cafecito's entrance. Sample creations such as grilled pineapple and brie salad, wild boar with baked apple, or *galinhada* (chicken stew with saffron rice served in a bubbling soapstone pot). Pizzas baked in a firewood oven are less adventurous but equally tasty. **Aprazível** (Rua Aprazível 62, tel. 21/2508-9174, www.aprazivel.com.br, noon-11pm Tues.-Sat., noon-6pm Sun., R$50-80)—the name is Portuguese for "delightful"—is the perfect name for this restaurant occupying a bucolic villa. Polished jacaranda tables spill out onto the veranda and lush tropical garden, which overlooks the Baía de Guanabara. The wine menu, designed by American expat and indie filmmaker Jonathan Nossiter, focuses on unsung local vintages. Reservations recommended.

Glória and Catete

Adega Portugália (Largo do Machado 30, Catete, tel. 21/2558-2821, 8am-midnight daily, R$20-35) is a friendly neighborhood restaurant-bar whose no-nonsense menu traffics in favorites such as grilled sardines and a legendary lamb risotto (served only on weekends), served in robust portions.

Flamengo and Laranjeiras

The most interesting eating options in this *bairro* are the handful of alluringly retro *botequins* and restaurants that have survived from the area's early 20th-century heyday.

CAFÉS AND SNACKS

Famed for its chocolate-covered carrot-cake, **Maya Café** (Rua Ortiz Monteiro 15, Laranjeiras, tel. 21/2205-4950, www.mayacafe.com.br, 9am-9:30pm daily) is a tranquil neighborhood nook that serves mouthwatering croissants, cakes, gourmet sandwiches, and salads as well as coffee. At night, caffeinated customers switch to wine and a delicious assortment of antipasti.

BRAZILIAN

Walking into ★ **Tacacá do Norte** (Rua Barão do Flamengo 35, Flamengo, tel. 21/2205-7545, 8:30am-11pm Mon.-Sat., 9am-9pm Sun., R$25-35) is like taking a trip to the Amazonian state of Pará. The standout is the namesake *tacacá*, a shrimp-filled broth flavored with *tucupi* (a yellow sauce made from wild manioc root) and *jambu* leaves, which leave your mouth tingling. Juices made from unpronounceable Amazonian fruits are ambrosial.

CHURRASCARIAS

The classic unfussy decor of **Majórica** (Rua Senador Vergueiro 11-15, Flamengo, tel. 21/2205-6820, noon-midnight Sun.-Thurs., noon-1am Fri.-Sat., R$40-60), where slabs of meat and a massive charcoal *churrasqueira* are prominent features, belie the fact that this is one of Rio's most traditional, and best, *churrascarias*. Traditional garnishes such as potato soufflé, french fries, *farofa* (toasted manioc flour) with eggs and banana, and *arroz maluco* ("crazy rice" that features bacon, parsley, and matchstick potatoes) are served separately. On weekends, avoid the immense family lineups by arriving after 3pm.

LOCAL COMFORT FOOD

At **Lamas** (Rua Marquês de Abrantes 18, Flamengo, tel. 21/2556-0799, www.cafelamas. com.br, 9:30am-2am Sun.-Thurs., 9:30am-4am Fri.-Sat., R$40-60), which originally opened in 1874, everything from the food and suave bow-tied waiters to the retro ambience is suffused with an aura of Rio's dining past. The food is honest, solid fare without surprises; try the famous filets mignons or the *filé à francesa*, served with matchstick potatoes and green peas flavored with diced ham and onions.

Botafogo, Cosme Velho, and Urca

These traditional residential neighborhoods are best known for their old *botequins* and Portuguese *tascas* that serve up tried-and-true *comida caseira*, but as Botafogo's nightlife has blossomed, so has the culinary scene.

CONTEMPORARY

With a name that's the Brazilian equivalent of "yum yum," **Miam-Miam** (Rua General Góes Monteiro 34, Botafogo, tel. 21/2244-0125, www.miammiam.com.br, 7pm-midnight Tues.-Fri., 8pm-1am Sat., R$35-45) is a tiny but very romantic café-bar owned and operated by Roberta Ciasca. At 21, Ciasca went backpacking through Europe and ended up at Paris's Cordon Bleu cooking school. In 2006, when she decided to convert her grandmother's turn-of-the-20th-century house into a restaurant, her creative comfort food—such as arugula rolls stuffed with roast beef and parmesan, or chicken pancakes with asparagus, mushrooms, emmental, and tarragon—quickly seduced the city's gourmets.

VEGETARIAN

Chácara is Portuguese for a rural estate, which is what it feels like when you arrive at **Vegana Chácara** (Rua Hans Staden 30, Botafogo, tel. 21/8599-7078, noon-3pm Mon.-Fri., R$20-30). Operated by two macrobiotic vegans who live on the second floor, the restaurant's daily options are so delicious that many carnivores stop by to savor meatless versions of Brazilian classics such as *feijoada* and *moqueca*. There's even a vegan caipirinha (the cachaça is replaced by ginger). Meals are paid for in cash, which you place in a box (make your own change).

Copacabana and Leme

Although the views from the tourist-flooded restaurants along Avenida Atlântica are incomparable, the food is usually overpriced and lackluster. Otherwise, Copa's most edible options are divided between the five-star kitchens of its most luxurious hotels and a few traditional restaurants and *botequins*.

CAFÉS AND SNACKS

Just around the corner from the Copacabana Palace, **La Fiducia Café** (Rua Duvivier 14, Copacabana, tel. 21/2295-7449, 7am-10pm daily) is a lively little café with sidewalk tables that make excellent perches for people-watching. Even if you have breakfast in your hotel, the pastries and coffee are so good you might want seconds. In the evening, it's a languorous spot for a glass of wine and a plate of pasta.

INTERNATIONAL

Considered by many to be Rio's top Japanese restaurant, **Azumi** (Rua Ministro Viveiros de Castro 127, Copacabana, tel. 21/2541-4294, 7pm-midnight Sun.-Thurs., 7pm-1am daily, R$35-75) emphasizes substance—and sushi—over style. Classic recipes are expertly prepared and presented in a pared-down, multilevel space. Slip off your shoes in one of the bamboo-screened rooms and Zen out before the check snaps you back to reality.

The ornate Middle Eastern trappings at **Amir** (Rua Ronald de Carvalho 55-C, Copacabana, tel. 21/2275-5596, www.amir-restaurante.com.br, noon-11pm Sun.-Fri., noon-midnight Sat., R$25-40) appear to be ripped out of a tale from *One Thousand and One Nights*. Despite the richness of the colors and fabrics on display, the Lebanese fare on Amir's menu is quite affordable, and portions are generous. A Leblon tentacle of Amir, **Yalla** (Rua Dias Ferreira 45, Leblon, tel. 21/2540-6517, www.yallabistro.com.br, noon-midnight daily, R$30) offers salads, shawarmas, falafels, and other light fare.

LOCAL COMFORT FOOD

The pioneer of the "favela-dining" phenomenon, the plastic chairs at ★ **Bar do David** (Ladeira Ary Barroso 66, Chapéu Mangueira, tel. 21/7808-2200, noon-5pm Tues.-Fri., noon-8pm Sat.-Sun., R$15-25) are as likely to seat local residents as Zona Sul foodies and foreign tourists. Owner David Vieira Bispo serves classic Brazilian homecooking with inventive twists. Pacific Chapéu Mangueira is just a quick, if steep, walk from Leme.

VEGETARIAN

Hidden in a little alley, **Naturaleve** (Rua Miguel Lemos 53, Loja B, Copacabana, tel. 21/2247-2900, 11am-8pm Mon.-Fri., 11am-4pm Sat., R$20-30) is a cheery, pistachio-green hole-in-the-wall. The vegetarian per-kilo restaurant serves a diverse selection of daily dishes as well as lots of organic, healthy goodies to go.

Ipanema and Leblon

The svelte and sun-kissed residents of these beach *bairros* dress up (casually chic) and go all out at international and contemporary restaurants, where the decor is as tasteful as the fare on the (usually pricey) menus. For lighter, more affordable sustenance, head to the neighborhoods' *botequins*, cafés, and delicatessens.

CAFÉS AND SNACKS

Armazém do Café (Rua Maria Quitéria 77, Ipanema, tel. 21/2522-5039, www.armazem-docafe.com.br, 8:30am-8:30pm Mon.-Fri., 8:30am-7pm Sat., 10am-6pm Sun.), a chain of gourmet cafés, currently has eight locations around Rio, including four in Ipanema. Armazém, which takes its beans quite seriously, is a great place to learn about and savor different Brazilian blends. For noshing, there are sandwiches as well as sweet and savory pastries.

Talho Capixaba (Av. Ataulfo de Paiva 1022, Loja A/B, Leblon, tel. 21/2512-8750, www.talhocapixaba.com.br, 7am-10pm daily) originally opened as a neighborhood butcher shop in the 1950s. Over the years it kept expanding, adding a fine-food delicatessen, a cheese shop, and one of the best bakeries in town. Choose from more than 20 types of bread and then design the sandwich of your dreams. If you have a sweet tooth, you won't be able to resist **Mil Frutas Café** (Rua Gárcia d'Avila 134, Ipanema, tel. 21/2521-1384, www.milfrutas.com.br, 10:30am-12:30am Mon.-Fri., 9:30am-1:30am Sat.-Sun.), whose all-natural gourmet sorbets are made from native fruits such as *açai, bacuri, and cupuaçu.* Though there are not yet *mil* (1,000) flavors, there are close to 200. Although there are several locations around town, Ipanema's café also serves snacks and light meals.

BISTROS AND LIGHT FARE

A mere block from Ipanema beach, **Delírio Tropical** (Rua Gárcia d'Ávila 48, Ipanema, www.deliriotropical.com.br, tel. 21/3624-8164, 9am-9pm daily, R$20-35) is a great place for a healthy meal after soaking up the sun. Choose from an array of colorful and unusual salads along with hot daily specials, then take a seat in the upstairs dining area, where glass walls afford a tree house-like view of the comings and goings of beach below.

Tucked down a narrow alley from Ipanema's main drag, **Market Ipanema** (Rua Visconde de Pirajá 452, Ipanema, tel. 21/3283-1438, www.marketipanema.com.br, R$20-40) is a vibrant refuge. The décor is as fresh, light, and colorful as the healthy and tasty dishes, which appeal to both herbivores (red quinoa risotto) and carnivores (baby beef in a mustard-wine sauce). The caipirinha (made with passion fruit, lychees, strawberries, and basil) is wicked.

Located on the mezzanine of Ipanema's Livraria da Travessa, there's nothing at all bookish about sleek and sophisticated **Lado B** (Rua Visconde de Pirajá 572, Ipanema, tel. 21/2249-4977, www.bazzar.com.br, 10am-11pm Mon.-Fri., 9am-11pm Sat., noon-11pm Sun.). Serving breakfast, creative sandwiches, and bistro-style meals with Brazilian touches along with desserts, coffee, and drinks, it's an appealing place to hang out. Smaller versions are at Travessa branches in Shopping Leblon and Centro (Av. Rio Branco 44).

BRAZILIAN

Although Rio's most traditional dish—*feijoada*—is eaten on Saturday, **Brasileirinho** (Rua Jangadeiros 10, Loja A, Ipanema, tel. 21/2513-5184, www.cozinhatipica.com.br, noon-11pm daily, R$25-40) has been serving up this quintessential stew for those (mainly gringos) who crave it any day of the week. The menu also traffics in succulent regional fare such as *carne seca com abóbora* (sun-dried beef with pumpkin) and *tutu à mineira,* a hearty stew of pork and pureed beans from Minas Gerais. The woodburning stove and rustic ambiance typical of the Interior décor comes as a refreshing shock.

CHURRASCARIAS

Son of Carioca superstar chef Claude Troisgros, Thomas Troisgros oversees the butchering and preparation of succulent meats at family-owned **CT Boucherie** (Rua Dias Ferreira 636, Leblon, tel. 21/2529-2329, www.ctboucherie.com.br, noon-4pm and 7pm-1am Mon.-Fri., noon-1am Sat.-Sun., R$60-90). Veggies and garnishes are given equal VIP treatment. An excellent wine list and contemporary decorative take on a classic French *boucherie* ensure an all-around appetizing experience.

CONTEMPORARY

Zaza Bistrô Tropical (Rua Joana Angêlica 40, Ipanema, tel. 21/2247-9101, www.zazabistro.com.br, 7:30pm-12:30am Mon.-Thurs., 7:30pm-12:30am Fri., 1:30pm-1:30am Sat., 12:30pm-6pm Sun., R$40-60) is a funky hippie-chic eatery where the organic and tropical (Asian, African, and American) rule. Red velvet flowers dangle from the ceiling of an upstairs room, where silk pillows litter the floor and shoes are optional. On the breezy, candlelit terrace, romance and relaxation are assured.

Foodie favorite **Zuka** (Rua Dias Ferreira 233, Loja B, Leblon, tel. 21/3205-7154, www.zuka.com.br, 7pm-1am Mon.-Fri., noon-4pm and 7pm-1am Sat., 1pm-midnight Sun., R$50-60) is presided over by Ludmila Soeira, one of Brazil's most exciting young contemporary chefs. Among her culinary fetishes is an old-fashioned charcoal grill; every hot dish passes over the grill's flames in some manner.

INTERNATIONAL

Spanish tapas are perfect for the Zona Sulistas' preoccupation with lithe figures and small portions. **Venga!** (Rua Dias Ferreira 113, Leblon, tel. 21/25129826, http://venga.com. br, 6pm-midnight Mon., noon-midnight Tues.-Wed. and Sun., noon-1am Thurs.-Sat., R$15-40) delivers with such aplomb that a second location opened in Ipanema (Rua Garcia D'Ávila 147b, 21/2247-0234, noon-1am daily). Tapas are as delectable as the people-watching from the terrace tables.

The penchant for small portions is so contagious that neighboring **Stuzzi** (Rua Dias Ferreira 48, Leblon, tel. 21/2274-4017, www. stuzzibar.com.br, 7pm-2am Mon.-Sat., 7pm-midnight Sun., R$28-38) jumped on the bandwagon—only in Italian. Rio is full of pricey *alta cocina* and pizza temples, but this subtle bar, with dim lighting and soft grey walls, is the real deal: Chef Paula Prandini did time at a Michelin-starred *ristorante* in Lombardy. The wine list focuses on Italian and Argentinian vintages.

The sushi chefs at **Sushi Leblon** (Rua Dias Ferreira 256, Leblon, tel. 21/2512-7830, noon-4pm and 7pm-1:30am Mon.-Wed., noon-1:30am Thurs.-Sat., 1pm-midnight Sun., R$50-75) are from the northeastern coastal state of Ceará, a region with a strong fishing tradition. Once they acquired Japanese preparation techniques, there was no stopping them—the sushi is sublime. While waiting for a table, do so in the company of a lychee caipisake (sake substitutes cachaça).

PER-KILO BUFFETS

Fellini (Rua General Urquiza 101, Leblon, tel. 21/2511-3600, www.fellini.com.br, 11:30am-4pm and 7:30pm-midnight Mon.-Fri., 11:30am-6pm and 7:30pm-midnight Sat.-Sun., R$25-40) offers one of Rio's most extensive and refined self-service buffets. There's no need to splurge at a five-star restaurant when you can savor the likes of lobster and

escargots for a price only slightly higher than your average per-kilo joint. There are dishes for vegetarians and diabetics, and the dessert table is a world unto itself. On weekends, avoid prime time or you'll have to stand in line for some time.

One of Ipanema's organic pioneers, **New Natural** (Rua Barão da Torre 173, Ipanema, tel. 21/2287-0301, 7am-11pm daily, R$20-30) captures the healthy Zona Sul ethos to the hilt with offerings that appeal to both hard-core vegans and veggie-loving carnivores. The GLS community has claimed the place as a healthy hangout, and an onsite food store offers goodies to go.

VEGETARIAN

The tiny **Vegetariano Social Clube** (Rua Conde de Bernadote 26, Loja L, Leblon, tel. 21/2294-5200, www.vegetarianosocialclube. com.br, noon-midnight Mon.-Sat., noon-6pm Sun., R$20-25) opened when a group of health-conscious pals from Leblon decided to do something about the lack of hard-core vegan restaurants in the hood. Choose from buffet (lunch only) or à la carte options. To drink, there are lots of organic juices and even caipirinhas made with organic *cachaça* or sake. Sunday's tofu *feijoadas* (also served Wed.) have a large vegetarian following.

Lagoa and Jardim Botânico

The dozen sophisticated kiosks scattered around the Lagoa Rodrigo de Freitas offer a wide range of delicious fare, ranging from Arabian to Amazonian, both day and night. The reserved, upscale residential neighborhood of Jardim Botânico is second only to Ipanema and Leblon when it comes to gourmet eating experiences.

CAFÉS AND SNACKS

The lush tropicality of the Jardim Botânico became even more seductive with the opening of **La Bicyclette** (Rua Jardim Botânico 920, Jardim Botânico, www.labicyclette.com.br, tel. 3594-2589, 8:30am-9pm Mon.-Sat., 8:30am-4pm Sun.), a fetching French *boulangerie* that has become *le lieu* for flaky croissants, *pains au chocolat, croque monsieurs,* and gourmet sandwiches. The main location is nearby at Rua Pacheco Leão 320d.

Within the arcaded central courtyard of the Parque Lage are a sprinkling of tables that belong to ★ **D.R.I. Café** (Rua Jardim Botânico 414, Jardim Botânico, tel. 21/2226-8125, www.driculinaria.com.br, 9am-5pm daily), which offers an enticing selection of quiche, sandwiches, and pastries. Wines provide sustenance while you kick back and contemplate Christ the Redeemer's looming reflection in the courtyard's blue pool. Come on weekends for delicious brunch and live music.

INTERNATIONAL

One of Brazil's most stellar chefs, Claude Troisgros migrated from Paris to Rio 25 years ago and started a (culinary) revolution by marrying sophisticated French cooking techniques with Brazilian produce. You can savor Troisgros's original creations at ★ **Olympe** (Rua Custódio Serrão 62, Jardim Botânico, tel. 21/2537-6582, www.claudetroisgros.com.br, 7:30pm-12:30am Mon.-Sat., noon-4pm Fri., R$80-120). The restaurant's decor is as unpretentious and refined as the menus themselves (Troisgros offers several). Adventurous souls can splurge on the five-dish tasting feast (daily, R$260) that Troisgros dreams up according to the ingredients at hand.

INFORMATION AND SERVICES

Riotur (www.rioguiaoficial.com.br) is the city travel association. Pick up maps and brochures at its tourist centers as well as the excellent free *Rio Guide* (in English), with exhaustive listings, updated bimonthly. You can also consult the guide and even download it, along with city maps, from their website, and take advantage of its 24-hour tourist information hot line, Central 1746 (tel. 1746). The main center is in Centro (Praça Pio X 119, 9th Floor, tel. 21/2271-7048, 9am-6pm Mon.-Fri.). There are also branches in Copacabana (Av. Princesa Isabel 183, tel. 21/2541-7522,

9am-6pm, Mon.-Fri.) and at the Aeroporto Internacional Tom Jobim (7am-11pm daily). Small kiosks at various locations include Centro (Rua Candelária 6), Pão de Açúcar (Praça General Tibúrcio, Urca), and Ipanema (Rua Visconde de Pirajá at the corner of Rua Joana Angélica).

Exchange currency at **Banco do Brasil,** with branches at Aeroporto Internacional Tom Jobim, as well as in Centro (Rua Senador Dantas 105, tel. 21/3808-3900) and Copacabana (Av. Nossa Senhora da Copacabana 1292, tel. 21/3202-4400). The city has many ATMs; Banco do Brasil, HSBC, Bradesco, and Citibank also accept international bank cards. The largest concentrations of banks are on Avenida Rio Branco (Centro), Avenida Nossa Senhora da Copacabana (Copacabana), and Rua Visconde de Pirajá (Ipanema).

The main **post office** is in Centro (Rua 1 de Março 64), but there are branches at Aeroporto Internacional Tom Jobim (open 24 hours), in Copacabana (Av. Nossa Senhora de Copacabana 540), and in Ipanema (Rua Prudente de Morais 147). Hours are 8am-6pm Monday-Friday, 8am-noon Saturday.

Emergency Services

In the event of a medical emergency, dial **193** for Pronto Socorro (First Aid). If you need to visit a hospital in Copacabana, **Clínica Galdino Campos** (Av. Nossa Senhora de Copacabana 492, tel. 21/2548-9966, www.galdinocampos.com.br) is a private clinic that has a tradition of treating foreigners. It is open 24 hours and has English-speaking staff.

Rio is filled with pharmacies; many stay open 24 hours. Two 24-hour locations of **Drogaria Pacheco** are in Copacabana (Av. Nossa Senhora de Copacabana 534 A/B, tel. 21/2255-5222) and Catete (Largo do Machado 29, tel. 21/2205-8572).

In the event of a crime, call **190** to reach the police. There is a special **Delegacia Especial de Atendimento ao Turista** (Tourist Police) unit whose Leblon headquarters (Av. Afrânio de Melo Franco 159, tel. 21/2332-2924) is open

24 hours daily. Agents are generally helpful and speak English.

TRANSPORTATION

Most international travelers arrive in Rio by air, although if you're traveling from another city in Brazil, you'll likely arrive by bus or car.

Air

Rio has two airports. International flights and the majority of domestic flights arrive and depart from the **Aeroporto Internacional Tom Jobim** (Av. 20 de Janeiro, Ilha do Governador, tel. 21/3398-5050, www.aeroportogaleao.net). Also known as Galeão, it is in the Zona Norte, around 20 minutes from Centro and 45-60 minutes from Zona Sul. Right in Centro, adjacent to the Parque de Flamengo, is Rio's oldest airport, **Aeroporto Santos Dumont** (Praça Senador Salgado Filho, Centro, tel. 21/3814-7070, www.aeroportosantosdumont.net), where flights are basically limited to the Rio-São Paulo air shuttle.

Both airports have kiosks for special airport taxis, where you pay your fare in advance based the distance of your destination. These are often more expensive (fare to Ipanema is R$105) than just hailing one of the yellow and blue *rádio taxis* available at the taxi stands (expect fare to Zona Sul to cost R$70-80). Make sure you use a bona fide taxi company, since there are a lot of "pirate" taxis. It should take around one hour to reach Ipanema, but if traffic is bad (as is frequently the case), it could take almost two.

From Galeão, the **Real** (www.realautoonibus.com.br) bus company offers regular *executivo* service for R$13.50 to Rio. Departing every 20 minutes between 5:30am-11:30pm, buses cut through Centro (along Av. Rio Branco) and then stop at Aeroporto Santos Dumont before continuing along the oceanfront *avenidas* of Flamengo (Av. Beira Mar), Copacabana (Av. Atlântica), Ipanema (Av. Vieira Souto), and Leblon (Av. Delfim Moreira) and then to Barra, including stops at all the major hotels along the way. For hotels that are inland, just ask the driver in advance

to let you off at the nearest cross street (*"Por favor, pode me deixar na Rua. . .?"*). To get to the airport, you can grab the same bus (on the reverse route) or ask your hotel to call you a cab and settle on a fixed rate in advance. Depending on the traffic, it can take between 90 minutes and two hours to reach Ipanema.

Bus

Close to Centro's port district, Rio's main bus station, **Rodoviária Novo Rio** (Av. Francisco Bicalho 1, São Cristóvão, tel. 21/3213-1800, www.transportal.com.br/rodoviaria-novo-rio), is a major transportation hub. Buses arrive from and depart to all points in Brazil and to other South American countries. Getting to and from the Rodoviária from anywhere in the city is easy. Just hop on any bus with "Rodoviária" posted as its destination on the front. A taxi will set you back around R$20 to Centro and R$40 to Copacabana. The area around the terminal is dodgy; exercise care.

MUNICIPAL BUS

Rio's municipal buses are not the safest form of locomotion due to pickpockets and occasional armed holdups. If you leave your valuables at the hotel and limit yourself to daytime trips between points in the Centro, Zona Sul, and the western beaches of Barra and Recreio, you'll be fine. Do take care to have your change already counted out beforehand, and always keep bags (including knapsacks) or other belongings closed (with a zipper or button) and close to your chest, especially when it's crowded. By day, buses run with great frequency. By night, you can risk taking buses between main stops in Flamengo, Botafogo, Copacabana, Ipanema, and Leblon, which are usually quite busy until around 9pm or 10pm. Otherwise, stick to taxis.

Final destinations are written on the front of the bus, and along the side are the main stops along the routes. Make sure you check this out. From Centro, for example, there are buses whose final destination is Leblon that careen along the coast through Copacabana and Ipanema, while others go inland via

Botafogo and Jardim Botânico. After paying your fare (R$3) to the *cobrador* at the back of the bus, make your way to the front, so you can make an easy exit when you get to your stop. If a bus stop is not clearly marked, look for a clump of people waiting. You can signal for a bus to stop by sticking out your arm.

Minibuses (or vans) have joined the traffic fray. They are often quicker for zipping between Centro and the Zona Sul since they can weave through traffic more easily. Destinations are listed on the windshield; fares hover between R$2.50-4.50.

Metrô

Rio's **Metrô** subway system (tel. 0800/595-1111, www.metrorio.com.br) is clean, efficient, and safe (and gloriously air-conditioned). The only problem is its size; spurred on by the 2014 World Cup and 2016 Olympic Games, Linha 1 is slowly expanding south, but currently it only goes to Ipanema/General Osório. Parts of the Zona Norte (Maracanã, for instance) and Centro are well served. In the meantime, MetrôRio has streamlined things considerably by adding "surface" Metrôs and express buses that depart from Metrô stations. For instance, to get from Ipanema to Leblon, Gávea, and Jardim Botânico, you can hop "subway buses" from Ipanema/General Osório station. From here, you can also transfer to a Barra Express bus. Express buses also leave from Largo do Machado, Botafogo, and Cardeal Arcoverde stations for Cosme Velho, Urca, and Leme, respectively. Tickets can be purchased in the stations. Fare is R$3.20, which includes a transfer to the "surface Metrô"; if transferring to an express bus, the fare for an *integração expressa* costs R$4.35. You can also purchase a prepaid Metrô card (the minimum charge is R$5) to which you can add as much credit as you want; not only is this cheaper than paying for individual fares, but you'll avoid lineups. The Metrô runs 5am-midnight Monday-Saturday, 7am-11pm Sunday. On weekends, you can board the trains with bikes and surfboards.

Taxis

Taxis are often the best way to get around Rio. Taxi service is reasonably priced, and for specific trips you can often bargain a fixed price with your driver (if language is a problem, ask someone at your hotel or hostel for help as well as approximate prices). There are two kinds of taxis in Rio. Yellow cabs with blue stripes are the most common. They can be hailed in the street and are cheaper. Large, white, air-conditioned radio cabs are usually ordered by phone and are more expensive. Two reliable companies are **Central Táxi** (tel. 21/2195-1000) and **Coopacarioca** (tel. 21/2518-1818). Most Carioca cab drivers are friendly and honest (although very few speak English), but there are a few who specialize in scamming gringo tourists. Unless you've agreed on a set fare, check to make sure the meter is always running. During daytime and until 8pm, the "Bandeira 1" rate is cheaper than at night and on holidays and weekends, when the rate is "Bandeira 2."

Car Rental

Driving in Rio de Janeiro is not exactly recommended. It's not that Cariocas are poor drivers, but they tend to forget they're not at the Indy 500. Then there are the rush-hour traffic jams, which are stressful and stiflingly hot. One-way streets, poorly marked turnoffs, and holdups—at stoplights and when you're parked—are further dissuading factors. In truth, renting a car only makes sense if you're going to be doing lots of day trips in and around the state of Rio de Janeiro. Major companies include **Avis** (www.avis.com.br), with agencies at Tom Jobim Airport (tel. 21/3398-5060) and Copacabana (Av. Princesa Isabel 350, tel. 21/2542-9937), and **Localiza Rent a Car** (www.localiza.com.br), with agencies at the Tom Jobim Airport (tel. 21/3398-5445), Santos Dumont Airport (tel. 21/2220-5604), Leme (Av. Princesa Isabel 150, tel. 21/2275-3340), and Barra (Av. das Américas 679, Loja C, tel. 21/2493-4477).

City Tours

An increasing number of organized tours allow you to explore Rio's diverse neighborhoods and natural attractions and to experience different aspects of Carioca life and culture.

Lisa Rio Tours (tel. 21/9894-6867, www.lisariotours.com, from R$120) is run by friendly, well-informed German expat Lisa Schnittger. Lisa offers a wide variety of tours in and around Rio including customized walking tours for individuals and small groups. Among her most popular outings are shopping in historic Centro, exploring Santa Teresa's bohemian life, and Afro-Brazilian culture in Rio.

Rio 4 Visitors (tel. 21/9355-9585, www.rio-4visitors.com) is run by multilingual Carioca native Daniel Cabral. Danny's car is comfy and air-conditioned and his enthusiasm is contagious whether he's introducing standard tourist attractions or little-known secret gems. Customized tours are based on the number of people, hours, days, and interests. He can pack a lot of Rio into one day.

Be a Local (tel. 21/9643-0366, www.bealocal.com) matches foreign visitors with English-speaking locals in an attempt to show them aspects of Carioca life—a funk party in a Rio *favela,* a soccer game at Maracanã—that they could never experience otherwise. A half-day trip with a *moto-boy* to a *favela* costs R$65.

Friendly British expat and foodie Tom Lemesurier gives **Eat Rio Food Tours** (http://eatrio.net/eat-rio-food-tours, email foodtours@eatrio.net), which combine historical and cultural anecdotes with walking and eating your way around the city.

Rio de Janeiro State

ILHA DE PAQUETÁ

Located in the Baía de Guanabara, the small Ilha de Paquetá (www.ilhadepaqueta.com.br) has been a favorite Carioca getaway since Dom João VI began coming here in the early 19th century. He was responsible for building the Capela de São Roque, around which the lively five-day **Festival de São Roque** takes place in August. On most weekends and holidays, the island is packed with families from the Zona Norte who crowd the seaside bars and (polluted) beaches (the cleanest are Moreninha, Imbuca, and José Bonifácio). During the week, though, the island offers splendid views of Rio and the bay and makes for a relaxing day trip. Tranquility reigns and the colonial buildings, although somewhat faded, retain their allure.

Transportation

Ferries leave at two-to-three hour intervals (5am-11pm daily) from the **Estação das Barcas** (tel. 0800/7211-0126, www.grupoccr.com.br/barcas, R$4.80) at Praça XV de Novembro. The trip takes a little over an hour. If you're in a hurry, hydrofoils (tel. 21/2533-4343) will get you there in half the time at double the price, with several departures and returns a day. Although no vehicles are allowed on the island, you can easily (and cheaply) rent a bike and pedal around.

NITERÓI

Only 17 kilometers (10.5 mi) across Baía de Guanabara, this well-to-do suburb-like city sports long white-sand beaches and space-age Niemeyer buildings, including the iconic *Star Trek*-worthy Museu de Arte Contemporânea.

Sights

The fantastic, UFO-shaped **Museu de Arte Contemporânea** (MAC; Mirante da Boa Viagem, Boa Viagem, tel. 21/2620-2400, www.macniteroi.com.br, 10am-6pm Tues.-Sun., R$4, free Wed.), designed by Oscar Niemeyer and inaugurated in 1996, sits on a slender cylindrical base of just 9 meters (30 feet). Since the museum overlooks the Baía de

Rio de Janeiro State

© AVALON TRAVEL

SÃO PAULO

MINAS GERAIS

ESPÍRITO SANTO

RIO DE JANEIRO

ATLANTIC OCEAN

Parque Nacional da Serra da Bocaina

PARATY

ILHA GRANDE

Baía da Ilha Grande

Costa Verde

Angra dos Reis

Baía de Sepetiba

Itaitaia

Parque Nacional do Itatiaia

Volta Redonda

Vassouras

Valença

Caxambu

Minduri

Bom Jardim de Minas

Lima Duarte

São João del Rei

Barbacena

Juiz de Fora

Leopoldina

Piraúba

Muriaé

Itaocara

Itaperuna

Cachoeira de Itapemirim

Marataízes

Barra de Itabapoana

Rio

Rio Muriaé

Paraíba do Sul

Campos dos Goitacazes

Barra Seca

São João da Barra

Farol de São Tomé

Quissamã

Macaé

Parque Nacional da Restinga de Jurubatiba

BÚZIOS

Cabo Frio

Arraial do Cabo

Saquarema

Araruama

Maricá

Rio Benito

Costa do Sol

Niterói

ILHA DE PAQUETÁ

RIO DE JANEIRO

AEROPORTO INTERNACIONAL ANTÔNIO CARLOS JOBIM

Itaguaí

Petrópolis

MUSEU IMPERIAL

Teresópolis

Parque Nacional da Serra dos Órgãos

Parque Estadual dos Três Picos

Pico da Caledônia

Nova Friburgo

Parque Nacional da Restinga de Jurubatiba

BR 101

BR 116

BR 101

BR 393

BR 40

BR 116

BR 492

BR 101

BR 267

BR 267

BR 383

BR 265

BR 40

BR 40

BR 265

BR 120

BR 356

BR 101

BR 116

Costa Verde

0   20 mi
0   20 km

ATLANTIC OCEAN

Guanabara, its 360-degree views are spectacular, often rivaling hit-or-miss art exhibits. To reach the museum from Niterói's ferry terminal, as you leave the terminal take a right and walk 50 meters (160 feet), then catch the 47B minibus.

The MAC was the first construction of the Caminho Niemeyer (Niemeyer Route). Other projects include the striking Teatro Popular and the Fundação Oscar Niemeyer. When (and if) completed, Niterói will be second only to Brasília as a showcase for the vanguard architect's constructions.

Beaches

The beaches close to Niterói's center are polluted, but take a bus due south—from the ferry terminal, any bus marked Itacoatiara—to encounter some surprisingly unspoiled and very attractive beaches, among them **Piratininga, Camboinhas, Itaipu,** and the most spectacular of them all, **Itacoatiara,** about 45 minutes from Niterói's center. From here, you have unrivaled views of Pão de Açúcar and Corcovado across the bay. All are well equipped with *barracas* where you can feast on fresh fish and seafood.

Transportation and Services

The municipal tourist office, **Neltour** (tel. 0800/282-7755, www.niteroiturismo.com. br), has several information kiosks, including one at the ferry terminal and another at the Mirador Boa Viagem, the lookout point adjacent to MAC (both open 9am-6pm daily).

Although you can take a bus or drive across the Ponte Rio-Niterói, one of the world's longest bridges, the most scenic way to get to Niterói is by taking the ferry that leaves from the Estação das Barcas at Praça XV de Novembro. Boats operated by **Barcas S.A.** (tel. 0800/7211-0126, www.grupoccr.com. br/barcas)—often jammed with commuters during rush hour—leave at 15-30-minute intervals 7:30am-midnight and at 60-minute intervals midnight-6am. Ferry rides take 20 minutes. In Niterói, ferries and catamarans either dock at the Estação Niterói in the center

of town (fare is R$4.80) or at the Estação Hidroviária at Charitas (R$13).

PETRÓPOLIS

When the going gets hot, Cariocas have historically headed for the cool, forest-clad mountains surrounding Rio, where charmingly rustic resort towns conjure up a tropical version of the Alps. Only an hour's drive north from Rio, the summer getaway of the Brazilian emperor and his family provides a welcome refuge, offering cool respite, fine food, and mountain scenery. Upon discovering this idyllic region, Dom Pedro I was so enchanted by the majestic landscapes and moderate temperatures that he drew up plans for a villa. However, it fell to his son, Pedro II—who founded Petrópolis (named after his imperialness) in 1843—to actually build his dream house, which ended up as a full-fledged royal palace. Not wanting to be out of the loop, barons, counts, and marquises came flocking. The town's alpine climes also attracted numerous German immigrants, which explains the Bohemian influence present in the architecture and cuisine.

Exploring Petrópolis by foot is easy, but if you're feeling lazy, romantic, or both, hire a horse-drawn carriage (R$50 for up to five, 45 min.), available in front of the Museu Imperial. Having a car, while not essential, is a bonus, since you can easily go zooming off to nearby towns and take in a fuller range of natural attractions. Many appealing (and luxurious) lodges are hidden in beautifully remote spots, as are gourmet restaurants.

Sights

Most of historic Petrópolis lies beyond the somewhat congested commercial center, concentrated in a bucolic cluster of streets lined with 19th-century mansions and laced with tree-shaded canals. Many of the most splendid *casas* are on the main street of Avenida Koeler.

★ MUSEU IMPERIAL

Amid landscaped gardens, the elegant neoclassical pink edifice that served as Dom

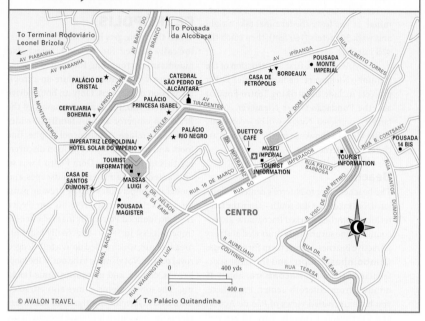

Petrópolis

To Terminal Rodoviário Leonel Brizola

To Pousada da Alcobaça

AV PIABANHA

AV. PIABANHA

AV. BARÃO DO RIO BRANCO

AV IPIRANGA

RUA ALBERTO TORRES

PALÁCIO DE CRISTAL

CERVEJARIA BOHEMIA

RUA MONTECASEROS

RUA ALFREDO PACHÁ

CATEDRAL SÃO PEDRO DE ALCÂNTARA

PALÁCIO PRINCESA ISABEL

AV TIRADENTES

CASA DE PETRÓPOLIS

BORDEAUX

POUSADA MONTE IMPERIAL

AV. DOM PEDRO I

IMPERATRIZ LEOPOLDINA/ HOTEL SOLAR DO IMPÉRIO

PALÁCIO RIO NEGRO

DUETTO'S CAFÉ

TOURIST INFORMATION

RUA MNS. BACELAR

CASA DE SANTOS DUMONT

MASSAS LUIGI

R. DR. NELSON DE SÁ EARP

POUSADA MAGISTER

AV KOELER

RUA DA IMPERATRIZ

MUSEU IMPERIAL

RUA 16 DE MARÇO

RUA DO IMPERADOR

TOURIST INFORMATION

RUA PAULO BARBOSA

RUA B. CONTSANT

POUSADA 14 BIS

TOURIST INFORMATION

RUA SANTOS DUMONT

CENTRO

R. VISC DE BOM RETIRO

R. DR. SÁ EARP

RUA WASHINGTON LUIZ

R. AURELIANO COUTINHO

RUA DR. SÁ EARP

RUA TERESA

0   400 yds
0   400 m

© AVALON TRAVEL

To Palácio Quitandinha

Pedro II's summer digs now houses the **Museu Imperial** (Rua da Imperatriz 220, tel. 24/2245-5550, www.museuimperial.gov. br, 11am-5:30pm Tues.-Sun., R$8). After replacing your shoes with soft-soled slippers, you can glide around the gleaming parquet floors and inspect the myriad regal trappings, whose highlights include Dom Pedro I's golden scepter and Dom Pedro II's fairy tale-like crown, encrusted with 639 diamonds and 77 pearls. The palace offers a rare day-in-the-life glimpse of an emperor in the tropics.

CATEDRAL DE SÃO PEDRO DE ALCÂNTARA

The imposing French neo-Gothic **Catedral de São Pedro de Alcântara** (Rua São Pedro de Alcântara 60, tel. 24/2242-4300, 8am-6pm daily), with its 70-meter (230-foot) tower (you can climb to the top—169 stairs—for R$8), wasn't completed until 1939. Its somber aura exterior houses lovely stained-glass windows, depicting scenes from poems written by the multitalented Dom Pedro II; the main attraction here is the marble, bronze, and onyx Imperial Mausoleum housing containing the mortal remains of Dom Pedro II, his wife, Dona Teresa Cristina, and their daughter, Princesa Isabel.

CASA DE SANTOS DUMONT

Brazilians have long snubbed their noses at the Wright Brothers. As far as they're concerned, the first human being to take to the skies in a plane was Alberto Santos Dumont, who in 1906 completed the first nonassisted flight in his plane, which he baptized *14-Bis*. Flying machines aside, Santos Dumont was an avid builder and inventor. He designed the gracious house known as **Casa de Santos Dumont** (Rua do Encanto 22, tel. 24/2247-3158, 9:30am-5pm Tues.-Sun., R$5). The house displays personal effects and various other inventions, among them an alcohol-heated shower and a bed that can be transformed into a desk.

PALÁCIO QUITANDINHA

Slightly outside of the center, most easily reached by car or taxi, the **Palácio Quitandinha** (Av. Joaquim Rola 2, tel. 24/2245-2020, 9am-6pm Tues.-Sat., 9am-5pm Sun., R$6) was built in the 1940s to house the largest and most glamorous hotel-casino in all of Latin America. While it attracted the likes of Marlene Dietrich, Orson Welles, and Lana Turner, its days as a luxury gaming den were short-lived; in 1946 gambling was outlawed in Brazil, and the casino was transformed into a posh apartment complex. Today, it functions as an SESC events center. You can explore its surprisingly vibrant interior—the work of famed American decorator and Hollywood set designer Dorothy Draper, who irreverently colored the walls in tones of shocking pink, scarlet, and turquoise, reminiscent of a Technicolor movie. Note that the lagoon out front is shaped like Brazil.

CASA DE PETRÓPOLIS

The former home of José Tavares Guerra, nephew of the Barão de Mauá (one Brazil's most famous entrepreneurs, he founded the Banco do Brasil), the **Casa de Petrópolis** (Rua Ipiranga 716, tel. 24/2231-8718, 1pm-6pm Fri.-Sun. and daily Jan. and July, R$8) is a Victorian mansion whose architecture was inspired by Guerra's early years spent living and studying in England. Guided tours are offered; the lovely gardens were a favorite strolling spot of Dom Pedro II.

Other Petrópolis palaces of note aren't open to visitors, but their exteriors are worth a look. These include the pretty pink **Palácio Princesa Isabel** (Av. Koeler, 42), home of the imperial princess, and the grand **Palácio Rio Negro** (Av. Koeler, 255), built by the Barão do Rio Negro, a rich coffee planter. After he sold it, the house became the official summer residence of Brazil's presidents. The **Casa do Barão de Mauá** (Praça da Confluência 3) was home to the Barão de Mauá.

Accommodations

There are a handful of basic accommodation options in Petrópolis's commercial center, as well as several nice hotels in the older, residential neighborhoods. An even larger number of *pousadas*—often quite posh and set in the midst of gorgeous landscapes—are located in the surrounding mountains, but you'll need a car to reach them. Sunday-Thursday, rates can be 20-50 percent lower.

Pousada 14 Bis (Rua Buenos Aires 192, tel. 24/2231-0946, www.pousada14bis.com.br, R$170-250 d), named after Santos Dumont's historic plane, is centrally situated and fetchingly rustic to boot. The lounge pays homage to the homegrown aviator-inventor with a smattering of engaging artifacts related to his life and times. Rooms are cozy and comfortable. Occupying an attractive European-style manor built in 1814, **Pousada Magister** (Rua Monsenhor Bacelar 71, tel. 24/2242-1054, www.pousadamagister.com.br, R$230-250 d) is in the midst of all of Petrópolis's historic attractions. The comfortable rooms lack much of a decorative scheme, but all boast soaring ceilings, immense windows, and polished wood floors. A steep uphill walk from the center of town, the **Pousada Monte Imperial** (Rua José de Alencar 27, tel. 24/2237-1664, www.pousadamonteimperial.com.br, R$215-370 d) is worth the physical exertion. With friendly service and compact, cozy rooms offering views of the town below, this *pousada* is an enchanting rural retreat within spitting distance of Petrópolis proper.

Surrounded by mansions that once belonged to barons and counts, **Hotel Solar do Império** (Av. Koeler 376, tel. 24/2103-3000, www.solardoimperio.com.br, R$440-700 d) will make you feel quite regal. This ornate 1875 mansion provided refuge for Princesa Isabel while her own *palácio* down the street was undergoing renovation. Stately rooms offer modern conveniences, and there's a swimming pool and a spa. The hotel's well-regarded restaurant, **Imperatriz Leopoldina** (7:30am-10pm Sun.-Thurs., 7:30am-midnight Fri.-Sat., R$40-70), specializes in elegantly presented dishes that draw on both European and Brazilian influences.

Food

Petrópolis is something of a gourmet destination, but many of the finest area restaurants are located along the Estrada União-Indústria, which winds from the Centro through the rural districts of Corrêas, Araras, and Itaipav—far from the city center and requiring a car. One of the best is ★ **Pousada da Alcobaça** (Rua Agostinho Goulão 298, Estrada do Bonfim, tel. 24/2221-1240, www.pousadaalcobaca.com.br, noon-10pm daily, R$45-65), located in the bucolic region of Corrêas (11 km, or 7 mi, from the center of Petrópolis, heading toward the Parque Nacional Serra dos Órgãos). This charming *pousada* occupies an early 20th-century Norman country house, surrounded by fragrant herb and vegetable gardens that supply produce for the excellent breakfasts, lunches, and teas prepared by 84-year-old owner and chef Laura Góes. Reservations are a must. You can also stay in exquisitely furnished comfortable rooms (R$385-550 d) occupying the main house or mill house.

In Centro and occupying a lovely old house with vaulted ceilings, **Massas Luigi** (Praça da Liberdade 185, tel. 24/2244-4444, www.massaluigi.com.br, 11am-midnight daily, R$20-35) is a fine place to go for tasty homemade pasta and pizzas. For a light meal or snack in imperial surroundings, the Museu Imperial's **Duetto's Café** (Av. Imperatriz 220, tel. 24/2243-2952, www.bistroimperatriz.com.br, 10am-6pm Sun. and Tues.-Wed., 10am-10pm Thurs.-Sat., R$15-25) is a great option, with a few entrées, salads, and sweet and savory pastries. In an irresistible setting in the shadow of the Casa de Petrópolis, **Bordeaux** (Rua Ipiranga 716, tel. 24/2242-5711, www.bordeauxvinhos.com.br, noon-midnight Mon.-Sat., noon-7pm Sun., R$15-25) is an emporium and bistro with delicious beers and wines to wash down nicely priced appetizers and gourmet sandwiches.

Beer lovers should head to the headquarters of **Cervejaria Bohemia** (Rua Alfredo Pachá 166, tel. 24/2247-5222, www.bohemia.com.br), home of Brazil's first beer. Considered one of Brazil's most quaffable brews (Pedro II was a fan), Bohemia was invented by a German immigrant who arrived in Petrópolis in 1853 and used the pure mountain water to craft this pale lager. In 2012, the historic brewery was transformed into a beer research center and **museum** (11am-6pm, Wed.-Fri., 11pm-8pm Sat.-Sun., R$20). At the adjacent **Boteco Bohemia** (tel. 24/3064-9127, noon-10pm Wed.-Thurs. noon-midnight Fri.-Sun.), sample the wares along with bar snacks that harmonize with individual labels.

Transportation and Services

Petrotur (tel. 0800/024-1516, http://destinopetropolis.com.br) operates several kiosks throughout town, including at Praça da Liberdade (9am-6pm daily) and across from the Museu Imperial (Praça Visconde de Mauá 305, 9am-6:30pm daily).

From Rio's Rodoviário Novo, **Única-Fácil** (tel. 0800/886-1000, www.unica-facil.com.br, 90 min., R$21) buses depart every 30 minutes from 5:30am-midnight to Petrópolis's long distance **Terminal Rodoviário Leonel Brizola** (tel. 24/2249-9856). From here, connect to a local bus (no. 100) to get to the downtown Terminal de Integração station in Centro (R$2.85) or take a cab (R$30). Buses leave approximately every 15 minutes. By car from Rio, take BR-040, which offers a splendid, if hair-raising, hour-long drive through the mountains; beware of rain and crowded weekend rush hours.

PARQUE NACIONAL DA SERRA DOS ÓRGÃOS

Created in 1939, **Parque Nacional da Serra dos Órgãos** (8am-5pm daily, R$25) owes its name to early Portuguese explorers, who thought that its strangely shaped rocky peaks bore an uncanny resemblance to a church pipe organ. Stretching between Petrópolis and Teresópolis, the park comprises 12,000 hectares (30,000 acres) of exuberant Atlantic forest with waterfalls, hiking trails, and the postcard-worthy **Dedo de Deus** (Finger of God), rising 1,692 meters (5,551 feet) above sea level. Higher but less dramatic is the **Pedra do Sino** (Bell Rock, 2,263 meters/7,425 feet). There are plenty of other peaks to marvel at and even scale—from the uppermost summits, on a clear day you can see all the way to Rio de Janeiro and the Baía de Guanabara.

The park is 5 kilometers (3 mi) from the center of Teresópolis on BR-116 leading to Rio. The entrance close to Petrópolis is 16 kilometers (10 mi) from the center of town on the Estrada União-Indústria.

Hiking

Numerous trails range from easy strolls to taxing but spectacular multiday treks. Since most trails are unmarked, hire a guide if you're thinking of doing more than a short hike. Guide information is available online and at the park's main entrance and headquarters in **Teresópolis** (Av. Rotariana, tel. 21/2152-1100, www.icmbio.gov.br/parnaserradosorgaos). There is also an entrance from **Petrópolis** (tel. 24/2236-0475). Entrance fees allow access to easier trails in the lower reaches of the park. For trails higher up the mountain, the fee is R$40 for the first day; an additional fee is charged on weekdays (R$4) and weekends (R$20). The longest and most challenging hike is the spectacular three-day trek between Petrópolis and Teresópolis (42 km/26 mi); consider starting from Petrópolis to get the hardest part out of the way first. Most guides charge around R$200 pp. For longer hikes and excursions such as rappelling and canyoneering, contact **Trekking Petrópolis** (tel. 24/2235-7607, www.rioserra. com.br/trekking). May-October is the best time for trekking; barring rain, November-February is more conducive to bathing in the park's many icy streams and waterfalls.

TERESÓPOLIS

Nowhere near as charming nor as imperial as Petrópolis, Teresópolis is a modern, upscale alpine resort whose name pays homage to Empress Teresa Cristina, wife of Dom Pedro II, who was taken by the area's magnificent mountain scenery and refreshing climate. Its main attraction lies in its proximity to the Parque Nacional da Serra dos Órgãos.

Accommodations and Food

Most of Teresópolis's worthy accommodations are tucked amid the mountains. The **Hotel Rosa dos Ventos** (RJ-130 Km 22.5 to Nova Friburgo, tel. 21/2644-9900, www.hotelrosa-dosventos.com.br, R$520-760 d) offers rustic yet luxuriously accessorized chalets with fireplaces and balconies. Nature lovers need never leave the hotel complex, which includes countless walking and biking trails, two swimming pools, a lake for kayaking, and stables for horseback riding. Also on the premises are three gourmet restaurants (full-board rates are higher) and an English bar.

More central and much cheaper is the **Várzea Palace Hotel** (Rua Prefeito Sebastião Teixeira 41, tel. 21/2742-0878, hotelvarzea@ bol.com.br, R$65-125 d). Although its early 20th-century elegance has faded, this formerly grand hotel offers clean and comfortable rooms with sky-high ceilings, parquet floors, and lots of retro character.

Manjeiricão (Rua Flávio Bortoluzzi de Sousa 314, Alto, tel. 21/2642-4242, 6pm-11pm Thurs.-Fri., noon-midnight Sat., noon-11pm Sun., R$25-35) serves a delicious thin-crust pizza baked to perfection in a wood-burning oven. Herbs and vegetables come from the restaurant's garden.

Transportation and Services

For maps and information about the surrounding area, head to the centrally located **tourist office** (Praça Olímpica, tel. 21/2742-5661, 8am-6pm daily) or visit www.teresopolis.rj.gov.br (in Portuguese).

Viação Teresópolis (tel. 21/2742-0606, ww.viacaoteresopolis.com.br) offers hourly bus service from 6am-10pm between Teresópolis and Rio de Janeiro (2 hours, R$27) and every 2-3 hours between Teresópolis and Petrópolis (2 hours, R$17). The bus station is close to the central main square. To reach Teresópolis directly from Rio by car (1.5 hours), take BR-040 and BR-116. The driving time by car between Petrópolis and Teresópolis is about 45 minutes.

NOVA FRIBURGO

Although it's hard to imagine, in the early 1800s Switzerland was so (temporarily) poor that 100 Swiss families left their hometown of Fribourg to settle in these mountainous climes. This explains the prevalence of wooden chalets, chocolate shops, and restaurants serving cheese fondue and raclette here, one of Brazil's oldest and only Swiss colonies. What it doesn't explain: Nova Friburgo is the Brazilian capital of lingerie. In the downtown *bairros* of Olaria and Ponte da Saudade (near the bus station), dozens of fine lingerie manufacturers export nationally and throughout the world, and discriminating shoppers can pick up fancy underthings for a song.

To survey the surrounding countryside, from the Alto do Cascatinha neighborhood (accessible via local bus to "Cascatinha-Interpass," R$3) take a steep but gratifying 6-kilometer (3.5-mi) hike up to the 2,310-meter (7,579-foot) summit of **Pico da Caledônia;** the top provides breathtaking views and also serves as a launching pad for hang gliders.

Within close proximity is the **Parque Estadual dos Três Picos** (Estrada do Jequitibá 145, Cachoeiras de Macacu, tel. 21/2649-5847, www.inea.rj.gov.br, 9am-4:30pm daily, free), Rio de Janeiro's largest state park. Easy trails are near the entrance; for more ambitious treks and climbs, a guide is required. Serious mountain climbers will want to hike to the top of the *três picos* (three peaks)—the two loftiest, Pico Maior and Montanha do Capacete (which measures 2,316 meters/7,598 feet), can only be scaled with climbing gear. Entrance to the park is at Km 46.5 on RJ-130 going to Teresópolis. At the entrance is the Refúgio da Águas, where you can contract a guide.

Accommodations and Food

In Centro, **Hotel São Paulo** (Rua Monsenhor Miranda 41, tel. 22/2523-5984, www.hotelsaopaulo.com.br, R$180 d) is a simple yet atmospheric 1940s hotel with original fixtures and details that cast a vintage spell, although the décor veers toward Spartan.

If you want to be surrounded by mountain greenery, there are multiple options in the surrounding area. One of the nicest is **Hotel Akaskay** (Estrada Eduardo Francisco do Canto 643, RJ-116 Km. 71.5, Mury, tel. 22/2542-1163, www.akaskay.com, R$280-320 d), some 8 kilometers (5 mi) from Friburgo. Owned by a landscaper and conservationist, the grounds are beautiful, as are the cozy wood cabins built from reforested wood and outfitted with quilts and fireplaces. A natural swimming pool, walking trails, and waterfalls ensure you never have to leave the property.

One of Friburgo's finest and most centrally located restaurants, the petite and charming ★ **Crescente Gastronomia** (Rua General Osório 21, tel. 22/2523-4616, www.crescenterestaurante.com.br, 11:30am-11pm Mon. and Thurs.-Sat., 11:30am-5pm Sun., R$40-70) has an eclectic, French-inflected menu. For cheaper, heartier fare, try **Dona Mariquinha** (Rua Monsenhor Miranda 110, tel. 22/2522-2309, noon-3:30pm Tues.-Sun., 7pm-9pm Mon.-Fri., R$35 pp). This 50-year-old institution specializes in homecooked Brazilian comfort food, which does the rounds of the dining room *rodízio* style in an all-you-can-eat rotating buffet.

Transportation and Services

The **tourist office** (Praça Doutro Demervel B. Moreira, tel. 22/2543-6307, www.pmnf.rj.gov.br/turismo, 8am-8pm daily) has maps and hotel listings as well as information about hikes and walks. **Viação 1001** (tel. 21/2516-3797, www.autoviacao1001.com.br) has hourly departures from Rio's Rodoviária Novo to Nova Friburgo via Niterói (3 hours, R$36-45) from 5am-11pm. Buses arrive at the Rodoviária Sul (Ponte de Saudade), 4 kilometers (2.5 mi) south of the center of town. If you're coming from Teresópolis via **Viação Teresópolis** (tel. 21/2742-0606, www.viacaoteresopolis.com.br, 2 hours, R$18, five daily departures), you'll arrive at the

Rodoviária Norte (Praça Feliano Costa), about 2 kilometers (1.2 mi) north from the center. If you're driving from Rio, you'll need to head across the Rio-Niterói bridge and then follow BR-101, BR-104, and BR-116.

PARQUE NACIONAL DO ITATIAIA

Brazil's oldest national park, **Parque Nacional do Itatiaia** (tel. 24/3352-1292, www4.icmbio.gov.br/parna_itatiaia, 8am-5pm daily, R$25 for foreign visitors), founded in 1937, spans the state frontiers of Rio de Janeiro, São Paulo, and Minas Gerais. The easily accessible lower regions are covered with lush native Atlantic forest, wild orchids, and begonias, and spectacular waterfalls such as **Itaporani, Véu de Noiva,** and **Maromba,** all of which are easy to reach and boast beckoning (if chilly) pools for bathing. Numerous easy hiking trails can be easily explored by families, without a guide, and are readily accessible from the pretty mountain towns of **Itatiaia** and **Penedo.** The upper part of the park—dominated by a stark and imposing landscape of sculpted rocks—also has its attractions, among them the dramatic peaks of **Agulhas Negras** (2,548 meters/8,360 feet) and **Prateleira** (2,791 meters/9,157 feet). To scale them, you'll have to be in superb shape and be accompanied by a guide (consult the park's website for a list). Prices for hikes on the lower portion cost around R$60 pp, while scaling Prateleira and Agulhas Negras is R$120 pp (group rates are cheaper).

The entrance to the lower portion of the park is easily reached by following the 5-kilometer (3-mi) stretch of BR-116 that links the town of Itatiaia to the park entrance. This is where you'll find the visitors center, which offers information and maps. The upper portion of the park is accessed via the town of Itamonte in Minas Gerais, 65 kilometers (40 mi) from Itatiaia. The best times to visit the lower parts of the park are January-February and October-December, when it's warmer for bathing. For climbing Agulhas Negras and Prateleira, May-August is better due to the clear skies and low rainfall (although temperatures can get chilly).

Accommodations and Food

The town of **Itatiaia** is the best and most convenient base for visiting the park. Its many hotels are located on BR-116, which leads to the park's entrance. **Chalés Terra Nova** (Estrada Parque Nacional, Km 4.5, tel. 24/3352-1458, www.chalesterranova.com. br, R$240-290 d, full board) offers basic but comfortable accommodations split between a main house and individual chalets, which are ideal for groups or families. Amenities include a sauna, swimming pool, a small lake for trout fishing, a treetop walking course, and mountain bikes for pedaling around. The oldest and one of the finest hotels in the region, **Hotel Donati** (Estrada Parque Nacional, Km 9.5, tel. 24/3352-1110, www. hoteldonati.com.br, R$295-415 d full board) is located within the park itself. Since 1931, its charm-laden chalets have sheltered nature lovers, including composer and poet Vinicius de Moraes and modernist painter Alberto da Veiga Guignard (who was inspired to paint the doors and windows of the main cabin). Some chalets have jetted tubs; all have fireplaces. Among the restaurant's many offerings are fresh trout and fondues.

Sabor de Itatiaia (Estrada Parque Nacional, Km 3, tel. 24/3352-3050, 11:30am-3:30pm Mon., 11:30am-3:30pm and 7pm-11pm Tues.-Fri., 11:30am-11pm Sat.-Sun., R$20-30) is a per-kilo buffet featuring hearty fare bubbling over a wood-burning stove. On weekends *churrasco* joins in the offerings, and at night the oven turns out piping hot pizzas.

Transportation and Services

For information about Itatiaia, visit the **tourist office** (Praça Mariana Leão Rocha 20, tel. 24/3352-6777, 10am-6pm daily, closed off-season). **Cidade do Aço** (tel. 0800/886-1000, www.cidadedoaco.net) operates seven daily departures from Rio's Rodoviária Novo to Itatiaia (2.5 hours, R$35). By car from Rio, take BR-116.

Costa do Sol

Running east from Rio, the Costa do Sol lives up to its name by offering more than 100 kilometers (60 mi) of gorgeous coastline. In summertime, the main towns of Cabo Frio, Arraial do Cabo, and Búzios come alive with activity.

ARRAIAL DO CABO

Arraial do Cabo is only 6 kilometers (4 mi) south of overdeveloped Cabo Frio, yet this fishing port town is more tranquil than either Cabo or frenetically fashionable Búzios to the south. The crystalline waters off Arraial are a diver's paradise, and Praia de Farol, on nearby Ilha de Cabo Frio, is considered one of the most beautiful beaches in Brazil.

Beaches

Closest to town is **Praia dos Anjos,** an attractive strip of sand with enticing turquoise waters whose only flaw is that it can get a little packed with water-sports enthusiasts. In 1503, Amerigo Vespucci landed on these sands (a plaque above the beach marks the spot) and was so taken with the spot that he left 24 of his cohorts behind to start a colony. It's only a short walk to the beaches of **Prainha** (north of town) and the sweeping stretch of **Praia Grande** (to the west)—equipped with *barracas* serving fresh fish and seafood—that extends all the way up to the Brazilian surfers' paradise of Saquarema. You can also follow a steep 1-kilometer (0.6-mi) trail from Praia dos Anjos (or take a boat) to the lovely and deserted **Praia do Forno,** where you can snorkel and then relax at a floating restaurant-bar. **Praia do Pontal** is another exceptional beach whose calm waters are backed by small dunes and native vegetation. The 4-kilometer (2.5-mi) walk from Arraial involves a steep climb up the Morro do Atalaia; at the top, catch sight of migrating humpback whales in the winter. An alternative is to take a boat.

The most fantastic beach, **Praia do Farol,** is on Ilha do Farol, a sublime island paradise fringed with fine white sand and sculpted dunes, whose 390-meter (1,280-foot) peak offers magnificent views. Praia do Farol has been scientifically classified as "the most perfect beach in Brazil." Unfortunately, you won't be able to stay long: since the Navy controls the island, you can only spend a maximum of one (pre-authorized) hour basking on its shores. Most boat excursions (with the necessary permission) stop here.

Diving

Arraial is considered one of the best spots for recreational diving in Brazil. Its transparent blue waters are the only place where the ocean currents (which usually flow north-south along the Brazilian coast) flow east-west, provoking a phenomenon whereby the deep, cold currents from Antarctica rise to the surface. While this means that water temperatures are always quite cold, it also results in the presence of many nutrients, which in turn attract an unusually rich variety of marine life. Add to this more than 30 sunken galleons—the consequence of heavy pirate activity off the coast during the 17th and 18th centuries—and you're in for an underwater treat.

An outing, including equipment rental and a snack, should cost around R$160. For more information, contact **PL Divers** (tel. 22/2622-1033, www.pldivers.com.br) or **Arraial Sub** (Av. Getúlio Vargas 93, tel. 22/2622-1945, www.arraialsub.net).

Boat Excursions

A wonderful way to explore Arraial's marine splendors is by boat. **Arraial Tur** (Rua Dom Pedro II, 02 A, Praia dos Anjos, tel. 22/2622-1340, http://arraialtur.com.br) offers three-hour schooner excursions for R$40, with stops at the beaches of Pontal do Atalaia and Ilha do Farol. On the island, you can visit Gruta Azul,

Costa do Sol

(Rua Sérgio Martins 27, Praia dos Anjos, tel. 22/2622-1922, www.pousadadopilar.com.br, R$220-260 d) is a bit like staying in a tropical antiques store; the owners' taste for found objects and artworks mingle with salvaged materials and lush plants. Rooms are large and attractive, and the common spaces—pool, gardens, solarium, kitchen—are inviting.

Portuguese expat Tuga spent years hawking his legendarily crunchy *bolinhhos de bacalhau* before opening his own restaurant, **Bacalhau do Tuga** (Praia dos Anjos, tel. 22/2262-1108, 6pm-11pm Wed.-Fri., 1pm-11pm Sat.-Sun., R$20-35). The *pastéis de nata* (Portuguese custard tarts) are sublime. Al fresco tables and a dining room adorned with Asterix and Obelisk frescos are at French-run **Saint Tropez** (Praça Daniel Barretto 2, Praia dos Anjos, tel. 22/2262-1222, 6pm-midnight Mon.-Tues., noon-midnight Wed.-Sun., R$25-40). Along with very decent pizza at night, the local daily catch is served up in a diverse array of succulent dishes incorporating fresh fish, shrimp, squid, and mussels.

Transportation and Services

Located at the entrance to town, the **tourist office** (tel. 22/2262-1949, www.arraial.rj.com. br, 8am-5pm daily) has information about excursions as well as diving and boating trips. **Viação 1001** (tel. 21/2516-3597, www.autoviacao1001.com.br) has departures every 1-2 hours, 5am-11pm, from Rio's Rodoviária Novo to Cabo Frio via Niterói. The 2.5-hour journey costs R$59. The *rodoviária* (Praça da Bandeira) is in the center of town.

★ BÚZIOS

Búzios is the Gisele Bündchen of Brazilian beach resorts: internationally renowned, naturally beautiful, sophisticatedly chic. Before it became Brazil's most stylish beach getaway, Armação de Búzios was a tiny fishing village perched on the tip of a peninsula, 190 kilometers (118 mi) east of Rio de Janeiro. All of that changed in 1964, when sultry French starlet Brigitte Bardot happened upon it with her Brazilian boyfriend of the moment. Aided by

an underwater cavern that turns blue when illuminated by the sun.

Accommodations and Food

For cheap digs, it's hard to beat the pleasant **Hostel Marina dos Anjos** (Rua Bernardo Lens 145, Praia dos Anjos, tel. 22/2622-4060, www.marinadosanjos.com.br, R$160-185 d, R$55-65 pp). Dorm rooms are spotless if a little overpriced, as are double, triple, and quadruple rooms. Common rooms (including a well-equipped kitchen) have a more appealing, loungey beach house vibe; Praia dos Anjos is conveniently close, and an obliging staff is full of regional information. You can also rent bikes and diving equipment. Located on a quiet little street near the pier, family-owned **Pousada Canto da Baleia** (Rua Kioto 30, Praia dos Anjos, tel. 22/2622-1156, www.cantodabaleia.com.br, R$325-400 d) offers sunny and modern accommodations with attentive service. A small pool, plenty of hammocks, and the possibility of a home-cooked meal make this a great choice. **Pousada Pilar** the international paparazzi, the bikinied "B. B." singlehandedly put the place on the map. Before long, she had moved on to other boys and other beaches, but idyllic Búzios—the name by which both the village of Armação and the entire peninsula came to be known— quickly became a favorite stop on the global jet-setters' paradise party circuit.

Búzios's narrow cobblestoned streets, yacht-infested waters, and softly illuminated, cactus-studded landscapes are decidedly Mediterranean. As the little town has grown, both the permanent population and the tourists who flock here every summer are increasingly global and moneyed. Although the cachet of its Bardot days is long gone, those prepared to fork out big bucks will also gain a very considerable bonus: unlimited access to some of Brazil's most enchanting beaches. Time your visit to avoid the summer months, and you'll find a more pleasantly placid Búzios and a considerably more affordable one as well.

The peninsula of Búzios has three main settlements. Closest to the mainland on the isthmus, **Manguinhos** is the most commercial; from here, the principal thoroughfare of Avenida José Ribeiro Dantas cuts straight through the peninsula, morphing into the Estrada Usina Nova as it arrives in the village of **Armação dos Búzios.** The touristy and hedonistic center of Búzios, Armação clusters chic boutiques, hotels, restaurants, and night spots along the celebrated main drag of **Rua das Pedras** and its extension, the **Orla Bardot.** A 15-minute walk north along the coast from Armação brings you to the peninsula's oldest settlement, **Ossos** (the name "Bones" hints at its early whaling days), whose pretty harbor continues to charm.

Beaches

Visitors to Búzios may either take or leave its cosmopolitan trappings, but no one can resist its beaches. There are 24 of them, ranging in size from tiny isolated coves to mile-long sweeps of sand, each flaunting its own distinctive attributes and personality.

The beaches closest to the northern part of the isthmus at Manguinhos are **Praia de Manguinhos** and **Praia Rasa,** where high winds and low waves attract windsurfers and sailboats as well as families with kids. Going toward Armação, **Praia dos Amores** and **Praia das Virgens** are unspoiled, quite deserted, and framed by lush vegetation. **Praia da Tartaruga**'s limpid blue waters are

Praia da Armação, Búzios

the warmest on the peninsula and ideal for snorkeling.

While the beaches in Armação—**Praia do Canto** and **Praia da Armação**—are pretty to contemplate, they are too polluted for swimming. Picturesque **Praia dos Ossos** attracts sailors and windsurfers but also isn't recommended for bathing. Farther north, the tiny twin (and surprisingly primitive, if you arrive early) beaches of **Azeda** and **Azedinha** are framed by exuberant foliage and famed for their unofficial topless sunbathing. The clear blue waters are good for snorkeling, as are those of neighboring **João Fernandes** and **João Fernandinho.** Long and wide, trendy João Fernandes is framed by dozens of beach bars that serve fresh lobster and seafood. João Fernandinho is smaller and less crowded, with enticing natural pools for bathing.

On the easternmost tip of the peninsula lie wilder, windswept, and isolated beaches—reached by car or by following offshoots of the Estrada Usina Velha. With rugged cliffs and stormy seas, **Praia Brava** impresses with rosy pink sand and rough swells that attract surfers. **Praia Olho de Boi** is a seductive little cove favored by nudists, while **Praia do Forno** and **Praia da Foca** are picturesque and tranquil, their calm blue waters set off by rocks decorated with twisting cacti.

On the southern end of the peninsula, going toward the mainland, **Praia da Ferradura** consists of a large *ferradura* (horseshoe) bay ringed with mansions, condos, *pousadas,* and bars. Its protected waters are popular with families as well as fans of sailing and windsurfing. Pretty **Praia da Ferradurinha**'s transparent waters are good for diving.

Closest to the mainland, **Praia de Geribá** is a long, sweeping beach that is beautiful but quite urbanized. It's usually flooded with surfer boys and partying twentysomethings lured by electronic beats emanating from multiple beach *barracas.* Much more rustic and unspoiled are **Praia dos Tucuns, Praia José Gonçalves,** and **Praia das Caravelas,** all accessible via the road leading to Cabo Frio.

You can reach most beaches by municipal bus (R$2). Taxis and minivans regularly careen up and down the peninsula via Avenida José Ribeiro Dantas/Estrada Usina Nova. By day, *taxis marítimos* (R$5-20) shuttle passengers to and from the northern peninsula beaches from piers at Armação and Praia dos Ossos.

Diving

The limpid blue waters off the peninsula offer ideal conditions for diving. **Casamar** (Rua das Pedras 242, Armação, tel. 22/2623-8165, www.casamar.com.br) organizes daily excursions that include snacks and drinks for divers of all levels (as well as lessons) to the islands of Âncora and Gravatá, where you can see bright coral and fish, sea turtles, and, if you're lucky, dolphins. A four-hour beginner's course costs R$220, and a morning excursion with two tanks and equipment, R$160; it's also possible to rent snorkels, masks, and fins (R$25).

Sailing, Windsurfing, and Kite Surfing

The wind conditions at many of Búzios's beaches are excellent for sailing and windsurfing. **Búzios Vela Clube** (Praia de Manguinhos, tel. 22/2623-0508) offers lessons as well as equipment rental. Eight hours of windsurfing and sailing lessons cost around R$600 pp. Equipment rental costs R$50 (sailboats) and R$50 (windsurf board) per hour. Praia Rasa has become a mecca for aficionados of kite surfing. **Búzios Kitesurf School** (tel. 22/9956-0668, www.kitenews.com.br) offers lessons and rents equipment; a basic 8- to 10-hour course costs R$1,500.

Boat Excursions

Interbúzios (tel. 22/2623-6454, www.interbuzios.com) offers daily three-hour schooner trips (R$40 pp), with various departure times, that stop at 12 beaches and three islands. More rapid and more frequently booked are the daily catamaran excursions (R$60 pp) offered by **Tour Shop** (tel. 22/2623-4733, www.tourshop.com.br), which hit 15 beaches and four islands and provide snorkels and masks as well as drinks. Both depart from the pier at Praia de Armação.

Nightlife

Búzios's nightlife is concentrated along Armação's Rua das Pedras and Avenida José Bento Ribeiro Dantas. Whie the nocturnal scene fizzles off-season, during the summer months it boils over. Things don't get going until around 11pm, and the partying, which entails a lot of eating, drinking, and checking people out, is so intense that most of the area's hotels serve breakfast until noon and most boutiques don't open their doors until the afternoon.

Búzios institution **Chez Michou** (Rua das Pedras 90, tel. 21/2623-2169, www.chezmichou.com.br, noon-close daily) is famous for its mouthwatering crepes; choose from more than 40 sweet and savory fillings. At night, it becomes one of Búzios's major hot spots, as does **Pátio Havana** (Rua das Pedras 101, tel. 22/2623-2169, 6pm-close Thurs.-Sun., daily in summer), a sophisticated place with a whiskey club, bistro, tobacco shop, and stage that hosts live jazz, blues, and MPB performers. Once you've warmed up, it's time to dance the night away. **Pacha** (Rua das Pedras, tel. 22/2633-0592, www.pachabuzios.com, 10pm-7am Fri.-Sat., daily in summer) prides itself on importing top international DJs, while **Privilège** (Orla Bardot, tel. 22/2620-8585, www.privilegenet.com.br, 8pm-close Thurs.-Sun., daily in summer) is where you can work up a sweat, chill out on the terrace, or ramble its five bars (one serves sushi). Some clubs go into hibernation off-season.

Accommodations

To be near all the action in Búzios, stay in Armação or Geribá; if you prize tranquility and seclusion, consider accommodations at the peninsula's other beaches. Búzios is definitely not a bargain, especially in high season, when reservations are a must. If you choose to come during the off-season (anytime other than July and Dec.-Mar.) or during

the week, you can take advantage of discounts of up to 30-40 percent. The lower-priced options are small but homey *pousadas* in and around Armação and Ossos. Prices listed are off-season.

Located just off Praia de Geribá, **Marésia de Búzios Guest House** (Rua das Pitangueiras 12, Bosque de Geribá, tel. 22/2623-3876, www.maresiadebuzios.com.br, R$150-170 d, R$50-60 pp) is a hostel that feels more like a B&B. Rooms are in a gleaming white beach-style house with living rooms and shady lawns for sprawling or barbecueing. A quartet of private doubles have small patios.

Owned and operated by a charming French couple, **L'Escale Pousada Restaurant** (Travessa Santana 14, Praia dos Ossos, tel. 22/2623-2816, www.pousadalescale.com, R$160-220 d) offers simple but fetching rooms in a cozy house overlooking the placid Bay of Ossos. The nicest rooms sport terraces with picturesque sea views, and the main floor is occupied by a bistro.

Immersed in nature but only a stone's throw from Rua das Pedras, **Villa Balthazar** (Rua Maria Joaquina 375, Praia da Ferradura, tel. 22/2623-6680, www.villabalthazar.com.br, R$345 d) offers five lavish private rooms that mingle vintage and modern furnishings with flawless panache and attention to detail. A lounge, library, herb-scented garden, and small pool are invitations to unwind while nursing cocktails and listening to birdsong from the adjacent lake.

Checking into ★ **Casa Búzios** (Alta do Humaitá 1, Praia da Armação, tel. 22/2623-7002, www.pousadacasabuzios.com, R$300-540 d) is like visiting a friend's rambling, sunny beach house (albeit a friend with impeccable taste); each of the thematically decorated rooms has its own charismatic personality. Dining, drinking, and lounging take place in the charming main house surrounded by patios, gardens, and a pool with views toward the sea.

Casas Brancas Boutique Hotel & Spa (Alto do Humaitá 10, Praia da Armação, tel. 22/2623-1458, www.casasbrancas.com.br,

R$680-1610 d) has been around since 1973, long before the term *boutique hotel* had been uttered. The cluster of Andalusian-like white hilltop *casas* overlooking Praia da Armação possess none of the contrived sleekness of more contemporary design hotels. Yoga classes and treatments are offered at the on-site spa, and a delightful terrace restaurant serves up Brazilian-Mediterranean fare.

Cachoeira is Portuguese for waterfall, and at **Cachoeira Inn** (R. El, Lote 18, Praia da Ferradura, tel. 22/2623-2118, http://cachoeirainnbuzios.com, R$880-1,700 d), nine waterfalls wind their way down ingeniously landscaped cliffs to the blue waters of Ferradura Bay. The four luxurious suites are each named after a world-famous waterfall.

Food

Among the excellent and budget-saving per-kilo buffet palaces along Rua Manuel Turíbia, **Bananaland** (Rua Manuel Turíbia de Farias 50, Centro, tel. 22/2623-2666, www.restaurantebananaland.com.br, 11am-11pm daily, R$20-30) is the most charming and healthy. The more anonymously palatial **Buzin** (Rua Manuel Turíbia de Farias 273, Centro, http://buzinbuzios.com, tel. 22/2623-7051, 11:30am-11pm daily, R$20-30) offers greater diversity and a little more bang for your buck.

The Orla Bardot concentrates some of Búzios' most sophisticated and celebrated restaurants, all with romantic views of the sea. One of the most adventurous is **Salt** (Orla Bardot 468, Praia da Armação, tel. 22/2623-2691, www.restaurantesalt.com.br, 5pm-midnight Sun.-Thurs., 5pm-3am Fri.-Sat., R$65-80). The contemporary menu, conceived by Ricardo Ramos Ferreira (an able disciple of French superchef Alain Ducasse), draws upon global influences from Italian risottos and Moroccan couscous to Thai red curries. Bucking Orla's trendy (and pricey) eateries is **O Barco** (Orla Bardot 1054, Praia da Armação, tel. 22/2629-8307, 6pm-close daily Dec.-Feb., Tues.-Sun. Mar.-Nov., R$60-75).

Terrace and sidewalk tables are perfectly positioned for savoring generous portions while watching the sunset.

João Fernandes, Brava, Ferradura, and Geribá have idyllic palm-thatched bars that serve up grilled fish and seafood at reasonable prices. At **Fishbone Café** (Av. Gravatás 1196, Praia de Geribá, tel. 22/2623-7348, http://fishbonebuzios.com, 11am-5pm daily, R$25-45), you can enjoy salads and sandwiches. More secluded and clubby is the idyllic cliffside ★ **Rocka Beach Lounge** (Praia Brava, tel. 22/2623-6159, www.rockafishfish.com.br, 11am-5pm daily, R$40-60), where you can sink your teeth into fish and seafood delicacies while sprawling in lounge chairs and sofas.

Transportation and Services

A **tourist office** is just off the main square of Praça Santos Dumont in Armação (Travessia dos Pescadorees 151, Centro, tel. 22/2623-2099, www.visitebuzios.com, 8am-10pm daily). A good source of online information is the bilingual website www.buziosonline.com.

Búzios is a little more than two hours by car from Rio. **Viação 1001** (tel. 21/2516-3597, www.autoviacao1001.com.br) operates almost hourly daily buses (3 hours, R$47) between 6am-9:30pm from Rio's Rodoviária Novo to Búzios. Buses arrive at the virtually nonexistent Búzios Rodoviária (Estrada da Usina Nova 444, tel. 22/2623-2050), which is only a few minutes' walk from the Orla Bardot. By car, after crossing the Rio-Niterói bridge, turn onto BR-101 leading to Rio Bonito. Close to Rio Bonito, turn onto RJ-124 before turning onto RJ-106, which leads to Búzios. The journey is close to 200 kilometers (125 mi) and should take around two hours. Another alternative is to hitch a ride in an air-conditioned minivan. Búzios-based **Malizia Tour** (tel. 22/2623-1226, www.maliziatour.com.br) offers transportation between Rio and Búzios with pickup and deposit at your hotel or the airport for R$90 pp.

Costa Verde

Stretching south from Rio de Janeiro to the state of São Paulo, Costa Verde (Green Coast) is one of southern Brazil's most captivating and (for the time being) unspoiled coastlines.

★ ILHA GRANDE

Only 160 kilometers (100 mi) south of Rio, the port town of Angra dos Reis anchors a magnificent bay whose aquatic realm embraces 1,000 beaches and (supposedly) 365 islands. The largest, Ilha Grande, boasts more than 100 pristine beaches, including the breathtaking *praias* of **Lopes Mendes, Cachadaço, Saco do Céu, Aventureiro,** and **Parnaioca.** A 90-minute boat ride from Angra, Ilha Grande's 192 square kilometers (74 square mi) are entirely preserved and offer abundant walking trails and a wide range of accommodations.

Before becoming one of Brazilians' retreats from civilization, Ilha Grande went through phases as a pirate hangout and a leper colony. It also housed two penitentiaries, reserved for some of Brazil's most hardened and violent criminals. Although the second prison was demolished in 1994, opening the door to tourism, the not-yet-overgrown ruins of the original jail still cast a slightly haunting spell.

No motorized vehicles are allowed on the island. Ferries and launches all dock at the main village of **Vila do Abraão,** a picturesque, palmy, beachfront settlement of 3,000 people (the population swells in the summer months). Vila do Abraão, with its cobblestone streets and pastel-hued houses, provides the main base for exploring—on foot or by boat—the island's natural attractions.

Beaches

An hour's walk south of Vila do Abraão brings you to **Praia Grande das Palmas,** a tiny fishing village in the shade of a forest of swaying palms. Another 40 minutes away, the palms give way to mangroves at **Praia dos Mangues.** Despite the loveliness of both, most earnest beach pilgrims are loath to linger when they know that a mere 20-minute walk will bring them to **Praia Lopes Mendes,** considered by many to be the most beautiful beach in all of Brazil. Walking along its 3-km (2-mi) expanse, the shimmering bands of emerald and indigo sea are unearthly. To savor it by yourself, head toward the left, where you can relax in the shade of an almond tree; to the right is surfer central, where *surfistas* can rent boards and take lessons. The immaculate state of Lopes Mendes is guaranteed by its limited access: boats aren't allowed to dock in its inlet. Visitors who are loathe to hike from Vila do Abraão must catch one of three daily boats that shuttle between town and Praia dos Mangues (45 min.), then continue on by foot.

Further afield is **Cachadaço,** a small but shimmery jewel of a beach whose size (15 meters, 50 feet) is compensated for by a secluded setting of dramatic boulders and rain forest. Invisible from the open sea, it was a favorite pirate refuge. Divers can climb the rocks and plunge into the emerald pool below. To get here from Abrãao takes more than three hours on foot, two hours by boat.

A two-hour trek south from town along an old prison road leads to **Praia dos Dois Rios,** whose sands are bracketed by *dois rios* (two rivers). The rain forest behind the beach, near the village of Dois Rios, camouflages the vestiges of the Cândido Mendes penal colony. The small **Museu do Cárcere** (tel. 24/2334-0939, 10am-4pm Tues.-Sun.) pays homage to its checkered past. Among its illustrious captives were 20th-century novelist Graciliano Ramos, who wrote about his experience in the classic *Mémorias do Cárcere,* and legendary Lapa *malandro,* Madame Satã, who spent 16 years here for killing a policeman.

Far more remote (6 hours on foot from Abraão) is **Praia da Parnaioca,** where the Rio Parnaioca creates a freshwater lagoon that offers a sweet alternative to saltwater bathing. On the western end of the south coast, the unspoiled allure of **Praia do Aventureiro** stems from its location within a nature reserve (although it can be reached on foot and by boat). During periods when the waves swell to heights of 4 meters (13 feet), it becomes a surfers' paradise.

Diving and Boat Excursions

The best way to discover Ilha Grande's beaches, coves, and grottoes is by boat. **Ilha Grande Turismo** (tel. 24/3361-6426, www.ilhagrandeturismo.com.br) offers full- and half-day trips on large schooners (with 70 passengers, free-flowing caipirinhas, and pulsing musical soundtracks, R$30-50 pp for 6 hours) as well as on smaller, faster motorized launches for up to 20 people (R$120-180 pp for 6-8 hours). Trips usually include visits to 7-8 beaches with stops for snorkeling, diving, basking in the sun, and lunch. You can also hire a *táxi-boat* at the **Associação dos Barqueiros de Ilha Grande** (tel. 24/3361-5046, R$30-50 pp).

Elite Dive Center (tel. 24/3361-5501, www.elitedivecenter.com.br) offers lessons, equipment rental, and diving excursions to the most scenic underwater spots around the island. A beginner's course (R$200) includes a six-hour excursion with a 45-minute dive; a more intensive four-day course (R$960) includes five dives.

Rain Forest Hikes

Enthusiasts can tap into their inner Tarzan or Jane by tackling the numerous hiking trails that weave through the island. The rain forest is home to a variety of wildlife, including monkeys, parrots, hummingbirds, and (unfortunately) many mosquitoes—for your sanity, repellent is a *must*. Most trails are well signed, but it's best to take a few precautions, such as informing your *pousada* of your route and equipping yourself with water, snacks, and sunscreen. Also carry a flashlight, since night can fall quickly.

One of the easiest walks from town is along the road that leads to **Lazareto** (20 min.), the site of the late 19th-century hospital where leprosy and cholera patients were quarantined. Towering over the ruins is a 26-arch aqueduct that supplied the hospital with water. At one end of the aqueduct is a smooth, chair-shaped stone where Emperor Pedro II often sat to compose poetry and sketch. From the aqueduct, a 90-minute walk along a rain forest trail leads to the Cachoeira da Feiticeira, a

Praia Lopes Mendes

15-meter (50-foot) waterfall that plunges into natural pools fit for bathing. Since the trail is poorly marked, hire a guide.

For serious treks into the interior, such as the five-hour hike across the island to **Praia da Parnaioca** or the three-hour climb up to the summit of **Pico do Papagaio** (Parrot's Peak), it's wise to hire a guide (R$80). **Ilha Grande Turismo** organizes day trips (R$160 pp) as well as overnight camping and hiking excursions led by bilingual guides.

Accommodations

Most accommodations are located in or around Vila do Abraão, although some more exclusive *pousadas* are hidden in secluded natural settings. Camping sites abound, while *pousadas* tend to be fairly simple, although not always cheap.

There's no shortage of hostels in Ilha Grande, but small, tidy, and modern **Biergarten** (Av. Getúlio Vargas 153, tel. 24/3361-5583, http://biergartenhostel. blogspot.com, R$130 d, R$60-90 pp) is one of the nicest. Lots of exposed red brick and wood, along with bright colors, make it more homey than hostel-y. There are two communal kitchens; an on-site restaurant (lunch and dinner) mixes a mean cocktail and serves a cheap, delicious, and vegetarian per-kilo buffet.

At ★ **Pousada Naturália** (Rua da Praia 149, tel. 24/3361-5198, www.pousadanaturalia.net, R$170-210 d), double, triple, and quadruple suites are handsomely finished with polished natural wood and wide terraces where you can settle into a hammock and gaze out to sea. Cozy **Pousada Mara e Claude** (Rua da Praia 333, tel. 24/3361-5922, http://ilhagrande.org/maraeclaude, R$180-220 d) looks right onto the beach. The friendly French proprietors have decorated the modest guest rooms with homey touches that will make you feel like a prized houseguest.

The trump card at **Pousada Aratinga** (Rua das Flores 232, tel. 24/3361-9559, www.aratingailhagrande.com.br, R$280-350 d) is hands-on hostess and Scottish transplant Rennie, who is responsible for everything from the guest rooms' homey touches to the scrumptious cakes that accompany afternoon tea. A small pool and hammocks increase the relaxation factor, as does distance from the Vila's madding crowd. Set into a hillside overlooking the sea, the sprawling rooms at **Pousada Asalem** (Praia da Crena, tel. 24/3361-5602, www.asalem.com.br, R$460-580 d) offer maximum comfort and Edenic isolation, despite being only a 25-minute walk (or 15-minute boat ride) from town. If you feel stranded, hop into a complimentary kayak or canoe and contemplate your own private seascape.

Food

Vila do Abraão has lots of simple, rustic bar-restaurants to choose from. **Dom Mario** (Travessa Buganville, tel. 24/3361-5349, open Mon.-Sat., R$20-30) is a nicely priced favorite. Local chef Mario gets fancy with fresh seafood, yielding generously portioned creative fare such as octopus Provençal and fish doused in passion-fruit sauce. **Lua e Mar** (Rua da Praia 297, tel. 24/3361-5113, 11am-10pm Thurs.-Tues., R$25-45) provides tables and chairs spread out beneath a giant tree overlooking the beach. Located in the beachfront *pousada* of the same name, **O Pescador** (Rua da Praia, tel. 24/3361-5111, 5pm-11pm Mon.-Sat., R$50-70) offers tasty and inventive dishes, such as shrimp with leeks and gratiné pineapple, along with a small but well-chosen wine menu.

Information

Ilha Grande's **tourist office** (Rua da Praia, tel. 24/3367-7826, 7am-7pm daily) is located close to where the ferries dock. Nearby, the **Centro de Visitante do Parque Estadual** (Av. Beira Mar, tel. 24/3361-5540, 8am-5pm daily) has maps and information regarding the natural park covering much of the island. The bilingual website http://visiteangradosreis.com.br and the Portuguese www.ilhagrande.com and www.ilhagrande.org also have information about the area. There are no vehicles on Ilha Grande, nor bank machines—come equipped with cash (although many places accept credit cards). Internet service is sketchy to nonexistent in many places.

Transportation

Ilha Grande can be reached by boat via three towns along the Costa Verde: Angra dos Reis, Mangaratiba, and Conceição de Jacareí. **Viação Costa Verde** (tel. 21/3622-3123, www.costaverdetransportes.com.br) offers hourly bus service between 4am-9pm from Rio's Rodoviária Nova to Angra (3 hours, R$44); six daily buses to Conceição de Jacareí (2.5 hours, R$37) and four to Mangaratiba (2 hours, $R31). Angra-bound buses can also drop you in Conceição, if you ask the driver to do so. The advantage of going to Conceição is that the most frequent number of scheduled boats depart from here; speedboats (R$30, 25 mins.) and schooners (R$20, 45 min.) leave every 1-2 hours between 9am-6pm. Angra and Mangaratiba are the departure points for the cheaper but less frequent regular ferries operated by **CCR Barcas** (tel. 0800-721-1012, www.groupccr.com.br/barcas, R$4.80, 80 min. from both ports). Ferries depart from Angra 3:30pm weekdays and 1:30pm weekends and from Mangaratiba at 8am daily, with an extra ferry at 10pm Friday. **Ilha Grande Turismo** (tel. 24/3365-6426, www.ilhagrandeturismo.com.br) also operates speedboats from Angra to Ilha Grande (R$30, 45 min.) with departures at 8am, 11am, and 4pm. Tickets can be purchased at Angra's bus station.

A door-to-door shuttle service can save time and transfers. **Easy Transfer** (tel. 21/9386-3919, www.easytransferbrazil.com) operates vans that pick you up at your hotel in Rio and take you all the way to Ilha Grande (R$80, 4 hours). By car, follow the BR-101 (the Rio-Santos highway) to Angra, where you can leave your car in a parking area. Beware of weekend traffic.

★ PARATY

In the early 1700s, the Portuguese were looking for ways to transport gold found in neighboring Minas Gerais across the ocean and into their coffers. Traders widened an ancient Guaianá Indian trail that led through the Serra do Mar mountain range and down to the sea; at the end of the route sprouted the tiny port town of Paraty. Over the next few decades, Paraty grew into a modest yet stately town, its cobblestoned streets filled with single-story whitewashed mansions and austere but elegant churches. Yet it remained an isolated spot that was difficult to defend. Increasing bandit raids and pirate attacks took their toll and led to the building of a new gold route that linked Minas's gold towns directly with Rio de Janeiro.

As a consequence, Paraty's importance declined, and over the next two centuries the town, always remote, slowly fell into oblivion. Its faded architecture remained frozen in time, preserved by its very isolation. It wasn't until 1960 that the town was connected to both Rio de Janeiro and São Paulo by BR-101, the Rio-Santos highway. Shortly afterward, in 1966, its historic center was declared a national monument, and in the 1970s, Paraty began to attract a small trickle of hippies and artists drawn to its bucolic vibe and rich historic legacy. Artists and entrepreneurs transformed its 18th- and 19th-century houses, which in turn lured a steady stream of weekenders from Rio and São Paulo as well as international tourists and, more recently, an alternative GLS crowd.

In the summer and during July, Paraty can get quite busy, but so far it has managed to stave off hysteria and trendiness. During the off-season, the town is languorous without being dull, and it is easier to soak up its seductive atmosphere. Within close proximity are dozens of gorgeously primitive beaches and deserted islands, along with the majestic Serra do Mar mountain range.

Sights

Paraty's compact *centro histórico* is considered by UNESCO to be one of the world's most outstanding examples of Portuguese colonial architecture. Although the streets are laid out on a grid plan, the uniformity of the bleached houses coupled with streets' multiple names can make it somewhat of a challenge to find your bearings. The crazily paved streets—constructed by slaves out of large irregular stones known as *pés-de-moleque* ("street kids' feet")—mean that vehicles can't circulate, but also make getting around treacherous for those with disabilities or sporting high heels. During high tides, the sea actually swallows up some of the streets closest to the port, temporarily transforming them into tropical Venetian canals. While tides and rainwater can leave the streets slippery, they also keep them clean.

The best way to explore Paraty is by wandering. Among the town's most handsome *sobrados* (mansions) is the **Casa da Cultura** (Rua Dona Geralda 177, tel. 24/3371-2325, www.casadaculturaparaty.org.br, 10am-10pm Tues.-Sun., R$8). Built in 1758, it hosts cultural events and has a permanent exhibition tracing Paraty's history. Several baroque churches are also particularly interesting; due to ongoing renovations, opening hours are in flux. The town's oldest church, **Igreja de Santa Rita dos Pardos Libertos** (Largo de Santa Rita, R$3), dates from 1722. Built by freed slaves, its interior houses a small collection of religious artifacts. Constructed a few years later, **Igreja Nossa Senhora do Rosário** (Rua do Comércio) was built by and for Paraty's slave population but is the only church in town with gold decoration on its altars, added in the 20th century. Paraty's principal and most grandiose church, **Igreja Matriz de Nossa Senhora de Remédios** (Praça da Matriz, R$2) was where the bourgeoisie worshipped. Outside on the Praça da Matriz is a small, daily crafts market selling local handicrafts. The town's aristocrats held their services in the late 18th-century **Igreja Nossa Senhora das Dores** (Rua Fresca), which has a privileged view of the sea and access to cooling breezes.

Venturing outside the *centro histórico*, take a 15-minute walk past Praia do Pontal to reach the **Forte Defensor Perpétuo** (9am-noon

cobblestoned street in colonial Paraty

and 2pm-5pm Tues.-Sun, R$2). This fortress was built in 1703 to prevent Paraty's gold from being hijacked by pirates. Restored in 1822, it houses a small museum with a display of local artisanal objects.

Beaches

Paraty is rich in beaches: Some 300 can be found along the surrounding coastline and among some 65 islands. Most beaches can be visited by boat leaving from Paraty's Cais de Porto; those along the coastline can be reached by car or, to a lesser extent, bus. Although the town has its own beaches, they aren't that attractive. The closest, **Praia do Pontal,** is a 10-minute walk from the *centro histórico*. While its beach *barraca* scene is lively, swimming isn't recommended. Cleaner and more deserted are **Praia do Forte** and **Praia do Jabaquara,** a wide beach whose shallow waters are ideal for bathing and kayaking.

Some of the finest and most easily accessible beaches are at **Trindade,** a fishing village and former hippie hangout 25 kilometers

(16 mi) south of Paraty along the Rio-Santos highway that can easily be reached by hourly local Colitur buses (R$3.70, 45 min.) departing from Paraty's bus terminal. To the east, the stunningly wild beaches of **Cepilho** and **Brava** are ideal for surfing, while to the west **Praia do Meio** and **Praia Cachadaço** (also good for snorkeling) are prized for their calm waters and natural swimming pools. You can get to Cachadaço by a 20-minute hike through the forest or by boat from Praia do Meio. Trindade's most far-flung beaches—**Praia do Sono** and **Praia dos Antigos**—are gloriously unspoiled. Reaching them entails a 2-3-hour hike or 20-30 minute boat ride.

Located 18 kilometers (11 mi) southwest of Paraty (8 km/5 mi are on an unpaved road) is **Paraty-Mirim,** with a lovely bay and invitingly calm waters as well as beach *barracas* reachable by municipal Colitur bus (R$3.70, 45 min.) or by boat. From here, it's only a 30-minute boat journey to **Saco do Mamanguá,** a narrow, 8-kilometer (5-mi) bay that hides 30 completely deserted beaches. From Paraty, it's possible to organize an outing that includes canoeing and hiking.

Boat Excursions

Various schooners offer five-hour trips around Paraty's bay with stops at islands such as **Ilha Comprida** (known for its diving) as well as otherwise inaccessible and enticing beaches such as **Praia da Lula** and **Praia Vermelha.** Lunch is included, as are caipirinhas (and sometimes rambunctious live music that might grate on those who imagined a more bucolic outing). For information, contact **Paraty Tours** (Av. Roberto Silveira 11, tel. 24/3371-1327, www.paratytours.com.br), which also organizes kayaking, horseback riding, and hiking trips. A five-hour tour costs R$40 pp. Individuals and small groups can charter boats at an hourly rate (7-15 people, R$30-50 pp) from the *barqueiros* at Cais de Porto.

Trekking

At the **Associação de Guias de Turismo de Paraty** (tel. 24/3371-1783, R$130 pp per day, accommodations and food not included), individuals and small groups can hire guides to travel the forested coastline to secluded beaches, including those around Saco do Mamanguá, with stops for bathing in bays and waterfalls. An enticing journey is to follow the **Caminho do Ouro,** the route along which gold was transported over the mountains from Minas to Paraty during colonial times. The historical hike along a 2-kilometer (1.2-mi) stretch of irregular cobblestones can be done in the company of a guide from the **Centro de Informações Turísticas Caminho do Ouro** (Estrada Paraty-Cunha, tel. 24/3371-1222, 9am-noon and 2pm-5pm Wed.-Sun., R$25) as well as with ecotour agencies. Operated by an Irish transplant, **Paraty Explorer** (tel. 24/9952-4496, www.paratyexplorer.com) is an exceptional outfit that specializes in hiking trips as well as kayak and paddleboard outings—book a half-day outing (R$35-50) to the Caminho do Ouro with a time-out for waterfall plunging and cachaça sampling.

Entertainment and Events

Paraty has a vibrant and cosmopolitan nightlife and cultural scene, although most of the action takes place during the summer or July, and on weekends.

NIGHTLIFE

Charming bars with live music are concentrated along Rua Marechal Deodoro in Paraty. A traditional favorite with a loyal following, **Margarida Café** (Praça do Chafariz, tel. 24/3371-6037, www.margaridacafe.com.br, noon-midnight daily, R$25-35) is an atmospheric restaurant-bar; they feature live jazz and MPB every night. **Paraty 33** (Rua da Lapa 357, tel. 24/3371-7311, www.paraty33.com.br) has a low-key tavern atmosphere and lures a younger, more animated crowd. Beer lovers should visit the **Cervejaria Caborê** (Av. Otávio Gama 420, Caborê, tel. 24/3371-2248, www.cervejariacabore.com.br, 5pm-midnight Wed.-Fri., noon-midnight

Sat.-Sun.), a microbrewery where you can check out the production facilities and then sample the wares at the in-house pub.

You don't have to understand Portuguese to be enchanted by the plays performed by the Contadores de Estórias at the **Teatro de Bonecos** (Rua Dona Geralda 327, tel. 24/3371-1575, www.ecparaty.org.br, 9pm Wed. and Sat. year-round, plus 9pm Fri. Jan.-Feb. and July, R$50). This renowned troupe of actors are talented manipulators of a disarmingly lifelike cast of doll-like puppets (*bonecos*) who mutely act out poignant and hilarious dramatic sketches. Leave the kids (under 14) at home, since these puppet shows are for adults only, and buy tickets in advance.

FESTIVALS

Carnaval is a serious street party; a highlight is the **Bloco da Lama** (www.blocodalama.com.br), composed of mud-covered young things dancing through the streets.

Paraty comes alive in the winter months (May-Aug.) for several popular *festas*. The **Festa do Divino** takes place 40 days after Easter and lasts for two weeks. This colorful religious festival hosts parades and celebrations along with theatrical, dance, and musical performances that take place in the street. Also known for their ornate pageantry are **Semana Santa** (Easter) and **Corpus Christi** (June). Since 2009, a top-notch roster of international artists has lured jazz lovers to town for the **Bourbon Festival Paraty** (www.bourbonfestivalparaty.com.br) during the last week in May. During the third weekend in August, *cachaça* lovers from far and wide descend on the town for the **Festival da Pinga**. Not just for bookworms, the **Festa Literária Internacional** (FLIP, www.flip.org.br), which takes place for five days in August, lures more visitors to Paraty than Carnaval. Readings and debates are attended by the likes of Paul Auster, Salman Rushdie, Margaret Atwood, and Ian McEwan, and the town comes alive with cultural and culinary happenings.

Shopping

Paraty is famous for its *cachaças,* produced in the surrounding region. One of the most potent brands is Corisco; Paratiana and Maria Izabel are smoother and more discreet. At *cachaça* boutiques, you can sample the wares even if you don't want to purchase; try **Armazém da Cachaça** (Rua do Comércio, tel. 24/3371-7519) and **Empório da Cachaça** (Rua Dr. Samuel da Costa 22, tel. 24/3371-6329). You can also visit many of the *alambiques* (distilleries); many have been in operation for generations and are located relatively close to town. One of the better tours is to **Maria Izabel** (BR-101 Km. 568, Sítio Antonio, Corumbé, tel. 24/9999-9908, www.mariaizabel.com.br). Respected and artisanal, it is also the only *alambique* owned and operated by a woman, Maria Izabel Gibrail Costa. Advance reservations are necessary.

Paraty is full of ateliers and boutiques flaunting an endless variety of objets d'art. Among the most unique and hard to resist are the miniature *caiçara* fishing vessels, made from wood and painted in vibrant colors, sold at **Atelier da Terra** (Rua da Lapa 1, tel. 24/3371-3070).

Accommodations

In the summer and during holidays (including Carnaval, the Festival da Pinga, and the Festa Literária Internacional), finding a room can be tricky, so reserve in advance. You'll have more luck and cheaper rates at one of the many newer places outside the *centro histórico;* try the *bairros* of Caborê and Chácara or Jabaquara beach or nearby Trindade, where hostels have mushroomed. If you have a car, take advantage of many idyllic spots tucked away in the forest-clad mountains. During the off-season (particularly weekdays), you can often negotiate rate reductions of up to 30-40 percent.

One of the most attractive and affordable hotels in the *centro histórico* is the **Solar do Gerânios** (Praça da Matriz, tel. 24/3371-1550, www.paraty.com.br/geranio, R$120-160 d), which offers a homey atmosphere enhanced by the friendly owner and her cats. Guest rooms are small but spotless and cheery; the best ones have small balconies overlooking the square. Lacking in historic character, yet quaint and friendly, **Pousada Flor do Mar** (Rua Fresca 257, tel. 24/3371-1674, www.pousadaflordomar.com.br, R$190-220 d) is another good choice that offers clean and colorfully painted guest rooms.

Highly atmospheric, **Pousada do Ouro** (Rua da Praia 145, tel. 24/3371-4300, www.pousadaouro.com.br, R$370-480 d) possesses tastefully furnished colonial-style guest rooms in a beautiful 18th-century *sobrado* (and a less impressive annex). A sauna, fitness room, and pool round out the amenities. One of Paraty's oldest guesthouses, **Pousada Pardieiro** (Rua do Comércio 74, tel. 24/3371-1370, www.pousadapardieiro.com.br, no children under age 15, R$310-420 d) clusters 18th-century houses converted into apartments. Guest rooms are impeccably furnished and face a pool and tranquil gardens.

Upon arriving at the **Pousada de Arte Urquijo** (Rua Dona Geralda 79, tel. 24/3371-1362, www.urquijo.com.br, no children under age 12, R$420-590 d), guests are invited to remove their shoes and don comfortable Japanese slippers in which they can glide around the polished wood floors of this uniquely renovated 18th-century *sobrado*. Painter-proprietor Luz Urquijo has an artist's eye for detail, reflected in the unusual furnishings and bright bold canvases on the walls (many by Luz and her daughter).

Although it's a 10-minute walk from the *centro histórico*, distance is a small price to pay for the exceptional comfort and privacy at ★ **Vivenda** (Rua Beija-Flor 9, Caborê, tel. 24/3371-4272, www.vivendaparaty.com, R$320-370 d). Accommodations consist of two modern but exquisitely designed and decorated bungalows and an apartment, which look out onto a pool and garden. English owner and host John makes visitors feel as if they are house guests, with the result that

checking out is like leaving a second home. Also in Caborê is **Music Art Hostel** (Rua Rita Ribeiro da Gama, Caborê, tel. 24/3371-8345, www.musicarthostel.com, R$140 d, R$40 pp), offers performances, live music jams, and *festas*. Dorms, private rooms, and a large communal kitchen are scattered among a colonial house with lofty ceilings, vast shuttered windows, and a pool. Bikes are available for rent (R$5), and an on-site restaurant-bar slakes thirst and hunger.

Food

The majority of Paraty's restaurants occupy charming *sobrados* in the *centro histórico*. *Caiçara* is the name given to local specialties that draw on fish, game, fruits, and vegetables traditionally used by the Costa Verde's indigenous peoples.

Banana da Terra (Rua Dr. Samuel Costa 198, tel. 24/3371-1725, www.restaurantebananadaterra.com.br, 6pm-midnight Mon. and Wed.-Thurs., noon-4pm and 7pm-midnight Fri.-Sun. Mar.-Nov., noon-midnight daily Dec.-Feb., R$50-70) serves up *caiçara* fare with a touch of refinement prepared by Ana Bueno, considered one of Brazil's top chefs. True to its name, various varieties of bananas make frequent appearances on the (somewhat overpriced) menu in guises both savory (banana-and-cheese-stuffed squid gratiné with shrimp) and sweet (warm banana tart with cinnamon ice cream).

The location of **Sabor da Terra** (Av. Roberto Silveira 180, tel. 24/3371-2384, www.paraty.com.br/sabordaterra, 11am-10pm daily, R$15-25), just outside the *centro histórico*, may justify the low-wattage decor and equally low prices. However, this per-kilo restaurant earns high marks in terms of the variety, freshness, and tastiness of its buffet offerings. Another inexpensive option is **Le Castellet** (Rua Dona Geralda 44, tel. 24/3371-4649, http://lecastelletyveslepide.com.br, 6pm-midnight Tues.-Fri., noon-midnight Sat.-Sun., R$20-35). Chef Yves Lapide has outfitted this cozy little *crêperie* with attractive decorative touches from his native Provence, but his real forte is delicious sweet and savory crepes, along with other French fare.

Casa do Fogo (Rua Comendador José Luiz 390, tel. 24/3371-3163, www.casadofogo.com.br, 6pm-1am Thurs.-Tues., R$30-55) takes its name literally: A majority of its main dishes (even desserts and drinks) arrive at the table on fire (*fogo*). Taking advantage of the local *cachaça* supply, local chef "Caju" flambées everything from shrimp (served with guava rice) to mangoes and star fruit (served with passion fruit jelly). The romantic atmosphere is abetted by nightly performances of chorinho and MPB.

For centuries, many escaped and freed slaves fled into remote rural regions of Brazil, where they created their own settlements and maintained cultural and religious vestiges passed down from their African ancestors. Today, there are thousands of *quilombos* throughout Brazil, including **Quilombo do Campinho** (http://quilombocampinhodaindependencia.blogspot.com). Located just south of Paraty, off the Rio-Santos highway, this traditional community of 120 families is home to ★ **Restaurante do Quilombo** (BR-101 Km. 589, tel. 24/3871-4866, 11am-5pm daily, R$15-30), a community-operated restaurant. The emphasis is on fresh fish and locally farmed produce; portions are robust and prices are honest. You can explore the community via guided tours (R$20) given by residents.

COOKING CLASSES

Treat yourself to a night of cooking (and eating) at the **Academia de Cozinha e Outros Prazeres** (Rua Dona Geralda 288, tel. 24/3371-6468, www.chefbrasil.com, R$190). The "Academy of Cooking and Other Pleasures" is run by Yara Costa Roberts, a professional chef whose fluent English is a result of years spent in the United States. Several nights a week, Yara offers small groups a chance to learn how to prepare dishes from Bahia, the Amazon, the Cerrado region (in the Central-West), and her own home state of Minas Gerais.

Transportation and Services

The **Centro de Informações Turísticas** (Av. Roberto Silveira 1, tel. 24/3371-1222, 8am-8pm daily), located at the entrance to the *centro histórico*, has maps, bus schedules to other beaches, and other information. Two useful bilingual websites with lots of information are www.paraty.com.br and www.paraty.tur.br.

Viação Costa Verde (tel. 21/3622-3123, www.costaverdetransportes.com.br) offers almost hourly daily bus departures from 4am-9pm between Rio and Paraty (4.5 hours, R$63). **Viação Reunidas** (tel. 0300/210-3000, www.reunidaspaulista.com.br) offers four daily departures from 8am-10:30pm between São Paulo's Rodoviária Tietê and Paraty (6 hours, R$52). The Rodoviária (Rua Jango Pádua) is 500 meters (0.3 mi) from the *centro histórico*.

By car from Rio, simply follow BR-101, the Rio-Santos highway (236 km/147 mi). From São Paulo, take the Rodovia Ayrton Senna and then the Mogi-Bertioga highway to BR 101 and drive north to Paraty (338 km/210 mi). An alternative route is to take the Ayrton Senna to the Rodovia Carvalho Pinto and then take the Rodovia dos Tamoios to BR-101 (285 km/177 mi).

From Rio, **Easy Transfer** (tel. 21/9386-3919, www.easytransferbrazil.com) operates vans that pick you up at your hotel and take you all the way to Paraty (R$90, 5 hours).

São Paulo

Look for ★ to find recommended sights, activities, dining, and lodging.

Highlights

★ **Avenida Paulista:** Raw, vital, messy, and fascinatingly diverse, São Paulo's main drag is the city's vibrant nerve center (page 120).

★ **Museu de Arte de São Paulo:** One of Latin America's finest art museums is housed in an iconic modernist building that is an attraction in itself (page 121).

★ **Parque do Ibirapuera:** São Paulo's version of Central Park, this vast green urban oasis has some of the city's finest museums (page 124).

★ **Campos do Jordão:** With hiking trails, Swiss chalets, and abundant fondue and chocolate, Paulistanos' preferred mountain getaway evokes a tropical version of the Alps (page 153).

★ **Bananal:** In the 19th century, this colonial gem of a town was the center of the biggest coffee-growing region in the world. The surrounding plantations of the coffee barons are still intact and worth a visit (page 158).

★ **Ilhabela:** Brazil's biggest off-coast island is a nature lover's dream, with virgin rain forests and unspoiled beaches (page 164).

Teeming with noise, activity, and a certain degree of urban chaos, São Paulo is bewildering for those unfamiliar or unenamored with cities its size—and enchanting for those who are.

Brazil's economic and cultural powerhouse is overflowing with banks and megacorporations, along with world-class museums, theaters, and concert halls. Rife with contrasts and contradictions, São Paulo mingles First World sophistication with *favelas*. While the working rich rely on the world's largest fleet of private helicopters to commute from posh suburbs to glittery office buildings, the less fortunate—and far more numerous—working poor spend hours snarled in lengthy traffic jams caused by the world's largest fleet of municipal buses. If you're looking for Brazil's quintessential tropical paradise, you won't find it here. Instead, you'll encounter a unique and fascinating fusion of elements from all over the country—and the world.

The surrounding state of São Paulo is as diverse as its capital. The wealthiest and most populous of Brazil's states, as well as the most developed in terms of industry and agriculture, São Paulo is also rich in impressive natural attractions. The coastline north from the historic city of Santos up to Rio de Janeiro is lined with stunning white-sand beaches and native Atlantic forest. São Sebastião is teeming with every kind of water sport imaginable and nonstop nightlife. North of Ubatuba and on the island of Ilhabela, you'll find primitive beaches you can have all to yourself. Traveling inland offers similar contrasts: While the mountain resort of Campos do Jordão attracts a crowd with a penchant for fondues and fireplaces, the tiny colonial towns and century-old coffee plantations of the Serra da Mantiqueira range remain largely unknown even to many native Paulistas (natives of São Paulo state). Well-maintained highways and an extensive and efficient bus system mean that most attractions are easy to get to: All it takes is a 2-3-hour drive from the city and you're in another world.

PLANNING YOUR TIME

Many international travelers only spend enough time in São Paulo to change planes at its busy airport. Despite its vast size, beachlessness, and—some would say—lack of

Previous: São Paulo skyline; São Sebastião. **Above:** Luz train station.

São Paulo City

To Fundação Maria Luiza e Oscar Americano

UNIVERSIDADE DE SÃO PAULO

INSTITUTO BUTANTAN

Butantã

CIDADE JARDIM

JOQUEI CLUBE

ALTO DE PINHEIROS

VILA MADALENA

BRÁS

INSTITUTO TOMIE OHTAKE

Faria Lima

LAPA

ÁGUA BRANCA

Vila Madalena

Sumaré

PERDIZES

Palmeiras-Barra Funda

NEU CLUB

Praça da Água Branca

MEMORIAL DA AMÉRICA LATINA

ITAIM BIBI

SHOPPING IGUATEMI

MUSEU DA CASA BRASILEIRA

MANI

INSTITUTO ITAÚ CULTURAL

PINHEIROS

MUSEU DA IMAGEM E DO SOM (MIS)

SEE "AVENIDA PAULISTA AND JARDINS" MAP

CERQUEIRA CESAR

JARDINS

Clínicas

Paulista

AVENIDA PAULISTA

Consolação

Trianon-Masp

Parque Trianon

PACAEMBU

ESTÁDIO PACAEMBU/ MUSEU DO FUTEBOL

EL TRANVIA

Mal. Deodoro

CONSOLAÇÃO

CENTRO

SEE "CENTRO" MAP

BOM RETIRO

Tiradentes

Praça da Luz

Luz

Armênia

HOTEL UNIQUE/ SKYE

FUNDAÇÃO CULTURAL EMA GORDON KLABIN

MUSEU AFRO BRASIL

MUSEU DE ARTE MODERNA

PARQUE DO IBIRAPUERA

MONUMENTO ÀS BANDEIRAS

PARAÍSO

TENDA DO NILO

CASA DAS ROSAS

Brigadeiro

BELA VISTA

República

Santa Cecília

Anhangabaú

São Bento

Sé

Praça Dom Pedro I

VILA MARIANA

MUSEU DE ARTE CONTEMPORÂNEA

QUINTAL DO BRÁS

Ana Rosa

Paraíso

Vergueiro

ACLIMAÇÃO

São Joaquim

LIBERDADE

Liberdade

Pedro II

Brás

MUSEU LASAR SEGALL

IPIRANGA

MUSEU DO IPIRANGA

CAMBUCI

PARI

BRÁS

0   0.5 mi
0   0.5 km

© AVALON TRAVEL

visual appeal, the city of São Paulo is one of the world's most vibrant and surprising metropolises. For a dose of sophisticated urban living, with all the culture, fine dining, and shopping that entails, it is definitely worth spending a **couple of days** here. If you're a true urban soul, stick around for a whole week to explore the city's many neighborhoods and take advantage of its fantastic nightlife. In a pinch, you can always make a quick day trip or overnight getaway to the coast or mountains.

Summer months are often unbearably hot and sticky (a fact made worse by pollution), with sudden downpours that can cause flooding in the streets. On the other hand, summer—along with long weekends, "winter break," and other holidays—is also when millions of residents hightail it out of the city and migrate to the coast. Popular resorts get very crowded, meaning that advance reservations are a must. In **winter**, temperatures can plunge to 10°C (50°F). This isn't a big deal if you're equipped with the proper clothing, but many places don't have heating.

São Paulo City

In Brazil, they say that Rio is all play, while São Paulo is all work. Indeed, the world's seventh-largest city, with a (metropolitan area) population of 20 million, is an economic force that generates a significant portion of Brazil's wealth. When you climb to the 35th floor of the landmark Banespa building and glimpse an endless concrete jungle that extends a full 360 degrees, you might wonder what the appeal could be.

Few vestiges remain of São Paulo's early days as a Jesuit missionary settlement, or as a thriving 19th-century trade center where coffee barons lived it up in grand style. However, its bustling downtown, Centro, offers vibrant history and architectural styles, ranging from surviving colonial churches to belle epoque and art deco apartment buildings. The clean lines of Brazilian modernism are on display in the elegant residences of the neighborhood of Higienópolis. And the city's version of the Champs-Élysées, Avenida Paulista, offers a daunting collection of skyscrapers that are undeniably impressive.

night view of São Paulo

Just as varied as the city are its residents, known as Paulistanos. São Paulo boasts particularly large Italian, Japanese, and Lebanese communities. Working-class and "popular" *bairros* exist alongside posh, heavily guarded residential areas. The aptly named Jardins (Gardens) neighborhood is home to the city's rich and powerful as well as some of the most luxurious boutiques, galleries, and bistros on the planet. Indeed, "Sampa" (as it is lovingly referred to by residents) is all about highs and lows. If you're after foie gras, you'll find it, but you can just as easily enjoy a cheese-filled *pastel* washed down with sugarcane "juice" at a street market. This mixture is reflected in unparalleled eating opportunities as well as cultural offerings that rival those of New York and London. A vibrant arts scene, great museums, and an intense and varied nightlife ensure that Paulistanos play harder than anyone else in Brazil. And when they tire of both work and play, there is always Parque do Ibirapuera, a vast oasis that is the perfect place to recharge one's batteries.

ORIENTATION

It's best to think of São Paulo as an ensemble of villages, each of which can be explored individually. **Avenida Paulista** is the city's freeway-esque main drag. Running east-west along an elevated plateau, it divides the historic and central downtown core, **Centro**—along with the surrounding dense neighborhoods of Liberdade, Luz, Higienópolis, Barra Funda, and Bixiga— from the swanky, green neighborhoods of the **Zona Sul** (South Zone). At the eastern end of "Paulista" (as the area is often called), the artery composed by Avenida Brigadeiro Luís Antônio plunges down toward Parque Ipirapuera and the luxurious residential *bairros* that surround it.

Further east, and to the north, lie the sweeping **Zona Leste** (East Zone) and **Zona Norte** (North Zone), which mingle poor and working-class neighborhoods with industrial districts. At Avenida Paulista's western end, Rua da Consolação, which segues into

Avenida Rebouças, marks the beginning of the **Zona Oeste.** Within the "West Zone" lie the lively, largely middle-class neighborhoods of Pinheiros and Vila Madalena, as well as Butantã, home to the vast University of São Paulo campus.

SIGHTS

The majority of São Paulo's attractions are located within the central core and are easily reached by Metrô, bus, or foot.

Centro

Hidden in São Paulo's original downtown core are a few vestiges of the city's colonial past, which are all the more striking for being hemmed in by a forest of skyscrapers. Although you should always be on the alert for pickpocket types, wandering around Centro during the day is a fairly safe, if mildly chaotic, experience. At night, however, much of the area clears out, making taxis necessary.

The geographic, historic, and symbolic center of São Paulo is **Praça da Sé.** By day, this vast plaza is filled with thousands of Paulistanos hurrying to and from somewhere, small clusters of street kids, and *camelôs* (illegal sidewalk vendors) hawking cheap wares. Many protests and demonstrations have been held here; one of the most famous occurred in 1984, when 300,000 citizens demanded direct democratic elections following two decades of military rule.

CATEDRAL DA SÉ

Dominating the Praça da Sé is the **Catedral da Sé** (Praça da Sé, tel. 11/3107-6832, 8am-7pm Mon.-Fri., 8am-5pm Sat., 8am-6pm Sun., free, crypt R$5). The city's main cathedral, this imposing mid-20th-century neo-Gothic building is large enough to hold 8,000 people. Inside, sculpted columns feature tropical elements such as coffee beans, exotic fruits, toucans, and armadillos.

CAIXA CULTURAL

Directly across from the Cathedral da Sé, at the far side of the *praça*, the magnificently

Centro

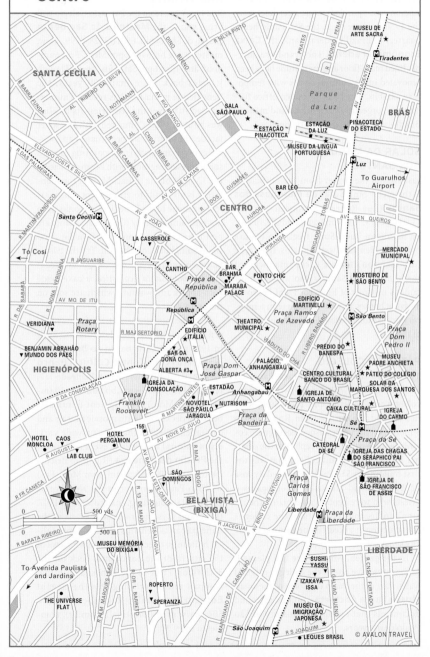

MUSEU DE ARTE SACRA

Ⓜ *Tiradentes*

SANTA CECÍLIA

Parque da Luz

BRÁS

SALA SÃO PAULO

★ ESTAÇÃO PINACOTECA

ESTAÇÃO DA LUZ

PINACOTECA DO ESTADO

MUSEU DA LÍNGUA PORTUGUESA

Ⓜ *Luz*

To Guarulhos Airport

▼ BAR LÉO

To Cosi ←

CENTRO

MERCADO MUNICIPAL ★

Ⓜ *Santa Cecília*

LA CASSEROLE

MOSTEIRO DE ★ SÃO BENTO

VERIDIANA ▼

▼ CANTHO

BAR BRAHMA ▼

PONTO CHIC

Praça de República

MARABÁ PALACE

EDIFÍCIO MARTINELLI ★

Ⓜ *São Bento*

Praça Ramos de Azevedo

Praça Dom Pedro II

Praça Rotary

Ⓜ *República*

EDIFÍCIO ITÁLIA

THEATRO MUNICIPAL ★

PRÉDIO DO BANESPA ★

MUSEU PADRE ANCHIETA ★ PÁTEO DO COLÉGIO ★

VERIDIANA ▼

R MAJ SERTORIO

BENJAMIN ABRAHÃO ▼ MUNDO DOS PÃES

BAR DA DONA ONÇA ▼

ALBERTA #3 ▼

PALÁCIO ANHANGABAÚ ★

CENTRO CULTURAL BANCO DO BRASIL ★

SOLAR DA MARQUESA DOS SANTOS ★

HIGIENÓPOLIS

Praça Dom José Gaspar

IGREJA DA CONSOLAÇÃO

ESTADÃO

Anhangabaú

IGREJA DE SANTO ANTÔNIO

Praça Franklin Roosevelt

NOVOTEL SÃO PAULO JARAGUÁ

▼ NUTRISOM

CAIXA CULTURAL

IGREJA DO CARMO

155 ●

Praça da Bandeira

Ⓜ *Sé*

Praça da Sé

HOTEL MONCLOA

CAOS ▲

HOTEL PERGAMON

CATEDRAL DA SÉ

IGREJA DAS CHAGAS DO SERÁPHICO PAI SÃO FRANCISCO

LAB CLUB ■

SÃO DOMINGOS ▼

IGREJA DE SÃO FRANCISCO DE ASSIS

BELA VISTA (BIXIGA)

Praça Carlos Gomes

Liberdade Ⓜ *Praça da Liberdade*

LIBERDADE

To Avenida Paulista and Jardins ←

MUSEU MEMÓRIA DO BIXIGA ■

SUSHI-YASSU ▼

● THE UNIVERSE FLAT

ROPERTO ▼

▼ SPERANZA

IZAKAYA ISSA ▼

MUSEU DA IMIGRAÇÃO JAPONESA ★

Ⓜ *São Joaquim*

● LEQUES BRASIL

© AVALON TRAVEL

0 — 500 yds
0 — 500 m

brooding art deco **Edifício Sé** (Praça da Sé 111, tel. 11/3321-4400, www.caixacultural. com.br, 9am-9pm Tues.-Sun., free) dates from the 1930s and serves as the São Paulo headquarters of Brazil's federal bank, the **Caixa Econômica Federal**. The grandiose, marble-lined main floor and mezzanine have been renovated into a cultural center with temporary exhibits. The bank's wooden office furniture—gorgeously streamlined and made in Brazil—will delight design aficionados.

SOLAR DA MARQUESA DOS SANTOS

Just around the corner from the Edifício Sé is the pretty pink **Solar da Marquesa dos Santos** (Rua Roberto Simonsen 136, tel. 11/3115-6118, www.museudacidade.sp.gov. br, 9am-5pm Tues.-Sun., free). São Paulo's oldest residential dwelling, this 18th-century mansion's former occupants included the Marquesa de Santos, who was the most famous mistress of Emperor Dom Pedro II. Today, it houses a small museum with temporary art exhibits devoted to different aspects of the city.

PÁTEO DO COLÉGIO

The **Páteo do Colégio** (Praça Páteo do Colégio 2, tel. 11/3105-6899, www.pateo-collegio.com.br, 9am-5pm Tues.-Sun., R$6) lies around the corner from Rua Roberto Simonsen. This whitewashed Portuguese colonial edifice is actually a replica of the original 16th-century Jesuit college that was the first building in São Paulo. Founded by José de Anchieta and Manuel da Nóbrega, two priests who were bent on catechizing the region's indigenous population, the college's construction marked the beginning of the city's history.

In the garden, where there is a pleasant café, you can see one of the college's original walls. Part of the Páteo do Colégio, the small **Museu Padre Anchieta** contains relics and documents that recount the history of São Paulo's early years.

MOSTEIRO DE SÃO BENTO AND VICINITY

Rua Boa Vista from the Páteo do Colégio will bring you to the **Mosteiro de São Bento** (Largo de São Bento, tel. 11/3328-8799, www. mosteiro.org.br, 6am-6pm Mon.-Fri., 6am-noon and 4pm-6pm Sat.-Sun., free). Though it dates back more than 400 years, the Benedictine monastery has received numerous facelifts over the centuries. Its basilica was built in 1912. Compared with the sober facade, the interior is more ornate—an interestingly pagan touch is the painting of a red sun (representing God) with beams radiating the 12 signs of the zodiac. Most of the monastery is off-limits to visitors since its quarters are home to the Benedictine monks, who not only sing divinely (Gregorian chants are performed at 7am Mon.-Fri., 6am Sat., and 10am Sun.) but also bake well: Try the *pão de mandioquinha* (a type of sweet-potato bread) and the *bolo Santa Ecolástica,* a cake made with apples and walnuts, which are sold on the premises.

Near the monastery is a trio of more modern but equally striking landmarks. Built in 1901 to house the Banco do Brasil's city headquarters, the **Centro Cultural Banco do Brasil** (CCBB; Rua Álvares Penteado 112, tel. 11/3113-3651, www.bb.com.br, 10am-9pm Wed.-Mon.) is an opulent beaux arts building decked out with mosaic murals and crystal chandeliers that hosts a wide variety of cultural and artistic events. Close by, the **Prédio do Banespa** (Rua João Bricola 24, tel. 11/3249-7180, 10am-5pm Mon.-Fri.) was São Paulo's answer to the New York's Empire State Building. Inaugurated in 1947, this grand skyscraper—headquarters of the Banespa bank—remains one of Sampa's tallest buildings; check out impressive views of the city from the panoramic deck on the 35th floor. Prior to the Banespa building, Sampa's tallest building was the elegant **Edifício Martinelli** (Rua Líbero Badaró 504, www.prediomartinelli.com.br), completed in 1929.

colorful Sampa

VIADUTO DO CHÁ

Rua Libero Badaró leads to the Vale do Anhangabaú, a narrow valley festooned with fountains and swaying palms and straddled by the **Viaduto do Chá**. Designed by 19th-century French architect Jules Martin, the Viaduto do Chá was the first of São Paulo's many overhead passes. Its original purpose was to facilitate transport among the coffee plantations that occupied the valley. In more recent times, viaducts have mushroomed throughout the city in an attempt to ease Sampa's crazy traffic flow.

From the Viaduto do Chá, you can get a sense of Sampa's intense activity as well as a great view of two of the city's most prestigious buildings. Inaugurated in 1939, the **Palácio Anhangabaú** (Viaduto do Chá 15) functions as São Paulo's city hall. A rooftop garden features more than 400 native plants, among them coffee bushes, sugarcane, and even a mango tree.

More dazzling is the **Theatro Municipal** (Praça Ramos de Azevedo, tel. 11/3397-0300, www.prefeitura.sp.gov.br, 10am-6pm Tues.-Sun.). Built at the turn of the 20th century, the theater reflects the opulence of the era and the art nouveau style of Paris's Opéra Garnier. Venetian mosaics, gold-leaf fixtures, and a chandelier with 7,000 crystals from Belgium are a few of the splendid trappings on display. To reserve a free guided tour, call 11/3397-0382.

LARGO DE SÃO FRANCISCO

Crowning the square of Largo de São Francisco is one of São Paulo's oldest churches, the **Igreja das Chagas do Seráphico Pai São Francisco** (tel. 11/3105-8791, 7am-5pm Mon.-Fri.). It is one of the city's finest examples of baroque architecture; construction began in 1676 and lasted for well over a century. The well-preserved interior features gold-leaf paneling, adding shimmers of light to this otherwise dimly lit church.

Also on the Largo is the **Igreja de São Francisco de Assis** (tel. 11/3291-2400, 8am-6pm Mon.-Fri., 8am-4pm Sat., 8am-1pm Sun.). Though it has undergone many alterations over the centuries, this church retains its original adobe walls from the 17th century.

MERCADO MUNICIPAL

São Paulo's **Mercado Municipal** (Rua da Cantareira 306, Parque Dom Pedro, tel. 11/3313-1326, www.mercadomunicipal.com.br, 6am-6pm Tues.-Sat., 6am-4pm Sun.-Mon.), within easy walking distance of the São Bento Metrô stop, is known affectionately by Paulistanos as the **Mercadão** (Big Market). Built in 1932, this vast neoclassical-style food hall is a major mecca for the city's restaurateurs and foodies. Each day, more than 1,000 tons of fresh produce and delicacies imported from all over Brazil and the world are purchased from its 300 stalls.

Should all the goods on display incite hunger pangs, head to the **Hocca Bar** (Rua G, Box 7), where you'll have to line up in order to savor the *pastéis de bacalhau* (deep-fried pastries filled with salted cod) that have been a favorite snack since 1952. Other traditional snacks can be found at the market's bars and *lanchonetes,* and at the mezzanine.

PRAÇA DA REPÚBLICA

At the tail end of the 19th century, **Praça da República** was hardly very republican—instead, it was a posh downtown square around which São Paulo's coffee barons built lavish city dwellings. However, as commerce—and its attendant trappings of noise, traffic, and riffraff—swept the city's center, the barons decamped and their mansions were replaced by modernist buildings, some quite striking, others sadly run-down. Today, Praça da República is a vibrant if somewhat forsaken square. On Sundays, it is the site of a colorful crafts and antiques market.

Two of the standout modernist buildings off of Praça da República have become Paulistano icons. Constructed between 1956 and 1965, **Edifício Itália** (Av. Ipiranga 344, www.edificioitalia.com.br) was built with the mission of surpassing the reigning Banespa building in height; indeed, for a long time, it held the title as tallest building not only in town but in all of Latin America. To take in the glorious view, ride the elevator up to the swank **Terraço Itália** (www.terraco-italia.com.br) piano bar on the 42nd floor. If you don't want to splurge for a mediocre meal or pay a cover charge at the bar, visits are free 3pm-4pm weekdays. Quite remarkable from the outside is the **Edifício Copan** (Av. Ipiranga 200), a curling S-shaped building that could only have been dreamed up by Oscar Niemeyer. The building is as famous as a living space as it is for its design—boasting more than 1,160 apartments and close to 6,000 residents, rare is the Paulistano who hasn't known someone who has lived here at some point in time.

Luz

Until the early 20th century, Luz wore its name—"Light"—well: It was one of São Paulo's more resplendent neighborhoods, with handsome buildings surrounding a bucolic park. In subsequent decades, it fell into disrepair, with areas given over to prostitution and drugs, but in the last decade there has been a successful effort to revitalize the area. After dark, Luz is still quite sketchy, but during the day its growing roster of top-notch museums, many housed in renovated historical buildings, have given a new shine to the *bairro.* All attractions in the area are easily reached by taking the Metrô to Luz station.

The crowning landmark of the neighborhood is **Estação da Luz,** a rosy redbrick train station, a portion of which houses the Museu da Língua Portuguesa. The rest functions as a busy station linking the capital to suburbs and surrounding towns.

MUSEU DA LÍNGUA PORTUGUESA

Even if you don't read or speak Portuguese, you'll likely enjoy the **Museu da Língua Portuguesa** (Praça da Luz, tel. 11/3322-0080, www.museudalinguaportuguesa.org. br, 10am-10pm Tues., 10am-6pm Wed.-Sun., R$6, free Tues. and Sat.). Fittingly located in the largest Portuguese-speaking city in the world, this original and imaginative museum relies on engaging interactive games and innovative multimedia to trace the fascinating history of the Portuguese language in Brazil.

PINACOTECA DO ESTADO

São Paulo's oldest art museum, the **Pinacoteca do Estado** (Praça da Luz 2, tel. 11/3224-1000, www.pinacoteca.org.br, 10am-6pm Tues.-Sun., R$6, free Sat.) has been around since 1905. Back then, its collection consisted of a mere 26 paintings. Today, it has swollen to an impressive 7,000 works, most of them representing major Brazilian painters and sculptors of the 19th and 20th centuries. The Pinacoteca hosts a permanent collection and some of São Paulo's most compelling temporary exhibitions featuring both national and international artists. Downstairs, a charming outdoor café serves pastries and light meals.

Purchasing a ticket to the Pinacoteca also gives you access to its nearby sister gallery, the **Estação Pinacoteca** (Largo General

Osório 86, tel. 11/3335-4990, 10am-6pm Tues.-Sun.). Built in 1914 as a railroad ware-house, during the military dictatorship it was converted into the headquarters of the DOPS (Department of Political and Social Order), a repressive organ that specialized in tortur-ing political prisoners. Following a renova-tion in 2003, it reopened as an extension of the Pinacoteca with a permanent collection of works by Brazilian modernists. Part of the building houses the Memorial da Resistência, where you can learn about Brazil's military dictatorship, view photos of political prison-ers, and even (rather morbidly) step into the cells in which they were held.

SALA SÃO PAULO

Of the four best concert halls in the world (from the point of view of acoustics), only one occupies a train station. The **Sala São Paulo** (Praça Júlio Prestes, tel. 11/3367-9573, www.osesp.art.br) is inside the grand hall of the re-stored Estação Júlio Prestes, an 1920s-era sta-tion whose sober and grandiose interior was designed in Louis XVI style. The auditorium roof is made from wooden panels that can be positioned to enhance the quality of whatever type of music is being played. The *sala* is the headquarters of the São Paulo State Symphony Orchestra; if you can't catch a performance, **guided visits** (tel. 11/3367-9500, 1pm and 4:30pm Mon.-Fri., 1:30pm Sat., 1pm Sun., R$5, free Sat. and Sun.) are available.

PARQUE DA LUZ

Parque da Luz (Praça da Luz, 9am-6pm Tues.-Sun.) is São Paulo's oldest public garden. Upon its completion in 1825, the park quickly became the favorite playground of the city's elite, who enjoyed strolling among its ponds, bandstands, fig trees, eucalyptus, and impe-rial palms. In more recent times, the park was taken over by homeless people, junkies, and prostitutes. A restoration—which included the introduction of a sculpture garden and beefed-up security—has brought renewed interest from families, couples in love, and those seek-ing some bucolic respite. The park is adjacent to the Pinacoteca do Estado and directly across the street from the Estação da Luz.

MUSEU DE ARTE SACRA

São Paulo's **Museu de Arte Sacra** (Av. Tiradentes 676, tel. 11/3326-1373, www.museuartesacra.org.br, 9am-5pm Mon.-Fri., 10am-6pm Sat.-Sun., R$6) showcases an im-pressive 5,000-piece collection that provides a wonderful overview of Brazilian baroque and rococo styles, including sculptures and sacred artifacts fashioned out of wood, terra cotta, silver, and gold. The museum is housed in the Mosteiro da Luz, a carefully conserved 18th-century monastery still inhabited by cloistered nuns.

Liberdade

In June 1908, a Japanese ship carrying 800 passengers docked at the port of Santos. Most of the immigrants on board made their way to the booming capital and settled in a central neighborhood known as Liberdade (Liberty). By the end of World War II, the *bairro* had consolidated its reputation as the city's Little Japan. Today, São Paulo boasts the largest Japanese population outside of Japan. Chinese and Korean immigrants have moved into Liberdade, but the heart and soul of the neighborhood—not to mention most of the stores and restaurants—are still Japanese. To get to Liberdade, take the Metrô to Liberdade station.

Liberdade's core is concentrated around the red lantern-lined streets of Rua Galvão Bueno, Rua dos Estudantes, and Rua da Glória. Here you'll find scores of great restaurants and su-permarkets along with emporiums display-ing a wide range of wares, from semiprecious stones, Buddhist oratories, and silk kimonos to Hello Kitty paraphernalia. On weekend days, the Praça da Liberdade is animated by the **Feira da Liberdade.** The stands at this open-air market sell everything from Japanese medicinal herbs to cheap and delicious bowls of stir-fried *yakissoba,* a mixture of noo-dles, meat, and vegetables that has become a Paulistano staple.

Those interested in the history of Japanese immigrants in Brazil can check out the **Museu da Imigração Japonesa** (Rua São Joaquim 381, 7th-9th Floors, tel. 11/3209-5465, 1:30pm-5:30pm Tues.-Sun., R$6). There is also a pleasant Japanese-style garden on the rooftop.

Higienópolis

The lovely residential *bairro* of Higienópolis, west of Praça da República, developed during the late 1890s. Relative to the increasingly congested and commercialized Centro, the elevated heights of this region offered a "hygienic" alternative to the frequent floods and epidemics in the city's downtown. By 1900, Sampa's wealthiest families were flocking to Higienópolis in droves. The opulent mansions they built in the early 1900s gave way to seductively streamlined art deco and modernist apartment buildings in the '30s, '40s, and '50s. Although only a few of the houses remain, many of the apartment buildings are still standing.

Higienópolis remains one of São Paulo's wealthiest and most traditional residential *bairros*. It possesses a significant Jewish population, both secular and orthodox, which accounts for the many kosher products available in the neighborhood's numerous delicatessens. Although there aren't many sights, there are quite a few pleasant little restaurants and cafés, and simply wandering around is an agreeable way to spend a low-key afternoon. Architecture buffs take note—among the most striking modernist buildings (in order of walkability) are the **Edifício Piauí** (Rua Piauí 428, at Rua Sabará), **Edifício Cinderela** (Rua Maranhão 163, at Rua Sabará), **Edifício Lausanne** (Av. Higienópolis 101), **Edifício Prudência** (Av. Higienópolis 265), **Edifício Parque das Hortênsias** (Av. Angélica 1106), **Edifício Bretagne** (Av. Higienópolis 938), **Edifício Louveira** (Rua Piauí 1081), and **Edifício Arper** (Rua Pernambuco 15). Close to Edifício Cinderela is the very charming **Praça Villaboim**, a tiny jewel of a park surrounded by restaurants, bars, and boutiques.

MUSEU DO FUTEBOL

While it would seem impossible to capture Brazil's passionate fanaticism for *futebol* within the confines of a museum, the **Museu do Futebol** (Praça Charles Miller, Pacaembu, tel. 11/3663-3848, www.museudofutebol.org.br, 9am-6pm Tues.-Sun., R$6, Tues. free) actually succeeds. It helps that the museum is located within Sampa's historic Estádio Pacaembu, which explains why it closes on game days. The permanent exhibition kicks off by stoking everyone's inner soccer fan with two interactive caverns. The first pays homage to Brazil's 25 greatest soccer gods. The second features panels that allow you to select footage of the greatest goals of all time, accompanied by commentators screaming *"go-o-ol!"* Other rooms trace the history of soccer in Brazil from its introduction in the late 1800s to the present day while making insightful parallels to what was going on in politics and culture at the time. Even if you don't read Portuguese (an English audio guide is available), the iconography is captivating. Kids in particular will love the final room, where they can play a simulated game of soccer projected on the floor or test the potency of their goal kicking abilities by firing a real ball against a virtual goalie. As the Louvre has the *Mona Lisa*, the Museu do Futebol has Pelé's retired No. 10 jersey, worn at the historic 1970 World Cup Game in which Brazil beat Italy to win their third World Cup in what many Brazilians claim was the most beautiful of the "beautiful games" ever played.

★ Avenida Paulista

Sampa's main drag of **Avenida Paulista,** a teeming multilane thoroughfare, is a shock: The roughly hewn skyscrapers that line it really do resemble a concrete jungle. It's hard to imagine that a little over a century ago, this 2.8-kilometer (1.7-mi) *mega-avenida* was a mere country road. In the late 1800s, it was widened into a European-style grand avenue by coffee barons and industrial magnates, who lived in sumptuous mansions built in wildly diverging architectural styles. Shortly after,

Avenida Paulista

most glamorous address. Those who lived in the coveted modernist apartments were treated to stunning views (the skyscrapers were yet to come) and could camp out at the swanky Restaurante Fasano, where the likes of Marlene Dietrich and Nat King Cole entertained international luminaries like Ginger Rogers, David Niven, and Fidel Castro. After falling into decay and suffering damage from a fire in the 1970s, it wasn't until the late 1990s that a restored Conjunto recaptured some of its former glory. Today it is a great place to have a *cafezinho,* take in a movie, or browse through the fantastic range of books at the Livraria Cultura.

PARQUE TRIANON

Back in the day when Avenida Paulista was the domain of the coffee aristocracy, **Parque Trianon** (Rua Peixoto Gomide 949, Cerqueira César, 6am-6pm daily) was *the* place to go strolling. Originally designed in 1892 by French landscaper Paul Villon, the park received a more tropical makeover in 1968 by Roberto Burle Marx, who played up the exuberant textures and colors of the native Atlantic forest. Today, this small but surprisingly lush oasis, punctuated with benches, sculptures, and fountains, provides a welcome contrast to the congested avenue. By day, the park attracts a colorful mixture of visitors, including bookworms and lunching tycoons. Its more jungly depths are a gay cruising area.

★ MUSEU DE ARTE DE SÃO PAULO

Paulistanos are justifiably proud of the **Museu de Arte de São Paulo** (MASP; Av. Paulista 1578, Cerqueira César, tel. 11/3251-5644, www.masp.art.br, 10am-6pm Tues.-Sun., 10am-8pm Thurs., R$15, free Tues.), considered one of Latin America's finest art museums. The top floor boasts Brazil's most important collection of European art, including multiple works by Flemish, Italian Renaissance, and French impressionist painters along with some wonderful Degas sculptures in bronze. Foreign visitors, however, might be more captivated by the leading

Avenida Paulista was the first of São Paulo's streets to be paved. It was also the first to go completely vertical in the 1940s, as São Paulo's industrial economy grew at rates of up to 60 percent a year. By the 1970s, the avenue had been widened to keep up with escalating traffic, and almost all of its beautiful mansions were replaced by skyscrapers.

In recent years, corporate headquarters have moved south to the new *bairros* of Brooklin and Berrini. However, Avenida Paulista still remains the city's symbol and vibrant nerve center, a place where commerce and culture thrive. Nowhere else in the city comes close to capturing and condensing the city's energy and adrenaline.

CONJUNTO NACIONAL

The elegant **Conjunto Nacional** (Av. Paulista 2073, Cerqueira César, tel. 11/3179-0000, www.ccn.com.br, 9am-10pm Mon.-Fri., 10am-9:30pm Sat., 2pm-8pm Sun.) was Latin America's first shopping center. Inaugurated in 1956, by the 1960s it had become Sampa's

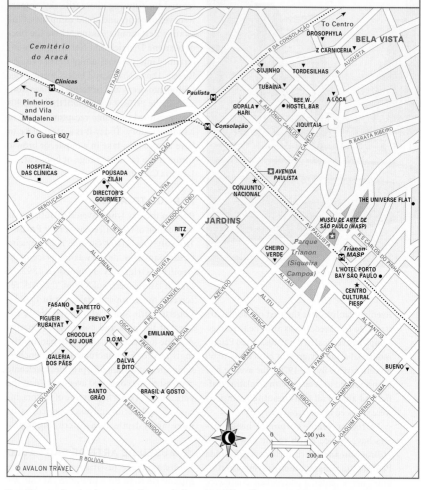

Avenida Paulista and Jardins

Brazilian modernists here, as well as works by foreign artists and adventurers. Among the most interesting of these were Jean-Baptiste Debret, a French artist and engraver who specialized in vivid portraits of African slaves and Indians in early 19th-century Rio, and Frans Post, a Dutch baroque painter whose Edenic renderings of Brazil inspired tapestries made by the famed French Gobelins factory.

Unfortunately, of the 7,000 works in MASP's collection, only around 500 are ever on display at a given time. In compensation, the temporary exhibitions are often of international caliber. As striking as the art on display is the MASP itself. The inspired creation of the vanguard architect Lina Bo Bardi (who was born in Italy and naturalized in Brazil), the building consists of a giant box suspended above the ground on four spindly, bright-red pillars. The effect is impressive, and it's hardly surprising that since its completion in 1968,

MASP has become one of São Paulo's most beloved and recognizable landmarks.

CASA DAS ROSAS

Near the end of Avenida Paulista, the **Casa das Rosas** (Av. Paulista 37, Bela Vista, tel. 11/3285-6986, www.casadasrosas.org.br, 10am-10pm Tues.-Fri., 10am-6pm Sat.-Sun., free) is one of the few remaining mansions that once lined the avenue. Designed by leading architect Ramos de Azevedo in the 1920s, the house is now devoted to poetry, hosting frequent readings and events among handsome wooden furnishings and stained-glass windows. Its library holds more than 30,000 volumes of verse.

Jardins

Avenida Paulista is the final frontier of Sampa's downtown area. Lying to the southwest is the leafy sprawl appropriately known as Jardins (Gardens). Modeled after the British garden suburbs of the early 20th century, Jardins is a wealthy and perennially fashionable residential neighborhood whose name conjures up lifestyles of Brazil's rich and famous. Jardins actually embraces four separate "gardens": Jardim Paulista, Jardim Paulistano, Jardim América, and Jardim Europa.

Bordering Avenida Paulista, the exclusive high-rise condos of **Jardim Paulista** (part of the district known as Cerqueira César that spills over onto both sides of Avenida Paulista) are interspersed with some of São Paulo's world-renowned and übertrendy restaurants, cafés, and bars. **Rua Oscar Freire** and the posh streets surrounding it contain a shopper's dream of upscale boutiques selling the fashionable wares of leading Brazilian and international designers.

Leading down to Avenida Brigadeiro Faria Lima, on the edge of Pinheiros, Jardim Paulista turns into **Jardim Paulistano,** an area with many restaurants and bars. Avenida Estados Unidos marks the beginning of **Jardim América** and **Jardim Europa**—two residential enclaves that are even more exclusive and wealthy, as evidenced by the opulent mansions that peek out from behind thickly hedged, electrically fenced estates. Three small, interesting museums are worth dropping into here.

MUSEU DA IMAGEM E DO SOM

The **Museu da Imagem e do Som** (MIS; Av. Europa 158, Jardim Europa, tel. 11/2117-4777, www.mis.sp.gov.br, noon-9pm Tues.-Sat., 11am-9pm Sun., free) usually hosts temporary exhibits that showcase some of the treasures in its vast archive of historic and contemporary Brazilian photographs. On weekends, international shorts and art films are screened in the theater.

FUNDAÇÃO CULTURAL EMA GORDON KLABIN

The **Fundação Cultural Ema Gordon Klabin** (Rua Portugal 43, Jardim Europa, tel. 11/3062-5245, www.emaklabin.org.br, guided visits 2pm, 3pm, and 4pm Tues. and Thurs.-Fri., 10am, 11am, and 2pm Sat., R$10) is located in a fabulous mansion inspired by Berlin's Palace of Sanssouci. This private home was built in the 1950s by heiress and philanthropist Ema Gordon Klabin, who amassed a significant Brazilian and international art collection. As you wander from room to room, you'll encounter everything from 6th-century BC Greek vases to paintings by Marc Chagall and Chaïm Soutine. A highlight of the beautiful garden is the orchid hothouse. Advance reservations are necessary. On alternate Saturdays, free concerts are held in the garden at 4:30pm.

MUSEU DA CASA BRASILEIRA

Housed inside a 1930s saffron-colored villa, the **Museu da Casa Brasileira** (Av. Brigadeiro Faria Lima 2705, Jardim Paulistana, tel. 11/3032-3727, www.mcb. sp.gov.br, 10am-6pm Tues.-Sun., R$4, free Sun.) displays an eclectic permanent collection of Brazilian and international furniture dating from the 17th century to the present. It also displays temporary exhibits focusing on various aspects of furniture and design.

A delightful place for lunch is the **Santinho** restaurant (www.restaurantesantinho.com.br).

Pinheiros and Vila Madalena

The major thoroughfare of Avenida Brigadeiro Faria Lima marks the southwestern frontier of Jardins. South lies the upscale commercial neighborhood of **Itaim Bibi,** where some of the city's trendy restaurants and bars open and close with impressive velocity. North are the adjacent *bairros* of Pinheiros and Vila Madalena. Pinheiros mixes a forest of commercial high-rises with boutiques, galleries, and a lively nightlife scene.

North of Pinheiros, Vila Madalena is Sampa's bohemian *bairro* par excellence. By day, Vila Madalena is a wonderfully laid-back place to wander around. Rua Aspicuelta and surrounding streets such as Rua Fradique Coutinho and Rua Fidalga are lined with funky boutiques, secondhand stores, and numerous art galleries where you can spend hours browsing. At night, the *bairro* buzzes with activity as its restaurants and clubs fill up with a mixed and alternative crowd.

INSTITUTO TOMIE OHTAKE

Pinheiros's most compelling attraction is the **Instituto Tomie Ohtake** (Av. Brigadeiro Faria Lima 201, Pinheiros, tel. 11/2245-1900, www.institutotomieohtake.org.br, 11am-8pm Tues.-Sun., free), which occupies the first two floors of a wildly flamboyant office tower whose curving facade is painted in tones of magenta and violet. The building showcases the signature style of one of Brazil's most daring architects, Ruy Ohtake, and features work by Ruy's mother, Japanese Brazilian artist Tomie Ohtake, whose paintings and engravings incorporate traditional Japanese brushstroke techniques in a range of early landscapes to later abstractions. Other galleries display temporary exhibits of contemporary art. In the Grand Hall, the gift store sells an array of objects, jewelry, and T-shirts by innovative Brazilian artists and designers. Time your visit to coincide with lunch at the sleek **Santinho** restaurant (www.restaurantesantinho.com.br).

★ Parque do Ibirapuera

Paulistanos' equivalent of Central Park is **Parque do Ibirapuera** (entrances on Av. Pedro Alvarés Cabral, Av. República do Líbano, and Av. IV Centenário, tel. 11/5573-4180, www.parquedoiberapuera.com, 5am-midnight Mon.-Fri., 24 hours Sat.-Sun., free), a 160-hectare (395-acre) expanse of green

view of Niemeyer's Oca, Parque do Ibirapuera

that Paulistanos unironically refer to as their *"praia"* (beach). Created in the 1950s to commemorate Sampa's 400th anniversary, the park project was headed by two stellar talents: Oscar Niemeyer and Roberto Burle Marx. Various curvy, concrete, well-illuminated Niemeyer pavilions today house a handful of top-notch museums, earning the area the nickname of "Museulândia." Contrasting with the futuristic buildings, Burle Marx's inspired landscaping mingles sweeping lawns with ponds, wooded areas, and bursts of flowers and tropical foliage. There is also a planetarium, a sculpture garden, and a Japanese pavilion modeled after the Katsura Imperial Palace in Kyoto. Music lovers can rock out at the free open-air concerts often held at a Roman-style amphitheater or enjoy more erudite melodies at the Niemeyer-designed **Auditório Ibirapuera.** The next best thing to a fireworks display is the sound and light show (8pm-10pm Mon.-Fri., 8:30pm-9:30pm Sat.-Sun. year-round) that erupts from the lagoon's 673 fountains.

The easiest way to get to the park is to take the Metrô to Brigadeiro station. Then take one of many buses or walk (around 30 minutes) down Avenida Brigadeiro Luís Antônio until you reach Portão 9, one of numerous entrances to the park. Dominating this area is the dramatic **Monumento às Bandeiras.** The work of renowned modernist sculptor Victor Brecheret, the imposing granite landmark pays homage to the intrepid 16th- and 17th-century adventurers of Portuguese origin (*bandeirantes*) who opened up much of Brazil's interior.

MUSEU DE ARTE CONTEMPORÂNEA

The Niemeyer-designed headquarters of the **Museu de Arte Contemporânea** (Av. Pedro Álvares Cabral 1301, tel. 11/5573-9932, www.mac.usp.br, 10am-9pm Mon., 10am-6pm Wed.-Sun., free) shelters one of Brazil's finest collections of contemporary art and hosts temporary exhibits.

MUSEU DE ARTE MODERNA

The first modern art museum to be founded in Latin America, the **Museu de Arte Moderna** (MAM; Portão 3, tel. 11/5549-9688, www.mam.org.br, 10am-6pm Tues.-Sun., R$6, free Sun.) actually focuses more on Brazilian contemporary works than modern art. Temporary exhibits from the permanent collection accompany visiting national and international exhibitions. The curving glass and concrete building was designed by Oscar Niemeyer and renovated by Lina Bo Bardi in the 1970s. A lovely minimalist restaurant serving contemporary fare looks out onto the sculpture garden.

MUSEU AFRO BRASIL

Niemeyer also designed the pavilion that houses the **Museu Afro Brasil** (Pavilhão Padre Manoel da Nóbrega, Portão 10, tel. 11/3320-8900, www.museuafrobrasil.org.br, 10am-5pm Tues.-Sun., free). This is a museum you shouldn't miss: Its three floors offer a compelling look at the rich historical, cultural, and artistic legacies of Brazil's Afro-descendent population from the 16th century to the present day. Highlights include finely crafted African artifacts along with objects and clothing used in Afro-Brazilian celebrations and rituals. Particularly harrowing is a room devoted to the slave ships that brought so many Africans to the New World. Insightful temporary exhibits by artists from Brazil and overseas offer more contemporary visions of the African diaspora.

PAVILHÃO DAS CULTURAS BRASILEIRAS

Yet another Niemeyer pavilion shelters the **Pavilhão das Culturas Brasileiras** (Portão 10, tel. 11/5083-0199, www.culturasbrasileiras.sp.gov.br, 9am-5pm Tues.-Sun., free). Devoted to Brazil's undeniably rich forms of *arte popular,* this dynamic museum juxtaposes unexpected dialogues between indigenous art, regional folk art, and contemporary urban design. You'd be surprised at the parallels between a wooden stool carved by Amazonian artisans and a chair dreamed up by the Campana brothers. For a glimpse at Brazilian creativity and ingenuity at its most beguiling, this museum is highly recommended.

Arredores (Outlying Neighborhoods)

If you have some extra time, São Paulo has several other attractions that are worth visiting, despite being slightly more far-flung.

MUSEU LASAR SEGALL

Although not well known outside of Brazil, Lasar Segall is one of the country's most singular modern artists. Many of his paintings, drawings, and engravings can be seen at the **Museu Lasar Segall** (Rua Berta 111, Vila Mariana, tel. 11/5574-7322, www.museusegall. org.br, 11am-7pm Wed.-Mon., free), where he lived and worked from 1932 until his death in 1957. To get to the museum, take the Metrô to Vila Mariana.

MUSEU DO IPIRANGA

Under renovation in 2014, the **Museu do Ipiranga** (Parque da Independência, Ipiranga, tel. 11/2065-8000, www.mp.usp. br, 9am-5pm Tues.-Sun., R$6) occupies a grand Renaissance-style palace built in 1890 to commemorate Brazilian independence, which took place in 1822 (it took decades for the final project to be approved). The museum is full of paintings, furnishings, and other artifacts that conjure up 19th- and early 20th-century Brazilian society. Fans of things royal can delight in the many knickknacks belonging to the Brazilian imperial family. The surrounding park is known as Parque da Independência, because it was here that Dom Pedro I proclaimed Brazil's independence. The spot where he dramatically cried out "Independence or Death!" is marked by a monument, beneath which lies his tomb and that of his wife, Empress Leopoldina. Many buses pass by the park, departing from Praça da Sé (4113), Praça da

República (4205, 4631), and Vila Mariana (4706) Metrô stations.

INSTITUTO BUTANTAN

Adults and kids with a fondness for reptiles will be in heaven at the **Instituto Butantan** (Av. Vital Brasil 1500, Butantã, tel. 11/3726-7222, www.butantan.gov.br, 9am-4:30pm Tues.-Sun., R$6, Thurs. free). The institute is one of the world's foremost research centers for poisonous snakes and insects, with the aim of creating antivenin serums. Located on the University of São Paulo's sprawling campus, it is home to some 54,000 slithering creatures, such as the Indian python, which can measure up to a spooky 6 meters (20 feet) in length. There is also a colorful collection of iguanas, scorpions, frogs, and lethal spiders. Also on the premises is the **Museu de Microbiologia,** where you can gaze through microscopes at everything from fleas and fungi to human blood samples. To get to the *instituto,* take the Metrô to Butantã or any bus marked Butantã-USP.

FUNDAÇÃO MARIA LUISA E OSCAR AMERICANO

Located in the wealthy suburban *bairro* of Morumbi, the **Fundação Maria Luisa e Oscar Americano** (Av. Morumbi 4077, tel. 11/3742-0077, www.fundacaooscaramericano. org.br, 10am-5pm Tues.-Sun., R$10) occupies an elegant streamlined house reminiscent of a Frank Lloyd Wright design. It was built in 1952 as a residence for wealthy engineer Oscar Americano and his wife, who were avid collectors of Brazilian art. The interior displays an impressive ensemble of paintings, furnishings, and religious art as well as objects belonging to Brazil's imperial family. Take a leisurely stroll through the beautifully landscaped gardens, and if you come in the afternoon, treat yourself to the lavish high tea (R$55), which includes brioches, croissants, tarts, and cakes.

MEMORIAL DA AMÉRICA LÁTINA

Niemeyer fans will either love or disdain this late 1980s ensemble of nine concrete buildings that comprise the **Memorial da América Látina** (Av. Auro Soares de Moura Andrade 664, Barra Funda, tel. 11/3823-4600, www. memorial.org.br, 9am-6pm Tues.-Sun., free). The absence of greenery accentuates the barrenness of the architecture. Of more interest is what's inside the buildings themselves. The Pavilhão da Criatividade contains an enticing permanent exhibition of traditional arts and crafts from all over Latin America, while the Salão de Atos houses Portinari's giant 1949 masterpiece, *Tiradentes,* painted to honor the 19th-century Mineiro freedom fighter. Contemporary art exhibits as well as dance, theater, and film events frequently take place here (take the Metrô to Barra Funda).

ENTERTAINMENT AND EVENTS

São Paulo boasts the most vibrant and varied cultural scene in Brazil. Surpassing even Rio (after all, Cariocas have the beach for entertainment), the city reunites the best of Brazil and a fantastic array of offerings from the rest of the world. Whether they were born or migrated here, Paulistanos are notoriously innovative, and the city pulses with creative energy that spills over into all the arts. As a result, Sampa is blessed with top-notch cultural centers, cinemas, theaters, and concert halls.

For information about what's going on, consult the arts sections of the leading paper, *Folha de São Paulo* (in Portuguese, http:// guia.folha.uol.com.br), which publishes a terrific cultural guide on Fridays featuring listings for the upcoming week. *Time Out* (www.timeout.com.br/sao-paulo) has a bilingual online version of its magazine with constantly updated, pithily written listings and reviews. Also pick up a copy of the weekly listings guide *Veja São Paulo*, which comes with *Veja* magazine (and see http://vejasp.abril. com.br). For upcoming events in English and Portuguese, visit www.guiasp.com.br. Tickets for concerts, shows, and other events can be purchased directly at theaters and concert halls; some will deliver tickets to your hotel for an extra fee.

Performing Arts

The splendid turn-of-the-20th-century **Theatro Municipal** (Praça Ramos de Azevedo, Centro, tel. 11/3397-0327, www. prefeitura.sp.gov.br) provides a magnificent backdrop for high-caliber classical music, dance, and opera performances. The Estação Júlio Prestes, a renovated train station, houses the **Sala São Paulo** (Praça Júlio Prestes, Luz, tel. 11/3367-9500, www.osesp.art.br), whose impeccable acoustics are enhanced by the auditorium's unique roof, which features adjustable wooden panels. Home to the acclaimed **Orquestra Sinfônica do Estado de São Paulo**, it also hosts other orchestras.

Named the "world's coolest building" by *Travel + Leisure* magazine, the futuristic **Auditório Ibirapuera** (Parque do Ibirapuera, Portão 2, tel. 11/3629-1075, www. auditorioibirapuera.com.br) could only have been designed by Oscar Niemeyer. During performances of erudite music, the enormous red door behind the stage often opens, allowing you to meditate on the greenery of Ibirapuera park.

Since its 2013 unveiling, cutting-edge **Praça das Artes** (Av. São João 281, Centro, tel. 11/3397-0327) has won international design awards for its bold integration of a former movie palace and conservatory into a series of concrete modular buildings tinted with pigments. It provided new homes to the highly reputed **Orquestra Sinfônica Municipal** and the city's classical ballet company, **Balé da Cidade.** Dance and music performances take place in the beautiful auditorium.

The state-of-the-art **Teatro Alfa** (Rua Bento Branco de Andrade Filho 722, Santo Amaro, tel. 11/5693-4000, www.teatroalfa. com.br) and the more traditional **Teatro Cultura Artística** (Rua Nestor Pestana 196, Cerqueira César, tel. 11/3256-0223, www. culturaartistica.com.br) are both top venues for concerts, theater, and dance. Two leading contemporary dance companies are **Ballet Stagium** (www.stagium.com.br) and **Cisne Negro** (www.cisnenegro.com.br). Even if your Portuguese is shaky, it's worth checking out the interactive offerings of vanguard dramaturge José Celso (Zé Celso) Martinez Corrêa, who operates the historical **Teatro Oficina** (Rua Jaceguai 520, Bela Vista, tel. 11/3104-0678, www.teatrooficina.com.br). Planned by architect Lina Bo Bardi, the landmark theater was designed to break down boundaries between actors and audience. Although performances of works by playwrights such as Euripides, Shakespeare, and Genet last for hours, the fact that audience members are encouraged to walk in and out of the narrative action ensures you won't be bored.

Cultural Centers

Along Avenida Paulista are several cultural centers; all host free art exhibitions. The FIESP (Federation of Industries of São Paulo State) building is easily recognizable by its wildly sloping ultramodern facade. It is home to the **Centro Cultural FIESP Ruth Cardoso** (Av. Paulista 1313, Cerqueira César, tel. 11/3146-7405, www.sesisp.org.br, 10am-9pm Tues.-Sat., 10am-7pm Sun.), which has an art gallery, theater, and cinema. Another major cultural center where something interesting is always going on is the **Instituto Itaú Cultural** (Av. Paulista 179, Cerqueira César,

tel. 11/2168-1777, www.itaucultural.org.br, 9am-8pm Tues.-Fri., 11am-8pm Sat.-Sun.).

Cinema

Paulistanos adore a *cineminha*. Lines are enormous on weekends and holidays, and prime-time screenings often sell out. The majority of the city's biggest and best theaters are conveniently concentrated on or around Avenida Paulista. Outfitted with a small bookstore and a cool café-restaurant that looks onto Avenida Paulista, the **Reserva Cultural** (Av. Paulista 900, Cerqueira César, tel. 11/3287-3529, www.reservacultural.com.br) shows high-minded commercial films on four large screens. Devoted cinephiles consistently flock to the **Espaço Itaú** (Rua Augusta 1470/1475, Consolação, tel. 11/3288-6780, www.itaucinemas.com.br), a complex of theaters across the street from each other that screen first-run Brazilian, international, and art films and host film festivals. Nearby, on the third floor of Shopping Frei Caneca, the **Espaço Itaú de Cinema Frei Caneca** (Rua Frei Caneca 569, Consolação, tel. 11/3472-2365, www.unibancocinemas.com.br) adds prestigious Hollywood pictures to its roster of indie and international films. **CineSesc** (Rua Augusta 2075, tel. 11/3087-0500, Jardim

Auditório Ibirapuera

The SESC System

Serviço Social do Comércio (www.sescsp.org.br) was created in 1946 to benefit workers from the trade and service industries. SESC cultural and recreational centers are all over Brazil. However, in São Paulo they're inextricably linked to the city's cultural life. Without SESC, Paulistanos would be cultural orphans—over 300,000 people a week turn out to see performances by top names in music, theater, and dance. They can afford to do so because SESC events are very reasonably priced or free. The city boasts 15 SESC centers, most of them occupying creatively renovated abandoned buildings or boldly modern constructions that have become architectural landmarks. The state-of-the-art theaters and concert halls share space with cafés, bars, galleries, and libraries.

Four of the most accessible SESC centers are **SESC Vila Mariana** (Rua Pelotas 141, Vila Mariana, tel. 11/5080-3000), **SESC Pinheiros** (Rua Paes Leme 195, Pinheiros, tel. 11/3095-9400), **SESC Belenzinho** (Rua Padre Adelinho 1000, Belenzinho, tel. 11/2076-9700), and **SESC Pompéia** (Rua Clélia 93, Pompéia, tel. 11/3871-7700).

Paulista, www.sesc.org.br) organizes retrospectives and screens repertory films on an enormous screen. A bar at the back of the theater allows you to sip cocktails while watching movies.

Festivals and Events
CARNAVAL
Somehow, the very notion of Carnaval seems at odds with São Paulo's hard-core urban image. Yet just like Rio, the city has its own neighborhood *escolas de samba* that spend all year rehearsing for the day in which their members dress up, mount extravagant floats, and parade through their very own Oscar Niemeyer-designed **Sambódromo** (Av. Olavo Fontoura 1209, tel. 11/2226-0400, Parque Anhembi, Santana, www.anhembi.com.br), located near the Tietê bus terminal. The results (televised on national TV) are less showy and spectacular than Rio de Janeiro's *desfiles*. However, it's also much easier and somewhat cheaper to get tickets for the festivities. Depending on how far away (high up in the stands) or close you are to the action—and how much pampering you demand—prices range R$90-600; you can also get group seats in boxes for 4, 10, and 25 people. Purchase tickets at the Sambódromo or Estádio Pacaembu (11am-5pm Mon.-Sat.), or by phone or online at Ingresso Fácil (tel. 11/3981-5188, www.ingressosligasp.com.br).

For more information, contact the Liga Independente das Escolas de Samba de São Paulo (tel. 11/2853-4555, www.ligasp.com.br).

There are dozens of roving street celebrations organized by neighborhood *blocos*, which are often fun, more alternative, and less crowded than their Rio counterparts. Among the most traditional revelers are **Bloco dos Esfarrapados** (in Bixiga) and LGBT favorites **Banda da Rendonda** (in Consolação) and Banda do Fuxio, in Centro's Largo do Arouche.

If you miss Carnaval, sit in on rehearsals at the neighborhood *escolas*. Admission ranges R$5-20. Schools worth checking out include **Vai Vai** (Rua São Vicente 276, Bela Vista, tel. 11/3266-2581, www.vaivai.com.br) and **Pérola Negra** (Rua Girassol 51, Vila Madalena, tel. 11/3812-3816, www.gresperolanegra.com.br), along with the far-flung hexa-champion **Rosa de Ouro** (Av. Colonel Euclides Machado 1066, Freguesia do Ó, tel. 11/3931-4555, www.sociedaderosasdeouro.com.br).

PAVILHÃO DA BIENAL DE ARTE
Designed by Oscar Niemeyer, the **Pavilhão da Bienal de Arte** is a vast rectangular building with glass windows and sky-high ceilings. It opened in 1957 to house the São Paulo Bienal de Arte, one of the world's largest and most important art biennials. Held

in even-numbered years during October-November, this event reunites more than 12,000 works by national and international artists. There are usually plenty of misses along with the hits, but since it is free (and arguing about the quality of the art in a bar afterward is a spirited Paulistano ritual), you can wander around to your heart's content, focusing on the provocative stuff and ignoring the rest. Many other events take place at the Pavilhão, among them the Bienal de Arquitetura (held in even-numbered years).

FILM FESTIVALS

São Paulo hosts some terrific and well-organized film festivals. **É Tudo Verdade** (It's All True) (www.itsalltrue.com.br) is an international documentary film festival held in late March-early April. **Anima Mundi** (www.animamundi.com.br), held in August, is Latin America's biggest animated film festival, featuring creative short and long features along with television cartoons, commercials, and cyber creations. Late October's **Mostra Internacional de Cinema de São Paulo** (http://mostra.org) has become one of the world's foremost film festivals, with screenings of more than 600 long features and 60 shorts.

NIGHTLIFE

Sampa lures the best performing arts Brazil—and the world—has to offer and has one of the hippest, most happening, and varied cultural and nightlife scenes in this hemisphere. Unlike other Brazilian cities, whose coastlines and tropical climes create nocturnal options that tend to be outdoors, Sampa's indoor night spots invest heavily in decor, ambiance, and vibe. The result is something for every urban *tribo* (tribe) under the moon.

Centro

While portions of Centro are deserted (and dangerous) after dark, a gradual revitalization of the area has seen up-and-coming hipster spots blossoming amidst some of the city's most traditional and authentic watering holes.

BARS

Bar Léo (Rua Aurora 100, tel. 11/3221-0247, www.barleo.com.br, 10am-8:30pm Mon.-Fri.) is a small, simple, and beloved old-style *boteco* (the bar dates back to 1940). You'll be hard-pressed to find sitting space during weekday happy hours and Saturday afternoons. However, the beer, bonhomie, and home cooking are worth standing for.

Part of the fame of **Bar Brahma** (Av. São João 677, tel. 11/3333-3030, www.barbrahma.com.br, 11:30am-1am Mon.-Wed., 11:30am-2am Thurs.-Fri., 11:30am-3am Sat., 11:30am-midnight Sun., cover R$5-45) is due to its location at the corner of São João and Ipiranga Avenues. This famous crossroads (a symbol of Paulistano glamour days) was eternalized by singer-composer Caetano Veloso in his paean "Sampa." Although the handsomely restored bar (which opened in 1948 and then closed for most of the 1990s) has lost some of its former bohemian cachet, it continues to be a classic address where old-guard singers still perform standards from yesteryear.

The **Estadão** (Viaduto 9 de Julho 193, tel. 11/3257-7121, www.estadaolanches.com.br, 24 hours daily) earned its name from the fact that São Paulo's first-ever 24-hour bar and luncheonette was conveniently located next to the offices of the *Estado de São Paulo* newspaper. When it first opened in the 1960s, it was a favorite haunt of journalists. They still frequent the place all night long, as do taxi drivers, politicians, office boys, rockers, and revelers of all stripes. Little has changed about the white-tiled, fruit-festooned bar since then—including customers' predilection for its famously gargantuan *pernil* (pork) sandwich, a Sampa classic.

NIGHTCLUBS

Named after a Bob Dylan song, **Alberta #3** (Av. São Luís 272, tel. 11/3151-5299, www.alberta3.com.br, 7pm-close Tues.-Sat., cover R$15-35) is the unpretentiously stylish, three-floor clubhouse of Sampa's arts-and-media crowd, who arrive for happy hour and stick around till 10pm, at which point the dance floor kicks into gear (and cover is charged). Those who don't want to rock out to classic indie and disco tunes can mellow out upstairs on comfy couches.

Avenida Paulista

Although there are few nightlife options right on Avenida Paulista, behind it—in the district known as Consolação (adjacent to Rua de Consolação)—bars and clubs run the gamut from sleazy dives, go-go clubs, and 24-hour fluorescent sidewalk bars to cutting-edge hot spots that attract a younger and extremely eclectic crowd. Over the last several years, the area known as **Baixo Augusta**—the middle and lower portions of Rua Augusta and surrounding streets—has easily become *the* most exciting and nocturnal destination in town.

BARS

Funky and offbeat **Drosophyla** (Rua Pedro Taques 80, Consolação, tel. 11/3120-5535, www.drosophyla.com.br, 7pm-2am Mon.-Wed., 8pm-3am Thurs.-Sat.) occupies a lovely 1940s house that features a backyard filled with lime, pear, and *jabuticaba* trees. An arty (and often older) crowd regularly gathers to converse amid the mellow tunes and visual kitsch (described as "contemporary baroque") that includes lamps made from macaroni and aquariums filled with dead cell phones. The caipirinhas—mango with *pimenta rosa*, and *carambola* (star fruit) with basil—are delicious.

Many Paulistanos actually hail from the surrounding state, and if they ever feel homesick, they can head to **Tubaína** (Rua Haddock Lobo 74, Consolação, tel. 11/3129-4930, www.tubainabar.com.br, 6pm-1am Mon.-Thurs., 6pm-3am Fri., 1pm-3am Sat.). This '80s-style, gay-friendly bar takes its name from a tutti-frutti-flavored cola whose taste conjures up images of life in São Paulo state's interior. More than 20 varieties are sold here—either straight up or mixed into very adult cocktails—along with comfort food such as *pamonhas* (a savory corn snack similar to a tamale).

On Baixa Augusta's cutting edge, **Z Carniceria** (Rua Augusta 934, Consolação, tel. 11/3231-3705, www.zcarniceria.com.br, 7pm-1am Tues.-Wed., 7pm-2am Thurs.-Sat., 7pm-midnight Sun.) occupies the street's first butcher shop—and has the original white tiling, scales, and hooks to prove it. Ironically, the menu is famed for vegetarian snacks such as the *buraco quente* ("hot hole") sandwich, which explains the general slimness and sexiness of the patrons.

Dating to 1947, **Riviera Bar** (Av. Paulista 2584, Bela Vista, tel. 11/3258-1268, http://rivierabar.com.br, noon-midnight Mon.-Thurs., noon-1am Fri.-Sat., noon-11pm Sun.) hit its stride during the darkest days of the military dictatorship, when artists and intellectuals used it as a clubhouse to swap ideas (and lovers). After a swank revamp by top architect Marcelo Kogan, it reopened in 2013 under the auspices of Sampa's reigning nightlife and culinary kings, Facundo Guerra and Alex Atala (who also devised the menu). The food and drinks are imaginative, the crowd surprisingly diverse, and the prices unsurprisingly inflated. Live jazz adds an extra touch of class (Wed.-Sat., cover R$20-35). Arriving early won't save waiting in a line.

Unpretentious neighborhood *boteco* **Veloso** (Rua Conceição Veloso 56, Vila Mariana, tel. 11/5572-0254, www.velosobar.com.br, 5:30pm-12:30am Tues.-Fri., 12:30pm-12:30am Sat., 4pm-11pm Sun.) draws its share of pilgrims due to the fame of its divine *coxinhas* (crisp chicken croquettes) and caipirinhas, in fruit flavors ranging from deep purple jabuticaba to punchy tangerine and *pimenta*.

NIGHTCLUBS

A Lôca (Rua Frei Caneca 916, Consolação, tel. 11/3159-8889, www.aloca.com.br, midnight-6am Thurs., midnight-10am Fri.-Sat., 7pm-6am Sun., cover R$25-40) is one of Sampa's most legendary underground *"inferninhos"* (little hells). Its dark, cavern-like innards attract a colorfully vanguard mix of (young) gays, lesbians, drag queens, rockers, and alternatives of all types itching to dance the night away to rock and electronica. Theme nights abound, so check the listings in advance.

A cluttered antique store by day, **Caos** (Rua Augusta 584, Consolação, tel. 11/2365-1260, http://caos584.com.br, 8pm-2am Tues.-Fri., 9pm-3am Sat., 1pm-8pm Sun., cover R$15-50) fills after dark with a crowd looking for fun in the guise of cool cocktails. Work up a sweat on the tightly packed dance floor, where tunes tend toward house and electro, but DJs have been known to administer everything from vintage Motown to surf rock.

In a stylishly renovated warehouse, **Lab Club** (Rua Augusta 523, Consolação, tel. 11/3231-3705, www.labclub.com.br, 11pm-close Tues.-Sat., cover R$25-35) has a sofa-strewn lounge and bar serving molecular cocktails, a smoking garden, and a basement disco (playing electronica and pop) bathed in a futuristic 3-D light show. The music is great, but the crowd might skew too young and trendy for some.

Jardins

The bars and lounges of Jardins generally attract an older, more sophisticated, and moneyed crowd as well as a significant international and gay and lesbian clientele.

BARS

For a drink with a view, there's nowhere sexier than Hotel Unique's rooftop **Skye** (Av. Brigadeiro Luís Antônio 4700, Jardim Paulista, tel. 11/3055-4702, www.hotelunique.com.br, noon-3pm and 6pm-12:30am Mon.-Sat., 7am-12:30am Sun.). By day, tables spill onto a wooden deck with lounge chairs and a cool blue pool overlooking the emerald expanse of Parque do Ibirapuera. At night the pool is lit up in red, the distant skyscrapers glow like fireflies, and DJs spinning electronic bossa nova and house music turn the rooftop into an achingly hip lounge. The indoor restaurant serves innovative Brazilian fusion cuisine.

More down to earth, **Balcão** (Rua Dr. Melo Alves 150, Cerqueira César, tel. 11/3063-6091, 6pm-1am daily) is an apt name for this ingeniously original bar whose 25-meter (82-foot) *balcão* (counter) curves and zigzags throughout the interior. The placement of barstools on both sides creates an atmosphere that is particularly conducive to conversing as well as neighbor gazing. The clientele is an older crowd (30s-50s) who sip wine and caipirinhas and tuck into sandwiches on *ciabatta* bread, while casting the odd gaze toward the original Roy Lichtenstein dominating one wall.

LIVE MUSIC

Baretto (Fasano Hotel, Rua Vitório Fasano 88, Jardim Paulista, tel. 11/3896-4000, www.fasano.com.br, 7pm-2am Mon.-Fri., 8pm-3am Sat., cover R$37 after 9:30pm) is the classiest bar in town. Subtle lighting, rustic wood floors, leather sofas, and velvet paneled walls cast a romantic spell. The mood is further enhanced by nightly performances of jazz and bossa nova. The cocktails (R$25), if not overly imaginative, are impeccably mixed.

Jazz nos Fundos (Rua João Moura 1076, Jardim Paulista, tel. 11/3083-5975, http://jazznosfundos.net, 8pm-2:30am Thurs.-Sat., cover R$20-25) is an intimate and unassuming little dive that benefits from live jazz accompaniment and the excellent roster of artists that perform here. Sets begin at 10pm and 1am.

Pinheiros and Vila Madalena

After dark, these two adjoining *bairros* are always hopping. Offering some of the city's biggest array of nightlife options, their bars and clubs attract a mixed clientele.

BARS

With a relaxed vibe and a classic 1950s bar atmosphere, **Astor** (Rua Delfina 163, Vila Madalena, tel. 11/3815-1364, www.barastor.com.br, 6pm-2am Mon.-Wed., 6pm-3am Thurs., noon-3am Fri.-Sat., noon-6pm Sun.) is one of the Vila's most popular watering holes. If you see a lot of good-looking people seemingly disappear into the basement, it's not because you've knocked back one too many; rather, they're heading to **SubAstor** (tel. 11/3615-1364, www.subastor.com.br, 8pm-3am Tues.-Thurs, 8pm-4am Fri.-Sat.), an ultracool speakeasy famed throughout town for both its classic and unconventional (though hardly cheap) cocktails.

The first bar to open on this now busy block, **São Cristovão** (Rua Aspicuelta 533, Vila Madalena, tel. 11/3097-9904, noon-1:30am daily) is the only one that has retained its street cred. Although the decor hasn't changed in a decade, it certainly has expanded; as a result, every square inch of wall space is covered with *futebol* paraphernalia. Those with an athlete's appetite won't be disappointed by the robust bar grub, which includes a mean Saturday *feijoada*. Musically, Sunday's *roda de samba* and Monday's jazz sessions also draw a crowd.

Heavy on neighborhood atmosphere, **Mercearia São Pedro** (Rua Rodésia 34, Vila Madalena, tel. 11/3815-7200, 8am-1am Mon.-Sat., 8am-6pm Sun.) is a former combination grocery, book, and video rental store turned neighborhood *boteco*. The fact that it still sells books—and serves cheap, delicious meals—is an obvious draw for the crowd of hipster intellectuals that have adopted it en masse. The liveliest nights are Tuesday and Thursday.

LIVE MUSIC

Ó do Borogodó (Rua Horácio Lane, Pinheiros, tel. 11/3814-4087, 9pm-3am Mon.-Fri., 1pm-3am Sat., 7pm-midnight Sun., cover R$25) looks and feels as if it were magically transported out of Rio's Lapa *bairro*. The relaxed vibe is downright Carioca, as are the amazing samba and *chorinho* jams that explode off the tiny stage and have patrons pushing chairs out of the way to cut the rug. The best night is Sunday, but arrive early and be prepared for a line.

Occupying a handsomely preserved old house, **Piratininga** (Rua Wisard 149, Vila Madalena, tel. 11/3032-9775, www.piratiningabar.com.br, 6pm-2am Mon.-Thurs., 6pm-close Fri.-Sat., cover R$8-15) is a classic Vila

address frequented by a laid-back clientele. The warm, softly lit interior gives off a romantic vibe, aided by the strains of live jazz and bossa nova that waft down from the mezzanine stage. The refreshing house cocktail, *caipi-pira,* mixes vodka and Persian limes.

Arredores (Outlying Neighborhoods)

The Zona Oeste *bairros* of Barra Funda and Lapa serve as headquarters for a thriving alternative club scene. Consistently ranked by Britain's *DJ-Mag* in its list of top 100 clubs on the planet, **D-Edge** (Av. Auro Soares de Moura Andrade 141, Barra Funda, tel. 11/3665-9500, www.d-edge.com.br, midnight-close Mon. and Thurs.-Sat., 5am-noon Sun., cover R$30-120) lives up to the hype. A roster of international DJs keep the electronica pulsing (Monday's rock and roll is the exception to the rule), and the decor seems to go along for the ride, with 200 multihued rectangles of light paneling the floor, walls, and ceiling and three green LED screens. The club is close to Metrô Barra Funda.

In the vicinity, but more laid-back, the **NEU Club** (Rua Dona Germaine Burchard 420, Barra Funda, no phone, www.neuclub.com.br, 11pm-close Fri.-Sat. 4pm-10pm Sun., cover R$15-25) feels like a big party in your friend's basement with lot of favorite pop and rock ditties playing on the turntable. There's even a backyard with plastic chairs for the smokers. Bring cash, as credit cards aren't accepted.

SHOPPING

São Paulo is a shopper's paradise. In a country that takes great pride in its malls—affectionately known as *shoppings*—Sampa's are the biggest and glitziest, and a *very* far cry from suburban strip malls in the United States. Unlike many other Brazilian cities, São Paulo also has a large selection of boutiques, particularly concentrated in Jardins (a Brazilian version of Rodeo Drive) and Vila Madalena (more funky, alternative fare with lots of art).

Gay Sampa

Sampa's gay offerings are more numerous and much more eclectic than Rio's. For an in-depth guide, visit www.guiagaysaopaulo.com.br (in Portuguese) or www.cidadedesaopaulo.com.

CENTRO

At night, the area between Praça da República and Largo do Arouche attracts a mixed (but not fashionable or yuppie) gay crowd of all ages, as well as trannies and hookers. Most bars are on the once-elegant Avenida Vieira de Carvalho. The scene is kind of seedy but very vibrant.

Cantho (Largo do Arouche 32, tel. 11/3723-6624, www.cantho.com.br, 11pm-5am Wed. and Fri.-Sat., 9pm-3am Sun., R$20-30) reels in a 35-and-over bear-ish clientele with '70s and '80s tunes, glittery globes, lots of Cher and Madonna videos, and strategically placed sofas in dark corners.

AVENIDA PAULISTA

In the Consolação district, the bars and clubs on Rua Augusta and Rua Frei Caneca (nicknamed Rua Gay Caneca) attract a younger, more alternative GLS public. **A Lôca** attracts a big GLS crowd, especially on Sunday.

Club Yacht (Rua 13 de Maio 703, Bela Vista, tel. 11/3104-7157, midnight-7am Wed. and Fri.-Sat., cover R$30-50) is nautically glam with an aquarium and *La Querelle* sailors/waiters. Music runs from '80s (Wed.) to indie rock (Fri.) and techno (Sat.).

JARDINS

Jardins is the playground of an upwardly mobile, fashionable crew. **Director's Gourmet** (Alameda Franca 1552, Cerqueira César, tel. 11/3064-7958, 10pm-3am Tues.-Sat.) is a small, friendly bar with a director's chair suspended from the ceiling, classic movie posters plastered on the walls, and a menu of gourmet sandwiches named after famous directors.

VILA MADALENA

The L Club (Rua Luiz Marat 370, tel. 11/2604-3394, www.thelclub.com.br, 11pm-close Fri., cover R$20-40) is one of Sampa's rare lesbian clubs, a buzzing spot where girls warm up lounge-side while listening to live MPB before rocking out to techno.

ARREDORES

The Week (Rua Guaicurus 324, Lapa, tel. 11/3868-9844, www.theweek.com.br, midnight-close Sat., R$45-65) is one of the biggest and trendiest clubs, with two dance floors, three lounges, six bars, and a swimming pool.

FESTIVALS AND EVENTS

Films dealing with themes of sexual diversity permeate cinemas and cultural centers during the **Mix Brasil Festival** (www.mixbrasil.org.br, Nov.). São Paulo hosts the **Parada de Orgulho GLBT** (www.paradasp.org.br, May), one of the biggest gay pride parades. Millions of people flood Avenida Paulista, which is filled with *trios elétricos* blasting party music.

Twice a year, the city hosts **São Paulo Fashion Week** (http://ffw.com.br/spfw), a globally important industry event that showcases the latest trends from consecrated national designers and lures international media, buyers, and screaming fashion groupies. As Brazilian fashion has taken off, Sampa has come into its own as a *capital da moda*.

If cheap buys are what you're after, secondhand stores and the vibrant bazaar-like atmospheres of Bom Retiro and Rua 25 de Maio are full of surprising bargains.

Shopping Malls and Districts

Sampa's *shoppings* unite fantastic food courts, mega book-and-CD stores, movie theaters, and more. Hours are generally 10am-10pm Monday-Saturday, noon-8pm Sunday.

Inaugurated in 1966, **Shopping Iguatemi** (Av. Brigadeiro Faria Lima 2232, Jardim Paulistano, tel. 11/3816-6116, www.iguatemi-aopaolo.com.br) has been São Paulo's most sophisticated *shopping* for decades. Apart from 360 chic boutiques (with an enormous international presence ranging from Burberry to Tiffany's), it possesses several movie theaters, gourmet cafés and restaurants, and a gigantic Saraiva bookstore.

The discreetly hidden **Shopping Pátio Higienópolis** (Av. Higienópolis 618, Higienópolis, tel. 11/3823-2300, www.patio-higienopolis.com.br) is spacious and airy, with a great mix of stores, eating options, and a cinema. Just off Avenida Paulista, the super-trendy **Shopping Frei Caneca** (Rua Frei Caneca 569, Consolação, tel. 11/3472-2075, www.freicanecashopping.com.br) is nicknamed "Shopping Gay Caneca" due to its popularity with fashion-forward gays and lesbians. Boutiques skew toward a younger, more alternative clientele. There is a food court, a gourmet supermarket, a great cineplex (the Unibanco Arteplex), and two theaters.

Shopping in São Paulo doesn't have to be synonymous with shelling out wads of cash. There are some amazing bargains to be found, particularly in two areas of Centro. **Rua 25 de Março** (www.guiada25.com.br) is not unlike a modern-day souk. On a slow day, an average 400,000 shoppers cram the 400 stores lining the street and hidden within small *galerias,* which hawk everything from housewares, toys, fabrics, and Carnaval paraphernalia to clothing, jewelry, and shoes. The prices are stupendously cheap (which accounts for the crowds), but part of the fun is bargaining for even further discounts. Shopping here—as well as on the surrounding streets of Rua Comendador Abdo Sahahin, Rua Barão de Duprat, and Rua Cavalheiro Basílio Jafret—can be a lively experience, but a chaotic and exhausting one. Avoid Saturdays and holidays, when the number of shoppers can hit the 1 million mark,

and don't bring small kids. Easiest access is via São Bento Metrô.

Great deals are also to be found in the *bairro* of **Bom Retiro** (www.omelhordobom-retiro.com.br), adjacent to Luz (take the Metrô to Luz station). Sampa's traditional garment district was originally inhabited by Jewish immigrants. Today, it is largely Korean and boasts hundreds of wholesale stores selling clothing and accessories that are up to 40 percent cheaper than they would be in shopping centers. Less hectic and more organized than Rua 25 de Março, Bom Retiro also has the advantage of an abundance of great, inexpensive Korean restaurants (open for lunch only).

Antiques

A classic Sunday afternoon activity is to browse through the small but colorful selection of antiques and collectibles on display at the **Feira de Antiguidades do MASP** (Av. Paulista 1578, Cerqueira César, www.aaesp.art.br, 10am-5pm Sun.), which takes place beneath the museum's suspended structure. Also lots of fun is the **Feira de Antiguidades e Artes** (Praça Benedito Calixto, Pinheiros, www.pracabeneditocalixto.com.br, 9am-7pm Sat.), where you'll find a colorful collection of bric-a-brac of varying quality. Held in a pretty square, the market itself—with lots of food and drink kiosks—is a gathering place for a young and alternative crowd.

Arts and Crafts

The proprietors of **Amoa Konoya** (Rua João Moura 1002, Jardim América, tel. 11/3061-0639, www.amoakonoya.com.br, 9am-7pm Mon.-Fri., 9am-6pm Sat.) travel throughout Brazil, visiting remote indigenous communities whose artisans create the pottery, basketry, artwork, and musical instruments sold in this charming boutique. **Galeria Brasiliana** (Rua Cardoso de Almeida 1297, Perdizes, tel. 11/3086-4273, www.galeriabrasiliana.com.br, 10am-6pm Mon.-Fri., 10am-5pm Sat.) is widely reputed for its impressive collection of contemporary Brazilian folk art. These aren't cheap trinkets; the quality is exceptional.

Vila Madalena's boutiques, galleries, and ateliers are a treasure trove of more affordable and funky artistic and design objects. **Projeto Terra** (Rua Harmonia 150, tel. 11/3034-3550, www.projetoterra.org.br, 10am-7pm Mon.-Fri., 10am-6pm Sat.) has a terrific array of high-quality, environmentally conscious *artesanato* from around the country, all of whose proceeds go to support grassroots social projects. Founded by architects, **Ôooh de Casa** (Rua Fradique Coutinho 889, tel. 11/3815-9577, www.oohdecasa.com.br, 10am-6pm Mon.-Sat.) focuses on an array of Brazilian artisanal objects that can be used—often in ingenious ways—to decorate your home.

Books and Music

São Paulo has many bookstores, but best of all is the **Livraria Cultura** (Av. Paulista 2073, Cerqueira César, tel. 11/3170-4033, www.livrariacultura.com.br, 9am-10pm Mon.-Sat., noon-8pm Sun.). Located in the Conjunto Nacional building, this sprawling bookshop has a terrific selection covering all subjects as well as a considerable number of English-language titles and national and international magazines, CDs, and DVDs. Although there are several big book and music store chains in the city's *shoppings,* **Livraria da Vila** (Rua Fradique Coutinho 915, tel. 11/3814-5811, Pinheiros, www.livrariadavila.com.br, 9am-10pm Mon.-Fri. 10am-8pm Sat. 11am-8pm Sun.) also has several cozy neighborhood locations in Jardins and close to Vila Madalena.

Collectors with a penchant for rare and alternative Brazilian music should head to **Baratos Afins** (Av. São João 439, Lojas 314-318, Centro, tel. 11/3223-3629, www.baratosafins.com.br, 7:30am-7:30pm Mon.-Fri., 8am-6pm Sat.). Founded by Arnaldo Baptista, the guitarist of the 1960s rock group Os Mutantes, the record store and independent label has recorded and rereleased an impressive number of Brazilian underground and alternative artists. You'll find these and other treasures in a fantastic store located in the **Galeria do Rock** (www.portalgaleriadorock.com.br), a 450-store temple devoted to the religion of rock 'n roll.

Clothing

For an introduction to São Paulo fashion head to Jardins, where the majority of local designers have showrooms. São Paulo's **Rua Oscar Freire** boasts nine blocks of unadulterated luxury shopping, with more than 100 (heavily guarded) boutiques representing Brazilian designers and international brands from Diesel to Armani. Even if you're not in the mood to buy, many of the stores are creatively designed, and the window shopping is fantastic. While Oscar Freire is the main fashion drag, the surrounding streets of Rua Augusta, Alameda Lorena, Rua Dr. Melo Alves, Rua Bela Cintra, Rua Haddock Lobo, and Rua da Consolação are also teeming with stores.

STREET AND CASUAL WEAR

In terms of the coolest in Brazilian casual and street wear, Paulistano designers have long been in the vanguard. Although the following labels can be found in the most upscale *shoppings* around town and around the country, you'll find the flagship stores in Jardins.

Fórum (Rua Oscar Freire 916, tel. 11/3085-6269, www.forum.com.br) singlehandedly put Brazilian jeans on the map with high-quality, form-fitting jeans that have become a closet staple for Hollywood celebs. Responsible for introducing stonewashed jeans to Brazil, **Ellus** (Rua Oscar Freire 990, tel. 11/3061-2900, www.ellus.com.br) has since evolved considerably into one of Brazil's sexiest and most adventurous casual-wear labels. **Zoomp** (Rua Oscar Freire 995, tel. 11/3064-1556, www.zoomp.com.br) is extremely popular with hip young things, who proudly flaunt the brand's yellow lightning-bolt logo. **M. Officer** (Rua Oscar Freire 944, tel. 11/3065-6866, www.mofficer.com.br) showcases the flawlessly cut and original casual clothing line of Paulistano designer Carlos Miele, a darling of the international fashion press. **Iódice** (Rua Oscar

Freire 940, tel. 11/3085-9310, www.iodice. com.br) is another homegrown label for both men and women featuring pared-down, casual designs with refined details.

Hidden amidst the luxury labels on Oscar Freire, **Mercadinho Chic** (Rua Oscar Freire 720, tel. 11/3088-2348, www.mercadinhochic. com.br) is a covered mini-market where a rotating selection of local indie designers showcase clothing, jewelry, accessories, and design pieces. Also great for alternative street wear is nearby **Galeria Ouro Fino** (Rua Augusta 2690, tel. 11/3082-7860, www.galeriaourofino.com), where more than 100 boutiques have something for urban style junkies of every type. Choose from clothing and shoes by up-and-coming designers, tattoos and body piercings, or get a radical new haircut. Because it is popular with DJs and musicians—there are a few great vinyl stores—the place is littered with flyers announcing shows, *festas,* and events.

PRÊT-À-PORTER

Jardins is also a great place to check out the ready-to-wear collections of Brazil's most renowned designers. Brazil's bad boy of design, **Alexandre Herchcovitch** (Rua Melo Alves 561, tel. 11/3063-2888, herchcovitch.uol.com. br), grew up in São Paulo's Orthodox Jewish community, where his mother, a lingerie seamstress, taught him the basics of sewing. Mixing elements from sources as diverse as punk rock, Judaism, Disney, and drag, his clothes have gone from seducing denizens of Sampa's underground scene to luring international jetsetters. Today, Herchcovitch shows collections in Paris and New York as well as São Paulo.

Brazil's "First Lady of Fashion," **Gloria Coelho** (Rua Bela Cintra 2173, tel. 11/3083-1079, www.gloriacoelho.com.br) has built an acclaimed career by fusing the most disparate references into clean, modern, smart designs with a futuristic edge. Her former assistant and present husband, **Reinaldo Lourenço** (Rua Bela Cintra 2167, tel. 11/3085-8151, www.reinaldolourenco.com.br) is known as

the "poet" of Brazilian fashion due to the lyrical sensibility that informs his contemporary clothing. **Adriana Barra** (Alameda Franca 1243, tel. 11/2925-2300, www.adrianabarra. com.br) specializes in fluid, feminine designs that recapture retro glamour and romance while remaining firmly grounded in modern times.

SHOES

Back in the days when Americans were wearing "jelly shoes," Brazilians were wedging their feet into "Melissas," the original "jelly" invented in Brazil in 1979. After more than 30 years on the market, these humble plastic shoes received a proper homage at **Galeria Melissa** (Rua Oscar Freire 827, Jardim Paulista, tel. 11/3083-3612, www.galeriamelissa.com.br). This wildly inventive design gallery and shoe temple sells cutting-edge versions of this surprisingly flexible and comfortable classic, reimagined by design gurus such as Alexandre Herchcovitch, the Campana brothers, and Vivienne Westwood.

The shoes at **Fernando Pires** (Rua Consolação 3534, Cerqueira César, tel. 11/3068-8177, www.fernandopires.com.br) are definitely not for conservative feet. With the goal of transforming women into "Greek goddesses," Pires specializes in flamboyant footwear such as high-heeled tie-up sandals encrusted in jewels and thigh-high metallic leather boots in Carnaval colors. Women in search of their inner drag queen will be in heaven. Men's shoes are slightly more discreet.

SPORTS AND RECREATION
Parks

São Paulo offers quite a few welcoming green oases in and around the city. Although the most famous and centrally located is **Parque do Ibirapuera,** near the southern outskirts of the city is the **Parque do Estado,** a vast expanse of native Atlantic rain forest with walking trails and picnic areas as well as a botanical garden and zoo. The easiest way to get to the park is to take the Metrô to Jabaquara.

From the station, it's only a quick taxi ride to the entrance.

JARDIM BOTÂNICO

One of the highlights of Parque do Estado is the **Jardim Botânico** (Av. Miguel Estéfano 3031, Água Funda, tel. 11/5073-6300, www. ibot.sp.gov.br, 9am-5pm Wed.-Sun., R$5), which specializes in the study and preservation of native plant and tree species. A large lagoon festooned with lily pads and other aquatic plants slices the park in two, separating shady woods from a tunnel of bamboo. Among the gardens' many scenic paths is a suspended treetop walking trail.

JARDIM ZOOLÓGICO

The other big draw at the Parque do Estado is the **Jardim Zoológico** (Av. Miguel Estéfano 4241, Água Funda, tel. 11/5073-0811, www. zoologico.sp.gov.br, 9am-5pm Tues.-Sun., R$18). São Paulo's very popular menagerie has more than 3,500 beasts and birds from all over the globe, including some extremely rare animals such as a white rhino and a Siberian tiger. Since the zoo is quite spread out, spring for the minibus (R$5), which will drive you around to visit all the animals. You can also get a minibus (R$23 includes entrance) at Jabaquara Metrô that whisks you to the zoo itself.

Soccer

Paulistanos boast three major teams—each with a mega-home-stadium of their own. São Paulo FC (www.saopaulofc.net) plays at **Estádio Morumbi** (Praça Roberto Gomes Pedrosa, Morumbi, tel. 11/3749-8000); reach it by taking the Metrô to Morumbi. Palmeiras (www.palmeiras.com.br) is set to move into the spanking new **Arena Allianz Parque** (Rua Turiassu 1840, Barra Funda, www.allianzparque.com.br), close to Metrô Barra Funda. Corinthians (www.corinthians.com. br), who played at the 1930s-era **Estádio Pacaembu** (Praça Charles Miller, Pacaembu, tel. 11/3664-4650), now have a new home at the state-of-the-art **Arena de Itaquera**

(Rua Miguel Inácio Cury 111, Itaquera, www. odebrechtarenas.com.br), completed for the opening game of the 2014 World Cup, close to Metrô Itaquera. Try to avoid finals—not only will the stadiums be sold out, but the fans' testosterone levels get dangerously high. Otherwise, catching a game is a heady experience. The well-funded teams boast some of the nation's top players, and the atmosphere among fans is an intoxicating mixture of gripping suspense and over-the-top melodrama—indeed, spring for covered seats that will protect you from the projectiles lobbed in anger by frustrated fans. Tickets can be purchased at the stadiums or online at www.futebolcard.com.br.

ACCOMMODATIONS

São Paulo attracts many more business travelers than tourists. As a result, many of its hotels are multinational and local chains that, while big on amenities such as work stations, are short on charm. A good number are located in far-flung business hoods such as Brooklin and Berrini, which are convenient for getting to and from airports and meetings but not so useful for exploring the city. You'll also find accommodations around Avenida Paulista (much better for exploring purposes) and adjacent Jardins. Still, the city boasts a surprising array of world-class, decadently luxurious hotels—even more than Rio—that are great for living it up. Hostels, including some cool designer options, have been mushrooming in the last couple of years in pleasant residential neighborhoods such as Vila Madalena and Vila Mariana, which have good Metro and bus access. Many of the fancier hotels offer great discounts—ironically, rates are often cheaper in the summer months of December-February, high season everywhere else in Brazil, since this is when Paulistanos head to the beaches. You can also get impressive discounts on weekends, when business travelers are scarce. In an attempt to fill rooms, many hotels offer weekend "honeymoon" specials that seduce couples, both married and otherwise.

Centro

Staying in Centro—around Praça da República—has the advantage of being cheaper and more convenient than other parts of São Paulo. The downside is that come nighttime, much of this area shuts down. To ensure your safety, rely on taxis.

R$200-400

A harbinger of the revitalization poised to transform Centro is the **Marabá Palace** (Av. Ipiranga 757, tel. 11/2137-9500, www.hotelmaraba.com.br, R$290-370 d), which opened in 2007 atop a splendid old cinema. While bringing some much-needed glamour back to the neighborhood, the hotel has opted for contemporary sophistication over nostalgic retro. Amenities such as a fitness room and sauna as well as soundproof guest rooms and impeccable service add to the comfort factor. Only two blocks from São Joaquim Metrô, ★ **Leques Brasil** (Rua São Joaquim, Liberdade, tel. 11/3019-4300, www.lequesbrasil.com.br, R$240-260 d) occupies a high-rise on the edge of Sampa's Japanese quarter. The fact that it functions as a hotel school means that every square centimeter is spotless and your every wish is the obliging student staff's command. Although rooms lack personality, amenities include a pool, cafés, and restaurants with good food.

R$400-600

Back in the '50s, the Jaraguá was one of Centro's most elegant hotels before falling on hard times. Purchased by the Accor chain, it got a stylish new lease on life as the **Novotel São Paulo Jaraguá** (Rua Martins Fontes 71, tel. 11/2082-7000, www.novotel.com, R$430-530 d). Airy rooms have muted wooden floors, soothing color schemes, and views that won't quit.

Higienópolis

Most tourists (and guidebooks) mysteriously overlook the elegant residential neighborhood of Higienópolis when it comes to hotel listings. Although accommodations here are sparse, there are some good bargains, and the *bairro* is not only attractive, tranquil, and safe, but is centrally located.

R$200-400

Tryp Higienópolis (Rua Maranhão 371, tel. 11/3665-8200, www.tryphotels.com, R$360-530 d) offers impressively large condo-style accommodations. Light, bright, and warmly accessorized, the guest rooms are a great value, particularly when you factor in the sundeck and swimming pool.

Avenida Paulista

Although hardly ultracheap, there are some bargains to be had in the generally large and modern hotels surrounding Avenida Paulista, and you're smack-dab in the middle of all the urban action. Ideally located in terms of bus and Metrô service, you are in walking distance of a number of neighborhoods and attractions, which means less time-consuming, stress-inducing exposure to infamous traffic jams. While located in the Consolação neighborhood, some of the cheaper options below are a good 10-15-minute walk from Avenida Paulista.

R$50-200

The slogan of **155** (Rua Martinho Prado 173, Consolação, tel. 11/3150-1555, www.155hotel.com.br, R$190 d) is that "price is just a detail." But what a sweet detail when you get box-spring mattresses, free Wi-Fi, silent air-conditioning, flat-screen cable TV, stark but attractively minimalist decor, and a to-kill-for location within spitting distance of Baixa Augusta. Request a room on a higher floor to escape street noise.

R$200-400

Offering good value along with a great location, **Hotel Moncloa** (Rua Augusta 646, Consolação, tel. 11/3256-2686, www.hotelmoncloa.com.br, R$200-260 d) possesses large, modern, and cozily if blandly decorated guest rooms (the nicest have wooden floors) that boast a surprising degree of comfort, including free Wi-Fi and flat-screen TVs, for this price range. Rooms on higher floors are quieter.

Hotel Pergamon (Rua Frei Caneca 80, Consolação, tel. 11/3123-2021, www.pergamon.com.br, R$260-330 d) brags that it was the first hotel in Brazil to introduce the concept of "chic and cheap" back in 1999. Its pioneering efforts have met with success, and this early boutique hotel is the darling of hip Rua "Gay" Caneca. The ultracontemporary decor resists being too cool by the occasional splash of tropical color, warm natural woods, and works by Brazilian artists. Rooms on the upper floors offer terrific panoramic views.

With a prime location just off Av. Paulista and behind MASP, **The Universe Flat** (Rua Pamplona 83, Bela Vista, tel. 11/3298-2686, www.intercityhoteis.com.br, R$315-425 d) is also a terrific bargain. Awash in wood, gloss, and soothing earth tones, quarters are outfitted with workstations, mini-kitchens and living areas (in the larger apartments). The higher you go, the bigger the rooms and the views get (the merely "luxo" ones are tight). Perks include an outdoor pool, sauna, fitness room, and a serviceable on-site café and restaurant.

OVER R$600

Mere meters from Avenida Paulista, **L'Hotel Porto Bay São Paulo** (Alameda Campinas 266, Bela Vista, tel. 11/2183-0500, www.portobay.com, R$605-845 d) bucks the trend of sleek yet soulless high-end business hotels by going for Old World refinement and discretion: a glass of bubbly at check-in, chocolates before bedtime, a 16th-century Flemish tapestry in the lobby, and Spanish marble bathtubs (and bidets!) in the bathrooms. For chilling out, there is a tiny rooftop pool and spa. Breakfasts are stand-outs, with *gauffres,* omelets, and flaky croissants redolent of Paris.

Jardins

Befitting the swankiness of the neighborhood, Jardins is where the crème de la crème of Sampa's luxury hotels are clustered—if you want to live it up in style and are prepared to spend big, this is the *bairro* for you. Low rollers need not despair: Although more modest digs are harder to come by, a handful of mid-range options do exist.

R$50-200

Bee W. Hostel Bar (Rua Haddock Lobo 167, Bela Vista, tel. 11/4328-6222, www.beew.com.br, R$200-250 d, R$45-65 pp) is pretty styling for a hostel. Ambiance, furnishings, and even the friendly, young staff are all as decidedly cool as is the lawn-covered rooftop lounge where guests can mingle with locals over snacks and *chupitos* (rainbow-hued cocktail shots). The location, just off Av. Paulista, is unbeatable.

R$200-400

Pousada Ziláh (Alameda França 1621, Jardim Paulista, tel. 11/3062-1444, www.zilah.com, R$250-450 d) is a rarity in São Paulo, let alone in the heart of chic Jardins: a welcoming B&B located in a charming old house. If the guest rooms are a little Spartan and amenities scarce, the cozy homelike atmosphere, great location, and affordable prices more than compensate.

OVER R$600

Bearing an uncanny resemblance to an ark or a watermelon, ★ **Hotel Unique** (Av. Brigadeiro Luís Antônio 4700, Cerqueira César, tel. 11/3055-4700, www.hotelunique.com.br, R$1,040-1,485 d) definitely lives up to its name. Designed by hot local architect Ruy Ohtake, the hipper-than-thou hotel doesn't even have its name advertised on its space-age exterior. What it does have are impeccably designed white-on-white guest rooms that are equally comfortable and high-tech. The rooftop **Skye** bar is (justifiably) one of the most coveted perches in town, not least because of its swimming pool, which glows with red lights and throbs with soothing underwater DJ tunes at night.

A favorite of jet-setters—who often fly in directly by helicopter and land at the hotel's private heliport—is **Emiliano** (Rua Oscar

Freire 384, Cerqueira César, tel. 11/3069-4369, www.emiliano.com.br, R$1,760-4,000 d). The most exclusive—and most expensive—of Sampa's designer hotels, Emiliano is reputed for its stellar service, which begins the minute you arrive and receive a welcome massage. A butler to pack and unpack your luggage, complimentary glasses of wine, and toiletries customized to your skin type are just a few of the pampering details that will leave you feeling utterly spoiled.

Famous throughout São Paulo for their gourmet restaurants, the enterprising Fasano family added world-class hoteliers to their impressive résumé when they opened **Fasano** (Rua Vitório Fasano 88, Cerqueira César, tel. 11/3896-4000, www.fasano.com.br, R$1,550-5,470 d), which is discreet and clubby with a streamlined 1930s edge. This sophisticated hotel is appealingly understated in comparison with most of the city's five-star options, and service is outstanding. As an added bonus, you don't have to step outside for a bite. Within the hotel you'll find **Fasano,** considered one of the finest restaurants in Brazil; **Nonno Ruggero,** a second multistar restaurant, where breakfast is served; and **Baretto,** a refined bar featuring live music.

Pinheiros and Vila Madalena

Accessible by Metrô, Vila Madalena and Pinheiros are safe. Each possesses a relaxed, alternative vibe that makes a compelling base.

R$50-200

One of the few options, and nicest of the new crop of hostels, to take advantage of the Vila's cachet is **Giramondo Hostel** (Rua Girassol 471, Vila Madalena, tel. 11/2369-3619, www.giramondohostel.com.br, R$160 d, R$45-55 pp), whose inviting atmosphere captures the laid-back, creative vibe of the hood. Well-maintained rooms are spread throughout the villa; dorm beds are top-of-the-line and, in keeping with the hostel's sustainable ethos, made of recycled peroba rosa, a beautiful tropical wood. Charming common rooms include a kitchen, living room, and cobblestoned courtyard. The young owners and staff are more than willing to share tips and hints that will make your stay memorable.

★ **Guest 607** (Rua João Moura 607, Pinheiros, tel. 11/3264-3015, guest607.com.br, R$150-255 d, R$60 pp) is a cool and crazily colorful B&B that looks and feels as though you walked into a Pedro Almódovar film. Rooms are small(ish) but funky, as are the gardens, professionally equipped gourmet kitchen, and Resto 607, which dishes up three innovative meals daily.

FOOD

São Paulo is a food lovers' haven that few other cities in the world can rival. At the high end of the scale are world-class kitchens ruled over by innovative chefs who offer both traditional and contemporary cuisine (if your purse strings are tight, many offer weekday lunchtime *executivo* menus where you can sample toned-down versions of master chefs' creations). At the other end of the price spectrum, numerous bakeries, cafés, and bars offer sustenance for every occasion and appetite. Due to its diverse immigrant population, the city is also rich in international cuisine, with special mention going to Lebanese, Japanese, and Italian. In terms of the latter, Sampa's *ristorantes,* cantinas, and pizzerias offer some of the best *cocina italiana* this side of the Atlantic. In São Paulo, pizza is as much a staple as *feijoada,* and many claim you can get a better pizza here than in Italy.

Centro
CAFÉS AND SNACKS

Ponto Chic (Largo do Paissandu 27, tel. 11/3222-6528, www.pontochic.com.br, 10am-8pm Mon.-Sat.) earned its name from the fact that when this now-famous luncheonette first opened in 1922, it immediately became the "chic point" for the city's intellectuals, artists, and soccer stars to meet. Then, as now, the most popular item on the menu was the *sanduíche Bauru,* a hefty sandwich of roast beef with tomato, cucumber, and a deliciously gooey melted mixture of four cheeses served on French bread. Invented here, it has since gone on to become a São Paulo culinary icon.

BRAZILIAN

Located on the ground floor of Niemeyer's iconic curvaceous Copan building, ★ **Bar da Dona Onça** (Av. Ipiranga 200, Lojas 27-29, tel. 11/3257-2016, www.bardadonaonca.com.br, noon-11pm Mon.-Wed., noon-midnight Thurs.-Sat., noon-5:30pm Sun., R$20-30) serves up inspired reworkings of hearty Brazilian classics such as *cuzcuz paulista* (a polenta-based recipe stuffed with olives, peppers, peas, hearts of palm, and sardines) and liver served with *jiló* chips (a slightly bitter green vegetable). Both appetizer and full-blown meal portions are available.

INTERNATIONAL

★ **La Casserole** (Largo do Arouche 346, tel. 11/3221-2889, www.lacasserole.com.br, noon-3pm and 7pm-midnight Tues.-Fri., 7pm-1am Sat., noon-5pm Sun., R$50-70) has hardly changed at all since it first opened in 1954. A quintessential Parisian bistro, its retro charm and bonhomie have long made it a favorite for discreet VIPs in search of classic French fare such as onion soup, duck à l'orange, and steak frites, prepared to perfection and served with flair by the attentive *garçons*. If you come for lunch during the week, take advantage of the R$49 three-course *menu executivo*.

VEGETARIAN

Hidden on the second floor of a nondescript office building, **Nutrisom** (Viaduto 9 de Julho 160, tel. 11/3255-4263, www.nutrisom.com.br, 11am-3pm Mon.-Fri., 11:30am-4:30pm Sun., R$25-30) is light, bright, and a little Spartan—the better with which to showcase the extensive vegetarian buffet of hot and cold dishes that attracts a diverse array of veggie lovers. Included in the all-you-can-eat price are fresh fruit juices and dessert.

Liberdade

Although Liberdade has an increasing number of Chinese and Korean eateries, the standouts remain the neighborhood's traditional Japanese restaurants.

JAPANESE

Izakaya Issa (Rua Barão de Iguape 89, tel. 11/3208-8819, 6:30pm-11:30pm daily) is a small Japanese *boteco* with a traditional decor where, after taking a seat at the bar or on a tatami mat, you can order a wide array of delicious portions—the crunchy octopus balls (*takoyaki*) and shrimp frittata with grated ginger and dried fish are a good place to start. Wash them down with a variety of sakes. Tiny **Aska** (Rua Galvão Bueno 466, tel. 11/3277-9682, 11am-2pm and 6pm-10pm Tues.-Sun., R$20-30) serves rich, fragrant bowls of ramen at this atmospheric, authentic hole in the wall.

Sushi-Yassu (Rua Tomás Gonzaga 98, www.sushiyassu.com.br, tel. 11/3209-6622, 11:30am-3pm and 6pm-11pm Tues.-Fri., noon-4pm and 6pm-11:30pm Sat., noon-10pm Sun., R$35-45) boasts more than 100 menu offerings; most focus on sushi, sashimi, and classic recipes such as stir-fried Japanese spinach with smoked fish shavings. An all-you-can-eat-buffet (R$58) nurses more severe hunger pains. For privacy, there are seven screened-off rooms with tatami mats.

Higienópolis
CAFÉS AND SNACKS

Benjamin Abrahão Mundo dos Pães (Rua Maranhão 220, tel. 11/3258-1855, www.benjaminabrahao.com.br, 6am-8:30pm daily) is considered one of the best *padarias* (bakeries) in town. Delicious baked goods and more than 50 varieties of bread emerge from its ovens daily. The freshly made sandwiches are very tasty, as are the *chipas*—golf ball-size baked dough stuffed with fillings such as guava jelly and white cheese with herbs.

CONTEMPORARY

Housed in a creamy brick mansion with a pretty veranda and a warmly furnished lounge, **Carlota** (Rua Sergipe 753, tel. 11/3661-8670, www.carlota.com.br, noon-4pm

Tues.-Sat., noon-6pm Sun., 7pm-midnight Mon.-Sat., R$50-70) is owned and operated by one of Brazil's most innovative contemporary chefs, Carla Pernambuco. Pernambuco's trademark dishes feature unusual multicultural combinations of flavors and textures; her warm guava soufflé bathed in Catupiry cream has become something of a local legend.

INTERNATIONAL

In a town with no shortage of extravagantly priced (and decorated) temples devoted to sophisticated *alta cocina*, **Cosi** (Rua Barão do Tatui 302, Santa Cecília, tel. 11/3826-5088, www.restaurantecosi.com.br, noon-3pm and 7pm-11pm Mon.-Fri., noon-4pm and 7pm-midnight Sat., noon-5pm Sun., R$45-60) is a refreshing exception to the rule. Although the small dining space can get crowded and noisy (reserve a table on the veranda), the unpretentious but expertly executed dishes—meat, fish, pasta, and especially the risottos—will win you over. The three-course weekday lunchtime *menu executivo* is a real bargain. The restaurant is located in the working-class *bairro* of Santa Cecília, which straddles Higienópolis and Centro.

Carnivores will be happy to stumble upon **El Tranvía** (Rua Conselheiro Broteiro 903, Santa Cecília, tel. 11/3664-8313, www.eltranvia.com.br, noon-3pm and 6-midnight Mon.-Fri., noon-midnight Sat., noon-5pm Sun., R$40-55), an authentic Uruguayan *churrascaria* where succulent cuts of beef (try the *vacio* and *bife de chorizo*) are sprinkled with fine salt and grilled over coals. Robust portions feed two and are best savored in the interior courtyard.

PIZZA

Veridiana (Rua Dona Veridiana 661, tel. 11/3120-5050, www.veridiana.com.br, 6pm-12:30am Sun.-Thurs., 6pm-1:30am Fri.-Sat., R$30-40) is named after Dona Veridiana, a baron's daughter and early feminist who scandalized late 19th-century Sampa when she divorced her husband and turned her palatial mansion into a famous literary salon, where she also entertained her lovers. Today the cathedral-like interior is home to the city's most sumptuous pizzeria—toppings include delicacies such as escarole, imported anchovies, and wild boar. Exposed brick walls lit by candlelight cast a warm glow on the tables, often filled by celebs.

VEGETARIAN

Housed in a grand old mansion with a soothing atmosphere, the all-you-can-eat buffet of hot and cold vegetarian offerings at **Bio Alternativa** (Rua Maranhão 812, tel. 11/3825-8499, www.bioalternativa.com.br, noon-3pm Mon.-Fri., noon-4pm Sat.-Sun., R$32-38) are attractively presented and downright delicious, and include a table of gluten-free breads and crackers accompanied by pâtés and spreads. There is a second location in Jardins (Alameda Santos 2214, tel. 11/3898-2971).

Avenida Paulista
BRAZILIAN

Jiquitaia (Rua Antônio Carlos 268, Consolação, tel. 11/3262-2366, www.jiquitaia.com.br, noon-3pm Mon.-Fri., 7pm-midnight Tues.-Fri., noon-midnight Sat., R$25-40) seduces one's pocketbook and palate in equal portions. Ignore the à la carte menu and focus instead on the three-course prix fixe lunch (R$39) and dinner (R$59) offerings, which riff on regional recipes from all over Brazil. Options range from barbecued ribs in tamarind sauce to penne with pupunha (the fruit of an Amazonian palm).

Tucked on a quiet residential street just a few blocks from Ana Rosa Metrô, **Sobaria** (Rua Áurea 343, Vila Mariana, tel. 11/5084-8014, www.sobaria.com.br, noon-11pm Mon.-Fri., noon-midnight Sat., R$20-30) dishes up rare-to-come-by specialties of Mato Grosso do Sul, a Wild West state where cowboy culture mingles with a significant Japanese immigrant population. The culinary consequences explain why *cupim ao leite* (strips of beef from the hump of zebu cows served with manioc fries) share menu space with steaming

Little Italy

Between Avenida Paulista and Centro, in a cluster of hilly streets known officially as **Bela Vista** (and popularly as **Bixiga**) is São Paulo's "Little Italy." In the early 20th century, Italian immigrants, primarily from Calabria, flocked to this *bairro*. Italian traditions are still strong, especially when it comes to food. A large number of decades-old bakeries and cantinas line Rua 13 de Maio and surrounding streets. Many are geared to tourism, but there are a few simpler (and calmer) traditional ristorantes where you can savor tasty authentic fare in charmingly rustic surroundings.

São Domingos (Rua Santo Domingos 330, tel. 11/3104-7600, www.paoitalianosaodomingos. com.br, 7am-8pm Mon.-Sat., 7am-3pm Sun.) is a *traditionalíssimo* Italian neighborhood bakery and emporium that has been around for close to a century. Enjoy freshly baked bread or build your own antipasto. Weekends feature fresh focaccia and *empadas*. The cannoli and *pastiera de grano* are divine.

Roperto (Rua Treze de Maio 634, tel. 11/3288-2573, www.cantinoroperto.com.br, 11:30am-midnight Sun.-Thurs., 11:30am-1am Fri.-Sat., R$35-50) has been in operation since 1942 and is still considered one of the best and most authentic of Bixiga's cantinas. The southern Italian fare ranges from scrumptious lasagna Bolognese to gnocchi with a pesto sauce. The house specialty is a tenderly roasted kid with potatoes and broccoli.

Speranza (Rua Treze de Maio 1004, tel. 11/3288-8502, www.pizzaria.com.br/speranza, 6pm-1:30am Mon.-Fri., 6pm-2am Sat., 6pm-1am Sun., R$25-40) has been seducing pizza lovers with a secret Neapolitan recipe for crunchy medium-crust pies since 1958.

bowls of soba noodles and meat in a ginger and scallion broth. Afterward, head next door to **Frutos do Brasil** (Rua Áurea 35, www.frutosdobrasil.com.br, 10am-11pm Sun.-Thurs., 10am-midnight Fri.-Sat.) for a palate-cleansing *picolé* (popsicle) made with typical fruits from the Central-West Cerrado such as mangaba, taperobá, and pequi.

CHURRASCARIAS

After close to a century of existence, **Sujinho** (Rua da Consolação 2078, Consolação, tel. 11/3231-5207, www.sujinho.com.br, noon-5am daily, R$25-35) is still a notorious all-day and after-hours hangout where Paulistanos meet, mingle, and dig in to reasonably priced and deliciously tender barbecued meat. A wide array of side dishes allows you to assemble a meal according to your appetite. Try to nab one of the sidewalk tables so you can observe the people passing by.

A discerning carnivore's paradise, **Baby Beef Rubaiyat** (Alameda Santos 86, Paraíso, tel. 11/3170-5100, www.rubaiyat. com.br, noon-3pm and 7pm-midnight Mon.-Fri., noon-midnight Sat., noon-6pm Sun., R$60-80) is a family-owned chain famed for its sublimely tender cuts of meat. Quality is ensured because the Iglesias family raises all its own cattle on a ranch in Mato Grosso do Sul, as well as chickens, wild boar, Dorper lambs, and a special breed of pig. An impressive wine list complements the food, and the service is excellent, although the ambiance is a bit dim and business-y. Lunch is served buffet-style. Friday's offerings include grilled fish, seafood, and paella, while Wednesdays and Saturdays feature a mean *feijoada*.

INTERNATIONAL

Tenda do Nilo (Rua Coronel Porto 638, Paraíso, tel. 11/3885-0460, www.tendadonilo.com.br, noon-3:30pm Mon.-Sat., R$20-30) is one of the tiniest and least expensive Middle Eastern restaurants in São Paulo. It is also one of the best. The simple yet mouthwatering Lebanese dishes are prepared according to recipes passed down by the cook's mother. Try the *fatte:* toasted Syrian bread topped with beef, chickpeas, and creamy white cheese steeped in garlic. Then cleanse your palate with "1001 Nights," a moist cake of semolina bathed in a pistachio cream.

PIZZA

For the last few years, **Bráz** has consistently been crowned one of the city's best pizzerias. The most recent and inviting of its several locations is ★ **Quintal do Bráz** (Rua Gandavo 447, Vila Mariana, tel. 11/5082-3800, www.quintaldobraz.com.br, 6:30pm-midnight Sun.-Thurs., 6:30pm-1:30am Fri.-Sat., R$30-40), where tables are scattered throughout a relaxing green *quintal* (garden). This location offers truly outstanding pizzas, a wonderful selection of antipasti, and the recently invented *pizza carola*, a hybrid that is part calzone and part pizza.

VEGETARIAN

Lactovegetarianism goes Indian at **Gopala Hari** (Rua Antônio Carlos 413, Consolação, tel. 11/3283-1292, www.gopalahari.com. br, 11:30am-3pm Mon.-Fri., noon-3pm Sat., R$25-30). Incense wafts through the interior, rose petals are scattered on the floor, and the constantly changing daily fixed-price menu features healthy fare flavored with spices from the Orient.

Jardins
CAFÉS AND SNACKS

Galeria dos Pães (Rua Estados Unidos 1645, Jardim América, tel. 11/3064-5900, www.galeriadospaes.com.br, 24 hours daily) is a mélange of bakery, delicatessen, wine shop, and café. It never closes, and this *superpadaria* is always packed, although the clientele changes hourly. The breakfast buffets, featuring more than 50 items, are a great start to any day, while creative sandwiches (named for famous painters) make for practical lunches.

Chocoholics will go cocoa *louco* at **Chocolat du Jour** (Rua Haddock Lobo 1421, Cerqueira César, tel. 11/3168-2720, www.chocolatdujour.com.br, 9am-9pm Mon.-Sat., noon-7pm Sat.). The interior of this celebrated Paulistano chocolatier resembles a swanky jewelry shop, except that the coveted bling on display in glass cases is edible. The outstanding truffles are made with a secret mixture of Belgian and Brazilian chocolate. Kids will love the *chocopop* (chocolate-covered popcorn). A small café serves espresso and hot chocolate.

If São Paulo had an equivalent of Paris' Deux Magots, it would be **Santo Grão** (Rua Oscar Freire 413, Jardim Paulista, tel. 11/3062-9494, www.santograo.com.br, 9am-1am Mon., 8am-1am Tues.-Sat., 8am-midnight Sun.), except that this clubby, modern café is frequented by a hipper, less touristy clientele than its Left Bank doppelgänger. As a people-watching scene, it is unparalleled. The extensive variety of gourmet *cafés* (including an aromatic house-grown blend) are prepared and served with the utmost care. Salads, sandwiches, and light gourmet meals are available, as is breakfast.

A charmingly retro diner-luncheonette, **Frevo** (Rua Oscar Freire 603, Jardim Paulista, tel. 11/3082-3434, www.frevinho.com.br, 10:30am-1am Sun.-Wed., 10:30am-2am Thurs.-Fri., 10:30am-3am Sat.) has been serving up snacks, sandwiches, and decadent sundaes since 1956. The pièce de résistance is the legendary *beirute* sandwich. The traditional version combines cheese, tomatoes, oregano, and a hearty slab of roast beef.

BRAZILIAN

Having steeped herself in culinary traditions from all over Brazil, chef Ana Luiza Trajano revisits classic recipes at **Brasil a Gosto** (Rua Professor Azevedo do Amaral 70, Jardim Paulista, tel. 11/3086-3565, www.brasilagosto.com.br, noon-3pm and 7pm-midnight Tues.-Thurs., noon-5pm and 7pm-1am Fri.-Sat., noon-5pm Sun., R$45-60), revitalizing them with unpredictable and delightfully contemporary twists. Shrimp with heart of palm in orange vinaigrette and *badejo* fish, encrusted with *baru* (a rare type of cashew) and served with a creamy *banana da terra* puree, are examples of the inspired fare served in the tastefully appointed and relaxed dining room. During the week, take advantage of a R$44 lunch menu.

An inspired chef devoted to the cause of Brazilian cuisine is Mara Salles of **Tordesilhas** (Alameda Tietê 489, Consolação, tel. 11/3107-7444, www.tordesilhas.com, 7pm-1am Tues.-Fri., noon-5pm and 7pm-1am Sat., noon-5pm Sun., R$50-70). While Salles tackles traditional regional dishes with gusto, she also goes out on creative limbs with the unusual likes of carpaccio of *carne-de-sol* (sun-dried beef) and pork ribs with *mulato* risotto, and, for dessert, *crème anglaise* made with pequi, an exotic fruit of the Cerrado.

CONTEMPORARY

Internationally celebrated chef Alex Atala has garnered extraordinary success with ★ **D.O.M.** (Rua Barão de Capanema 549, Jardim Paulista, tel. 11/3088-0761, www.dom-restaurante.com.br, noon-3pm and 7pm-midnight. Mon.-Fri., 7pm-1am Sat.). Atala's forte is applying classic and cutting-edge cooking techniques (the more molecular, the merrier) to unusual Brazilian ingredients and culinary traditions. The resulting creations are all about contrasting textures and inspired flavors that challenge the most jaded taste buds. The seductively modernist dining space was designed by architect Ruy Ohtake and includes an open kitchen where you can see the master chef at work. Avoid the dinner tasting menus (R$495, R$375, and R$242) and opt instead for the pared-down, more wallet-friendly *executivo* lunch menu (R$59) served during the week. Reservations are essential.

Across the street, **Dalva e Dito** (Rua Padre João Manuel 1115, Jardim Paulista, tel. 11/3068-4444, www.dalvaedito.com.br, noon-3pm and 7pm-midnight Mon.-Fri., noon-4:30pm and 7pm-10:30pm Sat., noon-5pm Sun., R$45-85) is Atala's inspired take on the kind of no-nonsense, regional Brazilian comfort food he grew up savoring in his grandmother's kitchen. *Rabada com agrião* (oxtail stew with watercress) and pork with pureed potatoes and fragrant *pequi* fruit are all cooked over low heat for hours to ensure amazing textures and flavors. On Saturdays, a late-night, midnight-3am feast is accompanied by samba jams.

Sporting scarlet leather banquettes and a casually urbane New York-like vibe, the **Ritz** (Alameda França 1088, Cerqueira César, tel. 11/3062-5830, www.restauranteritz.com.br, noon-3pm and 8pm-1am Mon.-Fri., 12:30pm-1am Sat.-Sun., R$25-40) has long been a favorite haunt of Sampa's art, fashion, and gay and lesbian crowd, who swear by its gourmet diner fare. Aside from inventive salads and pastas, the star of the menu is the hamburger (charbroiled over volcanic rocks) served with rice balls and garnished with horseradish, hollandaise, and spicy tamarind sauces.

★ **Maní** (Rua Joaquim Antunes 210, Jardim Paulistano, tel. 11/3085-4148, www.manimanioca.com.br, noon-3pm and 8pm-midnight Tues.-Fri., 1pm-4pm and 8:30pm-12:30am Sat., 1pm-5pm Sun., R$85-100) is operated by what many claim to be the hottest chef in Latin America, Helena Rizzo, along with her culinary coconspirator and husband, Daniel Redondo. Their unpretentious restaurant—all warm wood and cool white stucco—serves to highlight food that is not only daring but delicious. "Perfect Eggs" are cooked for two hours and served with a froth of *pupunha* (the heart of an Amazonian palm), while *feijoada* consists of glazed chunks of tender pork, carpaccio of pig's foot, and bean-shaped spheres containing a distilled essence of Brazil's national dish. Even the caipirinhas—with ginger ice cubes—will blow your mind. Tasting menus are available at dinner only, while weekday lunch offers more moderately priced daily specials.

JAPANESE

Prior to 2012, **Bueno** (Alameda Santos 835, Jardim Paulista, tel. 11/2386-8035, www.izakayabueno.com.br, 11:30am-2:30pm and 6pm-10:30pm Mon.-Sat., R$25-40) was a tiny Liberdade hideaway owned by a former sumo wrestler and frequented by a largely Japanese clientele who swore by the robust traditional fare on offer. While the move to Jardins has resulted in more seating (and a prix fixe lunch special for execs), don't expect sushi or sashimi; dishes run more along the lines of *okonomiyaki*, a fried pumpkin and cabbage pancake topped with shaved fish, and *chanko nabe,* a calorie-laden stew of meat and vegetables.

SEAFOOD

★ **Figueira Rubaiyat** (Rua Haddock Lobo 1738, Jardim Paulista, tel. 11/3087-1399, www.rubaiyat.com.br, noon-midnight Sun.-Thurs., noon-1am Fri.-Sat., R$60-85) is owned by the Rubaiyat restaurant chain. The *figueira* refers to the immense 100-year-old fig tree that spreads its great green limbs throughout much of this beautiful restaurant. Although the menu features all the delectable meats of its Rubaiyat siblings, the specialty here is fish and seafood. The signature dish is the *caixote marinho:* a re-imagined paella cooked in a brick oven.

VEGETARIAN

One of the best vegetarian restaurants in the city, **Cheiro Verde** (Rua Peixoto Gomide 1078, Jardim Paulista, tel. 11/3289-6853, www.cheiroverderestaurante.com.br, 11:30am-3pm Mon.-Fri., noon-4:30pm Sat.-Sun., R$15-30) serves fresh, creative, and inexpensive ovolactovegetarian salads, tarts, pastas, and pizzas in a relaxing environment.

Pinheiros and Vila Madalena
CAFÉS AND SNACKS

Lá da Venda (Rua Harmonia 161, Vila Madalena, tel. 11/3037-7702, www.ladavenda.com.br, 11am-8pm Mon.-Fri., 10am-8pm Sat., 10am-5:30pm Sun.) offers a beguiling 21st-century take on an old-fashioned café-emporium, offering an intoxicating cornucopia of edibles and *artesanato* from all over Brazil. It also serves lunch, homemade ice cream, and popsicles throughout the day on the sidewalk patio, internal courtyard, or upstairs mezzanine.

Java junkies who take their caffeine seriously should check into the **Coffee Lab** (Rua Fradique Coutinho 1340, Vila Madalena, tel. 11/3375-7400, www.coffeelab.com.br, 10am-7pm Mon.-Fri., 11am-8pm Sat.), owned by queen barista Isabel Raposeiras. Within the lab are some of the best beans, roasters, and brewers available, served up by a suitably geeky staff in white coats.

A favorite neighborhood hangout, **Empanadas Bar** (Rua Wisard 489, Vila Madalena, tel. 11/3032-2116, www.empanadasbar.com.br, noon-2am Mon.-Fri., noon-3am Sat., noon-1am Sun.) keeps expanding, both in size (it currently takes up an entire block) and in the number of delicious oven-baked empanadas it serves (25,000-30,000 a month!). Whether you opt for a classic filling such as spicy ground beef or the more unorthodox likes of heart of palm, roquefort, and guava with cheese, you'll find it impossible to eat just one.

BRAZILIAN

If you can't get to Minas to try its much-vaunted regional cuisine, a popular Paulistano alternative is **Consulado Mineiro** (Praça Benedito Calixto 74, Pinheiros, tel. 11/3064-3882, www.consuladomineiro.com.br, noon-midnight Tues.-Sun., noon-11pm Sun, R$25-35). Dishes are hearty, no-nonsense affairs such as *galinhada,* a risotto made with saffron, rice, chicken, and vegetables and served with *tutu,* a rich puree of beans with pork. Generous portions easily feed two, if not three.

INTERNATIONAL

Saj (Rua Girassol 523, Vila Madalena, tel. 11/3032-5939, www.sajrestaurante.com.br, noon-4pm and 7pm-11pm Mon.-Fri., noon-midnight Sat., 12:30pm-10:30pm Sun., R$20-35) serves up inexpensive and deliciously authentic Lebanese food. Its substantial menu runs the gamut from appetizers and salad to grilled dishes in airy minimalist surroundings. For dessert, try sesame ice cream or a glass of pomegranate-rose petal juice.

Señor Guatón and his wife preside over **El Guatón** (Rua Artur Azevedo 55, Pinheiros, tel. 11/3088-6019, noon-3pm and 5pm-midnight Mon.-Fri., noon-midnight Sat., noon-4:30pm Sun., R$20-40) a cozy and unpretentiously Chilean neighborhood restaurant. Prices are as honest as the specialties, which range from tangy fish ceviche and succulent baked empanadas to *pastel de choclos* (a chicken pie topped with gratinéed puree of corn).

Arredores (Outlying Neighborhoods)

It's worth making the trek to Vila Medeiros, a working-class neighborhood in the Zona Norte, to experience what many consider the best Brazilian eating in the city: **Mocotó** (Av. Nossa Senhora de Loreto 1100, Vila Medeiros, tel. 11/2951-3056, www.mocoto.com.br, noon-11pm Mon.-Sat., noon-5pm Sun., R$30-40). To get there, take the Metrô to Tucuruvi station and then hop the 121G-10 bus to the corner of Av. Gustavo Adolfo and Av. Nossa Senhora de Loreto.

This down-to-earth *boteco/cachaçaria* has been around since 1974, but it wasn't until 2004, when Rodrigo Oliveira took over from his father, that Mocotó began luring well-heeled gourmets accustomed to dropping small fortunes. Oliveira serves flawlessly inspired renditions of traditional Northeastern cuisine of the Sertão: Beloved examples include *bode atolada* (a rich stew of goat's ribs) and *escondidinho de carne seca* (shredded sun-dried beef "hidden" beneath a puree of gratinéed manioc). Due to the robustness of the food, and the inevitable lines (particularly severe on weekends), arrive with both hunger and patience.

In 2013, Oliveira opened **Esquina Mocotó** (tel. 11/2949-7049, www.esquinamocoto.com.br, noon-3pm and 7:30pm-11pm Mon.-Sat., noon-5pm Sun., R$40-55) right next door. The menu plays more freely with homegrown ingredients and yields surprising but delicious results such as grilled pork belly with fava beans and lime *farofa*.

INFORMATION AND SERVICES

A highly efficient and organized city, São Paulo is better equipped than many places in Brazil to deal with foreign visitors, even though the city receives more business travelers than tourists. Staff at airports, bus stations, and major hotels are quite informative and usually speak at least a little bit of English. Banks that accept foreign ATM cards are easy to find, especially on Avenida Paulista.

São Paulo Turismo (Praça da República, tel. 11/3331-7786, www.cidadedesaopaulo.com) is the city travel association. It operates a terrific bilingual website and more than a dozen tourist information kiosks scattered around the city, where you can pick up maps (including guided walks of different neighborhoods), a handy guide (published monthly) that lists events, and a guide that caters specially to LGBT travelers. The most useful locations are the **CIT Ólida** (Av. São João 473, Centro, 9am-6pm daily) and the **CIT Paulista** (Av. Paulista 1853, 7am-6pm daily). There are also branches at the Tietê bus station (6am-10pm daily), and at Guarulhos airports (8am-8pm daily). For more information, you can also visit the bilingual website www.saopaulo.sp.gov.br/conhecasp/turismo.

Exchange money at major branches of **Banco do Brasil** in Centro (Rua São Bento 465) and on Avenida Paulista (Av. Paulista 2163). Other major banks such as Citibank, Bank Boston, HSBC, Bradesco, and Santander Banespa accept international cards with Visa/Plus or MasterCard/Cirrus logos. You'll find branches of these banks concentrated around Avenida Paulista and Avenida Brigadeiro Faria Lima in Jardins.

The main **Correios** (post office) is at Rua Libero Badaró 595 in Centro (8am-10pm Mon.-Fri.). There are another 300 or so agencies throughout the city, including several along Avenida Paulista; to find one, access www.correios.com.br.

Emergency Services

In the event of a medical emergency, dial **192** for an ambulance. Two of the most distinguished private hospitals in the country are **Hospital Albert Einstein** (Av. Albert Einstein 627, Morumbi, tel. 11/2151-1233, www.einstein.com.br), which has several units around town, and **Hospital Sírio Libanês** (Rua Dona Adma Jafet 91, Bela Vista, tel. 11/3155-0200, www.hospitalsiriolibanes.org. br). São Paulo has three major pharmacy chains, each with numerous locations that are open 24 hours. Check websites for locations: **Droga Raia** (www.drogaraia.com.br), **Drogaria São Paulo** (www.drogariasaopaulo.com.br), and **Drogasil** (www.drogasil. com.br).

In the event of a crime, you can contact police by dialing **190**. There is a special unit, **Delegácia Especializada em Atendimento ao Turista** (Deatur, Rua Consolação 247, Centro, tel. 11/3257-4475, 8am-8pm Mon.-Fri.), that deals specifically with crimes involving foreign tourists.

TRANSPORTATION
Air

São Paulo has two airports. **Guarulhos International Airport** (Rodovia Hélio Smidt, Guarulhos, tel. 11/6455-2945), also known as Cumbica, is 30 kilometers (20 mi) northeast of the center of the city. The larger of the two airports, it is used for all international flights and a large portion of domestic flights. The majority of international flights land in Guarulhos before continuing on to other major cities—this usually involves a connecting flight. Much closer to the center is the older and smaller **Congonhas Airport** (Av. Washington Luís, Vila Congonhas, tel. 11/5090-9000). Limited to domestic flights, it also operates frequent air shuttles that connect São Paulo with Rio de Janeiro (a speedy 30-minute jaunt).

At both airports, you will find kiosks for taxis that can take you into the city for a fixed price, calculated according to your final destination. Expect to pay around R$120 from Guarulhos (since the Guarucoop taxi service has a monopoly on the route) and R$35-50 from Congonhas. A cheaper alternative is to take an *executivo* bus. **Airport Bus Service** (tel. 0800/770-22877, www.airportbusservice.com.br, R$38) offers regular service from Guarulhos to Praça da República,

the major hotels around Avenida Paulista, the Tietê and Barra Funda bus stations, and Congonhas. Buses leave at 30- to 60-minute intervals 6am-11pm daily, with less frequent service throughout the night to Praça da República. Cheapest, though challenging if you have a lot of luggage (and during rush hour), is to take the Metrô to Tatuapé station and from there grab a suburban bus (R$4.45) that will have you at Guarulhos in 30 minutes. Municipal bus 875A-10 links Congonhas with Metrô São Judas.

Bus

São Paulo has three major bus terminals. All are conveniently connected to Metrô stations that bear the same names as the bus terminals and can easily be reached by numerous municipal buses. To the north, **Rodoviária Tietê** (Av. Cruzeiro du Sul, Santana, tel. 11/3235-0322) is the second-largest bus terminal in the world. From here, you can catch a bus for anywhere in Brazil as well as Argentina, Chile, Uruguay, and Paraguay. You can also take express buses to Rio, which leave at roughly 15-minute intervals during the day and at 30-minute intervals at night. The 5.5-hour trip costs R$75 (conventional buses) and R$150-160 (buses with seats that fold into beds). **Autoviação 1000** (tel. 11/2252-3401, www. autoviacao1001.com.br) and **Expresso Brasil** (tel. 11/2221-0155, www.expressobrasileiro. com) offer service between the two cities.

Near the Memorial da América Látina, **Rodoviária Barra Funda** (Rua Maria de Andrade 664, Barra Funda, tel. 11/3235-0322) has buses that service the interior of São Paulo state and the state of Paraná (including Iguaçu Falls).

Close to Congonhas airport, **Rodoviária Jabaquara** (Rua dos Jequitibás, Jabaquara, tel. 11/3235-0322) is the departure point for buses to the region surrounding Santos and the southern coast of São Paulo state.

Socicam (www.socicam.com.br) is a private company that operates all of São Paulo's bus terminals. Its website lists all bus companies, routes, and schedules. It's advisable to purchase tickets in advance during weekends and holidays.

MUNICIPAL BUS

Buses go everywhere in São Paulo—except when they're stuck in rush-hour traffic (usually worst 7am-9am and 5pm-7pm). Despite a fleet of more than 10,000 vehicles, buses can get very crowded. Figuring out which bus goes where is a bit confusing, especially if you don't speak Portuguese. Final destinations are marked on the front of the bus, while major stops are listed along the side. You can pay for your fare in cash (R$3) or purchase the *bilhete único*. For information about itineraries, **Transporte Público de São Paulo** (www.sptrans.com.br) offers a free number to call (156). The website also lets you type in a starting point and final destination and then provides you with possible buses and routes to take.

Metrô

São Paulo's **Metrô** (tel. 0800/770-7722, www.metro.sp.gov.br, 4:40am-midnight Sun.-Fri., 4:40am-1am Sat., R$3) is clean, efficient, and safe. The only problem is its small size, although its five principal lines are slowly being extended and others are under construction. Beware of the Metrô during rush hour, when crowds can be really daunting. Tickets are sold in the station; for security reasons, kiosks are only open 6am-10am. Lineups to purchase tickets can also be pretty long; multiple purchases are a good idea. You can buy a rechargeable *bilhete único* (single ticket, R$3) card that allows four trips/transfers via Metrô and bus within three hours. For updated prices and a map of lines, check out the Metrô's bilingual website or visit www.vademetro.com.br to find out how to navigate sights throughout the city by Metrô.

Taxis

Taxis are the best and safest way of navigating São Paulo by night. By day, they can be useful for getting to specific destinations off the Metrô or main bus lines, although like other vehicles, they can get stuck in traffic during rush hour. Considering São Paulo's immensity, if you start shuttling back and forth across the city, you will rack up a small fortune in cab fares. *Taxis comuns* are the least expensive taxis. You can either hail one in the street (unless it's raining) or find one at a *posto* (taxi stand). *Rádio taxis* are a bit larger and a bit more expensive. Major companies include **Coopertax** (tel. 11/2095-6005) and **Ligue Taxi** (tel. 11/2101-3030).

Car Rental

Although São Paulo is definitely a city in which cars rule, you'll have to possess vast amounts of patience (and a certain degree of insanity) to consider renting a car here. Traffic is a nightmare, parking is a nightmare, and rainstorms (when streets are instantly inundated due to poor drainage) create nightmarish flooding. Add carjackings, the exhaust fumes of thousands of idling buses, and the hundreds of daredevil *"motoboys"* who weave in and out of traffic on scooters, and you'll really appreciate sidewalks. If you rent a car, you'll have to learn the *rodízio* ("rotation") system; to ease traffic during rush hour (7am-10am and 5pm-8pm Mon.-Fri.), cars with license plates ending in certain numbers must stay off the roads during these times: Monday, 1 and 2; Tuesday, 3 and 4; Wednesday, 5 and 6; Thursday, 7 and 8; and Friday, 9 and 0.

Renting a car only makes sense if exploring the coast or mountains of São Paulo state, particularly small towns or isolated beaches that are hard to reach by bus. Major companies include **Avis** (www.avis.com.br), with offices at both airports and in Centro (Rua da Consolação 335, Centro, tel. 11/3259-6868), and **Hertz** (www.hertz.com.br), also with branches at the airport and in Centro (Rua da Consolação 439, Centro, tel. 11/3258-9384).

City Tours

A serious Sampa specialist, multilingual **Flavia Liz Di Paolo** (tel. 11/3032-2692, www.flavializ.com.) offers a vast array of customized and theme-based half-day tours that go off the beaten track to expose you to Sampa behind the scenes, in milieus ranging from fashion to *favelas*. Expect to pay R$200/hour. Less exclusive (and expensive) **Go In São Paulo** (tel. 11/3289-3814, www.goinsaopaulo.com.br) runs custom-made city tours designed for individuals and small groups that are led by English-speaking guides. A five-hour city tour for two costs R$400. Excursions around the state—to north coast beaches or coffee plantations—are also available.

AROUND SÃO PAULO
Embu

The quickest and easiest day trip you can take from São Paulo is to the small colonial town of Embu, 27 kilometers (17 mi) west of the city. Founded in 1554, many of its historic white-washed houses and churches have been preserved. Make sure to visit the **Igreja Nossa Senhora do Rosário** (Largo dos Jesuítas 67, tel. 11/4704-2654, 9am-noon and 1pm-5pm Tues.-Sun., R$3), an impressive late 17th-century baroque church. Inside the adjacent monastery, the **Museu de Arte Sacra dos Jesuítas** houses a highly reputed collection of sacred art that includes intricately carved wooden saints (sporting human hair) and an 18th-century organ made by local Indians.

SHOPPING

Embu is famous (perhaps overly so) for its many artisans' studios—specializing in wood and stone carving, leatherwork, furniture-making, and decorative arts—as well as its numerous antiques stores. On weekends, the small town hosts an antiques fair and handicraft market that lures day-trippers and bargain-hunters from the city (to avoid the crowds, arrive early; better yet, come during the week). You could easily spend all day browsing. Note that in terms of antiques, many are not originals but replicas.

Malyla's Artes e Antiguidades (Rua Nossa Senhora de Rosário 116, tel. 11/4704-3984) specializes in original certified antiques from the 18th, 19th, and 20th centuries. **Empório King** (Rua Joaquim Santana 41, tel. 11/4704-3469) sells works crafted out of wood, ceramic, and iron from Minas Gerais and the Northeast. At **Guarani Artesanatos** (Largo dos Jesuitas 153, tel. 11/4704-3200), you'll find sculptures fashioned out of precious *pau brasil* (brazilwood) and carvings made from soapstone and semiprecious stones. Shops are usually open 9am-5pm daily; some close Monday.

FOOD

Hidden in a charming little alley off Rua Siqueira Campos, **Empório São Pedro** (Viela das Lavadeiras 28, tel. 11/4781-2797, noon-5pm Wed.-Fri., noon-midnight Sat., noon-6pm Sun., R$40-60) occupies an antiques store, where you can browse while feasting on dishes such as asparagus tortellini and roast lamb with sun-dried tomato risotto. For a less expensive snack or light meal, bite into one or more **Empanadas do Ramon** (Largo dos Jesuítas 97/99, 2pm-10pm, Tues.-Sun.), which come in sweet and savory versions.

TRANSPORTATION AND SERVICES

The **tourist office** (Largo 21 de Abril, tel. 11/4704-6565, www.embu.sp.gov.br, 8am-5pm Mon.-Fri., 9am-6pm Sat.-Sun.) is right in the center of town. Getting to Embu from São Paulo is easy. Embu Cultural *executivo* buses operated by **Miracatiba** (tel. 11/4165-9000) leave at 60-minute intervals from in front of Metrô Anhangabau in Centro (40 minutes, R$4.90). You can also catch a municipal bus from Campo Limpo Metrô station.

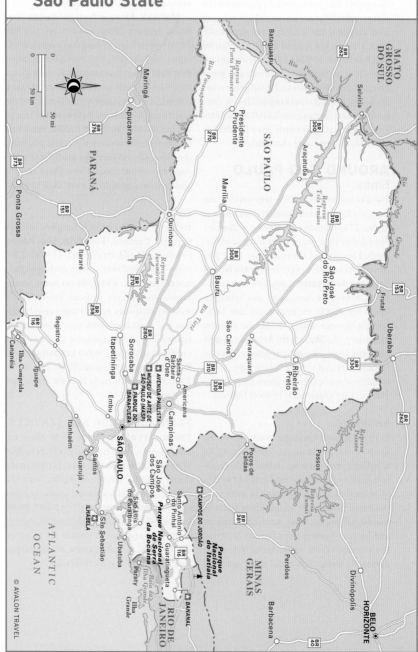

São Paulo State

MATO GROSSO DO SUL

SÃO PAULO

PARANÁ

MINAS GERAIS

RIO DE JANEIRO

ATLANTIC OCEAN

© AVALON TRAVEL

0 50 km
0 50 mi

BR 262

BR 300

BR 270

BR 310

BR 300

BR 153

BR 330

BR 262

BR 381

BR 116

BR 40

BR 376

BR 373

BR 151

BR 270

BR 258

BR 116

BR 280

BR 310

Bataguassu

Selvíria

Maringá

Apucarana

Ponta Grossa

Itararé

Ourinhos

Presidente Prudente

Marília

Bauru

São José do Rio Preto

Frutal

Uberaba

Araçatuba

São Carlos

Araraquara

Ribeirão Preto

Passos

Perdões

Barbacena

Divinópolis

BELO HORIZONTE

Registro

Cananéia
Ilha Comprida

Iguape

Itanhaém

Itapetininga

Sorocaba

Embu

Santos

Guarujá
ILHABELA

SÃO PAULO

São Sebastião

Ubatuba

Paraty
Ilha Grande

São Luís do Paraitinga

Guaratinguetá

São José dos Campos

Santo Antônio do Pinhal

Campos do Jordão

Campinas

Americana

Santa Bárbara d'Oste

Poços de Caldas

Bananal

Parque Nacional da Serra da Bocaina

Parque Nacional do Itatiaia

Baía da Ilha Grande

AVENIDA PAULISTA

MUSEU DE ARTE DE SÃO PAULO (MASP)

PARQUE DO IBIRAPUERA

CAMPOS DO JORDÃO

Represa Porto Primavera

Represa Primavera

Rio Paranapanema

Rio Paraná

Rio Grande

Rio Tietê

Represa Três Irmãos

Represa Jurumirim

Rio Paranapanema

Represa Peixoto

Represa de Furnas

Represa Jaguari

Serra da Mantiqueira

São Paulo is a small state with excellent roads and transportation systems. Whether you head for the mountains or take to the coast, most attractions are only 2-3 hours from the capital, making them ideal weekend or overnight excursions. An excellent way to explore the coast or the mountains is to make them part of a Sao Paulo-Rio itinerary, in which you leisurely stop at the destinations that appeal to you between Brazil's two megacities.

Only a couple of hours northeast of the city, in the Serra da Mantiqueira mountain range, is the tony resort town of Campos do Jordão, with its Swiss-style chalets and matching alpine scenery. If the fashion mavens who frequent "Campos" are a bit too much, seek refuge at nearby Santo Antônio do Pinhal, a smaller, more down-to-earth version. Both towns have numerous hiking trails through the mountains and are refreshingly cool in the summer. The Serra da Mantiqueira is the favorite winter playground of upscale Paulistanos and Brazilian celebs. Although snow is unheard of, in July temperatures can go as low as 0°C (32°F). In warmer months, they hover around 15°C (60°F).

★ CAMPOS DO JORDÃO

Brazil's loftiest town—at 1,628 meters (5,341 feet) above sea level—Campos do Jordão is somewhat of a Gstaad, Switzerland, wannabe. With its high-fashion boutiques, hotels equipped with down quilts and crackling fireplaces, and refined eateries serving hot chocolate and fondue, you'd swear you were anywhere other than Brazil. If you prefer nature to nurture, you'll find it in the surrounding mountain ranges, along with plenty of adventure-sports options. Winter months are when things (and prices!) really heat up in Campos, culminating with the **Festival de Inverno** (www.festivaldeinverno.gov.sp.br), an internationally renowned classical musical festival held in July.

The rest of the year—when everything but the temperature cools off—can be equally pleasant, and less crowded.

Sights

Campos consists of three districts: Abernéssia is the most commercial part of town; more central Jaguaribe is where you'll find the bus station; and Vila Capivari is the bustling, touristy epicenter. Outside Capivari, attractions are far-flung, and you'll need a taxi or car to get to them.

Palácio Boa Vista (Av. Ademar de Barros 3001, Alto da Boa Vista, tel. 12/3663-3762, www.palacioboavista.com.br, 10am-noon and 2pm-5pm Wed.-Sun.) is the grand English-style official winter residence of the state governor, which is open to visitors. Amid the marble fireplaces and shiny mahogany furniture is a collection of paintings by leading Brazilian modernists, such as Tarsila do Amaral, Cândido Portinari, and Di Cavalcanti.

Casa da Xilogravura (Av. Eduardo Moreira da Cruz 295, Jaguaribe, tel. 12/3662-1832, 9am-noon and 2pm-5pm Thurs.-Mon., closed Dec., R$4) exhibits woodcuts and engravings.

Sports and Recreation

Horto Florestal (Av. Pedro Paulo, tel. 12/3663-3762, 8am-4pm Thurs.-Tues., daily in Jan. and July, R$9) is a state park 12 kilometers (7.5 mi) east from Capivari, with easy hiking trails that wind through one of the state's few remaining forests of striking *araucária* pines. Waterfalls, a river brimming with trout, and the presence of squirrels, parrots, butterflies, and chattering *macacos-prego* ("nail" monkeys) round out the natural attractions. If you don't have a car, you can hop aboard a municipal bus. Rent bikes on site for R$25 for the first hour.

For a rigorous physical challenge and

360-degree views, tackle the rocky peak of **Pedra do Baú,** situated within a park 25 kilometers (16 mi) north of Campos that can be explored on horseback or on foot. To climb to the lofty (1,950-meter/6,400-foot) summit—a four-hour journey that includes trekking and climbing metal rungs set into the cliff face—it's recommended that you hire a guide. **Altus Turismo** (tel. 12/3663-8375, www.altus.tur.br) offers hiking, climbing, and mountain biking tours to Pedra do Baú as well as the surrounding Serra da Mantiqueira. The popular hiking tour to Pedra do Baú costs R$95. An easier excursion is to visit the much smaller Bauzinho. If you're driving, follow the Estrada São Bento do Sapucaí 18 kilometers (11 mi) and then turn onto a dirt road and follow it 6 kilometers (4 mi) to the parking lot. From here it's an easy 10-minute hike to the top of this giant rock, which also affords spectacular views.

Accommodations

Hotel prices are not cheap in Campos, and during the winter months of June and July they skyrocket. Advance reservations are essential. The more nights you stay, the cheaper the rate; during July there is often a three-day minimum stay. Prices below are for low season during the week.

Canadá Lodge (Rua Deputado Pl 358, Capivari, tel. 12/3663-6640, www.canadalodge.com.br, R$260-380 d) plunges you into a deliciously kitsch ambiance of maple leaves, mooses, and mounties without skimping on comfort or service.

Located just off the bucolic Estrada do Horto Florestal, surrounded by lush hills and wild hydrangeas, charming and intimate ★ **Pousada da Pedra** (Rua Alecrim 53, Jardim Embaixador, tel. 12/3663-6262, www.pousadadapedra.com.br, R$230-290 d) is a welcome alternative to Capivari's urban Alpine scene. Guest rooms sport soaring ceilings and fireplaces; common spaces, awash in light, are decorated with flair. The staff goes all out to make you feel at home, even delivering bowls of popcorn when you're tucked under your quilt watching a DVD. A smashing afternoon tea is included in the price.

Nestled in rolling hills 4 kilometers (2.5 mi) south of Abernéssia, **Hotel Toriba** (Av. Ernesto Diedricksen 2962, tel. 12/3668-5000, www.toriba.com.br, full board R$450-620 d) is one of Campos's most traditional hotels. Inaugurated in 1943, the guest rooms in this Alpine-style villa are suffused with a rustic elegance (although there are some newer units as well). Amenities range from a fitness spa and golf course to ice-skating and a small farm for children. Three on-site gourmet restaurants—including **Toribinha,** which serves the best fondue in town—mean you never have to leave the premises.

Food

Among Campos's local culinary specialties are fresh rainbow trout and *pinhões* (pine nuts), which turn up in everything from cakes and cookies to savory dishes. In keeping with the climate and recurring allusions to things Swiss, you'll also find an abundance of fondue and chocolates. Note that all the listings below have extended hours and are usually open daily in July.

Só Queijo (Av. Macedo Soares 642, Capivari, tel. 12/3663-7585, www.soqueijo.com.br, noon-11pm Thurs.-Sun., R$40-60) is a romantic eatery with red tablecloths, candlelight, and roaring fireplaces where you can feast on trout, cheese raclette, and a variety of fondues. The homemade pâtés served as starters are addictive enough to ruin your appetite for the main course. Cheaper and less Alpine, the **Myriam Café** (Av. Macedo Soares 191, Capivari, tel. 12/3663-1544, 10am-9:30pm Sun.-Thurs., 10am-midnight Fri.-Sat.), serves pastries, healthy sandwiches, and a decent bowl of soup. Across the street, **Pastelão do Maluf** (Av. Macedo Soares 134, Capivari, tel. 12/3663-3590, 11am-11pm daily) sells a giant-size version of Paulistanos' beloved deep-fried *pasteis* stuffed with a variety of fillings. One of these seemingly steroid-induced treats is big enough for a meal. Check out the fabulous pizza served at **Arte da Pizza** (Av. Frei

Orestes Girardi 3549, Capivari, tel. 12/3668-6000, www.grandehotelsenac.com.br, 7pm-11:30pm Thurs.-Sun. and daily July, R$30-40). Choose from exotic toppings such as shitake, trout, and brie, or a variety of olive oils (one is infused with tangerine) that "harmonize" with your pizza.

On the road to Horto Florestal, ★ **Harry Pisek** (Av. Pedro Paulo 857, tel. 12/3663-4030, www.harrypisek.com.br, noon-5pm Mon.-Fri., noon-11pm Sat., noon-6pm Sun., R$25-40) is considered one of the finest German restaurants in Brazil. Of Austrian descent, owner Harry Pisek spent five years in Stuttgart studying the art of sausage making. You can put his expertise to the test by ordering the Harry Pisek Wurst, featuring five homemade varieties that include sausages with herbs, emmental, and a mixture of beef and pork. Equally renowned is the stuffed pork cheek.

Chocoholics are in for a treat due to the town's chocolate-making tradition. At **Araucária** (Av. Macedo Soares 199, Capivari, tel. 12/3663-4306, www.chocolatearaucaria. com.br), you can watch and smell the chocolates being made. Popular enough to warrant four locations, **Montanhês** (Praça São Benedito 5, Capivari, tel. 12/3663-1979, www. chocolatemontanhes.com.br) is sought after for its spiked hot-chocolate drinks and 100 varieties of truffles. Relative newcomer **Bruno Alves** (Av. Macedo Soares 135, Capivari, tel. 12/3663-9045, www.brunoalveschocolatier. com.br) uses only the finest bars of Brazilian and Belgian chocolate.

Transportation and Services

Campos do Jordão's **tourist office** (tel. 12/3668-1098, 9am-8pm Mon.-Sat., 8am-2pm Sun.) is on the main highway, 2 kilometers (1.2 mi) before Abernéssia. For online information, check out www.camposdojordan.com. br and www.guiadecamposdejordao.com.br.

The *rodoviária* (Rua Benedito Lourenço 285, tel. 12/3662-1995) is between Jaguaribe and Capivari. **Pássaro Marron** (tel. 11/3775-3856, www.passaromarron.com.br) has six buses daily to Campos leaving from Tietê terminal (3 hours, R$40). Campos do Jordão lies 167 kilometers (104 mi) northwest of São Paulo. By car, take BR-116, SP-070, or SP-123. The travel time from São Paulo is roughly two hours.

TRAIN TO SANTO ANTÔNIO DO PINHAL

The highest and one of the most scenic train journeys in Brazil is the 20-kilometer (7.5-mi) ride between Campos do Jordão and Santo Antônio do Pinhal, which winds through forest-covered mountains at altitudes of 1,740 meters (5,710 feet). The railroad was inaugurated in 1914 to carry passengers with lung ailments from São Paulo to healthy mountainous climes. Make sure you sit on the right-hand side from Campos for the most breathtaking views. In Campos, climb aboard at the **Estação Emílio Ribas-Ferrovia de Capivari** (Av. Emília Ribas, Capivari, tel. 12/3663-1531). In Santo Antônio, the quaint whitewashed **Estação Eugénio Lefèvre** is in the center of town. A round-trip lasts 2.5 hours and costs R$45 with departures at 10am and 2pm. In Campos itself, it's possible to take a 50-minute tram tour around town (R$11), with hourly departures from the station.

SANTO ANTÔNIO DO PINHAL

A mere stone's throw (or scenic mountain train ride) from "Campos" is the much quieter, more bucolic, and less trendy Santo Antônio do Pinhal, where the emphasis is more on nature and sports than creature comforts. If you're after R&R without the ballyhoo, you can bypass Campos altogether.

Sports and Recreation

The area surrounding Santo Antônio is an important orchid-producing region. Just outside of town, the **Jardim dos Pinhais** (Rodovia SP-046 1645, tel. 12/3666-2021, 9am-5pm Wed.-Fri., 8am-6pm Sat.-Sun. and daily in July, R$18) is a botanical garden with a dazzling array of orchids and other exotic plants from the tropics and all over the world. Guided walks end with a rest stop at a gazebo surrounded by native forest.

Accessible by car, the **Cachoeira do Lageado** is a 15-meter (50-foot) waterfall 8 kilometers (5 mi) from town. **Pico Agudo** (1,700 meters/5,577 feet), whose summit offers impressive views of the Pedra do Baú and Paraíba valley, is 9 kilometers (5.5 mi) out of town. Pico Agudo is a popular launching pad for hang gliders and paragliders. To try these adventurous activities, contact **Xénios Ecoturismo** (Av. Ministro Nelson Hungria 12, tel. 12/3666-1815, www.xeniosecotur. com.br), which charges R$90 for trekking up to Pedra do Baú. It operates rappelling (R$90-120), cascading excursions (around R$90 for a three-hour outing), and hang gliding from the top of Pico Agudo (R$220).

Also worthwhile is the train trip to Campos de Jordão, with departures from the pretty **Estação Eugénio Lefèvre.** Even if you don't ride the rails, stop to snack on the legendary *bolinhos de bacalhau* served at **Bolinho de Bacalhau & Cia** (tel. 12/3666-1332, 8am-7pm daily), located in the station.

Accommodations and Food

Most accommodations in Santo Antônio are in the countryside, several kilometers from the center of town, but easily accessible by taxi. One of the closest to the center is the lovely and quite affordable **Pousada Mirante** (Rua José Cândido Machado 128, tel. 12/3666-1443, www.mirantepousada. com.br, R$150-180 d). Surrounded by greenery, the four cozy stone chalets are outfitted with fireplaces, roughhewn wooden furniture, and hand-embroidered sheets and quilts. Also close by, along the road leading to Pico Agudo, is the ★ **Pousada Vento Verde** (Estrada do Pico Agudo Km 1, tel. 12/3666-1114, www.pousadaventoverde. com. br, R$260-560 d), whose chalets (which range in size and price) are set along a steep mountainside with magnificent views overlooking

the valley toward the Pedra do Baú. Bonuses include pine cones for the fireplace and tap water served by a natural spring. Farther along the same road, the utterly charming **Pousada Quinta dos Pinhais** (Estrada do Pico Agudo, tel. 12/3666-2030, www. quintadospinhais.com.br, R$560-1,200 d) shares similarly breathtaking views, which can be contemplated from your room's private wooden jetted tub, the lounge chairs surrounding the pool, or the rambling gardens and fruit orchards. Lavish breakfasts are served anywhere on the grounds.

An atmospherically rustic restaurant with a thatched roof, **Santa Truta** (Av. Antônio Joaquim de Oliveira 267, tel. 12/3666-2764, statruta.com.br, noon-6pm Mon.-Thurs., noon-midnight Fri.-Sat., noon-10pm Sun., R$25-35) does justice to the region's favorite fish with mouthwatering recipes such as trout in Roquefort sauce with sautéed potatoes or trout with almond risotto in a red grape sauce. Right in the center of town, **Canto da Gula** (Av. Ministro Nelson Hungria 328, tel. 12/3666-1312, www.cantodagula.com. br, noon-4pm and 7:30pm-11:30pm Thurs.-Sun. and daily in July, R$20-30) is a cozy little jazz-infused bistro with an eclectic menu that runs the gamut from pastas and myriad trout dishes to house specialties such as salmon stroganoff.

Transportation and Services

For information about Santo Antônio (in Portuguese), visit the **Tourist Information Center** (12/3666-2595) located at the entrance of town; make sure to pick up the Caminho das Artes map, which indicates ateliers of local artisans and craftspeople that can be visited. **Pássaro Marron** (tel. 0800/285-3047, www. passaromarron.com.br) buses make three daily trips from Campos de Jordão to Santo Antônio (30 minutes, R$6) and two from São Paulo's Tietê terminal (2.5 hours, R$31). Santo Antônio is only 20 kilometers (12.5 mi) from Campos by car.

Serra do Mar

Traveling east, in the direction of Rio de Janeiro, lies the Serra do Mar. Covered with increasingly rare native Atlantic forest, the mountain range spans the northern coast of São Paulo state and the southern coast of the state of Rio de Janeiro. Surprisingly isolated, this region is sprinkled with towns that have remained largely untouched by time. The main draw, however, is the countryside itself—hikers, climbers, rafters, and waterfall junkies will not be disappointed. The Parque Nacional da Serra da Bocaina, a patch of native Atlantic forest with numerous cascades and hiking trails, is the highlight for outdoor enthusiasts.

SÃO LUÍS DO PARAITINGA

Nestled in the mountains, São Luís is a colonial town that has preserved its many handsome 18th- and 19th-century mansions and churches as well as the popular traditions of the Vale do Paraíba. Although flooding in early 2010 wreaked havoc on the town, renovations continue to recuperate damaged buildings. This valley was an important passageway for São Paulo's *bandeirantes* as they forged their way north to Minas Gerais. Later, São Luís emerged as an important trading post for *tropeiros*—roving merchants who carried supplies to and from São Paulo and the wild frontier towns of the interior. The crops that supplied sustenance—*feijão*, manioc, corn, and sugar (distilled into fine *cachaças*)— were instrumental in the development of the town as well as the elaboration of a robust *tropeiro* "cuisine," which is still very alive today.

Parque Estadual da Serra do Mar

São Luís is within the boundaries of the vast Parque Estadual da Serra do Mar, a nature preserve that encompasses 17,000 hectares (42,000 acres) of native Atlantic forest dotted with rivers, waterfalls, and natural pools. The **Núcleo Santa Virgínia** (Rodovia Osvaldo Cruz Km 78, tel. 12/3671-9266, 8am-5pm Tues.-Sun.)—located 36 kilometers (23 mi) from São Luís—administers the area of the park around São Luís leading all the way to Ubatuba on the coast and offers guides to the handful of hiking trails. The three main trails range 5.5-14 kilometers (3.5-9 mi) in length; advance reservations of one week are necessary.

Cia de Rafting (tel. 12/3671-2665, www.ciaderafting.com.br) operates rafting and kayaking trips down the Rio Paraibuna (4-6 hours, R$80-205) as well as hiking and horseback eco-excursions (2 hours, R$60).

Festivals and Events

São Luís is famous throughout Brazil for its traditional street **Carnaval.** Instead of the fervent rhythms of samba and *frevo* (banned by official decree), you'll hear only old-fashioned *marchinhas* (marching band songs) that recall Carnavals of yesteryear. With gigantic papier-mâchê dolls, festive decorations, and colorfully costumed residents organized into *blocos,* the atmosphere is festive without being out of control.

Held 40 days after Easter, the **Festa do Dívino Espírito Santo** includes a weeklong celebration involving traditional music, processions, fireworks, and public feasting. If you're planning on visiting during either of these festivals, you'll need to book a hotel months in advance, or hope you can luck into a local room last-minute.

Accommodations and Food

One of the nicest options in town is the **Pousada Vila Verde** (Rua Benfica 63, tel. 12/3671-1720, www.vilaverdeparaitinga.com.br, R$160-200 d). Large, attractively furnished rooms occupy a faux-colonial cluster of pastel-painted houses surrounded by gardens.

A *tropeiro* legacy, the local culinary specialty is *afogado,* a none-too-lean stew of beef and pork cooked over a low flame with cumin, parsley, and onions. It's served with a generous dusting of manioc flour as well as a shot or two of local *cachaça.* You'll find this dish at many restaurants in town, among them the cheery **Cantinho dos Amigos** (Rua Coronel Domingues de Castro 121, tel. 12/3671-1466, www.cantinhodosamigos. com.br, 11am-10pm Mon.-Thurs., 11am-midnight Fri.-Sun., R$20-30), which specializes in home-cooked regional fare as well as pizzas baked in a wood-burning oven. Occupying a colorful old house owned by a local musician, **Tempero da Terra** (Rua Coronel Domingues de Castro 178, tel. 12/3671-1574, 11am-4pm and 6pm-9pm Mon.-Fri., 11am-midnight Sat., 11am-6pm Sun., R$20-25) is known for its appetizing local fare and weekend music jams.

Transportation and Services
Paraitinga Turismo (tel. 12/3671-1179, www.paraitinga.com.br), across the street from the bus station, has maps and information about the town and region and organizes outings. You can also check out www.saoluizdoparaitinga.sp.gov.br.

São Luís do Paraitinga is 180 kilometers (112 mi) from São Paulo. From Tietê bus station, **Pássaro Marron** (tel. 11/3775-3856, www.passaromarron.com.br) operates hourly buses to Taubaté (2.5 hours, R$31), where you can hop a **São José** bus (tel. 12/3132-3666), with eight departures daily, to São Luís (1 hour, R$12). If you're driving, take BR-116 to Taubaté and then turn off onto Rodovia Dr. Oswaldo Cruz (SP-125). If you're arriving from the coast, the town is only 42 kilometers (26 mi) inland from Ubatuba. The travel time to São Luís do Paraitinga from São Paulo is roughly 2.5 hours by car.

★ BANANAL
Lying at the foot of the Serra da Bocaina mountain range, this seductive colonial town was a major hub during the coffee boom that swept through São Paulo state in the 19th century. An architectural gem, the town's elegant squares and *solares* (mansions) are still intact, as are the surrounding plantations built by the region's coffee barons.

Sights
CENTRO HISTÓRICO
Bananal's main square is the elegant, tree-shaded Praça Pedro Ramos. Perched on the square, the early 19th-century **Igreja de Matriz** is simple but picturesque. Nearby, the **Pharmácia Popular** (Rua Manuel de Aguiar 156) lays claim to being Brazil's oldest pharmacy; inside, little has changed since it was founded in 1830 by a French chemist. The polished pine shelves and cabinets are stuffed with wonderful old porcelain and glass vials containing bromides, remedies, powdered blood, and morphine.

Jarringly out of place is the European-style **Estação de Estrada de Ferro** (Praça Dona Domiciana), an abandoned train station built in 1889 that now houses the municipal library. Beside the station is a mildly rusting steam train from the same era.

COFFEE *FAZENDAS*
During the 1850s, Bananal was the world's primary producer of coffee, and the hills surrounding the town are still dotted with grand plantation mansions, although the coffee has given way to eucalyptus. Within close proximity to the town, several of these *fazendas* (estates) can be visited, although you must reserve by phone in advance.

Built in 1855, **Fazenda dos Coqueiros** (Rodovia dos Tropeiros km 309, tel. 12/3116-1358, www.fazendadoscoqueiros.com. br, R$6)—named after the swaying coconut palms that lead up to the gracious main house—is 5 kilometers (3 mi) from Bananal. The *fazenda* has been in the family of the friendly Carioca owners for over a century—their life amid the original furnishings brings history to life. And there is a lot of history: from the original fixtures (including an antique toilet) to more harrowing effects, such as the dungeon-like *senzala* where slaves were herded at night.

The region's most opulent estate is the elegant **Fazenda do Resgate** (SP-064 km 324, tel. 12/3116-1577, www.fazendaresgate. com.br, 8am-noon Tues., 8am-4pm Wed.-Fri., R$10), 8 kilometers (5 mi) from Bananal. Built in 1818, the interior features splendid murals painted by noted Spanish painter José Maria Villaronga as well as a chapel. The *fazenda* was the first plantation in São Paulo to cultivate coffee on a large scale. At its most productive the owner, Manual de Aguiar Valim, was among the richest men in Brazil.

CHÁCARA SANTA INÊZ
A 20-minute walk from the center of Bananal will bring you to the **Chácara Santa Inêz** (Av. João Barbosa de Camargo 1494, tel. 12/3116-1591, www.chacarasantainez.com. br, 9am-6pm daily, advance reservations advised), where Engels Maciel, a German chemist, distills some of the most ambrosial *cachaça* in the country. *Cachaça* has a long history in the region; before turning to coffee, 18th-century planters cultivated sugar. Its precious by-product, *cachaça,* was not only tippled by the aristocracy of the day but also used to barter for the slaves needed to work the plantations. Using a completely organic process and barrels made with precious Brazilian woods, *cachaça de Minuca* (named for Engels's wife) has won numerous awards. Tour the facility and sample the wares before purchasing some of the homemade organic vinegars, jams, and jellies made by Minuca from fruits planted on the property.

Sports and Recreation
Bananal is nestled amid the Serra da Bocaina, a region of mountains covered in dense Atlantic forest. Exploring the region is difficult without a car or guided excursion. However, you can still get a small taste of what the area has to offer. From town, you can walk through the hills along a 6-kilometer (4-mi) stretch of the Estrada da Turva to the **Recanto da Cachoeira** (tel. 12/3116-5527,

R$8). Privately owned by a local couple, this small patch of tamed wilderness—with the Rio Turva running through it—is open to visitors. After getting a hydromassage in the cascades, you can relax with beer and snacks at a small shaded bar or on a tiny island in the middle of the river.

More impressive waterfalls can only be reached by car. The nearby **Cachoeira da Usina** (Rodovia SP-247 Km 12) is on the premises of the Fazenda Cachoeira. Farther along, the **Cachoeira Sete Quedas** (Rodovia SP-247 Km 15, tel. 12/3116-2008) has natural slides and pools to swim in. Advance reservations are necessary, and after turning off the highway, be prepared for 10 kilometers (6 mi) along a bumpy dirt road. More distant, the **Cachoeira do Bracui** (Rodovia SP-247 Km 38) lies on property belonging to the **Pousada da Terra** (tel. 12/3361-1774, www. pdterra.com.br). A 3.5-kilometer (2-mi) trail leads to a series of five separate falls and magnificent views stretching as far as the bay of Angra dos Reis. The R$25 entrance fee includes a map and lunch.

PARQUE NACIONAL DA SERRA DA BOCAINA
Encompassing much of the Serra da Bocaina, the **Parque Nacional da Serra da Bocaina** (Estrada da Bocaina Km 27, tel. 12/3117-2143, www.icmbio.gov.br/parnaserradabocaina) spans the states of São Paulo and Rio de Janeiro, embracing the coastal towns of Angra, Paraty, and Ubatuba. Although access is difficult (you need a 4WD vehicle) and infrastructure virtually nonexistent, this national park offers more than 100,000 hectares (250,000 acres) of virgin Atlantic forest brimming with wild orchids, hydrangeas, bromeliads, waterfalls, and the chance of catching a glimpse of rare beasts such as the spotted jaguar and *mono-carvoeiro* monkey. The park's entrance is 27 kilometers (17 mi) from the pretty colonial town of **São José do Barreiro,** 45 kilometers (28 mi) from Bananal in the direction of São Paulo.

The best way to visit the park is by

guided tour. Several *pousadas* line the steep dirt road leading to the park. In São José, **MW Trekking** (Rua Siqueira Reis 19, tel. 12/99726-7976, www.mwtrekking.com.br) offers day trips (R$100) that include hiking, with stops for lunch and bathing in waterfalls. For more intrepid souls, the company offers longer trips, such as a three-day trek (R$490) that follows the **Trilha do Ouro** over the hills to the Praia de Mambucaba, a gorgeous beach located between Paraty and Angra. The excursion includes food and lodging supplied by local residents, who offer rooms in their simple homes (without electricity) and home-cooked meals prepared in wood-burning ovens.

Accommodations

On a quiet street in the historical center, the simple **Pousada Amiga** (Rua Leopoldo Carneiro 41, tel. 12/3116-0142, www.pousadaamiga.com, R$160 d) lives up to its name with a friendly reception, homey suites and common rooms, and home-baked breakfasts. For those with wheels, a handful of coffee *fazendas* around Bananal have been converted into reasonably priced hotels. Located 12 kilometers (7.5 mi) from Bananal, **Fazenda Boa Vista** (SP-068 Km 327, tel. 12/3116-1539, www.hotelfazboavista.com.br, R$230-280 d) lies in a forested conservation area ribboned with walking trails that lead to waterfalls. Constructed in 1780, the estate mansion has often been used by TV crews filming period dramas. Guest rooms in the main house and outlying *casas* are rustic but cozy, and kitchens are equipped with wood-burning stoves.

Food

In town, there are several options for honest home-style cooking. **Padaria Paremol** (Rua Manuel de Aguiar 60, tel. 12/3116-1136,

11am-3pm daily, R$15-20) is a retro-style bakery that serves up hearty lunches such as roasted pork with *feijão*, salad, and macaroni. **Restaurante 418** (Praça Pedro Ramos, tel. 12/3116-5418, lunch and dinner daily, R$10-20) is a cozy combination bar and restaurant where all the locals hang out. It's a perfect spot for tasty sandwiches as well as filet mignon and french fries. For al fresco dining, head to the **Restaurante Estação** (Av. Rubem de Melo 53, tel. 12/3116-1391, lunch and dinner daily, R$20-30), facing Bananal's train station. For dessert, try the homemade *doces*—preserved fruits such as green papaya and orange served with a slab of creamy white cheese.

Transportation and Services

For maps and information, visit the local tourist association **Abatur** in the Sobrado Aguilar Vallim (Praça Rubião Júnior 27, tel. 12/3116-1602), which isn't always open, or visit www.bananal.net.br. For information on the entire region, with an emphasis on historical towns, drives, and coffee *fazendas*, the website www.caminhosdocorte.com.br is a great source. If you don't have a car, you can hire taxis to take you to *fazendas* and waterfalls or have Abatur or your *pousada* recommend a local guide.

Bananal is 330 kilometers (205 mi) from São Paulo and 150 kilometers (93 mi) from Rio de Janeiro. From São Paulo's Tietê terminal, **Pássaro Marron** (tel. 11/3775-3856, www.passaromarron.com.br) operates buses departing every 30-60 minutes to Guaratinguetá (2.5 hours, R$42); from here you can catch one of three daily Pássaro Marron buses to Bananal (3.5 hours, R$31). By car from São Paulo, take BR-116 north to Queluz, then SP-068 to Bananal. Travel time is around 3.5 hours. From Rio, take BR-116 to Barra Mansa and follow it to SP-064. Travel time to Bananal from São Paulo is roughly 3.5 hours by car.

Litoral Norte

Although few foreigners are aware of it, São Paulo state boasts one of the most attractive and popular coastlines in Brazil. Known as the Litoral Norte (North Coast), it extends for more than 250 kilometers (155 mi) from Santos, passing through the resort towns of São Sebastião and Ubatuba up to the frontier of Rio de Janeiro state. Natural attractions include beckoning white-sand beaches and majestic mountains covered in dense rain forest. In recent years, the urban development of some of the larger resort towns has taken on a frightening aspect. Fortunately, there are still many smaller towns and isolated beaches where you can get away from it all. During the summer, long weekends, and holidays, the *litoral* is mobbed by millions of Paulistanos fleeing the city. If you visit off-season or during the week, you'll be treated to tranquility at significantly discounted prices.

The Litoral Norte officially begins at Santos, 70 kilometers (43 mi) from São Paulo. The largest maritime port in Latin America, Santos was founded (as São Vicente) in 1545. During the 19th century, it prospered as a result of São Paulo's coffee boom. Its recently restored historical center may hold some interest for fans of 19th-century architecture. Otherwise, the town is best avoided—it's rundown, and the beaches are unappealing. Equally unimpressive is nearby Guarujá, 15 kilometers (9 mi) away. This terrifically crowded and excessively built-up resort town has long been Paulistanos' favorite getaway, despite beaches that are nothing to write home about. Things start to get interesting as you make your way north toward the town of São Sebastião, which is only a boat ride from the island paradise of Ilhabela.

SÃO SEBASTIÃO

When Paulistanos say they are "going to São Sebastião," they're not actually referring to the busy seaside town with the colonial center located 220 kilometers (137 mi) from São Paulo, but to the 100-kilometer (62-mi) expanse of beaches and resort towns around it, included in the municipality of São Sebastião. Very few people visit São Sebastião itself. Despite a pleasant colonial center, the presence of a large oil refinery and lack of good beaches mean that its primary interest is as an access point to the stunning natural beauty of Ilhabela, a 15-minute ferry ride away.

More likely, "going to São Sebastião" means traveling to Maresias, Camburi, Juqueí, or any of the other couple of dozen beaches that precede it along SP-055, the highway linking Santos and Rio de Janeiro. The beaches themselves (most have *pousadas* and restaurants) are incredibly varied. You'll find tiny secluded coves as well as long sweeps of sand lined with fancy vacation homes and stylish bars. While some beaches have calm waters that are ideal for toddlers, others boast awesome waves that seduce surfers. Ultimately, whether you're in search of a family vacation, a flirtation fest, or a relaxing retreat, you'll likely find what you're looking for.

Beaches

Traveling east from Santos and Guarujá along the coast toward São Sebastião, after about 65 kilometers (40 mi) you'll reach **Barra da Una,** the first beach of interest and a major nautical center. Only 3 kilometers (2 mi) west of Barra da Una is secluded **Juréia,** backed by exuberant vegetation and blessed with a bewitchingly green sea. Farther along, **Juqueí**'s wide sandy beaches and calm waters are popular with families, as is the horseshoe-shaped **Praia da Barra do Saí.** The supertrendy beautiful beaches of **Camburi** and **Camburizinho** are magnets for a toned and tanned crowd.

If you're young, on the loose, and looking for even more action, avoid the excessively overdeveloped **Boiçucanga** and continue east until you hit **Maresias**. Big swells attract surfers, but a dangerous current makes bathing risky (although the blue-green sea is certainly seductive). Maresias's wild nightlife, with multiple bars and discos, mirrors its ocean. Another 5 kilometers (3 mi) east, **Santiago** is much more tranquil, as are neighboring **Toque-Toque Pequeno,** a quiet little fishing town with a relaxed vibe and view of the setting sun, and **Toque-Toque Grande.** Both Toque-Toques offer beckoning sands and good snorkeling. Hidden between them is the tiny, wild, and quite deserted **Praia de Calhetas.**

Sports and Recreation

To explore the islands off the coast, take a half-day schooner trip with **Green Way** (Av. Mãe Bernarda 2332, Juqueí, tel. 12/3863-2422, www.greenway.com.br), an operator specializing in ecotourism. Departing from Barra da Una, trips (minimum four people, R$150-250) include stops for diving and swimming. Equipment and snacks are included. Green Way offers kayak trips on the Rio Una (R$70 pp) as well as hiking, biking, and Jeep excursions into the native Atlantic forest. It also offers surfing and stand-up paddle classes (R$100 per hour).

Nightlife

Sirena (Rua Sebastião Romeo César, Maresias, tel. 12/3077-0020, www.sirena.com. br, 10pm-7am Fri.-Sat., daily summer cover R$80-160) bills itself as the best club in Brazil and regularly features some of the top DJs on the international circuit. Its phenomenal fame reels in beautiful young revelers from all over São Paulo state seduced by the electronic music and casual beach vibe. Its most serious rival is **Galeão** (Estrada de Camburi 79, Camburi, tel. 12/3865-1515, www.ogaleao. com.br, 10pm-6am Fri.-Sat. daily summer, cover R$30-50). Although it's not as hip as it once was, you'll hear a more eclectic mix of electronica, funk, and hip-hop.

Accommodations

Accommodations along this coast are not cheap, especially in the summer, when most places have a two- to three-night minimum. You'll find the greatest concentration of hotels in Juqueí, Camburi, Camburizinho, Boiçucanga, and Maresias, with the latter two offering the widest selection in terms of quality and price. If you're looking for something more affordable, try São Sebastião itself.

In São Sebastião, a great bargain is the simple but utterly charming ★ **Pousada da Ana**

Toque-Toque beach near São Sebastião

Doce (Rua Expedicionário Brasileiro 196, São Sebastião, tel. 12/3892-1615, www.pousadaanadoce.com.br, R$160-200 d), which occupies a colorful old house in São Sebastião's historical center. The owners are welcoming, and the small but quaint guest rooms feature verandas overlooking a tropical internal garden.

Pousada Porto Mare (Rua Sebastião Romão César 400, Maresias, tel. 12/3865-5272, www.pousadaportomare.com.br, R$290-480 d) is a welcome addition to Maresias's sometimes less-than-inspiring choice of hotels. The large garden featuring a pool and sauna offers respite, as do the modern, nicely appointed guest rooms.

On beautiful Praia da Barra do Saí, **Pousada da Foca** (tel. 12/3863-6880, www.pousadadafoca.com.br, R$280-460 d) has comfortable, attractively decorated guest rooms (including a few with mezzanines for families or groups). The bar serves drinks on the beach, as well as around a lovely pool overlooking a thick patch of rain forest.

Wonderfully secluded, the spacious and tastefully appointed bungalows at ★ **Ilha de Toque Toque Boutique Hotel** (Rod. Rio-Santos 1285, km 143.5, tel. 12/3864-9110, www.ilhadetoquetoque.com.br, R$420-630 d) are built into a lush hillside overlooking Praia Toque-Toque Grande, with access to Praia de Calhetas as well. Rambling grounds boast a pool, a hot tub, and patios. A launch takes small groups snorkeling and diving. The owners also rent out simple chalets nearby, ideal for small groups in the mood for a housekeeping holiday (although a car is necessary).

The spa is not the only antistress tonic you'll encounter at the alluring **Villa Bebek** (Rua Zezito 251, Camburizinho, tel. 12/3865-3320, www.villabebek.com.br, R$370-690 d), located on hip Camburizinho beach. The prettily decorated bungalow rooms are soothing enough, as are the landscaped gardens. However, the real treat is stepping out of your room and into the courtyard swimming pool shaped like a long, curvy river—a distraction so enticing you may be hard-pressed to make it to the beach.

Food

The best restaurants along the coast are concentrated in Camburi (sophisticated and pricy) and Juqueí (more casual and beachy). Dining at **Manacá** (Rua do Manacá 102, Camburizinho, tel. 12/3865-1566, www.restaurantemanaca.com.br, 6pm-11pm Thurs., 1pm-11pm Fri.-Sat., 1pm-9pm Sun., R$65-80) will put a dent in your budget, but you'll be

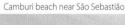
Camburi beach near São Sebastião

well rewarded with creatively refined dishes such as shrimp in a ginger tangerine sauce with wasabi. Equally seductive is the ambiance—built on stilts in the midst of tropical forest, the restaurant resembles an elegant tree house. Advance reservations are a must. Somewhat surprisingly, Maresias is rather bereft of good eating options. However, for great pizza, head to **A Firma** (Rua Sebastião Romão César 419, tel. 12/3865-6142, 7pm-midnight Thurs. and Sun.-Mon., 7pm-2am Fri.-Sat., R$25-35).

To keep costs down while soaking up the sun, beach *barracas* are the way to go. In Maresias, **Barraca do Alê** (Praia de Maresias 26 km, 10pm-6pm Sat.-Sun. and daily Jan.-Feb.) is a magnet for bronzed and buffed youths who swear by the healthy salmon wraps with yogurt and ginger. In Camburi, **Barraca do Alê** (Praia de Camburi 38 km, 9pm-6pm Sat.-Sun. and 9pm-8pm daily Jan.-Feb.) is famed for its savory tortes filled with shrimp, palm hearts, and zucchini.

For those passing through, **Atobá** (Praça Major João Fernandes 210, tel. 12/3892-4748 11pm-4:30pm daily, R$20-30) is a superior self-service buffet occupying a secular mansion in the colonial center.

Transportation and Services

In São Sebastião, the **tourist office** (Rua Altino Arantes 174, tel. 12/3892-2620, www.turismo.saosebastiao.sp.gov.br, 9am-8pm daily) offers information on the entire coastline.

From São Paulo's Tietê terminal, **Litorânea** (tel. 11/3775-3856, www.passaromarron.com.br) operates daily buses departing every two hours, from 6am-9:30pm daily, for São Sebastião's centrally located *rodoviária* (Praça da Amizade 10, tel. 12/3892-1072). The 3.5-hour trip costs R$50. If you're driving from São Paulo, take the Rodovia Aryton Senna (SP-070) to the São José dos Campos turnoff, then the Rodovia Tamoios (SP-099), followed by the Rio-Santos highway (SP-055), which leads to São Sebastião. For the southernmost beaches

(Juqueí onward), instead of the Tamoios, take the Rodovia Mogi-Bertioga (SP-098) to the Rio-Santos. You will pass all the other beaches along the way. Travel time is roughly three hours.

If you don't have a car, it's quite easy to go up and down the coast between São Sebastião and Barra do Una by flagging down the bright yellow buses, operated by **Eco-bus** (tel. 0800/771-0507, www.ecobus.com.br), that regularly travel up and down the Rio-Santos.

★ ILHABELA

Brazil's largest off-coast island is only a 15-minute ferryboat ride from São Sebastião. Once you're there, it's utter relaxation all the way (provided you're armed with mosquito repellent—85 percent of the volcanic island is covered in damp virgin Atlantic forest, and extremely annoying bloodsuckers called *borrachudos* are usually out in full force). With dozens of beaches, more than 300 waterfalls, and constant breezes (which make the surrounding waters a sailor's and windsurfer's dream), the island is a magnet for every kind of nature enthusiast, ranging from hikers and deep-sea divers to indolent, hammock-swinging, Robinson Crusoe types. It also draws a fair amount of fancy folk from São Paulo—many of whom have luxurious villas tucked away on beaches, along with private piers and helicopter pads. This explains the high number of eco-chic hotels and gourmet restaurants as well as the somewhat high prices. Things get especially astronomical on holiday weekends and in January, and it gets crowded, with traffic jams on the island's main coastal road.

Vila Ilhabela

The island's main settlement is the pretty little town of Vila Ilhabela. It is located on the sheltered west coast of the island, a 20-minute drive north from the ferry dock. Aside from a small (fairly touristy) commercial center, the town has some attractive vestiges of its colonial past, including the charming whitewashed **Igreja Matriz.** Several kilometers before the entrance to town, on the

Ilhabela

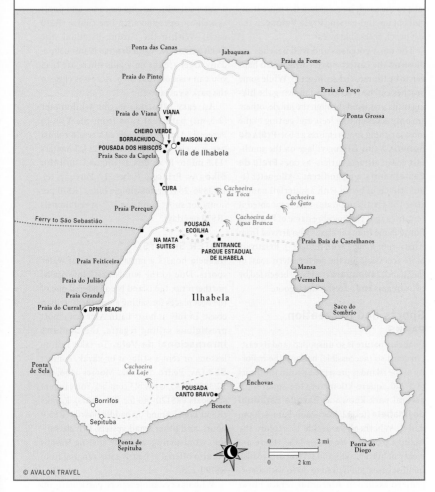

© AVALON TRAVEL

way to the ferry, is an impressive 18th-century mansion belonging to the **Fazenda Engenho d'Agua,** one of the most important of Ilhabela's many former sugar plantations. This history of cane cultivation explains the fine *cachaças* on the island.

Beaches

Ilhabela has no shortage of stunning beaches. Those on the west coast facing São Sebastião have calmer waters, but they are also smaller and often more crowded; they are easily reached by car, as well as municipal bus. A road extends along the western coast from **Porto do Frade** in the south to **Ponta das Canas** at the northern tip, where strong breezes attract windsurfers and kite surfers.

South from Ponta das Canas, among the nicest beaches are tiny **Praia do Viana, Feiticeira,** and **Praia do Julião;** all are relatively tranquil and popular with families. The young and restless tend to congregate on

Praia do Curral, known for its restaurants, bars, and nightly *festas* where DJs and dancers take to the sand. Its neighbor, the more tranquil but up-and-coming **Praia Veloso,** is the last beach accessible by car.

The most gorgeous and wild beaches are those on the eastern coast—which also happen to be the most tricky to get to. While some beaches can be reached by following the hiking trails that wind through the jungle, others are only accessible by Jeep, and getting to the most far-flung spots requires a boat. **Praia do Bonete,** a tiny fishing village on the southeast coast, attracts surfers, as does **Praia de Castelhanos,** a magnificent 2-kilometer (1-mi) stretch of beach with a waterfall named after the Castilian pirates that frequented it centuries ago. The macabre name of **Praia da Fome** came from the slaves who arrived from Africa *com fome* ("with hunger"). Relatively more accessible, on the northeastern coast of the island, **Jabaquara** is a lovely beach fed by two streams and a freshwater lagoon.

Sports and Recreation
PARKS
Ilhabela's nature is so unspoiled (and its eastern coast so inaccessible) because the majority of the island is preserved within the limits of a 270-square-kilometer (104-square-mi) natural park known as **Parque Estadual de Ilhabela** (tel. 12/3896-2660, 9am-4:30pm daily). Whether you decide to explore the island's treasures by sea or land (there are plenty of hiking trails and several dirt roads), in most cases you'll need to do so with an organized excursion. **Maremar** (Praça Elivar Storace 12, Pequeá, tel. 12/3896-1418, www.maremar.tur.br) offers boat, Jeep, and trekking tours around the island for R$60-150. Among the most popular trips are a bumpy Jeep ride across the park to beautiful Praia de Castelhanos, trekking to **Cachoeira da Laje,** a spectacular waterfall near Praia do Bonete, and climbing up the **Pico do Baepi,** a difficult three-hour ascent with incredible views of the mountainous mainland.

To explore on your own, hike 3-kilometers

(2-mi) inland from Praia de Feiticeira to **Cachoeira da Toca** (8am-5pm daily, R$10), a waterfall with various cascades and pools as well as ropes and a zip-line course (R$10 each). Within the Parque Estadual, the **Cachoeiras da Água Branca** (9am-4:30pm daily, free) are the only falls (there are five) you can visit on your own. Access is close to the park's entrance.

An easy bike ride is the 4-kilometer (2.5-mi) path that runs from the Vila to Perequê. Ambitious souls can rent a robust two-wheeler and venture the 22 kilometers (13.5 mi) to Praia de Castelhanos. **Juninho Bike** (Av. Princesa Isabel 217, Perequê, tel. 12/3896-2847) rents simple bikes (R$10 per hour) for short jaunts and 27-speed models (R$70 per day).

WATER SPORTS
Ilhabela boasts a fantastic array of water sports. Due to the winds that blow off its northern tip, the island is considered one of the best places for sailing along the Brazilian coast. In July, it hosts Latin America's most prestigious sailing regatta, the **Semana Internacional da Vela.** To take sailing lessons or rent a sailboat or kayak, contact **BL3** (Av. Pedro de Paula Moraes 1166, tel. 12/3896-5885, www.bl3.com.br). You can rent sailboats (R$120-140 for five hours), kayaks (R$30/hour), stand up paddle boards (R$50/hour), and other small vessels. Private sailing, windsurfing, and kite surfing lessons are also offered at hourly rates ranging from R$190-225.

With its crystalline waters, particularly off the east coast, Ilhabela boasts excellent diving and snorkeling opportunities. Beginners can get their feet wet at the **Reserva Marinha da Ilha das Cabras,** an island off Perequê, where you can view coral, anemones, and a parade of colorful fish or explore the handful of sunken ships. **Colonial Diver** (Av. Brasil 1751, Pedra Miúdas, tel. 12/3894-9459, www.colonialdiver.com.br) offers diving lessons and excursions and rents equipment. A two-hour dive for beginners costs R$230.

Accommodations

Ilhabela is one of the most expensive places to stay along the Litoral Norte, especially in the summer (when reservations are essential and minimum stays are required). Although stylish eco-chic guesthouses are a dime a dozen, budget bungalows are harder to come by. The vast majority of lodgings are in Vila Ilhabela, but there are an increasing number of options along the entire western coast of the island. Of good value in Vila is the charming **Pousada dos Hibiscos** (Av. Pedro de Paula Moraes 720, tel. 12/3896-1375, www.pousadadoshibiscos.com.br, R$185-240 d), whose jungly internal courtyard features a bar, pool, sauna, and bursts of flowers. Guest rooms are standard but pleasant whitewashed affairs with dark wood furniture, tile floors, and whirling ceiling fans.

A brisk walk from the center of town is a patch of rain forest domesticated by Tom and Silvia, the welcoming British/Brazilian couple who operate **Na Mata Suites** (Rua Benedicto Mariano Leite 167, Barra Velha, tel. 12/3896-8020, www.namatasuites.com.br, R$180-280 d). A quartet of lovely bungalows features comfy beds and hammocked decks, one with a kitchen.

If well-equipped with bug spray, hard-core jungle enthusiasts will adore the **Pousada Ecoilha** (Rua Benedito Garcêz 164, Água Branca, tel. 12/3896-3098, www.ecoilha.com.br, R$160-190 d), on the edge of the Parque Estadual de Ilhabela, just off the road leading to Praia de Castelhanos. Bird calls provide a constant soundtrack, while the backdrop includes views of the Pico do Baepi. Simple guest rooms have verandas and hammocks, and there is a nice pool for cooling off. It's no exaggeration to say that ★ **Maison Joly** (Rua Antônio Lisboa Alves 278, tel. 12/3896-1201, www.maisonjoly.com.br, R$450-670 d) is fit for royalty. Built right into a hilltop overlooking Vila Ilhabela, this exclusive luxury guesthouse has hosted everyone from the Swedish monarchy to the Rolling Stones. With a certain Italian Riviera flavor, the individually furnished bungalows are understated yet refined and boast private verandas overlooking the sea. Amenities include a classy piano bar, a "Zen" space, an Anti-Jet Lag Spa, and a romantic restaurant serving delicious Mediterranean-inspired cuisine.

Ilhabela's grooviest hotel is **DPNY Beach** (Av. José Pacheco de Nascimento 7668, Praia do Curral, tel. 12/3894-3000, www.dpny-beach.com.br, R$620-990 d) on trendy Praia do Curral. Almost overly designed, the guest rooms, in various sizes, boast richly colored walls, zebra motifs, and mosaic tiles made by the staff. The beds are king-size, TV screens are plasma, and everybody gets an iPod (laptops are available at the bar). For privacy, request a *casa caiçara,* renovated fishermens's bungalows sheltered beneath a forest of palms. Also take a look at the many off-season promotions and packages. An island hot spot, the hotel's private **Hippie Chic** beach club doubles as a lounge where house music plays day and night (day rates include lunch, drinks, and use of the fabulous spa). The contemporary restaurant, **Tróia,** has one of the most inventive kitchens on the island.

For splendid isolation (minus some creature comforts), head to the other side of the island (4 hours by foot or 1 hour by boat). Checking into **Pousada Canto Bravo** (tel. 12/3896-5111, www.pousadacantobravo.com.br, R$140-360 d) gives you private access to the island's most stunning beach, **Praia Bonete,** as well as surrounding nature. Accommodations can best be described as primitive chic. Leave your gadgets at home; there's no electricity (although a solar generator supplies essentials).

Food

Restaurants on Ilhabela are not cheap, although you can always spend the day nibbling at *barraca* fare on the beaches. Vila Ilhabela has a few *lanchonetes* and some scenic bars along the waterfront, where you can fill up on *petiscos* and ice-cold beer. **Cheiro Verde** (Rua da Padroeira 109, tel. 12/3896-3245, www.cheiroverdeilhabela.com.br, 11:30pm-5pm Mon. and Wed.-Thurs., 11:30am-11pm

Fri.-Sun. and daily Dec.-March and July, R$15-25) offers honest home-cooking for great prices. The lunchtime PFs (*pratos feitos*)—consisting of a choice of fish, shrimp, squid, chicken, or beef with *feijão*, fries, and salad—inspire lines during high season. For lunch, a decent inexpensive option is **Cura** (Rua Princesa Isabel 337, tel. 12/3896-1311, 11am-4pm Mon.-Fri., 11am-6pm Sat.-Sun. and Jan., R$15-25), which lays out a tasty and varied self-service buffet.

Popular with local residents is 50-year-old **Viana** (Av. Leonardo Reale 1560, Praia do Viana, tel. 12/3896-1089, www.viana.com.br, 1pm-6pm Mon.-Thurs., 1pm-11:30pm Fri.-Sun.; open daily July and Dec.-Feb. R$40-60), where you can eat inside or right on the sand while watching the sunset. The menu features fresh fish and seafood cooked with Brazilian seasoning and flair. The main attractions are *camarão* with mango risotto and Bahian-style *moqueca*.

In Vila Ilhabela, satisfy beer cravings at **Borrachudo** (Rua Dr. Carvalho 20, tel. 12/3896-1499, www.borrachudo.com.br, 4pm-12:30am Tues.-Thurs., 4pm-2am Fri.-Sun., and daily Dec.-Feb.), a perennially cool bar where a giant iron sculpture of the dreaded island insect guards the entrance. More than 100 brands of brew are accompanied by exotic sandwiches and burgers, including salmon and ostrich. Satisfy ice cream cravings with a cone or *picolé* (popsicle) at **Sorveteria Rocha** (Rua São Benedito 23/31, tel. 12/3896-1793, www.sorveteriarocha.com.br, 9am-1am Sat.-Sun., daily Dec.-Feb.), whose factory in São Sebastião has been churning out fantastic, flavor-packed ice cream since 1948.

Transportation and Services

At the ferry landing in Barra Velha there is a **Posto de Turismo** (Praça Vereador José Leite dos Passos 14, tel. 12/3895-7220, www.ilhabela.sp.gov.br/turismo, 9am-6pm Mon.-Fri., 10am-4pm Sat., 10am-2pm Sun.), where you can pick up detailed maps of the island. Check out the beaches yourself at photo-laden websites such as www.ilhabela.com.br.

Balsas (ferries; tel. 0800/773-3711, www.dersa.sp.gov.br, pedestrians free, cars R$14 weekdays, R$21 weekends) make the 20-minute crossing from São Sebastião to Ilhabela every half hour 6am-midnight, and hourly midnight-6am. There's no fee back to the mainland aside from a R$5 environmental tax. It's possible to reserve your crossing in advance, but it will cost you R$48 (to the island) and R$34.50 (to São Sebastião). If you rent a car on the mainland, it will give you great mobility on the island, but be aware that traffic lineups are insane on weekends and in summer. From the ferry terminal in Barra Velha, municipal buses (R$2.70) leave regularly for Vila Ilhabela and Praia do Curral.

UBATUBA

Nearing the state of Rio de Janeiro, Ubatuba and its surrounding coastline offer some of southern Brazil's most varied and attractive sand beaches in one of Brazil's largest remaining areas of native Atlantic rain forest. Like many towns along this coast, Ubatuba rocks hard during the summer months, when it is invaded by vacationing Paulistanos and Cariocas, then settles down during the rest of the year.

As is the case with São Sebastião, when Brazilians talk about going to "Ubatuba," they are actually referring less to the town than to the surrounding 90 kilometers (56 mi) of coastline that stretches along the Rio-Santos highway from Praia da Figueira to Camburi.

The town of Ubatuba holds few attractions other than the local branch of the **Projeto Tamar** (Rua Antônio Athanasio da Silva 273, Itaguá, tel. 12/3832-6202, www.projetotamar.com.br, 10am-6pm Sun.-Tues. and Thurs., 10am-8pm Fri.-Sat., daily Dec.-Feb. and July, R$12), a refuge and study center for Brazil's endangered species of sea turtles that will especially appeal to curious kids.

Beaches

Ubatuba's beaches pale in comparison to the more unspoiled sheltered coves and sandy expanses north and south of town. The majority are easily accessible by car and municipal buses as well as by boat.

Going south from Ubatuba, the initial stretch of coastline is fairly built up and gets quite crowded in the summer. Things only begin to get more interesting 15 kilometers (9 mi) from town as you arrive at tiny **Praia da Sununga,** whose big waves attract surfers. Here you can also see the legendary **Gruta que Chora,** a cavern where trickling water gives the illusion that the walls are "crying." Adjacent **Praia do Lázaro**'s placid waters are a favorite with families, while **Domingas Dias,** the next beach over and accessible on foot, is a beckoning cove with soft, sugary sand. Fronting a condo complex 24 kilometers (15 mi) south of Ubatuba, **Vermelha do Sul** is a well-preserved beach with reddish sands that is popular with water-sports enthusiasts.

Farther south, the beaches are even more pristine, although access is more difficult. From Vermelha do Sul, a sinuous road leads to the lovely **Praia da Fortaleza,** where there are only a few hotels, restaurants, and summer homes. A 40-minute walk away is the beautifully deserted **Praia do Cedro,** where the ocean is transparent and you can float in natural pools.

The beaches to the north of Ubatuba are generally less developed—and even more seductively wild—than those to the south. Some 15 kilometers (9 mi) north of Ubatuba, **Itamambuca** is a surfer's mecca whose *barracas* are always crowded. A more tranquil surfing spot is neighboring **Praia do Félix,** where forested mountains come right down to the sea. Farther north, **Praia do Prumirim** and **Praia de Puruba** are beautiful beaches where you can bathe in waterfalls and rivers as well as the sea. **Ubatumirim** boasts a long stretch of hard-packed sand that is ideal for walking to the secluded **Praia da Justa.**

Farther north, a scenic 30-minute walk from busy Praia da Almada brings you to idyllic **Brava da Almada,** which is part of the Parque Estadual da Serra do Mar. The coastal headquarters of the park are at nearby **Praia da Fazenda,** a lovely beach where you can swim in rivers and the sea. Bordering on the state of Rio are **Picinguaba,** a picturesque fishing village, and **Camburi,** a seductively wild beach whose only signs of civilization are a few primitive *barracas.*

Sports and Recreation

The beaches and rain forest surrounding Ubatuba are preserved within the coastal boundaries of the **Parque Estadual da Serra do Mar,** which has headquarters at the **Núcleo Picinguaba** (BR-101 Km 11, Praia da Fazenda, tel. 12/3832-9011, 8am-5pm daily), 40 kilometers (25 mi) north of Ubatuba. To explore the park—with its myriad cascades, rivers, hummingbirds, and rare orchids—you need to get in touch in advance with the **visitors center** (agendamento@gmail.com, 12/99707-2426). Staff can provide you with maps as well as guides that can lead you along the hiking trails that cut through the rain forest; prices vary. One of the most popular activities is to descend the Rio Fazenda in an inflatable dinghy (R$75 for 90 minutes and a minimum of 10 people) with stops for bathing. Home to more than 300 exotically feathered species, the park is also a major destination for birders. For trekking excursions into the park and along the coast, contact the **Associação de Monitores de Ubatuba** (tel. 12/9145-9015) or **Santa Cruz Adventure** (tel. 12/9740-8065).

A compelling feature of Ubatuba's coastline is its many offshore islands. One of the largest, **Ilha Anchieta,** is a short boat ride from the central beaches of Itaguá and Saco da Ribeira. Before becoming a natural park, the island housed a jail where political prisoners whiled away their days during the Vargas years; its ruins are still visible. The island is crisscrossed by trails leading to various deserted beaches, and its clear waters offer great diving. **Mykonos Turismo** (Rua Flamenguinha 17, Praia Saco da Ribeira, tel. 12/3842-0329, www.mykonos.com.br) organizes excursions to Anchieta (with stops at beaches along the way) and to **Ilha do Prumirim,** north of

Ubatuba

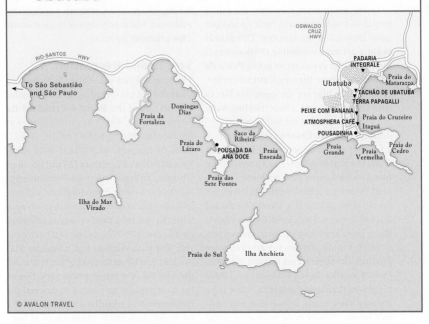

OSWALDO CRUZ HWY

RIO-SANTOS HWY

To São Sebastião and São Paulo

Ubatuba

PADARIA INTEGRALE

Praia do Matarazzo

TACHÃO DE UBATUBA

TERRA PAPAGALLI

PEIXE COM BANANA

ATMOSPHERA CAFÉ

POUSADINHA

Praia do Cruzeiro

Itaguá

Domingas Dias

Praia da Fortaleza

Saco da Ribeira

Praia do Lázaro

POUSADA DA ANA DOCE

Praia Enseada

Praia Grande

Praia Vermelha

Praia do Cedro

Praia das Sete Fontes

Ilha do Mar Virado

Praia do Sul

Ilha Anchieta

© AVALON TRAVEL

Ubatuba, for around R$60 pp. **Omnimare** (Rua Guaicurus 30, Itaguá, tel. 12/3832-2005, www.omnimare.com.br) offers diving courses as well as six-hour diving excursions (R$220) to Anchieta and other islands.

Accommodations

The hotels in and around Ubatuba are generally more affordable than those in other resorts along the Litoral Norte. Without a car, you run the risk of being confined to your own pre-chosen paradise, unless you opt to stay in Centro.

For bargain-seekers, **Pousadinha** (Rua Guarani 536, Itaguá, Ubatuba, www.ubatuba.com.br/pousadinha, tel. 12/3832-2136, R$90-140 d) is a convenient option in the center of town. Basic but clean guest rooms occupy an appealing old villa whose exterior is painted a bright shade of watermelon pink. Groups or families of four can rent chalets with fully equipped kitchens. A culinary bonus is **Spaghetto** (lunch and dinner daily,

R$30-40), a seafood and Italian restaurant located on the main floor.

South of town, **Pousada da Ana Doce** (Travessa JK 54, Praia do Lázaro, tel. 12/3842-0102, www.pousadaanadoce.com.br, R$160-200 d) is a pretty, intimate, and comfortable choice with a pool and nine guest rooms that each house up to four people. The *pousada* has kayaks and sailboats available for guest use.

North of Ubatuba, Praia Itamambuca specializes in back-to-nature lodgings for a clientele more intent on chasing perfect waves than admiring hotel decor. One of the more pleasant affordable options, **Pousada Canto de Itamambuca** (Rua Manoel Soares da Silva 1060, tel. 12/3845-3421, www.cantodeitamambuca.com.br, R$190-260 d) offers large, clean, and well-maintained rooms for two, three, and four surfers. Although it's a half-kilometer from the beach, there's a decent pool for lounging.

More remote **Casa Milá** (Rod. BR-101 km. 34, tel. 12/3832-9021, www.casamila.

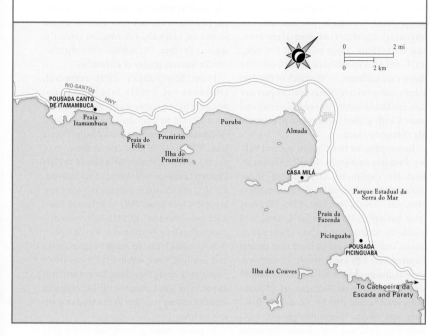

com.br, R$250 d) offers access (via a 1-km trail), to Praia Brava da Almeida, is one of the most sublime beaches along this coast. Towering above the sea are eight well-cared-for, simple, but private suites; all feature decks offering hypnotic views of beaches, mountains, rain forest, and sunsets. Hosts Milá and Rafa can help organize outings and recommend restaurants in the tiny nearby fishing village.

Further north along the coast, the refined ★ **Pousada Picinguaba** (Av. Beira Mar 183, Praia de Picinguaba, tel. 12/3836-9105, www.pousadapicinguaba.com, R$950-2,800 d with dinner) is a favorite getaway of gringos in the know who can live without TVs, phones, or Internet for at least three days (the minimum stay). Accommodations are in a beautiful colonial house and separate villa, both exquisitely decorated. A lush garden, pool, and panoramic views of the placid bay conspire to make real life seem an afterthought. All food, even the morning coffee and cachaça served in creative caipirinhas, is organic and locally sourced.

Food

Ubatuba has lots of casual restaurants where you can gorge on fresh fish and seafood. The local specialty is a dish called *azul-marinho* ("marine blue"). This evocatively named fish stew mixes fresh fish with *bananas-nanicas* (dwarf bananas), which, when cooked in a cast iron pot together with tomatoes, onions, and cilantro, take on an unusual bluish tinge due to oxidization. Served in a clay casserole, the dish is accompanied by *pirão* (a mush of manioc flour mixed with the stew's juices) and pureed banana. In Ubatuba, a good place to sample this and other regional seafood dishes is ★ **Peixe com Banana** (Rua Guarani 255, Praia do Cruzeiro, tel. 12/3832-1712, noon-10pm Mon. and Wed.-Thurs., noon-11pm Fri.-Sun., daily Jan. and July, R$25-40), a casual eatery where generous portions serve at least two people. There's a second location (SP-055 Km 62, tel. 12/3842-1338) at Saco de Ribeira beach. **Terra Papagalli** (Rua Xavantes 537, Itaguá, tel. 12/3832-1488, 6pm-11pm Mon. and Wed.-Thurs., noon-midnight Fri.-Sun., R$30-40) also specializes in seafood. The menu changes based on the catch of the day; simple but inventive dishes such as *pescada* fish cooked in mint-flavored olive oil and served with grilled tomato and mango are big enough to share.

Rumored to be Brazil's first natural bakery, **Padaria Integrale** (Rua Dr. Esteves da Silva 360, Centro, tel. 12/3836-1836, www. padariaintegrale.com.br, 7:30am-8:30pm Mon.-Sat., 7:30am-7pm Sun., R$15-25) offers fresh, healthy, and delicious cakes, tortes, and breads (including divine whole wheat *pão de queijo* and organic cocoa loaf) that can be lingered over in a lovely tropical courtyard. Sweeter cravings can be satiated at **Tachão de Ubatuba** (Rua Javaés 20, Itaguá, tel. 12/3836-1481, www.tachao.com.br, 10am-8pm Sun.-Tues. and Thurs., 10am-midnight Fri.-Sun., daily Dec.-Feb. and July). Savor all-natural local sweets and pastries on the wooden deck with an espresso or take them to go. The house specialty, *doce de bananas,* comes in various guises, such as crystalized and covered with chocolate.

Transportation and Services

The **tourist office** (Av. Iperoig 365, Centro, tel. 12/3833-9123, 8am-4pm daily) is a good source for maps and information about the region's beaches. The website www.ubatuba. com.br features photos of all beaches.

From São Paulo's Tietê terminal, **Litorânea** (tel. 11/3775-3856, www.litoranea.com.br) operates eight daily buses (4 hours, R$60) to Ubatuba's centrally located **Rodoviária Litorânea** (Rua Maria Vitória Jean 381, tel. 12/3832-3622), on the edge of Centro. From the **Rodoviária São José** (Rua Thomas Galhardo 513, Centro), **São José** (tel. 12/3832-6912, www.rodotursaojose.com. br) offers four buses daily to Paraty (1 hour, R$12), while **Útil** (tel. 12/3832-5361, www.util. com.br) has four departures to Rio de Janeiro (5 hours, R$53-73). To reach beaches north and south of town, municipal buses (R$3) pass hourly along Rua Hans Staden and will let you off at stops along the BR-101; note that actually setting your feet in the sand may involve a hike.

If you're driving from São Paulo (235 km/146 mi), take the Rodovia Aryton Senna (SP-070) to the São José dos Campos turnoff, then take the Rodovia Mogi-Bertioga (SP-098) to the Rio-Santos (BR-101/SP-505). Travel time by car is roughly 3.5 hours.

The South

174

Look for ★ to find recommended
sights, activities, dining, and lodging.

Highlights

this environmentally protected island in the Baía de Paranaguá, known for its deserted beaches and rugged, windswept landscapes (page 188).

★ **Iguaçu Falls:** One of the most spectacular natural wonders on the planet, these 275 roaring falls are set against an iridescent backdrop of lush Atlantic rain forest (page 191).

★ **East Coast Beaches of Florianópolis:** Facing the open Atlantic, Santa Catarina's cool island capital's east coast beaches are the island's longest and most dramatic, attracting a crowd of surfers, sand boarders, and hipsters (page 203).

★ **Reserva Biológica Marinha da Ilha do Arvoredo:** Off the coast of the Porto Belo peninsula, the clear azure waters surrounding this island offer the best diving in southern Brazil (page 211).

★ **Praia do Rosa:** On most Brazilian travel gurus' top 10 beach lists, this beautifully unspoiled beach, backed by verdant hills and lagoons, is ideal for swimming, surfing, and whale-watching (page 214).

★ **Gramado:** Seemingly ripped from an out-take of *The Sound of Music,* charming Gramado is an upscale mountain resort surrounded by majestic landscapes that rival the Alps (page 223).

★ **The Serra Verde Express:** One of the world's most breathtaking train trips is the vertiginous, adrenaline-charged three-hour journey from Curitiba to the coast, past the cloud-shrouded peaks and deep canyons of the jungle-covered Serra do Mar (page 186).

★ **Ilha do Mel:** No vehicles are allowed on

★ **Parque Nacional de Aparados da Serra:** This park's hiking trails weave through a series of dramatic canyons—including the spectacular Cânion de Itaimbezinho—as well as lush forests and waterfalls (page 226).

Brazil's Sul, or "South," consists of three states—Paraná, Santa Catarina, and Rio Grande do Sul—which stretch south from São Paulo toward Brazil's frontier with Uruguay and Argentina.

This region is not what most international travelers have in mind when they think of Brazil. The climate and vegetation are more Mediterranean than tropical, and the population—descendants of German, Italian, Polish, and Ukrainian immigrants—is distinctly European (which accounts for so many natural blonds).

Life is more organized and efficient than in other parts of the country, and because it has Brazil's highest standard of living, you'll see fewer *favelas* and a lot less of the have and have-not reality so visible in the rest of the country. The South may lack the pungent history and exoticism of the rest of Brazil, but the pretty patchwork farming communities of its interior and the attractive capitals of Curitiba, Florianópolis, and Porto Alegre provide pleasant distractions. The South also boasts some spectacular natural getaways unlike anywhere else in Brazil.

The coastline of Paraná entices with its handful of colonial towns, luxuriantly forested mountains, and the idyllic islands of the Bay of Paranaguá. The sweeping coastline of Santa Catarina is one of the most captivating in Brazil, and the dozens of beaches that rim the picturesque and increasingly hip island city of Floripa have made the Catarinense capital a radical-sports mecca for surfing, paragliding, windsurfing, and sand boarding.

As for Rio Grande do Sul, while its coastal pleasures are scant, it more than compensates with the attractions of its interior. Its varying landscapes run the gamut from the magnificently rugged Aparados da Serra National Park—a hiker's heaven—to the alpine charms of Gramado and Canela, which, in winter, are reminiscent of quaint Swiss villages. Land of the proud Gaúcho, Rio Grande do Sul is also known for its unique cowboy culture. Barbecued beef—the famous *churrasco*—is in abundance and will send carnivores' salivary glands into overdrive. Local wines are also as good as some of those from neighboring Argentina and Chile.

Of course, the No. 1 reason most tourists visit the South is to glimpse the world's largest

Previous: Florianópolis; surfing at Praia da Joaquina. **Above:** Barra da Lagoa, Florianópolis.

The South

MATO GROSSO
DO SUL

SÃO PAULO

To Brasília

BR
310

BR
330

BR
270

Ourinhos

BR
280

SÃO
PAULO

BR
463

Ponta Porã

5

BR
276

Londrina

Maringá

BR
116

BR
376

PARANÁ

Ponta
Grossa

Morretes

Guaraqueçaba

ILHA DO MEL

Prudentópolis

CURITIBA

THE SERRA
VERDE EXPRESS

Paranaguá

Antonina

PARAGUAY

BR
277

Itrati

BR
277

Mallet

BR
476

São Francisco
do Sul

Foz do Iguaçu

IGUAÇU FALLS

Ciudad del Este

União da
Vitória

Joinville

Puerto
Iguazú

Dionísio
Cerqueira

BR
116

Blumenau

Itajaí

SANTA
CATARINA

Caçador

RESERVA BIOLÓGICA
MARINHA DA ILHA
DO ARVOREDO

EAST COAST
BEACHES OF
FLORIANÓPOLIS

São Miguel
do Oeste

Videira

Chapecó

Joaçaba

FLORIANÓPOLIS

Rio Paraná

Lages

BR
282

BR
158

Erixim

PRAIA
DO ROSA

BR
153

São
Joaquim

Laguna

ARGENTINA

São Miguel

BR
285

Passo
Fundo

Vacaria

BR
116

PARQUE NACIONAL DE
APARADOS DA SERRA

São Borja

Caixias do Sul

Torres

GRAMADO

São Francisco de Paula

RIO GRANDE
DO SUL

Santa
Maria

PORTO ALEGRE

SOUTH
ATLANTIC
OCEAN

Rio Uruguay

BR
472

BR
290

Lagoa
dos Patos

Uruguaiana

BR
290

BR
392

Tavares

Santana
do Livramento

Pelotas

BR
293

Tacuarembó

Bagé

Aceguá

BR
116

Rio Grande

3

26

26

Paysandú

5

Jaguarão

0   50 mi

0   50 km

URUGUAY

Chuí

© AVALON TRAVEL

and most impressive waterfalls: Iguaçu Falls. Words don't do justice to this natural extravaganza. Iguaçu is not just one big cascade but a series of 275 falls that rush over a 3-kilometer-wide (2-mi) precipice. In comparison, Niagara Falls is but a piddling stream.

PLANNING YOUR TIME

If you love nature and the outdoors, it is worth exploring this compact trio of states. The tourist infrastructure is among Brazil's best, and poverty and crime are much less of a problem than in other parts of the country. Exploring the region's attractions can easily be added on to a trip to neighboring Rio de Janeiro and São Paulo. Indeed, many tourists head directly from Rio or Sampa to spend a day or two at the area's biggest draw: Iguaçu Falls. However, an easy excursion would be

4-5 days spent in either Curitiba, including side trips to Paranaguá Bay and Ilha do Mel, or in Florianópolis, with its surrounding region's beach resorts.

If you have a week or more, drive or take a bus down the coast from Curitiba to Porto Alegre, exploring cities and beaches along the way and making side trips into the interior. In the South, the roads are excellent, and distances between attractions are relatively small (for Brazil). From Curitiba, you can fit in a side trip—via bus or plane—to Iguaçu Falls.

Note that while summers can be hot, winters are quite chilly, with temperatures plunging to 5-10°C (40-50°F) in coastal regions and to the freezing point in the interior. Autumn (March-May) is quite a nice time in terms of weather.

Paraná

The wealthiest of all Brazil's states, Paraná is an agricultural and industrial powerhouse. Although Paraná was once part of Portugal's Brazilian colony, aside from a few coastal outposts and the tiny settlement of Curitiba (founded in 1693 as a gold mining camp), the territory was neglected. Things began to change in 1853, when Paraná separated from the state of São Paulo and the new provincial government started a massive campaign to lure immigrants to the region in order to develop the economy and open up the interior. From the late 1800s to the early 1900s, Germans, Italians, and Poles planted coffee and, later, soybeans. The efficiency of their small-scale farms contrasted with the vast slave-driven plantations that were the norm in other parts of Brazil. They also opened up businesses in and around the new capital of Curitiba, which—having emerged from its isolation due to the newly constructed railroad—grew in leaps and bounds. Today, Paraná's prosperity is based on state-of-the-art agribusinesses and highly

modern industries, while Curitiba has blossomed into a dynamic, ecofriendly city of 1.8 million that has become a model for other urban centers throughout Latin America. European cultural and culinary traditions are quite pronounced, especially in the small, isolated agricultural settlements of the interior.

CURITIBA

The efficiency, safety, and general air of well-being of the Paranaense capital provide an example of enlightened urban planning. City mayor (and later state governor) Jaime Lerner was a visionary architect who first took office in the 1970s. Concerned with the traffic pollution that was already afflicting large Latin American cities, Lerner inaugurated a modern, inexpensive municipal bus system and turned much of the small but carefully preserved historic center into a pedestrian district. Recycling and anti-pollution programs were adopted, and vast tracts of land were transformed into public green spaces. This emerald city now boasts more than 30 municipal parks and wooded areas with plenty of walking and biking trails. Though small, Curitiba is definitely refreshing (located high up on a plateau, it is Brazil's coolest state capital) and provides a good base for exploring the rest of Paraná.

Orientation

Curitiba's downtown core and historic center are compact and easy to explore on foot. To get to outlying attractions and the majority of the city's parks, you can rely on the municipal bus system. Better yet is the very handy **Linha Turismo** (tel. 41/3352-8000, www.urbs.curitiba.pr.gov.br/transporte/linha-turismo, 9am-5:30pm Tues.-Sun.), which departs from Praça Tiradentes. This bus line was created especially for tourists, with double-decker buses that circulate at 30-minute intervals throughout the day with short stops at 23 major and minor attractions throughout the city and suburbs. The entire tour takes around 2.5 hours; a daily pass (R$27) allows you to get off at any four stops. You can then continue the tour on a later bus. To take advantage of this option, it's best to start out early in the morning.

Sights

CENTRO HISTÓRICO

Curitiba's small but well-preserved historic center consists primarily of handsome 19th- and early 20th-century civic buildings. You'll find the majority clustered around the **Largo da Ordem,** the adjacent **Praça Garibaldi,** and the surrounding pedestrian-only cobblestoned streets.

On the Largo da Ordem are Curitiba's two oldest buildings. The city's first church, the **Igreja da Ordem Terceira de São Francisco das Chagas,** was built in 1737 and is one of the finest examples of Portuguese colonial architecture in southern Brazil. It is noteworthy for its blue-and-white Portuguese azulejo panels and its baroque-style altars doused in gold leaf. Inside, the small **Museu de Arte Sacra** (tel. 41/3321-3265, 9am-noon and 1pm-6pm Tues.-Fri., 9am-2pm Sat.-Sun., free) displays a small collection of baroque relics fashioned out of wood and terra cotta. Across the street from the church is Curitiba's oldest surviving dwelling, the **Casa Romário Martins** (tel. 41/3321-3255, 9am-noon and 1pm-6pm Mon.-Fri., 9am-2pm Sat.-Sun.). Also dating from the 18th century, this colonial-style house has become a cultural

Curitiba

Curitiba

SÃO FRANCISCO

BATEL

CENTRO

To Shopping
Crystal Plaza
and Manu

To Slaviero
Full Jazz Hotel

To Curitiba
Eco Hostel

To Praça 29 de Março
and Motter Home Hostel

To Centro Cívico

To
Jardim Botânico

RUA C. ARAÚJO
RUA C. EMILIANO PERNETA
RUA 24 HORAS
R. V. DE NÁCAR
RUA VICENTE MACHADO
RUA SALDANHA MARINHO
RUA VOLUNTÁRIOS DA PÁTRIA
RUA DAS FLORES
R. PEREIRA
RUA DAS FLORES
AV. DR MURICY
RUA DR PEDROSA
RUA DES. WESTPHALEN
AV MAL FLORIANO
RUA LOURENÇO PINTO
RUA ANDRE DE BARROS
RUA BR DO RIO BRANCO
RUA PEDRO IVO
RUA JOSÉ LOUREIRO
AV LUIS XAVIER
RUA MATEUS LEME
RUA PRES. FARIA
RUA RIACHUELO
RUA 13 DE MAIO
RUA KELLERS
AL. CABRAL
DR. MURICY
JOÃO NEGRÃO
TR DE LAPA
AV. V DE GUARAPUAVA
RUA C. LAURINDO
RUA TIBAGI
RUA MARIANO TORRES
RUA NILO CAIRO
RUA COM. MACEDO
RUA DR FÁVERE
RUA B. CONSTANT
RUA UBALDINO DO AMARAL
RUA XV DE NOVEMBRO
RUA AMINTAS DE BARROS
AV PRES. AFFONSO CAMARGO
RUA SETE DE SETEMBRO
RUA GENERAL CARNEIRO
AV SILVA JARDIM

MADERO
BURGER & GRILL

BOUQUET
GARNI

Praça
General
Osório

Praça
Zacarias

Praça
Rui Barbosa

MUSEU DE
ARTE SACRE

Praça
Tiradentes

CONFEITARIA
DAS FAMÍLIAS

LINHA
TURISMO
TICKETS

MUSEU
PARANAENSE

CURITIBA
MEMORIAL

Praça
João
Garibaldi

Praça
Garibaldi

SOLAR DO
ROSÁRIO

IGREJA DO
ROSÁRIO

MADERO PRIME
DURSKI
STEAKHOUSE

O TORTO BAR

MUSEU ALFREDO
ANDERSON

Praça 19 de
Dezembro

Passeio
Público

CASA ROMÁRIO
MARTINS

Largo da Ordem

IGREJA DA ORDEM
TERCEIRA DE
SÃO FRANCISCO
DAS CHAGAS

CATEDRAL
METROPOLITANA

Praça
Carlos Gomes

BAR
PALÁCIO

SAN JUAN
JOHNSCHER

NIKKO

RESTAURANTE-
ESCOLA DO SENAC

Praça
Santos
Andrade

UNIVERSITY
OF PARANÁ
(UFPR)

TEATRO
GUAÍRA

Praça Senador
Correia

Praça Eufrásio
Correia

SHOPPING
ESTAÇÃO

HOTEL
VILLÁGIO

RODOFERROVIÁRIO
(TRAIN STATION)

MERCADO
MUNICIPAL

0   200 yds
0   200 m

© AVALON TRAVEL

foundation with a gallery space that exhibits works by contemporary Paranaense artists.

Walking up Rua Claudino dos Santos brings you to the colorful **Praça Garibaldi;** the square is anchored by the **Relógio das Flores,** a sundial fashioned out of shrubbery. Among the more interesting buildings is the palatial pink **Solar do Rosário** (tel. 41/3225-6232, www.solardorosario.com.br, 10am-8pm Mon.-Fri., 10:30am-1pm Sat.-Sun.), a cultural center that houses an art gallery, a café, and a pretty garden.

One museum worth checking out is the **Museu Paranaense** (Rua Kellers 289, tel. 41/3304-3300, www.museuparanaense.pr.gov.br, 9am-5pm Mon.-Fri., 11am-3pm Sat.-Sun., free). Occupying a beautifully restored turn-of-the-20th-century neoclassical mansion that was the former state governor's residence, its collection traces Paraná's history from precolonial days to the present. There are temporary exhibits, a tea salon, and a shop selling books and local handicrafts.

Equally intriguing is the small **Museu Alfredo Andersen** (Rua Mateus Leme 336, tel. 41/3323-5148, www.maa.pr.gov.br, 9am-6pm Mon.-Fri., 10am-4pm Sat.-Sun., free), located in the former home and atelier of Norwegian-born local painter Alfredo Andersen, considered the "father of Paranaense painting." The striking landscapes and portraits on display conjure up Curitiba of the late 19th and early 20th centuries.

RUA DAS FLORES AND VICINITY

In 1971, Curitiba's mayor, Jaime Lerner, closed off a section of Rua 15 de Novembro, one of the commercial center's main streets, renamed it Rua das Flores, and transformed it into Brazil's first open-air pedestrian mall. To underscore his vision, the city's children were invited to gather on Saturday mornings to paint and draw on the sidewalks (a tradition that continues to this day). The bars and cafés occupying the restored pastel buildings became end-of-day gathering points for Curitibanos of all stripes.

Just off the eastern end of Rua das Flores

are a few other landmarks. Praça José Borges de Macedo is dominated by an impressive art nouveau building that used to be the city hall. From here, if you head three blocks north along Rua Barão do Rio Branco, you'll arrive at the **Passeio Público** (Rua Luiz Leão, 6am-8pm Tues.-Sun.). Inaugurated in 1886, the city's first park is a peaceful oasis with lakes for boating, walking paths, and shady oak, sycamore, and purple-blossomed *ipê* trees.

CENTRO CÍVICO

Famed Brazilian architect Oscar Niemeyer has had many hits and misses throughout his long career, but the **Museu Oscar Niemeyer** (Rua Marechal Hermes 999, tel. 41/3350-4400, www.museuoscarniemeyer.org.br, 10am-6pm Tues.-Sun., R$6) has definitely been a hit since its unveiling in 2002. The museum consists of two concrete buildings: a long, gleaming rectangle and the famous *"Olho"* ("Eye"), which resembles an enormous eye suspended in the air. Multiple stained-glass windows suffuse the interior with colored light. A small permanent exhibition documents Niemeyer's career and various galleries host high-quality temporary exhibits of contemporary art. The museum is in the Centro Cívico, a sprawling modern complex of state government buildings. If you don't want to walk the 3 kilometers (2 mi) from downtown, take the Linha Turismo bus, or any bus marked "Centro Cívico."

PARKS

Curitiba is overflowing with parks and wooded areas. The Museu Oscar Niemeyer overlooks the **Bosque Papa João Paulo** (6am-8pm daily), a wooded area named in honor of Pope John Paul II's 1980 visit to Curitiba. The popular **Jardim Botânico** (Rua Engenheiro Ostoja Roguski, Jardim Botânico, tel. 31/3264-6994, 6am-8pm daily, free) features winding trails that lead though formal French gardens shaded by peach trees and *araucárias* as well as a patch of native Atlantic rain forest. The highlight is the elegant steel and glass hothouse modeled after

London's Crystal Palace, featuring a collection of rare Brazilian plants.

The **Parque Tanguá** (Rua Dr. Bemben, Pilarzinho, tel. 41/3353-7607, 24 hours daily) occupies two former stone quarries linked by a tunnel through the rocks. There is a lake, an artificial waterfall, a panoramic lookout, and numerous hiking and biking trails through the greenery. Curitiba's equivalent of New York's Central Park is **Parque Barigüi** (Rodovia do Café/BR-227, Santo Inácio, tel. 41/3339-8975, 24 hours daily).

Parque da Pedreira (Rua João Gava, Abranches, 8am-8pm Tues.-Sun.) also used to be a rock quarry before it was converted into a green space with a lake and two theaters. The outdoor Pedreira Paulo Leminski amphitheater is the stage for large shows and concerts, but the park's true highlight is the **Ópera de Arame** (tel. 41/3355-6072)—a superbly designed "wire" opera house designed by local architect Domingos Bongestabs. Its delicate structure of tubular steel and wire mesh features walls of glass that allow you to contemplate the surrounding lakes and woodlands.

Entertainment and Events

Curitiba has a lively arts scene for a city of its size. One of Brazil's premier theaters, **Teatro Guaíra** (Rua 15 de Novembro, Centro, tel. 41/3304-7900, www.teatroguaira.pr.gov.br) has three auditoriums where you can often see high-caliber theater, dance, and classical music performances. Although the acoustics are less than impressive, in terms of aesthetics it is worth your while to check out a concert at the **Ópera de Arame.**

The majority of Curitiba's most interesting bars are divided between the historic center and the trendy *bairro* of Batel, whose nickname of "Batel Soho" betrays the hip-ification of the hood (particularly the area surrounding Praça da Espanha). Among Batel's bars du jour is **Le Voleur de Vélo** (Alameda Presidente Taunay 543, Batel, tel. 41/3079-6750, 4pm-10pm Tues.-Wed., 4pm-2am Thurs.-Fri., 3pm-2am Sat.); its name (French for "The Bicycle Thief") pays homage to its diurnal existence as a bike store. For live music, head to **Santa Marta** (Rua Bispo Dom José 2030, Batel, tel. 41/3343-2803, www.santamartabar.com.br, 6pm-2am Tues.-Sun., noon-4pm Sat., no cover), located in an 80-year-old house whose deck is shaded by an enormous *jabuticaba* tree. Nightly performances run the gamut from samba rock to *música sertanejo*. Santa Marta being the patron saint of cooks, it's not surprising that the food is tasty.

Museu Oscar Niemeyer

Beer aficionados will be in malt heaven at the **Hop 'N Roll Beer Club** (Rua Mateus Leme 950, Centro Cívico, tel. 41/3408-4486, www.hopnroll.com.br, 11am-1am daily). Choose from 150 brands of homegrown and international bottled brews or the 27 drafts on tap on any given night. Or, with three hours and R$450 at your disposal, you can concoct 40L of your own signature brand under the supervision of a master brewer.

For a cheap and atmospheric neighborhood *boteco,* stop at **O Torto Bar** (Rua Paula Gomes 354, São Francisco, tel. 41/3027-6458, 5pm-12:30am daily). "Torto" (Portuguese for "crooked") was the nickname of bow-legged soccer legend Mané Garrincha, an idol of the owner as attested to by the 250 photographs adorning the walls. In between shooting the breeze and some billiards, try the famous chicken and palm heart *empadinhas.*

Shopping

Shopping Estação (Av. Sete de Setembro 2775, Centro, tel. 41/3094-5300, www.shoppingestacao.com.br) is built around Curitiba's original 19th-century railroad station. It has more than 100 stores, including a movie theater, and a small museum devoted to the history of Paraná's railroads. **Shopping Crystal Plaza** (Rua Comendador Araújo 731, Batel, tel. 41/3883-3000, www.crystalplaza.com.br) is Curitiba's chic *shopping,* with upscale boutiques as well as restaurants and a cineplex. *Shopping* hours are 10am-10pm Monday-Saturday, 2pm-8pm Sunday.

The vibrant **Feira de Artesanato** (9am-2pm Sun.), which takes place in the Largo da Ordem and Praça Garibaldi on Sunday, is a good place to go hunting for arts and crafts and regional delicacies, as well as to soak up the atmosphere in a café.

Accommodations

Curitiba gets more business travelers than tourists. Hotels are mostly located in the center and the nearby *bairros* of Centro Cívico and Batel. Although prices are quite affordable, many hotels offer discounts during low season and weekends.

The ★ **Curitiba Eco Hostel** (Rua Luís Tramontin 1693, Campo Comprido, tel. 41/3274-7979, www.curitibaecohostel.com.br, R$40 pp, R$100-150 d) is much more of a bucolic country retreat than your average urban youth hostel. Guest rooms (with small balconies) and common spaces are warm and rustic, and there is a large heated pool, free Wi-Fi, and a 24-hour restaurant. The only

Curitiba's Jardim Botânico

drawback is its location—8 kilometers (5 mi) from the center of town; however, it is easily reached by bus from Praça Rui Barbosa. In terms of urban hostels, the **Motter Home Curitiba Hostel** (Rua Desembragador Motta 3574, Mercês, tel. 41/3209-5649, www.motterhome.com.br, R$40 pp, R$120 d) occupies a lemon-hued 1950s mansion with sophisticated trappings such as hardwood floors, art-hung walls, and a fragrant herb garden. Be warned; what you save on transportation costs (it's only a 15-minute walk from Largo da Ordem) you'll spend on extras such as towel fees (R$4!).

Occupying an early 20th-century edifice, the **Hotel Villaggio** (Rua Tibagi 950, Centro, tel. 41/3074-9100, www.villaggio.com.br, R$165 d) has airs of an Italian villa with its warm rosy brick facade and charming interior garden. Guest rooms are on the simple side and a bit tight, but well equipped and terrifically priced. ★ **Nikko** (Rua Barão Rio Branco 546, Centro, tel. 41/2105-1808, www.hotelnikko.com.br, R$190-220 d), hidden behind a 19th-century facade, offers a refined and modern Japanese hotel in a soothing atmosphere complete with sushi bar and goldfish pond. Guest rooms are small but relaxing oases.

Located in a historic landmark building where Curitiba's very first hotel opened in 1917, the **San Juan Johnscher** (Rua Barão do Rio Branco 354, Centro, tel. 41/3302-9600, www.sanjuanhoteis.com.br, R$280-380 d) is all about retro elegance combined with modern comfort. The palatial-size luxury suites feature soaring ceilings, polished wooden floors, king beds, and swimming pool-size bathtubs. Jazz aficionados will warm to the coolest member of Curitiba's ubiquitous Slaviero chain, the **Slaviero Full Jazz Hotel** (Rua Silveira Peixoto 1297, Batel, tel. 41/3312-7000, www.hotelslaviero.com.br, R$320-380 d). One of the city's rare boutique hotels, its minimalist yet stylish and comfortable decor jives nicely with the jazz theme, which extends from a jazz CD and DVD library to a cool piano bar.

Food

Curitiba has a fairly varied restaurant scene, and it is possible to eat well and quite affordably. European cuisine representing Paraná's major immigrant groups is a strong point—you'll find many options in the center. Contemporary eateries are clustered in the chic *bairro* of Batel.

One of the most delicious consequences of Paraná's late 19th-century coffee and immigration booms is the abundance of European-style cafés and tea salons. Located on and around Rua das Flores, several still draw (largely mature) crowds around tea time. **Confeitaria das Famílias** (Rua das Flores 374, Centro, tel. 41/3223-0313, 7:30am-11pm daily) has been satisfying Curitibanos' sugar cravings since 1945 with a mouthwatering array of pastries. Full afternoon tea for two costs R$20. In a pretty wooden house at the entrance to Bosque Papa João Paulo, **Kawiarnia Krakowiak** (Travessa Wellington de Oliveira Vianna 40, tel. 41/3026-7462, 10am-9pm daily) serves a "colonial tea" with scrumptious Polish cakes.

For delicious inexpensive fare, check out the organic food court at the **Mercado Muncipal** (Av. 7 de Setembro 1865, Centro, tel. 41/3363-1000, www.mercadomunicipaldecuritiba.com.br, 7am-2pm Mon., 7am-6pm Tues.-Sat., 7am-1pm Sun., R$15-25). **Ohana Restaurante** (Box 518) is particularly recommended. A nicely priced, sustainable option is **Bouquet Garni** (Alameda Dr. Carlos de Carvalho 271, Centro, tel. 41/3223-8490, www.restaurantebouquetgarni.com, 11am-3pm daily, R$15-25), which offers a self-serve vegetarian buffet featuring organic produce grown at the restaurant's farm outside Curitiba. **Restaurante-Escola do Senac** (Rua André de Barros 750, 2nd Floor, Centro, tel. 41/3219-4854, 11:30am-2pm Mon.-Sat., R$25-30) is run by the Curitiba branch of the Senac restaurant school, which means that the apprentice chefs are highly motivated and the waitstaff is on their best behavior.

A favorite haunt of journalists, artists, and bohemians since the 1930s, the atmospheric

Bar Palácio (Rua André de Barros 500, Centro, tel. 41/3222-3626, 7pm-1:30am Mon.-Thurs., 7pm-3am Fri.-Sat., R$25-40) satiates late-night munchies by serving its famous *churrasco paranaense* (grilled filet mignon and strip loin with rice) and *farofa,* as well as other lip-smacking grub.

Slightly removed from the center, **Cantinho do Eisbein** (Av. dos Estados 863, Água Verde, tel. 41/3329-5155, www.cantinhodoeisbein.com.br, 11:30am-3pm and 7pm-11:30pm Tues.-Sat., 11:30am-3pm Sun., R$25-40) is a highly recommended German restaurant. The owners themselves greet you and serve the generous portions of *eisbein* (pork knees), *kassler* (smoked pork loin), and a delicious stuffed duck, accompanied with garnishes such as apple puree, sweet red cabbage, and white sausage.

Durski (Av. Jaime Reis 254, São Francisco, tel. 41/3225-7893, www.durski.com.br, 7:45pm-11pm Thurs., 7:45pm-11:30pm Fri.-Sat., R$70-100) is one of the best restaurants in the South. Self-taught chef Junior Durski's menu is broadly international, the wine cellar is impressive, and the setting is dauntingly rococo (as are the prices). Durski's rapidly expanding culinary empire includes **Madero Prime Steakhouse** (Av. Jaime Reis 262, São Francisco, tel. 41/3013-2100, www.restaurantemadero.com.br, noon-2:30pm and 7pm-11pm Tues.-Thurs., noon-3:30pm and 7pm-midnight Fri.-Sat., noon-10pm Sun., R$35-50), a classily rustic dining room serving up the city's best cuts of locally sourced angus beef, and **Madero Burger & Grill** (Rua Comendador Araújo 152, Centro, tel. 41/3092-0021, www.restaurantemadero.com.br, noon-2:30pm and 6pm-11:30pm Mon.-Fri., noon-midnight Sat.-Sun., R$20-25), a much-lauded gourmet burger chain with more than a dozen locations.

The coolest contemporary chef in town, 30-year-old Manoella Buffara, presides over **Manu** (Alameda Dom Pedro II 317, Batel, tel. 41/3224-8244, www.restaurantemanu.com.br, 11:30am-3pm and 7pm-midnight Tues.-Sat., noon-5pm Sun.) when she isn't off scoping out fresh, local, unsung produce for the daily menus that feature four (R$84), six (R$128), and eight dishes (R$164). Since the intimate dining room only seats 30, reservations are a must.

Information and Services

The municipal **tourist office** (www.turismo.curitiba.pr.gov.br) is an efficient place. You'll find information centers with helpful staff and plenty of maps at the airport (tel. 41/3381-1153, 7am-11pm daily), *rodoferroviária* (tel. 41/3320-3121, 8am-6pm daily) and the Palacete Wolf (Praça Garibaldi 8, Centro, 41/3321-3206, 9am-6pm Mon.-Sat., 9am-4pm Sun.). There is a 24-hour tourist information hotline (tel. 156). The state tourist office, **Paraná Turismo** (Rua Deputado Mário de Barros 1290, Centro Cívico, tel. 41/3313-3500, www.turismo.pr.gov.br, 9am-noon and 1pm-6pm Mon.-Fri.), has information about attractions throughout Paraná, including transportation schedules and maps. The website is bilingual.

Main **bank** branches can be found around the commercial hub of Centro near Praça Osório and Rua das Flores. The main **post office** is at Rua XV de Novembro 700, near Praça Santos Andrade. In the event of an emergency, dial **192** for an ambulance, **193** for the fire department, and **190** for the police. **Hospital Universitário Cajuru** (Av. São José 300, Cristo Rei, tel. 41/3271-3000, www.hospitalcajuru.org.br) is a centrally located hospital.

Transportation

Curitiba is easily reached from all other Brazilian cities by air. There are numerous daily bus connections from Rio, São Paulo, Florianópolis, and Porto Alegre. Getting around town is easy—from the two central municipal bus terminals at Praça Tiradentes and Praça Rui Barbosa, you can get a bus (R$2.70) for anywhere in the city, the suburbs, and to nearby towns (the destination is clearly marked on the front). Taxis are also easy to flag down.

AIR

Curitiba's modern **Aeroporto Internacional Afonso Pena** (Av. Rocha Pombo, São José dos Pinhais, tel. 41/3381-1515) is 21 kilometers (13 mi) east of the city center. To get to the center of town, a taxi will set you back around R$50. A much better bargain is the excellent **Aeroporto Executivo** (tel. 41/3381-1326, www.aeroportoexecutivo.com. br), a minibus that runs between the airport, the *rodoferroviária*, Teatro Guaíra, Shopping Estação, and Rua 24 Horas. It costs R$12, and shuttles leave at 15-20-minute intervals. You can also hop a regular municipal bus to the *rodoferroviária*.

BUS

The main bus station and train station are located adjacent to each other, hence the hybrid moniker of *rodoferroviária* (Av. Presidente Afonso Camargo 41/330, tel. 41/3320-3000). Buses travel to destinations throughout the state and country as well as to Argentina, Paraguay, and Chile. **Cometa** (tel. 4004-9600, www.viacaocometa.com.br) offers frequent service to and from São Paulo (6 hours, R$72-112). **Catarinense** (tel. 4004-5001, www.catarinense.net) offers multiple departures to both Florianópolis (4.5 hours, R$53-71) and Foz do Iguaçu (10 hours, R$133).

CAR RENTALS

In Curitiba, traffic is lighter than in other major Brazilian cities. To rent a car, try **Avis** (www.avis.com.br), with locations at the airport (tel. 41/3381-1370) and **Batel** (Rua Teixeira Coelho 108, tel. 41/3333-5544). **Hertz** (tel. 4003-7368, www.hertz.com.br) also has a branch at the airport.

Around Curitiba

Less than 100 kilometers (62 mi) northwest of Curitiba, in the midst of a rolling green plateau region known as Campos Gerais, the **Parque Estadual de Vila Velha** (tel. 42/3228-1138, www.pontagrossa.pr.gov.br, 8:30am-5:30pm Wed.-Mon., tickets available until 3:30pm, R$15-25) is an easy day

trip from Curitiba, or a stop on your way to Foz do Iguaçu. There are small lakes, including a crater lake where you can swim, but the park's stellar attractions are the two-dozen fantastically shaped rock formations hewn out of reddish sandstone. Dating back 300 million years, they are the result of glacial activity combined with subsequent erosion. Their lifelike aspect has earned many of these sculptures nicknames, such as "The Boot," "The Sphinx," and "The Camel's Head." You can visit the area on foot, following a clearly marked 2.5-kilometer (1.5-mi) trail, or by taking tractor-pulled wagons with guides (R$10). The park has a visitors center, a restaurant, and food-and-drink kiosks.

From Curitiba, Vila Velha is a two-hour bus ride. **Princesa dos Campos** (tel. 0800-42-1000, www.princesadoscampos.com.br) has multiple daily departures beginning at 6am and continuing at 45- to 60-minute intervals throughout the day from the *rodoferroviária* to the town of Ponta Grossa; ask the driver to let you off at the entrance to the park. One-way fare is R$30. Make sure you check the schedule for return buses so you can flag down a ride back to Curitiba in the late afternoon. By car, follow the BR-376.

CURITIBA TO PARANAGUÁ

Between Curitiba and the coastal town of Paranaguá is 120 kilometers (75 mi) of spectacular mountainscape, part of the Serra do Mar. The height of the peaks and density of the vegetation has ensured the preservation of one of the largest remaining patches of the native Atlantic rain forest that once covered the entire Brazilian coast. Although you can drive or take a bus to Paranaguá, neither compares with four hours spent aboard the Serra Verde Express train. Stop-off points along the way include the colonial town of Morretes and the Parque Estadual do Marumbi, an unspoiled idyll that draws hikers, rafters, and those hardy enough to climb the 1,500-meter (4,920-foot) rocky Marumbi peak. Along the way are the charming towns of Antonina and

Morretes, and in the port city of Paranaguá you can catch a boat for Ilha do Mel.

★ The Serra Verde Express

Many of Brazil's railroads were financed and built by European (mostly British) companies, but the Curitiba-Paranaguá line was a 100 percent Brazilian project. A masterful engineering feat, the **Serra Verde Express** (tel. 41/3888-3488, www.serraverdeexpress. com.br) route features 67 bridges and viaducts and 13 tunnels. Tracks are sometimes perilously close to sheer cliffs, which makes for an adrenaline-charged journey. However, it's hard to be anxious when surrounded by so much natural beauty. As you plunge from Curitiba's highlands down to the blue Atlantic, you'll be treated to visions of cloud-shrouded peaks, deep canyons ribboned with waterfalls, and increasingly lush and tropical vegetation.

When you buy your ticket, try to reserve a seat on the left side (and on the right side on the return trip). Wagons come in various levels of comfort (prices listed are for one-way fare): *Econômico* (R$65) is the most basic. *Turístico* (R$84, with Portuguese guides), *executivo* (R$123, with large windows and bilingual guides), and *camarotes* (R$376-752 per wagon—private wagons accommodate 4-8) all include snacks as well as bar service. On weekends, the air-conditioned, luxury *Litorina* takes to the rails with opulent *luxo* (R$270) wagons; perks include velvet upholstery, continental breakfast, champagne, and bilingual guides. It's worth forking out an extra R$20 for a tour of both Morretes and Antonina and a typical *barreado* lunch. All trains depart from Curitiba's *rodoferroviária* at 8:15am Monday-Saturday and 9:15am Sunday. Return trains leave from Morretes at 3pm Monday-Saturday and 2:30pm Sunday. On Sundays, the Litorina normally goes all the way to Paranaguá and returns to Curitiba at 1:30pm. Although return fare is cheaper, you can also opt to return by bus. It's advisable to reserve in advance.

If you're driving from Curitiba to Morretes,

follow the **Estrada Graciosa**, a stunning 33-kilometer (21-mi) stretch of road that leads off BR-116. Although the sinewy route will take an hour longer than the alternative BR-277 highway, the views of the surrounding peaks of Marumbi and Paraná are well worth it. Along the way, you can purchase locally produced honey, *cachaça,* and *balas de banana* (chewy banana candies).

Parque Estadual do Marumbi

Both the railroad line and the Estrada da Graciosa pass right through the **Parque Estadual do Marumbi** (tel. 41/3462-3598, www.cosmo.org.br, 8am-6pm daily, free). The park offers plenty of well-marked hiking trails; many were carved out of the wilderness centuries ago by Indians and early settlers. One of the easiest is a 45-minute trail that leads to the hilltop of Rochedinha, with stops for bathing in natural pools created by the Rio Taquara. More adventurous souls can climb to the summit of Monte Olimpo, which at 1,539 meters (5,049 feet) is the highest peak in Paraná.

The Serra do Mar Express stops at Marumbi station, which is within the park. At the entrance is a **visitors center** with maps of the trails and other information. The park is also accessible by bus from Morretes.

Morretes

Straddling the Rio Nhundiaquara, this pretty colonial town at the foot of the Serra do Mar was founded by Jesuits in 1721. Filled with cobblestone streets and colorful old houses, the town is famous for its fine *cachaças* and artisan-produced *balas de banana*—the surrounding area boasts several colonial sugar plantations, and *bananeiras* (banana trees) are everywhere. Its languorous small-town atmosphere makes it a nice place to stay if you want a base for exploring the Parque Estadual do Marumbi—local buses go to nearby São João de Graciosa, which is 2 kilometers (1.2 mi) from the entrance to the park—and the nearby town of Antonina, 18 kilometers (11 mi) away.

ACCOMMODATIONS AND FOOD

The nicest hotel in town is the charming **Hotel Nhundiaquara** (Rua General Carneiro 13, tel. 41/3462-1228, www.nundiaquara.com.br, R$80-120 d), located in a whitewashed 17th-century mansion perched on a scenic bend in the river. The simple but appealing guest rooms feature soaring ceilings, but tiny bathrooms. Reserve in advance for a room overlooking the river. The hotel's **Restaurante Nhundiaquara** (lunch daily, plus dinner Sat., R$20-30) has been serving up *barreado* along with seafood dishes for more than 60 years. **Armazém Romanus** (Rua Visconde do Rio Branco 141, tel. 41/3642-1500, 11am-3pm Sun.-Wed., 11am-3pm and 7pm-10:30pm Thurs.-Sat., R$20-30) serves up a notoriously good traditional *barreado* accompanied by grilled local bananas.

A bucolic alternative is to stay outside of town. **Pousada Graciosa** (Estrada da Graciosa Km 8, tel. 41/3462-1807, www.pousadagraciosa.com, R$240 d) offers six homey, hammock- and fireplace-equipped chalets set amidst a lush, carefully preserved landscape. The surrounding forest can be easily explored on foot or by bike.

TRANSPORTATION AND SERVICES

The **tourist office** (Casa do Caboclo, tel. 41/3462-1024, 10am-5pm daily) has information about the town and the surrounding region, including the Parque Estadual do Marumbi. **Calango Expedições** (Estação Ferroviária, tel. 41/3462-2600, www.calangoexpedicoes.com.br) offers hiking, biking, mountain climbing, and rafting trips into the Parque Estadual do Marumbi and along the coast. A full-day excursion, with stops for bathing in waterfalls, costs R$180 for up to three people. A three-hour guided biking trip around the region costs R$60.

You can get to Morretes from Curitiba, 70 kilometers (43 mi) away, by the Serra Verde Express train or via eight daily buses operated by **Viação Graciosa** (tel. 41/3213-5511, www.viacaograciosa.com.br, R$19). Only one bus a day travels via the Estrada Graciosa. By car, the fastest route is BR-277 and then PR-408. A slower but more scenic route is to take BR-116, followed by the Estrada Graciosa. Frequent Graciosa buses also pass through Morretes to and from Antonina and Paranaguá.

Antonina

From colonial times to the 1940s, Antonina was Paraná's most important port. Since its role was usurped by Paranaguá, Antonina has slipped into something of a backwater, albeit an appealing one, full of preserved but faded 18th- and 19th-century buildings that gaze out over the blue waters of the Baía de Paranaguá. Drowsy Antonina comes to life during Carnaval. As in neighboring Morretes, its charms can be easily soaked up in a couple of hours. However, if you plan on spending more time in the region, Antonina makes a pleasant base. At the nearby Rio Cachoeira, you can go swimming in waterfalls or rafting down the river.

ACCOMMODATIONS AND FOOD

Sharing space with formerly grand colonial houses on the town's pretty main hilltop square, **Pousada Atlante** (Praça Colonel Macedo 266, tel. 41/3432-1256, www.atlante.com.br, R$165 d) offers comfortable lodgings in a beautiful historic house with a small pool. Get a room with a balcony that overlooks the 18th-century Igreja Matriz Nossa Senhora do Pilar and the Baía de Paranaguá. **Caçarola do Joca** (Praça Romildo G. Pereira 42, tel. 41/3432-1286, 11:30am-2pm Mon.-Wed., 11:30am-5pm and 7:30pm-10pm Sat., 11:30am-6pm Sun., R$20-35) is located in an atmospheric old house whose walls were constructed by the Jesuits who founded the town. The restaurant is acclaimed for seafood and its *barreado*, whose traditional preparation involves 20 hours of slow cooking over a low flame. In summer, it opens for lunch daily.

TRANSPORTATION AND SERVICES

The **tourist office** (tel. 41/3978-1080, 9am-6pm Mon.-Sat., 10am-6pm Sun.) is located in the old train station. **Icatu Rafting** (tel. 41/3432-1178) offers rafting trips down the Rio Cachoeira; a 90-minute trip costs R$65.

Antonina is 86 kilometers (53 mi) from Curitiba and 18 kilometers (11 mi) from Morretes. **Viação Graciosa** (tel. 41/3213-5511, www.viacaograciosa.com.br) operates eight daily buses to Curitiba (R$22) and Paranaguá (R$4) via Morretes.

Paranaguá

One of Brazil's oldest urban settlements, Paranaguá was founded in the 1550s on the banks of the lazy Rio Itiberê where it meets the Baía da Paranaguá. The town's importance as a major commercial port has destroyed much of its charm, however its small historical center has some handsome old houses and Portuguese-style colonial churches. These, together with a low-key atmosphere and some unassuming but very decent seafood restaurants, make it a worthwhile place to kill a few hours while you're waiting for a boat to Ilha do Mel or for the Sunday Serra Express train to Curitiba.

SIGHTS

Among Paranaguá's handful of churches, the oldest and most imposing is the **Igreja Nossa Senhora do Rosário** (Largo Monsenhor Celso), parts of which date back to 1578. Nearby, built by and for the town's slave population, the modest 18th-century **Igreja de São Benedito** (Rua Conselheiro Sinimbu) still retains all its original features. Construction of the imposing stone Colégio dos Jesuítas began in the late 1600s, when the city's elite invited Jesuit priests to set up a school for their sons. After later serving as a military barracks and a customhouse, it is now occupied by the **Museu de Arqueologia e Etnologia** (Rua XV de Novembro 575, tel. 41/3423-2511, 9am-6pm Tues.-Fri., 9am-4pm Sat.-Sun., free) and has an engaging collection of local Tupi-Guarani artifacts and regional folk art created by Paraná's earliest European settlers.

FOOD

Casa do Barreado (Rua José Antônio da Cruz 78, tel. 41/3423-1830, www.

casadobarreado.com.br, noon-3pm Sat.-Sun., R$25-35) has the best food in town, combined with a lovely garden setting. The highlight of the prix fixe self-service regional buffet is *barreado;* locally produced *cachaças* and delicious homemade desserts are included.

Overlooking the river, **Danúbio Azul** (Rua 15 de Novembro 95, tel. 41/3423-3255, www.restaurantedanubioazul.com.br, 11am-3pm and 7pm-11pm Mon.-Sat., 11am-3pm Sun., R$15-25) offers both à la carte and buffet service featuring a variety of salads, meat, and seafood dishes. For cheap and tasty seafood, head to the **Mercado Municipal do Café** (Rua General Carneiro, 8am-6pm Mon.-Sat., 8am-3pm Sun.), a former coffee market where you'll find a string of rustic restaurants and bars.

TRANSPORTATION AND SERVICES

The main **tourist information center** (Av. Arthur de Abreu 44, tel. 41/3420-2940, 8am-6pm Mon.-Sat., 8am-2pm Sun.) is adjacent to the Estação Ferroviária, the grand train station where you can catch the Sunday *Litorina* Serra Verde Express train to and from Curitiba and Morretes. You'll also find one at the *rodoviária* (Rua João Estevão, 8am-6pm Mon.-Sat., 8am-2pm Sun.).

Paranaguá is 92 kilometers (57 mi) from Curitiba. **Viação Graciosa** (tel. 41/3213-5511, www.viacaograciosa.com.br) offers almost hourly bus service (both direct and indirect) to Curitiba (2 hours, R$24). By car, the fastest route is to follow BR-277 (90 minutes); longer and more scenic is to take the Estrada da Graciosa (PR-110) before turning off on BR-116.

★ Ilha do Mel

Paraná's beaches aren't much to write home about, with the very notable exception of Ilha do Mel, a 10-kilometer-long (6-mi) island that is the Baía de Paranaguá's main attraction. A two-hour boat ride from Paranaguá, its deserted beaches and rugged landscapes are protected as part of an ecological reserve; the well-marked roads and walking trails that crisscross the island are all sand, and no cars are allowed. Accommodations, while comfortable, are fairly basic. During the summer months, the island's five settlements—Encantadas, Fortaleza, Farol, Praia Grande, and Nova Brasília—fill with young *surfistas* and eco-hippies. The rest of the year, a languorous tranquility holds sway.

BEACHES

Straddling two sheltered bays, **Nova Brasília,** in the middle of the island, is the largest of Ilha do Mel's settlements and home to most of its 1,000 residents. An easy 40-minute walk north leads to one of the island's most beautiful beaches, the 4-kilometer (2.4-mi) stretch of white sand known as **Praia da Fortaleza.** The *fortaleza* in question is **Fortaleza Nossa Senhora dos Prazeres,** an 18th-century Portuguese fortress that offers wonderful views of the bay along with the islands of Superagüi and Ilha das Peças.

A 15-minute walk south along the coast from Nova Brasília will bring you to the **Farol das Conchas.** Perched on a verdant hilltop straddling the **Praia do Farol** and the sheltered cove of **Praia de Fora,** this 19th-century lighthouse offers wonderful views that are worth the steep climb, particularly before sunset.

From Praia de Fora, it's a two-hour walk (best undertaken at low tide and not when it's rainy, due to slippery rocky patches) along the mountainous southeast coast to **Encantadas,** a pretty little fishing village. Along the way, you'll pass some of the island's most attractive white-sand beaches. **Praia Grande** and **Praia do Miguel** are surfers' paradises. Closer to Encantadas (and less deserted), **Praia de Fora das Encantadas** is home to the **Gruta das Encantadas,** a cavern set in the cliffs that is a hot spot for mermaids, according to local legend.

PARQUE NACIONAL DO SUPERAGÜI

From Nova Brasília and Encantadas, boats can be hired to take you to various beaches as well as to the nearby islands of Ilha das Palmas, Ilha das Peças, and Ilha do Superagüi. The latter two compose the **Parque Nacional do Superagüi.** This protected region of mangrove swamps and native Atlantic forest is home to a rich diversity of flora and fauna, including *mico-leões-de-cara-preta* (black-faced lion monkeys) and *chauás* (red-faced parrots), whose late-afternoon return to their tree canopy roosts is a scarlet sight to behold. Ilha do Superagüi also boasts the aptly named 37-kilometer (23-mi) **Praia Deserta.** From Nova Brasília, Superagüi is only a 40-minute trip by high-speed motorboat through dolphin-riddled waters; while you can navigate around the island, it's prohibited to venture on foot through the protected forest. You can, however, lounge away part of a day at the traditional fishing settlement of Barra do Superagüi, home to the island's only lodging, the welcoming but bare-bones **Pousada Superagüi** (Praia do Farol, tel. 41/3482-7149, www.pousadasuperagui.com.br, R$60-70 d), whose owners, Dalton and Olga, are great resources. For information about excursions or to hire a boat, consult with your *pousada* or the Ilha do Mel tourist offices. Expect to pay around R$400 to hire a private boat for a day.

SPORTS AND RECREATION

The rough Atlantic waters of Ilha do Mel are worshipped by surfers, particularly in the winter months. Rent a board at the **Galo Surf Shop** (Praia de Fora, R$40 per day), which also offers lessons to novices (R$55 an hour). Hiking the island's 20-km/12.5-mi circumference usually takes around eight hours. Local guides are available (R$150); ask your *pousada* for recommendations. Near Nova Brasília's pier, **Pura Vida** (tel. 41/3426-8138, R$60 per day) rents bikes.

ACCOMMODATIONS AND FOOD

Accommodations in Ilha do Mel tend toward rustic, although modern amenities such as DVD players and Internet access are ubiquitous. Encantadas's *pousadas* are more modern, while those in Nova Brasília are simpler but more charming. For more seclusion, try the handful of basic offerings on Praia da Fortaleza. In summer and during holidays, reservations are a must. Often, there is a minimum stay of 2-3 nights. Although you'll find no shortage of restaurants in both Nova Brasília and Encantadas, the most memorable meals can often be found in *pousadas*.

Just off Nova Brasília's pier, **Pousadinha** (Praia do Farol, tel. 41/3426-8026, www. pousadinha.com.br, R$70-160 d) offers attractive wooden lodgings (the newest apartments are the nicest) nestled in a nicely landscaped garden. The staff is friendly, and you can rent surfboards, bikes, and boats. The pretty **Restaurante Pousadinha** (noon-9pm daily, R$15-25) serves tasty local fare for lunch and Italian dishes at dinner. A more romantic option is the **Pousada das Meninas** (Praia do Farol, tel. 41/3426-8023, www.pousadadas-meninas.com.br, R$170-280 d). Ingeniously constructed from organic and recycled materials and decorated with whimsical flair, these charming though somewhat cramped bungalows house 2-6 people. Guests can use the kitchen, access free Wi-Fi, and rent bikes, surfboards, and other water-sports equipment.

On deserted Praia Grande, more than just serious wave aficionados will appreciate the **Grajagan Surf Resort** (Praia Grande, tel. 41/3246-8043, www.grajagan.com.br, R$190-460 d), owned and operated by a die-hard surfer. Accommodations in brick bungalows are fairly modest, especially considering the hefty prices. The best (and most expensive) face the sea and boast great verandas that look out over the jungle and the beach.

Located on the trail that leads to the Praia de Fora das Encantadas, the **Pousada Fim da Trilha** (tel. 41/3426-9017, www.fimdatrilha. com, R$330-500 d) is one of the island's most alluring (and ecologically correct) addresses. Seven small but relaxing rooms and one bungalow sit immersed in jungly gardens whose soothing spell is bolstered by a lounge, bar, and the **Restaurante Fim da Trilha** (noon-4pm and 8pm-10:30pm daily, R$20-35), which serves up some of the best seafood on the island. Closer to Nova Brasília, **Restaurante Sol e Mar** (Praia de Fora, tel. 41/3426-8021, www.restaurantemaresol.com.br, 9am-10pm daily, R$25-35) is renowned for inventing *moqueca da Ilha do Mel,* a local version of the classic Bahian fish and seafood stew.

INFORMATION

There are two small **tourist information** kiosks at the piers at both Nova Brasília and Encantadas that are usually open 7:30am-6pm daily. Eight daily ferries (20 minutes, R$8) shuttle between Nova Brasília and Encantadas should you not be up to the 90-minute walk between the two villages. There are no banks on the island, so make sure you stock up on cash before leaving the mainland. There is an Internet café, **Ilha do Mel Café** (tel. 41/3426-8065, www.ilhadomelonline.com.br, 9am-9pm daily), located in a pretty house on the trail between Nova Brasília and the Farol, which also rents out rooms. In addition to purchasing coffee and snacks and trading books, you can get information about boat trips.

TRANSPORTATION

From Paranaguá's dock, only two boats daily make the trip (R$32 round trip) from the Estação Nautica, stopping first at Nova Brasília (90 minutes) and then at Encantadas (2 hours). Current departure times are 9:30am and 3:30pm, but schedules can change according to tides and weather conditions (avoid making the trip in poor weather). Extra ferries are added in the summer. You'll have more options from the town of Pontal do Sul, where ferries (30 minutes, R$27 round trip) leave hourly 8am-7pm and every 30 minutes on weekends and in summer (leaving your car parked costs R$15 per day). **Viação Graciosa** (tel. 41/3213-5511, www.viacaograciosa.com. br) operates five buses daily from Curitiba to Pontal (2.5 hours, R$30), which drop you in front of the port. By car, Pontal can be reached by following BR-277; 10 kilometers (6 mi) before Paranaguá, turn onto PR-412 and follow

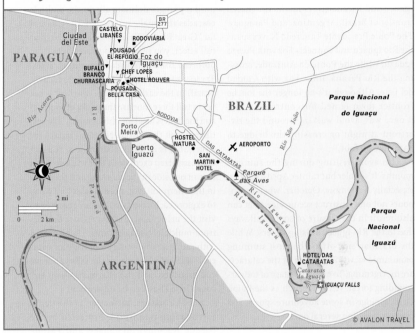

Iguaçu Falls and Vicinity

© AVALON TRAVEL

the signs to Pontal. For more information, contact **Abaline** (tel. 41/3455-2616, www.abaline.com.br), which operates the ferries. Upon arrival, local porters at both docks will cart your luggage to your hotel.

★ IGUAÇU FALLS

The Iguaçu Falls are one of the most spectacular natural wonders on the planet. Their sheer scale is so tremendous that no words or photos can do justice to the experience of actually seeing them. Set amid a primitive landscape of dazzlingly green rain forest, Iguaçu Falls consists of 275 cataracts that are 80 meters (260 feet) high, thundering over a 3-kilometer-wide (2-mi-wide) precipice. The sound is deafening, and the sight absolutely unforgettable. Eleanor Roosevelt summed up the spectacular sight of these famous falls when she declared: "Poor Niagara! This makes it look like a kitchen faucet."

Orientation

The falls straddle Brazil's border with Argentina and are located within the parameters of Brazil's Parque Nacional do Iguaçu and Argentina's Parque Nacional Iguazú. Both the Brazilian city of **Foz do Iguaçu** and the smaller Argentinean town of **Puerto Iguazú** are about 20 kilometers (12 mi) from the falls. Also close by is **Ciudad del Este,** a run-down Paraguayan frontier town where Brazilians flock in massive numbers to buy cheap duty-free goods (many of them counterfeit).

Of the three border towns, Foz do Iguaçu attracts the largest number of tourists (in 2012, it was Brazil's third-most popular destination for foreign tourists). A modern city, home to Brazil's second-largest Arab community (and Muslim population) after São Paulo, "Foz" grew in leaps and bounds during the 1970s and 1980s; its unbridled development was propelled by the construction of the monumental and controversial Itaipu Dam. South of town, the meeting of the Iguaçu and Paraná rivers marks the shared frontier of Brazil, Argentina, and Paraguay. The Ponte Presidente Tancredo Neves spans the Rio Iguaçu and connects Foz with Puerto Iguazú, while the Ponte da Amizade, crossing the Rio Paraná, links Foz with Ciudad del Este. Although it's no longer the louche frontier town famed for contraband that it once was, avoid walking around the riverfront at night or crossing the bridge to Paraguay on foot.

Also avoid visiting during the summer months. It's cooler but rainier April-October, especially September-October, when downpours not only obstruct scenic views but can also result in the closure of some walkways due to the Rio Iguaçu's rising waters. While the Brazilian side offers the most stunning panoramic views, 70 percent of the cataracts are in Argentina. To take advantage of the surrounding forest, visit sites such as the Itaipu Dam, indulge in some adventure sports, and plan on spending several days.

Sights

The Rio Iguaçu's source is in the coastal mountains near Curitiba. Fed by tributaries, the river winds west for 1,200 kilometers (750 mi), growing wider and increasing in force until it plunges dramatically in the multiple cascades that make up the Iguaçu (Guarani for "Great River") Falls. To be treated to their full effect, you really need to see them from both the Brazilian and Argentinean sides. Try to visit the Parque Nacional do Iguaçu (in Brazil) in the early morning—the heat is not yet in full force (nor are the packs of tourists) and the light is ideal for photographs. The best time to visit the Parque Nacional Iguazú (in Argentina) is in the late afternoon. You can take organized excursions that will allow you to visit one side in the morning and the other in the afternoon (you need at least half a day to explore each), but two days are required to visit the many sights and experience the falls from multiple vantage points. Come armed with rain gear and waterproof bags for cameras—the cold spray from the falls can leave you drenched, and the aftermath, in an air-conditioned bus, can be unpleasant.

A major natural attraction is the dense surrounding rain forest. Protected by the Parque Nacional do Iguaçu and Parque Nacional Iguazú, most of the forest is off-limits to visitors. However, even the trails leading to the falls allow you to experience

Iguaçu Falls

this unique ecosystem, whose lushness extends from the giant ferns covering the forest floor to the treetop canopies festooned with Tarzan-esque vines and wild orchids. Insect lovers will be enchanted by iridescent spiders, giant ants carrying bright leaves on their backs, and more than 250 types of butterflies. When hiking through the forest, make sure to bring sunscreen, insect repellent, and water. Most large animals (including the rarely sighted jaguar) are shy and nocturnal; your best shot at glimpsing them is in the early morning hours.

PARQUE NACIONAL DO IGUAÇU

The Brazilian side of the falls and the surrounding rain forest are contained within the **Parque Nacional do Iguaçu** (Rodovia das Cataratas Km 17, tel. 45/3521-4400, www.cataratasdoiguacu.com.br, 9am-5pm daily, R$48.80, Brazilians R$28.80, R$7.50 under age 12); the entrance is 15 kilometers (9 mi) southwest of downtown Foz, accessible by bus and car by following the Rodovia das Cataratas. Buses marked "Parque Nacional" leave at 30-minute intervals from the local *rodoviária* in downtown Foz. If driving, you'll have to leave your car at the main visitors center (parking R$15), where you'll find lockers and ATMs. After paying the admission fee, you board a double-decker bus that departs at 15-minute intervals, traveling along an 11-kilometer (7-mi) road. First stop is at the entrance to the **Trilha do Poço Preto,** a 9-kilometer (5.5-mi) trail that cuts a swath through the forest and along the river. Guided tours (tel. 45/3529-9626, 9:30am, noon, and 2pm daily, 3-4 hours, R$130) are on foot or by bike along the trail and include a jaunt along the river in an inflatable kayak. Subsequent stops include the entrance to Macuco Safari and then the Hotel das Cataratas, where you should get off. From here a panoramic 1.5-kilometer (1-mi) trail winds through the forest to lookout points and catwalks that take you over—and practically *into*—the falls; you can also descend in a panoramic elevator. At the end of the trail

at Porto Canoas (which is also the last stop if you stay on the tour bus) is a smaller visitors center with a souvenir stand and a food court. The **Restaurante Porto Canoas** (tel. 45/3521-4446, noon-4pm daily) serves up a varied self-service buffet lunch (R$45 pp) with terrace tables overlooking the falls.

Many swear that the most breathtaking view of Iguaçu Falls is from above. Departing from a heliport next to the Parque das Aves, **Helisul** (Rodovia das Cataratas Km 16.5, tel. 45/3529-7327, 9am-5:30pm daily) operates 10-minute helicopter tours (R$255) that fly thrillingly close to the falls.

Even more thrilling is tackling the falls head-on by boat. **Macuco Safari** (tel. 45/3529-4244, www.macucosafari.com.br, R$140) offers an adrenaline-filled foray into the cataracts themselves. The two-hour adventure begins with a guided Jeep tour, followed by a short hike through the forest to the Rio Iguaçu. After waterproofing yourself and your belongings, you'll board an inflatable motorboat that sails up the river to the Cachoeira dos Mosqueteiros, where amidst the deafening roar of crashing water, you'll receive the most invigorating bath of your life.

The falls also provide a backdrop to various radical sports. Located within the park (near Hotel das Cataratas), **Cânion Iguaçu** (tel. 45/3529-6040, www.campodosdesafios.com.br) is an ecofriendly company that organizes outings and provides guides and equipment for adventure sport enthusiasts of all levels and ages. Activities include rappelling (R$70), tree-trekking (R$70), and white-water rafting down the Rio Iguaçu (R$80).

PARQUE NACIONAL IGUAZÚ

The Argentinean side of the falls and the surrounding rain forest are contained within the **Parque Nacional Iguazú** (tel. 37/5742-0722, www.iguazuargentina.com, 8am-6pm daily, $170 pesos). Although it receives fewer visitors than its Brazilian counterpart, it boasts a larger number of cataracts as well as more vantage points from which to observe them up close. Make sure to bring a bathing suit, as there are pools in the river that are ideal for taking a dip. Entrance fees and other costs must be paid in Argentinean pesos.

Near the park entrance is a visitors center with a restaurant, lockers, and ATM, as well as the **Centro de Interpretación de la Natureza,** a natural history museum that provides a good introduction to the region's flora and fauna. From here, at 30-minute intervals, mini trains shuttle you through the forest to the falls (you can also walk the 1 km/0.6 mi yourself). The first stop is the **Estación Cataratas,** point of departure for two easy walking trails. The 900-meter (2,950-foot) Circuito Superior trail is at eye level with the top of the falls—catwalks allow you to actually walk behind some of them. The Circuito Inferior is a 1.5-kilometer (1-mi) circular trail that meanders through the forest and gives you a vision of the falls from below. A highlight is the free boat trip that takes you across the river to the Isla San Martín, where a lookout point offers a terrific view of the Argentinean falls. You'll also find natural pools where you can swim. The second train stop is the **Estación Garganta del Diablo.** From here, a 2-kilometer (1.2-mi) trail follows the Rio Iguaçu upstream to the Garganta del Diablo (Devil's Throat), a long and narrow chasm through which the highest and deepest of Iguaçu's falls rushes.

Located within the visitors center, **Iguazú Jungle Explorer** (tel. 54-3757-421-696, www.iguazujungle.com) is an ecotourism agency that offers guided hiking tours through the park along with boat trips up the Rio Iguaçu rapids that will bring you close to the falls. The **Gran Aventura** (1.5 hours, 360 pesos) is a longer, more thrilling, and less expensive version of Macuco Safari. A much briefer and somewhat cheaper version, **Aventura Náutica** (12 min., 180 pesos) exists for those with less time or money to spare.

If you have a car, getting to the Argentinean

Moonlight Tours

If your trip to the falls coincides with a full moon, don't miss the mesmerizing moonlit tours available on both sides of the falls. Brazil's Parque Nacional do Iguaçu offers a **Luau das Cataratas** (8pm-11:30pm, R$45 or R$115 with dinner at Porto Canoas restaurant overlooking the falls). Across the border in Argentina, the Parque Nacional Iguazú hosts the **Paseo Luna Llena** (tel. 37/5749-1469, 2.5 hours, 300 pesos or 450 pesos with dinner at La Selva restaurant). There are three departures (7:45pm, 8:30pm, and 9:15pm) of up to 40 people on each night. Tours may be canceled due to weather.

park is quick. The distance from Foz to Puerto Iguazú is 23 kilometers (14 mi); then follow Ruta 12 for 5 kilometers (3 mi) to the park entrance. Without a car, it's easy but somewhat time-consuming to get to the park from Foz. You might be better off joining a Brazilian excursion organized by some of the travel agencies and hotels in Foz. Alternatively, buses make the 30-minute trip to Puerto Iguazú, leaving at 45-minute intervals from the local *rodoviária* in Foz. From Puerto Iguazú's bus station, hourly buses make the 30-minute trip to the park's entrance.

You will need to have a valid passport and possibly a tourist visa to cross the border from Foz do Iguaçu into Argentina or Paraguay. Even if only crossing the border for the day to visit the Parque Nacional Iguazú, you'll need to pay a reciprocity tax in advance.

PARQUE DAS AVES

Located just before the entrance to Parque Nacional do Iguaçu, the **Parque das Aves** (Rodovia das Cataratas Km 16.5, tel. 45/3529-8282, www.parquedasaves.com.br, 8:30am-5pm daily, R$20) boasts a colorful collection of more than 900 types of tropical birds, most of them from Brazil and many of them quite rare, that are housed in enormous walk-in aviaries within the forest.

USINA HIDRELÉTRICA DE ITAIPU

The largest generator of hydroelectricity on the planet, **Itaipu Dam** (Av. Tancedro Neves 6731, tel. 0800/645-4645, www.turismoitaipu.com.br) supplies 20 percent of Brazil's electricity and 90 percent of Paraguay's. An amazing feat of engineering—measuring 8 kilometers (5 mi) in length and 200 meters (657 feet) in height—the dam cost a whopping US$18 billion.

The damming of the Rio Paraná is as controversial as it is impressive. On one hand, Itaipu has been lauded as a safe and non-polluting energy source that has helped fuel southern Brazil's incredible economic growth. However, the dam's social and environmental impact—the loss of Indian settlements, displacement of 40,000 families, and destruction and damage of 700 square kilometers (270 square mi) of rain forest—has been severely criticized, despite efforts of Itaipu Binacional (the Brazilian-Paraguayan company that administers the dam) to fund reforestation and relocate animals. Polemics aside, if you decide to visit Itaipu, located 10 kilometers (6 mi) from Foz, its sheer monumentality is undeniably impressive (although visit when the spillway is open—otherwise you're wasting your time).

There are three ways of **touring the dam.** The standard *Visita Panorâmica* (hourly 8am-4pm daily, R$24) begins with a 15-minute video showing the dam's construction followed by an hour-long guided bus tour. The longer and far more fascinating *Circuito Especial* tour (eight 2.5-hour tours daily, R$60) allows you to visit the inside of the plant (no sandals, shorts, or children under age 14 permitted). The *Visita Noturna* (8pm Fri.-Sat., R$14) includes a sound and light show. Other sights on the premises include an ecological museum and a biological nature reserve where animals (including a spotted jaguar) rescued during the building of the dam can be seen (call for times of guided walking tours, R$20). Buses marked "Conjunto C" (R$2.90) depart every 15 minutes from the central Terminal Urbano bus station and take you right to the dam's visitors center.

Accommodations

There is no shortage of accommodations in Foz. The more expensive (often overpriced) tourist-oriented resorts are located along the Rodovia das Cataratas. Surrounded by greenery and recreational areas, they are ideal for families, even though some are in sore need of refurbishing. In Foz itself, you'll find more basic options geared toward business travelers and Brazilian shoppers in search of cheap duty-free goods in Ciudad del Este. During off-season, you can get very good discounts.

Conveniently located in the center of town, friendly and family-owned **Pousada Bella Casa** (Rua Bellarmina de Mendonça 509, tel. 45/3097-2954, www.pousadabellacasa.com.br, R$155 d) six cheery rooms (from double to quadruples) offer a great value. Amenities include a small garden with hammocks and a pool, a bar, and free Wi-Fi. A bonus is proximity to oodles of restaurants and bars, a perk shared by the equally well situated **Hotel Rouver** (Av. Jorge Schimmelpfeng 872, tel. 45/3754-2916, www.hotelrouver.com.br, R$100-160 d). This small, innocuous, no-frills hotel offers great bang for your buck—from a pool and sauna to free airport pickup. Quieter rooms are at the back. For a home away from home, try to snag one of the two attractively decorated rooms tended to by the charming, multilingual Brazilian/Danish owners of **Pousada El Refúgio** (Rua Rio de Janeiro 853, tel. 45/3572-2038, R$370 d). You'll have the run of the entire pousada/villa, including the pool-dotted gardens where breakfast is served.

One of the best and most bucolic bargains on the Rodovia das Cataratas is **Hostel Natura** (Alameda Burri 333, Rodovia das Cataratas Km 12.5, tel. 45/3529-6949, www.hostelnatura.com, R$105-140 d, R$40 pp). Immersed in greenery, with a pool and two lagoons, the setting is relaxing, particularly when soaking up the sunset armed with a killer caipi from the small bar. Dorm and guest rooms are clean, if bare, and the multilingual staff is helpful. Close to the airport, it is easily accessible by municipal bus by day, although otherwise somewhat isolated (and chilly in the winter). **The San Martin Hotel** (Rodovia das Cataratas Km 21, tel. 45/3521-8088, www.hotelsanmartin.com.br, R$290-430 d) is one of the nicer 1970s-style resorts and is closest to the entrance of the Parque Nacional do Iguaçu. Attractive rooms sport white linens and hardwood floors, but an upgrade gets you more space and comfort along with forest views. The best feature is the surrounding expanse of green space: a mixture of landscaped gardens with recreational facilities and untamed jungle with a walking trail to the Rio Iguaçu.

In operation since the 1950s, the ★ **Hotel das Cataratas** (Rodovia das Cataratas Km 24.5, tel. 45/2102-7000, www.hoteldascataratas.com.br, R$1000-1,400 d) is the oldest hotel in Foz. It is also the only one actually *in* the Parque Nacional do Iguaçu, offering privileged access to the spectacular falls (especially in the precrowd early morning, when you can stroll around with a glass of breakfast champagne). Stylish rooms are steeped in character and retro charm. Only the wildly expensive Catarata Rooms and Suites actually offer views of the cataracts. Amenities include a large pool, tennis courts, forest walking trails, and a spa. The **Restaurante Itaipu** serves a delicious lunch buffet.

Food

Nobody really comes to Iguaçu Falls for the food, and although there is no shortage of sustenance, don't count on having a serious gourmet experience. Since you're in frontier land, *churrasco* is the way to go. **Bufalo Branco Churrascaria** (Rua Engenheiro Rebouças 530, tel. 45/3523-9744, www.bufalobranco.com.br, noon-11pm daily, R$35-45) is popular for succulent cuts of barbecued beef, pork, chicken, lamb, and even turkey testicles. Noncarnivores can opt for grilled *surubim* (a local fish), as well as the varied buffet

of salads and desserts. The enormous dining room of **Chef Lopes** (Rua Almirante Branco 1713, tel. 45/3025-3334, www.cheflopes.com.br, 11:30am-3:30pm daily, 6pm-11pm Mon.-Sat., R$30-45) serves prime Argentinean beef in various guises along with local river fish, exotic game, and an array of salads, sides, and pastas. At night, the per-kilo lunch banquet morphs into an à la carte menu. The variety, high quality, and sheer deliciousness justify the mildly lofty prices.

Foz has a large Arab community, and Middle Eastern cuisine is common. Serving up some of the finest Lebanese fare in town is **Castelo Libanês** (Rua Vinícius de Morais 520, Jardim Central, tel. 45/3526-1218, noon-midnight Tues.-Sun., 4pm-midnight Sat., R$25-35), a modest eatery with expertly prepared specialties that is conveniently adjacent to a halal butcher who supplies quality cuts of meat. **Barbarela** (Av. Brasil 1119, tel. 45/3028-2251, 9am-8pm Mon.-Fri., 9am-6pm Sat., R$5-10) is a great place for a snack or quick and healthy meal.

To savor fish from the region's mighty rivers, head to the banks of the Rio Paraná. Fish dishes and river views are equally appetizing at the **Clube Maringá** (Rua Dourado 111, tel. 45/3527-9683, www.restaurantemaringa.com.br, 11:30am-10:30pm Mon.-Sat., 11:30am-3pm Sun., R$25-40), a simple cantina-style restaurant with a large buffet. One of the specialties is grilled *dourado*, a large fish known as the "golden salmon" that is particularly abundant in the Rio Paraná's waters around Iguaçu.

Information and Services

There are many **tourist information** centers around Foz. Staff speak English, and you will find lots of information, including bus schedules and maps. The main **Teletur** office is at Av. das Cataratas 2330 (7am-11pm daily), which operates a bilingual hotline (tel. 0800-45-1516, www.iguassu.tur.br.). There are also locations at the airport (tel. 45/3521-4276, 8am-10pm daily), the international *rodoviária* (tel. 45/3522-1027, 7am-6pm daily), and the

Terminal Urbano local bus station (tel. 45/3523-7901, 7am-6:30pm daily).

Avenida Brasil is lined with numerous banks where you can withdraw money with your ATM card or exchange currency. In the event of a medical emergency, go to the Hospital Municipal (Adoniran Barbosa 370, Jardim Central, tel. 45/3521-1951).

Transportation

You can fly to Foz do Iguaçu directly from Curitiba and São Paulo. The Aeroporto Internacional Foz do Iguaçu (Rodovia das Cataratas Km 13, tel. 45/3523-4244) is on BR-469, halfway (13 km/8 mi) between the park and downtown Foz. A taxi to the park will cost around R$20; expect to pay R$50 to reach downtown. Buses marked "Aeroporto/Parque Nacional" (5am-midnight daily, R$2.90) leave at 20-minute intervals (45-minute intervals on Sun.) from the Terminal Urbano local bus station (TTU) in Centro, passing along Av. Juscelino Kubitschek and stopping at the airport en route to the park. To get from the airport to Centro, take the bus marked Centro/TTU.

Buses from cities throughout south and southeastern Brazil as well as Buenos Aires and Asunción arrive and depart from the Rodoviária Internacional (Av. Costa e Silva 1601, tel. 45/3522-3366), which is 5 kilometers (3 mi) from the center of Foz. Catarinense (tel. 4004-5001, www.catarinense.net) has eight daily buses that link Curitiba to Foz (10 hours, R$133). Pluma (tel. 0800/646-0300, www.pluma.com.br) operates three buses to and from São Paulo (16 hours, R$180) and two buses to and from Rio (23 hours, R$250). To get from the rodoviária to the TTU, take the 105 or 115 municipal bus, or a taxi (R$15). From here, Parque Nacional buses leave at 20-minute intervals 8am-6pm daily to the entrance of Parque Nacional do Iguaçu. From a stop on Av. Mem de Sá, across the street from the TTU, buses for Puerto Iguazú (R$4) depart at 15-minute intervals (30-minute intervals on Sunday) between 7am-7pm. It takes about an hour to get to Puerto Iguazú's bus station, where you need to transfer to a Rio Uruguay bus (30 pesos) that makes the 30-minute trip to the Parque Nacional Iguazú. To get to Foz from Curitiba—a 640-kilometer/398-mile (8-9 hour) drive—follow BR-277.

It is easy to get around Foz and visit surrounding attractions by bus (R$2.90) and taxi. To do some exploring on your own, rent a car at Avis (Rodovia das Cataratas Km 16.5, tel. 45/3529-6160, www.avis.com.br) or Localiza (Av. Juscelino Kubitschek 2878, tel. 45/3522-1608, www.localiza.com.br).

BORDER CROSSINGS

To cross the border from Foz do Iguaçu into Argentina or Paraguay, you will need to have a valid passport and—depending on your nationality—a tourist visa if you're going to leave Brazil for longer than a day trip. Most EU citizens don't need a visa, but Americans, Canadians, and Australians do. Even if only crossing the border for the day to visit the Parque Nacional Iguazú, you'll need to pay a reciprocity tax in advance if you're from the United States (US$160, valid 10 years), Canada (US$150, valid 5 years), and Australia (US$100, valid for 1 entry); this can be done online at Provincia Pagos (www.migraciones.gov.arg). If you're crossing the border by bus, some drivers may not wait while you complete immigration formalities, and you might end up asking for a pass to board the next bus that comes along. Also carry your Brazilian entry card, which you'll need to present to Brazilian immigration authorities when returning to Foz.

For Paraguay, visas are required for Americans (US$100), Canadians (US65), and Australians (US$75) traveling beyond Ciudad del Este. For information, contact the Argentinean Consulate (Rua Travessa Vice Consûl E. R. Bianchi 26, tel. 45/3574-2969, www.mrecic.gov.ar, 10am-3pm Mon.-Fri.) and the Paraguayan Consulate (Rua Marechal Deodoro 901, tel. 45/3523-2898, 8:30am-12:30pm and 1:30pm-5:30pm Mon.-Fri.). Get visas before you leave home.

Santa Catarina

The smallest of Brazil's southern states, Santa Catarina is famed for its beautiful coastline, which draws sun- and surf-seeking visitors from neighboring Argentina and Uruguay as well as Paulistanos and even Cariocas. Rough open seas lure surfers from around the world, but there are also plenty of sheltered coves for soakers and floaters. Some of the best beaches in the South surround the pretty island capital of Florianópolis, a vibrant, youthful, and prosperous city on the Ilha de Santa Catarina, whose beaches range from highly developed to practically deserted. Base yourself in "Floripa," and then spend 2-3 days (or more) beachcombing. On the mainland, highlights north of Florianópolis include the clear turquoise waters of Porto Belo and Bombinhas, whose Reserva Biológica Marinha da Ilha do Arvoredo offers excellent deep-sea diving. Heading south, you'll discover Garopaba, an Azorean fishing village famed for surfing, whale-watching, and the highly coveted Praia do Rosa. The pretty town of Laguna also offers some fine beaches as well as the best-preserved colonial architecture in the state.

Coastal Santa Catarina has a subtropical Mediterranean-like climate that translates into hot, humid summers and cool (as in 15°C/60°F) winters. The mountainous interior, however, is a different story, with snow being common in the highest areas during June-July; southern winds (from down Antarctica way) make the air temperature seem 10°C cooler. If you're looking for crowds and a party atmosphere, January-February is the best time to enjoy Santa Catarina's beaches. Otherwise, try to visit during November-December or March-April, when prices and temperatures decrease and you'll have the beaches to yourself.

ILHA DE SANTA CATARINA

Florianópolis, capital of the state of Santa Catarina, is located on the island of Santa Catarina. If you worry that the state and island sharing the same name might have confusing ramifications, don't. More confusing is that when Brazilians refer to "Florianópolis," they aren't just referring to the city but to the entire 420-square-kilometer (162-square-mi) Ilha de Santa Catarina, all of which lies under the municipal jurisdiction of Florianópolis. That said, the city is invariably and affectionately referred to as "Floripa."

Nomenclature aside, the island is a microcosm unto itself; officially, the island boasts 42 *praias,* but when the tides are low, there are closer to 100. Contrasting with Floripa's modern urban bustle are centuries-old Azorean fishing villages, where you can watch *pescadores* haul in the day's fresh catch and then savor the fruits of their labor while seated at *barracas* overlooking the sea.

Roads (most of them single-lane) are excellent, and bus service is extensive. Nonetheless, in view of its length—54 kilometers (34 mi) from the northern tip to the south—exploring its many beaches in a short time can involve an inordinate amount of traveling, particularly if you don't have a car.

Florianópolis

Founded in 1726 and settled largely by Azorean immigrants, Florianópolis was little more than a small fishing town until the early 19th century, when, having benefited enormously from the region's thriving whaling trade, it became the capital of Santa Catarina. Most of the Centro's fetching pastel-hued buildings—those that remain—are from this era. Yet despite Floripa's modern skyline and dynamic growth, this city of 420,000 retains a laid-back, small-town flavor. Its urban sights can be easily seen in half a day.

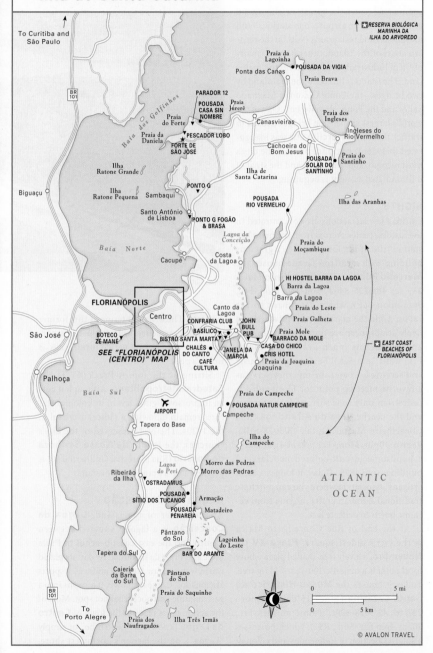

Ilha de Santa Catarina

To Curitiba and
São Paulo

Reserva Biológica
MARINHA DA
ILHA DO ARVOREDO

BR
101

Praia da
Lagoinha

POUSADA DA VIGIA

Ponta das Canas

Praia Brava

Baía dos Golfinhos

PARADOR 12

POUSADA
CASA SIN
NOMBRE

Praia
Jurerê

Praia
do Forte

Canasvieiras

Praia dos
Ingleses

PESCADOR LOBO

Praia da
Daniela

FORTE DE
SÃO JOSÉ

Cachoeira do
Bom Jesus

Ingleses do
Rio Vermelho

Ilha
Ratone Grande

Ilha
Ratone Pequena

Sambaqui

PONTO G

Ilha de
Santa Catarina

POUSADA
SOLAR DO
SANTINHO

Praia do
Santinho

Biguaçu

Santo Antônio
de Lisboa

POUSADA
RIO VERMELHO

Ilha das Aranhas

Baía Norte

PONTO G FOGÃO
& BRASA

Lagoa da
Conceição

Cacupé

Costa
da Lagoa

Praia do
Moçambique

FLORIANÓPOLIS

Centro

Canto da
Lagoa

HI HOSTEL BARRA DA LAGOA
Barra da Lagoa

Barra da Lagoa

Praia do Leste

CONFRARIA CLUB

JOHN
BULL
PUB

Praia Galheta

São José

BOTECO
ZE MANÉ

BASÍLICO

Praia Mole

BISTRÔ SANTA MARTA

BARRACO DA MOLE

SEE "FLORIANÓPOLIS
(CENTRO)" MAP

CHALÉS
DO CANTO

JANELA DA
MÁRCIA

CASA DO CHICO

CRIS HOTEL

Palhoça

CAFÉ
CULTURA

Praia da Joaquina
Joaquina

EAST COAST
BEACHES OF
FLORIANÓPOLIS

Baía Sul

Praia do Campeche

POUSADA NATUR CAMPECHE

AIRPORT

Campeche

Tapera do Base

Ilha do
Campeche

ATLANTIC

OCEAN

Lagoa
do Peri

Morro das Pedras
Morro das Pedras

Ribeirão
da Ilha

OSTRADAMUS

POUSADA
SÍTIO DOS TUCANOS

Armação

POUSADA
PENAREIA

Matadeiro

Pântano
do Sol

Lagoinha
do Leste

Tapera do Sul

BAR DO ARANTE

Caieriá
da Barra
do Sul

Pântano
do Sul

BR
101

Praia do Saquinho

0   5 mi

0   5 km

To
Porto Alegre

Praia dos
Naufragados

Ilha Três Irmãs

© AVALON TRAVEL

ORIENTATION

Although most of Floripa—its historic and commercial center, the upscale neighborhood of Beira Mar, the airport, bus stations, and most hotels and restaurants—sits on the western coast of the island, other *bairros* (many of them industrial) are located on the mainland. The island is linked to the mainland by two bridges—the Ponte Colombo Machado Salles and the Ponte Hercílio Luz. One of the world's largest suspension bridges (closed to traffic), the **Ponte Hercílio Luz** was inaugurated in 1926. It has since become the city's most recognizable landmark and the sight of it illuminated at night is beguiling.

SIGHTS

Floripa's few attractions are concentrated in the historic center. Across from the main bus station (site of the former port), a gracious building with a saffron facade houses the **Mercado Público** (Rua Conselheiro Mafra 255, tel. 48/3225-8464, 9am-7pm Mon.-Fri., 9am-noon Sat.), which dates back to the 1890s. Amid the market's colorful stalls and lively atmosphere are numerous patio bars and restaurants (open until 10pm Mon.-Fri., until 3pm Sat.). Featuring live music and serving beer and shrimp, they serve as a favorite meeting point for Floripanos. A pedestrian-only zone surrounds the market and the nearby **Casa da Alfândega** (Rua Conselheiro Mafra 141, tel. 48/3028-8102, 9am-6:30pm Mon.-Fri., 9am-1pm Sat.), a handsome biscuit-colored neoclassical building from 1875. Today, it lodges a local artisans' association where you can purchase traditional Azorean crafts ranging from ceramic bowls to delicate lace.

At the end of Rua Conselheiro Mafra is the city's oldest square, **Praça XV de Novembro,** a lovely tree-shaded plaza whose focal point is a majestic 100-year-old fig tree. Today it houses the **Museu Histórico de Santa Catarina** (Praça 15 de Novembro 227, tel. 48/3028-8091, 10am-6pm Tues.-Fri., 10am-4pm Sat.-Sun., R$2), which possesses a small collection of indigenous and colonial

Santa Catarina

artifacts. The ornate interior of this former governor's residence, with its lustrous parquet floors and elegant period furnishings, is worth a peek.

Sitting at the top of Praça XV is the **Catedral Metropolitano.** Although it cuts an impressive figure, few of its colonial features remain following a radical overhaul in the 1920s. The best-preserved of the city's churches, the **Igreja de Nossa Senhora do Rosário** (Rua Marechal Guilherme 60) is perched atop a grand flight of stairs.

Lagoa da Conceição

At the center of the island, **Lagoa da Conceição** is a lagoon situated between Centro and the east coast beaches of Praia Mole and Praia da Joaquina. By day, its placid warm waters draw families and water sports aficionados. Come sundown, it morphs into a gastronomic and nocturnal hot spot. Most of the action takes place in the town of **Centro da Lagoa** (known as "Centrinho" or simply "Lagoa"), on the lagoon's northwest shore.

Florianópolis (Centro)

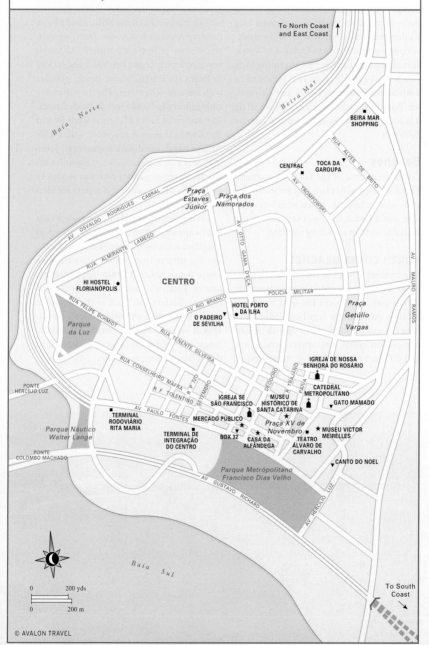

To North Coast
and East Coast

Baía Norte

Beira Mar

BEIRA MAR
SHOPPING

RUA ALVES DE BRITO

CENTRAL   TOCA DA
GAROUPA

AV TROMPOWSKI

AV OSVALDO RODRIGUES CABRAL

*Praça
Esteves
Júnior*

*Praça dos
Namorados*

AV OTTO GAMA DE ÇA

RUA ALMIRANTE LAMEGO

AV MAURO RAMOS

HI HOSTEL
FLORIANÓPOLIS

CENTRO

POLÍCIA MILITAR

*Praça
Getúlio
Vargas*

RUA FELIPE SCHMIDT

AV RIO BRANCO

*Parque
da Luz*

HOTEL PORTO
DA ILHA

O PADEIRO
DE SEVILHA

RUA TENENTE SILVEIRA

IGREJA DE NOSSA
SENHORA DO ROSÁRIO

R. TRAJANO

PAIVA

RUA CONSELHEIRO MAFRA

DEODORO

CATEDRAL
METROPOLITANO

PONTE
HERCILIO LUZ

R. P. 10

SETEMBRO

R. F. TOLENTINO

IGREJA SE
SÃO FRANCISCO

MUSEU
HISTÓRICO DE
SANTA CATARINA

GATO MAMADO

AV PAULO FONTES

TERMINAL
RODOVIÁRIO
RITA MARIA

MERCADO PÚBLICO

*Praça XV de
Novembro*

MUSEU VICTOR
MEIRELLES

*Parque Náutico
Walter Lange*

PONTE
COLOMBO MACHADO

TERMINAL DE
INTEGRAÇÃO
DO CENTRO

BOX 32

CASA DA
ALFÂNDEGA

TEATRO
ÁLVARO DE
CARVALHO

AV HERCILIO LUZ

CANTO DO NOEL

*Parque Metrópolitano
Francisco Dias Velho*

AV GUSTAVO RICHARD

Baía Sul

0   200 yds

0   200 m

To South
Coast

The Lagoa also possesses some nice swimming beaches. If you crave a little peace and tranquility, you can catch a boat (40 min.) that leaves hourly from the dock (or brave a long 7-kilometer/4.5-mi walk around the undeveloped western shore) to **Costa da Lagoa.** Surrounded by nature, this charming little village on the southern shore is inhabited by a mixture of fisherfolk, artists, and *alternativos.* Boasting beaches and a nearby waterfall, it is a relaxing spot to kick back and feast on fresh fish.

Beaches

Considered some of the finest in southern Brazil, Floripa offers beaches for every age, style, and inclination. If you want lots of action, you'll find it, but quiet seclusion is also available without searching too hard.

NORTH COAST BEACHES

The beaches along the island's north coast boast the warmest and calmest waters. For this reason, they were the first to attract tourists, particularly families. Today, most have become incredibly built up with numerous soulless hotels, restaurants, condos, and tacky T-shirt shops. At the extreme western tip, **Daniela** is one of the nicer beaches, with aquamarine waters and soft sand backed by greenery. Facing the beach is Ilha Ratones, with its medieval-looking 18th-century Forte de Santo Antônio de Ratones. Traveling west, you'll come to **Praia de Jurerê.** Although very developed, it has a fine beach and is close to **Praia do Forte,** whose beach, popular with families, is dominated by the impressive 18th-century Forte São José da Ponta Grossa. **Canasvieiras** is out of control while **Ponto das Canas** is more manageable, with a wide strip of beach lined with restaurants. From here, it is a 20-minute walk to **Lagoinha do Norte,** an enticing little beach surrounded by green hills whose calm, cold waters are ideal for snorkeling.

Facing the open Atlantic, trendy **Praia Brava** attracts surfers and hangers-on with its rough seas. Unfortunately, this pretty beach has also attracted some extreme condos. Even worse is neighboring **Praia dos Ingleses,** one of Floripa's most heavily urbanized beaches. Surfers also flock to the somewhat wilder **Praia do Santinho,** which is bracketed at one end by the Costão do Santinho megaresort and at the other by deserted sand dunes fringed with vegetation.

Floripa

★ EAST COAST BEACHES

Facing the open Atlantic, Floripa's east coast beaches are the island's longest and most dramatic. A combination of cold water, rough waves, and undercurrents keeps families (and package tours) at bay but attracts a crowd of surfers and young, tanned singles (both gay and straight).

Praia do Moçambique is the longest and most primitive of the island's beaches. Due to its inclusion in the Parque Estadual do Rio Vermelho, its 8 kilometers (5 mi) of dunes framed by pine forests are unmarred by human construction. The continuation of Moçambique is **Praia Barra da Lagoa,** which is anchored by **Barra da Lagoa,** a fishing colony. A canal links the Lagoa da Conceição to the sea.

From Barra da Lagoa, a hilly trail leads to **Praia da Galheta,** whose waters are warmer and more placid than elsewhere along the coast and where nude sunbathing is permitted. Another trail leads south to hip **Praia Mole,** whose name (*mole* means soft) derives from the large grains that make this sand so invitingly fluffy. Many of the younger crowd who frequent this beach are surfers, or wish they were. Most are also single, giving Mole a reputation for being the flirtiest beach on the island. The stretch of sand nearest to Galheta is a gay and lesbian hot spot.

Extremely popular (although somewhat overblown) is neighboring **Praia da Joaquina.** Famed for having the best waves on the island, major surfing competitions are held at "Joca." Although the beach is quite wide, in summer it is invaded by so many beach bars, frescoball games, and sunbathers that it's challenging to actually glimpse a patch of sand.

The continuation of Joaquina is the more deserted (if you ignore the encroaching upscale condos), but equally stunning **Praia do Campeche,** which gazes out toward the **Ilha do Campeche.** From the pier of the nearby village of Armação, it's only 30 minutes in a fishing boat (R$40 pp for a minimum of six) to the tiny island, where, when you're not busy snorkeling in emerald waters (R$40), you can kick back at one of two beach *barracas* that serve grilled fish. Ilha do Campeche is also famed for its glyphs—mysterious symbols and inscriptions carved into more than 160 stones—that date back more than 5,000 years. On the island, monitors are available to guide you along different trails (R$6-15) and explain the archaeological sites. To hire a boat, contact the Associação de Pescadores da Armação (48/8814-4364).

SOUTH COAST BEACHES

The south coast beaches are the most untamed on the island. Some say they are also the most beautiful, although the water is *frio!* Tourism has made few inroads, and even asphalt has yet to reach the most remote strips of sand. In compensation, countless walking trails lead along the coast.

South of Campeche, the quaint fishing village of **Armação** nestles against a rugged backdrop of green hills. Although the waters of **Praia da Armação** are rough and dangerous, signed trails lead to nearby coves and natural pools that offer safer swimming. A handful of charming *pousadas* makes this an excellent place to stay.

From Armação, you can walk along a trail to **Praia do Matadeiro,** then continue on for another three hours through native forest to what many consider the most dropdead gorgeous beach on the island: **Praia da Lagoinha do Leste.** The turquoise waters and white sand framed by lush mountains are spectacular, and an added bonus is the *lagoinha,* a beautiful freshwater lagoon that sits just behind the beach. The area is preserved within the Parque Municipal da Lagoinha do Leste, and as such you'll find no signs of civilization. Easier access is via a steep trail from Pantâno do Sul (1.5 hours) or by boat. If you choose to hike, it's wise to do so with a guide.

Pântano do Sul is one of the island's most active fishing villages, and it is an ideal place to tuck into raw oysters or the fresh catch of the day. The beach isn't the best along this coast, but swimming conditions in the protected bay are safe. A more beautiful beach is **Praia de Solidão,** whose name, "Solitude Beach," is quite fitting for this out-of-the-way spot that can only be reached by a steep 40-minute hike from Praia do Saquinho, farther south. At one end, a waterfall cascading into a natural pool offers freshwater bathing. Farther off the beaten track is **Praia dos Naufragados,** at the southern tip of the island. Although it can only be accessed by boat (25 minutes) or by an hour-long mountain hike from Caieiras da Barra do Sul, your efforts will be amply rewarded by paradisiacal landscapes and bewitching views out to sea.

WEST COAST BEACHES

Facing the mainland of Santa Catarina, the beaches north and south of Florianópolis are less spectacular (and less touristy) than other parts of the island. The main attractions are a trio of the island's oldest and most atmospheric Azorean fishing colonies. Between 1748 and 1756, as a result of natural disasters and overpopulation, more than 6,000 Azorean immigrants crossed the Atlantic and settled on the protected west coast of the Ilha de Santa Catarina, where they survived by fishing, cultivating manioc, and hunting whales (whose blubber and oil was a precious fuel). **Ribeirão da Ilha** (south of Floripa) and **Santo Antônio de Lisboa** and **Sambaqui** (to the north) all have simple Portuguese colonial churches and typical Azorean whitewashed houses with blue trim. Residents still make their living by fishing—Ribeirão and Santo Antônio da Ilha are renowned for mussels and oysters farmed offshore—and continue a centuries-old tradition of intricate lace-making, which you can purchase in both villages. Although the beaches are quite small (appealingly sprinkled with fishing nets and brightly painted wooden boats), the villages themselves are pleasantly languorous. It goes without saying that the fresh fish and seafood are fantastic.

Sports and Recreation
SURFING

The east coast is legendary for its surfing scene, particularly on the beaches of Joaquina, Mole, and Moçambique. On Praia da Joaquina, near the Cris Hotel, **Easy Surf** (Rua Pres. Acácio Garibaldi São Thiago 2367, Loja 8, tel. 48/3232-2082, www.easysurf.com. br), a surfing school operated by Brazilian surf champ Karina "Kika" Abramov, offers lessons

one of Floripa's east coast beaches

for all ages and levels (R$70 for 90 minutes) as well as outings and rental of boards (R$15-25 per hour/R$50-75 per day). During the *tainha* fishing season (Apr.-June), surfing is prohibited on the island.

SAND BOARDING

For those who fear wiping out in the waves, much softer landings are in store when you and your board take to the Sahara-like dunes behind **Praia da Joaquina.** You can rent boards (R$20 per hour) along the access road to Joaquina.

SURF RAFTING

The latest hybrid variation of surfing and water rafting involves riding the waves of Praia dos Ingleses in an inflatable raft. **Adrenailha** (tel. 48/3284-3585, www.adrenailha.com.br) charges R$70 for an adrenaline-charged hour.

PARAGLIDING

The east coast beaches and Lagoa da Conceição boast ideal wind conditions for paragliding (*parapente*). Based in Centro da Lagoa, **Parapente Sul** (Rua José Antônio da Silveira 201, tel. 48/3232-0791, www.parapentesul.com.br, R$150 for a 15-minute flight) is a reputable sports outfitter that offers lessons on the dunes of Joaquina before you take to the skies at heights of up to 1,200 meters (4,000 feet). If you lack experience, you can also fly tandem (*vôo duplo*) with an instructor.

WINDSURFING AND KITE SURFING

Windsurfers and kite surfers who want the challenge of rough winds and waves take to the east coast beaches, while calmer souls stick to the placid waters of the north coast beaches and the lagoon. In Lagoa, **Wind Center** (Rua Rita Lourenço da Silveira 673, tel. 48/3232-2278, www.windcenter.com.br) offers courses and equipment rental. A basic six-session windsurfing course costs R$350, and a two-hour kite-surfing course will set

you back R$250. Equipment rentals cost R$50 per hour.

DIVING

An hour's boat ride from the island's north coast, the waters surrounding Ilha do Arvoredo boast some of the best diving in the South. In Canasvieiras, **Acquanauta** (Rua Antenor Borges 324, tel. 48/3266-1137, www.acquanautafloripa.com.br) rents diving and snorkeling equipment, offers lessons, and runs numerous trips to Arvoredo for R$200 (divers) and R$90 (snorkelers).

BOAT EXCURSIONS

Two of the most popular boating trips are to islands off the coast of Ilha de Santa Catarina. **Scuna Sul** (Av. Oswaldo Rodrigues Cabral, Centro, tel. 48/3225-1806, www.scunasul.com.br) operates schooner excursions (boats carry 70-200 passengers) from Canasvieiras via the dolphin-inhabited Baía dos Golfinhos to **Ilha de Anhatorim.** Here you can visit the region's oldest fort, **Forte de Santa Cruz do Anhatorim,** built in 1744. An alternative route from Floripa takes you beneath the Hercílio Luz bridge and stops at the **Ilha de Ratones Grande,** where you can clamber around the 18th-century **Fortaleza de Santo Antônio de Ratones.** Both half-day outings fit in stops for lunch (not included in the R$50 cost).

GUIDED HIKES

Hiking from deserted beach to deserted beach through the forest-clad mountains is an excellent way to immerse yourself fully in Floripa's natural attractions. **Adrenailha** (tel. 48/3284-3585, www.adrenailha.com.br) offers a handful of guided day trips (R$250-R$350 for 2 people) that include guides, transportation, and snacks. Ambitious souls with plenty of time on their hands can undertake the seven-day around-the-island trekking tour. Designed for a maximum of six people, the cost (around R$2,000 depending on accommodation choices) includes all transportation and accommodation fees.

Entertainment and Events
NIGHTLIFE

During summer, Floripa's biggest parties unfold under the sun—and on the beach—at sophisticated beach *barracas,* where you can spend the day alternating between basking in beach chairs and grooving to DJ-spun tunes, with time out for ocean dips and multifruit *caipis.* Among the trendiest clubs is swanky **Parador 12** (Servidão José Cardoso de Oliveira, tel. 84/3284-8156, www.parador12.com.br, 10am-10pm daily, Dec.-Mar., cover R$80), with a restaurant, a pool, and white canopy beds where chic-sters sip champagne. Praia Mole attracts a hipper, more alternative crowd whose headquarters is the rustic **Barraco da Mole** (center of Praia Mole, tel. 84/3232-5585, www.barracodamole.com.br, 9am-8pm daily, closed June-Sept.), a happening haunt of *surfistas* and lithe young hangers-on who groove to electronica while pounding back healthy açaís.

Less sandy but no less sizzling offerings can be found in Lagoa da Conceição. With great lagoon views, **John Bull Pub** (Av. das Rendeiras 1046, tel. 48/3232-8535, www.johnbullfloripa.com.br, 10pm-4am Thurs.-Sat. off-season, 10pm-4am daily Dec.-Feb., cover R$15-20) is a perennially happening place with good live music, especially national and local rock, reggae, and blues bands. Lagoa's Grand Hipster Central is the belle epoque mansion housing the **Confraria Club** (Rua João Pacheco da Costa 31, tel. 48/3232-2298, www.confrariaclub.com.br, 11pm-5am Thurs.-Sat.), a pulsing club/lounge tricked out with vintage furniture.

Centro has some great watering holes. Around since the 1950s, **Canto do Noel** (Av. Tiradentes 186, tel. 48/3225-8821, cantodonoel.webnode.com.br, 1pm-midnight Mon.-Fri., noon-7 Sat.) is an unpretentious old-school *boteco* where politicos and bohos have gathered for decades. Savor live samba on Thursday and

Friday nights or during the coveted Saturday afternoon feijoadas (R$25 pp).

A favorite happy-hour haunt of Floripa's artist crowd, tiny **Gato Mamado** (Rua Saldanho Marinho 351, tel. 48/3371-9069, www.gatomamado.com.br, 6:30pm-4am Tues.-Sat.) explodes on Thursday and Friday nights, when the street closes to traffic, allowing live jazz, rock, and blues (not to mention the crowd) to spill onto the cobblestones. It's well worth a quick trip to the mainland neighborhood of Coqueiros to savor the inspired concoctions at **Boteco Zé Mané** (Rua Desembargador Pedro Silva 2360, tel. 48/3204-8562, 6pm-midnight Sun.-Thurs. 6pm-1pm Fri.-Sat.). Among the mouth-watering appetizers is tainha fish fried in crunchy manioc flour and suspended from a miniature fishing net. Drinks are equally innovative; try the watermelon, ginger, and basil caipirinha.

FESTIVALS AND EVENTS

Floripa's **Carnaval** has become one of the most flocked-to festivals of the South. Even Cariocas abandon Rio to join in the festivities, which feature a significant gay and lesbian contingent. Between May and mid-July is *tainha* fishing season, a period during which great schools of this delectable fish swarm the coasts of Floripa. It's customary for residents—and visitors—to help fishermen haul their overflowing nets up to shore. The ritual is especially popular at the beaches of Barra da Lagoa, Ingleses, Santinho, and Pântano do Sul. This is also the best period to sample fresh *tainha* in Floripa's restaurants.

Shopping

For regional folk art and handicrafts, particularly ceramics and Azorean lace, check out the **Casa da Alfândega** (Rua Conselheiro Mafra 141, tel. 48/3028-8102, 9am-6:30pm Mon.-Fri., 9am-1pm Sat.) and the **Casa Açoriana** (Rua Cônego Serpa 30, tel. 48/3235-1262, 10am-8pm daily) in Santo Antônio de Lisboa. For clothing, especially cutting-edge beach- and surf wear, head to **Beira Mar Shopping** (Rua Bocaiúva 2468, tel. 48/3212-4600, www.

shoppingbeiramar.com.br, 10am-10pm Mon.-Sat., 2pm-8pm Sun.), where you'll also find cinemas and a food court.

Accommodations

Most Floripa visitors have beaching on the brain and choose to stay on one of the coasts. Although Centro has few budget options, rates throughout the island fall significantly when summer crowds disperse. December through March, prices are high and reservations are essential. The seasonal migration of surfers, party animals, and back-to-nature buffs has resulted in a flood of hostels and other budget options.

CENTRO

Since downtown hotels are primarily geared to business travelers, prices are lower on weekends. The cheapest option is the cheery, well-kept **HI Hostel Florianópolis** (Rua Duarte Schutel 227, tel. 48/3225-3781, www.floripahostel.com.br), a 10-minute walk from the *rodoviária*. It has spotless dorm rooms (R$48 pp) and private guest rooms (R$110 d) for couples and families, a communal kitchen, pleasant dining area, and an outdoor terrace. Unbeatable in terms of cost-benefit, the **Hotel Porto da Ilha** (Rua Dom Jaime Câmara 43, tel. 48/3229-3000, www.portodailha.com.br, R$190-280 d) is a gleaming business hotel with a great location 10 minutes from the local bus station (known as TICEN) and five minutes from the seashore.

LAGOA DA CONCEIÇÃO

To be close to east coast beaches by day and all the action at night, stay in the town of Centro da Lagoa. The conveniently located **HI Hostel Barra da Lagoa** (Rua Inelzyr Bauer Bertolli, tel. 48/3232-4291, www.floripahostel.com.br) offers simple dorm rooms (R$45-60 pp) with decent mattresses and lots of storage space, and double guest rooms (R$115-170 d) that are spare but roomy. Perks include free Wi-Fi and lending of bikes and surfboards, along with friendly, helpful staff. An art curator living in Texas, Márcia Pirmez

returned to her hometown of Floripa to open ★ **Janela da Márcia** (Rua Dr. Alfredo Dauro Jorge 131, tel. 48/9958-1782, www.janeladamarcia.com, R$220-280 d). Located within a private residential complex, this three-room B&B is as warm, personable, and artistic as the *dona* herself.

If you feel like doing some cottage-keeping, check into one of the old-fashioned wooden A-frame bungalows at **Chalés do Canto** (Rua Laurindo da Silveira 2212, tel. 48/3232-0471, www.chalesdocanto.com.br, R$140-220 d). To ensure privacy, the chalets—which sleep up to five—are scattered amid the woodlands surrounding the pretty fishing village of Canto da Lagoa, 3 kilometers (2 mi) from Centro da Lagoa. Each cozy unit is equipped with a full kitchen, fireplace, and TV; far more watchable are the *lagoa* views from hammocks on the wooden decks.

NORTH COAST

Amid the urban development and *movimento* of Praia de Jurerê, **Pousada Casa Sin Nombre** (Rua dos Polvos 58-A, tel. 48/3282-1379, www.casasinnombre.com.br, R$200-300 d) is a lovely exception. Built and decorated in the style of a whitewashed Mediterranean villa, this cozy guesthouse, three blocks from the beach, exudes a homey warmth.

Located on an eco-estate overlooking Santinho beach, **Pousada Solar do Santinho** (Estrada Vereador Onildo Lemos 2197, tel. 48/3284-1789, www.pousadasolardosantinho.com.br, R$280-370 d) offers 14 sizable and well-appointed apartments with kitchenettes. The English-speaking owners are as efficient as they are eco-conscientious; notice the use of reforested wood and solar panels. Grounds are studded with fruit trees and Buddha statues; there's a pool and even a climbing wall. Children under age 12 are not allowed.

Located at the absolute northern tip of the island, only a footpath from beautiful Lagoinha beach, the pretty pink ★ **Pousada da Vigia** (Rua Conselheiro Walmor Castro 291, tel. 48/3269-4168, www.pousadadavigia.

com.br, R$300-700 d) is an enchanting and intimate hotel with eight apartments and two luxury suites nestled against a backdrop of Atlantic forest. Although hardly spacious, guest rooms are breezy and tastefully furnished with fine linens and local handicrafts as well as private balconies. A pool, Jacuzzi, and sauna, combined with the hotel's remoteness, are conducive to romance.

EAST COAST

Sitting within a vast green area between the Lagoa and the wild deserted sands of Praia de Moçambique, the well-run **Pousada Rio Vermelho** (Rodovia João Gualberto Soares 8479, tel. 48/3269-7337, www.pousadariovermelho.com.br, R$120-180 d) offers a total getaway. The main lodge is a paragon of rustic chic with hardwood floors, patchwork quilts, throw pillows, and handwoven carpets. Individual chalets are more basic and equipped with kitchens. There is also a lovely pool.

Surf junkies should consider the **Cris Hotel** (Av. Prefeito Acácio Garibaldi S Thiago 2399, tel. 48/3232-5380, www.crishotel.com.br, R$130-240 d), with a prime location overlooking Praia Joaquina. The sizable, unassuming rooms (which sleep up to five) aren't rave-worthy, but they're clean and a good value; plus, you'll fall asleep listening to the sound of waves.

SOUTH COAST

Just off Praia do Campeche, **Pousada Natur Campeche** (Servidão Família Nunes 59, tel. 48/3237-4011, www.naturcampeche.com.br, R$250-340 d) is a welcoming little oasis. The friendly owner, Talmir, knows how to treat travelers, as he is one himself: each guest room is decorated with artifacts gathered during his roaming. A small pool, verdant garden, and swinging hammocks reinforce the relaxing vibe.

Nature lovers will be smitten with the ★ **Pousada Sítio dos Tucanos** (tel. 48/3237-5084, www.pousadasitiodostucanos.com, R$170-260 d), which sits on a private

nature reserve on the edge of the Parque Municipal da Lagoa do Peri and offers sweeping views of Praia da Armação. The country-style chalet accommodations are simple but cozy and include hammock-strung balconies. The friendly German owner organizes eco-outings from mountain hikes to whale-watching excursions. A few steps from a secluded stretch of Praia da Armação, **Pousada Penareia** (Rua Hermes Guedes de Fonseca 207, tel. 48/3338-1616, www.pousadapenareia.com.br, R$180-270 d) offers modern and attractively appointed guest rooms with verandas, sea views, and lots of peace and tranquility (no children under 12). Guests are pleasantly pampered—the hotel offers everything from beach chairs and volleyballs to inflatable kayaks and bikes.

Food

Florianópolis is a seafood lover's paradise. The island is the biggest producer of oysters in Brazil, which are served fresh and deliciously raw (accompanied by lime wedges) at many beachside eateries and in rustic restaurants in the Azorean fishing villages on the west coast. You'll know an oyster is fresh if it glistens and smells slightly of the sea. Also popular are shrimp—pink and white—prepared in myriad ways, and local *tainha,* whose tender meat melts in your mouth.

CENTRO

By day, Centro boasts many inexpensive eating options. At night, however, most people head to the chic Beira Mar neighborhood or to the Lagoa. Downtown, the **Mercado Público** (Rua Conselheiro Mafra 255, tel. 48/3225-8464, 9am-7pm Mon.-Fri., 9am-noon Sat.) is a classic spot to eat and hang out. **Box 32** (tel. 48/3244-5588, www.box32.com.br, 9am-7pm Mon.-Fri., 9am-1pm Sat., R$10-25) is a Floripa institution that draws locals and tourists for its delicious fish and seafood.

One of the best per-kilo joints in town, **Central** (Rua Bocaiuva 2180, Beira Mar, tel. 48/3222-0089, 11am-2:30pm daily, R$15-25) has an appetizing spread of hot and cold dishes and salads with organic vegetables. For baked goods, **O Padeiro de Sevilha** (Rua Esteves Júnior 418, Centro, tel. 48/3025-3402, www.opadeirodesevilha.com.br, 7am-8:30pm Mon.-Fri., 7am-2pm Sat.) offers a mouthwatering assortment of focaccias, sandwiches, pastries (sweet and savory), cookies, and cakes (including dairy- and gluten-free options).

Toca da Garoupa (Rua Alves de Brito 178, Beira Mar, tel. 48/3223-1220, www.tocadagaroupa.com.br, noon-3pm and 7pm-midnight daily, R$55-80) was founded by a group of friends who share a love for deep-sea fishing. While the ambiance is stodgy (and sometimes noisy) and the prices (and portions) hefty, the seafood is dependably rave-worthy.

LAGOA DA CONCEIÇÃO

Lagoa possesses a variety of restaurants. You'll find many casual places serving fish and seafood as well as the traditional *sequência de camarões,* in which waiters circulate, *rodízio*-style, offering dish after dish of shrimp prepared in a variety of ways, such as steamed, grilled, breaded, stuffed with creamy Catupiry cheese, and *au vinaigrette.* With panoramic views of the lagoon, **Casa do Chico** (Av. das Rendeiras 1620, tel. 48/3232-5132, www.casadochico.com, 11:30am-11:30pm daily, R$30-45) is a simple and much-loved institution.

Located in a historic Azorean *casa* along the "Via Gastronômica" leading to Canto da Lagoa, **Bistrô Santa Marta** (Rua Laurindo Januári da Silveira 1350, tel. 48/3371-0769, www.bistrosantamarta.com.br, 8am-midnight Mon.-Sat., R$50-65) is a tiny gem whose Gaucho owners go all out in forging an unforgettable and intimate dining experience. With only seven highly coveted tables, reservations are a must.

For a break from seafood, head to **Basílico** (Rua Laurindo Januário da Silveira 649, tel. 48/3232-1129, www.pizzariabasilico.com.br, 7pm-midnight daily, R$30-40) for pizzas that are baked to crisp perfection in a wood-burning oven. There's also a branch in Centro (Rua Rafael Bandeira 328, tel. 84/3225-5574). **Café**

Cultura (Rua Manuel Severino 669, Loja 3, tel. 48/3334-0483, www.cafeculturafloripa.com.br, 9am-12:30am daily, R$15-30) will fix up those in need of a java jolt. The house blend is made from Arabica beans grown in the Alta Mogiana region of São Paulo (the *terroir* of Brazilian coffee). Snacks, light bistro food, breakfast, and even waffles (one of the owners—a former Starbucks barista—is American) are also served. A second location in Centro (Praça XV de Novembro 352, tel. 48/3364-3323) is open Monday-Saturday.

NORTH COAST

As developed as it is, the north coast is not an easy place to find good eating options. One of the few exceptions to this rule is the family-style **Pescador Lobo** (Rua José Cardoso de Oliveira, Praia do Forte, tel. 48/3282-0631, 10am-6pm daily, Mar.-Nov., 10am-midnight daily, Dec.-Feb., R$25-35). Overlooking the sea and the Fortaleza de São José da Ponta Grossa, it's owned by a local fisherman whose nickname is Lobo ("Wolf"). Robust seafood dishes (portions feed two) include specialties such as gratiné sole with cream corn and shrimp cooked in a pumpkin.

SOUTH COAST

★ **Bar do Arante** (Rua Abelardo Otacílio Gomes 254, Pântano do Sul, tel. 48/3237-7022, 11:30am-midnight daily, R$25-35) has been around since 1958, when Arante and his wife, Osmarina, opened a little shack in Pantâno do Sul. In the 1960s, after relocating to the beach, the bar became headquarters for students who came to camp on the deserted south coast. In those pre-cell phone days, they left written messages to each other—which explains the thousands that are still taped all over the walls and ceiling (to leave one, just ask the waiter for paper and a pen). The sheer number of these notes also attests to the popularity of Osmarina's cooking. Dishes feed at least two.

WEST COAST

When faced with serious seafood cravings, Floripanos head to the island's traditional

Azorean fishing villages of Sambaqui, Ribeirão da Ilha, and Santo Antônio.

★ **Ostradamus** (Rodovia Baldocero Filomeno 7640, Ribeirão da Ilha, tel. 48/3337-5711, www.ostradamus.com.br, noon-11pm Tues.-Sat., noon-5pm Sun., R$50-70) is the island's high temple of oysters. In a pretty pumpkin-colored colonial house overlooking the sea, oyster junkies gather to savor these freshly farmed jewels, served by the dozen (and carefully prepared—ultraviolet radiation is used to neutralize bacteria). For dessert, cross the street to **Tens Tempo,** owned by the same proprietors, where you can cap off the meal with a traditional Portuguese pastry.

Considered the finest gourmet dining experience on the island, **Ponto G** (Rua Padre Rohr 1717, Santo Antônio de Lisboa, tel. 48/8815-0618, www.pontoggastronomia.com.br, 7pm-midnight Wed.-Sat. noon-5pm Sun., R$80-100) is located on the remote (and tricky to find) property of chef-of-the-moment Victor Gomes. Gomes opens his home (literally) to a nightly handful of guests eager to experience his freshly sourced, innovative cuisine (and able to fork out some serious *reais*). The multicourse menus change weekly and mingle local ingredients with French culinary techniques. Reservations are essential. In late 2013, Gomes opened the more accessible **Ponto G Fogão & Brasa** (Rua Quinze de Novembro 18, Santo Antônio de Lisboa, tel. 48/3235-2623, noon-3pm Tues.-Sun., 7pm-11pm Tues.-Sat., R$60-80), specializing in expertly grilled seafood and meat and offering bewitching sea views.

Information and Services

There are several branches of the **tourist office** around Floripa and the island, including one at the Terminal Rodoviário Rita Maria (Av. Paulo Fontes 1101, tel. 48/3228-1095, 9am-7pm). Also check out the sites www.guia-floripa.com.br and http://portal.pmf.sc.gov.br/entidades/turismo (in Portuguese). For information about Santa Catarina, check out the state's bilingual site, www.santacatarina-turismo.com.br.

For exchanging currency and withdrawing money from ATMs, head to the banks along Rua Felipe Schmidt and the streets surrounding Praça 15 de Novembro, where you'll also find the main post office and Internet cafés.

In an emergency, dial **192** for an ambulance, **190** for the police, and **193** for the fire department. For medical treatment, go to the **Hospital Universitário** (Av. Beira-Mar Norte, Trindade, tel. 48/3721-9100, www.hu.ufsc.br).

Transportation

By air, Florianópolis can be reached directly from Rio, São Paulo, Curitiba, and Porto Alegre. The **Aeroporto Internacional Hercílio Luz** (Av. Diomício Freitas, tel. 48/3331-4000) is 12 kilometers (8 mi) south of the city center. Taking a taxi into town costs around R$45; to the north coast, around R$85. To call a cab from anywhere on the island, call **Central Radio Taxi** (tel. 48/3240-6009). Between 5:30am and 12:30am, regular municipal buses (183 and 186) link the airport with the local bus terminal (TICEN) in Centro.

Buses from around the state and the country arrive at the modern **Terminal Rodoviário Rita Maria** (Av. Paulo Fontes 1101, tel. 48/3212-3100), located between the Hercílio Luz and Colombo Machado Sales bridges. **Catarinense** (tel. 48/4004-5001, www.catarinense.net) operates 10 daily buses from São Paulo (10 hours, R$120) and hourly departures from Curitiba (4.5 hours, R$55).

Close to the main *rodoviária* is the **Terminal de Integração do Centro (TICEN).** From here buses serve Florianópolis and points along the south coast. From another terminal at the corner of Rua José da Costa Moelmann and Avenida Mauro Ramos, buses depart to beaches on the north, east, and south coasts via (respectively) the local terminals of Canasvieiras (TICAN), Lagoa (TILAG), and Rio Tavares (TIRIO). Regardless of your destination, you can usually choose from simple (often crowded) municipal buses (R$2.90, which includes the right to one transfer) and more expensive, air-conditioned *executivo* minibuses (R$3.50).

Although bus service around the island is extensive, buses themselves are infrequent and service can be slow. If you're going to be moving around a lot, you're better off renting a car (bear in mind that in summer, traffic jams to popular beaches are common). **Hertz** (www.hertz.com.br) has offices at the airport (tel. 48/3236-9955) as well as multiple locations around the island. For competitive rates, try **Le Mans** (tel. 48/3222-9999, www.lemansfloripa.com.br), which has offices at the airport but will deliver and pick up cars throughout the island. Based in Lagoa, **Loco Motos** (Av. das Rendeiras 1462, tel. 48/3232-1717, www.locomotos.com.br) rents scooters and motorcycles; both are an excellent way to explore the island.

NORTH OF FLORIANÓPOLIS

The coastline running north from Florianópolis is spectacular. It is also insanely mobbed in the summertime by tourists from São Paulo, Paraná, and Argentina. Unfortunately, its many natural attractions are marred by the type of unbridled urbanization epitomized by the resort town of Balneário Camboriú. Billed as the South's "Pequena Copacabana," this tourist mecca 80 kilometers (50 mi) north of Florianópolis possesses the Rio neighborhood's high-rises without any of its charm. To date, the area that has best fended off development is the peninsula of Porto Belo, 60 kilometers (37 mi) north of Floripa. Here, you'll find some of the state's loveliest beaches, along with emerald waters that are ideal for snorkeling and diving. The small town of Porto Belo is the departure point for exploring the neighboring beaches of Bombas and Bombinhas, which, although crowded by families in the summer, still have not been completely overwhelmed. Close by—accessible only by boat or on foot—a dozen small, deserted coves offer peace and tranquility.

Bombas and Bombinhas

Situated 5 kilometers (3 mi) from Porto Belo, separated by a promontory, lie the twin beaches of **Bombas** and **Bombinhas.** Visit during off-season, when you can take better advantage of the sheltered bay. East of Bombinhas, emptier but easily accessible beaches include the small, very pretty **Lagoinha** and **Sepultura,** with calm waters that are ideal for swimming and snorkeling. Facing the open sea, **Quatro Ilhas** and **Mariscal** are prized by surfers in search of swells. The continuation of Mariscal is **Canto Grande,** from which a 4-kilometer (2.5-mi) trail (a dirt road) leads to the beautiful and secluded **Praia da Tainha.**

For guided hikes to even more far-flung beaches, contact **Caminhos e Trilhas** (tel. 47/9973-0584, www.caminhosetrilhas.com.br) in Bombinhas; a five-hour trip costs around R$80.

★ Reserva Biológica Marinha da Ilha do Arvoredo

The best place for diving in the entire South is the clear azure Atlantic waters surrounding the Ilha do Arvoredo, a biological reserve accessible from both Bombinhas and Florianópolis. The coral reefs surrounding the southern part of the island are teeming with brightly colored fish, dolphins, and sea turtles. Both **Patadacobra** (Av. Vereador Manoel José dos Santos, tel. 47/3369-2119, www.patadacobra.com.br) and **Acquatrek** (tel. 47/3369-2137, www.acquatrek.com.br) offer diving courses and half-day outings for divers of all levels. Excursion rates are R$170-230 (diving) and R$50-70 (snorkeling). Offered daily in the summer, during the off-season outings are often only scheduled for weekends.

Accommodations and Food

Stylish *pousadas* are scarce around Porto Belo (family accommodations rule), and even basic accommodations don't come cheap during summer. Most hotels are situated along Bombas and Bombinhas.

Somewhat less crowded than Bombinhas is the adjacent beach of Mariscal, where you'll find the appealing and ecofriendly **Pousada Arágua** (Rua Amoreira 786, tel. 47/3393-4687, www.pousadaragua.com.br, R$220-280 d). Guest rooms (some accommodate up to five) are handsomely designed with natural fibers, lots of light, and furnishings fashioned out of reforested woods. Perks include private decks, kitchens, and flat-screen TVs. A pool and gardens are sprinkled with futons and hammocks, while you can even rock out in a fully equipped music studio (the owner, René, is a professional musician).

Occupying a renovated fisherman's house on beautiful Canto Grande beach, **Tatuira Petisqueira** (Av. João José da Cruz 1700, tel. 47/3369-6338, www.tatuirapetisqueira. com.br, 11:30am-10pm Thurs.-Sat., 11:30am-6pm Sun. Mar.-Nov., 11:30am-11pm daily Dec.-Feb., R$25-40) is a delicious spot to while away the sunset hours with stir-fried squid and seared pink shrimp with herbs.

Transportation and Services

In Bombas, the **tourist office** (Av. Leopoldo Zarling 2072, tel. 47/3393-7320, 8am-noon and 1:30pm-5:30pm daily Mar.-Nov., 8am-10pm daily Dec.-Feb.) has information about the entire peninsula. You can also visit www. portobelo.com.br and www.bombinhas. sc.gov.br/turismo.

Porto Belo is easy to get to from Florianópolis, only 55 kilometers (34 mi) away. **Navegantes** (tel. 47/3342-1183, www. viacaonavegantes.net) has six daily departures during the week and 2-3 departures daily on weekends. The 75-minute trip costs around R$14. Hourly buses (R$3) operated by **Praiana** (tel. 0800-647-8400, www.via-caopraiana.com.br) connect Porto Belo with Bombinhas. By car, just follow BR-101 north. Whether traveling by bus or car, try to avoid "rush hour" (9am-11am and 4pm-6pm) in high season.

SOUTH OF FLORIANÓPOLIS

The beaches in and surrounding the settlements of Guarda do Embaú, Garopaba, and Praia do Rosa have become a less-than-secret getaway for bikinied young backpackers. In recent years, a burgeoning number of gourmet eateries and eco-chic *pousadas* have expanded the region's lure, transforming it into one of the hippest summer seaside spots on the Brazilian coast without sacrificing its aura of rusticity. In off-season, things are much more tranquil, but with the vanishing of the crowds, many accommodations and restaurants close.

Guarda do Embaú

Sporting some of the most well-known surfing swells in the South, this fetching fishing village 44 kilometers (27 mi) south of Floripa lures plenty of back-to-nature bohemians and, in the summer, plenty of partiers, along with families who paddle around in the calm water beaches of **Praia da Pinheira** and **Praia de Baixa,** closer to town. To reach the sweeping stretch of sand that comprises the village's namesake beach involves wading, swimming, or taking a canoe-ride (R$0.50) across the waters of the Rio Madre, which runs parallel to the ocean. To the north, accessible via a 30-minute trail, the deserted **Prainha** beach is particularly prized by surfers. From here, another trail climbs to Pedra do Urubu, whose heights offer panoramic views of the coastline.

ACCOMMODATIONS AND FOOD

Set back 400 meters from the beach, **Pousada Zululand** (Rua Emerenciana, tel. 48/3283-2093, www.zululand.com.br, R$150-500 d) is the prettiest place in town. It's also surprisingly well-priced, with standard suites as well as more "luxurious" (spacious and comfortable) split-level bungalows outfitted with partial or full kitchens. The vast green estate offers plenty of chill spots, including pools for adults and kids and a massage space. The on-site restaurant (1pm-8pm daily Dec.-Mar.,

R$30-50) serves fresh, organic food. Less pricy organics—from fish and artisanal pasta to salads and microbrew lagers—are offered at **Big Bamboo** (Rua Cândida Maria dos Santos 48, tel. 48/3283-2814, www.bigbamboo.com.br, 11am-midnight daily Dec.-Mar., Thurs.-Sun. Apr.-Nov., R$25-35). The proprietor is the father of soccer star Fernando Prass, which explains the décor of proud papa clippings mingled with the sweeping beach views.

TRANSPORTATION AND SERVICES

For more information (in Portuguese), visit www.guardadoembau.com.br/canoa. From Florianópolis's Rodoviária Rita Maria, **Paulotur** (tel. 48/3244-2777, www.paulotur. com.br) operates daily bus service down the coast, with departures every 1-2 hours during the week (fewer on weekends). The 1.5-hour trip costs R$11. If you're driving from Floripa, take BR-101 south.

Garopaba

Located 95 kilometers (59 mi) south of Florianópolis, Garopaba is one of the country's major surfing meccas during the summer months. Between June and November, it is also the best place on the Brazilian coast for whale-watching.

While Garopaba's small beach is pleasant enough, the real attractions are the wilder beaches within close proximity of the village. **Praia Siriú,** 10 kilometers (6 mi) to the north, is backed by 40-meter (130-feet) dunes that are excellent for sand boarding (boards can be rented for R$10 a day). Although the waves are rough, you can swim in the calm waters of the Rio Siriú. Surfers, however, are lured by the beaches to the south, the most famous being **Praia do Silveira,** 3 kilometers (2 mi) from Garopaba. Another 5 kilometers (3 mi) south, happening **Praia da Ferrugem** has bars along the shore that attract visiting young Paulistanos and Gaúchos in the summer. Natural ocean pools offer a calmer alternative to otherwise big waves, but the water here is usually pretty chilly.

ACCOMMODATIONS AND FOOD

Lodgings in Garopaba are generally no-frills affairs, and many are only open in summer. Choose between Garopaba, more popular with families, and Ferrugem, favored by young *surfistas*. In Garopaba's Centro, three blocks from the beach and adjacent to the bucolic Lagoa das Capivaras, **Pousada da Lagoa** (Rua Rosalina de Aguiar Lentz 325, tel. 48/3354-3201, www.pousadadalagoa. com.br, Oct.-Mar., R$220-340 d) is the nicest option in town. Apartments and common rooms are inviting, with high ceilings, warm wooden fixtures, and walls carefully draped with art. A lush surrounding garden boasts a pool and sauna. If views could kill, **Morada Prainha** (Estrada Geral da Silveira 1265, Praia da Silveira, tel. 48/3354-1182, www.moradaprainha.com.br, R$400-600 d) would be deadly: Its seven airy and sparklingly modern apartments (studio, one-bedroom, and two-bedroom, all with kitchens and verandas) and stunning infinity pool take advantage of breathtaking views overlooking the coast. It's one of the few options that remains open year-round.

Garopaba and the surrounding beaches have a fair number of basic fish and seafood restaurants. Among the most highly recommended is **Algarve** (Av. Prefeito João Orestes de Araújo 222, Centro, tel. 48/3354-1440, 11am-11pm Mon.-Sat. Apr.-Nov., 11am-midnight daily Dec.-Mar., R$20-30), which specializes in Portuguese dishes.

TRANSPORTATION AND SERVICES

For more information (in Portuguese), visit www.garobapa.com.br and www.garopaba. sc.gov.br/turismo. From Florianópolis's Rodoviária Rita Maria, **Paulotur** (tel. 48/3244-2777, www.paulotur.com.br) operates daily bus service down the coast, with departures every 1-2 hours during the week (and fewer on the weekends). The two-hour trip costs R$19. Driving from Floripa, take BR-101 south, then turn onto SC-434.

★ Praia do Rosa

Just 18 kilometers (11 mi) south of Garopaba, Praia do Rosa is routinely touted as one of the most photogenic beaches in southern Brazil. It's also the only stretch of Brazilian coast that's a member of the exclusive Most Beautiful Bays in the World Club (www.world-bays.com). Although its big waves draw surfers, Praia do Rosa has also become an eco-sophisticated resort renowned for its gourmet restaurants and handful of posh *pousadas* tucked in the hills. May-June is the period for *tainha* fishing, while July-November is whale-watching season. Plan on doing a lot of steep hiking up and down the forested hills. Nearby lagoons (where windsurfing is the rage), waterfalls, and beaches such as Praia Vermelha and Praia do Luz can only be reached by foot or on horseback.

ACCOMMODATIONS AND FOOD

You'll be tempted to spoil yourself by checking into one of Praia do Rosa's alluring hilltop *pousadas*. ★ **Pousada Quinta do Bucanero** (Estrada Geral do Rosa, tel. 48/3355-6056, www.bucanero.com.br, closed June, R$540-850 d) is a refined and romantic affair (no children under age 14) where beautifully furnished rooms with wooden verandas offer hypnotic views of the rain forest-fringed bay below. A little more country, but no less charming, is the equally lofty **Pousada Caminho do Rei** (Caminho do Alto do Morro, tel. 48/3355-6062, www.caminhodorei.com.br, R$290-490 d), whose decor mixes local folk art, hand-woven carpets, and patchwork quilts. Each of the eight airy guest rooms is individually furnished, and all boast views.

Amenities include a pool, sauna, games and reading room, and a cozy candlelit restaurant.

Simple, warm, and welcoming, the **Regina Guest House** (Caminho do Alto do Morro, tel. 48/3355-6247, www.reginagh.com.br, R$160-220 d) is close to the beach. Choose between individual bungalows nestled in the forest and the main building, a renovated manioc flour mill decorated with colorful local handicrafts. All guests receive a *"kit praia"* that includes a beach chair, towel, and parasol. The restaurant, ★ **Bistrô Pedra da Vigia** (2pm-11pm Tues.-Sat. Mar.-Nov., 2pm-12:30am daily Dec.-Feb., R$20-30) serves delicious French-inspired bistro fare with an emphasis on local fish and seafood.

Although you might be surprised to come across pad Thai in these parts, **Tigre Asiático** (Estrada Geral do Rosa, tel. 48/3355-7045, www.restaurantetigreasiatico.com.br, 7pm-11pm daily, R$45-60) is famed for being one of the best Thai restaurants in Brazil. Purists will note that traditional dishes have been adapted slightly for Brazilian palates. Soft lighting and Asian flourishes enhance the mood.

TRANSPORTATION AND SERVICES

For more information (in Portuguese), visit www.praiadorosa.com.br. There are no banks or ATM machines in Praia do Rosa. Most establishments (hotels and restaurants) accept cards, but it's wise to bring some cash as well.

From Florianópolis, take a bus operated by **Paulotur** (tel. 48/3223-7424, www.paulotur.com.br) to Garopaba. From Garopaba, transfer to one of the frequent local buses (R$3.60, 40 min.) that serve Praia do Rosa. By car from Garopaba, follow the Estrada Geral do Rosa.

Rio Grande do Sul

Brazil's southernmost state, bordering Argentina and Uruguay, Rio Grande do Sul is also one of Brazil's most distinctive regions, with a climate and regional identity all its own—it is the only Brazilian state where a separatist movement exists. With some good restaurants and top-notch cultural venues, the capital, Porto Alegre, is a pleasant-enough city, but much more interesting is the mountainous Serra Gaúcha region of the

European Immigrants

In the 19th century, southern Brazil was a magnet for immigrants from Europe: Italy, Poland, Ukraine, Germany, and Austria. In fact, Dona Leopoldina, the Austrian-born first wife of Brazilian emperor Dom Pedro I, must have been rather homesick when she embarked on a mission to lure her countrymen to the unfarmed territories of subtropical southern Brazil. Accordingly, agents were sent to central Europe to hype the fertile fields (actually tangled Atlantic forests home to indigenous peoples) to adventurous farmers, who subsequently showed up in droves and settled regions of central and eastern Rio Grande do Sul and eastern Santa Catarina.

To this day there is a surprising number of fair-skinned people in the region—Gisele Bündchen is only the most famous—along with a Viennese café culture, folk dances reminiscent of the polka, a significant number of Lutheran churches, and a fondness for draft beer, potato salad, sauerkraut, and, of course, pork sausages. If you're in the vicinity of traditional German towns such as **Blumenau** and Joinville **(Santa Catarina)** or **Novo Hamburgo, Gramado,** and **Santa Cruz do Sul** (Rio Grande do Sul), you're sure to encounter more than a little bit of Bavaria.

interior. Only two hours from Porto Alegre are the picturesque resort towns of Gramado and Canela, renowned for their alpine landscapes and German immigrant traditions. Those in search of all-out wilderness can take to the hiking trails that crisscross the Parque Nacional de Aparados da Serra. If you're on your way to or from Argentina or exploring all of the South from São Paulo on down, 3-5 days spent in this unique Brazilian region are definitely worth your while.

The fierce independence and distinctiveness of the modern-day Gaúcho—an inhabitant of Rio Grande do Sul—dates back to the region's beginnings as a type of Wild West frontier zone between the Spanish and Portuguese colonial empires. As early as the 18th century, cowboys traveling solo or in small bands earned their livelihoods driving immense herds of cattle across the high plains of the Pampas. Fearless and ruthless, they also worked as mercenaries for powerful landowners and colonial governments, who were constantly seeking to expand and defend their territories. A mix of Indians, Spanish, and Portuguese settlers and African slaves, these "Gaúchos"—a pejorative term of indigenous origin—became the stuff of legend, as emblematic of Rio Grande do Sul as cowboys in Texas.

The term *Gaúcho* became synonymous with all residents of Rio Grande do Sul during the Guerra dos Farrapos, a failed war of independence that pitted Rio Grande do Sul's freethinking rebels against imperial forces. Lasting from 1835 to 1845, this series of battles constituted the longest war ever fought in the Americas. During this period, Rio Grande do Sul became an autonomous republic, and its citizens defiantly adopted the "Gaúcho" moniker used as an insult by monarchists in Rio. After the war, the courageous Gaúcho became a symbol of the state and a popular hero that came to be idealized in local literature, music, and art.

By the beginning of the 20th century, the Gaúcho way of life had already begun to disappear. In the mid- to late 19th century, German and Italian immigrants arrived en masse, establishing efficient farms and bustling towns. As the 20th century wore on, cattle farming became increasingly industrialized, and the Pampas was taken over by cash crops such as soybeans. Today, Gaúcho traditions—rodeos, *bombachas* (baggy trousers), ponchos, felt hats, and leather boots—still persist only in small towns deep in the hinterlands. Yet other legacies, such as drinking bitter *erva maté* and eating *churrasco* (the wandering cowboys' staple of slow-cooked, charcoal-grilled cuts of beef seasoned with rock salt) are now part of the proud lifestyle of all 21st-century Gaúchos.

PORTO ALEGRE

Stretched out along the eastern shore of the Rio Guaíba, Rio Grande do Sul's prosperous Gaúcho capital of 1.5 million resembles a somewhat generic European or North American city. Although it has a respected gastronomic scene (particularly if you're a card-carrying carnivore) and a very dynamic cultural life, in terms of attractions, Porto Alegre is not really worth going out of your way to visit. However, there is definitely a day's worth of sights and activities to keep you agreeably occupied if you end up here.

Founded in 1755, "Porto" began life as a Portuguese outpost whose mission was to defend the Brazilian colony from its Spanish rivals to the south. Throughout the 20th century, the city grew at breakneck pace, becoming the largest and most economically important of Brazil's southern capitals. More recently, as the host of events such as the controversial World Social Forum—which has provided a counterpoint to the First World elitism of the World Economic Forum—and the distinguished Bienal de Artes do Mercosul, Porto Alegre has proved to be a progressive and cosmopolitan place.

Orientation

Most of Porto Alegre's attractions are located within the old city center (Centro) next to the river, a compact region easily explored on foot. Although a late 20th-century building boom resulted in a sea of nondescript office towers and busy thoroughfares, a significant number of grand neoclassical buildings have happily survived the wrecking ball. Be careful at night (take a taxi).

Sights
MERCADO PÚBLICO

The city's geographic and symbolic heart is the **Mercado Público** (Praça XV de Novembro, Centro, tel. 51/3289-4000, www.portoalegre.rs.gov.br/mercadopublico, 7:30am-7pm Mon.-Fri., 7:30am-6pm Sat.). Completed in 1869 (and undergoing restoration), this rather grand, biscuit-colored neoclassical building has an array of stalls proffering everything from food, wine, cookware, and herbs to handicrafts from all over the state. For refreshments, do like the locals and stop for an icy *chope* at **Naval** or an icy *suco* or *sorvete* at **Banca 40,** which has been selling homemade ice creams for more than 50 years. The **Café do Mercado** (Loja 103, tel. 51/3029-2490) serves up one of the best espressos in the city, a nice accompaniment to a traditional *doce de Pelotas*. The market is a favorite gathering place during happy hour (bars and restaurants stay open later than the market's stalls).

PRAÇA DA ALFÂNDEGA

From the market and Praça XV, a labyrinth of pedestrian streets running parallel to Rua Sete de Setembro lead uphill toward the **Praça da Alfândega,** where you'll immediately notice a trio of very handsome neoclassical buildings. Built in the late 1920s, **Santander Cultural** (Rua Sete de Setembro 1028, tel. 51/3287-5500, www.santandercultural.com.br, 10am-7pm Mon.-Fri., 11am-7pm Sat.-Sun.) is a former bank headquarters that was purchased by the Spanish Banco de Santander and converted into an excellent cultural center. A main-floor gallery hosts important exhibits of national art. There is a cinema and a charming café located inside the former safe.

The palatial turn-of-the-20th-century Correios (post office) building now houses the **Memorial do Rio Grande do Sul** (Rua Sete de Setembro 1020, tel. 51/3225-7580, www.memorial.rs.gov.br, 10am-6pm Tues.-Sun., free). This is the place to bone up on Rio Grande do Sul's history, peruse illustrated timelines, and learn about famous Gaúchos (among them President Getúlio Vargas and beloved diva Elis Regina). Occupying the former customhouse is the **Museu de Arte do Rio Grande do Sul** (MARGS; Av. Sete de Setembro 1010, Centro, tel. 51/3227-2311, www.margs.rs.gov.br, 10am-7pm Tues.-Sun., free), with a collection of works by Brazilian and Gaúcho artists as well as temporary exhibits and a rooftop café with great views of the city.

Porto Alegre

© AVALON TRAVEL

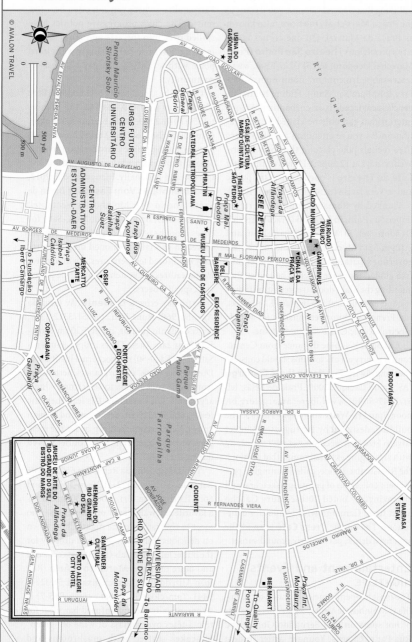

Rio Guaíba

USINA DO GASOMETRO

AV. PRES. JOÃO GOULART

Parque Maurício Sirotsky Sobr

AV. EDVALDO PEREIRA PAIVA

0   500 yds
0   500 m

AV. LOUREIRO DA SILVA

URGS FUTURO CENTRO UNIVERSITÁRIO

AV. AUGUSTO DE CARVALHO

R. DOS ANDRADAS

R. RIACHUELO

R. DUQUE DE CAXIAS

Praça General Osório

CASA DE CULTURA MARIO QUINTANA ★

AV. SETE DE SETEMBRO

R. CEL. FERNANDO MACHADO

CATEDRAL METROPOLITANA ★

PALÁCIO PIRATINI

R. DR. FLORES RIBEIRO

R. DE TIO RIBEIRO

R. WASHINGTON LUIZ

THEATRO SÃO PEDRO ★

Praça Mal. Deodoro

SANTO

R. ESPIRITO

MUSEU JÚLIO DE CASTILHOS ★

AV. BORGES

MEDEIROS

SEE DETAIL

Praça da Alfândega

AV. MAUÁ

AV. SIQUEIRA

CAMPOS

PALÁCIO MUNICIPAL

MERCADO PÚBLICO

GAMBRINUS ★

CHALÉ DA PRAÇA 15 ★

R. VOLUNTÁRIOS DA PÁTRIA

AV. JÚLIO DE CASTILHOS

AV. MAUÁ

CENTRO ADMINISTRATIVO ESTADUAL-DAER

Praça Batalhão Suez

Praça dos Açorianos

AV. BORGES DE MEDEIROS

To Fundação Iberê Camargo

Praça Isabel a Católica

AURELIANO DE F. GUERREIRO PINTO

MERCATTO D'ARTE

R. DA REPÚBLICA

R. LUIZ AFONSO

OSSIP ●

R. MAL. FLORIANO PEIXOTO

DEL BARBIERE ▼

R. PROF. ANNES DIAS

EKO RESIDENCE ●

Praça Argentina

AV. LOUREIRO DA SILVA

R. INDEPENDÊNCIA

AV. ALBERTO BINS

COPACABANA ▼

AV. VENÂNCIO AIRES

R. OLAVO BILAC

Praça Garibaldi

PORTO ALEGRE ECO HOSTEL ●

AV. JOÃO PESSOA

AV. E. ENGLER

Parque Paulo Gama

Parque Farroupilha

AV. OSVALDO ARANHA

AV. JOSÉ BONIFÁCIO

OCIDENTE ▼

R. FERNANDES VIERA

R. DR. BARROS CASSAL

R. IRMÃO JOSÉ OTÃO

AV. INDEPENDÊNCIA

VIA ELEVADA CONCEIÇÃO

RODOVIÁRIA ■

AV. FARRAPOS

AV. CRISTÓVÃO COLOMBO

R. RAMIRO BARCELOS

NABRASA STEAK ▼

R. CASEMIRO DE ABREU

R. MOSTARDEIRO

Praça Int. Montaury

BIER MARKT ■

To Quality Porto Alegre

R. DR. VALE

R. F. GOMES

R. 24 DE OUTUBRO

To Barranco

UNIVERSIDADE FEDERAL DO RIO GRANDE DO SUL

R. MARIANTE

Praça da Montevidéu

R. URUGUAI

R. GEN. ANDRADE NEVES

R. DOS ANDRADAS

R. GEN.

MUSEU DE ARTE DO RIO GRANDE DO SUL/ BISTRO DO MARQS ★

R. CAP. MONTANHA

R. CALDAS JUNIOR

MEMORIAL DO RIO GRANDE DO SUL ★

R. SETE DE SETEMBRO

R. SIQUEIRA CAMPOS

Praça da Alfândega

SANTANDER CULTURAL ★

PORTO ALEGRE CITY HOTEL ●

PRAÇA MARECHAL DEODORO

Heading south from Praça da Alfândega, uphill along Rua General Câmara, you'll come to the **Praça Marechal Deodoro** (also known as Praça da Matriz). On one corner is the city's prestigious **Theatro São Pedro** (Praça Marechal Deodoro, tel. 51/3227-5100, www.teatrosaopedro.com.br, noon-6pm Mon.-Fri., 4pm-6pm Sat.-Sun.). Hiding behind its neoclassical facade is an enchanting baroque interior that can only be visited by reservation unless you're attending a performance (free recitals take place in the Foyer Nobre, Wednesdays at 12:30pm). However, the lovely **Café do Theatro** is open daily to the public and serves a lavish tea (4pm-7pm Wed., R$40).

Flanked by Roman columns, the rather imperious **Palácio Piratini** (Praça Marechal Deodoro, tel. 51/3227-4170, 9am-11am and 2:30pm-5pm Mon.-Fri.) is home to the state governor's palace. At half-hour intervals, free guided tours are given. The two statues guarding the main doors (representing industry and agriculture) are by Paul Landowski, the French sculptor responsible for Rio de Janeiro's iconic *Cristo Redentor* statue.

Although it's some distance from Centro, contemporary art aficionados should consider checking out the **Fundação Iberê Camargo** (Av. Padre Cacique 2000, Praia de Belas, tel. 51/3247-8000, www.iberecamargo.org.br, noon-7pm Fri.-Wed., noon-9pm Thurs.). The building, designed by Portuguese architect Álvaro Siza Vieira, combines white concrete with zigzagging external ramps that overlook the Rio Guaíba. Inside, galleries mingle a permanent collection of paintings, sketches, and engravings by noted 20th-century Gaúcho artist Iberê Camargo with temporary exhibitions. The on-site **Press Café** is an idyllic spot for a drink, particularly around sunset.

Entertainment and Events
NIGHTLIFE

The most happening neighborhood for nightlife is Moinhos de Vento, where there are lots of hot spots on Rua Fernando Gomes and Rua Padre Chagas. Younger, artier student types frequent the more alternative bars in Cidade Baixa—surrounding the Parque Farroupilha—where you can often hear live music. The city's progressive politics have spilled over into the arts and music scene, making Porto a surprisingly vanguard place with a fairly active gay and lesbian community.

Opened by a local trio of beer buddies, **Bier Markt** (Rua Castro Alves 442, Rio Branco, tel. 51/3013-2300, www.biermarkt.com.br, 6pm-midnight Mon.-Sat.) takes brewksy seriously, giving prime consideration to artisanal microbrews made locally (Abadessa and Coruja) and nationally. Inaugurated in 2012, sister **Bier Markt Vom Fass** (Rua Barão de Santo Angelo 442, Moinhos de Vento, tel. 51/3286-0927, 6pm-11:30pm Mon.-Sat.) focuses more heavily on draft beer; brews are served in specially fashioned mugs at carefully monitored temperatures. An innovative menu features edible items that can be paired with specific beers.

Extremely eclectic **Ocidente** (Av. Osvaldo Aranha 960, Bom Fim, tel. 51/3312-1347, www.ocidente.com.br, noon-2:30pm Mon.-Sat., 9pm-2am Tues.-Thurs., 10pm-6am Fri.-Sat., cover R$10-50) is a nocturnal institution. During the week, performances here range from indie rock bands to "electronic" literary salons. On weekends, DJs lead thematic *festas*, and Friday attracts a gay and lesbian crowd. Vegetarians can drop by for the inexpensive lactovegetarian lunch buffet served during the week.

Tiny **Ossip** (Rua da República 666, Cidade Baixa, tel. 51/3224-2422, 11:30am-2:30pm and 6pm-1:30am Mon.-Fri., noon-1:30am Sat.) is a favorite sidewalk haunt of Alegrenses, who meet to chat late into the night. Chow down on delicious thin-crust pizzas or drop by for the buffet lunch specials (R$13). Less crowded and more intimate, **Mercatto D'Arte** (Rua João Alfredo 399, Cidade Baixa, tel. 51/3224-9441, 7pm-close Tues.-Sat., cover R$5-7) is a romantically lit, jazz-infused bar ideal for tête-à-têtes over a glass of wine or "green" pancakes stuffed with mushrooms and gorgonzola. The owners love trolling Uruguay for antiques, and much of the eclectic decor is for sale.

CULTURAL CENTERS

Before being transformed into one the city's foremost cultural centers, the pale pink **Casa de Cultura Mario Quintana** (Rua dos Andradas 736, Centro, tel. 51/3221-7147, www.ccmq.rs.gov.br, 2pm-9pm Mon., 9am-9pm Tues.-Fri., noon-9pm Sat.-Sun.) was the formerly grand belle epoque Hotel Majestic, where renowned local poet Mario Quintana resided for some time (his room is now a museum). Today, the building houses various art exhibition spaces along with a bookshop, candy store, theater, art-house cinema, and—for fans of MPB—the Elis Regina gallery, with photos and recordings of the great singer. In the ground-floor courtyard, the lovely **Café Catavento** serves snacks and light meals. At 7pm Wednesday-Friday, there are always free musical performances. On the seventh floor, the **Café Santo de Casa** offers sweeping views over the Rio Guaíba as well as a per-kilo lunch buffet (Mon.-Fri.) and happy-hour specials accompanied by live jazz and classical music.

Porto Alegre's other major cultural hub is the **Usina do Gasômetro** (Av. Presidente João Goulart 551, Centro, tel. 51/3289-8140, 9am-9pm Tues.-Fri., 10am-9pm Sat.-Sun.). Built in the 1920s on the banks of the Rio Guaíba, the towering redbrick smokestack of this former coal-fired power plant has become a city landmark. The renovated interior has various galleries and a cinema, theater, and bookstore, along with a café that features one of the finest views of Porto's legendary sunsets over the river.

FESTIVALS AND EVENTS

In late September, **Semana Farroupilha** (www.semanafarroupilha.com.br) commemorates September 20, 1835, which marked the beginning of the Revolução Farroupilha, the popular uprising that led to the declaration of the short-lived Republic of Rio Grande do Sul as well as a 10-year war of independence (the Guerra dos Farrapos). The weeklong festivities include parades, traditional Gaúcho music and dancing, and, of course, lots of food.

Shopping

Any day is a good day to troll the **Mercado Público.** On Sundays, however, head to the centrally located **Parque Farroupilha** (also known as Redenção) for the lively **Brique da**

Usina do Gasômetro

Redenção (9am-6pm), a flea market featuring a mix of art, antiques, and regional handicrafts. For sophisticated shopping, check out glitzy **Moinhos Shopping** (Rua Olavo Barreto 36, Moinhos de Vento, tel. 51/2123-2000, www.moinhosshopping.com.br, 10am-10pm Mon.-Sat., 1pm-7pm Sun.), which also boasts a fancy food court and cineplex.

Accommodations

There are some decent budget accommodations options in Centro, and a new crop of hostels has sprouted in the boho hood of Cidade Baixa. Posher options can be found in upscale Moinhos de Vento, home to the city's fashionable restaurant and bar scene. Since Porto attracts far more business travelers than actual tourists, hotels offer weekend discounts. The quasi-continental climate ensures that most hotels have heating in the winter and air-conditioning in the summer.

Those with sustainable sensibilities will approve of **Eko Residence** (Av. Des. André da Rocha 131, Centro, tel. 51/3225-8644, www.ekoresidence.com.br, R$180-230 d). This "green" hotel's energy needs are partially met by wind and solar power, and it recycles rainwater and garbage. Appealingly modern guest rooms are spacious and feature free Wi-Fi along with kitchenettes, while an in-house restaurant serves healthy fare. Eco-backpackers on a budget can opt for the cheery private rooms and dorms of the **Porto Alegre Eco Hostel** (Rua Luiz Afonso 27, Cidade Baixa, tel. 51/3019-2449, www.portoalegreecohostel.com.br, R$120-140 d), where bunks are made of demolition wood. When not cooking in the kitchen or grilling on the barbecue, guests can chill out in a garden shaded by grape vines or check out one of the rental bikes.

Reasonably priced and well located, the **Quality Porto Alegre** (Rua Com. Caminha 42, Moinhos de Vento, tel. 51/3323-9300, www.atlanticahotels.com.br, R$260-390 d) is a sleek and attractive, if generic, high-end choice. The large guest rooms are nicely appointed. The best have sweeping views across the treetops of the Parcão, a neighborhood park whose entrance faces the hotel.

Food

Vegetarians beware! In Rio Grande do Sul's capital, *churrasco* is an art form, and the city's *churrascarias* are temples where carnivores fervently worship the most succulent cuts of red meat on the planet. Although you'll find *churrascarias* and *rodízios* throughout Brazil, the best and cheapest are in Porto Alegre. Although all *churrascarias* serve salads and vegetable dishes on the side (a tendency disdained by the "Old Guard"), if meat really isn't your thing, there are also some fine eateries representing Rio Grande do Sul's major immigrant groups: Italians, Germans, and Poles. Centro has many options during the day, but at night, when the area closes down, you'll have to search for sustenance in surrounding regions, such as swanky Moinhos de Vento.

CAFÉS AND SNACKS

Located in the Museu de Arte do Rio Grande do Sul (MARGS), the **Bistrô do Margs** (Praça da Alfândega, tel. 51/3018-1380, 11am-10pm Mon.-Fri., 11am-7pm Sat.-Sun., R$20-30) is conveniently situated if you're sightseeing. You can choose to sit in the warmly minimalist dining room or on the outside terrace, which is ideal for people-watching. This is a popular happy-hour meeting point, especially on Thursday and Friday when live music is played. For lighter and cheaper fare, such as freshly made sandwiches as well as desserts and coffee, visit the **Café do Margs** on the first floor.

CHURRASCARIAS

Coming to Porto Alegre and not indulging in the sublime melt-in-your-mouth cuts of Pampas-raised beef is akin to traveling to Japan and never partaking in sushi. Flaunting the convention of swank *superchurrascarias* with their cavernous dining rooms, **Portoalegrense** (Av. Pará 913, São Geraldo, tel. 51/3343-2767, www.

Drinking *Erva Maté* the Gaúcho Way

Throughout Rio Grande do Sul, you'll notice the common sight of locals using a silver straw to sip what appears to be a hot potion from a rather primitive-looking polished gourd. The straw is known as a *bomba,* the gourd is a *cuia,* and the bitter, pungent, and addictive drink is a strong tea known as **chimarrão,** made from the ground-up leaves of a small local evergreen tree known as **erva maté.** Guarani Indians were the first to partake of this medicinal drink, and it subsequently caught on with roving Gaúchos on the Pampas.

Today Gaúchos of all ages and backgrounds regularly indulge in this favorite beverage. The leaves are brewed in hot (not boiling) water in the *cuia* itself, and then passed around communally until the empty *cuia* is refilled by the last slurper. This communal ritual continues slowly, so that the tea and accompanying conversation can be richly savored. Etiquette requires the person who prepares the *erva maté* to take the first sip (usually more bitter); adding sugar or sweetener is definitely against the rules.

churrascariaportoalegrense.com.br, 11:30am-2pm and 7pm-11pm Mon.-Sat. Mar.-Jan., closed Feb., R$20-30) is a traditional family-run restaurant in a large, rustically furnished house where the focus is all on the meat. Delicious *picanha* (rump cut), *costelas* (spare ribs), and *costeletas de carneiro* (lamb chops) are particularly well regarded.

Equally traditional is ★ **Barranco** (Av. Protásio Alves 1578, Petrópolis, tel. 51/3331-6172, www.churrascariabarranco.com.br, 11am-2am daily, R$20-30). In a given month, some 15,000 local carnivores devour 8,000 tons of prime cuts of beef, pork, and lamb here. Those craving variety should head to **Nabrasa Steak** (Rua Ramiro Barcelos 389, Floresta, tel. 51/3225-2205, www.nbsteak.com.br, 11:30am-3pm and 7pm-midnight Mon.-Fri., 11:30am-midnight Sat.-Sun., R$65 pp), where both classic and more exotic cuts—ostrich, quail, and *javali* (wild boar)—are served *rodízio* style (a 1960s innovation frowned upon by traditionalists).

INTERNATIONAL

Young chef Marcelo Schambeck subdivided his father's 1940s-era barber shop and occupied his half with ★ **Del Barbiere** (Rua Jerônimo Coelho 188, Centro, tel. 51/3019-4202, www.delbarbiere.com.br, 9am-3pm Mon.-Fri., 11am-3pm Sat.), a bistro whose three-course daily lunch menus (R$46) rely upon fresh ingredients and simple preparation but yield original dishes such as spaghetti carbonara with okra and collard greens. Saturday's Menu de Feira (R$68) draws upon Schambeck's early morning market forays and includes dessert (optional other days). Reservations are necessary.

Serving authentic southern Italian cuisine, **Copacabana** (Praça Garibaldi 2, Cidade Baixa, tel. 51/3221-4616, www.restcopacabana.com.br, 11:30am-3pm and 7pm-1am Tues.-Sun., R$20-30) has been around for three family generations. The faithful diners who clustered around its wooden tables in their student days still swear by the homemade pastas and delicious veal and lamb dishes served in this cozy trattoria.

REGIONAL

Located in the Mercado Público, **Gambrinus** (Av. Borges de Medeiros 85, tel. 51/3226-6914, www.gambrinus.com.br, 11am-9pm Mon.-Fri., 11am-4pm Sat., R$25-35) is the oldest restaurant in the city and a culinary and cultural institution. With a tavern-like décor that is simple and welcoming, the forte here is fish and seafood. Since there is no dessert, head across to Banca 40 for *sorvete.* **Chalé da Praça XV** (Praça XV de Novembro, tel. 51/3225-2667, 11am-midnight Mon.-Fri., 11am-11pm Sat.-Sun., R$15-20) is another atmospheric restaurant, located in a historic art nouveau-ish building whose steel structure was sent over in pieces from England. This is a good place to try regional specialties or come for a happy-hour drink and snack.

Information and Services

The **municipal tourist office** (tel. 0800/51-7686) has detailed information as well as free city maps. You'll find branches at the airport (8am-10pm daily), the Mercado Público (9am-6pm Mon.-Sat.), and the Usina de Gasômetro (9am-6pm Tues.-Sun.). The municipal website (www.portoalegre.rs.gov.br/turismo), in Portuguese, is very thorough. For (some) English information, try www.poaconvention.com.br.

For money changing and ATMs, the greatest concentration of banks is in Centro, along Rua dos Andradas and Avenida Senador Salgado Filho near Praça da Alfândega. The post office is at Rua Siqueira Campos 1100.

In an emergency, dial **192** for an ambulance, **190** for the police, and **193** for the fire department. For medical treatment, go to the **Hospital Pronto Socorro** (Largo Teodoro Herzl, tel. 51/3289-7999).

Transportation

Porto Alegre is directly connected to Rio, São Paulo, Curitiba, and Florianópolis by air. There are also flights to Buenos Aires, Santiago, and Montevideo. The ultramodern **Aeroporto Internacional Salgado Filho** (Av. Severo Dulius 9010, tel. 51/3358-2000, www.aeroportoportoalegre.net) is only 8 kilometers (5 mi) northeast of the city center. Taking a prepaid taxi into town will cost around R$30. An easy alternative (if you don't have much luggage and are staying in Centro) is walking over a viaduct to take the Metrô (R$1.70), which will take you to the Mercado.

Buses from around the state and the country arrive at the rather forlorn **Estação Rodoviária de Porto Alegre** (Largo Vespasiano Veppo, tel. 51/3210-0101). **Itapemirim** (tel. 0800/723-2121, www.itapemirim.com.br) operates two daily buses from São Paulo (18 hours, R$230), while **Santo Anjo** (tel. 48/3621-5000, www.santoanjo.com.br) offers eight daily buses from

Florianópolis (6.5 hours, R$75-135). For schedules and prices of bus services throughout Rio Grande do Sul, visit www.rodoviaria-poa.com.br. Although the bus station is within walking distance of Centro, it is surrounded by highways and bypasses; it's easier (and safer) to take a taxi, bus, or the Metrô to your destination.

Although getting around central Porto Alegre is easily done on foot, the city also has an extensive municipal bus service (fare is R$2.85) as well as a one-line **Metrô** (tel. 51/3363-8000, www.trensurb.gov.br, 5am-11pm daily)—although quite limited, it is a convenient option for travel between the airport, *rodoviária*, and the Mercado Público.

Roads in Porto Alegre and throughout Rio Grande do Sul are well maintained. To rent a car, **Avis** (tel. 51/3358-2260, www.avis.com.br) and **Hertz** (tel. 51/3358-2472, www.hertz.com.br) both have offices at the airport.

CITY TOURS

For city tours, the **Linha Turismo** (Travessa do Carmo 84, Cidade Baixa, tel. 51/3289-0176) is an open-roof double-decker bus that follows two different routes. The *"Tradicional"* (9am-4pm, R$18-20) weaves hourly through the Centro Histórico along the banks of the Rio Guaíba to the Fundação Iberê Camargo and includes five stops. The less "touristy" *"Zona Sul"* (3pm Wed.-Fri., R$18, 10am and 3:30pm Sat.-Sun., R$20) passes along the shores of Praia de Ipanema and in front of the house of legendary soccer star Ronaldinho Gaúcho. To view Porto from the Rio Guaíba, two boats—the *Cisne Branco* (departing from the port at Av. Mauá 1050, tel. 51/3224-5222, www.barcocisnebranco.com.br, Tues.-Sun., R$25) and the *Porto Alegre 10* (departing from the Usina do Gasômetro, tel. 51/3211-7665, www.barcoportoalegre10.com.br, Tues.-Sun., R$20), offer several hour-long outings a day.

SERRA GAÚCHA

The landscape surrounding Porto Alegre is pancake-flat, but driving north, the land starts to rise into a series of hills that gradually morph into the Serra Gaúcha mountain range. In the 1820s and 1830s, Germans arrived and built farming communities in the lower hills. They were followed a few decades later by Italians from the wine-growing regions of Veneto and Trento who traveled farther into the interior, where the soil and climate proved ideal for vine cultivation. Continuing due north, the mountains take on an Alpine allure. The mountain resort towns of Gramado and Canela have become favorite destinations for Brazilian tourists in search of exotica such as strudel and even snow.

★ Gramado

From fondue restaurants to faux ski lodges that wouldn't be out of place in Gstaad, Gramado's Swiss connection is played to the hilt (sometimes to excess—such as during Christmas, when the whole town is lit up like a kitschy theme park). You might find this Alpine aspect excessively quaint or charming, but it attracts Brazilian tourists in droves, making it somewhat of a mob scene. For this reason, winter (when artificial snowstorms are the rage) and summer (when moderate temperatures attract sweltering city dwellers, especially those dreaming of a "white" Christmas) are less than ideal; instead, plan to visit in the spring (October-November), when tourism is down and wild hydrangeas are in full bloom.

SIGHTS

Gramado has a few natural attractions. At the end of Rua Bela Vista, **Parque Knorr** (9am-6pm daily) offers magnificent views of the Vale do Quilombo, a dramatic valley that runs along the road between Gramado and Canela. Around 1.5 kilometers (1 mi) from the center of town, amid a wooded park, the **Lago Negro** is a bucolic artificial lake ringed by hydrangeas where you can pedal around in swan-shaped boats (R$20). Exploring the mountains on your own from Gramado is difficult without a car. However, a quick bus or taxi ride can take you the 8 kilometers (5 mi) from Gramado's center to the **Ecoparque**

Sperry (Linha 28, tel. 54/9629-8765, www.ecoparquesperry.com.br, 9am-5pm Tues.-Sun., R$12). Located in the Vale de Quilombo, this organic farm, surrounded by native forest and waterfalls, has well-marked nature trails you can explore. On weekends, an on-site restaurant serves delicious lunches using local produce.

In an increasing effort to entice families to Gramado, the town has invested in a wealth of oddly themed museums, ranging from the Harley (Davidson) Motor Show to Latin America's only wax museum and over-the-top winter theme parks such as Santa's Home and Workshop. **Snowland** (RS-235 9009, Carazal, tel. 54/3286-5007, www.snowland.com.br, 9am-6pm Sun.-Thurs., 9am-10pm Fri.-Sat., R$60-200) opened in 2013 some six kilometers (4 mi) from the center of town. The winter wonderland bills itself as the only indoor artificial snow park in the Americas. Visitors can ice skate, snowboard, ski, and even indulge in snowball fights.

FESTIVALS AND EVENTS

During the second week in August, celebs, paparazzi, and cinephiles flock to Gramado's **Festival de Cinema** (www.festivaldegramado.net), one of the oldest and most prestigious film festivals in Latin America.

ACCOMMODATIONS

Gramado tends to be on the pricy side, especially during high season (Christmas and winter), when prices double and 2-3-day minimums are common. In off-season and during the week you can find some good discounts. Prices below are for low and between seasons.

Located in a leafy upscale neighborhood only slightly removed from the bustling center, **Recanto da Lua** (Rua Antônio Accorsi 322, Bavária, tel. 54/3286-2463, www.pousadarecantodalua.com.br, R$160-230 d) is a very good bargain. The guest rooms inside the large A-frame lodge are pleasant and cozy (standard rooms are in the attic with sloping ceilings) with lots of wood and farmhouse accents. In the same neighborhood, **Pousada**

Vovó Carolina (Av. das Hortênsias 677, Bavária, tel. 54/3286-2433, www.vovocarolina. com.br, R$230-360 d) is slightly more plush. Except for the master suites, the sedately decorated guest rooms are a bit small but possess a nice retro flavor. The lounge has an enormous fireplace, and there is a thermally heated pool.

Perched graciously on the shores of Lago Negro, ★ **Estalagem St. Hubertus** (Rua da Carrière 974, Planalto, tel. 54/3286-1273, www.sthubertus.com, R$350-850 d) is a stately white palace of a hotel surrounded by thick forest and splashes of hydrangeas. Although standard rooms are a bit cramped, you can definitely stretch your legs out in the fireplace lounge or the glassed-in salon overlooking the lake, where afternoon tea is served. Extras range from a thermal pool to swan-shaped boats in which you can pedal around the lake.

Varanda das Bromélias (Rua Alarisch Schulz 158, Planalto, tel. 54/3286-6653, www. varandadasbromelias.com.br, R$610-1,180 d) boasts a privileged location amid a private woodland on the town's highest summit. Billing itself as the region's first boutique hotel, it is a sophisticated departure from the faux Alpine chalets that are the norm. Each of the exquisitely furnished apartments has its own fireplace and veranda. Amenities include a glassed-in pool, a spa, and a fitness center. Rates include afternoon tea.

FOOD

In Gramado, you'll find no shortage of fondues (beef and cheese), fresh river trout, and chocolates (the town is home to 28 chocolatiers!). Although plenty of cheap fondue *rodízios* have sprung up, if you want the real cheesy deal, you'll have to pay for it. Often touted as one of Brazil's finest Swiss restaurants, **Belle du Valais** (Av. das Hortênsias 1432, tel. 54/3286-1744, www.belleduvalais. com.br, 7pm-midnight daily, noon-5pm Sat.-Sun., R$50-70) is decidedly romantic. Try the ubiquitous fondues or the *pierrade* (filet mignon and chicken cooked over volcanic rocks and served with sauces).

You'll find fondues as well as traditional German dishes at **Gasthof Edelweiss** (Rua da Carrière 1119, Lago Negro, tel. 54/3286-1861, www.restauranteedelweiss.com.br, noon-3pm and 7pm-11pm daily, R$45-60), the godfather of Gramado's Alpine eateries; the wine cellar here is so vast that it doubles as a dining room. A more unusual dining experience can be had at **La Caceria** (Av. Borges de Medeiros 3166, tel. 54/3295-1305, www.casadamontanha.com.br, 7pm-midnight daily, R$50-70), located in the luxurious (and kitschy) Hotel Casa da Montanha. The dining room, decorated with hunting rifles and stuffed animal heads, is the perfect setting for tucking into game such as partridge, duck, wild boar, and even capybara. The wine list features an impressive array of regional vintages. Reservations are essential.

Of Italian origin, *galeterias* are Gaúcho institutions second only to *churrascarias* in terms of gastronomic popularity. Instead of red meat, the star here is a *galeto* (i.e., a chicken that is only a month old), which, after being marinated in sage and white wine, is roasted over hot coals. Those served at ★ **Casa Di Paolo** (Rua Garibaldi 23, Centro, tel. 54/3286-7799, www.casadipaolo. com.br, 11am-3pm and 7pm-11pm Tues.-Sat., 11:30am-3pm and 7pm-11pm Sun., daily July and Dec., R$53), are golden and tender. Traditional accompaniments include homemade pastas and *capeletti in brodo*.

Centro has innumerable cafés, including those along the Rua Coberta, a covered passageway leading from Avenida Borges de Medeiros and Rua Garibaldi. Particularly inviting is **Josephina Café** (Rua Pedro Benetti 22, Centro, tel. 54/3286-9778, www.josephinacafe.com.br, 11:30am-11pm Tues.-Sun.), which is located in the owners' own charmingly decorated house. To nosh, there are tasty homemade sandwiches and pastries.

TRANSPORTATION AND SERVICES

The helpful **tourist office** (Av. Borges de Medeiros 1647, tel. 54/3286-1475, www.

gramado.rs.gov.br, 9am-7pm daily) has maps as well as hotel and restaurant listings. Also check out www.gramadosite.com.

Gramado is 115 kilometers (72 mi) northeast of Porto Alegre. From the *rodoviária* (Av. Borges de Medeiros 2100, tel. 54/3286-1302), frequent buses arrive and depart from Porto Alegre. **Citral** (tel. 0800/979-1441, www.citral.tur.br) has bus service from Porto Alegre's *rodoviária* and airport to Gramado and on to Canela. Buses leave nearly every 30-60 minutes, but not all are direct. The two-hour journey costs R$24-31. By car, the shortest route is to follow RS-020 to Taquara before turning onto RS-115. Frequent buses (R$2.10) connect Gramado and Canela, 20 minutes away.

Canela

Canela is smaller, lower in altitude, and less touristy, as well as more down-to-earth than its ostentatious sister city, Gramado, 8 kilometers (5.5 mi) away. It also makes a better base for adventure-sports enthusiasts since it is much closer to Parque Ferradura and Parque Estadual do Caracol. If you don't have your own wheels, **JM Rafting e Expedições** (Av. Osvaldo Aranha 1038, tel. 54/3282-1255, www.jmrafting.com.br) offers offers half-day tours to the parks as well as full-day trips to the magnificent canyons of the Parque Nacional de Aparados da Serra.

PARQUE ESTADUAL DO CARACOL

Canela's main draw is the **Parque Estadual do Caracol** (Estrada do Caracol Km 9, tel. 54/3278-3035, www.parquedocaracol.com.br, 8:30am-6pm daily, R$12). Within its borders is the stunning 131-meter (430-foot) Cascata do Caracol, the tallest waterfall in Rio Grande do Sul. You can gaze on this spectacle from a lookout point, or climb 927 very steep stairs (which takes about 40 minutes, and isn't for the faint of heart) to the top of the falls—take comfort in the fact that there's also a panoramic elevator that will whisk you to the top for R$9. Various hiking trails weave through the park's wooded

landscape. If you don't have a car, you can get to the park on the "Caracol Circular" bus that leaves from Canela's *rodoviária*. Be prepared for dozens of tour buses to accompany you during high season.

PARQUE DA FERRADURA

Parque da Ferradura (Estrada do Caracol Km 15, tel. 54/9972-8666, 9am-5:30pm daily, R$8) is a natural park that offers incredible views into the immense canyon, shaped like a *ferradura* (horseshoe) formed by the Rio Caí. Two easy trails lead to lookout points, while a more challenging 2-kilometer (1-mi) trail leads down to the river.

SPORTS AND RECREATION

Canela has become an eco-adventure destination. **JM Rafting e Expedições** (tel. 54/3282-1255, www.jmrafting.com.br) offers reasonably priced half-day excursions that include rappelling (R$85), rafting (R$75), and horseback riding (R$35). Daredevils will particularly enjoy pendulum jumping (R$75)—that is, throwing themselves off the 30-meter-high (98-foot) Ponte Passo do Infirmo (which spans the Rio Cará waterfall) and swinging wildly in the air. Another Canela-based company that offers similar activities is **Black Bear Adventure** (tel. 54/9939-7191).

ACCOMMODATIONS

From basic rooms to luxury suites, accommodations in Canela offer better value for your money than in trendy (often overpriced) Gramado. Close to the central hub, cozy **Pousada Encantos da Terra** (Rua Tenente Manoel Corrêa 282, Centro, tel. 54/3282-2080, www.pousadaencantosdaterra.com.br, R$140-190) is an apartment-style *pousada* in a wooded setting with bright, attractive, and comfortable rooms and a sustainable ethos. Less central but more alluringly rustic is **Aldeia dos Sonhos Pousada** (Rua Santa Terezinha 334, Santa Terezinha, tel. 54/3282-0000, www.pousadaaldeiadossonhos.com.br, R$160-220 d), whose simple, cozy cabins are scattered amid a country estate dating back to the 1930s.

Located in the former governor's mansion and built in the 1950s, ★ **Pousada Cravo e Canela** (Rua Ten. Manoel Corrêa 144, Centro, tel. 54/3282-1120, www.pousadacravoecanela.com.br, R$285-570 d) is one of Canela's most charming accommodation options. Breakfasts (served till noon) are lavish; afternoon tea and contents of the minibar are both on the house. With the pool, day spa, games room, bar, and lounge complete with crackling fireplace, you'll have plenty to keep you relaxingly engaged.

FOOD

On the road from Canela to Gramado, **Cantina 28** (Rua Jacob Adamy 528, tel. 54/3282-0628, noon-3:30pm Thurs.-Sun., R$25-35) is a necessary stop for those with a penchant for polenta. In their welcoming house and garden, the owners serve a buffet of 28 Italian dishes; since only 28 guests are seated on any given day, reservations are a must. Equally nourishing are the culinary creations at cozy **Café Canela** (Rua Altenor Teles de Souza 15, tel. 54/3282-4422, www.cafecanela.com.br, R$20-30), whose signature soups and salads are served in hollowed-out bread bowls, while pastas and risottos come to the table in carved-out blocks of cheese.

Canela is famed for its apple strudel. Aside from traditional German cuisine such as *kessler* and sauerkraut, **Schnitzelstubb** (Rua Baden Powell 246, tel. 54/3282-9562, noon-3pm and 7:30pm-11pm Tues.-Sat., noon-4pm Sun. July-Aug. and Dec., R$15-25) serves up a tasty version with ice cream. One of the finest recipes to be had in the center of town is at **Confeitaria Martha** (Av. Júlio de Castilhos 151, tel. 54/3282-4190, 10am-8:30pm daily, R$8-20), a bakery that also makes good sandwiches. The best of all is served at ★ **Castelinha Caracol** (Estrada do Caracol Km 3, tel. 54/3278-3208, 9am-1pm and 2:20pm-5:40pm daily, R$8-20). Built by family of German immigrants, this historic early 20th-century house was constructed entirely from native *araucária* pine without using a single nail. It's the perfect place to savor the family recipe for strudel alongside homemade fruit jams and waffles.

TRANSPORTATION AND SERVICES

The **tourist office** (Largo da Fama, tel. 54/3282-2200, www.canelaturismo.com.br, 8am-7pm daily) is in the center of town. During the day, a Canela-Gramado bus circulates between the two towns at regular 20-minute intervals (R$2.10). From Porto Alegre, the same **Citral** (tel. 0800/979-1441, www.citral.tur.br) buses that stop in Gramado continue onto Canela.

★ PARQUE NACIONAL DE APARADOS DA SERRA

Some 40 kilometers (25 mi) northeast of Canela, straddling Rio Grande do Sul's frontier with Santa Catarina, lies the **Parque Nacional de Aparados da Serra** (tel. 54/3251-1277, 8am-5pm Wed.-Sun., R$6), a magnificent natural park that encompasses some 60 canyons as well as breathtaking waterfalls and one of the only remaining *araucária* forests in Brazil. The most dramatic highlight of the park is the 6-kilometer-long (4-mi) **Cânion de Itaimbezinho.** Carpeted in *araucárias,* its steep walls plunge to vertiginous depths of 720 meters (2,360 feet) and are adorned by two magnificent waterfalls, Andorinha and Véu de Noiva. From the visitors center at the main park entrance, 18 kilometers (11 mi) along RS-429 from the town of Cambará do Sul, three trails allow you to explore the canyon (though the park prohibits swimming). The easiest 45-minute, 1.5-kilometer (1-mi) path leads to the canyon's rim, passing by the Cachoeira das Andorinhas, while a second 2.5-kilometer (1.5-mi) trail skirts the Véu de Noiva waterfall. A more difficult, 2.5-hour, 6-kilometer (3.5-mi) route descending into the canyon requires a guide and trekking gear and departs from the Rio do Boi entrance.

The best time to visit the region is during

the winter (although temperatures are chilly), when visibility is best due to the lack of mist, or in the spring (October-November) in order to see wild blossoms. The months of April, May, and September can be very rainy. Call Cambará do Sul's tourist office (tel. 54/3251-1557) or check its website (www.cambaraonline.com.br) for weather conditions. Although the visitors center at Parque Nacional da Serra Geral is equipped with a tourist office, maps, and a restaurant, there are no guides at either of the parks—to hire one, contact the **Associação de Condutores Locais de Eco-Turismo (Acontur)** (tel. 54/9916-1583/9964-1033, http://acontur.wordpress.com), whose headquarters is in Cambará do Sul's Centro Cultural. Depending on the length of the trail, guides charge between R$40-125 pp to hike within the Parque de Aparados da Serra and the Parque da Serra Geral (based on a minimum of five people). Somewhat more expensive, **Cânion Turismo** (Av. Getúlio Vargas tel. 54/3251-1027, www.canionturismo.com.br) is a highly specialized and much-recommended ecotour outfit offering myriad single and multiday hiking, biking, horseback and camping adventures, with customized outings geared to families.

Accommodations and Food

The best base for visiting the park is the traditional cattle town of **Cambará do Sul,** whose surrounding flat plains betray no hint of the breathtaking topography nearby. Accommodations in Cambará do Sul are generally basic but atmospheric. One of the nicer and more central choices is **Pousada João de Barro** (Rua Padre João Francisco Ritter 631, tel. 54/3251-1352, www.joaodebarropousada.com.br, R$150-175 d), a family-style place with small, well-appointed guest rooms, which sleep up to five; guided tours are offered. Also close to the center is the highly atmospheric **Pousada Estalagem da Colina** (Av. Getúlio Vargas 80, tel. 54/3251-1746, www.estalagemdacolina.com.br, R$190-240 d), where accommodation is in individual wooden chalets adorned with simple, homey

touches. The main chalet features inviting common rooms along with a Jacuzzi, Internet access, and a boutique selling local *artesanato* and delicacies.

Well-heeled ecotourists will prefer the luxuries offered by the ★ **Parador Casa da Montanha** (Fazenda Camarinhas Km 9.5, tel. 54/3504-5302, www.paradorcasadamontanha.com.br, R$279-675 d), set amid a rolling landscape between Cambará and the entrance to the Parque Nacional de Aparados da Serra. Accommodations consist of chic thermal tents engineered to battle the elements and seduce your senses. To keep you warm and relaxed, there are saunas and jetted tubs. The hotel organizes trips to the park as well as hiking, horseback-riding, and mountain-bike excursions. Prices include all meals at the *pousada*'s charming restaurant. Lunch and dinner feature typical regional dishes, such as *carreteiro de charque* (seasoned cured beef with rice) and *doce de abóbora* (candied pumpkin). Noon-2:30pm on weekends, the restaurant serves a delicious regional buffet that can be enjoyed by nonguests. There's a two-night minimum on weekends and a three-night minimum during holidays and July; packages are available if you stay more than one night.

For proximity to the Parque da Serra Geral, **Refúgio Pedra Afiada Ecológico** (Estrada da Vila Rosa, tel. 48/3532-1059, www.pedraafiada.com.br, R$190-460 d) is a wonderful, secluded option near the town of Praia Grande in Santa Catarina. Accommodations are in charming bungalows plunged into the steep and exuberantly green midst of Cânion Malacara. Take advantage of outdoors activities ranging from rafting to horseback riding; at night, get warm and cozy in front of a crackling fireplace, or at the communal wooden tables of the on-site bistro (dinner included).

Resembling the set of a Hollywood Western, **Restaurante Galpão Costaneira** (Rua Dona Úrsula 1069, tel. 54/3251-1005, 11:30am-3pm daily and 7:30pm-10pm Mon.-Sat, R$15-30) is heavy on atmosphere. Inside, the walls are decorated with Gaúcho artifacts, and a copious buffet of regional dishes and sizzling grilled meats is served at your table with traditional accompaniments of melted cheese and sausages. On weekends, Gaúcho music is performed live. Warm, wood-paneled **O Casarão** (Rua João Francisco Ritter 969, tel. 54/3251-1711, 11:30am-3pm Mon.-Fri., 11:30am-10:30pm Sat.-Sun, Dec.-Feb. and July, R$20-30) specializes in hearty Italian food of the Gaúcho interior. Accompanying the succulent fare are local wines and grappa.

Transportation and Services

In Cambará, the **tourist office** (Av. Getúlio Vargas 1720, tel. 54/3251-1557, www.cambara-dosul.rs.gov.br, 8am-6pm daily) is in the center of town in a historic wooden house. Aside from providing maps and information, the staff can help you find guides or join an organized excursion.

There is no bus service. If you don't have a car, getting to the Parque Nacional de Aparados da Serra or Parque da Serra Geral

requires hiring a taxi or minivan to take you to the entrances and pick you up again. Or, take a guided excursion offered by ecotour outfits in Cambará, Gramado, or Canela; many offer full-day excursions to the parks.

Getting to Cambará by bus is not that easy. From Porto Alegre, 193 kilometers (120 mi) away, **Citral** (tel. 0800/979-1441, www.citral.tur.br) has one daily bus (R$33) that departs at 6am and takes 5.5 hours—due to numerous stops—to get to Cambará's *rodoviária* (Rua Dona Úrsula 840, tel. 54/3251-1567). Otherwise, from Porto Alegre—as well as from Gramado and Canela—you have to go to the town of **São Francisco da Paula,** 60 kilometers (37 mi) from Cambará; from here there is also a 5pm departure (1.5 hours, R$14).

If you're driving from Porto Alegre, take BR-166 to Taquara and then follow RS-020, straight north. Be aware that many of the roads around Cambará are not paved and can be particularly difficult to navigate when it rains.

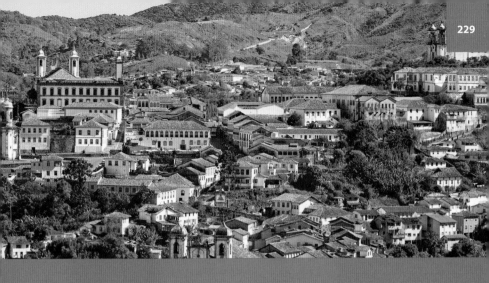

Minas Gerais

Highlights

★ **Nightlife in Belo Horizonte:** With more bars per capita than any other Brazilian city, Belo Horizonte's *boteco* scene is in a class of its own (page 239).

★ **Igreja de São Francisco de Assis:** Ouro Preto is stuffed with magnificent churches, but this jewel created by sculptor Aleijadinho and master painter Manuel da Costa Ataíde is Mineiro baroque at its finest (page 254).

★ **Basílica e Santuário do Bom Jesus de Matosinhos:** Aleijadinho's final masterpiece, the *12 Prophets,* is the highlight of this monumental 18th-century sanctuary in the *cidade histórica* of Congonhas. It's one of the greatest and most moving examples of baroque art (page 262).

★ **Igreja Matriz de Santo Antônio:** Perched on a steep hill, Tiradentes's main church has a dazzling interior plastered with half a ton of pure gold (page 267).

★ **Caminho de Escravos:** This road was cut into the mountains by thousands of African slaves; wandering along it offers striking views of colonial Diamantina and the surrounding peaks and valleys (page 277).

Locked within steep mountain ranges and with no coast of its own, the vast state of Minas Gerais is a country unto itself.

As a result, Mineiros have a different style and rhythm, with their own distinctive accents, expressions, and *jeitos*, or ways of doing things. They also have their own cuisine—*comida mineira*—with mouthwatering specialties ranging from *tutu à mineira* (a thick bean puree) to *frango ao molho pardo*, chicken cooked in a pungent sauce made from its own blood. Just as varied as the main courses are its infinite desserts and more than 4,000 regionally produced *cachaças* (alcohol made from fermented sugarcane); the best rival world-class whiskeys.

Minas is a forward-looking place. An economic powerhouse, its dynamic capital, Belo Horizonte, is a cosmopolitan city with an impressively varied cultural scene and a diverse range of restaurants, bars, and nightlife options. "BH," as locals refer to it (pronounced "BAY ah-GAH"), is also surrounded by some great getaway destinations, including caves with prehistoric paintings, national parks replete with canyons and waterfalls, and charismatic historical towns.

Minas first gained attention in the 1700s, when Portuguese adventurers discovered its lush mountains were abundantly stocked with precious stones, diamonds, and especially gold. During the subsequent gold rush, mining towns sprung up amid the valleys of central Minas. Although these towns prospered, Portugal profited the most from the tremendous quantity of gold that was mined by African slaves and shipped off to Europe. Of the gold that remained in Brazil, much was used to fund the building and decoration of baroque churches, whose richness is unparalleled in the New World. Today, these *cidades históricas* (historic cities) afford a glimpse into Brazil's colorful past as boom-and-bust frontier towns that once possessed the largest deposits of gold and diamonds on the planet. Although some—Ouro Preto, Tiradentes, and Diamantina—have weathered the centuries more successfully and with more charm than others (Sabará, Congonhas, and São João del Rei), all offer a wealth of artistic and cultural diversions as well as exposure to authentic Mineiro life.

Previous: view of Ouro Preto; Minas Gerais landscape. **Above:** church in Ouro Preto

Minas Gerais

To Salvador

BR 116

Rio São Francisco

BR 122

BR 251

Montes Claros

Itaobim

Araçuaí

Rio Jequitinhonha

BR 365

To Brasília
and Goiânia

BR 135

MINAS GERAIS

Biribiri

CAMINHO DE ESCRAVOS ✚

Diamantina

BR 116

Serro

Governador
Valadares

Represa
Três Marias

Curvelo

ESPÍRITO
SANTO

BR 354

Parque Nacional da
Serra da Cipó

BR 259

Colatina

Sete Lagoas

NIGHTLIFE IN
✚ BELO HORIZONTE

BR 262

BELO HORIZONTE

Sabará

Santa
Bárbara

Manhuaçu

VITÓRIA

Ouro
Preto

BR 262

BASÍLICA E SANTUÁRIO DO
BOM JESUS DE MATOSINHOS ✚

Congonhas

Mariana

Manhumirim

✚ IGREJA DE SÃO
FRANCISCO DE ASSIS

BR 354

IGREJA MATRIZ
DE SANTO ANTÔNIO ✚

Tiradentes

Barbacana

BR 101

São João
del Rei

BR 381

BR 116

Poços de Caldas

Três Corações

Cambuquira

Juiz de Fora

Campos dos
Goitacazes

Lambari

Caxambú

Pouso Alegre

São Lourenço

RIO DE
JANEIRO

BR 116

SOUTH
ATLANTIC

OCEAN

SÃO PAULO

RIO DE
JANEIRO

Niterói

Cabo Frio

SÃO PAULO

0   50 mi

0   50 km

© AVALON TRAVEL

PLANNING YOUR TIME

With the exception of Diamantina (five hours north of Belo Horizonte), most of Minas's colonial treasures and a good many of its natural attractions are close together in southern Minas, within easy striking distance of Belo Horizonte (2-4 hours by bus or car). São João del Rei and Tiradentes, the *cidades históricas* farthest south, are equidistant from Belo Horizonte and Rio de Janeiro. Roads are in top condition and buses run frequently, making traveling between the various destinations easy.

With **three days,** focus on Ouro Preto and Mariana (14 km/9 mi apart) or São João del Rei and Tiradentes (12 km/7.5 mi apart); either will easily satiate your appetite for colonial history, baroque magnificence, steep cobblestoned hills, and mouthwatering Mineiro cuisine. **One week** will allow you time to explore more of the *cidades* (including the far-flung Diamantina), the surrounding mountains and waterfalls, and to stop in Belo Horizonte for a shot of big city life.

Minas can get hot and crowded in the summer months. Although the historic towns tend to be livelier in the summer, accommodations (particularly in Ouro Preto and Tiradentes) fill up quickly and are more expensive, particularly during Carnaval and Semana Santa. July coincides with winter vacation, which means high prices but also misty mornings, chilly nights, and roaring fireplaces—enticing if you bring warm clothing. In **August-September,** you'll find the climate dry and the historic cities delightfully tranquil. October is usually when the rainy season starts, which lasts four months.

Belo Horizonte

Built in the late 1800s, Belo Horizonte was planned as a progressive new capital that could replace Ouro Preto, whose fortunes had dwindled after the gold rush. Although it is one of Brazil's largest and most important cities (population 2.6 million), the planned metropolis, with its scores of nondescript high-rises and industrial outskirts that reflect its economic clout, doesn't offer much in the way of history or charm. BH is nonetheless a compelling city with a varied cultural and culinary scene and a sizzling nightlife that easily offers a couple days' diversion. Although colonial architecture is nonexistent, fans of modernism are in for a treat: The city is brimming with houses and buildings from the 1950s and quite a few art deco gems from the preceding decades. In the 1940s and early 1950s, Belo Horizonte served as a three-dimensional drafting board for an ambitious young architect by the name of Oscar Niemeyer. His earliest and still surprisingly vanguard buildings can be seen in the city center as well as in the well-to-do neighborhood of Pampulha.

Belo Horizonte is also a useful base for exploring the surrounding region. Located in a deep valley ringed by the majestic Serra do Espinhaço mountain range—which explains the name Belo Horizonte (Beautiful Horizon)—the city is close to a wealth of natural attractions that can be visited in under an hour. It is also near three of Minas's most impressive colonial towns: Sabará (30 minutes away), Ouro Preto and Mariana (2 hours away), as well as Congonhas (1 hour away), the site of master baroque sculptor Aleijadinho's final—and arguably greatest—works.

ORIENTATION

Although Belo Horizonte is sprawling, most central neighborhoods are contained within a 12-kilometer (7.5-mi) ringed road known as Avenida do Contorno. With the exception of Oscar Niemeyer's Pampulha Complex, almost all sights and attractions are located in either **Centro** or the leafy upscale neighborhood of **Savassi.** Along lively Avenida Cristovão Colombo is Praça da Savassi, the

Belo Horizonte

R BERNARDO MASCARENHAS

SANTO AGOSTINHO

Praça da Assembléia

★ MUSEU HISTÓRICO ABÍLIO BARRETO

AV DO CONTORNO

AV OLEGARIO

GONÇALVES DAS

BERNARDO

R DOS AMORES

R GUIMARÃES

MACIEL

SANTA

CATARINA

CURITIBA

SANTO ANTÔNIO

PROF ANTONIO

FELIPE

DOS SANTOS

ALEIXO

GONÇALVES

SÃO

PAULO

PELOCIO

LOURDES

AV BIAS FORTES

AV ALVARES CABRAL

FERNANDES

TOURINHO

R ALBIQUERQUE

R DE

ESPIRITO

SANTO

R DA BAHIA

AV DO CONTORNO

LEVINDO LOPES

CCCP ■

DONA DERNA ■

TEATRO IZABELA HENDRIX ■

MEMORIAL MINAS GERAIS VALE ★
MUSEU DAS MINAS DE DO METAL ★
ESPAÇO TIM UFMG ★

CENTRO DE ARTE POPULAR ★

Praça da Liberdade

PALÁCIO DA LIBERDADE ■

EDIFÍCIO NIEMEYER ■

AV CRISTOVÃO COLOMBO

CAFÉ COM LETRAS ▼

DONA LUCINHA ▼

CENTRO CULTURAL BANCO DO BRASIL ★

CLAUDIO

SANTA RITA

DURÃO

ALAGOAS

AV JOÃO PINHEIRO

SERGIPE

DOS TIMBIRAS

R MANOEL

CATEDRAL DA BOA VIAGEM ♦

ARMAZÉM DONA LUCINHA ▼

PÁTIO SAVASSI ▼

A OBRA BAR DANÇANTE ▼

Praça Savassi

SAVASSI

R PERNAMBUCO

● ROYAL SAVASSI BOUTIQUE HOTEL

SANTA FÉ

R PARAIBA

HOTEL BOULEVARD PARK ●

BERNARDO

DAS

R PARAIBA

AV BRASIL

To Salsa Parrilha,Mercearia Lili, and Via Cristina →

To Hermengarda →

SION

AV DO CONTORNO

PROF

MORAIS

R TOMÉ DE SOUZA

DOS INCONDENTES

DOS CEARÁ

AV GETULIO VARGAS

RIO GRANDE DO NORTE

AV AFONSO PENA

GUIMARÃES

DOS AMORES

DOS TIMBIRAS

AV BERNARDO

GUAJAJARAS

PIAUÍ

SÃO PEDRO

MARANHÃO

COZINHA MINEIRA ▼

PIAUÍ

CEARÁ

To Parque das Mangabeiras →

AV DO CONTORNO

0   200 yds
0   200 m

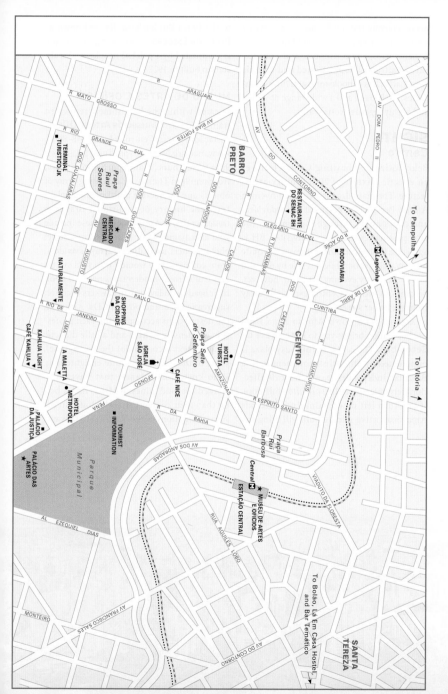

R MATO GROSSO
ARAGUARI
R RIO GRANDE DO SUL
R DOS GUAJAJARAS
TERMINAL TURISTICO JK
Praça Raul Soares
AV GOTACAZES
AV DOS ANDRADAS
R DOS TUPIS
R DOS TAMOIOS
R DOS CARIJOS
MERCADO CENTRAL
R AUGUSTO DE LIMA
NATURALMENTE
R SAO PAULO
R RIO DE JANEIRO
SHOPPING DA CIDADE
AV AFONSO PENA
IGREJA SAO JOSE
CAFÉ NICE
Praça Sete de Setembro
KAHLUA LIGHT
CAFÉ KAHLUA
A MALETA
HOTEL METROPOLE
PALACIO DA JUSTICA
PALACIO DAS ARTES
Parque Municipal
TOURIST INFORMATION
AL EZEQUIEL DIAS
MONTEIRO
AV FRANCISCO SALES
AV DO CONTORNO

BARRO PRETO
AV OLEGARIO MACIEL
RESTAURANTE DO SENAC BH
AV BIAS FORTES
R TUPINAMBAS
R DOS CAETES
CURITIBA
CENTRO
AV AMAZONAS
HOTEL TURISTA
R ESPIRITO SANTO
R DA BAHIA
Praça Rui Barbosa
R GUAICURUS
R 21 DE ABRIL
RODOVIARIA
R DO ACRE
AV DO CONTORNO
Lagoinha
AV DOM PEDRO II
To Pampulha
To Vitoria
Central
MUSEU DE ARTES E OFICIOS
ESTAÇÃO CENTRAL
VIADUTO DA FLORESTA
RUA AQUILES LOBO
To Bolão, Lá Em Casa Hostel, and Bar Tematico
SANTA TEREZA

nerve center for the area known as Savassi that roughly incorporates the neighborhoods of Funcionários, Santo Antônio, and Lourdes. Savassi attracts a sophisticated and eclectic crowd, with lots of bookstores and funky boutiques, lively bars, and a wide range of varied and highly regarded restaurants.

SIGHTS
Centro

Belo Horizonte's bustling Centro features an eclectic mixture of 20th-century architecture. The main drag is tree-lined Avenida Afonso Pena, which begins at the *rodoviária* and cuts straight through the center of the city, passing several interesting sites. BH is agreeable to stroll around; however, it is quite hilly. Walking around Belo is safe by day and even in the early evening. At night, however, be cautious around Centro, especially away from the busier streets.

A short walk down Afonso Pena from the bus station brings you to **Praça Sete de Setembro.** The center of this busy plaza is punctuated by an obelisk commemorating Brazilian independence, which locals affectionately refer to as the *pirulito* (lollipop). If you turn left down palm-lined Avenida Amazonas, a five-minute walk will bring you to the Praça Rui Barbosa. Better known as **Praça da Estação**, this rather grand square is dominated by a palatial neoclassical train station built in 1922.

MUSEU DE ARTES E OFÍCIOS

Located within the handsomely renovated train station is the **Museu de Artes e Ofícios** (Estação Central, Centro, tel. 31/3248-8600, www.mao.org.br, noon-7pm Tues.-Fri., noon-9pm Wed.-Thurs., 11am-5pm Sat.-Sun., R$4, free 5pm-9pm Thurs.). A fascinating array of objects and interactive multimedia displays trace the history of traditional Brazilian trades, crafts, and professions. These include gold and diamond miners, stevedores, street photographers, and a diverse array of vendors, from colonial slave women who sold sweets and fruits from wooden trays perched upon their heads to today's urban hawkers of coffee, sugarcane juice, and pirated CDs. Although the descriptions accompanying each profession are densely written and a little didactic (English text accompanies the Portuguese), some of the details are quite enlightening. Who knew, for instance, that slaves who worked the gold mines in Minas had it better than their counterparts who toiled in the sugar plantations of the Northeast? This was

Belo Horizonte

because bosses gave slaves a quota of gold they had to mine; any surplus nuggets were theirs to keep and used to purchase their freedom. Some of the objects on display are also quite astonishing. Particularly shocking is the enormous metal scale that was used to weigh slaves.

PARQUE MUNICIPAL

Parque Municipal (Avenida Afonso Pena) is a verdant oasis that conjures up a mildly tropical version of the fin de siècle public parks of Paris upon which it was modeled. There are 50 varieties of century-old trees, a lake, fountains, rose gardens, and an "orchidarium." This lovely park also shelters Belo Horizonte's most important arts and cultural center, the **Palácio das Artes** (Av. Afonso Pena 1537, Centro, tel. 31/3236-7400, www.fcs.mg.gov.br). Designed by Oscar Niemeyer and inaugurated in 1971, this gleaming white building houses two theaters, a cinema, art galleries, a bookstore, a café, and a large boutique that sells traditional handicrafts from all over Minas.

PRAÇA DA LIBERDADE

The **Praça da Liberdade** lies south of the Palácio das Artes, along Rua Sergipe. The immaculately landscaped gardens of this large plaza—with its fountains, bandstands, and Greco-Roman sculptures—were modeled after those at the Palace of Versailles, and a distinctly European elegance reigns. At night there are often free theatrical or musical performances. The park is surrounded by impressive buildings that range in style from grand neoclassical palaces (the **Palácio do Governo**) to the fluid modernism of the **Biblioteca Pública** and the fantastically curvy **Edifício Niemeyer,** a striking residential building designed by Oscar himself and completed in 1955. Since 2010, a handful of palaces have transformed into cutting-edge museums and cultural centers (an ongoing process); most host myriad happenings and house cool boutiques and cafés. Together, this ensemble of attractions constitutes the Circuito Cultural Liberdade (http://circuitoculturalliberdade.com.br), making the area a dynamic cultural hub.

Housed inside the palatial former state Ministry of Education, geology buffs can get their rocks off at the **Museu das Minas e do Metal** (tel. 31/3516-7200, www.mmm.org.br, noon-6pm Tues.-Wed. and Fri.-Sun., noon-10pm Thurs., R$6, free Thurs.). This shiny museum pays homage to the activity that's synonymous with Minas itself—mining—with a host of high-tech interactive exhibits (including an elevator to the replica of the state's deepest mine), distributed amid marble columns and centuries-old azulejo panels. The neighboring **Espaço TIM UFMG do Conhecimento** (tel. 31/3409-8350, www.ufmg.br/espacodoconhecimento, noon-6pm Tues.-Wed. and Fri.-Sun., noon-10pm Thurs., free) is a natural history museum whose exhibits are less interesting than its state-of-the-art planetarium (R$6) and rooftop terrace outfitted with telescopes (7pm-9pm, Wed.-Thurs., free).

More worthy of a visit is the **Memorial Minas Gerais Vale** (tel. 31/3343-7317, www.memorialvale.com.br, 10am-5:30pm Tues-Wed. and Fri.-Sun, 10am-9:30pm Thurs., free). Occupying a palace that once housed the state Ministry of Finance, this museum does an admirable job of capturing Minas's essence with creatively curated displays devoted to the state's history and culture. Most are organized by key themes such as celebrations, baroque, and Afro-Mineiro culture, while others are dedicated to prominent Mineiros ranging from 18th-century rebel Tiradentes to 20th-century photographer Sebastião Salgado.

Directly across the park, the **Centro Cultural Banco do Brasil** (tel. 31/3343-7317, http://culturabancodobrasil.com.br, 10am-5:30pm Tues-Wed. and Fri.-Sun, 10am-9:30pm Thurs., free) occupies the beautifully restored former state Ministry of Public Health and Safety, built in 1926. Amidst cavernous ceilings and glossy parquet floors, it plays host to some of the city's art exhibits and music, dance, and theatrical performances.

A block from the *praça*, but still part of the Circuito da Liberdade, the **Centro de Arte Popular** (Rua Gonçalves Dias 1668, Funcionários, tel. 31/3222-3231, www.centrodeartepopular.mg.gov.br, 10am-7pm Tues.-Wed. and Fri.-Sun., noon-9pm Thurs., free) has a modest but diverse permanent collection of folk art from throughout the state. Exhibits are attractively displayed throughout three floors of a 1920s mansion. Among the highlights are the expressive ceramic bridal *bonecas* (dolls) fashioned by women of the remote north.

Beyond Centro

If you have extra time to spare in Belo Horizonte, there are a couple of worthwhile sights located beyond the limits of Avenida Contorno (which rings the central core of the city).

MUSEU HISTÓRICO ABÍLIO BARRETO

South of Savassi in the pretty suburban neighborhood of Cidade Jardim is the **Museu Histórico Abílio Barreto** (Av. Prudente de Morais 202, Cidade Jardim, tel. 31/3277-8573, 10am-5pm Tues. and Fri.-Sun., 10am-9pm Wed.-Thurs., free). Inside this renovated colonial farmhouse, photographs and artifacts recount the development of the Mineiro capital. Overlooking a garden shaded by century-old trees, the museum's lovely café (www.cafedomuseu.com.br) serves lunch and dinner as well as coffee and snacks.

PARQUE DAS MANGABEIRAS

For a dose of nature, head to **Parque das Mangabeiras** (Av. José Patrocínio Pontes 580, Serra do Curral, tel. 31/3277-8277, 8am-5pm Tues.-Sun.), a 230-hectare (570-acre) expanse of native vegetation only partially tamed by noted Brazilian landscape architect Roberto Burle Marx. Carpeting the steep hills of the Serra do Curral, the park is easily reached by taking the No. 4103 Aparecida/Mangabeiras municipal bus from Avenida Afonso Pena (between Av. Amazonas and Av. Tamóios) in Centro. The views of the city are really quite stunning. The best vantage point is from the Mirante da Mata, a lookout that's a 20-minute walk from the entrance. Park maps are available at the visitors kiosk.

Pampulha

Juscelino Kubitschek was elected mayor of Belo Horizonte in 1940, 20 years before he became one of Brazil's most beloved presidents. At the time, Belo was a provincial and conservative town. Kubitschek was a dreamer who believed that mayors shouldn't concern themselves just with practical matters, but with beauty as well. One of his ambitions was to create an entirely new and modern neighborhood surrounding a lake, with facilities for leisure and recreation, some 15 kilometers (9 mi) from Centro.

To carry out this task, he called upon the talents of a number of notable Brazilian artists. Among them were landscaper Roberto Burle Marx, the celebrated modernist painter Cândido Portinari, and a young architect who had only recently graduated by the name of Oscar Niemeyer. Excited by the proposal, Niemeyer traveled to Belo Horizonte from Rio to meet with Kubitschek, and during dinner sketched plans on a napkin for the modernist constructions that would ultimately become the Pampulha neighborhood.

To get to Pampulha, take the No. 2004 Bandeirantes/Olhos d'Água bus that leaves from the stop in front of the Hotel Financial on Avenida Afonso Pena in Centro. Ideally (without traffic), the trip takes about 20 minutes, and the bus lets you off right in front of the Igreja de São Francisco de Assis.

IGREJA DE SÃO FRANCISCO DE ASSIS

The highlight of Niemeyer's contributions to Pampulha is the **Igreja de São Francisco de Assis** (Av. Otacílio Negrão de Lima 3000, tel. 31/3427-1644, 9am-5pm Mon.-Sat., noon-5pm Sun., R$2). The eye-popping church with its sensual curves and bold lines was constructed between 1943 and 1945. Its exterior is covered with tiny blue ceramic tiles; the highlights are a mural depicting scenes from the life of Saint Francis of Assisi and 14 canvases that illustrate scenes from the Passion of Christ, both painted by Portinari. There's also a none-too-private cylindrical confessional—due to the church's fantastic acoustics, it has never been used. When the church was completed, conservative Belo Horizonte was shocked by its vanguard design and subversive aesthetic. Many members of the city's elite called for a boycott, and the clergy refused to recognize the modernist temple because Niemeyer was not only an atheist but a communist. It wasn't until 1959 that Belo Horizonte's bishop came around to allowing marriages and baptisms in the church.

IATE TÊNIS CLUBE AND CASA DO BAILE

There is a trio of Niemeyer buildings in Pampulha. Although they are of minor interest, two of them can be visited by taking a pleasant half-hour stroll around the bucolic Lagoa de Pampulha, which is lined with opulent mansions. The **Iate Tênis Clube** (Av. Otacílio Negrão da Lima 1350) was built in 1943 and is now a favorite hangout of Belo Horizonte's sail-hoisting, racket-swinging elite (although it's not open to visitors). Close by is the **Casa do Baile** (Av. Otacílio Negrão da Lima 751, tel. 31/3277-7433, 9am-6pm Tues.-Sun.), whose curved lines mirror the outline of the lake. Originally a dance hall where couples could waltz the night away, today it houses a reference center for urban design and architecture.

MUSEU DE ARTE DE PAMPULHA

Hard to get to (if you're already in Pampulha, you'll need to take a car or taxi) due to its location on the far shore of the *lagoa* is the **Museu de Arte de Pampulha** (Av. Otacílio Negrão da Lima 16585, tel. 31/3277-7953, 9am-7pm Tues.-Sun., free). Niemeyer's first Pampulha construction, this modern art museum (whose exhibits can be hit or miss) reveals the strong influence of his mentor Le Corbusier. Originally built to be a glamorous casino, it served its original purpose for only three years before being closed down in 1946, when Brazil banned gambling houses. The surrounding gardens, designed by Burle Marx, are quite lovely.

SPORTS AND RECREATION

Belo Horizontinos take their soccer very seriously. Minas's most famous stadium is the **Minerão** (Av. Abraão Carã 1001, Pampulha, tel. 31/3499-4300, www.minasarena.com.br), whose overhaul for the 2014 World Cup left it with fewer seats, but with a small Museu de Futebol, souvenir stores, and a food court where you can stuff your face with Mineiro specialties such as *tropeirão*, a hearty post-game concoction of manioc flour-coated beans, steak, collard greens, and fried egg. The two major state rivals are Cruzeiro and Atlético (avoid games in which they face off). To get to the stadium from Centro, take the No. 2004 municipal bus that passes in front of the Hotel Financial on Avenida Afonso Pena.

ENTERTAINMENT AND EVENTS
★ Nightlife

In BH, a popular saying is *"não tem mares, tem bares"* ("we don't have beaches, we have bars"), which explains a lot about the way the natives spend their idle hours. At last count, the city boasted more than 8,000 *botecos*, or tavern-like bars. Indeed, Belo Horizontinos love nothing more than bar hopping in the pursuit of beer, *cachaça, petiscos*, and conversation. Lots of no-nonsense inexpensive options exist in Centro, such as simple sidewalk bars along Avenida Amazonas that stay open until the wee hours. For a bit more atmosphere and a more eclectic, upscale mix of people, head to the sophisticated *bairros* of Savassi, Lourdes, Funcionários, and Santo Antônio. It's also worthwhile to check out the funky residential neighborhood of Santa Tereza, popular with a bohemian crowd.

Inhotim

The **Instituto de Arte Contemporânea Inhotim** (tel. 31/3571-9700, www.inhotim.org.br, 9:30am-4:30pm Tues.-Fri., 9:30am-5:30pm Sat.-Sun., R$20 Wed.-Fri. R$30 Sat.-Sun., free Tues.) assembles Brazil's largest collection of contemporary art amid the rolling hills of the country's largest botanical garden. Located near the small town of Brumadinho 60 kilometers (37 mi) from Belo Horizonte, this 1,200-hectare (3,000-acre) open-air museum is the brainchild of local iron magnate Bernardo Paz, who spent more than US$90 million acquiring the fantastic collection. It includes audacious large-scale sculptures and installations by Brazilians such as Hélio Oiticica, Tunga, and Adriana Varejão as well as Chris Burden, Matthew Barney, Jorge Macchi, and Doug Aitken, whose Sonic Pavilion is a real trip.

Shuttle buses operated by **Saritur** (0800-039-8846, www.saritur.com.br, 90 min., R$24) leave Belo's *rodoviária* (platform F2) at 8:15am Tuesday-Sunday and return at 4:30pm Tuesday-Sunday. By car, from Savassi follow the Rodovia Fernão Dias (BR-381); at Km 500, take exit 501 in the direction of Inhotim. With a half-dozen alluring cafés and restaurants nearby, you can easily spend a whole day here. To spend the night, **Pousada Estalagem da Villa** (Av. Casa Branca 524, Brumadinho tel. 31/3575-3220, www.pousadaestalagemdavilla.com.br, R$140) is a nice option.

BARS

A Maletta (Edifício Maletta, Av. Augusto Lima 245, Centro) is a once-elegant building in the center of town that still has a certain dilapidated charm. While people live on the upper floors, the bars and crowded second-hand bookstores on the main floor and the mezzanine have been a mainstay of BH's left-wing intelligentsia, along with the prerequisite *marginais* and eccentrics, since the swinging '60s and '70s. From early afternoon on into the wee small hours, this is a fun place to soak up a slice of bohemian BH of yore. Bars include **Arcangelo Bar Café** (tel. 31/3237-1351, 6pm-midnight Tues.-Sun.), where the homemade Argentinian empanadas go nicely with both beer and the house brand of coffee; **Cantina do Lucas** (tel. 31/3226-7153, www.cantinadolucas.com.br, 11:30am-2am Mon.-Thurs., 11:30am-4am Fri.-Sat., 11:30am-1am Sun.), an early '60s hangout famed for its comfort food; and hip newcomer **Dub** (tel. 31/3222-3527, 6pm-1am Tues.-Sat.), whose creative cocktails have taken the city by storm.

Beer aficionados will go into serious overdrive at **Krug Bier** (Rua Major Lopes 172, São Pedro, tel. 31/2535-1122, www.krug.com.br, 6pm-4am Mon.-Fri., 1pm-4am Sat.-Sun.), home of a pioneering microbrewery. Choose between the vast, gymnasium-sized beer hall

inside or the breezier outdoor decks to sample the numerous house draft and bottled pilsens, goldens, and weisses.

Mercearia Lili (Rua São João Evangelista 696, Santo Antônio, tel. 31/3293-3469, 5pm-midnight Mon.-Fri., 11am-6pm Sat.) is an actual *mercearia* (general store) with a warm neighborhood feel that also happens to be a bar. It's been around since 1949, which means that the clientele is very loyal and the decor authentically retro. Try the delicious *sacolão* vegetable soup and the justly famous *maça de peito,* melt-in-your-mouth tender chunks of beef grilled and served with sautéed onions and crispy fries, from the terrific menu. Also in the vicinity is **Salsa Parrilha** (also known as Bar da Taninha; Rua São Domingos do Prata 453, Santo Antônio, tel. 31/3225-7758, 6pm-2am Mon.-Fri., noon-2am Sat.), a relaxing neighborhood *boteco* with tables that spill out onto the sidewalk. The inviting interior is spacious and features an ever-changing roster of works by local artists.

Minas is *cachaça* country, and the towering shelves at **Via Cristina** (Rua Cristina 1203, Santo Antônio, tel. 31/3296-8343, www.viacristina.com.br, 6pm-midnight Tues.-Fri., 11am-midnight Sat., 11am-6pm Sun.) display more than 700 brands of the stuff—the vast majority produced in state and artisanally, with some rarities from the owner's home region of Vale de Jequitinhona. If you have a passing interest in *"pinga,"* you could do worse than a trip to this lively *boteco* that also doubles as a *churrascaria.*

Since 1961, **Bolão** (Praça Duque de Caxias 288, Santa Tereza, tel. 31/3463-0719, 7am-3am Mon.-Thurs., 24 hours Fri.-Sun.) is the classic last stop on the party circuit. The last-call atmosphere is so convivial that it's rare revelers don't stick around till the sun comes up, fortified by a heaping plate of Bolão' famous spaghetti Bolognese. A nearby boho fave is **Bar Temático** (Rua Perite 187, Santa Tereza, tel. 31/3481-4646, www.bartematico.com.br 5pm-midnight Tues.-Fri., 10:30am-midnight Sat., 10:30am-6pm Sun.). Indulge in the heady likes of pancakes stuffed with *carne de sol* and *queijo mineiro.*

LIVE MUSIC

Café Com Letras (Rua Antônio de Albuquerque 781, Savassi, tel. 31/3224-9973, www.cafecomletras.com.br, noon-midnight Mon.-Thurs., noon-1am Fri.-Sat., 5pm-11pm Sun., cover R$1 Thurs.-Fri., R$3-12 Sat.-Sun.) is a wonderfully hybrid space—an inspired mixture of bookstore, bar, gallery, and live-music venue that has become a major cultural mecca. Located in a charming old house in the heart of Savassi, the café plays host to national and international musical performers with a predilection for DJs (Thurs.-Sat.) and jazz (Sun.). While the 4,000 titles on the shelves might assuage your hunger for knowledge, the imaginative menu will take care of your empty stomach.

A Savassi stalwart with no tables or chairs, **A Obra Bar Dançante** (Rua Rio Grande do Norte 168, Savassi, tel. 31/3261-9431, www. aobra.com.br, 8pm-close Wed.-Thurs., 10pm-close Fri.-Sat., cover R$10-25) is an alternative club started by the members of As Meldas, a local rock band who dreamed of a place where the city's various indie artist tribes could all hang out together.

Spot of the moment **CCCP** (Rua Levindo Lopes 356, Savassi, tel. 31/3582-5628,

6pm-2am Sun. and Tues.-Wed., 6pm-4am Thurs.-Fri., 8pm-4am Sat., cover R$10-25) stands for Cult Club Cine Pub, summing up the eclectic offerings at this renovated cinema. CCCP's stage hosts some of the best and most eclectic live music in the city. Genres range from jazz and soul to electronica, rock, and Western. A handsome tiled bar offers regional handcrafted brews.

Performing Arts

Belo Horizonte has earned a reputation as an innovative center for the performing arts, particularly with respect to theater and dance. **Grupo Corpo** (www.grupocorpo.com.br) is an internationally renowned troupe that fuses modern dance forms with Brazilian music and cultural influences. **Uakti** (www.uakti. com.br) is a musical group that creates highly original rhythms and melodies using their own ingeniously designed instruments. The **Grupo Galpão** (www.grupogalpao.com.br) is a theatrical company that specializes in giving universal classics a new twist by adding elements of street theater. Instead of human actors, **Giramundo** (www.giramundo.org) relies on a company of more than 600 handcrafted puppets (not all appear at the same time) in the staging of its own works.

Festivals and Events

Belo Horizonte hosts several renowned festivals, including the **Festival Internacional de Teatro Palco e Rua** (www.fitbh.com.br, May in even-numbered years); the **Forum Internacional de Dança** (www.fid.com.br, Oct.-Nov.), where free and low-priced theatrical and dance performances are held throughout the city; and the **Festival de Arte Negra** (mid-late Nov.), which celebrates black arts and culture. For programs of events, check out the Belotur tourist office. Foodies and tipplers alike should definitely check out the **Comida di Buteco** festival (www.comidadibuteco. com.br, Apr.-May), in which 40 of the city's top *botecos* compete against each other in an attempt to gauge who is capable of concocting the most lip-smacking *petiscos.* The most delicious part is that the judges consist of the public, and voting takes place in bars.

SHOPPING
Shopping Malls

Belo Horizonte has scads of shopping centers. The most central of them all is **Shopping da Cidade** (Rua Tupis 337, Centro, tel. 31/3279-1200, www.shoppingcidade.com.br, 9am-10pm Mon.-Sat., 10am-4pm Sun.), with a wide variety of fairly low-priced shopping and eating options as well as a multiplex theater. More trendy and chic are **Shopping Pátio Savassi** (Av. do Contorno 6061, Funcionários, tel. 31/4003-4172, www.patiosavassi.com) and **Diamond Mall** (Av. Olegário Maciel 1600, Lourdes, tel. 31/4003-4136, www.diamond-mall.com.br); both house upscale boutiques and eateries along with multiplexes and share the same hours (10am-10pm Mon.-Sat., 2pm-8pm Sun.)

Boutiques

The Savassi area is home to most of Belo's avant-garde clothing and jewelry boutiques. Belo Horizonte has earned a certain amount of national renown for nourishing the unique talents of a handful of young designers. **Ronaldo Fraga** (Rua Fernandes Tourinho 81, São Pedro, tel. 31/3282-5379, www.ronaldofraga.com.br, 9am-7pm Mon.-Fri., 10am-2pm Sat.) is considered one of the most original and imaginative young fashion designers working in Brazil today. His whimsical boutique features a room with clothing from past collections available at discounts of up to 40 percent.

Graça Ottoni's hippie-chic women's clothing is sold at her flagship store, **Graça Ottoni** (Rua Santa Catarina 1471, Lourdes, tel. 31/3335-9008, http://gracaottoni.com.br, 9am-7pm Mon.-Fri., 10am-2pm Sat.). Designs rely heavily on appliqué, embroidery, and patchwork. The cool but impeccably cut casual clothes made by designer Zepa for **Ave Maria** (Rua Padre Odorico 98, São Pedro, tel. 31/2555-2564, www.lojaavemaria.com.br, 9am-7pm Mon.-Fri., 10am-2pm

Sat.) are cult favorites with young urban Brazilians.

Markets

The nonprofit **Centro de Artesanato Mineiro** (CEART) is inside the Palácio das Artes (Av. Afonso Pena 1537, Centro, tel. 31/3272-9513, 9am-8pm Mon.-Fri., 9am-2pm Sat., 9am-1pm Sun.) and offers a wide range of traditional Mineiro art and handicrafts from all over the state at surprisingly decent prices. The **Feira de Arte e Artesanato** (8am-2pm Sun.) is a big open-air market that spills out along Avenida Afonso Pena. Although it purports to sell arts and handicrafts, traditional examples of either are in short supply. More compelling is the people-watching.

A more satisfying market experience can be had at the **Mercado Central** (Av. Augusto de Lima 744, Centro, tel. 31/3274-9434, www.mercadocentral.com.br, 7am-6pm Mon.-Sat., 7am-1pm Sun.). This covered market is the place to stock up on Mineiro foodstuffs and cooking ware. It might be a challenge to carry them back on the plane, but it's hard to resist the copper and soapstone pots and pans available at ridiculously low prices along with fudge-like *doce de leite,* organic coffee beans, and bottle after bottle of fine *cachaça.* **Ronaldo Licores e Cachaças** (Lojas 34 and 141, tel. 31/3274-9674, www.ronaldocachacas.com.br) is the best place to pick up a bottle. Its shelves stock more than 450 varieties of Mineiro *pinga* ("drop"—slang for *cachaça*), ranging from the most basic brands to the king of *cachaças,* Havana (an aged bottle goes for R$480). After you've scoped out the produce, stop for an icy cold beer at one of the many traditional white tiled bars, such as **Casa Cheia** (Loja 167, tel. 31/3274-9585) and sample the local market grub: grilled liver (or beef) accompanied by sautéed *jiló.*

ACCOMMODATIONS

Belo Horizonte doesn't attract too many sightseers. It does, however, play host to a large number of business travelers. Consequently, unless there are a few major conventions taking place, accommodations are easy to find, and you can negotiate some attractive rates, especially on the weekends. Although stylish boutique hotels are nonexistent, there are some nicely priced modern options as well as a few plush hotels where you can spoil yourself for far less than you'd be able to in other major Brazilian cities. Most hotels are conveniently situated in Centro or Savassi.

R$50-200

Run by a friendly English-speaking Franco-Brazilian couple, **Lá Em Casa Hostel** (Rua Eurita 30, Santa Tereza, tel. 31/3653-9566, www.laemcasahostel.com, R$110-140 d, R$32-48 pp) occupies a woody and warm 1930's villa in the tranquil boho hood of Santa Teraza. Dorms and private rooms are homey but basic, as are the common areas—a living room, garden, and kitchen where you can rustle up your own *tutu à mineira*. If you're too lazy to cook, *botecos* are minutes away, while Centro is only a 15-minute walk. **Hotel Turista** (Rua Rio de Janeiro 423, Centro, tel. 31/3273-7282, www.hotelturista.com/bh, R$180-195 d) is a good bargain in Centro. Located in a 1950s building that lends it an appealing retro edge, it offers clean and simple guest rooms with the advantage of leafy trees peering in through the windows. It's practically next to the *rodoviária*, which makes it ideal if you're just passing through. Drawbacks include urban noise and a certain dodginess after dark.

R$200-400

From the exterior, the landmark art deco **Hotel Metrópole** (Rua da Bahia 1023, Centro, tel. 31/3273-1544, www.hotelmetropolebh.com.br, R$220-240 d) looks like South Miami, but inside modern fixtures coexist with retro features (some newly renovated, others shabby). It's worth upgrading to "luxury" rooms if you want more space; to avoid noise, ask for a room overlooking the "winter garden." For those who prefer tidy modernity to fading atmospherics, **Hotel Boulevard Park** (Rua Bernardo Guimarães 925, Savassi, tel. 31/3261-7000, www.hotelboulevardparkbh.

com.br, R$179-259 d) is a pleasant option that feels more like moving into an apartment building than checking into a hotel. Offering spotless standard guest rooms, it is located on a quiet, tree-shaded street within walking distance to everywhere. "Boutique" may be a misnomer, but the sleek and modern **Royal Savassi Boutique Hotel** (Rua Alagoas 699, Savassi, tel. 31/2138-0000, www.royalsavassi.com.br, R$227-349 d) possesses large, attractive guest rooms with refined contemporary furnishings and mega TVs. Although there's no pool and the fitness room is closet-like, being among Savassi's bars and restaurants more than compensates.

FOOD

Belo Horizonte has a thriving restaurant scene, and it's possible to eat very well without spending too much. Eateries in Centro are often inexpensive, self-service per-kilo places that cater to the daily working crowd; options in and around Savassi are more varied, atmospheric, and upmarket. *Boteco* fare is really tasty (and inexpensive); consider the bar listings as possible ways of assuaging your hunger.

Cafés and Snacks

Café Nice (Av. Afonso Pena 727, Centro, tel. 31/3222-6924, 7am-9pm Mon.-Fri., 8am-3pm Sat., 9am-1pm Sun.) opened its doors in 1939. Step inside and you'll feel as if you've entered one of those coffee shops from an early 1940s Warner Brothers film. When he was mayor of Belo Horizonte, Juscelino Kubitschek often scored his caffeine fix here; since then it has become *the* place for campaigning politicos to drop by.

Café Kahlúa (Rua das Guajajaras 416, Centro, tel. 31/3222-5887, www.cafekahlua.com.br, 8am-9:30pm Mon.-Fri., 10am-9pm Sat.) is a sleek café with more than 60 different kinds of coffee drinks as well as lip-smacking sandwiches and desserts. For a major pick-me-up, try *café bruna*—java mixed with açai and *guaraná*, liqueur, and milk. The crowd who frequents this place is urban and professional with an artsy edge. If you're in need of a bona fide lunch, try the light fare (omelets, salads, grilled meats) served around the corner at **Kahlúa Light** (Rua da Bahia 1216, Centro, tel. 31/3214-2648, 11:30am-3:30pm Mon.-Fri., R$15).

Minas is renowned for its coffee and cafés, which is why those fervently devoted to both should make a pilgrimage to the **Academia do Café** (Rua Grão Pará 1024, 2nd floor, Funcionários, www.academiadocafe.com.br, tel. 31/3225-3268, 7pm-midnight Tues.-Thurs., 10am-7pm Mon.-Fri., 10pm-4pm Sat.). This is the headquarters of Minas' Coffee Academy, and the baristas know what they're talking about when they recommend different homegrown blends (also available for purchase). If you're in town on the last Thursday of the month, don't miss the "latte-art" competitions (7pm, R$8), where pros and amateurs vie to see who can top their cappuccinos with the most stunning designs.

Contemporary

Although the name **Hermengarda** (Rua Outono 314, Carmo Sion, www.hermengarda.com.br, tel. 31/3225-3268, 7pm-midnight Tues.-Thurs., 7pm-1:30am Fri.-Sat., noon-5pm Sun., R$45-60) pays homage to the grandmother who taught chef Guilherme Melo the basics of cooking, at his unpretentious country-house of a restaurant Melo revels in experimenting with Brazilian ingredients. The results are unorthodox but inspired pairings that combine basics such as manioc, Brazil nuts, and the *pupunha* palm hearts with fish, meat, and exotic game such as capybara. When reserving, request a table outside beneath the jaboticaba tree.

Italian

Dona Derna (Rua Tomé de Souza 1343, 1st Floor, Savassi, tel. 31/3223-6954, www.derna.com.br, 11am-midnight Mon.-Sat., 11am-6pm Sun., R$35-45) is a city institution that has been serving up robust Tuscan Italian cuisine since 1960. Meats, pastas, fish, and seafood are all exceptionally flavorful at this family-owned trattoria.

Per-Kilo Buffets

It's little wonder the lines are long to get into **Santa Fé** (Rua Pernambuco 800, Savassi, tel. 31/3261-6446, www.redegourmetbh.com.br/casas-santafe, noon-3pm and 6pm-midnight Mon.-Fri., noon-5pm and 6pm-1am Sat., noon-5pm Sun., R$20-40). The banquet of more than 60 creative salads and antipasti—along with à la carte options—is both delicious and diverse, and the attractive atmosphere (especially if you nab a patio table) is conducive to lingering. The dinner menu is pricier and strictly à la carte.

Naturalmente (Rua Rio de Janeiro 1197, Centro, tel. 31/3213-7029, 11am-3pm Mon.-Fri., 11:30am-3pm Sat., R$15-25) offers delicious and nutritious per-kilo buffet lunches. Although the choices aren't endless, they are fresh, imaginative, and inexpensive. There are also some 20 fresh juice options. On Saturday—Brazilians' traditional *feijoada* day—a vegetarian version is served. The unassuming yet modern interior is pleasantly soothing.

A well-kept secret, **Restaurante do SENAC BH** (Rua Tupinambás 1038, 3rd Floor, Centro, tel. 0800-724-4440 or 31/3057-8600, 11am-3pm Mon.-Fri., R$45) is the classy restaurant of the SENAC hotel and restaurant school, where students go all out to make customers feel pampered and well-fed (after all, they're being graded). Monday and Tuesday are reserved for daily à la carte menus (reservations recommended); the rest of the week features an all-you-can-eat buffet. Both options mingle international and regional recipes. Bonuses include a free welcome drink and live piano accompaniment.

Regional

Belo Horizonte has its share of top addresses for Mineiro cooking in all its succulent glory. One of the most traditional is ★ **Dona Lucinha** (Rua Sergipe 811, Savassi, tel. 31/3261-5930, www.donalucinha.com.br, noon-3pm and 7pm-11pm Mon.-Fri., noon-5pm Sat.-Sun.). Dona Lucinha began life cooking delicacies she sold in the market of her hometown, Serro (in northern Minas near Diamantina), and brought her experience and many recipes with her when she came to the capital. For R$56 you have unlimited access to a mouthwatering buffet of close to 40 dishes—including crisp barbecued pork ribs bathed in caramel and chicken cooked in fragrant *ora-pró-nobis* leaves—that serve as a fine introduction to Mineiro cooking. An equally diverse array of desserts and liqueurs are included. Both this restaurant and the original in the neighborhood of São Pedro (Rua Padre Odorico 38, São Pedro, tel. 31/3227-0562) conjure up the warm kitchens of rural Minas. If you're not up to stuffing yourself, head across the street from the latter address to **Armazém Dona Lucinha** (Av. do Contorno 6283, São Pedro, tel. 31/3281-9526, www.armazemdonalucinha.com.br, 7am-8pm Mon.-Fri., 8am-3pm Sat.), an emporium where you can indulge in a seemingly endless variety of traditional baked goods (including what many claim to be the best *pães de queijo* in the city) or dig into a lunch special (R$12-15) on the spot.

Located on a vast estate but with airs of a typical Mineiro farm, **Xapuri** (Rua Mandacaru 260, Pampulha, tel. 31/3496-6198, www.restaurantexapuri.com.br, 11am-11pm Mon.-Sat., noon-8pm Sun., R$35-50) is more a transporting experience than a mere restaurant. Guests (there's room for 500) are invited to sit down at the benches that line rustic wooden tables and partake of riffs on Mineiro classics such as pork in bathed in honey and *mexerica* (a local tangerine). Portions feed 2-4 people; the larger the group, the more you can sample. Plan to while away a few hours among shots of *cachaça*, portions of homemade *linguiça* (sausage), the decadent buffet of *doces*, and the lure of strung-up hammocks.

INFORMATION AND SERVICES

Belotur (tel. 31/3429-0405 24-hour hotline, http://visitbh.pbh.gov.br) is the city travel association, and its staff is very knowledgeable. It publishes a free trilingual monthly guide, *Guia Turística* with a good city map distributed throughout the city. Its tourist listings are extensive, even including instructions on what buses to take to different attractions and where to get them. Belotur kiosks are at Confins airport (tel. 31/3689-2557, 8am-10pm Mon.-Sat., 8am-5pm Sun.), the *rodoviária* (Praça Rio Branco, Centro, tel. 31/3277-6907, 8am-6pm daily), and at the Parque Municipal (Av. Afonso Pena 1055, Centro, tel. 31/3277-7666, 8:30am-6:30pm Mon.-Fri., 8am-3pm Sat.-Sun.).

You'll find plenty of **banks** with ATMs along Avenida Afonso Pena in Centro—among them are Banco do Brasil (Rua Rio de Janeiro 750) and Citibank (Rua Espírito Santo 871)—as well as on and around Avenida Contorno in Savassi. The main **post office** (Av. Afonso Pena 1270, Centro) is opposite the Parque Municipal.

In the event of a medical emergency, dial **192** for Pronto Socorro (First Aid). The **Hospital das Clínicas** (Av. Alfredo Badalena 190, Santa Efigênia, tel. 31/3409-9300, www.hc.ufmg.br) is affiliated with UFMG, the federal university. In the event of a crime, call **190** to reach the police.

TRANSPORTATION
Air
Most flights arrive at **Tancredo Neves International Airport** (Rodovia MG, km 39, Confins, tel. 31/3689-2700, www.aeroportoconfins.net). More popularly known as **Confins** (after the suburb where it is located), it is around 40 kilometers (25 mi) from the center of Belo Horizonte; count on an hour if traffic is light. Much closer is the older and smaller **Pampulha Airport** (Praça Bagatelle 204, São Luiz, tel. 31/3490-2000), which is around 15 kilometers (9 mi) from Centro, a journey that should ideally take 20 minutes. If you don't want to take a taxi, **Airport Conexão** (tel. 31/3224-1002, www.conexaoaeroporto.com.br) offers *executivo* bus service between Confins airport and Centro (R$20). Buses arrive at and depart from the entrance to the Belo Horizonte Palace Hotel

(Av. Alvares Cabral 387) and run every 15-30 minutes 5:15am-11:15pm and hourly 12:30am-5:30am. **Expresso Unir** (tel. 31/3663-8020, www.expressounir.com.br, R$9) offers conventional bus service between Confins and Pampulha airports from the *rodoviária* with departures every 15-45 minutes, 5:30am-1am. A taxi to Centro or Savassi will set you back around R$95 from Confins and R$40 from Pampulha.

Bus

The main *rodoviária* (Praça Rio Branco 100, Centro tel. 31/3271-3000) is right in the heart of the city. From here, buses serve destinations throughout Minas Gerais and the rest of Brazil.

Belo's municipal buses are operated by **BH Trans** (www.bhtrans.pbh.gov.br); the website lists all routes and provides search options. From Centro and Savassi, it is easy to get anywhere quickly. Route numbers are usually listed at bus stops; the numbers and the final destinations are listed on the front of the bus and the major stops along the routes are listed on the sides. Fare is R$2.80 for both the blue buses that serve major downtown avenues and the green express buses, and R3.40 or more for the red buses that cover the suburbs as well. At night, it's wiser to take a cab. Major taxi companies include **Ligue Táxi BH** (tel. 31/3421-3434) and **Coopertáxi BH** (tel. 31/3421-2424).

Car

Because of its many one-way streets, driving a car in Belo Horizonte is tricky, and traffic is deadly. The rules of which street goes which way are always changing (even the taxi drivers have trouble keeping up). Since most sights are in Centro, getting around on foot is easy. There is a subway, but you'll likely never use it, since it is more useful for workers getting in and out of the suburbs than for tourists.

Renting a car can come in handy for day trips to sites around Belo Horizonte. **Hertz** (tel. 31/3689-2150, www.hertz.com.br) is at Confins and **Localiza** (www.localiza.com)

is at both airports and in **Funcionáiros** (Av. Bernardo Monteiro 1567, tel. 31/3247-7956).

AROUND BELO HORIZONTE
Caverns

Of the supposedly 3,000 grottoes and caverns that exist in Brazil, 2,000 are located in Minas, and 500 are within striking distance of Belo Horizonte. Rei do Mato, Lapinha, and Maquiné all make easy day trips north from the capital. For more information about the "Circuito das Grutas," visit www.circuitodasgrutas.com.br.

GRUTA DA LAPINHA

Located on the outskirts of the town of Lagoa Santa, **Gruta da Lapinha** is famous for its fantastically shaped stalactites and stalagmites and the Véu de Noiva, a crystal formation that resembles a "bride's veil." The cavern is situated within the **Parque Estadual do Sumidouro** (tel. 31/3661-8171 www.pesumidouro.blogspot.com.br, 9am-4pm Tues.-Sun, R$15 entrance). The state park features lakes, caves painted with petroglyphs (which can be explored via a trio of hiking trails), and two small museums. Visits must be reserved in advance and are guided; trails are open weekends and can book up in July and August. **Atual** buses (tel. 31/3272-6104, www.ciaatual.com.br, R$6) leave from Belo Horizonte's bus station hourly to Lagoa Santa; from Lagoa Santa, there are almost hourly buses to Lapinha (check the park website for schedules). By car, take MG-010 north of BH for 40 kilometers (25 mi).

GRUTA REI DO MATO

Gruta Rei do Mato (tel. 31/3773-0888, 8am-4:30pm daily, R$10) earned its name (King of the Bush) from a legend about a fugitive who once lived in this palatial cave. Today, the cavern is well illuminated and equipped for the visitors who wander through its otherworldly environs decorated with stalactites, stalagmites, and marvelous prehistoric paintings. The cave is 5 kilometers (3 mi) from the turnoff to the town of Sete Lagoas, 70 kilometers (43 mi) north of Belo Horizonte along BR-040. Buses (75 minutes, R$19) operated by **Expresso Setealagoano** (tel. 31/3073-7575, www.passaroverde.com.br) leave at 6:30am daily from the *rodoviária*; many more pass hourly along BR-040. All stop in front of the park's entrance.

GRUTA DO MAQUINÉ

The entrance to the **Gruta do Maquiné** (tel. 31/3715-1310, 8am-5pm daily, R$16) is home to cave paintings that date back more than 6,000 years. Wander deeper in the cave to encounter seven vast chambers, all dripping with stalactites. Adjacent is the **Museu da Gruta** (R$3), which exhibits replicas of prehistorical fossils uncovered in the region, and **Chero's** (tel. 31/9903-0677), a restaurant specializing in Mineiro home cooking. The cave is 5 kilometers (3 mi) from the town of Cordisburgo along the Via Alberto Ramos. **Expresso Setealagoano** (tel. 31/3073-7575, www.passaroverde.com.br) and **Viação Sertaneja** (tel. 31/3201-2604, www.viacaosertaneja.com.br) offer several daily departures from BH's *rodoviária* (2.5 hours, R$36) daily from Belo Horizonte to Cordisburgo. By car, take BR-040 for 90 kilometers (56 mi) and then MG-231 for another 20 kilometers (12 mi).

Parque Nacional da Serra do Cipó

Located 100 kilometers (62 mi) northeast of BH, **Parque Nacional da Serra do Cipó** possesses breathtaking scenery, with flowers, waterfalls, and hiking trails that make it a favorite with ecotourists. The most impressive waterfall is the Cachoeira da Farofa. At the park entrance (which closes at 2pm) is the **visitors center** (tel. 31/3718-7151, 8am-5pm), where you can rent bikes or horses. There isn't much in the way of food, though, so bring a snack or picnic. The best times to visit are during the winter or spring months. Only the lower part of the park can be visited without a guide. Guides and park maps are supplied by the **Associação Comercial da Serra do Cipó** (tel. 31/3718-7017). The website www.circuitoserradocipo.org.br (in Portuguese) has lots of information, including accommodation options.

The park can be accessed via the towns of Jaboticatubas and Santana do Riacho; for overnight options, there are lots of simple but charming *pousadas* scattered along highway MG-101. If pressed for time, you might be better off driving here (take MG-010 north from Belo Horizonte) or taking an excursion from Belo Horizonte. **Cipoeiro Expedições** (Rodovia MG-0101, km 95, tel. 31/3718-7396 or 31/9611-8878, www.cipoeiro.com.br) offers hiking, climbing, canoeing, and other outings. Their easy four-hour "adventure circuit" (R$125 pp) features trekking, rappelling, a zipline, and canoeing along the Rio Cipó.

Parque Natural do Caraça

Situated 120 kilometers (75 mi) southeast of BH, near the fetching colonial town of Santa Bárbara (www.santabarbara.mg.gorv.b), the private nature reserve **Parque Natural do Caraça** (7am-5pm daily, R$10 per vehicle) is a botanist's dream, with an unusual mixture of native Atlantic forest and Cerrado vegetation that carpets the scenic Serra do Espinhaço mountain range. The park's name, Caraça (Big Face), stems from one slope's uncanny resemblance to a giant's head in repose. Within the park's boundaries are lakes, waterfalls, and various hiking trails, along with the **Gruta do Centenário,** one of the world's largest quartzite caves.

From Belo Horizonte, **Pássaro Verde** (tel. 31/3073-7575, www.passaroverde.com.br) offers four daily buses to Santa Bárbara (3 hours, R$52). The park entrance is 25 kilometers (16 mi) from town, so you'll have to take a taxi. If driving, take BR-381 from BH and turn off at the exit to Barão de Cocais and Santa Bárbara; the road to the park (19 km/12 mi) is signed, and the turnoff is 5 kilometers (3 mi) after Barão, 7 kilometers (4.3 mi) before Santa Bárbara. There's a cafeteria and a restaurant, but it's a good idea to take a snack and a warm sweater regardless of the time of year. Walking trails are well signed and begin right from the entrance; monks at the nearby Hospedaria do Caraça can also supply maps and directions.

Situated near the park's entrance is the **Santuário do Caraça** (www.santuariodocaraca.com.br), a former 18th-century seminary. From the late 1700s to 1911, it housed a school where the sons of Minas's most distinguished families were sent to study (five Brazilian presidents are alumni). After a catastrophic fire in 1968, the buildings were restored in the 1990s. Apart from the impressive neo-Gothic Igreja Nossa Senhora Mão dos Homens, with its French stained-glass windows, grandiose organ, and baroque altars, other buildings were subsequently transformed into a museum (R$10), a restaurant

with a self-service buffet (R$22 pp), and simple but atmospheric apartments that comprise the **Pousada do Caraça** (tel. 31/3837-2698, 8am-4pm Mon.-Fri, pousadadocaraca@gmail.com, reservations required 6 months in advance, R$170-270 d full board), which is run by the remaining members of the monastery. Several kilometers from the main complex, more bucolic accommodation is available in the main house of the **Engenho da Fazenda** (tel. 71/3809-3904, faz.engenho@gmail.com, R$187-206), a rural estate where the seminary produces its own milk, butter, and produce.

While the park can be visited year-round, the altitude means it can get fairly chilly at night and in the winter. Summer is the best season to visit if you're intent on plunging into otherwise icy waterfalls and natural pools.

Sabará

Sabará is a mere 20 kilometers (12 mi)—a local bus ride—from Belo Horizonte and makes a great day trip. Nestled in a valley where the Rio das Velhas runs into the Rio Sabará, Sabará produced more gold in one week than the rest of Brazil's mining towns in one year at the height of Minas's 18th-century gold flush. Unsurprisingly, for a while it was one of the richest cities in the world. Testifying to this fact are the mansions lining its steep cobblestoned streets as well as a handful of baroque churches whose modest exteriors hide a dazzling array of gold-clad treasures. Although centuries of mining have stripped the surrounding hills of their foliage, and the town's recent rapid expansion has saddled it with none-too-attractive urban sprawl, if you stick to the cobblestones, it's still possible to get the sense that you're stepping back in time. Today you won't find any large chunks of gold in Sabará's rocks, but fortune-seekers continue to pan the rivers in search of precious flakes and slivers (you can see them in action at the tiny Carmo stream running alongside the far end of town going toward Caeté).

SIGHTS

The main square and lovely colonial center of the town is **Praça Santa Rita.** From here, signs point the way to Sabará's main attractions; on Monday, almost all sights are closed. Closest to the *praça* is the **Teatro Imperial** (Rua Dom Pedro II, tel. 31/3672-7728, 8am-noon and 1pm-5pm Tues.-Sun., free). Built in 1770, it is the second-oldest theater in Brazil still in operation. The elegant interior boasts not only excellent acoustics but crystal chandeliers and beautiful woodwork. Adjacent to Praça Santa Rita, the Praça Melo Viana is dominated by the imposing stone walls of the strikingly simple **Igreja de Nossa Senhora do Rosário dos Pretos** (9am-11am and 1pm-5pm Tues.-Sun., R$12). Construction on this church for Sabará's significant black slave population commenced in 1766 but was never completed. The building still houses the original adobe chapel from 1713. To ensure that one day you return to town, make sure to take a refreshing sip of water from the **Chafariz do Kaquendé** (Rua Kaquendé), the only one of

Sabará's public fountains whose water is still drinkable.

Sabará has three other churches that are worth seeing. Since they are a bit of a trek from the center, you might want to take a municipal bus to the furthest, Igreja Nossa Senhora do Ó, and then visit the other two as you walk back toward town.

Museu de Ouro

Near Praça Santa Rita, the **Museu de Ouro** (Rua Intendência, tel. 31/3671-1848, 10am-5pm Tues.-Fri., noon-5pm Sat.-Sun., R$1) is an engaging museum in a sprawling stone house that was the former foundry and deposit for all of Sabará's gold. According to the museum guards, the place is haunted by the ghosts of former slaves who toiled in the rivers and mines. Miners' tools and equipment help you get a sense of the many exacting activities related to the mining and processing of gold. There are some examples of period furniture (many featuring hidden drawers and cabinets used to conceal people's private stashes of gold) as well as domestic and religious objects that conjure up life in colonial Sabará.

Igreja Nossa Senhora do Ó

Three kilometers (1.8 mi) from Praça Santa Rita along the main road to Caeté is the **Igreja Nossa Senhora do Ó** (Largo Nossa Senhora do Ó, tel. 31/3674-1724, 8am-noon and 1:30pm-5pm daily, R$2). From the outside, it resembles a humble colonial church. In this case, however, appearances are extremely deceiving: The magnificently adorned interior is considered one of the best of Minas's baroque churches.

Igreja Matriz de Nossa Senhora de Conceição

Built between 1700 and 1710, the **Igreja Matriz de Nossa Senhora de Conceição** (Praça Getúlio Vargas, tel. 31/3671-1724, 9am-11:30am and 1pm-5pm Sat.-Mon., 8am-5pm Tues.-Fri., R$2) is Sabará's oldest church. While its exterior is quite plain, the interior

offers up a rich feast of intricately sculpted decoration, all completely bathed in gold. This church also offers an example of an intriguing mixture of Portuguese baroque and Asian styles. Especially stunning are the doors leading to the sanctuary, which are exquisitely festooned with painted gold and scarlet pagodas and cranes. Also take note of the fantastically lifelike Christ figure chained and leaning on a column of blue marble.

Igreja da Ordem de Nossa Senhora do Carmo

Constructed in the mid-1700s, the **Igreja da Ordem de Nossa Senhora do Carmo** (Rua do Carmo, tel. 31/3671-2417, 9am-11:30am and 1pm-5pm Tues.-Sat., 1pm-5pm Sun., R$2) is the only church in Sabará with works by the great baroque master sculptor Aleijadinho. You can glimpse his expressive genius in certain details of the facade, as well as in the choral, pulpits, and images of São Simão and São João da Cruz that adorn the lateral altars.

FESTIVALS AND EVENTS

Belo Horizontinos flock to two lively festivals that animate Sabará's colonial streets. In May, the **Festival Ora-Pró-Nobis** pays homage to the humble *ora-pró-nobis* leaf that is a favorite ingredient in many savory Mineiro stews made with chicken and pork. Early November (dates depend on the harvest) coincides with the **Festival da Jabuticaba,** in which delicious drinkables and edibles inspired by the black currant-like *jabuticaba* fruit are celebrated.

ACCOMMODATIONS AND FOOD

It isn't necessary to stay overnight in Sabará and there are prettier and more bucolic colonial cities to choose from in Minas. However, if you're looking for a relaxing alternative to Belo Horizonte, it's hard to resist the rustic charms of **Pousada Solar dos Sepúlvedas** (Rua Intendência 371, tel. 31/3671-2705, www. sepulveda.com.br, R$160 d), situated in a gracious old colonial mansion next to the Museu de Ouro. Guest rooms have massive wooden beds that could easily sleep 3-4 people and are furnished with antiques and colorful ceramic tiles. Most bathrooms claim the luxury of bathtubs with feet (or paws), although if you actually take a hot bath, you'll be charged extra. Terraces, walkways, and a swimming pool are surrounded by an oasis-like garden of tropical flowers and fruit trees.

For some good home-style cooking, a local favorite is **314 Sabarabuçu** (Rua Dom Pedro II 279, tel. 31/3671-2313, 11am-midnight Mon.-Thurs., 11am-2am Fri.-Sat., 11am-1pm Sun., R$12-20), which, along with a self-service per-kilo lunch buffet, offers *churrasco*. At night, dig into pizzas baked in the restaurant's wood-burning oven.

TRANSPORTATION AND SERVICES

The **tourist office** is at the entrance to town. Unless you're coming by car, it's quite a walk to and from the center, and Sabará's sights are so few and well indicated that you probably don't need a map. Two useful websites are www.sabara.mg.gov.br and www.sabaranet.com.br.

Sabará is practically a suburb of Belo Horizonte. It can be reached easily by municipal buses (No. 5509 and No. 1059), which leave around every 15 minutes from Centro, at stops along Rua Rio de Janeiro and Rua dos Caetés. *Executivo* buses also leave frequently from a stop adjacent to the main bus station. If you're driving, follow Avenida Cristiano Machado and take highway MG-262 leading east out of Belo Horizonte.

Ouro Preto

Minas's first capital, Ouro Preto, is easily the most magnificent of Minas's *cidades históricas*. The picturesque town is hemmed in by the Serra do Espinhaço mountains, which effectively saved the former gold town from modern development.

It was in 1698 when a roving *bandeirante* named Antônio Dias de Oliveira came upon some chunks of shiny black metal, which on close inspection revealed themselves to be gold. As a result, the mining camp that sprang up on the spot came to be known as Ouro Preto (Black Gold). The surrounding region proved to possess more gold than any other part of the western hemisphere.

Eventually, gold supplies dwindled and in 1897, the capital of Minas Gerais moved to Belo Horizonte. While Ouro Preto lost both political and economic clout, both "losses" were instrumental in helping to preserve the colonial center, which was declared an UNESCO World Heritage Site in 1981. In recent times, an aluminum industry has lured migrant workers to the area, creating *favelas* that are mushrooming on the outskirts

of town. The town also thrives—for better or worse—on tourism, which means that it can get quite crowded.

While Ouro Preto's (very) precipitous cobblestoned streets may induce a certain degree of huffing and puffing, the very steepness of these hills means that most vehicles can't enter the colonial center, making it a pedestrian-only zone ideal for savoring its architectural gems. Baroque aficionados will feel as if they've died and gone to heaven when they lay eyes on the many extraordinary works on display, particularly the creations of genius sculptor Aleijadinho and master painter Manuel da Costa Ataíde. Ouro Preto, however, is far from being a living museum. The presence of one of the country's oldest federal universities and a thriving student population ensures a buzzing nightlife and plenty of popular *festas* (most notably Carnaval and the Semana Santa processions).

Although Ouro Preto can be visited as a day trip from Belo Horizonte, you need at least two full days to take in the number of

Ouro Preto

To Lavras
Novas

ROSÁRIO

PILAR

IGREJA DE
N S ROSÁRIO
DOS PRETOS

R BENEDITO VALADARES

R B GUIMARÃES

RODOVIÁRIA

ACASO 85

R ANTÔNIO ALBUQUERQUE

R CONS SANT'ANNA

R HENRIQUE AGEODATO

R DR G VARGAS

IGREJA
SÃO FRANCISCO
DE PAULA

R S FRANSICSO DE PAULA

MUSEU DA ARTE SACRA

R C FOUREAUX

CHOCOLATES
OURO PRETO

R S JOSÉ

CHAFARIZ

CASA DOS
CONTOS

CENTRO

To Belo Horizonte

R PE ROLIM

IGREJA N S
DO PILAR

R DO PILAR

HOSPEDERIA
ANTIGA

R PACÍFICO HOMEM

AV VITORINO DIAS

R X DA VEIGA

TEATRO MUNICIPAL

MUSEU CASA
GUIGNARD

ESCADABAIXO

R SEN ROCHA LAGOA

CAFÉS
GERAIS

GRAND HOTEL
OURO PRETO

VIDE
GULA

ESCOLA
DE MINAS

R HENRIQUE GORCEIX

Rio
Funil

BARRA

R M CABRAL

R COSTA SENA

R DIREITA

POUSO DO
CHICO REI

MUSEU DO
ORATÓRIO

IGREJA N S
DO CARMO

MUSEU DA
INCONFIDÊNCIA

CAFÉ E LIVRARIA
CULTURAL

NELLO
NUNO

R DOS PAULISTAS

CONTOS
DE REIS

R BARÃO DE CAMARGOS

R SALVADOR TROPIA

R PREF NASHINGTON DIAS

R DAS MERCÊS

IGREJA DE
SÃO FRANCISCO
DE ASSIS

R CARLOS THOMAZ

POUSADA
DOS MENINOS

R DA CONCEIÇÃO

R VASCONCELOS

R CONSELHEIRO QUINTILIANO

ANTÔNIO DIAS

R PE TOBIAS

R CEL SERAFIM

R BÁRBARA HELIODORA

IGREJA DA
CONCEIÇÃO DE
ANTÔNIO DIAS

R D SILVÉRIO

MINA DO
CHICO REI

RUA STA EFIGÊNIA

BENZADEUS

IGREJA DE NOSSA
SENHORA DA SANTA
EFIGÊNIA DOS PRETOS

R DR JOÃO VELSO

MINA JEJE

R CHICO REI

R RESENDE

MINA DO
SANTA RITA

To Mariana

© AVALON TRAVEL

0   200 yds
0   200 m

churches (23), museums, and monuments and to simply wander around.

ORIENTATION

Barring the steepness of its streets, Ouro Preto is compact enough that it is easy to get around. It's also easy to get confused by the street names; there are usually two sets, an official name and one used by residents. For instance, the main street of Rua Conde de Bobadela is more frequently known as Rua Direita. What complicates things even further is that generally neither set of names is posted in the streets themselves. So you're often better off aiming for various churches and landmarks when navigating the town.

Surrounded by imposing colonial buildings, **Praça Tiradentes** is Ouro Preto's elegant main square and the geographical and spiritual heart of the city, a fact punctuated by the statue of local hero Tiradentes in the center of the square. From here, a labyrinth of roads lead to the town's various attractions, which are all in close proximity.

SIGHTS

The sheer number of churches in Ouro Preto may give you a serious case of baroque burnout. For this reason, you might want to prioritize in advance which to visit. Not to be missed are the Igreja de São Francisco de Assis, the Matriz de Nossa Senhora do Pilar, the Igreja de Nossa Senhora do Carmo, and the Igreja de Nossa Senhora do Rosário dos Pretos.

Museu da Inconfidência

Housed in the former municipal government building and city jail, the **Museu da Inconfidência** (Praça Tiradentes 139, tel. 31/3551-1121, noon-5:30pm Tues.-Sun., R$8) contains a grandiose Vargas-era shrine with the mortal remains of the leaders of the Inconfidência Mineira. Upstairs is a collection of religious and secular objects and furnishings that evoke daily life in 18th- and 19th-century Ouro Preto. Among the more unique objects is a seal used by the bishop to brand

MINAS GERAIS
OURO PRETO

colonial street, Ouro Preto

his herald on sweet cakes. Also on display are some fine works by Aleijadinho and Manuel da Costa Ataíde.

Igreja de Nossa Senhora do Carmo

Adjacent to the Museu da Inconfidência stands the beautiful **Igreja de Nossa Senhora do Carmo** (Rua Brigadeiro Musqueira, tel. 31/3551-2601, 8am-11:30am and 1pm-5:15pm Tues.-Sat., 10am-3pm Sun., R$2), which kicked off the rococo (late) phase of baroque in Ouro Preto. It was designed by Aleijadinho's father, Manoel Francisco Lisboa, and construction began in 1776. It is the only church in Minas that features panels fashioned out of Portuguese azulejos (ceramic tiles), a request of its largely Portuguese congregation. When his father died, Aleijadinho took over the construction and decoration of the church. The soapstone baptismal font and lateral altars were sculpted by Aleijadinho, and the sacristy paintings were created by Manuel da Costa Ataíde.

The Art of Aleijadinho

Aleijadinho ("Little Cripple") was a fascinating figure, a genius sculptor and a leading representative of the artistic style known as Brazilian baroque. He was born in the 1730s in Ouro Preto to a Portuguese carpenter-turned-architect and his mistress and slave, Isabel. Named **Antônio Francisco Lisboa,** he began sculpting while still a boy. He specialized in carving religious images out of native soapstone and wood that were used to adorn the magnificent churches of his hometown. An architect like his father, he also designed churches.

In his early 40s, Lisboa was afflicted with a chronic illness that left him increasingly crippled and deformed. Over time, he lost some of his fingers and toes. As his deformities grew more hideous, he stopped going out in public. He would leave for work before sunrise and return home long after dark. At work, he labored behind curtains. In spite of his disabilities, he continued to sculpt with a passion. Even during his lifetime, Aleijadinho was recognized as one of the finest artists of the rococo (late baroque) style that was then in vogue, and all the *cidades históricas* competed fiercely to have him design and decorate their churches. By the time he was called on to create the sculptures for Congonhas's Basílica, Aleijadinho was in his 70s. Not long after completing his oeuvre at Congonhas, he succumbed to his illness and died in 1815.

Museu do Oratório

Aleijadinho spent his final years in what is now the **Museu do Oratório** (Rua Brigadeiro Musqueira, tel. 31/3551-5369, www.oratorio.com.br, 9:30am-5:30pm daily, R$4). This three-story colonial house is packed full of a stunning variety (162, to be precise) of oratories devoted to various saints. The range in decorative style is amazing: from simple (made by African slaves) to ornate (owned by aristocrats), including some exquisite specimens resembling miniature baroque churches with altars blanketed in gold. Among the most unusual examples are those fashioned out of tiny seashells and the *oratório-balas* ("bullet oratories"): rounded oratories whose compact, projectile-shaped casing allowed them to be closed up and easily transported by voyagers who didn't want to leave home without their personal saints. Beautifully displayed, the oratories, along with a rich array of other religious objects, are accompanied by informative bilingual descriptions.

Museu de Ciência e Técnica da Escola de Minas

On the far side of Praça Tiradentes, facing the Museu de Inconfidência, is a rather grand 18th-century building that was formerly Minas's Palácio de Governadores. When the capital moved to Belo Horizonte, the Escola de Minas (School of Mineralogy) moved into the palace. Part of the school is occupied by the **Museu de Ciência e Técnica** (Praça Tiradentes 20, tel. 31/3559-3119, www.museu.em.ufop.br, noon-5pm Tues.-Sun., R$8 includes entrance to Igreja Matriz de Nossa Senhora do Pilar). Geology aficionados will enjoy the impressive collection of 20,000 rocks and gemstones, while natural history buffs will get chills viewing the oldest human skull in the Americas, unearthed in nearby Lagoa Santa. Astronomers and romantics alike should check out the observatory: Stargazing is open to the public on Saturday nights.

Museu Casa Guignard

Although celebrated Brazilian painter Alberto da Veiga Guignard (1896-1962) was born in Rio and educated in Europe, he spent most of his life in Minas and his final years in Ouro Preto. The town's landscapes, colors, and textures are all very much present in his vibrant canvases, housed in the **Museu Casa Guignard** (Rua Conde de Bobadela 110, tel. 31/3551-5155, www.museuguignard.mg.gov.br, noon-6pm Tues.-Fri., 10am-3pm Sat.-Sun.).

Teatro Municipal and Casa dos Contos

Built in 1769, Ouro Preto's charming **Teatro Municipal** (Rua Brigadeiro Musqueira, tel. 31/3559-3224, http://casadaoperaop.wordpress.com, noon-6pm Mon.-Sat., noon-4pm Sun., R$2) is not only the oldest theater still in operation in Brazil (both Pedro I and Pedro II were audience members), it also boasts some of the finest acoustics. Nearby is the **Casa dos Contos** (Rua São José 12, tel. 31/3551-1444, 2pm-6pm Mon., 10am-5pm Tues.-Sat., 10am-4pm Sun.), whose name—the "House of Accounts"—evokes one of its original functions as the headquarters of the Intendência do Ouro, the crown entity responsible for the weighing and melting of all gold into bars. You can still see the immense furnace from which the royal fifth was promptly confiscated. In 1789, this house served as a prison for leaders of the Inconfidência Mineira. The dark and gloomy basement was a *senzala,* in which slaves were kept in far from comfortable conditions. Today, it displays some decidedly gruesome instruments of torture. More pleasant are the lovely internal courtyard and the panoramic views of the surrounding rooftops from the fourth floor. The *casa* houses a public library and a study center specializing in the gold-rush era.

Igreja Matriz de Nossa Senhora do Pilar

One of Ouro Preto's most magnificent churches, the **Igreja Matriz de Nossa Senhora do Pilar** (Praça Monsenhor João Castilho Barbosa, tel. 31/3551-4735, 9am-11am and noon-5pm Tues.-Sun., R$8, fee also covers the Museu de Arte Sacra) is easily the most opulent of Minas's baroque churches. It's difficult to take in so much glitter: The angels, seashells, and floral motifs that adorn the altars and pulpits are doused in 400 kilograms (880 pounds) of pure gold, and the effect is of having stepped into someone's jewelry box. This was done by covering the wood with a special type of glue, which was then coated with the finest gold dust; even the walls are painted in gold. Responsible for the exquisite sculptures was the talented Francisco Xavier de Brito, an important mentor of Aleijadinho. The basement's **Museu de Arte Sacra** houses religious icons and vestments embroidered with silver and gold.

Igreja de Nossa Senhora do Rosário dos Pretos

The modest **Igreja de Nossa Senhora do Rosário dos Pretos** (Largo do Rosário, 1pm-4pm Tues.-Sun.) was built by and for Ouro Preto's significant slave population with profits made from after-hours mining. The simplicity of the interior is supposedly due to the fact that the slaves ran out of gold after spending heavily on the lavish exterior, which is striking with its unusual curved design. Note that the sculpture depicting Santa Helena, attributed to Aleijadinho, has "two faces": one masculine and one feminine.

★ Igreja de São Francisco de Assis

Close to Praça Tiradentes is the Igreja do Pilar's rival for title of Ouro Preto's most magnificent church. The **Igreja de São Francisco de Assis** (Largo do Coimbra, tel. 31/3551-4661, 8:30am-noon and 1:30pm-5pm Tues.-Sun., R$8, fee also covers the Igreja de Nossa Senhora da Conceição and Museu Aleijadinho) is a tour-de-force by Aleijadinho and his greatest work after the 12 Prophets in Congonhas. Built between 1767 and 1800, it represents the apex of Mineiro baroque. Aleijadinho himself designed the church and supervised its construction. He carved the entire facade, including the marvelous soapstone medallion, and is responsible for most of the exquisite cedar and soapstone carvings on the inside. The ceiling panels that adorn the interior are the work of master painter Manuel da Costa Ataíde and reveal Aleijadinho's frequent collaborator at the height of his powers. The rich colors made from natural pigments have admirably stood the test of time. Note the African features of the Virgin and the cherubs surrounding her: They were inspired by the painter's *mulata* wife and their many offspring.

Igreja Matriz de Nossa Senhora da Conceição de Antônio Dias and Museu de Aleijadinho

From the outside, the grandiose **Igreja Matriz de Nossa Senhora da Conceição de Antônio Dias,** named after Ouro Preto's founder, bears a striking resemblance to the equally flamboyant Igreja Matriz de Nossa Senhora do Pilar. This similarity is hardly surprising: Since its founding, Ouro Preto has been divided into two rival parishes, Pilar and Antônio Dias, each with its own church, that vied to outdo the other in magnificence. To this day, the rivalry is played out during the famous Semana Santa processions, which in even years depart from the Matriz do Pilar and in odd years from the Matriz de Santo Antônio. Antônio Dias died a wealthy man, bequeathing part of his fortune to have the church built on the site of his original mining camp. The church is also famed for being the burial place of Aleijadinho and his architect father, Manuel Francisco Lisboa, who designed it.

Unfortunately, the exquisite interior has been closed for renovation since 2013, an undertaking expected to last three years. In the interim, the small **Museu Aleijadinho** (www.museualeijadinho.com.br), formerly housed in the sacristy, has moved to the Igreja São Francisco de Assis. The collection pays homage to the great sculptor with a collection of extraordinary baroque and rococo works, among them a quartet of fierce lions— Aleijadinho carved them from his imagination, and they resemble mythical monsters more than large felines.

Mina do Chico Rei

Along Rua Dom Silvério, from the Matriz de Antônio Dias, is the **Mina do Chico Rei** (Rua Dom Silvério 108, tel. 31/3551-1749, 8am-5pm daily, R$10), one of the oldest visitable Minas gold mines. According to local legend, Chico Rei was an African king who was sold into slavery along with most of his people in the early 18th century. With the extra nuggets he was allowed to harvest at night and on Sundays, he eventually bought his freedom. Sometime later, he acquired his own gold mine and, with its profits, promptly set to work buying the liberty of the other slaves from his tribe. Today you can visit 360 meters (1,200 feet) of underground tunnels that still show the traces of the miners' activities.

Many mines exist beneath Ouro Preto. Among the most visitable are **Mina do Jeje** (Rua Chico Rei 371, Alta da Cruz, tel. 31/8591-8375, 9am-5:30pm daily, R$15) and **Mina de Santa Rita** (Rua Santa Rita 171, Padre Faria, tel. 31/3552-3363, 8am-6pm daily, R$20).

Igreja de Nossa Senhora da Santa Efigênia dos Pretos

Chico Rei's mine yielded so much gold that he was able to fund a church of his own, and it was here that Ouro Preto's black population was able to worship. Construction on the **Igreja de Nossa Senhora da Santa Efigênia dos Pretos** (Rua Santa Efigênia 396, tel. 31/3551-5047, 8:30am-4:30pm Tues.-Sun., R$3; fee also covers the Capela do Padre Faria) began in 1733 and continued until 1785. Along the way, many of the slaves who helped build the church contributed financially with gold dust smuggled in their hair. The soapstone baptismal fonts came in very handy as basins in which donors could rinse the gold out of their hair. Although not much gold was left over for decorative purposes, this understated church boasts some fine art. The altar was sculpted by Aleijadinho's mentor, Francisco Xavier de Brito; the external figure of Nossa Senhora do Rosário is by the master sculptor himself.

Capela do Padre Faria

Padre João de Faria was among the first

bandeirantes who settled Ouro Preto and, although getting there is a bit of a walk, it's worthwhile to glimpse this beautifully ornate chapel built in the early 1700s. (If you're pressed for time, take a municipal bus marked Capela do Padre Faria.) The oldest religious edifice in town, the **Capela do Padre Faria** (Rua Nossa Senhora do Parto, 8:30am-4:30pm Tues.-Sun., R$3; fee also covers the Igreja da Santa Efigênia) was erected on the site of the improvised chapel where the padre preached the town's first mass. Defying royal decree, its bells were the only ones in Ouro Preto to toll upon receiving news of the execution of Tiradentes in 1792.

Parque Estadual do Pico do Itacolomi

Back in the late 17th century, the 1,770-meter (5,800-foot) mountain peak of Itacolomi (a Tupi-Guarani expression for "rock-child") served as a beacon-like landmark for the *bandeirantes* who combed Minas's hills in search of precious stones. Part of the Serra do Espinhaço mountain range, the peak and surrounding region make up the **Parque Estadual do Pico do Itacolomi** (tel. 31/3551-6193, www.ief.mg.gov.br, 8am-5pm Tues.-Sun., R$10, trail to Pico R$10). Marking the transition phase between native Atlantic forest and Cerrado ecosystems, the vegetation is quite varied and supports a wide range of wildlife, including anteaters, jaguars, and numerous types of hummingbirds. Most of the hiking trails—ranging 8-16 kilometers (5-10 mi)—are quite easy and offer the bonuses of (icy) waterfalls and splendid views. If you're in the mood for a challenge, consider the 20-kilometer (12-mi) climb to the top of Itacolomi peak. The park is well-organized, with a visitors center, restrooms, and a café. To get there, follow highway BR-356 (Av. do Contorno) for 5 kilometers (3 mi) from the center of Ouro Preto.

ENTERTAINMENT AND EVENTS
Nightlife

Due to its large university population, Ouro Preto has quite a vibrant nightlife. Rua Conde de Bobadela (Rua Direita) is crammed with bars that are usually very lively during the week. To catch a local band playing jazz or MPB, follow the almost hidden passageway that leads to **Escadabaixo** (Rua Conde de Bobadela 122, tel. 31/3551-1482, 5pm-close daily), a cozy, dimly lit cellar with exposed stone walls. Nearby, **Acaso 85 Scotch Bar e Restaurante** (Largo do Rosário 85, tel.

Serra do Espinhaço, northern Minas

31/3551-2397, www.acaso85.com.br, 11am-3pm and 6pm-close Tues.-Sun., 11am-3pm Mon.) is even more atmospheric. The cavernous, candlelit stone interior was once a *senzala* (slaves' quarters), and the beguiling garden attracts late-night drinkers in search of a snack and a *saideira* ("last call"). By day, this is also a great place for a self-service lunch of *comida mineira*. Far from Rua Conde de Bobadela, **Benzadeus** (Largo Marília de Dirceu 41, tel. 31/8433-5167, 6am-1am Wed.-Sun.) is a cool neighborhood gastropub in the heart of Antônio Dias.

Festivals and Events

Ouro Preto is famous throughout Brazil for its traditional **Semana Santa** (Holy Week) celebrations, held during Easter, when windows are hung with white banners and the streets are carpeted with a trail of colored sawdust and flowers that links the two Matriz churches of Antônio Dias and Pilar. Highlights include open-air pageants depicting Christ's last days and splendid religious processions. The town is also known for its traditional **Carnaval** (www.carnavalouropreto.com), although the revelry is nowhere near the level of bacchanalia that explodes in Salvador, Recife, and Rio. In late July, when the weather is chilly, things heat up considerably during the **Festival de Inverno** (www.festivaldeinvernoufop.br) with a diverse array of artistic, musical, and cultural events. The second weekend in September, **Tudo É Jazz** (www.tudoejazz.com.br) brings national and international jazz attractions to bars, restaurants, and outdoor venues.

SHOPPING

Centuries after the gold rush, Ouro Preto is still a major destination for those in search of jewels and other precious stones. Although there are scores of boutiques selling gems and jewelry, to make sure you're getting the real deal and not a synthetic product, it's better to stick to larger and more traditional addresses with a solid reputation. Stores in Ouro Preto are generally open 9am-7pm Monday-Saturday.

One of Ouro Preto's mineral specialties is the imperial topaz, which ranges in hue from pink to apricot. You can find it along with other gorgeous rocks at **Ita Gemas** (Rua Conde da Bobadela 139, tel. 31/3551-4895) and **Imperial Brasil Gemas** (Rua Amélia Bernhouse 11, tel. 31/8596-2142), where you can visit the jewelers at work in their atelier.

Another specialty of Ouro Preto is soapstone (there are quarries nearby), which accounts for the plethora of carvings and objects ranging from pots to backgammon sets that you'll find around town. In front of the Igreja São Francisco de Assis is a handicrafts fair, the **Feira do Largo de Coimbra** (9am-7pm daily), which, despite its touristy nature, carries a lot of soapstone carvings. If the plethora of saints and oratories in Ouro Preto's churches stirs your cravings for sacred art, you may want to invest in the artifacts sold at the atelier of **Elias Layon** (Rua Getúlio Vargas 251, tel.31/3551-6577). The collective **Casa de Artes Ouro Preto** (Rua São Francisco de Assis, tel. 31/3551-5793) reunites the works of 20 local artists.

ACCOMMODATIONS

Ouro Preto has lots of accommodations options to suit all budgets, many of them in centuries-old dwellings. Reserve in advance during holiday periods. To save money, immerse yourself in Ouro Preto's legendary student culture by renting a simple room in a *república* (traditional student residence); a bed (and not much else) costs R$15-20. Among the options are **Formigueiro** (Rua Xavier da Veiga 178, tel. 31/3551-2239, www.republicaformigueiro.com.br), **Trem de Doido** (Rua Prefeito Washington Dias, tel. 31/3551-7638, www.reptremdedoido.com.br), and **Verdes Mares** (Praça Juvenal Santos 34, tel. 31/3551-1264, www.republicaverdesmares.com.br).

R$50-200

With a prime location and unbeatable prices,

the **Pousada Hospedaria Antiga** (Rua Xavier da Veiga 1, tel. 31/3551-2203, www.antiga.com.br, R$100-130 d) offers rustic yet sizable guest rooms in a historic building that was the former abode of renowned 19th-century poet and politician Xavier de Veiga. A stay here feels like going back in time thanks to the (well-used) antique furniture, lofty ceilings, and creaky wooden floors. Hearty breakfasts are served in the stonewalled dining room.

Book in advance for one of the six lovely guest rooms at **Pousada Nello Nuno** (Rua Camilo de Brito 59, tel. 31/3551-3375, www.pousadanellonuno.com.br, R$140-180 d), two blocks from Praça Tiradentes. This intimate *pousada* is owned by a printmaker and engraver whose works adorn the walls of the historic house. An internal courtyard exudes unpretentious charm.

R$200-400

While one can't say that Ouro Preto is short on hotels with history and charm, it's hard to outdo the ★ **Pouso do Chico Rei** (Rua Brigadeiro Mosqueira 90, tel. 31/3551-1274, www.pousodochicorei.com.br, R$160-240 d). One of the oldest *pousadas* in town, this palatial 18th-century villa sits next to the Teatro Municipal. The lovely guest rooms—all featuring rustic antiques and views—can accommodate 1-5 people and are named after some of the hotel's most illustrious guests, among them Pablo Neruda, Elizabeth Bishop, and Vinicius de Moraes.

Although it occupies a historic *solar*, the comfy rooms at **Pousada dos Meninos** (Rua Brigadeiro Mosqueira 90, tel. 31/3551-1274, www.pousadadosmeninos.com.br, R$240-370 d) favor a minimalist, whitewashed aesthetic interrupted by bright blue wooden shutters and Day-Glo prints by neo-Pop artist Romero Britto. Breakfast is lavish, since the owners also run the gourmet deli **Empório dos Meninos,** where guests are invited to linger.

For a complete break with things colonial,

check into the **Grande Hotel de Ouro Preto** (Rua das Flores 164, tel. 31/3551-1488, www.grandehotelouropreto.com.br, R$240-320 d), a jarring modernist block designed by Oscar Niemeyer back in the 1940s. Although its being plunked rather unceremoniously in the midst of the *centro histórico* hasn't endeared it to the locals, its wide-open interior spaces and ample use of glass offer guests a particularly stunning visual feast of Ouro Preto's baroque treasures, whether from the guest rooms, multiple terraces, or lovely swimming pool.

R$400-600

Located in a sprawling mid-18th-century mansion, the **Pousada do Mondego** (Largo de Coimbra 38, tel. 31/3551-2040, www.mondego.com.br, R$390-570 d) is both intimate and exquisite, a refined yet relaxed mix of rustic accents and modern Brazilian art along with 21st-century amenities such as cable TV and high-speed Internet. A lavish spread is served daily in the tea salon, and there is a bar, an art gallery, and a boutique selling local crafts.

FOOD

Ouro Preto is endowed with a wide variety of food options, ranging from simple snack bars to gourmet experiences. It is renowned for having some of the finest Mineiro cooking in the state.

There are a fair number of cheap eats along Rua Conde de Bobadela, where cafés and snack bars often fill up with the resident student population. The nicest is the coffee-scented **Café Geraes** (Rua Conde de Bobadela 122, tel. 31/3551-5097, 11am-11pm daily, R$15-25), a welcoming space with tiled floors, lots of wood, and a piano. Locals flock here to nosh on thick *caldos* (soups), delicious sandwiches, and *pratos executivos* such as a fillet with jabuticaba sauce (served at lunch and dinner). For those on a tight budget, unprepossessing **Vide Gula** (Rua Senador Rocha Lagoa 79, tel. 31/3551-4493, 11:30am-3pm

Mon.-Sat., R$15-25) offers a very reasonable per-kilo self-service buffet with an emphasis on Mineiro specialties.

Near the Casa de Contos, ★ **Chafariz** (Rua São José 167, tel. 31/3551-2828, 11:30am-4pm Tues.-Sat., R$44 pp) has served its self-service banquet of Mineiro specialties, including *doces* and *licores,* since the 1930s. Many claim this is the tastiest Mineiro fare in town. Others swear by the equally delicious offerings at **Contos de Reis** (Rua Camilo de Brito 21, tel. 31/3551-5359, www. restaurantecontosdereis.com.br, 11:30am-10pm Wed.-Sat., 11:30am-5pm Sun.-Tues., R$20-30), situated in the former *senzala* (slaves' quarters) of an 18th-century mansion. While lunch is a per-kilo buffet, dinner is à la carte. Especially good is the *frango ao molho pardo.*

Amidst 5,000 tomes, pillowed sofas, and exposed brick walls, the mellow **Café e Livraria Cultural** (Rua Claudio Manoel 15, tel. 31/3551-1361, cafeculturalop.com.br, 9am-7pm Fri.-Sun., R$15-25) serves serious homegrown Mineiro coffee along with delicious homemade soups, quiches, pastries, and artisanal beers. There are live jazz and MPB performances Saturday night.

Chocoholics beware: Next to the Igreja Nossa Senhora do Rosário dos Pretos, **Chocolates Ouro Preto** (Rua Getúlio Vargas 72, tel. 31/3551-7330, www.chocolate-souropreto.com.br, 9am-7pm Sun.-Thurs., 9am-9pm Sat.) offers serious temptation for chocolate lovers, especially those with a weakness for truffles. The bestsellers are those stuffed with a mousse of *maracujá* (passion fruit).

TRANSPORTATION AND SERVICES

The main **tourist office** is at Praça Tiradentes 41 (tel. 31/3559-3269, 7am-7pm daily); a second branch is at the *rodoviária* (Rua Padre Rolim, tel. 31/3551-5552, 7am-6pm daily). Staff at the adjacent **Associação dos Guias de Turismo** (Rua Padre Rolim, tel. 31/3551-2665, 8am-8pm) offer guided city tours and can organize treks and horseback-riding trips. The multilingual websites www. ouropreto.mg.gov.br and www.ouropreto.org. br offer more information about Ouro Preto. **Banco do Brasil** (Rua São José 189) accepts international bank cards, as does the Bradesco on Praça Tiradentes.

There is direct bus service to Ouro Preto from Belo Horizonte, Rio de Janeiro, and São Paulo. From Rio, **Viação Útil** (tel. 21/3907-3900, www.util.com.br) operates two daily buses leaving at 7:30am and 11:30pm (eight hours, R$84 and R$125). From Belo Horizonte, **Pássaro Verde** (tel. 31/3073-7575, www.passa-roverde.com.br) offers hourly buses (two hours, R$28) between 6am-11pm. The *rodoviária* (Rua Padre Rolim 661, tel. 31/3559-3252) is a 10-minute walk from Praça Tiradentes. If you don't want to deal with the hills, minibus service (R$2) runs into town. Driving from Belo Horizonte, the 90-kilometer (56-mi) journey is very quick. Take BR-040 in the direction of Rio de Janeiro, then turn off onto BR-356, following the signs to Ouro Preto.

Mariana

Only 12 kilometers (8 mi) from Ouro Preto, Mariana is smaller and less ornate—and less touristy—than its neighbor. Founded in 1696 on the site of a major gold deposit, and named after King Dom João's wife, Maria Ana of Austria, it proudly claims to be the oldest city in Minas Gerais. Although you can easily discover its attractions in a day trip from Ouro Preto, you might want to stay for a couple of days to fully appreciate its tranquility, scenic mountain backdrop, and pleasant streets lined with elegant colonial homes.

SIGHTS

Mariana's key sites are all clustered together, and thankfully, its streets are much less steep than those of other *cidades históricas*. The most impressive and stately colonial mansions are clustered on or around the principal street of Rua Direita. The main, and surprisingly verdant, colonial square, **Praça Minas Gerais,** is quite splendid. Here you'll find two baroque churches, the Igreja de São Francisco de Assis and the Igreja de Nossa Senhora do Carmo, as well as the stately 18th-century Casa de Câmara e Cadeia, the former city hall and jail, which today is the seat of the municipal government.

Churches

Mariana's handful of churches are all quite interesting, in part because Mariana was the headquarters of the bishop of Minas Gerais. One of the town's most famous native sons is the master painter Manuel Costa da Ataíde, the expressive artist and superb colorist who often collaborated with the sculptor Aleijadinho.

On Praça Minas Gerais, the **Igreja de São Francisco de Assis** (9am-noon and 1pm-4pm Tues.-Sun., R$2), constructed between 1763 and 1794, boasts an ornate medallion above its front door that was sculpted in soapstone by Aleijadinho. Inside is the burial place of Ataíde; unfortunately, the exquisite ceiling panels he painted depicting the life and death of Saint Francis of Assisi can't be viewed since the church is undergoing renovations. Not as impressive but still quite graceful is the **Igreja de Nossa Senhora de Carmo** (9am-noon and 2pm-4:30pm Tues.-Sun.), completed in 1784.

From Praça Minas Gerais, if you walk uphill along the pretty Rua Dom Silvério, you'll reach the **Basílica Menor de São Pedro dos Clérigos** (tel. 31/3557-1216, 9am-noon and 1pm-5pm Tues.-Sun., R$2). Begun in 1752, it was never entirely finished. More interesting than the actual church are the arresting panoramic views from its palmy hilltop perch. The oldest and most opulent church in town is undoubtedly the **Catedral Basílica de Nossa Senhora de Assunção** (Praça Claudio Manoel, tel. 31/3557-1216, 8am-6pm Tues.-Sun., R$5; fee also covers the Museu Arquidiocesano). Built in the early 1700s when the region was still flush with gold, this cathedral is among the most richly ornamented churches in Minas. Both Manoel Francisco Lisboa and his son Aleijadinho collaborated on the church, as did Ataíde. Concerts featuring a magnificent German organ with 969 pipes are held in the church (11:30am Fri. and noon Sun., R$15).

Museu Arquidiocesano

Considered one of the finest sacred art museums in Brazil, the **Museu Arquidiocesano** (Rua Frei Durão, tel. 31/3557-2581, 8:30am-noon and 1:30pm-5pm Tues.-Fri., 8:30am-2pm Sat.-Sun., R$5; fee also covers the Catedral) has an extensive collection of more than 2,000 religious objects, among them works by Aleijadinho and Ataíde, most of them dating from the 18th and 19th centuries.

Mina de Ouro da Passagem

Located 5 kilometers (3 mi) outside of

Mariana on the road to Ouro Preto, the **Mina de Ouro da Passagem** (Rua Eugénio Eduardo Rapallo 192, Passagem da Mariana district, tel. 31/3357-5000, 9am-5pm daily, R$30) is the largest gold mine in the world currently open to visitors. Between its founding in the early 1700s and its closure in 1985, more than 35 tons of gold were extracted from its dark subterranean tunnels. Today, only a fraction of its labyrinthine passageways are open to visitors, but the experience of wandering through them is deliciously eerie. To begin exploring the underground galleries, you'll have to brave a descent of 120 meters (390 feet) in a creaky cable car. Guided tours provide a history of mining techniques. Bring along a bathing suit to take advantage of the shallow, surprisingly blue (and very icy) underwater lagoon. All buses that run between Mariana and Ouro Preto pass by the *mina;* simply request that the driver let you off in front of the entrance.

ACCOMMODATIONS AND FOOD

Mariana has a number of attractive and affordable *pousadas* within walking distance of Praça Minas Gerais. Located in a handsome mid-19th-century edifice, **Hotel Providência** (Rua Dom Silvério 233, tel. 31/3557-1444, www.hotelprovidencia.com. br, R$120 d) combines historical ambiance with irresistible prices. Simple but cheery rooms occupy quarters formerly inhabited by the nuns who still run the adjacent school (guests can use the pool when school's out). Rooms overlooking the street can be noisy. A bit of a walk from the center, near the entrance to town, is the **Pousada Gamarano** (Rua Raimundo Gamarano 1, tel. 31/3557-1835, R$160 d). Perched on Colina São Pedro, it offers attractive views of Mariana and the surrounding mountains. Polished wood, a working fireplace, and original furnishings made by owner and artist Ladim Gamarano make guests feel decidedly at home.

Mariana's restaurant options are more humble than those in Ouro Preto. For a quick, tasty, and inexpensive lunch, **Lua Cheia** (Rua Dom Viçoso 23, tel. 31/3557-3232, 11am-3pm daily, 6pm-10pm Wed.-Sat., R$15-20) is a pleasant per-kilo self-service restaurant with stone walls, wooden floors, and a leafy garden. It offers salads and hot dishes as well as Mineiro specialties and *churrasco*. At night, the menu is à la carte. Another local favorite, **Dom Silvério** (Praça Gomes Freire 242, tel. 31/3557-2475, 6:30pm-midnight daily, R$20-30) is renowned for serving up the best pizzas in town as well as a very fine lasagna. Slightly more upscale but still down-to-earth is **Bistrô** (Rua Salomão Ibrahim 61-A, tel. 31/3557-4138, 11am-3pm and 6pm-close daily, R$20-30), a small, cozy restaurant that offers a little bit of everything on its menu, from Mineiro specialties to fish and meat dishes.

TRANSPORTATION AND SERVICES

There is a helpful **tourist office** (Praça Tancredo Neves, tel. 31/3557-1158, 8am-5pm daily) where you can get info and purchase a map. You can also consult www. mariana.mg.gov.br and www.mariana.org.br (Portuguese only).

Local **Transcotta** buses operating from Ouro Preto (leaving from a stop in front of the Escola de Minas) arrive and depart from Praça Tancredo Neves every 30 minutes (5:30am-11:30pm, R$3.20). The main bus station (Rodovia dos Inconfidentes, tel. 31/3557-1373) is a 2-kilometer (1.2-mi) hike from town. Buses leave and arrive from São João del Rei, Diamantina, and Belo Horizonte, which is serviced by **Pássaro Verde** (tel. 31/3073-7575, www.passaroverde.com.br) hourly (6am-11pm, R$32) for the two-hour journey.

If you plan to travel between Ouro Preto and Mariana on the weekend, take advantage of the **Maria Fumaça steam train** (Praça da Estação Ferroviária, tel. 31/3551-7705, www. tremdavale.org, Fri.-Sun., R$40 one-way, R$50 round-trip) with departures for Ouro Preto at 1pm and 4pm Friday-Saturday.

Congonhas

Although considered a *cidade histórica,* there is nothing very historical about Congonhas. Its main appeal is the magnificent Basílica e Santuário do Bom Jesus de Matosinhos, a national treasure that features the last and, according to many art experts, greatest work of Aleijadinho. During the master sculptor's lifetime, Congonhas was a flourishing gold-mining town. Two centuries later, when iron was discovered in the surrounding hills, the resulting industrial activity caused most of the town's colonial architecture to be wiped out. Untouched by the wrecking ball, the *basílica* features a magnificent staircase with sculptures of the 12 Old Testament prophets and six chapels with carved figures representing scenes from the Passion of Christ. Considered one of the high points of Brazilian baroque, the sanctuary is recognized by UNESCO as a World Heritage Site.

★ BASÍLICA E SANTUÁRIO DO BOM JESUS DE MATOSINHOS

Despite his compromised physical state, Aleijadinho was at the height of his talent when he was summoned to create sculptures for the **Basílica e Santuário do Bom Jesus de Matosinhos** (Praça da Basílica, 7am-6pm Tues.-Sun., free), which crowns the steep hill known as Morro de Maranhão.

The church itself—modeled after the church of Bom Jesus in Braga, Portugal—is simple on the outside but splendidly ornate on the inside. Construction began in 1757. Although the church was built in four years, it took another 55 years to complete the rest of this vast sanctuary. Aleijadinho himself was only brought on board in 1796. For the next decade, he would work obsessively.

Aleijadinho's life-size statues representing the 12 prophets of the Old Testament are the highlight of any visit. Carved out of native soapstone by Aleijadinho and his disciples, they dominate the majestic stone staircase that leads up to the church. When glimpsed close up, the prophets' faces, ravaged by the elements, are startlingly expressive and often fierce, particularly when viewed against the brooding mountain backdrop.

The other high point of Aleijadinho's oeuvre at Congonhas is the Passion of Christ: seven tableaux he sculpted representing the Last Supper, Calvary, Imprisonment, Flagellation, Coronation, the Carrying of the Cross, and the Crucifixion. In each scene, the carved human figures are rendered even more vivid by the talents of master painter Manuel da Costa Ataíde. The figures of Christ were carved by Aleijadinho himself and are disarmingly lifelike. Contemplation of them in the brutally dramatic later scenes is harrowing enough to raise goose bumps.

Before leaving the basilica, visit the small **sanctuary** adjacent to the church. Here, thousands of pilgrims from all over Brazil have left ex-votos, paintings, photographs, and letters, thanking Jesus for miraculous cures and divine intervention in the face of myriad tragedies. Even if you aren't religious and don't read Portuguese, it's difficult not to be moved by such powerful expressions of faith dating back well over two centuries.

ACCOMMODATIONS AND FOOD

Since Congonhas is so close to Belo Horizonte and the other *cidades históricas,* most tourists spend a couple of hours visiting the *basílica* before hightailing it out of town. To check out Aleijadinho's masterpiece lit up by early morning or late afternoon sunlight (or moonlight), check into the **Colonial Hotel** (Praça da Basilica 76, tel. 31/3731-1834, www. hotelcolonialcongonhas.com.br, R$120 d), right across the street from the sanctuary. This 100-year-old hotel has definitely seen better times, but it has retained a faded air of elegance. The hotel's cavernous basement restaurant, **Cova do Daniel** (9am-6pm Mon., 11am-11pm Tues.-Sun., 9am-6pm Sun., R$30-40) serves up reasonably priced, fine-tasting Mineiro food for both lunch and dinner.

TRANSPORTATION

Congonhas is only an hour from Belo Horizonte. **Sandra** (tel. 31/3201-22512, www.

viacaosandra.com.br) offers bus service from Belo Horizonte's *rodoviária* with a stop in Congonhas before continuing on to São João del Rei. There are buses daily between 6am-7pm, with fewer running on Sunday. The 75-minute trip costs R$24. If you're coming from São João, the 2-hour trip costs R$27. By car, take BR-040 south from Belo Horizonte or BR-265 from São João del Rei until you hit BR-040, leading north to Congonhas.

São João del Rei

The largest of the *cidades históricas*, São João boasts a colonial center flush with architectural treasures as well as a more developed commercial area that is less seductive. For better or worse, it is the only former gold-mining town that has made the successful transition into modern times. You can see most of São João's sights in a day, although the city is pleasant enough to warrant staying overnight. Otherwise, it is a convenient base for exploring the region, especially if you don't have a car. On the charm scale, however, its smaller neighbor, Tiradentes, only 12 kilometers (8 mi) away, is much prettier and more uniformly colonial.

SIGHTS

São João's most interesting attractions are clustered together in the *centro histórico*. Thankfully, there are fewer steep hills to clamber up and down than in Minas's other historic towns. As you walk around, you'll hear a lot of bells ringing: The bells of the city's churches are regulated to chime the hour at slightly different intervals, creating a symphonic effect.

Igreja de São Francisco de Assis

The **Igreja de São Francisco de Assis** (Praça Frei Orlando, tel. 32/3372-3110, 8am-4pm Mon., 8am-6pm Tues.-Sat., 8am-2pm Sun., R$3) is the most magnificent of São

João's attractions, and it is also one of the most splendid examples of late baroque rococo architecture in Minas. The exterior view of the church is quite striking. Monumental in stature, it dominates an elegantly landscaped square surrounded by colonial villas. The original design of the church was one of Aleijadinho's first projects; he also created the sculptures of the Immaculate Virgin and the angels on the building's facade. Inside, Aleijadinho contributed to the main altar and carved the statues of Santo Antônio and São João Evangelista. At 9am Sunday there is a mass at which the traditional Ribeiro Bastos women's choir performs baroque music.

Behind the church, the small cemetery is the final resting place of Tancredo Neves, who was Brazil's first democratically elected president, in 1985, following two decades of military dictatorship. Tragically, Tancredo died before he could take office, and ever since he has been somewhat of a martyr figure, particularly in São João, where he was born and grew up.

Catedral Basílica de Nossa Senhora do Pilar

Built in the 1720s, the **Catedral Basílica de Nossa Senhora do Pilar** (Rua Getúlio Vargas, tel. 32/3371-2568, 8am-10:30am and 1pm-5pm Mon., 8am-10:30am and 1pm-8pm Tues.-Thurs. and Sat.-Sun., 1pm-8pm

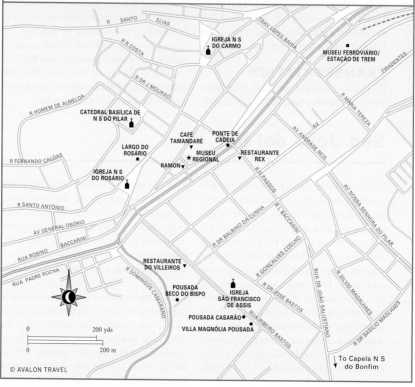

São João del Rei

Fri., R$8) is São João's (and one of Minas's) most sumptuous, since gold was in abundance during the time of its construction. The ceiling murals' distinctive coloring was achieved by the use of natural pigments. Note the figure of São Miguel encrusted with diamonds and emeralds.

Igreja de Nossa Senhora do Carmo

Perched on a triangular cobblestoned *praça* at the end of Rua Getúlio Vargas, the **Igreja de Nossa Senhora do Carmo** (Largo do Carmo, tel. 32/3371-7996, from 8am Mon.-Sat., R$1) was designed by Aleijadinho, who also sculpted the frontispiece. Construction on the church began in the 1730s and lasted throughout most of the century, which

accounts for the varying styles of baroque. The unusual sculpture of Christ here, unadorned and carved from cedar, was found beneath some rubble when the church was undergoing renovations in the early 20th century. Its origins are a mystery.

Igreja de Nossa Senhora do Rosário

Much simpler than the other churches, **Igreja de Nossa Senhora do Rosário** (Largo do Rosário, 8:30am-10:30am Tues.-Sun.) was built by and for São João's slave population and is the town's oldest church. Located at the beginning of Rua Getúlio Vargas, it is adjacent to the elegant Solar dos Neves, the traditional home of the Neves family, where future president Tancredo was born and raised.

Museu Regional

On Largo Tamandaré, the **Museu Regional** (Rua Marechal Deodoro 12, tel. 32/3371-7663, 9am-5:30pm daily, R$1) is housed in a handsome mansion built in 1859. Spread out among three floors, a collection of furniture (lots of great beds), religious icons, and various domestic items conjures up life in 18th- and 19th-century São João.

SHOPPING

São João is the pewter capital of Brazil and this is the place to pick up a decanter, a set of goblets, or a candlestick holder made of this alloy of tin and copper (although they don't come cheap). What may appear to be an age-old artisanal tradition actually only dates back half a century. While doing geological research, an Englishman named John Somers discovered that the hills surrounding São João were rich with tin. As a result, he moved to São João and started his own pewter factory. Over time, his apprentices opened their own ateliers, and today the city is flooded with them (ironically, most of the pewter now comes from the Amazonian state of Rondônia). Situated just behind the bus station, the original **John Somers** (www.johnsomers.com.br) factory is still highly regarded. Even if you're not in a purchasing mood, you can visit the small **Museu de Estanho John Somers** (Av. Leite de Castro 1150, tel. 32/3379-8101) located on the premises, which features pewter pieces from all over Brazil and Europe. Other recommended shops to stock up on pewter include **Ame Arte** (Rua Getúlio Vargas 73, tel. 32/3371-8109) and **Imperial Pewter** (Rua da Prata 132A, tel. 32/3372-1465, www.imperial-estanhos.com.br).

ACCOMMODATIONS

São João del Rei has some good options right in the heart of the *centro histórico*. Budget-minded travelers might want to consider basing themselves in São João instead of neighboring Tiradentes, where accommodations are considerably pricier, especially on the weekends and during holidays. Nonetheless, even in São João, take care to book ahead for stays during Carnaval and Semana Santa.

Pousada Casarão (Rua Ribeiro Bastos 94, tel. 32/3371-7447, www.pousadacasarao.com, R$160-170 d) is a great bargain in a spacious historic villa that gazes worshipfully onto the back of the Igreja de São Francisco de Assis. The interior is not as "colonial" as one might expect from the outside, but the hotel is welcoming. Guest rooms are cozy and comfortable and there's a pool.

Facing the Igreja de São Francisco de Assis is the **Villa Magnólia Pousada** (Rua Ribeiro Bastos 2, tel. 32/3373-5065, www.pousadavillamagnolia.com.br, R$220-290 d). It too occupies an attractive colonial manse, but here the charm factor is considerably higher; a lovely pool, internal courtyards, terraces, and greenery make this an oasis. Also nearby is the **Pousada Beco do Bispo** (Beco do Bispo 93, tel. 32/3371-8844, www.becodobispo.com.br, R$210-275 d). What this lovely *pousada* lacks in history it makes up for in warmth, comfort, and attention to detail. The pool area is quite posh, and breakfast is a lavish affair.

FOOD

It's much easier and cheaper to eat in São João than in nearby Tiradentes. ★ **Restaurante do Villeiros** (Rua da Prata 132A, tel. 32/3372-1034, www.villeiros.com.br, 11am-5:30pm Mon.-Sat., 11am-4pm Sun., R$15-35) is a charming eatery, with tables sprinkled throughout a prettily decorated colonial mansion and internal courtyard. The very reasonably priced per-kilo self-service buffet features delicious Mineiro specialties as well as a slew of creatively prepared alternatives and plenty of salads. The desserts are outstanding, and there is an à la carte menu. For lunch, **Restaurante Rex** (Av. Hermílio Alves 146, tel. 32/3371-1449, 11am-3pm daily, R$20-30) is another good and inexpensive per-kilo restaurant that specializes in home-cooked Mineiro fare.

Carnivores will appreciate the meaty fare at **Churrascaria e Restaurante Ramon** (Largo Tamandaré 52, tel. 32/3371-3540,

10am-10pm daily, R$30-45), which specializes in substantial portions of prime cuts of barbecued beef as well as chicken. This family-run cantina, featuring long wooden tables and dark blue tablecloths, has been in operation for 40 years and is something of an institution.

The heady scent of freshly ground coffee will overwhelm you before you even set foot on the patterned marble floors of atmospheric **Café Tamandaré** (Rua Marechal Deodoro 232, tel. 32/3371-7838, 8am-5pm Mon.-Fri., 8am-noon Sat.) where home-brewed Tamandaré coffee—grown in Minas Gerais—is ground and packaged in an adjacent room. When you finish getting your caffeine fix, purchase a bag or two to take with you.

TRANSPORTATION AND SERVICES

The **tourist office** (Praça Frei Orlando, tel. 32/3372-7338, 8am-6pm daily) offers free maps. For organized tours—by Jeep, mountain bike, or on horseback—throughout the region as well as information about sports activities such as rappelling and mountain climbing in the surrounding Serra do Lenheiro mountain range, get in touch with **Lazer e Aventura Turismo** (Rua Antônio Josino de Andrade Reis 232, tel. 32/3371-7956, www.lazereaventura.com). A four-hour hiking trip that ascends the nearby Serra do Lenheiro (whose summits are covered with prehistoric rock paintings) costs R$40.

Sandra (tel. 31/3201-2512, www.viacao-sandra.com.br) offers buses daily (fewer on Sun.) to São João from Belo Horizonte (3.5 hours, R$50). There is also a daily bus operated by **Útil** (tel. 0800-886-1000, 31/3551-3166, www.util.com.br) to and from Ouro Preto (4 hours, R$52) as well as three daily buses to and from Rio de Janeiro (7.5 hours, R$62-78) with **Paraibuna** (tel. 21/2253-0894, www.paraibunatransportes.com.br). Buses to Tiradentes, only 12 kilometers (8 mi) away, leave at regular intervals throughout the day. For information about all bus lines and schedules, call the *rodoviária* (Rua Cristovão Colombo, tel. 32/3373-4700), located 1.5 kilometers (1 mi) from the *centro histórico*. Unless you don't mind a long hike, catch a local bus out front or a taxi. A much cheaper and more fun way of getting around town is by *moto-taxi*. There is a stand outside the bus station. By car from Belo Horizonte, take BR-040 south and then turn onto BR-383.

São João del Rei's **train station** (Avenida Hermílio Alves, tel. 32/3371-8485, R$3) features a small Museu Ferroviário (9am-11am and 1pm-5pm, Wed.-Sun. R$3, free with train ticket) where you can gaze at train paraphernalia before jumping aboard the 19th-century **Maria Fumaça** (Smoking Mary) steam train to Tiradentes operated by **Ferrovia Centro-Atlântica** (tel. 0800/285-7000, www.trensturisticos.fcasa.com.br, one-way R$40, round-trip R$50). The train only operates Friday through Sunday with two daily departures in each direction.

Tiradentes

This small, incredibly charming colonial town has a historical center that is splendidly intact and a cinematographic backdrop of rolling green hills. Its steep cobblestoned streets are lined with gleaming churches, gracious mansions, and profusely blossoming bright pink and red tropical flowers. There are so many perspectives from which to admire the views that you can easily spend hours wandering around, despite the fact that the town consists of little more than a dozen streets. Tiradentes's drop-dead beauty and sophisticated cultural and culinary scene make it a favorite refuge for artists and intellectuals as well as upscale visitors from Rio and São Paulo, who descend on the town on weekends and holidays. To avoid the crowds, visit during the week, when you'll have the placid streets and baroque churches to yourself.

SIGHTS

The main square of **Largo das Forras** is flanked by the pretty chapel of Bom Jesus da Pobreza and other handsome 18th-century buildings that formerly served as administrative palaces. Today they have become hotels and restaurants; all gaze onto a park designed in 1989 by noted landscaper Roberto Burle Marx. At night, when the rest of town falls quiet, this square is where all the action takes place, especially on weekends.

Built in 1749, the **Chafariz de São José**—a well that long supplied the town's water—features three faucets protruding from the mouths of a trio of magnificently sculpted heads. Originally, one faucet supplied drinking water, another was used for washing clothes, and the third was reserved for thirsty livestock. Behind the well, a lush woodland area leads to the well's natural water source.

Museu Padre Toledo

The **Museu Padre Toledo** (Rua Padre Toledo 190, tel. 32/3355-1549, 10am-4:30pm Tues.-Sun., R$10) occupies a mansion whose sky-high ceilings are covered with frescoes. It belonged to Padre Toledo, a priest, an Inconfidente, and apparently a bon vivant, judging by the size and suggested former opulence of his none-too-humble abode. The museum's collection consists of a smattering of religious objects and domestic furnishings dating from Tiradentes's wealthy gold mining days.

★ Igreja Matriz de Santo Antônio

It's hard to miss the **Igreja Matriz de Santo Antônio** (Rua da Câmara, tel. 32/3355-1238, 9am-5pm daily, R$5), one of the most sumptuous baroque churches in Brazil. Perched on a steep hill, it is visible from myriad points throughout town, and you'll no doubt waste a lot of digital frames attempting to get the

"perfect" shot. Dedicated to Santo Antônio, patron saint of Tiradentes, church construction began in 1710 and was only completed some 40 years later. The interior is plastered with gold—half a ton, to be precise—resulting in seven richly detailed altars and a choir festooned with garlands and flowers. The organ is considered one of the most ornate examples of its kind in the world, and was specially made in Portugal; every Friday night (7:30pm, R$30) local musician Elisa Freixo brings it to life. Although the church facade was redesigned according to the drawings of Aleijadinho in 1810, the intricate soapstone carvings surrounding the main door were created by one of the master sculptor's pupils. The front patio offers mesmerizing views of the town and the Serra de São José mountains. The sundial, sculpted out of native soapstone, has become one the city's symbols.

If you keep walking up the steep Rua da Santíssima Trindade from the Igreja Matriz de Santo Antônio, you'll come upon the imposing **Igreja de Santíssima Trindade** (9am-4pm Mon.-Fri., 8am-5pm Sat.-Sun.). Built in 1810, its simple interior features some colorful trompe l'oeil details.

Igreja de Nossa Senhora do Rosário dos Pretos

The town's oldest church (dating from 1708), **Igreja de Nossa Senhora do Rosário dos Pretos** (Praça Padre Lourival, 10am-6pm Wed.-Sun., R$3) was where Tiradentes's slave population worshipped, which explains why the altars feature images of black saints. Slaves themselves built it during bright moonlit nights after having spent days toiling in the mines. The gold flakes they smuggled in their hair and beneath their fingernails were used to adorn the altars.

SPORTS AND RECREATION

Tiradentes lies at the foot of the region's principal natural attraction: the Serra de São José. The lower regions of this mountain range are thick with the lush fauna typical of native

Tiradentes

© AVALON TRAVEL

IGREJA
SANTÍSSIMA
TRINDADE

To Brisa da
Serra Pousada

RUA ANTÔNIA E. XAVIER

Córrego Santo Antônio

RUA PE LUVRAMENTO

LADEIRA SANTÍSSIMA TRINDADE

RUA JOSÉ LUIZ DE PAIVA

N

0   100 yds
0   100 m

IGREJA MATRIZ DE
SANTO ANTÔNIO

CASA DE CÂMARA
MUNICIPAL

IGREJA N.S DO
ROSÁRIO DOS PRETOS

R. DA
CÂMARA

R. DO JOGO
DE BOLA

Largo do
CHAFARIZ

POUSADA
DA BIA

R. DO CHAFARIZ

CHAFARIZ
DE SÃO JOSÉ

To Villa Paolucci

CENTRO CULTURAL
YVES ALVES

DIREITA

TRAGALUZ

CADEIA
PÚBLICA

ESTALAGEM
DO SABOR

Campo de
Futebol

VIRADAS
DO LARGO

MUSEO
PADRE TOLEDO

R. PE TOLEDO

POUSADA
PADRE TOLEDO

POUSO
FRANCÊS

TOURIST
INFORMATION

DONA XEPA

IGREJA
SÃO FRANCISCO
DE PAULA

POUSO ALFORRIA

CENTRO HISTÓRICO

RUA DOS CONFIDENTES

Largo das
Forras

CONTO
DE REIS

BAR DO
CELSO

RUA HENRIQUE DINIZ

SOLAR DA PONTE

Largo das
Mercês

R. SÍLVIO DE VASCONCELOS

IGREJA N.S
DAS MERCÊS

PARQUE DAS ABELHAS

Rio das Mortes

R. ANTÔNIO TEIXEIRA CARVALHO

R. FRANCISCO P. DE MORAIS

RUA JOAQUIM RAMALHO

POUSADA
VILLA BIZUCA

To São João del Rei;
Casa da Pedra Caves

ALTO DA
TORRE

ESTAÇÃO
DE TREM

Atlantic forest. Although hiking trails exist, locals recommend hiring a guide or taking an organized excursion. **Tiradentes Brasil** (Rua dos Inconfidentes 218B, tel. 32/3355-1270, www.tiradentesbrasil.com, 8am-8pm daily) is a well-organized tour operator with friendly staff. They offer reasonably priced half- and full-day guided walking, biking, and horseback-riding excursions to the Serra de São José, allowing time for dips in icy waterfalls and freshwater pools along the way. A medium-level five-hour hike costs R$75, with the possibility of renting knapsacks and purchasing snacks as well.

ENTERTAINMENT AND EVENTS

Tiradentes boasts an impressive cultural calendar for a town of its size. Apart from a lively music scene, it lures cinephiles to the **Mostra de Cinema** (www.mostratiradentes.com.br, end of Jan.), and chefs from all over Brazil and the world—as well as foodies eager to partake in their culinary creations—during the **Festival Internacional de Cultura e Gastronomia** (www.culturaegastronomia.com.br, end of Aug.). **Carnaval** and **Semana Santa** (Holy Week) festivities are also pretty lively.

SHOPPING

Many of the villages surrounding Tiradentes and São João del Rei have a long and rich tradition of craftsmanship. Generations of local artists create everything from wood sculptures and wrought-iron decorative objects to papier-mâché figures and hand-woven textiles. Consequently, one of the first things you'll notice about Tiradentes—for better or for worse—is the profusion of antiques shops, *artesanato* stores, and chic boutiques. The result is kind of quaint but also kind of consumerist. However, there are some finds, and various local artists sell directly from their ateliers. **Jango** (Rua Direita 32, tel. 32/8427-5703) is a local sculptor who creates beautifully carved religious figures. **Lyria Palombini** (Rua Direita 183, tel. 32/3355-2667) is known for her woodcuts and engravings. **Oscar Araripe** (Ladeira da Matriz 92, tel. 32/3355-1148, www.oscarararipe.com.br) is a prolific experimental painter. **Paula Spivak** (Rua Francisco Pereira de Morais 99, tel. 32/3355-1537) is famous for her handwoven shawls, carpets, and blankets. **Tereza Oliveira** (Rua Santíssima Trindade 50, tel. 32/3355-1978) makes unusual baroque-inspired decorative pieces featuring seashells. **Aolibama Brinquedos** (Rua Frei Veloso

Igreja Matriz de Santo Antônio

1000, tel. 32/3335-1954, http://aolibamabrinquedos.blogspot.ca) specializes in artisanally made educational, therapeutic, and classic children's toys using recycled, sustainable wood and other materials.

A trip to Bichinho, a dusty village 7 kilometers (4 mi) from Tiradentes (there are only two buses a day), is a good idea if you want to visit more ateliers where artists and craftspeople make all sorts of wonderful objects. Although many of them also turn up in Tiradentes, the prices are significantly marked up. Among the boutiques that sell art and antiques in Tiradentes are the **Empório Vanilce** (Largo das Forras 48, tel. 32/3355-1219, www.emporiovanilce.com.br), **Francisco Rodriguez** (Rua Direita 136, tel. 32/3355-1334), and **Cuia Brasil** (Rua da Câmara 83, tel. 32/3355-1521, www.cuiabrasil.com.br). **Inês Rabelo Arte** (Rua da Cadeia 38, tel. 32/3355-1329) carries the fantastic works of Toto, a famous Bichinho artist whose atelier, Oficina de Agosto, produces canvases, sculptures, and furniture ingeniously crafted from pieces of scrap wood.

ACCOMMODATIONS

Tiradentes is not a destination for the budget-minded, but with so many *pousadas,* there are deals to be found. If money is no object, Tiradentes has no shortage of truly unforgettable accommodations that marry colonial architecture, modern amenities, high style, and exquisite cuisine. Take note that prices are often up to 50 percent lower during the week and in the off-season (those listed below reflect these times). Weekends and holidays are not only more expensive but are often booked up. Reserving in advance is a must.

R$50-200

Pousada da Bia (Rua Frederico Ozanan 30, tel. 32/3355-1173, www.pousadadabia.com.br, R$120-160 d) is a welcoming and very affordable option with an ideal location. The simple guest rooms are enhanced by well-tended grounds that feature a sweet-smelling herb garden and a small pool. The staff is particularly friendly, and you can use the kitchen if you have a hankering to make a snack. The small rooms at romantic **Pouso Francês** (Rua Martin Paolucci 30, tel. 32/3255-2184, www.pousofrances.com, R$150 d) are offset by charming decorative elements, including artwork, antique *azulejos,* sherbet hues, two winter gardens, and the owner's hospitality. Only a 15-minute walk from Centro, ★ **Pousada Vila Bizuca** (Rua Alvarenga Peixoto 13, tel. 32/3355-1939, pousadavillabizuca@hotmail.com, R$160-200 d) feels like a world away. Its natural setting and Arcadian views are restive, but owner Erika goes the extra step with thousands of tiny details and a killer regional breakfast. Basic lodgings ooze warmth, with rustic wood furnishings and artisanal accessories.

R$200-400

Pousada Padre Toledo (Rua Direita 260, tel. 32/3355-2132, www.padretoledo.com.br, R$250 d) boasts a rustic country-style ambiance enhanced by its location in an 18th-century mansion. Some guest rooms—particularly 1 and 2, which are spacious and have terrific views of the tiled rooftops and mountains—are quite a bit nicer than others (a few are cramped and windowless), so ask to check them out beforehand. Out back are a pool and a stone deck for sunning yourself. The bread served at breakfast is baked fresh from the Padre Toledo bakery around the corner. In the evenings, *caldos* (hearty soups) are served to guests. Seek refuge from the colonial aesthetic at ★ **Pouso Alforria** (Rua Custódio Gomes 286, tel. 32/3355-1536, www.pousoalforria.com.br, R$285 d), which cleverly integrates 18th-century architectural elements into a contemporary house that is classy and cool. Rooms are airy and spacious, filled with an eclectic mix of antique, rustic regional, and contemporary furnishings and feature balconies that overlook the gardens and Serra do São José. Artwork dots the lovely common rooms, and a pool heightens the relaxation factor.

R$400-600

Although it's a steep climb to the **Brisa da Serra Pousada** (Rua Santíssima Trindade 520, tel. 32/3355-1838, www.brisadaserra. com.br, R$390-600 d), having the impossibly lush Serra de São José mountains staring you in the face more than compensates. The breathtaking scenery is accentuated by the inspired design, which features multiple gardens and terraces as well as plenty of natural stone, adobe, wood, and even thousands of dried flowers (which cover the ceiling of the sprawling lounge). The guest chalets are often booked up by honeymooning couples. Rates include a smashing afternoon tea.

Pousada Villa Paolucci (Rua do Chafariz, tel. 32/9981-8003, www.villapaolucci.com.br, R$340-698 d) resembles the fabulous film set of a colonial country estate, idyllically ringed by woods and mountains. A 15-minute stroll from the center of town, the main house and surrounding buildings of this former cattle ranch have been converted into luxury lodgings, with a pool and tennis courts set amid the expansive grounds. Sumptuous guest rooms are awash with dark shiny wood, antiques, gilt, and deep-red velvet, while the living and dining pavilions are quite regal. Although it doesn't have its own restaurant, the *pousada* is known for the owner's *leitão de pururca,* a Mineiro specialty of pork roasted to crispy perfection (orders must be made in advance). Unlike some of Tiradentes's other luxury accommodations, Villa Paolucci allows children.

Over R$600

Owned by a British-Brazilian couple, ★ **Solar da Ponte** (Praça das Mercês, tel. 32/3355-1255, www.solardaponte.com.br, R$520-875 d) is a reconstructed colonial villa that is routinely cited as one of the finest hotels in Brazil. Mineiro art and artifacts blend harmoniously with a discreetly English sense of style and comfort, creating a guesthouse that is refined yet unpretentious. The English influence extends to the gorgeously landscaped gardens surrounding the villa, replete with a swimming pool and a lavish afternoon tea. Service is flawless and friendly. If you're in the mood to splurge, the Solar da Ponte is definitely worth it. Children under 12 aren't allowed.

FOOD

Tiradentes is famous for its culinary scene. Although it offers some fine regional Mineiro cooking, in recent years it has become equally renowned as a mecca for haute cuisine and possesses an impressive number of upscale, romantically lit, critically acclaimed eateries serving experimental contemporary options that seduce foodies from Rio and São Paulo. The downside is that prices are inflated across the board.

Dona Xepa (Rua Ministro Gabriel Passos 26A, tel. 32/3355-1767, 11am-9pm Thurs.-Tues., R$25-35) is a warm and welcoming local eatery off the Largo das Forras where you can whet your appetite for hearty Mineiro dishes by sampling one (or several) of the delicious *cachaças* listed on the extensive drink menu. Try the house specialty *Dona Xepa com arroz,* an aromatic stew of chicken, corn, and seasonal vegetables. **Bar do Celso** (Largo das Forras 80, tel. 32/3355-1193, 11:30am-9pm Mon. and Wed.-Sat., 11:30am-6pm Sun., R$15-20) serves tasty home-cooked fare such as *costelinha* (pork ribs) with *linguiça* (pork sausage), *torresmo* (pork rinds), and collard greens (yes, this comprises one dish). Neighboring **Conto de Réis** (Largo das Forras 62, tel. 32/3355-1790, 6pm-11pm Sun.-Thurs., 11am-1am Fri.-Sat., R$15-25) is a mellow bar with ample windows that offer a great view of the action taking place on the Largo das Forras and which serves traditional *petiscos* such as *pastéis de angu* (a corn-flour pastry stuffed with braised banana stems) along with beer and *cachaça* against a backdrop of jazz and blues.

★ **Viradas do Largo** (Rua do Moinho 11, tel. 32/3355-1111, www.viradosdolargo. com.br, noon-10pm Wed.-Mon., R$30-45) is considered to be one of the best Mineiro restaurants in the country. The fruits and vegetables that don't come from the restaurant's back garden are purchased fresh from neighboring organic farms. Then they are cooked on a traditional wood-burning stove that has a privileged place in the cozy, country-style dining room. *Viradinha* (a stew featuring beef, beans, kale, pine nuts, and bacon) and *lombo com tutu* (pork with pureed beans) are among the most popular dishes. A worthy rival, **Estalagem do Sabor** (Rua Ministro Gabriel Passos 280, tel. 32/3355-1144, 11am-4pm and 7pm-10pm Mon.-Fri., 11:30am-10pm Sat., 11:30am-5pm Sun., R$30-45) is a warm, unassuming family-style operation. Two or more can dig into hefty portions of *frango com quiabo* (chicken stew with okra) and *porco religioso* (pork ribs in a sauce of *ora-pro-nobis*). For dessert, try the notoriously velvety and not-too-sweet *doce de leite* made by local legend **Dona Bolota** (Rua Bias Fortes 77, tel. 32/3355-1561, 10am-7pm Mon.-Sat., 10am-2pm Sun.).

Tragaluz (Rua Direita 52, tel. 32/3355-1424, www.tragaluztiradentes.com, 7pm-10:30pm Sun.-Mon. and Wed.-Thurs., 7pm-12:30am Fri.-Sat., R$50-60) specializes in creative adaptations of regional cuisine. The results—such as smoked *surubim* (a freshwater fish) with stuffed zucchini and *banana-da-terra* (a type of plantain)—are inspired. Burnished wood, candles, and Nina Simone purring in the background are downright romantic. Leave room for dessert.

TRANSPORTATION AND SERVICES

The **tourist office** (tel. 32/3355-1212, 9am-6pm Sun.-Thurs., 9am-8pm Fri.-Sat) is right on Largo da Forras. Free detailed maps with listings are available, as are lists of guides for hikes into the nearby Serra de São José. Online, check out www.tiradentes.mg.gov.br and www.guiatiradentes.com.br (both in Portuguese). A **Bradesco** bank (Rua Ministro Gabriel Passos 43) has ATMs that accept international cards.

Tiradentes is only a 25-minute bus ride from São João del Rei. Buses operated by **Presidente** (tel. 32/3371-5767) and **Vale de Ouro** (tel. 32/3371-5119) depart at 30-minute intervals. The tiny *rodoviária* is centrally located, just across the narrow river from Largo das Forras. By car, São João is only 10 minutes along BR-265. A taxi will cost around R$55.

If you're traveling Friday-Sunday or on a holiday, take advantage of the **Maria Fumaça** steam train (Smoking Mary), a 19th-century steam train running on one of the first railroad lines built in Brazil. Trains depart from the Tiradentes station (tel. 32/3371-8485, 1pm and 5pm Fri.-Sat., 11am and 2pm Sun. R$50 round-trip), a 10-minute walk from the center of town along Rua do Inconfidentes. Departing from São João (10am and 3pm Fri.-Sat., 10am and 1pm Sun.), sit on the left for the best views.

Diamantina

Diamantina is the only *cidade histórica* to the north of Belo Horizonte. Unlike Minas's other colonial towns, whose wealth was derived from gold, Diamantina's fortunes were sealed by the astonishing quantity of diamonds waiting to be harvested from the rocky Serra de Espinhaço mountains surrounding the town. Outcrops of these were discovered in the 18th century; once the word got out, this isolated region was mobbed by fortune seekers. For the next 150 years—until diamonds were found in South Africa—Diamantina was the largest producer of these glittery rocks in the world. What many don't know is that Diamantina is still the largest producer of diamonds in Brazil. Generations

Diamantina

Diamantina's colonial mansions and churches are encrusted into a precipitous mountain slope paved with enormous stones. Descents are marvelous, while ascents will leave you cursing, gasping, and wondering how the locals deal (they walk slowly and rely heavily on cars and motorcycles). However, the colonial historical center is quite compact. Make sure you come equipped with good walking shoes.

Churches

The nucleus of the *centro histórico* is the **Praça Conselheiro Mota,** which is dominated by the **Catedral de Santo Antônio** (8am-6pm daily). Striking from a distance, the mid-20th-century cathedral, devoted to the city's patron saint, is less inspiring close up. Diamantina's churches are simpler and less adorned than their glittery baroque counterparts in southern Minas. Their exteriors, with trims outlined in deep blues, ochers, and scarlets, are often more striking than the interiors.

Diamantina's oldest church, built in the 1720s, **Igreja Nossa Senhora do Rosário** (Largo do Rosário, 9:30am-11:30am and 1:30pm-5pm Tues.-Sat., 9:30-11:30 Sun., R$2) is curious for its slanted walls, floor, and altar columns; their crookedness is due to the fact that most of the construction was undertaken by slaves, who worked at night under terrible lighting conditions. The **Igreja São Francisco de Assis** (Rua São Francisco, 8am-noon and 2pm-5pm Tues.-Sat.) features a rococo interior as well as a bell tower from whose summit you have incomparable views of the *centro histórico.* The **Capela Imperial do Amparo** (9:30am-11:30am and 1:30pm-5pm Tues.-Sat., 9:30-11:30 Sun., R$2) mixes baroque and rococo elements. Don't leave without examining the wonderful nativity scene (on the right-side altar); made of tiny shells, it's more than 200 years old.

The most ornate of the lot is the **Igreja Nossa Senhora do Carmo** (Rua do Carmo, 2pm-5pm Tues. and Thurs-Sat., 9am-noon Sat.). Built in the 1760s, it has managed to

of miners, cutters, and jewelers still prosper, and the dream of striking it rich continues to nourish the locals, who were raised on tales of fortunes made and lost. The town is also very proud to be the birthplace of Brazil's eternally loved "bossa nova" president, Juscelino Kubitschek, the man responsible for building Brasília.

Instead of the lush slopes that surround Minas's other colonial towns, Diamantina is set against an arid, rocky landscape. It is also the gateway to the Jequitinonha Valley, a barren and isolated region that is dirt-poor but culturally rich, as can be seen by the famous clay sculptures and handicrafts that are sold in Diamantina's boutiques and market. Although its colonial treasures are much less ostentatious, Diamantina—declared a UNESCO World Heritage Site in 1999—is one of the most traditional and best preserved of the *cidades históricas.* While it has no stellar individual attractions, the town and surrounding landscape cast a captivating spell.

preserve its original gold leaf-covered organ, with 549 pipes.

Casa da Chica da Silva

Chica da Silva, former slave and then mistress of a wealthy diamond contractor named João Fernandes de Oliveira, was one of Brazil's most beloved heroines. Between 1763 and 1771 she lived in the handsome mansion João built for her across the street from the Igreja Nossa Senhora do Carmo. Known as **Casa da Chica da Silva** (Praça Lobo Mesquita, tel. 38/3531-2491, noon-5:30pm Tues.-Sat., 9am-noon Sun., free), the house disappointingly has few vestiges of its former resident, once the most powerful woman in Diamantina (the bell tower of the church was placed at the back so that the ringing bells wouldn't wake her). If you can, see Cacá Diegues's 1976 film *Xica da Silva,* with the incomparable singer/actress Zezé Mota in the title role.

Museu do Diamante

Offering more insight into Diamantina's past is the **Museu do Diamante** (Rua Direita 14, tel. 38/3531-1382, 10am-5pm Tues.-Sat., 9am-1pm Sun., R$1), in the former residence of Diamantina's bishop. A modest but intriguing display of objects ranges from diamond mining tools and some nasty torture equipment to colonial furnishings and a room full of beautifully wrought religious altars and saintly icons (some of the latter carved from local stone).

Casa de Juscelino Kubitschek

For a slice of more recent history, brave the steep climb up the Rua São Francisco to the **Casa de Juscelino Kubitschek** (Rua São Francisco 241, tel. 38/3531-3607, 8am-5pm Tues.-Sat., 8am-1pm Sun., R$3). This humble home is where Brazil's most beloved president (1902-1976) spent his childhood along with his strict but loving mother, Julia, and his older sister (his father died of tuberculosis when Juscelino was only three). It displays original furnishings, including a narrow bed, desk, and the books "Nono" (his childhood

nickname) pored over nightly in an attempt to better himself. Photos and some biographical info offer a surprisingly moving glimpse into Kubitschek's early life. Although the museum is fairly basic, it is Diamantina's most visited attraction.

Passadiço da Glória

One of Diamantina's architectural highlights is the **Passadiço da Glória,** a striking wooden passageway painted a rich blue that spans the steep Rua da Glória. It links two 18th-century buildings known collectively as the Casa da Glória, formerly the residence of diamond supervisors as well as the first bishop of Diamantina.

ENTERTAINMENT AND EVENTS

Both musical and religious traditions remain strong in Diamantina. Throughout the year, on certain Friday evenings, *serestas* are held, with bands of musicians parading through the *centro histórico* (beginning at Praça Juscelino Kubitschek and ending in front of the Mercado Municipal). *Vesperatas* (which take place two Saturdays a month May-October) is another musical event that dates back to the 19th century and attracts tourists from all over Brazil. They reserve tables at the outdoor bars in the Rua da Quitanda, which offer a view of traditionally clad musicians and singers who perform in the windows of the street's mansions while a maestro conducts them from the cobblestones (if you want a table, book one in advance with your hotel). Spurred on by the city's mushrooming student population, Carnaval has become a big draw for partying Mineiro youth. During Easter, **Semana Santa** festivities and processions are lively events (don't miss Easter Sunday, when the streets are decorated with tapestries of colored sand and sawdust) and in the first weekend in October, the city fills up with revelers who pay homage to **Nossa Senhora do Rosário.**

SHOPPING

Diamantina is a good place to buy jewels. More interesting—and infinitely more affordable—than diamonds is a local specialty known as *coco e ouro* (coconut and gold). This unusual confection came about as a result of the diamond rage that drew so many jewelers to Diamantina that there weren't enough buyers for their expensive wares. In response, some jewelers went down-market by cutting coconut husks, polishing them to a lustrous black, and encrusting them with gold, which was a by-product of more lucrative diamond mining. The most traditional place to buy stunning *coco e ouro* earrings and necklaces is at **Pádua** (Rua Campos Carvalho 43, tel. 38/3511-1116, 8am-6pm Mon.-Fri., 8am-1pm Sat.), a family-owned jewelry store that has been in business since 1888.

As the gateway to the Vale de Jequitinhona, Diamantina is also an ideal place to purchase the unique and much-celebrated artisanal work made by the craftspeople of this isolated valley region. Enormous ceramic dolls representing brides—most often hand-painted in tones of ocher and cream—are arresting, not only because of their size but also because of the expressions on the women's faces (said to be self-portraits of their makers). Also prized are ceramic vases, dried flower arrangements, and woven *arraiolo* carpets made from lamb's wool. **Relíquias do Vale** (Rua Macau do Meio 401, tel. 38/3531-1353) has an extensive selection of local art and handicrafts. In terms of quality, prices, and friendly service, the family-run **Arte do Vale** adjacent to the Mercado Municipal (Praça Barão de Guaicui 135, tel. 38/3531-6482) is also recommended.

Located in the always-lively central square of Praça Barão de Guaicui, it's hard to miss the **Mercado Municipal.** Painted blue and red, the wooden arches of this 19th-century market inspired Oscar Niemeyer's design of the presidential palace in Brasília. On Friday nights and Saturdays, the market buzzes with activity. Fresh produce, local handicrafts, homemade baked goods and other *mineiro* delicacies including *cachaças* are sold here. A local singer is usually on hand to supply a folksy background soundtrack.

ACCOMMODATIONS

Although there are some cheap hotels surrounding the bus station, due to the painfully steep climb from the *centro histórico,* your feet will thank you for forking out a little more money and opting to stay in the colonial thick of things.

R$50-200

Pousada Capistrana (Rua Campos Carvalho 35, tel. 38/3531-6560, www.pousadacapistrana.com.br, R$140 d) offers one of the best bargains in the *centro histórico* with small but spotless sunny rooms overlooking the Mercado Municipal and generous dollops of family-style hospitality. Also a good bargain is the **Pousada dos Cristais** (Rua Jogo da Bola 53, tel. 38/3531-3923, www.pousadadoscristais.com.br, R$90-130 d). Whether you choose a guest room in the main colonial house or one from the more recently constructed "panoramic" wing—which lives up to its name by offering private verandas with stunning views—the atmosphere is appealingly rustic.

For a complete and utter contrast to Diamantina's reigning colonial style, you can't do better than **Hotel Tijuco** (Rua Macau do Meio 211, tel. 38/3531-1022, www.hoteltijuco.com.br, R$150-200 d). In 1952, Juscelino Kubitschek—then governor of Minas Gerais—invited his friend and future Brasília collaborator, Oscar Niemeyer, to design a hotel for his home town. The result is this spacious, minimalist, and utterly stylish example of Brazilian modernism featuring luminous spaces, lots of natural woods, and original furnishings. Make sure to reserve a guest room with a veranda and (very impressive) view.

R$200-400

Carmen, the owner of ★ **Pousada Relíquias do Tempo** (Rua Macau de Baixo

104, tel. 38/3531-1627, www.pousadareliquias-dotempo.com.br, R$210-230 d) is the great-granddaughter of a Portuguese goldsmith who immigrated to Diamantina in the 19th century. She grew up in the rambling house he built and has kept its original furnishings intact while combing the region for antiques. Guests are invited to peruse her grandfather's leather-bound books in the library and marvel at the display of diamond mining paraphernalia in the Garimpeiro (miner) museum. One of the loveliest features is the open courtyard kitchen with its wood-burning oven. At the end of the afternoon, a bell summons guests to tea made from local herbs and leaves, served with homemade biscuits.

A comfortable marriage of past and present is found at **Pouso da Chica** (Rua Macau de Cima 115, tel. 38/3531-6190, www.pousodachica.com.br, R$265-370). The polished wooden floors and exposed adobe walls of the main colonial house create a traditional atmosphere, as does the smoke-scented wood-burning oven upon which cauldrons of hearty homemade soup and toasted bread greet guests every evening. Guest rooms, whether in the main house or one of seven charming bungalows built in the fruit orchard behind, offer more contemporary creature comforts: 400-thread-count cotton sheets, fluffy over-sized towels, and marble bathroom counters. Single and multiday Jeep outings can be organized to remote historic towns, splendid state parks, and waterfalls.

FOOD

Diamantina is a good place to sample *comida mineira*. You'll find a mélange of homecooked regional and globalized fare at **Apocalipse** (Praça Barão Guaicuí, tel. 38/3531-3242, 11:30am-3pm daily, R$15-25), a self-service per-kilo restaurant on the second floor of a light-suffused mansion overlooking the Mercado Municipal. For a light meal or snack amid what passes for urban fray, pull up a chair or bar stool at **Café A Baiuca** (Rua da Quitanda 13, tel. 38/3531-3181, 8am-midnight Mon.-Wed., 8am-2am Thurs.-Sat.,

9am-1pm Sun.). Choose from pancakes, omelets, sandwiches, or exotic local concoctions such as *linguiça com jiló* and *bolinhos crème de milho com carne seca* (creamed corn and sun-dried beef fritters). There are also delicious beers on tap. More charming and intimate is ★ **Espaço B Café** (Beco da Tecla 31, tel. 38/3531-6005, 9am-midnight Mon.-Sat., 10am-2pm Sun.), a laid-back bookstore where tomes and periodicals share shelf space with coffee beans and *cachaça* bottles; local bohos of all ages browse and converse over gourmet stuffed *paes de queijos* and other delicacies.

Occupying the *pousada* of the same name, **O Garimpeiro** (Av. da Saudade 265, tel. 38/3531-1040, 6pm-10pm Mon.-Fri., 11am-10pm Sat., 11am-4pm Sun., R$25-40) serves exceptional local dishes prepared with great flair. After learning how to cook from his grandmother as a boy, in his teenage years the chef, Vandeca, honed his skills by cooking grub for diamond miners up and down the Jequititonha Valley. He pays homage to his past in the mines with recipes such as *bambá do garimpo,* a robust stew of pork, collard greens, and pureed beans as well as *costelinhas com brotas de samambaia,* in which pork ribs are cooked with delicately pungent giant fern sprouts. Outdoor tables offer terrific panoramic views.

Al-Arabe (Praça Dr. Prado 124, tel. 38/3531-2281, 10am-2am Mon.-Sat., R$25-35) is a decent Middle Eastern restaurant that does the standard recipes proud. Appetizers and mains are best enjoyed at the scenic outdoor tables with views of the large square backed by jagged mountains.

TRANSPORTATION AND SERVICES

The municipal **tourist office** (Praça Antônio Eulálio 53, tel. 38/3531-9532, 9am-6pm Mon.-Sat., 9am-2pm Sun.) provides free city maps and information about events in Diamantina as well as how to contact a guide to surrounding attractions. Online resources include www.diamantina.mg.gov.br and www.diamantina.com.br (both in Portuguese).

Curralinho

unfailingly delicious homecooked Mineiro specialties. Spending a night is an ideal way to come into contact with traditional rural Mineiro life and lifestyles (and delicious local moonshine). All are surrounded by stunning mountain landscapes carpeted with striking Cerrado vegetation, much of which is preserved within a quartet of natural parks: Parque Estadual do Biribiri, Parque Nacional dos Sempre-Vivas, Parque Estadual do Rio Preto, and Parque Estadual do Pico do Itambé. The possibilities for hiking, climbing, and waterfall plunging are endless.

Buses here are few, slow, or nonexistent. Rent a car (although many roads are unpaved and mountainous) or take a guided single or multiday tour with **Minhas Gerais** (Rua Direita 68, tel. 38/3531-1667, www.minhagerais.com).

From Belo Horizonte's *rodoviária*, **Pássaro Verde** (tel. 31/3073-7575, www.passaroverde.com.br) offers eight buses daily to Diamantina (5 hours, R$80). In Diamantina, the bus station is a very steep 15-minute walk (or cab ride) from the center. By car, follow highways BR-040 and BR-105 north from Belo Horizonte to Curvelo, then take BR-259 and BR-367, which pass through the town of Gouveia.

AROUND DIAMANTINA

The area surrounding Diamantina is extremely rich in both natural and cultural attractions. Within close proximity are charmingly bucolic historical towns and villages such as Biribiri, São Gonçalo do Rio Preto, São João da Chapada, Mendanha, São Gonçalo do Rio Preto, Curralinho, São Gonçalo do Rio das Pedras, Milho Verde, and Serro. All possess preserved colonial architecture and languourous rhythms, with simple yet comfortable B&B-style *pousadas* and restaurant/bars serving humongous portions of

★ Caminho de Escravos

The **Caminho de Escravos** is an old slave road, part of the Estrada Real that was cut into the mountains by thousands of African slaves who were also used to transport loads of diamonds down to Rio de Janeiro and Paraty on the Atlantic coast. Although the road weaves through the mountains for 20 kilometers (12 mi) to the historic hamlet of Mendanha, you need only walk 3-4 kilometers (2-2.5 mi) to take advantage of stunning views of the town and surrounding peaks and valleys. The road begins in a steep descent from the Mercado Municipal; if you plan anything longer than a stroll, do so in the company of a local or guide.

Gruta do Salitre and Curralinho

Gruta do Salitre (9am-noon and 2pm-5pm Sat.) sits 9 kilometers (5 mi) south of Diamantina on the dusty road leading to the historic village of Curralinho. This ancient quartzite cave sits hidden amidst a fantastical landscape of sculptural rocks whose rough-hewn towers resemble a gothic cathedral. Although you can inspect the cave and surrounding terrain, it's best to get tips (and if possible a guide) from **Instituto Biotrópicos**

(Praça Juscelino Kubitschek 25, tel. 38/3531-2197, www.biotropicos.org.br), the NGO that administers and studies the Gruta. It's worth going the extra mile (literally) to picturesque **Curralinho,** where you can kick back with a cachaça and some lipsmacking *comida caseira* specialties at **Pousada do Tropeiro** (Rua Mestre João Coimbra 15, tel. 38/3531-2418).

Biribiri

A popular full- or half-day trip is a visit to **Biribiri** (www.biribiri.com.br). This 19th-century village grew up around a now-defunct fabric factory and features a collection of warehouses, workers' residences (some can be rented by tourists), a school, and a church. A small but still thriving restaurant, **Ramiundo Sem Braço** (10am-6pm, Tues.-Sun.) serves food and drink throughout the day while the Rio Biribiri supplies refreshing waters for bathing. Biribiri is 18 kilometers (11 mi) north from Diamantina; take BR-367 to Km 587 and turn onto the signed dirt road. Along the way, stop off for a refreshing dip at the **Cachoeira da Sentinela** (9 km/6 mi) and **Cachoeira dos Cristais** (16 km/10 mi), two waterfalls that cascade into very cold natural swimming pools. If you don't have a car, you can take a taxi, moto-taxi, or an organized excursion.

Garimpo Real

If all the allusions to fortunes found incite treasure-seeking urges, do some diamond mining of your own with a guide using traditional panning techniques. The **Garimpo Real** (BR-367, km 10, tel. 38/3531-1557, 8am-3pm, R$30) is some 25 kilometers (16 mi) from town. Advance reservations are necessary; call the owner, Belmiro.

Brasília, Goiás, and the Pantanal

Look for ★ to find recommended sights, activities, dining, and lodging.

Highlights

Niemeyer in Brasília comprises gleaming masterpieces of modernist architecture (pages 289 and 290).

★ **Parque Nacional da Chapada dos Veadeiros:** Fantastic rock outcrops, myriad waterfalls, and lots of positive energy emanating from quartz crystals make this national park an invigorating eco-retreat (page 302).

★ *Centro Histórico* **of Goiás Velho:** The former gold mining town and first capital of Goiás is one of the best-preserved and most atmospheric colonial towns in Brazil (page 305).

★ **Parque Nacional da Chapada dos Guimarães:** This park offers natural grandeur, with scores of waterfalls, tropical foliage, and a wealth of colorful birdlife (page 314).

★ **The Pantanal's** *Fazenda* **Lodges:** The best way of getting up close to the amazing wildlife that inhabits the planet's largest wetlands is to check into one of the cattle ranch eco-resorts within its depths (pages 317, 323, and 324).

★ *Flutuação* **in Bonito:** The highlight of this ecological hot spot is donning snorkeling gear and "floating" down rivers so clear and crammed with fish that you'd swear you'd fallen into an aquarium (page 330).

★ **Esplanada dos Ministérios and the Praça dos Três Poderes:** The futuristic complex of government palaces designed by Oscar

sília

ital located in the heart of the country is as old as the Brazilian republic,
it as early as the dawn of the 19th century. In the 1890s, Congress once
went so far as to send an expedition into the Planalto (high plains) of
sisted of little more than decaying gold-mining towns, cattle ranches,
until the 1950s that **Juscelino Kubitschek,** former mayor of Belo
inas Gerais, made the new capital a central tenet of his 1955 campaign
zil's president. When the victorious Kubitschek took power in early 1956,
work. Through aerial surveys, a site was quickly chosen. An international
g plan submitted by **Lucio Costa,** a young urban designer. Working
ngtime collaborators of Kubitschek's who had contributed to daring
andscaper Roberto Burle Marx (responsible for Copacabana's famous
ct Oscar Niemeyer, who was a former pupil of Le Corbusier, the brilliant
ate of geometrically planned cities.

ilia followed Le Corbusier's precepts of rectilinear order while playing
w buildings, wide boulevards, and vast green expanses. His goal was to
less horizon, drawing the eye to the point at which the red earth meets
a once commented: "The sky is the sea of Brasília." Indeed, what makes
ast of gleaming white buildings set against green lawns and azure skies.
adhered to Le Corbusier's principles, he also subverted (and improved)
ves to otherwise linear buildings. Softening what could have otherwise
an uniformity, he imbued his buildings with an organic, even playful
ith a tropical aesthetic and with the Brazilian personality as a whole.

Brasília into a
icated gastro-
by that of Rio
offerings are
nding number
he surround-
ngular vegeta-
and countless

turistic as its
plane (as most
's-eye view of
an airplane or
s. Lucio Costa
to (Pilot Plan).
o matter how
it helps if you
of the city into
and tail.

the **Eixo**
xis), is an 8-ki-
ne boulevards

that runs east-west from the **Praça do
Cruzeiro** (the plane's tail) to **Praça dos
Três Poderes** (the head, or cockpit). Running
north-south and intersecting with the Eixo
Monumental, the **Eixo Rodoviário** (known
as the "Eixão") is a curving artery that forms
the wings of the bird or plane. At the intersection of the two Eixos is the city's transportation hub: the municipal **Rodoviária do
Plano Piloto.**

Another signature feature of Brasília is its
organization into zones. For instance, the
Eixo Monumental is lined with government
buildings, monuments, and museums, but is
also divided into specific *setores* ("S") that
concentrate clusters of banks (Setor Bancário),
hotels (Setor Hoteleiro), and commercial areas
(Setor Comércio). Sectors themselves are further subdivided into *blocos* ("Bl."), which are
large buildings; *conjuntos* ("Cj."), which are
building subdivisions; *lojas* ("Lj."), or stores;
and *lotes* ("Lt."), or lots.

The two "wings" of the bird or plane that
branch off either side of the Eixo Monumental

More than 50 years ago, Juscelino
Kubitschek was elected Brazil's
president, largely as a result of his wildly
ambitious plans to construct a capital from scratch right in the
middle of Brazil (i.e., in the middle of nowhere).

To carry out this endeavor, he hired architect Oscar Niemeyer and urban planner Lúcio
Costa. Construction began in 1957, and three
years later, Brasília—the world's most famous
and controversial planned city—was unveiled.
Over the years, Brasília's unearthly charms
have seduced architecture buffs from around
the globe.

One of Brasília's raisons d'être was to facilitate the opening up of the vast and isolated
interior of Brazil's Central-West, a region of
elevated plains whose unique landscape,
the Cerrado, conjures up the muted colors
and scrubby foliage of East Africa's savannas. As a result, the city is an ideal departure point for exploring natural and cultural
treasures located in the surrounding state of
Goiás. Highlights include the Chapada de
Veadeiros, whose surreal rock formations,
bathed by numerous waterfalls, are a hiker's
paradise, as well as the charming colonial

towns of Pirenópolis and Goiás Velho, which
are largely overlooked by foreign visitors.

Beyond Goiás, straddling the Wild West
frontier states of Mato Grosso and Mato
Grosso do Sul, lies one of the most fantastically diverse ecosystems on the planet. Larger
than Great Britain, the Pantanal (which
means "swamp") is an ecotourist's dream.
Caimans, jaguars, anacondas, capybaras (the
world's largest rodents), and brilliantly hued
exotic birds are just a few of the fauna you're
likely to meet. The more than 200 species of
fish that live in the Pantanal's rivers make it
one of the best places in the world for freshwater fishing—and for eating (make sure to
try the piranha soup). Rivaling the flocks of
birds and schools of fish are great herds of cattle whose presence accounts for vast ranches;
some, nestled deep within the Pantanal, double as wildlife reserves and eco-resorts.

Close to the Mato Grosso capital of
Cuiabá lies the Chapada dos Guimarães, a

Previous: Parque Nacional da Chapada dos Guimarães; a cobblestone street in Goiás. **Above:** Congresso
Nacional building, Brasília.

Brasília, Goiás, and the Pantanal

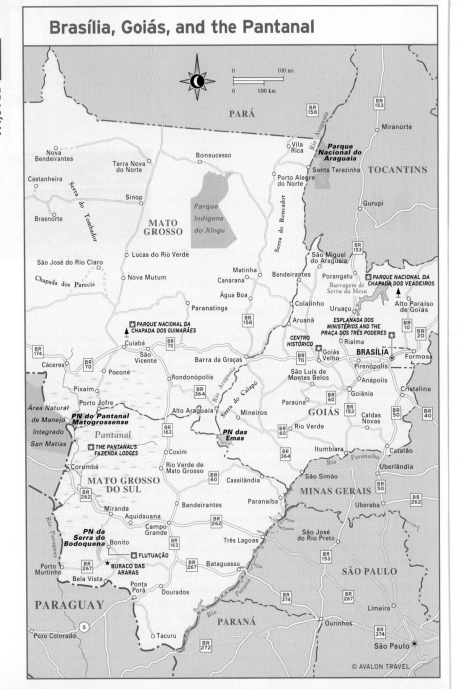

© AVALON TRAVEL

magnificent series of c
falls that offers great
of the oldest tectonic
Grand Canyon gone
Mato Grosso do Sul's
the unspoiled nature
of Bonito constitutes
example of sustainab
pure, crystalline wa
flutuação, a sport th
snorkel, mask, and li
the current carry you
shoulders with a da
tropical fish. Since
are off the proverbia
and traveling throug
an adventure in itsel

PLANNING

Despite the fact that
than any other reg
cally it is in the m
linking major citic
shape, but distance
is easily reached
more remote cities
Grosso do Sul (Cu
Corumbá) are rarel
and nearby attrac
and the Chapada d
you could comfort
(unless you're a di
chitecture, you ca
attractions in one
to have substanti

Brasília

Some people go g
ers find it arid a
most famous pl
mecca of modern
different. Indisp
the most stunni
chitecture on th
recognition as a

Building

The idea of a new Braz
and was being bandie
again resurrected the
Goiás, which, at the ti
and Indian territory. It
Horizonte and govern
platform to get electec
he lost no time in gett
competition yielded a
alongside Costa were
projects in Belo Horizc
mosaic walkway), and a
French modernist and

Lucio Costa's plan fc
up the element of space
emphasize the Planalto
the luminous blue skies
the city so striking is the
As for Niemeyer, althou
them by adding sensuo
taken on shades of tota
sensibility more in keepi

dignitaries, has transform
cosmopolitan place. Its sop
nomic scene is surpassed o
and São Paulo and its cult
world-class. There are an as
of parks within the city, ar
ing Cerrado beckons with it
tion, unusual rock formatio
waterfalls.

ORIENTATION

Brasília's urban design is as
architecture. If you arrive b
do), you'll be treated to a bi
the city's layout in the shape
a bird with outstretched win
referred to this as the Plano Pi
Once you're on the ground,
confusing Brasília might seer
keep in mind this organizatio
the bird or plane's head, body

The body, known a
Monumental (Monumental
lometer (5-mi) strip of multi

More than 50 years ago, Juscelino Kubitschek was elected Brazil's president, largely as a result of his wildly ambitious plans to construct a capital from scratch right in the middle of Brazil (i.e., in the middle of nowhere).

To carry out this endeavor, he hired architect Oscar Niemeyer and urban planner Lúcio Costa. Construction began in 1957, and three years later, Brasília—the world's most famous and controversial planned city—was unveiled. Over the years, Brasília's unearthly charms have seduced architecture buffs from around the globe.

One of Brasília's raisons d'être was to facilitate the opening up of the vast and isolated interior of Brazil's Central-West, a region of elevated plains whose unique landscape, the Cerrado, conjures up the muted colors and scrubby foliage of East Africa's savannas. As a result, the city is an ideal departure point for exploring natural and cultural treasures located in the surrounding state of Goiás. Highlights include the Chapada de Veadeiros, whose surreal rock formations, bathed by numerous waterfalls, are a hiker's paradise, as well as the charming colonial towns of Pirenópolis and Goiás Velho, which are largely overlooked by foreign visitors.

Beyond Goiás, straddling the Wild West frontier states of Mato Grosso and Mato Grosso do Sul, lies one of the most fantastically diverse ecosystems on the planet. Larger than Great Britain, the Pantanal (which means "swamp") is an ecotourist's dream. Caimans, jaguars, anacondas, capybaras (the world's largest rodents), and brilliantly hued exotic birds are just a few of the fauna you're likely to meet. The more than 200 species of fish that live in the Pantanal's rivers make it one of the best places in the world for freshwater fishing—and for eating (make sure to try the piranha soup). Rivaling the flocks of birds and schools of fish are great herds of cattle whose presence accounts for vast ranches; some, nestled deep within the Pantanal, double as wildlife reserves and eco-resorts.

Close to the Mato Grosso capital of Cuiabá lies the Chapada dos Guimarães, a

---

Previous: Parque Nacional da Chapada dos Guimarães; a cobblestone street in Goiás. **Above:** Congresso Nacional building, Brasília.

Brasília, Goiás, and the Pantanal

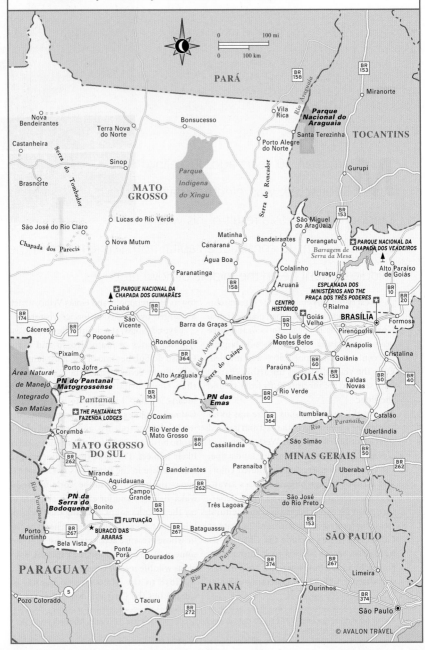

magnificent series of cliffs, gorges, and water-falls that offers great hiking. Located on one of the oldest tectonic plates, it resembles the Grand Canyon gone tropical. Not far from Mato Grosso do Sul's capital, Campo Grande, the unspoiled nature surrounding the town of Bonito constitutes Brazil's most successful example of sustainable ecotourism. Bonito's pure, crystalline waters have given rise to *flutuação,* a sport that involves donning a snorkel, mask, and lifejacket and then letting the current carry you downriver while you rub shoulders with a dazzlingly colorful array of tropical fish. Since many of these attractions are off the proverbial beaten track, getting to and traveling through these unique regions is an adventure in itself.

PLANNING YOUR TIME

Despite the fact that Brasília is growing faster than any other region in Brazil, geographically it is in the middle of nowhere. Roads linking major cities are actually in decent shape, but distances are enormous. Brasília is easily reached by plane; flights to the more remote cities of Mato Grosso and Mato Grosso do Sul (Cuiabá, Campo Grande, and Corumbá) are rarely direct. Excluding Brasília and nearby attractions such as Pirenópolis and the Chapada dos Veadeiros—all of which you could comfortably fit into a **5-6-day trip** (unless you're a die-hard fan of modernist architecture, you can see most of Brasília's top attractions in one very full day)—you'll need to have substantial time at your disposal. It's

well worth spending **3-4 days** in Goiás Velho, one of the loveliest of Brazil's historic towns—not only because of its distance, but also to soak up its languid colonial atmosphere and immerse yourself in its unspoiled landscapes. Reserve at least a week for Mato Grosso, where you can spend **2-3 days** in the Chapada dos Guimarães and the remaining time exploring the northern Pantanal. Similarly, a week is recommended for Mato Grosso do Sul; aside from the southern Pantanal, you might want to explore Bonito, whose natural attractions deserve at least **2-3 days**.

Brasília and Goiás are best visited during the dry season, **April-October**. During this time, skies are impossibly blue, and during the winter months of June-early August, temperatures tend to be comfortable (around 22°C/75°F), but can be considerably cooler in the mountains and even in the Pantanal, especially at night. April-June, the blooming wildflowers turn the normally scrubby, dun-colored Cerrado into a patchwork of color. In late August-October things heat up considerably, with temperatures easily hitting 38°C (100°F), although nights are usually a little cooler. In Brasília, the Saharan heat and dryness can become quite unbearable; even locals complain of parched throats and nosebleeds. As for the Pantanal, the rainy season (Nov.-Mar.) turns the wetlands into a lush landscape, but makes both wildlife observation and transportation difficult. For this reason, the dry season (May-Sept.) is usually preferred for travel.

Brasília

Some people go gaga over Brasília, while others find it arid and alienating. The world's most famous planned city and undisputed mecca of modernism doesn't leave anyone indifferent. Indisputably, Brasília concentrates the most stunning ensemble of modernist architecture on the planet, a fact that earned it recognition as a UNESCO World Heritage Site

in 1987. If you are interested in 20th-century architecture, a pilgrimage to this meticulously planned city—a decidedly retro 1950s and 1960s futuristic version of utopia—is an absolute must.

Brasília does hold other attractions. The presence of the nation's political elite, along with international diplomats and visiting

Building Brasília

The idea of a new Brazilian capital located in the heart of the country is as old as the Brazilian republic, and was being bandied about as early as the dawn of the 19th century. In the 1890s, Congress once again resurrected the plan. It went so far as to send an expedition into the Planalto (high plains) of Goiás, which, at the time, consisted of little more than decaying gold-mining towns, cattle ranches, and Indian territory. It wasn't until the 1950s that **Juscelino Kubitschek,** former mayor of Belo Horizonte and governor of Minas Gerais, made the new capital a central tenet of his 1955 campaign platform to get elected as Brazil's president. When the victorious Kubitschek took power in early 1956, he lost no time in getting to work. Through aerial surveys, a site was quickly chosen. An international competition yielded a winning plan submitted by **Lucio Costa,** a young urban designer. Working alongside Costa were two longtime collaborators of Kubitschek's who had contributed to daring projects in Belo Horizonte: Landscaper Roberto Burle Marx (responsible for Copacabana's famous mosaic walkway), and architect Oscar Niemeyer, who was a former pupil of Le Corbusier, the brilliant French modernist and advocate of geometrically planned cities.

Lucio Costa's plan for Brasília followed Le Corbusier's precepts of rectilinear order while playing up the element of space—low buildings, wide boulevards, and vast green expanses. His goal was to emphasize the Planalto's endless horizon, drawing the eye to the point at which the red earth meets the luminous blue skies. Costa once commented: "The sky is the sea of Brasília." Indeed, what makes the city so striking is the contrast of gleaming white buildings set against green lawns and azure skies. As for Niemeyer, although he adhered to Le Corbusier's principles, he also subverted (and improved) them by adding sensuous curves to otherwise linear buildings. Softening what could have otherwise taken on shades of totalitarian uniformity, he imbued his buildings with an organic, even playful sensibility more in keeping with a tropical aesthetic and with the Brazilian personality as a whole.

dignitaries, has transformed Brasília into a cosmopolitan place. Its sophisticated gastronomic scene is surpassed only by that of Rio and São Paulo and its cultural offerings are world-class. There are an astounding number of parks within the city, and the surrounding Cerrado beckons with its singular vegetation, unusual rock formations, and countless waterfalls.

ORIENTATION

Brasília's urban design is as futuristic as its architecture. If you arrive by plane (as most do), you'll be treated to a bird's-eye view of the city's layout in the shape of an airplane or a bird with outstretched wings. Lucio Costa referred to this as the Plano Piloto (Pilot Plan). Once you're on the ground, no matter how confusing Brasília might seem, it helps if you keep in mind this organization of the city into the bird or plane's head, body, and tail.

The body, known as the **Eixo Monumental** (Monumental Axis), is an 8-kilometer (5-mi) strip of multilane boulevards

that runs east-west from the **Praça do Cruzeiro** (the plane's tail) to **Praça dos Três Poderes** (the head, or cockpit). Running north-south and intersecting with the Eixo Monumental, the **Eixo Rodoviário** (known as the "Eixão") is a curving artery that forms the wings of the bird or plane. At the intersection of the two Eixos is the city's transportation hub: the municipal **Rodoviária do Plano Piloto.**

Another signature feature of Brasília is its organization into zones. For instance, the Eixo Monumental is lined with government buildings, monuments, and museums, but is also divided into specific *setores* ("S") that concentrate clusters of banks (Setor Bancário), hotels (Setor Hoteleiro), and commercial areas (Setor Comércio). Sectors themselves are further subdivided into *blocos* ("Bl."), which are large buildings; *conjuntos* ("Cj."), which are building subdivisions; *lojas* ("Lj."), or stores; and *lotes* ("Lt."), or lots.

The two "wings" of the bird or plane that branch off either side of the Eixo Monumental

are actually referred to as wings: curving south is the Asa Sul (South Wing) and swinging north is the Asa Norte (North Wing). Both of these sweeping districts are largely residential, with numbered apartment blocks known as **quadras** ("Qd.") and **superquadras** ("SQ"). Instead of names, roads are numbered according to their distance from the main Eixo and whether they are north ("N") or south ("S") of the Eixo Monumental and east ("L") or ("W") west of the Eixo Rodoviário.

Despite this precision, Brasília can be both easy and incredibly confusing to navigate. The problem isn't so much the uniformity of the buildings but trying to decipher addresses.

SIGHTS

It will take you a full day at minimum to visit Brasília's architectural marvels. Although most are located along the Eixo Monumental, its length, coupled with the inevitably scalding sun, means you'll have to combine walking with buses (104 and 108) and taxis to get from one end to the other. Even so, wear sunscreen, carry mineral water, and dress lightly (although no flip-flops, shorts, or tank tops, since many of the sights are government buildings with dress codes).

Eixo Monumental

It's best to start at the tail end of the **Eixo Monumental.** From the lofty height of Praça do Cruzeiro, you are treated to an impressive view down the Eixo toward the Esplanada dos Ministérios. Surveying the scene is a monumental bronze statue of Juscelino Kubitschek inside a curving half-shell.

MEMORIAL JK

An appropriate beginning to your exploration of Brasília is to pay homage to its founder at Niemeyer's **Memorial JK** (Praça do Cruzeiro, tel. 61/3225-9451, www.memorialjk.com.br, 9am-6pm Tues.-Sun., R$10). Constructed out of white marble, its resemblance to an Egyptian pyramid is hardly coincidental. This reverential museum and shrine was inaugurated in 1981, five years after Kubitschek's

untimely death in a car accident. You can inspect Kubitschek's personal objects, clothing (JK was a notorious dandy), and library. Photographs of the president's life and the construction of his dream capital provide an excellent overview of the city's foundation and early years. Upstairs is the mortuary chamber where Kubitschek's body rests in a black marble sarcophagus, illuminated by colorful beams filtered through a roof of stained glass. This striking piece was designed by artist Marianne Peretti, who contributed many works to Brasília. Particularly moving is the simple epitaph engraved on JK's tomb: "O Fundador" (The Founder).

MEMORIAL DOS POVOS INDÍGENAS

Niemeyer's cylindrical **Memorial dos Povos Indígenas** (Praça do Buriti, tel. 61/3344-1154, 9am-5pm Tues.-Fri., 10am-5pm Sat.-Sun., free) imitates the traditional round dwellings of the Yanomami Indians. The curving interior shelters an impressive collection of indigenous art—baskets, jewelry, weapons, hammocks, and feather headdresses—the majority made by groups from the surrounding Planalto region, especially around the Rio Xingu. Particularly striking are the ceramic vessels made by the Warao people, intricately decorated with bird and animal motifs.

TORRE DE TELEVISÃO

Grab a bus or taxi down the Eixo Monumental to reach the **Torre de Televisão** (tel. 61/3323-7944, 8am-8pm daily, free), the tallest metallic structure in Latin America. A third of the way up Lucio Costa's 224-meter (735-foot) television tower is the viewing deck, with incredible 360-degree views of the city—particularly bewitching around sunset. On the main floor is the *feira hippie* (a small crafts market, weekends), a good place to pick up regional handicrafts.

TEATRO NACIONAL CLÁUDIO SANTORO

Cross the Eixo Rodoviário, and on the north side of the Rodoviária do Plano Piloto you'll

Brasília

© AVALON TRAVEL

Jardim Zoológico de Brasília

Jardim Botânico de Brasília

AEROPORTO INTERNACIONAL DE BRASÍLIA

DF-047

DF-025

QI-1
QI-2
QI-3
QL-2
QL-3
QL-4
QL-5
QL-6
QL-10

ESTRADA PARQUE PENÍNSULA SUL

PENÍNSULA SUL DOM BOSCO

QI-11

SETOR DE HABITAÇÕES INDIVIDUAIS SUL

SETOR DE CLUBES ESPORTIVOS SUL

0   1 km
0   1 mi

TEMPLO DA BOA VONTADE ★

Cimitério da Esperança

Parque da Cidade

913 SUL SESC HOTEL ●

316 116 315 115 314 114 313 313 312 312 311 311 310
216 275 214 273 213 212 211 210
416 475 414 413 412 411
616 615 614 613 612 611
815

VIA W5 SUL
915 914 913 912 911 910
VIA W3 SUL 712 711 710 709 708 VIA W5 SUL 706 705 704
SMHS
VIA W1 SUL BAR 108 107 106 105 BRASÍLIA 305 SHS
EIXO RODOVIÁRIO BAR BEIRUTE 110 TUPINIQUIM ▼ VERSÃO ▼
209 INÁCIA 202 DON DÚRICA
409 408 207 208 205 POULET 404 ROTI 402
608 VIA LT SUL 204 GATE'S PUB 602
603 VIA L2 SUL

SANTUÁRIO DOM BOSCO ✠
MUSEU NACIONAL ▲
GRENAT CAFÉS ▼
SBS
CATEDRAL METROPOLITANA ✠
SAS
MUSEU DE VALORES
MANGAI ●

AV. DAS NAÇÕES

PIER 21 ■

MONUMENTAL

SEE DETAIL

To Ermida Dom Bosco

SEE DETAIL

0   200 yds
0   200 m

PALÁCIO ITAMARATY ★
ESPLANADA DOS MINISTÉRIOS ✚
PALÁCIO DA JUSTIÇA ★
VIA N UM LESTE
VIA N UM LESTE
OS CANDANGOS ★
VIA N DOIS LESTE
CONGRESSO NACIONAL ★
VIA S UM LESTE
CENTRO CULTURAL TRÊS PODERES ★
VIA S DOIS LESTE
PRAÇA DOS TRÊS PODERES ✚
PALÁCIO DO PLANALTO ★
SUPREMO TRIBUNAL FEDERAL ★
PANTEÃO DA PÁTRIA ★

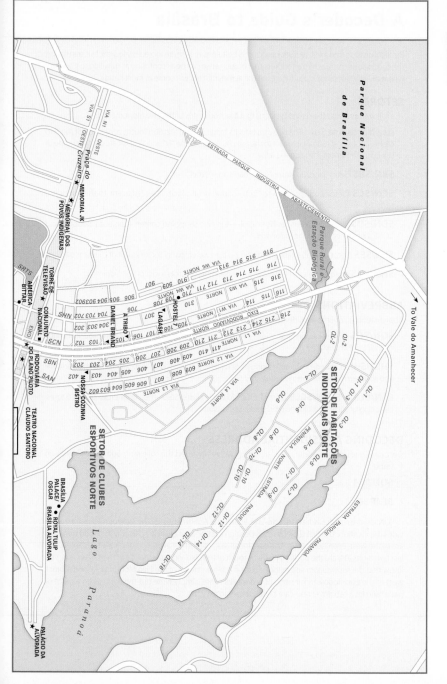

Parque Nacional de Brasília

Parque Rural e Estação Biológica

ESTRADA PARQUE INDUSTRIA E ABASTECIEMENTO

→ To Vale do Amanhecer

VIA ST
VIA N1
OESTE
OESTE Cruzeiro
Praça do
MEMORIAL JK ★
POVOS INDÍGENAS
MEMORIAL DOS

SRTS
AMÉRICA
BITTAR ■
TORRE DE
TELEVISÃO ★
CONJUNTO
NACIONAL ■
SCN
EIXO
RODOVIÁRIA
DO PLANO PILOTO ★
★
SBN
SAN
NVS
★
TEATRO NACIONAL
CLÁUDIO SANTORO

916 915 914 913 VIA W5 NORTE
716 715 714 713 712 711 VIA W4 NORTE
910 909 907
906 905 904 903 902
316 315 VIA W3 NORTE 710 709 708
116 115 114 VIA W1 NORTE 709 708
310 HOSTEL ●
A TRIBO ▼ 307 LAGASH ▼
DANIEL BRIAND ▼ 706
705 704 703 702 NHS
304 303 302
103 102
216 215 214 213 212 211 210 VIA L1 EIXO RODOVIÁRIO NORTE 108 109
402 NOSSA COZINHA BISTRO ▼ 403 404 405 406 407 408 409 410 411 VIA L2 NORTE
202 203 204 205 206 207 208 209
607 606 605 604 603 602 608 609 VIA L3 NORTE
VIA L4 NORTE

SETOR DE CLUBES
ESPORTIVOS NORTE

SETOR DE HABITAÇÕES
INDIVIDUAIS NORTE

QI-1
QI-2
QL-1 QI-3
QL-3
QL-4
QL-6 QI-5
QI-7
QI-9 QL-5
QL-7
QI-11
QI-13
QL-9
QI-8 PENÍNSULA NORTE
ESTRADA PARQUE NORTE
ESTRADA PARQUE PARANOÁ
QL-10
QL-12
QI-14
QI-16
QL-14
QL-16

Lago
Paranoá

BRASÍLIA
PALACE/ ●
OSCAR
BRASÍLIA ALVORADA
ROYAL TULIP
BRASÍLIA ALVORADA

PALÁCIO DA
ALVORADA ★

A Decoder's Guide to Brasília

Brasília's division into axes, sectors, blocks, and buildings may seem incredibly logical, but translating the coded abbreviations into an address that makes sense can be as confusing as traveling to a country where only Cyrillic script is used. Here are the acronyms that will come in most handy.

SETORES

The following refer to the *setores* (sectors) that line both sides of the Eixo Monumental.

- **Asa Norte/Asa Sul**—The two *asas* (wings), Norte (North) and Sul (South), curving off of the Eixo Monumental and running parallel to the Eixo Rodoviário. The "N" and "S" indicate on which side of the Eixo Monumental an address falls.

- **SBN/SBS** (Setor Bancário Norte/Sul)—banking sectors

- **SCN/SCS** (Setor Comercial Norte/Sul)—commercial office areas (adjacent to the shopping centers)

- **SDN/SDS** (Setor de Diversões Norte/Sul)—the two shopping centers (Conjunto Nacional and CONIC) on either side of the *rodoviária*

- **SEN/SES** (Setor de Embaixadas Norte/Sul)—the two embassy sectors (east of the bank sectors)

- **SHN/SHS** (Setor Hoteleiro Norte/Sul)—the two hotel sectors (west of the *rodoviária*)

ABBREVIATIONS

Abbreviations in the main residential areas are as follows:

- **SQN/SQS** (Superquadras Norte/Sul)—the individual *superquadras* in the main residential wings of Asa Norte and Asa Sul

- **SHIN/SHIS** (Setor de Habitações Individuais Norte/Sul)—residential zones around the northern and southern banks of Lago Paranoá

- **CLN/CLS** or **SCLN/SCLS** (Setor Comércio Local Norte/Sul)—the commercial blocks (stores, bars, restaurants) set amid the residential *superquadras*

DECODING A RESIDENTIAL ADDRESS

Decoding a residential address can be tricky. We've decoded the following address below as an example.

- **SQN 204**

- **Bl. B-303**

SQN refers to *superquadra* north, No. 204, Building B, Apartment 303. The *superquadra* number provides the location: The first digit (2) is the position east or west of the Eixo Rodoviário (odd numbers are to the west, even numbers to the east, increasing the farther away you get from the center). The last two digits (04) are the position north or south of the Eixo Monumental. So in the case of 204, you know that the *superquadra* you're looking for is 4 blocks north of the Eixo Monumental and 1 block west of the Eixo Rodoviário. If none of this makes sense, simply write out the address on a piece of paper and let a cab driver take care of the decoding for you.

come face to face with another Niemeyer pyramid housing Brasília's prestigious **Teatro Nacional Cláudio Santoro** (tel. 61/3325-6277, 3pm-5pm daily). Dazzling from the outside, its glass-covered surface permits natural light to suffuse the lobby, where art exhibitions are displayed. The lateral facades embossed with a sea of white cubes and rectangles are the work of Athos Bulcão, while the surrounding gardens featuring native plants are by Roberto Burle Marx. In the foyer, the lyrical bronze statue *O Contorcionista* (*The Contortionist*) is by noted sculptor Alfredo Ceschiatti. Three separate auditoriums host theatrical productions as well as concerts, dance, and ballet performances. Guided tours are available.

MUSEU DE VALORES

An easy 15-minute walk south from the *rodoviária*, you can't miss the towering skyscrapers of concrete and dark glass that house the Edifício-Sede do Banco Central. At the rear of the Central Bank building, the **Museu de Valores** (SBS, Qd. 3, Bl. B, tel. 61/3414-2099, 10am-5:30pm Tues.-Fri., 2pm-6pm Sat., free) traces Brazilian history via its many monies: from the first coins minted in Portugal to today's remarkably stable *real*. The

most fascinating section is devoted to a history of gold in different forms, ranging from the ingots featuring the emperor's official stamp to the largest gold nugget ever found in the world, a 61-kilo (135-pound) chunk that was uncovered in the Amazon region.

★ ESPLANADA DOS MINISTÉRIOS

Approaching the Praça dos Três Poderes along the Eixo Monumental, you'll be confronted with the **Esplanada dos Ministérios,** an enormous corridor of 17 identical government buildings facing each other from opposite sides of the street. At the very beginning of the Esplanada, you'll find two of Niemeyer's most recent works, the **Biblioteca Nacional** (National Library) and the **Museu Nacional** (tel. 61/3325-5220, 9am-6:30pm Tues.-Sun., free). Completed in 2006, both buildings were part of Niemeyer's original plans for the Eixo. The gleaming dome-shaped museum, whose cavernous interior features the architect's signature swirling ramps, is only open for temporary art exhibitions.

CATEDRAL METROPOLITANA

One of Niemeyer's undisputed masterpieces is the **Catedral Metropolitana de Nossa Senhora da Aparecida** (tel. 61/3224-4073,

Catedral Metropolitana de Nossa Senhora da Aparecida

8am-6pm Sun.-Fri., 8am-5pm Sat.). Built on the spot where Brasília was inaugurated, the cathedral's graceful hourglass structure consists of 16 reinforced concrete columns whose thorny tips thrust skyward. The columns provide support for the immense panes of stained glass designed by Marianne Peretti that make the subterranean church seem bathed in heavenly light. The cathedral seems small from the outside. However, once inside, you'll be amazed by the soaring spaciousness enhanced by the clean lines and use of white marble. Paintings by Athos Bulcão and a panel depicting the Way of the Cross by modernist painter Emiliano Di Cavalcanti are on display, but the most striking contribution is three floating angels suspended in the air. They are the work of Alfredo Ceschiatti, who also designed the statues of the four apostles near the entrance. Try to contain any oohs and aahs—the acoustics are such that a word muttered in a low voice can be clearly heard from 25 meters (80 feet) away.

PALÁCIO ITAMARATY

At the end of the Esplanada dos Ministérios lie two of Niemeyer's most famous works: the Palácio Itamaraty and the Palácio da Justiça. Housing the Ministry of Foreign Affairs, the **Palácio Itamaraty** (Esplanada dos Ministérios, tel. 61/3411-8051, www.mre.gov. br, guided visits daily, free) is a disarmingly elegant fusion of classicism and modernism. The exterior is impressive enough: Its raw concrete arcades sheltering a glittering glass box are reflected in pools of water that surround the construction like a moat. The island gardens featuring Amazonian plants were designed by Roberto Burle Marx, while the striking abstract sculpture *O Meteoro* (*The Meteor*), whose interlocking pieces represent the earth's continents, was carved by Bruno Giorgi from four tons of Carrara marble. Don't neglect to take a tour inside. The sprawling, open interior and its garden courtyards house a veritable who's who of 20th-century Brazilian artists: Sculptures by Alfredo Ceschiatti, Victor Brecheret, and Lasar Segall

and paintings by Cândido Portinari and Alfredo Volpi are a few of the works in the vast salons. Guided visits are 40 minutes long and need to be reserved in advance. If you can only tour one government building, this is one you shouldn't miss.

Facing the Palácio Itamaraty, the **Palácio da Justiça** is similar in style but less impressively grand than its counterpart. Housing the Ministry of Justice, its architectural highlight is six waterfalls pouring down from the building's facade into a surrounding pool.

★ PRAÇA DOS TRÊS PODERES

At the western end of the Eixo Monumental, the Praça dos Três Poderes corresponds to the head of the bird (or cockpit of the airplane) as laid out in the Plano Piloto. The nexus of government power is concentrated around the vast plaza in the buildings housing the *três poderes* (three powers)—the executive (Palácio Planalto), legislative (Congresso Nacional), and judicial (Supremo Tribunal Federal) branches. The fantastic Niemeyer constructions in which they are housed are widely considered to be the most splendid examples of modernist architecture in the world.

Before exploring, take a quick glance at the small trio of museums that comprise the **Centro Cultural Três Poderes** (tel. 61/3325-6244, 10am-5pm Tues.-Sun., free). The **Espaço Oscar Niemeyer** displays the architect's sketches, while the **Espaço Lucio Costa** possesses the original plans (in Portuguese and English) that won Costa the commission to design Brasília, along with a gigantic maquette of the city that gives a great overview of the Plano Piloto. The **Panteão da Pátria e da Liberdade Tancredo Neves** honors national heroes in a building shaped to resemble a dove.

Guarding the *praça* is Bruno Giorgi's famous bronze sculpture, *Os Candangos,* which has become a symbol of the city. *Candango* was an expression that referred to the thousands of poor workers, mostly from the Northeast, who were hired to build Brasília and who subsequently settled in the

favela-like suburbs that surround the city. Originally it was a derogatory term African slaves applied to the Portuguese during colonial times. Over the years, however, the pejorative connotation has evaporated, and today all native residents of Brasília are called Candangos.

CONGRESSO NACIONAL

Between the Esplanada dos Ministérios and the Praça dos Três Poderes lies Brasília's most instantly recognizable symbol: the 28-story twin towers flanked by two giant bowl-shaped cupolas that make up the **Congresso Nacional** (tel. 61/3216-1771, 9:30am-5pm daily). The convex (right-side-up) bowl is where the 500-member Câmara de Deputados (House of Representatives) convenes, while the concave (upside-down) bowl houses the 80 members of the Senado (Senate). Both were originally designed so the public could hang out on top of them; these days only the Polícia Militar have this privilege. You can, however, take an hour-long tour of the sweeping marble and granite salons decorated with tile panels by Athos Bulcão and paintings by Di Cavalcanti. If the chambers are in session, you can check out the senators and deputies in action. A gift shop in front sells surprisingly cool Congresso T-shirts and souvenirs.

SUPREMO TRIBUNAL FEDERAL

On the southern side of the Praça dos Três Poderes, the elegant **Supremo Tribunal Federal** (tel. 61/3217-4037, 10am-5:30pm Sat.-Sun.) houses the Brazilian Supreme Court. Guarding the entrance is the striking granite sculpture *A Justiça* (*The Justice*) by Ceschiatti. Tours of the interior last 30 minutes.

PALÁCIO DO PLANALTO

On the northern side of the Praça dos Três Poderes, the **Palácio do Planalto** (tel. 61/3411-2042, 9:30am-2:30pm Sun.) is where the president works, which is why you can only visit the interior (including her office) on Sunday during 30-minute free guided tours. The majestic exterior is notable for its mingling of straight and curving lines and for the ramp leading up the entrance, by which newly inaugurated presidents literally ascend to power (on a day-to-day basis, they enter through a back door). During the week, you can observe the changing of the guard at two-hour intervals and take in temporary exhibits in the main hall.

Congresso Nacional

PALÁCIO DA ALVORADA

To see where the president lives, visit the **Palácio da Alvorada** (SHTN, tel. 61/3411-2317, 3pm-5pm Wed.), a quick 15-minute taxi ride north from the Praça dos Três Poderes. It sits along the northern shore of Lago Paranoá. The name (*alvorada* means "dawn") was supplied by Kubitschek himself, who often referred to Brasília as a "new dawn in Brazil's history." The first of Niemeyer's Brasília buildings to be completed (in 1958), the president's official residence is also one of the most beautiful: The harmonious fusion of glass, white marble, and mirrorlike pools is offset by expansive green gardens and an immaculate soccer field (added at the request of President Lula). Tours (including a visit to the chapel, dining room, library, and gardens) are only available on Wednesday (tickets are distributed from 2pm onward). Otherwise, you'll have to be content to gaze at the ensemble from behind the guarded gates (make sure you get your taxi to wait for you).

Beyond the Plano Piloto

There are several attractions located off the main axes of the Plano Piloto. They are linked to Brasília's notorious mystical element, which adds a counterpoint to its culture of political wheeling and dealing. The city's mysticism stems from the 1883 vision that came to an Italian priest named Dom João Bosco of a new civilization that would rise up around a lake situated between the 15th and 20th parallels. Kubitschek was a big Bosco devotee, and when his gleaming city of the future rose up (somewhat miraculously) on the shores of an artificial lake, it wasn't long before various cults and New Age groups claimed the area as their utopia.

SANTUÁRIO DOM BOSCO

Often eclipsed by the Catedral Metropolitana, the **Santuário Dom Bosco** (W-3 Sul, Ad. 702, Bl. B, tel. 61/3223-6542, www.santuariodombosco.com.br, 7am-7pm Mon.-Sat., 7am-8pm Sun.) is equally splendid. The slender concrete columns of its boxlike shell function as frames for the floor-to-ceiling stained-glass windows, whose intricate mosaic motifs are rendered in 12 blue tones. During the day, the effects of the sun's rays shining through the azure glass are quite dazzling. At night, an equally impressive spectacle is provided by the gargantuan central chandelier fashioned out of 7,400 individual crystals of Murano glass. To get here, take the 107 bus, which departs from the Rodoviária do Plano Piloto.

Palácio do Planalto

TEMPLO DA BOA VONTADE

Located 8 kilometers (5 mi) south of the Eixo Monumental, the **Templo da Boa Vontade** (SGAS, 915, Lt. 75/6, tel. 61/3114-1070, www.tbv.com.br, temple 24 hours daily, Egyptian room and gallery 10am-6pm daily, R$2) is a pyramid topped with an enormous 21-kilogram (46-pound) crystal. Created by the Legião da Boa Vontade (Goodwill Legion) with the objective of promoting peace and unity among "earthly and celestial beings of all races, philosophies, religious and political creeds, and even atheists and materialists," the temple includes a meditation space, an art gallery, a sumptuously outfitted Egyptian Room, and a sacred fountain whose healing natural waters are believed to receive the energies of the giant crystal. To get here, take the 105 or 107 buses from the Rodoviária do Plano Piloto.

SPORTS AND RECREATION
Parks

Once you get off the beaten Plano Piloto, you'll find a surprisingly vast number of parks that make Brasília one of the greenest cities in Brazil. Central and easy to get to is the **Parque da Cidade** (Eixo Monumental Sul, 5am-midnight daily). Officially known as the Parque Sarah Kubitschek, it features wooded areas and a large artificial lake as well as bars and food kiosks.

A favorite recreational destination, the **Lago Paranoá** is an immense artificial lake surrounded by walking trails, sports clubs, restaurants, and bars. Most attractions are around the Lago Sul (southern part of the lake), with many concentrated in the well-to-do lakeside development of **Pontão do Lago Sul** (SHS Qd. 5, www.pontaodolagosul.com.br), where Brasília's sporty young wine, dine, and indulge in water sports. For in-your-face views of the triple-arched **Ponte Juscelino Kubitschek,** take to the waters in front of the Clube Naval's **Clube do Vento** (SCES, Trecho 2, Conj. 13, tel. 61/3532-5009, www.clubedovento.com),

which offers lessons (R$60 per hour) and rents equipment (R$35).

The **Ermida Dom Bosco** (Estrada Parque Dom Bosco, Lago Sul, Cj. 12, tel. 61/3367-4505, 8am-9pm daily) is a sanctuary devoted to Italian priest Dom João Bosco that features a futuristic pyramid-shaped chapel and gardens designed by Burle Marx. The locale offers one of the best vantage points for watching Brasília's legendary sunsets. From the *rodoviária*, both the 123 and 125 buses circle around the southern shore.

The Cerrado

In only a few decades, rampant urban development and the clearing of surrounding land for the planting of lucrative cash crops such as soybeans has led to the destruction of the majority of the native Cerrado vegetation that once covered the Planalto. Despite this tragic devastation—of roughly 10,000 Cerrado plant species, only 44 percent exist elsewhere in the world—several parks preserve this unique mixture of grassland, dry forest, and *buriti* palms. In Brasília, you can follow various hiking trails through a preserved swatch of typical Cerrado vegetation at the well-organized **Jardim Botânico** (SMDB, Cj. 12, Lago Sul, tel. 61/3366-2141, www.jardimbotanico.df.gov.br, 9am-5pm Tues.-Sun., R$2), located along the southern shores of Lago Paranoá. To get here, take the 147 bus from the Rodoviária do Plano Piloto. Farther away, along the city's northern fringes, is the vast **Parque Nacional de Brasília** (BR-040 Km 9, Setor Militar Urbano, tel. 61/3233-4553, 8am-4pm daily, R$15), known popularly as "Água Mineral" due to its abundant freshwater springs and natural pools in which you can take a dip. Several walking trails lead through preserved Cerrado vegetation, including trees bearing *pequi* and *mangaba* fruits and *ipês* sprayed with yellow and violet blossoms. During the week, when the park receives fewer visitors, your chances of glimpsing armadillos, monkeys, and capybaras are higher. A visitors center offers maps and snacks. To get here, take a cab or the W3 Norte Circular bus, which passes along W3 and can let you off near the park entrance.

Two hours (115 km/72 mi) northeast of the city, the town of Formosa is the base for visiting the **Salto de Itiquira** (tel. 61/3981-1234, www.itiquira.tur.br, 9am-4:30pm daily, R$10), a spectacular, 170-meter-high (560-foot-high) waterfall, surrounded by a park with lush tropical vegetation and natural swimming pools. You can take a bus from the *rodoferroviária* to Formosa, but getting a taxi to the falls, 40 kilometers (25 mi) away, is tricky and expensive. If you have a car, just follow BR-020 and BR-030 to Formosa and then follow GO-44 along to Itiquira. On site are a restaurant and snack bar along with restrooms.

ENTERTAINMENT AND EVENTS
Nightlife

Although hardly wild, Brasília has a fairly varied nightlife. Many of the best options are concentrated in and around the Asa Sul. Some of Brasília's restaurants also have bars and even host live music performances. Among the more classic watering holes, **Bar Beirute** (SCLS, Qd. 109, Bl. A, Lj. 2-4, tel. 61/3244-1717, 11am-1am Sun.-Wed., 11am-2am Thurs.-Sat.) is a local institution that has barely changed since it first opened its doors in 1966. Over the years, major political and cultural figures have engaged in often heated discussions at the tables scattered beneath a canopy of trees. A happy-hour favorite during the week, on Saturday nights it draws a gay and lesbian crowd. **Bar Brasília** (SCLS, Qd. 506, Lj. 15, tel. 61/3443-4323, www.barbrasilia.com.br, 5:30pm-close Mon.-Thurs., 11:30am-close Fri.-Sat., 11:30am-5pm Sun.) is a popular old-style *boteco* where you can get the best *chope* in town. Art deco light fixtures and a handsome wooden bar salvaged from a 1950s pharmacy add to the retro atmosphere. Although the rocker scene isn't what it used to be, at the dim, dusky, and vaguely Britlike **Gate's Pub** (SCLS, Qd. 403, Bl. B, Lj. 34, tel. 61/3244-0222, www.gatespub.com.br,

10pm-close Tues.-Sun., cover R$15-30), you can catch some live bands and then continue dancing the night away to DJ-spun music.

Performing Arts

Brasília receives the best of national and international musicians, theatrical productions, and dance companies. The **Centro Cultural Banco do Brasil** (SCES, Trecho 2, Lt. 22, tel. 61/3108-7600, www.culturabancodobrasil.com.br, 9am-9pm daily) is a Niemeyer-designed cultural center with a theater that hosts art exhibitions and screens films. A free CCBB shuttle bus departs at 90-minute intervals from the Biblioteca Nacional and the **Teatro Nacional Claudio Santoro** (tel. 61/3325-6277); check the website for times. Every September, Brasília hosts the important **Festival de Brasília de Cinema Brasileiro** (www.festbrasilia.com.br). **Cine Brasília** (EQ Sul, 106-107, tel. 61/3244-1660) is a government-operated cinematheque that screens art and repertory films at subsidized prices. Designed by Niemeyer and inaugurated in 1960, it boasts a big screen, a modernist lobby, and very comfy seating.

For more information, check out the cultural listings in the daily *Correio Brasiliense* newspaper or visit the (Portuguese) site www.brasiliagenda.com.br.

SHOPPING

Shopping malls reign supreme in Brasília. The oldest and most central *shopping* is the **Conjunto Nacional** (SDN, tel. 61/2106-9700, www.cnbshopping.com.br, 10am-10pm Mon.-Sat., noon-8pm Sun.). A massive hulk of concrete on the north side of the Rodoviária do Plano Piloto, it's more democratic than average Brazilian malls, which are usually either chic or "popular." This one is both, with stores, a supermarket, and a wide range of eating options. The Siciliano bookstore has English-language books and magazines. More upscale and glossy, with fancier boutiques, food options, and cineplexes, are **Brasília Shopping** (SCN, Qd. 5, Bl. A, tel. 61/2109-2136, www.brasiliashopping.com.br,

10am-10pm Mon.-Sat., 2pm-10pm Sun.) and **Pátio Brasil Shopping** (SCS, Qd. 7, Bl. A, tel. 61/4003-7800, www.patiobrasil.com.br, 10am-10:30pm Mon.-Sat., 2pm-8pm Sun.), which is conveniently close to the hotel sectors.

Tucked away in an innocuous commercial building, the **Fundação Athos Bulcão** (CLN, Qd. 208, Bl. D, tel. 61/3322-7801, www.fundathos.org.br) preserves the legacy of one of Brasília's signature artists, whose memorable sculptures, stained glass windows, and azulejo panels adorn many of the city's iconic buildings. Its boutique sells authorized replicas of Athos Bulcão's azulejos and usable and wearable *objets d'art*.

ACCOMMODATIONS

When Congress is in full swing (Mon.-Thurs.) hotel rooms fill up, prices rise, and reservations are a must. On weekends, when deputies return to their home states and the city clears out, you can get discounts of up to 50 percent. Since business execs and politicos are much more common than backpackers, no-frills budget accommodations are harder to come by. The cheapest *pousadas* in town are on and around Via W3 Sul and are usually down-and-out, unsafe, and inconvenient. Hotels in Brasília are concentrated in the central Hotel Sector.

R$50-200

One of Brasília's secret bargains is the **913 Sul SESC Hotel** (W4 Sul, Qd. 713/913, Lote F, tel. 61/3445-4401, www.sescdf.com.br, R$152 d), located on a quiet street within a couple of blocks' walk of the Parque da Cidade and the Santuário Dom Bosco. The hotel accommodates SESC members (SESC is a type of trade union); tourists can take advantage of the 16 spotless apartments, all equipped with basic amenities, including air-conditioning. Advance reservations are necessary. Those not averse to a dorm experience will appreciate bunking down at the intimate and expertly run **Hostel 7** (SCLRN 708, Bloco I, Loja 20, tel. 61/3033-7707, www.hostel7.com.br, R$80-95 d). The only drawback is its somewhat

out-of-the-way location, though it is easily reached by bus.

R$200-400

The nicest of the Bittar group's "economic" hotels, the revamped **América Bittar** (SHS, Qd. 4, Bl. B, tel. 61/3704-4000, www.hoteisbittar.com.br, R$190-290 d) is one of the capital's more attractive budget options. The sizable guest rooms are nicely, if innocuously, decorated and many have handsome hardwood floors. Wi-Fi is extra.

Reopened in 2007 after 30 years of inactivity following a devastating fire, the ★ **Brasília Palace** (SHTN, Trecho 1, Lt. 1, tel. 61/3306-9000, www.brasiliapalace.com.br, R$180-270 d) was Brasília's first hotel. A modernist box designed entirely by Niemeyer (down to the furniture), the Brasília Palace was built in an incredible eight months, down to the enormous, egg-shaped pool. Upon its completion, "Brazil's Waldorf Astoria" served as President Kubitschek's private clubhouse. From here he entertained VIPs from far and wide, who flew into the dusty middle of nowhere to watch as the space-age capital rose to life before their eyes. The first visiting dignitary to check in was Paraguayan dictator Alfredo Stroessner, followed by Indira Gandhi, Fidel Castro, Che Guevara, and Dwight D. Eisenhower. Jean-Paul Sartre and Simone de Beauvoir also showed up and soundly dissed the plans for the new capital. However, when the city was inaugurated in 1960, the Palace was so overpacked that hotel tycoon Conrad Hilton had to bunk in the barber shop. Today, this architectural gem has once again become a hot spot, not only as a hotel but as place to listen to live jazz, performed at the swanky restaurant and piano bar, **Oscar.**

R$400-600

Brasília's only 5-star hotel, the **Royal Tulip Brasília Alvorada** (SHTN, Trecho 11, Lt. 1-B, Bl. C, tel. 61/3424-7000, www.royaltulipbrasiliaalvorada.com, R$540-820 d) isn't really luxurious (and taxis are a necessity), but it's definitely worth the bucks. Designed by vanguard Brazilian architect Ruy Ohtake, the lipstick-red, horseshoe-shaped hotel is eye-poppingly futuristic. The inspiration for the lobby—"a Zeppelin floating above a garage"—says it all. The guest rooms traffic in sleek modernism, with Ohtake riffing on Niemeyer (and actual Niemeyer panels hanging above the beds). Most feature small balconies overlooking a fabulous pool and the Lago Paranoá—you'll appreciate both after a hot day in the sun. A spa, gym, pub, and two restaurants round out the amenities.

FOOD
Cafés and Buffets

The **Daniel Briand Pâtissier & Chocolatier** (CLN, Qd. 104, Bl. A, Lj. 28, tel. 61/3326-1135, 9am-10pm Tues.-Fri., 8am-10pm Sat.-Sun.), a Parisian-style café, serves the finest pastries (and croissants) in town. Indulge in mouthwatering sweets and light bistro fare such as smoked salmon crepes with lime and cream. **Grenat Cafés Especiais** (CLS, Qd. 201, Bl. A., Lj. 5, tel. 61/3322-0061, www.grenatcafes.com.br, 9am-10pm Mon.-Fri., 1pm-10pm Sat.) is a tiny, cozy place that takes the art of espresso seriously. To lessen the java jolt, indulge in a pastry or ice cream. This is an inviting place for a laptop break; Wi-Fi is available.

Considered the top per-kilo restaurant in town, **Don'Durica** (CLS, Qd. 115, Bl. C, Lj. 36, tel. 61/3346-8922, www.dondurica.com. br, 11:30am-3pm and 6pm-11pm Mon.-Fri., noon-3:30pm and 6pm-11pm Sat., R$15-25) offers an array of appetizing dishes for a reasonable price in agreeable surroundings. This convenient location is just off the Eixo Monumental, and there are two others (CLS, Qd. 201, and CLN, Qd. 201); the latter's buffet is a fixed-price (R$37) all-you-can-eat version.

For a tasty all-natural lunch at a nice price, head to **A Tribo** (CLN, Qd. 105, Bl. B, Lj. 52-59, tel. 61/3039-6430, 11am-3pm Tues.-Fri., noon-4pm Sat.-Sun., R$20-25), a laid-back and rustic per-kilo retreat that offers an organic spread of salads and hot dishes prepared on a wood-burning stove.

Brazilian

Chef Alexandra Alcoforado and her mother Maria do Socorro serve up robust, decently priced helpings of succulent roasted and stuffed chicken, quail, and duck at **Inácia Poulet Rôti** (CLS 103, Bl. B, Lj. 34, tel. 61/3225-4006, www.inaciapouletroti.com.br, noon-10:30pm Tues.-Sat., noon-3:30pm Sun., R$20-30). The cozy setting is as heartwarming as the food.

The bewitching views of Lago Paranoá are a mere bonus at **Mangai** (SCES, Trecho 2, Cj. 41, tel. 61/3224-3079, www.mangai. com.br, noon-3pm and 6pm-10pm Mon.-Fri., noon-10pm Sat.-Sun., R$20-30). More than 100 hearty, no-nonsense dishes of the Sertão laid out at this self-service banquet will make your taste buds believe you've died and gone to Nordestino culinary heaven.

Contemporary

Centrally located **Versão Tupiniquim** (CLS, Qd. 302-B, Bl. C, Lj. 2, tel. 61/3322-0555, noon-4pm and 6pm-midnight Tues.-Sat., noon-4pm Sun., R$50-70) offers surprising 21st-century riffs on traditional Brazilian recipes dreamed up by chef Fabiana Pinheiro. Offerings are available à la carte, as a 12-tapa menu (R$39), or assembled into seven-course tasting menus (R$100).

International

Lagash (CLN, Qd. 308-309, Bl. B, Lj. 11/17, tel. 61/3273-0098, noon-4pm and 7pm-11pm Mon.-Sat., noon-5pm Sun., R$25-35) is renowned for its refined and immaculately prepared Moroccan, Lebanese, and Syrian fare. For a medley of flavors, try the tasting menu (R$55), which offers a sampling of 15 dishes.

The small, unpretentious dining room of ★ **Nossa Cozinha Bistrô** (CLN, Qd. 402, Bl. C, Ljs. 60/64, tel. 61/3443-2089, www. nossacozinhabsb.blogspot.com.br, 11:30am-2:30pm and 7:30pm-11:30pm Mon.-Fri., 11:30am-3pm and 7:30pm-midnight Sat., R$30-40) belies the worldly scope of its innovative dishes, such as Colombian-inspired steak braised in wine and bitter chocolate and killer barbecued spareribs. Chef Alexandre Albanese did serious culinary time in the United States and now offers one of the capital's best dining experiences.

INFORMATION AND SERVICES

There are **tourist offices** at the airport, Rodoviária Interestadual, and Praça dos Três Poderes; all are open daily from 8am-6pm. For online information, visit the government's multilingual tourism website (www.vemviver-brasilia.df.gov.br) or www.aboutbrasilia.com. In Portuguese, a good site is www.candango. com.br.

Banco do Brasil has 24-hour ATMs at the airport and on the second floor of the Conjunto Nacional shopping center. The main **post office** (SBN, Qd. 6, Bl. A, Suite 1A) is in the Northern Banking Sector, just off the Eixo Monumental.

For emergencies, dial **192** for an ambulance, **193** for the fire department, or **190** for police. Hospitals are all in the hospital sector (SHLS and SHLN); **Hospital Santa Lucia** (SHLS, Qd. 76, Conj. C, tel. 61/3445-0000, www.santalucia.com.br) is recommended.

TRANSPORTATION

Once you get the hang of Brasília's "sectors" (which could take a while), you will see how orderly it all is. Roads are numbered instead of named. Digits represent positions and distances north or south of the Eixo Monumental and east or west of the Eixo Rodoviário. Each sector has its own acronym. The central Rodoviária do Plano Piloto—the main urban bus station—is also the city's nucleus. The Eixo Rodoviário crosses over the *rodoviária*, while the Eixo Monumental passes around it.

Air

Most travelers arrive in Brasília by air and there is no shortage of flights from most state capitals, including numerous flights from Rio and São Paulo. Make sure to request a window seat, since the view of the Plano Piloto from above is truly unforgettable. The **Aeroporto**

Internacional de Brasília—Presidente Juscelino Kubitschek (tel. 61/3364-9000, www.aeroportobrasilia.net) is a high-tech and futuristic place, located 10 kilometers (6 mi) west of the Eixo Monumental. A taxi from the airport to the hotel sectors costs about R$40-50. **Ônibus Executivo Aeroporto** (tel. 61/3344-2769, www.tcb.df.gov.br, 6:30am-11pm daily, R$8) is an executive bus that links the airport to the Rodoviária do Plano Piloto passing by the Esplanada dos Ministérios and the Hotel Sector at 30-minute intervals.

Bus

Buses arrive and depart at the long-distance **Rodoviária Interestadual** (SMAS, Trecho 4, Conj. 5/6, tel. 61/3234-2185), at the western edge of the Eixo Monumental. Aside from destinations in neighboring Goiás, traveling anywhere else involves an exhaustingly long haul: Brasília is 930 kilometers (580 mi) from Rio, 870 kilometers (540 mi) from São Paulo, and 1,000 kilometers (620 mi) from Salvador. **Itapemirim** (tel. 0800-723-2121, www.itapemirim.com.br) offers daily service to Rio (17 hours, R$190), while **Real Expresso** (tel. 0800-280-7325, www.realexpresso.com.br) offers numerous daily buses to São Paulo (14 hours, R$80-R$180) and Salvador (20 hours, R$140).

Although not that useful for tourists, Brasília's **Metrô** (www.metro.df.gov.br, 6am-11pm Mon.-Fri., 7am-7pm Sat.-Sun., R$3) is a cheap and useful way to get from the Rodoviária Interestadual (the Shopping station) to the more local Rodoviária do Plano Piloto (Central station) and vice versa.

The **Plano Piloto Circular** buses (notably 104 and 108) stop at most monuments, hotels, and *shoppings* along the Eixo Monumental. Bus fare varies between R$2 and R$3, depending on the distance. Otherwise, you're best off taking a taxi.

Car

Although it's possible to drive to Brasília from other Brazilian regions, distances are enormous and you'll waste a lot of time on the road. Highway BR-050 connects Brasília with São Paulo. BR-060 goes west to the Pantanal, where it intersects with BR-153, which stretches north to the Amazon and Belém. Running east to the coast, BR-020 cuts through the Sertão of Bahia all the way to Salvador.

Brasília is a sprawling city custom-made for cars (and buses), so forget about wandering around town unless you're in a strolling zone (such as a park). The most convenient buses run along the major axes of the Eixo Rodoviário and the Eixo Monumental, all of them stopping at the Rodoviária do Plano Piloto, located at the crossroads of the two.

Brasília's thoroughfares were designed to make traffic lights unnecessary through the use of roundabouts at intersections. Although some traffic lights do exist, roundabouts rule—if driving, remember that the car that's already in the roundabout has the right of way. Otherwise, driving here is smoother than in other large Brazilian cities. Renting a car is useful for visiting the Cerrado around Brasília. **Avis** (tel. 61/3364-9904, www. avis.com.br) and **Hertz** (tel. 61/3365-5151, www.hertz.com.br) both have agencies at the airport. Renting a car in the city can be cheaper—try **Via Rent A Car** (SHS, Qd. 6, Conj. A, Bl. F, Lj. 50, tel. 61/3322-3181, www. viadfrentacar.com.br).

Taxis

Taxis are usually easy to hail, and if you can't make sense of Brasília's sometimes confusing system of *setores* and *quadras,* your cab driver can. You can also call a taxi—**Rádio Táxi Alvorada** (tel. 61/3321-3030) or **Brasília Rádio Taxi** (tel. 61/3344-3060).

City Tours

Most hotels offer information about city tours. For a more do-it-yourself approach, assume your touristic identity and jump aboard the double-decker bus operated by **Catedral Turismo City Tour** (tel. 61/9304-3201-1222, R$30), which hits most of the city's architectural hot spots in two hours. Buses depart from Brasília Shopping. For a splendid bird's-eye perspective of Brasília, splurge for a helicopter ride with **Esat Aerotaxi** (Eixo Monumental at the Torre de TV, tel. 61/9981-1915). A 10-minute whiz costs R$500 for three passengers.

Goiás

Surrounding Brasília and the Distrito Federal is the state of Goiás. Brazil's "heartland," this state is often overlooked by foreign, and even many Brazilian, visitors, which is both a blessing and a shame since it has some unique attractions. One of the most spectacular destinations is the Parque Nacional da Chapada dos Veadeiros, which lies in the mountainous region north of Brasília. This vast natural park offers landscapes you're unlikely to see anywhere else in Brazil, with outcrops of coppery red rock, plunging canyons, myriad waterfalls, and an impressive array of flora and fauna.

The gradual development of ecotourism in Goiás has brought focus on the need to preserve the Cerrado. Sadly, it is estimated that close to 70 percent of this unique ecosystem has already been devastated—compared to 15 percent of the much more lamented Amazon rain forest—to make way for big agro-business such as cattle-raising and cultivation of cash crops. Such prosperity is apparent in the state's two major cities, Goiânia (the state capital) and Anápolis, both thriving modern boomtowns that hold little interest for travelers.

However, Goiás does have its historical attractions. Long before the region struck it rich with agriculture, it experienced a gold boom similar to, but more timid than, that of its neighbor Minas Gerais. In the late 1600s, fortune-hunting *bandeirantes* discovered that the region's hills were riddled with gold. The subsequent gold rush that lasted until the early 1800s saw the birth of Goiás Velho and Pirenópolis, two prosperous mining towns whose colonial architecture and rich cultural and culinary traditions have been carefully preserved to this day.

Goiás has a good highway system, and most attractions are easily reached by bus or car from Brasília, although distances are considerable. The climate is fairly hot year-round, although the winter months tend to be dry, and rain is frequent in the summer months.

PIRENÓPOLIS

This atmospheric historic town dates back to 1727, when gold was discovered in the riverbed of the Rio das Almas, at the foot of the Serra dos Pireneus. Named for the surrounding mountains, Pirenópolis thrived for a century and then turned into a ghost town when the source of its wealth dried up. In the 1980s, enchanted with its preserved colonial buildings and the abundance of natural crystals and waterfalls in the surrounding region, latter-day hippies, New Agers, and artists arrived to set up alternative communities, open organic restaurants, and begin producing jewelry and handicrafts. After it was declared a National Heritage Site in 1989, the town was discovered by Brasilienses (residents of Brasília) and became a favorite getaway where the nation's power brokers unwind.

Sights

Exploring the historical center is easily done on foot. If you notice a glint in the cobblestones, it is because they contain quartzite from the surrounding hills. Particularly charming is Rua Direita (Main Street), which is lined with whitewashed 18th-century mansions trimmed with green and blue, along with an art deco cinema whose powder-blue facade dates to 1936. At Praça da Matriz, the **Igreja Matriz de Nossa Senhora do Rosário** (7am-5pm daily, R$2) is Goiás's oldest church. Constructed in the early 1730s, it

was severely damaged as the result of a 2002 fire and is slowly being restored to its former glory. Dating back to 1750, the nearby hilltop **Igreja de Nosso Senhor do Bonfim** (Rua do Bonfim) is the town's only church whose original interior has survived. Equally old, the **Igreja Nossa Senhora do Carmo** (Rua do Carmo, 11am-5pm Wed.-Sun., R$2) shelters the small Museu de Arte Sacra.

Pirenópolis is famed for having one of the most original and spectacular religious pageants in Brazil: the **Cavalhadas** features horsemen dressed to represent medieval Moors and Christians, who recreate a battle fought by Charlemagne during the Crusades. The elaborate costumes are astonishingly sumptuous—the Christian *cavalheiros* (knights) wear scarlet, the Moors blue, and a third, more surreal group of characters, the Mascarados, wear fantastic masks fashioned out of papier-mâché. The pageantry lasts for three days and includes parades, tournaments, and a mock battle in which the Moors are vanquished (of course) and later converted to Christianity. Of Portuguese origin and dating back to the Middle Ages, Cavalhadas have been played out in Pirenópolis since 1826 as part of a larger popular and religious festival, the 12-day-long **Festa do Divino Espírito Santo,** which begins 40 days after Easter Sunday. Leading up to the Cavalhadas are numerous celebrations ranging from parades and masked balls to fireworks displays. If you miss the main event, you can at least get a dose of the festivities by visiting the **Museu das Cavalhadas** (Rua Direita 39, tel. 62/3331-1166, 10am-5pm daily, R$2). Operated out of a private home owned by the Pina family (all of whom have historically been fervent participants), it has a splendid collection of costumes, masks, and photographs. Also worth checking out is the **Museu do Divino** (Rua Bernardo Sayão, tel. 62/3331-1166, 11am-5pm Wed.-Sun., R$4), housed in the former city hall and municipal prison. The small permanent exhibition breaks down the various aspects of this complex *festa* and whets your appetite to take part yourself. A compelling video rounds out the experience.

Sports and Recreation

The hilly countryside surrounding Pirenópolis boasts more than 70 cascades and waterfalls, which can be reached by nature trails. Five kilometers (3 mi) north of town on a continuation of Rua do Carmo, the **Cachoeiras de Bonsucesso** (tel. 62/3321-2145, 7am-5pm daily, R$10) are the closest—and most crowded on the weekends—place to take a cool plunge, with six falls dispersed along a 1.5-kilometer (0.9-mi) trail. At the entrance, you can buy homemade snacks and drinks at the *fazenda* (ranch house). There is also a restaurant serving *comida caseira* (home-cooked specialties).

Around 6 kilometers (3.5 mi) north of town is the **Santuário de Vida Silvestre Vagafogo** (tel. 62/3335-8515, www.vagafogo.com.br, 9am-5pm daily, R$12), an ecological reserve with short hiking trails and tree-trekking platforms that wind through a magnificent patch of Cerrado forest teeming with black howler and brown capuchin monkeys, armadillos, deer, and various birds. There is a waterfall with a refreshing pool as well as beckoning hammocks near the visitors center. The café serves a delicious weekend and holiday brunch (R$38 pp) featuring typical farm products and preserves made from native Cerrado fruits (these can be purchased as well).

Both attractions can be easily reached by taxis or *moto-taxis* around town. If you have a car, there are plenty of other attractions in the vicinity. Only 11 kilometers (7 mi) from town, the **Reserva Ecológica Vargem Grande** (Estrada dos Pirineus, tel. 62/3331-3071, www.vargemgrande.pirenopolis.tur.br, 9am-5pm daily, R$20) is a private nature reserve containing two of the region's most smashing waterfalls along with river beaches and natural pools. The spectacular **Cachoeiras dos Dragões** consists of eight waterfalls scattered along a 4-kilometer (2.5-mi) trail in the countryside, located

colonial Pirenópolis

40 kilometers (25 mi) from town along the Estrada pra Goianésia.

Also worth a visit is the **Fazenda Babilônia** (G0-431 Km 3, tel. 62/9294-1805, 9am-4pm Sat.-Sun., R$8), a historic 18th-century sugarcane plantation that gives a glimpse into colonial life in rural Goiás. Tours through the main plantation house are conducted by owner Telma Machado, whose family has owned the property for more than 100 years. The pinnacle is a lavish and irresistible spread featuring typical Goiana delicacies (R$50). During the week, group visits are possible with advance reservations.

Taking a guided tour or organized excursion is a good alternative, and is imperative if you want to hike along the trails that weave through the **Parque Estadual dos Pireneus** (Estrada dos Pireneus 20 km, 8am-5pm daily, free) past waterfalls, swimming holes, and up to the 1,385-meter (4,544-foot) summit of the Pico dos Pireneus. The reference to Pireneus (Pyrenees)—and the origin of the name Pirenópolis—allude to the region's supposed resemblance to Europe's homonymous mountain chain. **Morro Alto** (Rua Direita 71, tel. 62/3331-3348, www.morroalto.tur.br) offers a wide array of ecotours throughout the region as well as cultural and history-themed outings, such as a trip to Fazenda Babilônia. Adventure sports such as rappelling, canyoneering, and white-water rafting are also offered. Expect to pay R$100-140 for a full-day guided trip.

Accommodations

There are lots of good hotel options in Pirenópolis. Not only are they reasonably priced (particularly during the week), but many are located in colonial homes. On weekends, and during the Festa do Divino Espírito Santo and Carnaval, reservations are necessary. You can also easily rent a room in a local home.

A great budget choice is **Pousada SESC Pirenópolis** (Rua Pireneus 45, tel. 62/3331-1383, www.sescgo.com.br, R$60-140 d). Although built to accommodate SESC members (SESC is a type of trade union), mere tourists can check into these spacious, spotless, though style-challenged guest rooms. The swimming pools are welcome on hot days, but expect lots of splashing during school holidays. Advance online reservations are necessary. **Pousada Arvoredo** (Av. Abércio Ramos, Qd. 7, Lt. 15, tel. 62/3331-1305, www. arvoredo.tur.br, R$150-290 d) makes the best of its location on a residential dirt road off Rua Direita with an intimate cluster of apartments surrounding a lush garden and pool. Guest rooms are fairly simple but nicely finished, and the staff is friendly.

Pouso Café e Cultura (Rua Santa Cruz 32, tel. 62/3331-1206, www.pousocafeecultura. tur.br, R$180-280 d) occupies a historic house, behind which sprawls a hammock-strung garden scattered with seven spacious, modern chalets. Helpful English-speaking owner, Rodrigo, spent time in the United States. More upscale, ★ **Pousada O Casarão** (Rua Direita 79, tel. 62/3331-2662, www.ocasarao. pirenopolis.tur.br, R$170-270 d, rates include dinner) is a particularly lovely option in a renovated 19th-century house. Sizable guest rooms feature ceramic tile floors and period furnishings, and there is an outdoor pool surrounded by 100-year-old fruit trees.

Cloaked in Cerrado vegetation 4 kilometers (2.5 mi) out of town, ★ **Pousada Villa do Comandador** (GO-431, tel. 62/3331-2424, www.viladocomandador.com.br, R$260-580 d) is ideal for families and nature lovers. The large and comfortable apartments are exquisitely furnished, while luxurious bungalows (outfitted with hot tubs, saunas, and wine cellars) are located in prime waterfall country. This stylish, ultra-green resort (vouched for by environmental watchdogs as the real deal) offers many perks—pools, playgrounds, spas, and stables.

Food

Many of the town's restaurants and bars can be found along Rua do Rosário (also known as Rua do Lazer), but some are only open on weekends. Overlooking Praça do Coreto, **Forneria Pireneus** (Rua Pireneus 41, tel. 62/3331-3047, 3pm-11pm Mon.-Thurs., 10am-1am Fri.-Sat., 10am-11pm Sun., R$20) is a favorite hangout for those in search of gourmet focaccia sandwiches and a serious java jolt. For sustenance of a more resolutely Goiana nature, **Pamonharia Souza** (Av. Pref. Sizenando Jayme 24, tel. 62/3331-2615, 8am-10pm daily, R$10) serves fresh corn *pamonha* (sweet and savory versions) as well as *empadão,* an oversized *empada* stuffed with everything from chicken and sausage to hearts of *guariroba* (a local palm). Reputed for its tasty regional fare, **Restaurante Pensão Padre Rosa** (Rua Aurora 14, tel. 62/3331-3577, noon-5pm daily Jan. and July, noon-5pm Sat.-Sun. Feb.-June and Aug.-Dec., R$20-30) is a local favorite. A copious lunch buffet includes specialties such as *carne ao molho de café* (beef in a coffee sauce) and *paçoca de pilão* (sun-dried meat with manioc flour) as well as plenty of salads. Leave room for dessert—there are more than 40 types of homemade *doces*.

For a bucolic setting, head to **Restaurante Dona Cida** (Rua do Carmo 22, tel. 62/3331-2233, 11am-5pm Mon.-Thurs., 11am-10pm Fri.-Sun., R$25-35), where wooden tables are spread amid a wide veranda and garden filled with the chatter of birds and monkeys. Dona Cida herself oversees the preparation of hearty traditional dishes such as *galinha à cabidela* (chicken cooked in its own blood) and *arroz com pequi* (rice cooked with the aromatic *pequi* fruit).

Vegetarians will appreciate the healthy fare prepared by Edna Lucena, the town's pioneering hippie-mystic, who first opened **Aravinda Bar e Restaurante** (Rua do Rosário 25, tel. 62/3331-2409, www.restaurantearavinda.com.br, 11am-close daily, R$20-30) in the early 1980s as a boutique that sold East Indian garb. On weekends, this mellow hangout features live music. For a sweet conclusion, **Sorvetes Naturais** (Rua Nova 16, tel. 62/3331-1327) serves more than 80 flavors of homemade ice cream; indulge in those made from Cerrado fruits such as buriti, pequi, and mangaba.

Transportation and Services

Pirenópolis's **Centro do Atendimento ao Turista** (Rua Bonfim 14, tel. 62/3331-2633, 8am-6pm daily) has lots of information about the region and can put you in touch with local guides. It also sells local *artesanato* and *doces*. You'll find a Banco do Brasil and Bradesco on Rua Direita. In Portuguese, two useful websites with plenty of photos are www.pirenopolis.com.br and www.pirenopolis.tur.br.

Pirenópolis is 160 kilometers (100 mi) from Brasília. **Viação Goianésia** (tel. 61/3323-6593, www.viacaogoianesia.com.br) offers four buses daily from Brasília (3 hours, R$22) and one bus daily from Goiânia (2 hours, R$15). In Pirenópolis, the *rodoviária* (Rua Neco Mendonça, tel. 62/3331-1080) is a five-minute walk from the center of town. If you're driving from Brasília, take BR-070, followed by BR-414 and BR-225.

CHAPADA DOS VEADEIROS

Situated in northern Goiás, the Parque Nacional da Chapada dos Veadeiros and its environs constitute one of the most unusual natural ecosystems in South America. Access to the park is via two towns: Alto Paraíso de Goiás, a magnet for mystics and alternative communities, is 38 kilometers (24 mi) from the park, while right next to entrance, the small village of São Jorge is renowned for its fantastic scenery and hiking trails.

★ Parque Nacional da Chapada dos Veadeiros

The **Parque Nacional da Chapada dos Veadeiros** (Rod. GO 239 km 36, tel. 62/3455-1114, www.icmbio.gov.br/parnachapadadosveadeiros, 8am-5pm daily Dec.-Jan. and July, 8am-5pm Tues.-Sun. Feb.-June and Aug.-Nov., visitors must enter before noon) is situated on what is considered to be one of the oldest parts of the American continent. According to NASA, when observed from outer space, the Chapada's high plateaus are the most luminous point visible on earth. Although the region's esoteric pilgrims chalk it up to a variety of supernatural forces, the scientific explanation is the vast quantity of quartz crystals embedded in the soil and fantastic outcrops of rock that make hiking through the park such a breathtaking experience. Add to the mixture plummeting canyons, crystal-clear cascades, Cerrado vegetation, and wildlife such as giant armadillos, anteaters, deer, extremely rare maned wolves, rheas, and green-beaked toucans, and you're in for an eco-treat.

The park's four trails can only be explored in the company of a guide. You can hire one easily in Alto Paraíso de Goiás or São Jorge, or at the park's entrance. Guides usually charge around R$100 per day for groups of up to 10 people. In Alto Paraíso, many ecotourism outfits run full-day excursions into the park and offer adventure-sports outings. Make sure your guide has been officially registered with ICMBio, the federal environmental protection agency. Also make sure to bring plenty of sunscreen, water, and food. The park can be visited year-round, but the May-October period coincides with the dry season, which ensures sunshine. In May-June, you can witness the blooming of delicate Cerrado flowers. In August-September, things can get hot; waterfalls can shrink or dry up, and brush fires are a risk. In December-March, heavy rains can make hiking slippery and even dangerous.

Alto Paraíso de Goiás

The Chapada dos Veadeiros's capital of ecotourism and esotericism, Alto Paraíso de Goiás is a trippy, incense-scented place haunted by a surprisingly international collection of astrologists, mystics, and latter-day hippies drawn by the abundance of sublime landscapes, natural crystals, and reports of UFO and extraterrestrial sightings. Many buildings are pyramid-shaped, the better to capture the energies in circulation. One of the classic pastimes is to hang out at the **Aeroporto de UFO**, 4 kilometers (2.5 mi) north of town. This deactivated airstrip was supposedly built by a wealthy mystic as a welcoming gesture to receive any extraterrestrial craft that wanted to land. These days it is the stage for meditation sessions, New Age rituals, and live concerts; it is especially popular when the moon is full. *Esoturismo* aside, the immediate surrounding area has lots of striking natural features and many waterfalls that you can easily hike to.

ACCOMMODATIONS AND FOOD

The town offers a wide range of accommodations, mostly concentrated around the main drag of Avenida Ary Valadão. To take advantage of Alto Paraíso's holistic vibes, check into **Pousada Alfa e Ômega** (Rua Joaquim de Almeida 15, tel. 62/3446-1225, www.pousadaalfaeomegasite.com.br, R$150-220 d). Although the guest rooms' dark brick walls are hardly conducive to levitation, East Indian ornaments, a meditation room, a sauna, and surrounding gardens have more

mellowing influences. Ayurvedic massages and alternative therapies are also available. Set amid a bucolic farm filled with fruit orchards and flowers, the **Pousada Casa Rosa** (Rua Gumercindo Barbosa 233, tel. 62/3446-1319, www.pousadacasarosa.com.br, R$160-260 d) is a pleasantly tranquil haven. Choose from spacious guest rooms in the renovated pale pink main *casa* or surrounding chalets with verandas overlooking the Vale do Moinho. Offering more luxury and sublime Cerrado views, the **Pousada Maya** (Rua 11, Qd. 10, Lt. 4/5 tel. 62/3446-2062, www.pousadamaya.com.br, R$240-560 d) has more expensive suites featuring decks with hot tubs and private gardens. Service is highly personalized.

For creative vegetarian fare, head to lively **Oca Lila** (Av. João Bernardes Rabelo 449, tel. 62/3446-1006, noon-4pm and 6:30pm-midnight Wed.-Sun., extended hours Jan. and June, R$10-20) for salads (self-service buffet lunch), sandwiches, and pizzas. The hangout is popular with healthy youth, who flock to the place on weekends for live music.

TRANSPORTATION AND SERVICES

Located near the *rodoviária*, the **Centro de Atendimento ao Turista** (Av. Ary Valadão 1100, tel. 62/3446-1159, 8am-noon and 1pm-6pm daily) is quite helpful. You can pick up park maps and inquire about guides and excursions. On the Internet, check out www.altoparaiso.com and www.chapadados-veadeiros.com, both featuring bilingual content.

Excursions are recommended, particularly if you're short on time or without a car. **Travessia Ecoturismo** (Av. Ary Valadão 9799, tel. 62/3446-1595, www.travessia.tur.br) and **Alternativas Ecoturismo** (Av. Ary Valadão 1331, tel. 62/3446-1000, www.alternativas.tur.br) offer numerous hiking, mountain biking, and horseback riding trips as well as canyoneering and rappelling. **Ecorotas** (Rua das Nascentes 129, tel. 62/3446-1820, www.altoparaiso.com) offers a wide variety of eco-excursions and organizes alternative therapy and bird-watching outings.

Alto Paraíso de Goiás is 220 kilometers (137 mi) from Brasília. **Real Expresso** (tel. 0800-280-7325, www.realexpresso.com.br) at 10am and 9pm and **Santo Antônio** (tel. 61/3234-3997) at 3pm offer daily buses each from Brasília's Rodoviária Interestadual and Rodoviária do Plano Piloto, respectively. The 4.5-hour journey costs R$38. If you're driving from Brasília, follow BR-020 in the direction of Sobradinho and turn onto GO-118, which leads to Alto Paraíso.

São Jorge

Smaller and quite a bit prettier than Alto do Paraíso, the village of São Jorge is a former quartz-mining town that has given itself over to ecotourism. Despite the influx of nature-loving Brazilian youth in high season, it has retained its small-town flavor. Apart from the advantage of being only 1.5 kilometers (1 mi) from the entrance to the Parque Nacional da Chapada dos Veadeiros, São Jorge boasts a wealth of other natural attractions within close proximity that involve easier hikes than those in the park. The most easily accessible and spectacular is the appropriately named **Vale da Lua** (7am-5:30pm, R$10), or Moon Valley, 6 kilometers (3.5 mi) east toward Alto do Paraíso, where over the course of millions of years the jade green Rio São Miguel has sculpted a canyon out of a lunar landscape of granite. A little further afield and more challenging for hikers, but no less spectacular is the five-hour trek to and from the gigantic waterfall known as the **Cachoeira do Segredo** (Estrada para Colina do Sul, R$15), which is nonetheless alleviated by multiple bathing opportunities in the crystal water of the Segredo and São Miguel Rivers.

ACCOMMODATIONS AND FOOD

While São Jorge has fewer hotel options than Alto do Paraíso, the village's *pousadas* have considerably more charm. **Pousada Trilha Violeta** (Rua 12, Qd. 7, Lote 5, tel. 62/3455-1088, www.trilhavioleta.com.br, R$100-135 d) has simple guest rooms housed in attractive bungalows painted pale violet (the owners are staunch believers in chromotherapy), with verandas gazing out onto a tranquil garden and a "Zona Zen" for meditation. Friendly staff can help you with guides and excursions. A little more upscale is the enchanting **Pousada Bambu Brasil** (Rua 1, Qd. 1, Lt. 8, tel. 62/3455-1044, www.bambubrasil.com.br, R$190-250 d). Comfortable guest rooms sleep 1-4 people and are housed in chalets painted in rich mango and pumpkin hues, offset by exuberant greenery. Hammocks and lounge chairs abound, and there is an inviting pool and a cafe. Children under 12 aren't allowed. The most "luxurious" of São Jorge's accommodations, **Baguá Pousada** (Rua 3, Qd. 16, Lt. 2, tel. 62/8264-0748, www.baguapousada.com.br, R$320-400 d) possesses a quartet of primitive-chic bungalows on stilts that boast king-sized beds, fireplaces, and private decks with hot tubs and hammocks. An alluring restaurant/lounge overlooks gardens with the rocky Chapada mountainscape as a hypnotic backdrop. The entrance to the park is only a 5-minute walk; on request, the kitchen prepares snack boxes for hikers.

For a mixture of local and international fare, head to **Papalua** (Rua 12, Qd. 7, Lt. 8, tel. 62/3455-1085, 5pm-midnight Fri.-Wed., daily in July, R$15-25), celebrated for its homemade pasta and crepes as well as its tasty "trail kit" lunch boxes. **Nenzinha** (Rua 6, Qd. 11, Lt. 2, tel. 62/3455-1085, noon-6pm daily, R$15-20) operates out of the humble home of a former quartz miner, Dona Nenzinha. The local dishes served for breakfast and the buffet lunch feature fresh produce from Nenzinha's own garden.

TRANSPORTATION AND SERVICES

Located at the entrance to town, the **tourist office** (9am-6pm Mon.-Sat.) is where you can pick up park maps and inquire about hiring local guides. For information in Portuguese, visit www.portaldesaojorge.com.br. São Jorge has no banks, so make sure you stock up on cash (credit cards are not usually accepted).

Goiás Velho is surrounded by the Serra Dourada, a region of hills and forests sprinkled with waterfalls and natural pools. The falls closest to town are **Cachoeira Grande,** 7 kilometers (4.3 mi) to the east, and the more spectacular **Cachoeira das Andorinhas,** 1 kilometer (0.6 mi) farther. You can easily get to them by hiring a *moto-taxi.*

★ *Centro Histórico*

Goiás Velho's streets meander haphazardly; if this lack of urban planning wreaks havoc on today's traffic, it also adds considerably to the town's charms and makes wandering a pleasure. For a fine panoramic view, climb up to the threshold of the Igreja de Santa Bárbara. This adobe and soapstone church is one of the more modest of Goiás Velho's seven colonial churches. The most impressive is the **Igreja de São Francisco de Paula** (Praça Zaqueu Alves de Castro, 8am-noon and 2pm-6pm Mon.-Fri., 9am-noon Sat.-Sun.). Dating back to 1760, it features some lovely murals depicting the life of São Francisco.

MUSEU DE ARTE SACRA DA BOA MORTE

The Igreja de Nossa Senhora da Boa Morte now houses the **Museu de Arte Sacra da Boa Morte** (Rua Luiz do Couto, tel. 62/3371-1207, 8am-5pm Tues.-Fri., 9am-5pm Sat., 9am-1pm Sun., R$3). The expressive cedar sculptures, carved by José Joaquim da Veiga Valle, are the pride of its small collection. Veiga Valle was a local baroque artist whose talent earned him comparisons to the legendary Mineiro sculptor Aleijadinho.

PALÁCIO CONDE D'ARCOS

Among the town's secular buildings is the **Palácio Conde d'Arcos** (Praça do Coreto, tel. 62/3371-1200, 8am-5pm Tues.-Sat., 8am-1pm Sun., R$4). Dating to 1755, it was seat of the state government before the capital moved to Goiânia in 1937 (with the condition that every year, on July 25, the governor would return to rule from Goiás for a day). Part of the building currently functions as a cultural

Goiás Velho

From Alto Paraíso to São Jorge, **Santo Antônio** (tel. 61/3234-3997) operates only one bus daily, which leaves at 4pm. By car, follow GO-239 for 36 kilometers (22 mi). A taxi will set you back around R$100.

GOIÁS VELHO

A well-kept secret, Goiás Velho, a UNESCO World Heritage Site, is quite simply one of the most attractive and best-preserved colonial towns in Brazil. Founded in 1726 by fortune-hunting *bandeirantes* who struck gold in the surrounding hills, over the next century Vila Boa (or "Good Town," as it was originally known) evolved from a rugged mining town into a gracious state capital. With the end of the gold rush and subsequent transfer of the capital to Goiânia, Goiás Velho reverted to a certain languor that still envelops the town. The surrounding countryside beckons with its many waterfalls and trails meandering through the Cerrado. Although the town is small, you could easily spend a few days here just soaking up the tranquil atmosphere.

center, but a guided tour takes you through the governor's rooms, which are handsomely appointed with furniture dating back to the 18th century.

MUSEU DAS BANDEIRAS

The former city hall and municipal jail now houses the impressive **Museu das Bandeiras** (Praça Brasil Ramos Caiado, tel. 62/3371-1087, 9am-3pm Tues.-Sat., 9am-1pm Sun., R$4). This museum traces the history of the region's gold rush and sits atop the bucolic Praça Brasil Caiado, its shaded lawns surrounded by picturesque houses and anchored by an impressive 18th-century fountain.

CASA DE CORA CORALINA

Goiás Velho's most popular—and moving—attraction is the **Casa de Cora Coralina** (Rua Dom Cândido Penso 20, tel. 62/3371-1990, 9am-5pm Tues.-Sat., 9am-1pm Sun., R$5). One of Goiás's most beloved poets, Cora Coralina (1889-1985) grew up in the same house in which her mother and grandmother had been raised. Although she had to drop out of school in her early adolescence, Cora loved to read and began composing her first poems at age 14. At 22 she left Goiás for São Paulo and only returned following the death of her husband. By then she was 66. To survive, she made and sold crystallized fruits, or *doces* (her specialty was candied oranges), but she never stopped writing. At the age of 75, Cora published her first book of poetry—minute observations of Goiás and the rhythms of its daily life—and completed two more books before she died at the age of 95. Built in the 1770s, along the banks of the Rio Vermelho, her house is one of the oldest in town. In the bedroom, kitchen, and room where Cora wrote, her possessions are arranged exactly as she left them. A frequent guest at the house was Cora's friend Maria Grampinho, a local black woman who by day wandered the streets and at night slept at Cora's. Her name (*grampinho* means "bobby pin") comes from the fact that Maria wore about 1,000 pins in her hair at any given time.

A cult figure, you'll see Maria Grampinho rag dolls all over town.

Entertainment and Events

Every Easter, Goiás Velho is the stage for one of Brazil's most traditional and haunting religious events, the **Procissão de Fogaréu.** At midnight on Ash Wednesday, all the lights in town are extinguished, and pounding drums and blazing torches accompany a procession of 40 robed and hooded figures as they set off from the Igreja da Boa Morte. While chorales sing Latin hymns and residents brandish candles, these *farricocos* parade around town with the mission of finding and crucifying Christ. The scene is quite medieval and attracts thousands of spectators. Another big draw is the **Festival Internacional de Cinema Ambiental** (www.fica.art.br), held in early June, which brings together environmentally themed films and videos from all over the world.

Accommodations

Right in the heart of town, **Pousada do Ipê** (Rua do Forum 22, tel. 62/3371-2065, www.pousadadoipego.com.br, R$140-180 d) is a welcoming choice steeped in rural charm. Simpler guest rooms face onto an inner courtyard, while newer, more spacious ones gaze onto an oasis-like garden with a pool. **Hotel Casa da Ponte** (Rua Moretti Foggia, tel. 62/3371-4467, R$100-150 d) is another very affordable choice located in a stylish baby-blue 1950s building overlooking the river. Basic guest rooms are a bit cramped and stuffy, but good service and retro allure compensate. A 10-minute walk from the center, the simple bungalow-style apartments at **Pousada Chácara da Dinda** (Praça do Asilo 10, tel. 62/3371-4327, www.chacaradadinda.com.br, R$100-140 d) are set amid a rambling garden shaded by fruit trees that overlook a babbling brook. To cool off, there's a small pool, and to fill up, a gargantuan breakfast buffet.

Food

Goiás Velho is an ideal place to savor

traditional Goiana cooking. Although most restaurants are simple, the fare—usually prepared over wood-burning stoves—is rife with colors and textures. Portions are inevitably whopping. The town is especially famed for its *empadões*—tortes made with a robust filling of chicken, sausage, cheese, potatoes, and *guariroba,* the slightly bitter heart of a local palm. Among other Cerrado fruits you'll encounter, the most ubiquitous is the pungently perfumed *pequi,* which accompanies rice and chicken dishes but also turns up in sweets. (Warning: Don't ever bite into a whole *pequi*—the inner nut is protected by a layer of tiny thorns that will leave you feeling as if you had bitten into a porcupine.) The more exotic likes of *murici, mangaba, cagaita, aracá,* and *buriti* all make appearances in preserves, liqueurs, *sorvetes,* and the *doces* and crystallized fruits sold by women out of their homes (and displayed on windowsills).

One of the best restaurants in town is **Flor do Ipê** (Rua Boa Vista 32-A, tel. 62/3372-1133, noon-3pm and 7pm-midnight Tues.-Sat., noon-4pm Sun., R$20-30), whose tables are scattered around a relaxing tree-shaded garden. Also good for local fare is **Dalí** (Rua 13 de Maio 26, tel. 62/3372-1640, 11:30am-11:30pm Tues.-Sun., R$20-30). Its *empadão* is legendary, as are its typical sweets, including *pastelinho,* a cake made with caramel-like *doce de leite* and cinnamon. If you can only choose one, make it ★ **Braseiro** (Praça Brasil Caiado 3, tel. 62/3371-2892, noon-4pm Tues.-Sat.), a simple but atmospheric family-style restaurant occupying an old house whose high ceilings are papered with mats of woven palm. The all-you-can-eat lunch buffet (R$22) features delicious local dishes and organic vegetables overflowing with flavor.

Once you've finished, you'll lament the fact that there's only one hammock strung from the trees outside.

A good way to ease the digestion process is to head to the lovely wooden 1920s **Bar do Correto** (Praça do Correto, from 7am daily) to indulge in the mouthwatering artisanal ice cream made from local Cerrado fruits. You can also order a beer and drink it on the rooftop.

Transportation and Services

The **tourist office** (Rua Moretti Foggia, tel. 62/3371-7714, www.cidadegoias.com.br, 8am-noon and 1:30pm-5:30pm, Mon.-Fri.) has irregular hours, but you can get help at **Ourotur** (Praça do Correto 15, tel. 62/3371-3346, www.ourotur.tur.br), which also organizes guided day treks into the surrounding Serra Dourada with stops at waterfalls.

Goiás is 320 kilometers (200 mi) from Brasília. However, the only city with easy access is Goiânia, 140 kilometers (87 mi) away. If you're driving, follow BR-070 from Brasília to Goiânia, and then take GO-070. Several bus companies frequently make the three-hour journey from Brasília to Goiânia, among them **Viação Goiania** (tel. 62/3523-8600, www.viacaogoiania.com.br) and **Viação Araguarina** (tel. 62/3253-8600, www.araguarina.com.br). The fare ranges from R$35-45. **Moreira** (tel. 62/3255-1459, www.empresamoreia.com.br) offers hourly service between 6am-8pm, from Goiânia to Goiás Velho. A direct bus will take three hours, and a *"pinga pinga"* (literally "drop drop") bus will take four hours. The fare is R$26. Note that all buses arrive and depart from the newer *rodoviária,* but only some use the old central *rodoviária.*

The Pantanal

The Amazon rain forest may get all the media attention, but it is Brazil's Pantanal region (which spills over into neighboring Bolivia and Paraguay) that has all the wildlife. This unique ecosystem of lakes, rivers, grasslands, and forests is overwhelmingly vast—the size of Great Britain—and amazingly unspoiled. The largest wetlands on the planet, the Pantanal (*pântano* is Portuguese for "swamp") is actually not a marsh but a floodplain of the giant Rio Paraguai and its tributaries. The fact that most of it is underwater for six months of the year means there is little human encroachment aside from traditional cattle *fazendas* (farms). As a result, native fauna have the run of the 130,000-square-kilometer (50,000-sq-mi) territory. *Jacarés* (caimans), for instance, far outnumber both human beings and cattle, but there are also 30 frog, 500 butterfly, 400 fish, 650 bird, and 75 mammal species—all in fantastic abundance and largely unfazed by human presence.

The creatures often seem to have emerged from a mythological menagerie—giant anteaters, armadillos, and river otters. You'll also encounter the world's largest rodent (the *Alice in Wonderland*-worthy capybara, which can weigh up to 45 kilograms (100 pounds); largest stork (the red-necked *jaribu*); largest flightless bird (the greater rhea, an American cousin of the ostrich whose eggs alone are things of wonder); and largest snake (the infamous anaconda—which, although it grows to lengths of 9 meters/30 feet, defies its Hollywood reputation by being something of a shy loner). Rarely seen but avidly sought after are the spotted jaguar and jewel-like hyacinth macaw, which can measure up to a 1 meter (3 feet) from tail to beak. The bird's size and stunning cobalt-blue and banana-yellow plumage have earned it the going rate of tens of thousands of dollars on the black market as well as endangered status.

Fishing enthusiasts: be warned that the Pantanal is one of the best places in the world to go fishing (season lasts Apr.-Oct.). To this day new species are being discovered. Trying sinking your hooks into the highly prized *piraputanga* and *dourado,* as well as *pacu, pintado,* and *surubim.* The most classic catch is the infamous (and surprisingly delicious) piranha, which can easily be lured by baiting a hook with a chunk of raw steak.

Although many of the indigenous groups that originally occupied the area were largely wiped out by colonists, descendants survive on reservations, and their cultural and culinary influence is quite pronounced. Other notable influences include those of the intrepid Paulistano *bandeirantes,* the first non-natives to explore the area; the ranch owners of Spanish and Portuguese descent; and the Gaúchos who emigrated from the south to take care of their herds. Although cattle ranching has become increasingly mechanized, the cowboy remains a strong presence despite the fact that an increasing number of *fazenda* owners are finding ecotourism to be more profitable (and sustainable). The states of Mato Grosso and Mato Grosso do Sul still retain a rugged Wild West flavor.

Planning Your Time

Spanning the states of Mato Grosso and Mato Grosso do Sul, the Pantanal is a difficult region to travel through. Distances are enormous, and roads are scarce. Although the highways linking the major towns are in reasonable shape and have ample bus service, the dirt tracks that approach (but don't enter) the Pantanal are often only navigable by 4WD vehicles—in the dry season. "Doing" the Pantanal on your own is only for the very brave and Tarzanic. The best option is to organize an eco-safari—either individually (more expensive) or as a group (cheaper) out of one of the major access towns: **Cuiabá** and **Cáceres** (Mato Grosso) or **Campo Grande** (Mato Grosso do Sul). Make sure to do this

The Pantanal

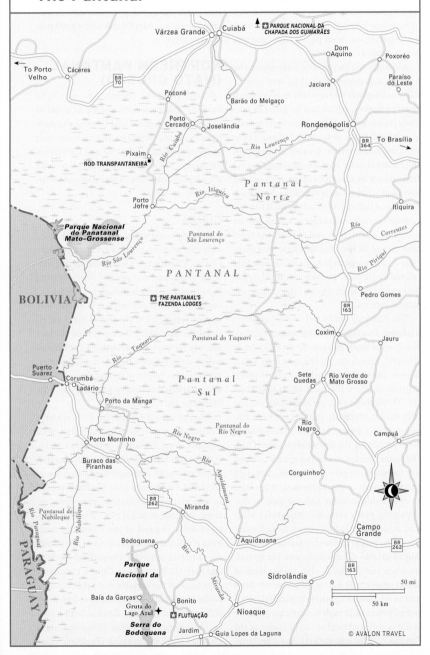

To Porto Velho

Cáceres

Várzea Grande Cuiabá

★ PARQUE NACIONAL DA
CHAPADA DOS GUIMARÃES

Dom Aquino

Poxoréo

BR 70

Poconé

Barão do Melgaço

Jaciara

Paraíso do Leste

Porto Cercado Joselândia

Rondonópolis

Rio Cuiabá

Rio Lourenço

BR 364 To Brasília

Pixaim
ROD TRANSPANTANEIRA

Pantanal Norte

Rio Itiquira

Itiquira

Porto Jofre

Parque Nacional do Panatanal Mato–Grossense

Rio São Lourenço

Pantanal do São Lourenço

Rio Correntes

PANTANAL

Rio Piriqui

BOLIVIA

★ THE PANTANAL'S FAZENDA LODGES

Pedro Gomes

BR 163

Pantanal do Taquarí

Coxim

Jauru

Rio Taquari

Puerto Suárez

Corumbá
Ladário

Pantanal Sul

Sete Quedas Rio Verde do Mato Grosso

Porto da Manga

Pantanal do Río Negro

Rio Negro

Porto Morrinho

Rio Negro

Rio

Campuã

Buraco das Piranhas

Rio Aquidauana

Corguinho

BR 262

Miranda

Pantanal de Nabileque

Rio Nabileque

Rio Paraguai

Bodoquena

Aquidauana

Campo Grande

BR 262

Rio Miranda

PARAGUAY

Parque Nacional da

Sidrolândia

BR 163

0   50 mi

0   50 km

Baía da Garças

Gruta do Lago Azul ★ FLUTUAÇÃO

Bonito

Nioaque

Serra do Bodoquena

Jardim Guia Lopes da Laguna

© AVALON TRAVEL

with only *recommended* outfits; there are lots of scammers and poorly run agencies with incompetent guides with little knowledge of nature or English. Know in advance what you're paying for, never pay up front, and talk to other Pantanal pilgrims.

Although you can explore some regions by Jeep, truck, and horseback, to go deep into the Pantanal requires taking to the rivers in small boats or canoes, which can be hired in outposts such as **Porto Jofre.** Most tours include accommodations at *fazenda* lodges. These working cattle farms, located deep within the Pantanal, offer accommodations ranging from simple to luxurious along with guided tours and activities such as boating, horseback riding, and fishing. Another option is to book yourself into a *fazenda* lodge in advance (often a cheaper alternative) and then let the hotel take care of all your needs. Those with extra time and money can indulge in the ecotours offered by "luxury" houseboats, which is the best way to see more elusive larger mammals such as jaguars.

The Pantanal can be wet or downright inundated. During the **rainy season** (Nov.-Mar.), river levels can rise by up to 3 meters (10 feet), transforming the area into a vast lagoon interspersed with islands of green vegetation where the local fauna take shelter. Throughout this period, boats are the only means of access, animals are harder to glimpse, and mosquitoes are unbearable. In contrast, during the **dry season** (Apr.-Oct.), the water recedes, revealing grasslands and dry forests in coppery earth tones. Although the vegetation is less exuberant, it is easier to spot wildlife, since fish trapped in disappearing pools provide banquets for birds and other animals that gather in vast numbers. The height of the dry season—and the **high season**—is July-September, but no matter when you choose to visit, bring plenty of insect repellent as well as long-sleeved shirts and pants made of lightweight material. You'll need them, even though the daily temperature is hot year-round (nights can be cooler in the "winter"). Although malaria isn't a problem,

you do need to get a yellow fever shot. Since the Pantanal is a remote region, make sure you come equipped with sunscreen, any medication you might need, and a good pair of binoculars.

NORTHERN PANTANAL (MATO GROSSO)

Located in Mato Grosso, the northern Pantanal is accessed via the state capital of Cuiabá. Although Cuiabá is some distance from the Pantanal proper, two highways lead to the settlements of Poconé and Cáceres on the edge of the wetlands. From here, you can get a quick taste of the Pantanal or venture by boat into its depths.

Cuiabá

A thriving commercial center, Cuiabá is the only city of note in the vast state of Mato Grosso. Visually it is a somewhat jarring mélange of colonial vestiges and mushrooming high-rises, but there is enough to keep you occupied here for a day or two. With the only airport connected to the rest of the country, Cuiabá is also Mato Grosso's most obvious gateway for trips to the northern Pantanal as well as to the nearby Chapada dos Guimarães, a spectacular region of mountains, canyons, and waterfalls that rises up suddenly out of the otherwise flat Cerrado.

Cuiabá was founded in 1719 when a Paulistano *bandeirante* stumbled on gold deposits along the banks of the Rio Cuiabá. Fortune seekers immediately set out in search of instant wealth, although the 3,000-kilometer (1,900-mi) journey from São Paulo proved so long and treacherous that many never arrived, let alone struck it rich. When gold petered out at the end of the 1700s, the small town remained an isolated outpost in the middle of Indian territory. Throughout the 19th and early 20th centuries, Cuiabá's economy depended on the region's vast cattle ranches. In the 1890s, an enterprising Brazilian army officer named Cândido Rondon built a telegraph system from Goiás Velho to Cuiabá and then south to Corumbá. (Rondon's forays north into the Amazon inspired the western Amazonian state's name of Rondônia). However, it wasn't until the 20th century that trains, planes, and finally paved highways connected Cuiabá to São Paulo in the south, Brasília and Goiás to the west, and the Amazon to the north, transforming the city into a major crossroads. As a result, Cuiabá is a lively place with a bit of a frontier feel to it. While it is one of Brazil's fastest-growing cities, it is also its hottest. Average temperatures are 27°C (81°F) and can hit highs of 45°C (113°F).

SIGHTS

The two parts of the city—Cuiabá and Várzea Grande (where the airport is located)—are separated by the Rio Cuiabá. The town's main square is the vibrant **Praça da República.** Here you'll find one of the town's most attractive old mansions, the Palácio da Instrução, which houses the **Museu Histórico de Mato Grosso** (Praça da República 131, Centro, tel. 65/3613-9234, 8am-6pm Mon.-Fri., 8am-3pm Sat., free); it traces Cuiabá's colorful past via photos and paintings. Those with a penchant for geography and controversy should walk three blocks south along Rua Barão de Melgaço to the obelisk marking the "supposed" **Centro Geodésico de América do Sul** (Praça Moreira Cabral); according to early calculations, this is the exact center of the South American continent (the residents of the nearby town of Chapada do Guimarães beg to differ).

It's worth checking out the renovated west bank of the Rio Cuiabá. Along the waterfront, pass on the **Aquário Municipal** (Av. Beira Rio) a dank space with depressingly small aquariums; more appealing specimens are at the bustling new **Mercado do Porto** (Av. Oito de Abril, Porto, tel. 65/3313-3332, www.mercadodoportocuiaba.com.br, 6am-6pm Mon.-Sat., 6am-noon Sun.). Not to be missed is the nearby **SESC Casa do Artesão** (Rua 13 de Junho 315, Porto, tel. 65/3611-0500, www.sescmatogrosso.com.br, 8:30am-5:30pm Tues.-Fri., 8:30am-1pm Sat.). Each

room inside this charming yellow villa is devoted to a specific type of Mato Grosso *artesanato*—ceramics, woodwork, weaving and embroidery, bio-jewelry, and indigenous objects. Not only does the ensemble provide a terrific overview of the state's rich artisanal legacy, but everything is for sale (at very decent prices). Temporary exhibits highlight aspects of Mato Grossense culture and an air-conditioned café-emporium allows you to cool off with a *guaraná* juice and savor deliciously moist *bolos de arroz* (rice cakes), a local specialty. Made from local fruits, the *licores* and *doces* on sale are ideal gifts. On Thursday night (6pm-10pm, free) *festas populares* allow you to sample local delicacies and regional music.

NIGHTLIFE

The city's bar scene is concentrated in the center, around Avenida Getúlio Vargas and Avenida Mato Grosso and Praça Popular. Most bars serve food, and you can count on them for dinner as well as drinks. **Choppão** (Praça 8 de Abril, Goiabeiras, tel. 65/3623-9101, www.choppao.com.br, 11am-2am Mon. and Wed.-Thurs., 11am-4am Fri.-Sat.) is a classic hangout. The cavernous restaurant-bar has a wood-beamed ceiling and an outdoor patio that's great for people-watching. Praça Popular is where Cuiabá's young cool off. The coolest bar here is **Ditado Popular** (Rua Senador Villas Boas 86, Goiabeiras, tel. 65/4141-3655, www.ditapop.com.br, 4pm-4am daily), featuring live music nightly and a circulating *rodízio* of finger-licking appetizers. For unpretentious local charm (and the odd breeze), head to **Praça da Mandioca.** By day, this picturesque little square in the heart of the Centro Velho is where Cuiabanos come to purchase manioc flour at a small market. After dark, it's where they come to drink, chat, and listen to music. The **Bar e Restaurante Conde de Azambuja** (tel. 65/8401-1234, 7pm-close), whose walls are decorated with naïf-style local paintings, also has a sprinkling of tables and chairs outside beneath a shady tree. The caipirinhas are appropriately fierce.

SHOPPING

For regional handicrafts, your best bet is the **SESC Casa do Artesão** (Rua 13 de Junho 315, tel. 65/3611-0500, www.sescmatogrosso.com.br). Since this is cowboy country, invest in some authentic *vaqueiro* boots—or some rugged leather sandals—at **Sapataria Barão** (Calçadão da Ricardo Franco 214, tel. 65/3623-8764, 8am-6pm Mon.-Fri., 8am-1pm Sat.), a traditional boot maker located in the heart of the Centro Velho that uses the finest local leather. Close by, get your rocks off at **Vera Forte** (Calçadão do Galdino Pimentel 195, tel. 65/3623-1591, 8am-6pm Mon.-Fri., 8am-1pm Sat.), where you'll encounter precious *pedras* from all over Brazil in both raw and polished states. Among the more enticing finds are gigantic Bahian rubies, brilliant blue apatite, and enchanting Mato Grossense crystals shot through with strands of gold.

ACCOMMODATIONS

There are several good choices near the center of town. Operated by local English-speaking eco-guide Joel Souza, **Pousada Ecoverde** (Rua Pedro Celestino 391, tel. 65/3624-1386, www.ecoverdetours.com, R$40-60 pp) offers simple and worn guest rooms (bathrooms are communal, as is the kitchen) that open onto the courtyard of a rambling old house belonging to Souza's family. Borrow Pantanal books from the library and retire to a hammock in the gardens shaded by fruit trees. A halfway house for Pantanal pilgrims, this is a great place to trade tales and tips with fellow travelers. A more organized budget option with a friendly family vibe is the **Hotel Ramos** (Rua Campo Grande 487, tel. 65/3624-7472, R$50-80 d). Guest rooms are simple but clean, and perks include free Wi-Fi and mineral water. More upscale and comfortable is the **Amazon Plaza** (Av. Getúlio Vargas 600, tel. 65/2121-2000, www.hotelamazon.com.br, R$280-380), one of the nicer modern hotels in the center. Although the large, nondescript guest rooms are blessedly air-conditioned, you can also cool off in the small pool and *redário* (hammock area). A restaurant features great breakfasts as well as regional fare. While somewhat removed from the center, **Gran Odara** (Av. Miguel Sutil 8344, Ribeirão da Ponte, tel. 65/3616-2014, R$310-370 d) gives you considerable bang for your buck. Equipped with a spa, gym, and (small, but cool) pool as well as surprisingly stylish rooms, this is the place to come for a little luxury after roughing it in the wetlands.

FOOD

Cuiabá has a good range of restaurants, most of them very affordable. One of the favorite local traditions is to eat at a *peixaria*, a typical eatery that serves fresh river fish such as *piraputanga, pintado,* and *pacu.* **Peixaria Popular** (Av. São Sebastião 2324, Goiabeiras, tel. 65/3322-5471, 11am-3pm and 7pm-midnight Mon.-Sat., 11am-5pm Sun., R$15-25) is a perennial favorite, where you can try the Mato Grossense specialty known as *mojica de pintado.* The generous portions easily feed two. Another good place for local cuisine is **O Regionalíssimo** (Av. Beira Rio, Porto, tel. 65/3623-6881, 11am-2:30pm Tues.-Sun., R$15-25). Located next in the faded blue Mercado Municipal, this self-service buffet specializes in local fare. Fish is the mainstay, but there are also meat and vegetable dishes. Located next to the SESC Casa do Artesão, the SESC-operated **Mangaba** (Rua 13 de Junho 315-A, Porto, tel. 65/3611-0530, 11:30am-2pm Tues.-Sun), offers a soothing white dining room decorated with local artwork. Stuff yourself on delicious *matogrossense* specialties at the all-you-can-eat buffet (R$44 pp). For decent home-cooking in the Centro Velho, help yourself to the lunch buffet fixings at **Mistura Cuiabana** (Rua Pedro Celestino 8, Centro, tel. 65/3624-1127, 11am-2:30pm Mon.-Fri., R$8-12), a cafeteria-style restaurant housed in the back of a gracious old *galeria* with cathedral ceilings and plenty of whirring fans.

Although *guaraná* (the wonder berry known for its energy-giving properties) is most often associated with its home turf, the Amazon, Mato Grossenses swear by the stuff and use it for a quick pick-me-up on a daily basis. In *casas de guaraná* throughout Cuiabá, you can buy big *bastões* (sticks) of dried *guaraná,* sold in various weights and thicknesses. *Guaraná* in this form is more potent than prepackaged *pó* (powder), and it can be grated into your juice (*guaraná* graters resembling large nail files are sold separately). At **Ranchinho do Guaraná** (Rua 27 de Dezembro 30, Centro, tel. 65/3321-8986), a cool little cavern on one of the city's oldest and most picturesque *praças,* you can buy *guaraná* sticks, powder, seeds, and syrup to go and also down refreshing glasses of *guaraná* juice while sitting at the counter. Those in need of a more serious kick can opt for heavy-duty cocktails such as the "Overdose," whose ingredients include *guaraná* juice, powdered *guaraná, catuaba* (an infusion of native tree barks that jolts the nervous system and your libido), and ginseng.

INFORMATION AND SERVICES

The state **tourist office** (Rua Voluntários da Pátria 118, Centro, tel. 65/3613-9313, www. sedtur.mt.gov.br, 8am-noon and 2pm-6pm Mon.-Fri.) supplies information and maps. Municipal tourist offices are at both the airport and the bus station. Major banks such as Banco do Brasil and HSBC are on Avenida Getúlio Vargas as well as at the airport. The main post office is at Praça da República.

TRANSPORTATION

Cuiabá is linked by air to Brasília, Rio, and São Paulo. **Aeroporto Marechal Rondon** (Av. João Ponce de Arruda, tel. 65/3614-2511) is 7 kilometers (4.3 mi) south from the city center in Várzea Grande. A taxi to the center will cost around R$45. If you booked a tour to a *fazenda* lodge in the Pantanal, airport transfers may be included. The modern *rodoviária* (Rua Jules Rimet, Senhor dos Passos, tel. 65/3621-3629) is 3 kilometers (2 mi) north of the city center. If you don't want to take a cab, there are various municipal buses marked Centro that will get you downtown. Bus fare is R$2.95.

Although the roads are not bad, Cuiabá is *very* far from everywhere by bus—Brasília, for instance, is 1,100 kilometers (680 mi) away. **Motta** (tel. 65/3927-9898, www.motta.com.br) and **Andorinha** (tel. 65/3621-3201, www.andorinha.com) run several buses a day to Campo Grande (11 hours, R$95-115), gateway to the southern Pantanal. Renting a car is useful to drive to the Chapada das Guimarães. Driving along the Transpantaneira is possible in the dry season, but you'll need a tough vehicle such as a Fiat Uno (and keep in mind that there are no gas stations). **Localiza** (Av. Dom Bosco 965, tel. 65/3624-7979, www.localiza.com), in Centro, and **Unidas** (tel. 65/3682-4052, www.unidas.com.br) at the airport are two car-rental options.

PANTANAL TOURS FROM CUIABÁ

Cuiabá is full of tour operators that can organize trips and offer excursions into the northern Pantanal as well as to the nearby Chapada dos Guimarães. For the Pantanal, operators offer different itineraries that include transportation to a *fazenda* lodge combined with guided excursions into the wetlands. Tour operators usually work with specific lodges, but in terms of the itineraries there is flexibility to customize, depending on your budget, interests, and the amount of time available. Prices vary widely, but generally begin at around R$300 per day pp, including all food, lodgings, transportation, guides, and excursion costs. An average price is around R$400. Associated with the Araras Eco Lodge, **Pantanal Explorer** (Av. Governador Ponce de Arruda 670, Várzea Grande, tel. 65/3682-2800, www.pantanalexplorer.com.br) is a highly recommended operator that offers a range of Pantanal excursions led by bilingual guides that include canoe and horseback riding excursions as well as hiking. It also offers trips to the Chapada dos Guimarães, the Cerrado, and the southern portion of the Amazon rain forest.

Operated by knowledgeable local guide Ailton Lara, **Pantanal Nature** (Rua Professor Francisco Torres 48, Araés, tel. 65/9994-2265, www.pantanalnature.com.

br) is another highly regarded outfit whose expertly led tours of the northern Pantanal (and southern Amazon) get raves from travelers as well as TV documentary makers. June-November it operates a jaguar camp at Porto Jofre, which practically guarantees a glimpse of this elusive feline.

Recommended for people who want to build and customize their own tour over the Internet is **Pantanal Tours** (www.pantanaltours.com). A division of Brazil Nature Tours, a Dutch-managed Brazilian tour operator with an office in Campo Grande, the professional English-speaking team is practiced at helping you create a trip—combining the Pantanal with other Brazilian natural attractions—that caters to precisely your needs and budget (their prices are very competitive).

Avian aficionados should check out the bird-watching excursions offered by **Boute Expeditions** (tel. 79/3223-1791, www.bouteexpeditions.com), whose knowledgeable guides are all professional birders.

Chapada dos Guimarães

Only an hour from Cuiabá, the Chapada dos Guimarães is a startlingly beautiful mountainous region situated on one of the planet's oldest tectonic plates. While the tiny eponymous town is pretty—and the nexus for Brazilian New Age types—the surrounding region, with its rugged cliffs, plunging canyons, and abundant waterfalls, is the real draw. Arid scrubland and coppery red rock formations reminiscent of the Grand Canyon alternate with lush patches of tropical foliage that sprout around the many rivers and natural pools. Much of the area is preserved within the Parque Nacional da Chapada dos Guimarães, a park with breathtakingly scenic (though often unmarked) hiking trails and numerous waterfalls that you can swim in. Take note that in the winter months (July-August), temperatures can go down to freezing at night. Summer months are better for bathing and for taking advantage of the marvelous vistas (in the winter, mist is common),

but there are also more crowds and frequent rains. Avoid the weekends, when the region is packed with Cuiabanos in search of a quick nature fix.

★ Parque Nacional da Chapada dos Guimarães

Coming from Cuiabá, the entrance to the **Parque Nacional da Chapada dos Guimarães** (tel. 65/3301-1133, www.icmbio. gov.br/parnaguimaraes, 9am-4:30pm daily) is on MT-251 about 15 kilometers (9 mi) before the town of Chapada dos Guimarães. The park's visitors center is about 8 kilometers (5 mi) past the park entrance and is equipped with a restaurant, snack bar, a store selling *artesanato,* and maps of the park. From here, it's only a five-minute walk to a lookout point, where you'll come face-to-face with the park's star attraction: the **Cachoeira Véu da Noiva,** the 86-meter (282-foot) "Bride's Veil" waterfall that goes plunging straight over a sandstone cliff into a pool (access to the bottom of the falls, where it's possible to bathe, is indefinitely closed). Other popular trails (which require the accompaniment of a hired guide) include the **Circuito das Cachoeiras,** a six-hour hike that passes seven waterfalls (with stops for swimming), and the strenuous eight-hour trek that leads to the **Morro de São Jerónimo,** the highest point of the region, from whose summit the views are astounding.

Beyond the park's boundaries are some worthy attractions. Hailed as the largest sandstone cave in Brazil, the **Caverna Aroe Jari** is an enormous 1,550-meter-long (5,085-foot) cavern whose walls are decorated with primitive paintings dating back 8,000 years. The cave is 40 kilometers (25 mi) northeast of town; getting here involves driving along a dirt road and then hiking 8 kilometers (5 mi). A guided tour is essential.

A 30-minute walk brings you to the **Gruta da Lagoa Azul,** whose crystalline waters turn brilliant blue when hit by the midday rays of the sun (bathing is prohibited). After another 30-minutes, you arrive at the **Caverna**

Kyogo Brado, where you can succumb to the pummeling waters of a small waterfall. These three sights are located on the Fazenda Água Fria (R$35), a private estate. Ecotourist outfits offer a full-day outing (R$160 pp), with a stop at a typical rural restaurant (R$25 pp).

Easier to visit on your own is the **Mirante da Geodésia,** 8 kilometers (5 mi) from town on an extension of the Rua Cipriano Curvo. The *mirante* (lookout) is at the edge of a canyon and offers spectacular sweeping views of the distant towers of Cuiabá and the Pantanal beyond.

CHAPADA DOS GUIMARÃES

The Chapada's geodesic centrality and the positive energies associated with it are partially responsible for a certain mystical, neo-hippie aura that permeates the charming little town of Chapada dos Guimarães. The pretty main square, Praça Dom Wunibaldo, conserves the baroque **Igreja de Nossa Senhora de Santana do Sacramento,** Mato Grosso's oldest church, which dates to 1779. If you visit in late June-early July, take advantage of the **Festival de Inverno,** a lively arts and music festival with an alternative edge. The town is also a good place to pick up locally produced art and handicrafts; several ateliers/shops are located on Praça Dom Wunibaldo.

ACCOMMODATIONS

You'll find a range of places to stay, both in town and in the surrounding countryside. Make advance reservations on weekends and during the summer months. Central and simple but also very welcoming is the **Hotel Turismo** (Rua Fernando Correa 1065, tel. 65/3301-1366, www.hotelturismo.com. br, R$280-320 d). That the town's pioneering *pousada* resembles an Alpine chalet is hardly surprising in view of the owners' German origins, manifested in the general tidiness and coziness of the (smallish) guest rooms and common spaces as well as the amazing array of fresh-baked breads (including rye, pumpernickel, and potato) and cakes served at breakfast. A 15-minute walk from Praça Dom Wunibaldo, the **Pousada Cambará** (Alameda dos Anjos, Florada da Serra, tel. 65/3301-1130, http://sitiocambara.chapadadosguimaraes.tur.br, R$140-200) is enticingly friendly, rural, and rustic. Lodgings are in simple yet cozy rooms in a ranch style house with shady verandas. Further out of town, ★ **Pousada do Parque** (MT-251 km 51, tel. 65/3391-1346, www.pousadadoparque.

Parque Nacional da Chapada dos Guimarães

com.br, R$330-360) takes ample advantage of the fact that it's the only accommodation option on the fringes of the park. Contemplate the Chapada's natural rock sculptures and exotic avians from the observation tower or wander into its midst via nature trails that weave through the Cerrado. The pleasant rooms are a tight fit, but with hammock-slung verandas, a small pool, an al fresco restaurant, and so much sublime Cerrado in such close proximity, you'd be crazy to do anything more than sleep in them. Advance reservations are necessary.

FOOD

Dining options revolve around simple regional fare. You'll find several restaurants and bars on and around Praça Dom Wunibaldo. For lunch, **Passarão** (Praça Dom Wunibaldo, tel. 65/3301-2801, 11am-2pm and 6pm-close Wed.-Mon., R$10-20) offers an all-you-can-eat buffet of delicious, robust fare (with lots of veg options), along with a prime sidewalk vantage point. Dinner is à la carte. At the lovely, laid-back **Pomodori Café** (Rua Quincas Caldas 60, tel. 65/3301-3061, 4pm-10pm Mon.-Fri., 8am-midnight Sat., 8am-10pm Sun., R$10-25), you can get light fare such as salads and *empadas* (try the chicken with pequi) along with soups and homemade pastas. There's even a wine cellar so you can sip a glass at the outdoor tables.

For food with a view, there are several amazingly scenic options. When not mobbed by tour buses (avoid weekends), ★ **Morro dos Ventos** (Estrada do Mirante Km 1, tel. 65/3301-1030, www.morrodosventos.com.br, 9am-5pm daily, R$20-30) is definitely worthwhile. Robust portions of Mato Grossense dishes such as *galinhada* (chicken stew) and *maria-isabel* (a local version of risotto with sun-dried beef, rice, and herbs) are almost as unforgettable as the stunning views. The restaurant is located within a private condominium complex; the entrance fee (R$10 per vehicle) is subtracted from the check.

Only 10 kilometers (6 mi) from Chapada, on the highway to Cuiabá, is the Cachoeirinha waterfall (R$10 entrance fee). After taking a dip, use the R$5 coupon for food and drinks at the rustic **Restaurante Cachoeirinha** (tel. 65/9216-3497, 9am-5pm daily, R$25-40). Dig into enormous portions dishes of *peixe na telha,* a stew in which chunks of *pintado* fish in a seasoned manioc sauce are cooked and served in a curved ceramic roofing tile.

Don't leave town with slurping your way through at least one *picolé* (popsicle) or *sorvete,* artisanally made by **Mazinho** (Rua das Palmeiras 236, 9:30am-6pm daily), which takes advantage of fresh Cerrado fruits such as *buriti, bocaiuva,* and *pequi.*

TRANSPORTATION AND SERVICES

The **tourist office** (Rua Penn Gomes, tel. 65/3301-2045, www.chapadadosguimaraes. mt.gov.br, 7am-6pm Mon.-Sat.) has maps of the park and Chapada along with a list of guides. **Chapada Explorer** (Praça Dom Wunibaldo 57, tel. 65/3301-1290), a friendly and helpful tour operator run by knowledgeable and eco-minded locals, organizes guided day trips as well as longer, multiday itineraries through the Chapada as well as the Pantanal and Mato Grosso's Amazon. Outings include transportation and guides, but not food or entrance fees.

Chapada dos Guimarães is 74 kilometers (46 mi) north of Cuiabá. **Expresso Rubi** (tel. 65/3621-1764) buses at hourly intervals between 6:30am and 7:30pm from the *rodoviária.* The scenic trip takes about one hour and costs R$11. By car, follow MT-251.

Poconé and Porto Jofre: The Rodovia Transpantaneira

The easiest way to enter the Pantanal from Cuiabá is via the town of Poconé, 100 kilometers (62 mi) to the south. The Pantanal begins as you continue south from Poconé along the Rodovia Transpantaneira. Back in the 1970s, when megaprojects were in vogue throughout Brazil, the plan was to build a highway that plowed all the way through the Pantanal from Poconé to Corumbá. Fortunately, neither human beings nor human technology were any match for this aquatic ecosystem—the project was aborted after 145 kilometers (90 mi), at Porto Jofre, a fishing village on the shores of Rio Cuiabá. Over the years, the former highway has metamorphosed into a decidedly bumpy road connected by 126 wooden bridges in varying states of disrepair. However, despite the fact that it is quite overgrown in spots, it is still the only road that actually leads into the Pantanal. The earth that was cleared for the highway's construction left holes that have become ponds, canals, and lagoons. These watering holes attract a wealth of wildlife, making the journey along the Transpantaneira into a fantastic safari (although one that can only be undertaken in the dry season).

The first stretch of the Transpantaneira, between Poconé and the Rio Pixaim, is lined with numerous *fazenda* lodges (cattle are often driven along the *rodovia*). Even if you don't check in as an overnight guest, you can visit these ranch-hotels during the day and partake of the facilities and activities they offer. The second stretch, leading to Porto Jofre, is wilder and more remote (neither electricity nor cell phone coverage have arrived). Make sure you leave Poconé with a full tank of gas and drive slowly—not only due to the precariousness of the road but to avoid running over any *jacarés*, deer, or capybaras that may be crossing. Also make sure to stock up on mineral water (not included in all-inclusive packages, and expensive when you're chugging umpteen little bottles a day).

From Porto Jofre, you can venture farther into the Pantanal by boat, either by sailing up the Cuiabá and Piquiri Rivers or, if you're feeling very adventurous and have lots of time on your hands, by catching one of the infrequent cargo boats that cut all the way through the Pantanal to the town of Corumbá in Mato Grosso do Sul (which could take 2-5 days).

★ *FAZENDA* **LODGES**

Although there are several small and basic hotels in Poconé, you're better off staying at one of the 20 or so *fazenda* lodges scattered along the Transpantaneira highway down to Porto Jofre and the Rio Corumbá. They offer full-board accommodations, recreational activities, and a variety of guided excursions into the wilder regions of the Pantanal. Package trips to the Pantanal usually involve guides taking travelers up and down the Transpantaneira with stops at various *fazenda* lodges, and this is a good strategy if you're traveling on your own, allowing you to experience the region in more depth and improving your chances of seeing a greater range of wildlife.

Closest to Poconé, **Pousada Piuval** (Rod. Transpantaneira Km 10, tel. 65/3345-1338, www.pousadapiuval.com.br, R$440-520 d) is an appealing place located on a sprawling cattle ranch with lakes and patches of forest that attract birds galore. Guest rooms are a little tight but inviting, and there is a large pool. Included in the daily rate are guided hikes and the choice of an excursion by boat or horseback as well as cayman feeding. **Curicaca Eco Lodge** (Rod. Transpantaneira Km 28, tel. 65/3345-2335, www.curicaca.com, R$440-540 d) is also the only one that is no longer a *fazenda*. Taking its eco-mission seriously (many scientific researchers also shack up here), the well-designed and spacious bungalows of recycled wood are hidden in the midst of a wooded reserve along the shores of the Rio Novo (along which guided canoe trips are offered). Adding to the ambiance are the anteaters and coatis that casually amble by the pool, bar, and rustic restaurant serving outstanding Pantaneira food. Farther along, the **Pousada Araras Eco Lodge** (Rod. Transpantaneira Km 32, tel. 65/9983-8633, www.araraslodge.com.br, R$480-670 d) is one of the Pantanal's eco-pioneers, and the owner's conservation efforts ensure that there is plenty of wildlife in close proximity. Bilingual nature guides offer myriad excursions (all included in the daily rate) on horseback and in canoes (by day and night) as well as photo safaris, piranha fishing, and overnight trips. The lodge is stylishly rustic and makes creative use of organic materials. There is a lovely pool, and wooden walkways lead across the lagoons to lofty wildlife observation decks. Reflecting regional culinary traditions, the menu relies on local fish, meats, and organically grown fruits and vegetables. The minimum stay is two days, and its international reputation means you'll need to reserve in advance. The Bar do Araras, located at the entrance, is the only place to get a caipirinha along the entire Transpantaneira.

Way down at the end of the Transpantaneira, along the riverbanks near Porto Jofre, you have the best chance at catching a glimpse of what everyone comes to the Pantanal to see: an *onça pintada* (jaguar). For some years now, U.S. conservationist Charles Munn has made it his mission to help visitors glimpse the rare cats. Munn operates the ecotourism agency **SouthWild** (Travessa da Liberdade 70, Várzea Grande, Cuiabá, tel. 65/3682-3175, www.southwild.com), whose flagship conservation tourism program, SouthWild Jaguar, racked up 3,700 jaguar sightings between 2006 and 2012. SouthWild operates the **SouthWild Pantanal Lodge** (Rod. Transpantaneira Km. 66, R$480 d), an attractively outfitted eco-lodge along the nature-rich shores of the Rio Pixaim. The lodge makes creative use of the former Fazenda de Santa Tereza cattle ranch, along with two rustic (but mercifully air-conditioned) "flotels" in Porto Jofre, where you're guaranteed to see big cats frolicking along the riverbanks during day trips on silent-motored boats. SouthWild offers various multiday Pantanal packages, including a 7-day "Jaguar Extreme" option, where guests divide their time between both outposts.

TRANSPORTATION AND SERVICES

In Poconé, the **Secretaria de Turismo e Meio Ambiente** (Praça Menino Jesus, tel. 65/3445-1575, 7am-1pm Mon.-Fri.) has tourist information and Transpantaneira maps. For cash withdrawals, you'll find a Banco do Brasil at Rua Campos Sales 449.

From Cuiabá's *rodoviária,* **Tut** (tel. 65/3317-2100, www.tut.com.br) has six daily departures to Poconé (2.5 hours, R$26). If you're driving, follow BR-070. If you don't have a car, expect a taxi from Cuiabá to cost around R$200. On the way back, consider taking a *taxi coletivo* (1.5 hours, R$30 pp) departing from Praça Matriz, which will deposit you wherever you want in Cuiabá.

Cáceres

The other access point into the northern

the gateway to the Transpantaneira highway

Pantanal is via Cáceres, a drowsy little town 220 kilometers (137 mi) west of Cuiabá on the banks of the Rio Paraguai. Although farther than Poconé, it offers another alternative for exploring the Pantanal via the river, one that is generally cheaper than the Rodovia Transpantaneira. Lots of boat excursions (including infrequent and inexpensive cargo boats to Corumbá) depart from here. March-October the fishing is fantastic—in September, the town plays host to the **Festival Internacional de Pesca,** the biggest freshwater fishing competition in the world. During mating and hatching season (Nov.-Feb.), fishing is prohibited, and many *hotéis de pesca* (geared specifically to anglers) close for the season.

ACCOMMODATIONS AND FOOD

Cáceres has several simple and inexpensive hotels that offer a great base for exploring the Pantanal. Fishing enthusiasts should try one of the region's *hotéis de pesca*. Only 8 kilometers (5 mi) from Cáceres (access from BR-070 Km 728), the **Pousada Fordinho** (Rua dos Quidás 950, tel. 65/3224-1080, www.pousada-fordinho.com.br, R$360-420 d full-board) offers fairly basic but well-maintained lodgings right on the banks of the Rio Paraguai. Expert fishing guides can take you out on the river so you can land yourself a whopper; other boats are available for ecotours. The restaurant serves typical Mato Grossense fare, taking full advantage of the daily catch.

If your pockets are deep enough, the ideal way for anglers and ecotourists to take advantage of the region's bounty is to book a passage on an exclusive *"barco-hotel"* (also known as a *"botel"*). These generally feature 5-10 cabins and range in comfort from standard to fairly luxurious. Although everything (excluding gear)—from meals and liquor to bait and small boat excursions into the wilds—is included in the price, the price is usually hefty, ranging from R$3,500-5,000 pp for a weeklong trip (usually the minimum). Advance reservations are a must. **Lenda Turismo** (tel. 65/3027-5600, www.lendaturismo.com.

br) operates two of the newer *botels* with air-conditioned bunk-bed cabins and private bathrooms on two decks. It offers both fishing and ecotourism excursions up and down the Rio Paraguai.

TRANSPORTATION AND SERVICES

The local **tourist office** (Rua Riachuelo, tel. 65/3222-3455) has information on hiring boats and finding accommodations. **Leão Tour** (Rua Colonel José Dulce 304, tel. 65/3223-7357) can help with transportation needs and also runs shorter 2-3-day eco-trips up and down the river.

Cáceres is 220 kilometers (137 mi) from Cuiabá. **Verde Transportes** (tel. 65/3316-7500, www.viagemverde.com.br) offers four daily bus departures (4 hours, R$52). By car, follow BR-174, generally in fairly good condition.

SOUTHERN PANTANAL (MATO GROSSO DO SUL)

The southern Pantanal lies within the state of Mato Grosso do Sul. From the rest of Brazil, the main access city is the modern capital of Campo Grande. While Campo Grande is some distance from the wetlands, well-paved BR-262 leads to the smaller towns of Aquidauana and Miranda, where many of the southern Pantanal's *fazenda* lodges—some of them extremely sophisticated—are located. It then continues on to the colonial city of Corumbá, close to the Bolivian border, which is actually located within the wetlands. Due to widespread cattle ranching, the Pantanal's untamed regions are more difficult to access from the south than from Mato Grosso in the north, and encroaching human development means there are fewer of them. Some of the best *fazenda* lodges are tricky to get to. During the rainy season, you can only reach them by chartering a small airplane, which can be very costly (upward of R$2,000 for an hour-long round-trip flight).

Campo Grande

The prosperous and sprawling capital of Mato

Grosso do Sul is an agreeable (albeit often sweltering) city that warrants a day's exploration. Owing to its proximity to Paraguay and Argentina, it is suffused with a distinct Gaúcho flavor, reflected in customs such as drinking *tereré* (iced *maté*) and eating *sopa paraguaia* (actually not a soup at all, but an omelet-like torte made with eggs, corn, smoky cheese, and onion). With the state's only airport connected to the rest of the country, Campo Grande is also Mato Grosso do Sul's most obvious gateway for trips to the southern Pantanal as well as the pristine rivers and lush landscapes surrounding the eco-mecca of Bonito.

Founded in 1889, Campo Grande is a fairly new city that only became the state capital in 1978. Until quite recently, it was little more than a market center for the region's vast cattle ranches. Despite many brash new high-rises, its rural past hasn't entirely rubbed off, and cowboy culture still lingers. Increasingly, however, the crops cultivated in Mato Grosso do Sul have become as important, and profitable, as cattle. Indeed, farmland was what originally drew many immigrants from São Paulo and southern Brazil. With the inauguration, in 1914, of a railroad that stretched from São Paulo to the frontiers of Bolivia and Paraguay, Campo Grande became an important crossroads and thriving boomtown that drew immigrants from far and wide, including a number of Arabs and Japanese, whose presence is still felt today.

SIGHTS

There is just enough in Campo Grande to keep you pleasantly occupied for a day if you don't mind leaving the compact city center. Taxis are plentiful and cheap. The most useful bus route goes along the main street of Avenida Afonso Pena and will get you to the Parque das Nações Indígenas, a sweeping green space housing a resident population of capybaras, toucans, and macaws and two museums. The more interesting of the two is the **Museu das Culturas Dom Bosco** (Av. Afonso Pena 7000, Chácara Cachoeira, tel. 67/3326-9798,

www.mcdb.org.br, 8am-5pm daily, R$5). The fascinating geology section has fossils of everything from gigantic sand dollars to prehistoric fish as well as some multicolored quartz specimens. It's hard not to be knocked out by the rooms lined floor-to-ceiling with display cases of thousands of gorgeously iridescent butterflies (and creepy-crawly insects). The ethnology section features a splendid collection of artifacts made and used by regional indigenous groups such as the Bororo, Xavante, and Carajá. Temporary exhibits round out the offerings, and there's also a small boutique. Also in the park is the **Museu de Arte Contemporânea** (Rua Antônio Maria Coelho 6000, Caranda, tel. 67/3326-7449, http://marcovirtual.wordpress.com, noon-6pm Tues.-Fri., 2pm-6pm Sat.-Sun., free), whose temporary exhibits are worth wandering through.

To get a feel for local culture, hit the **Feira Central** (Rua 14 de Julho 3351, tel. 67/3317-4671, www.feiracentralcg.com.br, 4pm-midnight Wed.-Fri. and noon-1am Sat.-Sun.). The market is full of the exotic scents and colors of local fruits and vegetables, Paraguayans hawking toys and trinkets, and Indians from the countryside selling medicinal plants, seed jewelry, and handicrafts. Should you want a bite to eat, you'll find everything from skewers of barbecued meat to *sobá* at the food section (11:30am-3pm and 5pm-2am).

NIGHTLIFE

Campo Grande has several universities, and a large student population makes for a surprisingly fertile nocturnal scene. Options are concentrated east of Centro along Av. Afonso Pena. Among them is **Café Mostarda** (Av. Afonso Pena 3952, tel. 67/3301-9901, 5pm-1am Sun.-Thurs., 5pm-3am Fri.-Sat.), an upscale urban café-bar with sleek metallic furniture and young folk who lounge around to DJ-spun tunes at discreet volumes. The sprawling outdoor patio is ideal for cocktail sipping and sharing *petiscos* or light meals. More romantic and retro is **Bar Mercearia** (Rua 15 de Novembro, Centro, tel. 67/3384-9622, www.

Campo Grande

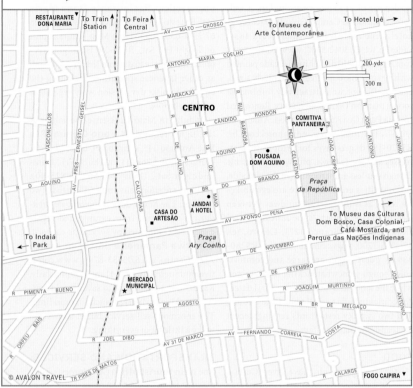

To Train Station
To Feira Central
RESTAURANTE DONA MARIA
To Museu de Arte Contemporânea
To Hotel Ipê

AV MATO GROSSO

R ANTONIO MARIA COELHO

R MARACAJÚ

CENTRO

R VASCONCELOS
AV PRES. ERNESTO GEISEL

R MAL. CÂNDIDO

RONDON

COMITIVA PANTANEIRA

RUA 14 DE JULHO
R 13 DE
R DE
AQUINO

POUSADA DOM AQUINO

R JOSÉ ANTONIO
R 13 DE JUNHO

R PEDRO CELESTINO
R JOÃO CRIPPA

R D AQUINO

AV CALÓGERAS

DO RIO BRANCO

Praça da República

CASA DO ARTESÃO

JANDAIA HOTEL

R BR

MAIO

AV AFONSO PENA

To Museu das Culturas Dom Bosco, Casa Colonial, Café Mostarda, and Parque das Nações Indígenas

To Indaiá Park

Praça Ary Coelho

R 15 DE NOVEMBRO

R 7 DE SETEMBRO

MERCADO MUNICIPAL

R PIMENTA BUENO

R 26 DE AGOSTO

R JOAQUIM MURTINHO

R BR DE MELGAÇO

R JOSÉ ANTONIO

R ORFEU BAIS
R JOEL DIBO
AV 31 DE MARCO
AV FERNANDO CORREIA DA COSTA

© AVALON TRAVEL
TR PIRES DE MATOS
R CALARGE
FOGO CAIPIRA

0   200 yds
0   200 m

barmercearia.com.br, 5pm-1am Mon.-Thurs., 5pm-2am Fri., 11:30am-2am Sat., 11:30am-8pm Sun.), a cozy and classic old-school *boteco* (in terms of ambiance and décor), with a more daringly diverse selection of nibbles and beers.

SHOPPING

Campo Grande is a great place to purchase indigenous art and handicrafts. The **Casa do Artesão** (Av. Calogeras 2050, Centro, tel. 67/3383-2633, 8am-6pm Mon.-Fri., 8am-noon Sat.) possesses an impressive array of works by local groups with some enticing seed jewelry as well as ceramics, wood carvings, and weavings, all for reasonable prices. Another option for souvenirs (from homemade *doces* to cowboy hats) is the lively **Mercado Municipal** (Rua Sete de Setembro 65, tel. 67/3383-3151, 6:30am-6:30pm Mon.-Sat., 6:30am-noon Sun.). While browsing, stop for a classic market snack of a *pastel* filled with cheese washed down with *guaraná* juice. Across from the market, the **Feira Indígena** (Praça Oshiro Takemori, 8am-5pm Tues.-Sun.) is where Terena Indians sell local produce and handmade artifacts.

ACCOMMODATIONS

Centrally located and nicely priced, **Pousada Dom Aquino** (Rua Dom Aquino 1806, Centro, tel. 67/3384-3303, www.pousadadomaquino.com.br, R$126 d) is a friendly, relaxing place to lay your head and catch your breath after a Pantanal trip. Rooms are clean but a little frayed despite some nice retro accents. A pleasant living area and courtyard garden are nicer to lounge around in. A welcome addition to Campo Grande's lackluster hotel scene is **Hotel Ipê** (Rua Ceará 1834, Santa Fé, tel. 67/3042-5000, www.hoteleipems.com.br, R$190-210 d). Behind a façade painted with a giant yellow *ipê* tree are 70 nicely sized, energy-efficient, and attractively minimalist rooms that don't skimp on quality. Renovated **Indaiá Park** (Av. Afonso Pena 354, Amambai, tel. 67/2106-1000, www.indaiahotel.com.br, R$220-360 d) gets raves for orthopedic mattresses and goose-down pillows in its sizable though soulless guest rooms. On the plus side, the amenities are good (there are even bikes for rent!) as is the location, midway between Centro and the airport. At the **Jandaia Hotel** (Rua Barão Rio Branco 1271, Centro, tel. 67/3316-7700, www.jandaia.com.br, R$280-380 d), guest rooms are large and comfortable though somewhat lacking in character, while the lobby and lounges are posh if dated. Amenities include a small pool, fitness room, and two swanky restaurants serving decent local and international fare.

FOOD

History and geography have given Campo Grande a distinctive culinary culture. Due to its cow-town legacy, it is an excellent place to dig into succulent chunks of grilled beef. Among the many high-quality carnivore temples is **Casa Colonial** (Av. Afonso Pena 3997, Centro, tel. 67/3383-3207, www.casacolonial.com.br, 11am-2:30pm Tues.-Sun., 6:30pm-midnight Mon.-Sat., R$25-45), offering an all-you-can-eat *churrasco rodízio*, a salad buffet, and à la carte options in atmospheric surroundings. Thanks to the city's significant Japanese community, decent sushi isn't hard to come by. More popular is *sobá*, a tasty soup of wheat noodles, shredded omelet, and cilantro. Traditionally eaten on New Year's Eve to ensure prosperity in the coming year, *sobá* has become a local staple, spawning *sobarias* where grilled meats, ginger cream, and lots of soy sauce are added to the original

recipe. Apart from the various *barracas* at the Mercado Central (try Barraca da Amélia), the unpretentious **Restaurante Dona Maria** (Av. Ernesto Geisel 5915, Carbreúva 776, tel. 67/3321-0305, 6pm-11pm Mon.-Thurs., 6pm-midnight Fri.-Sat., R$20-30) is a highly recommended place to dig into this broth as well as other Japanese specialties, including the equally popular dry version with vegetables called *yakissoba*.

Indulge in Mato Grossense specialties at the highly reputed ★ **Fogo Caipira** (Rua José Antônio 145, Centro, tel. 67/3324-1641, 11am-3pm and 7pm-11pm Thurs.-Fri., 11am-midnight Sat., 11am-4pm Sun., R$25-40). Portions are enormous and easily satisfy two or three. The house dessert, *bolinho de rapadura* (a cake made from caramelized sugarcane) is accompanied by *sorvete de cachaça*. **Comitiva Pantaneira** (Rua Dom Aquino 2221, Centro, tel. 67/3383-8799, www.comitivapantaneira.com.br, 11am-2:30pm daily, R$20-30) is a good place to savor local farm-style cooking in colorful ranch surroundings. The enormous self-service buffet allows you to try a little bit of everything.

TRANSPORTATION AND SERVICES

The main **tourist office** (Av. Noroeste 5140, Centro, tel. 67/3314-9968, 8am-6pm Tues.-Sat., 9am-close Sun.) offers city maps as well as information about destinations throughout the state. There are also branches at the airport (tel. 67/3363-3116, 6am-midnight daily) and the *rodoviária* (tel. 67/3314-4488, 6am-10pm daily). For online information, visit www.turismo.ms.gov.br.

Banks with ATMs are plentiful at the airport, bus terminal, and in the center of town along Avenida Afonso Pena. You'll find a **Banco do Brasil** (Av. Afonso Pena 2202) and an **HSBC** (Av. Afonso Pena 2440). In Centro, there is a post office at the corner of Avenida Calógeras and Rua Dom Aquino.

Campo Grande has regular flights to São Paulo and Rio, as well as to Cuiabá and Corumbá. The **Aeroporto Internacional** (Av. Duque de Caxias, Vila Serradinho, tel.

All Aboard

Imagine riding through the Pantanal by rail. The Trem do Pantanal, connecting Campo Grande with Corumbá, was inaugurated in 1914 as part of the Estrada de Ferro Noroeste do Brasil, a railroad that enabled people and produce to travel all the way from São Paulo to Bolivia. But from the early 1990s on, only cargo had the pleasure of passing through *pantaneira* landscapes by train. Happily, since 2009, passengers can relive the experience.

Operated by **Serra Verde Express** (tel. 67/3043-2233, www.serraverdeexpresss3029-0759, http://serraverdeexpress.com.br/pantanal), the Trem do Pantanal's signature red train cars operate between Campo Grande and Miranda. Trains depart Campo Grande (8am Sat., R$90-150) for the 10-hour journey, stopping in Taunay and Piraputanga with a pause for lunch in Aquidauana; you can return to Campo Grande by van (R$200) or take the night train in Miranda (R$380 d).

To get around Campo Grande by bus, you'll need to buy a bus pass sold at bus stop kiosks, news *barracas*, and pharmacies. Both single-trip and rechargeable multitrip options are available.

67/3368-6000) is 7 kilometers (4.3 mi) west of the center. A taxi (R$30-35) is the easiest way to get downtown.

The long-distance *rodoviária* (Av. Gury Marques 1215, Universitário, tel. 67/3313-8708) is 6 kilometers (4 mi) from downtown. **Andorinha** (tel. 67/3323-4848, www.andorinha.com) has four daily buses to São Paulo (16 hours, R$170), three to Cuiabá (10 hours, R$110), and nine to Corumbá (7 hours, R$94), as well as to other major towns in Mato Grosso do Sul. **Cruzeiro do Sul** (tel. 67/3321-8797, www.cruzeirodosulms.com.br) offers five buses daily to Bonito (4.5 hours, R$64). For rental cars, try **Localiza** (Av. Afonso Pena 318, Amambai, tel. 67/3382-8786, www.localiza.com.br) or **Unidas** (tel. 67/3368-6120, www.unidas.com.br) at the airport. A taxi to Centro will cost around R$25.

TOURS

The Pantanal is too far from Campo Grande to be explored in a day trip. However, it's possible to organize 3-5-day **ecotours** with city-based operators. With an office in the Hotel Nacional, **Pantanal Discovery** (Rua Dom Aquino 610, Amambai, tel. 67/9163-3518, www.gilspantanaldiscovery.com.br) is one of the oldest and most experienced tour operators in Campo Grande. A division of Brazil Nature Tours, a Dutch-managed Brazilian tour operator, **Pantanal Tours** (Rua Terenos

117, Amambai, Sala 15, tel. 67/3042-4659, www.pantanaltours.com), specializes in trips throughout the Pantanal as well as other natural attractions in Brazil. Even before boarding your plane, their English-speaking team can help you customize a trip that suits your desires and budget.

Aquidauana and Vicinity

Heading west from Campo Grande to Corumbá, BR-262 passes through the towns of Aquidauana and Miranda; both serve as gateways to the southern Pantanal and its many *fazenda* lodges. The sleepy town of Aquidauana is a popular fishing destination with a few sandy beaches, but it's not really worth staying. Instead, check into the *fazenda* lodges (cattle ranch-eco-resorts) in the vicinity of Aquidauana.

★ *FAZENDA* LODGES

At **Fazenda Pequi** (BR-262 Km 497.5, tel. 67/3245-0949, www.pousadapequi.com.br, R$680 d), get behind-the-scenes insight into life on a (very friendly) family-owned *pantaneiro* cattle ranch that dates back to 1850. Guests can stay in fairly basic but comfortable guest rooms in the main house (built in 1920) or rent bungalows for groups of five or six. Other permanent residents of the property include *jacarés*, capybaras, and various bird species. The wide range of activities includes piranha fishing, night forays, and horseback riding. Only 48 kilometers (30 mi) from Aquidauana, this *fazenda* is less expensive and easier to get to than most in the southern Pantanal.

The remote **Recanto Barra Mansa** (tel. 67/3325-6807, www.hotelbarramansa.com.br, R$970 d) can only be reached by Jeep in the dry season (July-Nov.); otherwise you'll have to take an aero taxi (round-trip flight from Aquidauana, 120 kilometers/75 mi, R$600 pp). The subsequent price is hefty, but this *fazenda* is owned by the conservation-minded Rondon family, descendants of Marechal Rondon, who "opened up" Brazil's Central-West. Built in the 1940s, the traditional *fazenda* boasts an enviable setting along the banks of the Rio Negro, which makes it ideal for boat trips in native *ximbuva* wood canoes, fishing, and wildlife watching (particularly birds), as well as relaxing (in dry season, sandy white river beaches appear). The comfortable guest rooms all gaze on the river. A family atmosphere reigns, making service warm and personalized.

FOOD

You could do far worse than tucking into a hearty meal at **O Casarão** (Rua Manuel A. Paes de Barros 533, tel. 67/3241-2219, 11am-2pm and 6pm-11pm Tues.-Sun., R$10-20). Although the specialty is *pintado,* you can also savor *pacu* and *jacaré*. The self-service per-kilo lunch buffet allows you to sample a little (or a lot) of everything.

TRANSPORTATION

Aquidauana is 148 kilometers (92 mi) from Campo Grande; **Andorinha** (tel. 67/3323-4848, www.andorinha.com) has five daily departures (2 hours, R$33). The neighboring town of Anastácio, on the other side of the Rio Aquidauana, is a regional transport hub with bus service to Bonito, Miranda, and Corumbá.

Miranda and Vicinity

Around 70 kilometers (43 mi) west of Aquidauana, the small town of Miranda is a good base for exploring the Pantanal or Bonito, 130 kilometers (80 mi) south. Nestled in the foothills of the Serra da Bodoquena, the surrounding region is the traditional territory of the Terena Indians. Considered one of the best "integrated" of Brazil's indigenous groups, many still live in the area, and you'll encounter a lot of traditional handicrafts, particularly at the **Centro Referencial da Cultura Terena** (BR-262, km 558, 7am-6pm Mon.-Sat., 8am-6pm Sun.) on BR-262 at the entrance to town.

In recent years, Miranda has given itself over to ecotourism. The Miranda, Salobra, and Agachi Rivers offer excellent fishing and are favorite refuges of magnificent and increasingly hard-to-glimpse jaguars.

★ FAZENDA LODGES

Fazenda **Refúgio da Ilha** (tel. 67/3306-3415, www.refugiodailha.com.br, R$405-460 d) is exceptionally located on an island in the Rio Salobra completely surrounded by water and dense greenery. Although fishing is prohibited, masks and snorkels are de rigueur. Bilingual guides share all sorts of fish lore and lead Jeep, canoe, and horseback excursions to spots where it's possible to catch sight of the elusive jaguar. Accommodations are simple but quaint and comforting, and there are plenty of areas for relaxation and reflection. The food is outstanding. There is a three-day minimum stay June-October and a two-day minimum December-May. Access is at Km 573 of BR-262, between Miranda and Corumbá.

One of the Pantanal's most established, luxurious, and expensive *fazenda* lodges, **★ Refúgio Ecológico Caiman** (tel. 67/3242-1450, São Paulo tel. 11/3706-1800, www.caiman.com.br, R$2,100-2,500 d) is well-regarded for its outings, led by excellent bilingual guides and local Pantaneiros, who know the wetlands inside out. Despite the fact that Caiman isn't deep into the Pantanal and its landscapes have been somewhat tamed by intensive cattle farming (guests are encouraged to take part in ranch activities), there is a wealth of wildlife. Accommodations are quite plush—choose from guest rooms inside the original main house or in two outlying *pousadas*. All are exquisitely furnished and equipped with swimming pools. The meals are also quite outstanding and include a traditional outdoor *churrasco pantaneiro* featuring beef raised on the ranch. Canoe, bike, and horseback trips, photo safaris, and night outings are all included, and there is a three-day minimum stay. The *fazenda* is 37 kilometers (23 mi) from Miranda on the road to Agachi; transfers are available.

More affordable and highly regarded is the intimate and efficiently run **Pantanal Ranch Meia Lua** (tel. 67/3242-1450, São Paulo tel. 67/9686-9064, www.caiman.com.br, R$170 d not including activities), located a 15 kilometers (9 mi) from Miranda. This working ranch is presided over by Swiss conservationist and Shamanistic healer Mirjam Goring, who leads meditation sessions along with other activities to relieve stress and get in sync with nature. Multilingual local guides can help you explore the diverse area. The locally sourced food is so good you'll be inspired to take an on-site Pantaneira cooking class. A major bonus is a breezy location that discourages mosquitos.

ACCOMMODATIONS AND FOOD
An alternative to expensive *fazenda* lodges is staying in town and taking tours to surrounding farms and into the Pantanal. The **Pousada Águas do Pantanal** (Av. Afonso Pena 367, tel. 67/3242-1242, www.aguasdopantanal.com.br, R$140-180 d) is a lovely budget choice located in a historic house. Bright, air-conditioned guest rooms are warmly furnished, the ambiance is very welcoming, and there is a pool. The friendly owner operates an ecotourism agency that can organize sports activities and fishing excursions, day visits to *fazendas,* and outings into the Pantanal and to Bonito.

Zéro Hora (BR-262 Km 55, tel. 67/3242-4200, 11am-4pm and 6pm-11pm daily, R$15-25) is a restaurant-bar with a varied menu, ranging from *pintada belle meunière* to cream of piranha, where you can also buy *pantaneiro* souvenirs.

TRANSPORTATION AND SERVICES
For tourist information, your best bet is to consult with the knowledgeable and bilingual staff at the **Águas do Pantanal Tour** agency (Av. Afonso Pena 367, tel. 67/3242-1242, www.aguasdopantanal.com.br). They can provide information about Miranda and the Pantanal and arrange excursions—eco-outings, day trips to *fazendas* and *fazenda* lodges, and packages to the Pantanal and nearby Bonito.

Miranda is 210 kilometers (130 mi) from Campo Grande and 200 kilometers (124 mi) from Corumbá along BR-262. **Andorinha** (tel. 67/3323-4848, www.andorinha.com) offers daily bus service to and from both towns. Both trips last roughly three hours and cost around R$47. Miranda is also only 120 kilometers (75 mi) from Bonito. If you're driving, take the paved road to Bodoquena for 70 kilometers (43 mi), followed by a dirt road that leads to Bonito.

Estrada Parque do Pantanal
Before the construction of highway BR-262, there was only one land route that connected Campo Grande with Corumbá: a dirt road winding through the southern edge of the Pantanal that was laid by the intrepid Cândido Rondon in the early 1900s as part of his mission to extend telegraph lines all the way to Brazil's border with Paraguay. With the inauguration of the highway, Rondon's route was abandoned and forgotten until nascent ecotourism brought it back to life, rebaptized as the Estrada Parque do Pantanal. The Estrada consists of 120 kilometers (75 mi) of dirt road linked by 71 precarious wooden bridges that cut through a wild and beautiful patch of the wetlands where you're likely to see wildlife (although not nearly as much as along the Transpantaneira). The stretch between Buraco das Piranhas and Curva do Leque is where you'll find most *pousadas* as

well as access to some of the region's best *fazenda* lodges.

ACCOMMODATIONS

On the shores of the Rio Miranda, **Passo do Lontra Parque Hotel**'s (tel. 67/3231-6569, www.passodolontra.com.br, R$315-390 d) multitude of wooden walkways stretched over the marshes and bogs make you feel as if you're walking on water, and the accommodations themselves, in wooden chalets, are all on stilts. The budget prices make this the definitive backpackers' choice—there are main bungalows and an *apart-hotel* complex that offers basic guest rooms (up to six people). For those who don't mind roughing it, there is a *redário* (where you can crash in a rented hammock) on a nearby farm along with camping facilities. There are activities and packages geared both toward ecotourism and fishing here. The hotel is 120 kilometers (75 mi) from Corumbá (access is from Km 8 of Estrada Parque via Buraco das Piranhas). There is also a landing strip for airplanes.

One of the more charming and comfortable options in the region, **Pousada Xaraés** (tel. 67/9906-9272, www.xaraes.com.br, R$610-730 d) boasts an idyllic location on the banks of the Rio Abobral, a region flooded with feathered creatures (including hyacinth macaws) as well as some larger mammals. The large air-conditioned guest rooms are handsomely furnished with recycled wood and red ceramic tiles; for cooling off, there's a scenic pool. Tours by boat, horseback, and on foot are conducted by two guides: a Pantaneiro and a biologist-zoologist. This *pousada* is 130 kilometers (80 mi) from Corumbá (access is from Km 19 of the Estrada Parque via Buraco das Piranhas).

TRANSPORTATION

The Estrada Parque do Pantanal extends from Buraco das Piranhas, a settlement located at Km 664 of BR-262, 100 kilometers (60 mi) northwest of Miranda, to Porto da Manga, a fishing village on the banks of the Rio Paraguai where a barge transports vehicles (6am and 6pm daily, R$25). Porto da Manga is 12 kilometers (7.5 mi) from Corumbá. Although a 4WD vehicle is essential during the rainy season (and even so, you should always check weather conditions beforehand), the Estrada Parque is the only portion of the southern Pantanal that you can explore on your own. The Estrada's sole gas station has closed.

Corumbá

Although getting to Corumbá involves quite a journey, once you're here, as you can see from the heights of the city's upper town, the Pantanal is literally at your feet. Subsequently, exploring the wetlands involves less traveling and can be done more inexpensively. Languid and incredibly humid, Corumbá is only 20 kilometers (12 mi) from the Bolivian border and 400 kilometers (250 mi) west of Campo Grande (a seven-hour bus ride). Founded in 1776, by the mid-1800s remote Corumbá surprisingly held the title as the largest river port in the *world*. Ships from the Atlantic would sail up the Rio de la Plata to the Rio Paraná and then continue along the Rio Paraguai to what was, at the time, a thriving city. By the early 20th century, however, spurred on by the arrival of the São Paulo-Paraguay railroad, the town's fortunes had declined. Only recently, with the development of ecotourism and sports fishing (the region is considered one of the best freshwater fishing destinations in Brazil), has it begun to shakily get a new lease on life.

SIGHTS

Although its setting is fairly exotic, there's really not that much to see or do in Corumbá. The oldest and most colorful part of town is the port area, which is lined with some handsome 19th-century colonial buildings. Other sights are a few blocks up from the riverfront. The shady **Praça da Independência** is an elegant square that offers welcome respite from the heat. Nearby, occupying an elegant peach-colored 19th-century mansion is the **Museu de História do Pantanal** (Rua

Manoel Cavassa 295, tel. 67/3231-0303, www. muhpan.org.br, 1pm-6pm Tues.-Sat., free) which, with the aid of panels and objects such as indigenous artifacts and Paraguay War paraphernalia, traces 8,000 years of human existence in the Pantanal.

In a restored old house, the **Estação Natureza Pantanal** (Ladeira José Bonifácio 111, tel. 67/3231-9100, 8am-noon and 2pm-6pm Tues.-Fri., 2pm-6pm Sat., R$3) is operated by O Boticário, one of Brazil's largest and most environmentally engaged cosmetics and beauty products companies (you'll see stores throughout the country). The company is renowned for its research into and sustainable use of products from the Amazon and the Pantanal. This museum features engaging interactive exhibits that highlight the richness of the region's ecosystem.

Corumbá's only surviving legacy of its role as defender of Brazil's western frontier is the octagonal **Forte Junqueira** (Rua Cáceres 425, 8am-11am and 2pm-4:30pm Mon.-Fri.). Occupied by local army recruits, who are happy to give guided tours to Portuguese speakers, it's worth checking out if only for the splendid views of the Rio Paraguai.

SHOPPING

For a selection of locally made art and handicrafts, visit the **Casa do Artesão** (Rua Dom Aquino Correia 405, tel. 67/3231-2715, 7am-11am and 2pm-5pm Mon.-Fri.), located in a former prison, where each cell showcases the work of an individual artist. Common materials you'll come across include fish skin and palm fibers. **Casa de Massabarro** (Rua da Cacimba, tel. 67/3231-0518, 8am-11:30am and 1pm-5pm Mon.-Fri., 8am-noon Sat.) sells clay figures representing the flora and fauna of the Pantanal along with icons of São Francisco (patron saint of ecology) and of Our Lady of the Pantanal.

ACCOMMODATIONS

Although there's no reason to stay in Corumbá (it's more of a convenient base than a destination in itself), the town has a large number of hotels, particularly cheap budget choices; most are located near the bustling (and sometimes noisy) port. Other options include the more "luxurious" houseboats that travel up and down the Rio Paraguai regions and the *fazenda* lodges of the surrounding region (particularly along the Estrada Parque do Pantanal).

The organized and efficient **Santa Mônica Palace Hotel** (Rua Antônio Maria Coelho 345, tel. 67/3234-3000, www.hsantamonica.com.br, R$185 d) is fairly dated (late 1950s), but it is one of the more comfortable hotels in town. Tidy guest rooms are uninspiring, but those higher up have enticing views. A sizable pool (with a slide!) is surrounded by a garden patio. The once grand **National Palace Hotel** (Rua América 936, tel. 67/3234-6000, www.hnacional.com.br, R$230 d), if not exactly stylish, is also comfortable. Neat, modern guest rooms are smart though bland, and the pool is welcome.

FOOD

"When in the Pantanal . . ." eat fish. **Migueis Peixaria** (Rua Frei Mariano 700, tel. 67/3231-4798, 11am-2:30pm and 6pm-11pm daily, R$20-30) may be modest in appearance, but this lively, family-run eatery serves up some of the best prepared dishes in town, along with a per-kilo buffet and à la carte menu. The surprisingly intimate and innovative **Avalom Bistro** (Rua Frei Mariano 499, tel. 67/3231-4430, 6pm-11pm Mon.-Fri., noon-11pm Sat.-Sun, R$10-20) offers refined riffs on local fish and other regional ingredients, often mixing them up with Euro-gastronomic staples such as pasta, risotto, and pizza. At **Ceará** (Rua Albuquerque 516, tel. 67/3231-1930, 11am-2:30pm and 7pm-11pm Tues.-Sun., R$20-30), *pintado* reigns in many guises (some lighter than others); try the classic *pintado à urucum* or fried *à pantaneira,* which comes accompanied with bananas and manioc and can be eaten in the garden. For regional specialties, head to **Vila Moinho,** a snack bar located inside the **Instituto Moinho Cultural** (Rua Comendador Domingos Sahib 300, tel. 67/3232-9981, www.moinhocultural.org.br, 7:30am-5pm, Mon.-Fri.). The cultural center is worth checking out for musical and dance performances by local kids and teens as well as locally designed T-shirts and accessories in the boutique.

TRANSPORTATION AND SERVICES

Located on the waterfront, the **tourist office** (Rua Manuel Cavassa 275, tel. 67/3231-5221, 1:30pm-6pm Mon., 8:30am-11:30am and 1:30pm-6pm Tues.-Fri.) is a good place for information about accommodations, tour companies, and boat trips. Close by, you'll find most of the fishing and tour operators. You can also check out www.corumba.com.br, a site in Portuguese. **Banco do Brasil** (Rua 13 de Junho 914) and **Bradesco** (Rua Delamere 708) have ATMs that accept international cards.

Corumbá is awash with **tour operators** (and some rather aggressive representatives who will approach you in the street) offering fishing excursions, boat trips, and Jeep trips that range from budget to super-luxurious and last from half a day to a week. **Joice Pesca e Tur** (Rua Manuel Cavassa 1, tel. 67/3232-4048, www.joicetur.com.br) specializes in fishing excursions on a wide variety of vessels and *barco-hotels.* **Canaã Viagens e Turismo** (Rua Colombo 245, tel. 67/3231-3667, www.pantanalcanaa.com.br) organizes both fishing trips and ecotourism packages into the Pantanal.

Corumbá's **Aeroporto Internacional** (Rua Santos Dumont, tel. 67/3231-3322) has few regular flights other than those to Campo Grande via Bonito. Small planes depart from here to airfields within the Pantanal. The airport is 5 kilometers (3 mi) north from the center of town; a taxi will cost around R$20-25. The long-distance *rodoviária* (Rua Porto Carrero, tel. 67/3231-2033) is around 3 kilometers (2 mi) west from the center of town. **Andorinha** (tel. 67/3231-2033, www.andorinha.com) operates a daily bus to Campo Grande (7 hours, R$92) via Aquidauana and Miranda (3 hours). **Cruzeiro do Sul** (tel. 67/3231-9318, www.cruzeirodosulms.com.br) offers one daily departure at 7am to Bonito (5 hours, R$72). Municipal buses connect the *rodoviária* with the local bus station in the center of town. Alternatively, you can take a taxi or *moto-taxi.*

BONITO

In Portuguese, *bonito* means "beautiful," an apt name for this patch of paradise on the southern fringe of the Pantanal. One of Brazil's hippest ecotourist destinations, Bonito and the surrounding area offers visitors a range of magnificent natural attractions, including caverns, waterfalls, rivers with bright fish-filled waters as clear as glass, and the verdant forests of the Serra da Bodoquena mountain range.

Although Bonito has been discovered, the crowds haven't marred this unspoiled spot thanks to careful vigilance, which has transformed it into a model of sustainable tourism. Strict rules abound: No one can set foot on any trail or enter any river without making a reservation, paying an eco-charge, and hiring a guide. Each attraction has a limit on the number of visitors at any given time. Paradise doesn't come cheap—guides and entrance fees cost upward of R$150 per day, and the farther-flung attractions involve spending a frustrating amount of time on the road. However, most admit that the distances and costs involved are a small price to pay for experiencing Bonito's natural marvels. Winter (with the exception of July) is recommended for travel; not only will you avoid summer crowds (and score low-season discounts), but reduced rainfall means increased visibility in the region's rivers. The downside is that bathing in the waterfalls is an icy experience.

Sights

Bonito is surrounded by grottos, forests, rivers, and wildlife sanctuaries, most located on private *fazendas* which can be visited by guided tours. Most involve half-day or full-day trips in small groups, which need to be reserved and paid for in advance at one of the town's many tour agencies. Often lunch is included in the price. Besides hiking, sports include horseback riding, climbing, rappelling, white-water rafting, and the activity that is synonymous with Bonito: "floating." Independent-minded adventure-sports enthusiasts will probably chafe at all the rules and the guidance of monitors; however, for kids, elderly travelers, and more reticent or nonathletic types, Bonito provides an ideal and safe environment to indulge in such diversions.

GRUTA DO LAGO AZUL

One of Bonito's most popular attractions, the **Gruta do Lago Azul** (Rodovia Três Morros Km 22, R$60 for a four-hour tour) is a deep cavern (accessed by 287 precarious stairs) adorned with stalactites and stalagmites. At the bottom lies an impossibly blue lagoon whose depth has never been measured; its age is estimated at 10 million years. When illuminated by the sun's rays, the *lagoa* turns a piercing turquoise, a truly magical phenomenon that only occurs November-January 8:30am-9am.

BURACO DAS ARARAS

Fazenda Alegre hosts the **Buraco das Araras** (BR-267 Km 58, tel. 67/3255-4344, http://buracodasararas.tur.br, 7am-5pm daily, R$45 for 1-hour visit), a favorite roosting spot for more than 40 exotic bird species, among them the gaudily colored *arara vermelha* (red macaw). Now an ecological refuge, the Buraco can be visited with an excursion (the tour lasts an hour). The best time to see the macaws is in the morning when they rise from their nests and start to sing in unison. Bring binoculars. The Fazenda Alegre is some 50 kilometers (30 mi) from Bonito; it's often combined with a trip to the Recanto Ecológico do Rio Prata, a top *flutuação* destination located nearby.

Recreation

HIKING

There are wonderful opportunities for hiking in the Serra da Bodoquena. The **Parque das Cachoeiras** (Estrada Aquidauana Km 18, tel. 67/3225-3910, www.parquecachoeiras.com.br, R$115 includes lunch and snack) boasts six fabulous cascades, all of which can be visited during a 3-hour trek, as well as small grottoes and refreshing springs that are ideal for bathing. At a former cattle ranch, **Estância Mimosa** (Estrada Bodoquena Km 26, www.estanciamimosa.com.br, R$105 includes lunch), encounter eight falls during a 3.5-hour hike; at the end, enjoy a delicious home-cooked lunch at the *fazenda* house.

A popular trek along the banks of the Rio Olarias stops at the **Cachoeiras do Rio do Peixe** (Estrada Bodoquena Km 33, R$165 includes lunch). The guided hike (three hours) ends at a high point—dive off a three-meter-high (10-foot) rock into the Poço do Arco-Iris, the source of the Rio do Peixe. The expedition is capped off with a return to the ranch house; after a hearty Pantaneira lunch and sampling of regional sweets, relax in a hammock.

At 157 meters (515 feet), the Boca da Onça (Mouth of the Jaguar) waterfall is the highest *cachoeira* in Mato Grosso do Sul. Yet it's only one of a dozen scattered throughout the vast **Boca da Onça Ecotour** (Estrada Bodoquena, Km 65, tel. 67/3268-1711, www.bocadaonca.com.br, R$123 includes lunch, R$275 includes rappelling) nature reserve. A 3.5-hour trek allows you to explore them all and dive into a few. Afterward, tuck into a traditional meal at the main *casa,* then laze around a natural pool. Those who undergo a previous day's course at a training center in town can plunge off a 90-meter (295-foot) rappel platform (the highest in Brazil) overlooking the spectacular Rio Salobra canyon.

RAPPELLING

There are several places you can rappel in Bonito (including Buraco das Araras and the Boca da Onça), but the most breathtaking is the **Abismo Anhumas** (Estrada Campo dos Índios Km 24, Fazenda Anhumas). If you've never rappelled before, this is the perfect initiation; a day prior, you'll have a 30-minute practice session at a climbing wall in town. After monitors teach you the ropes, get geared up to leap into a narrow crack in the earth. You'll plunge 72 meters (236 feet) into an abyss that widens into one of the largest underground caves in Brazil; the walls are adorned with fantastical stalactites and stalagmites. At the bottom lies an underground lake the size of a soccer field, where you can snorkel or dive in water whose visibility extends 30 meters (90 feet). The outing lasts four hours, with 30 minutes spent in the water. Rappelling with snorkeling costs R$465, and with diving costs R$650. Reserve in advance since only two groups of eight people can visit per day.

★ FLUTUAÇÃO

Bonito is famous for its *flutuação* (flotation). Don a mask, snorkel, wetsuit, and life jacket and let yourself be carried down Bonito's rivers, whose unearthly transparency allows astonishing close-up interaction with more than 80 varieties of fish. The sensation is akin to being let loose within a giant tropical aquarium (don't show up without an underwater camera). The fantastic visibility extends to 50 meters (165 feet) and is due to the water's high limestone content, which acts as a natural filter, leaving the rivers exceptionally pure. You don't need any diving experience

to "float": After a few practice sessions with monitors, just let yourself literally go with the flow. Among the colorful fish you'll see are *piraputangas, dourados,* and *curimbatás*—rest assured that piranhas prefer other aquatic pastures.

The **Aquário Natural** (Estrada Jardim Km 7, www.aquarionatural.com.br) is the highlight of the **Reserva Ecológica Baía Bonita,** a wildlife sanctuary whose crystalline rivers can be explored with snorkeling equipment or glass-bottomed boats. Recommended for beginners (there is a training session before you hit the river), this 500-meter (1,600-foot) underwater excursion is dazzling but all too brief—its popularity limits float time to one hour. The price (R$132) includes access to hiking trails and lunch. An extra R$30 buys access to the Trilha dos Animais, an open-air wildlife refuge.

Longer yet equally stunning floating experiences can be had on other rivers. Close to Bonito, **Bonito Aventura** (Estrada Jardim Km 6, www.bonitoaventura.com.br, R$170 with lunch) offers a 1.5-kilometer forest hike amidst toucans and monkeys followed by a two-hour aquatic journey down the Rio Formoso that involves sailing over mini-waterfalls.

snorkeling in Recanto Ecológico, Rio da Prata, Bonito

At **Barra do Sucuri** (Estrada São Geraldo Km 17, www.sucuri.com.br, R$168 includes lunch), a boat travels up the jungle-fringed Rio Sucuri to the Rio Formoso and then lets you glide all the way back down again on your own. Rio Sucuri's riverbed is composed of calcified snail shells; the waters are particularly blue and transparent, with clear views of the swaying jungle of aquatic plants.

Bonito's latest flotation destination is **Nascente Azul** (Estrada Bodoquena Km 29, www.nascenteazul.com.br, R$132 with lunch). A 2-kilometer (1-mi) forest trek is an idyllic prelude to entering the Eden-esque and terribly blue *nascente* (spring); from here, you'll float beneath a jungle canopy until reaching Praia da Capela, a beautiful sandy beach.

Bonito's furthest *flutuação* option is also its best. Located on a reserve 50 kilometers (30 mi) from Bonito, **Recanto Ecológico Rio da Prata** (BR-267 Km 518, Fazenda Cabeceira da Prata, www.riodaprata.com.br, R$162 with lunch) offers various activities. The most unforgettable is floating down the astonishingly clear Rio Olho d'Água (and slightly less clear Rio da Prata) in the colorful company of more than 50 species of fish, including the enormous, sinister-looking *dourado* and extended families of *pacu*. A 40-minute hike through tropical forest precedes the hour-long aquatic journey.

It is possible to go scuba diving in Rio Formoso, Rio da Prata, the Abismo Anhumas, and the aptly named **Lagoa Misteriosa** (www.lagoamisteriosa.com.br), a bottomless underwater lagoon close to the Rio da Prata. Expect to pay between R$200-300 per dive.

SWIMMING

Most of Bonito's attractions involve a certain amount of travel, physical exertion, and considerable outlay of cash. To stay closer to home, head to the beaches, natural pools, and waterfalls around town, accessible via car or moto-taxi (R$7-10). Bonito's local swimming hole is **Balneário Municipal** (Estrada Jardim, tel. 67/3255-1966, 8am-6pm daily,

R$20), only 6 kilometers (3.5 mi) away, and consists of numerous pools and falls fed by the Rio Formoso. Popular with families, it can get packed on weekends and holidays. There are restaurants, bars, picnic areas, a zip line, and even a giant chess board. It's only 8 kilometers (5 mi) to **Balneário Monte Cristo** (Estrada Rio Sucuri, tel. 67/3255-1008, R$30), which, in addition to natural pools and a large waterfall, offers floatation in the clear waters near the source of the Rio Formosinho. An on-site restaurant serves typical dishes, and there are vast lawns for picnics.

Nightlife

Taboa Bar (Rua Colonel Pilad Rebuá 1837, tel. 67/3255-3598, www.taboa.com.br, 5pm-2am daily) is Bonito's big nocturnal hangout. Locals and tourists alike fill the tables inside and on the sidewalk to converse over a beer or a Taboa, the house specialty of *cachaça* infused with honey, cinnamon, herbs, and an energetic twist of *guaraná* powder (manufactured at a nearby distillery).

Accommodations

Even in high season, there are lots of places to stay in Bonito. For the backpacking crowd, you can't beat the **Pousada São Jorge** (Rua Colonel Pilad Rebuá 1448, tel. 67/3255-1645, www.pousadasaojorge.com.br, R$90 d, R$30 pp), a welcoming place that's more of a hostel with dorms (four, six, and eight people) and private rooms. Pros include a strategic location on the main drag, a communal vibe (and kitchen), and a helpful on-site ecotour agency. Cons are the rather stark (sometimes dark) aspect of the basic rooms. Perched on a hill overlooking town, the **Chale do Bosque** (Rua Lício Borralho 100, tel. 67/3255-3213, www.chaledobosque.com.br, R$215-265 d) is an idyllic getaway. Seven stone bungalows are decked out in rough-hewn unpolished wood and sport verandas with panoramic views and visiting toucans.

Artist and world traveler Maria Pires transformed her plans for a local art gallery into the lovely ★ **Pousada Galeria Artes** (Rua Luiz da Costa Leite 1053, tel. 67/3255-4843, www.pousadagaleriaartes.com.br, R$160-220 d). The four homey suites and surrounding gardens, patios, and pool are suffused with warmth; Maria and her husband, Frank, serve lavish breakfasts. On the northwest edge of town, some 3 kilometers (2 mi) from the center, the **Pousada Olho d'Agua** (Rodovia Três Morros, tel. 67/3255-1430, www.pousad-aolhodagua.com.br, R$190-280 d) offers a deliciously tranquil retreat. A lodge constructed out of "eco-bricks" is set in the middle of a wooded estate dotted with ponds, a lovely pool, and a bar. The simple, appealing guest rooms are ensconced in bungalows, and you can take advantage of an in-house tour operator. A taxi to Centro costs around R$15.

Bonito also has its share of *fazenda* hotels in the countryside. The advantage is that many have private access to rivers. The downside is their isolation from town (although some may see this as a plus). Most charming is the ★ **Santa Esmeralda** (Estrada Guia Lopes Km 17, tel. 67/3255-2683, www.hotel-santaesmeralda.com.br, R$430-620 d), a stellar example of eco-chic—from the spacious private bungalows (accommodating up to six people) with living rooms and verandas to the enticing restaurant, bar, and lounge areas. However, the real attraction is the estate itself: a vast area of verdant rolling hills with nature trails, natural pools, and access to the Rio Formoso (the hotel provides *flutuação* gear as well as kayaks). Prices include dinner as well as breakfast.

Food

It's impossible to go hungry in Bonito. Located in an atmospheric wooden house, **Casa do João** (Rua Colonel Nelson Felício dos Santos 664, tel. 67/3255-1212, 11am-2:30pm and 6pm-11:30pm Wed.-Mon., daily Dec.-Feb. and July, R$20-35) serves hearty portions of *pantaneiro* fish dishes; save room for the *petit gâteau* made from guavira, a local fruit. The adjacent Armazém do João sells purchase-worthy

artesenato. The varied menu at **Castellabate** (Rua Colonel Pilad Rebuá 2168, tel. 67/3255-1713, 11:30am-3pm and 6pm-11pm Mon.-Tues. and Thurs.-Sun., 11am-midnight daily Jan.-Feb. and July, R$20-35) includes pizzas, pastas, and regional dishes.

Although fish is the common thread running through the menu at **Sale e Pepe** (Rua 29 de Maio 971, tel. 67/3255-1822, 6pm-11pm Tues.-Sun., daily Dec.-Feb. and July, R$15-30), recipes run the gamut from *pantaneiro* to Japanese and Chinese. **Vício da Gula** (Rua 29 de Maio, tel. 67/3255-2041, noon-midnight Tues.-Wed. and Thurs-Sat., 3:30pm-midnight Sun., R$10-15) is a great place for a snack, sandwich, burger, or light meal. For late-night sweet cravings, head to the **Palácio dos Sorvetes** (Rua Coronel Pilad Rebuá 1915, 9:30am-midnight daily). Its 45 flavors of ice cream range from classics such as chocolate to the rarefied likes of *jaracatiá* and *bocaiúva,* two of the sweetest and most succulent fruits of the Cerrado.

Transportation and Services

All ecotour agencies and hotels offer loads of information. For more information, check out www.portalbonito.com.br and www.tur-ismo.bonito.ms.gov.br (both in Portuguese). A **Banco do Brasil** is at Rua Luiz da Costa 2279.

Unless you're on a package, on-site tours of natural attractions don't include transportation and there is no bus service. One alternative is to share costs of the vans operated by local tourist agencies (around R$35 pp per day). The only disadvantage is you'll have to adhere to the vans' schedules. Another option is to take a taxi. While there is no shortage of taxis, they have all made a pact to charge the same rather extravagant rates (upward of R$130 per day). You might find it more economical to rent a car in Campo Grande (there are no car rental agencies in Bonito).

Cruzeiro do Sul (tel. 67/3255-1606, Bonito, www.cruzeirodosulms.com.br, four hours, R$64) runs four daily buses between Campo Grande and Bonito. If you're driving, from Campo Grande take BR-060 and then MS-382; both are paved.

ECOTOURS

Bonito's tourism is highly organized. Many of the larger hotels have their own tour companies or can organize guides and excursions. However, there is no lack of tour agencies in town. All excursions and activities in Bonito have set prices (although they can be lower across the board during off-season). Recommended agencies include **Ygarapé Tour** (Rua Colonel Pilad Rebuá 1956, tel. 67/3255-1733, www.ygarape.com.br), which offers excursions, guides, and scuba diving for beginners, and **H20 Turimso** (Rua 24 de Fevereiro 2101, tel. 65/3255-3535, www.h2o-ecoturismo.com.br). December-January and June, make reservations at least three months in advance.

Bahia

I t's the rare visitor who isn't mesmerized by São Salvador da Bahia dos Santos. With its flood of baroque churches in an idyllic setting overlooking the shimmering Bay of All Saints, Brazil's first capital is magical.

Bahians refers to it as *axé*, or "good energy." But the truth is that in Salvador, life flows in a different rhythm. Like the warm Atlantic waters that lap its shores, time is more liquid here. Its balmy climate, sea breezes, and enticing beaches are constant companions. Music, too, is everywhere—from the chants of the beach vendors hawking grilled shrimp to the twang of the one-string *berimbaus*, a bow-shaped instrument of African origin that accompanies spinning *capoeiristas* as they practice their graceful combination of dance and martial art. African elements seep into every facet of Bahian culture: from language and music to religion and food. Fused together with Catholic elements, this African legacy is vibrantly on display in the dozens of popular *festas* that invade the streets in the summer. Of course, Soteropolitanos (as the capital's inhabitants are known) are never hard-pressed to find an excuse for a party.

It would be a crime not to visit Bahia's capital city of Salvador, but it would be pure sin to miss the many natural, historic, and cultural attractions within the largest of Brazil's northeastern states: the gentle hills and decaying sugarcane plantations of the Recôncavo region that ring the Baía de Todos os Santos; the colonial towns of Santo Amaro and Cachoeira, both known for their religious celebrations; and a long string of idyllic beach towns stretching along the coast.

PLANNING YOUR TIME

For some travelers, Salvador is a complete destination in itself. Certainly the city offers a rich local culture, dazzling baroque architecture, a pulsing nightlife, relaxing beaches, and (in summer) some of the most colorful and popular *festas* in Brazil. To get a taste of the place, spend at least **3-4 days**. Toss in the easily accessible surrounding area with its idyllic beaches, the colonial towns of the Reconcâvo region, the spectacular natural attractions of

Previous: Praia dos Coqueiros, Trancoso; Igreja Rosário dos Pretos in Pelourinho, Salvador; **Above:** Praia do Forte.

Highlights

★ **Carnaval:** Billed by the *Guinness Book of World Records* as the world's biggest street party, Salvador's mind-blowing Carnaval is also Brazil's longest, lasting a full seven days (page 356).

★ **Mangue Seco:** On Bahia's northern coast, Mangue Seco is a deserted paradise of dunes, palms, rivers, and ocean (page 371).

★ **Cachoeira:** This sleepy colonial town on the banks of the Rio Paraguaçu preserves some of the African diaspora's oldest religious and musical traditions (page 373).

★ **Parque Nacional da Chapada Diamantina:** In the heart of Bahia's arid interior, this lush, mountainous plateau region is filled with hiking trails, waterfalls, and colonial diamond-mining towns (page 376).

★ **Barra Grande:** Perched on Brazil's third largest bay, the Baía de Camamu, Barra Grande boasts a laid-back vibe and stunning beaches, including the Taipu de Fora (page 388).

★ **Trancoso:** The ultimate in hippie chic, the village of Trancoso is cosmopolitan yet rustic, and blessed with stunning beaches (page 401).

★ **Pelourinho:** The winding streets of Salvador's colonial center are awash in museums, music, magnificent baroque churches, and faded treasures that conjure up its glory days as Brazil's first capital (page 338).

★ **Igreja e Convento de São Francisco and the Igreja da Ordem Terceira de São Francisco:** The adjoining church and convent devoted to St. Francis are some of the most glorious examples of baroque art in all Brazil (page 343).

★ **Caraíva:** For an idyllic, away-from-it-all beach experience, it's hard to beat the rustic charms of this tiny fishing village surrounded by some of Bahia's most gorgeous and deserted beaches (page 404).

★ **Parque Nacional Marinho dos Abrolhos:** This offshore marine reserve is a diver's delight; both Charles Darwin and Jacques Cousteau were impressed by the spectacle of sea life here (page 407).

Bahia

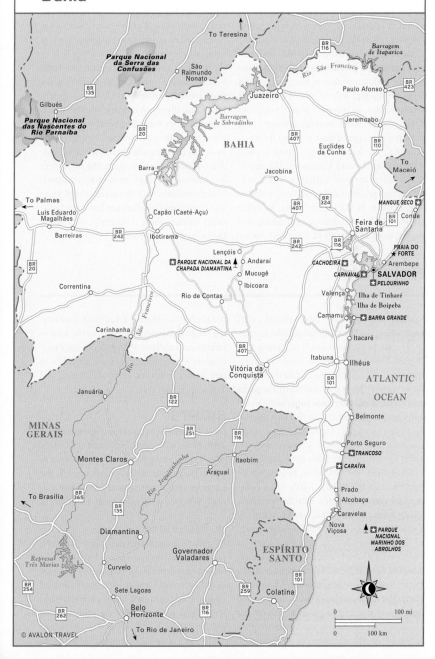

To Teresina

Parque Nacional
da Serra das
Confusões

São
Raimundo
Nonato

Barragem
de Itaparica

Rio São Francisco

BR
116

Juazeiro

Paulo Afonso

BR
423

BR
135

Gilbués

Parque Nacional
das Nascentes do
Rio Parnaíba

Barragem
de Sobradinho

BR
20

Jeremoabo

BAHIA

BR
407

Euclides
da Cunha

BR
110

Barra

Jacobina

To
Maceió

To Palmas

Luís Eduardo
Magalhães

Capão (Caeté-Açu)

BR
407

BR
324

Feira de
Santana

MANGUE SECO

BR
101

Conde

Barreiras

BR
242

Ibotirama

BR
242

BR
116

PRAIA DO
FORTE

BR
20

Lençóis

Andaraí

PARQUE NACIONAL DA
CHAPADA DIAMANTINA

Mucugê

CACHOEIRA

Arembepe

SALVADOR

Correntina

Rio de Contas

Ibicoara

CARNAVAL

PELOURINHO

Valença

Ilha de Tinharé
Ilha de Boipeba

Carinhanha

Camamu

BARRA GRANDE

BR
407

Itacaré

Januária

Vitória da
Conquista

Itabuna

Ilhéus

ATLANTIC

BR
101

OCEAN

BR
122

MINAS
GERAIS

BR
251

BR
116

Belmonte

Montes Claros

Itaobim

Porto Seguro

TRANCOSO

Araçuaí

CARAÍVA

To Brasília

BR
365

BR
135

Prado
Alcobaça

Caravelas

Diamantina

Governador
Valadares

Nova
Viçosa

PARQUE
NACIONAL
MARINHO DOS
ABROLHOS

Represa
Três Marias

Curvelo

ESPÍRITO
SANTO

BR
354

Sete Lagoas

BR
101

BR
262

Belo
Horizonte

BR
116

BR
259

Colatina

To Rio de Janeiro

0   100 mi
0   100 km

© AVALON TRAVEL

the Parque Nacional da Chapada Diamantina, and a pilgrimage to one or several of the famed beaches along Bahia's northern or southern coasts, and you could easily spend 2-3 weeks in Bahia, using Salvador as a base.

Bahia can be visited year-round. The summer months of **December-March** are the hottest, with temperatures hovering around 35°C (95°F) and lots of sun. This is high tourist season, as travelers from throughout Brazil and the world descend on many of the most popular coastal resorts (Praia do Forte, Morro de São Paulo, Itacaré, Porto Seguro, Arraial d'Ajuda, and Trancoso). The upside is an endless array of festivities. The downside is that prices usually rise along with the temperature. In the summertime, Salvador sizzles with lively ambiance, myriad musical shows, open rehearsals of Carnaval *blocos,*

and especially the "season" of popular *festas.* If revelry, combined with relaxation, is what you're looking for, you've come to the right place. With the end of Carnaval comes what Soteropolitanos refer to as the post-Carnaval *ressaca* (hangover), which means a halt in the partying until June and a return to work. Mother Nature also seems to know that the party is over, because the period from April to June is usually rainy. Bahian "winter," which stretches from **June-September,** is a great time to visit the city and the coastal regions as well as the Chapada. Although short, sudden downpours are common, the sun shines less intensely. Except for mid-July-August, which coincides with Brazilian school vacation, hotels and beaches are less crowded— many Bahians think it odd to lie on a beach in the "middle of winter."

Salvador

Salvador was originally built around a cliff overlooking the Bay of All Saints, which effectively split the city into two. The Cidade Alta (Upper Town) was home to ornate administrative palaces and churches, while the Cidade Baixa (Lower Town) sheltered maritime docks and markets and later grew into the financial and commercial district. To this day, the two are linked by a series of tortuously steep roads, two funiculars, and one of Salvador's most famous monuments: the Elevador Lacerda.

Over time, the city grew, following the extension of the Cidade Alta's main commercial avenue, Avenida Sete de Setembro, which leads from the Praça do Sé in the colonial Pelourinho district to the main square of Campo Grande—an area that today is the Centro district. From Campo Grande, Avenida Sete de Setembro continues down to the lively beach neighborhood known as Barra; Barra's iconic black-and-white striped lighthouse marks the point at which the placid Bay of All Saints meets the rougher waters of the Atlantic open sea. At this point,

the main coastal road takes over, continuing for 20 kilometers (12.5 mi) to the former fisherman's enclave of Itapuã, whose rustic charms were romanticized in the lyrics of two former residents, Dorival Caymmi and Vinicius de Moraes.

SIGHTS

Most of Salvador's sights are conveniently located in the old colonial center of the Cidade Alta, known as the Pelourinho (a reference to one of the neighborhood's main squares, the Largo do Pelourinho, where slaves were routinely whipped at the *pelourinho,* or "pillory").

★ Pelourinho

Despite its inauspicious past, the Pelourinho provides a feast for architecture buffs, with the largest concentration of baroque architecture in the Americas. Replete with richly adorned churches and convents, its hilly cobblestoned streets also reflect a lot of the vibrancy and color of Bahian life. Until the 1990s, the "Pelô" was a crumbling mess. After being declared a UNESCO World Heritage Site in 1985, the area underwent a massive restoration that saved many of the historic buildings and somewhat unceremoniously removed the former inhabitants, replacing them with boutiques, restaurants, bars, and open-air spaces for musical shows. What it lost in terms of gritty authenticity, it made up for in terms of heightened security and animation.

The Pelô has since become increasingly forsaken by locals, with the exception of vendors and beggars who approach anybody resembling a tourist. Nonetheless, there is no denying the rich history and magnificence of its restored edifices. While the *bairro* can be explored on foot in a couple of hours, in order to take advantage of all the church interiors and museums, boutiques, and lazy outdoor bars, you'll need a full day. The labyrinthine layout of the neighborhood is conducive to wandering. Just make sure you don't venture off the beaten police-patrolled track, especially at night; tourist *assaltos* (muggings) are not unheard of.

PRAÇA MUNICIPAL

The seat of colonial Brazil for over two centuries, the Pelourinho is dominated by the monumental **Palácio do Rio Branco** (tel. 71/3316-6928, 10:30am-1:30pm and 2:30am-5:30pm Mon.-Fri., 1pm-6pm Sat.-Sun., free). Guarded by soaring eagles and topped by an impressive dome, the palace is fondly known by Bahians as the *bolo de noiva* ("the wedding cake"), an appropriate nickname considering its resemblance to the baker's confection. Constructed by Tomé de Souza in 1549 as the governor's palace, over time the building suffered partial demolitions and makeovers, which explains its eclectic style—a mixture of neoclassical, Byzantine, and Renaissance elements. Having housed the Portuguese royal family when they fled Napoleon's troops in 1808, and later a prison, it now houses Bahia's ministry of culture. Step inside for a guided tour and you'll find rococo plasterwork, frescoes, and a small museum. More interesting is the view from the palace's verandas, which takes in the Cidade Baixa and the Bay of All Saints.

ELEVADOR LACERDA

The streamlined, art deco **Elevador Lacerda** (6:30am-11pm daily, R$0.15), to the right of the Palácio do Rio Branco, has shuttled lines of Soteropolitanos between the Cidade Baixa and the Cidade Alta since the 1930s. It takes only 20 seconds for each of its four elevators to transport more than 50,000 passengers a day. To visit the Mercado Modelo, catch a local bus to Bonfim, or grab a boat to Itaparica, the Elevador comes in handy. Otherwise, have a seat at **Sorveteria Cubana** (tel. 71/3322-7000, 9am-10pm), a 1930s landmark, and indulge in an icy treat such as a *coco espumante* (a fizzy old-fashioned coconut ice cream soda).

MUSEU DA MISERICÓRDIA

Down the Rua da Misericórdia, past City Hall, is the **Museu da Misericórdia** (Rua da Misericórida 6, tel. 71/3322-7355, 10am-5pm Mon.-Fri., 9am-1pm Sun., R$6). A religious complex dating from 1549, it was converted into a museum as part of an ongoing project to renovate the architectural treasures on this strip. A permanent exhibition of artwork, religious objects, and furniture from the 17th-19th centuries conjures up Salvador's colonial history, as do its magnificent cloisters, church, and living quarters.

GALERIA FUNDAÇÃO PIERRE VERGER

The **Galeria Fundação Pierre Verger** (Portal da Misericórdia 9, tel. 71/3321-2341, www.pierreverger.org, 9am-8pm Mon.-Sat., 9am-3pm Sun., free), across from the Museu da Misericórdia, shows a small rotating collection of black-and-white photographs by French photographer, ethnographer, and adopted Bahian Pierre Verger. Born into a wealthy Parisian milieu in which he never felt at home, in 1932 Verger took off at the age of 30 to explore the world. With a camera in hand to fund his journeys (his pictures were published in magazines such as *Life* and

Pelourinho and Centro

R VISCONDE DE MAUÁ
R DO SODRE
R DO SODRE
BECO C MARIA DA PAZ
MUSEU DE ARTE SACRA DA BAHIA
AMADO
To Museu de Arte Moderna (MAM), Museu de Arte da Bahia, and Museu Carlos Costa Pinto
LAD DA PREGUIÇA
LAD CONCEIÇÃO
AV CONTORNO
IGREJA N S DA CONCEIÇÃO DA PRAIA
Praça Cairu
MERCADO MODELO
BELGICA
SANTOS DUMONT
CORPO SANTO
Praça Castro Alves
R BARBOSA
R DO TESOURO
BARROQUINHA
MOSTEIRO DE SÃO BENTO
To Campo Grande and Barra
HORTAS
R DO PARAISO
R DA CASTANHEDA
MOURARIA
MANGUEIRA
BENGALA
R DA INDEPENDENCIA
R TINGUI
PALMA
KOISA NOSSA
CIDADE ALTA
MINI CACIQUE
PALACIO RIO BRANCO
RUA CHILE
CENTRO
AJUDA
SALDANHA
DA GAMA
CURRACHITO
R S FRANCISCO
LAD DA PRAÇA
R DA ORAÇÃO
R DE SÃO BRITO
R GUEDES DE BRITO
Praça Tomé de Sousa
GALERIA FUNDAÇÃO PIERRE VERGER
MUSEU DA MISERICÓRDIA
ELEVADOR LACERDA
LA PE DA MONTANHA
NOBREGA
Praça da Sé
CATEDRAL BASILICA
O CRAVINHO
Terreiro de Jesus
CRUZEIRO S FRANCISCO
R DO BISPO
TRÊS DE MAIO
DOMINGOS DE GUSMÃO
IGREJA DA ORDEM TERCEIRA DE SÃO
MUSEU AFRO-BRASILEIRO
IGREJA SÃO PAULO DOS CLÉRIGOS
ALFREDO DE BRITO
CASA DO AMARELINDO
AXEGO
JOÃO DE DEUS
DAS LARANJEIRAS
R GREGORIO DE MATOS
GLACIER LAPORTE
HOTEL VILLA BAHIA
ALAIDE DO FEIJÃO
LA FIGA
HOSTEL GALERIA 13
PONTO VITAL
MUSEU DA CERÂMICA UDO KNOFF
MUSEU TEMPOSTAL
MUSEU ABELARDO RODRIGUES
IGREJA E CONVENTO DE SÃO FRANCISCO
IGREJA DA ORDEM TERCEIRA DE SÃO FRANCISCO
SANTANA
SEABRA
BARRO DO DESTERRO
PRAÇA
R DO CARRO
R DO DESTERRO
STA. CLARA
PIE DO DESTERRO
R DA POEIRA
JOGO DO LOURENÇO
JENIPAPEIRO
LAD DA SAÚDE
JOANA ANGELICA

0   200 yds
0   200 m

© AVALON TRAVEL

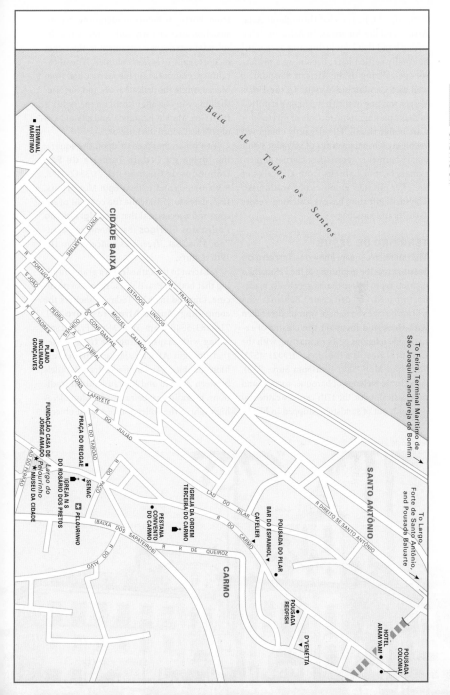

Paris Match), he traveled throughout Asia, Africa, and the Americas. In Bahia, he felt a strong bond that kept luring him back until he finally settled here, becoming a professor specializing in the African diaspora as well as a Candomblé initiate. In the 1940s Verger was one of the first people permitted to make photographic records of mysterious Candomblé rituals. His elegantly composed yet highly sensual portraits of Salvador's sailors, fishermen, *capoeiristas,* Carnaval merrymakers, and Bahians from all walks of life offer precious glimpses of a world past. The small gift store has eye-catching Verger T-shirts and handbags.

TERREIRO DE JESUS

The impressive square known as **Terreiro de Jesus** marks the beginning of the Pelourinho district. Try to ignore the exaggeratedly made-up, turbaned, and petticoated Bahianas who will encourage you to have your picture taken with them and focus on the cluster of remarkable religious edifices, starting with the **Catedral Basílica (Sé)** (tel. 71/3321-4573, 9am-5pm Mon.-Sat., 1pm-5pm Sun., R$3). An eclectic mélange of baroque, rococo, and neoclassical styles, the 17th-century cathedral was built out of sandstone shipped in blocks

from Portugal before undergoing reconstruction after an early 20th-century fire. Its splendid interior is a testament to the riches of Portugal's overseas colonies. The 16th-century ceramic tiles in the sacristy hail from Macau, while the delicate ivory and tortoiseshell inlay in one altar (third on the right) is from Goa. Marble, jacaranda, and lots and lots of gold leaf adorn the interior.

Two other churches sit upon the square: the **Igreja da Ordem Terceira de São Domingos de Gusmão** (tel. 71/3242-4185, 8:30am-noon and 1:30pm-6pm Mon.-Thurs, R$2) dates to 1731, while the cocktail of rococo and neoclassical that is the **Igreja São Pedro dos Clérigos** (8am-noon and 2pm-7pm Mon.-Sat., free) was conceived in the 19th century.

Adjacent to the cathedral is a grand building that housed Brazil's first school of medicine, founded in 1833. Today, it shelters the compelling **Museu Afro-Brasileiro** (tel. 71/3283-5540, 9am-5pm Mon.-Fri., R$6). Along with maps tracing the trade routes that brought African slaves to Bahia, exhibits of objects and artifacts draw parallels between African and Bahian cultural traditions, including capoeira and Candomblé. A highlight is the collection of sacred objects

Terreiro de Jesus

and apparel—as well as photos—related to Candomblé and the cult of individual *orixás,* or divinities, which provide an informative introduction to the Afro-Brazilian religion that is such a strong cultural reference in Bahia. Depicting the *orixás* are the exquisitely carved wooden panels, inlaid with shells and shiny metals, sculpted by one of Bahia's most famous artists, Carybé.

★ IGREJA E CONVENTO DE SÃO FRANCISCO

Looming magnificently at the far end of Largo do Cruzeiro de São Francisco is the finest example of Bahian baroque architecture: a religious complex dedicated to Saint Francis of Assisi comprising two churches and a convent. Constructed between 1686 and 1750, the **Igreja e Convento de São Francisco** (tel. 71/3322-6430, 9am-5:30pm Mon. and Wed.-Sat., 9am-4pm Tues., 10am-3pm Sun., R$5) will take your breath away with gold leaf paneling—800 kilograms (1,760 pounds), to be exact—that covers its intricately carved and sumptuously painted ceilings and altars. Carefully wrought scenes depict the life of Saint Francis on 55,000 blue-and-white Portuguese azulejos in the chapel and cloister. Tuesday mass is followed by the distribution of food to the poor, which then morphs into a Pelô-wide celebration of a more profane nature, known as *terça do Benção* (Tuesday of the Blessing).

★ IGREJA DA ORDEM TERCEIRA DE SÃO FRANCISCO

Next door to the Igreja e Convento de São Francisco, the **Igreja da Ordem Terceira de São Francisco** (tel. 71/3321-6968, 8am-5pm daily, R$5), completed in 1703, is remarkable for its striking high-relief facade: a sandstone tapestry of saints, angels, and organic and abstract motifs. This unique exterior was "hidden" for 150 years until, in 1936, a painter accidentally discovered it when he chipped off a piece of the plaster facade. Inside the church, azulejo panels narrate the marriage of the king of Portugal's son to an Austrian princess and offer a rare portrait of Lisbon before it was devastated by the Great Earthquake of 1755.

MUSEU DA CERÁMICA UDO KNOFF

The **Museu da Cerámica Udo Knoff** (Rua Frei Vicente 3, tel. 71/3117-6389, noon-6pm Tues.-Fri., noon-5pm Sat.-Sun., free) displays a resplendent collection of ceramic tiles from Portugal, Spain, Belgium, and Mexico as well as Brazil. They are from the personal collection of Horst Udo Knoff, a German expat ceramicist whose own works, inspired by azulejos covering facades of Salvador's buildings, are also featured. To get here from the Igreja, follow Rua Inácio Acciole and take a left on Rua Frei Vicente.

MUSEU TEMPOSTAL

The "artwork" in the **Museu Tempostal** (Rua Gregório de Matos 33, tel. 71/3117-6383, noon-6pm Tues.-Fri., noon-5pm Sat.-Sun., free) consists of thousands of postcards that trace Salvador's surprisingly rapid transformation over the last century. The entire collection of more than 35,000 works includes some amazing belle epoque specimens—postcards decorated with embroidery as well as watercolors, feathers, and strands of human hair.

MUSEU ABELARDO RODRIGUES

The gracious 17th-century mansion known as the Solar do Ferrão houses the **Museu Abelardo Rodrigues** (Rua Gregório de Matos 45, tel. 71/3117-6467, 10am-6pm Tues.-Sun., R$1), a collection of more than 800 icons of saints, altars, engravings, and other religious objects (not all on display). The works were amassed by Pernambucano collector Abelardo Rodrigues, who resided here, and are considered to be one of the finest collections of sacred art in Brazil. Also on permanent display are architect Lina Bo Bardi's fine collection of Northeast Brazilian folk art and an equally impressive ensemble of African masks and statues donated by Italian magnate Claudio Masella.

LARGO DO PELOURINHO

When you first set foot in this picturesque square, you'll likely be overwhelmed by the baroque landscape of church spires and faded pastel mansions, as well as the Cubist-like image of houses rising up and down the Pelô's steep hills. Although its official name is Praça José de Alencar, it is known as **Largo do Pelourinho** due to its dubious past as the site of the city's *pelourinho* (whipping post; public flogging was legal in Brazil until 1835).

Today the *largo* buzzes with less nefarious activities. By day, vendors hawk *naïf* canvases and coax gringos to put Afro braids and corn-rows in their hair. Nights are filled with the pounding drums of traditional Afro-Bahian *blocos* such as Olodum, whose rhythms defy people to dance.

Housed in a handsome colonial mansion, the **Museu da Cidade** (Largo do Pelourinho 3, tel. 71/3321-1967, 9am-6pm Mon. and Wed.-Fri., R$1) serves up an eclectic mix of things Soteropolitano. Depictions of Catholic saints and ex-votos mingle with sculptures of *orixás* and other objects related to Candomblé. More secular offerings include works by local artists and artisans and a room devoted to Castro Alves, one of Brazil's great romantic poets and famously eloquent abolitionists.

Next door, the **Fundação Casa de Jorge Amado** (Largo do Pelourinho 49, tel. 71/3321-0122, www.fundacaojorgeamado.com.br, 10am-6pm Mon.-Sat., free) is a small museum and shrine devoted to the life, times, and writing of Jorge Amado, one of Bahia's (and Brazil's) most cherished and internationally renowned writers. With photos, book covers, and other media featuring the author of *Dona Flor and Her Two Husbands* and *Gabriela, Clove and Cinnamon,* the museum provides an overview of Amado's life and career, also touching on that of his lifelong love and companion, Zélia Gattai, a renowned writer in her own right to whom homage is paid at the homonymous, and pleasant, café.

Halfway down the Largo, the strikingly blue-tinged **Igreja Nossa Senhora do Rosário dos Pretos** (tel. 71/3326-9701, 8:30am-6pm Mon.-Fri., 8:30am-3pm Sat.-Sun.) is a symbol of black pride and resistance. After the king of Portugal gave the site to the Irmandade dos Homens Pretos, a brotherhood of local black men, it took slaves most of the 18th century to construct this church. While the façade is classic rococo, the unusual tiled towers bear Indian influences, a consequence of Portugal's colony in Goa. Services in which Catholics hymns merge with traditional African percussion instruments (mass 6pm Tues.) reflect Bahia's unique religious syncretism.

IGREJA DA ORDEM TERCEIRA DO CARMO E CONVENTO DO CARMO

The climb up the Ladeira do Carmo might leave you huffing and puffing, but great views of the surrounding Pelô compensate. Halfway up, the majestic Escadas do Carmo staircase leads to the sadly dilapidated Igreja Santíssimo Sacramento do Passo. Both the staircase and the church were immortalized in the first Brazilian film to win the Cannes Festival's Palme d'Or, *O Pagador de Promessas* (1962).

Towering above the Ladeira do Carmo is the dramatic whitewashed complex that houses the **Igreja da Ordem Terceira do Carmo** (tel. 71/3481-4169, 8am-noon and 2pm-6pm Mon.-Sat., 8am-10am Sun., R$1) and the Convento do Carmo. Constructed in 1636 and rebuilt in neoclassical style after a fire in 1786, the church is worth a visit for its eerily expressive cedar carving of Christ, sculpted in 1730 by Francisco Xavier Chagas. A slave nicknamed "O Cabra" ("The Goat"), Chagas has been compared to the great *mulato* baroque sculptor of Minas Gerais, Aleijadinho. If the drops of blood on the reclining Christ figure seem to glint and glisten as if they were transparent liquid, it is because they are assembled out of 2,000 encrusted rubies. Chagas is also responsible for the statue of Nossa Senhora do Carmo, whose features were said to be inspired by Isabel, daughter of

Garcia d'Ávila, the largest landowner in the Northeast during colonial times.

Adjacent to the church is the **Convento do Carmo** (Rua do Carmo 1, www.pestana.com/en/pestana-convento-do-carmo). Built in 1586, this convent has been converted into a hotel. Wander in and examine the stylishly furnished interior, then stop for a drink at the bar-lounge that sprawls around a palmy, arcaded cloister.

Santo Antônio

Santo Antônio Além do Carmo is the name given to the narrow neighborhood that stretches from the church and convent of Carmo down to the open square of Largo do Santo Antônio. Neither as old, splendid, nor reupholstered as the Pelourinho, tranquil Santo Antônio hints at what the Pelô could have been had the strategies accompanying its makeover—expulsion of residents and pandering to tourists—not been so brutal. In the last few years, many of its crumbling belle epoque-era mansions have been saved by enterprising hoteliers who have opened up restaurants, galleries, and *pousadas*. Instead of radically transforming the 'hood, these newcomers spruced it up and then integrated themselves into the fabric of what is still, at heart, a traditional *bairro popular*. As you make your way down the main street, Rua Direito de Santo Antônio, highlights include the **Cruz do Pascoal**, a giant cross planted in the middle of the road, and the beguiling 18th-century **Igreja Nossa Senhora do Boqueirão** (Rua Direito de Santo Antônio 60).

Largo de Santo Antônio is framed at one end by a belvedere overlooking the ocean and at the other by the neoclassical **Igreja de Santo Antônio Além do Carmo.** The church is almost always open due to Santo Antônio's popularity—not only a protector of the poor, he also intercedes on behalf of lonely hearts and bachelors (as the patron saint of marriage) and specializes in finding lost valuables.

At the far side of the square, the **Forte de**

Santo Antônio Além do Carmo (Largo de Santo Antônio, tel. 71/3321-7587, 7:30pm-9:30pm Tues., Thurs., and Sat., 5:30pm-7:30pm Sun., free) was constructed in the 16th century by the Portuguese as a defensive measure against invading Dutch troops. During the years of military dictatorship, the abandoned fort served as a detention center for political prisoners who spoke out against the government. Today it shelters the Capoeira Preservation Center, dedicated to safeguarding this traditional martial art while providing new headquarters for some of the city's oldest capoeira schools.

Cidade Baixa

Sadly, the Cidade Baixa, Salvador's port and commercial district, has seen better days. The area is a mélange of decaying historic buildings and decaying high-rises built before Salvador's commercial center moved to the neighborhoods surrounding Shopping Iguatemi. Today, "Comércio" (as it is known) is fairly bustling during the day but dangerous at night. Take a bus, the Elevador Lacerda to Praça Visconde de Cairu, or a taxi. Don't even think about walking up or down the steep roads linking the two *cidades*—they are unsafe, even by day.

IGREJA DE NOSSA SENHORA DA CONCEIÇÃO DA PRAIA

The stately, baroque **Igreja de Nossa Senhora da Conceição da Praia** (Rua Conceição da Praia, tel. 71/3242-0545, 7am-noon and 3pm-7pm Mon., 7am-5pm Tues.-Fri., 7am-11:30am Sat.-Sun., free) rises to the left upon emerging from the Elevador Lacerda. Built in Portugal in 1736, the deconstructed church was shipped piece by piece to the site of Salvador's first chapel. The patron saint of Salvador, Our Lady of Conception, is also linked to the wildly popular Candomblé *orixá* Iemenjá, goddess of the sea. Accordingly, the saint's feast day (Dec. 8) is the occasion for one of the city's most traditional religious and popular *festas*.

IGREJA DE NOSSO SENHOR DO BONFIM

If you hop a bus with the destination Bonfim or Ribeira from Praça Cairu, or Campo Grande, you will find yourself sailing through the length of the Cidade Baixa, following the 8-kilometer (5-mi) route taken by worshippers and revelers who, on the second Thursday of January, make their way in a procession to one of Brazil's most famous churches: the **Igreja de Nosso Senhor do Bonfim** (Praça Senhor do Bonfim, tel. 71/3316-2196, 6:30am-noon and 2pm-6pm Tues.-Sun.).

Sacred to Catholics as well as followers of Candomblé (for whom Senhor do Bonfim is equated with both Christ and one of the most important *orixás,* Oxalá), the *igreja* is an important pilgrimage site. Morning mass is large, especially on Friday—Oxalá's day of the week. Rising up from a hilltop and accessorized by swaying imperial palms, it's an eye-catching example of Portuguese rococo. In front, you'll likely be accosted by a few vendors plying you with brightly colored *fitas de Bonfim.* If you choose to follow tradition and tie one of these ribbons around your wrist, make sure you tie three knots and make a wish on each one. You'll be stuck wearing it for weeks, months, or even years (don't tie it too tight); when it naturally falls off, your wishes will come true. With the exception of the resplendent panels of blue-and-white Portuguese tiles, the interior of the church is relatively unadorned by Bahian standards. The real interest lies in its importance to Bahians, which becomes clear when you visit the church's small but fascinating **Museu dos Ex-Votos do Senhor do Bonfim** (Largo do Bonfim, tel. 71/3312-4512, 9am-noon and 2pm-5pm Tues.-Sat., R$2).

Your visit begins in the Sala dos Milagres (Room of Miracles), whose walls are covered from floor to ceiling with thousands of photographs and handwritten notes accompanied by *fitas de Bonfim.* These heartfelt supplications to Senhor do Bonfim—be it pleading for the life of a child, the safe return of a fisherman, or even victory in a soccer championship—are incredibly moving. So are the photos, newspaper clippings, and paintings of miracles, depicting believers being saved from tragedies such as car accidents and fires. Dangling from the ceiling are wooden and plastic heads, limbs, and even organs. These are the offerings of worried patients seeking protection before surgery. The second floor houses older and more precious ex-votos in display cases—including silver heads, arms, hearts, eyes, noses, even livers and intestines—offered in thanks by miraculously cured patients. The presence of soccer uniforms indicates that both of Salvador's major teams wouldn't dream of starting *futebol* season without first visiting the church for a blessing.

FORTE DE MONTE SERRAT AND PONTA DE HUMAITÁ

If you walk uphill from the Largo de Bonfim and take the road that swerves to the left, you'll be treated to sweeping panoramic views of the entire city. Follow the road for another five minutes, which will lead you downhill to the popular beach of **Boa Viagem.** A favorite *praia popular,* on weekends it is so packed with residents of surrounding neighborhoods you can barely see the sand. Crowning the beach is the 16th-century **Forte de Monte Serrat,** whose cannons chased off invading Dutch. Today, its functions are decidedly less bellicose—it is a favorite place for smooching couples to get a glimpse of the sunset over the Bay of All Saints. Another great vantage point is the nearby **Ponta de Humaitá,** whose striped lighthouse, tiny 17th-century **Igreja de Nossa Senhora de Monte Serrat,** and sweeping sea views provide a romantic spot for a late-afternoon drink.

Centro

Salvador's Centro encompasses a somewhat loosely defined neighborhood that more or less consists of the old "downtown" of the Cidade Alta, which follows Avenida Sete de Setembro (the main drag) from its beginning at Praça Castro Alves to Campo Grande and the sweeping tree-lined Corredor da Vitória. Chaotic, crowded, and oddly provincial for such a major city, Centro remains an interesting place to walk around. Filled with museums, churches, shops, markets, and *ambulantes* (street vendors), by day it hums with activity but at night empties out and is dangerous to stroll around in.

From the Praça Municipal, the once elegant **Rua Chile** still displays some grandiose buildings that formerly housed department stores and hotels. Restoration projects are underway in an attempt to regain at least some of its former glory. Rua Chile leads onto the **Praça Castro Alves,** a semicircular plaza where Bahia's famous Romantic poet (Antônio Frederico de Castro Alves) stares out at the Bay of All Saints.

MUSEU DE ARTE SACRA DA BAHIA

A block from Praça Castro Alves, Ladeira de Santa Teresa is a steep little alley that plunges down to the imposing 17th-century convent of Santa Teresa de Ávila, which was once occupied by the Ordem das Carmelitas Descalços (Barefoot Carmelites Order). Overlooking the sea and surrounded by shady courtyards, its tranquil church, cloisters, and monks' cells are part of the **Museu de Arte Sacra da**

Bahia (Rua do Sodré 276, tel. 71/3243-6511, 11:30am-5pm Mon.-Fri., R$5). One of the most important and impressive museums of sacred religious art in Brazil, its collection of 1,400 pieces includes a wealth of paintings, sculptures, icons, and furniture from Bahia's glorious colonial past.

MOSTEIRO DE SÃO BENTO

Along Avenida Sete de Setembro, a few meters from Praça Castro Alves, is one of the oldest monasteries in the Americas. The grandiose **Mosteiro de São Bento** (Largo de São Bento, tel. 71/2106-5200, 11:30am-5pm daily) has undergone numerous renovations since its founding in 1582. Pop in for a quick look at its interior and museum of religious art or take a cab here on Sunday to hear the monastery's 30 cloistered monks sing Gregorian chants.

MUSEU DE ARTE MODERNA

Take a quick taxi ride up the coastal road to one of the city's finest and most beautifully situated museums, the **Museu de Arte Moderna** (MAM; Av. Contorno, tel. 71/3117-6139, www.bahiamam.org, 1pm-7pm Tues.-Fri. and Sun., 1pm-10pm Sat., free). Originally titled the Solar do Unhão, this 17th-century complex hovering over the Bay of All Saints

Barra lighthouse

was a sugarcane plantation complete with a mansion (*solar*), slave quarters, and a chapel. In the 1960s, the well-preserved ensemble got an inspired refurbishment courtesy of São Paulo modernist architect Lina Bo Bardi that transformed it into Bahia's Museum of Modern Art. A permanent collection boasts token works of major Brazilian modernist painters, and the museum showcases temporary exhibitions of contemporary artists from all over Brazil.

The buildings and setting are captivating. A sculpture garden, featuring works by local talents such as Carybé and Mario Cravo Jr., winds along a shady path overlooking the sea. In the late afternoon, the wooden pier above the ocean is a magical place to watch the sun set behind the Ilha da Itaparica. Shaded by flamboyant trees, it is the scene of Saturday night jazz jams (from 6pm, R$6) that are mobbed by young Soteropolitanos.

CAMPO GRANDE

This elegant oasis of a park boasts carefully tended flower patches, century-old trees, playgrounds, goldfish ponds, and plenty of benches from where you can take it all in. At the center of Campo Grande, the **Monumento ao Dois de Julho,** featuring a statue of a fierce-looking Caboclo (a mythical figure, part Indian, part African, who is a symbol of Bahian independence from the Portuguese), pays homage to July 2, 1823, the date Bahian troops achieved autonomy by expelling Portuguese troops. The monument—and Campo Grande—has a strong symbolic significance for Soteropolitanos. Accordingly, a large number of important official and cultural events are often held here.

Corredor da Vitória

From Campo Grande onward, Avenida Sete de Setembro is known as the Corredor da Vitória. Lined with wonderfully overgrown trees and less wonderful luxury apartment complexes, "Vitória" is where Salvador's elite have traditionally lived. The small but economically important British community

that founded this posh hood in the late 19th century and constructed some of its lavish mansions (a few still survive) is now home to a handful of small museums and cultural centers.

MUSEU DE ARTE DA BAHIA

Occupying a stately 1920s mansion, the **Museu de Arte da Bahia** (Av. Sete de Setembro 2340, tel. 71/3117-6903, 2pm-7pm Tues.-Fri., 2:30pm-6:30pm Sat.-Sun., R$5, free Thurs. and Sun.) houses a hit-and-miss collection of Bahian paintings and furnishings as well as some curiosities, such as a sewing machine that transforms into a small piano.

MUSEU CARLOS COSTA PINTO

In a gracious private villa that still belongs to Salvador's traditional Costa Pinto family, the **Museu Carlos Costa Pinto** (Av. Sete de Setembro 2490, tel. 71/3336-6081, 2:30pm-7pm Wed.-Mon., R$5, free Thurs.) features a rare and magnificent collection of Bahian art and artifacts that offer a glimpse into the grandeur of the Bahian elite during colonial times. Apart from some exquisite European furnishings and finery, you're likely to be most impressed by the fantastic collection of *balangandãs:* ornate bracelets with glittery, dangling "charms" ranging from tropical fruits to *figas* (clenched fists symbolizing power). Made of silver and gold, these were gifts given by rich masters to their female slaves, who used them to accessorize their traditional attire of white petticoats and turbans. After feasting your eyes, retire to the lovely courtyard **Balangandan Café** and savor some of the menu's delicious French tarts.

PALACETE DAS ARTES

In the early 20th century, businessman Bernardo Catharino was the richest man in Bahia. In 1912, he built this gracious mansion in the still swanky neighborhood of Graça (just off the Corredor da Vitória). Known today as the **Palacete das Artes** (Rua da Graça 284, Graça, tel. 71/3117-6910, www.

palacetedasartes.ba.gov.br, 10am-6pm Wed.-Mon., free), it's worth checking out for the intricate parquet floors, jewel-hued stained glass windows, belle epoque frescoes, and the exhibits of modern and contemporary Brazilian art displayed in the villa as well as an adjacent modern annex. Shaded by giant mango trees, the gardens can be savored from the outdoor **Solar Café.**

Barra

At the end of Corredor de Vitória, the descent from Avenida Sete de Setembro begins a steep plunge toward the neighborhood and beaches of Barra. On the way down, you'll pass Bahia's yacht club, with its swan-like array of sailboats, the Cimetério dos Ingleses, where Bahia's Brit expat community encountered a scenic resting place, and, perched on a verdant hill, the 16th-century Igreja de Santo Antônio da Barra.

PORTO DA BARRA

Salvador's small but famous urban beach, **Porto da Barra,** is dramatically framed by two 17th-century Portuguese fortresses: Forte São Diogo and Forte Santa Maria. More than just a small crescent-shaped golden sand beach, "Porto" is an entire microcosm uniting families, gays, tourists, locals, vendors, hustlers, lovers, celebrities, sun worshippers, and volleyball and frescoball aficionados on one vibrant and colorful strip of sand bathed by the calm and surprisingly clear sea. Barring the rainy season, no matter how overpopulated it gets, Porto's waters are always miraculously crystalline.

Although Porto has a small-town feel to it—aided by the fact that the only vessels bobbing on its waters are brightly painted wooden fishing boats—it packs a surprisingly urban wallop. You'll be bombarded by the songs and chants of passing vendors hawking everything from handmade jewelry to fresh fruit popsicles called *picolés* (the best are made by a company called Capelinha). You'll also be spoiled: After renting a beach chair and giant parasol, you'll have your feet regularly refreshed with a watering can and all your drink requests attended to.

Porto is the classic place to watch the sunset—applause rings out the moment the glowing orange-red disk descends below the Ilha da Itaparica, bathing both sky and sea in a painterly blaze of colors. (On Friday nights in summer, sunset is accompanied by free outdoor concerts). Since the beach is lit at night, it is possible to take a moonlight dip. However, be very careful with your valuables (even more so than during the day), since tourists are often targeted by thieves.

FAROL DA BARRA

Walking along the breezy seaside promenade—past small coves and the increasing number of hotels, gyms, cybercafés, and bars that are turning Barra into a small-scale Copacabana—you'll soon reach the iconic black-and-white striped **Barra lighthouse.** Jutting out into the sea at the point where the Bay of All Saints meets the Atlantic, the Farol da Barra is lodged within the 17th-century Forte de Santo Antônio. Although the current lighthouse, constructed of iron, was built in 1836, the original wooden one—dating from 1696—operated using whale oil and was the first lighthouse in all of the Americas. Inside the fort, the **Museu Naútico da Bahia** (tel. 71/3264-3296, www.museunauticodabahia. org.br, 9am-7pm Tues.-Sun., R$6) displays maps, navigation instruments, model ships, and other seafaring paraphernalia. Just as interesting is the secluded bar situated within the lighthouse's sun-bleached walls. During the year, the Farol and surrounding area are the setting for various shows and concerts; the biggest occur on New Year's Eve and New Year's Day.

Rio Vermelho and Vicinity

Rio Vermelho is a bohemian enclave, more lively at night when its bars, squares, and restaurants fill with the city's artistic and intellectual crowd. Although its beaches aren't good for swimming, the hidden **Praia do Buracão** ("Big Hole") functions as a hip

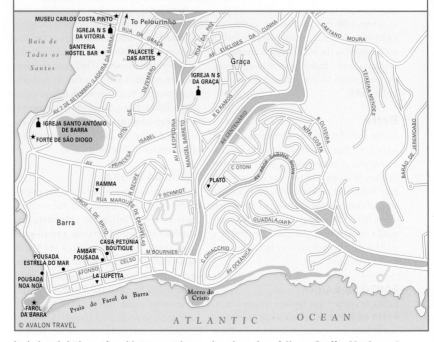

Barra and Rio Vermelho

little beach hideout for old-time residents and young *alternativos*. The neighborhood is enhanced by cobblestoned squares where the city's triumvirate of reigning Bahianas sell their famed *acarajés* and *abarás*.

Rio Vermelho is followed by the rather soulless Pituba, where the city's yuppies live. From there, the beaches keep coming until **Itapuã,** which only a couple of decades ago was a bucolic palm-fringed fishing village that captivated the imaginations of residents such as Dorival Caymmi and Vinicius de Moraes, both of whom immortalized its languorous vibe in their unforgettable musical compositions. Today, the neighborhood is more developed and scruffy; it's not the best beach in town for a swim. Nonetheless, the languorous vibe has somehow survived—as have the fishermen, the swaying palms, and the pretty candy cane-striped lighthouse.

More popular with middle-class patrons (who have cars) are the more unspoiled beaches that follow: **Stella Maris** and **Flamengo** (municipal buses whose final destination is marked Praia de Flamengo depart from Campo Grande or along the *orla*). These beaches offer more shade, water-sports equipment, and natural pools that are ideal for kids.

Baía de Todos os Santos

It's the biggest bay in Brazil—even bigger than Rio's famous Guanabara Bay—and the beckoning blue and always warm waters of the Bay of All Saints are ideal for swimming, sailing, diving, and contemplation.

ILHA DE ITAPARICA

The largest of the bay's 30-plus islands is the 35-kilometer-long (22-mi) narrow strip called Itaparica, whose lithe silhouette bisects the sea and the sky for those gazing out over the bay from Salvador. A favorite getaway for Soteropolitanos, Itaparica's beaches are lined with many weekend and holiday homes—a

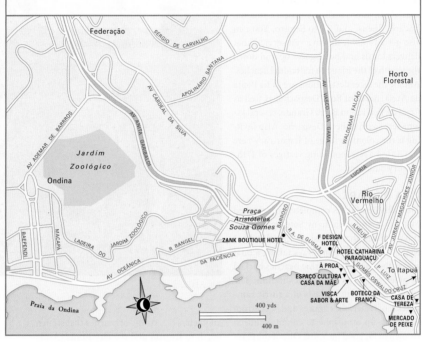

few quite old and grand, others resembling *favelas*. Avoid holiday weekends; getting there and back means lining up for hours to catch a boat (make sure you buy your return ticket), and once there, you'll be immersed in a sea of people. However, during the week or in off-season, the *"ilha"* has a laid-back atmosphere. Although the beaches are inferior to those north of Salvador, soaking in the calm blue water is as relaxing as taking a bath, and the view of the glimmering white city across the bay is quite enchanting. The island's major crop is mangoes, and once you sink your teeth into the real thing (depending on the season, they'll be literally raining down on you), you'll be in heaven.

There are two ways of getting from Salvador to Itaparica. The nicest, and simplest, is to grab a boat bound for **Mar Grande** at the **Terminal Náutico da Bahia** (Av. da França 757, tel. 71/3242-3180, R$4.20), behind the Mercado Modelo. The scenic trip across the bay takes 45 minutes with departures every 30 minutes 6:30am-8pm daily (depending on the tides). On the other side, Mar Grande is a lazy beach resort town with some languid old summer homes, tree-lined streets, and lots of seafood restaurants. You can easily explore the beaches by foot or rent a bike. The return trip at the end of the day almost always offers the bonus of a fantastic sunset.

Another way to get to Itaparica is to grab a catamaran or ferryboat from the **Terminal Marítimo de São Joaquim** (Av. Oscar Pontes 1501, tel. 71/3032-0475, www.agerba. ba.gov.br/transporteHidroviarioFerry.htm, R$3.95-5.20), near the Feira de São Joaquim. Although you can take a bus marked Ribeira or Bonfim, the easiest way to get to the ferry terminal is by taxi. Ferries will take you to Itaparica's main bus and boat terminal, aptly named Bom Despacho (Good Send-off). Ferry crossings take about an hour with departures every hour 5am-11:30pm daily.

From Bom Despacho, buses travel to cities on the Recôncavo as well as southern coast destinations such as Valença, Camamu, Itacaré, Ilhéus, and Porto Seguro. You can also get a *kombi* (collective van service) that delivers locals and beachgoers up and down the length of the island to individual beaches. Among the nicer destinations are Praia Ponta de Areia, north of Bom Despacho, as well as Praia da Penha and Barra Grande, several kilometers south of Bom Despacho. Also inviting is the colonial village of Itaparica, where you'll find a few remaining vestiges of 17th-century buildings.

ILHA DE MARÉ

Tiny Ilha de Maré is completely overlooked by tourists and even many Soteropolitanos. It hasn't been that long since the island got electricity, and in many ways taking a boat across the bay to its pristine beaches backed by green hills is like going back in time. The island's settlement consists of a rustic ramshackle of fisherfolk's houses and beachfront bars with an atmospheric colonial church thrown in for good measure. One of the main commercial products is the delicious *doce de banana*, a banana sweet made in wood ovens, then wrapped in banana-fiber packages and sold by the dozen by children roaming up and down the sand. On the beaches away from town, *barracas* serve delicious fried fish and *moqueca* as the tide comes in and laps at your legs.

To get a boat to Ilha de Maré, grab a bus with the destination Base Naval/São Tomé, which passes in front of the Teatro Castro Alves at Campo Grande; ride to the end of the line and then get a boat from the São Tomé de Paripe terminal (tel. 71/3307-1447). The R$3 trip takes 20 minutes with departures every 45 minutes 8am-5:30pm daily.

SPORTS AND RECREATION
Beaches

Barra marks the beginning of the *orla*, or coastline; a long string—roughly 20

Porto da Barra

kilometers (12.5 mi)—of beaches that stretch north to **Itapuã** and the city limits. Aside from Rio Vermelho, the adjoining neighborhoods themselves are of little interest. For good beaches, the ones farther away (beginning at **Boca do Rio**) are the only worthy candidates for bathing. Loads of buses leave from the center (Campo Grande and Lapa) or from Barra and speed up and down the coast all the way to Itapuã. On the weekends, particularly in the summer, all of these beaches get packed. It's best if you can go early and come back around 3pm to beat the crush.

Parks

Salvador is not a very green city. The only area resembling a park in the center of town is the **Dique de Tororó,** an urban lagoon out of whose calm waters rise gigantic statues of *orixás*. Surrounding the Dique is a walking and jogging path shaded by gigantic trees (and traffic). Kiosks sell *água de coco,* and it's possible to rent a pedal boat and glide around the water. The Dique's shores are flanked by

Avenida Presidente Silva e Costa and Avenida Vasco da Gama, and the lagoon is on the edge of the *bairros* of Nazaré and Tororó (behind the Lapa bus station).

Boat Excursions

Boats trips around the Bay of All Saints leave from Porto da Barra and from the ferry dock in front of the Mercado Modelo. The full-day excursions (around R$70 pp) stop at the larger islands, including Ilha dos Frades, Itaparica, and Ilha de Maré. Specific information is available at Salvador's largest hotels and at Bahiatursa, or contact a travel operator such as **Privê Tur** (tel. 71/3205-1400, www.privetur.com.br), which also runs various city tours.

Diving

If you want to search for buried treasure, there are about a dozen sunken ships in the Bay of All Saints. **Dive Bahia** (Porto da Barra 3809, tel. 71/3264-3820, www.divebahia.com.br) offers diving courses and rents out equipment, as does **Bahia Scuba** (Av. do Contorno 1010, Bahia Marina, tel. 71/3321-0156, www.bahiascuba.com.br). Dive excursion rates range R$150-210 pp (for certified divers) and R$250-280 (for beginners, which includes two dives).

Capoeira

This uniquely Brazilian activity is a graceful, but vigorous mix of dance and martial arts. Regular displays are held at the Mercado Modelo and the Terreiro de Jesus, but if it's an authentic experience you're after, head to one of the city's Academias de Capoeira.

One of the oldest capoeira schools, the **Associação de Capoeira Mestre Bimba** (Rua das Laranjeiras 1, Pelourinho, tel. 71/3322-0639, www.capoeiramestrebimba.com.br) offers demonstrations as well as classes open to visitors. The Forte de Santo Antônio Além do Carmo is occupied by the **Centro Esportivo de Capoeira Angola** (Largo de Santo Antônio, Santo Antônio, tel. 71/3117-1488), which houses seven different academies; apart from classes and demonstrations, capoeira-related events are always hosted here.

ENTERTAINMENT AND EVENTS
Nightlife

Salvador's nightlife is somewhat of an enigma. Contrary to its fame as a party place, when the sizzling summer season comes to an end, many bars and clubs close early or shut down altogether. Supposedly, the blame falls to the

Barra beach

fickleness of Soteropolitanos. There is always something happening in Barra and Rio Vermelho, and the Pelô and Centro offer a few old standbys that never go out of style. For listings, check out the entertainment sections of the two daily papers, *A Tarde* and *O Correio da Bahia*, or pick up the free monthly *Agenda Cultural* booklet available at tourist offices and cultural venues.

BARS

Most of Salvador's bars are at least partially outdoors and pretty basic. What makes them special is their strategic setting, located in a hidden garden or a colonial mansion, overlooking the ocean, or in a lively cobblestoned *praça*.

Although there's no lack of action in the Pelô, with vendors and beggars going after gringos some of it can be trying. Ubiquitous bars are sprinkled around the Praça Tereza Batista, Praça Pedro Archango, and Praça Quincas Berro D'Água. A traditional watering hole with a largely local clientele is **O Cravinho** (Terreiro de Jesus 3, Pelourinho, tel. 71/3322-6759, www.ocravinho.com.br, 11am-11pm daily). *Cravinho,* meaning "little clove," refers to the house specialty of *cachaça* infused with cloves, lime, and honey. This deceptively explosive concoction goes down nicely and costs next to nothing (which is why the bar is always packed). More than 200 such *cachaça* infusions (using herbs, flowers, roots, fruits, and seeds) are left to steep in the great wooden barrels lining the walls.

In Santo Antônio, a favorite place to watch the sunset over the Baía de Todos os Santos is the **Bar do Espanhol,** also known as **Bar Cruz do Pascoal** (Rua Direita de Santo Antônio 2, Santo Antônio, tel. 71/3243-2285, 11am-close Mon.-Sat.), where any hunger pangs can be assuaged by an *arrumadinho* (bite-size chunks of sun-dried beef mixed with black-eyed beans, toasted manioc flour, and diced tomatoes and peppers). A well-kept secret unknown to most locals, **D'Venetta** (Rua dos Adobes 12, tel. 71/3243-0616, www.dvenetta.com.br, 6pm-close Wed.-Sat.,

11am-6pm Sun.) is owned by a young local couple who had the insight to buy an enormous old house and transform it into the kind of bar where customers feel like family. Expect live samba and chorinho on the weekends and delicious home cooking all the time. The back garden with its wild roses and banana trees is an oasis.

Just behind the Pelourinho, **Mouraria** is a vibrant old neighborhood that is completely off the tourist path. For years, Thursday has been the customary night to head to one of the sidewalk bars clustered around Mouraria's cobblestoned square and dig into a ceramic pot steaming with *lambretas*. A local clam-like mollusk reputed to be an aphrodisiac (and a great hangover cure), the *lambretas* are steamed with cilantro and onions, then served piping hot. Traditionally, the city's "Old Guard" indulges at the square's largest bar, called **Koisa Nossa** (Travessa Engenheiro Alione 3, Mouraria, tel. 71/3266-5596, 5pm-close Mon.-Fri., noon-8pm Sat. More recently, a younger crowd has caught *lambreta* fever, and newer bars have opened to keep up with the demand.

Similar to Mouraria, **Dois de Julho** is another lively old residential neighborhood in the center of town where you can find authentic watering holes. One of the most happening is the **Mocambinho Bar** (Rua da Faisca 12, Dois de Julho, tel. 71/3328-1430, from 6pm Tues.-Sat.), a friendly place that draws in a bohemian and alternative crowd and where the home-cooked bar food—sun-dried beef and pumpkin puree, for example—is a few steps above usual bar fare.

In Barra, the biggest concentration of nocturnal activity takes place near the residential streets of Rua Belo Horizonte, Rua Florianópolis, and Rua Recife—a neighborhood known as **Jardim Brasil.** Although quiet enough during the week, the place sizzles on weekends. This is when a rather yuppie-ish university-age crowd flocks to the multiple bars and eateries in the area (which close early, at 1:30am). For a quieter and less collegiate option, drop by **Platô** (Rua Plínio

Moscoso 25, Barra, tel. 71/3273-1604, 5pm-close Tues.-Fri., noon-2am Sat., noon-10pm Sun.), an appealingly laid-back *boteco* with scrumptious food and killer drinks such as *pinha* (sugar apple) *caipis*. The tables sprinkled beneath the 50-year-old mango tree are a fine perch from which to zone out to live MPB and jazz on weekend afternoons.

The most eclectic nightlife destination in town is the bohemian *bairro* of Rio Vermelho. Unless it's pouring, the outdoor bars on Largo de Santana and Largo de Mariquita have always long lines of people waiting. The bars and restaurants on Rua da Paciência and Rua do Meio are always pulsing with activity. Considered one of the best traditional *botecos* in the *bairro,* the always popular but not too trendy Boteco da França (Rua Borges dos Reis 24-A, Rio Vermelho, tel. 71/3334-2734, 6pm-1am Mon., noon-close Tues.-Sun.) was opened in 2002 by a former waiter who toiled for many years at two other classic Rio Vermelho haunts. He obviously learned his trade well, because the Boteco offers attentive service, an extensive food and drink menu, including *chope de vinho* (wine on draft), and a mellow jazzy-bossa soundtrack that has made it a favorite with intellectuals, artists, and journalists. Cozy A Proa Bar (Rua Guedes Cabral 81, Rio Vermelho, tel. 71/8888-8315, 6pm-close Tues.-Sat.) is funkier, with a whitewashed porch that overlooks the sea and a narrow but homey interior that feels like a living room. If everything is closing down, the sun is coming up, and you're still raring to go, make a beeline for the Mercado de Peixe (Largo de Mariquita). Open 24 hours, this market's many lively bars are a classic "last call" option. Despite a soulless makeover, you'll still find plenty of traditional grub—try a thick, chowder-like bean soup, *caldo de feijão,* or *caldo de sururu* (similar to a mussel)—to stave off a hangover.

LIVE MUSIC

Salvador is justly famous for its music scene. There are limitless possibilities for hearing music, often for free. In the summertime,

especially, the Pelourinho throbs with the beat of drums as the city's Carnaval *blocos* (traditional Carnaval groups associated with organizations or neighborhoods) hold open weekly rehearsals, often with special guests in attendance. Usually beginning in November, these *ensaios* are either free or ridiculously expensive (to gouge tourists). Locales change yearly. Taking part will not only ensure you rub shoulders with Salvador's young blood but will also allow you to witness firsthand how summer musical hits—which eventually captivate all of Bahia and Brazil—are generated. Think of it as a taste of the sheer exuberance and intense musicality of Carnaval, should you not be around for the main event itself. The hottest *ensaios* around include the *tradic'onalíssimo* Afro *blocos* Ilê Aiyê (whose rehearsals take place at its headquarters in the *bairro* of Curuzu), Filhos de Gandhy, Olodum, Muzenza, and Cortejo Afro (all of whom perform in the Pelô).

There is usually always something going on at the Pelourinho's Praça Tereza Batista and Praça Pedro Archango (both off Rua Gregório de Matos) as well as Praça Quincas Berro D'Água (off Rua Frei Vicente). In the summer, these three outdoor areas, surrounded by bars, host musical repertories ranging from samba-reggae to *pagode* that jive with the feverish public's desire to get down, get close, and samba till they drop. In the winter, the tempo slows down, switching to MPB, bossa nova, and *chorinho*. Not to be missed are the Tuesday-night jams on the steep steps of the Igreja do Santíssimo Sacramento do Passo on Rua do Passo, hosted by the terrific homegrown singer and composer Gerónimo. From the top of the stairs the view across the Pelourinho is enchanting, especially if there is a full moon. Also wildly popular are the traditional *rodas de samba* (samba circles), which take place in Largo de Santo Antônio at 7pm on the last Friday of the month.

Up and running since 1958, the beloved Concha Acústica (Ladeira da Fonte, Campo Grande, tel. 71/3535-0600, www.tca.ba.gov.br), or simply *a Concha,* is part of the Teatro

Castro Alves complex. Since day one, this outdoor amphitheater, which seats 5,000, has hosted the biggest names in Brazilian music and continues to do so, all at affordable prices.

On a much smaller scale, the **Espaço Cultural Casa da Mãe** (Rua Guedes Cabral 81, Rio Vermelho, tel. 71/3017-9041, 7pm-2am Tues.-Sat., 1pm-11pm Sun., cover R$5) is a cozy bar situated in a whitewashed house with ocean views. Operated by Roda Bahiana (an organization based in the Recôncavo town of Santo Amaro that promotes local artists and musicians), it is a great place to catch some very fine and authentic musical performances. For more space, stretch your legs or dance the night at neighboring **Visca Sabor & Arte** (Rua Guedes Cabral 123, Rio Vermelho, tel. 71/3034-1688, 6pm-2am Tues.-Sat.), a cool alternative with healthy bar grub.

NIGHTCLUBS

When Soteropolitanos want to let their hair down and samba the night away, they tend to favor the balmy outdoors over being cooped up between four walls. Because of this, the club scene can be rather uninspiring.

On a small street off Avenida Sete de Setembro (near Campo Grande), the **Tropical** (Rua Gamboa de Cima 24, Centro, tel. 71/3487-1213, www.boatetropical.com, 11pm-6am Fri.-Sat., cover R$10-20) is the third and latest incarnation of a gay club called Holmes whose nocturnal happenings were legendary throughout Brazil in the 1980s. The decor is festive, gaudy, and heavy on Carmen Miranda tributes. There are two bars, a lounge, the requisite dance floor, and a stage where local drag queens entertain the mixed yet largely gay audience.

Opened in 2013, **Commons Studio Bar** (Rua Odilon Santos 224, Rio Vermelho, www.commons.com.br, tel. 71/3022-5620, 10pm-5am Fri.-Sat. cover R$15-25) has been anointed one of the most scaldingly hot destinations to trip the night fantastic. A mixture of cutting-edge live bands and DJ-hosted *festas* keep the city's young *alternativos* grooving on the wood-paneled dance floor until dawn.

Performing Arts

Salvador is famed for its rich cultural scene, particularly when it comes to music. For major musical, dance, and theatrical events—featuring big-name performers from both Brazil and abroad—check out the offerings at Salvador's **Teatro Castro Alves** (Campo Grande, tel. 71/3535-0600, www.tca.ba.gov.br), a gleaming modernist theater directly in front of Campo Grande. Don't miss the nightly dance performances given by **Balé Folclórico da Bahia,** held at the Teatro Miguel Santana (Rua Gregório de Matos 49, Pelourinho, tel. 71/3322-1962, www.balefolcloricodabahia.com.br, 8pm Mon. and Wed.-Sat., R$40). Although not strictly "folkloric," the graceful and acrobatic choreographies are inspired by capoeira, Candomblé, and many other Afro-Bahian traditions, and the dancers themselves are breathtakingly fluid.

Festivals and Events

Salvador has all the prerequisite ingredients for a good party: an idyllic climate, a powerful musical and cultural heritage, the mix of Catholic and Candomblé, and a population that loves an excuse to take to the streets and display their *ginga* (graceful moves).

★ CARNAVAL

Billed as the biggest street party on the planet (it's listed in *Guinness Book of World Records* as such), Salvador's Carnaval lures an estimated 2 million local and international revelers to the streets of the Centro, Barra, and Ondina for madness, mayhem, and plenty of dancing.

Carnaval begins on a Thursday in February or early March (it's the week prior to Lent; the date changes every year according to the Catholic calendar). The merrymaking gets underway timidly (although in Salvador, "timid" is very relative) on Thursday night, when keys to the city are handed over to the Rei Momo (Carnaval King). It then continues until noon on Ash Wednesday, when the leader of the Timbalada *bloco,* Carlinhos Brown, leads a procession of *trios elétricos*—massive stages on wheels outfitted with mega speakers (as well as dressing rooms, lounges, bars, and restrooms)—along Avenida Oceânica. The stages propel Carnaval's major musical artists and their guests around the 25 kilometers (16 mi) of closed-off thoroughfares. Each *trio* belongs to a *bloco,* a type of closed club, which is literally cordoned off from the masses on the sidewalks. For a fee (ranging R$300-3,000, payable at Central do Carnaval stands), you can join a *bloco.* You'll get a festive costume (known as an *abadá*), unlimited beverages, use of the toilet, and protection, courtesy of the *cordeiros,* who are (very poorly paid) to (wo)man the ropes separating *blocos* from the rest of the populace, known as the *pipoca* ("popcorn").

Although being part of a *bloco* allows you to be right in the center of things, you can also leave your valuables at home and take to the streets. This will give you a chance to wander around more freely and fully experience the variety of offerings. There are many *blocos:* indigenous, African—such as **Olodum** (tel. 71/3321-5010, www.olodum.com.br) and **Ilê Aiyê** (tel. 71/2103-3400, www.ileaiyeoficial.com)—and transvestite. *Afoxés,* such as **Filhos de Gandhy** (tel. 71/3321-7073, www.filhosdegandhy.com.br), whose all-male members dress in long white robes and turbans, are religiously oriented. There are even hip-hop and reggae groups and DJ-led raves.

Carnaval unfolds in three areas, known as "circuits." While the **Dôdo Circuito** in Barra and Ondina tends to attract the big names associated with *axé* music (Bahia's signature style of throbbing commercial pop), the **Osmar Circuito** between Campo Grande and Praça Castro Alves features the more traditional and less commercial *blocos.* The Circuito Batatinha in the Pelourinho, with its small samba groups and marching bands, is perfect for children and families.

Whether you indulge for one night or all six, as an unadulterated sensory hedonistic experience, Salvador's Carnaval is beyond comparison. If you can't take the heat (or the blaring music and chaotic crowds), get out of the city. But if you're in the mood to dance, sing, *pular* (jump up and down), and *paquerar* (flirt) from dusk till dawn and back again, you'll be absolutely thrilled.

Considering the possible mayhem when you throw a couple of million drunken people together in 35°C (95°F) heat, Carnaval is surprisingly peaceful, thanks to heavy police presence. That said, it's best to use caution. Certainly, don't party alone. Pickpockets abound. Be smart and carry photocopied documents and just enough money for snacks, beers, and a cab ride.

For more information about joining a *bloco,* contact **Central do Carnaval** (tel. 71/3535-7000, www.centraldocarnaval.com.br). For information about Carnaval, check out www.carnaval.salvador.ba.gov.br.

FESTA DOIS DE JULHO
While the rest of Brazil celebrates independence on September 7, for Bahians independence is all about July 2, when courageous local forces expelled Portuguese troops from Bahian soil. The festivities begin on the morning of July 2, with a procession from the Igreja of Lapinha through the historic center and the Pelourinho, then finishing up in the afternoon at Campo Grande. Politicians of all parties show up, as do traditional marching bands and baton twirlers, but the quasi-mystical Caboclo figures, effigies of mixed indigenous and European race that are carried through the streets in ornate chariots, are the main draw.

FESTA DE SANTA BÁRBARA
One of the most moving celebrations is held on December 4 in honor of the patron saint of markets and firefighters, Santa Bárbara. Due to her association with the fiery and feisty Iansã, devotees, in large part women (including many transsexuals), dress in red and white, the symbolic colors of the *orixá.* There's a mass in front of the Igreja de Nossa Senhora do Rosário dos Pretos in the Largo do Pelourinho, then a procession passes through the historic center, stopping at the main fire

station and the Mercado de Santa Bárbara, where free *caruru* (made from more than 5,000 okra) is distributed. Throughout the day and into the night, the streets resemble a dancing sea of red.

FESTA SENHOR DOS NAVEGANTES
In Salvador, New Year's Day is synonymous with this beautiful celebration in which the effigy of Nosso Senhor dos Navegantes is transported around the Bay of All Saints by a fleet of decorated boats. From Praia da Boa Viagem, religious music and lots of samba accompany landlubbers watching the procession.

LAVAGEM DO BONFIM
The most important religious and popular *festa* on the calendar takes place on the second Thursday in January. Dressed in traditional white garb and strings of beads, Bahianas lead an 8-kilometer (5-mi) procession of similarly white-attired and perfumed devotees and partyers from Comércio to the Igreja de Bonfim for the washing (*lavagem*) of the church steps. The *festa* honors Senhor do Bonfim (associated with the important *orixá* Oxalá, whose color is white). After the crowd is doused with blessed water and perfume, the party really gets going, lasting long into the night.

FESTA DE IEMENJÁ
As the sun rises on February 2, Candomblé worshippers and Bahians from all walks of life begin arriving at the Casa do Peso in Rio Vermelho, where they leave offerings of flowers and perfumes for Iemenjá, the beloved queen of the seas. At the end of the afternoon—when the presents are transported by a fleet of hundreds of decorated fishing boats and tossed into the sea—the streets of Rio Vermelho erupt in major partying.

SHOPPING
Salvador isn't a big shopping mecca. The Mercado Modelo (Praça Visconde de Cairu 250, tel. 71/3241-2849, 9am-7pm Mon.-Sat., 9am-2pm Sun.) sells Bahian trinkets and

souvenirs, jewelry, and handicrafts. The city's oldest and biggest daily outdoor *mercado* is Feira de São Joaquim (in Calçada), best for authentic Candomblé artifacts. Most purchases are concentrated in the Pelourinho and Barra. The Pelô has an assortment of boutiques and galleries (and tourist traps).

Didara (Rua Gregório de Matos 20, Pelourinho, tel. 71/3321-9428, www.didara.com.br, 10am-6pm Mon.-Sat.) is the boutique of clothing and housewares designer Goya Lopes. After studying the history of African textiles, Lopes began making clothes for local musicians. Over time, her designs—sold under the name Didara, which means "good" in Yoruba—have attracted an international following who seek out her bold and colorful yet refined clothing and housewares inspired by African design motifs.

Another homegrown talent who has made a mark on the national fashion scene is Márcia Ganem (Rua das Laranjeiras 10, Pelourinho, tel. 71/3322-2423, www.marciaganem.com.br, 9am-7pm Mon.-Sat.). Her contemporary designs for women are mostly made of polyamide fibers recycled from rubber tires—a surprisingly delicate material that has become her trademark. Equally original is her line of jewelry. Natural fibers derived from regional palms (such as piaçava and ouricuri) inspire Marta Muniz (Rua João de Deus 17, Pelourinho, tel. 71/3321-4728, www.lojamartamuniz.blogspot.com.br, 11am-8pm Mon.-Sat.) to weave tropically textured eco-housewares and decorative objects.

Few CD stores remain in the city, yet Cana Brava Records (Rua João de Deus 22, tel. 71/3321-0536, www.canabrava.org, 9am-close Mon.-Sat.), run by a knowledgeable American expat, is a great place to listen to and purchase Brazilian music. Among its offerings, Cana Brava specializes in traditional music of the Bahian Reconcâvo region.

Cultuarte (Rua das Laranjeiras 48, tel. 71/3495-1736, www.cultuartebahia.com, 9:30am-5:30pm Mon.-Fri.), in the Pelô, is an association of local artists and artisans who earn their living by creating compellingly original clothing, accessories, and decorative objects that draw upon and seek to strengthen Afro-Bahian culture. For art, housewares, and handicrafts made by artists from all over the state of Bahia, a great source is the **Instituto de Artesanato Visconde de Mauá** (Rua Gregório de Matos 27, tel. 71/3116-6712, www.maua.ba.gov.br, 9am-6pm Mon.-Fri., 9am-2pm Sat.). Although pricy, the quality of the work is high. There is a second boutique at Porto da Barra (tel. 71/3116-6190, 9am-6pm Mon.-Sat.). Also in Barra is Salvador's largest centrally located shopping mall. Just off the Praia do Farol, **Shopping Barra** (Av. Centenário 2992, Barra, tel. 71/3264-7128, www.shoppingbarra.com, 10am-10pm Mon.-Sat., 3pm-9pm Sun.) offers three gloriously air-conditioned levels featuring Brazilian designer boutiques, food courts, bookstores, and a cineplex.

ACCOMMODATIONS

Where you decide to stay in Salvador depends on your priorities and personal taste. To soak up lots of colonial atmosphere, the Pelourinho and neighboring *bairro* of Santo Antônio offer all sorts of options, from backpacker-filled hostels to sophisticated boutique hotels in restored 17th- and 18th-century mansions. Beach bunnies will prefer to be in Barra (still very central) or at the more traditional hotel chains in Ondina and Rio Vermelho. Though other options exist farther along Salvador's coast, particularly in Itapuã, their distance from the center and lack of neighborhood attractions make them impractical.

Pelourinho and Santo Antônio

The Pelourinho is always humming (or drumming) with activity. It can also be noisy and touristy. Off the beaten path and only reachable by taxi or on foot—factor in a steep climb up the Ladeira do Carmo—are the many *pousadas* in tranquil Santo Antônio, where many foreigners have purchased and converted 18th- and 19th-century houses into stylishly, intimate lodgings.

R$50-200

Occupying a biscuit-colored colonial mansion, the well-run and air-conditioned **Hostel Galeria 13** (Rua da Ordem Terceira 23, Pelourinho tel. 71/3266-5609, www.hostelgaleria13.com, R$100-140 d, R$32-38 pp) functions as the unofficial headquarters for the young and the sleepless (it's not exactly quiet). Compensating for the lack of cooking facilities are a tapas bar, pool, Moroccan lounge, free happy hour caipis, and breakfast until noon.

Tucked away on a tranquil residential street, **Pousada Baluarte** (Ladeira do Baluarte 13, Santo Antônio, tel. 71/3327-0367, www.pousadabaluarte.com., R$140-180 d) is a welcoming and flawlessly run Bahian B&B with a quintet of small but cozy rooms. Charming owner Zelina doles out everything from homemade breakfasts to insider tips.

R$200-400

With a great location near the Terreiro de Jesus, the French-owned **Casa do Amarelindo** (Rua das Portas do Carmo 6, tel. 71/3266-8550, www.casadoamarelindo.com, R$350-530 d) offers 10 elegant and spacious guest rooms in a 19th-century mansion. Don't worry about noise; windows and doors are insulated from the bustle outside, ceiling fans and mini fridges are equipped with silencers, and kids under 14 aren't allowed. The swimming pool and rooftop lounge, as well as most guest rooms, boast wonderful views of the surrounding baroque architecture and the Bay of All Saints. A small gym offers morning capoeira classes, and there is an innovative restaurant on site.

On Rua Direita de Santo Antônio, you will find a handful of attractive *pousadas* located in colonial mansions. Many have terraces with sweeping views of the Baía de Todos os Santos, and charming bars where you can have a drink should you decide not to check in. Owners and staff are invariably multilingual.

Pousada Colonial (Rua Direita de Santo Antônio 368, Santo Antônio, tel. 71/3243-3329, www.colonialpousada.com, R$190-280

d) offers good value. Large, spotless guest rooms come in a variety of prices and sizes. The top floor suite, with a private balcony and splendid views, is marvelous.

Pousada do Pilar (Rua Direita de Santo Antônio 24, Santo Antônio, tel. 71/3241-2033, www.pousadadopilar.com, R$260-430 d) is a particularly pleasant option. The 12 immense guest rooms are handsomely furnished and flooded with natural light. Only seven have sea views, but everyone can partake of the lavish breakfast served on the panoramic terrace overlooking the bay.

Owned by an English artist with a penchant for red fish (all the wooden furnishings are decorated with bright scarlet fish swimming against a sea-blue background) **Pousada Redfish** (Rua Direita de Santo Antônio 442, Santo Antônio, tel. 71/3241-0639, www.hotelredfish.com, R$220-350 d) inhabits a vast, beautifully renovated colonial building beside the 18th-century Igreja Nossa Senhora de Boqueirão. Exterior and interior have been painted in watery shades of green; guest rooms—both standard and the luxury suites—are clean, cool, and quite sizable (the largest ones easily sleep six).

R$400-600

The **Pestana Convento do Carmo** (Rua do Carmo 1, tel. 71/3327-8400, www.pestana.com/br, R$490-820 d) occupies a 16th-century convent that, aside from some discreet and very handsome trappings of luxury, is remarkably faithful to its religious roots. Cells that once housed Carmelite nuns have been converted into 80 tasteful (if rather neutral) guest rooms. Arcaded cloisters shelter a bar and Portuguese restaurant that face a profusion of tropical plants and a swimming pool. Amenities include a library, L'Occitane spa, fitness center, theater, and, of course, chapel.

OVER R$600

Housed in two 17th-century colonial mansions that overlook the Largo de Cruzeiro São Francisco, the French-owned **Hotel Villa Bahia** (Largo de Cruzeiro São Francisco 16/18, Pelourinho, tel. 71/3322-4271, www.lavillabahia.com, R$530-730 d) pays heavy homage to both Brazil's and Portugal's past. Each of the 17 luxurious guest rooms is inspired by former colonies ranging from Macau to Madagascar. Colonial antiques abound, as do baroque accessories, jacaranda, and Portuguese ceramic tiles (even the staff wears period getups). Inner courtyards and a pool offer respite from the hustle and bustle outside. The on-site restaurant serves fresh local produce with a marvelously French twist.

★ **Hotel Aram Yami** (Rua Direita de Santo Antônio 132, Santo Antônio tel. 71/3242-9412, www.hotelaramyami.com, R$520-900 d), whose name is Tupi for "sun and night," alludes to the trouble you'll have *not* spending 24 hours a day here. A Brazilian-Spanish couple, both architects, purchased this colonial mansion as a second home and then decided it was too large to keep to themselves. Now this seductive hotel offers five roomy apartments, each a private oasis; restored colonial features fuse harmoniously with contemporary furnishings, while Bahian *artesanato* mingles with Chinese silk pillows and jewel-hued Japanese lanterns. Two swimming pools (one belongs to the two-bedroom master suite), a bewitching bar, and multiple verandas with sea views are further conducive to an utter sense of well-being.

Barra

Barra has tons of accommodations. Apart from the soulless chain hotels, a few enterprising souls are converting the neighborhood's surviving villas, tucked away in tranquil residential streets, into appealing B&Bs and *pousadas.*

R$50-200

Santeria Hostel Bar (Av. Sete de Setembro 2914, tel. 71/3012-7030, www.santeriahostelbar.com.br, R$120-150 d) occupies a renovated three-story house perched at the top of Ladeira da Barra; offsetting the steep climb up from the beach is the sunset over the Bay of All Saints gleaned from the lounge/terrace.

A Frida Kahlo color scheme, accessorized by popular Bahian saints and *orixás,* brightens up the two small dorm rooms (R$50 pp) and three doubles.

A pretty tree-lined residential street, Rua Afonso Celso has dozens of still-surviving villas, and a handful have been converted into *pousadas.* **Âmbar Pousada** (Rua Afonso Celso 485, tel. 71/3264-6956, www.ambar-pousada.com.br, R$140-160 d, R$43-53 pp) is a mixture of *pousada* and hostel that prides itself on its familial atmosphere. Staff are gracious and helpful, and the homey common rooms and verandas are conducive to hammock-swinging, journal-writing, Web surfing, and checking out the next day's itinerary (or lack thereof) in your guidebook. The guest rooms (located off the courtyard) are well maintained and feature portable boom boxes for sampling the eclectic CD collection. Be sure to visit the bar, where you can get a mean caipirinha.

Only a block from the beach is the low-key and attractive **Pousada Estrela do Mar** (Rua Afonso Celso 119, tel. 71/3264-4882, www.estreladomarsalvador.com, R$150-225 d). The friendly Scottish owners have transformed two houses into nine apartments (the upstairs ones are nicer), decorated in maritime-inspired shades of blue and white. A laid-back vibe reigns. **Pousada Noa Noa** (Av. Sete de Setembro 4295, tel. 71/3264-1148, www.pousadanoanoa.com, R$160-200 d) has a privileged beachfront location in a hibiscus-colored mansion next to Barra's lighthouse. Its 12 guest rooms—named after 12 European (mostly French) artists—are simple but nicely finished and accessorized. If you can't get one with ocean views, toast your "bad" luck by adjourning to the terrace bar, which, libations aside, is an idyllic spot to watch the sunset. Be forewarned that during Carnaval and New Year's, the place will be one big *festa.*

R$200-400

The brother-sister team at ★ **Casa da Vitória** (Rua Aloísio de Carvalho 95, Vitória, tel. 71/3013-2016, www.casadavitoria.com,

R$270-350 d) converted their handsome two-story family residence, on a quiet cul-de-sac off swank Corredor da Vitória, into a casual guesthouse that feels just like home (albeit one with a fabulous collection of artworks by contemporary Bahian artists). Seven pretty and personalized guest rooms feature antique and modern wood furnishings and marble bathroom fixtures; the largest room boasts a private veranda with sea views, while those at the back are a bit dim. Closer to the beach, **Casa Petúnia Boutique** (Rua Engenheiro Milton Oliveira 217, tel. 71/3264-5458, R$190-325 d) is a terrific B&B-style option that receives raves for the Bahian hospitality of English-speaking hosts Marcos and Petúnia. Seven spotless white and soothing rooms offer modern comfort.

Rio Vermelho

Salvador's top-of-the-line big chain beach hotels are concentrated in the middle-class neighborhoods of Ondina and Rio Vermelho. Rio Vermelho is picturesque and full of transportation options, although not as central as Barra. The beaches are not good for swimming, but the location is perfect for its vibrant nightlife.

R$50-200

Since opening in 2012, **F Design Hostel** (Travessa Prudente de Moraes 65, tel. 71/3035-9711, www.fdesignhostel.com, R$200-220 d, R$55-65 pp) has been touted as not only the best hostel in Salvador, but in all of Brazil. The brainchild of celebrated Brazilian actor/comic and Salvador-lover Luiz Fernando Guimarães, this uber-cool, gay-friendly hostel treats everything—from bunks to the communal bathrooms—with generous dollops of sophisticated design. There's a film screening room and a rooftop bar with a pool.

R$200-400

Located in a charming pink colonial house overlooking the sea, the **Hotel Catharina Paraguaçu** (Rua João Gomes 128, tel. 71/3334-0089, www.hotelcatharinaparaguacu.

Acarajé

One of the most distinctive fragrances you'll encounter in Salvador is the scent of *acarajés* sizzling in cauldrons of amber-colored *dendê* (palm oil). Made of pounded black-eyed beans, these round fritters are fluffy on the inside and crunchy on the outside. Once the *acarajé* is cut in half, you have the option of several traditional fillings: dried shrimp, *vatapá* (a puree of bread, shrimp, ginger, coconut milk, and cashews), *caruru* (a puree of diced okra), *salada* (a mixture of chopped tomatoes and cilantro), and spicy *pimenta*. *Acarajé* (along with *abarás*) is the city's favorite snack food. Enjoy it at these favorite Bahianas:

- **Acarajé da Neinha** (Av. Sete de Setembro, Centro, 2:30pm-9pm Mon.-Fri., 10:30am -7pm Sat.) at the entrance to Rua Politeama

- **Acarajé do Gregório** (Av. Centenário 2992, Barra, 2pm-10pm Mon.-Fri., 10am -8pm Sat.) in front of Shopping Barra

- **Dinha** (Largo de Santana, Rio Vermelho, 4:30pm-midnight, Mon.-Fri., noon-midnight Sat.-Sun.)

- **Regina** (Largo de Santana, Rio Vermelho, 3pm-10:30pm Tues.-Fri., 10am-10pm Sat.)

- **Cira** (Largo da Mariquita, Rio Vermelho, 10am-11pm daily), with an original Itapuã location (Rua Aristides Milton, 10am-10pm Tues.-Thurs., 10am-midnight Fri.-Sat.)

com.br, R$210-250 d) is a favorite of both Brazilian and foreign travelers who appreciate the intimate atmosphere. The 32 guest rooms are cozy if not stylish; more alluring are the common spaces and surrounding gardens.

R$400-600

The **Zank Boutique Hotel** (Rua Almirante Barroso 161, tel. 71/3083-4000, www.zankbrasil.com.br, R$350-570 d) offers a Bahian boutique experience with a welcome shot of contemporary. The 16 elegant guest rooms are divided between a 100-year-old villa and a sleek annex with floor-to-ceiling windows. Both buildings share a courtyard garden and overlook the sea. It's worth springing for a room with a view. A spa, lounge, reading room, and rooftop pool compensate for the lack of a nearby beach.

FOOD

A potent mixture of African, Portuguese, and indigenous influences, and with an emphasis on fish and seafood, Bahian cuisine is justly celebrated for its colorful presentations and sophisticated flavors. Palm oil, coconut milk, peppers, cilantro, lime, dried shrimp, and cashews create dishes that are both suave

and piquant, and often as fragrant as they are delicious.

Soteropolitanos are famous nibblers. Many meals are enjoyed communally around a bar table (many bars double as restaurants) or on the beach, and delicacies such as *acarajé* and *cocada* are savored in the street. The largest concentrations of eateries tend to be in tourist areas such as the Pelourinho and Barra as well as in Rio Vermelho.

Pelourinho and Santo Antônio

There is no shortage of restaurants in the Pelourinho. A longtime favorite for Bahian fare that's frequented by locals is **Axego** (Rua João de Deus 1, Pelourinho, tel. 71/3242-7481, noon-10pm daily, R$25-35). The restaurant is hidden on the second floor of an old building and serves excellent *moqueca* and *bobó de camarão* without a lot of fuss. Vital Abreu, the owner of **Ponto Vital** (Rua das Laranjeiras 23, Pelourinho, tel. 71/3215-3225, 11:30am-11:30pm Tues.-Sun., R$20-30), serves exotic dishes from his hometown of Santo Amaro da Purificação (in the Recôncavo). Those eager to try an authentic *feijoada* (innards and all) should grab a seat at the small and simple **Alaíde do Feijão** (Rua 12 de Outubro 2,

Pelourinho, tel. 71/3321-6775, 11:30am-10pm daily). Local institution Alaíde Conceição learned how to make this classic Brazilian bean-and-meat stew from her mother, who sold *feijoada* on the streets of the Cidade Baixa. *Feijoadas* cost R$25 and easily serve two; choose between *mulata* and *preta* (black) versions (which refer to the color of the beans).

The **Restaurante do SENAC** (Largo do Pelourinho 13, Pelourinho, tel. 71/3324-8107, www.ba.senac.br, 11:30am-3:30pm Mon.-Sat., R$40) is a touristy but terrific option for its diversity of Bahian cuisine. The restaurant is located in a spacious colonial mansion and is operated by the Senac restaurant school, so the (somewhat formal) service is extremely attentive. The food is carefully prepared and presented by professors and students—an all-you-can-eat buffet features more than 40 regional dishes. For the less culinarily adventurous, a second per-kilo restaurant on the main floor offers a conventional (non-Bahian) but equally tasty buffet.

La Figa (Rua das Laranjeiras 17, Pelourinho, tel. 71/3322-0066, www.ristorantelafiga.com, noon-midnight Mon.-Sat., noon-6pm Sun., R$25-35) is a laid-back yet stylish Italian eatery whose vibrant owner-chef hails from Padua and makes all his fresh pasta by hand. Other strengths are the seafood dishes and pizzas (served at night). For something lighter, tuck into a salad, sandwich, or pastry at **Cafelier** (Rua do Carmo 50, Santo Antônio, tel. 71/3241-5095, www.cafelier.com.br, 2:30pm-9:30pm Thurs.-Tues., R$10-20), occupying an atmospheric mansion teetering over the Bay of All Saints.

Facing onto the Igreja e Convento de São Francisco, French-owned **Le Glacier Laporte** (Largo do Cruzeiro 21, Pelourinho, tel. 71/3266-3649, 10am-9pm daily) serves wonderful sorbet made from local ingredients that packs a Parisian wallop of distilled flavor.

Cidade Baixa

Almost immediately upon opening in 2005, **Amado** (Av. do Contorno 660, Comércio, tel. 71/3322-3520, noon-midnight Mon.-Sat.,

noon-5pm Sun., www.amadobahia.com.br, R$65-85) was crowned as Salvador's undisputed king of contemporary cuisine. Self-taught Brazilian chef Edinho Engel holds court in a spacious modernist warehouse suspended above the Bay of All Saints, where the ocean fuses perfectly with the restaurant's wood, glass, and jungle of potted plants. Local ingredients—with an emphasis on seafood and fish—receive daring and sophisticated treatment, and the impressive wine cellar features more than 3,000 bottles. Unfortunately, service can be exasperatingly slow.

If you visit the Igreja de Bonfim, take advantage of its proximity to the **Recanto da Lua Cheia** (Rua Rio Negro 66, Monte Serrat, tel. 71/3315-1275, 11am-11pm Wed.-Sat., 11am-5pm Sun., R$20-30). The ocean views are just as mesmerizing (if not more so), but the food, ambiance, and clientele are completely different at this typically Soteropolitano restaurant, whose tables are shaded by a canopy of tropical fruit trees. The house specialty is the *moqueca de peguari,* made with shellfish from the island of Itaparica, famed for its aphrodisiac qualities. There's often live music at night, and things can get slow and cacophonous on weekends. Nearby **Sorveteria da Ribeira** (Praça General Osório 87, Ribeira, tel. 71/3316-5451, www.sorveteriadaribeira.com.br, 9am-10:30pm Mon.-Fri., 9am-midnight Sat.-Sun.) is an ice cream parlor in the pretty seaside neighborhood of Ribeira that has been around since 1931. Local tour buses make the trip out here just so out-of-towners can sample a scoop or two of the 50 homemade flavors, including toasted coconut, guava and cream, tapioca, and tamarind.

Centro

There are lots of cheap eats in the bustling Centro, although not so many good ones. However, several long-standing Soteropolitano institutions—which have been offering up delicious *comida caseira* (home cooking) for decades—are definitely worth your while. Close to the Pelourinho and just off the Praça Castro Alves, **Mini Cacique**

(Rua Ruy Barbosa 29, tel. 71/3243-2419, 11am-3:30pm Mon.-Fri., R$15-30) is a favorite lunch destination for businesspeople, which means it can get a little noisy. The elderly waitresses in pumpkin-colored uniforms are atypically brisk, so you won't have to wait long to dig into the well-seasoned dishes. The daily specials are the cheapest and often the most succulent.

Facing a flower market in the lively neighborhood of Dois de Julho, the small and somewhat claustrophobic **Porto do Moreira** (Rua Carlos Gomes 486, Dois de Julho, tel. 71/3322-4112, 11:30am-4pm Mon.-Sat., 11am-3pm Sun., R$20-30) is a throwback to Bahia of yesteryear with its tiled walls and whirring fans. If it seems as if the place was ripped from the pages of a Jorge Amado novel, know that Bahia's favorite author was an assiduous fan of the 70-year-old family restaurant's delicious *bacalhaus* (Portuguese salted cod, prepared in various manners) and *moquecas* (including the unusual *moqueca de carne,* made of beef meat seasoned with dried shrimp and palm oil).

A practical and pleasant option for lunch or dinner is the fresh and varied per-kilo buffet at the Teatro Castro Alves's **Café Teatro** (Rua Leovigildo Figueiras 18, Campo Grande, tel. 71/3328-5818, 11:30am-3pm daily, 5pm-11pm performance nights, R$15-20). Local and visiting musicians, dancers, and thespians performing at Salvador's premiere theater eat here, making it a great place for people-watching.

Barra

Barra has its own share of eating options (and the more obvious tourist traps). For a light and wholesome lunch between bronzing sessions, head over to the jasmine-scented **Ramma** (Rua Lord Cochrane 76, tel. 71/3264-0044, www.rammacozinhanatural.com.br, 11:30am-3:30pm daily, R$15-25), which serves a healthy yet appetizing per-kilo and largely vegetarian menu with Asian leanings. It's a favorite with Salvador's yoga and Pilates crowd. You'll find a second location

in the Pelourinho (Largo do São Francisco 7, tel. 71/3321-0495, noon-4pm Mon.-Sat.). Another per-kilo favorite that draws a more businesslike crowd is **Spaghetti Lilas** (Rua Professor Fernando Luz 75, tel. 71/3237-9592, 11:30am-2:30pm Mon.-Fri., noon-4pm Sat.-Sun., R$20-30). Low ceilings and an excess of stucco aside, the decor is cool and clean and the mouthwatering buffet has plenty of appetizing local and international choices to fill up on.

Seemingly just another innocuously laid-back sidewalk *boteco,* **La Lupetta** (Rua Marquês de Leão 161, tel. 71/3264-0495, 6pm-close Mon.-Sat., noon-11pm Sun., R$20-30) is actually operated by the owner of what was once Salvador's best Italian restaurant. The menu offers very decent Italian fare, from creative antipasti to irresistible pizzas and pastas.

Rio Vermelho

The boho hood of Rio Vermelho comes to life at night with dozens of restaurants where one can drink, and even more bars where one can eat. The rest of the *orla* is less interesting, although a few legendary seafood restaurants make great lunch stops after a morning spent lolling on the beaches between Barra and Itapuã.

Catering to Rio Vermelho's significant vegetarian fringe, **Manjeiricão** (Rua Fonte de Boi 3B, tel. 71/3565-8305, noon-3pm Mon.-Sat., R$15-25) has a diverse and nicely priced per-kilo buffet and an oasis-like ambiance.

Dona Mariquita (Rua do Meio 178, tel. 71/3334-6947, www.donamariquita.com.br, noon-5pm and 6pm-midnight daily, R$25-40) specializes in "Northeastern recipes in extinction"—that is, the kind of honest grub that used to be found on street corners, marketplaces, and kitchens throughout Brazil's Northeast. The menu is helpfully divided into *pesada* (hardcore heavy dishes) and *levinho* (lighter fare that won't put you in a coma).

Trendy and more upscale (but no less Bahian) **Casa de Tereza** (Rua Odilon Santos 45, tel. 71/3329-3016, www.casadetereza.com.

br, noon-midnight Mon.-Sat., noon-5pm Sun., R$60-80) is named after, and presided over by, local superchef Tereza Paim. Paim uses sustainable ingredients (fish supplied by Rio Vermelho's fishermen's colony, hand-pressed *dendê* oil) to revisit Bahian classics in surprising and sophisticated ways. Results run from crunchy manioc shrimp bathed in passion fruit nectar and lobster moqueca to tapioca soufflé topped with a champagne-ginger coulis. Exposed wooden beams and brick walls covered with local art create a warm, let's-stay-a-while ambiance.

For a light bite and a strong dose of culture, drop by **Ciranda Café** (Rua Fonte do Boi 131, tel. 71/3012-3963, www.ciranda-bahia.com.br, noon-10pm Mon.-Thurs., noon-midnight Fri.-Sat., noon-10pm Sun.), an inviting space that's a combination gallery, café, emporium, and performance space where you can take in an exhibit, listen to live music, buy organic Bahian chocolate (or an organic cotton T-shirt), and have a bite to eat. Reflecting the Australian chef's devotion to slow food, the creative menu takes advantage of fresh local fish and lots of organic fruit and veg.

INFORMATION AND SERVICES

The state tourist office, **Bahiatursa** (www.bahiatursa.ba.gov.br), has various locations in the Pelourinho (Rua das Laranjeiras 12, tel. 71/3321-2133, 8:30am-9pm daily), at the airport (tel. 71/3204-1244, 7:30am-11pm daily), and in the *rodoviária* (71/3450-3871, 7:30am-9pm daily). Staff are helpful and friendly. There's also a 24-hour tourist hotline with English service (tel. 71/3103-3103). Pick up the free pocket guide *Agenda Cultural Bahia* for monthly events and entertainment listings. The official Bahian tourism website (www.bahia.com.br) is a great resource, but the Portuguese links are more complete than those in English.

There is a **Banco do Brasil** (Cruzeiro de São Francisco 11) in the Pelourinho. Others are at Shopping Barra, in front of the Mercado Modelo, at Porto da Barra, and at the airport. **HSBC** has a branch in Barra (Avenida Marquês de Caravelas 355). **Citibank** has a branch close to the Farol da Barra (Rua Marques de Leão 71).

You'll find post offices at the airport, as well as in Shopping Barra, at Campo Grande (Rua Visconde de São Lourenço 66), and in Pelourinho (Largo do Cruzeiro de São Francisco 20).

For medical emergencies, dial **192** for Pronto Socorro (First Aid). In Barra, there are two conveniently located hospitals: the **Hospital Espanhol** (Av. Sete de Setembro 4161, Barra, tel. 71/3264-1500, www.hospitalespanhol.com.br) and the **Hospital Português** (Av. Princesa Isabel 914, Barra tel. 71/3203-5555, www.hportugues.com.br). In the event of a crime, call **190** to reach the police. For crimes involving tourists, you'll have to deal with the special tourist police force (they're the ones patrolling the Pelourinho wearing Polícia Turistica armbands). The **Delegacia do Turista** (DELTUR) is on the Largo de Cruzeiro do São Francisco (tel. 71/3116-6817).

TRANSPORTATION

Most international travelers arrive in Salvador by air, although if you're traveling from another city in Brazil, you'll either arrive by bus or car. Salvador is also a popular stop for international cruises.

Air

The **Aeroporto Deputado Luís Eduardo Magalhães (Dois de Julho)** is the city's main airport (tel. 71/3204-1010, www.aeroportosalvador.net). Located inland from Itapuã, in the *bairro* of São Cristovão, it is around 30 kilometers (19 mi) from the city center. A taxi will cost around R$70 (if you bargain hard). There are also *executivo* air-conditioned buses (R$3) that pass along the coast and head to Praça da Sé, and regular municipal buses (R$2.80), which aren't recommended unless you have very little luggage and an awful lot of time (around 90 min.).

Bus

Salvador's long distance bus station, **Rodoviária Central** (Av. Tancredo Neves, Iguatemi, tel. 71/3616-8300) is across the street from Shopping Iguatemi. From here you can catch buses to destinations throughout Bahia and Brazil. In front of the *rodoviária*, amidst the daunting traffic and chaos, you can grab city buses to all destinations or (more sagely) hail a cab; a trip to the Pelourinho or Barra will cost you around R$40.

The main municipal bus station in Centro is Lapa, but many buses also pass through Campo Grande en route to the rest of the city. Regular municipal buses cost R$2.80, whereas plush, air-conditioned *executivo* buses (which link Praça da Sé, the Atlantic coast, and the airport) are R$3. The final destination is written on the front of the bus, and the main stops are listed on the side near the back door. If in doubt, ask the *cobrador* (who takes money at the back of the bus), since some buses have very circuitous routes. As a rule, don't carry a lot of valuables since robberies are common. However, don't be surprised if a seated passenger offers to take your bags and hold them safely on his or her lap. This is simply a courtesy.

Taxi

At night, bus service dwindles and it's safer to take a cab. Taxi drivers rarely speak English but are friendly. If you want, bargain with them, but before the meter starts running. Major companies include **Chame Táxi** (tel. 71/3241-8888) and **Ligue Táxi** (tel. 71/3357-7777).

Car

Driving in Salvador can be a challenge: Soteropolitanos have a penchant for not adhering to rules of the road. That said, for exploring the surrounding region, especially the beautiful north coast, which boasts an excellent (privatized) highway, having a car is a big bonus. **Hertz** has an airport office (tel. 71/3377-3633), as does **Localiza** (tel. 71/3377-4227), which has another in Ondina (Av. Oceânica 3057, tel. 71/3173-9292).

City Tours

Privé Tur (tel. 71/3205-1400, www.privetur. com.br) and **Tatur** (tel. 71/3114-7900, www. tatur.com.br) specialize in city and regional tours in English; rates run R$150-200 pp for a half-day guided tour. **Salvador Bus** (tel. 71/3356-6245, www.salvadorbus.com.br, R$45), a (rather conspicuous) double-decker bus, will take you to all the city's far-flung sights with briefs stops at landmarks such as the Igreja do Bonfim and the Barra lighthouse, along with 90 minutes at the Mercado Modelo/Pelourinho. Audio guides in English accompany the tour, which lasts four hours. Four buses make the trip over the course of the day, so you can hop off and on with the same ticket.

North of Salvador

ESTRADA DO COCO

The coast north from Salvador to Praia do Forte is known as the Estrada do Coco, or the Coconut Road (in honor of the coastline's abundance of swaying coconut palms). Although increasingly subject to the whims of real estate developers, the alarmingly urbanized villages boast lovely beaches.

Arembepe

Arembepe, 50 kilometers (31 mi) north of Salvador, was a hippie haven in the 1960s. The actual "village" consisted of ingeniously constructed palm-frond cottages set amid sand dunes; it was so swinging that it attracted the likes of Janis Joplin, Mick Jagger, and Roman Polanski. Some hippies still live (without electricity) in the village, making and selling jewelry and macramé and living off shrimp and fish. The placid lagoons attract a mellow crowd smoking reefer in idyllic surroundings. Show up at the end of the afternoon to catch the sunset and moonrise while floating in the warm waters of the Rio Capivara. The town of Arembepe attracts weekending and summering Soteropolitanos and has been filling up with condos. Despite the recent development, the beaches are attractive (especially if you walk far from town itself).

A languid place to while away the hottest hours of the day, **Mar Aberto** (Largo de São Francisco 43, tel. 71/3624-1257, www.mara-bertorestaurante.com.br, 11:30am-9pm Mon.-Thurs., 11:30am-11pm Fri.-Sat., noon-7pm Sun., R$45-55) is easily the best and prettiest (and priciest) of Arembepe's beachfront restaurants. For dessert, try *manjar,* a creamy pudding topped with a peppery mango coulis.

TRANSPORTATION

Arembepe is easily reached from Salvador via highway BA-099. Buses leave throughout the day every 30-60 minutes from the main Lapa bus station (final destination Monte Gordo) and the Terminal França near the Cidade Baixa's Mercado Modelo. The trip takes about an hour and costs R$6.

Praia do Forte

The country's first eco-resort in the 1980s (long before the prefix "eco" even existed), Praia do Forte drew international tourists to its beautiful beaches and surrounding natural attractions: a mixture of native Atlantic forest, lagoons, and mangroves. Before you could say "environmental," the sandy main road became a carefully landscaped and paved thoroughfare, Alameda do Sol, flanked by chic bikini-filled boutiques, jewelry shops, *creperias,* cafés, and even a *shopping.* Though tastefully designed, the commercial strip transformed the flavor of the place. Today, Praia do Forte is lovely and lively, but quite touristy—and becoming more developed by the day.

SIGHTS

One reason for the town's success as a thriving eco-resort is the presence of Brazil's acclaimed **Projeto Tamar** (an abbreviation of the Portuguese phrase for sea turtles, *tartaruga marinha).* Founded in 1980 by the Brazilian Environmental Agency (IBAMA), this non-profit research organization works to preserve the lives of the giant sea turtles living along Brazil's Atlantic coast, which is home to five out of seven of the world's sea-turtle species. Until recently, many were facing extinction as a result of rampant overfishing and urbanization that destroyed nesting sites. At Praia do Forte, Projeto Tamar's mission is not only to save the turtles (and their eggs, traditionally a staple food for local fisherfolk), but to actively involve the population in their plight in a sustainable manner. This is done both directly (by patrolling the beach at night to move eggs or hatchlings at risk of being harmed), and indirectly (through the increased tourism the project has brought to the region).

Eggs, hatchlings, and turtles of all ages find refuge at **Projeto Tamar** (Al. do Sol, tel. 71/3676-0321, www.tamar.com.br, 9am-5:30pm daily, R$16), located on the beach just behind the pretty whitewashed Igreja de São Francisco. It's filled with pools and aquariums where you can observe the turtles at various stages of their existence—from cute, tiny hatchlings to gigantic full-grown creatures capable of living to the ripe old age of 200. The center includes bilingual information and a gift shop selling the infamous turtle-themed paraphernalia (all proceeds go to Projeto Tamar). There's also a shady café on the premises.

Praia do Forte is also the headquarters of the **Instituto Baleia Jubarte** (Av. do Farol, tel. 71/3676-1463, www.baleiajubarte.org.br, noon-6pm Tues.-Sat., R$6), a research station for studying humpback whales. Between July and October, these 40-ton mammals trade the frigid waters of Antarctica for warm currents more conducive to reproductive activities. **Portomar** (Rua da Aurora 1, tel.

71/3676-0101, www.portomar.com.br, 4 hours, R$155 pp) offers boat excursions that allow you to get a close-up glimpse at these fascinating giants.

Back on land, an important historical landmark is the **Castelo Gárcia d'Ávila** (tel. 71/9985-3371, www.fgd.org.br, 9am-5pm Tues.-Sun., R$10). Originally a lowly clerk for the Portuguese monarchy, the ambitious Gárcia d'Ávila, as a reward for his services to the crown, received the *capitânia* of Bahia (which back in the 16th century embraced a large portion of the Brazilian Northeast stretching up to Maranhão). Built between 1551 and 1624 on a strategic hilltop overlooking the sea, his castle—now in ruins—is one of the first stone structures and the only medieval-style fortress in Brazil. The recently renovated **Capela de Nossa Senhora da Conceição** houses a tiny museum. The castle can be reached by walking along a 2.5-kilometer (1.5-mi) stretch of dirt road known as Rua do Castelo that branches off from the entrance to Praia do Forte, or else via rental bike, quadricycle, or taxi.

SPORTS AND RECREATION

Praia do Forte and the surrounding area offer lots of activities. First and foremost are its palm-fringed beaches, which offer the shelter of crescent-shaped coves and natural pools framed by coral reefs. The clear blue waters of **Praia do Papa-Gente**—a 20-minute walk north—are perfect for snorkeling (masks and fins can be rented at Projeto Tamar). You can also venture into the **Reserva de Preservação Ambiental Sapiranga** (Linha Verde, tel. 71/3676-1133, 9am-5pm daily, R$10). Located 2 kilometers south of Praia do Forte (enter from the Linha Verde), this nature reserve unites rivers, lagoons, and virgin Atlantic forest inhabited by endangered creatures such as the *mico-estrela-de-tufos-brancos* (miniature white tufted star monkey) and the *preguiça-de-coleira* (a type of sloth). Various trails weave through the brush, and there are plenty of opportunities for bathing in the Rio Pojuca. Young local guides can be hired at the entrance to take you on trails (price depends on the distance; the longest and most difficult trail takes five hours). Aside from hiking, you can explore the park by horse (R$120 pp for 1 hour) or the popular quadricycle (built for two, R$240 for a 2.5-hour excursion). With a canoe, you can paddle around the **Lagoa Timeantube,** a haven for close to 200 exotic bird species (R$30 for 1.5 hours). For more information,

Praia do Forte

contact **Portomar** (tel. 71/3676-0101, www.portomar.com.br)

ACCOMMODATIONS

Increasingly upscale and Eurocentric, Praia do Forte is not the cheapest place to stay along Bahia's north coast. However, in off-season and during the week, it's possible to find some good discounts.

Praia do Forte Hostel (Rua da Aurora 3, tel. 71/3676-1094, www.albergue.com.br, R$170-220 d, R$45-60 pp) offers clean rooms and facilities, including a kitchen and attractive garden courtyard. It's ideal for budgeting backpackers seeking dorm accommodations (and bikes and surfboards for rent). A few more *reais* will buy a nicer double room, more privacy, and tranquility (noise can be a factor here) in a *pousada*. **Casa Verde Apart** (Rua do Peixe Espada 100, tel. 71/3676-1531, www.praiadoforteapart.com.br, R$180-220 d) is ideal for families and those who want to keep house. Friendly owners/hosts Marcelo and Mirian rent six spotless and ecofriendly apartments that sleep up to four and include kitchens, hammock-strung verandas, and private parking. Fusing affordability and aesthetics, **Pousada Rosa dos Ventos** (Al. da Lua, tel. 71/3676-1271, www.pousadarosadosventos.com, R$210-310 d) offers six charmingly decorated guest rooms, each outfitted with flat-screen TVs and private terraces. Breakfast and a free afternoon tea service show off the virtuosity of the kitchen staff.

More upscale is **Pousada Refúgio da Vila** (Lot. Aldeia dos Pescadores, tel. 71/3676-0114, www.refugiodavila.com.br, R$400-570 d), whose lofty living and dining areas are beautifully designed and decorated to take advantage of the light and vivid colors of the surrounding gardens and pool. Guest rooms are less spectacular but well appointed—too bad some of the balconies overlook more "urbanized" parts of Praia do Forte—but the breakfasts are out of this world. If you feel like splurging, check into the place that put Praia do Forte on the ecotourist map way back in the 1980s: the **Tivoli Eco Resort Praia do Forte** (Av. do Farol, tel. 71/3676-4000, tel. 0800/71-8888, www.tivolihotels.com, R$840-1,615 d). Set amid beautifully groomed gardens—with swimming pools, bars, and lounge chairs and overlooking a crescent-shaped beach—this sprawling resort is hardly intimate, yet it definitely makes you feel spoiled and relaxed. All the bright and spacious guest rooms have ocean views. The prices might seem a bit steep, but they include a welcome drink, breakfast and dinner (the spreads are marvelous), sports and leisure equipment, and lots of activities for both adults and children. The thalassotherapy sessions featuring algae and heated seawater are a big bonus.

FOOD

Among the array of less enthralling and often overpriced eateries along the main drag of Alameda do Sol, **Sabor da Vila** (Al. do Sol 159, tel. 71/3676-1156, 11:30am-midnight daily, R$25-40) offers a diversity of dishes with some well-executed fish and seafood options. Prettier and pricier is **Terreiro da Bahia** (Al. do Sol 188, tel. 71/3676-1754, www.terreirobahia.com.br, noon-11pm Thurs.-Tues., R$50-70), where owner/chef Tereza Paim uses fresh, locally sourced produce to riff on classic Bahian recipes. Results include shrimp in mangaba coulis and coconut rice. A break from Bahian fare, **Tango Café** (Al. do Sol 269, tel. 71/3676-1637, 2pm-11pm Mon.-Fri., 11am-midnight Sat.-Sun., R$10-20) serves empanadas, sandwiches, and delicious desserts. This is one of the few places in Bahia where you can get a real cappuccino.

TRANSPORTATION AND SERVICES

On Alameda do Sol (near the bus stop) are several ATMs that accept international cards. For more information, visit www.praiadoforte.org.br. Buses leave from Terminal da França, in the Cidade Baixa, stopping at Salvador's Rodoviária Central, approximately every hour between 5am and 6pm with the **Expresso Linha Verde** (tel. 71/3460-3636, R$10). The trip takes around 90 minutes along highway BA-099. Informal vans (R$8) offer more frequent service, but prepared to be squished like sardines.

LINHA VERDE

Up the coast from Praia do Forte, the Estrada do Coco morphs into the Linha Verde (Green Line), stretching all the way to Bahia's frontier with the state of Sergipe. With the exception of the megaresort complex of Costa do Sauípe—with its umpteen international hotels surrounded by a fake theme-park likeness of the Pelourinho—the little fishing villages that dot this beautiful stretch of coast are (for the time being) largely untouched by mass tourism.

Imbassaí

Only 10 kilometers (6 mi) past Praia do Forte, this low-key village is a welcome antidote to Praia do Forte. It attracts a mix of locals, families, gays, and a few fashionistas (bikini spreads for Brazilian *Vogue* are often shot here). The main draw is the beach, which straddles a windswept blue Atlantic on one side and the warm Coca-Cola-colored Rio Imbassaí on the other side. The upshot is that you can spend your day alternating between two utterly relaxing watery worlds.

ACCOMMODATIONS AND FOOD

There are quite a range of good *pousadas* and restaurants in Imbassaí. The most charming of the lot is the ★ **Eco Pousada Vilangelim** (Al. dos Angelins, tel. 71/3677-1144, www.vilangelim.com.br, R$320-390 d). Although the cozy bungalow guest rooms are a little snug, you can always hang out in the main dining and lounge areas (children under 12 aren't allowed). Common spaces extend to the wooden decks, where a tiled swimming pool is framed by lush foliage (including namesake *angelim* trees). The food (especially the lavish breakfasts) is excellent, and the staff is terrifically attentive. You'll get a friendly welcome at **Pousada Cajibá** (Al. das Bromélias, tel. 71/3677-1111, www.pousada-cajiba.com.br, R$180-220 d), set amidst an exuberant garden with a pool frequented by *mico* monkeys. Accommodations are in two-story bungalows; those on the second floor look out onto a canopy of fruit trees. **Casa Viola** (Al. dos Cajueiros, tel. 71/3677-1017, casaviola.wix.com, R$160-200 d) combines atmosphere with affordability in six colorful chalets, whose rusticity is offset by well-chosen decor. Delicious homemade breakfasts and a romantic on-site bistro, verdant garden, and tiny pool up the oasis factor.

barracas facing the beach in Imbassaí

For Bahian specialties such as fish, seafood, and *moquecas,* plant yourself beneath the enormous *mangaba* tree that shelters the **Santana Restaurante** (Rua da Igreja 1, tel. 71/3677-1237, noon-10pm Thurs.-Tues., R$25-40). Aside from the welcome shade, when ripe the tree's *mangabas* yield a succulent nectar (it will make your lips stick together slightly). Also famed for *moquecas* is **Vânia** (Al. dos Hibiscos, tel. 71/3677-1040, 11:30am-7:30pm Tues.-Sun., R$25-35), located just off the main drag.

At night, what laid-back action there is unfolds on the main street of Rua das Amendoeiras. **É Massa** (tel. 71/3676-1067, R$15-25) is an Italian restaurant-bar owned by an Argentinean expat; it serves tasty salads, empanadas, and homemade pizzas and pastas and offers free Wi-Fi for those with laptops. Always abuzz with an older crowd is **Nega Fulo** (Al. das Amendoeiras, tel. 71/3677-1019, 5:30pm-11pm Mon.-Tues. and Thurs., 5:30pm-midnight Fri., 1pm-midnight Sat.-Sun., R$20-35), a romantically lit pizzeria fused with the equally enticing **Jerimum Café,** which has elaborate drinks and mouthwatering desserts.

TRANSPORTATION
Imbassaí is 10 kilometers (6 mi) north of Praia do Forte along BA-099. Buses leave from Terminal da França, in the Cidade Baixa, stopping at Salvador's Rodoviária Central, hourly between 5am and 6pm with the **Expresso Linha Verde** (tel. 71/3460-3636, R$14). The trip takes close to two hours along highway BA-099. Informal vans (R$10) offer more frequent service.

Diogo

Diogo, 4 kilometers (2.5 mi) north of Imbassaí, is more bucolic and less visited. Its most "sophisticated" accommodation is the Belgian-owned **Too Cool na Bahia** (tel. 71/9952-2190, www.toocoolnabahia.com, R$120-200), whose eight simple but comfortable bungalows (with and without air-conditioning) are set in sand dunes and shaded by large fruit trees. It's a 20-minute walk to reach the beach of Santo Antônio, which, aside from a couple of simple *barracas,* is inevitably deserted. In the village, **Caminho do Rio** (tel. 71/9964-4087, 10am-5pm daily, R$15-30) excels at Bahian specialties such as seafood moqueca.

Getting to Diogo is easy; the Expresso Linha Verde buses and vans that stop in front of Imbassaí also stop in front of the BA-099 turn-off to Diogo. From there, it's a 1-km hike to the village; or take one of the *moto-taxis* usually parked at the entrance.

★ Mangue Seco

At the end of the Linha Verde, 70 kilometers (43 mi) north from Sítio do Conde, is the secluded Mangue Seco. Ever since its otherworldly dunescape made a cameo appearance in *Tieta,* a 1989 *novela* based on the Jorge Amado's novel *Tieta do Agreste,* Brazilians have been flocking to this slice of palmy paradise wedged between the Rio Real and the open Atlantic. Aside from the rustic little fishing village, you'll find yourself surrounded by coconut plantations, mangroves, and snowy white sand beaches whose big waves attract surfers. Thankfully, despite its fame, Mangue Seco's remoteness keeps the crowds at bay.

ACCOMMODATIONS AND FOOD
Mangue Seco has a handful of comfortably rustic accommodations. The nicest of all is **Eco Pousada O Forte** (tel. 75/3455-9039, www.pousadaoforte.com, R$250-310 d), located along the river between town and the beach. The owner, Yves, is a French adventurer (who sailed solo across the Atlantic from France to Salvador) with a flair for decorating as well as running a restaurant (which has the best wine cellar in town). In town, **Pousada Fantasias do Agreste** (tel. 75/3455-9011, www.pousadafantasiasdoagreste.com.br, R$150-210 d) offers modern guest rooms and a leafy green central courtyard. Overlooking the river, the cheaper and simpler **Pousada Suruby** (tel. 75/3455-9061, www.pousadasuruby.com.br, R$120-140 d) boasts a breezy veranda hung with hammocks, along with a restaurant that serves delicious fish and seafood dishes. Also good

for deliciously prepared fish and seafood is **Frutos do Mar** (tel. 75/3455-9049, 7am-9pm daily, R$20-35), which also offers river views. A Mangue Seco specialty is the delicious crab-like *aratú,* which are used to make *moquecas.* On the beach, you'll also encounter *moque-quinhas,* tasty slices of cured fish wrapped in palm leaves and sold by local boys on the beach for R$1. Don't leave town without trying the amazing homemade *doces,* fruit *licores,* and *sorvetes* at ★ **Recanto Dona Sula** (tel. 75/3455-9008, 8:30am-8:30pm daily), located right on the sandy main square. Sula's daughter, Ana Flora Amado (a relative of novelist Jorge Amado), presides over the most idyllic ice cream parlor—and best ice cream—you'll ever encounter. Sandwiches and light meals are also available.

To really experience Mangue Seco's dunes you need to rent a dune buggy. A standard one-hour tour costs R$70 for up to four people with stops for pictures and to partake in *esqui-bunda* ("butt-skiing"). Sunset is particularly bewitching. You'll find *bugueiros* in the main square.

TRANSPORTATION

Getting to Mangue Seco is a bit tricky: Take a 15-minute ride in a motorboat (R$45 for up to four people or R$3 pp in a larger boat) from Pontal on the Sergipe side of the Rio Real. **Expresso Linha Verde** (tel. 71/3460-3636) has three daily buses departing at 7am, 11am and 2pm from Salvador to Indiaroba (five hours, R$35)—from there you'll have to take a taxi (R$40) or minibus (20 minutes) to Pontal. If driving, follow SE-368 (continuation of the Linha Verde) to the Pontal turnoff, then drive another 12 kilometers to the town, where you can stash your car (many villagers offer parking in their gardens for R$15 a day). If the tide is high, ask the boatman to take you directly to your *pousada.* If not, you'll have to lug your bags along a sandy trail.

The Recôncavo

Named after the concave-shaped Bay of All Saints, the Reconcâvo refers to the former sugarcane region surrounding Salvador. Once the major purveyor of Bahia's great wealth, the colonial cities of Santo Amaro and Cachoeira were prosperous regional capitals whose prominence is reflected in the impressive array of baroque churches and gracious mansions that line their sleepy cobblestoned streets and squares. Despite a certain air of dilapidation, the towns retain a distinctive charm. The Reconcâvo is also known for its rich cultural traditions, linked to the African heritage of the largely black population descended from the slaves who worked the sugar plantations. Both towns are within a two-hour drive from Salvador and can be easily visited in a day trip. To soak up the region's history and distinctive flavor, consider staying overnight in Cachoeira.

SANTO AMARO

Only 70 kilometers (43 mi) from Salvador, this typical Recôncavo town—the hometown of Brazilian musical sibling superstars Caetano Veloso and Maria Betânia—is attractive and unpretentious. With elegant squares framed by baroque churches and a couple of ruined plantation manors, it's a pleasant place to wander around for a couple of hours if you're on your way to or from Cachoeira. Highlights include the colonial buildings around the **Praça da Purificação,** among them the 17th-century **Igreja Matriz de Nossa Senhora da Purificação,** with its Portuguese tiles, and the imposing 18th-century **Convento dos Humildes** (9am-1pm Tues.-Sun.), at Praça Padre Inácio Teixeira dos Santos Araujo, which houses a small museum of religious art. Don't leave without sampling the *sequilhos,* crisp buttery biscuits made by the nuns at the convent.

Entertainment and Events

Santo Amaro hosts two *festas populares* in the Recôncavo. On January 6 is the **Festas dos Reis,** during which the town's squares are given over to music and merrymaking. On May 13, **Bembé do Mercado** celebrates the abolition of slavery in Brazil in 1888. Offerings are given to the *orixá* Iemanjá, and there are plenty of traditional African-inspired songs and *samba-de-roda* dancing.

★ CACHOEIRA

Two hours from Salvador, this atmospheric town on the banks of the languid Rio Paraguaçu is a small treasure trove of colonial architecture that is slowly being restored. Cachoeira is also a center of Afro-Brazilian culture; there are a large number of traditional Candomblé *terreiros* as well as the Irmandade da Boa Morte (Sisterhood of Good Death)—a female religious order created by freed slaves more than 200 years ago. The order's annual **Festa da Boa Morte** has become a major event, attracting loads of *afro-descendentes* in search of their ancestral roots.

During the 17th and 18th centuries, Cachoeira was one of the wealthiest and most populous cities in the Brazilian colony. Its strategic location upriver from the Paraguaçu's entrance into the Bay of All Saints made it an important crossroads for the riches—particularly the gold mined in the Chapada Diamantina—that were being shipped from the interior down to the coast and off to Portugal. Its fertile soil lured Portuguese colonists to cultivate sugarcane in the surrounding hills and led to the importation of thousands of African slaves who worked the plantations. While the slaves toiled, their rich masters poured money into the embellishment of the thriving town, bequeathing a legacy of fine baroque churches.

By the early 19th century, colonial rule was being increasingly challenged, and as a hotbed of revolt, Cachoeira achieved national prominence. Cachoeirenses led the battle for independence against Portuguese troops. When Brazil subsequently won its independence, it

was in Cachoeira that Dom Pedro I chose to be crowned as Brazil's first emperor.

At the end of the 19th century, sugar prices had diminished and slavery had been abolished. Cachoeira and its neighboring town, São Félix (across the river) still prospered due to the cultivation of tobacco (its quality renowned throughout the world), but today tobacco's importance has dwindled. The glory of former times is but a distant memory preserved in the town's rich architectural and cultural heritage.

Sights

You can discover Cachoeira's treasures in a half-day of pleasant wandering around, which can also include a boat trip along the Rio Paraguaçu.

CENTRO

Praça da Aclamação is a grand square lined with impressive edifices. The **Casa da Câmara e Cadeia** is the town's 17th-century jailhouse and currently functions as its city hall. You can't miss the splendidly baroque **Igreja da Ordem Terceira e Convento do Carmo** (tel. 75/3425-4853, 9am-5pm daily). The church is richly decorated with Portuguese ceramic tiles, an ornate gold altar, and an exquisitely paneled ceiling. A side gallery features polychrome Christ figures, produced in the Portuguese colony of Macau, whose gory realism is enhanced by a mixture of bovine blood and rubies. Inside, the **Museu de Arte Sacra do Recôncavo** (R$5) has a collection of religious art and objects. It can be accessed via the cloister of the magnificent convent, which operates as a *pousada* with a restaurant.

Housed in a handsome civic building, the **Museu Regional** (tel. 75/3425-1123, 8am-noon and 2pm-5pm Mon.-Fri., 8am-noon Sat.-Sun., R$2) has an unassuming collection of 18th- and 19th-century furniture and decorative objects.

A couple of blocks away, on Rua 13 de Maio, is the coral-colored building that is the headquarters of the **Irmandade da Boa Morte**

(10am-6pm daily, donation suggested). Inside, a small museum displays photographs detailing the sisterhood's history and traditions, including the famous Festa da Boa Morte. From the museum, a steep ascent leads to the **Praça da Ajuda,** where you'll come face-to-face with the **Igreja de Nossa Senhora da Ajuda,** a simple stone church built in the 1590s that happens to be Cachoeira's oldest (sadly, it can't be visited). Descending an equally steep alley in the other direction will bring you to Rua Ana Nery, where you can visit the 17th-century **Igreja Matriz Nossa Senhora do Rosário,** renowned for its wonderful blue-and-white ceramic tile panels.

SÃO FÉLIX

When through wandering around Cachoeira, cross the rickety British-built wooden bridge that leads across the river to the town of São Félix. Aside from some attractive pastel-colored riverfront buildings, the main interest of São Félix is the **Centro Cultural Dannemann** (Av. Salvador Pinto 29, tel. 75/3438-3716, www.dannemann.com, 8am-5pm Tues.-Sat.), a warehouse that has been converted into a contemporary art center. Apart from temporary shows, the center hosts the prestigious **Bienal do Recôncavo** in November of even-numbered years. Famed throughout the world for its fine cigars, Dannemann still produces its heavily perfumed smokes on the premises. To catch a glimpse—and a whiff—of the process, make your way to the rear of the building, where women dressed in white sit at ancient wooden tables, rolling cigars as if it were still 1873. Even if you don't inhale yourself, you might want to buy a few to take home as the ultimate gift for the smokers in your life. Also in São Félix is the **Museu Casa Hansen** (Ladeira dos Milagres, tel. 75/3245-1453, 9am-5pm Tues.-Fri., 9am-1pm Sat., free). This museum is devoted to the expressive woodcuts and paintings of Hansen Bahia, a German engraver who fled Nazi Germany for Cachoeira (changing his last name along the way) and is located in his former home. Hansen's work reflects a strong local woodcarving tradition that you'll notice as you wander around town.

Festivals and Events

Without a doubt, the most famous event in Cachoeira is the three-day **Festa de Nossa Senhora da Boa Morte,** held every year in August. If you want to stay in Cachoeira, reserve a hotel *months* in advance. Should you miss this unforgettable celebration, try to make the **Festa de Nossa Senhora da Ajuda** (mid-Nov.), which features the washing of the steps of the Capela de Ajuda as well as plenty of traditional *samba-de-roda* music and dancing.

Accommodations and Food

The most comfortable and atmospheric—and really quite affordable—place to stay in town is the **Pousada Convento do Carmo** (Praça da Aclamação, tel. 75/3425-1716, R$90-140 d), with 26 guest rooms that are distributed among the town's 18th-century Carmelite convent. Ceilings are cathedral-high, dark wood is in abundance, and the plain decor is bereft of worldly goods. Slightly more hedonistic are the outdoor pool and an elegant restaurant. It serves a mean *maniçoba,* a heady local stew invented by slaves; the main ingredients include sun-dried beef and pork as well as stewed manioc leaves that must be boiled for three days beforehand to expel their natural toxins. For appetizing home-cooked Bahian fare, head to **Beira-Rio** (Rua Manuel Paulo Filho 19, tel. 75/3425-5050, 9am-11pm daily, R$10-20), a simple place whose outdoor tables and chairs overlook the river.

Transportation

Santana (tel. 71/3450-4951) provides hourly bus service between Cachoeira and Salvador (R$20) via Santo Amaro, with departures from Salvador's *rodoviária.* If you're driving, take BR-324 from Salvador for 60 kilometers (37 mi) until it meets BA-026 near Santo Amaro. From Santo Amaro, follow BA-026 for 38 kilometers (24 mi) to Cachoeira.

Candomblé Rituals

African slaves who arrived in Bahia came armed with the divinities of their homeland. After Portuguese slave masters banned practices that strayed from Catholicism, many slaves pretended to adopt Christian dogmas and rituals. In reality, they merged Catholic symbols with age-old beliefs preserved from their religious heritages. The result was the syncretic Afro-Brazilian religion known as **Candomblé.**

As Candomblé developed, the *orixás* (traditional African divinities representing various natural forces) became associated with Catholic saints: Oxalá the Creator with Jesus Christ; Iemanjá queen of the seas with Nossa Senhora da Conceição (Our Lady of Conception); Ogum, the great warrior and blacksmith, with both Santo Antônio and São Jorge; and Iansã, goddess of fire and thunderbolts, with Santa Bárbara.

This clever strategy ensured Candomblé's survival for more than four centuries. Still it was brutally repressed, not only by clerical authorities but by the ruling elite. In fact, to this day, there is a lingering prejudice against worshippers, who were known derogatorily as *macumbeiros* (practitioners of *macumba*, or witchcraft).

Terreiros are sacred casas (houses) where rituals and celebrations take place; these are presided over by *mães* and *pais de santos* (venerated Candomblé priests and priestesses). Among the most famous and traditional *terreiros* are Gantois, Ilê Axê Opô Afonja, and Casa Branca.

Although visitors are welcome, Candomblé rituals are sacred events. If you go, dress simply but formally (long pants and shoes for men, a long skirt and modest top for women), inquire beforehand about using a camera, and never join the dance. Candomblé festivities take place on the specific days associated with various *orixás*. The majority of *terreiros* are located in poor suburbs best reached by taxi:

- **Gantois** (Rua Alto do Gantois 23, Federação, tel. 71/3321-9231): Founded in 1849, the most important *festa* is held in honor of Oxossi (June 19).

- **Ilê Axé Opô Afonja** (Rua Direita de São Gonçalo do Retiro 557, Cabula, tel. 71/3384-3321): This traditional *terreiro* houses various *casas*, each devoted to a specific *orixá*. The most important *festas* take place in June-July and September-October.

- **Casa Branca** (Avenida Vasco da Gama 463, Vasco da Gama, tel. 71/3335-3100): Brazil's oldest surviving *terreiro* (dating from 1830) is recognized as a National Cultural Heritage. The most significant *festas,* held in honor of Oxossi and Xango, take place in May-June.

- **Irmandade da Boa Morte** (Sisterhood of Good Death): A religious order founded in the early 19th century by elderly black women of Cachoeira, the sisterhood has become a symbol of Brazilians' black heritage and culture. Members must be women, black, and at least 60 years old (the oldest *irmã* is over 100). The most important festival is the three-day **Festa de Nossa Senhora da Boa Morte** (Aug. 13-15) in honor of the Virgin Mary.

Chapada Diamantina

Due west from Salvador, the dry and dusty landscape of the northeastern Sertão region segues to mountains, and the vegetation turns surprisingly lush, with an abundance of orchids and bromeliads. The transformation signals the beginning of the Chapada Diamantina (Diamond Plateau), a vast and ancient geological region filled with canyons and gorges and crisscrossed by rivers and waterfalls, whose spectacular beauty has made it the No. 1 ecotourist destination in Brazil. Much of this unique and spectacular area is preserved as a national park. If you find yourself in Salvador with three days or more to spare, visiting the Chapada Diamantina is an adventure you won't regret.

★ PARQUE NACIONAL DA CHAPADA DIAMANTINA

The **Parque Nacional da Chapada Diamantina** is one of the most gorgeous natural regions in Brazil. Within its borders is the Cachoeira da Fumaça, the highest waterfall (380 meters/1,250 feet) in Brazil and the fifth highest in the world, as well as Pico dos Barbados (2,000 meters/6,560 feet), the highest peak in Bahia. Grottoes hide lagoons whose waters turn to piercing blue when touched by the sun. The striking vegetation ranges from giant ferns to the rarest of orchids—and there is always the chance of stumbling on a tiny nugget of gold or a diamond in the rough.

Only one paved road cuts through the 152-square-kilometer (59-square-mi) park, and there is no official entrance. The Chapada can be visited year-round; in summer, the sun can be scorching hot and rain (sometimes lasting for several days) can put a damper on hiking plans. In winter, cooler temperatures (which can become downright chilly at night) coincide with the dry season (Mar.-Oct.), when waterfalls can thin and even dry up.

One of the main bases for exploring the area is Lençóis, a former diamond-mining town now occupied by a lively mix of locals and ecotourists. Mucugê, Andaraí, and Vale do Capão are equally enticing diamond towns offering their own access to several of the park's natural attractions, and their surrounding areas are also worth exploring.

Hiking

The trails that cut through the valleys, plateaus, and canyons of the Parque Nacional da Chapada Diamantina make for some of the most spectacular hiking in Brazil. There are plenty of trails of varying difficulty; many were carved out of the landscape by slaves and gold and diamond miners in the 19th century. These are best traveled with a guide or on an excursion, since many are unmarked. Hire a guide directly via your hotel or through the local **Associação de Condutores de**

Chapada Diamantina

Gruta Azul · Gruta da Torrinha · Poço do Diabo · Lapa Doce · MORRO DO PAI INÁCIO · BR 24 · To Salvador · Tanquinho · Gruta do Lapão · CACHOEIRA PRIMAVERA · Lençóis · Palmeiras · CACHOEIRA DA FUMAÇA · Rio Santo Antônio · RA 142 · Rio São José · Caeté Açu · CACHOEIRA DO SOSSEGO · Vale do Capão · Barra · Rio Roncador · Marimbus Wetlands · ★ PARQUE NACIONAL DA CHAPADA DIAMANTINA · CACHOEIRA DO RAMALHO · Rio Baiano · Guiné · Rio Preto · Andaraí · Poço Azul · Igatu · Mucugê · Poço Encantado

© AVALON TRAVEL — SCALE NOT AVAILABLE

Visitante (ACV). The guide association is based in the region's main towns and offers a cheaper option, ideal for those who want a personalized, customized hiking tour. Guided tours cost R$80 (up to four people); overnight trips cost R$150-200 per day (up to six people), which includes food and lodgings. Specialized excursions include transportation and are the way to go for those short on time. Most full-day excursions cost R$130-170 and include transportation, entrance fees, and snacks; optional activities are extra.

LENÇÓIS

Lençóis means "sheets" in Portuguese. The name alludes to the town's early 19th-century origins as a camp for thousands of avid diamond and gold miners, who slept beneath

Parque Nacional da Chapada Diamantina

makeshift tents of white cotton fabric after long days combing the region's river in search of precious stones. Although many struck it rich, by the end of the 19th century most of the big rocks had been found. Over the next 100 years, the former boomtown was abandoned and its population shrank significantly. Lençóis's fortunes only revived in 1985, with the creation of the Chapada Diamantina National Park. Despite its size and relative isolation, Lençóis possesses a surprisingly cosmopolitan flavor due to the collection of nature lovers, adventure-sports enthusiasts, and New Age groupies who linger in its cobblestoned streets.

Sights

Tourism has been a catalyst for the ongoing renovation of Lençóis's 19th-century homes and civic buildings, which number more than 200. Among the most splendid traces of its former grandeur are the **Igreja Nossa Senhora do Rosário,** the wealthy home of the Sá family, which later became the **Prefeitura** (city

hall), and the **Subconsulado Francês,** the former French consulate building. **Capela de Santa Luzia** (Morro Alto da Tomba, tel. 75/3425-4853, 8am-noon and 2pm-5pm Mon.-Sat., 9am-1pm Sun.) is a small chapel whose interior became a minor work of contemporary art when internationally renowned São Paulo graffiti artist Stephan Doitschinoff decorated the walls with vivid frescos of saints (look for other "interventions" by the artist around town).

Sports and Recreation

Lençóis is close to many of the Chapada Diamantina's most popular sights. One great walk is to follow the Rio Lençóis. After 15 minutes, you'll find yourself at the **Poço Serrano,** a series of freshwater pools where you can dip your toes or swim and enjoy a panoramic view of the town. Another 15 minutes brings you to the **Salão de Areias Coloridas,** an area with caves carpeted in multicolored sands sought after by local artists, who layer them in bottles and sell them to tourists. Hire a local youth as a guide (your hotel can do so) to take you to these attractions and to the nearby **Cachoeirinha** and **Cachoeira da Primavera,** two small waterfalls where you can swim.

Heading out of town to the southwest (follow the signs), a marked 4-kilometer (2.5-mi) trail leads to the **Escorregadeira,** a natural rock waterslide that sends you careening down into swimming pools (wear shorts to avoid scraping the skin off your bottom). If you keep going (with a guide, since access is tricky), the trail gets more difficult and involves serious rock climbing. After 8 kilometers (5 mi), you'll reach the impressive **Cachoeira do Sossego** waterfall, with rock ledges from which you can dive into a deep pool.

A challenging 5-kilometer (3-mi) trek (guide recommended) north from Lençóis brings you to the fantastic **Gruta do Lapão,** considered to be the largest sandstone cave in South America.

Having a car or being part of an organized

excursion is necessary to discover some of the more far-flung and dramatic natural highlights of the Chapada. The **Poço do Diabo** (Devil's Well), 20 kilometers (12.5 mi) from Lençóis, consists of a series of swimming pools crowned by a majestic 25-meter (82-foot) waterfall. Only 30 kilometers (19 mi) away is **Morro do Pai Inácio,** a striking 300-meter-high (980-foot) mesa formation. From its cacti-covered summit, you are treated to amazing 360-degree views of the countryside. According to local legend, Inácio was a fugitive slave who scaled the great rock in search of refuge. When cornered by his pursuers, he jumped from the top. Miraculously, he was saved from a fatal fall by the umbrella he opened in midflight. If you can, make the trip in the late afternoon—the sunset viewed from the top is a sight to behold.

Heading west in the direction of Seabra from Lençóis are a number of caverns, all clustered close together. The truly spectacular **Gruta da Torrinha** (Estrada da Bandeira Km 64, 1-2-hour guided tour R$35 pp) and cavernous **Gruta da Lapa Doce** (Estrada da Bandeira Km 68, 90-minute guided tour R$20 pp) boast surreally sculptural ensembles of stalactites and stalagmites. Located within walking distance from each other on the Fazenda Pratinha are the **Gruta da Pratinha** and **Gruta Azul** (Estrada da Bandeira Km 75, R$20 pp). The latter more than lives up to its name: When lit up directly by the sun (2:30pm-3:30pm daily, Apr.-Sept.), the lagoon at its bottom glows an unearthly azure. At Pratinha, you can rent a flashlight and snorkeling gear (R$20) and plunge right into the clear waters, which are inhabited by 24 species of fish.

Festivals and Events

The two biggest events in Lençóis take place in the winter. Throughout most of mid-late June, the town gets into the swing of things with the typically northeastern **Festas Juninas.** The feverish high point is the **Festa de São João** (June 23-24). Expect lots of corn-based delicacies, homemade fruit liqueurs, smoking bonfires, processions, and *forró* music. In August, the town resembles a latter-day Woodstock when it hosts the **Festival de Inverno de Lençóis,** a musical festival that lures some of the biggest names in Brazilian popular music. January 23 marks the beginning of the **Festa de Senhor dos Passos,** whose week-long festivities pay homage to the patron saint of miners.

Accommodations

Lençóis has a wide variety of accommodations, and given its backpacking ethos, there is no shortage of cheap lodgings. Simple and downright affordable, the small but quaint **Hostel Chapada** (Rua Urbano Duarte 121, tel. 75/3334-1497, www.hostelchapada.com.br, R$115-155 d, R$45-55 pp), located in a 19th-century house, has only seven rooms and 27 beds, but lots of greenery, swinging hammocks, and laundry facilities—everything a backpacker dreams of. Budget travelers will also feel at home at the welcoming **Pousada da Lua Cristal** (Rua dos Patriotas 27, tel. 75/3334-1658, www.pousadaluadecristal.com.br, R$120-130 d), a colonial house with modest but fetching rooms ranging from singles to quintuplets (bathrooms are shared). The great value is enhanced by attentive service and copious breakfasts. Unusual and alluring, **Alcino Atelier Estalagem** (Rua Tomba Surrão 139, tel. 75/3334-1171, www.alcinoestalagem.com, R$190-290 d) occupies a lovingly restored old house. Owner/artist Alcino Caetano makes guests feel right at home with cozy guest rooms decorated with antiques, glazed tiles, and shards of ceramic painted by local artists. Verandas with hammocks, a garden with fruit trees, and lavish homemade breakfasts, featuring exotica such as taioba quiche, complete the picture.

Ingeniously integrated into its natural surroundings is the ★ **Canto das Águas** (Av. Senhor dos Passos 1, tel. 75/3334-1154, www.lencois.com.br, R$370-630 d). A river literally runs through the property, providing the gardens, pool, café and celebrated **Azul** restaurant (open to the public for lunch and dinner) with a constantly soothing soundtrack. More intimate and affordable is the holistic and harmonious **Pousada Vila Serrano Pousada** (Alto do Bomfim 8, tel. 75/3334-1486, www.vilaserrano.com.br, R$190-260 d). Occupying a faux-colonial manse, its nine highly sustainable apartments, designed according to the rules of feng shui, emphasize natural textures, soft lighting, and a fusion between indoor and outdoor environments.

Food

Considering the global tribes that pass through and settle down in Lençóis, the mix of good eating options here is hardly surprising. A great place to sample regional fare is **O Bode** (Praça Horácio de Matos, tel. 75/3334-1600, noon-5pm daily, 7pm-10:30pm daily Dec.-Jan., R$15-25), where you'll find a buffet of local dishes as well as many options featuring the house specialty, *bode* (goat). Among the more exotic local recipes you should try are *godó* (a stew of green bananas and sun-dried beef), *cortado de palma* (diced cactus with ground beef), and a salad of *batata-da-serra*, a local potato found only in the Chapada.

   Natora (Praça Horácio de Matos 20, tel. 75/3334-1646, 4pm-1am Sun.-Wed., 10am-1am Fri.-Sat., and daily from Dec-Mar. and July, R$15-20) serves up a crisp, thin-crust Armenian pizza at outdoor tables that allow you to savor all the action. The freshly made pastas and gnocchis at **Os Artistas da Massa** (Rua da Baderna 49, tel. 75/3334-1886, noon-10pm daily, R$20-30) are as addictive as the cozy ambiance. Note that opening and closing hours (and days) can be irregular. More eclectic is ★ **Cozinha Aberta Slow Food** (Rua da Baderna 111, tel. 75/3334-1066, 12:30pm-11pm daily, R$25-35), where an open kitchen allows diners to watch the preparation of organic local comfort food that draws on Thai, Indian, and Mediterranean cuisines. Service can be as slow as the food. For sweets, head to **Pavé e Comé** (Rua da Baderna 99, tel. 75/3334-1963, 7:30pm-midnight daily). You'll be hard-pressed to choose between the

homemade desserts made by Dona Sonia and served inside her lavishly decorated home.

Information and Services

Visit the **Associação dos Condutores de Visitantes de Lençóis** (Rua 10 de Novembro 22, tel. 75/3334-1425, 8am-noon and 2pm-8pm daily) for information and hiring guides. You can also check out the bilingual website www.guialencois.com as well as www.guiachapadadiamantina.com.br (Portuguese only) and www.chapada.org, which offer information about the entire Chapada region along with useful maps. **Guia Turística Chapada Diamantina** (www.guiachapada-diamantina.com.br) is an excellent and very thorough English-language guide filled with maps. Purchase one online or at a tour agency if you plan on spending more than a few days.

   Lençóis brims with ecotourism agencies that organize excursions and hire guides. **H20 Adventures** (Rua do Pires, tel. 75/3334-1229, www.h20traveladventures.com) offers a wide variety of excursions; its knowledgeable, English-speaking guides routinely receive raves from adventurous gringos. Aside from trekking, **Nas Alturas** (Praça Horácio de Matos 130, tel. 75/3334-1054, www.nasalturas.net) offers customized expeditions tailored to families, foodies, and birdwatchers. **Fora da Trilha** (Rua das Pedras 202, tel. 75/3334-1326, www.foradatrilha.com) specializes in rock-climbing and rappelling for all levels.

   The **Banco do Brasil** at Praça Horácio de Matos is one of the only ATMs in the Chapada Diamantina that accepts foreign cards.

Transportation

You can fly from Salvador to **Aeroporto Coronel Horácio de Matos** (tel. 75/3625-8100), 20 kilometers (12.5 mi) from Lençóis, although flights, with the airline Trip (www.voetrip.com.br, 0800/887-1118), are only offered on Saturday and Sunday mornings. From Salvador's Rodoviária Central, **Real Expresso** (tel. 71/3450-9310, www.realexpresso.com.br, 6.5 hrs, R$60) has four buses at 7am, 1pm, 5pm, and 11pm daily. Extra buses are added during high season. If driving, take BR-324 until Feira de Santana, where you can choose between taking BR-116 until it meets BR-242 or taking BA-052 until Ipirá, following BA-488 until Itaberaba. From this point on, both ways follow BR-242. Whichever route you choose, driving to Lençóis is not for the faint of heart. The roads are often full of potholes and slow-moving trucks.

MUCUGÊ

Smaller and less touristy than Lençóis, Mucugê (named after a native fruit used to make a knockout local liqueur) is another pretty colonial diamond-mining town with its share of nearby natural attractions.

Sights

Aside from pretty 19th-century buildings such as the **Prefeitura** (city hall) and the **Igreja de Santa Isabel,** Mucugê possesses the extremely unusual **Cimitério Bizantino.** Built in 1855 following an outbreak of cholera, the Byzantine style of the snow-white gravestones and monuments of this windswept hillside cemetery is explained by the presence of Turkish diamond traders who lived here. The ensemble is particularly haunting when illuminated at night.

Sports and Recreation

Situated in the heart of the Chapada, Mucugê is at close proximity to numerous natural attractions. Only 5 kilometers (3 mi) away is the **Parque Municipal do Mucugê** (access via BA-142 toward Andaraí, tel. 75/3338-2156, www.projetosempreviva.com.br, 8am-6pm daily, R$10), a research and cultivation center that doubles as a wildlife reserve. One of the park's main activities is the Projeto Sempre-Viva. The *sempre-viva* ("forever alive") is a delicate local flower that became a cash cow for locals after the gold rush. Threatened with extinction, commercialization of this delicate blossom was prohibited in 1985; you'll see many growing in the park along with a Museu Vivo do Garimpo, which traces the history of diamond mining in the

region. Within the park, short and easy trails lead to the waterfalls of Piabinhas, Tiburtino, and Andorinhas (the furthest away at one hour), all with natural pools for bathing. Also within 15 kilometers (9 mi) of Mucugê are more waterfalls—Três Barras and Cristais (which together form one of the Chapada's largest swimming holes), Cardoso, Córrego de Pedra (which only flows during the rainy season), Sibéria, and Martinha—all worthy of whiling away a few hours.

Entertainment and Events

Mucugê is reputed for its vibrant **Festa de São João** (June 23-24) festivities, which include smoky bonfires in the streets, neighbors serving homemade fruit liqueurs from their homes, lots of *forró* music, and dancing from dusk till dawn. Book accommodations in advance and bundle up, since the longest night of the year can get chilly.

Accommodations and Food

The nicest place to stay in Mucugê is the **Pousada Mucugê** (Rua Dr. Rodrigues Lima 30, tel. 75/3338-2210, www.pousadamucuge. com.br, R$80-120 d). Well-equipped guest rooms occupy a restored 19th-century mansion in the center of town with a respected restaurant. For delicious regional specialties, try **Dona Nena** (Rua Direita 140, tel. 75/3338-2143, 11:30am-4pm daily, R$15-25) and **Pé de Salsa** (Rua Cel. Propércio, tel. 75/3338-2290, 11:30am-2:30pm and 6pm-10:30pm daily, R$8-15).

Information and Services

To book tour guides, visit the **Associação dos Condutores de Visitantes de Mucugê** (Praça Cel. Propércio, tel. 75/3338-2414, 8am-noon and 2pm-9pm daily), whose building also houses the tourist information center (tel. 75/3338-2255). **Km Viagens e Turismo** (Praça Cel. Douca Medrado 126, tel. 75/3338-2152, www.kmchapada.com) offers guides as well as taxis and rental cars and motorcycles. **Terra Chapada** (Rua Dr. Rodrigues Lima, tel. 75/3338-2284, www.terrachapada.com.br)

is a travel agent that can put you in touch with guides and arrange excursions.

Transportation

From Salvador, **Águia Branca** (tel. 71/4004-1010, www.aguiabranca.com.br) provides direct bus service (8 hours, R$55-71) to Mucugê on weekends; otherwise, you have to change in Itaberaba, where there are two daily departures, in the morning and at night. Driving from Salvador, take BR-324 to Feira de Santana, then BR-242 to the town of Itaberaba, where BA-142 leads to Andaraí and then continues another 50 kilometers (31 mi) to Mucugê.

ANDARAÍ

Between Lençóis and Mucugê, pastel-hued Andaraí is humbler than the other two diamond towns. However, it is surrounded by its share of fantastic natural sights and is the easiest way to get to Igatu, a once-thriving diamond mining town now reduced to a tiny but terribly charming mountain village only 5 kilometers (3 mi) away.

Sights and Recreation

Andaraí is a great point of departure for many of the Chapada Diamantina's star attractions. On the eastern edge of the Sincorá mountain chain, it is perfectly situated for those who want to go trekking through the **Vale do Paty.** It is also less than 10 kilometers (6 mi) from **Marimbus,** a swamp-like ecosystem created by the Rio Santo Antônio. The best way to get around the area is by hiring a guide with a canoe (2.5 hours, R$20), then gliding through the waters adorned with oversized *Victoria amazonica* lily pads and giant water ferns. A few kilometers outside of town is the **Cachoeira de Ramalho,** a medium-to-difficult trek along an ancient miners' trail surrounded by natural pools. Farther afield (20 km/12.5 mi) is the **Cachoeira do Roncador,** featuring pools sculpted out of rose quartz, reached after an easy hike.

Those with a penchant for the color blue should visit **Poço Encantado.** (8pm-4pm daily, R$20), 40 kilometers (25 mi) from Andaraí on the road to Itaeté. When illuminated by sunlight (10am-1:30pm daily Apr.-Sept.), the intense cobalt hue of its waters is truly "enchanting." The added advantage of **Poço Azul** (8pm-5pm daily, R$15)—whose waters also turn dazzling blue when hit by the sun's rays (12:30pm-2:30pm daily Feb.-Oct.)—is that you can swim or snorkel (R$15). Before you take the plunge, make sure to reserve a delicious home-cooked meal prepared by Dona Alice (tel. 75/8163-8292), whose home lies at the entrance to the property. Poço Azul is around 50 kilometers (31 mi) from Andaraí on the road to Itaeté.

Accommodations and Food

The **Pousada Sincorá** (Av. Paraguassu 120, tel. 75/3335-2210, www.sincora.com.br, R$115 d) is a warm and appealingly decorated old house that is rightly proud of its hearty "colonial" breakfasts. The owners also have a farm in the Marimbus wetland where guests can camp or go on guided canoe tours. For light food and delicious homemade ice cream featuring rare flavors such as *jenipapo, cachaça,* and *rapadura* (caramelized sugar cane), visit the **Sorveteria Apollo** (Praça Raul Dantas 1, tel. 75/3335-2256, 9am-8pm).

Transportation and Services

For guides and tourist information, contact the **Associação dos Condutores de Visitantes de Andaraí** (Rua Dr. José Gonçalves Cincorá, tel. 75/3335-2225, 8am-noon and 2pm-5pm daily).

Andaraí is about 100 kilometers (62 mi) from Lençóis (to the north, via BR-242 and BA-142) and around 50 kilometers (31 mi) from Mucugê (to the south along BR-142). From Salvador, **Águia Branca** (tel. 71/4004-1010, www.aguiabranca.com.br) provides direct bus service (7 hours, R$66) to Andaraí on weekends; otherwise you'll need to change in Itaberaba. Driving from Salvador, take BR-324 to Feira de Santana, then BR-242 to the town of Itaberaba, where BA-142 leads to Andaraí.

IGATU

During the height of its 19th-century diamond rush, thriving Igatu had a population of 3,000. Today it's a small village of 350 where *Flintstones*-like stone houses alternate with pretty pastel villas, all of which are surrounded by the lush fruit and vegetable gardens that supply much of the local produce. As for the splendor of its past, it has been reduced to a bewitchingly haunted area of ruined stone mansions overgrown with mango trees and wild orchids.

Sights

Amid Igatu's ruins, the **Galeria Arte & Memória** (Rua Luís dos Santos, tel. 75/3335-2510, 9am-6pm daily, R$2) exhibits found objects and equipment used by the diamond miners as well as contemporary artwork by regional artists inside a beautiful space built on the ruins of a stone house. A garden shelters local flora, contemporary sculptures, and an enticing café where you can linger over crepes and cappuccino. For more insight into the town's diamond legacy, tour the nearby **Mina Brejo-Verruga** (7am-5pm daily, R$5), the biggest mine in the region, where—helmeted and armed with a flashlight—you can snake your way through a hand-dug tunnel stretching 400 meters (1,300 feet) into the side of a mountain. In the main chamber, 20 clay markers, each with a candle, pays homage to the miners who died here. The return to daylight will be a shock, which you can alleviate with a swim in the **Poço do Brejo.** Back in town, visit **Ponto do Amarildo** (Rua Sete de Setembro, tel. 75/3335-7017, noon-2pm and 5pm-10pm Mon.-Fri., 8am-10pm Sat.-Sun.), an eccentric emporium that local character Amarildo dos Santos has created in the living room of his house. The shelves are crammed with everything from homemade *doces* and *licores* to odd bits of local memorabilia and Amarildo's own hand-painted books recounting tales of Igatu.

Accommodations and Food

The best *pousada* here is the lovely and very comfortable **Pousada Pedras de Igatu** (Rua São Sebastião, tel. 75/3335-2281, R$120-170), which has a swimming pool and a sauna (but no TV) and terrific views of the surrounding countryside. Cheaper but charming is **Hospedagem Flor de Açucena** (Rua Nova, tel. 75/3335-7003, R$80-120), located in a rustic stone house whose guest rooms overlook a garden and pool. A kitchen and bathrooms are available for those who want to camp in the garden. Also ask around for rooms to rent with locals; many will cook local specialties for you on their wood stoves using produce grown in their gardens. A great option for home-cooked fare is **Água Boa** (Rua Nova 13, tel. 75/3335-7013, 10am-10pm daily, R$15-25), a family-run spot where you can dig into *godó* (finely diced and cooked green banana flavored with sun-dried beef) and *galinha caipira* (a rich chicken stew).

Transportation

Igatu can only be reached by a rocky trail that turns off BA-142 from Mucugê or from Andaraí. In either case, you'll need a 4WD vehicle or the stamina required for a couple of hours of uphill hiking. However, when you arrive at this remote town suspended in the mountains, you'll be more than compensated for the hardships of the journey.

CAPÃO (CAETÉ-AÇU)

Hugging the northwest edge of the Parque Nacional da Chapada Diamantina, Caeté-Açu (commonly referred to as Capão, after the valley in which it sits) is a tranquil village that in recent years has attracted a mellow expat community of New Agers, artists, hippies, and gringos who live in harmony with the spectacular surroundings. Aside from its bucolic air, it's a starting point for treks to some of the park's most impressive natural attractions, including the Cachoeira da Fumaça.

Sights and Recreation

One of the indisputable highlights of the Chapada, the **Cachoeira da Fumaça** is a waterfall so high that most of its water evaporates to mist before hitting the ground (hence its name, "Smoke Waterfall"). Looking down on the cascading water from above involves a long but scenic 6-kilometer (3.7-mi) hike from Capão. Getting right beneath it is even more arduous, involving a three-day trek (with a guide, supplies, and camping gear) through the breathtakingly beautiful **Vale do Capão.**

An easier outing is to **Poço Angélica**, a natural pool surrounded by lush vegetation that's only a 15-minute walk from Vila do Bomba, a village 8 kilometers (5 mi) from Capão (whose narrow road can be difficult to navigate). Closer to town is the **Cachoeira do Rio Preto,** a small cascade with a pool, located 4 kilometers (1.5 mi) from the center of town.

Accommodations and Food

There are a handful of pleasantly rustic places to stay in Capão. **Pousada Vila Esperança** (Rua dos Gatos, tel. 75/3344-1384, www.vilaesperanca.com.br, R$100-150 d) is an appealing choice set amid an orchard of fruit trees with a small creek in back. Tatami mats and the presence of *yakkissoba* on the menu betray the owner's Japanese origins. Close to the main square, **Pousada Pé No Mato** (tel. 75/3344-1105, www.penomato.com.br, R$100-140 d, R$40-50 pp) is a friendly combo hostel/ecotour agency with accommodations for two, three, and four people in individual chalets, sustainably fashioned out of adobe and reforested native woods and surrounded by native vegetation. It's popular with foreign backpackers for its organic breakfasts made with garden produce. The most luxurious option is **Pousada Vila Lagoa das Cores** (Rua da Lagoa, tel. 75/3344-1114, www.lagoadascores.com.br, R$280-480 d), located 2.5 kilometers (1.6 mi) outside of town in an idyllic natural

setting with views of Morro Branco mountain. Charmingly decorated bungalows, soap made with aromatic herbs grown on the premises, a holistic spa, and organic produce at the superb restaurant all complement the personalized service.

Capão's famed culinary specialty is the *pastel de palmito de jaca,* a pastry stuffed with "green" (i.e., unripe) jackfruit cooked and seasoned with herbs. You'll find it all over town, but the woman who invented it is **Dona Dalva** (Praça São Sebastião, tel. 75/3344-1140, 9am-9pm daily). Also famous is the healthy (and gigantic!) whole-wheat crust pizza served at **Pizza Integral do Capão** (Praça São Sebastião, tel. 75/3344-1138, 4pm-11pm daily, R$15-20). For a tasty home-cooked meal, head to the welcoming house of **Dona Beli** (Rua do Folga 140, tel. 75/3344-1085, noon-8pm daily, R$15-20), where dishes of the day are accompanied by local exotica such as sautéed *palma* (cactus) and *jaca; e*xpect lines on holidays.

Transportation and Services

To book tour guides, visit the **Associação dos Condutores de Visitantes do Vale do Capão** (Rua Campos, 75/3344-1087) or contact **Tatu na Trilha** (Rua da Vila, tel. 75/3344-1124), which also organizes trekking expeditions. There are no banks with ATMs in Capão; for cash withdrawals you'll need to go to Palmeiras.

From Salvador, **Real Expresso** (tel. 71/3450-9310, www.realexpresso.com.br) provides four daily departures to Palmeiras (7 hours, R$67). Buses also leave from Lençóis (1 hour, R$6). From Palmeiras, local vans for Capão cost R$10 pp. Driving from Salvador, take BR-324 to Feira de Santana, then BR-242 to Palmeiras (passing Itaberaba and Lençóis), from which a 21-kilometer (12-mi) dirt road leads to Capão.

The Southern Coast

The coast leading south from Salvador down to Bahia's border with Espírito Santo is the longest—and perhaps most beautiful—coastline in Brazil. Beaches, beaches, and more beaches are the big draw. From the party scenes of Porto Seguro and Morro de São Paulo, passing through the drowsy colonial charms of Ilhéus and Caravelas, to the sensation of being lost in paradise provoked by the likes of Boipeba and Caraíva, reserve a week (or two), stock up on SPF 60, and start exploring.

MORRO DE SÃO PAULO

For more than 20 years, this once-tiny fishing village on the Ilha de Tinhare has been the most popular destination along the Dendê Coast—named after the *dendê* palm, whose fruit produces the amber-colored oil used in traditional Bahian cooking—that stretches from Valença south to Itacaré. During the summer, it is mobbed by sand- and sun-worshippers from all over, and "Morro" (as it is called) becomes party central. If this isn't your scene, don't completely give up on Morro de São Paulo. In the off-season, especially during the week, it's possible to surrender to the simpler pleasures offered by swaths of native Atlantic forest, coral reefs, and warm ocean pools. And there are no cars, a big plus (you can hire a wheelbarrow to lug your baggage for R$10 per piece).

Beaches

Most visitors arrive by boat in Morro and are greeted by the grandiose stone gates of an early 17th-century ruined fortress and a 19th-century lighthouse, from whose lofty heights sunset gazing (and applauding) has become a ritual. The rest of the village is urbanized, densely packed with restaurants, *pousadas,* and stores. Follow the main drag of Rua Caminho da Praia to arrive at the beginning of a quintet of nameless but distinctive numbered beaches. **Primeira Praia** (First Beach) is the closest to the village and is where most of the local families hang out. **Segunda Praia** (Second Beach) is lined with restaurants, clubs, and beach bars that throb with raves and luaus all night. By day it's full of hip young things knocking around soccer balls, volleyballs, and frescoballs. **Terceira Praia** (Third Beach) is somewhat more tranquil and has some of the best water for diving. Boat excursions depart from here. Half an hour from the village, **Quarta Praia** (Fourth Beach) offers 4 kilometers (2.5 mi) of coconut-fringed sand, which starts out developed and peters out into delicious seclusion. The best-preserved (and most gorgeous) of them all, **Quinta Praia** (Fifth Beach), also known as Praia do Encanto, involves a long two-hour trek that can only be undertaken at low tide (or by mule-drawn carts from Terceira Praia, R$30 for 2 people). Aside from a small handful of upscale *pousadas,* its sands are deserted.

Sports and Recreation

The best way to take advantage of Morro's natural attractions is by boat. The most popular trip is a full-day outing (R$80) around Tinhare island: stops include the offshore reefs of **Garapuá** and **Moreré,** the beaches of **Cueira, Tassimirim,** and **Boca da Barra** (all on the island of **Boipeba**), and then the pretty town of **Cairu** with its 17th-century **Convento de Santo Antônio** (the second oldest convent in Brazil). Throughout the day, there are ample opportunities for swimming, snorkeling, and feasting on fresh oysters from floating oyster bars anchored in the Rio do Inferno. Another highlight is diving amidst the reefs in the clear, shallow waters off Primeira and Terceira Praias, which you can do by day or night for R$75-130 pp with an instructor. For more information about excursions or diving, contact **Itha do Mar** (Rua da Prainha 11, tel. 75/3652-1104).

An easy 40-minute hike (during low tide) from Morro leads to the tranquil fishing village of **Gamboa,** from where you can easily reach the **Fonte do Céu** waterfall. The trail passes by cliffs of colored clay, where you can give yourself a purifying facial—or "claycial." You can rent a boat to sail in the bay at **Clube de Vela de Gamboa** (tel. 75/3653-7131, R$45-95/hour), with or without an instructor.

Accommodations

There's no shortage of accommodations on Morro de São Paulo. Rates listed are for the off-season, but high-season prices are much steeper. Although Morro is famed for its beaches, it's worth trading beachfront access for one of the trio of simple yet fetching private guest rooms at **Villa-Bahia Apartments** (Rua Porto de Cima, tel. 75/8169-6532, www.vila-bahia.com, R$120-180 d), an expertly run B&B perched on a hilltop above Morro's main square. German owner Werner plays tropical host to the hilt, dishing up advice as well as lavish homemade breakfasts on a balcony with spectacular views. Boasting the same spectacular views is neighboring **Pousada Aquarela** (Rua Porto de Cima, tel. 75/3652-1509, www.pousadadoaquarela.com, R$110-150 d), whose bright and breezy guest rooms boast hammock-strung verandas and sleep up to four. An enticing on-site restaurant overlooking the jungle is a bonus. To be right in the middle of the action on Segunda Praia (but still get some shut eye), try **Pousada Villa dos Graffitis** (tel. 75/3652-1803, www.villadosgraffitis.com.br, R$240-360 d). At this funky newcomer, graffiti adorns the sleekly minimalist rooms (which sleep up to five). Its off-beach location ensures sleep, while the pool, lounge, and fresh breakfasts are ideal hangover cures. On Terceira Praia, **Hotel Fazenda Vila Guaiamu** (tel. 75/3652-1035, www.vilaguaiamu.com.br, July-Apr., R$180-230 d) feels miles from the nearby mayhem. A sprinkling of whitewashed chalets scattered amid the rustling palms of a former coconut plantation are home to clean, if somewhat worn guest rooms as well as namesake

guiamus, blue-hued crabs who emerge from their holes to feed at the beginning and end of the day. The on-site restaurant does a mean *moqueca.*

For a resort experience, head to the **Pousada Villa dos Corais** (tel. 75/3652-1560, www.villadoscorais.com.br, R$430-490 d) with an enviable location straddling both Terceira and Quarta Praias. The 40 bungalows are spacious, airy, and comfortable, with king beds, noiseless air-conditioning, and verandas with hammocks. Two restaurants, a pool bar and beach bar, tennis courts, a games room, library, sauna, and steam room round out the amenities. Located on utterly dreamy Quinta Praia, the nine fully equipped eco-chalets at ★ **Anima Hotel** (tel. 75/3652-2077, www.animahotel.com, July-May, R$340-410 d) are the epitome of back-to-nature chic, though you might feel a little isolated. The hotel offers snorkel masks and binoculars so you can commune with the exotic fish and birds sharing your ecosystem.

Food

During the day, food options are mostly geared toward classic Bahian beach fare, such as the fried fish, crab, shrimp, and *moquecas* served at many *barracas.* For some of the best fish and seafood dishes around, try **Club do Balanço** (10am-7pm daily Mar.-June and Aug.-Dec., 10am-midnight daily Jan.-Feb. and July) on trendy Segunda Praia. Fans of Quarta Praia swear by **Bar das Piscinas** (9am-6pm daily) and **Pimenta Rosa** (10am-5pm daily).

At night, culinary pleasures are taken more seriously. For both lunch and dinner, **Sabor da Terra** (Rua Caminho da Praia, tel. 75/3652-1156, noon-midnight daily, R$20-30), on the town's main drag, beckons with its wide veranda, perfect for people-watching, and the fragrance of well-seasoned Bahian fish and seafood dishes such as *moqueca* and *bobó de camarão.* The wafting scent of freshly baked pizza emerging from a wood oven will lure you to **Restaurante e Pizzeria Bianco e Nero** (Rua Caminho da Praia, tel. 75/3652-1097, lunch Tues.-Sun., dinner daily, R$20-30).

For the perfect finishing touch, stop by **Dona Bárbara's** sweet stand (in front of Sabor da Terra) and stock up on homemade goodies such as *brigadeiro, cocadas,* and *quejadinhas.*

Information

There is a **tourist office** at Praça Aureliano Lima (tel. 75/3652-1083, www.morrosp.com. br, 8am-10pm daily). You can also check out www.morrodesaopaulobrasil.com.br. Although there are a few ATMs, they can run out of money during holidays; while it's a good idea to have some spare cash, many places accept credit cards.

Transportation

Both high-speed catamarans and *lanchas rápidas* offer daily transportation from Salvador's Terminal Marítimo in front of the Mercado Modelo. The trip (2.5 hrs, R$80) is scenic, but the ocean can be quite choppy. In Salvador, contact **Catamarã Biotur** (tel. 75/3641-3327, www.biotur.com.br), **Catamarã Farol da Barra** (tel. 71/3319-4570, www.faroldomorrotour.com), **Lancha Lula Lu** (tel. 75/9917-1975), **Lancha Ilha Bela** (tel. 71/3326-7158, www.ilhabelatm.com.br), or the Terminal Marítimo (tel. 71/3319-2890). From Salvador, you can take a small eight-seater plane (20 min., R$320 pp) operated by **Addey Taxi Aéreo** (tel. 71/3204-1393, www.addey.tur. br). You must pay a visitor's tax (R$15) upon arrival on the island.

Águia Branca (tel. 71/4004-1010, www. aguiabranca.com.br) and **Viação Cidade Sul** (tel. 71/3682-1791, www.viacaocidadesol. com.br) both provide hourly bus service from Bom Despacho (the bus station located at the ferry terminal on the island of Itaparica) to the nearby town of Valença (2 hours, around R$18). From Valença's docks, numerous boats (1.5 hours, R$7) and *lanchas* (30 min., R$16) make the trip to Morro daily 7am-6pm.

ILHA DE BOIPEBA

Although only the Rio do Inferno (River of Hell) separates Ilha de Boipeba from the Ilha do Tinhare, where Morro de São Paulo is

located, Boipeba is Morro as it was 20 years ago before an influx of tourism blew everything out of proportion. Its beautiful unspoiled beaches are framed by lush jungle and crisscrossed by warm rivers that are ideal for bathing. Although Boipeba is becoming a hip beach resort for those in the know, it has managed to retain a bucolic tranquility along with some 20 kilometers (12 mi) of secluded white-sand beaches protected by coral reefs.

Sights and Recreation

The most "developed" of Boipeba's beaches—which, thankfully, isn't saying much—is **Boca da Barra.** Here, where the Rio do Inferno meets the sea, you'll find lots of *barracas* where you can dig into fresh fish and seafood while soaking in fresh water. Heading south, a half-hour walk brings you to the sugary white sands of **Tassimirim,** followed by the blissfully deserted **Praia de Cueira,** the island's best swimming beach. Another 1.5 hours' walk (easier undertaken during low tide) brings you to idyllic **Morerê,** where the shade of a giant almond tree offers respite from the sun, and an hour more brings you to **Bainema,** a deserted beach fringed by coconut palms and lush vegetation. Another 30 minutes away is **Ponta dos Castelhanos,** a great diving destination with coral reefs and a 16th-century Spanish shipwreck to explore. Apart from walking, it's possible to take boat trips to all of these beaches from the docks at Boca da Barra. A trip to Ponta de Castelhanos costs around R$40, while a journey around the entire island will set you back R$60. You can also sail up the Rio do Sapé and around the surrounding mangroves in a dug-out canoe (R$30 for 2 hours). It's possible to journey overland via bumpy tractor-trucks between Velha Boipeba and Morerê; depending on the number of passengers, expect to pay R$5-10.

Accommodations and Food

The languorous village of **Velha Boipeba,** whose epicenter is the 17th-century Igreja do Divino Espírito Santo, offers both simple and more sophisticated accommodations for visitors, as does **Moreré,** a tiny fishing village that's a 90-minute walk or 40-minute boat or tractor ride away.

Owned by two American brothers from Queens, **Pousada Santa Clara** (tel. 75/3653-6085, www.santaclaraboipeba.com, R$140-170 d, closed June) offers a dozen cozily minimalist guest rooms set amidst a lush tropical garden. Brother Mark is the culinary genius behind the romantic **Restaurante Santa Clara;** he plans internationally inspired daily dinner options based on the fresh catch available (lobster, shrimp, fish). Practically next door, **Pousada Vila Sereia** (tel. 75/3653-6045, www.vilasereia.com.br, R$280-350) is more intimate but equally well run by Chris, a São Paulo transplant. A quartet of private, ingeniously outfitted, and candy-colored palm-thatched bungalows (sleep up to four) are situated right on Boca da Barra beach. Wake in the morning to a tropical breakfast banquet arrayed upon your private veranda.

At ★ **Eco-Pousada Casa Bobô** (tel. 75/9930-5757, www.pousadacasabobo.com, R$180-280 d), Catalan/Brazilian owners Myriam and Nilton preside over a trio of sustainably built, eco-chic bungalows nestled atop the jungly slopes of Monte Alegre with views of the jade waters of Morerê beach, 15 minutes away. For those who can't get enough of Nilton's organic cuisine, half-board accommodation is available. Right on Moreré beach, **Restaurante Mar e Coco** (tel. 75/3653-6094, 10am-6pm daily, R$25-35) offers an idyllic setting in which to take shelter from the midday sun in the crustacean company of succulent shrimp and plantain *moquecas* and seafood stroganoffs. In the same vein, but more primitive, is the **Barraca do Guido** (tel. 75/9907-7049, 8am-5pm daily, R$20-30), located on Praia da Cueira, where the specialty is freshly caught lobster cooked over an open flame and served with butter or pineapple. Back in town, don't leave Boipeba without trying the island's most famous *sorvete,* made out of local *mangaba* fruit at **Picolé do Pinto** (Rua do Areal, tel. 75/3653-6119, noon-10pm daily), in the village of Velha Boipeba.

Information

Many hotels can organize guides or trips, including activities such as canoeing, horseback riding, taking nature walks through the Atlantic forest, or snorkeling in the tidal pools. For boating trips, talk to local fishermen down at the docks. For more information, consult the multilingual website www.

Ilha de Boipeba

ilhadeboipeba.org.br and www.boipeba.tur. br. There are no banks on the island, so stock up on cash.

Transportation

Difficult access to Boipeba has helped keep the tourist crush at bay. From Valença's docks you can take a boat (4 hours, R$14), with one daily departure at noon, or smaller, motorized *lanchas* (30 minutes, R$38), with more frequent daily departure (especially during high season). Another option is to take a bus to the town of Torrinhas and then board a ferry (1.5 hours, R$15) or *lancha* (20 minutes, R$80) for Boipeba, which stops in the colonial town of Cairu. From Morro de São Paulo, tour operators offer daily boat trips that stop at Boipeba; you can organize it so that you can stay for more than a day. Another alternative is to take a one-hour Jeep ride and then a quick boat across the river to Boipeba, a service offered by **Bahia Terra** (Segunda Praia, 75/3653-6017, www.boipebatur.com.br, R$95 pp). Quicker, more comfortable, and more expensive is to fly directly from Salvador to Boipeba in a small plane operated by **Addey Taxi Aéreo** (tel. 71/3204-1393, www.addey. tur.br, 30 minutes, R$370 pp).

PENÍNSULA DE MARAÚ

Squeezed between the Bay of Camamu and the open Atlantic, the Maraú peninsula is a region of great natural beauty composed of islands, lagoons, dunes, and mangrove swamps. The easiest way to explore the area is by traveling to the mainland city of Camamu, 330 kilometers (205 mi) south of Salvador, and then taking a boat across the Bay of Camamu to the fishing village and main resort town of Barra Grande.

★ Barra Grande

Despite the increase of *pousadas*, restaurants, and trendy young vacationers from southern Brazil who flock here in the summer for some hippie-flavored R&R, this relaxing fishing village, with its main drag of soft sand leading down to fluffy beaches, is still deliciously unspoiled. Barra Grande is a great place to unwind as well as explore Brazil's third largest bay (after Salvador's Baía de Todos os Santos and Rio's Guanabara). From the town, you can wander endlessly along the coast.

Sights and Recreation

Praia do Barra Grande all but disappears during high tide; other, more secluded beaches are reachable by foot. Walk toward the open Atlantic to reach **Ponta do Mutá,** which marks the northern tip of the peninsula before veering south and passing reef-lined **Três Coqueiros** and idyllic **Bombaça** with both rough waves and protected natural pools. A 2.5-hour walk from Barra, **Taipu de Fora** routinely racks up accolades as one of Brazil's most stunning beaches due to a combination of shimmering turquoise waters and coral-lined pools flooded with brightly hued fish (rent snorkel equipment from beach vendors). Taipu is often packed with tourists; if you continue another 6 kilometers (3.5 mi), you'll find a remote refuge amidst the more secluded sands of **Cassange.** Open trucks known as *jardineiras* shuttle passengers between Barra Grande and Taipu (R$10 pp).

Apart from beachcombing, you can explore the Baía de Camamu's more far-flung attractions by land or by sea. In the absence of paved roads, the former involves walking or catching a ride with a dune buggy or *jardineiras,* which leave from Rua Vasco Neto. Road-trip excursions stop at Taipu de Fora as well as **Morro Bela Vista,** a lush hilltop with panoramic views and terrific sunset watching; and **Lagoa de Cassange,** a freshwater lake in the midst of Sahara-like dunes. An equally unforgettable experience is taking a full-day boat trip around the bay with stops at many islands. Excursions usually leave early in the morning and cost R$30 for a boat and R$60 for a high-speed *lancha.* For information, contact **Camamu Adventure** (Av. Beira Mar, tel. 73/3258-6236, www.camamuadventure.com.br).

Accommodations

For a great location with access to the beach

and the village, try simple and friendly **Pousada Tubarão** (Rua Vasco Neto 92, tel. 73/3258-6006, pousadatutti.com.br, R$140-220 d), whose casual restaurant also serves delicious fare in the tropical garden or on the beach. Owned by a friendly young Italian couple, **Denada Posada** (Rua Vasco Neto 10, tel. 73/3258-6444, www.denadaposada.com, R$250-350 d) features eight clean and stylish bungalows decked out in wood and natural fibers; a small pool and restaurant serve up views and Italian food. **Flat Bahia** (Rua José Melo Pirajá, tel. 73/3258-6124, www.flat-barra.com.br, R$115-140 d) offers 10 cheery and spacious apartments with verandas, living rooms, and equipped kitchens—rustle up your own freshly caught fish 24/7, but still have your sheets changed. Common areas include a lounge, pool, barbecue area, and garden, where breakfast is served.

Taipu de Fora's stunning beach lures its own share of (somewhat upscale) eco-accommodations. Among the nicest is appropriately named **Dreamland Bungalows** (tel. 73/3258-6087, www.dreamland-brasil.com, R$320-360 d), with breezy, modern two-story villas within spitting distance of the sand. Even closer is the beach bar/restaurant decked out with rustic lounge furniture where friendly Norwegian owner/lapsed rock 'n roller Yan takes time out from hosting duties to flaunt his guitar skills. Those seeking serious yet sustainable seclusion will fall hard for the ★ **Butterfly House** (tel. 73/3258-6087, www.dreamland-brasil.com, R$420-800 d). Located on a lush estate just off unspoiled Cassange beach, this eco-boutique *pousada* is the brainchild of Chloe Gibbs, a former British nurse and fervent ecologist who spent close to a decade turning her dream into reality (she even fashioned the bathroom sinks herself at a local ceramics factory!). The results wed environmentalism (grass thatched roofs, solar-heated water, recycled everything) with an exquisite decorative sensibility that deftly fuses French, Moroccan, Indian, and local elements throughout the pool area, bar, gazebo, and

Anna Banana, an organic fusion restaurant serving delicious meals.

Food

Near the main square, **A Tapera** (Rua Dra Lili, tel. 75/3258-6119, www.atapera.com.br, 1pm-11pm daily Dec.-Feb., 1pm-10pm Wed.-Mon. Mar.-Nov., closed May, R$25-40) is a favorite for fish and a delicious squid and octopus *moqueca*. At her pretty namesake outdoor restaurant, **Donanna** (Rua do Anjo, tel. 75/3258-6407, noon-10pm Mon.-Sat., noon-midnight daily Dec.-Feb., closed June, R$25-35), owner-chef Dona Ana concocts unusual seafood delicacies such as ginger-mango fish and shrimp in coconut sauce. Scrumptious pizza and other freshly made Italian dishes are served at **Pinocchio** (Praça do Tamarindo, tel. 73/3258-6248, dinner daily, R$20-30), whose outdoor candlelit tables are spread beneath an enormous tamarind tree. At secluded Bombaça beach, just before the more touristy Taipus de Fora, the **Tocossauro Bar** (tel. 73/3528-6047, 9am-6:30pm daily) is an enticing "surf" bar-restaurant belonging to the Pousada Kaluana, where you can chill out beneath whispering palms.

Information

Head to the **Secretaria de Turismo de Maraú** (Av. José Melo Pirajá, tel. 73/3258-2131) for info about Barra Grande and the surrounding peninsula. For information in English, www.barra-grande.net is a great website with lots of listings and maps. Bring lots of cash since there are no banks or ATMs (the closest are in Camamu).

Transportation

The easiest, but longest, way to get to Barra Grande is to take a ferry from Salvador's Terminal Marítimo to Bom Despacho on the Ilha da Itaparica. At the docks, there is a bus station where companies such as **Águia Branca** (tel. 71/4004-1010, www.aguiabranca.com.br) and **Viação Cidade Sol** (tel. 71/3682-1791, www.viacaocidadesol.com.br) have buses departing almost hourly between 5am-6pm to Camamu (3.5 hours, R$31). At Camamu's dock, during the day frequent slow boats (1.5 hours, R$6) and fast *lanchas* (40 minutes, R$30) make the scenic trip across the Rio Acarai to Barra Grande. It is also possible to reach Barra Grande by land, going north along a dirt road from Itacaré. This requires chartering a Jeep or other 4WD vehicle, which is expensive (around R$100 pp) and slow-going.

ITACARÉ

Until 1998, when a paved highway opened up access to Itacaré from Ilhéus, 70 kilometers (43 mi) to the south, Itacaré was a remote fishing village straddling the mouth of the Rio de Contas. Its stunning beaches backed by native Atlantic forest were a well-guarded secret known to only a few hard-core surfers and getaway artists. Since then, the secret has gotten out, and Itacaré has become one of the biggest "it" beaches on the Bahian coast.

Beaches

Itacaré's 15 pristine beaches are set off by dramatic hillsides carpeted in lush green vegetation. Many—such as the urban beaches of **Resende, Tiririca, Praia do Costa** and **Praia do Ribeira**—are only a few hundred meters' walk from Itacaré's center. Those closest to town—especially the nerve center that is **Praia da Concha**—can get pretty crowded in the summer, littered as they are with *pousadas* and bars playing trance-inducing electronic music. However, the farther you get, the more deserted the beaches become. Hiking through virgin forest to the best of these *praias de fora* (outer beaches)—such as the idyllic **Prainha,** reached by a 45-minute jungle trail that begins at Praia do Ribeira—is part of the unique Itacaré experience.

The bustling main drag of Rua Pedro Longo and its continuation (known as the Caminho das Praias) links the urban beaches. You can reach more far-flung beaches on foot or by the municipal bus (R$2.50) that leaves Centro hourly and runs along highway BA-001 in the direction of Ilhéus. Some trails to the beaches pass through private property, and you'll be charged a small access fee. Due to poor signage and isolation (and security issues), it's best to go in the company of a guide or a local. Many tour agencies run "best of" beach day trips for around R$50 pp.

Itacaré has some of the finest waves in the Brazilian Northeast. Surfers will go gaga over **Prainha** (3 km/2 mi) and its neighbors, **Praia São José** (6 km/3.5 mi) and **Praia Jeribucaçu** (7 km/4 mi), as well as the particularly beautiful **Praia Havaizinho** and **Praia de Engenhoca,** roughly 12 kilometers (7.5 mi) from town. If you don't want complete seclusion, **Itacarezinho,** 15 kilometers (9 mi) away and accessible by bus, has a sprinkling of beach *barracas* where you can kick back with a caipirinha and refresh yourself in the sparkling freshwater pool formed by the Tijuípe waterfall. **Easy Drop** (Rua João Coutinho 140, tel. 73/3251-3065, www.easydrop.com) is a surf school where a four-day package, including transportation and equipment, costs R$225 per day. To rent your own gear, contact **Thor Surf Point** (Rua Pedro Longo 574, tel. 73/3251-2057).

Sports and Recreation

Tree-trekking aficionados will enjoy channeling Tarzan at the activities circuit located in the middle of Praia da Ribeira's Atlantic rain forest. **Conduru Ecoturismo** (Praça da Bandeira 89, tel.73/3251-3089, www.conduruecoturimso.com.br) offers various radical sports activities on Praia do Ribeira, including ziplining over the beach (four rides, R$40). Rappelling at the Noré waterfall (R$40) is another popular adrenaline-charged outing, as is rafting down the Rio de Contas; **Ativa Rafting** (Rua Pé da Pancada, tel. 73/3257-2083, www.ativarafting.com.br) charges R$75 for a full-day outing. Those seeking more mellow vibes can rent a canoe and paddle through the coastal mangrove swamps to the Cachoeira do Engenho waterfall (6 hours, R$55). **EcoTrip** (Rua João Coutinho 235, tel. 73/3251-2191, www.ecotrip.tur.br) offers many of these outings throughout the region.

Accommodations

Since the paved highway to Ilhéus opened, Itacaré has been flooded with *pousadas*, from backpackers' refuges to tropically chic eco-resorts. Prices listed are for off-season. Some of the most inexpensive options—and also those closest to the action—are along the Rua Pedro Longo. More upscale options are sheltered within the confines of the leafy Condomínio Conchas do Mar complex.

The **Casarão Verde Hostel**'s (Av. Praça Castro Alves 7, tel. 73/3251-2037, www.casaraoverdehostel.com R$60-70 d, R$26-38 pp) renovated dorms and private rooms occupy a turn-of-the-20th-century mansion overlooking the harbor. Aside from cathedral-high ceilings, polished wood floors, and stained glass windows, guests can take advantage of a kitchen, barbecue area, mini-gym, and elegant gardens. At **Pousada Casa Tiki** (Rua C 30, Conchas do Mar, tel. 73/9810-6098, www.pousadadacasatiki.com.br, R$100-150 d), outgoing young expats, Kevin and Pati, instill a casual vibe and a Polynesian tiki bar aesthetic at their tropical B&B. Guests are invited to sit around a big log table swapping stories over fresh fruit juice and petting the *pousada* pooches. More boutiquey than tiki is the lovely **Pousada Burundanga** (Qd. D. Lot. 6, Conchas do Mar, tel. 73/3251-2543, www.burundanga.com.br, R$215-275 d). Spacious bungalows are tastefully decorated with local *artesanato* and furnishings hewed out of local wood. From the hammock on your private deck, gaze onto a tangle of jungle visited by birds and monkeys

Pousada Tãnara (tel. 73/3251-3423, www.pousadatanara.com, R$150-290 d), around 2 kilometers (1.2 mi) from town, is a favorite with the international and surfing crowd. In indigenous Pataxó, Tãnara means "nature," evidenced by six rustic rooms that sit immersed in greenery, tumbling onto the surfer's paradise of Praia de Tiririca. Lodgings are attractive, but some are quite tight. It's a quick walk to town by day, but a taxi is recommended at night. ★ **Art Jungle Eco Lodge** (Rod. Ilhéus-Itacaré km 63, tel. 73/9905-7775, artjungle.com.br, R$120-220 d) consists of a handful of magical storybook-come-to-life tropical bungalows (including a couple of bonafide tree houses!) near the shores of Rio de Contas, yet only a five-minute drive from Itacaré. Transportation can be organized, while renting a car keeps you from feeling cut off from civilization— but if that's your mission, you'll be in heaven. There are no phones, TV, air-conditioning, or Internet, just hummingbirds, silence, sea views, and a pool and sauna.

Live it up and wind down at the same time at the happily un-resorty **Txai Resort** (tel. 73/2101-5000, www.txai.com.br, R$1,100-2,200 d). Located 16 kilometers (10 mi) from Itacaré, the rambling palmy grounds of this former cocoa plantation gaze onto the unspoiled white sands of Itacarezinho beach. Its 40 spacious, simple bungalows and creatively decorated main lounges merge traditional architecture and organic materials with understated luxury. There is a pool as well as yoga and alternative healing therapies at a stunning hilltop spa. While service is attentive, food is hit-and-miss.

Food

Take a seat (and be prepared to wait) at **Estrela d'Alva** (Rua Pedro Longo 568, tel. 73/9909-1191, lunch and dinner daily, R$15-25) and **Flor do Cacau** (Rua Pedro Longo 4800, tel. 73/9945-4800, lunch and dinner daily, R$15-25) for tasty, authentic Bahian fare such as *bobó* and *moqueca de camarão,* served in robust portions with *farofa, banana da terra,* and *feijão*. The hot and cold buffet offerings at **Casa de Taipa** (Rua Pedro Longo 345, tel. 73/3251-3510, noon-10pm daily, R$22) are more diverse, and you can refill your plate as many times as you want. For Arab, vegetarian fare, try **Alamaim** (Rua Pedro Longo 203, 73/3251-3462, www.restaurantealamaim.com. br, 2:30pm-10pm Mon.-Sat., R$15-25).

Come sundown, a popular stop for the young and famished is **Tio Gu Caféça** (Rua Pedro Longo 488, 73/3251-2084, www.tiogu. com, 5pm-midnight Wed.-Mon., R$15-25), specializing in fresh fruit juices, salads, and generously stuffed, sweet and savory crepes named after the region's beaches. At the fare end of the harbor is a colonial blue mansion home to **Café e Boteco da Vila** (Rua Castro Alves 35, tel. 73/9915-3574, 6pm-midnight Sun.-Thurs., 5pm-2am Fri.-Sat., R$15-30). Listen to music while munching on New York-style pizza and scrumptious brownies made with chocolate from the nearby plantation. American expat owner Alan Slesinger also organizes excursions to his nearby cocoa farm.

Most of Bahia's best cocoa has been exported, but you can get a sublime taste of the homegrown product at ★ **Itacaré Cacau** (Praça Santos Dumont 16, tel. 73/3251-3349, http://itacarecacau.com, 1pm-10pm daily), where local chocolate maker Maria Joanita sells artisanally crafted cocoa liqueurs and truffles (including a to-die-for version filled with cucuaçu jelly and cashews).

Transportation and Services

Itacaré has no tourist office, but it does have a terrific English and Portuguese bilingual website, www.itacare.com. There's a Bradesco ATM that accepts international cards, but no banks, so stock up on cash.

Itacaré is 70 kilometers (43 mi) north of Ilhéus along highway BA-001. Ilhéus's airport has daily flights from Salvador, Porto Seguro, and São Paulo. **Rota** (tel. 73/3251-2181, www.rotatransportres.com.br) offers hourly buses 5am-7:45pm from Ilhéus. The 90-minute trip costs R$12, and the bus station (tel. 73/3251-2200) is only a short distance from the center. A taxi to your hotel costs R$15; a wheelbarrow taxi costs R$7. Or take a taxi from Ilhéus (usually the airport); most hotels have their own trusted drivers, or you can contact **PC Taxi** (tel. 73/3086-3072, R$150). It's also possible to reach Itacaré from Salvador via BA-001, heading south from Bom Despacho on the island of Itaparica. From Bom Despacho, **Águia Branca** (tel. 71/4004-1010, www.aguiabranca.com.br) and **Cidade Sol** (tel. 71/3682-1791, www.viacaocidadesol.com.br) provide a half-dozen daily bus departures (4 hours, R$40).

ILHÉUS

Ilhéus is the main city along what's known as Brazil's Cocoa Coast. The town dates back to the early 1500s; during colonial times, it thrived due to the sugarcane trade. Its true boom came in the late 19th-century with the introduction of *cacau* (cocoa) by Jesuits from the Amazon. Plummeting world prices and the abolition of slavery caused the sugar plantations to go into decline. However, cocoa—which earned the nickname *ouro branco* (white gold)—drew freed slaves and entrepreneurs to the hills surrounding Ilhéus, all of them seized by the desire to strike it rich (or at least earn a decent living). A handful of cocoa barons (known as *coronéis*, or colonels), with vast plantations, did indeed become immensely wealthy and powerful. They ruled over their workers and the region as a whole until the 1980s, when a fungus known as *vassoura de bruxa* ("witch's broom") decimated the cocoa trees and left the region's economy in ruins, from which it has only recently begun to recuperate. Today, traces of the legacy of the "colonels" can be glimpsed by wandering among the handful of grandiose mansions and civic buildings of Ilhéus's small historical center. You can also read about their exploits in the novels (particularly *The Violent Land*) of famous Brazilian author Jorge Amado (1912-2001), Ilhéus's most illustrious son. The loss in revenue from cocoa has been somewhat offset by the development of tourism. Ilhéus is surrounded by native Atlantic forest and, to the north and south, it boasts attractive white-sand beaches—all of which make it well worth exploring.

Sights

Ilhéus's tiny historical center makes for a pleasant morning or afternoon stroll. Many of its landmarks have become renowned throughout Brazil due to their presence in Jorge Amado's novels. On Praça Luiz Viana Fialho, the **Teatro Municipal,** built in 1932, was formerly a cinema where an adolescent Amado frequently went to watch movies. On a corner of the square, the **Casa de Cultura**

Jorge Amado (Rua Jorge Amado 21, tel. 73/3634-8986, 9am-noon and 2pm-6pm Mon.-Fri., 9am-noon Sat., R$4) is housed in the family mansion, built by the author's father in 1920 after he struck it rich with a winning lottery ticket; guided tours are offered. Nearby, the **Praça J. J. Seabra, Praça Rui Barbosa,** and **Rua Antônio Lavigne** contain early 20th-century homes and palaces that attest to the wealth of the cocoa barons. Built in 1534, the **Igreja de São Jorge** on Praça Rui Barbosa is Ilhéus's oldest church, while the towering mid-20th-century **Catedral de São Sebastião,** on Praça Dom Eduardo, displays an unusual blend of architectural styles.

There are still cocoa plantations in operation near Ilhéus. Since cocoa trees require shade to grow, farms preserve many taller tree specimens of native Atlantic forest, which makes a stroll through these estates a pleasurable outing. Visitors can taste the cocoa and sample the succulent nectar made from its fruit. **Fazenda Yrerê** (tel. 73/3656-5054, R$25) is 11 kilometers (7 mi) from town on highway BR-415, which links Ilhéus to Itabuna. Another 9 kilometers (6 mi) out of Ilhéus on the same road is **Fazenda Primavera** (tel. 73/3231-3996, R$20). Advance reservations are necessary. Trips can be organized through **Órbita Turismo e Expedições** (Rua Fernando Leite Mendes 71, tel. 73/3234-3250, www.orbitaexpedicoes. com.br), which offers city tours as well as outings to hidden beaches, waterfalls, forest reserves, and a sloth rehabilitation center.

Beaches

The beaches within Ilhéus are neither very clean nor appealing; most locals head north toward Itacaré or to the beaches south of the city. After **Praia do Sul,** one of the closest and most popular is **Praia dos Milionários.** Only 7 kilometers (4.5 mi) from the center of town, its name alludes to its past as the favored beach of Ilhéus's wealthy cocoa barons. You don't have to be rich to sit at the many *barracas* along this coconut-shaded beach.

Wilder, more enticing beaches include **Praia de Cururupe,** along with **Backdoor** and **Batuba,** both in the vicinity of **Olivença,** a little fishing village 16 kilometers (10 mi) from Ilhéusare. Large waves make swimming dangerous, though they attract surfers. Backdoor is a well-kept secret of hardcore surfers, who worship its exceptionally long point breaks. Another well-kept secret is Olivença's natural hot springs; its medicinal properties are claimed to not only hydrate and rejuvenate skin, but leave you with a tan. Municipal buses serve all these beaches and depart at 30-minute intervals between 6pm-10pm from the local *rodoviári.*

Accommodations

While hotels in the center of Ilhéus are usually good bargains, they tend to be older and not in mint condition; a handful retain some historical character. The **Ilhéus Hotel** (Rua Eustáquio Bastos 144, tel. 73/3634-4242, www.ilheushotel.com.br, R$80-180 d) is a case in point. Inaugurated in 1930, the block-long hotel was the brainchild of one of the area's richest cocoa barons, who dreamed of building the most modern and luxurious hotel in all of Bahia. At the time, his architectural plans consisted of such novelties as separate bathrooms for men and women, as well as the state's first elevator, still in operation today. Long since overhauled, the guest rooms are modern and modest, but stylish remnants of its glory days compensate.

Beach bums, nature buffs, and getaway artists will find refuge along the still-wild coastline north of Ilhéus. ★ **Casa Paraíso Verde** (Rod. BA-001 km 30, tel. 73/9971-7371, www.casaparaisoverde.com.br, R$275-500 d; add R$100 pp full-board) is located 30 kilometers (19 mi) north of Ilhéus amidst a tangle of rain forest that is truly a "verdant paradise." Owned by American artist Kenny Scharf and his Ilhéus-born wife, Tereza, the quintet of beautifully crafted treehouse style eco-bungalows is a homey retreat. Back in the '80s, close friend Keith Haring created several art installations on the premises. Just a short walk away are waterfalls and deserted, palmed-lined beaches ideal for endless shelling, bathing, and surfing. Back at the *casa,* indulge in a yoga session, watch a film, or relax in a breeze-swung hammock.

Food

On Praia dos Milionários, **Armação** (tel. 73/3632-1817, 8am-5pm daily, R$20-30) offers delicious fish and seafood as well as heady Bahian *moquecas.* In town, an Ilhéus classic is **Bar Vesúvio** (Praça Dom Eduardo 190, tel. 73/3634-2164, www.barvesuvio.com.br, 10am-midnight Mon.-Sat., 6pm-midnight Sun., R$25-40). Built in 1919, it appeared in several of Jorge Amado's novels and is a local institution. The menu is a mix of Arab and Bahian specialties. Take a seat at one of the sidewalk tables, order a beer, and engage in some people-watching; live music is played nightly.

Information and Services

Tourist information is available at the *rodoviária* and the airport. **Bahiatursa** (Rua Estáquio Bastos 308, tel. 73/3231-8679, 7:30am-5pm Mon.-Fri.) and **Setur** (Av. Soares Lopes 1741, tel. 73/3634-6008, www.ilheusdabahia.tur.br) are both located in the historic center. A good Portuguese and English website is www.brasilheus.com.br. A convenient Banco do Brasil ATM that accepts international cards is near the cathedral (Rua Marquês de Paranaguá 112).

Transportation

The **Aeroporto Jorge Amado** (tel. 73/3234-4000) is 4 kilometers (2.5 mi) south from the center of town and close to the beaches south of the city. There are daily flights to Ilhéus from Salvador, Porto Seguro, Rio de Janeiro, and São Paulo. The long-distance *rodoviária* (tel. 73/3634-4121), in Pontal, is also only 4 kilometers (2.5 mi) west from the center and easily accessible by taxi or municipal bus. **Águia Branca** (tel. 71/4004-1010, www.aguiabranca.com.br) operates numerous daily buses from Salvador's *rodoviária* (7 hours, R$70-170) and two a day (at 9am and

1pm from Bom Despacho (5.5 hours, R$46). **Rota** (tel. 73/3634-3161, www.rotatransportres.com.br) has four daily connections to Porto Seguro (five hours, R$50-67). Driving to Ilhéus from either the north or south, take BR-101 to Itabuna, and then take coastal BR-415 for 40 kilometers (25 mi) to Ilhéus.

TO CANAVIEIRAS

The pretty little colonial town of Canavieiras, located 120 kilometers (68 mi) south of Ilhéus, has a surprisingly well-preserved historic center with candy-colored mansions built by local sugar and cocoa barons. There are deserted beaches as well as mangrove swamps, where you can treat yourself to a mud bath. The surrounding coastline is one of the best places for blue marlin fishing; the mighty fish can measure up to 5 meters (16 feet) in length and 500 kilograms (1,100 pounds) in weight; for this reason, landing one is a true battle. **Bahia Pesca Esportiva** (tel. 11/3284-1137, www.bahiapescaesportiva.com.br) organizes fishing trips. A day of marlin fishing costs R$3,800 for four people. To spend the night, the German-owned **Bahiadomizil** (Av. Beira Mar 1065, tel. 73/3284-2902, www.bahiadomizil.com, R$120-180 d) offers a quintet of laid-back beach bungalows beneath the palms with kitchens and living rooms. **Cidade Sol** (tel. 73/3231-3392, www.viacaocidadesol.com.br) operates 10 daily buses from Ilhéus to Canavieiras (2.5 hours, R$20). For more information, check out www.canavieiras-ba.com.br.

PORTO SEGURO

When you arrive in Porto Seguro, you'll be greeted by banners touting the fact that this is where Brazil "began." Indeed, Porto's claim to fame as the nation's first city stems from the fact that it was here in 1500 that Brazil's "discoverer," Pedro Alves Cabral, planted his wooden cross in the name of the Portuguese crown. Half a millennium later, Porto Seguro is better known as the birthplace of the 1980s dance craze known as the *lambada* and as one of the biggest and most ballyhooed beach resorts in all of Brazil. Indeed, despite a few colonial vestiges and some attractive beaches, Porto Seguro is all about packing in the tourists. Synonymous with two words, *package tour,* in the summertime, the place is downright Floridian in its touristic fervor as Brazilian families check into condos and crowds of young party animals crash in fleabag hotels after drinking and dancing the night away. As a party capital, Porto is known for two merrymaking institutions: the Passarela do Alcool, or "Alcohol Catwalk," a seaside promenade filled with stands hawking near-explosive fruit cocktails, and sprawling, sophisticated beach bars known as "mega-*barracas*": By day they function like fully equipped adult playgrounds, while at night they metamorphose into raucous clubs that are home to luaus and raves. Although Porto's heyday has passed, leaving the place a little beat-up and seedy around the edges, if you want to party hearty—and then nurse your hangover on some fine beaches—this is the place to be. However, those seeking something with more natural beauty and charm are best advised to take a quick look around and then head north to Santo André or south to Arraial d'Ajuda, Trancoso, and lovelier points further down the coast.

Sights

Perched strategically on a verdant bluff overlooking the ocean, the handful of colonial buildings that compose Porto Seguro's *centro histórico* mark the beginning of Brazil's official history. A five-minute walk from the *rodoviária* or a fast but steep climb up a staircase from the main traffic circle at the end of Avenida 22 de Abril is all it takes to rewind time a few centuries. A couple of hours can be easily spent—with or without the guidance of eager (and expensive) local guides—wandering among the pastel-painted houses and gleaming churches. Arrive early in the morning when the light is golden or in the late afternoon to catch the sunset.

Begin at the foot of Brazil's oldest monument, the **Marco da Posse.** Brought over from Portugal in 1503, this marble column, worshipfully encased in glass, is tattooed with the insignia of the Portuguese crown and the cross of the Order of Christ. In the lovely Praça Pero de Campos Tourinho, the simple **Igreja de Nossa Senhora da Penha** (9am-noon and 2pm-5pm daily) dates back to 1535 and boasts an impressive icon of São Francisco de Assis. In the same green square is the **Casa de Câmara e Cadeia,** the former town hall and Brazil's first public jail. Today, its polished interior houses the small **Museu de Porto Seguro** (tel. 73/3288-5182, 9am-5pm Tues.-Sun. and daily Jan.-Feb., R$6), with a collection of maps and indigenous artifacts. Nearby, in the Praça da Misericórdia, stands the **Igreja de Nossa Senhora da Misericórdia.** Built in 1526, it is the oldest church in Brazil. Among the treasures inside its modest **Museu de Arte Sacra** (9am-5pm Tues.-Sun., R$2) are a ruby-encrusted statue of Senhor dos Passos and a life-size Christ on the crucifix, both dating from the late 16th century. More understated is the tiny, whitewashed **Igreja São Benedito** (1549), which now lies in atmospheric ruins.

Beaches

Porto Seguro's beach culture is concentrated on the 20 kilometers (12.5 mi) of low scrub and palm-flanked coastline that spread north from the city center. As far as urban beaches go, you could do a lot worse. The sand is sugary and white and the water, protected by reefs, is not only child-friendly but comes in unreal shades of jade and aqua. The **Curuípe, Itacimirim, Mundaí, Taperapuã, Ponta Grande,** and **Mutá** beaches reach up from Porto to Coroa Vermelha, 13 kilometers (8 mi) to the north. The first few are packed with *barracas,* including the famous mega-*barracas* that are entertainment complexes. By day, these offer *lambada* and *"lambaérobica"* classes, water sports, and Internet access as well as food and drink. By night, their multiple stages host musical performers and DJs that whip the crowd into a sweat to the throbbing strains of *axé, forró,* pop, and techno.

Porto Seguro

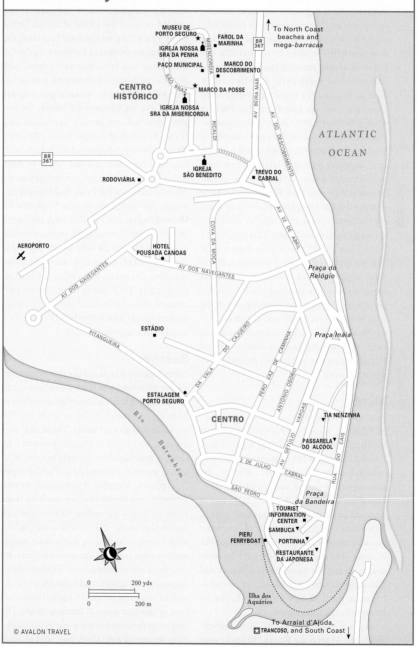

MUSEU DE
PORTO SEGURO

IGREJA NOSSA
SRA DA PENHA

FAROL DA
MARINHA

PAÇO MUNICIPAL

MARCO DO
DESCOBRIMENTO

CENTRO
HISTÓRICO

MARCO DA POSSE

IGREJA NOSSA
SRA DA MISERICORDIA

BR 367

To North Coast
beaches and
mega-*barracas*

ATLANTIC
OCEAN

IGREJA
SÃO BENEDITO

TREVO DO
CABRAL

RODOVIÁRIA

BR 367

AV BEIRA MAR

AV DO DESCOBRIMENTO

AV 22 DE ABRIL

COVA DA MOCA

AEROPORTO

HOTEL
POUSADA CANOAS

AV DOS NAVEGANTES

Praça do
Relógio

AV DOS NAVEGANTES

DO CAJUEIRO

ESTÁDIO

Praça Inaia

PITANGUEIRA

PERO VAZ DE CAMINHA

DA VALA

ANTONIO OSORIO

ESTALAGEM
PORTO SEGURO

VARGAS

CENTRO

TIA NENZINHA

AV GETULIO

RUA DO CAIS

PASSARELA
DO ALCOOL

Rio Buranhém

2 DE JULHO

CABRAL

SÃO PEDRO

Praça
da Bandeira

TOURIST
INFORMATION
CENTER

PIER/
FERRYBOAT

SAMBUCA

PORTINHA

RESTAURANTE
DA JAPONESA

0   200 yds

0   200 m

Ilha dos
Aquários

To Arraial d'Ajuda,
TRANCOSO, and South Coast

© AVALON TRAVEL

The biggest, loudest, and hippest of these are **Tôa-Tôa** (Av. Beira Mar km 5, Taperapuã, tel. 73/3679-1714, www.portaltoatoa.com), **Axé Moi** (Av. Beira Mar 6500, Taperapuã, tel. 73/3679-1248, www.axemoi.com.br), and the granddaddy of them all, **Barramares** (Av. Beira Mar km 68.5, Taperapuã, tel. 73/3679-2980, www.barramares.com.br). More sedate is the relatively distant beach of Mutá. From the traffic circle in the center of town, municipal buses go north along to coast to the sleepy town of Santa Cruz de Cabrália. At night, you're better off taking a cab.

Entertainment and Events
NIGHTLIFE
Porto Seguro's sizzling nightlife begins in town along the legendary **Passarela do Alcool**, an ultratouristy and pretty garish seaside promenade of bars, restaurants, and hundreds of stands hawking tacky T-shirts, "indigenous" trinkets, and the potent local cocktail, *capeta*. This is both an energizing and intoxicating potion made from pure cocoa powder, Amazonian jolt-providing *guaraná* powder, vodka, sugar, and ice. As a final touch, sweet condensed milk is added to make the medicine go down nice and easy. The many drink stands along the Passarela—most of them more flamboyantly decked out than a Carmen Miranda tutti-frutti hat—also serve up everything from caipirinhas to *batidas* mixed with *cachaça* and fresh fruit.

The Passarela serves as a warm-up for the nightly extravaganzas held at the mega-*barracas* along the northern beaches of Mundaí and Taperapuã as well as **Ilha dos Aquários** (Ilha do Pacuico, access from Praça do Pataxó, tel. 73/3268-2828, www.ilhadosaquarios.com.br), located on a private island in the Rio Buranhém; its attractions include various immense aquariums filled with glitzy fish. Each *barraca* (some operate during normal business hours) has its own *festa* night (widely advertised by fliers along the Passarela). The weekday action is more exciting than on the weekends; bear in mind that it's all geared to young Brazilian party animals. Free buses usually head up and down the coast from the traffic circle off Avenida 22 de Abril. The cover for most shows is R$30-60.

FESTIVALS AND EVENTS
Porto Seguro's summer festivities come to a head during **Carnaval.** Although much smaller than Salvador's celebration, the *axé*-throbbing merrymaking lasts for a lot longer—until the Saturday following Ash Wednesday. This gives Salvador's megastars a chance to migrate south and whip the party into full swing. A more traditional celebration is the **Festa de São Benedito** (Dec. 25-27), held in the *centro histórico,* in which traditional African music and dances are performed.

Accommodations
Accommodation options range from very basic closet-size rooms to megaresorts dripping with amenities. Off-season coincides with high vacancies and discounts galore, but as early as October things starting going up, and by December even the prices of fleabags will have doubled. During New Year's and Carnaval, prices are astronomical, and throughout the summer, it's best to make reservations. Prices below are for off-season.

If you are happy with the simple combination of a bed and clean digs, there are many choices, although these budget *pousadas* are very tiny, often dark and a bit musty, and devoid of any decorative scheme. One of the nicer inexpensive options is **Hotel Pousada Canoas** (Av. Navegantes, tel. 73/3288-2205, pousadahotelcanoas.jimdo.com, R$100-140 d). The small but Spartan whitewashed guest rooms with wooden accents have basic amenities including cable TV and air conditioning and are clustered around a garden with a swimming pool. Its prime location is close to all the action. Overlooking the Rio Buranhém, **Estalagem Porto Seguro** (Rua Marechal Deodoro 66, tel. 73/3288-2095, www.hotelestalagem.com.br, R$100 pp, R$80-170 d) is simple but atmospheric. Housed in a 200-year-old inn once frequented by traveling cocoa barons, the building's original walls were constructed out of stone and whale oil; ceiling beams of brazil wood are still apparent. Rooms in the new wing are less charming, but compensate with verandas hung with hammocks and a small pool.

Food

Amidst the tourist traps in central Porto, there are a handful of surprisingly good eateries to choose from. A culinary touchstone, **Tia Nenzinha** (Pássarela do Alcool 170, tel. 73/3288-1846, noon-midnight Tues.-Sun. and daily from Dec.-Feb., R$20-30) has been dishing up *moquecas* and other traditional Bahian fish and seafood dishes since the mid-1970s. Sugar fiends can top off their meal with a succulently moist *cocadas* (freshly grated coconut and sugar mixed with honey, chocolate, or guava). The best pizza in town is in a pretty coral-colored house with a cozy white interior called **Sambuca** (Praça dos Pataxós 216, tel. 73/3288-2366, 6pm-midnight daily, R$20-30), located right beside the pier. Directly opposite, **Restaurante da Japonesa** (Praça dos Pataxós 38, tel. 73/3288-5606, 7am-midnight daily, R$20-40) possesses an eclectic menu—everything from Bahian *moqueca* and Portuguese *bacalhau* to cheeseburgers and chop suey. The sushi and sashimi are made with fresh fish locally caught by Ju—reputed to be the Discovery Coast's one and only sushiwoman—and are excellent (and reasonably priced). A small emporium on the premises is a great place to load up on Japanese snacks. For cheap, fast, and delicious *comida por quilo*, head to **Portinha** (Rua Saldanha Marinha 43, tel. 73/3288-2743, www.portinha.com.br, noon-5pm and 6pm-10pm daily, R$15-20). Pick and choose from a mouthwatering buffet of fresh salads and hot dishes warmed over a wood oven, then savor your meal at wooden picnic tables in the leafy garden or out on the cobblestoned street.

Transportation and Services

There are **tourist offices** at the *rodoviária* and at Praça Manoel Ribeiro Coelho 10 (on the Passarela do Alcool, 9am-11pm Mon.-Sat.). International bank cards are accepted at the Banco do Brasil and HSBC ATMs in the center of town.

There are usually numerous and often inexpensive (if booked in advance) flights available to Porto Seguro from Rio, São Paulo, and Salvador. The international **airport** (Estrada do Aeroporto 1500, tel. 73/3288-1880) is a five-minute taxi ride from the city center.

Buses from all over Brazil also serve Porto. **Águia Branca** (tel. 73/3288-1039, www.aguiabranca.com.br), whose night bus has reclining sleepers, offers two daily buses north to Salvador (11 hours, R$150). **São Geraldo** (tel. 73/3288-1198, www.saogeraldo.com.br) has one daily bus to Rio (19 hours, R$186). The *rodoviária* (tel. 73/3288-1914) is a five-minute taxi or bus ride to the center of town.

If you're traveling by car, turn off BR-101 at Eunápolis and take the Porto Seguro turnoff (BR-367) for roughly 70 kilometers (43 mi).

North of Porto Seguro

North along the coast from Porto Seguro, the beaches become more deserted and unspoiled. From Santa Cruz de Cabrália, 25 kilometers (16 mi) north, a boat trip across the Rio João de Tiba brings you to the rustic and surprisingly undervisited fishing settlement of **Santo André** (www.santoandrebahia.com). Santo André's long coastline of empty beaches and swaying palms makes a nice antidote to Porto's urban beach scene. Farther north, you'll hit the surfer's paradise of **Guaiú** and **Mojiquiçaba,** followed by the atmospherically decaying town of **Belmonte,** with its faded mansions once owned by cocoa barons. To stay a while in Santo André, there are a handful of *pousadas,* although no banks or gas stations. **Pousada Ponta de Santo André** (Rua Beira-Rio, tel. 73/3671-4031, www.stoandre.com.br, R$150-235 d) is a pleasant riverside option with tropically rustic apartments and bungalows set amid greenery. Guests can take advantage of kayaks, sailboats, and windsurfers.

From Santa Cruz de Cabrália, ferries (tel.

73/3282-1094) leave every half-hour from the port; the 10-minute crossing costs R$1 for pedestrians and R$11 for cars. Buses operated by **Expresso Brasileiro** (tel. 73/3288-3650, www.expressobrasileiro.com.br) travel from Porto Seguro's airport and bus terminal at 20-minute intervals to Santo Cruz (R$4.40) between 5am-midnight and from the far side of the river to Santo André at hourly intervals between 6:30am-7:15pm (R$2.50).

ARRAIAL D'AJUDA

Despite being only a 10-minute boat ride across the Rio Buranhém from Porto Seguro, Arraial is another world. A major tourist destination in its own right, the town is much more charming than Porto. Aside from its splendid beaches, Arraial's winding streets, shaded by lofty trees and overflowing with atmospheric bars and restaurants, give off a pleasurable vibe that proves quite addictive. While Arraial boasts a Central Park and its main downtown drag is known as **Rua da Broadway** (or "Bróduei," as it's spelled locally), much more in keeping with New York City is the town's cosmopolitan air and edible fare. Both can be sampled on the **Rua do Mucugê,** a bustling artery lined with boutiques, bars, and restaurants that magically springs to life come sundown. Proof of how international this thoroughfare has become is in the number of multilingual menus and the 24-hour Internet cafés touting Hebrew keyboards. Indeed, in the summer, Arraial can get as packed as Porto, although the crowd is more alternative and upscale, as are the parties. Most of these all-night affairs are luaus or raves that take place at the sophisticated *barracas* and in the surrounding white sands of Mucugê and Parracho beaches. During the off-season, however, the town is deliciously tranquil. Although it was founded in the early 16th century, aside from the pretty **Igreja Matriz de Nossa Senhora de Ajuda,** built on a cliff and offering stunning views of the beaches below, there are few remnants of its colonial past. However, the present is certainly inviting.

Beaches

A quick and steep descent down the Rua do Mucugê will bring you right onto the soft white sands of Arraial's closest beach, **Praia do Mucugê.** If you turn left, you will pass **Apaga-Fogo,** lined with *pousadas,* from which you can rent equipment for water-sports activities such as kayaking and windsurfing. More popular with locals than tourists is tranquil **Araçaipe,** which has some great beach bars. Turning right will take you past the trendy **Praia do Parracho,** with its many *barracas,* to the startlingly beautiful **Praia da Pitinga,** whose sugary sands are backed by jagged red and white stone cliffs. Continuing onward, you'll reach the equally beautiful and deserted **Praia de Taípe,** where sunbathing in the nude is de rigueur. During low tide you can continue on to Trancoso, a 12-kilometer (7.5-mi) stroll, then take a bus back.

Sports and Recreation

Arco Íris Turismo (Rua do Mucugê 199, tel. 73/3575-1672) offers full-day outings in which a van picks you up at your hotel and takes you to the sublime beaches of Praia de Espelho and Trancoso (R$50) or Praia do Espelho and Caraíva (R$55). Other fun ways of exploring the coastline are by quadricycle or on horseback. **Bahia Eco Adventure** (tel. 73/3575-8568, www.bahiaeco.com) organizes half-day quadricycle outings (R$150 per vehicle) for small groups to Praia de Taípe as well as full-moon nocturnal outings that include a luau on the beach. The **Centro Equestre** (Praia dos Pescadores, tel. 73/3575-3965) offers several excursions on horseback, both on the beach and in the native Atlantic forest (R$70 for 90 minutes). You can also rent a bike (R$35 a day) at **Arraial Trip Tur** (tel. 73/3575-2805, www.arraialtriptur.com.br).

Although the coral reefs make for safe swimming on most of these beaches, it may be hard to resist the aquatic options at **Arraial d'Ajuda Eco Parque** (Estrada da Balsa Km 4.5, tel. 73/3575-8600, www.arraialecoparque.com.br, 10am-5pm Thurs.-Fri. and daily in

Jan., closed May-June, adults R$85), located on Praia do Mucugê. Supposedly the biggest water park in Latin America, its attractions include a wave pool, twisting water slides, and rappelling and tree-climbing in the jungle.

Between July and October, humpback whales are busy mating and giving birth along the Bahian coast. To see the great mammals in action, **Cia do Mar** (tel. 73/3575-2495) offers five-hour outings (R$150), departing from the *balsa*, in the company of a marine biologist.

Accommodations

The vast majority of accommodation options in Arraial are quite enticing. Prices are reasonable in the off-season, but come summertime, they can double and you'll need to reserve in advance. Rates listed are for off-season.

One of Arraial's nicest affordable options is the **Tubarão Pousada** (Rua Bela Vista 210, tel. 73/3575-3379, www.pousadatubaraoarraial.com, R$60-90 d). On a pretty cobblestoned cul-de-sac, facing a cliff with stupendous beach views, the hotel offers pleasant, guest rooms that open onto a shady oasis with a pool. Also a good bargain is the attractive **Hotel Pousada Saudosa Maloca** (Alameda da Eugênias 31, tel. 73/2105-1200, www.saudosamaloca.tur.br, R$180-230 d). Located on a tranquil sandy street, its modern guest rooms with verandas and swinging hammocks overlook a garden with a pool and a cheery breakfast area. Its more recently constructed neighbor, **Hostel Maloca** (Alameda da Eugênias 10, tel. 73/3575-1473, www.maloca.hostel.br, R$115-180 d, R$40-50 pp), offers a budget version with basic, spotless dorms and private rooms. Amenities include a cool pool, plenty of greenery, and delicious breakfasts. **Pousada Bucaneiros** (Rua do Mucugê 590, tel. 73/3575-1105, www.pousadabucaneiros.com.br, R$120-160 d) has a terrific location only two minutes from Mucugê beach. Although tightly packed within a garden complex, the simple guest rooms harbor a beach house vibe, enhanced with warm decorative touches. The friendly owners can organize walking trips and excursions. Three bungalows come with fully equipped kitchens and are ideal for families or big groups. For sublime sea views, go across the street, where the massive windows and generous verandas of the tropically swank **Hotel Paraíso do Morro** (Rua do Mucugê 471, tel. 73/3575-3330, www.paraisodomorro.com, R$320-380 d) will leave you gasping in awe. Other standouts include a beckoning pool and attentive service. Those seeking a home-away-from-home will find it at ★ **Casa Natureza** (Rua dos Coqueiros 27, tel. 73/3575-10701, www.casanaturezabrasil.com.br, R$176-220 d). Reni Azevedo transformed his family's abode in the leafy residential *bairro* of São Francisco into a welcoming B&B. Four beautifully furnished suites spread between two villas are equipped with living areas, a kitchen, and even a yoga room. The jungly grounds include a pool as well as myriad monkeys.

Pousada Pitinga (Praia de Pitinga, tel. 73/3575-1067, www.pousadapitinga.com.br, no children under age 12, closed May-June, R$390-590 d) is set in a lush jungle area that spills right onto the sand. Tropically chic guest rooms rely on raw and polished natural materials, lulling you into a state of total harmony with nature. There is a pool for lounging. For a loftier, more removed vision of Arraial's seascapes, ★ **Casarão Alto do Mucugê** (Estrada Alto Mucugê 17, tel. 73/3575-1490, www.casaraoaltomucuge.com, R$230-350 d) features eight appealingly rustic guest rooms divided between a main house *(casarão)* and bungalows dispersed throughout a garden. Perched upon a cliff overlooking Praia de Pitinga, the intoxicating views and soundtrack of crashing waves are constant companions. Enjoy a lavish al fresco breakfasts or sunset-watching from the Japanese hot tub. Despite the seclusion, it's only a five-minute walk to the center of town.

Food

By day, beach *barracas* also offer all sorts of fish, seafood, and other beach-worthy delicacies that can assuage hunger pangs of all sizes throughout the day. Especially good are **Barraca do Nel** (Praia dos Pescadores, tel. 73/3575-2816, 10am-5pm daily) and the sophisticatedly loungey **Flor do Sal** (Praia de Pitinga, tel. 73/3575-3078, 9am-5pm Tues.-Sun. Mar.-Nov. and daily Dec.-Feb.), whose options bear a distinctive Thai influence.

In Arraial, most restaurant kitchens don't get going until the end of the day. When they do, the options are very eclectic. Bahian food is the exception among the sushi bars, Italian cantinas, Argentinean steak houses, and other international eateries (concentrated on the Rua do Mucugê). When you can't take any more fish or seafood, **Boi nos Aires** (Rua do Mucugê 200, tel. 73/3575-2554, www.boinosairesrestaurante.com, 5pm-midnight daily, R$25-45) will have you back in carnivore heaven with its prime cuts of beef flown in from Buenos Aires (although it does grill fish as well). **Manguti** (Rua do Mucugê 99, tel. 73/3575-2270, www.manguti.com.br, noon-11pm daily, R$35-50) is another local favorite that serves up meat, fish, pasta, and its famous gnocchi in a variety of sauces. The setting, in a cozy little house that is slightly removed from Rua do Mucugê's buzz, is quite romantic. You've never seen a food court quite as fetching as the **Beco das Cores,** an open-air galleria that groups together a series of bewitchingly lit boutiques, bars, and restaurants serving everything from crepes and pizza to sushi. An alluring ambiance is also one of the attractions of ★ **Rosa dos Ventos** (Alameda dos Flamboyants 24, tel. 73/3575-1271, 4pm-midnight Mon.-Tues. and Thurs.-Sat. and daily Dec.-Feb., 1pm-10pm Sun. Mar.-Nov., R$50-60), located in a gracious house lit by candles and surrounded by tropical foliage. The surprising menu pairs tropical dishes such as fish baked in banana leaves with wonderfully rich Viennese desserts.

For less expensive sustenance, brave the lineups (in summer) at **Paulo Pescador** (Praça São Brás 116, tel. 73/3575-1242, noon-10pm Tues.-Sun. and daily Dec.-Feb., closed May, R$15-25). The simple Bahian fish dishes rely on fresh ingredients at this unassuming local eatery in the main square, a great vantage point for watching the hippies selling their wares at the nightly craft market. Nearby, in a chalet-style house looking onto "Central Park," is the pioneering per-kilo restaurant **Portinha** (Rua do Campo, tel. 73/3575-1289, www.portinha.com.br, noon-10pm daily, R$10-15). Like its siblings in Porto Seguro and Trancoso, the buffets feature a tasty assortment of varied salads and main dishes kept hot over a wood oven.

To satisfy sweet cravings, head to the charming Praça Brigadeiro Eduardo Gomes. **Café da Santa** (Rua Brigadeiro Eduardo Gomes 134, tel. 73/3575-1078, 7am-10pm Tues.-Sun.) serves delicious, freshly ground coffee along with plenty of pastries (including flaky croissants).

Transportation and Services

Many hotels have tourist information about Arraial, as does the tourist office in Porto Seguro and a small but well-stocked kiosk at the beginning of Rua Mucugê. You can also check out the Portuguese website www.arraialdajuda.tur.br. The local Bradesco ATM on the Praça São Braz accepts international cards.

Balsas (ferries) leave from Porto Seguro to Arraial at 30-minute intervals throughout the day. After midnight, they leave at hourly intervals. Round-trip fare is R$4 for pedestrians, R$13 (weekdays)/R$20 (weekends) for cars. The *balsas*—some allow cars, while others are strictly for passengers—leave from Praça dos Pataxós in Porto Seguro. Tickets can be purchased at **Rio Buranhém Navegação** (tel. 73/3288-2516). Once you arrive at the other side of the river, buses, vans (R$3), and *moto-taxis* (R$6) transport you along the 6-kilometer (3.5-mi) coastal road to the center of Arraial d'Ajuda. A taxi from Porto Seguro's airport will cost close to R$100.

★ TRANCOSO

Only 12 kilometers (7.5 mi) south of Arraial is lovely Trancoso, an upscale yet not too developed former hippie haven whose magical vibe, beautiful surroundings, and eco-chic ethos is a magnet for Brazilian and international magnates, celebs, and jetsetters with money to burn and stress to alleviate. Instead of the hard-core partying that goes on at Porto Seguro and Arraial, pilgrims to Trancoso often prefer an evening of fine dining followed by drinks at the candlelit al fresco restaurants sprinkled around the Quadrado (although the surrounding beaches offer their share of hedonistic nocturnal activities, particularly when the moon is full).

The **Quadrado** (Square), an immense open-air plaza carpeted in thick grass and framed by trees, is the historical, spiritual, and nerve center of Trancoso. On three sides, it is surrounded by colonial homes painted in vibrant colors, many of which now house stylish boutiques, *pousadas,* and restaurants. On the far side is the incandescent **Igreja de São João Batista,** built in the 18th century on the ruins of a Jesuit convent. As you approach the church, you also near the edge of the cliff behind it, which plummets down to a green tangle of native Atlantic forest, an endless strip of beach, and a great sweep of the Atlantic in shades of bright turquoise-green. The ensemble is intoxicating, and more than a little dreamlike.

Beaches

Only a five-minute descent from the Quadrado lie a series of gorgeous beaches, fed by rivers and bordered by mangrove swamps and rain forest-carpeted cliffs. At strategic intervals are funky *barracas* where you can catch the sun's rays while electronica, bossa nova and lounge music wafts through the air. Closest to Trancoso is **Praias dos Nativos;** the more deserted stretches attract the odd nudist. With calmer seas are the ultra-trendy **Praia dos Coqueiros** and **Praia do Rio Verde,** ideal for bathing. By horseback, buggy, or on foot, you can continue south along these primitive beaches, which stretch all the way to Caraíva.

Sports and Recreation

Natural Ecobike e Aventura (tel. 73/3668-1955, www.naturalecobike.com) operates excursions (R$150 for 2.5 hours) for various skill levels by day and at night. Another possibility is to go galloping down the beaches on horseback or kayaking down the crystal-line waters of the Rio Trancoso to Praia dos Nativos, with stops for swimming. **Trancoso Receptivo** (tel. 73/3668-1183, www.trancoso-receptivo.com) charges R$150 for two hours of both pursuits. Golfers are in for a treat if

Trancoso

they choose to play the stunning 18-hole **Terravista Gold Course** (tel. 73/2105-2104, www.terravistagolfcourse.com.br, 8am-5pm Mon.-Sat., R$230 for 9 holes), located 18 kilometers (11 mi) from Trancoso on a cliff overlooking the Praia de Taípe.

Entertainment and Events

Trancoso's nightlife is less than wild, particularly in the off-season. There is usually a group playing live *forró,* samba, or rock music in the main square off the Quadrado or along the bars that lead down **Rua Principal** such as Para-Raio and São Brás, famed for its Friday night forró jams. In the summer, things heat up on the beaches of **Praia dos Coqueiros** and **Praia do Rio Verde** with parties, luaus, and even raves that last for days and draw a young, beautiful crowd. In summer, many of Trancoso's chicest hotels possess their own lounge barracas on **Praia dos Nativos**, among them Estrela d'Água, Uxua, and Bahia Bonita; all are open to the public.

Festa de São Sebastião (Jan. 20) is the town's most traditional *festa,* complete with processions, fireworks, and the raising of the two decorated masts that can be viewed in front of the church of São João Batista.

Accommodations

Trancoso's charming hotels tend to be on the pricy side, although some affordable options are available, particularly in and around the Bosque *bairro,* not far from the Quadrado. During the summer, prices double and reservations are a must. Prices listed are for off-season.

On the Quadrado, a lovely option is the **Pousada Porto Bananas** (Quadrado 234, tel. 73/3668-1017, www.portobananas.com.br, R$220-495 d). Various bungalows that sleep up to four are spread throughout a jungly garden that will make you feel as if you just checked into Eden. The tastefully simple guest rooms are decorated with harmonious colors and textures. You might find it hard to believe that there's anything but luxury on the Quadrado, but those on a budget can take refuge at the **Albergue Café Esmeralda** (Quadrado, tel. 73/3668-1527, www.trancosonatural.com, R$90-130 d). Although guest rooms are dark and cramped (only some have bathrooms), they are clean, and the owners are terribly friendly.

A little off the beaten track but also of great value is the **Pousada Encantada** (Rua João Vieira de Jesus, tel. 73/3668-2024, www.pousadaencantada.com.br, R$250-400 d). Although the bungalows are in close proximity and the garden is more residential backyard than tropical paradise, the guest rooms themselves are in mint condition and the staff makes you feel at home. Another fine choice, only 150 meters (500 feet) from the Quadrado, is the **Pousada Mundo Verde** (Rua João Vieira de Jesus, tel. 73/3668-2024, www.pousadamundoverde.com.br, R$220-310 d). The comfortable guest rooms aren't stylish, but the verdant surroundings are bucolic. From the pool at the edge of a bluff, you'll be treated to captivating views of the forest and beaches below.

There is no shortage of fabulous, eco-chic designer hotels in Trancoso. One of the first to rear its lovely head was ★ **Etnia Pousada** (Rua Principal 25, tel. 73/3668-1137, www.etniabrasil.com.br, R$510-630 d). This vast, hilly, and wooded property feels miles from the Quadrado. Immersed within the jungle are eight cleverly designed and beautifully appointed bungalows. Creature comforts include a humungous pool, terrace restaurant, and guests' access to the Etnia's private beach club on secluded Praia do Rio Verde. Located 2 kilometers south of town, **Etnia Clube de Mar** (Estrada Trancoso-Itaquena 300, tel. 73/3668-2065, www.etniaclubedemar.com.br, R$930-1,140 d) boasts a quintet of comfortable yet casual two-story beach houses ideal for couples and families in search of reclusion, relaxation, pampering, and privileged beach access. A hallmark of both Etnia properties is the extremely attentive service. If you have the urge to splurge, the most fabulous of Trancoso's accommodations options is ★ **Uxua Casa** (Quadrado, tel. 73/3668-2277, uxua.com, R$1,100-3,300 d)—the name, a Pataxó term for "marvelous," says it all. Dutch owner Wilbert Das applied his sensibility and impeccable taste to the 10 primitive bungalows (one is a treehouse), spread out beneath a canopy of native fruit trees. All were built using local construction techniques and recycled materials and are decorated with a captivating mélange of *artesanato* and antiques, as well as fixtures designed by Das himself. Open-sky bathrooms, full kitchens, private gardens, and indoor-outdoor living rooms make it hard to leave. The public spaces include a restaurant, lounge, and lagoon-shaped pool lined with 40,000 green aventurine quartz crystals supposed to possess healing properties. Uxua's beach club bar is made from recycled fishing boats. Service is superb yet casual and includes a 24-hour personal concierge.

Food

Just as sophisticated as its accommodations are Trancoso's range of culinary choices. During the day, you can take advantage of the fare served at the beach *barracas*. One of the nicest is the Italian-owned ★ **Cabana do Andrea** on Praia de Coqueiros. The Italian salads and pizzas are flavorful, as are the more tropical selections, including shrimp cooked in coconut milk and served in a coconut and grilled shrimp and squid with mango chutney. The service is attentive and the mellow soundtrack will put you in a sweet trance, aided by beach chairs and hammocks galore.

The restaurant scene in town doesn't get hopping until sundown. One of the best options, day or night, is the per-kilo buffet at **Portinha** (Quadrado, tel. 73/3668-1054, www.portinha.com.br, noon-8pm daily Mar.-Dec., noon-10pm daily Jan.-Feb. and July, R$15-20). The deliciously fresh salads and hot dishes kept sizzling over a wood oven can be savored at picnic tables right on a tree-shaded patch of the Quadrado. Come sundown, if you don't want to repeat the experience, try another Quadrado favorite: **Silvana & Cia** (Quadrado, tel. 73/3668-1122,

1pm-10pm daily, R$40-50). Beneath a giant almond tree magically lit up with lanterns and candles, Trancoso-born Silvana prepares typical Bahian dishes such as grilled fish, shrimp *bobós*, and *moquecas*. It's nicely priced by Trancoso standards; locals often dine here.

Natives of both Italy and São Paulo (where pizza is king) swear by the crunchy pies prepared in the large open kitchen of **Maritaca** (Rua do Telégrafo 388, tel. 73/3668-1702, 7pm-11pm Tues.-Sun., 7pm-2am daily Jan.-Feb., R$25-35). The ambiance is casual, but toppings include the more refined likes of asparagus and brie. For a respite from Trancoso's lofty prices, head to **Lá No Dom** (Rua da Gameleira 43, 6pm-1am Mon.-Sat. and daily Jan.-Feb.), where Dom prepares robust pita sandwiches layered with his secret eggplant sauce.

Transportation and Services

Tourist information and reservations for excursions are available at **Trancoso Receptivo** (Rua Carlos Alberto Parracho, off the Quadrado, tel. 73/3688-1333, www.trancosoreceptivo.com). For information online, check out www.trancosobahia.com.br. Also on Rua Carlos Alberto Parracho are ATMs that accept international cards. In front is a taxi stand with service to surrounding destinations.

Hourly **Águia Azul** (tel. 73/3575-1175) buses run between Trancoso and the *balsa* at Arraial d'Ajuda from 6am-7pm. The 50-minute trip, most of it through papaya plantations, costs R$6. By car, follow the 38-kilometer (24-mi) Estrada Arraial-Trancoso. After 7 kilometers (4 mi), you can turn onto the Estrada Velha de Trancoso, a dirt road that is only 15 kilometers (9 mi) to Trancoso.

★ CARAÍVA

Off the beaten track—which has left it gloriously intact from developers—Caraíva is most people's fantasy of an idyllic tropical getaway. On the banks of the Rio Caraíva, this tiny fishing village is surrounded by the thick vegetation of mangroves as well as deserted white beaches that extend for kilometers in both directions. Its few roads are paved with silky sand instead of asphalt, which hardly matters since no cars exist here. You can hire a donkey-driven wooden chariot or jump into a dugout canoe to get around. After a 10-year battle with the national energy company, Caraíva finally received electricity in 2007. However, since residents are used to lanterns and candles, you'll still be able to wander around at night with little more than moonlight and starlight to guide you. There isn't much to do in Caraíva, but if all you want to do is completely relax in idyllic natural surroundings, it is incomparable.

Beaches

You can walk for hours along Caraíva's beautiful coastline, and there is barely any construction in sight to break the brilliant green of native Atlantic forest and swaying coconut palms. Going south from the **Praia da Caraíva,** the beaches will take you past the **Parque Nacional Monte Pascoal** (tel. 73/3288-1613, www.icmbo.gov.br, R$5), a nature preserve that is also partially occupied by the **Barra Velha Pataxó** reservation (guided excursions can be organized from Caraíva for R$40 pp for groups of eight), all the way down to the splendidly isolated beaches of **Barra do Cai** and **Ponta do Corumbau,** where there is wonderful diving.

Once you take a canoe across the Rio Caraíva, you can also make your way north along the coast. A 4-kilometer (2.5-mi) walk brings you to the **Praia de Satu.** Cutting into the red cliffs crowned with jungle are freshwater lagoons where you can swim. An alternative to walking is to hire a boat from the quays (R$20).

Day outings by boat (R$60) or high-speed *lanchas* (R$100-130) to beaches north or south of Caraíva depart from the quays along the river and include snorkels and masks to check out fish amidst the reefs; reserve in advance with *barqueiros* or at the Boteco da Pará. Also fun is taking a *lancha* or kayak up the Rio Caraíva and then spending 90 dreamy

minutes floating back down the river in an inflated rubber tire.

Accommodations and Food

Caraíva hotels are pretty rustic, although they range from very basic to atmospheric. One of the most centrally located and attractive is ★ **Pousada da Lagoa** (tel. 73/3668-5059, www.lagoacaraiva.com.br, R$180-315 d). Brightly painted cabins are nestled among abundant foliage and around a small lagoon. The restaurant serves up nicely prepared meals (including garden-grown fruits and veg), and on summer nights it serves as bohemian headquarters to the mellow crowd that congregates to listen to great canned and live music. For immediate beach access, a nice option is the **Pousada Casa da Praia** (tel. 73/3274-6833, casadapraiacaraiva.com. br, R$180-270 d), which has a vast gazebo and lawn-chair studded garden as well as a lively bar. Guest rooms are simple but airy, with sea-facing verandas, and stepping outside means literally stepping into soft sand. The best bargain in town is **Memoan Hostel** (tel. 73/9275-7649, www.memoanhostel.com.br, R$70-100 d, R$35-40 pp), whose rustic dorm and double rooms (no TVs) are distributed amidst a spacious watermelon-colored *casa* surrounded by tropical gardens and overlooking the river. Guests are encouraged to cook in the communal kitchen and share the fruits of their labor at communal picnic tables.

Pará, the owner of ★ **Boteco do Pará** (Rua Beiro-Rio, tel. 73/9991-9804, 11am-6pm Tues.-Sun., 11am-10pm daily Dec.-Feb., R$20-35) has his own fishing boat, which guarantees the freshness of the fish and *moquecas* at this traditional eatery overlooking the Rio Caraíva. Tables are shaded by an immense almond tree and adjacent to the Ponto dos Mentirosos (Liars' Spot), where fishermen traditionally congregate to tell tall tales.

Transportation and Services

For information about Caraíva, check out www.caraiva.com.br. The **Associação dos Nativos de Caraiva** (near the church) offers contact info for local guides. Two buses daily (three daily in summer) operated by **Águia Azul** (tel. 73/3575-1175) connect Arraial d'Ajuda and Trancoso to Caraíva along a dirt road (that's difficult to navigate during the rainy season). The boat from Nova Caraíva to the village is R$4. From Arraial, the journey takes two hours and costs R$16. If you're driving, follow BR-101 to Monte Pascoal, then continue 42 kilometers (26 mi) along a dirt road to Nova Caraíva, where you'll have to leave your car.

Around Caraíva

Close to Caraíva are two of the most stunning and remote beaches along the Bahian coast: Praia do Espelho and Ponta do Corumbau. In recent years, despite (or because) of their seclusion, several rustically chic hotels have opened along their sands, allowing you to bed down in paradise—for a price.

PRAIA DO ESPELHO

With its coral-framed pools of limpid blue and flour-white beaches backed by dramatic red cliffs, it's no wonder that Praia do Espelho ranks at the top of the "Best Beaches" lists frequently compiled by Brazilian travel writers and hard-core beach aficionados. This means frequent boatloads of tourists show up from Porto Seguro and Arraial d'Ajuda. However, given Caraíva's 9-kilometer (6-mi) proximity, you can beat the crowds and enjoy the sheer beauty of the place in splendid isolation. An early arrival coincides with low tide. Reserve a boat from the **Boteco do Pará** (tel. 73/3274-6829); an outing costs R$60 and includes a stop at the Ilha de Tatuaçu for snorkeling. To stay a while and be pampered, a wonderful choice is ★ **Hotel Fazenda Cala & Divino** (tel. 73/9191-5183, www.divinoespelho.com.br, R$500-770 d). The former beach house of local ceramicist João José Calazans (a.k.a. Cala) boasts eight breezy guest chalets, beautifully decorated by the artist, that gaze out over the sea (you can even see the ocean from

bed). This is the only *pousada* with direct access to Praia do Espelho; others are located on the neighboring Praia do Curuipe. For a delicious lunch with a view, make advance reservations at **Restaurante da Sylvinha** (tel. 73/9985-4157, noon-3:30pm Mon.-Sat. Mar.-Nov., noon-6pm daily Dec.-Feb., R$50-65). Delicious fresh fish and seafood is prepared using regional fruits (mangaba, mango, passionfruit) and global influences (Moroccan, Thai, Mediterranean).

To get to Praia do Espelho from Arraial d'Ajuda, take the same **Águia Azul** (tel. 73/3575-1175, R$12.50) bus that goes to Caraíva, which will let you off at the entrance to town, 800 meters (0.5 mi) from the beach. By car, follow BR-101 to Monte Pascoal, and then continue 42 kilometers (26 mi) along a dirt road to Nova Caraíva; turn off at the sign indicating Praia do Espelho and then follow signed-turn offs to Praia do Espelho or to individual *pousadas*. If you plan to stay overnight, most *pousadas* can arrange transfers from Porto Seguro, Arraial, Trancoso, and Caraíva.

PONTA DO CORUMBAU

Corumbau remains one of the most unspoiled beaches along the Bahian coast. It's also one of the most alluring, with jade green water sheltered by coral reefs, a long white sand bar and endless beaches shaded by coconut palms and almond trees. From Caraíva, hire a boat at the Boteco do Pará to bring you here for the day (R$60, includes snorkel gear) or get Jonathan (tel. 73/9994-3371) or Nel (tel. 73/9901-8329) to zoom you here and back by buggy (R$150 for up to four people). To stay, ★ **Vila Naia** (tel. 73/3573-1006, www. vilanaia.com.br, R$1,400-1,800 d) is a stunning example of sustainable luxury. Four rustic fishermen's bungalows are scattered within a private reserve with trails that wind through mangroves and beaches, punctuated with wooden decks. Accommodations are comfortable and equipped with all modern amenities. There is also a spa with yoga classes, a pool, and an organic garden that supplies produce for delicious meals, included in the room rates. Much more affordable is **Pousada Corumbau** (tel. 73/3573-1190, www.corumbau.tur.br, R$150-290 d), which gives you a choice of apartments, bungalows, or an apartment with a kitchen and a living room. The clean, modern guest rooms are pretty modest, but the location is great, on a quasi-private strip of beach with its own *barraca*. Kids will love the hotel mascot: a large red macaw that wanders around as if he owns the place.

There is no bus service to Corumbau; driving takes forever and involves taking the BR-101 from the inland city of Itamaraju. The fastest and easiest way to get here is by boat or buggy via Caraíva.

CARAVELAS

Depending on which direction you're coming from, the last (or first) resort town of consequence in Bahia's extreme south is Caravelas. A decidedly low-key place, the colonial town's biggest draw is its proximity to the fantastic Parque Nacional Marinho de Abrolhos. Located 70 kilometers (43 mi) offshore, this marine reserve encompasses an archipelago of five islands whose crystalline waters and coral reefs make up one of the world's best diving spots.

★ Parque Nacional Marinho dos Abrolhos

Abrolhos comes from the Portuguese command *abre os olhos* ("open your eyes"), and visitors to the archipelago of volcanic islands and coral reefs will feel guilty if they so much as take time out to blink. Both Charles Darwin and Jacques Cousteau were impressed by the sheer diversity of colorful fish, surreally shaped coral, giant sea turtles, and rare marine birds that make their home in this live aquarium. December-March, when visibility is at its best, it's possible to see to depths of 20 meters (65 feet). Between July and November, an added bonus is watching the spectacle of humpback whales—16 meters (50 feet) in length and 40 tons in weight—who mate and

give birth in the warm waters. September and October are the best months to see them in action. In July-August, rainy weather can result in excursions being canceled.

From Caravelas, it takes a little more than 2.5 hours to reach the Abrolhos archipelago by speedboat, and four hours by catamaran. Full-day excursions, with a minimum of 10 people, are offered by small operators, registered with the Instituto Chico Mendes environmental agency, such as **Catamarã Horizonte Aberto** (Av. das Palmeiras 313, tel. 73/3297-1474, www.horizonteaberto.com.br) and **Catamarã Sanuk** (Rua das Estrelas 80, tel. 73/3297-1344, www.abrolhos.net) for around R$350 per day. If you have time to spare (and money to spend), both companies also offer three-day overnight trips with accommodations and meals on schooners. Diving and snorkeling equipment can be rented for an extra fee. Advance reservations are advised. Beginners diving lessons are also available starting at R$150.

Accommodations and Food

In Caravelas, **Pousada Liberdade** (Av. Adalício Nogueira 1551, tel. 73/3297-2415, www.pousadaliberdade.com.br, R$170-200 d) is a low-key choice with bungalows sitting in a garden shaded by palm, mango, and cashew trees. More upscale and with a privileged beach location 7 kilometers (4.5 mi) from town is the **Hotel Marina Porto Abrolhos** (Rua da Baleia 333, Praia de Grauça, tel. 73/3674-1060, www.marinaportoabrolhos.com.br, R$190-275 d). The breezy, attractive guest rooms are in individual bungalows crowned by palm thatching and surrounded by plenty of swaying trees.

Carenagem (Rua das Palmeiras 210, tel. 73/3297-1280, 11:30am-11pm Mon.-Sat., R$25-35) is a lively restaurant/bar that serves up classic Bahian *moquecas* and unpretentious fish and meat dishes as well as live music.

Transportation and Services

For information about Caravelas and

Abrolhos, visit www.abrolhos.net. **Águia Branca** (tel. 71/4004-1010, www.aguiabranca.com.br) offers one daily direct bus to Caravelas from Salvador (15 hours, R$130) and three from Porto Seguro (4 hours, R$37) to the town of Teixeira de Freitas. From Teixeira de Freitas, **O Brasileiro** (tel.

73/3291-2529) operates five daily buses to Caravelas (2 hours, R$16). By car, turn off highway BR-101 at Teixeira de Freitas and continue along BA-290 for around 54 kilometers (33 mi) in the direction of the coastal town of Alcobaça. Head south for another 24 kilometers (15 mi) along the BA-001 to Caravelas.

Pernambuco
and Alagoas

Highlights

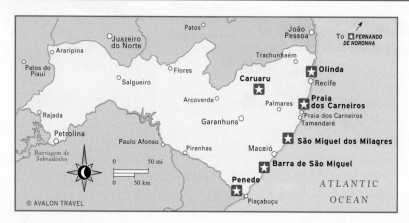

★ **Olinda:** Although most are lured by its wealth of splendid baroque churches, Pernambuco's first capital is no living museum but a vibrant colonial town pulsing with art and life (page 426).

★ **Caruaru:** Host of the biggest open-air market in the Northeast—and together with the surrounding villages of Alto do Moura and Bezerros—Caruaru provides an unforgettable taste of the Sertão's rich artistic, musical, and culinary culture (page 433).

★ **Praia dos Carneiros:** Straddling the green waters of the Rio Ariquindá and the transparent blue Atlantic, this secluded beach is a largely undiscovered haven for those in search of sun, sand, and snorkeling (page 437).

★ **Fernando de Noronha:** The archetype of everyone's fantasy tropical island,

carefully preserved Fernando de Noronha is a paradise for divers, surfers, dolphin-lovers, and escapists (page 439).

★ **Barra de São Miguel:** The star attraction of this stretch of coast is drop-dead gorgeous Praia do Gunga, whose impossibly white sands are bathed by a turquoise sea and freshwater lagoon (page 453).

★ **Penedo:** This picturesque colonial town perched above the Rio São Francisco offers a captivating glimpse of life along Brazil's largest national river (page 453).

★ **São Miguel dos Milagres:** Simultaneously unspoiled and exclusive, the idyllic palm-lined beaches and coral-protected waters surrounding this charming fishing village provide the ultimate getaway (page 456).

The northeastern state of Pernambuco may be fairly small, but its cultural and historical importance is gigantic.

Its capital city, Recife, and the adjacent town of Olinda possess an impressive array of colonial architecture and lay claim to some of the richest artistic and musical traditions in Brazil. Come summertime, both cities host exuberant, highly colorful street Carnavals that attract revelers from all over the world.

Founded by the Dutch in the 1500s and with a historical center dissected by a series of canals flowing into the sea, Recife is known as Brazil's Amsterdam. The similarities, however, end there. Recife is humid, somewhat ramshackle, and poor—yet it is also a subtly alluring place with numerous historical buildings, a Copacabana-worthy strip of white sand, and a distinctive cultural scene. Close by is Pernambuco's original capital, Olinda. Its hilltop churches, cobblestoned streets, and placid squares make it one of the most beautiful examples of colonial architecture in the Americas. No mere ode to the glorious past, Olinda is also home to a thriving artist community, which accounts for its numerous ateliers, galleries, and boutiques.

North and south of Recife, Pernambuco's coast is lined with magnificent white-sand beaches, including those surrounding the famous resort of Porto de Galinhas. Traveling inland, the landscape gives way to the dry, rugged desert-like Sertão, known for its blazing blue skies, red earth, thorn trees, and cattle. Many towns of this vast region are reputed for their traditional crafts, such as ceramics and woodcuts. The most famous of these inland towns, Caruaru, has the largest and one of the most colorful outdoor markets in Brazil.

Wedged between Pernambuco and Bahia are Brazil's smallest states, Alagoas and Sergipe, often overlooked by travelers to the Northeast. However, the coast of Alagoas, both north and south of its seaside capital of Maceió, lays claim to some of the most drop-dead gorgeous tropical beaches in Brazil. Clear turquoise-green lagoons and coral reefs are ideal for snorkeling and diving or simply floating around. On Alagoas's border with Sergipe, the charming colonial town of Penedo overlooks the mighty Rio São Francisco, Brazil's longest national river.

Despite the beauty of Pernambuco's and Alagoas's beaches, none of them compare

Previous: Praia dos Carneiros; **Above:** Praia de Ponta Verde, Maceió.

Pernambuco and Alagoas

© AVALON TRAVEL

ATLANTIC OCEAN

with those you'll encounter if you fly to the island archipelago of Fernando de Noronha, 550 kilometers (340 mi) off the coast of Pernambuco; these pristine beaches are considered the most sublime in Brazil. Fernando de Noronha is proof that you don't need to die to get to paradise.

PLANNING YOUR TIME

Pernambuco is jam-packed with treasures of every type: from baroque churches and stunning beaches to distinctive regional culture that can easily keep you engaged for days. To soak up some local flavor and see the sights of Recife and Olinda, you need a minimum of **3 days.** For some fun in the sun, the beaches of both Pernambuco and neighboring Alagoas are in very close proximity (Recife and Maceió are only four hours apart by bus). Many can be enjoyed as day trips from either capital. If you have more time, spend **2-3 days** or more traveling from one city to the other, stopping overnight at such places as Cabo de Santo Agostinho, Porto de Galinhas, and Praia dos Carneiros (southern Pernambuco)

or Maragogi, São Miguel dos Milagres, and Barra de Santo Antônio (northern Alagoas). A trip inland to Penedo from Maceió merits a couple of days, as does a pilgrimage to the market town of Caruaru. If you're prepared to splurge on a trip to the island paradise of Fernando de Noronha, set aside at least **4-5 days,** as you'll want to wallow in its sheer idyllic beauty.

Both Recife and Maceió are easily reached by plane and bus from cities around the country. Along the coast, main highways are generally in good shape, and due to the relatively short distances involved, you can easily explore other parts of the Northeast from either state. Temperatures are consistently tropical and there is lots of sun to go around, although rains can be intense April-July. In **summer months,** beaches tend to fill up with vacationing Brazilians. The sun is also hottest at this time, and temperatures are routinely in the 30s Celsius (90s Fahrenheit). If you're venturing into the Sertão, days can be furnace-like in summer, while nights can cool down (becoming quite cold in June-July).

Pernambuco

Along with Bahia, the state of Pernambuco is the other economic, demographic, and cultural powerhouse of the Northeast. With a rich history all its own, it boasts some of Brazil's most unique and fascinating cultural events and traditions, particularly in the realms of art and music. Highlights include the historic cities of Recife and Olinda, along with a beautiful coastline of beaches and the parched, rugged landscape of the Sertão, where the poverty of the soil contrasts with the richness of the popular culture.

RECIFE

Although its river canals and bridges sometimes (rather optimistically) earn it the nickname "Amsterdam of the Northeast," not much of a colonial Dutch legacy remains in

Pernambuco's capital. Aside from the partially revamped colonial center, known as Recife Antigo, and a handful of impressive 17th- and 18th-century churches in the otherwise built-up downtown neighborhoods of Santo Antônio, São José, and Boa Vista, there is not much of a colonial Portuguese legacy either. For baroque treasures, visit the state's first capital of Olinda, across the bay. Many visitors prefer to stay in Olinda, which is smaller and certainly prettier.

However, beyond the sprawling chaos, humidity, and mishmash of architectural styles, Recife is a city that grows on you, with a rhythm and flavor all its own. By day, there is lots to see and do, and if you get a sudden urge to be horizontal on a white-sand beach with a cooling caipirinha, you can make for Boa

Recife

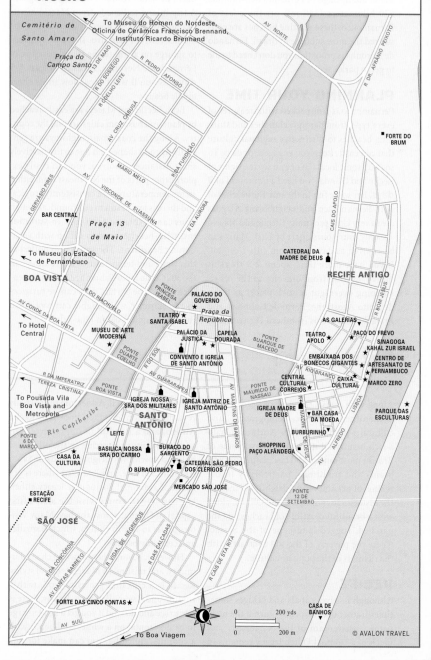

Cemitério de
Santo Amaro

To Museu do Homen do Nordeste,
Oficina de Cerâmica Francisco Brennand,
Instituto Ricardo Brennand

AV. NORTE

R. DR. AFRÂNIO PEIXOTO

Praça do
Campo Santo

R. 13 DE MAIO
R. DO SOSSEGO
R. COELHO LEITE
R. PEDRO AFONSO

FORTE DO
BRUM

AV. CRUZ CABUGÁ
AV. MÁRIO MELO
R. DA FUNDIÇÃO

VISCONDE DE SUASSUNA
R. DA AURORA

R. GERVÁSIO PIRES
AV.

CAIS DO APOLO

BAR CENTRAL

Praça 13
de Maio

CATEDRAL DA
MADRE DE DEUS

R. BOM JESUS

To Museu do Estado
de Pernambuco

RECIFE ANTIGO

BOA VISTA

R. DO RIACHUELO

AV. CONDE DA BOA VISTA

PONTE
PRINCESA
ISABEL

PALÁCIO DO
GOVERNO

Praça da
República

AS GALERIAS

To Hotel
Central

MUSEU DE ARTE
MODERNA

TEATRO
SANTA ISABEL

PALÁCIO DA
JUSTIÇA

CAPELA
DOURADA

PONTE
BUARQUE DE
MACEDO

TEATRO
APOLO

PAÇO DO FREVO

SINAGOGA
KAHAL ZUR ISRAEL

R. DA IMPERATRIZ

PONTE
DUARTE
COELHO

R. DO SOL

CONVENTO E IGREJA
DE SANTO ANTÔNIO

EMBAIXADA DOS
BONECOS GIGANTES

CENTRO DE
ARTESANATO DE
PERNAMBUCO

TEREZA CRISTINA

PONTE
BOA VISTA

AV. GUARARAPES

PONTE
MAURÍCIO DE
NASSAU

CENTRAL
CULTURAL
CORREIOS

CAIXA
CULTURAL

MARCO ZERO

To Pousada Vila
Boa Vista and
Metropole

IGREJA NOSSA
SRA DOS MILITARES

IGREJA MATRIZ DE
SANTO ANTÔNIO

AV. MARTINS DE BARROS

IGREJA MADRE
DE DEUS

R. MADRE DE DEUS

R. BRANCO

R. DO SOL

LISBOA

PARQUE DAS
ESCULTURAS

Rio Capibaribe

SANTO
ANTÔNIO

BAR CASA
DA MOEDA

PONTE
6 DE
MARÇO

LEITE

BURBURINHO

CASA DA
CULTURA

BASÍLICA NOSSA
SRA DO CARMO

BURACO DO
SARGENTO

AV. ALFREDO

SHOPPING
PAÇO ALFÂNDEGA

O BURAQUINHO

CATEDRAL SÃO PEDRO
DOS CLÉRIGOS

ESTAÇÃO
RECIFE

MERCADO SÃO JOSÉ

PONTE
12 DE
SETEMBRO

SÃO JOSÉ

R. VIDAL DE NEGREIROS

R. DAS CALÇADAS

R. CAIS DE STA RITA

R. DA CONCÓRDIA

AV. DANTAS BARRETO

FORTE DAS CINCO PONTAS

CASA DE
BANHOS

AV. SUL

0   200 yds

0   200 m

To Boa Viagem

© AVALON TRAVEL

Viagem, the longest urban beach in Brazil. Recife has a surprisingly good restaurant scene and varied nightlife, spurred on by one of the most creative music scenes in Brazil, responsible for the birth of rhythms such as *frevo, maracatu,* and *mangue beat.*

Recife has considerable poverty and, unfortunately, is renowned for a high incidence of violent crime. Stay clear from the Centro at night and weekends and if you go to Recife Antigo or bars in the area, take a taxi. At night, taxis are a must.

Orientation

With its winding river canals and twisting old streets, crowded sidewalks cluttered with vendors, and indistinguishable modern high-rises, Recife's downtown is somewhat of a puzzle to navigate. Fortunately, most of its historical attractions are within walking distance of each other. Spread out among three small islands that form the *bairros* of **Recife Antigo** (also called Bairro do Recife), **Santo Antônio,** and **Boa Vista,** the center is connected to the mainland by numerous bridges that cross the Beberibe and Capibaribe Rivers. You can see most of these sights easily in a day or less; add a second day for the fantastic museums in the outlying suburbs, and a third to lounge on Boa Viagem's beach.

Getting around Recife is somewhat tricky: There are many one-way streets and bridges, the urban layout is rather haphazard, and it is hard to identify streets in the center. Meanwhile, the bus system is complicated, and routes change frequently. When in doubt, take a taxi—especially at night.

Sights
RECIFE ANTIGO
(BAIRRO DO RECIFE)
Founded by the Dutch in the 1630s, the historic core of Recife, or Recife Antigo, is the oldest part of town. For years its glorious edifices were left in a tragically dilapidated state until Recife's authorities decided to restore and revitalize its historic quarter (an ongoing process). Although the makeover is a little garish (the paint on its buildings is *very* bright), these efforts succeeded in breathing new life into an area that was once avoided like the plague. At night and on weekends, its many bars and cobblestoned squares teem with Recifenses and tourists alike, who gather to drink and check out live music performances.

The heart of Recife Antigo is the Praça Barão do Rio Branco, more commonly known as **Marco Zero.** From here you can look out across the ocean and see the coral reef that inspired the city's name. Jutting up from the reef are a series of phallic sculptures by renowned local ceramicist and artist Francisco Brennand. Should you have the urge to gaze at them up close, you can hop a boat (R$5) for the **Parque das Esculturas,** leaving from in front of the *praça.*

Overlooking Praça do Marco Zero is an imposing and impossibly yellow neoclassical palace. Built in 1912 to house the Bank of London and South America, it then served as the Pernambuco stock market before undergoing a major renovation. Now the **Caixa Cultural** (Av. Alfredo Lisboa 505, tel. 81/3425-1906, www.caixacultural.com.br, 10am-8pm Tues.-Sat., 10am-6pm Sun.), it hosts art exhibits and musical and theatrical performances. A former shipping warehouse now shelters the **Centro do Artesanato do Pernambuco** (Av. Alfredo Lisboa, tel. 81/3181-3450, www.artesanatodepernambuco.pe.gov.br, 2pm-8pm Mon., 9am-8pm Tues.-Sun.). A collection of more than 15,000 sculpted, embroidered, carved, and woven objects provide a terrific overview of Pernambuco's rich artisanal traditions along with plenty of prime purchasing possibilities.

One block behind the square, lively **Rua do Bom Jesus,** now filled with bars and boutiques, was one of the main streets of Recife Antigo. For a short while, it was also the center of a small but thriving Jewish community. The first Jews arrived in Olinda in 1537, and under Dutch occupation the community flourished. Unlike the Portuguese, who persecuted Jews, the Dutch tolerated Judaism.

It was during this period that the first synagogue in the Americas—the **Sinagoga Kahal Zur Israel-Centro Cultural Judaíco** (Rua do Bom Jesus 197, tel. 81/3224-2128, www.arquivojudaicope.org.br, 9am-4:30pm Tues.-Fri., 2pm-5:30pm Sun., R$6) was constructed on what was then known as Rua dos Judeus (Street of the Jews). When the Portuguese finally routed the Dutch from Recife in 1654, most of Pernambuco's Jews fled to New Amsterdam, where they founded what would become the future New York's first Jewish community (others remained in Brazil under the guise of "New Christians"). The synagogue was abandoned and forgotten until excavations in the 1990s uncovered the *mikveh,* a ritual fountain used for purification. After major renovations, it reopened as a museum that traces the history of Jews in Pernambuco. On the ground floor, you can still see vestiges of the original synagogue, including the floor of Dutch tiles and parts of the walls. On the third floor, an excellent video (with English subtitles) describes the Jewish experience in Brazil.

The **Embaixada dos Bonecos Gigantes** (Rua do Bom Jesus 183, tel. 81/3441-5102, www.bonecosgigantesdeolinda.com.br, 8am-6pm daily, R$10) exhibits more than 50 gigantic dolls traditionally paraded through the streets of Olinda. Housed in a surreal and somewhat spooky display are heroes such as Pelé, Carmen Miranda, Michael Jackson, and Barack Obama.

Paço do Frevo (Praça do Arsenal da Marinha 91, tel. 81/3355-8142, www.pacodofrevo.org.br, 9am-8pm Tues.-Sun.) pays homage to a trademark Pernambucano cultural tradition. Interactive exhibits offer an engaging introduction to the 19th-century musical style, which emerged during Recife's Carnaval processions. The electric mélange includes influences from military marching bands, *maxixe,* and capoeira. Derived from the Portuguese *ferver* (to boil), *frevo* is aptly named; both the pulsating music and vigorous dancing (performances are often held here) tend to leave both participants and observers in a state of effervescence. Frevo was declared a Cultural Heritage of Humanity site by UNESCO.

A handsome old building of particular note is the **Teatro Apolo** (Rua do Apolo 121), a grand mid-19th-century theater constructed out of Portuguese limestone that now houses a cinema, theater, and concert hall. Housed in a 1921 building that was formerly Recife's main post office, the **Centro Cultural Correios** (Av. Marquês de Olinda 262, tel. 81/3224-5739, www.correios.com.br, 9am-6pm Tues.-Fri., noon-6pm Sat.-Sun.) is worth popping into for some art—and you can still mail a letter. Close by, one of Recife's oldest churches, the **Igreja Madre de Deus** (Rua Madre de Deus, tel. 81/3224-5587, 8am-noon and 2pm-5pm Tues.-Fri., 8am-11am Sat., 8am-noon Sun.) is remarkable for its facade featuring stone sculptures carved out of local coral and an interior filled with golden columns and flocks of baroque angels.

SANTO ANTÔNIO

Across the river from Recife Antigo, the *bairro* of Santo Antônio was also originally settled by the Dutch. A block from the Ponte Buarque de Macedo sits the stately **Praça da República,** surrounded by grand 19th- and early-20th-century buildings such as the pale pink Teatro Santa Isabel, the Palácio da Justiça, and the Palácio do Governo, seat of the state government. The park was once the site of Dutch governor Maurits van Nassau's estate, and its current design—by a 19th-century French landscaper with later embellishments by Roberto Burle Marx—has maintained an air of bucolic languor thanks to a fountain, myriad palms, and a gigantic African baobab whose origin is a mystery.

A block from Praça da República is the most impressive baroque architectural ensemble in Recife. Built in 1606, the **Convento e Igreja de Santo Antônio** (Rua do Imperador Dom Pedro II 206, 8am-noon and 2pm-4:30pm daily) is distinctive for its cupola lined with Dutch ceramic tiles and blue-and-white Portuguese azulejo panels. More panels depicting Old Testament scenes line the walls of the small cloister. Most splendid of all is the **Capela Dourada** (tel. 81/3224-0530, www.capeladourada.com.br, 8am-11:30am and 2pm-5pm Mon.-Fri., 8am-11:30am Sat., R$3), an early baroque extravaganza of dazzling gold. Gold leaf covers the sculpted cedar altars and columns and frames the religious paintings that adorn the walls and ceilings. You are left with the impression of having walked into a jewel box.

Avenida Dantas Barreto is home to three colonial churches. The **Basílica e Convento de Nossa Senhora do Carmo** (Praça do Carmo, tel. 81/3224-3341, 6:30am-7pm Mon.-Fri., 6:30am-noon Sat., 8am-noon and 5pm-8pm Sun.) offers another shining example of baroque, with carvings, gold-covered altars, and azulejo panels depicting biblical scenes. The mid- to late-18th-century **Igreja Matriz de Santo Antônio** (Praça da Independência, tel. 81/3224-9494, 7am-noon and 2pm-6pm Mon.-Fri., 4pm-6:30pm Sat., 7am-noon and 4pm-6pm Sun.) features a mixture of styles. The simple facade of the **Igreja Nossa Senhora da Conceição dos Militares** (Rua Nova 309, tel. 81/3224-3106, 8am-4pm Mon.-Fri., 8am-1pm Sat.-Sun.) hides exuberantly sculpted columns and altars covered in gold leaf, along with a ceiling fresco depicting a pregnant Virgin Mary.

Rua do Sol runs along the waterfront, and will bring you to the **Casa da Cultura** (Rua Floriano Peixoto, tel. 81/3184-3151, www.casadaculturape.com.br, 9am-6pm Mon.-Fri., 9am-5pm Sat., 9am-2pm Sun.), which occupies a prison that dates back to the 1860s. While one of the cells gives you an impression of 19th-century life behind bars, the others have been converted into claustrophobic shops selling art and handicrafts from all over the state of Pernambuco.

SÃO JOSÉ

Avenida Dantas Barreto leads from Praça da República through the maze of bustling shop-lined streets that stretches from Santo Antônio to the adjacent *bairro* of São José. A few blocks south along Dantas Barreto brings you to the **Catedral de São Pedro dos Clérigos** (Pátio de São Pedro, tel. 81/3224-2954, 8am-noon and 2pm-5pm Mon.-Fri.), one of Recife's most striking churches. Dating to 1728, the facade is modeled after the church of Santa Maria Maggiore in Rome. Inside, admire the beautifully detailed woodwork, including likenesses of the 12 apostles set against a splendid trompe l'oeil background on the ceiling.

The church dominates the **Pátio de São Pedro,** a charming rectangular plaza surrounded by restored and brightly painted 18th- and 19th-century houses, many of which are now restaurants, bars, and boutiques. Tuesday nights, the Pátio becomes a stage for Terça Negra, featuring music and dance performances related to Pernambuco's African heritage. Don't leave without quick stops (all that's required) at a series of micro-museums devoted to key figures and aspects of Pernambucano culture (all are open 9am-5pm Mon.-Fri.). "Memorials" pay homage to **Luiz Gonzaga** (Casa 35, tel. 81/3232-2965, www.recife.pe.gov.br/mlg) and **Chico Science** (Casa 21, tel. 81/3355-3158, www.recife.pe.gov.br/chicoscience), the patron saints of *forró* and *mangue beat*, respectively. The **Museu de Arte Popular** (Casa 47, tel. 81/3355-3110) presents temporary exhibits of the state's rich folk art traditions, while the tiny **Casa do Carnaval** (Casa 52, tel. 81/3355-3302) displays Carnaval paraphernalia. Not to be missed is the **Centro de Design do Recife** (Casa 10, tel. 81/3355-3148), which showcases fabulous contemporary designs by Recifenses; many involve inspired takes on artisanal traditions. Tragically, the bags, lamps, jewels, and housewares are *not* for sale (although you can get in touch with the artists).

The name of the impressive **Forte das Cinco Pontas** (Praça das Cinco Pontas, tel. 81/3355-3107, 9am-6pm Tues.-Fri., 1pm-5pm Sat.-Sun., R$4) alludes to the original five-pointed adobe fort erected by the

Dutch. Although the Portuguese razed it and then rebuilt a more traditional four-pointed fortification out of stone, the name stuck. Inside, a rather musty (and not at all essential) **Museu da Cidade** traces Recife's history through a series of engravings and paintings.

BOA VISTA

Along Rua do Sol is the pretty Ponte Duarte Coelho, Recife's oldest remaining Dutch-built bridge. On the other side of the river, in the *bairro* of Boa Vista, is **Rua da Aurora.** Its brightly painted neoclassical buildings, radiant when lit by the early morning sun, are reflected in the waters of the Rio Capibaribe. At No. 175, **Cine São Luiz,** the oldest and grandest cinema in town, dates to 1952. It's worth dropping by the **Museu de Arte Moderna** (Rua da Aurora 256, tel. 81/3355-6870, www.mamam.art.br, noon-6pm Tues.-Fri., 1pm-5pm Sat.-Sun., free) to check out key works and temporary exhibits featuring modern and contemporary Pernambucano art.

BOA VIAGEM

Flanked by gleaming yet rather dauntingly massive apartment buildings, Boa Viagem as a neighborhood is certainly nowhere near as interesting as Copacabana, to which it is often compared. Aside from hotels and some good restaurants and bars (mostly centered around the area known as Segundo Jardim and the northern stretch, Pina), the only attraction is the very urban—albeit attractive—**white-sand beach**. Although on weekends it can get mobbed, Boa Viagem is otherwise relaxing (and very well equipped, with vendors hawking everything from grilled shrimp to icy beer). The waters are calm and warm for bathing (there is an offshore reef visible at low tide, which is the best time to swim). Do *not* venture far, since Boa Viagem is the Brazilian capital of shark attacks; there have been instances of careless bathers going out too far and being injured or even killed. If you stay close to shore, however, there's no reason to worry.

ARREDORES (OUTLYING NEIGHBORHOODS)

A quick bus or taxi ride from the center, the leafy, residential neighborhoods of Graças, Casa Forte, Poço da Panela, Casas Amarelas, and Várzea are situated on land formerly occupied by sugar plantations. Although out of the way, these *bairros* offer a glimpse at more tranquil side of Recife and contain several unusual museums.

Located in a gracious 19th-century neoclassical villa, the **Museu do Estado de Pernambuco** (Av. Rui Barbosa 960, Graças, tel. 81/3184-7174, 9am-5pm Tues.-Fri., 2pm-5pm Sat.-Sun., R$5) displays an engaging collection of fine colonial furniture along with engravings and paintings of Recife from the 17th to 20th centuries. For an overview of Pernambucano culture, head to the **Museu do Homem do Nordeste** (Av. 17 de Agosto 2187, Casa Forte, tel. 81/3073-6340, www.fundaj.com.br, 8am-5pm Tues.-Sun., free). Extremely well-organized, the museum relies on objects to depict the rich singularity of traditional life in the Brazilian Northeast. Sugarcane cultivation, Sertanejo cattle culture, Catholicism, Candomblé, and Carnaval are only a few of the themes touched on. Although it's all highly compelling stuff, the most striking section is devoted to popular art forms of the interior, where there is a strong tradition of making clay figurines that illustrate scenes from daily life. One of the greatest practitioners of this art form was Mestre Vitalino, a poor farmer from the village of Alto do Moura, who in the 1920s began sculpting highly expressive vignettes—often doused with humor—of the changing rural world around him.

Recife's two most fascinating and original museums both bear the name of Brennand. The renowned artist and ceramicist Francisco Brennand transformed the old brick, tile, and ceramic factory that made his family millionaires into the **Oficina de Cerâmica Francisco Brennand** (Av. Caxangá, Várzea, tel. 81/3271-2466, www.brennand.com.br, 8am-5pm Mon.-Thurs., 8am-4pm Fri., R$10).

Forró

One of the most popular musical traditions throughout the Northeast is *forró*, a lively form of country-style dance music mixed with a bit of rumba, whose resulting swing is very infectious. *Forró* is associated with the dance (a two-step with swing) and the music (a wilder version of the *baião*), played by a trio of accordion, triangle, and *zabumba* drum that swept the Northeast and was given a major boost by the late great *forró* pioneer and poet, **Luiz Gonzaga** (1912-1989). As *forró* evolved, it took on new repertoires and new instruments, such as the *pifano* (wooden flute) and *rabeca* (a Brazilian fiddle). It has now caught on in hip pockets of urban centers such as Rio and São Paulo, where the addition of electronic keyboards has endeared it to DJs and clubbers.

Recife has many traditional *casas de forró*, which really get hopping on Friday and Saturday nights (more so after midnight). Most are in *arredores* (outlying neighborhoods), easily reachable by taxi. Visit the **Sala de Reboco** (Rua Gregório Junior 264, Cordeiro, tel. 81/3228-7052, www.saladereboco.com.br, 10pm-close Thurs.-Sat.), a very atmospheric dance hall-bar that works hard to capture the flavor of the northeastern interior with authentic decorative details and food. The stage attracts the biggest national names in *forró* as well as up-and-coming local talents.

In this atelier-museum, Brennand, a white-bearded, biblical-looking personage, exhibits his fantastic, often monumental sculptures and paintings, drawings, and engravings. Inspired by mythical, historical, and literary figures, many of his sculptures have a surreal flavor and a distinct erotic charge. The atelier is surrounded by exuberant gardens, designed by Roberto Burle Marx, with lagoons and fountains; there's also a café and a boutique. Instead of making art, Fernando's no less colorful cousin, Ricardo, collects it. In 2002 he opened the nearby **Instituto Ricardo Brennand** (Alameda Antônio Brennand, Várzea, tel. 81/2121-0352, www.institutoricardobrennand.org.br, 1pm-7pm Tues.-Sun., R$20, free last Tues. of the month) in order to share his eclectic finds with the public. A stately alley of imperial palms leads through a sculpture garden and up to a complex of buildings dominated by a crazily out-of-place medieval castle with an on-site café. The highlights of Brennand's art collection are the paintings by European artists who traveled to Brazil between the 16th and 20th centuries. Particularly well represented is talented Dutch painter Franz Post (1612-1680), who was officially commissioned to depict the otherworldly tropical landscapes, fauna, and inhabitants of Pernambuco. Precious maps, manuscripts, and money from the Dutch occupation can also be seen. The 3,000 pieces of medieval armor and weaponry located in the castle are another high point of Brennand's collection.

Nightlife

Much of the city—including the center and Boa Viagem—shuts down at night. However, there are definitely urban pockets where Recifenses gather to have fun until the wee hours. Indeed, of the northeastern cities, Recife's nightlife is one of the most eclectic, although its nocturnal pleasures aren't always obvious, especially for foreigners. Contributing to Recife's singularity is the diversity of homegrown music styles—ranging from traditional *forró* and *maracatu* to the postmodern strains of *mangue beat*—that provide the soundtrack to its bars, clubs, and dance halls.

RECIFE ANTIGO

Recife Antigo is a major nocturnal haunt for Recife's youth. Come sunset, the place starts to buzz, although recent security issues have put a bit of a damper on proceedings. You'll find lots of bars in Rua do Apolo, Rua do Bom Jesus, and Praça Arsenal da Marinha. A favorite is the warm and funky **Bar Casa da**

Moeda (Rua da Moeda 150, tel. 81/3224-7095, www.casadamoedabar.com.br, 7pm-1am Tues.-Sun.), a gallery-bar where artists and hipsters listen to live jazz, bossa, and MPB. The sidewalk tables are great for checking out the flow of revelers. More removed from the main sizzle is laid-back **Burburinho** (Rua Tomazina 106, tel. 81/3224-5854, 11am-2pm and 5pm-10pm Mon.-Thurs., 11am-2pm and 5pm-2am Fri., 7pm-2am Sat.), which draws an eclectic crowd of all ages to its sidewalk tables. Inside, a small stage often hosts local rock and blues bands.

SANTO ANTÔNIO, SÃO JOSÉ, AND BOA VISTA

This area is pretty dead (and spooky) at night. Classic bohemian bars such as **Buraco do Sargento** (Pátio de São Pedro 33, São José, tel. 81/3224-7522, 9:30am-10pm Mon.-Sat.) are the exception. In existence since 1955 (and headquarters to the Batutas de São José Carnaval *bloco*), it attracts a cachaça-sipping, *carne-do-sol*-munching crew that invades the tables overlooking charming **Pátio São Pedro,** where live music is often performed in the evenings. Come Tuesday nights for Terça Negra, an event featuring performances of Afro-Brazilian music such as *afoxé, maracatu,* samba, and reggae. The Pátio gets a lot of happy-hour traffic, as does the generically named **Bar Central** (Rua Mamede Simões 144, Santo Amaro, tel. 81/3222-7622, 11am-2am Mon.-Fri., 8pm-2am Sat.), which lures an attractive and eclectic mix of artists, musicians, and ad execs who mellow out to the customized soundtrack

Boa Vista is where you'll find most of Recife's gay offerings. **Metrópole** (Rua da Ninfas 125, Boa Vista, tel. 81/3423-0123, www.clubeemetropole.com.br, 10pm-6am Fri.-Sat., R$20-30) is Recife's temple of gaydom, a megaclub with two thematic bars (New York and Brasil), each with their own dance floors, vibes, and soundtracks (and swimming pools and showers). A third rooftop bar has a telescope for romantic stargazing. Other gaze-worthy items include go-go boys and drag queens.

PINA

Boa Viagem's northern strip of Pina (also known as Polo Pina) was the city's happening nocturnal circuit back in the 1990s. After falling out of favor, it has crept back in style with a vengeance. Hipster HQ is **Galeria Joana D'Arc** on Avenida Herculano Bandeira, a cluster of bars, restaurants, and vintage clothing boutiques haunted by a youngish, alternative, GLS crowd. Check out **Anjo Solto** (Av. Herculano Bandeira 513, Loja 14-A, tel. 81/3325-0862, www.anjosolto.com. br, 5:30pm-close daily) and **Boratcho** (Av. Herculano Bandeira 513, tel. 81/3327-1168, www.boratcho.com.br, 7pm-close Tues.-Sun.), which brings a little bit of Mexico to Recife with bright Frida Kahlo colors and a menu featuring tacos and *tequiroskas* (tequila cocktails made with crushed local fruits such *siriguela* and *umbu-cajá*). This creative bar—owned by a tattoo artist—is also known for its eclectic musical tastes. These run the gamut from *chorinho,* jazz, and samba-rock to events such as Thursday's *"sem noção"* (without notion) nights, in which a DJ gets the arty crowd dancing till dawn.

Two popular northeastern bar snacks are *caldinhos,* hearty chowders, and *guaiamuns,* blue-shelled crabs that live in mangroves. Both delicacies reel in customers at the laid-back **Socaldinho Guaiamum** (Av. Conselheiro Aguiar 112, tel. 81/3326-3766, 11:30am-close daily). A special chef watches over the cauldrons of eight bubbling *caldinhos,* ranging from classic black bean to *mocotó* (calves' hoofs), popularly known as "Viagra." Live MPB performances on weekdays give way to chorinho on Saturday and *samba de roda* on Sunday. Just footsteps from the sand, **Biruta Bar** (Rua Bem-Te-Vi 15, Brasília Teimosa, tel. 81/3326-5151, www.birutabar. com.br, 11am-close Tues.-Sun.) resembles a rustic beach house. With soft MPB playing in the background and moonlight reflecting on the water, it's a romantic one at that. The extensive menu offers plenty of sea fare.

BOA VIAGEM
After dark, this modern stretch of high-rise condos and hotels pulses with upscale options. **UK Pub** (Rua Francisco da Cunha 165, tel. 81/3465-1088, www.ukpub.com.br, 7pm-close Tues. and Thurs.-Sun., cover R$30-50) is a sophisticated pub (the menu includes fish 'n chips as well as champagne) that attracts an upscale crowd of dressed-to-kill 20- to 40-somethings who don't mind long lines. Aside from the flirt-fest, the two main draws are the extensive drink menu featuring more than 50 types of beer and the great live music, which tends toward rock and samba-rock. On the cusp of Pina and Boa Viagem, the breezy **Boteco Maxime** (Av. Boa Viagem 21, tel. 81/3456-1491, 5pm-midnight, Mon.-Fri. noon-2am daily) has a great wooden deck overlooking Boa Viagem's palms. Feast on seafood delicacies such as buckets of fresh oysters and fried soft-shelled crab.

Entertainment and Events
PERFORMING ARTS
The elegant **Teatro de Santa Isabel** (Praça da República, Santo Antônio, tel. 81/3355-3323, www.teatrosantaisabel.com.br) is the city's premier venue for theater, dance, and musical performances. In Recife Antigo, the **Cinema Apolo** (Rua do Apolo 121, tel. 81/3355-3220) is an old art house cinema occupying the renovated Teatro Apolo. For schedules, pick up *Agenda Cultural,* a free monthly calendar of events available at tourist information kiosks and some cultural venues. Also visit www.agendadorecife.com for cultural listings.

FESTIVALS AND EVENTS
Recife's **Carnaval** is one of the big triumvirate of Brazilian Carnavals. While Rio is legendary for its parades and samba schools and Salvador pulses with *axé* music blasted from the tops of gigantic *trios elétricos,*

Recife's frenetic street Carnaval draws on Pernambuco's rich multiplicity of rhythms. The classic soundtrack to Recife's Carnaval is the pulsing *frevo.* Quite appropriately, the word is said to be a derivation of *ferver*—meaning "to boil." An unlikely but characteristically inventive mixture of African capoeira and Portuguese marches, *frevo* has been around since the 19th century. It is accompanied by dervish-like dancers who twirl around with multicolored parasols, creating an intoxicating aural and visual kaleidoscope that has become Recife's trademark. To see the best *frevo* performances during Carnaval, plant yourself at the Pólo de Todos os Frevos, on Avenida Guararapes, where you'll have the privilege of seeing the Orquestra Spok Frevo do Recife along with dozens of other traditional groups. Otherwise, *freviocas*—trucks with electric *frevo* groups on board—also ride around the center inciting the multitudes to get their groove on.

In an attempt to diversify its Carnavalesque attractions and rescue musical traditions, other local African-influenced rhythms such as *maracatu, ciranda, afoxé,* samba, *caboclinho, coco-de-roda,* and even rock and techno are increasingly given space during the festivities. Check out the Pólo Mangue, on Avenida Caís da Alfândega, where you can rock out to *mangue beat,* a musical movement that emerged in Recife in the 1990s, when vanguard bands such as Chico Science & Nação Zumbi and Mundo Livre began creatively fusing regional musical traditions with pop, rock, rap, and electronica.

Two groups that are especially remarkable are the *maracatu* and *caboclinhos. Maracatu* groups originally consisted of *nações* (nations) of slaves, whose leaders were crowned as symbolic kings and queens. Descendants of these nations, many with links to Afro-Brazilian religion, still perform the ritual crowning in groups of sumptuously costumed singers, dancers, and percussionists that often number up to 100 people. *Caboclinho* groups date back to early colonial times, when Indians presented elaborate dances to the Portuguese during official ceremonies. Today's *caboclinho* dancers dress up as Indian warriors complete with feather headdresses, loin cloths, bows, and arrows and dance to the haunting music played with flutes, drums, and rattles.

Recife's Carnaval kicks off Friday night, and over the next five days the entire Centro shuts down to traffic and becomes one enormous *festa*. The party gets started early on Saturday morning with the parade of the Recife's largest *bloco* (Carnaval group), the Galo da Madrugada, flooding the center with 1 million dancing souls. Another highlight is Sunday night, when the Pátio do Terço is invaded by the Noite dos Tambores Silenciosos (Night of the Silent Drums). At 11pm, traditional *maracatu* nations pay homage to Pernambuco's former population of African slaves—you can imagine the shock when the 300-plus drummers suddenly stop for a minute of silence.

If you're in town at this time, you get the bonus of experiencing two Carnavals at once: only 7 kilometers (4 mi) away is Olinda's smaller but equally famous street celebration. For Carnaval dates, information, and attractions, visit www.programacaocarnavalrecife.com.br. If you're already in town, the tourist office can supply you with detailed info and maps. If you come to Recife at other times of the year, you can get a taste of the festivities by attending one of the weekly shows featuring **Galo da Madrugada** (Rua da Concórdia 984, São José, tel. 81/3224-2899, www.galodamadrugada.org.br, R$20) and musical guests, which take place beginning at 7pm most Thursday nights (Jan.-Feb. and Sept.-Dec.).

Shopping

Recife is a great place to load up on local *artesanato,* ranging from *literatura de cordel* and ceramics to leatherwork, embroidery, and lace. The **Mercado São José** (Praça Dom Vital, São José, tel. 81/3355-3398, 6am-5:30pm Mon.-Sat., 6am-noon Sun.) and the shops in the surrounding labyrinth of streets

have wonderful finds if you don't mind the fun of hunting around a bit. In Recife Antigo, check out the **Centro do Artesanato do Pernambuco** (Av. Alfredo Lisboa, tel. 81/3181-3450, www.artesanatodepernambuco.pe.gov.br, 2pm-8pm Mon., 9am-8pm Tues.-Sun.) and the lively outdoor **Feira de Artesanato** (Praça do Arsenal da Marinha, 2pm-8pm Sun.).

Overlooking the Rio Capibaribe, the **Shopping Paço Alfândega** (Rua da Alfândega 65, Recife Antigo, tel. 81/3194-2100, www.pacoalfandega.com.br, 10am-10pm Mon.-Sat., noon-9pm Sun.) is a former convent and customhouse that now houses a designer shopping center filled with cool boutiques, cafés, and restaurants. Overlooking a branch of Rio Capibaribe, in Pina, Recife's swankiest *shopping* is **Shopping RioMar** (Av. República do Líbano 251, Pina, tel. 81/3878-0000, www.riomarrecife.com.br), a glitzy, mercifully air-conditioned mall frequented by local fashionistas. You can buy a bikini, take in a movie, or even go bowling.

Accommodations

Visitors to Recife have three options: staying in the Centro (cheap and well-located, but less safe at night), Boa Viagem (more secure and upscale—and bland—with beach access for which you'll pay a price), or across the bay in lovely Olinda (if you want immerse yourself in colonial atmosphere and charm).

SANTO ANTÔNIO, SÃO JOSÉ, AND BOA VISTA

Hotels in Centro tend to be geared toward not-so-well-heeled business travelers rather than tourists. Some are a little down and out, while others are sorely lacking in style. Most are concentrated in Boa Vista, which is where you'll find one of the nicer bets, the **Pousada Vila Boa Vista** (Rua Miguel Couto 81, Boa Vista, tel. 81/3223-0666, www.pousadavillaboavista.com.br, R$220-260 d). Rare among the city's hotels, it has the welcoming intimacy of an old country house, an atmosphere bolstered by the regional art and vast communal table where a typical breakfast banquet is served. Rooms are standard but clean and cheery. A courtyard garden and house plants prettify the proceedings. Although it has seen better days, the **Hotel Central** (Av. Manuel Borba 209, Boa Vista, tel. 81/3222-42353, R$145-175 d) is a good budget choice. Built in 1931, it was Recife's version of the Plaza as well as its first (eight-story!) skyscraper. In its heyday, guests included Orson Welles, Carmen Miranda, and Getúlio Vargas. Aside from fixtures and the cage-like elevator, not much of the glamour has survived, but the place is clean, cheap, and oozing with atmosphere.

BOA VIAGEM

Pousada Casuarinas (Rua Antônio Pedro Figueiredo 151, tel. 81/3325-7048, www.pousadacasuarinas.com.br, R$180-210 d) is a homey guesthouse set back from the beach. Run by a pair of friendly sisters, basic no-nonsense guest rooms (with or without verandas) are fairly pleasant, and a shady courtyard is outfitted with hammocks and a pool. Cheaper still is **Piratas da Praia Hostel** (Av. Conselheiro Aguiar 2034, 3rd floor, tel. 81/3326-1281, www.piratasdapraia.com, R$140-160 d, R$40-50 pp), probably the nicest and best located of Boa Viagem's hostels. Located just off the beach with scads of amenities, this backpacker mecca with a communal kitchen and rental bikes is located on the third floor of an elevator-less residential apartment building. Private rooms and small flats are available along with colorful but basic dorms.

Amidst Boa Viagem's overpriced high-rise hotels, one of the more styling options is **Beach Class Suites** (Av. Boa Viagem 1906, tel. 81/2121-2626, www.atlanticahotels.com.br, R$430-550 d). Perched on a prized stretch of Boa Viagem, this shiny tower is awash with light, from the sleekly polished lobby to the cool white guest rooms. There is silent air-conditioning and Wi-Fi in all guest rooms, and some have microwaves and coffeemakers. A pool, fitness room, and restaurant round out the amenities.

Food

Typical Pernambucano cuisine is an intoxicating mixture of indigenous, African, and European (mainly Portuguese and Spanish) influences. Along the coast, dishes such as *peixada* and *moqueca* feature fish and seafood in stews that are seasoned with cilantro, lime, and coconut milk. From the interior come robust dishes such as *carne-de-sol* (sun-dried beef) and *bode assado* (roasted goat), cooked with *macaxeira* (manioc) and beans. Ubiquitous throughout Pernambuco are *frango à cabidela* (chicken cooked in a fragrant sauce of its own blood) and *feijoada pernambucana,* which distinguishes itself from *feijoadas* in the rest of Brazil by the rare appearance of vegetables among the obligatory beans and meat. And then there are the desserts: simple but inspired creations such as tangy *coalho* cheese dripping with *mel de engenho* (sugarcane molasses) and *cartola,* in which a fried banana is topped with creamy Sertanejo cheese and a dusting of sugar and cinnamon. You can savor all of these specialties in Recife, along with some outstanding contemporary cuisine dreamed up by a few of the most daring young chefs on the Brazilian restaurant scene.

RECIFE ANTIGO

You can't get more Recifense than having lunch or a late-afternoon drink on the actual reef that inspired the city's name. Take the boat (10 min. R$10) from Marco Zero (or get a cab to take you via the *bairro* of Brasília Teimosa) to the **Casa de Banhos** (Arrecifes do Porto do Recife, tel. 81/3075-8776, 11am-4pm Wed.-Thurs., 11am-6pm Fri.-Sun. May-Aug.; 11am-5pm Tues.-Thurs., 11am-7pm Fri.-Sun. Sept.-Apr., R$20-30), a former 19th century bath house. Today it is a restaurant-bar with exceptional views of Recife and a small seafood menu of dishes such as *peixada* and shrimp in mango sauce.

Sentimental Recifenses love **As Galerias** (Rua da Guia 183, 8am-10pm Mon.-Fri., 2pm-10pm Sat.-Sun.), a fixture since 1928, as much as first-time tourists do. While gringos are bedazzled by the variety of juices made from exotic fruits such as *graviola* and *acerola,* locals swear by a frothy concoction known as the *maltado,* a revisited American milk shake that, along with baked goods such as peanut and cashew cake, tastes of childhood. On weekends, the place functions as a bar.

SANTO ANTÔNIO, SÃO JOSÉ, AND BOA VISTA

The oldest restaurant in operation in Brazil, ★ **Leite** (Praça Joaquim Nabuco 147, Santo Antônio, www.restauranteleite.com.br, tel. 81/3324-7997, 11:30am-3:30pm Sun.-Fri., R$45-55) has been around since 1882. Although the service is old-school impeccable and the decor is classically refined (all polished wood and linen table cloths), such staying power is ultimately explained by the food: international fare with a strong Portuguese influence that results in specialties such as *frutas do mar gratinadas* (shrimp, langoustine, octopus, and fish bathed in olive oil, white wine, and herbs) and various forms of *bacalhau* (salted cod). The *cartola* is considered to be the best in town. Following in the footsteps of Juscelino Kubitschek and Jean-Paul Sartre, this is a favorite pilgrimage of politicos, business execs, and visiting celebs.

Situated on the lively Pátio de São Pedro, **O Buraquinho** (Pátio de São Pedro 28, Santo Antônio, tel. 81/3224-6431, 11am-3pm daily, R$10-15) is a traditional favorite for inexpensive "popular" dishes such as *feijoada* and *carne-de-sol* served with manioc puree, beans, rice, and fresh corn. Enormous portions can feed three.

PINA

This tiny beach neighborhood has an assortment of restaurants and bars, and comes to life at night. Considered the finest Italian restaurant in town, **Vittorina Pomodoro Café** (Rua Capitão Rebelinho 418, tel. 81/3326-6023, www.pomodorocafe.com.br, 7pm-midnight Mon.-Thurs., 7pm-1am Fri.-Sat.,

noon-3:30pm and 7pm-10:30pm Sun., R$35-50) is a charmingly unpretentious trattoria. It's presided over by hot local chef Duca Lapenda, who has a knack for creatively revisiting classic cantina dishes. The homemade pastas are particularly outstanding.

Severino Reis worked his way up from dishwasher to owner of **Pra Vocês** (Av. Herculano Bandeira 115, tel. 81/3326-3168, 11am-midnight daily, R$25-35), one of the most traditional seafood restaurant-bars in the city. The menu ranges from simple fare such as fried *agulinhas* (sardine-size swordfish) to lobster in coconut sauce. The *peixadas* (fish stews) are legendary. Outside tables are great for icy beer and snacks.

One of the perennially popular gay, lesbian, and hipster hangouts in town, **Anjo Solto** (Av. Herculano Bandeira 513, Loja 14-A, tel. 81/3325-0862, www.anjosolto.com.br, 5:30pm-close daily, R$20-30) seduces not just with its intimate quintet of discreetly lit spaces (which include a wine bar), but with its outstanding crepes. The menu features close to 100 of them—all named after friends and faithful clients—in versions both sweet and savory. There are also terrific salads and some wildly inventive house cocktails.

BOA VIAGEM

Boa Viagem has the most varied and cosmopolitan eating options, but due to the flashiness of the 'hood, the prices tend to be higher as well.

Refined, unpretentious, and beautifully decorated **Nez Bistrô** (Rua Amazonas 40, tel. 81/3032-08488, www.nezbistro.com.br, 6:30pm-midnight Mon.-Sat., noon-4pm Fri.-Sat., R$50-70) specializes in meticulously prepared contemporary fare that draws ingeniously on French and Italian influences. Typical entrees include cannelloni stuffed with guinea hen and mushrooms, while bananas stuffed with banana sorbet, cheese crumble, and cinnamon meringues are an irresistible dessert. The wine list is more than decent, as is the service.

If you don't have time to travel into

Pernambuco's interior, you can get a taste of it at **Parraxaxá** (Av. Fernando Simões Barbosa 1200, tel. 81/3463-7874, www.parraxaxa.com. br, 11:30am-11pm daily, R$20-30), whose dining area is decked out to look like a typical country house from the Sertão. The decor is appealing (if a little overdone—and the waiters dressed like the outlaw Lampião are a tad goofy), but the real attraction is the per-kilo buffet that allows you to sample every type of Sertanejo dish under the blazing sun—from grilled *bode* and *carne-de-sol* to *baião-de-dois* (a mixture of beans and *coalho* cheese) and fried, pureed, and boiled manioc. Don't miss the weekend breakfast buffet with *tapiocas,* umpteen loaves and cakes, and *café* with *leite* from a nearby farm.

Those with a fondness for sweets will be sorely tempted by Pernambuco's sugary specialties. Two particular favorites are *bolo Sousa Leão,* a cake made with manioc flour, eggs, and coconut milk and topped with a warm sugar syrup, and *bolo-de-rolo,* in which spiraled layers of soft cake are lined with creamy guava paste. The best place to sink your teeth into these and many other delicacies is at **Casa dos Frios** (Av. Engenheiro Domingos Ferreira 1920, tel. 81/3327-0612, www.casadosfrios.com.br, noon-11pm Mon.-Wed., noon-midnight Thurs.-Sat.). Recife's most traditional (and most swanky) delicatessen, it has been around since 1957 (the original deli is in the *bairro* of Graças). There is also a small (and rather pricy) restaurant, and its state-of-the-art wine cellar is the best in the city. You can buy a bottle and then drink it at one of the tables in the cellar itself. If the climate-controlled atmosphere gives you goose bumps, the waiter will cover you with a woolen wrap.

A healthier way to beat the heat is to head to **Usina de Força** (Av. Conselheiro Aguiar 3553, Galeria Alameda Center, tel. 81/3463-7136, 10am-11pm Mon.-Sat., 4pm-11pm Sun.). Boa Viagem's favorite juice bar serves up more than 30 varieties of *suco* made from fruit delivered fresh every day. For extra sustenance, there are healthy sandwiches.

Information and Services

Tourist offices are located throughout the city. Aside from the airport (tel. 81/3355-0128, 7am-11pm daily) and the main TIP bus terminal (tel. 81/3182-8298, 7am-7pm daily), you'll find branches in Boa Viagem (Praça Boa Viagem, tel. 81/3182-8297, 8am-8pm daily) and in Recife Antigo (Praça Arsenal da Marinha, tel. 81/3355-3402, 8:30am-8:30pm daily). Online, www.recifeguide.com is an English-language guide to the city, while www.pernambuco.com/turismo is a good source of information in Portuguese.

There are plenty of **banks** with ATMs—including Banco do Brasil branches in Santo Antônio (Av. Dantas Barreto 451), in Boa Vista (Rua Sete de Setembro 128), and in Boa Viagem (Rua Barão de Souza Leão 440). Also try the main *shoppings.* The main **post office** is in Santo Antônio (Av. Guararapes 250).

In the event of an emergency, dial **193** for an ambulance or the fire department, or **190** for the police. There is a special tourist police (tel. 81/3322-4088) unit at the airport. For medical treatment try the **Centro Hospitalar Albert Sabin** (Rua Senador José Henrique 141, Ilha do Leite, tel. 81/3131-7400, www.hospitalalbertsabin.com.br).

Transportation
AIR

Recife's **Aeroporto Internacional dos Guararapes** (Praça Ministro Salgado Filho, Imbiribeira, tel. 81/3464-4188, www.aeroportorecife.net) is at the far end of Boa Viagem, conveniently close to beach hotels; it is about 12 kilometers (7.5 mi) south of the city center and just a few kilometers from the beachside hotels in Boa Viagem. A taxi to Boa Viagem will cost around R$30, while one to Olinda will set you back around R$70. Municipal buses—both the more circuitous 040 executivo bus, which departs from the arrivals terminal, and the more direct 042 bus that passes by the stop on Av. Mascarenhas de Morais—go from the airport through Boa Viagem (one block behind the beach) on their way to Avenida Dantas Barreto in the center of town. Another option is to take the Metrô from the Aeroporto station to Recife station in Santo Antônio.

BUS

Buses arrive at the **Terminal Integrado de Passageiros** (TIP; Rodovia BR-232 Km 15, Curado, tel. 81/3452-9400, http://rodorecife. blogspot.com.br), 14 kilometers (8.5 mi) from the center. The Metrô—via the *rodoviária* station—links the TIP with Centro (get off at Recife station) and Boa Viagem (buy an *integração 1* ticket, which will allow you to get off at Joana Bezerra station and transfer to a Boa Viagem-bound bus). A taxi from the TIP to Centro will cost around R$40 and R$60 to Boa Viagem.

By day, taking buses between Santo Antônio and Boa Viagem, and from both of these neighborhoods to Olinda, is fairly straightforward; visit www.granderecife. pe.gov.br for specific itineraries. From the Terminal Cais de Santa Rita municipal bus station (in São José) to Boa Viagem (with stops along Av. Engenheiro Domingos Ferreira), take any bus marked Boa Viagem, Aeroporto, or Iguatemi. From Boa Viagem (with stops along Av. Conselheiro Aguilar) to the center, grab any bus going to Conde da Boa Vista or Terminal Cais de Santa Rita. Bus fare is R$2.15. The gradually expanding Metrô (R$1.60) is useful for getting to and from the bus station and the airport, but that's about it.

TAXIS

Taxis are a great idea, especially at night. Flag them down in the street or call **Tele-Taxi** (tel. 81/2121-4242) or **DiskTaxi** (tel. 81/3419-9595). Renting a car is not a great idea due to traffic and security; but to hit the beaches north or south of town, rent a car from **Avis** (tel. 81/3322-4016, www.avis.com.br) or **Hertz** (tel. 81/3338-2102, www.hertz.com.br); both have offices at the airport.

CITY TOURS

Take advantage of Recife's scenic waterways with a tour along its rivers. **Catamaran Tours** (tel. 81/3424-2845, www.catamaran-tours.com.br, R$40) runs hour-long tours in the afternoon (4pm) and evening (8pm) in comfortable catamarans that drift by the city's major historic attractions. Expeditions up and down the coast, such as to Ilha da Itamaracá and Praia dos Carneiros, are available. Departures are from the quays at Cinco Pontas.

★ OLINDA

Pernambuco's original capital is a baroque treasure and one of the highlights of the Northeast. Perched on a series of green hills overlooking the sea (and the disparately modern sprawl of Recife), the colonial town is home to nuns and monks, artists and expats, bohemians, and, understandably, a steady (but not overwhelming) stream of tourists. While the lower, modern "Novo Olinda" has grown into a none-too-attractive (and unsafe) extension of Recife, the historic center—declared a World Cultural Heritage Site by UNESCO—offers a captivating mix of churches, artists' ateliers, boutiques, bars, and restaurants.

Sights

Olinda's main attractions are clustered together in its *centro histórico*. Although the area is compact, visiting involves climbing some steep but picturesque cobblestoned streets (the payoff is in the views from the summits). Thanks in part to a large artist population, Olinda's historic quarter is an authentic neighborhood where locals work, play, and contribute to the city's rich cultural life.

CHURCHES

Olinda is famed for is its stunning collection of baroque churches—18 of them—scattered among several hills. Although many were originally constructed in the 1500s, when the Dutch invaded Olinda in 1630, most were torched to the ground. Those you see today are the results of reconstructions undertaken by the Portuguese in the 17th and 18th centuries. Opening hours are notoriously erratic, so take the hours listed below with a grain of salt.

Olinda

Map labels: OFICINA DO SABOR, IGREJA N S DO AMPARO, POUSADA DO AMPARO, AMPARO, MUSEU REGIONAL, BODEGA DE VEIO, IGREJA N S DA MISERICÓRDIA, LICOTERIA NOCTIVAGOS, CASA DOS BONECOS, MUSEU DE ARTE SACRA, PATUÁ, POUSADA DOS QUATRO CANTOS, DON FRANCESCO, ALTO DA SÉ, Horto d'El Rey, MUSEU DE ARTE CONTEMPORÂNEA, SKINA DO SABOR, CATEDRAL DA SÉ, MUSEU DO MAMULENGO, PALÁCIO DOS GOVERNADORES, TRAVESSA DE SÃO FRANCISCO, CREPERIA, MAISON DO BONFIM, HOTEL 7 COLINAS, CONVENTO DE SÃO FRANCISCO, Praça Monsenhor Fabrício, TOURIST INFORMATION, CARMO, Praça da Abolição, MOSTEIRO DE SÃO BENTO, VARADOURO, POUSADA SÃO FRANCISCO, XINXIM DA BAIANA, OLINDAPART, IGREJA DE N S DO CARMO, RUA DO SOL, MILAGRES, Praça Rio Branco (Jacaré), RUA MANOEL BORBA, AV BEIRA MAR, To Recife, Praia do Carmo, To Itamaracá and Maria Farinha, Praia dos Milagres, ATLANTIC OCEAN, © AVALON TRAVEL, 0 200 yds, 0 200 m

You can survey most of churches from the loftiest *praça* in the city, the **Alto da Sé,** which offers bewitching views of white towers and red tiled roofs nestled in a tangle of palms and set against a backdrop of blue-green ocean and Recife's glimmering skyline. Alto da Sé is a lively place with a daily and somewhat touristy arts and crafts market. The square is dominated by Olinda's main church, the **Catedral da Sé** (Alto da Sé, 8am-noon and 2pm-5pm daily). The original church, built in 1540 out of wood and palm thatching, was the first ever constructed in Brazil.

What you see today is the reconstructed version from the 17th century. Less ornate than some of the town's other churches, it possesses some attractive azulejo decorative panels, but its most striking feature is the postcard-perfect views of Olinda's other churches from the patio.

A church that is sure to catch your eye is the spectacular **Convento de São Francisco** (Rua de São Francisco 280, tel. 81/3429-0517, 9am-noon and 2pm-5:30pm Mon.-Fri., 9am-noon and 2pm-4:30pm Sat., R$3), Brazil's oldest Franciscan convent, dating to 1577. The buildings, only partially destroyed by the Dutch, are awash in beautiful azulejo murals. Those paneling the cloisters portraying the life and death of Saint Francis in tones of blue, yellow, and red are particularly striking. Other highlights include the ornately carved jacaranda furnishings in the sacristy and the exquisitely painted ceiling frescoes in the church. The cross in front of the convent is made of pulverized coral from local reefs. Equally splendid is the **Igreja e Mosteiro de São Bento** (Rua de São Bento, tel. 81/3316-3290, 6:30am-11:30am and 2pm-6:30pm daily), which dates to 1582. From the outside, the monastery is striking, with swaying palms adding tropical flourishes to the more austere bleached baroque facade. The main altar is exquisitely carved cedar doused in gold, and the sacristy is richly outfitted with gold leaf, crystal mirrors, and panels depicting the life of Saint Benedict. Show up at Sunday mass from 10am-noon to hear Gregorian chants.

A particularly steep climb will bring you to the **Igreja de Nossa Senhora da Misericórdia** (Largo da Misericórdia, tel. 81/3494-9100, open daily), whose delicately sculpted altars, ornamented in gold leaf, and clever trompe l'oeil paintings are particularly

sumptuous examples of Brazilian rococo. Visiting hours coincide with mass (6:30am Mon.-Sat., 7:30am Sun.) and prayers (11:30am and 5pm daily) of the Benedictine nuns; silence is a must. The captivating **Igreja de Nossa Senhora do Amparo** (Largo do Amparo) was originally built as a place of worship for single men and musicians in the 1550s, which explains the painted panels to the right of the main altar, depicting the life of Saint Cecilia, patron saint of musicians. The twisting gold-doused columns, ornate altars, religious paintings, and French and Portuguese tile work are all superb. Visits are only possible during Sunday mass (10am-11:30am).

Less splendid, but also noteworthy, are the atmospheric **Igreja de Nossa Senhora do Carmo** (Praça do Carmo, 8am-5pm Mon.-Sat.), the oldest Carmelite church in Brazil, and the **Igreja de Nossa Senhora do Monte** (Praça Nossa Senhora do Monte, tel. 81/3429-0317, 9am-11am and 2:30pm-5pm daily). Built in 1540, the latter survived the Dutch invasion largely intact. It has been a refuge for Benedictine monks since the 16th century, and 30 monks still reside here; you can hear them singing at 5pm daily.

Convento de São Francisco, Olinda

Olinda

MUSEUMS

Housed in a 17th-century building that formerly served as a bishop's palace, a nunnery, and city hall, the **Museu de Arte Sacra de Pernambuco** (Rua Bispo Coutinho 726, tel. 81/3184-3154, 10am-4pm Mon.-Fri., 10am-2pm Sat.-Sun., R$2) shelters a fine collection of religious art from throughout the state dating from the 16th to the 20th centuries. Particularly fascinating is the collection of regional folk art: Note the manger with baby Jesus asleep in a hammock, Mary and Joseph as *mulatos,* and the presence of local legends such as the outlaw Lampião.

The **Museu Regional de Olinda** (Rua do Amparo 128, tel. 81/3184-3159, 8am-1pm and 2pm-5pm Tues.-Fri., R$2) offers a glimpse into Olinda's glorious past, mainly via an opulent array of jacaranda furniture, imported Baccarat crystal, and English porcelain that attests to the lush life derived from sugarcane cultivation—if you had the luck to be a planter and not a slave. The **Museu de Arte Contemporânea** (Rua 13 de Maio 128, tel.

81/3184-3153, 9am-5pm Tues.-Sun., R$5) occupies an 18th-century public jail, with a permanent (if piecemeal) collection of works in various media by modern and contemporary Brazilian artists as well as some engaging temporary exhibitions.

Pernambuco is famous for *mamulengo,* a form of popular theater in which expressive handmade puppets act out traditional folk tales, often based on *literatura de cordel.* Although many of the stories are slapstick, they also have a subversive political edge. They pit a cast of clever Indians, cunning Africans, and trickster peasants as well as animals and supernatural spirits against repressive authority figures such as wealthy landowners or military figures. Dramatic and comic moments are punctuated by dance and music (courtesy of *forró* musicians). The puppets themselves, made from wood and cloth, are quite wonderful. They can be viewed at the **Museu do Mamulengo** (Rua de São Bento 344, tel. 81/3493-2753, 9am-5pm Tues.-Sat., R$2), which has a vast collection of more than 1,200 puppets as well as a theater, the Espaço Tiridá, where performances are often held.

Nightlife

Olinda has a relaxed bohemian vibe that mixes artists, tourists, local residents, and Recifenses. Lots of bars are set up on sidewalks and in the lovely *praças,* and there are many hidden in private leafy gardens. Aside from Alto da Sé, there is also a good range of bars and musical venues along the beach. Music is literally in the streets, especially homegrown specialties such as *forró* and *maracatu.* Samba rehearsals (6pm-10pm Sun.) are held by the *bloco* Grêmio Preto Velho at their Alto da Sé headquarters. Saturday and Sunday in the late afternoon, you can catch *maracatu* at Praça do Carmo. And on the first Saturday of the month, don't miss the *sambada do coco* performed on the Largo da Igreja de Guadalupe.

Olinda's favorite neighborhood hangout, **Bodega de Veio** (Rua do Amparo 212, tel. 81/3429-0185, 9am-11pm Mon.-Sat.) is a simple family-run convenience store where locals go to buy their beans, rice, and *carne-de-sol,* and usually end up stopping off for a cool *cerveja.* The beer is cheap, and so are the portions of salami and *coalho* cheese. The vibe is laid-back and very friendly. On Thursday and Saturday nights, live *chorinho* is performed, and *forró* jams are frequent. **Licoteria Noctívagos** (Rua 13 de Maio 3, tel. 81/3439-6248, 5pm-close Thurs-Sun.) is a fine place to sample addictive homemade *licores* made from ingredients such as ginger or banana. Music is supplied by faithful clients who bring in their CDs or records. One of the cooler haunts in town, **Xinxím da Baiana** (Av. Sigismundo Gonçalves 742, Carmo, tel. 81/3439-8447, 7pm-close Tues.-Sun.) is owned by a Bahian couple, which explains the presence of *pesticos* such as *acarajé* on the menu. From Wednesday through Saturday, live performances of *forró,* soul, and national rock lure an alternative crowd intent on dancing up a storm.

Festivals and Events
CARNAVAL
Of all Brazil's major street **Carnavals** (www.carnaval.olinda.pe.gov.br), Olinda's is the most picturesque and the most democratic. There are no Sambódromos with costly seats, nor are there cordoned-off areas or bleachers that afford privileged access to samba schools and *blocos* while the poorer masses are crushed together on the sidelines. Olinda's highly colorful festivities draw people of all ages, colors, and inclinations together. The mass of merrymakers flood the lavishly decorated *praças* and narrow streets of the historic center to dance and weave among riotous *blocos* that blast the pulsing rhythms of *frevo,* samba, *afoxé,* and *maracatu.* Costumes are whimsical and outrageous and masks are de rigueur. Gigantic *bonecos* (dolls), representing folk heroes or political figures, are the trademark of Olinda's Carnaval. Made of papier-mâché and painted in festive colors, they go twirling and dancing through the streets along with the throngs.

Other highlights include the appearances of traditional *blocos* such as Elefante, Lenhadores, and Enquanto Isso na Sala da Justiça; the meeting of the dazzlingly costumed *maracatu* groups in the *bairro* of Cidade Tabajara (Mon.); and the always wildly attired transvestite groups. On the final day of festivities (Mardi Gras), the meeting of all the *bonecos,* some of which have been around since the 1930s, brings the celebrations to a close with much fanfare and *alegria.*

ARTE EM TODA PARTE
Olinda's prolific artists generally open the doors of their ateliers to the public during the last two weeks of November (though in 2013, the event occurred in May). Not only does this give you a privileged opportunity to view some (mostly) terrific art, but it also allows a rare glimpse into some wonderful historic houses.

SERESTA
Every Friday night, the members of Luar de Olinda (a group of singing Olindenses) wander the streets serenading their hearts out to people in windows, attracting a charmingly ragtag collection of tourists, kids, drunks, and beer vendors in their wake. The group departs (more or less) at 10pm from the Igreja de São Pedro and heads up Rua Prudente de Morais.

Shopping
Olinda is an excellent place to peruse and purchase both original works by local artists and regional crafts. The **Mercado da Ribeira** (Rua Bernardo Vieira de Melo, 9am-6pm daily) has a hit-and-miss mix of local handicrafts and also houses the **Casa das Bonecas,** where giant Carnaval dolls are stashed (somewhat eerily) when not in use. Around Alto da Sé, aside from vendors with kiosks, you'll find a pair of shops that specialize in quality *artesanato.* **Ecological** (Rua Bispo Coutinho 799, tel. 81/3429-1187, www.ecologicalartesanato.com) has a fine collection of woven and embroidered items and ceramics along with cotton T-shirts whose colors are derived from natural pigments.

Among the unique items at **Imaginário** (Rua Bispo Coutinho 814, tel. 81/3439-4514, www.imaginariobrasileiro.com) are wooden objects intricately adorned with hand-painted scenes by artist Geraldo Andrade. Check out **Período Fértil** (Rua 15 de Novembro 164, tel. 81/3439-8926, www.atelieperiodofertil.com) for cool clothing by young Olindense designers. **Ateliê da Barbearia** (Rua Sete de Setembro 109, tel. 81/9949-5147) is a multipurpose artistic-cultural space where you'll find a dreamy collection of delicately hand-embroidered pajamas and nightgowns, among other home-crafted creations. Simply wandering amid the dozens of galleries and ateliers is a pleasurable experience.

Accommodations

Although hotels in the modern Novo Olinda are cheaper, the area is soulless. Since you came to Olinda for the history, pay a little more and stay in the colonial center (good discounts in off-season). If you plan to be here during Carnaval, book months in advance.

Tucked behind the Igreja do Carmo, ★ **Olindapart** (Rua 10 de Novembro 90, tel. 81/3429-4183, olindapart.com, R$95-120 d) is the private home of a friendly local artist who rents a number of spacious, simple, and well-tended apartments for researchers, artists, and tourists on a long-term and daily basis. Excellent value accommodations include kitchenettes, breezy terraces, a garden where breakfast is served (and art films are screened), and an atelier where you can indulge your artistic inclinations. **Pousada São Francisco** (Rua do Sol 127, tel. 81/3429-2109, www.pousadasaofrancisco.com.br, R$235-285 d) is another decent bargain with tropical gardens and a nice-size pool. Although the red tile roofs and pastel hues reflect Olinda's colonial architecture, this hotel—a stone's throw from the Convento de São Francisco—is uninspiringly modern. Guest rooms are standard, but the walls are adorned with works by local artists; many are outfitted with balconies offering sweeping views toward Olinda or the sea.

Pousada dos Quatro Cantos (Rua Prudente dos Morais 441, tel. 81/3429-0220, www.pousada4cantos.com.br, R$200-280 d) is located in a vast 19th-century mansion that was formerly a posh weekend residence. Polished parquet floors, lofty ceilings, and eclectic, tasteful decor combined with welcoming staff and lavish breakfasts make you feel as if you're a privileged guest in a home. There is also a terrace pool.

Set amid the leafy gardens of a former sugarcane plantation, ★ **Hotel 7 Colinas** (Ladeira de São Francisco 307, tel. 81/3493-7766, www.hotel7colinas.com.br, R$290-380 d) offers a tranquil refuge after a day of steep cobblestoned streets. The pleasant, air-conditioned guest rooms have verandas that open onto the garden. Surrounded by tropical foliage is a beautiful pool, and the restaurant and bar areas are very attractive. Immerse yourself in the spirit of colonial Olinda at the **Pousada do Amparo** (Rua do Amparo 199, tel. 81/3439-1749, www.pousadadoamparo.com.br, R$260-480 d), whose apartments are distributed between adjoining 200-year-old buildings. Most are heavy on charm, with exposed beams and antique furnishings, while others are cramped (or noisy if they face the street). Choose with care: Those at the back are enchanting, overlooking a secluded garden pool and a sea of palms. The romantic **Restaurante Flor de Coco** serves delicious food.

Food

Olinda has a serious gastronomic scene, enhanced by the fact that many of its eateries occupy centuries-old colonial houses, many with palmy gardens. On the weekend, it is a favorite dining destination for Recifenses.

Patuá (Estrada do Bonsucesso 399, tel. 81/3055-0833, www.restaurantepatua.com.br, noon-3pm daily, 7pm-11pm Mon.-Sat., R$20-30) is a case in point. The menu features regional fare—fish, seafood, and *carne-de-sol*—with some unusual contemporary twists, including *pescada* fish in a shiitake cream served with crab risotto and flambéed banana. ★ **Oficina do Sabor** (Rua do Amparo 335, tel. 81/3429-3331, www.oficinadosabor.com, noon-4pm and 6pm-midnight Tues.-Fri., noon-1am Sat., noon-5pm Sun., R$35-50) is renowned for the preparation of Pernambucano culinary specialties with uncommon flair. *Carne-de-sol, macaxeira,* seafood, coconut milk, and fresh *feijão* are all flawlessly combined with local fruits and spices. If you can, grab a veranda table with spectacular panoramic views.

Maison do Bonfim (Rua do Bonfim 115, tel. 81/3429-1674, noon-4pm Tues.-Sat., 6pm-1am Mon. and Wed.-Sat., noon-9pm Sun., R$30-45) serves traditional French recipes, often livened with startling fusions of tropical fruit. Fish and seafood are especially tasty— the "bucket" of *moules marinières* (marinated mussels) is one of the best you'll taste this side of the Equator—and, *bien sûr,* the wine list is good. Delicious Italian food can be found at **Don Francesco** (Rua Prudente de Morais 358, tel. 81/3429-3852, noon-3pm and 6:30pm-11pm Mon.-Fri., 6:30pm-midnight Sat., 11:30am-4pm Sun., R$20-30), an intimate place with a terrace looking onto a back garden that supplies fresh herbs and vegetables for the kitchen. The Italian chef's homemade pastas, topped with the likes of organic pesto made with sheep ricotta, basil, and crushed Brazil nuts, are his forte.

For a light bite, **Creperia** (Praça Conselheiro João Alfredo 168, tel. 81/3429-2935, 11am-11pm daily, R$10-20) is a cozy option with works by local artists on the walls and a breezy outdoor terrace. Aside from a vast array of tasty crepes both savory and sweet (try the *Olinda,* filled with chocolate, bananas, ice cream, raisins, and rum), the menu features salads and crunchy thin-crust pizzas. For a more local version of a crepe, head to Alto da Sé, where, every day from morning to midnight, 30 *tapioqueiras* prepare *tapiocas,* made with crunchy manioc flour. The queen of them all is Tia Lu, who has been preparing this favorite snack for more than 40 years. The classic *tapioca* filling is freshly grated coconut and melted cheese,

but alternative (and more filling) variations abound, such as cheese mixed with *carne-de-sol,* shrimp, and even guava jelly. Don't leave town without a stop at **Skina do Sabor** (Rua Prudente de Morais 210, 11am-10pm daily) to sample the amazing *sorvete* made by Fri-Sabor, a Recife ice cream maker around since the 1950s. The *abacaxi vinho* (pineapple red wine) will blow you away.

Transportation and Services

The **tourist office** (Rua Prudente de Morais 472, tel. 81/3305-1060, www.olindaturismo.com.br, 9am-6pm daily), at Praça do Carmo, has free maps and lots of info. You can also visit www.olinda.pe.gov.br (in Portuguese). There are no banks in Olinda's historic center; the closest ATM is at the **Banco do Brasil** (Av. Getúlio Vargas 1470, Bairro Novo).

Olinda is basically a neighborhood of Recife. As such, municipal bus service (R$3.45) is very regular and quite fast (30 minutes from the center of Recife). The final stop is the terminal at Praça do Carmo, from where you can begin your ascent to the town's various colonial treasures. Buses depart from stops along Av. Conselheiro Aguiar in Boa Viagem and the Terminal Cais de Santa Rita municipal bus station in São José; from either, take any bus marked "Rio Doce" or "Casa Caiada." Springing for a taxi—essential at night—will set you back R$40 from Boa Viagem and R$70 from the airport.

INLAND FROM RECIFE

The major inland destination from Recife is the town of Caruaru, 135 kilometers (85 mi) from Recife. Lying on the edge of the Sertão, it contains the biggest open-air market in the Northeast, where you can find locally produced *artesanato.* As you head west from the palmy coastal region, the countryside begins to change. A series of undulating hills blanketed in jade green sugarcane offers a visual reminder of the crop that made Pernambuco so rich. Gradually, the lushness of the hills fades into sepia tones, giving way to a harsher landscape of ruddy brown earth populated by herds of cattle and fields of thorny *palma,* a type of cactus that serves as sustenance for both cattle and humans during the frequent droughts that plague the Sertão. This region, known as the *agreste,* gives you a foretaste of the Sertão itself, which begins after Caruaru and is much starker and more desertlike.

★ Caruaru

Famous throughout Brazil for its massive outdoor market, its animated Festa de São João, and its rich cultural and artistic traditions that reflect the vivid culture of the Sertão, Caruaru is definitely worth a day trip from Recife. If you hop an early bus from Recife, you have ample time to wander through the market, dawdle over lunch, and check out the ceramicists' ateliers at Alto do Moura.

SIGHTS

The highlight of a visit to Caruaru is the traditional **Feira de Caruaru** (Parque 18 de Maio, 6am-5pm daily). Seeming to engulf the entire town, this daily market lures buyers from all over the Northeast, who arrive to purchase everything from cheap clothing and made-in-China electronics to great creamy blocks of *coalho* cheese, bottles of herb-infused *cachaça,* and popular folk remedies to cure every ailment under the sun. The market is divided into sections; some are quite unusual. At the bird market, multicolored warblers (some of them illegal to sell) preen from hand-built wooden cages, while at the *troca-troca* market (*trocar* means "to swap" or "to exchange"), you'll encounter people bartering donkeys for bicycles and CDs for cooking gas. Tuesday is an especially big day due to the cattle market and Feira da Sulanca, a clothing bazaar that lures thousands of bargain hounds eager to swipe up articles for as little as R$1. Friday and Saturday are also packed. For visitors, the Feira de Artesanato is where you'll find a vast array of regional handicrafts made of everything from cotton and leather to polished coconut shells.

Although you can't purchase them, you'll definitely be impressed by the ceramic

figures, many by Mestre Vitalino, on display at the **Museu do Barro** (Praça Colonel José de Vasconcellos 100, Pátio de Eventos, tel. 81/3721-2545, 8am-5pm Tues.-Sat., 9am-1pm Sun., R$2). Along with other examples of traditional ceramic work and pottery from all over the Sertão, this museum houses one of the finest collections of folk art in Brazil. Next door, the small **Museu do Forró** pays homage to the Sertão's most famous musical style along with one of its greatest artists, Luiz Gonzaga.

FESTIVALS AND EVENTS

The interior's equivalent of Carnaval, **Festa de São João** takes place all over the Northeast, but the biggest and most legendary celebration takes place in Caruaru (although the town of Campina Grande, in neighboring Paraíba, begs to differ). Every night, square dances, known as *quadrilhas* (a descendant of the ballroom quadrilles popular in 19th-century France), bring together thousands who stomp and twirl and then refresh themselves at *barracas* serving typical food commemorating the harvest. Most delicacies are made with corn, including *pamonha,* a dense corn pudding, and *canjica,* a creamy dessert made with white corn. Streets are decorated with colorful paper banners and balloons, and residents dress up in country-style gear with lots of plaids, ginghams, and straw hats. Caruaru's Festa de São João is particularly famed for its *bandas de pifanos*—marching bands led by a fife (*pifano*) player, whose members don Napoleonic-style leather hats typical of the *cangaçeiro*).

Although the official Festa de São João festivities take place June 23-24, in Caruaru the whole month of June is one big São João celebration, with *forró* balls and feasting that lead up to the main event. If you plan to stay in town during this time, be warned you'll need to book accommodations far in advance.

ACCOMMODATIONS AND FOOD

Most people visit Caruaru as a very full day trip from Recife. If you want to soak up a little atmosphere and catch some nightly *forró*, consider checking into the **Hotel Central** (Rua Vigário Freire, Centro, tel. 81/3721-5880, www.citihoteis.com.br, R$110-130 d), which, as its name implies, has the advantage of being quite central (other hotels are closer to the bus station). Recently renovated, air-conditioned guest rooms are fairly basic but sizable, and breakfasts feature lots of regional goodies. During São João, prices multiply fivefold.

To sample regional cuisine, try **Bar da Perua** (Rua Aliança 105, Boa Vista, tel. 81/3722-3266, 11am-4pm daily, R$15-25), where you can stuff yourself on roasted *bode, carne-de-sol,* and *galinha ao molho pardo* (chicken cooked in its own blood). For a drink or a snack, the Feira de Caruaru has a whole section of *barracas* where you can sample local fare ranging from *carne-de-sol* with *macaxeira* (pureed manioc) to sweeter options such as *pamonha* and *arroz doce* (rice pudding). This is a lively place to hang out and have a beer or *cachaça* while listening to local *forró* musicians jamming. You'll often here *repentistas* as well—northeastern troubadours who make their living singing verses of poetry, which they wittily improvise on the spot.

TRANSPORTATION AND SERVICES
In Caruaru, the **tourist office** (Praça Colonel José de Vasconcelos 100, tel. 81/3723-4010, 8am-1pm Mon.-Fri.) is centrally located. Online, check out www.caruaru.com.br.

Although the *rodoviária* (Av. José Pinheiros dos Santos, tel. 81/3721-1930) is on the outskirts of town, on the road to Alto da Moura, all buses make stops in the center. From Recife, **Progresso** (tel. 81/2121-9000, www.progressoonline.com.br) offers bus service to Caruaru (2 hours, R$24) with departures every 60-90 minutes; the ride includes a stop in Bezerros. If you're driving, follow BR-232.

One option is to take an organized day trip from Recife. **Luck Viagens** (tel. 81/3366-6222, www.luckviagens.com.br, R$130 pp) runs trips to Caruaru that include a visit to the market and the ateliers in Alto do Moura,

with time out for an atmospheric lunch in Nova Jerusalém.

Around Caruaru
ALTO DO MOURA
Only 6 kilometers (4 mi) from Caruaru is the village of Alto do Moura (www.altodomoura.com), whose claim to fame is being the hometown of Mestre Vitalino (1909-1963). The main street is named after him, and the first house on the left, the **Casa de Mestre Vitalino** (Rua Mestre Vitalino, tel. 81/3725-0805, 8am-noon and 2pm-5pm Mon.-Sat., 9am-5pm Sun.), has been converted into a small museum where you can view the artist's home with his personal objects and *figurinhas de barro* (clay figures). Reproductions of his clay figurines, produced by his son Severino, are for sale. Many of the humble houses along Rua Mestre Vitalino are also ceramics studios; some are operated by Mestre Vitalino's talented children and grandchildren (his granddaughter Marliete makes miraculous miniature figures).

For a meal in Alto do Moura, *bode* is the undisputed specialty at **Bode Assado do Luciano** (Rua Mestre Vitalino 511, tel. 81/3722-0413, 11am-4pm Tues.-Fri., 11am-6pm Sat.-Sun., R$15-25). To get here from Caruaru, take a taxi (around R$25) or *moto-taxi* or hop the "Alto do Moura" bus (R$2) on Rua Duque de Caixias, in front of the Catedral Nossa Senhora das Dores.

BEZERROS
Woodcuts are the other major type of *artesanato* that is synonymous with the Pernambucano Sertão. An ancient Chinese tradition, this art arrived in the Northeast in the 19th century as a means to illustrate the little booklets of stories known as *literatura de cordel*. Famous for its woodcut traditions is the small town of Bezerros (www.bezerrosonline.com), located 25 kilometers (16 mi) from Caruaru along BR-232, which leads to Recife. Renowned throughout Brazil, the town's most famous printer is J. Borges, whose bold, expressive illustrations constitute mini portraits

of Sertanejo life. You can view (and purchase, for ridiculously low prices) his works printed on paper, ceramic tiles, and even T-shirts at his atelier, the **Memorial J. Borges** (BR-232 Km 99, tel. 81/3728-0364, 7am-11am and 1pm-5pm Mon.-Fri., 7am-noon Sat.); a whole section is devoted to *literatura de cordel*.

For a terrific overview of popular art from all over the state, visit the **Centro de Artesanato de Pernambuco** (BR-232 Km 107, tel. 81/3728-2094, www.artesanatodepernambuco.pe.gov.br, 9am-6pm Tues.-Sat., 9am-1pm Sun., R$2), which contains a boutique. Among the many objects on view are colorful papier-mâché Carnaval masks; see even more of them at the **Casa de Cultura Popular Lula Vassoureiro** (Rua Otávia Bezerra Vila Nova 64, tel. 81/9102-0665, 8am-noon and 1pm-4pm daily), a museum and atelier operated by Lula Vassoureiro, who has been making masks since he was eight years old.

SOUTH OF RECIFE

The beautiful coral-lined beaches south of Recife are some of the finest in the Northeast. Stretching from Cabo de Santo Agostinho to Tamandaré, 113 kilometers (70 mi) from the capital, this coastline, nicknamed the Costa dos Arrecifes (Coast of Reefs), can be explored in day trips from Recife or by checking into a rustic beachfront *pousada* or a more comfortable Porto de Galinhas resort.

Cabo de Santo Agostinho

Only 33 kilometers (21 mi) from Recife, Cabo de Santo Agostinho consists of three main seaside villages. **Gaibu** is an overly popular resort with lots of palms and sand and tons of mellow beach bars framed by rocky hills. While the rough waves—great for surfing—are dangerous, there is a calmer area that's more propitious for bathing. For a seafood lunch, **Opará** (Av. Beira-Mar 79, tel. 81/3512-0954, 11am-10pm Mon.-Sat., 8am-4pm Sun., R$20-30) is highly recommended. Prettier and more deserted is the small crescent-shaped bay of **Praia de Calhetas.** Framed by a dramatic backdrop of primitive boulders

sprouting lush vegetation, it is 3 kilometers (2 mi) from Gaibu. The beach hot spot is **Bar do Artur** (Rua dos Carneiros 17, tel. 81/3522-6382, 10am-6pm daily, R$20-30), where you can feast on *peixada* and *lagosta na telha* (lobster grilled on a ceramic tile). For more information on Cabo de Santo Agostinho and photos, visit www.cabo.pe.gov.br.

TRANSPORTATION

Cruzeiro (tel. 81/2101-9037, R$6-10) offers frequent daily buses to the bus terminal in Cabo (some continue onto Porto de Galinhas) departing from Recife's Terminal Cais de Santa Rita and passing through Boa Viagem (along Av. Domingos Ferreira); from Cabo's terminal you can transfer to buses to Gaibu, Calhetas, and other beaches. By car, follow BR-101 and then PE-060. From Recife, many hotels and travel agencies offer day trips to Gaibu and Calhetas.

Porto de Galinhas

Porto de Galinhas's beaches are so enticing, it's no wonder it has turned into a destination renowned throughout Brazil for its soft white sands and warm natural pools that you could easily float in for a week. Dangerously popular and increasingly (over)developed, this former fishing village is nicer in off-season (at least during the week—on weekends, it is still mobbed by Recifenses). Coral reefs off the coast are ideal for snorkeling and diving. Within close proximity of Porto are the somewhat more tranquil beaches of Maracaípe, famed for its surfing, and Serrambi, with placid waters for bathing, both to the south. To the north are Cupe and Muro Alto, which are lined with hotels and resorts.

SPORTS AND RECREATION

The thing to do in Porto de Galinhas is simply to float in the warm, bath-like water. To get out close to the reef, hire a *jangada*. In the busiest times, you'll often have to line up to do so—and the reefs themselves can get ridiculously packed. A one-hour trip costs R$15 and includes a mask and fish food.

Most *pousadas* and hotels can organize trips by *jangada* and dune buggy to nearby beaches such as Praia de Serrambi and Praia de Muro Alto (a three-hour buggy trip costs around R$160 for up to four people) as well as Praia dos Carneiros (R$170). Buggies depart at 8am from the **Associação dos Bugueiros** (Rua da Esperança, Centro, tel. 81/3552-1930).

Snorkeling outings are popular. Aside from Porto de Galinhas, there are plenty of underwater attractions off the more tranquil reefs of Maracaípi and those surrounding **Ilha de Santo Aleixo,** an island with fabulous deserted beaches that can be reached by *jangada,* boat, or catamaran. **Cavalo Marinho** (tel. 81/3552-2180, www.catamaracavalomarinho.com.br) charges R$100 (including lunch) for a six-hour outing on a big, super-modern catamaran that includes stops at Ilha de Santo Aleixo, Praia dos Carneiros, and the mangroves of Rio Formoso. You can also take a *jangada* trip (R$10) through the mangroves around **Pontal de Maracaípe,** where you may catch a glimpse of extremely rare Brazilian sea horses frolicking in their native habitat. You'll see them for sure in the aquariums at the **Projeto Hipocampo** (Rua da Esperança 700, tel. 81/3552-2191, www.projetohippocampus.org, 9am-1pm and 2:30pm-5pm Tues.-Sun., R$4), a reserve dedicated to studying and protecting these mythical-looking creatures.

ACCOMMODATIONS

Porto de Galinhas accommodations options range from five-star, all-inclusive megaresorts (most of them on the beaches of Cupe and Muro Alto) to more basic small and medium-sized *pousadas* near the bustle of Centro. Surfer-friendly eco-offerings can be found on Maracaípe. Prices rise significantly during high season, sometimes by up to 50 percent.

Station yourself right in the middle of Porto at fetching budget option **Pousada Porto Verde** (Praça 1, Porto de Galinhas, tel. 81/3552-1410, www.pousadaportoverde.com.br, R$145-155 d). The clean, basic, and warmly outfitted guest rooms overlook a tropical garden with a pool and attention-seeking cats. A friendly, homey atmosphere reigns. Slightly removed from the village but right on a fabulous stretch of beach, **Pousada Canto do Porto** (Av. Beira Mar, Praia de Porto de Galinhas, tel. 81/3552-2165, www.pousadacantodoporto.com.br, R$150-250 d) offers a variety of attractive accommodations. The best are the deluxe beach bungalows with wraparound verandas, where the ocean is a major part of the decor. Though considerably smaller, the "economic" apartments aren't bad, though they have neither verandas nor nice views. Bonuses include a vast lawn sprinkled with chaise longues and a restaurant.

Around 6 kilometers (4 mi) north of Porto along PE-009, the **Pousada Tabapitanga** (Praia do Cupe, tel. 81/3352-1037, www.tabapitanga.com.br, R$280-510 d) sets itself apart from the more aggressive Club Med-style resorts. Large bungalows are decked out with natural fibers, wood, and even seashells and furnished with king beds and hammock-strung verandas. A lavish breakfast features regional food. Lunch and dinner are also available, as are *caipifrutas,* served on the beach or around the gorgeous pool.

Only 4 kilometers (2.5 mi) south of Porto de Galinhas, access by a dirt road has ensured Praia de Maracaípe's semiseclusion, although there are a handful of attractive bars and restaurants. The **Pousada Maracabana** (Av. Beira Mar, tel. 81/3552-3417, www.maracabana.com.br, R$180-330 d) plays up the getaway factor, with spotless, tastefully furnished apartments with full or partial sea views. Hammocks and beach chairs make it easy to flake out, as do the swimming pools.

FOOD

Considered one of the finest restaurants in the region, ★ **Beijupirá** (Rua Beijupirá, Vila, tel. 81/3552-2354, www.beijupira.com.br, noon-midnight daily, R$40-60)—named after a delicious local fish—is also one of the most romantic, especially after dusk when lanterns glow and hundreds of candles are lit. Don't be alarmed if you can't find the items listed on the menu in your pocket dictionary; the hybrid names are as creative as the dishes themselves, which mix fish, seafood, and meat with tropical fruits.

For a meal with a view, head to **Peixe na Telha** (Av. Beira-Mar 40B, Praia de Porto de Galinhas, tel. 81/3552-1877, 10am-4:30pm and 6:30pm-10pm daily, R$25-40), whose patio faces right onto the beach. While admiring the bright sails of the *jangadas,* you can down a beer or dig into copious fish and shrimp *moquecas.* The house specialty, *peixe na telha,* consists of fish grilled on a red roof tile. Portions are monstrous, serving two or even three. **Barcaxeira** (Rua da Esperança at the corner of Rua das Piscinas Naturais, Vila, tel. 81/3552-1913, www.barcaxeira.com.br, noon-midnight daily, R$15-25) is a brightly hued, kid-friendly bar that serves eight varieties of *escondidinhos,* a Northeastern specialty in which a blanket of pureed and gratineed manioc hides (*esconde*) delicacies ranging from classic *carne de sol* to shrimp.

TRANSPORTATION AND SERVICES

The **tourist office** (Rua Beijupirá, tel. 81/3552-1728, noon-6pm Mon., noon-8pm Tues.-Fri., 2pm-7pm Sat., 9am-noon Sun.) is easy to find. You can also visit www.

portodegalinhas.com.br. You'll find ATMs at the Banco do Brasil (Vila Porto de Galinhas) and the Banco 24 Horas inside the Petrobras gas station on Rua da Esperança.

Porto de Galinhas is 70 kilometers (43 mi) south of Recife. During the day and early evening, **Cruzeiro** (tel. 81/2101-9000) buses leave hourly from Recife's **Terminal Cais de Santa Rita,** via Boa Viagem (along Av. Domingos Ferreira) and the airport. The trip takes two hours and costs R$11. You can cut your time in half if you take a taxi from the airport or downtown (you should be able to bargain a price of around R$120 for up to four people—paying by the meter will cost far more). If you rent a car, follow BR-101, PE-060, and then PE-038 to Porto de Galinhas (on weekends, traffic can be heavy).

Visiting surrounding beaches from Porto de Galinhas is easy. Minivans (R$2) leave from the Petrobras gas station on the corner of PE-009 and Rua Esperança for Praia Maracaípe at 15- to 30-minute intervals, stopping at *pousadas* along the way. Grab a *moto-taxi* (R$5) or dune buggy taxi (R$20) to Cupe, Maracaípe, and other beaches.

★ Praia dos Carneiros

The remote beach of Praia dos Carneiros lies

church of São Benedito, Praia dos Carneiros

hidden amidst mangroves and a preserved tropical forest, 8 kilometers (5 mi) north of the bustling beach town of Tamandaré. Far more secluded than Porto de Galinhas (60 km, 37 mi) to the north, its unspoiled beaches are lined with coconut palms. For utter respite, this is the place. The only decision you'll have to make is whether to float in turquoise sea pools or the equally lulling green waters of the Rio Ariquindá.

SPORTS AND RECREATION

You probably won't want to do much of anything in Carneiros, but it's worthwhile to take the two-hour boat trip that departs in the mornings from the Bora Bora or Sítio da Prainha beach bars here. The trip takes you to Praia de Guadalupe, where you can rub exfoliating clay all over your body; the Cruzeiro, a 17th-century cross that marks the spot where the Portuguese battled the Dutch; and to Morro do Reduto, for a bird's-eye view of the surrounding land and waterscapes. On the way back, you'll pass by mangrove swamps and the charming 18th-century chapel devoted to São Benedito before heading to the reefs for some snorkeling. Catamarans cost R$30 pp, but for privacy hire your own boat (R$15 pp). Snorkel gear (R$5) can be rented at the reefs.

ACCOMMODATIONS AND FOOD

Although Praia dos Carneiros's beach is public, the coconut plantations facing the water all belong to one local family, whose descendants own most of the (somewhat overpriced) *pousadas* and restaurants. At the northernmost end of the beach, **Bangalôs da Prainha** (tel. 81/3676-1681, www.sitiodaprainha.com.br, R$350-450 d) offers accommodations in private bungalows (sleeping up to four) with a breezy beach-house vibe. A row of five "apartments" are newer and cheaper, but offer less privacy. The grounds are wonderfully shady; hammocks strung from the palms catch the trade winds, and there's a pool. The rustic beachside Sítio da Prainha

snorkeling at Praia dos Carneiros

restaurant offers lunch and dinner. More airy and upscale are the lovely two-story, very private bungalows at ★ **Pousada Pontal dos Carneiros Beach Bungalows** (tel. 81/3676-2365, www.pontaldoscarneiros.com.br, R$490-660 d) with multiple verandas and a Jacuzzi. Ideal for families or groups of friends, those that sleep up to six are equipped with kitchens, although you'll be sorely tempted to eat all your meals at the neighboring ★ **Beijupirá** (tel. 81/3676-1461, www.beijupira.com.br, 9am-5pm Sun.-Mon. and Wed.-Thurs., 9am-8pm Fri.-Sat., R$35-50). An outpost of the Porto de Galinhas eatery whose fame is for mixing fish with fruit, this restaurant boasts an unbeatable setting with tables sprinkled beneath the coconut palms.

A cheaper, less isolated option is to stay in Tamandaré, where the beach is nothing to scoff at. A great central option is **Pousada Recanto dos Corais** (Rua Hermes Samico 317, tel. 81/3676-2215, www.pousadarecantodoscorais.com.br, R$120 d), efficiently operated by a charming Gaúcho couple. The modest rooms and common spaces are decorated with a winsome mélange of homey and beachy bric-a-brac.

TRANSPORTATION AND SERVICES

The Banco do Brasil has an ATM that accepts international cards. Visit www.guiatamandare.com.br, a Portuguese site with info and photos of Carneiros and Tamandaré's other beaches.

Cruzeiro (tel. 81/2101-9000) offers infrequent bus service from Recife (100 km/62 mi away) to Tamandaré (three hours, R$10), after which you'll have to get a buggy taxi for the 5 kilometers (3 mi) to Carneiros. If you're driving, follow BR-101 and PE-060. An easier but more expensive alternative is to have hotels arrange pickup in Recife, which will cost around R$150.

★ FERNANDO DE NORONHA

Fernando de Noronha, an archipelago of 21 islands 550 kilometers (340 mi) from Recife, easily lives up to the wildest dreams of both escapists and ecotourists. Aside from offering great hiking, surfing, and snorkeling, Fernando de Noronha is considered one of the foremost diving spots due to spectacularly clear waters with visibility of up to 50 meters (165 feet).

In 1988, Fernando de Noronha was transformed into Brazil's first ecological marine reserve (known as the Parque Nacional Marinho), with more than 70 percent of its territory administered by the Instituto Chico Mendes de Conservação da Biodiversidade (ICMBio), the Brazilian environmental agency. All visitors to the island (the daily entrance limit is 450 people) must pay a daily environmental tax, and there are limits on where you can go and when. Development is tightly controlled and ecological rules prevail (on some beaches even polluting sunscreen is a no-no), but since the island caught on as the ultimate honeymoon destination for Brazilian celebs, there has been an influx of eco-chic

pousadas decked out with hot tubs, plasma TVs, and gourmet restaurants. Even the most modest bungalow accommodations now charge upward of R$200 for the privilege of bunking down in paradise. Once you've factored in the airfare, the idyll becomes quite a costly one—although if you can afford it, you won't be disappointed.

There are a limited number of daily flights, so plan in advance for your trip, especially during Brazilian high season (Dec.-Feb. and July-Aug.). In Recife and Natal, many travel agencies sell all-inclusive packages that include airfare, accommodations, and tours. Although there are package tours for 2-3 days, if you're going to travel so far (and pay so much), it's worth staying a week. The best time to visit is in the dry period (Aug.-Nov.), when the offshore waters are at their clearest (visibility is best in Sept.-Oct.). Surfers should know that the biggest waves hit December-February. Prices soften between March and June, when the otherwise eternal sun is interrupted by frequent rains.

Sights

The main town of Vila dos Remédios comprises the island's "historical" center. Colonial vestiges consist of the **Igreja Nossa Senhora dos Remédios,** a pretty baroque hilltop church; **Palácio São Miguel,** which houses the island's administrative offices; and the atmospheric ruins of the **Forte dos Remédios,** an 18th-century Portuguese fortress littered with cannons. At the foot of the church, the tiny **Museu Histórico** (8am-4pm daily, free) traces the island's history.

Beaches

Fernando de Noronha's main draw is its spectacular beaches. The west coast of the island, known as Mar de Dentro (Inside Sea) has calmer waters. The more turbulent east coast waters are referred to as the Mar de Fora (Outside Sea). The island has 18 beaches, all of them stunners. The three unanimous contenders for the title of most beautiful beach in Brazil—according to Brazilian travel writers and tourist polls—are Baía do Sancho and Baía dos Porcos (both on Mar do Dentro) and Praia do Leão (Mar de Fora).

The approach to **Baía do Sancho** is fittingly dramatic: A steep metal staircase descending a rugged cliff requires you to squeeze through a hole carved out of rock in order to reach the soft sands. The ruddy red cliffs overgrown with primitive rain forest provide a hypnotic backdrop for the beach. It's equally hard to take your eyes off the jade waters blossoming with coral that make Sancho one of the best snorkeling sites in Brazil. From the top of the cliffs, where the view is equally fantastic, a trail leads to the ruins of the Dois Irmãos fortress. If you continue along the rocky trail, you'll arrive at **Baía dos Porcos,** an incandescently blue bay framed by sculpted volcanic rocks whose beach vanishes during high tide. At low tide, rocks form natural pools where you can sit amid glittering fish and gaze at the twin cones of the Ilha dos Dois Irmãos rising out of the water. The largest beach of all, **Praia do Leão,** is mysteriously (and mercifully) the least visited. Untamed and windswept, its sweeping reddish-tinged sands are the favored hatching grounds of numerous birds and sea turtles. During mating season, access is controlled by ICMBio.

On the Mar de Dentro side, standout beaches include **Praia do Boldró** and **Praia Cacimba do Padre.** November-April, waves of up to 5 meters (16 feet) transform these beaches into a surfers' delight. Otherwise, at low tide, sheltered pools appear that are ideal for snorkeling. Overlooking the beach, the ruins of Forte São Pedro do Boldró are a popular spot for watching the sunset. More "urban" due to their proximity to Vila dos Remédios are **Praia do Cachorro, Praia do Meio,** and **Praia da Conceição.** Locals hang out at the sprinkling of *barracas* set against the imposing backdrop of Morro do Pico.

On the Mar de Fora side, **Praia da Atalaia** is a snorkeler's dream. The Instituto Chico Mendes allows only 120 people on the beach per day (six groups of 20—each of which is allowed a frustratingly brief 30 minutes in the

water). Lineups form at the adjacent beach of **Baía do Sueste,** where you can rent masks and snorkels (R$15 per day) and cool your heels in the tranquil, island-dotted waters while waiting for your turn at Atalaia.

Sports and Recreation

The quickest way to tour of the island is take the eight-hour Ilhatur. Choose between a 4x4 with **Atalaia** (tel. 81/3619-1328, R$115) or a dune buggy with **Nortax** (tel. 81/3619-1314, R$300 for up to three people). Then let yourself spend the day being whisked around to Noronha's most famous beaches and the Caieira and Boldró lookout points.

DIVING

Fernando de Noronha is one of the best diving spots. The average water temperature is a balmy 28°C (82°F), visibility extends to a depth of 50 meters (165 feet), and the profusion of brightly colored sea fauna will give you the impression of swimming through an award-winning National Geographic documentary. The only drawback is the price: a 30-minute monitored "baptismal" plunge goes for R$320, while guided excursions for experienced divers begin at R$360 for four people. Diving companies offer lessons and outings, including **Atlantis** (tel. 81/3619-1371, www.atlantisnoronha.com.br), with friendly English-speaking staff, and **Águas Claras** (Alameda do Boldró, tel. 81/3619-1225, www.aguasclaras-fn.com.br). Diving on your own is prohibited by ICMBio.

SNORKELING AND *PLANASUB*

Snorkeling can be done during low tide at many of the beaches around the island, with honorable mention going to Baía do Sancho, Baía dos Porcos, Praia do Boldró, and Praia de Atalaia. You can rent a mask, snorkel, and fins for around R$15 at **Santuário** (tel. 81/3619-1247), a tour operator in Porto de Santo Antônio that also runs snorkeling outings as well as at various outfits in town, at the harbor, and Baia do Sueste. You can also *planasub:* snorkel while gripping an acrylic swimming board attached to a boat, which then takes you offshore where you can see fish swimming around coral banks and wrecked ships. From Porto de Santo Antônio, various boat operators offer *planasub* trips; **Na Onda** (tel. 81/3619-1307, www.barconaonda.com.br, R$110) takes small groups of up to 10 out on three-hour excursions (each person gets one hour of planasubbing), with daily departures at 9am and 2pm.

SURFING

The Mar de Dentro beaches of Praia de Conceição, Boldró, Cacimba do Padre, and do Meio offer some of the best surfing in Brazil during November-March (the rest of the year, you'll be disappointed) when terrific barrels and breaks form, measuring up to 5 meters (16 feet). Make sure to bring your own gear, since there are no surf shops, although you can rent boards at **Locadora Solymar** (Rua São Miguel 169, tel. 81/3619-1965) for between R$30-50 per day. Rentals are also available at **ATM Esportes de Aventura** (Rua Eurico Cavalcante de Albuquerque, tel. 81/3619-0447), where a 90-minute lesson costs R$100.

BOAT EXCURSIONS

Boat excursions depart from the harbor of Porto de Santo Antônio, near Vila dos Remédios. Aside from trips to various beaches, the most popular destination is the **Baía dos Golfinhos,** at the southern tip of the island, where you can see large schools of *golfinhos* (dolphins) come to feed and frolic in the calm bay waters. Both **Na Onda** and the local association of boat-owners **Abatur** (tel. 81/3619-1360) offer three-hour excursions (daily departures leave in the morning and in the afternoon, R$90) with stops for snorkeling at Baía do Sancho; you're likely to see more dolphins in the afternoon. You can also view the dolphins from the **Mirante dos Golfinhos,** a lookout point above the bay (the beach is off-limits). The best time here is in the early morning, when they are cavorting around and leaping in and out of the water. A 2-kilometer (1.2-mi) trail leads to the Mirante from the parking lot above the Baía do Sancho.

HIKING

Hiking is a great way to discover Noronha, although the majority of the island's trails can only be explored in the company of an ICMBio-accredited guide. One of the most popular routes is the 5-kilometer (3-mi), four-hour trek from Vila do Trinta to Praia da Atalaia, which leads past dramatic cliffs overlooking two peninsulas as well as natural pools where you can swim and snorkel. **Atalaia** (tel. 81/3619-1328, R$85) offers this trek. To go on your own (less expensive), ask your *pousada* to recommend a guide, which should cost around R$60. For a knowledgeable English-speaking guide, contact biologist and photographer **Lisandro de Almeida** (tel. 81/3619-1539, Lisandro@atairubrasil.com.br, R$80).

WILDLIFE-WATCHING

The local ecoguide association is located in a building shared by ICMBio and the **TAMAR** project (Av. do Boldró, tel. 81/3619-1174, www.tamar.org.br, 9am-10pm daily), which is dedicated to the preservation of Brazil's sea turtles. Aside from nightly nature talks (in Portuguese), TAMAR has a small café and boutique selling turtle paraphernalia. During nesting season (Mar.-July) and hatching season (Jan.-May), when baby turtles emerge from their eggs and migrate en masse into the ocean, you can accompany the biologists who track and study them.

Accommodations

Accommodations range from Spartan simplicity to eco-chic luxury. The one thing you can count on is extremely inflated prices (discounts are available outside of high season). Most basic "budget" *pousadas* are modest affairs operated out of local residences, with small guest rooms and friendly but sometimes improvised service. It's worth getting in touch with **YourWay** (tel. 81/9949-1087, www.yourway.com.br). This small, English-speaking ecotourism outfit works with a select ensemble of accommodation options in all price ranges, including a handful of private homestay options; it's ideal if you're on a budget and want to feel like part of a Noronhense family. You'll find most options split between Vila da Trinta and Floresta Nova, both suburban areas close to Vila dos Remédios's historic center.

For those counting their *reais,* **Pousada Monsieur Rocha** (Rua Dona Juquinha 139, Vila da Trinta, tel. 81/3619-1227 www.pousadamrocha.com, R$250-340 d) is a basic, well-run choice with bright, whitewashed air-conditioned guest rooms. Only a three-minute walk from Vila dos Remédios, it's also across the street from the local bus stop. **Casa Joãb** (Praia da Conceição, tel. 81/3619-1267, R$340-380 d) is far off the beaten track; getting there involves a bus and a 10-minute walk along a bumpy road. It's Noronha's only lodging on a (splendid) beach. Some may balk at the cost for such humble dwellings, but the locale and common areas combined with the warm ministrations of Joab and his wife Monica (who will even prepare lunchboxes for guests) are priceless.

In Floresta Nova, the **Pousada Maratlântico** (Quadra M, Lote 6, tel. 81/3426-8398, www.pousadamaratlantico.com.br, R$398 d) is simple, but atmospheric—a pleasantly faux rustic lodge with lots of dark wood paneling and furniture set amid a pretty garden. The hotel serves afternoon tea (unusual in these parts) and rents snorkeling equipment. ★ **Pousada Naiepe** (Alameda das Acácias 555, Floresta Nova, tel. 81/9783-5080, www.pousadanaiepe.com.br, R$415-460 d) racks up major raves for its family-style ambiance and hospitality. A quartet of cozy rooms boasts hardwood floors and quality bedding, but you'll spend more time lounging in the hammocks ensconced amid a vast garden planted with fruit trees. The very pretty **Pousada Beco de Noronha** (Rua das Acácias, Floresta Nova, tel. 81/3619-1568, www.becodenoronha.com.br, R$520-700 d) goes for the rustic lodge look,

although the trappings are more polished and refined. Sizable guest rooms are seductively furnished with earthy colors, organic fibers, and clever artisanal elements. Buggies can be rented on-site.

Seeing as a trip to Fernando de Noronha is already busting your budget, you might want to go all out (at least for one romantic night) at ★ **Pousada Maravilha** (BR-363, Praia de Sueste, tel. 81/3619-0028, www.pousadamaravilha.com.br, R$1,430-1,700 d). This luxurious *pousada* is a secluded oasis perched above the Praia de Sueste where everything is exquisitely designed to harmonize with the sublime natural environs. The guest rooms (private bungalows or in the main lodge) are soothing refuges decked out in white and natural woods. Terraces and decks are outfitted with hammocks and futons. A sauna and the infinity pool add to the sense of hedonism. The restaurant is considered one of the best on the island, and service is top-of-the-line. Children under 10 aren't permitted.

Food

Since everything is imported, food tends to be more expensive on Noronha. One of the main island staples is *tubarão* (shark). Rest assured that you won't be sinking your teeth into any of the friendly (and protected) sharks you swim up against during the day—the edible sharks come from Natal. The island's favorite *petisco* is *bolinhos de tubalhau,* crunchy fried fish balls in which shark fills in for the more traditional *bacalhau* (cod). It is also a presence in *tubalhoada,* in which slivers of shark meat, doused in olive oil, are baked along with tomatoes, peppers, potatoes, and olives. You can sample such concoctions at the terrace snack bar-restaurant of the **Museu do Tubarão** (Porto Santo Antônio, tel. 81/3619-1365, 10am-7:30pm daily, R$20-30), which pays homage to the 11 species that reside in the island's waters.

Varanda (Av. Major Costa, Vila do Trinta, tel. 81/3619-1546, noon-11:30pm daily, R$35-50) specializes in creative dishes such as shrimp in creamy pumpkin sauce and an elaborate seafood risotto known as "Sinfonia do Mar." It's worth reserving a table on the namesake *varanda* with garden views. The small, family-style **Tricolor**'s (Rua do Sol 145, Vila dos Remédios, tel. 81/3619-1119, noon-3:30pm and 7pm-11:30pm, Thurs.-Tues, R$25-40) forte is simple yet succulent fish and seafood. An equally good deal (especially if you want to avoid slow service) is **Lanchonete Ousadia** (Rua São Miguel, tel. 81/3619-1725, 11:30am-3pm and 6:30pm-10pm daily, R$15-30), a per-kilo buffet whose fresh if unambitious offerings include lots of salads and fresh fish.

It's a bit out of the way (behind the airport), but extremely simple ★ **Ecologiku** (Estrada Velha do Sueste, tel. 81/3619-1807, 7pm-10:30pm daily, R$30-40) serves some of the best food on the island. A menu of fish and seafood dishes is inspired by the daily catch. The view of Morro do Pico from the plastic tables mesmerizes. Free pick-ups are offered (minimum groups of four); otherwise, you'll need to cab it. Another place with great sunset views is the laid-back **Bar Duda Rei** (tel. 81/3619-1679, 10am-6:30pm, R$25-40), located on the island's most "urban" beach, Praia da Conceição. A more multifaceted hot spot is **O Pico** (Rua Nice Cordeiro, Floresta Nova, tel. 81/3619-1377, noon-midnight daily, R$20-45), a combination bar-restaurant, boutique, and cultural center. Every night offers a different attraction, from Monday's innovative "native dinners" (sample creative recipes, such as passion fruit ceviche) to Thursday's outdoor cinema screenings and Sunday's spirited *samba de roda* sessions.

Information and Services

There are small **tourist offices** at both the port and airport, but you're better off consulting the state of Pernambuco's excellent bilingual website (www.noronha.pe.gov.br). Information is extensive and up-to-date, and there are lots of seductive photos as well as handy maps. For information about the Parque Nacional Marinho, visit the park's **Centro de Visitantes** (Vila de Boldró) and the well-equipped **PICs** (Postos de Informação e Controle) at Praia do Sancho and Baia do Sueste. There are bathrooms, showers, lockers, snack bars, and bike and snorkel equipment for rent.

YourWay (tel. 81/9949-1087, www.yourway.com.br) is a small, but highly professional ecotourism agency run by the savvy, English-speaking Adriana Schmidt Raub. This excellent resource on Noronha can help with airline bookings, buggy and bike rentals, and accommodations as well as plan outings and expeditions.

ATMs at the airport and Centro de Visitantes accept international cards, although it's best to have some backup currency in case they run dry. Although *pousadas* and diving operators accept credit cards, other places do not. Since everything on the island is imported, come equipped with sunscreen, mosquito repellent, flip-flops, and other sundries to avoid paying heavily inflated prices.

Transportation

Measuring 17 square kilometers (6.5 square mi), Fernando de Noronha is quite manageable to get around. Its one paved road, 7-kilometer (4.5-mi) BR-363, might be Brazil's shortest federal highway, but it links Vila dos Remédios, the port, the airport, and most of the beaches and *pousadas*.

AIR

There are two flights a day to Fernando de Noronha from both Recife (2 hours) and Natal (50 minutes). During high season (Dec.-Feb. and July), these are often booked far in advance. From Recife both **Azul** (tel. 0800/887-1118, www.voeazul.com.br) and **Gol** (tel. 0800/704-0465, www.voegol.com.br) offer daily flights. A round-trip usually costs upward of R$900. Current flight schedules are listed on www.ilhadenoronha.com.br. In Recife, you can buy tickets and packages at **Ilha de Noronha Turismo e Ecologia** (Rua Ernesto de Paula Santos 1368, Sl. 202, Boa Viagem, tel. 81/3076-9777, www.ilhadenoronha.com.br), which specializes in Noronha tourism. The **Aeroporto Fernando de Noronha** (tel. 81/3619-0950) is located in the center of the island. A taxi ride to Vila dos Remédios (or most other places) is around R$20, although most *pousadas* offer free pick-ups.

All visitors to Fernando de Noronha must pay an environmental tax (2014 rates begin at R$48.20 per day) before arriving based on the duration of their stay. Save yourself a line at the airport and pay online at www.noronha. pe.gov.br. The Parque Nacional Marinho charges a visitors' fee (valid for 10 days) of R$75 for Brazilians and R$150 for foreigners, which you can buy at the Centro de Visitantes or at either of the PICs.

DUNE BUGGIES

The main way of getting around the island is by buggy. Renting one gives you the freedom to visit all the beaches you want. Just remember that gas is imported and much more expensive than on the mainland. The two main companies are **LocBuggy** (tel. 81/8688-4128, www.locbuggy.com.br) and **Locadora Morro do Farol** (tel. 81/3619-0127, www.locadoramorrodofarol.com.br); both rent out Jeeps, motorbikes, and motorboats. Daily rental fees start at around R$150 for buggies and R$100 for motorbikes; try to reserve in advance due to high demand (this can be done online). You can also easily take advantage of the island's many buggy-taxis, which are quite easy to hail (or hitchhike—islanders and tourists alike are generous with rides). A more economic option is take the microbus that runs up and down BR-363 from Porto Santo Antônio to Baía Sueste. It circulates at 30-minute intervals 5am-11pm and only costs R$3.10.

Alagoas

Alagoas is one of the smallest and poorest states in the Northeast. It is also one of the most enchanting, largely due to its absolutely stunning white-sand beaches, which rank among the most beautiful and unspoiled in Brazil. The presence of coral reefs along much of the coastline ensures that the captivating blue-green waters are ideal for bathing as well as snorkeling and diving. The laid-back capital, Maceió, has its share of terrific beaches and makes a good base for exploring the coasts both north and south. Although Maceió has preserved relatively few vestiges of its past, the colonial towns of Marechal Deodoro and Penedo, on the banks of the Rio São Francisco, are well worth visiting for a taste of regional traditions and a glimpse into Alagoas's past.

MACEIÓ

Like Pernambuco, Alagoas began colonial life as a major producer of sugarcane. Maceió grew up around an 18th-century sugarcane plantation strategically situated between the open sea and the Lagoa Mundaú, an immense inland lagoon that provided a sheltered natural harbor for the shipping of sugar and, later, tobacco, coconut, and spices. In 1839, Maceió became the state capital, but it wasn't until the latter part of the 20th century that it shook off its small-town languor. In the last few decades, the city has gone on a building spree, disfiguring much of its pretty colonial center with generic modern edifices and overdeveloping its coastline, which in recent years has experienced a tourist boom. Although Maceió is a pleasant enough town, what really lures visitors are the turquoise waters and white-sand beaches located right in the city as well as north and south along the coast.

Sights

Maceió is pretty much a beach town with little in the way of historic or cultural sights. However, in the compact (and chaotic) Centro, behind Praia da Avenida, a

Maceió

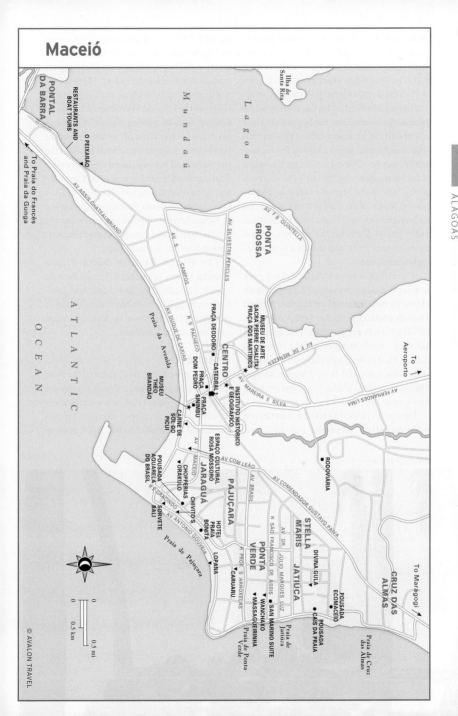

© AVALON TRAVEL

smattering of handsome neoclassical government palaces, colonial churches, and monumental *praças* hint at an elegant architectural past. The **Praça dos Martírios** (also known as Praça Marechal Floriano Peixoto) is an attractive square flanked by the creamy white Palácio do Governo and the Igreja Bom Jesus dos Martírios, an eclectically styled church with a resplendent blue-and-white Portuguese azulejo facade. Adjacent to Centro, the *bairro* of **Jaraguá,** sheltering the city's 19th-century port, is one of the Maceió's oldest neighborhoods. Many of its century-old mansions and warehouses have undergone restoration. Sadly, grand plans for the *bairro*'s revival haven't borne fruit, and the area is increasingly abandoned.

If strolling around Centro, take a peek at several modest museums. Occupying an imposing onion-domed palace, the **Museu Théo Brandão** (Av. da Paz 1490, Centro, tel. 82/3214-1713, 9am-5pm Tues.-Fri., 2pm-5pm Sat.-Sun., free) provides insight into local culture via its engaging collection of folk art and crafts, most of it from Alagoas. At 8pm Thursday nights, folkloric groups perform music from throughout the state.

The pale pink **Instituto Histórico e Geográfico** (Rua do Sol 382, tel. 82/3223-7997, www.ihgal.al.org.br, 8am-noon and 2pm-5pm Mon.-Fri., R$4) has a rather musty collection of documents and artifacts associated with Alagoan history. However, it's worth stopping in to check out the personal effects of the infamous local bandit Lampião, accompanied by riveting photos of him and his not-so-merry band of outlaws. Included is the iconic image of the severed heads of the *cangaçeiro* and his crew, taken after the police finally gunned them down in 1938. The photo was circulated throughout the Northeast—along with the heads themselves (preserved in formaldehyde)—in order to prove that the greatly feared (and equally revered) bandits were indeed out of commission.

The **Museu de Arte Sacra Pierre Chalita** (Praça Marechal Floriano Peixoto 44, tel. 82/3223-4298, 8am-noon and 2pm-5:30pm daily, free) has a modest collection of religious art and colonial furnishings culled from around the Northeast.

Beaches

Maceió is famed for having some of the most splendid urban beaches in Brazil. Impressive as they are, they don't compare with the more pristine and undeveloped versions located north and south of the city. Since most of

Praia de Ponta Verde, Maceió

The Bonnie and Clyde of Brazil

Lampião and **Maria Bonita**—the scourge of the Sertão—were charismatic and funkily dressed folk heroes. Lampião was the nickname of Virgulino Ferreira da Silva, born in 1895 into a peasant family living in the arid Sertão of Pernambuco. Until the age of 21, Virgulino worked as a leatherwork artisan. He also possessed an uncommon literary bent. But after his father was killed by police, Lampião swore to wreak vengeance. His nickname supposedly comes from the fact that he customized a shotgun to shoot so fast that the resulting flash resembled the sudden flare of a gas lantern (*lampião*).

For the next 20 years, together with his wife, Maria Déa (nicknamed Maria Bonita, or "Pretty Mary"), and a band of loyal but ruthless outlaws known as *cangaçeiros,* Lampião went on a violent rampage, brazenly stealing police weapons and using them to attack, terrorize, and steal from wealthy landowners and small towns throughout the Northeast. To protect themselves from the merciless sun and sharp thorns of the Caatinga's thorn trees, the *cangaçeiros* decked themselves out from head to toe in leather, which they embellished with intricate and colorful embroidery, coins, and metal scraps resembling chunks of medieval armor. These desert dandies also had a weakness for French perfume—Lampião, in particular, stole great quantities of it from the wealthy homes he broke into. Both vain and charismatic, Lampião and Maria Bonita were early media darlings—they courted their fame, inviting reporters to photograph them in their stylish leather finery.

Their cunning ability to elude capture for so long, coupled with their outrageous crimes, turned Lampião and his band into front-page material. Wealthy landowners lived in fear and entreated the federal government to send a special force of soldiers to hunt them down. They did so, to no avail—until 1938, when Lampião was ambushed by police with machine guns. After a shootout, Lampião, Maria Bonita, and their gang of nine were killed and their heads cut off.

Although brutal Lampião was certainly no saint, his defiant rebel stance against the establishment and the wealthy landowners who treated the Sertão's peasants as feudal serfs turned him into a Robin Hood-esque legend during his lifetime. Following his death, he became a national folk hero, the subject of poems, stories, songs, TV miniseries, films, comic books, and thousands of the mimeographed stories illustrated with woodcuts, known as *literatura de cordel,* which remain popular throughout the Northeast interior.

Maceioenses' urban life revolves around the *orla* (coast), the city beaches are definitely worth checking out.

Only 2 kilometers (1.2 mi) east of Centro, crescent-shaped **Praia de Pajuçara** is Maceió's most urbanized beach, lined with high-rises, hotels, bars, and *barracas* hawking *água de coco* (coconut water) and caipirinhas. The beach is wide with calm emerald waters that are good for swimming. When the tide is low, you can hire a *jangada* (R$22 for 1 hour) to take you out to the *piscinas* (swimming pools) offshore, where you can snorkel and wallow around to your heart's content and sip on cocktails served from floating bars.

Continuing east is the more trendy and upscale **Praia de Ponta Verde**, where the most luxurious hotels and restaurants are located. Until the 1950s, this pretty beach, framed by dense foliage and coconut palms, was so untamed that its vegetation served as camouflage for modest society youths to come and bathe in private, a practice that earned it the name of Praia das Acanhadas (Shy People Beach). There is still a profusion of palms as well as sophisticated *barracas* where you can kick back with a *chope* and listen to live music.

Farther along, the beaches of **Jatiúca** and **Cruz das Almas** are sought after by Maceió's *surfista* crowd but are still fairly urban. If you're seeking less crowded sands, continue north along the *orla* (there are plenty of buses that leave from Centro), stopping at any stretch of sugary white sand that takes your fancy. **Jacarecica, Guaxuma, Garça Torta,** and **Riacho Doce** are all seductive. The last beach on the municipal bus line is **Praia de Pratagi,** a wide expanse of fluffy sand with natural pools 15 kilometers (9 mi) from Centro. The mermaid statue erected on one of the coral reefs honors the Candomblé *orixá* Iemanjá, whose title is "Queen of the Seas." For this reason, this beach is often referred to as **Praia do Mirante da Sereia** (*sereia* is Portuguese for "mermaid").

Sports and Recreation

Aside from its beaches, Maceió is known for the **Lagoa Mundaú,** a freshwater lagoon fed by the Rio Mundaú that feels like another world. It's a lovely place for a drink and a portion of fresh crab or shrimp while watching the sunset. During the day, boat excursions sail around the lagoon and its handful of islands. For information about departures, visit the *barracas* at Pontal da Barra, where traditional lace-makers make and display their wares. Boats usually leave at 9am and 1:30pm; outings last four hours and cost around R$35.

Entertainment and Events
NIGHTLIFE

Most of Maceió's nightlife takes place in the upscale beach neighborhoods of Pajuçara, Ponta Verde, and Jatiúca. Aside from a late-afternoon beer at the rustic waterfront *barracas* surrounding Lagoa Mundaú, all beaches have *barracas* where you can sip caipirinhas and feast on crab, oysters, and *sururu*. Among the most sophisticated beach bars in town is **Lopana** (Av. Sílvio Carlos Viana, Ponta Verde, tel. 82/3231-7484, www.lopana.com.br, 10am-midnight Tues.-Sun. and daily in summer). Straddling Pajuçara and Ponta Verde beaches, this *barraca* has it all—air-conditioning, Wi-Fi, and even catamaran excursions up and down the coast. DJs spin mellow tunes by day; on weekends, live MPB, blues, and rock performances transform it into one of the city's' hottest night clubs.

A few blocks inland, **Massagueirinha** (Av. Dep. José Lages 1105, Jatiúca, tel. 82/3327-1027, 11am-1am Tues.-Sun. and daily in summer) is a simple little bar with plastic tables and chairs that are always full due to the amazing seafood specialties served here. Absolute musts are the *pata de carangueijo* (crab claws) with vinaigrette and the *casquinha de siri gratinada,* in which fresh crab cooked in coconut milk is served gratiné with parmesan. Live MPB and rock often provide a soundtrack.

As the weekend approaches, Jaraguá heats up, particularly the streets surrounding Rua Sá de Albuquerque. Occupying a renovated warehouse, **Chopperia Orákulo** (Rua Barão

jangadas along Maceió's Praia de Pajuçara

de Jaraguá 717, tel. 82/3326-7616, www.oraku-lochopperia.com.br, 9pm-3am Wed. and Fri.-Mon., cover R$15-20) hosts some of the hottest and most varied live-music performances in town. While listening to rock, *forró, chorinho,* and *"swingueira,"* you can knock back nicely priced beers in an open courtyard. Jaraguá is also home to one of Maceió's favorite GLS bars, **Espaço Cultural Rosa Mossoró** (Praça Arthur Ramos 181, tel. 82/8836-6834, 7pm-close daily). The proprietress, Rosa, has quite a pedigree; her father, Mossoró, owned one of the 'hood's oldest and most legendary cabarets. Cheap eats and drinks, a jukebox, and an eclectic crowd make this a fun place to start or end an evening.

FESTIVALS AND EVENTS

In the third week of November, the city celebrates **Maceió Fest;** *trios elétricos* blast ear-splitting *axé* music in an out-of-season Carnaval that is a watered-down version of Salvador's.

Shopping

Alagoas is rich in artisanal traditions, and Maceió is a great place to pick up well-made local crafts. The city is especially famous for its *rendas,* or lacework, and specifically for *filé,* a style that bears a resemblance to fish netting (*filé* means "net"). Often dyed in tropical colors, *filé* items range from towels and tablecloths to hippie chic blouses and skirts. You can view a traditional community of *rendeiras* at work at the **Núcleo Artesanal do Pontal da Barra,** on the shores of the Lagoa (8am-6pm daily). More than 200 shops and ateliers, most located in the homes of fisherfolk, sell beautifully made wares at very good prices. Although lace-making is traditionally women's work, 40-year-old Guilherme dos Santos has been making *rendas* since he was a tween. To check out his wares—rumored to be among the finest in the 'hood—visit his **atelier** (Rua Alípio Barbosa da Silva 176).

Other places to check for regional handicrafts are the **Mercado do Artesenato** (Rua Melo Morais 617, Centro, 8am-5pm daily), where prices are cheaper and you'll find locally made Sertanejo-style leather sandals, and the **Feira do Artesanato da Pajuçara** (Av. Dr. Antônio Gouveia 1447, Pajuçara, tel. 82/3231-3901, 9am-10pm daily), a touristy place with wood carvings, ceramics, and coconut-fiber baskets decorated with intricate geometric patterns. The main mall in town is **Shopping Maceió** (Av. Gustavo Paiva 2990, Mangabeiras, tel. 82/2126-1010, www.maceio-shopping.com, 10am-10pm Mon.-Sat., 3pm-9pm Sun.), behind Jatiúca.

Accommodations

There's no compelling reason to stay in Centro, which has only a few budget hotels. A considerable array of both standard and luxury options are in the beach neighborhoods of Pajuçara, Ponta Verde, and Jatiúca. Most are quite modern, somewhat pricey, and lacking in personality.

R$50-200

The only decent budget *pousada* in town that has the privilege of being right on the beach is **Pousada Cais da Praia** (Av. Álvaro Otacílio 4353, Jatiúca, tel. 82/2121-3636, www. caisdapraia.com.br, R$120-190 d), within spitting distance of Ponta Verde's hub. The boxlike brick exterior seems out of place on a tropical beach, but the guest rooms have sea views and are clean and modern, if basic. Outside beneath swaying palms is a modest blue pool surrounded by shrubbery. Only a block back from the beach, but way cooler (and greener), ★ **Pousada EcoMaceió** (Av. Desembargador Valente Lima 204, Jatiúca, tel. 82/3317-8551, www.pousadaecomacieo.com. br, R$135-170 d) fuses a clean, contemporary style with environmental friendliness. The 20 guest rooms and common areas are light and alluring and the English-speaking staff are pros.

A block in from Pajuçara beach, **Pousada Aquarela do Brasil** (Rua Desembargador Almeida Guimarães 367, tel. 82/3231-0113, www.pousadaaquareladobrasil.com, R$130-200 d) is an appealing budget choice with pleasing modern design and friendly service. Small but attractive guest rooms are immaculate and open onto tiny private gardens with hammocks. A good choice nearby is **Hotel Praia Bonita** (Av. Dr. Antônio Gouveia 943, Pajuçara, tel. 82/2121-3700, www.praiabonita. com.br, R$170-220 d), a refreshingly stylish place with large sunny guest rooms whose blond wood fixtures conjure up an Ikea showroom. Rooms with sea views are more expensive. A small pool overlooks the ocean (and sea of passing cars).

R$200-400

Just off Ponta Verde beach, **San Marino Suite** (Rua Dr. Noel Nutels 437, tel. 82/2121-9000, www.sanmarinosuite.com.br, R$240-340 d) is one of Maceió's more attractive and comfortable hotels. Sizable guest rooms, painted in soothing tones, have flat-screen TVs and gorgeous designer bathrooms. Melding modern design with rustic wooden furnishings earns **Ritz Coralli** (Rua Eng. Mário de Gusmão 4201, Ponta Verde, tel. 82/3177-6400, www. ritzcoralli.com.br, R$220-380 d) serious style points. Modest amenities include a tiny pool, fitness room, and sauna.

Food

Maceió is the meeting point of two major culinary influences: the sea and the Sertão. A legacy of the fishing communities that line the coast is the abundance of lobster, shrimp, and crabs (both fresh and saltwater) along with fish such as *dourado, cavala,* and *beijupira,* traditionally served with rice and *pirão* (a puree made with manioc flour). A source of revenue for many families is *sururu,* a little mollusk harvested from the mud surrounding freshwater lagoons such as Lagoa Mundaú. You'll find *sururu* everywhere (it is believed to be an aphrodisiac) in forms ranging from the chowder-like *caldo de sururu* served in bars to entrées such as *sururu de capote,* in which it's cooked in its shell along with tomatoes, peppers, and garlic (not unlike French mussels). From the hot and barren Sertão comes a predilection for *carne-de-sol,* prepared in a variety of ways, usually with fried or pureed manioc. Don't leave town without trying the local version of a crepe. Made from crunchy white manioc flour (not tapioca) mixed with grated coconut, *tapiocas* are cooked on hot plates and stuffed with a variety of fillings, both sweet and savory. You'll find *tapioqueiras* (the women who make them) along the beaches of Pajuçara, Ponto Verde, and Jatiúca.

CAFÉS AND SNACKS

Chivito's (Av. Dr. Antônio de Gouveia 759, Pajuçara, tel. 82/3111-9102, 11am-5am Mon.-Sat., 4pm-11pm Sun., R$5-15) offers Northeastern takes on classic meat and cheese sandwiches. The most popular *sandubas* are stuffed with *carne de sol* and *coração de galinha* (chicken hearts). For a sweet heat antidote, head to **Sorvete Bali** (Av. Dr. Antônio de Gouveia 481, Pajuçara, tel. 82/3231-8833, www.sorvetesbali.com.br, 10am-midnight Sun.-Thurs., 10am-1am Fri.-Sat.), with locations on the beaches of Ponta Verde as well as Pajuçara. The 70 ice-cream flavors include fruits such as *bacuri, jaca,* and *sapoti,* as well as exotica—caipirinha, papaya with cassis, and honey with pollen (made from regional honey).

BRAZILIAN

Some of the best *carne-de-sol* in town can be savored at **Carne de Sol do Picui** (Av. da Paz 1140, Jaraguá, tel. 82/3223-5313, www. picui.com.br, 11am-11pm Mon.-Sat., 11am-4pm Sun., R$25-40). Seven types of *carne-de-sol* are served here, from the classic filet mignon and *picanha* (rump steak) to more unorthodox buffalo and ostrich. *Galeto* (charcoal-roasted spring chicken) is the star at **Caruaru** (Rua Carlos Tenório 350, Ponta Verde, tel. 82/3227-0782, www.picui.com.br, 11:30am-11pm Mon.-Sat., 11:30am-7:30pm Sun., R$20-30), where it arrives whole (deboned) and accompanied with typical Sertanejo fixings ranging from buttery *feijão verde* to crunchy farofa.

For fish and seafood, try simple but welcoming **O Peixarão** (Av. Alípio Barbosa da Silva 532, Pontal da Barra, tel. 82/3351-9090, www.opeixarao.com.br, 11am-5pm Sun.-Thurs., 11am-11pm Fri.-Sat., R$20-30), overlooking the Lagoa Mundaú. The house specialty is *peixarão,* an aromatic stew of fish cooked in a sauce of shrimp and coconut milk.

★ **Divina Gula** (Rua Engenheiro Paulo Brandão Nogueira 85, Jatiúca, tel. 82/3235-1016, www.divinagula.com.br, 11:30am-midnight Sun. and Tues.-Thurs., 11:30am-2am Fri.-Sat.) is an immensely popular restaurant-bar serving some of the most appetizing food in the city. The Mineiro owners daringly mix hearty Minas classics with Alagoan produce such as *carne-de-sol,* shrimp, and manioc. The rustic, ranch-style interior is very welcoming, but at night, the sidewalk tables are the coveted place to kick back.

INTERNATIONAL

While Alagoan cuisine is hardly humdrum, even more exotic is the Japanese-tinged Peruvian fare served at ★ **Wanchako** (Rua São Francisco de Assis 93, Jatiúca, tel. 82/3377-6024, www.wanchako.com.br, noon-3pm and 7pm-11:30pm Mon.-Sat., R$40-60). Peruvian fare is hard to come by in Brazil. This soothingly attractive restaurant corrects this culinary lapse with ceviches galore—the lime-marinated seafood is ideally refreshing in the hot climate—as well as crunchy coconut shrimp with tangerine salsa and grilled fish with green risotto and *aguaymanto* (an Andean fruit) jelly.

Information and Services

There are **tourist offices** at the airport (tel. 82/3036-5313, 9am-5pm daily) and *rodoviária* (9am-5pm daily) as well as Maceió Shopping (Av. Gustavo Paiva 2990, Mangabeiras, tel. 82/2126-1010, www.maceioshopping.com, 10am-10pm Mon.-Sat., 3pm-9pm Sun.). You can also visit www.turismo.al.gov.br (in Portuguese).

In Centro, you can withdraw cash at the **ATMs** of Banco do Brasil and HSBC, both located near the Instituto Histórico on Rua

do Livramento. You'll also find ATMs at Shopping Iguatemi. The main **post office** is also in Centro (Rua João Pessoa 57).

Transportation

Maceió is connected by air to most major Brazilian cities, including São Paulo, Salvador, and Recife. The **Aeroporto Zumbi dos Palmares** (BR-104 Km 91, tel. 82/3036-5200) is on the outskirts of town, 25 kilometers (16 mi) from Ponta Verde. A taxi will cost around R$50 (fixed rate). **Tropical** (tel. 82/3354-2043) operates a bus (every 30 min. Mon.-Fri., hourly Sat.-Sun. R$2.50) that goes to and from the airport along the coast, with stops in Pajuçara, Ponta Verde, and Jatiúca. Much closer to Centro is the **Terminal Rodoviário João Paulo II** (Av. Leste-Oueste, Feitosa, tel. 82/3221-4615), where you can catch buses for points up and down the coast as well as to Recife (four hours) and Salvador (eight hours). From the *rodoviária* there is also no shortage of municipal buses (R$2.50) to Centro and the beaches of Pajuçara, Ponta Verde, Jatiúca, and others farther north.

Maceió and the surrounding coastline are served by bus, but the faster and easier way of getting where you want to go is by flagging down *taxi comuns;* these vans and cars pick up passengers and deposit them at points up and down the coast with much greater frequency than buses. Another alternative is to rent a car at **Avis** (tel. 82/3036-5341, www.avis.com.br) or **Hertz** (tel. 82/3342-0033, www.hertz.com. br); both have branches at the airport. Try to stay clear of Centro with a car, since it gets clogged with traffic.

CITY TOURS

Maceió Turismo (Rua Firmínio de Vasconcelos 685, Pajuçara, tel. 82/3327-7711, www.maceioturismo.com.br) offers city tours (two hours, R$50) as well as day excursions to surrounding beaches north and south of the city. Expect to pay around R$30 pp to take in the sandy marvels of Praia do Francês, Barra de São Miguel, and Praia da Gunga, south of the city, and around R$65 for a day of soaking, sailing, and snorkeling along the reefs of Maragogi, to the north.

SOUTH OF MACEIÓ

The beaches south of Maceió along AL-101 are close enough to be almost suburban, as is the famous Praia do Francês. Only a few extra kilometers brings you to more languid fishing villages and deserted sands backed by plantations of swaying coconut palms. Highlights include Barra de São Miguel and gorgeous Praia de Gunga.

Praia do Francês

Around 22 kilometers (14 mi) south of Maceió, Praia do Francês is known for its white sands, hypnotic blue-green seas, and Tahiti-worthy coconut palms. A major tourist mecca, it gets crowded in the summer and on weekends, when its beachside bars and restaurants are stuffed to the gills with day-tripping Maceioenses, many of whom have vacation houses in the vicinity, and sun worshippers from all over Brazil. While the rough waves at the southern end are the fiefdom of surfers (and the site of international competitions), the calm waters protected by coral reefs are popular with families and enthusiasts of water sports such as sailing, Jet Skiing, and banana boating.

MARECHAL DEODORO

Alagoas's first capital of Marechal Deodoro lies 6 kilometers (4 mi) from Praia do Francês. A National Heritage Site, this atmospheric colonial town was founded in 1611. It was known as Vila Madalena de Sumaúna until 1939, when it received a new name in honor of homegrown son Marechal Manuel Deodoro da Fonseca (1827-1892). A trained soldier, Deodoro not only staged Brazil's first military coup—supplanting Emperor Dom Pedro II and officially proclaiming Brazil a republic—but also became the nation's first president in 1889. His disastrous tenure proved an inauspicious start to Brazil's republican era; after unsuccessfully dissolving Congress and declaring a state of siege, Deodoro resigned after only two years in power.

Marechal Deodoro is quite small, but you can easily spend a couple of hours ambling around its cobblestoned streets, pretty pastel houses, and colonial churches (many in state of decay). You'll find the most splendid architecture on the elegant Praça Comendador Firmo Lopes, where you'll see the **Igreja de Santa Maria Magdalena,** an imposing mid-18th-century church, which sits adjacent to the late-17th-century **Convento de São Francisco** (closed for restoration).

ACCOMMODATIONS AND FOOD

Although you can easily commute to Praia do Francês in a day trip from Maceió, there are a fair number of reasonably priced hotel options. Tucked on a quiet street near the beach, **Taba Brasil** (Rua Maresia 4, tel. 82/3260-1910, www.pousadatababrasil.com. br, R$100-140 d) has eight cute and compact, whitewashed rooms with small hammocked verandas. For housekeeping accommodations, the modern but pleasant **Residenza Casa Del Sole** (Rua São Pedro 699, tel. 82/3260-1870, www.residenzacasadelsole.com, R$120-170 d) offers a large pool and tidy condo-like apartments that sleep up to four; the larger ones feature kitchens and living rooms.

Aside from beach *barracas,* a good place for fish and seafood is **Parada de Taipas** (Av. Caravelas, tel. 82/3260-1609, 11am-10pm daily, R$15-25). The owner claims to be the inventor of a dish that has become synonymous with Praia do Francês—*chiclete de camarão* (which translates into "shrimp bubblegum"). Shrimp is sautéed with garlic, green peppers, and tomato sauce and then mixed with melted mozzarella and sour cream (this is the gummy part).

TRANSPORTATION

Getting here from Maceió is easy. Hourly **Real Alagoas** (tel. 82/3356-1324, www.realalagoas. com.br) buses (30 min. R$3) and even more frequent minibuses and *taxi comuns* leave from the *rodoviária* and make stops along Praia da Avenida, passing through Praia do Francês on their way to Marechal Deodoro.

★ Barra de São Miguel

Located 38 kilometers (24 mi) south of Maceio, Barra de São Miguel is a favorite Maceioense beach getaway. Aside from the stunning but more urbanized **Praia de Barra de São Miguel** (closest to the small town of Barra and its port), and **Praia do Niquim** (where many hotels are located), this long beach pales in comparison with **Praia do Gunga.** Often included in rankings of Brazil's most enchanting beaches, Gunga is around 3 kilometers (2 mi) from Barra's village, on the far side of the Rio São Miguel. It's most easily accessible by boat (20 minutes, R$30) from the village quay or from Praia de Barra (though you can also get there by buggy in the summer). The beach consists of an impossibly white stretch of sand that is shaded by whispering palms (the land behind it is a vast coconut farm) and bathed on one side by a warm turquoise sea, and on the other by the equally bath-like waters of the freshwater Lagoa do Roteiro. During low tide, you can take a boat or kayak out to the reefs and snorkel. Gunga's fame means it gets packed with excursions from Maceió, particularly during holidays, when *barracas* jack up prices sky high (Macieoenses in the know often bring their own coolers filled with icy beer).

ACCOMMODATIONS AND FOOD

At **Lua Pousada** (Av. Moema Cavalcante 385, tel. 82/3272-1359, www.luapousada.com.br, R$130-160 d), guest rooms are basic but spotless, and there is a pool even though the beach is just two blocks away. At the other end of the spectrum is one of the most buzzed-about luxury getaways in the Northeast, **Kenoa Resort** (Rua Escritor Jorge de Lima, tel. 82/3272-1285, www.kenoaresort.com, R$1,270-1,920 d). Designed by Pernambucano architect Osvaldo Tenório, the beachfront suites and bungalows feature exquisitely worked stone and wood furnishings. For relaxing, take your pick of a wine bar, a golf range, a spa, and a gorgeous infinity pool lined with stones that reflect the sky. The pricy, beautiful restaurant, **Kaamo,** serves fresh fish and seafood creations that imaginatively mingle Northeastern and Portuguese influences.

TRANSPORTATION AND SERVICES

For information about Barra, check out www.barradesaomiguel.net (in Portuguese). For cash, the Banco do Brasil in the village center accepts international ATM cards. **Real Alagoas** (tel. 82/3356-1324, www.realalagoas.com.br) has hourly bus service (1 hour, R$3) beginning at 5:30am, with departures from Praça Afrânio Jorge in Centro as well as the *rodoviária.* By car, merely follow the AL-101 south from Maceió.

★ Penedo

One of the most picturesque colonial towns of the Northeast, Penedo, situated 170 kilometers (106 mi) south of Maceió, sits dramatically atop a cliff overlooking Brazil's longest national river, the Rio São Francisco (2,800 km/1,740 mi). The river is a source of livelihoods, legends, and transportation that colors Penedo's rich culture; taking jaunts up and down its deep blue waters makes for a scenic outing (you may see dugout canoes whose bows are adorned with monstrous figureheads known as *carrancas*). The town, overlooked by most tourists, is an architectural jewel with a handful of majestic baroque churches and colonial buildings in faded shades of rose, blue, and saffron.

Penedo was founded in the mid-1500s as a defensive outpost on the Rio São Francisco. The Portuguese weren't happy with French traders' use of the river to transport valuable *pau brasil* wood, nor were they pleased with the local Caeté Indians who had killed (and supposedly eaten) Brazil's first bishop, who bore the appetizing name of Sardinha (Sardine). In 1637, the town was conquered by invading Dutch troops as part of a plan to stake out a colony in the Brazilian Northeast. The Dutch erected an imposing fortress before being expelled in 1645. In 1660, the first Franciscan monks arrived in Penedo and kicked off a baroque building frenzy of ornate churches, convents, and chapels along with an educational tradition that left its mark on the town's social and cultural traditions for centuries to come.

SIGHTS

Penedo possesses a fine collection of colonial architecture, including several baroque churches (with unstable opening hours). Construction of the **Igreja de Nossa Senhora da Corrente** (Praça 12 de Abril, 8am-5pm Tues.-Sat., 10am-4pm Sun.) began in 1764 but wasn't completed until the late 19th century. It's considered a masterpiece of Brazilian rococo; there are some strikingly beautiful blue-and-white azulejo panels, but most impressive is the main altar, a sumptuous feast of burnished gold that contrasts with pale blue and pink marble trompe l'oeil. Next to it is an alcove where slaves were hidden before escaping to freedom via a secret passageway (Penedo was a hotbed of abolitionism).

Older still is the complex consisting of the **Igreja de Nossa Senhora dos Anjos** and the **Convento de São Francisco** (Praça Rui Barbosa, 8am-11:30am and 2pm-5pm Tues.-Fri., 8am-11am Sat.), built during the 17th and 18th centuries on the site of the Dutch Forte Nassau and inhabited by Penedo's Franciscans. The austere facade hardly prepares you for the interior's baroque exuberance, which features gold leaf and lots of delicious trompe l'oeil as well as a palmy cloister. A small museum with antique furnishings traces the history of the Franciscan order. Built in 1758, the restored **Igreja de São Gonçalo Garcia dos Homens Pardos** (Av. Floriano, 8am-5pm Mon.-Sat., 8am-4pm Sun., free) is striking for its neo-gothic bell towers and its limestone facade.

The **Casa do Penedo** (Rua João Pessoa 126, tel. 82/3551-5443, 8am-noon and 2pm-6pm Tues.-Sun., R$3) traces the history of the town via a collection of photographs and artifacts, many belonging to Penedo's most illustrious families. The **Museu do Paço Imperial** (Praça 12 de Abril 9, tel. 82/3551-2498, 11am-5pm Tues.-Sat., 8am-noon Sun., R$3) is located in an 18th-century mansion

that earned its name, the Paço Imperial, when Dom Pedro II stayed here during an 1859 visit. Today it houses a collection of 17th- and 18th-century religious art as well as furniture and decorative objects.

SPORTS AND RECREATION

To get a feel for the mighty Rio São Francisco, hop a boat (R$2) to the towns of **Neópolis** or **Santo do São Francisco** on the Sergipe side of the river. Although there isn't anything much to see, you can have a drink, check out the local pottery made from riverbank clay, and take panoramic pictures of Penedo. For more of an adventure, head by bus or car down to the little fishing village of **Piaçabuçu**, 22 kilometers (14 mi) away; from here, you can take a boat (four hours, R$140, minimum four people) down to the mouth of the river. You can also easily find boats for hire at the riverside dock and the surrounding wild dune beaches of **Pontal do Peba.** **Farol da Foz Ecuturismo** (tel. 82/3552-1298, www.faroldafozecoturismo.com) runs three-hour buggy excursions (R$160 for up to four people) along the wild dune beaches of Pontal do Peba.

FESTIVALS AND EVENTS

Held on the second Sunday in January, the **Festa do Bom Jesus dos Navegantes** is a splendid fluvial procession in which more than 100 decorated boats take to the river accompanying a sculpted effigy of Bom Jesus. The event is the highlight of several days of merrymaking that includes performances of traditional dance and music..

ACCOMMODATIONS AND FOOD

Pousada Colonial (Praça 12 de Abril 21, tel. 82/3551-2355, R$90-120 d) is a simple but atmospheric guest house occupying a whitewashed colonial building. Guest rooms sport dark wood floors and antique furnishings; although they're smaller, request a room whose wooden shutters open to offer lovely views of the river framed by flamboyant trees. The **Hotel São Francisco** (Av. Floriano Peixoto

237, tel. 82/3551-2273, www.hotelsaofrancisco.
tur.br, R$160-280 d) is an early 1960s attempt
at luxury with an ugly exterior but spacious
and comfortable interior. Air-conditioned
guest rooms offer fantastic views; the more
expensive 4th- and 5th-floor rooms have been
renovated. There's a pool with fountains and a
vast dining area for the lavish daily breakfast.

Forte da Rocheira (Rua da Rocheira 2,
tel. 82/3551-3273, 11am-4pm daily and 6pm-
10:30pm Fri.-Sat., R$20-30) has a location on a
rocky cliff overlooking the Rio São Francisco
that makes it the most scenic eatery in town.
It's a fine place for river fare such as tilapia in
white wine sauce and the more exotic *jacaré*
(caiman) cooked in palm oil, lime juice, and
grated coconut.

TRANSPORTATION AND SERVICES
The **tourist office** (Praça Barão de Penedo,
8am-11am and 2pm-5pm Mon.-Fri.) has
maps of the town. Banks with ATMs are located behind the riverfront. To get to Penedo
from Maceió, follow coastal AL-101 south and
then west from Piaçabuçu. **Real Alagoas** (tel.
82/3356-1324, www.realalagoas.com.br) operates four daily buses (three hours, R$15) that
will put you right in the center of town.

NORTH OF MACEIÓ
The northern coast of Alagoas, much of it still
undeveloped by tourism, dishes up some of
Brazil's most paradisiacal beaches. Protected
by coral reefs that are a snorkelers' delight, a
large stretch of the coastline is actually a series
of natural pools whose Caribbean blue waters
are as placid as a lagoon's and as warm as a
lulling bath. The blindingly white sands are
as soft as sugar and are idyllically framed by
a sea of coconut palms. Although settlements
such as Barra de Santo Antônio and particularly Maragogi—a snorkeling paradise—have
mushroomed into tourist resorts, human encroachment on nature rarely extends beyond
simple fishing villages here. The string of
beaches start right in Maceió itself, extending up the coast from Praia do Mirante da
Sereia all the way to Alagoas's frontier with

Pernambuco. Although infrequent buses and
taxis comuns from Maceió journey up the
coast, for the freedom of beach-hopping and
exploring more remote spots off the beaten
track, you might consider renting a car.

Barra de Santo Antônio
Around 40 kilometers (25 mi) north of
Maceió, Barra de Santo Antônio is a pretty
fishing village. Founded by the Dutch in
the 17th century, it has a smattering of colonial buildings and is also known for its lively
Carnaval. However, its greatest lures are its
natural attractions. Bisected by the Rio Santo
Antônio, Barra is surrounded by stunning
beaches and natural ocean pools. A five-minute ride to the other side of the river by fishing
boat, ferry, or car (over the newly inaugurated
bridge) brings you to the **Ilha da Crôa,** which
is actually a narrow sandy peninsula dotted
with natural pools. You can loll around in the
warm, clear blue water or take a boat to the
nearby **Praia do Carro Quebrado,** a truly
wild and gorgeous beach backed by sandy
cliffs whose name (Broken Car Beach) is a
testament to the difficulty of getting here (although you can take a dune buggy or *moto-
taxi* for around R$25 for two round-trip). The
subsequent beaches of **Pedra do Cebola**
and **Praia da Ponta do Gamela** are equally
dreamy and even more remote. Also close to
Barra de Santo Antônio (and accessible by
boat or *taxi comum*) is the attractive crescent
beach of **Praia de Tabuba.**

ACCOMMODATIONS AND FOOD
Pousada Arco-Íris (Loteamento Tabuba, tel.
82/3291-1250, www.tabuba.tk, R$125-150 d),
a breezy, well-kept guesthouse right off Praia
de Tabuba, is the best of the few accommodations around. The guest rooms are cool
and comfortable, and the restaurant serves
up tasty local and international fare. Kayaks,
mountain bikes, and windsurfing boards are
available for rent.

In town, **Estrela Azul** (Lote Paraíso 54, tel.
82/3291-1599, 11am-9pm Tues.-Sun., R$25-
40) is particularly well regarded for its shrimp

dishes. During the day both Praia do Carro Quebrado and Ilha da Crôa have rustic *barracas* that serve icy beer along with the fresh catch of the day (be forewarned that none have restrooms). Particularly friendly is **Bar do Piú** on Ilha da Crôa, where you can feast on a plate of fresh butter-fried shrimp sautéed in onions.

TRANSPORTATION

Real Alagoas (tel. 82/3356-1324, www.realalagoas.com.br) operates buses (R$5) to Barra de Santo Antônio from Maceió, although much faster is taking a *taxi comum* (R$10) from the Terminal Mercado da Produção. A normal taxi costs around R$50. By car, follow AL-101 north.

★ São Miguel dos Milagres

A tranquil fishing village 110 kilometers (70 mi) north of Maceió, **São Miguel dos Milagres** (www.saomigueldosmilagres.net.) is one of Alagoas's oldest settlements. With a whitewashed colonial church and a charming cluster of historic houses, it is completely surrounded by thick palm forests. This whole stretch of coastline is rife with coconut plantations (a bonus is that sweet, refreshing *água de coco* is cheaper and more plentiful than water). Aside from its utterly relaxing vibe, the beaches in the vicinity of São Miguel—among them Toque, Porto da Rua, Tatuamunha, Patacho, Lages, and Porto de Pedras—are stunners, and their reef-protected waters (the reefs themselves can be reached by boat) are flooded with colorful fish. While São Miguel remains deliciously untrampled by tourism, a number of extremely charming and quite sophisticated *pousadas* have opened on remote beaches, making this an ideal destination for a stylish getaway.

ACCOMMODATIONS AND FOOD

São Miguel's accommodation offerings are truly some of the most attractive on the whole Northeast coast (with fine restaurants to boot; owners will happily shuttle you from one to another). To get to these *pousadas*—located amid tiny fishing villages or on secluded beaches—you'll need a car (or need to brave multiple collective vans), although if you call ahead, staff will pick you up in Maceió.

The most luxurious option on this coast is the gorgeously secluded ★ **Pousada do Toque** (Rua Felisberto de Ataíde, Praia do Toque, tel. 82/3295-1127, www.pousadadotoque.com.br, R$680-1,580 d), located on the Praia do Toque, only 2 kilometers (1.2 mi) from São Miguel. Set amid an Edenic garden right off the deserted beach, the hotel features solar-energized cabanas outfitted with fine Italian linens, DVD players, and jetted tubs. The sprawling estate features swimming pools, a tennis court, a wine cellar, a bar, and plenty of decks and verandas for lounging. Two gourmet restaurants (dinner is included in the rate) and a sushi bar serve up divine creations with fresh produce harvested from the sea as well as the on-site organic garden.

Another 2 kilometers (1.2 mi) up the coast, near the pretty little fishing village of Porto da Rua, ★ **Pousada Côté Sud** (Praia do Porto da Rua, tel. 82/3295-1283, www.pousadacotesud.com.br, R$295-495 d) is owned by a Belgian couple who brought their refined sense of craftsmanship to the design of this beautiful beachside guesthouse. Accommodations are in cool bungalows creatively and thematically decorated with works by local artisans. The lush grounds include an elevated pool with a stunning view of the beach and a romantic gourmet restaurant (dinner is included in the rate). The owners can arrange a variety of outings, from horseback riding and snorkeling to shrimp and crab fishing (after which you can have your catch cooked for you). Children under 16 aren't allowed.

Most hotels in São Miguel don't accept kids, but if you have a few in tow, you'll be more than welcome at **Borapirá** (Praia de Tatuamunha, tel. 82/3298-6233, www.borapira.com.br, R$270-300 d), which has multiple kiddie pools, sprawling grounds, a charming indoor playroom filled with artisanal toys, and a mini zoo (with mini ponies and some Crayola-colored toucans). Even the delicious restaurant features a kid's menu. No matter what your age, the fetching bungalows (with porches and hammocks) and splendidly isolated beach seduce. For true romance, the owners operate the equally secluded **Pousada Aldeia Beijupirá** (Praia do Lage, tel. 82/3298-6520, www.aldeiabeijupira.com.br, R$485-750 d), whose palm-thatched buildings are modeled after indigenous *malocas*. Back-to-nature accoutrements range from shrimp-net light fixtures to polished sea shells in the beautiful bathrooms (a little less aboriginal are the home theaters and jetted tubs). Simple, more affordable **Pousada Riacho dos Milagres** (Praia do Riacho, tel. 82/3295-1206, www.riachodosmilagres.com.br, R$300-400 d) is a small, tranquil beachfront option with airy, comfortable rooms; all sport quality amenities and overlook a garden with a pool. Multiple decks, hammocks, and a reading gazebo gaze right onto beckoning Praia do Riacho (only a couple of kilometers from São Miguel).

TRANSPORTATION

From Maceió, **Real Alagoas** (tel. 82/3356-1324, www.realalagoas.com.br) operates five daily buses to Porto de Pedras (3.5 hours, R$20) with stops in São Miguel dos Milagres and Porto do Rua. You can also flag down any number of minibuses or *taxi comuns* heading north along the coast; have a city taxi let you off at the Mar Azul gas station on the northern outskirts of Maceió, which is a main pick-up point. Fare is around R$14. By car, follow AL-101 north to Usina Santo Antônio and then turn off onto AL-435. Easier, but more expensive, is to ask your *pousada*—all of whom work with trusted *motoristas*—to pick you up in Maceió. Expect to pay around R$150-200.

Maragogi

Halfway between Maceió and Recife, and 130 kilometers (80 mi) from both, **Maragogi** (www.maragogionline.com.br) is the most popular beach destination in Alagoas. The village sits between the banks of the Rio Maragogi and an unbelievably turquoise sea. Tourism has hit hard and fast, and the beach is an increasingly lively place. Those in search of peace and tranquility need merely venture a few kilometers to the more rustic beaches of São Bento, Japaratinga, and Bitingui to the south or Barra Grande, Ponta de Manga, and Peroba to the north. Although they are accessible by car, bus, and collective minivans, you can also get to them by boat, dune buggy, on horseback, or even by mountain bike (the hard-packed sand is a delight to stroll, ride, or pedal).

Part of the Costa dos Corais (Coral Coast), this coastal stretch is renowned for its immense ocean pools framed by coral reefs, which can be reached by boat. In many places, during low tide you can walk far out toward the reefs. The most famous and fabulous of all the natural pools along Alagoas's coast are known as the Galés and are located off Maragogi. The entire coastal region is part of an environmentally protected area of reefs that extends for 135 kilometers (84 mi).

SPORTS AND RECREATION

The big thing in Maragogi is hitting the reefs for snorkeling and diving. Most regular excursions to the Galés last two hours and cost R$65 (add an extra R$10 for snorkel gear); you can also hire your own private boat. To avoid the crush of Maragogi's reefs, boats also travel to the smaller but more remote and better preserved Barra Grande, Taoca, and Barreira de Peroba. The majority of outings are organized by beachfront restaurants such as **Ponto de Embarque** (Av. Beira Mar 327, tel. 82/3296-1400) or by hotels.

Costazul (tel. 82/3296-2125, www.costazulturimso.com.br) is an ecotour outfit that organizes excursions along the coast and into the *mata atlântica* (where you can nestle in the trunk of a 500-year-old *visgueiro* tree). They also rent cars so you can explore the coast on your own. Many hotels have their own private *piscinas* and organize outings.

ACCOMMODATIONS AND FOOD

Most lodgings in Maragogi are uninspiring, but **Pousada Olho d'Água** (Rua José Machado Carvalho Raposo 156, Praia do Maragogi, tel. 82/3296-1263, www.pousadaolhodagua.com.br, R$190-260 d) is a fairly nice beachfront option facing the sand. Tidy guest rooms are comfortable and modern, with large beds and air-conditioning; some have sea views, but noise can be an issue. For more seclusion, the ★ **Praiagogi Boutique Pousada** (Praia Camacho, tel. 82/3296-1510, www.pousadapraiagogi.com.br, R$320-380 d) is a great choice. It sits on a practically deserted beach 2 kilometers (1.2 mi) south of Maragogi. Owned by a charming Dutch-Brazilian couple, the cozy and carefully decorated suites feature private verandas. At the on-site restaurant **Tuyn** (lunch and dinner), meals are prepared with fresh produce in an open kitchen and eaten at a communal table.

There are plenty of places for fish and seafood along Av. Senador Rui Palmeira. It's far more idyllic at **Restaurante Burgalhau,** where (after a considerable wait) you can tuck into the well-prepared seafood served in billowing beach tents overlooking the fluffy sands of Praia Burgalhau, a tranquil beach adjacent to Maragogi. Arrive early to score a good table.

TRANSPORTATION

There is a Banco do Brasil with an ATM that accepts international cards. From Maceió, **Real Alagoas** (tel. 82/3356-1324, www.realalagoas.com.br) operates seven daily buses to Maragogi (2.5 hours, R$20) via Recife. During the day, you can also hail a *taxi comum* heading north along the coast; have a city taxi let you off at the Mar Azul gas station on the northern outskirts of Maceió, a main pick-up point. Fare is around R$30. By car, follow the AL-101 north.

The Northeast Coast

Highlights

★ **Dune Buggying in Natal:** Natal is famed for its coastline of quasi-Saharan sand dunes, and the best way to navigate them is by dune buggy (page 467).

★ **Praia da Pipa:** Charming hotels, gourmet restaurants, and chic boutiques haven't spoiled the laid-back vibe or idyllic beauty of one of the most famous dolphin-studded beaches on Brazil's northeastern coast (page 476).

★ **Canoa Quebrada:** This hip beach town combines a mellow atmosphere with the high drama of crumbling red cliffs, immense white dunes, and luminous blue waters (page 490).

★ **Jericoacoara:** Remote and unspoiled Jericoacoara is more than just one of the planet's most revered and worshipped beaches—it's an otherworldly experience (page 494).

★ *Centro Histórico* **in São Luís:** Crammed with pastel-colored palaces and pulsing with reggae and pounding drums, São Luís's historic center is one of the most atmospheric colonial ensembles in Brazil (page 499).

★ **Lençóis Maranhenses:** One of Brazil's most spectacular national parks features immense snow-white sand dunes with valleys of jade-green lagoons (page 508).

T he 1,300-kilometer (800-mi) coastline that rises north from Pernambuco to the small state of Rio Grande do Norte is almost one long, spectacular beach.

Its endlessness should not be confused with monotony. Beaches along this stretch of Northeast coast range from fine white sands backed by rugged red cliffs to vast Sahara-like dunes where buggies reign supreme. While an abundance of coral reefs means that waves are often too puny for serious surfing (snorkelers, however, are in for a treat), strong and steady easterly trade winds blowing across the Atlantic from Africa have transformed much of the coastline into one of the world's best kite surfing spots. Many beaches, such as Galinhos, Icaraí de Amontada, and Jericoacoara, are quite remote and can only be reached by boat or after hours of four-wheeling through the dunes. Others, such as Pipa and Canoa Quebrada, have developed into charmingly sophisticated resorts without losing their palmy, hippie, flip-flop vibe. There are plenty of dunes to go around, but the biggest of all are located in the Parque Nacional dos Lençóis Maranhenses, a vast lunar landscape of stupendous 50-meter (165-foot) dunes dotted with thousands of green oasis-like lakes. All in all, it's impossible not to unwind. Should you require a dose of city life, the modern capitals of Natal and Fortaleza offer impressive beaches, an appealing mixture of urban energy and laid-back hospitality, and infectious *forró* music.

A transition state between the sunbaked aridness of the Northeast and the rainy lushness of the Amazon rain forest, Maranhão's island capital, São Luís, is one of Brazil's oldest and most fascinating cities. Often overlooked by tourists, São Luís possesses a striking colonial center awash in mansions and palaces whose facades are covered in ornately patterned Portuguese azulejos. The local culture, with its renowned reggae scene and *tambor de crioula* drumming and dances, was greatly influenced by African slaves who came to work in the region's colonial sugar plantations. African elements are also visible in the fantastically colorful Bumba-Meu-Boi festivities that take place in June. Across the bay of São Marcos from São Luís, Maranhão's first capital, Alcântara, is a wonderfully atmospheric

Previous: Fortaleza; hammocks on a northeastern beach; **Above:** dunes in Jericoacoara Beach.

The Northeast Coast

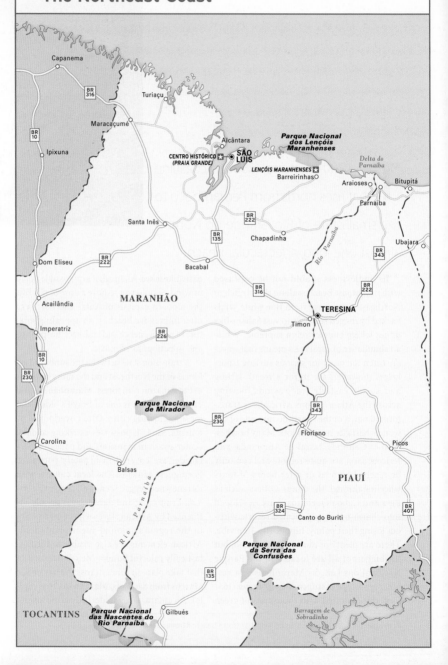

Capanema

BR 316

Turiaçu

Maracaçumé

BR 10

Ipixuna

Alcântara

Parque Nacional dos Lençóis Maranhenses

CENTRO HISTÓRICO (PRAIA GRANDE)

SÃO LUÍS

Delta do Parnaíba

LENÇÓIS MARANHENSES

Barreirinhas

Araioses

Bitupitá

Parnaíba

Santa Inês

BR 222

BR 135

Chapadinha

Rio Parnaíba

Ubajara

BR 343

Dom Eliseu

BR 222

Bacabal

BR 316

BR 222

MARANHÃO

TERESINA

Acailândia

Timon

Imperatriz

BR 226

BR 10

BR 230

Parque Nacional de Mirador

BR 230

BR 343

Carolina

Floriano

Picos

Balsas

PIAUÍ

Rio Parnaíba

BR 324

Canto do Buriti

BR 407

Parque Nacional da Serra das Confusões

BR 135

TOCANTINS

Parque Nacional das Nascentes do Rio Parnaíba

Gilbués

Barragem de Sobradinho

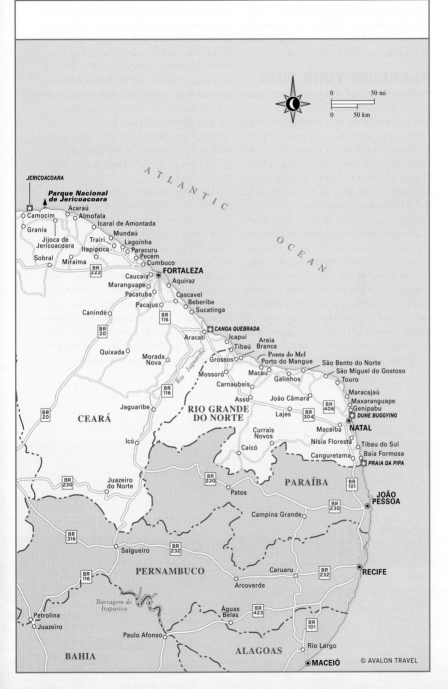

© AVALON TRAVEL

place. As you wander among its grand colonial mansions in varying states of decay, you'll be struck by how the town is being invaded by the dense tropical forest that surrounds it.

PLANNING YOUR TIME

With the exception of São Luís, the main draw of the Northeast coast is its beaches. So how you plan your time really depends on whether you're restless and want to beach-hop or would rather just choose one or two idyllic getaways where you can veg out. Rio Grande do Norte is a small state. By basing yourself in Natal, you can very easily spend **5-7 days** exploring the coastline north and south of the city while stopping for a couple of days at Praia da Pipa. Sprawling Ceará deserves a little more time. Fortaleza, while not beautiful, is a vibrant city that warrants a day or two; more for some day trips. You'll be disappointed if you don't stay over in Canoa Quebrada, and plan at least **4-5 days** for Jericoacoara (it takes close to a day just to get there). Some people end up staying in "Jeri" for weeks. As for São Luís, three days is the minimum you'd want to stay. Having come

so far, it would be a crime not to add another three days to explore the dunes and lagoons of the Lençóis Maranhenses. Traveling between Natal and Fortaleza is easy, and all of Ceará's beaches are quite accessible by bus and car (some of Rio Grande do Norte's are more difficult to access without wheels). São Luís is more remote. Bus service from other cities takes forever, and plane fare can be steep. Adventurous souls with time on their hands (a week or two) can travel by Jeep (and, in parts, by dune buggy) up the entire coastline, from Natal to São Luís.

Due to its proximity to the Equator, you'll find the Northeast coast **hot year-round**. Rio Grande do Norte and Ceará are notoriously sunny. Even during the so-called "rainy season," which generally occurs March-May, you're treated to quick downpours more than days of drizzle. Under the sway of the Amazon's climate, Maranhão is considerably wetter, particularly January-May. If you want the beaches to yourself, **avoid peak seasons of January-February and July,** when both Rio Grande do Norte and Ceará are mobbed by Brazilian and international tourists.

dunes of Ceará

Natal and Rio Grande do Norte

The tiny state of Rio Grande do Norte is known foremost for its vast sand-dune beaches (and the dune buggies required to navigate them).

NATAL

The main reason for visiting the small capital of Rio Grande do Norte is to take advantage of its endless amounts of sun and sand. In truth, Natal's beaches never stop. They just keep going for hundreds of kilometers in either direction.

In 1501, Portuguese navigator Amerigo Vespucci landed 32 kilometers (20 mi) north of Natal at the northeastern tip of South America (and the closest point to Europe from Brazil), a spot he christened Cabo São Roque. Despite this new discovery, for decades Portugal showed little interest in the sweeping coastline inhabited by the Potiguar Indians. But in 1597, annoyed by the growing *pau brasil* (brazilwood) trade between French pirates and the Potiguar, the Portuguese decided to get territorial. They proceeded to build the Forte dos Reis Magos, an imposing fortress that guarded the entrance to the Rio Potengi from the sea. Officially established on December 25, 1599, the village that rose up around the fort became known as Natal (Christmas). Once the French were expelled, subsequent Dutch invaders defeated, and the aggressive Potiguar subdued, Natal settled down into its role as a small outpost. Despite its coastline, for centuries the state's main source of revenue came from the cattle that were raised in the interior, but traded and shipped from Natal.

During World War II, Natal's strategic proximity to Western Europe and Africa led to the establishment of an American air base that became the Allies' military base for operations into North Africa. As a result, thousands of American pilots and soldiers flooded Natal's dunes, and Natalenses became the first

Brazilians to be introduced to ketchup, bubble gum, and blue jeans. However, it wasn't until later in the 20th century that the growth of the salt and petroleum industries—Rio Grande do Norte produces 95 percent of Brazil's salt and has some of the country's biggest inland oil reserves—coupled with nascent tourism caused the city to grow in leaps and bounds, acquiring a modern skyline of high-rise condos and hotels.

Sights

What few historical sights Natal possesses are located in the *bairros* of Ribeira and Cidade Alta, which fan out from the **Forte dos Reis Magos** (Av. Presidente Café Filho, Praia do Forte, tel. 84/3202-9006, 8am-4:30pm daily, R$3). The most impressive of the all-too-few vestiges of the past is the star-shaped fort itself. Poised majestically along a reef and built using a mixture of stone, sand, whale oil, and oyster shells, it is separated from the tip of the city by a sandbar. Construction on the fort began on January 6, 1598—the feast day of the Reis Magos (Three Kings). Inside, the most important historical artifact on display is the Marco de Touros, a limestone cross engraved with the herald of the Portuguese king. The cross, originally planted in the village of São Miguel do Gostoso in 1501, symbolizes the first claim to Portuguese territory in Brazil. In 1962, it was transferred to the fort because villagers—who had come to view it as a miraculous object—had taken to chipping pieces off to make curative teas for ailing family members. From its ramparts, the views of the city and coastline are stupendous.

A couple of leisurely hours is enough to explore the rest of what's left of historic Centro. The heart of the colonial city is **Praça André de Albuquerque.** It is flanked on one side by the 17th-century **Igreja Matriz de Nossa Senhora da Apresentação.** A block away lies the pretty baroque **Igreja de Santo**

Natal

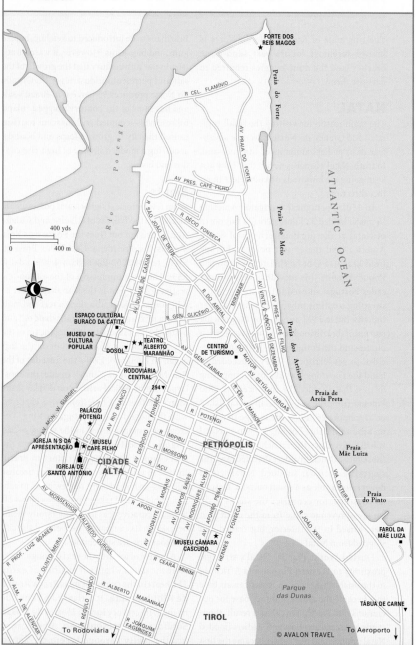

FORTE DOS
REIS MAGOS

Praia do Forte

R CEL. FLAMÍNIO

AV PRAIA DO FORTE

AV PRES. CAFÉ FILHO

R DÉCIO FONSECA

Praia do Meio

R SÃO JOÃO DE DEUS

ATLANTIC OCEAN

Rio Potengi

0   400 yds
0   400 m

AV DUQUE DE CAXIAS

R DO ARIAL

MIRAMAR

AV VINTE E CINCO DE DEZEMBRO

AV PRES. CAFÉ FILHO

Praia dos Artistas

R GEN. GLICÉRIO

ESPAÇO CULTURAL
BURACO DA CATITA

MUSEU DE
CULTURA
POPULAR

DOSOL

TEATRO
ALBERTO
MARANHÃO

CENTRO
DE TURISMO

R DO MOTOR

AV GETÚLIO VARGAS

RODOVIÁRIA
CENTRAL

AV GEN. FARIAS

294

PALÁCIO
POTENGI

AV MON. W. GURGEL

AV RIO BRANCO

AV DEODORO DA FONSECA

R POTENGI

R GEL. J MANUEL

Praia de
Areia Preta

IGREJA N S DA
APRESENTAÇÃO

MUSEU
CAFÉ FILHO

R MIPIBU

R MOSSORÓ

PETRÓPOLIS

Praia
Mãe Luiza

IGREJA DE
SANTO ANTÔNIO

CIDADE
ALTA

R AÇU

VIA CISTEIRA

Praia
do Pinto

AV MONSENHOR WALFREDO GURGEL

R APODI

AV PRUDENTE DE MORAIS

AV CAMPOS SALES

AV RODRIGUES ALVES

AV AFONSO PENA

AV HERMES DA FONSECA

R JOÃO XXIII

FAROL DA
MÃE LUIZA

MUSEU CÂMARA
CASCUDO

R CEARÁ MIRIM

R PROF. LUIZ SOARES

R QUINTO MEIRA

AV ALM. A DE ALENCAR

R ALBERTO

MARANHÃO

R RÉGULO TINOCO

Parque
das Dunas

TIROL

R JOAQUIM
FAGUNDES

To Rodoviária

TÁBUA DE CARNE

To Aeroporto

© AVALON TRAVEL

Antônio (Rua Santo Antônio 698), which houses a small museum. Surrounding the **Praça Sete de Setembro** is the **Palácio Potengi** (tel. 84/3211-7056, 8:30am-4:30pm Tues.-Sun., free), the Victorian-style former governor's palace, which displays a collection of period furniture along with temporary exhibits of works by local artists. The city's premier theater, the grandly neoclassical **Teatro Alberto Maranhão** (Praça Augusto Severo, tel. 84/3222-3669, www.teatroalbertomaranhao.rn.gov.br, 9am-5pm Mon.-Fri.), is located a few blocks west of the Palácio Potengi.

A trio of modest museums are worth popping into. The **Museu Café Filho** (Rua da Conceição 601, Ribeira, tel. 84/3232-9724, 9am-5pm Tues.-Sat., R$1) makes a big deal about the fact that its former inhabitant, João Fernandes Campos Café Filho, was once president of Brazil. In truth, the inept Natalense only lasted a year in power. He stepped in after Getúlio Vargas shot himself in 1954, and quickly stepped down again in early 1956, citing poor health. If you have time, take a quick spin through his elegant mansion. The small **Museu Câmara Cascudo** (Av. Hermes da Fonseca 1398, Tirol, tel. 84/3342-4914, 9am-4:30pm Tues.-Fri.) provides an informative hands-on overview of Rio Grande do Norte's social and natural history. Fun gimmicks include stepping into a typical fisherman's shack and investigating a recreated salt mine. Occupying the second floor of a renovated old bus station, the **Museu de Cultura Popular** (Praça Augusto Severo, Ribeira, tel. 84/3232-8149, 9am-4pm Mon.-Fri., 10am-4pm Sat., free) offers permanent and temporary exhibits that testify to the richness of Rio Grande do Norte's popular arts, both visual and musical.

Beaches

Natal is all about its beaches, but urbanization has taken its toll on the central ones of **Praia do Forte, Praia do Meio** and the formerly fashionable but increasingly seedy **Praia dos Artistas.**

A rocky headland separates Praia dos Artistas from **Praia de Areia Preta,** where

reefs make bathing dangerous. Rising up at the far end of the beach, the **Farol da Mãe Luiza** lighthouse marks the beginning point of **Parque das Dunas** (Av. Alexandrino de Alencar, Tirol tel. 84/3201-3985, 8am-6pm daily, R$1), an urban park situated amid the dunes that has a trio of hiking trails (guided walks depart at 8am, 8:30am, 2pm, and 2:30pm daily; advance reservations required) and *lanchonetes.* Lined with resort hotels, the Via Costeira coastal highway runs from Natal all the way to Praia de Ponta Negra 10 kilometers (6 mi) away, and passes through the park.

Ponta Negra is the nicest of Natal's beaches. Its most unique feature is the gigantic sand dune at the southern tip. Known as **Morro da Careca** (Bald Man's Hill), its nickname accurately evokes the dune's resemblance to a bald head (although the lush foliage surrounding the strip of white sand makes it look more like an inverted Mohawk). Over the last few years, all the action that used to take place at Natal's more central beaches has migrated to Ponta Negra. Although the beach is still attractive—featuring both calm and wavy waters—it has also become quite touristy. The southern strip of the beach is particularly full of hotels, trendy restaurants, and bars, along with a colorfully diverse mix of locals, foreigners, and *ambulantes* (vendors) hawking their wares along the sands. At night, Ponta Negra is one of the most happening places in the city. For more peace and tranquility, head to the more sedate and upscale northern tip. Ultimately, Ponta Negra is like a small city in itself, and you can easily spend all your days and nights here.

★ Dune Buggying

In Rio Grande do Norte, beaches and buggies are an inseparable pairing. Young buggy drivers, known as *bugueiros,* are rampant in Natal. Before setting off, however, a *bugueiro* will considerately inquire whether you want the jaunt to be *com emoção* or *sem emoção* (i.e., with or without emotional thrills). Respond at your own risk.

Some people take to buggy riding, while

others aren't so crazy about (literally) getting sand in their faces. However, racing madly through the dunes, with or without stunts, is an unforgettable experience. From Natal, you can take half-day and full-day trips along the north and south coastlines. This is an ideal way of getting an overview of the region's beautiful beaches, many of which you can't get to by bus. You can book buggy excursions through hotels and tour agencies as well as directly with the *bugueiros* themselves via the Genipabu-based **Associação de Proprietários e Condutores de Buggy** (APCBA; tel. 84/3225-2077, www. genipabudebuggy.com.br). Before taking off, ask to see the official SETUR certification of the *bugueiro*. Both the APCBA and **Marazul** (Rua Desportista José Leão de Oliveira 75, Ponta Negra, tel. 84/3219-2221, www.passeiodebuggy.com.br, R$100-120 pp) offer a full-day trip following the coastline north of Natal to Genipabu, with stops at beaches and the freshwater lagoons of Pitangui and Jacumã.

Entertainment and Events
NIGHTLIFE
Most of Natal's nightlife takes place in the lively beach neighborhood of Alto de Ponta Negra as well as in Centro. The old riverside *bairro* of Ribeira, adjacent to Cidade Alta, lures a young and alternative crowd. Since parts of Centro—Ribeira and Praia dos Artistas, in particular—can be a little louche, especially at night, taxis are recommended.

In Centro, the three airy, plant-festooned salons that compose **294** (Av. Deodoro da Fonseca 294, Cidade Alta, tel. 84/3211-1783, www.bar24.com.br, 6pm-midnight Thurs.-Fri., 11am-11pm Sat.-Sun.) make this laid-back bar a favorite happy-hour option. The seafood *petiscos,* such as crab with coconut, and the organic oysters are highly regarded, and you can easily make a meal of the shrimp and vegetables cooked in coconut milk.

The bars around Praça Pôr do Sol are ideal for watching the sunset over the Rio Potengi, while Rua Chile has alternative clubs and performance spaces such as the **Centro Cultural Dosol** (Rua Chile 40, Ribeira, tel. 84/3642-1520, www.dosol.com.br, 8pm-close Wed.-Sat., cover R$10-20), a renovated warehouse where you can rock out to local underground bands. The **Espaço Cultural Buraco da Catita** (Trav. José Alexandre Garcia 95, Ribeira, tel. 84/2010-9185, www.buracodacatita.com.br, 8pm-2am Thurs.-Sat.) is an

Morro da Careca

inviting place to listen to more mellow strains of live music, particularly jazz and *chorinho*.

Soak up some sand with your suds at **Old Five** (Praia Ponta Negra in front of Morro da Careca, tel. 84/3236-3696, 8pm-1am daily). Lounge in beach chairs by day, then enjoy the intimate ambiance at night (aided by a soundtrack of live reggae, MPB, and samba). Located within the cozy "dungeon" of the castle-like Lua Cheia Hostel, the **Taverna Pub Medieval** (Rua Dr. Manoel Augusto Bezerra de Araújo 500, Alto de Ponta Negra, tel. 84/3236-3696, www.tavernapub.com.br, 10:30pm-close Mon.-Sat., cover R$10-20) has long worn the crown of the most happening dance spot in town. Ever since he was a kid, the Paulistano owner has had a fondness for things medieval, which explains the mildly kitschy decorative scheme of shields, banners, and armor. However, the music, which leans toward pop, rock, and MPB, is definitely contemporary, as are the imaginative themed *festas* that occur nightly. To catch some *forró*, head to **Rastapé** (Rua Aristides Porpino Filho 2198, Alto de Ponta Negra, tel. 84/3219-0181, www.rastapecasadeforro.com.br, 10pm-4am Wed. and Fri.-Sat.), a relaxed and rustic place where you can sip *cachaça* and watch couples whirl each other around.

PERFORMING ARTS

Natal's premier theater is the opulent, neo-classical **Teatro Alberto Maranhão** (Praça Augusto Severo, Ribeira, tel. 84/3222-3669, www.teatroalbertomaranhao.rn.gov.br), which hosts dance, theater, and musical events. Occupying a beautifully restored old mansion, **Casa da Ribeira** (Rua Frei Miguelinho 52, Ribeira, tel. 84/3211-7710, www.casadaribeira.com.br, 4pm-10pm Tues.-Sun.) provides a charming venue for local artists. Alternative theatrical, dance, and musical performances are held here, along with film screenings and art exhibits. There is also an attractive café.

FESTIVALS AND EVENTS

Carnatal (tel. 84/4006-0990, www.carnatal.com.br) is the name of Natal's out-of-season Carnaval. For four days in late November-early December, the streets surrounding the Arena das Dunas stadium in the *bairro* of Lagoa Nova go crazy as the stars of Salvador's mega Carnaval whip the crowds into a frenzy with throbbing *axé* music sung from the tops of *trios elétricos* (massive stages on wheels).

Shopping

In Centro, a former 19th-century orphanage

buggy riding Rio Grande do Norte's dunes

and prison now houses the **Centro de Turismo** (Rua Aderbal de Figueiredo 980, Petrópolis, tel. 84/3211-6149, www.forrocomturista.com.br, 8am-6pm daily). Each cell is occupied by a vendor selling regional handicrafts such as lace, pottery, wood carvings, and blue-and-white painted azulejos, a tradition handed down from the Portuguese. There is a tourist office here as well as a dance hall, where live *forró* (10pm-2am Thurs., R$25) attracts both gringos and locals. In Ponta Negra, you'll find a wide array of handicrafts along with edible delicacies at the **Shopping do Artesanato Potiguar** (Av. Eng. Roberto Freire 8000, www.shoppingartesanatopotiguar.com.br, tel. 84/3219-3207, 10am-10pm Mon.-Sat., 9am-9pm Sun.). For more contemporary items, head next door to the mall at **Praia Shopping** (Av. Engenheiro Roberto Freire 8790, Ponta Negra, tel. 84/4008-0842, www.praiashopping.com.br, 10am-10pm Mon.-Sat., 3pm-9pm Sun.).

Accommodations

Although Natal has lots of hotels in the city, the beach at Ponta Negra is much nicer, and you'll find scads of options. Prices below are for the off-season.

R$50-200

Lua Cheia Hostel (Rua Dr. Manoel Augusto Bezerra de Araújo 500, Ponta Negra, tel. 84/3236-3696, www.luacheia.com.br, R$115-150 d, R$44-55 pp) defies expectations. The exterior resembles a medieval castle, complete with towers and a drawbridge. Inside, the Middle Ages theme continues with bunks located in cellar-like dorm rooms that sleep six. Despite the excess brick, the place has a kooky-spooky charm, and the staff is friendly. For party animals (which this place attracts), a bonus is that one of Natal's hottest nightspots is located in the "dungeon." Small and homey **Pousada Castanheira** (Rua da Praia 221, Ponta Negra, tel. 84/3236-2918, www.pousadacastanheira.com.br, R$150-190 d) is an inviting place with lively color

and a verdant garden surrounding the small pool and bar. Guest rooms are cheerful; the best and biggest, 201, has a terrace overlooking the sea.

R$200-400

Intimate and organic ★ **Pousada Manga Rosa** (Av. Erivan França 240, Ponta Negra, tel. 84/3219-0508, www.mangarosanatal.com.br, R$180-240 d) is a stylishly rustic hotel built around a mango tree. Located right on the beach, its multiple balconies and verandas gaze right on Morro de Careca. Guest rooms, while fairly standard, have nice decorative flourishes; the "master" rooms feature terraces.

OVER R$400

The most romantic and sophisticated hotel on the entire coast is the ★ **Manary Praia Hotel** (Rua Francisco Gurgel 9067, Ponta Negra, tel. 84/3204-2900, Ponta Negra, www.manary.com.br, R$390-790 d). *Manary* is a Potiguar term for "well-being," which is something of an understatement considering this exquisite complex of neocolonial villas set amid exuberant gardens. It has a prime beach location, two swimming pools, waterfalls, and fish ponds. The lofty guest rooms are luxurious, with fine linens, carefully chosen art, and wide balconies. Serving polished contemporary versions of regional cuisine, the restaurant is a gastronomic high point.

Food

Natal is a great place to indulge in regional *potiguar* specialties. Choose between hearty Sertanejo fare, such as sun-dried beef and roasted goat, and fresh fish and seafood dishes (lobster and shrimp are particularly abundant) from the coast.

CAFÉS AND SNACKS

Casa de Taipa (Rua Dr. Manoel Augusto Bezerra de Araújo 130-A, Alto de Ponta Negra, tel. 84/3219-5798, 5pm-midnight daily, R$5-15) is a delightfully laid-back hangout with a thatched palm roof, sandy floors, and adobe walls decorated with local art (for sale). The city's premier *tapiocaria* serves up a delicious array of this Northeast version of a crepe made with crunchy manioc flour.

BRAZILIAN

When migrants from Rio Grande do Norte's interior get homesick, they head to ★ **Mangai** (Av. Amintas Barros 3300, Lagoa Nova, tel. 84/3206-3344, www.mangai.com. br, 11am-10pm daily, R$20-30). A ranch-style decor coupled with waiters sporting straw hats and leather sandals conjure up a slightly hokey version of a typical Sertanejo farm. However, what really satiates customers' nostalgia is the vast buffet of regional specialties—*carne-de-sol na nata* (sun-dried beef in cream), *sovaco de cobra* (shredded *carne-de-sol* cooked with corn and manioc flour), and *gororoba* (*carne-de-sol* with manioc and cheese. There is also a large choice of salads as well as mouthwatering *doces* such as creamy *cocada* (a sweet coconut dessert) and *cartola oba-oba* (fried banana topped with Sertanejo cheese, caramelized sugar, cinnamon, and chocolate). Although slightly off the beaten track, this restaurant is highly recommended as an appetizing introduction to the culinary traditions of the northeastern interior.

The succulent *carne-de-sol* served at **Tábua de Carne** (Av. Eng. Roberto Freire 3241, Capim Maceio, tel. 84/3642-1236, www. tabuadecarne.com.br, 11:30am-3:30pm and 6:30pm-11pm daily, R$25-35) hails from Picuí, a town in the neighboring state of Paraíba that is as famous for its sun-dried beef as Bordeaux is for fine wines. At this carnivore's heaven, the *carne-de-sol* is made from filet mignon and comes accompanied with such fixings as green *feijão*, fried manioc, and pumpkin puree. À la carte portions serve three, but you can also choose the *rodízio* option (R$38-42 pp), which includes various meats along with a buffet of regional dishes. A second Via Costeira location (Av. Senador Dinarte Mariz, tel. 84/3202-7353), with only à la carte service, offers amazing seaside views.

INTERNATIONAL

Piazzale Italia (Av. Deputado Antônio Florêncio de Queiroz 12, Rota do Sol, Ponta Negra, tel. 84/3236-2697, www.piazzaleitalia.com.br, 6pm-midnight daily and noon-4pm Sun., R$25-35) is considered the finest Italian restaurant in town. Patrons swear by the homemade *grano duro* pasta, as well as imported ingredients such as skinless tomatoes, pine nuts, and porcini mushrooms. Thin-crust pizzas are topped with everything from classic prosciutto to local fresh lobster. The outdoor terrace is popular.

SEAFOOD

Occupying a stylishly modern adobe house with a view of the sea, ★ **Camarões Potiguar** (Rua Pedro da Fonseca Filho 8887, Ponta Negra, tel. 84/3209-2425, www. camaroes.com.br, 11:30am-3:30pm and 6:30pm-midnight daily, R$20-25) specializes in *camarões* (shrimp) cultivated at the restaurant's own aquatic farms. Influences are both regional (*camarão cajueiro* stars shrimp topped with crushed cashews in a passion-fruit sauce), and international (*camarão au gratin* features shrimp cooked in a stew of white wine, Dijon mustard, hearts of palm, and béchamel sauce with a gratin of gruyère).

Information and Services

The main tourist office is in the **Centro de Turismo** (Rua Aderbal de Figueiredo 980, Petrópolis, tel. 84/3211-6149, www.turismo. natal.rn.gov.br, 8am-7pm daily). You'll also find a branch at the airport (tel. 84/3087-1200, 9am-5pm daily). **Praia Shopping** (Av. Eng. Roberto Freire 8790, Ponta Negra, tel. 84/3219-4323, www.praiashopping.com.br) is where you'll find branches of Banco do Brasil and Banco 24 Horas with ATMs.

In the event of an emergency, dial **193** for an ambulance or the fire department, and **190** for the police. There is a special 24-hour **tourist police** unit at Praia Shopping (tel. 84/3232-7404). For medical treatment, try the **Hospital Monsenhor Walfredo Gurgel**

(Av. Hermes Fonseca 817, Tirol, tel. 84/3232-7530, www.walfredogurgel.rn.gov.br).

Transportation

AIR

Flights from all over Brazil arrive at the **Aeroporto Augusto Severo** (Rua Rio Xingu, Emaus, Parnamirim, tel. 84/3087-1200), which lies 15 kilometers (9 mi) from the center of town and 12 kilometers (7.5 mi) from Ponta Negra. A taxi costs around R$55 to Centro and R$45 to Ponta Negra. You can also take a municipal bus (R$2.90) marked Natal, which travels to Praça Cívica in Centro. Under construction since 1995, the **Aeroporto São Gonçalo do Amarante** (Rua Rio Xingu, Emaus, Parnamirim, tel. 84/3087-1200), located some 40 kilometers (25 mi) from Centro, is slated to open (at some undefined moment) in 2014 and will become the city's main air hub.

BUS

Long-distance buses arrive at the **Rodoviária Nova** (Av. Capitão Mor Gouveia 1237, Cidade de Esperança, tel. 84/3205-4377). From here, you can grab a cab to Centro (around R$25) or Ponta Negra (R$35) or take a municipal bus to municipal **Rodoviária Velha** in Ribeira (Centro). Buses also depart here (including the 54 and 56 buses) that run along the Via Costeira to Ponta Negra.

Getting to and from Centro and Ponta Negra is quick and simple by bus (R$2.40). From Centro to Ponta Negra, take any bus marked "Via Costeira" or "Ponta Negra"—from Ponta Negra, hop any bus bound for Centro or Cidade Alta (buses will take the coastal highway or inland avenues).

CAR AND TAXI

Driving is fairly stress-free, and a car is a great plus for exploring less accessible beaches north and south of Natal. **Localiza** (tel. 84/3643-1557, www.localiza.com) and **Avis** (tel. 84/3087-1403, www.avis.com.br) both have offices at the airport. Taxis are affordable

and easy to hail. You can also call **Disk Taxi Natal** (tel. 84/3223-7388).

CITY TOURS

Cariri Ecotours (Trav. Joaquim Fagundes 719, Tirol, tel. 84/9660-1818, www.caririecotours.com.br) has an assortment of guided tours throughout Rio Grande do Norte and the neighboring states of Ceará, Paraíba, and Piauí, including many into the Sertão. Lasting from one day to one week, trips are customized for small groups and led by multilingual guides.

BEACHES NORTH OF NATAL

Heading north from Natal, the beaches get increasingly wild and the dunes more impressive. Most people visit these fairly touristy destinations on all-day buggy tours from Natal, which tour the best of the closest beaches stretching from Redinha across the Rio Potengi to Mariú, 50 kilometers (31 mi) north. Bus service is mostly nonexistent—the other cheaper (but sometimes time-consuming) alternative is to flag down a van (*transporte coletivo*); ask around, but they usually pass along Rua Prudente de Morais in Centro.

Redinha

Just across the Rio Potengi from Natal, this former fishing village is now urbanized, and there are far nicer beaches up and down the coast. To soak up local atmosphere, head to the old **Mercado Municipal** (Largo João Alfredo, 7am-6pm daily), where you can feast on *ginga com tapioca* (*tapioca* stuffed with fried fish). For easy access, grab a bus passing along Praia do Meio and Praia do Forte and crossing the Ponte Newton Navarro (also known as the Ponte Forte-Redinha).

Genipabu

Genipabu is a fishing village 25 kilometers (16 mi) from Natal whose spectacular sand dunes have become iconic. Genipabu is the primary destination of Natal's *bugueiros* since the constantly shifting dunes practically cry out to be buggied over (if you come here on your own, there are also many local *bugueiros* who can take you for a spin; R$240/hour for four people). Equally fun is trying to run up and down the dunes, or traveling across them by mule or dromedary. Yes, dromedaries were long ago imported from the Sahara, and they hardly look out of place at all. It's hard to resist a ride, even if costs R$45 for 15 minutes. Another very fun way to get sand up your nose is to indulge in *esquibunda* (R$8 pp), in which you place your posterior on a wooden board and go tobogganing down the dunes.

You can also take advantage of the waters of the mesmerizingly blue Lagoa de Genipabu, a freshwater lagoon fringed by lush plants and cashew trees. For lunch amid the dunes, head to **Bar 21** (tel. 84/3224-2484, 10am-6pm Tues.-Sun.) for delicious fish and seafood. Getting there involves a 10-minute trek through the sand; if driving, cross the Ponte Forte-Redinha and follow BR-406 to Genipabu.

Pitangui and Jacumã

Located 45 kilometers (28 mi) north of Natal, Pitangui is a little fishing village with an enticing palm-fringed beach. You can swim in the ocean or float, kayak, and pedal around the Lagoa Pitangui. Set amid snow-white dunes, the lagoon is also a great place to try *aerobunda*—which involves attaching yourself to a cable and swinging (butt-first) across the sand and into the water. The same fun can be had at the adjacent beach of Jacumã. Each *aerobunda* descent costs R$10.

Maracajaú

Maracajaú, which lies 60 kilometers (37 mi) north of Natal, offers some of the best snorkeling in Rio Grande do Norte. When the tide recedes, the extensive coral reefs, located 6 kilometers (4 mi) offshore, form vast natural pools known as *parrachos,* whose warm and particularly limpid waters, reached by boat, are transformed into fantastic open-air aquariums

(albeit very crowded ones during high season). Depending on the tides, depths range 2-6 meters (6-20 feet). The shallower regions are equipped with floating bars. **Maracajaú Diver** (Praia da Maracajaú, tel. 84/3261-6200, www.maracajaudiver.com.br) offers 2.5-hour snorkeling excursions (R$75) out to the reefs, along with "baptismal" diving excursions (R$95). **Expresso Cabral** (tel. 84/3205-4041, www.expressocabral.com.br) operates two daily departures (10:15am and 1:15pm), with a single departure on Sunday (6:30am), from Natal's Rodoviária Nova (R$10). By car, follow BR-101 in the direction of Touros. You can easily hire a taxi or buggy to bring you here from Natal.

SÃO MIGUEL DO GOSTOSO

Still on the cusp of being "discovered," the friendly fishing village of São Miguel do Gostoso (110 km north of Natal) is often referred to as "Gostoso," which in Portuguese translates to "hot, luscious, tasty." This enticing escape possesses just enough quality *pousadas* and restaurants to ensure comfort and variety.

Sports and Recreation

Among the numerous unspoiled, empty *praias* ripe for strolling and bathing is the stellar **Praia de Tourinhos,** 8 kilometers (5 mi) away, whose calm reef-protected waters are decorated by a sculpted landscape of 2,500-year-old petrified dunes. Tourinhos and other beaches can be explored via buggy excursions. A full-day outing (R$350 for four people) passes a dozen splendid specimens on its way to Galinhos, 90 kilometers (60 mi) to the west, with a stop at Tourinhos on the way back to watch the sun set.

Gostoso's wind conditions are ideal for both wind- and kite-surfing. The best beach for both is Ponta do Santo Cristo, 2 kilometers (1.25 mi) west of town. **Clube Kauli Seadi** (tel. 84/9197-1297, www.clubekauliseadi. com) and **Dr. Wind** (tel. 84/9981-0583, www. drwind.com.br) offer lessons (expect to pay upwards of R$100/hour) and rent equipment (R$125-160 per day, reduced rates for multiple days), as well as surf and stand-up paddle boards and bikes. They also organize excursions.

Accommodations and Food

Located off a beach that doubles as kite-and-wind-surf central, **Ilha do Vento Pousada & Hostel** (Rua das Caraúnas 70, Praia do Santo Cristo, tel. 84/9428-9909, www.pousadarivas.com.br, R$120-150 d, R$50 pp) offers sunny, spotless, and comfortable dorm and private rooms in cozy beach bungalows. A barbecue pit and fully equipped kitchen provide a great excuse for guests to mingle with the helpful Italian-Brazilian owners. That the owners of the charming **Pousada Casa de Taipa** (Rua Bagre Caia Coco 99, Centro, tel. 84/3623-4227, www.pousadacasadetaipa.com.br, R$180 d) are artists comes as no surprise; both interiors and exteriors incorporate typical Sertanejo elements—from adobe walls, ceramics, and hand-woven hammocks to cacti and native fruit trees. The restaurant dishes up typical hearty fare and there is even an on-site mini-museum. The *pousada* lies some distance from the beach.

Authentic cooking with a sophisticated twist is on the menu at **Dio Gastronomia** (Av. dos Arrecifes 1397, Centro, tel. 84/9156-3606, noon-4pm and 7pm-11pm Tues.-Sun., R$20-35). Fresh greens are adorned with slivers of chicken and melon in a balsamic reduction, while sesame-crusted snook is paired with lime risotto. Even the caipirinhas are dressed up with fresh basil. Prices are as modest as the décor.

Transportation and Services

Banco do Brasil and Bradesco have ATMs that accept international cards; credit cards aren't always accepted. For online information, visit www.oportalsaomigueldogostoso.com.br and www.praiadogostoso.com. **Expresso Cabral** (tel. 84/3205-4041, www.expressocabral.com.br) operates one direct bus daily (2 hours) and several others via Touros (2.5-3.5 hours) from Natal's Rodoviária Nova (R$15). By car, follow BR-101 in the direction of Touros and keep going until the Gostoso turn-off.

GALINHOS AND GALO

It's difficult to imagine a more get-away-from-it-all beach than the twin fishing villages of Galinhos and Galo, located 160 kilometers (99 mi) from Natal. With a population of 1,200, Galinhos is perfectly perched on a dune-riddled sandbar straddling two "seas": the open Atlantic and a saltwater *lagoa* upon whose shores, 3 kilometers (1.8 mi) to the east, sits the even tinier and more bucolic village of Galo (pop. 500). Whiling away some days in either spot feels like stepping back in time. Galinhos' roads are lined with sand instead of asphalt and transportation is by boat and *jegues* (mules), which serve as taxis. (Cars must be left at the free parking lot on the far side of the *lagoa*.) The biggest high-tech concession is the giant screen erected in Galinhos' main square, where residents gather to watch nightly *novelas* and soccer games.

Sports and Recreation

The names of both villages are derived from *peixe galo* (moonfish), whose abundant schools provide a livelihood for many residents. A popular excursion is to hire a local fisherman (R$160 for two people for a half-day) to take you around the mangrove-fringed *lagoa,* with time-outs to catch your own crabs or fish (which can later be cooked for you). Or explore the beaches and dunes via mule-driven buggies or on horseback. Galinhos is also prime kite surfing territory; **Kite&Surf** (www.kiteesurf.com/camp.html), based at the Chalé Oásis, offers lessons (R$90 pp/1 hour) and rents equipment (R$100/hour).

Accommodations and Food

Hotels and restaurants are both scant and rustic. In Galinhos, **Chalé Oásis** (Rua Beira-Rio, tel. 84/3552-0024, www.oasisgalinhos.com, R$180-250 d) offers a half-dozen light and breezy bungalows right on the beach, with hammocks and mineral-water showers (there is no public water source in Galinhos). Amenities include a pool, Jacuzzi, and a restaurant (if you go fishing with local *pescadores*, the kitchen will cook your catch for you). For all-out-remoteness, check into **Pousada Peixe Galo** (Rua da Candelária 30, tel. 84/3552-0024, www.pousadapeixegalo.com.br, R$170-190 d). To date Galo's only accommodation option, this hospitable choice is only steps from the beach and features simple cheerful, color-coded rooms that all face a large pool.

Transportation and Services

Expresso Cabral (tel. 84/3205-4041, www.expressocabral.com.br) operates direct buses to Pratagil (three hours, 6am Sun.-Mon. and Fri.) from Natal's Rodoviária Nova (R$24) as well as more frequent buses to Macau (5-6 daily, 2.5 hours, R$16). Ask the driver to let you off at the "trevo de Galinhos" (Galinhos turn-off) on the BR-406 highway; you can then take a taxi (around R$30) to Pratagil. Ask your *pousada* to organize this for you; *pousadas* can also organize transportation all the way from Natal (around R$300). At Pratagil, boats depart to Galinhos (8am-5pm, 10 min., R$2.50 pp, R$10 per boat) and Galos (15 min., R$4 pp, R$40 per boat). During low tide, you can arrive in Galinhos from São Miguel do Gostoso by buggy. By car, follow the BR-406 in the direction of Macau and keep going until the Gostoso turn-off (15 km/9 mi) after Jandaíra. After another 25 kilometers (16 mi), you'll arrive at Pratagil, where you can park your car (free).

BEACHES SOUTH OF NATAL

The coastline south of Natal is a seductive mixture of dunes and lagoons, coconut groves, and dramatic red cliffs. Limpid ocean pools are protected by coral reefs where you can snorkel or indulge in dolphin watching. The relative remoteness of many of the beaches has kept most from becoming overly developed. Although a few can be reached by buses leaving from the local *rodoviária*, others require a car or hopping a ride in a van, buggy, or Jeep. Most *bugueiros* and travel agents in Natal offer half-day and full-day trips that go as far as the legendary Praia da Pipa. Along the way, you'll get a taste of numerous beaches, such as Cotovelo, Pirangi, Búzios, Tabatinga, and Tibau do Sul. You can also access them by car, driving south along RN-063 (Rota de Sol) from Natal, or take a bus.

Pirangi

Separated by the Rio Pirangi, the twin beaches of Pirangi do Norte and Pirangi do Sul are only 10 kilometers (6 mi) south of Ponta Negra. The calm waters are ideal for swimming and windsurfing, and their palm-fringed white sands are dotted with friendly little *barracas* as well as beach homes belonging to wealthy Natalenses. Boats can take you to the reefs 1 kilometer (0.6 mi) offshore, where you will encounter excellent snorkeling.

Pirangi do Norte has achieved *Guinness Book of World Records* fame as home to the world's most immense **cashew tree** (Av. Deputado Márcio Marinhos, tel. 84/3238-2975, www.omaiorcajueirodomundo.com, 7:30am-5:30pm daily, R$5). Planted in 1888, the tree is more than a century old and currently covers approximately 8,500 square meters (86,000 square feet). Around the tree, multiple kiosks sell cashew juice as well as bags of nuts harvested from its branches.

Búzios and Barra de Tabatinga

Búzios is another favorite getaway of upscale Natalenses. The northern stretch of the beach has limpid waters, while the southern end's wild waves lure surfers. Búzios segues into Barra de Tabatinga, another lovely beach framed by rugged reddish cliffs. From the summit's Mirante dos Golfinhos, you're treated to a spectacular view of the coastline, and of the dolphins that usually appear at low tide. If this coincides with lunchtime, 1pm-3pm, take advantage of the scattered bars and restaurants that offer fish and seafood dishes along with glorious views.

From Natal, **Campos** (tel. 84/3230-6133,

www.autoviacaocampos.com.br) operates buses from Natal to Barra de Tabatinga that pass through Pirangi and Búzios. Depending on the time of day (call or check the website) buses depart every 15-60 minutes (6am-10pm Mon.-Sat., reduced service Sun. and holidays) from the *rodoviária*, stopping at points along Avenida Eng. Roberto Freire in Ponta Negra. The fare to Barra da Tabatinga is R$4.80.

Tibau do Sul

Tibau do Sul is only 6 kilometers (4 mi) north of Praia da Pipa, and most travelers mistakenly bypass its series of small, empty, cliff-protected beaches en route to its more famous neighbor to the south. Its beaches are striking, and their natural beauty is enhanced by the proximity of the **Lagoa Guaraíras,** a freshwater lagoon that is an ideal spot for swimming, boating, kayaking, and watching a picture-perfect sunset.

Travelers in search of tranquility (and lower prices) are swapping Pipa for Tibau do Sul. The **Rio Mar Boutique Hotel** (Av. Gauraíras 56, tel. 84/3246-4103, www.pousadariomar. com.br, R$140-200 d) offers a half-dozen spacious and appealing chalets with living rooms and verandas featuring splendid views of the *lagoa* and its surrounding lushness. The attractive grounds include a pool and lots of greenery.

Even if you don't stay overnight, you can easily spend a whole day pampering yourself at **Ponta do Pirambu** (Rua Sem Pescoço 252, Praia do Giz, tel. 84/3246-4333, www. pontadopirambu.com.br, 9am-5pm daily, R$50 low season includes a drink, children under age 7 free), a fantastic leisure complex set amid an idyllic patch of nature. A complex made of palm fronds and recycled wood shelters a massage and therapy center, a lounge full of hammocks, and a gourmet restaurant. Wooden walkways lead to a swimming pool. If you're feeling a little too lazy to walk to the beach, you can always take the bamboo panoramic elevator.

Tibau do Sul is easily accessed by buggy or boat from neighboring Pipa, and vans

(5am-10pm daily) shuttle back and forth between the two. If you're driving from Natal, take BR-101 and then RN-003 from Goianinha. **Oceano** (tel. 84/3311-3333, www. expresso-oceano.com.br) offers bus service from the Rodoviária Nova. Buses depart more or less hourly (7am-6pm Mon.-Sat., reduced service Sun. and holidays) on their way to Pipa and Sibaúma. The fare is R$10.50. For more information, visit www.tibaudosul.com.br.

★ PRAIA DA PIPA

One of the most famous beaches on the Northeast coast is Praia da Pipa, which rivals Jericoacoara for the title of hippest tropical beach getaway. It is certainly the most happening. Surfers discovered the tiny fishing village, 80 kilometers (50 mi) south of Natal, back in the 1970s. Since then, an endless trail of both native and foreign paradise junkies has been seduced by the tiny town. Yet despite the onslaught of charming eco-*pousadas,* gourmet restaurants, and chic boutiques and the hordes of getaway artists and revelers that descend on it come summertime, Pipa hasn't lost its laid-back allure (or its dirt roads). Its beaches remain astonishingly beautiful, with sugary white sand offset by spectacular red cliffs. Although you can easily visit Pipa on a day trip from Natal, you'd be doing yourself a disservice if you didn't stick around for at least two or three days.

Beaches

Praia da Pipa is very attractive, but fairly urbanized. The water is a mesmerizing blue-green, and when the tide goes out, natural pools form amid the coral reefs. Within walking distance are more unspoiled and enticing beaches. Most are only accessible on foot during low tide—otherwise you'll need to take a van, buggy, or boat. Heading north, a 30-minute walk will bring you to **Praia do Curral,** followed by **Praia do Madeiro.** Both are splendid white-sand beaches whose emerald waters are known as the Enseada dos Golfinhos (Bay of Dolphins) due to these mammals' fondness for feeding here in the morning hours. Although Curral is completely secluded (with the exception of enterprising *agua de coco* vendors), you'll find *barracas* on Madeiro's beach, which is also popular with body boarders.

South from Pipa is the beautiful **Praia do Amor,** which can be reached along the beach at low tide as well as from the Rua da Praia do Amor, from which stairs lead from the scenic cliff tops known as Chapadão. While Amor's heart-shaped beach is popular with sunbathers, its waves are revered by surfers and body boarders. The *surfista* scene is at its fever pitch, and the beachside *barracas* are filled with ripped dudes and their lovely ladies. In contrast, neighboring **Praia das Minas** is wide, long, and empty. Excellent for walking, it's a hatching spot for the region's sea turtles. Also tranquil is **Praia de Sibaúma,** a tiny fishing village that was originally a *quilombo* community formed by runaway slaves. On the other side of the Rio Catu from Sibaúma, **Barra do Cunhaú** also has a fine beach and lots of great local fish and seafood restaurants.

Sports and Recreation
HIKING
Before colonial settlers began clearing the land to plant *feijão* and manioc, the southern coast of Rio Grande do Norte was covered with native Atlantic forest. Although only small patches have survived, a considerable swath has been preserved in the **Santuário Ecológico de Pipa** (Estrada Tibau do Sul, tel. 84/3211-6070, 8am-5pm daily, R$10), 2 kilometers (1.2 mi) north of town between Praia do Curral and Praia do Madeiro (you can access the park from Madeiro beach). Although maps are available at the entrance, the 14 easy hiking trails that lead through the forest are very well marked. A steep staircase leads to Praia do Madeiro; between January and June, you can accompany turtles hatching on the beach where **Projeto TAMAR** (www.tamar.org), devoted to the rescue and preservation of Brazil's sea turtles, has a base.

BUGGY AND JEEP TRIPS
Buggy excursions are a big deal in Pipa. However, unlike the beaches north of Natal where you actually careen around in sand dunes, Pipa's lack of dunes mean that buggies zoom along flat beaches, up and down hills, and over rivers. The most adventurous jaunt is a full-day outing (R$600 for four people) that goes south to the primitive Praia do Sagi, on the frontier of Paraíba, with stops at lagoons and beaches along the way. Half-day

Praia da Pipa

trips are also available to Sibaúma, Barra do Cunhaú, and Baía Formosa, 25 kilometers (16 mi) south. For more information, contact **Pipatour** (Av. Baía dos Golfinhos 673, Loja 2, tel. 84/3246-2234, www.pipatour.com) and **Pipa Aventura** (Av. Baía dos Golfinhos 654, Loja 2, tel. 84/3246-2008, www.pipaaventura.com.br).

A crowd-pleaser for adrenaline junkies is the full-day Jeep adventure tour run by Pipatour. *Pau de arara* is a Portuguese expression that refers to the open flatbed trucks in which poor northeastern migrants fled the drought and poverty of the Sertão and traveled south to Rio and São Paulo in search of a better life. With room for 13 eager adventure tourists, these modified Jeeps take you on a full-day adventure (R$95 pp) that includes stops for swimming in the natural pools of Praia de Sibaúma, sailing and kayaking at Barra do Cunhaú, sand board and *esquibunda* ("bum skiing") fun in the dunes of Tibau do Sul, and a final rest stop at the nearby Lagoa de Guaraíras, where you munch on crepes and watch the sunset.

BOAT EXCURSIONS

From Praia do Curral's beach, you can often see dolphins. To see them at close range, take a 90-minute boat trip (R$30), where (after donning a life jacket) you can swim among them as they perform their marine acrobatics. **Pipatour** (Av. Baía dos Golfinhos 673, Loja 2, tel. 84/3246-2234, www.pipatour.com) organizes daily outings. For a whole day trip, request Galego's boat. Aside from being a sailor, Galego is a chef. After mingling with dolphins, he'll take you to Tibau do Sul, where you can hang out around the Lagoa Guaraíras while he prepares a splendid seafood banquet that includes fresh oysters and grilled shrimp. The excursion, including lunch, costs R$130.

Nightlife

At night, Pipa literally lights up as visitors step into their finest flip-flops and take to the bars and clubs on and around Avenida Baía dos Golfinhos. Every summer brings a new slew of bars (or old ones with new names), but expect to hear every kind of music, from reggae and electronic to live *forró* and lots of beach *festas*, especially when the moon is full. For all-night partying, the classic address is **Calangos** (Rua das Gameleiras 1050, tel. 84/3246-2396, Thurs.-Sun., cover R$15-25), a rowdy nightclub that only starts buzzing after midnight.

Accommodations

Pipa is overflowing with accommodations. In summer, book in advance, and stay clear of the party zone surrounding Avenida Baía dos Golfinhos if you want to sleep.

Pousada Rivas (Rua das Araras 89, tel. 84/3246-2111, www.pousadarivas.com.br, R$140 d) is a basic but welcoming place where the service (and the breakfasts) are family-style. Despite the cliché tropical decor, double, triple, and quadruple guest rooms are spacious and spotless and feature porches hung with hammocks. Abundant shrubbery and a pool round out the amenities. A terrific bargain is **Pousada Xamã** (Rua dos Cajueiros 12, tel. 84/3246-2267, www.pousadaxama.com.br, R$100-120 d). Simple, pretty guest rooms are tricked out with quality mattresses, bedding, and towels. A ramshackle tropical garden with a nice pool is inhabited by iguanas, *mico* monkeys, and hummingbirds.

Perched on a hill with sweeping views of Praia da Pipa, **Pousada Mirante de Pipa** (Rua do Mirante 1, tel. 84/3246-2251, www.mirantedepipa.com.br, R$180-220 d) is the eco-dream of a couple of Carioca fugitives who replanted the property with native woods and fruit trees, then built 10 distinctive "eco-chalets" using only natural wood and stone. Completely integrated into the surroundings, each bungalow is rustic, sprawling, and extremely restful. An elegant escape awaits at ★ **Terra dos Goitis** on Praia do Amor (Rua das Acácias 290, tel. 84/3246-2261, www.tocadacoruja.com.br, R$390 d). Immense and imaginatively appointed bungalows are nestled amidst a forested garden, home to a cool pool, tons of lounging spaces, and birds and monkeys galore. Breakfast in bed (or on your veranda) is only one of myriad attentive services that make you feel pampered.

Although Pipa has no shortage of charming hotels, the most tropically luxe is **Toca da Coruja Pousada** (Av. Baía dos Golfinhos 464, tel. 84/3246-2226, www.tocadacoruja. com.br, R$610-930 d). In keeping with Pipa's green vibe, organic forms and materials reign in harmony with creature comforts such as swimming pools, an outdoor fitness room, and a romantic restaurant that serves fusion cuisine. All guest rooms are beautifully appointed, but the deluxe bungalows with four-poster king beds and a private solarium containing a jetted tub are definitely worth splurging for.

Food

Many travelers who visit Pipa decide they can't bear to leave. Instead, they open restaurants—which accounts for the town's gastronomic scene.

When world travelers Lucas and Nicole Kondo first arrived in Pipa, they only had R$100 between them. To earn money, they started selling organic sandwiches, which proved so popular that instead of continuing their travels, the couple stayed put and opened **Tapas** (Rua dos Bem-Te-Vis 8, tel. 84/9465-4468, 6:30pm-11:30pm Tues.-Sat. July-Apr., R$25-35), a relaxing little restaurant that serves up tapa-size portions of dishes inspired by their globe-trotting.

Born into a family of pizzaiolos in a small town in Veneto, Paolo Cappelari has pizza making in his veins. The 62 varieties of crispy discs served at **Pizzaria Dall'Italiano** (Rua do Céu 17, tel. 84/915286511, 6pm-midnight daily, R$20-30) will seduce even the most critical Italian tourist. Homemade pastas and antipasti also entice, and the Amaretto torte is a sublime footnote.

Housed inside a cozy yellow *casa* shaded by palms, the laid-back ambiance of ★ **Cruzeiro do Pescador** (Rua dos Concris 1, Chapadão, tel. 84/3246-2026, www.cruzeirodopescador.com.br, 1pm-4pm and 7pm-11pm daily, R$40-65) belies the fact that its Paulistano proprietor takes his cooking seriously. Fish and seafood are the menu's stars, and they are accessorized with unusual flair.

For a light and inexpensive meal, head to **Aruman** (Av. Baía dos Golfinhos 734, tel. 84/3246-2398, 2pm-midnight daily July-Apr., 4pm-midnight daily May-June). Amid the *movimento* of Pipa's main drag, you can chill out at the sidewalk tables and feast on a crepe (or two). An inspired savory filling blends shrimp and sun-dried tomatoes with pureed manioc and tangy *coalho* cheese.

Transportation and Services

Although there is no tourist office in Pipa, the bilingual website www.pipa.com.br is loaded with information. Many places accept credit cards, but it's wise to stash up on cash since the local Banco do Brasil's ATM has been known to run dry.

Pipa is easily reached by bus from Natal's Rodoviária Nova (2 hours). **Oceano** (tel. 84/3311-3333, www.expresso-oceano.com.br) offers hourly departures (7am-6pm Mon.-Sat., reduced service Sun. and holidays, 2.5 hours, R$12). By car, follow BR-101 from Natal to Goianinha, then take RN-003. You can also take a taxi directly from Natal's airport, which will cost around R$130. It's less expensive to book a transfer with **Pipatour** (tel. 84/3246-2344, www.pipatour.com.br), which offers airport pickup in Natal (R$50 pp).

There are buggies as well as vans and microbuses that shuttle between Pipa and surrounding beach towns such as Tibau do Sul to the north and Barra do Cunhaú to the south.

Fortaleza and Ceará

One of the largest and most arid of the northeastern states, Ceará has a distinctive identity of its own. Fortaleza, its bustling, modern capital, is a major tourist hub. Yet while Fortaleza's beaches are attractive, the coastline stretching north and south from the city offers some of the most fabulous and most distinctive beaches in Brazil. With the exception of eastern Rio Grande do Norte, nowhere else will you encounter the striking blend of crumbling red cliffs, gleaming white sand, and intensely blue waters that are particular to Ceará. Sprinkled with lazy little fishing villages, much of the coastline is framed by gigantic dunes are ideal for buggying, skiing, or tobogganing; breezes and waves beckon surfers, kite surfers, and windsurfers. Once you've spent a day or two exploring Fortaleza, hit the road and surrender yourself to this intoxicating cocktail of sand, sun, and surf.

FORTALEZA

After Salvador and Recife, Fortaleza is the largest and most important of the Northeast capitals. However, practically nothing remains of Fortaleza's colonial past. The city's signature skyline is crammed with multistory offices, apartment buildings, and tourist hotels. While lacking in charm, these high-rises lend the city an aura of modernity and dynamism that is unique in this part of the Northeast, and which spills over into the vibrant cultural scene and nightlife.

Fortaleza's saving graces are the photogenic urban beaches around which much of its social life revolves. They are both idyllic and urbane, especially Praia do Futuro, which mingles sweeping white sands and clean blue waters with a string of sophisticated *megabarracas* where you can surf the web (or the waves), get a massage or manicure, and feast on fresh lobster.

Sights

While Fortaleza has retained little of its history, the small heart of the city, Centro, is teeming with life. Despite the heavy traffic and numerous sidewalk vendors, it is an interesting place to explore. Its small size and grid-plan layout make it easy to walk around. The area is safe enough during the day, but be wary of pickpockets: keep your eye on your belongings.

The **Museu do Ceará** (Rua São Paulo 51, tel. 85/3101-2609, 9am-5pm Tues.-Sun., free) is housed in an impressive neoclassical building. The collection relies on diverse artifacts—including furniture, clothing, fossils, and *literatura de cordel* (traditional northeastern folk tales that are illustrated with woodcuts)—to evoke Ceará's rich history and culture. Particularly moving is the display dedicated to four fishermen who, in 1941, sailed by *jangada* (a rough-hewn and picturesque raft fitted with a sail) from Fortaleza to Rio de Janeiro with the mission of bringing Ceará's poverty to the attention of Getúlio Vargas's government. Their epic journey was captured beautifully by Orson Welles as part of his 1942 must-see documentary, *It's All True.*

Rua São Paulo also leads onto the highly animated **Praça José de Alencar,** which is dominated by what is easily the city's most stunning edifice. Named in honor of Ceará's most renowned poet and novelist, the early 20th-century **Theatro José de Alencar** (Praça José de Alencar, tel. 85/3101-2583, 9am-noon and 2pm-5pm Mon.-Fri., 1pm-5pm Sat.-Sun., R\$4) mixes a delicate neoclassical cast-iron structure (shipped over piece by piece from Scotland) with art nouveau stained-glass windows in rich jewel tones. Tropical embellishment is provided by the surrounding gardens designed by Roberto Burle Marx. If you can't take in a performance, it's worthwhile taking the guided tour.

Fortaleza

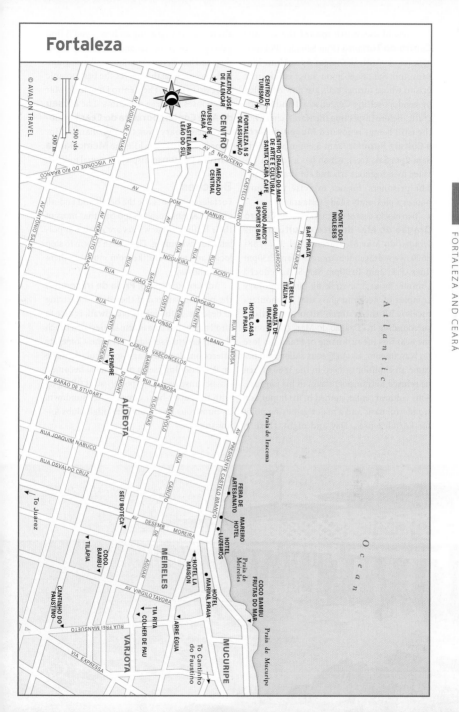

© AVALON TRAVEL

0   500 yds
0   500 m

Atlantic

Ocean

CENTRO

ALDEOTA

MEIRELES

VARJOTA

MUCURIPE

CENTRO DE TURISMO ★
THEATRO JOSÉ DE ALENCAR ★
MUSEU DE CEARÁ ★
FORTALEZA N.S. DE ASSUNÇÃO ■
PASTELARIA LEÃO DO SUL ★
CENTRO DRAGÃO DO MAR DE ARTE E CULTURAL/ SANTA CLARA CAFÉ ★
BUONO AMICI'S SPORTS BAR ▼
MERCADO CENTRAL ■
LA BELLA ITALIA ▼
SONATA DE IRACEMA ▼
HOTEL CASA DA PRAIA ●
PONTE DOS INGLESES
BAR PIRATA ▼

Praia de Iracema

FEIRA DE ARTESANATO
MAREIRO HOTEL ●
HOTEL LUZEIROS ●
COCO BAMBU FRUTAS DO MAR ▼
HOTEL LA MAISON ●
HOTEL MARINA PRAIA ●

Praia de Meireles

Praia de Mucuripe

SEU BOTECA ▼
COCO BAMBU ▼
TILAPIA ▼
CANTINHO DO FAUSTINO ▼
TIA RITA ▼
COLHER DE PAU ▼
ARRE ÉGUA ▼

To Juarez ←

To Cantinho do Faustino

AV DUQUE DE CAXIAS
AV VISCONDE DO RIO BRANCO
AV ANTONIO SALES
AV HERACLITO GRAÇA
RUA DOM MANUEL
AV NEPUCENO
RUA CASTELO BRANCO
RUA NOGUEIRA
RUA ACIOLI
RUA SANTOS
RUA JOÃO
RUA COSTA
RUA FERREIRA
RUA TENENTE
RUA CORDEIRO
RUA IDELFONSO ALBANO
RUA M. TABOSA
RUA CARLOS VASCONCELOS
RUA MADEIRA
ALPENDRE
DUMONT
AV RUI BARBOSA
RUA BARROS
RUA BENÉVOLO
RUA FIGUEIRAS
AV BARÃO DE STUDART
RUA JOAQUIM NABUCO
RUA OSVALDO CRUZ
RUA CANUTO
PRESIDENTE CASTELO BRANCO
AV DESEMB. MOREIRA
AV AGUIAR
AV VIRGILIO TAVORA
RUA FREI MANSUETO
VIA EXPRESSA
AV BARROSO
R TABAJARAS

A few blocks north toward the sea, the **Centro do Turismo** (Rua Senador Pompeu 350, tel. 85/3101-5507, 8am-6pm Mon.-Fri., 8am-4pm Sat., 8am-noon Sun.) is a former prison whose former cells are now occupied by vendors selling Cearense art and handicrafts. Before inspecting the wares, check out the (still being) renovated **Museu de Arte e Cultura Popular** (8am-5:30pm Mon.-Fri., 8am-2pm Sat., free), which has a section devoted to indigenous arts and culture of Ceará. The prisoners' former exercise yard now houses a pleasantly shady restaurant.

Two blocks east of the market is the **Centro Dragão do Mar de Arte e Cultura** (Rua Dragão do Mar 81, Iracema, tel. 85/3488-8600, www.dragaodomar.org.br, 9am-8:30pm Tues.-Fri., 2pm-10:30pm Sat.-Sun., reduced summer hours), a striking contemporary complex of steel and glass that harmonizes nicely with the restored historic buildings surrounding it. "Dragão do Mar" (Dragon of the Sea) was the nickname of Francisco José do Nascimento, a courageous sailor who became an abolitionist hero in the 1880s when he refused to transport slaves in his *jangada*. This cultural center, named in his honor, is a wonderful oasis and a major gathering point for Fortalezenses. Day and night, there is always something going on here—you'll find gallery spaces, cinemas and a theater, a bookshop and handicrafts boutique, a planetarium, and a scenic café that serves the best organic espresso in town. The Centro Dragão do Mar also houses two free museums: The **Museu de Arte Contemporânea do Ceará** exhibits its contemporary works by Brazilian and international artists, while the **Memorial da Cultura Cearense** displays regional folk art.

Beaches

Fortaleza's beaches are the be-all and end-all of the Cearense capital; too bad that most of their brilliant blue waters are often too polluted for swimming. That doesn't seem to stop locals and tourists alike from mobbing them night and day.

Adjacent to Centro, **Praia de Iracema** is the most urbanized of the city's long string of beaches. Although its boardwalk is nice to stroll along, Iracema is actually less of a beach than a perpetual seaside party zone. Come late afternoon, its many bars—particularly those on Ponte dos Ingleses, a pier that has become a classic sunset-watching point—start filling up with the happy-hour crowd. After sundown, its numerous restaurants and nightclubs follow suit.

Fortaleza

More attractive and upscale is **Praia de Meireles,** which lies east of Iracema, although its waters aren't recommended for swimming. The glittery high-rise hotels lining the main ocean boulevard of Avenida Beira Mar are reminiscent of Copacabana, as is the shady boardwalk that attracts joggers, walkers, and bikers. Just as nice as strolling is kicking back with a cool coconut water at one of the many *barracas* on the sand. Along the waterfront, a popular **Feira Noturna** (5pm daily) features a hit-and-miss array of handicrafts as well as local produce. Inland from Meireles, the upscale neighborhoods of Aldeota and Varjota concentrate many of Fortaleza's most fashionable restaurants, bars, and boutiques.

Praia de Meireles segues into the less busy but equally posh and built-up **Praia de Mucuripe.** A picturesque aspect of this beach is the presence of traditional fishing *jangadas,* their faded sails flapping in the wind. The southern stretch of the beach is where the fisherfolk haul their daily catch up to the **Mercado de Peixes** (2pm-10pm daily). Buy some glistening shrimp and fish and take them to the cluster of bars with kitchens; you can have your catch fried up right in front of you while you enjoy a cool beer.

From Mucuripe, the coast bends south and leads to **Praia do Futuro,** the only beach in Fortaleza where the water is truly clean enough for swimming. Unlike at the other beaches, the open sea has strong waves that attract surfers. Praia do Futuro is famed for its *megabarracas* offering food, drinks, restrooms, and showers as well as super-sophisticated extras ranging from kiddie water parks and jetted tubs to stages where live bands perform for hundreds of revelers. You should stick to these *barracas* or their more humble brethren if you come here on a weekday. During off-season the beach can empty out, and there have been reports of holdups. If you hang around until evening, make sure to take a taxi back to the center of town. Otherwise, from Centro, take any bus marked P. Futuro or Caça e Pesca.

Sports and Recreation

Although not the best for swimming, Fortaleza's urban beaches are good for surfing, windsurfing, and kite surfing. **Brothers Wind School** (Av. Beira Mar 4260, Mucuripe, tel. 85/9984-1967) offers lessons (beginners pay R$300 for 12 hours of windsurfing) and rents windsurfing equipment (R$50) and sailboats, as well as kayaks (R$15 per hour) and

statue of Iracema, on Praia de Iracema

stand-up paddleboards (R$30). Kite surfing take place on Praia do Futuro, where wind speeds can reach 40 kilometers per hour (25 mph). Also specializing in wakeboarding and surfing, **30 Knots** (tel. 85/8756-4206, www.30knots.com) offers lessons (R$240 for three hours) that continue at nearby beaches Aquiraz and Cumbuco.

For a wilder beach experience, consider a buggy outing to the beaches east of Fortaleza. **Top Tour Ecotourismo** (tel. 85/3278-1501, www.toptourecoturismo.com.br) and **Nordeste Off Road** (tel. 85/3032-3949, www.nordesteoffroad.com) offer customized guided day trips by Jeep to Cumbuco, Lagoinha, and Canoa Quebrada (R$300-600 for groups up to six). Longer trips last up to 10 days and travel the coastline of Ceará as far south as the dunes of Natal (R$1,600 pp for three days) and as far north as the Parque Nacional dos Lençóis Maranhenses (R$2,900 pp includes accommodations). Less expensive, but more "collective," are the full-day outings offered by **Felix Tur** (tel. 85/3082-2694, www.felixtur.com.br). Minivans hold up to 15 people, but cost only R$25-40 pp to hit most nearby beaches. This is almost as cheap and far less time-consuming than braving local buses, and you can negotiate one-way fares if you don't plan to return to Fortaleza.

Entertainment and Events

You'll find tons of bars in the beach neighborhoods of Iracema (particularly around Rua das Tabajaras) and Meireles. There are also scads of places where you can listen and dance to live music, especially *forró*, which Cearenses claim is more popular here than anywhere else in the Northeast (no mean feat).

NIGHTLIFE

Back in the 1950s, when Fortaleza's original port was located at Iracema, this neighborhood was boho central for journalists, artists, and literati. A few of their old-time haunts still survive, but many more have become rather tacky beer halls, pack-'em-in restaurants, and

megaclubs. In view of the number of tourists here, Iracema is also the notorious walking grounds for Fortaleza's working-girl population, many of whom are underage. Lively and colorful, but also somewhat seedy and overblown, Iracema's nightlife is at least worth checking out, even if you then decide to go elsewhere.

Begin the evening by watching the sunset at one of the *barracas* along the Ponte de Inglês, accompanied by cold beer and fried shrimp. Then stroll along lively **Rua Tabajaras,** home of the famous **Bar Pirata** (Rua da Tabajaras 325, tel. 85/4100-6161, www.pirata.com.br, 8pm-3:30am Mon., cover R$30-40), whose vertiginous Monday *forró* nights have been luring visiting gringos ever since the *New York Times* called them the wildest Monday nights on the planet. Those who survive until closing get free soup on the house.

The Centro Cultural Dragão do Mar and its immediate vicinity has a bustling happy-hour scene that continues late into the night. **Buoni Amici's Sport Bar** (Rua Dragão do Mar 80, tel. 85/3219-5454, www.buoniamicis.com.br, 4pm-close daily, cover R$15-20) is always a happening spot. Housed in a restored early 20th-century warehouse, it boasts soaring ceilings and lots of soccer paraphernalia. During the week, *futebol* fans gather to watch games and scarf down pizza and beer. From Friday onward, the bar hosts lively dance parties commanded by DJs who play an intoxicating mix of samba, MPB, and *carimbó*, a local musical style that mixes indigenous and African elements.

Upscale Meireles and the adjacent *bairros* of Aldeota, Dioníso Torres, and Varjota offer quieter nightlife options. Open since 2013, **Seu Boteco** (Av. Dom Luís 575, Meireles, www.seuboteco.com.br, tel. 85/3461-1691, 5pm-1am Tues.-Fri., 1pm-1am Sat.) quickly morphed into an instant hot spot on a privileged Meireles corner. The old-school *boteco* décor is energized by intense blue walls and a sea of dangling lights. On weekends, live MPB and chorinho provide musical accompaniment. More down-to-earth is **Alpendre** (Rua

Torres Câmara 160, Aldeota, tel. 85/3261-1525, 5pm-midnight Wed.-Fri., 9am-7pm Sat.). Every day around happy hour, the sidewalk tables fill with a neighborhood crowd in search of cold beer, *cachaça* (more than 600 varieties), and conversation.

For a taste of Ceará's Interior, head to **Arre Égua** (Rua Delmiro Gouveia 420, Varjota, tel. 85/3267-2325, www.arreegua.com.br, 8:30pm-3:30am Tues.-Fri., cover R$20-30), a cultural space whose architecture replicates the typical structures and materials of the Sertão. At the bar, you can feast on Sertanejo delicacies such as shredded *carne-de-sol* gratiné. The real fun begins when the band breaks into traditional *forró*.

PERFORMING ARTS

There is always something happening at the **Centro Dragão do Mar de Arte e Cultura** (Rua Dragão do Mar 81, Iracema, tel. 85/3488-8600, www.dragaodomar.org.br), which has a theater and cinema. It's also worthwhile checking to see what musical and dance events are being performed at the opulent **Theatro José de Alencar** (Praça José Alencar, Centro, tel. 85/3101-2583). For up-to-date listings, visit www.centrodefortaleza.com.br.

FESTIVALS AND EVENTS

Although Fortaleza has a Carnaval in the summer, it is nothing compared to the out-of-season "winter" Carnaval known as **Fortal.** Held during the last weekend of July, the festivities erupt along Praia de Meireles's Avenida Beira Mar. The event draws hundreds of thousands of skimpily clad and inebriated souls bent on dancing the days and nights away to the ear-shattering pulse of Bahia's biggest *axé* music stars. For detailed information, see www.fortal.com.br.

Shopping

Ceará is renowned for the variety and quality of its traditional *artesanato*, and Fortaleza is a good place to stock up on pieces to add to your burgeoning folk art collection. You'll find lots of wood carvings, ceramics, and leather goods, but two artisanal traditions that really stand out are woven hammocks and lacework.

No matter what Brazilian beach you happen to be on, if you ask the vendors hawking hammocks where their wares come from, the inevitable response will be "Ceará." The region's cotton cultivation, together with its weaving traditions, make this the best place in Brazil to pick up excellent gifts for layabout friends back home. You'll find ample proof of Cearenses' needle skills in the exquisite embroidery, lace, and crochet used to make everything from pillows and tablecloths to blouses and skirts.

The best places for *artesanato* include the **Mercado Central** (Av. Alberto Nepomuceno 199, tel. 85/3454-8586, 8am-6pm Mon.-Fri., 8am-4pm Sat., 8am-1pm Sun.), which is particularly good for hammocks, and the **Centro do Turismo** (Rua Senador Pompeu 350, tel. 85/3101-5507, 8am-6pm Mon.-Fri., 8am-4pm Sat., 8am-noon Sun.). **Ceart** (Av. Santos Dumont 1589, Aldeota, tel. 85/3101-1644, 9am-9pm Mon.-Sat., 2:30pm-8:30pm Sun.), which also has a boutique in the Centro Cultural Dragão do Mar, sells pricier but very good quality *artesanato*. You can also peruse the stands at the nightly **Feira Noturna** (Avenida Beira Mar, 5pm-close), although you'll have to search hard amid the profusion of souvenirs and tourist trinkets.

For contemporary fashion and beachwear (and a 12-screen Cineplex with food courts), head to upscale **Shopping Iguatemi** (Av. Washington Soares 85, Água Fria, tel. 85/3477-3560, www.iguatemifortaleza.com.br, 10am-10pm Mon.-Sat., 2:30pm-8:30pm Sun.).

Accommodations

Fortaleza is a major tourist destination with plenty of hotels to choose from, though they tend to be innocuous, modern high-rises strong on amenities (you'll want air-conditioning or a good fan to fight the heat) but light on character. Centro has some bargains, but while the area bustles during the day, it is pretty dead at night. Most people tend to stay in the beach neighborhoods where all the action takes place. For proximity to the city's restaurants and nightlife, Iracema and Meireles are good choices. Upscale Mucuripe tends to be a bit more tranquil. While Praia do Futuro is great for swimming during the day, it is far from the center and dangerous at night. In the summer months and July, prices can double.

IRACEMA

One of Iracema's best value options, **Hotel Casa de Praia** (Rua Joaquim Alves 169, tel. 85/3219-1022, www.hotelcasadepraia.com.br, R$140 d) offers innocuous guest rooms that are spacious and spotless with excellent mattresses, air-conditioning, and (Brazilian) cable TV; opt for one on a higher floor. Breakfast is served in a lovely area with lots of light and plants. More upscale but still a bargain is the beachfront **Sonata de Iracema** (Av. Beira-Mar 848, tel. 85/4006-1600, www.sonatadeiracema.com.br, R$205-240 d). Bucking the high-rise hotel trend, this hotel integrates a restored beachfront mansion. Modern rooms are large, bright, and blessed with sea views. There is an attractive pool area with a bar, as well as a restaurant and fitness room.

MEIRELES

The French-owned **Hotel La Maison** (Av. Desembargador Moreira 201, tel. 85/3048-4200, www.hotellamaison.com.br, R$120-150 d), a pretty budget hotel in a renovated house only a few blocks from the beach, is a favorite of French backpackers. Basic air-conditioned guest rooms are enlivened with colorful accents and hanging art, and there is a small, charming courtyard garden. The owner, Francis, is very helpful. **Hotel Marina Praia** (Rua Paula Barros 44, tel. 85/3242-7734, www.hotelmarinapraia.com.br, R$185-205 d) is another small-scale cozy hotel located in a residential building and surrounded by a pretty garden. The simple guest rooms have polished hardwood floors, good lighting, and brightly painted walls.

More luxe is the **Mareiro Hotel** (Av. Beira Mar 2380, tel. 85/3266-7200, www.mareiro.

com.br, R$280-570 d), a low-slung resort on a tranquil stretch of Meireles. It is sleek and tasteful, if a little lacking in warmth. The sizable guest rooms are awash in neutral tones with natural wood accessories. The wet bar, restaurant (with sea views), solarium, and pool areas are also stylish. **Hotel Luzeiros** (Av. Beira-Mar 2600, tel. 85/4006-8585, www.hotelluzeiros.com.br, R$280-380 d) is Fortaleza's attempt at an international-style design hotel. It succeeds very nicely in the achingly minimalist lobby, two restaurants, and bars. As for the guest rooms, the suites are quite posh, but standard rooms, while comfortable, are disappointingly basic. All guest rooms have at least partial sea views, and there is a nice pool and a fitness room.

Food

Fortaleza is Brazil's lobster capital; this crustacean is cheaper and more abundant here than in any other part of the country. But Ceará's coastline yields all sorts of other fish and seafood. Try *peixada cearense,* the classic fisherman's dish, which combines fresh fish such as *robalo, cavala,* and *beijupirá* with cabbage, carrots, potatoes, onions, and hard-boiled eggs. The ensemble is baked in an oven before receiving a last-minute drizzle of fresh coconut milk. Beach *barracas*—particularly those at Praia do Futuro—are a great place for fresh seafood snacks such as *carangueijo* crab, fresh oysters, and the ubiquitous *pargo assado,* grilled snapper sprinkled with sea salt.

CENTRO

Over the decades, it has become a long-standing tradition to pull up a stool at **Pastelaria Leão do Sul** (Praça do Ferreira, tel. 85/3231-0306, www.leaodosul.com.br, 9am-6:30pm Mon.-Fri., 9am-1:30pm Sat., R$2-4). It's a cramped but atmospheric little place decorated with old photos of Fortaleza, and locals swear by the crisp, deep-fried *pastéis* (turnovers) stuffed with chicken, beef, and cheese. The classic accompaniment is a glass of *caldo de cana* (sugarcane juice). Another favorite standby for a cheap local lunch with plenty

Beach *Barracas*

Beach-going would be unimaginable without the ever-present *barracas*, seaside restaurant-bars where friends and family settle in for a long day of chatting, drinking beer, and nibbling on portions of fried fish and seafood. The classic *barraca* is a basic shelter made from boards and palm thatch furnished with a smattering of tables and chairs. Over the years, the *barraca* has evolved along Fortaleza's Praia do Futuro into a series of sophisticated *megabarracas*. These private beach clubs are outfitted with restaurants and amenities ranging from personal lockers to playgrounds and aquatic parks for the kids. Open daily, the *barracas* really fill up on the weekends as well as Thursday nights, when legendary *carangueijadas* take place, along with shows of live rock, MPB, and *forró*. Among the most popular are:

- **Atlantidz** (Av. Zezé Diego 5581, tel. 85/3249-4606) with kitschy decor inspired by the lost city of Atlantis
- **Cabumba** (Av. Zezé Diego 3911, tel. 85/3262-4187) is the unofficial gay and lesbian headquarters
- **Chico do Carangueijo** (Av. Zezé Diego 4930, tel. 85/3262-0108), where fresh crab is king
- **Coco Beach** (Av. Zezé Diego 6421, tel. 85/3249-9879) is loved by families because of the water slide and weekend buffets (Sat. *feijoada* and seafood Sun.)
- **Crocobeach** (Av. Zezé Diego 3125, tel. 85/3521-9600) takes the mega concept to the max with a convenience store, Internet café, beauty salon, ice cream parlor, and surfing school
- **Vila Galé** (Av. Zezé Diego 4189, tel. 85/3486-4400) is the most tony and tranquil
- **Vira-Verão** (Av. Zezé Diego, tel. 85/3391-6200) is the headquarters of the bronzed and buff kite surfing and windsurfing set

of atmosphere are the various food stalls and per-kilo restaurants at the **Mercado Central** (Av. Alberto Nepomuceno 199, tel. 85/3454-8586, 8am-6pm Mon.-Fri., 8am-4pm Sat., 8am-1pm Sun.).

IRACEMA

If you get a craving for cheap and tasty Italian food, **La Bella Itália** (Av. Almirante Barroso 812, tel. 85/3219-2166, 6pm-midnight daily, R$25-40) is a casual little eatery owned by two Italian cousins who effortlessly cook up classic and inventive pasta dishes. Located in the tower of the Centro Cultural Dragão do Mar, **Santa Clara Café Orgânico** (Rua Dragão do Mar 81, tel. 85/3219-6900, 3pm-10pm Tues.-Sun.) is an ideal spot for an organic java jolt (you can buy beans to go as well).

MEIRELES

Meireles and the adjacent neighborhoods of Aldeota, Varjota, and Mucuripe make up

Fortaleza's gastronomic zone. **Coco Bambu** (Rua Canuto de Aguiar 1317, tel. 85/3242-7557, www.pizzariacocobambu.com.br, 11am-3pm and 5pm-midnight Mon.-Thurs., 11am-3pm and 5pm-2am Fri.-Sun., R$20-35) boasts sandy floors and a jungly decor. The restaurant began life as a fun place to enjoy a mouthwatering selection of crepes, *tapiocas,* and pizzas before adding a more intimate dining room with exposed brick and chandeliers where diners can enjoy more elaborate meat and seafood concoctions.

At **Tilápia** (Rua Vincente Leite 1131, Aldeota, tel. 85/3268-1734, www.tilapiarestaurante.com.br, 11am-3pm and 6pm-midnight Tues.-Thurs., 11am-midnight Fri.-Sat., 11am-6pm Sun., R$25-35), chef Valdir Nascimento shows how many culinary variations exist for his restaurant's namesake fish. He first began serving the traditionally dissed freshwater fish in a makeshift eatery in his garage; he has since designed 60 versions, including shrimp-stuffed tilapia in a panko crust and grilled tilapia topped with almonds, mushrooms, and cherry tomatoes. Leave room for homemade *sorvetes,* made of caramelized sugar cane and lemongrass.

★ **Colher de Pau** (Rua Ana Bilhar 1178, Varjota, tel. 85/3267-6688, 11am-midnight daily, R$25-35) is a classic address for regional dishes such as *arroz-de-carneiro* (a local version of a lamb risotto) and *peixada.* For dessert, sample the *doces* made with guava or *cajú.* The restaurant's cozy interior is reminiscent of a Cearense country house. Outdoor tree-shaded tables are also very pleasant.

You'll need at least two companions to devour the overly generous portions of home-cooked fish and seafood served at no-frills **Tia Rita** (Rua Frederico Borges 336, Varjota, tel. 85/3267-5879, 11am-11pm daily, R$20-30). The *pargo* with shrimp sauce is made using 1.5 kilograms (3.3 pounds) of fish, while the *mariscada* is a seafood stew overflowing with crab, octopus, mussels, shrimp, fish, and fish eggs.

Beat Fortaleza's heat with a scoop or two of *sorvete* from **Juarez** (Av. Barão de Studard 2023, Aldeota, tel. 85/3244-3848, 7am-10pm daily). Every day, owner João José Juarez heads to the market at 4am to buy the fresh *sapotis, graviolas, cajás,* and other fruity flavors that have tempted locals for more than 40 years.

MUCURIPE

Ensconced in simple but hard to find digs on a tiny street parallel to Avenue Beira Mar, **Cantinho do Faustino** (Rua Bauxita 58, tel. 85/3263-8766, www.cantinhodofaustino.com. br, 11:30am-4pm Sun.-Mon., 11:30am-midnight Tues.-Sat., 11:30am-5pm Sun., R$30-45) features contemporary regional dishes conceived around local produce, including herbs and vegetables culled from the garden of chef/owner José Faustino Paiva. Lobster in a sauce of *mororó* (a type of wild cashew) and roasted goat kid with broccoli rice are creative examples. For dessert, try the *sorvetes,* made from unlikely ingredients such as olives and *buriti* (the rich orange fruit of a native palm).

Overlooking Mucuripe beach, **Coco**

Bambu Frutas do Mar (Av. Beira Mar 3698, tel. 85/3198-6000, 11am-3pm and 5pm-midnight Mon.-Thurs., 11:30am-2am Fri.-Sat., 11:30am-midnight Sun., R$35-55) is a great place to stuff yourself with top quality seafood (many dishes feed 3-4 people). Despite the various ambiances (including multiple terraces and air-conditioned rooms—attractive, but not intimate), the place can get pretty packed; weekend lineups are de rigueur.

Information and Services

The main Ceará tourist office is the **Centro de Turismo** (Rua Senador Pompeu 350, Centro, tel. 85/3101-5508, 8am-6pm Mon.-Fri., 8am-4pm Sat., 8am-noon Sun.), where you can get city maps and staff can help you plan trips up and down the coast of Ceará, which can be tricky if you're trying to get to remote beaches without direct bus service. There is also a branch at the airport (tel. 85/3392-1667, 6am-11pm daily) and the *rodoviária* (tel. 85/3230-2670, 6am-10pm daily). The city tourist office, **Setur**, has a small outpost in Meireles (Av. Beira Mar, tel. 85/3105-2670, 9am-9pm Mon.-Sat., 9am-8pm Sun.). Online websites include www.fortaleza. ce.gov.br/turismo (the official Portuguese-only government site), www.fortalezabeaches. com, and www.visitfortaleza.com (both in English but not always up-to-date).

There are lots of banks in Centro and Meireles; branches of **Banco do Brasil** with ATMs are in Iracema (Av. Monsenhor Tabosa 634) and in Meireles (Av. Aboliçao 2308). The main post office is at Rua Senador 38 in Centro.

For emergencies, dial **193** (ambulance or fire department) or **190** (police). There is a special **tourist police** unit (Av. Almirante Barroso 805, Iracema, tel. 81/3101-2488) at Praia de Iracema. For medical treatment, visit **Hospital Batista Memorial** (Av. Padre Antônio Tomas 2058, Aldeota, tel. 85/3224-5417, www.hospitalbatistamemorial.com.br).

Transportation

The airport and *rodoviária* are both in the

southern suburb of Fátima. Transportation to Centro or the beaches is easy. Flights from most major Brazilian cities arrive at **Aeroporto Internacional Pinto Martins** (Av. Senador Carlos Jereissati 3000, Serrinha, tel. 85/3392-1200). Long-distance buses arrive at the **Rodoviária João Tomé** (Av. Borges de Melo 1630, Fátima, tel. 85/3230-1111). There are numerous buses daily to Natal (8 hours) and Recife (12 hours), and one a day to Salvador (22 hours), Rio (48 hours), and São Paulo (52 hours). Taxis from the airport to destinations along Avenida Beira Mar will cost R$40-50. You can also flag down a municipal bus bound for the local Papicu terminal (27, 66, and 87); from here you can transfer to a bus bound for Meireles and Iracema. From the *rodoviária* to Avenida Beira Mar, a taxi will cost between R$25-35. Exit the terminal, cross Avenida Borges de Melo, and walk to your right, where buses (73 and 78) travel to the Centro Dragão do Mar and along the coast to Iracema and Meireles.

Fortaleza is easy to navigate and offers good bus service. Buses that circulate between Centro and the closer urban beaches include those marked Grande Circular and Mucuripe. Bus fare is R$2.20. Taxis are cheap, easy to find, and recommended for getting around at night. To reserve one in advance, call **Coopertaxi** (tel. 85/3477-5549). Although driving within Fortaleza is a hassle due to traffic, renting a car is useful to get to far-flung beaches. Try **Avis** (tel. 85/3392-1369, www.avis.com.br) or **Localiza** (tel. 85/3308-8350, www.localiza.com.br); both have offices at the airport.

EAST OF FORTALEZA

Fortaleza's urban beaches look good and are certainly fun. When it comes to actually going swimming, however, it's better to head beyond the urban sprawl. The coastline running east of Fortaleza—from the town of Aquiraz to Ceará's frontier with Rio Grande do Norte—is known as the Costa do Sol Nascente (Coast of the Rising Sun). Its beachscapes are composed of white dunes, red cliffs, and fishing *jangadas*

that set off long before sunrise to bring in the daily catch. Those closest to town are increasingly developed and tourist-flooded, particularly on weekends.

Linked to Fortaleza by well-paved CE-040, the coastal highway, these beaches can be easily visited in a day trip by car, buggy, or organized excursion. Buses operated by **São Benedito** (tel. 85/3444-9999, www.gruposaobenedito.com.br) depart regularly from the *rodoviária*.

Aquiraz

The Costa do Sol Nascente begins with the beaches of **Porto das Dunas** and **Prainha,** located near the pretty historic town of Aquiraz, some 35 kilometers (22 mi) from Fortaleza. Founded in the early 1700s by Jesuit priests, Aquiraz served as Ceará's first capital. Sights here include the early 18th-century Igreja Matriz São José de Ribamar and an intriguing 19th-century meat market. The town is best known for the intricately detailed embroidery and lacework made by local *rendeiras* as well as **Beach Park** (Rua Porto das Dunas 2734, tel. 85/4012-3000, www.beachpark.com.br, hours vary, R$170), Latin America's largest aquatic theme park. Included among the umpteen water rides are giant slides to "river" pools with simulated currents, and "ocean" pools with simulated waves. Adults can veg out poolside in private cabanas or at the Champagne Bubble Lounge on the beach, which serves succulent crab along with national Chandon.

Departing from the Domingos Olímpio bus terminal at the corner of Avenida Domingos Olímpio and Avenida Aquanambi in Fátima, São Benedito bus No. 367 goes directly to Porto das Dunas and Beach Park, while No. 129 goes 3 kilometers (2 mi) farther to Aquiraz. Buses to Aquiraz depart every 30 minutes (R$3.90).

Beberibe

The town of Beberibe, 85 kilometers (53 mi) from Fortaleza, is known for the **Praia de Morro Branco,** home to the otherworldly

Labirinto das Falesias, a series of "labyrinths" formed by fissures in the dune-shaped cliffs behind the beach. Local guides will vie to lead you through the maze, but you can easily follow the twisting trails on your own. You'll be astonished by the colored sands, which range from creamy whites and fleshy pinks to oranges, yellows, russets, and purples. The wide array of tonalities inspires the local production of glass bottles containing scenes "painted" with colored sand. These can be kitschy but quite fascinating. Avoid weekends, when tour buses arrive en masse. While Morro Branco pulses with bars and restaurants, the nearby beach of **Praia das Fontes** is somewhat more tranquil. (The *fontes* in its name refer to the freshwater springs that bubble up from the red rock cliffs on the beach.) Popular activities on both beaches include dune buggy rides, *jangada* trips, and kite surfing.

São Benedito offers four daily bus departures from Fortaleza's *rodoviária* (2 hours, R$8.30). By car, follow CE-040, the coastal highway.

★ Canoa Quebrada

Three hours east of Fortaleza (160 km/100 mi), the poetically named Canoa Quebrada (Broken Canoe) is one of Ceará's most popular beach getaways. A former fishing village that became a 1970s hippie haven and is now (sadly) transitioning from hip to hysterically mobbed, Canoa Quebrada possesses a youthful yet cosmopolitan vibe that draws an international crew of sun and sand worshippers as well as, increasingly, Cearense families. By day, all the action takes place on the pinkish dunes, where buggies zoom around like roller coasters, and on the turquoise waters, which are dotted with kite surfers and triangle-sailed *jangadas*. But at night, the bars on Broadway (yes, Canoa has a Great White Way) start pulsing with tanned bodies intent on dancing until the sun comes up. You can visit Canoa Quebrada in a day trip from Fortaleza. However, to take advantage of its laid-back ambiance, you need to give yourself some time to unwind. Be warned: If you favor tranquility over a party scene, make sure to come during the week and off-season.

BEACHES

The main beach of **Praia da Canoa Quebrada** is quite dramatic, with its rusty cliffs, soft white-sand beach, and warm reef-protected waters. However, it is also quite busy. For more seclusion, go east and take

Canoa Quebrada

a buggy toward the more tranquil beaches of **Fontainha Retiro Grande** and **Ponta Grossa.**

The most popular buggy trip is a three-hour journey that takes you to the splendid **Praia da Ponta Grossa,** 54 kilometers (34 mi) away, with stops at other beaches along the way. This half-day outing costs around R$250 for up to four people. It's best undertaken in the afternoon, when it's not as hot and you can stop to watch the sunset from the dunes of Ponta Grossa. Stops along the way include Praia Majorlândia, a fishing village famed for artisans who fill bottles with colored sand arranged into surprising designs, and beach bars where you can stuff yourself on fresh fish and lobster. Buggy trips west to Fortim (R$200), on the shores of the Rio Jaguaribe, are more interesting for dune junkies than beach aficionados. Although you'll be approached by buggy drivers on the beach, book a licensed *bugueiro* through a hotel. You can also contact the **Associação dos Bugueiros de Canoa Quebrada** (tel. 88/3421-7175).

SPORTS AND RECREATION

When wind conditions are ideal (July-Dec.), Canoa Quebrada is a hotspot for wind- and kite surfers, particularly in the calm waters surrounding the mouth of Rio Jaguaribe, 12km west and accessible via buggy (R$25 pp). **Kite School Canoa Quebrada** (tel. 88/9960-6070, www.kitesurfcanoa.com) is one of several accredited schools that offers lessons as well as outings and rental equipment. A two-hour beginner's course costs around R$180.

NIGHTLIFE

Canoa Quebrada's nightlife sizzles on a stretch of Rua Dragão do Mar known as **Broadway.** If you're looking for action, you'll find it at places such as the mellow **Caverna Bar,** which reels in pool sharks, and **Bar Meu Xodó,** which attracts aficionados of *forró.* Dancing fiends can whip themselves into a frenzy at **No Name,** which plays a variety of tunes. During the height of the summer,

the festivities take to the beach, where reggae rules and various *barracas* such as **Freedom** sponsor luaus in the sand.

ACCOMMODATIONS AND FOOD

Canoa's *pousadas* are mostly basic and fairly affordable (eco-chic has yet to arrive). During off-season, you can easily find a room for under R$100. **Pousada Lua Estrela** (Rua Nascer do Sol 106, tel. 88/3421-7040, www.pousadaluaestrela.com, R$120-150 d) is an appealingly rustic, family-run *pousada* that has preserved its original hippie charms. Bonuses include a small pool and panoramic views of red tiled roofs, palms, and the beach beyond. **Pousada Aruanã** (Rua dos Bugueiros, tel. 88/3421-7154, www.pousadaaruana.com.br, R$140-180 d) boasts an attractive setting—two-story bungalows are set amid a palmy garden with a pool. Both standard and superior rooms are tastefully furnished with lots of wood, organic fibers, and soft lighting; all have verandas, and most overlook the sea. The bonus (or drawback) is the distance from the center of town (a 10-minute walk). **Pousada La Dolce Vita** (Rua Descida da Praia, tel. 88/3421-7213, www.canoa-quebrada.it, R$140-180 d) is a relaxing place with friendly staff, attractive grounds, and a great pool. The chalet accommodations, each named after a Fellini film, are nicely decorated (with vintage film posters, of course). The restaurant serves tasty Italian fare.

Canoa's restaurants are laid-back and light on the pocketbook. For lunch, dig into a plate of shrimp, lobster, or fresh fish served at the beach *barracas* and avoid the *megabarracas* close to town. The more atmospheric *barracas* farther east, such as **Freedom Bar, LazyDays,** and **Barraca Antônio Coco,** have good nibbles. For dinner, **Cabana** (Rua Dragão do Mar 52, tel. 88/3421-7018, 5pm-11pm Tues.-Thurs., 11am-11pm Fri.-Sun., noon-midnight daily Dec.-Jan and June; closed May, R$20-35) is one of the most decent and delicious deals in town. Generous portions of everything from giant shrimp to juicy steak are served with flair. At the attractive,

Spanish-run **Costa Brava** (Rua Dragão do Mar 2022, tel. 88/3421-7088, 5pm-midnight Mon.-Sat., R$20-35) you can feast on paella or the more unusual *fideoa,* a Catalonian version of paella with angel-hair spaghetti substituted for rice.

TRANSPORTATION AND SERVICES

Check out the informative and multilingual (in theory) website www.portalcanoaquebrada.com.br. Banks are located 15 kilometers (9 mi) away in Aracati. There are ATM machines in a small *shopping* at the end of Broadway. Minibuses (R$3) depart frequently, connecting the two towns, as do taxis (R$30).

São Benedito (tel. 85/3444-9999, www.gruposaobenedito.com.br) offers four direct daily departures to Canoa from Fortaleza's *rodoviária* (4 hours, R$17). If you're driving, follow CE-040 to Aracati and follow the turnoff to Canoa.

WEST OF FORTALEZA

The coastline running west of Fortaleza toward Maranhão is known as the Costa do Sol Poente (Coast of the Setting Sun). Its beaches tend to be more deserted but no less spectacular than those to the east. The star attraction is Jericoacoara, a primitive paradise set amid magnificent dunes that is routinely celebrated by international *travelistas* as one of the planet's most perfect beaches. Thanks to all the hype, "Jeri" is not as secluded as it was in its heyday. To recapture the remoteness that was, head to Icaraí de Amontada, a tiny fishing village with sandy splendors of its own. Linked to Fortaleza by the well-paved CE-085 coastal highway, most of the closer beaches can be easily visited in a day trip by car, organized excursion, or bus. Kite surfers take note: blessed by a steady dose of trade winds, this coast has morphed into one of the world's kite surfing hotspots, with an abundance of rental shops, schools, and safari outfits.

Cumbuco

Only 35 kilometers (22 mi) west of Fortaleza, popular Cumbuco offers endless activities on a palm-fringed beach. You can ride dune buggies, quadricycles, or horses through the sands, enjoy freshwater bathing in various lagoons, or take to the calm but murky ocean waters on a *jangada.* The major draws, however, are kite surfing and windsurfing. If you're feeling active, you'll love the place. However, if it's seclusion you're after, the crowds and insistent vendors coaxing you to rent a boat, bike, or buggy will become tiresome.

They say that Cumbuco is one of the best kite surfing destinations in the *world. . .* and if you're here June-December, you can test this claim for yourself. Many *pousadas* rent equipment and offer lessons. At **Pousada 0031** (Av. das Dunas 2249, tel. 85/8899-7153, www.0031.com, R$135-155 d), a certified instructor offers lessons in English, while private lessons and rental equipment cost R$75 per hour. Situated smack-dab in the middle of a Saharan dunescape, the charming apartments (one sleeps four) are airy and spacious and have hammock-hung terraces. In addition to a lovely pool, the friendly Dutch owners run a romantic on-site restaurant. The nicely priced hors d'oeuvre and dinner menu features a locally sourced, creative mishmash of international fare (including a kids menu with burgers and pancakes) that's hard to come by in these parts.

For information, check out www.portalcumbuco.com.br (although bilingual, the English translations are feeble). From Fortaleza, Cumbuco is easily reached by van or by taking a bus operated by **Vitória** (tel. 85/3342-1148, www.evitoria.com.br, departing 9am, 11am, 3:50pm, 6:20pm, 45 minutes, R$5.15), which stops along Avenida Beira Mar. If driving from Fortaleza, take Avenida Beira-Mar, which turns into CE-090 and leads to Cumbuco.

Lagoinha

Once one of the most idyllic beaches along the Sunset Coast, Lagoinha, located 100 kilometers (60 mi) west of Fortaleza, may have lost some of its unspoiled beauty to development, but it's still quite enticing. A pirate hideout turned fishing village, its palm-shaded beaches are backed by dunes that range in hue from creamy white to orange-pink. You can explore them by quadricycle or buggy. The most popular excursion leads to the Lagoa das Alméceges, where you can bathe in crystalline waters and snack on seafood at the *barracas* along the shore. Like Cumbuco, Lagoinha can get unbearably crowded on the weekends.

Pousada do Sol (Rua Antônio Cordeiro Filho 10, tel. 85/3363-5092, www.apousadadosol.com, R$110-140 d) is a modest but pretty overnight option in town. Basic rooms (only some with sea views) are livened up by colorful accents and local *artesanato*.

There are no direct buses to Lagoinha; instead, take a **Viação Paraipaba** (tel. 85/3256-4128) bus from Fortaleza's *rodoviária* to the nearby town of Paraipaba (2 hours, R$14). Buses run every hour. From Paraipaba, a communal taxi to Lagoinha will cost around R$2 pp. If you're driving, follow CE-085, and after crossing the Rio Curu, stop to buy fresh fruits such as *pitomba* and *sapoti* from roadside vendors.

Flexeiras, Mundaú, and Guajiru

If you're longing for more remote beaches, travel to the tiny fishing villages of Guajiru, Flexeiras, and Mundaú, around 130 kilometers (80 mi) from Fortaleza, near the town of Trairi. Along this stretch of coastline, tourism is still in its nascent stages. Flexeiras boasts sweeping white sands and reef-protected waters that are ideal for swimming and popular with kite surfers. Mundaú offers more of the same, with the addition of the freshwater pleasures of the Rio Mundaú, whose banks are lined with tangled mangroves. Guajiru is the most secluded of all.

The fishing villages possess friendly restaurants and modest *pousadas*. For simple, clean accommodations right on the beach, try **Pousada Cabôco Sonhadô** (Av. Beira Mar, Mundaú, tel. 85/9975-6720, www.caboco.com. br, R$110-130 d), where you'll be lulled to sleep

by the sound of the breeze in the surrounding palms. The ultrarelaxing **Rede Beach Resort** (Rua Principal, Guajiru, tel. 85/9156-0279, www.rede-resort.com.br, R$195-235 d) is a comfortable place with simple but pretty rooms. The British owners are warm and helpful; they can organize excursions, but it will be a struggle to abandon the premises with lures such as a pool, hot tub, and beachfront restaurant, along with spa treatments and your own private veranda strung with a soft hammock.

From Fortaleza's *rodoviária*, **Fretcar** (tel. 85/3256-4128, www.fretcar.com.br) operates six daily buses to Flexeiras (3.5 hours, R$14); three buses continue on to Guajiru, while the other three serve Flexeiras. If driving, follow CE-085 and the CE-163 to Trairi. From Trairi, Flexeiras, Mundaú, and Guajiru are all within 20 kilometers (12 mi) along the coast.

ICARAÍ DE AMONTADA

To travel back in time and get off the grid, get thee to Icaraí de Amontada. Icaraízinho, as it's known by the locals, is a well-kept secret of Fortalezenses, who find the deserted dunes, bisected by rivers running into a green sea, reminiscent of Jericoacoará back in the day. You'll be hard-pressed to find this remote little fishing village on any map, but you can access it via Jericoacoara as well as Fortaleza (although thankfully, not easily enough to make it accessible for day-trippers).

Sports and Recreation

Icaraizinho's seemingly endless curve of palm-fringed beach is swept by breezes that make its jade waters ideal for wind- and kite-surfing, particularly July-December. **Clubventos** (tel. 88/3636-3006, www.clubventos.com) offers lesson packages and rents gear as well as surfboards, kayaks, and stand-up paddle equipment.

For those eager to take to the dunes, **Eve** (tel. 88/3636-4005) offers various buggy outings to surrounding beaches, many even more remote than Icaraí. You can hit a number of them, including Almofala (a little fishing village whose 18th-century church spent centuries buried in the sand) and Preá on their own or via a day trip (R$450 for up to three people) or overnight (R$600) to Jericoacoara. Eve also organizes romantic full moon dune outings (R$60 pp) in which small groups gather to enjoy caipirinhas, fresh oysters, and lobsters while sitting around a camp fire fueled by palm fronds.

Accommodations and Food

Drawn by its paradisiacal pull, a sprinkling of enlightened entrepreneurs have opened small, seductive *pousadas*. Among the loveliest and best value is ★ **Pousada Casa Zulu** (Rua Francisco Gonçalves de Souza, tel. 88/3636-3016, www.casazulu.com, R$160-220 d), with a cluster of pseudo-primitive, beautifully outfitted bungalows in the center of town and right by the sea. Lush grounds are littered with shady spots, swaying hammocks, and poolside chairs. Set back from the beach, the more luxurious **Hula Hula Brazil** (Rua João Rafael Diniz, tel. 88/3636-3016, www.hulahulabrazil.com, R$350-450 d) consists of a trio of exquisitely designed and decorated private bungalows baptized "Peace," "Love," and "Life." Hosts Fabio and Nika go all out to make guests feel treasured—from organizing outings to delivering fresh croissants to your veranda in the morning. For cheaper digs, try **Pousada Hibiscus** (Rua Joaquim Alves Parente, tel. 88/3636-3076, www.pousadahibisco.com, R$150-200 d), a centrally located, rustic little spot amidst a coconut grove with modest but welcoming rooms. The on-site restaurant (lunch and dinner daily) serves delicious seafood, sandwiches, and wood oven-baked pizza. It is considered one of the best eateries in town.

Transportation and Services

Icaré is bereft of ATMs and other trappings of "civilization." From Fortaleza's *rodoviária*, **Fretcar** (tel. 85/3256-4128, www.fretcar.com.br) offers a single daily departure at 2:30pm (R$22) to Icaraí. To drive here from Fortaleza (190 km/120 mi), follow CE-085 to Barrento and then take the Praia de Baleia road to Veados; a 30-kilometer (18-mi) partially paved road leads to Icaraí. From Jericoacoara, 90 kilometers (55 mi) to the west, a full-day outing to Icaraí by buggy costs R$240 for up to four people. Contact the **Associação dos Bugueiros** (tel. 88/3669-2284) or **Agência By Boogie** to negotiate one-way rates.

★ JERICOACOARA

International travel writers have raved about Jericoacoara, explaining the presence of so many global beach worshippers at this remote (320 km/200 mi west of Fortaleza), rustic little fishing village. Of course, when you finally get to "Jeri," you'll also understand that it deserves such worship. However, the biggest mistake these travel writers make is calling Jeri a "beach." It's actually much more.

Jericoacoara is what you get when a desertscape of constantly shifting dunes—some of them more than 30 meters (100 feet) high—collides with the majesty of the open sea. Wandering or buggying through these dunes is mesmerizing. Depending on the hour of the day, the sun tints them burnished gold, searing yellow, deep orange, and purply pink. You're never quite sure if the ocean is swallowing up the desert, or vice versa. A 30-minute Jeep ride from the village of Jeri is the Lagoa de Jijoca, a turquoise lagoon surrounded by creamy white sand.

Jericoacoara is a popular package-tour destination. Until now its distance—a six-hour bus trip from Fortaleza to the village of Jijoca, followed by a 23-kilometer (14-mi) hour-long truck or buggy ride through the dunes—has left it happily free of the hordes that descend on Ceará's other beaches. Despite a new regional airport (slated for completion in 2014, but presently delayed), hopes are that the ebb and flow will remain manageable. Trappings of civilization—electricity, Internet access, and sushi—have already arrived. So have many foreigners, who have remained to open charming yet simple *pousadas* and restaurants. These new transplants are respectful of the unspoiled nature that reigns. The Brazilian government's designation of Jeri as an environmentally protected zone has strictly regulated development and enforced recycling. Nonetheless, Jeri does get booked up in the summer. To experience the full effect of its seclusion, visit during the off-season (Aug.-Nov. and Mar.-June); be aware that some hotels and restaurants close in May.

Beaches

Near the village, the **Praia de Jericoacoara** is a stunning sight, with its massive half-moon-shaped dune facing out onto the water. At the end of the day, tourists gather along the crest to watch the sunset (the dune's unofficial name is Duna do Pôr-do-Sol, or "Sunset Dune"). The moment is always accompanied by whistles and applause. . .and caipirinhas. The beach's shallow waters make swimming difficult but are ideal for windsurfing. To the right, a 10-minute walk leads to **Praia da Malhada,** which is much better for bathing. At low tide, you can continue on past Praia do Pontal to **Pedra Furada,** a striking rock formation with a hole in the middle (which, in July, is in perfect and photo-worthy alignment with the orb of the setting sun). Around 10 kilometers (6 mi) farther east, **Praia do Preá** has wind conditions that make it a mecca for kite surfers. For more seclusion, take a buggy

30 kilometers (20 mi) west up the coast to the tiny fishing village and beach of **Tatajuba.**

While Jeri's ocean is ideal for water sports, for sunning and splashing around many prefer the sugary sands and jade waters of the **Lagoa de Jijoca.** This freshwater lagoon consists of pure rainwater. So much of it evaporates during the dry season that it separates into two smaller lagoons. Closer to the town of Jijoca, the **Lagoa do Paraíso** is dotted with rustic *pousadas* and restaurants. A couple of palm-thatched bars are the only sign of civilization at **Lagoa Azul.** When winds are strong, windsurfing, kite surfing, and *jangada* outings are popular on both lagoons. Buggies and *jardineiras* (open-back trucks that serve as taxis) go back and forth from Jeri to Jijoca. The ride takes 30 minutes.

Sports and Recreation

Although Jeri feels as if it's at the end of the world, there is lots to keep you occupied apart from sprawling in a dune with a book. Sand activities range from yoga and capoeira classes to navigating the dunes by buggy, sand board, or on horseback.

A five-hour buggy outing west to the fishing village of Tatajuba includes a stop to view seahorses (R$10) and a fresh lobster lunch

Pedra Furada, Jericoacoara

followed by a refreshing siesta in hammocks slung amid the Lagoa da Torta. Heading east along a route less traveled takes you to beautiful Barrinha beach with stops at Lagoa da Pinguela, Lagoa Formosa, and the kite surfers' delight of Praia do Preá. Those with a full day (or more) at their disposal can head to secluded Praia de Icaraí de Amontada, located 90 kilometers (55 mi) away. The full-day outing allows you to savor dozens of other beaches as well. These and other outings last five hours and cost between R$180-200 for two and R$200-250 for four. Contact the **Associação dos Bugueiros** (tel. 88/3669-2284) or **Agência By Boogie**. Horses (R$20 per hour with an extra R$20 per hour for a guide) can be rented from the **Associação dos Cavaleiros** located near the Duna do Pôr do Sol.

For excursions even further off the beaten dunes, **Jeri Off Road** (Travessa da Rua do Forró, tel. 88/3669-2268, www.jeri.tur.br) is a knowledgeable and ecologically conscious outfit that operates various excursions, including multiday Jeep and buggy expeditions to locales such as the Delta da Parnaíba, the Lençois Maranhenses, and São Luís. Expect an all-inclusive three-day adventure to cost around R$3,000 for two.

Jeri's idyllic setting and wind conditions lure surfers of all stripes. The best period for kite- and wind-surfing is June-December, when tradewinds blow at an average of 46 kilometers per hour (28 mph). Ideal surf conditions are January-May. Hardcore practitioners who want to forgo the expensive rental fees can bring their own gear. Others can rely on **Jeri Kite School** (88/9693-7343, dani4401. wix.com/jks#!) for kite surfing and **TicoWind** (Rua das Dunas 30, tel. 88/9662-9291, www. ticowindjeri.com) for windsurfing. Located right on the beach, **Clubventos** (Praia de Jericoacoara, tel. 88/3669-2288, www.club-ventos.com.br) is a fantastic watersports and recreation complex that covers all forms of wave action. The latter provides lessons for beginners and rents equipment to fans of both kite surfing and windsurfing (R$180 a day);

rates decrease for rental packages over multiple days. Surf and stand-up paddle boards are also available for rent. Expect a three-day, nine-hour beginner's kite surfing course to begin at R$700. A basic windsurfing course of three 90-min. sessions costs around R$400. A one-hour surfing course is R$70 and boards can be rented for around R$60 for a day. For kite surfing courses, ensure your instructor has been certified by the International Kitesurfing Association (www.ikointl.com), even if it means forking out extra *reais*.

Nightlife

Jeri does have a nightlife, especially during the summer. Warm-up usually takes place around sundown on at the beach end of Rua Principal, fueled by *barracas* selling *caipis* and other mood-enhancing cocktails before branching out around various village venues. Standbys include *forró* at the *tradicionalíssimo* **Restaurant Dona Amélia** (Rua do Forró, Wed. and Sat. R$10), where locals are as numerous as tourists. The eclectic and electronic **Planeta Jeri** (Rua Principal, daily) is where most revelers begin and often end the night.

Movie nights are held on the beach in front of **Clubventos** (tel. 88/3669-2288, www.club-ventos.com) beachside clubhouse; Tuesday and Thursday are reserved for wind- and kite-surfing flicks, but Saturday features more general Hollywood fare.

Accommodations

Jeri's *pousadas* are all appropriately rustic, although many proprietors take advantage of organic materials and regional artistic traditions to create a seductive ambiance. Among Jeri's significant hostel population, **Hostel e Pousada Tirol** (Rua São Francisco 202, www.jericoacoarahostel.com.br, R$100-120 d, R$40-50) ranks ahead of the rest due to the great common areas—a kitchen, bar, and a chill area with hammocks—that promote a communal vibe. Rooms, while clean, can feel cramped and stuffy. **Pousada Ibirapuera** (Rua das Dunas S, tel. 88/3669-2012, www. pousadaibirapuera.com.br, R$160-200 d) is one of Jeri's original *pousadas* and offers good value. Guest rooms consist of small lofts with a bedroom upstairs and living room downstairs. The brick buildings are softened by a lush garden festooned with hammocks, shady cashew trees, and a curvy blue pool. Windsurfing boards are available for rent. If you're on a budget or find yourself stretching a week's stay into a month (it happens!), **Jeri Athome** (Rua Principal, tel. 88/3669-2078, www.jeriathome.com, R$100-140 d) is a great choice resembling a private beach house. Set amid a fruit tree-laden garden, guest rooms are simple but spotless. The real deals are the self-service apartments with kitchens that allow for cooking around the clock.

Operated by a former Oregon schoolteacher who stumbled into Jeri after riding around South America on a motorcycle, **Vila Bela Vista** (Rua dos Coqueiros 100, tel. 88/9962-9810, www.vilabelavista.com, R$180-290 d) is an inviting bed-and-breakfast 10 minutes' walk from the village. Enjoy lavish breakfasts, free classes (from capoeira to samba), and barbecues, musical jams, and horseback outings. Housed in charming bungalows overlooking the dunes, rooms sleep 1-4; all have lovely decks. A rambling garden shelters a pool, jetted tub, hammocks, and a tree house for kids.

It's almost impossible to get more primitive-chic than ★ **Vila Kalango** (Rua das Dunas 30, tel. 88/3669-2289, www.vilakalango.com.br, R$430-580 d). Nestled right on the beach, accommodations are divided between rustic brick bungalows and wooden huts suspended on stilts; all are creatively and beautifully decorated with natural fibers and ingeniously recycled objects. This is one place where you're actually encouraged to track around sand—a wonderful lounge of hammocks, pillows, and futons is located in a soft patch. The pool, restaurant, and palmy grounds overlook the Duna do Pôr-de-Sol.

Food

Jeri boasts a large selection of eating options, with an emphasis on healthy cooking. During the day, you might want to partake of the *barraca* fare served on the beach. Among the best and most diverse offerings are those served at the breezy beach-with-a view restaurant at **Clubventos** (tel. 88/3669-2288, www.clubventos.com, noon-5pm daily, R$15-25). Choose from healthy sandwiches, shakes, and salads, or pig out on an assortment of hot and cold dishes at the per-kilo buffet before flaking out for a shady siesta on a recliner or bean bag. The pizzas emerging from the wood-burning oven at **Nômade** (Travessa Ismael, tel. 88/9990-8142, 6pm-midnight daily, R$25-35) are considered the best in town, with unusual toppings such as leeks, zucchini, smoked ham, and chutney. The laid-back ambiance makes them all the more enjoyable.

Get here early to stake out one of the few cozy tables at ★ **Pimenta Verde** (Rua São Francisco, tel. 88/9916-0057, 3pm-11pm daily, R$25-40), a simple yet romantic spot that churns out some of the most creative fish and seafood dishes in Jeri. Desserts—especially the *petit gâteau*—are wickedly good. The rustic setting (with a lovely back garden) at **Carcará** (Rua do Forró 530, tel. 88/3669-2013, noon-11:30pm daily, R$25-40) belies its sophisticated menu. Dishes run from ceviche and sashimi to regional specialties such as *carne-de-sol com arroz de leite* (sun-dried beef with rice in melted *coalho* cheese). For a healthy light meal or snack, **Café Brasil** (Beco do Guaxelo 65, tel. 88/3669-2272, 9:30am-11pm Tues.-Sun.) serves thick sandwiches on homemade wheat bread stuffed with unusual fillings such as chicken, cashews, and pineapple. Also on the menu are sweet and savory *tapiocas* and fresh fruit juices. Those who wake up (or go to bed) at the crack of dawn swear by the fresh-baked coconut, cheese, and banana buns that emerge early from the ovens of charming little **Padaria Santo Antônio** (Rua São Francisco, 2am-5am daily).

Information and Services

Jeri doesn't have a tourist office. For information, visit www.jericoacoarasite.com.br, www.jeri-brazil.org, www.jericoacoara.com, and www.portaljericoacoara.com (all bilingual). There are no banks, so bring plenty of cash in small denominations; many restaurants and hotels do accept credit cards. There is a Banco do Brasil (Av. Manoel Teixeira 139) with ATMs in Jijoca.

Transportation

The easiest way to get here is by bus from Fortaleza's *rodoviária*. **Fretcar** (tel. 85/3256-4128, www.fretcar.com.br) operates three buses daily that will take you all the way to Jijoca and includes subsequent transport by small truck to Jeri (6.5 hours, R$48-63) as well as nine daily buses to Jijoca (6 hours, R$29-36) itself. Known as Jeri's parking lot, Jijoca is where people stash their cars before boarding the *jardineiras* (open trucks) that run back and forth across the dunes between Jijoca and Jeri (a breathtaking but bumpy 40-minute ride that costs R$10). *Jardineiras* usually run from 6am-9pm and depart once they have a full load. Another alternative is to flag down

a buggy (R$50 for up to four people). If you drive to Jeri via the CE-085, you'll have to leave your car in Jijoca and pay around R$10 a day for parking (vehicles aren't allowed in and around Jeri). A longer, more expensive, but unforgettably scenic alternative is to travel up the coast by Jeep, hitting all the beaches between Fortaleza and Jeri, which could take a day or even more. Adventure tour operators in Fortaleza such as **Top Tour Ecotourismo** (tel. 85/3278-1501, www.toptourecoturismo.com.br) and **Nordeste Off Road** (tel. 85/3032-3949, www.nordesteoffroad.com) specialize in such trips.

At the time of publication, the inauguration of the "Jeri airport" (slated for 2014) remained delayed. When it does open, it will be located in the town of Cruz (20 km from Jijoca) and will reduce travel time from Fortaleza to one hour. Authorities are considering developing a taxi, van, and Jeep network that links the airport directly with Jijoca and Jeri and the region's "other" kite surfing mecca of Preá.

Maranhão

Although Maranhão is considered to be a Northeast state, its wet climate, relatively lush vegetation, and significant indigenous influences announce your arrival into the threshold of the Amazon. Instead of parched Sertão, Maranhão's interior is marked by rivers and the omnipresent *babaçu* palm, which provides Maranhenses with everything from soap and cooking oil to charcoal and timber. Along the coast, particularly in the alluring if somewhat dilapidated colonial cities of São Luís and Alcântara, European and especially African influences are more palpable, creating an intoxicating local culture. Despite its relative poverty, the state capital of São Luís is one of Brazil's most beguiling historic cities. There are enough historic and cultural attractions to keep you well occupied for a couple of days—more if you come during June, when the city plays host to the sumptuous Bumba-Meu-Boi

festivities. Having traveled so far, it's worth adding an extra few days to take an unforgettable side trip from São Luís to the Parque Nacional dos Lençóis Maranhenses, where you'll be treated to a surreal landscape of endless white sand dunes dotted with thousands of tiny lakes. In terms of weather, Maranhão's rainy season lasts from January to June, but you can count on at least some rapid downpours year-round.

SÃO LUÍS

Somewhat crumbling but charismatic, Maranhão's island capital has a flavor quite unlike any other of Brazil's northeastern cities. Its very origins are unique, since São Luís was the only Brazilian city to be founded by the French. The city is bursting with cultural riches, which are a legacy of slavery that transformed São Luís—along with Rio and Salvador—into one of the Brazilian cities where African religion, culture, music, and cuisine are still strong. This influence is apparent in the city's many popular *festas* as well as the music that regularly fills the streets, be it the powerful drumming of *tambores de crioula* or the slower, more mellow rhythms of reggae.

Sights

The city of São Luís is spread out along an island peninsula. However, the oldest parts are concentrated on the island's tip, at the point where the Rio Anil flows into the Baía de São Marcos. Within Centro, the old city center, lies the neighborhood of Praia Grande. Almost all of São Luís's sights are concentrated in this dense, fascinating, and easy-to-wander-around area. However, many streets bear more than one name and become dodgy after dark and on weekends, when businesses close.

★ CENTRO HISTÓRICO (PRAIA GRANDE)

The *centro histórico,* a neighborhood known as Praia Grande or Reviver, is a long area bordered by Rua Afonso Pena to the east and Avenida Beira Mar to the west. A good place to begin exploring is at its northernmost edge, where you'll find two magnificent squares. **Praça Benedito Leite** is an elegant green park dominated by the **Catedral da Sé** (Praça Dom Pedro II, tel. 98/3222-7380, 8am-7pm Tues.-Fri., 8am-noon and 3pm-10pm Sat., 8am-noon and 4pm-9pm Sun.). The city's main cathedral, it was built in 1690 by Jesuits and Indians in honor of Nossa Senhora da Vitória, who had supposedly helped the Portuguese oust the French from São Luís. Inside, the main baroque altar is awash in gold, and you can detect some local *babaçu* palms depicted in the painted ceiling frescoes.

Adjacent to Praça Benedito Leite is the much grander **Praça Dom Pedro II,** whose far end gazes out over the Baía de São Marcos. Two particularly majestic palaces line the square. The **Palácio dos Leões**

(Av. Dom Pedro II, tel. 98/3232-9789, 2pm-5:30pm Mon., Wed., and Fri., free) was constructed in 1766 as the state governor's residence, on the site of the original Fortaleza de São Luís erected by the French. Guided visits (in Portuguese) allow you to view the elegant salons filled with 18th- and 19th-century paintings and furniture. Next door, the stately **Palácio La Ravardière,** built in 1689, is one of São Luís's oldest edifices. Still exercising its original function as City Hall, its name and the statue on its threshold pay homage to São Luís's dashing French founder, Daniel de La Touche, also known as the Sieur de la Ravardière.

On the opposite side of the *praça* from the palaces, a flight of steep limestone steps leads down the picturesque bar-lined street known as **Beco Catarina Mina.** Near the end of the stairs is the mansion of Catarina Rosa Ferreira de Jesus, an African slave of great beauty who, after purchasing her freedom, became a wealthy and successful merchant by supplying manioc flour to the Portuguese. The staircase marks the descent into the heart of colonial Praia Grande, where block after block of azulejo-encrusted mansions alternate with peeling buildings in blistered and faded pinks, blues, jades, and saffrons. Running parallel to each other are three main streets that cut lengthwise through the *bairro* and are home to most of its treasures: **Rua da Palma, Rua do Giz,** and **Rua da Estrela.**

Beco Catarina Mina ends on **Rua Portugal,** a street whose buildings showcase a dazzling array of colorful tile work. Close by, the arches of the early 19th-century **Casa das Tulhas** (Rua da Estrela 184, 7am-8pm Mon.-Fri., 7am-6pm Sat., 7am-3pm Sun.) give way to the Mercado Praia Grande, a traditional and very charming market hidden behind the Casa's colonial facade. It's worth wandering past the stands selling dried shrimp, medicinal herbs, exotic fruit, cotton hammocks, and Indian basketry. Sometimes on Fridays, at 7pm, there are performances of traditional *tambor de crioula* dancing.

São Luís is bereft of splendid colonial

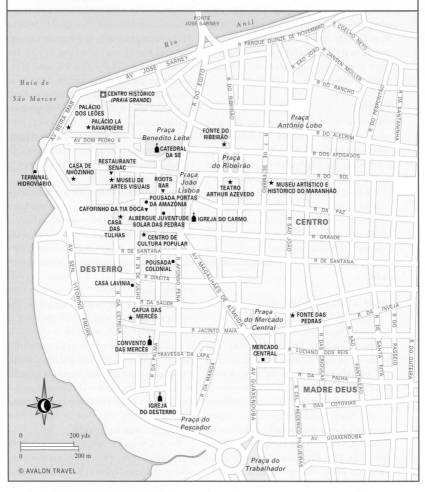

São Luís

PONTE JOSÉ SARNEY · Anil · Rio · AV. JOSÉ SARNEY · R PARQUE QUINZE DE NOVEMBRO · R COELHO NETO · R SÃO JOÃO · R JANSEN MÜLLER · R DE SANTANINHA · R DO RANCHO · R DO EGITO · R DO. RIBEIRÃO · R DO RESPONTÃO

Baía de São Marcos

★ CENTRO HISTÓRICO (PRAIA GRANDE)

PALÁCIO DOS LEÕES ★ · PALÁCIO LA ★ RAVARDIÈRE · AV. BEIRA MAR · AV. DOM PEDRO II

Praça Benedito Leite · FONTE DO RIBEIRÃO · Praça Antônio Lobo · R DO ALECRIM

🏛 CATEDRAL DA SÉ · Praça do Ribeirão · R DOS AFOGADOS · R DO SOL

CASA DE NHOZINHO ★ · RESTAURANTE SENAC ★ · ★ MUSEU DE ARTES VISUAIS · ROOTS BAR · Praça João Lisboa · TEATRO ★ ARTHUR AZEVEDO · ★ MUSEU ARTÍSTICO E HISTÓRICO DO MARANHÃO · R DA PAZ

TERMINAL HIDROVIÁRIO ■ · ● POUSADA PORTAS DA AMAZÔNIA · CAFOFINHO DA TIA DOCA ▼ · ● ALBERGUE JUVENTUDE SOLAR DAS PEDRAS · 🏛 IGREJA DO CARMO · CENTRO · R SÃO JOÃO · R GRANDE

CASA DAS TULHAS · ★ CENTRO DE CULTURA POPULAR · R DE SANTANA

DESTERRO · POUSADA COLONIAL ● · R 28 DE JULHO · R DIREITA · AV. MAGALHÃES DE ALMEIDA · R DE SANTANA

CASA LAVINIA ● · R DA SAÚDE · AV. AFONSO PENA · Praça do Mercado Central · ★ FONTE DAS PEDRAS · R DA INVEJA

AV. SEN. VITORINO FREIRE · R DA ESTRELA · CAFUA DAS ★ MERCÊS · R JACINTO MAIA · MERCADO CENTRAL · R LUCIANO DOS REIS · R DA PALHA · MADRE DEUS

CONVENTO 🏛 DAS MERCÊS · TRAVESSA DA LAPA · R DA PALMA · R DA MANGA · AV. GUAXENDUBA · R CEL. FREDERICO FIGUEIRAS · R DAS COTOVIAS

🏛 IGREJA DO DESTERRO · Praça do Pescador · AV. GUAXENDUBA · Praça do Trabalhador

0   200 yds
0   200 m
© AVALON TRAVEL

---

churches. Apart from the cathedral, the most striking is the early 18th-century **Igreja do Desterro** (Largo do Desterro, 9am-5pm daily), whose onion-like Byzantine domes are a strange but striking surprise. The **Convento das Mercês** (Rua da Palma 502, tel. 98/3231-0641, 2pm-6:30pm Mon., 8am-6pm Tues.-Fri., 8am-noon Sat.) was founded in 1654 by celebrated Jesuit preacher Antônio Vieira, whose sermons are highly regarded as some of Brazil's early literary writings.

The hibiscus-colored exterior is arresting. However, you can skip the museum inside—a worshipful collection of memorabilia honoring José Sarney, a former Brazilian president (1985-1990) and all-powerful former governor of Maranhão. On the edge of Praia Grande, the **Igreja do Carmo** (Praça João Lisboa 350, tel. 98/3878-0706, 7am-5pm Mon.-Fri., 7am-11:30am and 4:30pm-6pm Sat., 6:30am-9am and 4:30pm-6pm Sun.) dates to 1627 and originally served as a fortress against Dutch invaders. It has suffered various modifications over time, including the 1866 addition of the white and yellow Portuguese azulejos covering its facade. The convent formerly served as home to capuchin monks and now shelters a tiny **museum** (2pm-5pm Mon.-Fri., free).

São Luís has an impressive number of small museums. Most are located in Praia Grande's historic mansions and palaces. Many of the visits are guided, often only in Portuguese. The **Centro de Cultura Popular** (Rua do Giz 221, tel. 98/3218-9924, www.culturapopular.ma.gov.br/centrodecultura.php, 9am-6pm Tues.-Fri., 9am-5pm Sat.-Sun., free), also known as the Casa da Festa, boasts four floors of colorful displays that provide a wonderful overview of rich cultural traditions from around the state. Aside from a refresher in Bumba-Meu-Boi, captivating photographs and regalia explore festivals such as Carnaval, the Festa do Divino, and rituals linked to Tambor de Mina, Maranhão's important Afro-Brazilian religion (similar to Candomblé).

Lodged inside a splendid azulejo-covered house, the **Casa de Nhôzinho** (Rua Portugal 185, tel. 98/3218-9953, www.culturapopular. ma.gov.br/casadenhozinho.php, 9am-5:30pm Tues.-Sat., 9am-12:30pm Sun., free) showcases Maranhão's typical *artesanato* with a beguiling array of objects, including pottery, fishing implements, wonderful toys made from scrap materials, and artifacts from numerous indigenous groups. A special gallery is devoted to the works of Mestre Nhozinho (1904-1974), a Maranhense artisan renowned for the wood carvings he sculpted out of *buriti* palm. The toys he made and gave to poor children are ingenious.

The **Museu de Artes Visuais** (Rua Portugal 273, tel. 98/3218-9939, 9am-7pm Tues.-Fri., 9am-6pm Sat.-Sun., R$2) serves up an artistic mishmash culled from private collections that mixes centuries (17th-20th) and genres (baroque religious art, Brazilian modernism, works by contemporary Maranhense artists). Its overview of azulejo manufacturing is illustrated by some fine samples of glazed tiles from Portugal, Spain, Germany, and France.

The **Cafua das Mercês** (Rua Jacinto Maia 43, 9am-5pm Mon.-Fri., R$2) consists of a small house and courtyard, with a replica of a whipping post, that was formerly São Luís's slave market. The haunting, claustrophobic atmosphere and handful of chains and torture instruments leave more of an impact than the

the Praia Grande neighborhood of São Luís

The Pageantry of Bumba-Meu-Boi

São Luís is the definitive place to observe one of the country's most captivating spectacles. Drawing on indigenous, African, and Portuguese folk elements, Bumba-Meu-Boi consists of a series of theatrical dances performed over several nights in mid-late June. The visually stunning festivities feature troupes of well-known folk characters in brilliant costumes accompanied by musicians playing brass instruments and drums, the most unique of which is the deep, throbbing *bumba*.

The *festa* revolves around the magical tale of a plantation owner who leaves a slave to take care of his prize bull *(boi)*, which dies and then comes back to life with the help of forest spirits. Bumba-Meu-Boi troupes are like samba schools. There are many groups within the city, and rivalries exist as to who can put on the most dazzling spectacle featuring the story's characters. The *bois* are exceptionally resplendent—their costumes are festooned in ribbons, sequins, and embroidery fanciful enough to make a Parisian couturier's jaw drop. It's impossible to resist joining in the dancing and singing that invades the streets of Praia Grande and Centro. If you miss the main celebration, you can catch Bumba-Meu-Boi troupes performing throughout the month of July at the Convento das Mercês.

sprinkling of West African artifacts that aspire to constitute the Museu do Negro.

CENTRO

Beyond Praia Grande's frontiers lie a couple of other museums. Occupying a gracious early 19th-century mansion, the **Museu Artístico e Histórico do Maranhão** (Rua do Sol 302, tel. 98/3218-9922, 9am-5pm Tues.-Fri., 9am-4pm Sat.-Sun., R$2) conjures up the lifestyles of the rich and powerful in São Luís's economic heyday. Furnished as if lived in, the rooms are replete with lots of dark, gleaming wooden furniture, crystal chandeliers, and delicate English and French porcelain, most of which was donated by descendants of the former proprietors. Just around the corner, another grand mansion houses the **Museu de Arte Sacra** (Rua 13 de Maio 500, tel. 98/3218-9922, 9am-6:30pm Tues.-Fri., 2pm-6pm Sat.-Sun., R$2), which possesses a fine collection of 17th- to 19th-century religious art rescued from churches throughout Maranhão.

Built in the early 19th century with money from local cotton barons and homesick Portuguese merchants, the **Teatro Arthur Azevedo** (Rua do Sol 180, tel. 98/3218-9900, visits between 2pm-5pm Tues.-Fri., R$2) is the second-largest theater in Brazil. It is worth taking a guided tour to observe the opulence of its interior.

During the 17th and 18th centuries, São Luís had many public fountains that supplied water to the populace. Two that are still in existence are the **Fonte das Pedras** (Rua São João) and **Fonte do Ribeirão** (Largo do Ribeiro). The latter is truly splendid, with water pouring out of bronze spigots that are set into the mouths of a quintet of fierce-looking heads. The heads are set into a bright blue wall, behind which a series of subterranean tunnels lead to underground wells. According to local legend, these tunnels are inhabited by a giant serpent that, one day, will rise up with its tail and smash the city, causing it to sink to the bottom of the sea.

Beaches

Beaches are not a main attraction in São Luís. Although sweeping and wide, the sands are an uninspiring beige, and the water is murky. Due to the configuration of the sea and coastline, the city's tides are enormous. As a result, when the tide goes out, you have to walk for ages just to feel the ocean lapping against your knees. When the tide is high, rough waves and currents make swimming dangerous. Nonetheless, the beaches do offer a relaxing break. Crowded on weekends, they're almost deserted during the week.

It's easy to get to the beaches by bus or car from Centro. Just cross the Ponte José Sarney that spans the Rio Anil; on the other side is the modern commercial district of São Francisco. From here, Avenida Ana Jansen leads past the Lagoa de Jansen to **Ponta d'Areia,** the first of many tony but completely characterless beach neighborhoods that serve as residences and playgrounds for São Luís's middle class and elite. The main drag, Avenida Litorânea, then follows the ocean past the long beaches of **São Marcos, Calhau,** and **Olho d'Agua.** São Marcos has a pleasant boardwalk lined with animated bars that are popular with surfers. Equally nice is Calhau, with its many *barracas* where you can take refuge from the sun (or rain). Vendors sell various snacks, including fresh oysters, which they will open right in front of you and douse with lime juice.

Entertainment and Events
NIGHTLIFE
São Luís is a pretty quiet city. Although there are some options across the bridge in the beach *bairros* of Ponte d'Areia and Calhau, most nightlife takes place in Praia Grande's bars, specifically in the streets surrounding the Casa das Tulhas. Live music (Thurs.-Sat.) draws large crowds, and the bars on Beco Catarina Mina are quite picturesque at happy hour. For serious dancing, **Chez Moi** (Rua da Estrela 143, Praia Grande, tel. 98/3221-5877, 10pm-close Fri.-Sat.) is the place. While the upstairs dance floor throbs with an eclectic roster of styles ranging from samba to funk, downstairs VIP DJs from around Brazil set young Ludovicences whirling like dervishes.

São Luís is associated with two very distinctive types of music with strong African roots: *tambor de crioula* and reggae. **Tambor de crioula** is a traditional form of dance and music that dates back to the early colonial days of slavery. While men pound out frenzied rhythms of long drums (played horizontally), women dressed in bright, billowing hoop skirts and lace blouses dance in a circle. Associated with the cult of São Benedito (a black saint), *tambor de crioula* groups perform during Carnaval as well as in the streets of Praia Grande.

Few foreigners are aware that São Luís is South America's reggae capital. Back in the 1970s, the city's proximity to Jamaica allowed tunes by Bob Marley, Peter Tosh, and others to be picked up by shortwave radio, which were then adapted into Portuguese. In São Luís, reggae—live or played by DJs—is blasted through multiple speakers known as *radiolas.* Dancing is done in a romantic cheek-to-cheek style. The most authentic reggae *festas* are held in the poor suburbs, but a few take place in Praia Grande and the beach areas, which are safer for gringos. *Festas* usually occur Thursday-Saturday beginning at around 8pm. In Praia Grande, **Roots Bar** (Rua da Palma 85, 6pm-2am Wed.-Fri., tel. 98/3221-7580) attracts hard-core *regueiros.* **Bar do Nelson** (Av. Litorânea 135, Calhau, tel. 98/8776-2875, 9pm-close Thurs.-Sat.) is a "cleaner" but classic bar whose denizens are more well-to-do. Weekend nights are the most lively.

PERFORMING ARTS
Located in an attractively renovated old warehouse near the waterfront, the **Centro de Criatividade Odylo Costa Filho** (Rampa do Comércio 200, Praia Grande, tel. 98/3218-9930) is a worthwhile place to check out the local arts scene. There is a gallery space, a theater that hosts plays and dance performances, and a small art-house cinema that screens films. Also check for concerts at the ornate **Teatro Arthur Azevedo** (Rua do Sol 180, Centro, tel. 98/3218-9900).

FESTIVALS AND EVENTS
São Luís is a hothouse for popular and religious celebrations. While its **Carnaval** doesn't receive much attention, in recent years traditional *blocos* (groups) and *bandas* have been resurrected. The resulting festivities provide a real taste of the Brazilian Carnavals of yore. Brass bands play *marchinhas* (marches), and traditional Afro *blocos* pound out *tambor de crioula* rhythms while lithe dancers whirl like dervishes. Residents of all ages take to the streets of the *centro histórico* and Praia Grande in masks and sequins. Even bigger

and more spectacular than Carnaval are the not-to-be-missed **Bumba-Meu-Boi** festivities, which take place in June. One of Brazil's most ornate and moving popular celebrations, the *festa* combines African, Indian, and European melodies and rhythms and lots of pageantry.

Shopping

São Luís is a rich source of folk and indigenous art and *artesanato*. Located in a vast warehouse on the edge of Praia Grande, the state-run **CEPRAMA** (Rua São Pantaleão 1232, Madre de Deus, tel. 98/3231-6018, 9am-6pm Mon.-Sat.) reunites souvenir-style handicrafts from around Maranhão, including hand-painted azulejos and miniature Bumba-Meu-Boi bulls with embroidered costumes, lacework, and ceramics. You'll also find *doces* and liqueurs made from local fruits such as *buriti, bacuri,* and *cupuaçu*. In Praia Grande, there are lots of little shops. Check out the market stalls at the **Casa das Tulhas** (Rua da Estrela 184, 7am-8pm Mon.-Fri., 7am-6pm Sat., 7am-3pm Sun.). **Arte Indígena** (Rua do Giz 66, Praia Grande, tel. 98/3221-2940, 8:30am-5pm Mon.-Fri., 8:30am-2pm Sat.) features basketry, jewelry, and other objects made by Maranhense indigenous groups.

Accommodations

São Luís's real interest lies in its history, culture, and architecture, which makes Praia Grande and Centro the best places to stay. Although there are plenty of modern hotels in the beach neighborhoods of Ponta d'Areia and Calhau, the hotels range from bland to hideous and are overpriced.

An insanely inexpensive option, the **Albergue Juventude Solar das Pedras** (Rua da Palma 127, Praia Grande, tel. 98/3232-6694, www.ajsolardaspedras.com.br, R$70-80 d, R$30-35 pp) is a youth hostel located in an old building right in the middle of the historical center. The rich blue facade gives off cheery vibes, but the clean and functional guest rooms are a little spare and sad. Still, where else can you get a bed with breakfast (and access to Internet, a kitchen, and laundry facilities) for so little? More atmospheric are the common spaces, where exposed stone walls and wooden floors reveal the building's former character. At ★ **Casa Lavínia** (Rua 28 de Julho, Praia Grande, tel. 98/3221-4655, www.casalavinia.com, R$200-220 d), giant canopy beds anchor four palatial, second-floor suites flaunting glossy wood floors, sky-high ceilings, and eclectic furnishings culled from the Italian owners' world travels. Outside, the

Bumba-Meu-Boi in the streets of São Luís

beguiling lounge, dining room, and patio garden have been expertly refurbished to showcase the original features of this 19th-century villa (which once served as a bordello). Nearby **Pousada Portas da Amazônia** (Rua do Giz 129, Praia Grande, tel. 98/3222-9937, www. portasdaamazonia.com.br, R$180-250 d), hosts airy, cathedral-ceilinged rooms occupying a handsomely restored mansion dating to 1839. Large windows either overlook a sea of colonial rooftops (a little noisy) or tropical courtyard garden (more tranquil) where breakfast is served. There is a cybercafé on-site as well as a pizzeria (open evenings).

While not right in Praia Grande, the **Pousada Colonial** (Rua Afonso Pena 112, Centro, tel. 98/3232-2834, www.clickcolonial. com.br, R$125-210 d) is close enough. This atmospheric colonial building plastered in white, blue, and lemon azulejos has been carefully renovated. While the common spaces are bright, spacious, and well cared for, the basic guest rooms could use some TLC. The brightest and least cramped are those overlooking the street.

Food

São Luís is a seafood lover's paradise and Maranhão's specialty is *arroz-de-cuxá*. This rice-based dish is made with the mildly pungent leaves of a local plant called *vinagreira*, to which dried shrimp, toasted sesame, and manioc flour are added. Also try the *torta de camarão*, a type of frittata stuffed with dry or fresh shrimp, a recipe that was originally invented by slaves. Maranhão's proximity to the Amazon explains the presence of a couple of the most ambrosial fruits you'll ever taste: *cupuaçu* (whose popularity has spread throughout Brazil) and the much rarer *bacuri*. Savor them as thick juices or for dessert as mousse-like *cremes*, or else stop by any drugstore of the Extra Farma chain, which sells a local brand (Blaus) of *picolé* (popsicle) made using the aforementioned native fruits as well as *muruci* and *taperaba*.

Instead of Coca-Cola or *guaraná*, Maranhenses swear by Jesus. The name of this bright pink soft drink has no connection to the Son of God. Instead, it pays homage to local pharmacist Jesus Norberto Gomes, who invented it back in 1920. Jesus's ingredients include cinnamon, cloves, and the jolting presence of *guaraná*. In markets and bars, you'll also see plenty of bottles of a distilled substance that ranges in color from pale lilac to ultraviolet. Known as *tiquira,* this popular Maranhense version of *cachaça* is made from fermented manioc, and it packs quite a wallop.

Located on the second floor of a colonial building, the lavish spreads at the ★ **Restaurante Senac** (Rua de Nazaré 242, Centro, tel. 98/3198-1100, noon-3pm Mon. and Wed.-Thurs., noon-3pm and 7pm-11pm Fri.-Sat., R$30-40) are prepared and ceremoniously served by local students of the Senac restaurant school. The lunch buffet (R$30) changes daily; at night, the menu is à la carte. One of Praia Grande's few remaining eateries, **Cafofinho da Tia Doca** (Trav. Marcelino de Alveida, Praia Grande, tel. 98/3235-8971, noon-close daily, R$30-40) is a charmingly atmospheric and animated little hole-in-the-wall. Sit outside and nurse a coffee or cocktail, or enter to enjoy meals such as fresh fish and seafood risotto (you'll swear it serves six).

The vast majority of São Luís' restaurants are strung along the middle-class beach neighborhoods across the Rio Anil. **Maracangalha** (Rua Mearim 13, Quadro 3, Renascença II, tel. 98/3235-9305, 11:30am-midnight Mon.-Sat., 11am-5pm Sun., R$35-50) is a little hard to find but worth the trip; access is via Avenida dos Holandeses, km. 6. Chef Melquíades Dantas is the inventor of an addictive *geleia de pimenta* (pepper jelly) that accompanies the beef *pastéis,* a great starter. The breezy veranda is an ideal spot to sample the extensive menu of cocktails and *cachaças.* Closer to Centro (and easier on the pocketbook), **Feijão de Corda**'s (Rua Maracaçume 8, Farol de São Marcos, tel. 98/3233-4717, 11am-midnight daily, R$25-40) rustic décor complements regional specialties such as crab (plucked live from an aquarium) and melt-in-your-mouth *carne de sol,* all served in heaping portions with lots of fixings.

Information and Services

Tourist information is at the municipal tourist office, **Setur** (Praça Benedito Leite (Rua da Palma 53, Centro, www.visitesaoluis.com, tel. 98/3212-6215, 8am-7pm Mon.-Fri., 8am-1pm Sat.-Sun.) and at the Maranhão state tourist offices located in the *centro histórico* (Rua Portugal 165, Praia Grande, tel. 98/3231-4696, www.turismo-ma.com.br, 8am-7pm, Mon.-Fri. 9am-6pm Sat., 9am-1pm Sun.), the airport (tel. 98/3244-4500, 6am-10pm daily), and the *rodoviária* (tel. 98/3249-4500, 8am-7pm daily). **Lotus Turismo e Aventura** (Rua Marcelino Almeida 25, Praia Grande, tel. 98/3221-0942, www.lotusturismo.com. br) and French-owned **Terra Nordeste** (Rua do Giz 380, Praia Grande, tel. 98/8857-7408, www.terranordeste.com.br) offer tours of the coastline around São Luís as well as trips to Alcântara and the Parque Nacional dos Lençóis Maranhenses.

There is a **Banco do Brasil** in Praia Grande (Travessa Boa Ventura 26-B) and an HSBC in Centro (Rua do Sol 105). The main post office is on Praça João Lisboa 292, in Centro.

In an emergency, dial **193** (fire), **192** (ambulance), or **190** (police). The special **tourist police** headquarters is in Praia Grande (Rua da Estrela 427, tel. 98/3214-8682). For medical assistance, try the **Santa Casa de Misericórdia** (Rua do Norte 233, Centro, tel. 98/3232-0248).

Transportation

Airfare to São Luís is not cheap, but the alternative is long hours spent on buses. There are few direct flights from major Brazilian cities. You'll often need to make a connection in Fortaleza or Brasília. The **Aeroporto Marechal Cunha Machado** (Av. dos Libaneses, Tirirical, tel. 98/3217-6100), is 13 kilometers (8 mi) from the *centro histórico.* A taxi to Centro and Praia Grande costs R$35-40.

Long-distance buses to São Luís are much cheaper but take forever. There is no direct service along the coast from Fortaleza—instead you have to go via Piauí and change in Parnaíba or Teresina (ultimately, you'll spend 15 hours on the road). Coming from Recife, Salvador, or Brasília also usually entails a connection in Teresina. The long-distance *rodoviária* (Av. dos Franceses, Santo Antônio, tel. 98/3243-1305) is 10 kilometers (6 mi) from the Centro. A cab will cost R$25-30. You can also take a municipal bus marked "São Cristovão/Aeroporto," which stops at the *rodoviária,* to the **Terminal de Integração Praia Grande,** the local bus station located along the waterfront at Praia Grande. Be aware that due to traffic, getting from the airport and bus station to Centro can take well over an hour.

The only municipal buses you'll need to take are those that shuttle between the Terminal de Integração (marked "Praia Grande") and the beaches (marked "Ponta d'Areia" or "Calhau"). Bus fare is R$2.10. For other destinations, and after sundown, you should resort to taxis, which are easy to hail. You can also reserve one by calling **Ligue Taxi** (tel. 98/3222-2222). Renting a car is not really necessary, unless you want to drive to the Lençóis Maranhenses. If so, **Avis** (www. avis.com.br, tel. 98/4062-0633) and **Localiza** (www.localiza.com, tel. 98/3245-1566) both have offices at the airport.

ALCÂNTARA

Across the Baía de São Marcos from São Luís—about 1.5 hours by boat—lies the hauntingly beautiful colonial town of Alcântara. Founded in 1648, its picturesque hilltop was the favored dwelling place of Maranhão's wealthy sugar and cotton plantation owners. During its 18th- and 19th-century heyday, it was one of Brazil's most sumptuous colonial towns. The abolition of slavery resulted in the end of the high life. The ruined plantation owners decamped to São Luís, leaving their freed slaves in the abandoned town. Subsequently, like a city out of a Gabriel García Márquez novel, Alcântara slipped into oblivion. The road leading to São Luís (an eight-hour drive) became overgrown, as did the town itself. Indeed, its dilapidated baroque treasures—many now in ruins—seem to be on the verge of slowly being swallowed up by steamy tropical jungle. What Alcântara lacks in lost grandeur, it more than makes up for in atmosphere.

Sights

Approaching Alcântara by boat is an experience in itself: its church domes, red tile roofs, and lithe imperial palms slowly emerge from a swathe of emerald jungle. Despite the many ruins, there are more than 300 mansions dating to the 17th and 18th centuries spread around the hilltop in various states of disrepair. The main square of Praça da Matriz is truly impressive. Lined on three sides by once-grand palaces and with a splendid view overlooking the bay, the heart of the square is dominated by the rust-red brick ruins of the **Igreja Matriz de São Mathias.** In the center stands the *pelourinho* (whipping post used for slaves) tattooed with the Portuguese crown's coat of arms. On one side of the *praça* sits the **Museu Histórico de Alcântara** (tel. 98/8865-0215, www.museuhistoricodealcantara.com.br, 9am-3pm Tues.-Fri. 9am-1pm Sat.-Sun., R$2). Occupying an azulejo-covered mansion that belonged to one of Alcântara's aristocratic families, the museum displays a small collection of engravings, furnishings, and objects that evoke the city's days of glory. Included is the iron bed specially made for the visit of Emperor Dom Pedro II. Similar trappings from the past are at neighboring **Casa Histórica de Alcântara** (tel. 98/3337-1515, http://museucasaalcantara.blogspot.com.br, 9:30am-4:30pm Tues.-Fri., 9:30am-2:30pm Sat.-Sun., free).

On **Rua da Armagura** (Street of Bitterness) are the ruins of the Palácio Negro, which served as the slave market, and the Casa do Imperador. Alcântara's leading families fought tooth and nail over who would have the privilege of building the house that would lodge Imperador Pedro II during an official visit. To the townspeople's eternal disappointment, despite the lavish welcome they had prepared for him, the emperor never made it to Alcântara; rumor has it he was waylaid by a seductive Indian maiden. Rua Grande is also full of treasures, including the 17th-century **Igreja do Carmo** (9am-1pm daily, R$2), whose original baroque splendor has been restored to its former glory.

A short walk from the town brings you to the fairly primitive **Praia da Baronesa.** Framed by jungle, the beach is a nice place to sit at a *barraca* and feast on fresh fish and icy beer while watching for *guarás* (scarlet ibises). A diet of pink shrimp explains the lipstick-red plumage of these birds, and their appearance against the canopy of green foliage presents a shocking contrast.

Festivals and Events

One of Maranhão's legendary popular celebrations, the **Festa do Divino** mobilizes Alcântara's entire population during two weeks in May. A colorful fusion of African and Catholic elements, the *festa* also provides a resolution to the no-show of Dom Pedro II with celebrations revolving around the figures of a sumptuously attired emperor and empress (two local children) who are paraded through town to much fanfare. Commemorations include fireworks, music, and dancing to the pounding drums played by matriarchs of Tambor de Mina *terreiros.* Moist coconut tarts shaped like tiny tortoises, known as *doce-de-especies,* are distributed to all the children. For an off-season glimpse at the festivities, visit the **Casa do Divino** (9am-3pm Tues.-Sun, R$1).

Accommodations and Food

Most people visit Alcântara as a day trip. Should you be very struck by the place, there are several *pousadas* where you can spend the night, including the **Pousada dos Guarás** (Praia da Baronesa, tel. 98/3337-1339, R$85 d). Located right on the beach, these palm-thatched bungalows are simple but utterly tranquil. A seaside restaurant-bar serves up delicious fresh fish. For food in town, **Restaurante da Josefa** (Rua Direita 33, tel. 98/3337-1109, 10am-9pm daily) is a cozy home-style eatery where generous portions of local fish, seafood, and chicken dishes are served with myriad fixings.

Transportation

Ferries to Alcântara (R$12, 1.5 hours) depart from São Luís's **Terminal Hidroviário** (tel. 98/3232-0692) on Praia Grande's main waterfront. Schedules can be affected by the tides, but there are usually two departures in the morning and one in the afternoon. During low tide, you may need to depart or return via the Yacht Club in Ponto d'Areia (check first at the terminal); sometimes the crossing can be a little choppy. Alternatives are to take a faster but more expensive motorboat or a slower but more scenic catamaran. All boat and information schedules are available at the terminal.

★ LENÇÓIS MARANHENSES

One of Brazil's most spectacular natural attractions, the Lençóis Maranhenses, 250 kilometers (155 mi) east of São Luís, is a fantastic desert of immense white sand dunes that bear a striking resemblance to billowing *lençóis* (sheets). Some of the dunes are 50 meters (165 feet) high. Every year when the rains come (December-May), their valleys fill with water, forming a series of jade lagoons whose mirrorlike surfaces reflect the piercing blue sky, filled with drifting clouds and gliding egrets. The majesty of the landscape is impossible to express, but the sense of timelessness is impressive; particularly when trekking through the sand, you can turn around to see that the wind has wiped out the only sign of civilization—the footprints you made five minutes earlier.

Parque Nacional dos Lençóis Maranhenses

The Lençóis Maranhenses are within the Parque Nacional dos Lençóis Maranhenses, a protected area that is about the size of Rhode Island. No cars are allowed in the park, although Jeeps can take you within close proximity. To explore the dunes on foot, you'll need to hire a guide or go as part of an excursion. The closest town is nearby **Barreirinhas**, set along the Rio Preguiças and a six-hour bus ride from São Luís; here there are plenty of hotels and restaurants as well as guides, tour operators, ATMs, cellphone and Wi-Fi signals, and traffic jams. To experience the dunes up close and without crowds (or electricity and phone service), base yourself in two far more charming and rustic little villages. Off the beaten path but on the cusp of the dunes themselves are **Atins** (to the east, at the point at which the Rio Preguiças meets the Atlantic) and **Santo Amaro do Maranhão** (to the far—and remote—west). Plan to spend a minimum of three nights in the region. The best times to visit are the sunny days during June-September, when the lagoons are still full enough to bathe in (by December, they've often completely evaporated). Those based in Barreirinhas can explore the park by Jeep or by boat.

BY JEEP

The closest and easiest way to explore the dunes is by taking a half-day Jeep trip to visit nearby lagoons, including the particularly gorgeous **Lagoa Bonita** and **Lagoa Azul.** Try to go in the afternoon, when it's cooler and the light is more golden, since you'll be able to watch the sun set over the dunes. A full-day Jeep outing to the village of **Santo Amaro do Maranhão** allows you to visit the **Lagoa da Gaivota,** one of the largest and deepest of all the park's lagoons, whose colors change like a 1970s mood ring. **Tropical Adventure** (tel. 98/3349-1987, www.tropicaladventure.com) and **Rota das Trilhas** (tel. 98/3349-0372, www.rotadastrilhas.com.br) operate Jeep trips that start at around R$70 pp for a half-day trip. If you take a *jardineira* (an open-backed truck that fits 10), a trip to both *lagoas* costs around R$35 pp.

BY BOAT

The **Rio Preguiças** is a river that passes close to Barreirinhas. It winds through a landscape of *buriti* palm forests, mangrove swamps, and sand dunes, passing tiny palm-thatched villages until it finally flows into the ocean. With a guide, you can descend the river by launch or by a small motorboat known as a *voadeira*. Excursions include stops for swimming and lunch in the fishing village of **Caburé,** which lies on a sandbar between the river and the sea. You'll also stop in the village of **Mandacaru** to climb up the **Farol Preguiças,** a picturesque lighthouse that offers fantastic 360-degree views of the dunes. Another option is to hire a boat to take you downriver to **Atins,** an idyllic village ensconced in the dunes and surrounded by some stunning lagoons such as the Lagoa Tropical. Although you can visit Atins in a day trip, it's worthwhile staying overnight so you can explore the surrounding dunes and lagoons on foot (and soak up the relaxing vibes).

Tropical Adventure and **Rota das Trilhas** can organize these boat trips for you. A full-day excursion for up to four people costs around R$60 pp (not including lunch). You can also negotiate directly with a boat operator and guide (a private boat trip to Atins should cost around R$280 for four people).

Sports and Recreation

Take to the sands on a quadricycle (R$330 for two) and zoom 45 kilometers (28 mi) through the dunes, past an ecologically intoxicating mix of Cerrado, *restinga* and mangrove vegetation, all the way to Caburé. You can also float the dunescapes in a rubber inner tube known as *boia cross*. Half-day trips (R$60 pp) feature 90 minutes of floating down Rio Cardosa, an emerald colored river that's a 45-minute Jeep ride from Barreirinhas. Or splurge for the 30-minute flight (R$180 pp) for an unforgettable bird's-eye view over the dunes (reserve morning or late afternoon for best light). **Tropical Adventure** (tel. 98/3349-1987, www.tropicaladventure.com) and **Rota das Trilhas** (tel. 98/3349-0372,

www.rotadastrilhas.com.br) can organize trips.

Shopping

Barreirinhas is *buriti* country. Locals use the fibers from this palm to make everything from roofing thatch to baskets, hats, and handbags that are the epitome of organic chic. You'll find a wide array of items at the shops along Avenida Brasília and the **Centro de Artesanato** (Praça do Trabalhador). If you visit Lagoa Bonita, visit the *barraca* of Dona Maria do Buritizal, who sells beautifully made *buriti artesanato* along with freshly roasted cashews.

Accommodations and Food
BARREIRINHAS

Barreirinhas has been growing in disorderly leaps and bounds, spurred on by its role as the prime tourist hub of the Lençóis. There are plenty of *pousadas* in and around town, although some downtown options are a little on the tacky side.

Clean, cost-effective, and comfortable, **Pousada d'Areia** (Av. Joaquim Soeira de Carvalho 888, tel. 98/3349-0550, www.pousadadareia.com.br, R$120-150 d) is a nondescript but well-maintained option with all the basics intact, conveniently located on the main drag. Newer rooms, further from the reception, are the largest and quietest. A more atmospheric budget option is the **Pousada Sossego do Cantinho** (Rua Principal 2, Cantinho, tel. 98/3349-0753, www.sossego-do-cantinho.com, R$180-230 d). Located 15 minutes from the center of town in the village of Cantinho, this Swiss-owned *pousada* consists of four rustic but sprawling wooden bungalows set along the sandy white banks of the river (boats can shuttle you to and from town). While not central, it's very bucolic, and the hosts are very helpful. Also along the river but less basic is **Pousada Encantes do Nordeste** (Av. Boa Vista, tel. 98/3349-0288, www.encantesdonordeste.com.br, R$255-310 d), whose pretty coral chalets are nestled in a lush garden. Rooms are simple but homey, and the staff is friendly. For cooling off, there is a pool as well as the river. Although it's 4 kilometers (2.5 mi) from the center of town, most excursions will pick you up at the *pousada*. At night, you can easily take a cab or *moto-taxi* to the center. The **Bambaé** (tel. 98/3349-0691, noon-3pm and 6pm-10pm daily) riverside restaurant is one of the best around.

Various restaurants line Avenida Beira-Rio; all take advantage of the pretty river views. **Restaurante do Carlão** (Rua Coronel Godinho, tel. 98/3349-0016, 11am-10pm daily, R$20-30) wins kudos for having the most interesting menu in town: Fresh fish and seafood are all imaginatively prepared using exotic local fruits such as *muruci, cajá,* and *açaí.*

Be sure to sample some of the sweets made from the glossy amber fruit of the *buriti* palm. **Tá Delícia** (Travessa Vereador Zé Diniz, tel. 98/3349-0576) is a simple per-kilo joint. A small but well-executed buffet offers regional dishes, and there is a fantastic buffet of *sorvete,* among whose exotic flavors is buriti. **Doces Dagente** (Av. Brasília) sells *buriti* candies, preserves, and brick-like *doce de buriti* packed in wooden boxes to go.

ATINS

Located at the extreme eastern edge of the Parque Nacional dos Lençóis Maranhenses, where the Rio Perguiças runs into the ocean, Atins is a tiny, timeless, and completely untouristy fishing village surrounded by dunes and within close range of Lagoa Tropical and Lagoa Mário, easily reached by Jeep.

It was only a matter of time before a few intrepid gringos were lured to set down roots and open up *pousadas* at the end of the world. Sprinkled amid a cluster of palms, **Pousada Rancho do Buna** (Rua do Sol, tel. 98/3349-5005, www.ranchodobuna.com.br, R$168 d) offers enticingly rustic chalets that house up to four. An inviting restaurant serves fish and seafood dishes accompanied by organically grown vegetables and *doces* made from local fruits. There is a pool for dipping, and surrounding lagoons can be explored via Jeep and boat. Reservations are necessary. Owned by

Italian expats who tumbled into Atins seeking kiteboarding thrills, **Pousada Maresia** (Rua Principal, tel. 98/8816-7265, www.maresia-atins.com.br, R$130-160 d) began life as a pizzeria, then added charming apartments and beach bungalows built for two, three, and four. Kite surfing equipment and lessons are available. The garden restaurant serves traditional Neapolitan pizza and pesto made with organic basil and cashews.

It's worth the 25-minute Jeep ride (or one-hour guided walk) to the simple shack that houses **Restaurante da Luzia** (Canto de Atins, tel. 98/8709-7661). You'll understand why Luzia Diniz's cooking has achieved legendary status when faced with a massive portion of fresh shrimp barbecued over hot coals. Luzia claims her house is always open for business—helpful if you develop a sudden midnight craving for shrimp stroganoff.

Atins can be reached from Barreirinhas by Jeep or boat. If you negotiate a one-way voyage on the day trips offered by outfits such as **Tropical Adventure** and **Rota das Trilhas** (usually around R$60), you'll also get to visit other destinations along the route. Both outfits can arrange for private launch transportation as well; expect to pay R$250 for up to four people for a journey that will take one hour. Another alternative is to jump aboard the 4X4 Toyota (R$20, 2 hours) that leaves Barreirinhas at 9am from Rua Monsenhor Gentil.

SANTO AMARO DO MARANHÃO

Perched near the western extreme of the park, Santo Amaro is close to some of the highest dunes and most enchanting *lagoas* in the Lençóis Maranhenses. The town's several *pousadas* are all pretty basic. What **Pousada Cajueiro** (Rua Oswaldo do Cruz 2-A, tel. 98/3369-1119, www.pousadacajueiro.com.br, R$160 d) has going for it is a privileged site overlooking the Rio Alegre. The stark guest rooms are clean and have air-conditioning as well as balconies with hammocks. The on-site restaurant does local cuisine proud by serving up giant specimens of fresh local shrimp cooked in a variety of ways. The *pousada* also organizes Jeep outings to nearby attractions, including beautiful Lagoa da Gaivota, only 20 minutes away.

From Barreirinhas, **Tropical Adventure** offers transportation by Jeep to Santo Amaro (three hours, R$550 for four) and includes a stop at Lagoa da Gaivota. A cheaper option is to take one of four daily buses operated by **Cisne Branco** (tel. 98/3245-1233, www.cisnebrancoturismo.com.br, R$5). If coming directly from São Luis, take a Cisne Branco bus (3.5 hours, R$20), with four daily departures to the town of Sangue. From here, a Jeep taxi can take you 36 kilometers (22 mi) across the dunes to Santo Amaro; it's best to allow your accommodations in Santo Amaro to organize this for you. Cheaper and more convenient is to hire a taxi-van to pick you up in São Luís and drive you directly to Santo Amaro. **Denilson** (tel. 98/8808-9109) and **Tomás** (tel. 98/8836-4099) are two trusted local drivers who shuttle passengers daily between the two towns (5 hours, R$50 pp).

Transportation and Services

There is no tourist office in Barreirinhas. Local tour agencies have lots of information about the park, as does the local branch of the **Instituto Chico Mendes** (tel. 98/3349-1115), which administers the park. **Banco do Brasil** (Av. Joaquim Soeiro de Carvalho) has an ATM that accepts international Visa cards.

There are various ways of getting to Barreirinhas from São Luís. **Cisne Branco** operates four daily buses (4.5 hours, R$24) that depart from the *rodoviária*. Should you want more comfort (i.e., air-conditioning), contact **BRTur** (tel. 98/3236-6056, R$20), a minivan service that picks you up at your São Luís hotel in the morning. Fewer stops speed up the journey significantly to 3-4 hours.

A car is useless in the dunes, but should you want to drive, the MA-402 highway that leads to Barreirinhas is in good condition.

From São Luís, various tour agencies can organize your trip to the Lençóis Maranhenses—whether it's simply reserving transportation or customizing an entire package that includes Jeep and boat outings. **Lotus Turismo e Aventura** (Rua Marcelino Almeida 25, Praia Grande, tel. 98/3221-0942, www.lotusturismo.com.br) is recommended, as is **Ecodunas** (tel. 98/3349-0545, www.ecodunas.com.br), which organizes a variety of adventure excursions that depart from São Luís.

The Amazon

O ccupying an area roughly the size of the continental United States, the Amazon is the Earth's largest and most ecologically diverse rain forest and its greatest river system (with more than 1,000 tributaries).

Dense, green, wet, and full of the promise of adventure, the rain forest provides an unforgettable experience for those who venture to get there. Sail along one of the Rio Amazonas's many tributaries in a riverboat or dugout canoe that glides past caimans and cavorting pink dolphins. Hike through a jungle filled with the screams and squawks of hundreds of fluorescently colored birds, or climb up into the trees' canopy, where you'll be eye-level with monkeys. Swim amid piranhas (the chances of you eating them are greater than them eating you) in waters that range from creamy brown to jet black. Or stay in a jungle lodge—which can range from rustic to downright luxurious—and let the wildlife come to you. If time and money are no obstacle, consider trips far into the jungle: the Anavilhanas archipelago, with its 400 islands, or the Mamirauá Reserve, Brazil's first sustainable jungle park, home to the elusive scarlet-faced uakari monkey.

The region's two principal cities are Manaus and Belém. Manaus, capital of the state of Amazonas and gateway to the forest, is a busy river port humming with activity and markets. Manaus is famous as the birthplace of the Amazon River. It is here that the Meeting of the Waters takes place, a spectacle in which the dark clear waters of the Rio Negro flow beside and finally merge with the lighter hued Rio Solimões to form the world's mightiest river.

Midway between Manaus and Belém lies the town of Santarém, perched upon the Rio Tapajós. Steeped in Amazonian culture, Santarém is a languid, largely undiscovered place blessed with the white-sand river beaches of Alter do Chão. The surrounding region has a wealth of attractions ranging from the jungles of the Floresta Nacional do Tapajós to the 12,000-year-old rock paintings hidden amid the caves and grottoes of Monte Alegre.

Previous: a typical riverscape; Teatro Amazonas, Manaus. **Above:** waterfall near Manaus.

Highlights

© AVALON TRAVEL

★ **Mercado Ver-o-Peso:** For 300 years, Belém's fascinating riverside market has served as an essential and exotic link between this colonial capital and the jungle beyond (page 522).

★ **Ilha de Marajó:** Deserted beaches, exuberant vegetation, a centuries-old ceramics tradition, and thousands of water buffalo make this Switzerland-size island an idyllic and intriguing retreat (page 535).

★ **Alter do Chão:** In the middle of the Amazon, Alter do Chão is a mini beach resort with sugary white sands and clear green waters (page 542).

★ **Teatro Amazonas:** This sumptuous opera house in the middle of the jungle is a testament to the heyday of the Amazon's rubber boom (page 548).

★ **Reserva de Desenvolvimento Sustentável de Mamirauá:** This sustainable reserve is the hottest eco-spot along the Rio Solimões. Canoeing through the flooded forests in search of the red-faced uakari monkey is only one of the amazing activities available here (page 559).

★ **Jungle Lodges (Hotéis de Selva):** There's no better way to get a feel for the rain forest than by shacking up in its squawking, chirping, ribbeting depths (pages 560 and 562).

★ **Arquipélago de Anavilhanas:** The second-largest freshwater archipelago in the world boasts more than 400 deserted islands, virgin rain forest, and the possibility of swimming with pink dolphins (page 561).

★ **Riverboat Trips:** Set sail on the Rio Negro and Rio Solimões on a riverboat. Riverboat trips allow you to cover the most territory in the Amazon while enjoying the comforts of its rustic or luxury accommodations, depending on your budget (page 563).

The Amazon

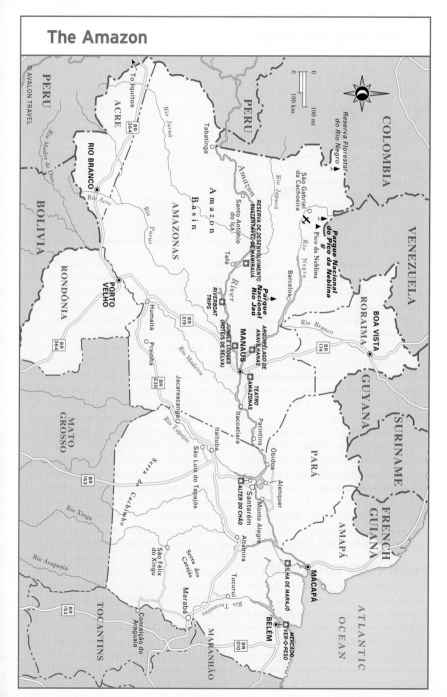

The Amazon River

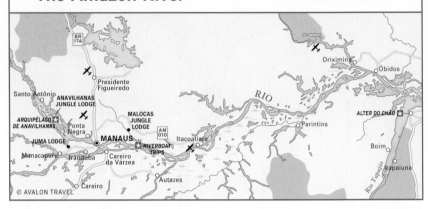

At the mouth of the Amazon, 1,600 kilometers (1,000 mi) downriver from Manaus, sits Belém, capital of the state of Pará and one of Brazil's most interesting capitals. Founded in the 1600s, Belém was little more than a sleepy colonial outpost until the rubber boom of the late 1800s. Overnight, Belém was transformed into a "tropical Paris" with palaces, plazas, and parks. Although the boom had gone bust by the early 20th century, this atmospheric city still retains considerable vestiges of its former wealth and elegance.

From Belém, it's a three-hour boat trip to Marajó, a vast island of secluded river beaches, water buffalo farms, and ceramics studios where local artisans make pottery based on the sophisticated techniques and designs used more than 1,000 years ago by their indigenous ancestors. The world's largest freshwater island, Marajó is an idyllic place to while away a few days at the tail end of a jungle trip.

PLANNING YOUR TIME

Unless you're a jungle junkie or a river rat, the best and most efficient way to explore the Amazon is to base yourself in either **Manaus or Belém**—or else to split your time between the two. **Two days in each city** is a minimum (although Belém offers more historical and cultural attractions than Manaus, which is more modern and less attractive).

From both, you can venture forth into the surrounding area. From Belém, set aside **3-4 days** for a trip to Ilha de Marajó, or to the beaches on Ilha de Mosqueiro or Ilha de Algodoal. From Manaus, spend a day or two in nearby Presidente Figueiredo, with its dozens of waterfalls, or **2-3 days** in rain forest lodges within a short distance of the city. To really get a feel for the rain forest, set aside a minimum of **4-5 days,** which could be spent on an organized excursion up the Rio Negro or Rio Solimões or at a far-flung forest lodge in an area such as the Mamirauá Reserve or the Anavilhanas archipelago.

If neither time nor comfort is a major issue, the classic Amazonian trip is a boat ride from Manaus to Belém, or vice versa, which will set you back 4-5 days, the price of a hammock (or cabin), and a lot of bug repellent. On the way, stop at Santarém, whose surrounding attractions (most notably the beaches of Alter do Chão) deserve at least three days. If you're pressed for time and don't want to miss Santarém, you can easily fly there from both Belém and Manaus. Flying between far-flung Amazonian destinations saves you an awful lot of time that could be spent on more varied and diverting activities than sitting on a crowded boat in the middle of the river. If booked in advance, airfare is often similar to the price of a cabin.

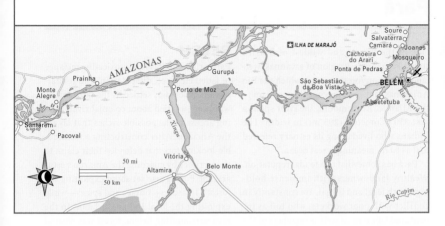

Despite a major drop in deforestation (approximately 80 percent of the jungle is still intact), the most recent threat has been global warming. Over the last decade, the Amazon has been hit by severe droughts and floods that have wreaked havoc upon traditional ecosystems. The Amazon is always fairly wet, humid, and hot, seeing temperatures of 35-40°C (95-104°F) and humidity levels of 80 percent. Belém is one of the rainiest cities on the planet (December-June is considered the wet season, and July-November is considered slightly less wet). Belém's rains are torrential, but they pass. Manaus and the Amazonian Basin possess a more pronounced dry season, which lasts roughly **July-November** and sees somewhat cooler temperatures (23-30°C/73-86°F). If you plan on traveling into the rain forest, the season you choose will have a significant impact on your trip due to the vast flooding of the Amazon and its tributaries. During the dry season, the water recedes, leaving beaches exposed and forest floors dry and hikable. Fishing is also better at this time.

However, the wet season's high waters give you access (by boat) to temporarily flooded forests known as *igapós,* where you'll see more wildlife. Although it's always hot during the day, nights in the forest can be cooler, so it's always a good idea to have long pants and a light jacket or sweater. A light blanket is recommended if you're going to be on a riverboat. Santarém receives less rain than either Belém or Manaus—the better with which to soak up sun on its inviting beaches.

A **vaccine for yellow fever** is necessary and proof is required. You can get these shots for free at public health clinics throughout Brazil, but you'll need to have the injection 10 days prior to entering the Amazon. Some tropical disease experts also recommend taking antimalarial pills, though they're not always effective and can have strong side effects. Bring lots of mosquito repellent and wear long sleeves, especially around the sunrise and sunset, when mosquitoes are on the prowl. Most accommodations offer mosquito netting.

Pará

One of the largest and wildest of Brazil's states, Pará is a vast region of savannas, wetlands, and rain forest through which the Rio Amazonas makes its journey downstream to the Atlantic. At its mouth, the river spans a vast 330 kilometers (205 mi) in width. The Indians who lived along its estuary referred to it as *pa'ra,* meaning "great ocean."

Pará has somewhat of a feudal reputation. Wealthy landowners with immense holdings, both legal and illegal, are constantly in conflict with poor workers, who toil as indentured laborers, as well as members of the *movimento sem terra* (landless movement) who occupy their lands. Conflicts are often resolved with guns. Both landowners and migrants have wreaked havoc on Pará's forests, particularly in the east, burning great swaths for the purposes of farming and raising cattle. Further devastation is the result of mineral excavation, logging, soybean cultivation, and hydroelectric projects (Pará's Tucuruí dam is one of the world's largest hydroelectric plants, and hotly contested plans are in the works to build Belo Monte, which would be the third largest dam on the planet). These activities have brought significant prosperity to the region in recent years.

Perched at the mouth of the Amazon in eastern Pará, the colonial capital of Belém is an evocative city. Apart from its considerable charms, it makes a good base from which to visit Ilha de Marajó. Western Pará—reached by plane or by sailing upriver from Belém—is considerably less developed. Surrounding the city of Santarém is a languorous port town along the Rio Tapajós, whose neighboring village of Alter do Chão boasts Caribbean-worthy beaches. Here you'll find large patches of unspoiled jungle as well as typical *caboclo* villages, where Amazonian river culture remains very much alive.

BELÉM

Pará's river capital is an intoxicating mélange of faded elegance, dilapidation, and revitalization. Belém was settled by the Portuguese, who were worried about colonial rivals having access to the possible riches that lay up the Amazon. After constructing a formidable-looking fort that defended their claim to the territory by guarding the Amazon's estuary, the Portuguese set about exploiting the forest's treasures—timber and spices—while exploiting the local Indians as labor. In the area surrounding Belém, forest was cleared to make way for sugar and rice plantations similar to those in neighboring northeastern states. Thought to be hardier than local Indians (who easily fell victim to European diseases), African slaves were imported to work the plantations. Despite the creation of a small elite, Pará's colonial economy never took off like that of neighboring Maranhão. By the late 1700s, the population had stagnated to the extent that the Portuguese crown was offering incentives for Portuguese settlers to marry Indian women (the result of this miscegenation is Pará's significant *caboclo* population).

Belém only came into its own in the late 19th century, when the onset of the rubber boom brought fabulous wealth to the city. Nothing was too good for the rich rubber barons, who poured their profits into making their city a best-of-Europe hybrid with grand Parisian-style avenues and squares, splendid Italian-influenced theaters and basilicas, and state-of-the-art English streetlamps and electric trolleys. The city went into fast decline when the Amazon's rubber industry went belly-up, but most of the ornate edifices from this grand era survived. Despite the decay that set in during the mid- to late 20th century, Belém remains the Amazon's most important port. The city's revitalized downtown

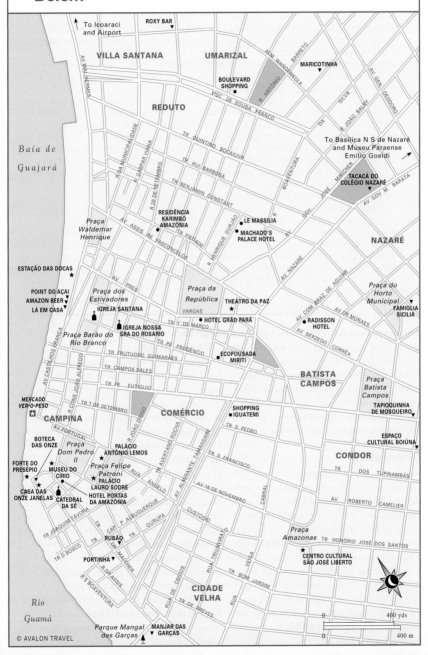

Belém

To Icoaraci and Airport

ROXY BAR

VILLA SANTANA

UMARIZAL

MARICOTINHA

BOULEVARD SHOPPING

REDUTO

AV. MAL HERMES

AV. ALM. WANDENKOLK

R. ANTÔNIO

BARRETO

AV. GEN. DEODORO

VISC. DE SOUSA BRANCO

DA

SILVA

R. JOÃO BALBY

TR. QUINTINO BOCAIÚVA

TR. RUI BARBOSA

Baía de Guajará

R. DA MUNICIPALIDADE

R. GASPAR VIANA

R. 28 DE SETEMBRO

TR. BENJAMIN CONSTANT

BOAVENTURA

JOSÉ

MALCHER

GOV.

To Basílica N S de Nazaré and Museu Paraense Emílio Goeldi

TACACÁ DO COLÉGIO NAZARÉ

AV. GOV. M. BARATA

RESIDÊNCIA KARIMBÓ AMAZÔNIA

LE MASSILIA

MACHADO'S PALACE HOTEL

NAZARÉ

Praça Waldemar Henrique

AV. ASSIS DE VASCONCELOS

TR. PIEDADE

R. HENRIQUE GURJÃO

AV. NAZARÉ

ESTAÇÃO DAS DOCAS

AV. IPIRES

Praça dos Estivadores

IGREJA SANTANA

Praça da República

THEATRO DA PAZ

Praça do Horto Municipal

FAMIGLIA SICILIA

POINT DO AÇAÍ
AMAZON BEER
LÁ EM CASA

AV. COM. BRAZ DE AGUIAR

AV. DR. MORAES

VARGAS

IGREJA NOSSA SRA DO ROSÁRIO

TR. 1º DE MARÇO

HOTEL GRÃO PARÁ

RADISSON HOTEL

Praça Barão do Rio Branco

AV. CASTILHOS FRANÇA

R. CONS. JOÃO ALFREDO

AV. ALFREDO

TR. PE. PRUDÊNCIO

AV. SERZEDO CORRÊA

TR. FRUTUOSO GUIMARÃES

ECOPOUSADA MIRITI

BATISTA CAMPOS

Praça Batista Campos

TR. CAMPOS SALES

TR. PE. EUTIQUIO

MERCADO VER-O-PESO

TR. 7 DE SETEMBRO

R. JOÃO DIOGO

COMÉRCIO

SHOPPING IGUATEMI

TAPIOQUINHA DE MOSQUEIRO

CAMPINA

AV. PORTUGAL

TR. S. PEDRO

BOTECA DAS ONZE

Praça Dom Pedro II

PALÁCIO ANTÔNIO LEMOS

AV. AVERTANO ROCHA

TR. S. FRANCISCO

ESPAÇO CULTURAL BOIÚNA

CONDOR

FORTE DO PRESÉPIO

MUSEU DO CÍRIO

Praça Felipe Patroni

RUA

ÂNGELO

AV. ALMIRANTE TAMANDARÉ

AV. 16 DE NOVEMBRO

CABRAL

TR. DOS TUPINAMBÁS

PALÁCIO LAURO SODRÉ

HOTEL PORTAS DA AMAZÔNIA

CASA DAS ONZE JANELAS

CATEDRAL DA SÉ

CUSTÓDIO

AV. ROBERTO CAMELIER

TR. JOAQUIM TÁVORA

TR. CAP. P. ALBUQUERQUE

GURUPÁ

RUA TRIUNVIRATO

Praça Amazonas

TR. HONÓRIO JOSÉ DOS SANTOS

RUBÃO

TR.

R. DE MALCHER

VEIGA

CENTRO CULTURAL SÃO JOSÉ LIBERTO

TR. D. BOSCO

PORTINHA

R. DR. ASSIS

RUA DE ÓBIDOS

TR. BOM JARDIM

RUA

CIDADE VELHA

Rio Guamá

R. S. BOAVENTURA

TR. DE BREVES

Parque Mangal das Garças

MANJAR DAS GARÇAS

0   400 yds

0   400 m

© AVALON TRAVEL

Brazil's Rubber Barons

It was an American innovation that completely transformed the Amazon in the 19th century. In the 1840s, Charles Goodyear invented vulcanization, a process by which natural rubber could withstand incredibly high and low temperatures and hence used to manufacture rubber goods. At the time, sources of natural rubber were scarce. Yet Amazonian Indians had been using the milky sap of the *Hevea brasiliensis* (the rubber tree) to make natural rubber for centuries. Once outsiders got hold of this Amazonian secret, all hell broke loose.

Fortune seekers descended on the Amazon, the only known source of the rubber tree. Conquering vast swathes of forests, they built complexes for processing rubber and lodgings for the masses of *seringueiros* (rubber tappers) who swarmed to the area in search of work. Aside from *caboclos* (local riverside dwellers of mixed Indian and European ancestry), many were poor immigrants who traveled from Brazil's Northeast. Most workers were treated like slaves—conditions were so brutal that many succumbed to numerous diseases and died. As for the fortune-seeking "rubber barons" (as they were called), some struck it rich. Steamships sailed down the Amazon and across the Atlantic carrying cargoes of rubber, and returned stocked with fine English porcelain, the latest French fashions, and Italian wines, allowing the barons to live it up as if they were in London or Paris. Imported materials were used to build and furnish both public and private palaces that sprang up amid the elegant new avenues and squares of Belém and Manaus. By the dawn of the 20th century, both cities were fabulously wealthy.

A decade later, the boom went bust. After *Hevea brasiliensis* seeds were smuggled out of the Amazon by a crafty Englishman, new plantations in the British colonies of Malaysia and Ceylon supplanted Brazil as a cheaper and more efficient source of rubber. The industry experienced a brief revival during World War II, when the Japanese interfered with East Asian rubber production. However, the subsequent popularization of synthetic rubber in the 1940s and 1950s brought the rubber era to a definitive end.

---

includes restored architectural treasures and the inspired revamp of its historic center and riverfront. Due to the mixture of European, Indian, and African influences, it also boasts one of Brazil's most distinctive regional cultures; elements are present in everything from the flavorful delicacies of Paraense cuisine to popular *festas* such as Círio de Nazaré.

Orientation

Belém sits at the intersection of the Rio Guamá with the Baía de Guajará. The river defines Belenense life, and along its banks you'll find many of the city's sights. Fanning out from the Forte do Presépio, the historic quarter known as **Cidade Velha** is rife with an unusual mishmash of old buildings that range in style from baroque to art deco. Cidade Velha's northern boundary is Avenida President Vargas, Belém's main boulevard, which stretches up from the waterfront to **Praça da República,** the city's elegant main square.

Sights
CIDADE VELHA

Cidade Velha is Belém's oldest neighborhood and it retains many colonial buildings with adobe walls and red-tiled roofs. Wandering around its narrow, atmospheric streets is a pleasure, although the area should be avoided at night and on Sunday. It was here—around the early 17th-century **Forte do Presépio** (Praça Frei Caetano Brandão 117, tel. 91/4009-8828, 10am-6pm Tues.-Sun., R$2, free Tues.)—that the city sprang to life. From this fortress overlooking the Rio Guamá, the Portuguese jealously guarded the entrance to the Amazon while launching conquests deeper and deeper into the rain forest. The enormous cannons perched on the ramparts are proof of their defensive zeal. Inside the fort, a small museum somewhat ironically pays homage to the local Tapajós and Marajoara Indians that thrived here before the arrival of the Portuguese. Among the artifacts unearthed in archaeological sites are some wonderful examples of pre-Columbian pottery, notably vessels made by the indigenous peoples of Ilha de Marajó.

It wasn't long before the Portuguese had settled in. With the wealth earned from the sugar trade, aristocrats built sumptuous mansions along the waterfront. One of the grandest was the **Casa das Onze Janelas** (Praça Frei Caetano Brandão, tel. 91/4009-8821, 10am-6pm Tues.-Sun., R$2, free Tues.), built by sugar baron Domingos da Costa Bacelar in the late 1600s. From the *onze janelas* (11 windows) of his pale yellow mansion, Bacelar and his rich cronies sipped tea and watched as slaves loaded up boats with sugar and unloaded European goodies that would allow them to live in the jungle without sacrificing style and comfort. Today, the mansion is a cultural center that juggles a permanent collection of Brazilian modernists with temporary exhibits of contemporary art. The sweeping balcony once haunted by sugar barons is now occupied by a fashionable bar, **Boteco das Onze** (tel. 91/3224-8559, www.botecodasonze.com.br), where Belenenses and tourists alike snack on *coxinhas de carangueijo* (tender crab pastries) and watch the sun set over the river.

Picturesque Praça Frei Caetano Brandão (also known as the Praça da Sé) is anchored by the twin-towered **Catedral da Sé** (Praça Frei Caetano Brandão, tel. 91/3223-2362, 7:30am-noon daily, 2pm-6pm Mon.-Sat., 4pm-8pm Sun.). It was designed by Italian architect Antônio José Landi, who had numerous commissions in Belém. The interior is an unremarkable mishmash of baroque and neoclassical styles with a lot of glossy marble imported from Italy. Also on the *praça* is the early baroque **Igreja de Santo Alexandre.** Built by local Indians, it features some delicate woodwork. The church, along with its annex, the former archbishop's palace, houses the **Museu de Arte Sacra** (Praça Frei Caetano Brandão, tel. 91/4009-8802, 10am-6pm Tues.-Sun., R$4, free Tues.), which exhibits a collection of religious paintings and carved wooden saints.

Just around the corner, the **Museu do Círio** (Rua Padre Champagnat, tel. 91/4009-8846, 10am-6pm Tues.-Sun., R$2, free Tues.) conjures up the pageantry and frenzy (both sacred and profane) of Círio de Nazaré, Belém's most important popular and religious festival. Gaze at photographs of the processions and admire the artistry of emblematic objects such as embroidered banners, images of Nossa Senhora de Nazaré, and feather-light toys made of *miriti,* an Amazonian palm, made especially for the *festa* by *caboclo* artisans from a tiny town in the Paraense interior.

Nearby, on Praça Dom Pedro II, are two magnificent palaces that conjure up Belém's late-19th-century days of rubber glory. Once the city hall, the **Palácio Antônio Lemos** is a stately neoclassical construction with a striking powder blue and white facade. After being abandoned, it later underwent restoration. It currently houses municipal government offices along with the **Museu de Arte do Belém** (Praça Dom Pedro II, tel. 91/3114-1024, 10am-6pm Tues.-Fri., 9am-1pm Sat.-Sun., free), whose permanent collection of paintings is less impressive than the palace itself. The interior is a Versailles-worthy series of courtyards and grand salons decked out in crystal chandeliers, bronze and marble statues, and belle epoque furniture. Slippers are provided so you won't scratch the glossy parquet floors.

Next door, the gleaming white **Palácio Lauro Sodré** is another edifice that was designed by Antônio Landi in the 1770s. The former residence of Pará's governors, it now lodges the **Museu do Estado do Pará** (Praça Dom Pedro II, tel. 91/4009-8838, 1pm-6pm Tues.-Fri., 10am-2pm Sat.-Sun., R$4, free Tues.). Aside from some exquisite furniture, the rather musty historical artifacts are less interesting than the palace interior. The ground floor reception salons overlooking the *praça* (where good temporary exhibits are often held) are particularly opulent, as is the grand marble staircase leading upstairs to older and more sedate rooms, where you'll find the permanent collection.

★ MERCADO VER-O-PESO

Synonymous with Belém is the sprawling **Mercado Ver-o-Peso** (Blvd. Castilhos França, Cidade Velha, 6am-6pm Mon.-Sat., 6am-1pm Sun.), which stretches out along the river. Just as Belém is the gateway to the Amazon rain forest, the market serves as an essential link between the city and the jungle. For more than 300 years, boats have sailed down the river from the depths of the Amazon to unload their wares at the Mercado, whose name, Ver-o-Peso ("See the Weight"), is derived from the Portuguese habit of weighing all merchandise in order to calculate tributes to the crown. The main building, with its twin neo-Gothic towers and cast-iron structure imported from Scotland in the late 1800s, was originally known as the Mercado de Ferro (Iron Market). Today, it is only one section of the immense bazaar, which also includes hundreds of *barracas* as well as a tented area containing bars and restaurants where you can sample Paraense specialties such as fried fish, *maniçoba*, and *açaí*.

The market is somewhat ramshackle and chaotic; keep an eye on your belongings at all times due to pickpockets. But the colorful jumble adds to the adventure of wandering through the labyrinth of stalls, where you'll encounter exotica ranging from cobra teeth and *pirarucu* tongues (used by Indians as a food grater) to herbal potions guaranteed to make you filthy rich or lucky in love. The initial assault on your senses is a little overwhelming. The liquid gold of bottled *tucupi* clashes with the deep green of ground manioc leaves, the soft rose blush of a *jambu* fruit, and the rich purple of *açaí*. The sweet perfume of *bacuri* and *graviola* mingles with the pungent saltiness of cured beef and fresh fish, and the merchants tout their wares with singsong cries.

One section is devoted to indigenous herbal remedies that will cure whatever ails you—physically or spiritually. The women who hawk these potions, known as *mandingueiras,* swear by the miraculous recipes that have been passed down through generations. They range from powdered vulture's liver (great for a hangover) to the bottled genitalia of a *boto,* or pink river dolphin, which is purported to be a foolproof love potion. Although it has no curative properties, a Ver-o-Peso bestseller is extract of *pau-rosa,* an Amazonian tree whose bark is one of the main ingredients in Chanel No. 5 perfume.

The best hours are 6am-9am, when wares

Mercado Ver-o-Peso, Belém

Açai

In the Amazon, *açai* is consumed by everyone. Cheap, bountiful, and an excellent source of calcium, minerals, and vitamins B1 and B2, it can easily serve as a meal on its own, and in many Amazonian river communities, it does. *Açai* is also a main source of livelihood for many families. The fruit comes from a palm species known as an *açaizeiro*. At a young age, many *caboclos* and Indians learn how to shimmy up the tree, a knife between their teeth, to cut down the dark berry-size fruit.

In Belém, *açai* consumption is three times higher than that of milk. (Many mothers prefer to give babies bottles filled with *açai*.) Unlike in the rest of Brazil, *açai* is not eaten with sugar. As an accompaniment to fish, *açai* is thickened with manioc flour and used as a substitute for *feijão*, which is the main staple in the rest of the country. This is the way you'll see it served at Belém's **Mercado Ver-o-Peso** (one whole section is reserved for *açai*). There are *açai* stores all over the city. Using machines, the pulp is stripped from the seeds and then sold in plastic pouches. Quality and price depend on the thickness of the pulp (the more diluted, the cheaper) and its origin (the crème de la crème comes from the Ilha das Onças, or Island of Jaguars).

are at their most abundant and the sun isn't too strong.

ESTAÇÃO DAS DOCAS

In 2001, an inspired renovation transformed the 19th-century steel cargo warehouses that lined Belém's seedy riverside port area into an airy and modern complex known as the **Estação das Docas** (Blvd. Castilhos França, Campina, tel. 91/3215-5660, www.estacaodas-docas.com.br, 10am-midnight Sun.-Mon., 10am-3am Tues.-Sat.). There is a theater,

cinema, and galleries along with boutiques, bookstores, a bar, a café (the famous Cairu *sorveteria*), and a cluster of gourmet restaurants. Featuring large glass walls overlooking the docks and the river, the Estação das Docas has become one of Belém's most happening hangouts. By day, it's a nice place to walk around (there is a scenic view of the bay from the boardwalk), quaff microbrewery beer, nibble on buffalo kebabs, and watch the sunset. At night, live music shows are often performed on a movable stage fashioned out

Estação das Docas, Belém

of a former loading trolley. Tourist excursions along the river depart from the dock's small *hidroviária*.

PRAÇA DA REPÚBLICA AND THEATRO DA PAZ

Belém's main square is the leafy Praça da República, an elegant green park with a small amphitheater that offers respite to Belenenses of all ages. On one side of the *praça* sits the **Theatro da Paz** (Praça da República, Campina, tel. 91/4009-8750, http://theatro-dapaz.com.br), a deep-rose-colored, white-pillared, neoclassical theater inaugurated in 1878. Inspired by Milan's La Scala, Belém's rubber barons financed the splendid building, whose interior is decked out in precious woods, gilt mirrors, crystal chandeliers, and glossy Italian marble. In the auditorium, note the ceiling mural of Apollo on his chariot being pulled through the Amazon. The **guided tours** (hourly 9am-5pm Tues.-Fri., 9am-noon Sat., 9am-11am Sun., R$4, free Wed.) are recommended. In August, the theater hosts the prestigious Festival de Ópera.

NAZARÉ

From Praça da República, Avenida Nazaré cuts through the upscale neighborhood of the same name. Belém is renowned for its centuries-old mango trees, and Nazaré's streets are lined with a dark-green leafy canopy. Watch out for the bright yellow pulp of mangoes on the sidewalks (much more slippery than a banana peel) and for them falling overhead (particularly Oct.-Dec.). Nazaré possesses many pastel-colored historic buildings, some of which house chic boutiques and restaurants.

On the corner of Avenue Nazaré and Avenue Generalíssimo Deodoro lies Belém's most famous church, the **Basílica de Nossa Senhora de Nazaré** (Praça Justo Chermont, Nazaré, tel. 91/4009-8400, 6am-8pm Mon.-Fri., 6am-noon and 3pm-9pm Sat.-Sun.). Completed in 1908, this majestic white church was modeled after Rome's Saint Peter's Basilica. This is where the image of Nossa Senhora de Nazaré, the patron saint

of Pará, is housed. The exterior is impressive for its simplicity, offset by the giant *samauma* tree in front. More awe-inspiring is the marble interior, which is accessorized with stained-glass windows, wooden ceiling carvings, and colored tile mosaics reminiscent of Moorish architecture. Every October the church and the statue of the saint are the focal point for Círio de Nazaré, one of Brazil's most lavish religious and popular festivals.

Avenida Nazaré turns into Avenida Magalhães Barata and two blocks farther is the not-to-be-missed **Museu Paraense Emílio Goeldi** (Rua Magalhães Barata 376, Nazaré, tel. 91/3182-3231, www.museu-goeldi. br, 9am-5pm Tues.-Sun., R$2). Founded in 1895, the museum was the world's first research center devoted to the flora, fauna, and cultures of the Amazon. To date, it is also considered one of the best. Located on a vast estate, the museum has an impressive collection of Indian artifacts, including a great display of the distinctive and delicate pre-Columbian ceramic vessels made by the indigenous groups that once inhabited the Ilha de Marajó. Better yet is the introduction it provides to the rain forest itself. Simply strolling amid towering mahogany and rubber trees, past lagoons strewn with giant *Victoria amazonica* water lilies, will get you in a jungly frame of mind. The art nouveau-style aquarium is full of electric eels, flying fish, *matamata* turtles, and black piranhas. You can familiarize yourself with mammals you may never see in the actual jungle, such as spider monkeys, tapirs, anteaters, and ultrarare spotted jaguars as well as more common but surreally Day-Glo toucans and macaws. Due to ongoing renovations of various pavilions, some attractions (such as the *serpentarium*) may be temporarily closed.

Two blocks from the museum, the **Parque da Residência** (Av. Magalhães Barata 830, São Braz, tel. 91/3229-8000, 9am-7pm Tues.-Sun.) is a small but very pretty park surrounding the former governor's residence. This handsome mansion is now headquarters to the Secretary of Culture. It functions as a cultural center with a gallery space, a theater, and the excellent Restô do Parque. Visit the nearby orquidarium, then reward yourself for walking in the heat with a refreshing ice cream at the 100-year-old train wagon that has been converted into a *sorveteria*.

CENTRO CULTURAL SÃO JOSÉ LIBERTO

A short cab ride from Cidade Velha, the **Centro Cultural São José Liberto** (Praça Amazonas, Jurunas, tel. 91/3344-3500, 9am-7pm Tues.-Sat., 10am-6pm Sun.) occupies an early 18th-century Franciscan monastery on Praça Amazonas. The square was once an execution ground, and the neighboring monks routinely accompanied criminals to their hangings. In the 18th century, the monastery was converted into a prison, which was then abandoned before a major overhaul in the 1990s gave it a happier reincarnation as a cultural complex. Most of the Centro's exhibits and activities revolve around Pará's abundance of precious and semiprecious stones (for this reason, it is also known as the Pólo Joalheiro, or Jewelry Zone). The colonial part of the complex houses the **Museu das Gemas do Estado** (R$4), which boasts a dazzling collection of Amazonian rocks and minerals in rough and polished states.

Having whetted your appetite for jewels, check out the **Casa do Artesão,** a series of ateliers where you can watch local artisans hard at work cutting, polishing, and creating intricate and original jewelry from the stones you saw in the museum. If you're struck by the urge to buy, the final products can be purchased in on-site boutiques. In an adjacent modern annex, you'll find a café and a Cairu *sorveteria* outlet as well as exhibition areas and stands selling handicrafts, including some very attractive ceramics in the tradition of Marajoara pottery.

PARKS

Belém has a number of parks, the most central of which is **Parque Mangal das Garças** (Passagem Carneiro da Rocha, Campina, tel. 91/3242-5052, www.mangaldasgarcas.com.br, 9am-6pm Tues.-Sun., R$4, R$12 for a passport to all attractions), located along the edge of Cidade Velha on the banks of the Rio Gaumá. The landscaping mixes plants and trees from different Amazonian ecosystems as well as lagoons dotted with bright white herons and scarlet ibises. Birders will have a field day at the **Aviário das Aningas.** At the entrance to the aviary, you're given an illustrated guide to all the feathered creatures inside. The fun

Parque Mangal das Garças, Belém

part is walking around the jungly atmosphere, keeping score of who can catch sight of a giant stork or bright red *guará* first. Once you've checked off all 150 birds, go for a rematch at the **Borboletário Márcio Ayres.** Upon entering this pavilion, you'll once again be furnished with an illustrated guide—only this time, your eyes will be peeled for the resplendent Amazonian *borboletas* (butterflies) and jewel-like *beija-flores* (hummingbirds) that flap and dart amid the misty environment. The park's main complex, an indigenous structure of *ipê* wood and palm fibers, houses the Mangal das Garças restaurant and the **Memorial Amazônico de Navegação,** a small museum that traces the Amazon's tradition of boat-building as well as the history of river transportation in Pará. For a terrific view of the river looking toward the Cidade Velha, walk along the wooden walkways that lead out to a viewing platform suspended above the muddy banks. For even better views, take the elevator to the top of the Farol de Belém, the rather odd-looking modern lighthouse located in the middle of the park. On your way out, stop by the **Armazém do Tempo,** a renovated shipbuilding warehouse converted into a gallery.

More untamed Amazonian foliage can be found at the **Bosque Rodrigues Alves** (Av. Almirante Barroso 2305, Bairro do Marco, tel. 91/3277-1112, 8am-5pm Tues.-Sun., R$2), an untamed 19th-century botanical garden filled with 2,500 regional species (most typical of virgin rain forest). Meandering trails lead past a lagoon brimming with fish and turtles to an orchidarium and a small aquarium. Among the rare and very weird mammals you can glimpse up close are the *jupará*—which resembles a cross between a cat, a bear, and a monkey—and the Amazonian manatee, whose Portuguese name, *peixe boi* ("fish-cow"), says it all.

Entertainment and Events
NIGHTLIFE

Much of Belém's nightlife is centered on the Estação das Docas as well as the area near Avenida Souza Franco, confusingly known as "Docas." On the weekends the bars along Avenida Almirante Wandenkolk, in Umarizal, get pretty lively.

Belém's bohemians congregate at **Rubão** (Travessa Gurupá 312, Cidade Velha, tel. 91/9122-4232, 8pm-1am daily), a classic *boteco* with cheap icy beer and tasty regional snacks (the shredded crab with *farofa* is excellent). Owner and local institution Rubão presides over an unpretentious atmosphere. The tables out in the street are great for people-watching. A magnet for bohemian Belenenses is **Meu Garoto** (Rua Senador Manoel Barata 928, Campina, tel. 91/3230-5413, 9am-11:30pm Mon.-Fri., 9am-3pm Sat.). Amidst a giant stuffed bull's head and improvised tables, lovers of conversation and cachaça tipple more than 200 varieties, including local concoctions infused with açaí, cupuaçu, and jambu leaves that leave your entire mouth deliciously tingly.

Beer connoisseurs will appreciate **Amazon Beer** (Estação das Docas, Blvd Castilho França, Campina, tel. 91/3212-5401, www.amazonbeer.com.br, 5pm-midnight Mon.-Thurs., 4pm-2am Fri., 11am-2am Sat., 11am-midnight Sun.), which brews its own beer without the use of additives. Among the seven varieties are "forest," a traditional pilsner, "black," an aromatic dark malt beer, and the exotic "bacuri," flavored with subtle hints of this delicious local fruit. The bar fills up during happy hour as well as on Saturday afternoon, when *feijoada* (R$48 pp) is accompanied by live samba.

Located in a fabulous art deco building, the **Roxy Bar** (Av. Senador Lemos 231, Umarizal, tel. 91/3224-4514, www.roxybar.com.br, 7:30pm-1am Tues.-Thurs., 7:30pm-close Fri.-Sat.) is a favorite haunt for those in search of a quieter, more intimate scene that continues into the wee hours. Walls are decorated with images of classic Hollywood stars, whose names inspire the menu's simple but creative dishes. **Maricotinha** (Rua Domingos Marreiros 279, Umarizal, tel. 91/3225-0125, www.maricotinhabar.com.br, 7pm-close Wed.-Fri., 4pm-close Sat.-Sun., cover R$4-10) occupies three floors of a 1920s house. Hangout spaces range from a garden adorned with potted ferns to a lounge whose ceiling features hanging umbrellas and another where walls are papered in photos of the owner's female relatives, many of them named Maria. Live *música sertaneja*, samba, and reggae are performed on weekends. To soak up Belém's indie music scene, head to **Espaço Cultural Boiúna** (Rua dos Pariquis 1556, Batista Campos, tel. 91/4141-3190, 8pm-4am Tues.-Sat.). Owned by a couple of musicians, it lures an artistic crowd who gather round the stage inside or the outdoor sidewalk tables to listen to live MPB, samba, chorinho and jazz music (sets begin at 10:30pm) while nibbling on delicious jambu and pirarucu *pastéis*.

One of the most seductive bars in town, **Boteco das Onze** (Praça Frei Caetano Brandão, Cidade Velha, tel. 91/3224-8559, www.botecodasonze.com.br, 5pm-2am Mon., noon-2am Tues.-Sun.) occupies the historic Casa das Onze Janelas. Outside, a wide terrace gazes out over the Baía de Guajará. The terrace is popular during happy hour, when Belenenses gather to drink *chope* or killer *tangirsoscas* (vodka and fresh tangerine juice), and nibble on *petiscos* such as *casquinha de caranguejo com jambu* (a fresh crab salad seasoned with *jambu*). On weekend, live bands playing "flashback" ditties inspire dance-a-thons.

PERFORMING ARTS

It's always worth taking a look to see what's on at the beautiful **Theatro da Paz** (Praça da República, Campina, tel. 91/4009-8750, http://theatrodapaz.com.br). If you're in the mood for a film, check out the schedule at the **Cinema Olympia** (Av. Presidente Vargas 918, tel. 91/3230-5380, www.cinemaolympia.com. br). Built in 1912, Belém's (and Brazil's) oldest movie theater is still in operation; it screens independent and art films (some free).

FESTIVALS AND EVENTS

One of the biggest, most spectacular festivals in Brazil is **Círio de Nazaré** (www. ciriodenazare.com.br), held the second Sunday of October. Millions of Paraenses throng the streets of Belém to join in the procession carrying the statue of Nossa Senhora de Nazaré from the Catedral da Sé to the Basílica de Nazaré.

Considered the patron saint of all Paraenses and protectress of Belém, the cult of Nossa Senhora de Nazaré dates back to 1700, when a *caboclo* named Plácido found a statue of the Virgin lying in a creek located in the present-day *bairro* of Nazaré. Plácido took the statue home with him. But when he woke up the next morning, he was astonished to discover that it had returned to its original spot. After taking the statue home once again, it reappeared at the creek. The amazed *caboclo* built a small chapel (later replaced by the Basílica de Nazaré) to house the Virgin. Word of the miracle got around, and pilgrims and supplicants from all over Pará came seeking Nossa Senhora's blessing and divine intervention.

By the end of the 1700s, her popularity had become so great that a public *festa*, the Círio de Nazaré, was organized so that the entire city could pay homage to the Virgin. The first procession took place in 1793. The image of Nossa Senhora de Nazaré, splendidly arrayed and covered in flowers, was carried in a chariot through the muddy streets by bulls. By the 20th century, Belém's streets had become paved and bulls were no longer necessary. Instead, the thick rope attached to the carriage—measuring 350 meters (1,150 feet)—was now pulled by penitents who, to this day, jostle ferociously for the chance to grip their hands around the rough sisal and literally bleed—by the procession's end, there is blood in the streets—for the honor of transporting the Virgin.

Although the Sunday procession constitutes the most important event, the *festa* actually kicks off on Friday afternoon with Nossa Senhora de Nazaré's departure from the Basílica to a church in the nearby town of Ananindeua. As the Virgin glides by in an open car, Belenenses hovering in decorated windows and spilling into the streets toss rose petals and confetti. The following dawn, the Virgin once again takes to the road, this time in an open truck surrounded by a cavalcade of cars and motorcycles, en route to the town of Icoaraci. Here, the image is loaded onto a spectacularly decorated boat. Since Nossa Senhora de Nazaré is also the patron saint of river navigators, the Virgin's crossing of the Rio Guamá to Belém is accompanied by a fleet of hundreds of festively adorned wooden boats. This river spectacle is best viewed from the ramparts of the Forte do Presépio. The Virgin's arrival in Belém is greeted with a fireworks display. Much merrymaking then ensues throughout the Cidade Velha, lasting all night, until the climactic procession that takes place on Sunday morning. The Virgin's return to the Basílica is usually completed by midday. Afterward, people get together with family and friends and feast on favorite dishes, such as *pato no tucupi* and *maniçoba*. If you want to be in town for Círio, make sure to book a hotel far in advance.

Shopping

Belém is a great source for Amazonian artifacts, from beautiful indigenous art to practical items such as energy-boosting *guaraná* powder and woven hammocks (essential for any boat trip or backyard porch). In Cidade Velha, Rua Gaspar Viana is home to stores where you can find hammocks for that boat trip up the Amazon. Located in the Parque Mangal das Garças, **Armazém do Tempo** (tel. 91/3242-5052, 9am-8pm Tues.-Sun.) sells books, CDs, and a good mix of local *artesanato,* such as indigenous jewelry made from the seeds of fruit and delicate toys made from *miriti* palm fibers. A stand-out boutique in the Estação das Docas, **Ná Figueredo** (Blvd. Castilho França, Armazém 1, loja 10, tel. 91/3212-3421, 10am-10pm Tues.-Sat., 9am-10pm Sun.) offers a cool mix of regional products—from CDs and DVDs of Paraense musical groups to funky Amazon-themed T-shirts.

For more contemporary items, try the city's most fashionable mall, **Boulevard Shopping** (Av. Visconde de Souza Franco 776, Reduto, tel. 91/3299-0500, www.boulevardbelem.com.br, 10am-10pm Mon.-Sat., 2pm-10pm Sun.). You'll find national boutiques, fast-food joints, and a state-of-the-art cinemaplex.

Recommended for anyone with a sweet tooth are the chocolates filled with Amazonian fruits such *bacuri, cupuaçu,* and *açaí* sold at **Bombom do Pará** (Av. Visconde de Sousa 1302, Campina, tel. 91/3241-2937, 7:30am-7:30pm Mon.-Sat.) along with jams and jellies.

Accommodations

Surprisingly, Belém doesn't have many decent hotels. Many of the more centrally located options are pretty down-and-out, and even standard mid- and upper-range options, concentrated in Nazaré and Batista Campos, can be disappointing. Fortunately, there are a few exceptions.

Apart from its ideal location on Praça da República, **Hotel Grão Pará** (Av. Presidente Vargas 718, tel. 91/3321-2121, www.hotelgraopara.com.br, R$120 d) is a recently renovated mid-1960s-era hotel that offers excellent value. The sizable rooms are bland but well-maintained (the higher the floor, the quieter it gets), and the staff is helpful. Another terrific deal is ★ **Le Massilia** (Rua Henrique Gurjão 236, Reduto, tel. 91/3222-2834, www.massilia.com.br, R$130-160 d). One of Belém's only intimate hotels, the standard but comfortable air-conditioned guest rooms are housed in low-slung brick villas with cool tile floors and polished wooden fixtures. There is a refreshing pool and courtyard and a decent French restaurant. The hotel also organizes city tours and fishing and boating excursions. On the same street is the modern and functional **Machado's Plaza Hotel** (Rua Henrique Gurjão 2000, Reduto, tel. 91/4008-9816, www.machadosplazahotel.com.br, R$240-270 d). The spotless, exec-friendly guest rooms lack views but have welcome splashes of color and nice lighting. There is also a small pool and a fitness room.

A great location and atmosphere are selling

points of **Hotel Portas da Amazônia** (Rua Dr. Malcher 15, Cidade Velha, tel. 91/3222-9252, www.portasdaamazoniabelempara. com.br, R$130-160 d), which occupies a 19th-century villa next to the Catedral da Sé (you better like the regular chiming of bells). The restored interior possesses lots of character, but choose your room with care: windowless rooms are claustrophobic, and only some boast lustrous wooden floors. Those overlooking the courtyard are quieter. Blocks from Praça da República, ★ **Residência Karimbo Amazônia** (Travessa Piedade 391, Reduto, tel. 91/3298-1373, www.rkamazoniabrasil. sitew.com, R$135 d) is an unexpected find: an extremely homey B&B operated by an obliging Franco-Brazilian couple. Rooms are cozily decorated (the nicest, on the top floor, has a large balcony) and common spaces include a garden, living room, and games room with a pool table almost the same size as the dinky outdoor pool. The vibrant neighborhood can be a little sketchy at night. In the same vicinity, the small-scale, 11-room **Ecopousada Miriti** (Travessa Padre Prudêncio 656, Campina, tel. 91/3252-2218, www.miritipousada.com, R$130 d) is a good choice for those on a small budget. Well-maintained rooms are minimalist to the point of being Spartan; those on the upper floors are less humid and receive more light. Pluses include tranquility, a certain degree of eco-consciousness, friendly staff, and lots of pretty shrubbery.

Belém's most upscale hotel, the **Radisson Hotel Maiorana Belém** (Av. Braz de Aguiar 321, Nazaré, tel. 91/3205-1399, www.radisson. com.br, R$320-480 d), is a gleaming, modern behemoth whose sleek, massive guest rooms boast comfy beds and more mod cons than anywhere else in Belém. Geared more toward execs than leisure travelers, the hotel is efficient and friendly, although the decor lacks personality. Amenities include a rooftop pool and fitness center.

Food

Paraense cuisine is gaining fame throughout Brazil. However, the best place to savor the region's cuisine is in Belém—either at an atmospheric restaurant (many are located in tourist attractions) or at the one of the street *barracas* where local women sell local delicacies such as the famous *tacacá*.

CAFÉS AND SNACKS

To savor the most typically Belenense of Pará's many delicacies, you'll have to head to a simple *barraca* across the street from the Colégio Nazaré known as **Tacacá do Colégio Nazaré** (Av. Nazaré, Nazaré, tel. 91/9142-0433, 4pm-8pm daily). From this spot, for the last four decades, Maria do Carmo has been serving up what many consider to be the most perfect *tacacá* in town. She attributes the success of her fragrant broth to quality ingredients such as the giant shrimp imported from Maranhão and *jambu* purchased daily from the Ver-o-Peso market.

An equally beloved snack is the *tapiocas* (crunchy crepes made from manioc flour) that Andreia Dias Gonçalves has been making since she was a young girl in Pará's interior. Locals flock to her stand, **Tapioquinha de Mosqueiro** (Rua dos Pariquis 1981, Batista Campos, tel. 91/3242-5240, 7am-noon and 3:30pm-9:30pm Tues.-Sun.) for their early morning and late-afternoon *tapioca* fix. There are more than 75 sweet and savory fillings; the most popular, however, is *molhada*, in which the *tapioca*, filled with freshly grated coconut, is dipped in coconut milk and then wrapped in a banana leaf.

Tucked amid the old mansions of Cidade Velha, **Portinha** (Rua Dr. Malcher 463, Cidade Velha, tel. 91/9115-2222, 5pm-10pm Fri.-Sun.) is easily identifiable by the locals who line up in front of this tiny *lanchonete* to feast on homemade pastries, all with an Amazonian twist. The Lebanese *esfihas* are stuffed with duck, *jambu*, and *tucupi*; turnovers filled with smoked sausage and *pupunha*; and rolls stuffed with sun-dried tomatoes, buffalo mozzarella, and Brazil nuts. Regional dishes, such as *maniçoba* and *tacacá*, are prepared daily.

Point do Açaí (Blvd. Castilhos França

Tacacá

The Amazon's rivers and rain forests provide an endless supply of exotic ingredients. Belém is the Amazon's culinary capital, and the city's signature dish, *tacacá*, is an intoxicating fusion of key ingredients that provides an excellent initiation to the region's cuisine. To some, tacacá is a broth; to others it is a drink, or even a stew. *Tacacá* mixes shrimp with *tucupi*, a thick yellow liquid extracted from the roots of the manioc plant, and *jambu*, a creeping plant whose leaves cause a pleasant tingling and numbness of your lips. It is cooked for 12 hours in order to remove poisonous components, then served piping hot in *cuias* (hollowed-out gourds). *Tacacá* gets an extra kick from the addition of *pimenta de cheiro*, a yellow pepper whose aroma is pungent and piquant, and *alfavaca*, a wild Amazonian version of basil.

Tucupi shows up in other specialties, such as the iconic **pato no tucupi,** an aromatic duck stew, and **maniçoba,** the Paraense equivalent of *feijoada* (pork and sausage cooked together with leaves from the manioc plant). Dishes are often accompanied by **arroz de jambu** (rice flavored with *jambu* leaves) and **farinha d'água** (manioc flour left to soak in the river), which has a soft, fluffy consistency.

744, Campina, tel. 91/3212-2168, www.point-doacai.net, 8am-4pm Sun.-Mon., 11am-11pm Tues.-Sat.) serves a sweet gringo version of the famous purple Amazonian power fruit with banana, granola, and *guaraná*. To savor *açai* like the locals do, order it as an accompaniment to fish, shrimp, or chicken.

★ **Cairu** (Travessa 14 de Março 1570, Nazaré, tel. 91/3242-2749, 9:30am-midnight daily) has been churning out its lip-smacking *sorvetes* for close to 50 years. Purists can indulge in Amazonian flavors made from local fruits such as *bacuri, murici, sapoti, graviola,* and *açai,* while novelty-seekers can try the *"mestiços"* (mixed breeds) such as *carimbó* (*cupuaçu* and Brazil nut) and *maria isabel* (*bacuri,* shortbread, and coconut). The ice creams are so delectable that five-star restaurants in Rio and São Paulo feature them on their dessert menus. There are 10 locations around Belém, including one at the Estação das Docas.

INTERNATIONAL

Some of the finest Italian food in town can be found at **Famiglia Sicilia** (Av. Conselheiro Furtado 1420, Batista Campos, tel. 91/4008-0001, www.famigliasicilia.com, 6pm-midnight Mon.-Sat., noon-3pm and 6pm-midnight Sun., R$35-55). Although recipes are devoutly Italian, the tastes are sharply enhanced by the use of ingredients supplied by local producers. The smooth, creamy mozzarella comes from regional buffalo herds, while the semolina used in the polenta is from a local manioc farm. Even the chocolate comes from cocoa grown in the interior of Pará. The wine list is impressive.

PER-KILO BUFFET

Restô do Parque (Av. Gov. Magalhães Barata 830, São Brás, tel. 91/3229-8000, noon-3:30pm Tues.-Sun, R$20-30) offers a delicious per-kilo spread featuring local standards such as *maniçoba* alongside more inventive creations. It's located in the former residence of Pará's state governors, with views overlooking the bucolic Parque da Residência.

REGIONAL

Paulo Martins, founder of ★ **Lá em Casa** (Blvd. Castilhos França, Estação das Docas, tel. 91/3212-5588, www.laemcasa.com, noon-midnight daily, R$25-40), was an ambassador of Paraense cuisine who traveled the world introducing foodies to the aromas and flavors of the Amazon. Since his death in 2010, his daughter Daniela has picked up where he left off, serving classic recipes along with the more innovative concoctions such as shrimp with *bacuri* and black *maniçoba* pasta with Paraense haddock in a curry sauce. Lunch features a best-of buffet (R$48-51).

Restaurants specializing in Amazonian fish (as opposed to meat or seafood) are hard to come by in Belém. A delicious exception to this rule is ★ **Remanso do Peixe** (Travessa Barão do Triunfo 2950, Casa 46, Marco, tel. 91/3228-2477, 11:30am-3pm and 7pm-10pm Tues.-Sat., 11am-3pm Sun., R$35-50). Despite this restaurant's off-the-beaten-path location—hidden in a pleasant villa in the residential *bairro* of Marco—both locals and tourists have no problem seeking it out to savor dishes made from fresh fish purchased daily at the Mercado Ver-o-Peso. The most popular dish is the *moqueca paraense,* a bubbling stew of local *filhote,* crab legs, and shrimp cooked in a broth of *tucupi, jambu,* tomatoes, and herbs and served piping hot in a cast-iron pot. (The owners patented the recipe.). In 2011, the brother chefs launched the sophisticated **Remanso do Bosque** (Av. Rômulo Maiorana 2350, Marco, tel. 91/3347-2829, www.restaurantemanso.com, noon-3:30pm and 7pm-11:30pm Tues.-Sat., 11:30am-4pm Sun., R$40-60), where they riff daringly on Amazonian ingredients, yielding surprises such as roast lamb with pequi mousseline.

Located within the Parque Mangal das Garças, ★ **Manjar da Garças** (Mangal das Garças, Campina, tel. 91/3242-1056, www.manjardasgarcas.com.br, noon-4pm and 8pm-midnight Tues.-Thurs., noon-4pm and 8pm-2am Fri.-Sat., noon-4pm Sun., R$35-50) consists of a vast *Swiss Family Robinson*-style bungalow on stilts with a palm thatched roof and stunning views of the Rio Guamá. Sophisticated dishes take advantage of local ingredients, such as crunchy almond-crusted *filhote* served with *jambu* risotto, and shrimp with leeks bathed in a sauce of apples and Brazil nuts. For dessert, the *bacuri* profiteroles swimming in melted chocolate are pretty sublime. Lunch features an all-you-can-eat buffet (R$55) of hot and cold dishes, while the dinner menu is à la carte.

Information and Services

In the center of town, you'll find the municipal tourist office, **Belémtur** (Av. Gov. José Malcher 257, Nazaré, tel. 91/3283-4850, www.belem.pa.gov.br/belemtur, 8am-noon and 1pm-6pm Mon.-Fri.), and the state tourist office, **Paratur** (Praça Maestro Waldemar Henrique, Reduto, tel. 91/3212-0575, www.paraturismo.pa.gov.br, 8am-2pm Mon.-Fri.). Both supply good free city maps. Staff rarely speak English, but are friendly. Each agency has an information booth at the airport with extended and weekend hours.

You'll find lots of banks on Avenida Presidente Vargas, including Banco do Brasil (No. 248), HSBC (No. 670), and Bradesco (No. 998); all have ATMs that accept international cards. The main **post office** is also on Avenida Presidente Vargas at No. 498. Estação das Docas (Blvd. Castilho França, Campina) and Shopping Boulevard (Av. Visconde de Souza Franco 776, Reduto) also have plenty of ATMs.

In the event of an emergency, dial **192** for an ambulance or the fire department, and **190** for the police. For medical treatment, try the **Hospital Ophir Loyola** (Av. Magalhães Barata 992, São Brás, tel. 91/3265-6500, www.ophirloyola.pa.gov.br). **Farmácia Big Ben** (Av. Gentil Bittencourt 1584, Nazaré, tel. 91/3084-4783, www.drogariasbigben.com.br) is a 24-hour pharmacy.

Transportation

Most visitors coming from southern Brazil choose to fly to Belém. There are many flights from major cities, although few are direct; airfare can be costly, however, if you don't book in advance. If you're traveling along the Northeast coast, you can easily hop a bus, which is comfortable and far more affordable, although it will take a while. And if you have time (and patience) to spare, you can indulge in the classic river journey—a 4-5-day voyage down the mighty Amazon—from Manaus.

Most of Belém's principal attractions are in the Cidade Velha or Nazaré and can easily be walked to. For farther-flung destinations there are plenty of buses (R$2.20)—major hubs include Avenida Presidente Vargas, Praça da República, and the Mercado Ver-o-Peso.

AIR

Flights from cities around Brazil, including Manaus and Santarém, arrive at the **Aeroporto Internacional de Val-de-Cans** (Av. Júlio César, Val-de-Cans, tel. 91/3210-6039), which is about 15 kilometers (9 mi) from the center of town. A taxi to downtown costs R$35-40. You can also take a municipal bus (R$2.20): Buses marked "Pres. Vargas" head to Praça da República, while those marked "Ver-O-Peso" head to Cidade Velha.

BUS

Long-distance buses arrive at the **Terminal Rodoviária de Belém** (Praça do Operário 1, São Brás, tel. 91/3266-3225), just east of Nazaré at the corner of Avenida Almirante Barroso and Avenida Gov. José Malcher. Taking a bus to Belém inevitably involves a long haul. The closest Brazilian capital, São Luís, is a 12-hour ride. **Transbrasilianaça** (tel. 91/3226-1942, www.transbrasiliana.com. br) offers two daily buses (R$130-150) and provides service to Fortaleza and Brasília. **Itapemirim** (tel. 91/3226-3458, www.itapemirim.com.br) operates buses to southern cities such as Salvador, Rio, and São Paulo.

BOAT

Taking a boat up the Amazon to Manaus (with a possible stop at Santarém, which cuts the voyage in half) is on many people's journey-of-a-lifetime lists. The reality is not quite as romantic as you might envision. Boats keep to the middle of the river, which makes seeing wildlife or even vegetation up close the exception. However, if you don't mind crowds, lots of basic rice-and-beans-style cooking, and a landscape that can grow a little monotonous, consider this trip. Treat it less like a sightseeing excursion and more as an authentic insight into life along one of the world's great waterways—complete with swinging hammocks,

blaring music, idle conversations, and lots of loading and unloading of exotic wares—and you'll be in for an adventure.

Cabins (with bunks and fans) and suites (with beds and air-conditioning) offer privacy, security, and the luxury of your own bathroom, but can be cramped and stuffy. A cheaper alternative is to buy a hammock and string it up among those of the other passengers on the ship's deck. The middle deck is the best place to string your hammock (away from the bottom deck's engine noise and the top deck's socializing noise). Bring some rope with which to tie it and to secure your belongings (keep within reach); you can also ask the captain to stow excess or valuable baggage in a safe hold. Avoid pitching your hammock near the common restrooms, which aren't always in pristine condition on long voyages (and bring a roll of toilet paper).

Try to purchase your ticket in advance (you can often negotiate a discount) and arrive on board several hours early to stake out hammock space. Also consider getting off at Santarém for a few days and then continuing your journey by plane.

For information about departures and tickets, visit the **Terminal Fluvial** (Av. Marechal Hermes, Umarizal, tel. 91/3224-6885). Located 1 kilometer (0.6 mi) downstream from the Estação das Docas, this is where all the riverboat companies have their offices. Boats also depart from here. Although the terminal is safe by day, be careful at night, and always take taxis. Different companies operate boats that travel upstream to Manaus with stops at Monte Alegre and Santarém on different days of the week, but not every day, and schedules are always changing. Expect fares for Manaus to hover around R$350 for hammock space, R$500pp for a cabin for two people, and R$600pp for a suite for two, which includes private bathrooms and TVs, while those to Santarém are R$160 for hammock space, R$350pp for a cabin for two, and R$370pp for a suite for two, although prices can vary. Highly recommended is local travel agency **Amazon Star Turismo** (Rua

Henrique Gurjão 236, Reduto, tel. 91/3241-8624, www.amazonstar.com.br), whose bilingual staff can book both boat and plane tickets in advance over the phone and via the Internet for no extra charge.

CAR AND TAXI

Driving in Belém is pretty easy, although there are a lot of one-way streets. To rent a car to get around the city or head to some nearby beaches, there is an **Avis** (tel. 91/3257-2257, www.avis.com.br) at the airport. Taxis are also easy to hail and quite inexpensive. It's recommended that you take them for getting around at night. To reserve one, call **Coopertaxi** (tel. 91/3257-1720).

CITY TOURS

For tours of Belém and the surrounding region, there are two reputable tour operators that have lots of experience with foreign tourists. Their outings and excursions are nicely priced, and many of the staff and guides speak English. Offerings include day outings, trips, and packages to destinations such as Ilha de Marajó and Santarém.

Amazon Star Turismo (Rua Henrique Gurjão 236, Reduto, tel. 91/3241-8624, www.amazonstar.com.br) offers a variety of tours. Particularly popular are the full-day hiking tours (including a guide and lunch, R$300) that take you across the Rio Guamá to a patch of rain forest. For bird-lovers who can get up at the crack of dawn, Amazon Star offers a unique excursion (R$100) to Ilha do Papagaio (Parrot Island), an island off the shore of Belém that is the roosting spot for hundreds of brightly colored parrots. After a hotel pickup, sail to the island to watch the birds awaken and fly away.

Valverde Turismo (Estação das Docas, tel. 91/3212-3388, www.valverdeturismo.com.br) is a reputable tour operator that offers half-day tours to the beach town of Icoaraci (R$90). Romantics should take the two-hour "sunset" boat tour (R$45) that departs at 5:30pm nightly from the Estação das Docas and navigates the river as the sun sinks below the horizon and the city lights come twinkling on.

Around Belém

There are several side trips you can make within the vicinity of Belém. The most popular destinations are the beaches along the banks of the region's rivers. Avoid the dirty and crowded ones closest to the city, and avoid weekends, when most beaches are swarmed by day-tripping Belenenses.

ICOARACI

Only 25 kilometers (16 mi) north of the city, **Icoaraci** (www.icoaraci.com.br) is a pleasant river town renowned for its ceramic workshops. Dozens of potters have kept alive the techniques and forms of the distinctive pottery made by the Marajoara Indians. Replicas of the creamy white and red vessels are adorned with strikingly original geometric and primitive motifs. Although the pieces are fragile, the potters are as good at packing as they are at sculpting. Also not to be missed is a meal at ★ **Na Telha** (Rua Siqueira Mendes 363, tel. 91/3227-0853, 11am-4pm and 6pm-10pm Mon.-Fri., 11am-10pm Sat.-Sun., R$20-35). This local restaurant is famed for its delectable fresh fish dishes—such as *filhote* bathed in a sauce of shrimp—cooked on a piping hot *telha* (red ceramic roofing tile). For starters, order the delicious *bolinhos de pira-rucu*. To get here, look for local buses marked Icoaraci passing along Av. Presidente Vargas.

ILHA DE MOSQUEIRO

For a beach trip you can do in a day, your best bet is **Ilha de Mosqueiro** (www.portal-mosqueiro.jimdo.com). Seventy kilometers (44 mi) east of Belém, it has some attractive sandy beaches, particularly once you get away from the little town of Vila Mosqueiro. From the town's main square, you can catch local buses to beaches such as Praia Morubira and Praia Marahú. The most unspoiled of all is Praia do Paraíso, where you'll encounter white sands fringed by green vegetation and clean, emerald waters for bathing.

The ★ **Hotel Farol** (Praça Princesa Isabel 3295, tel. 91/3771-2095, www.hotel-farol.com.br, R$120-160 d) is a once-grand early 20th-century hotel that was a favorite retreat of Belém's rubber barons. Facing the attractive Praia do Farol, the simple but spotless guest rooms are divided between the original building and a more modern annex. Opt for the former, with its curving walls, sweeping hallways, polished marquetry, and bay windows overlooking a tropical garden and the beach. An atmospheric restaurant with columns and wonderful tiled floors serves simple home-cooked dishes such as shrimp frittata.

Getting to Mosqueiro, connected by a bridge to the mainland, is easy from Belém. Frequent buses (45 min., R$3.60) leave daily from the *rodoviária*, with stops along Avenida Almirante Barroso. By car, just follow well-paved BR-316.

ILHA DE ALGODOAL

The finest beaches within reach of Belém are the primitive windswept dunes that ring the idyllic **Ilha de Algodoal** (www.algodoal.com). Due to its distance from Belém (a five-hour trip), visiting Algodoal involves staying at least one night. Once you arrive, though, you likely won't be in a hurry to leave. The island's name is inspired by the abundance of a native plant known as *algodão de seda* (silk cotton). Its pods release fluffy white down that often wafts around the island like stray snowflakes. Fishing communities only settled here in the early 20th century, and to this day, the island's quartet of tiny fishing towns (the largest is Algodoal) are terribly bucolic and laid-back. Water is pumped from natural wells, electricity only arrived in 2005, and transportation is by bike, boat, or horse (there are no motorized vehicles—or banks, for that matter, so stock up on cash before coming). There are, however, abundant idyllic beaches, freshwater lagoons, lily-pad covered marshes, and unspoiled native vegetation. Through your *pousada,* you can get local guides to take you on fishing and canoeing trips as well as nature walks to spot monkeys, tortoises, and wild orchids in bloom. The islanders are hospitable, and the only interruption to the tranquility that reigns is the infectious rhythm of *carimbó,* a local dance set to pounding log-like drums that originated with the African slaves that came to coastal Pará in the 17th century.

Various rustic *pousadas* and camping grounds have sprung up to meet the demands of young backpackers and savvy ecotourists. Most *pousadas* are located in and around the village of Algodoal itself, which is close to the island's most beautiful beaches—Praia do Farol and Praia da Princesa. One of the most central is the **Pousada Chalés do Atlântico** (Rua Bertoldo Costa 33, Quadra 12, Centro, tel. 91/3854-1114, R$120-160 d), whose apartments and individual chalets, which sleep up to four, are scattered amid a bucolic garden strewn with fruit trees and only three minutes from the beach. Accommodations are simple but cared for. The restaurant serves lip-smacking regional fare.

Ilha de Algodoal is 163 kilometers (101 mi) northeast of Belém. From Belém's *rodoviária,* **Rápido Excelsior** (tel. 91/3249-6365) operates five buses daily to the town of Marudá (3.5 hours, R$20), where you can catch a boat (tel. 91/8146-5091, 40 minutes, R$6) to the island. There are four departures daily during the week and five on weekends (9am-5pm) with an 8pm departure on Friday. Driving from Belém, take well-paved BR-316, PA-136, and PA-318 to Marudá; leave your car in a parking lot for R$10 per day.

Arriving at Algodoal, you'll be met on the beach by drivers with mules and carts ready to whisk you to a hotel (R$8). Drivers can be hired to take you around the island. Boat owners at the Associação de Barqueiros do Algodoal will take you on half-or full-day excursions around the island. If you choose to walk, be careful of the tides (which can leave you stranded) and the deceptively strong currents of the channels (*furos*) that link inland lagoons to the sea.

★ ILHA DE MARAJÓ

Bathed by waters of the Rio Amazonas, Rio Tocantins, and the Atlantic Ocean, this island some 90 kilometers (56 mi) northwest of Belém boasts deserted beaches and mangrove swamps teeming with exotic cranes, herons, ibises, and thousands and thousands of water buffalo. On the largest river island in the world, buffalo are a major source of food (providing succulent steaks and creamy cheese) and transportation. They are far better than horses or cars at wading through muddy wetlands—for this reason, buffalo tow the municipal garbage trucks. They outnumber the human population by a ratio of 3:1. Although at first glance they might appear a little ornery, the buffalo are actually very docile. Those that serve as transportation vehicles receive special training to deal with tourists.

There are various stories surrounding the water buffalo's arrival on Marajó. One version credits their introduction to 18th-century Franciscan monks, while another claims they were survivors of a capsized boat that was transporting buffalo from India to French Guyana. Buffalo aside, Ilha de Marajó is a fascinating place. Despite its relative accessibility, Ilha de Marajó is also somewhat of a secluded world unto itself. Geographically, its vegetation is split between the flat wetlands of the eastern coast, which conjure up the Pantanal of Mato Grosso (particularly during the floods that occur February-May) and the tangled forests of the remote western coast. Historically, the island has a rich heritage. Between 1000 BC and AD 1300, it was inhabited by a group of Indians who are believed to have had a very sophisticated culture. Evidence of this lost civilization came to light in the 19th century when, after the annual floods, local farmers began to find shards of pottery and funeral urns stuck in the thick matting of their buffalos. The pottery, which came to be known as *cerámica marajoara*, consisted of finely wrought vessels made of local white clay mixed with substances such as ground tree bark and tortoise shells. Color was added via charcoal (black) and *urucum*

(an ocher-colored powder used in cooking to this day). Before being baked and varnished, the pottery was decorated with intricate designs illustrating scenes from life such as marriage and hunting ceremonies. To this day, the island has maintained this ceramics tradition, with local artists continuing to create distinctive pieces inspired by the ancient Marajoara techniques and motifs.

Visitors to Ilha de Marajó stay on the island's eastern coast (closest to Belém). If you're traveling independently and without a car, base yourself in one of the picturesque villages of Soure, Salvaterra, or Joanes. It is difficult to get around the island on public transport, although you can easily rent a bike. To see more than beaches, arrange a tour out of Belém that includes a stay at a working buffalo *fazenda;* a number operate as ecotourist *pousadas.*

Sights

The two main towns on Ilha de Marajó are Soure and Salvaterra. **Soure** is the largest and liveliest of the two. Founded in the 17th century on the mouth of the Rio Paracauari, it is an enticing place with pastel-painted houses shaded by palms and mango trees. Most of the island's hotels, restaurants, and services (including the island's only pair of international-card-friendly ATMs) can be found here, along with the closest semblance to nightlife. During the second weekend of November, Soure hosts its own small but enchanting Círio de Nazaré.

Surrounding the town are some alluring beaches. A 3-kilometer (2-mi) walk or bike ride north brings you to **Praia Barra Velha,** and a little farther on—across the Rio Araruna—is the even more striking **Praia de Araruna.** Popular **Praia do Pesqueiro,** 9 kilometers (6 mi) away (accessible by bus), has blue-green waters dotted with fishing boats whose daily catch is served at palm-thatched beach *barracas.*

On the other side of the Rio Paracauari, facing the Baía de Marajó, equally pretty **Salvaterra** has a more languid air and boasts proximity to **Praia Grande,** a sweeping ocean beach backed by palms. Around 16 kilometers (10 mi) south of Salvaterra is **Joanes.** This tiny village is known for its golden-sand beach and the atmospheric ruins of a 17th-century church built by Jesuits, who were the first Europeans to settle the island. A historic source of contention between Spain and Portugal revolves around the fact that, in 1500, Spanish navigator Vicente Yáñez Pinzón landed on Joanes's beach—two months before Pedro Álvares Cabral "discovered" Brazil and claimed it as Portuguese territory.

Buffalo Farms

On Marajó, numerous buffalo *fazendas,* or farms, are open to visitors. Many of these farms are located on plains and wetland areas that are rife with wildlife and offer insight into the daily lives of Marajoanos and a behind-the-scenes look at a working buffalo farm. You can often even ride the buffalo. Wildlife includes monkeys, capybaras, *jacarés* (caimans), and the flamboyantly pink and scarlet ibises known as *guarás.* Advance reservations are necessary; while you can reserve directly with these *fazendas* (often cheaper), several agencies in Belém sell packages to them, including **Amazon Star** (tel. 91/3241-8624, www.amazonstar.com.br) and **Valverde** (tel. 91/3212-3388, www.valeverdeturismo.com.br).

Located 12 kilometers (7.5 mi) from Soure, **Fazenda Bom Jesus** (4a Rua Km 8, tel. 91/3741-1243) is owned by Eva Abufaiad, a veterinarian and agricultural engineer who really knows her buffalo (as well as birds such as blue storks, parrots, and *guarás,* all of which can easily be spotted here). During the day, three-hour visits cost R$45 (R$70 with transportation) and include a home-cooked Marajoara snack. Only 2 kilometers (1.2 mi) from Soure, **Fazenda Araruna** (tel. 91/9605-8674) has its own lovely river beach that is popular with *guarás* and can be reached by a two-hour ride on the back of a buffalo (R$30). Those who are buffalo-shy can explore the area by horseback (R$30) or canoe (R$50).

Some *fazendas* offer accommodations as well. Although no longer a working farm, **Fazenda São Jerônimo** (Rodovia Soure-Pesqueiro Km 3, tel. 91/3741-2093, www.marajo.tk, R$180 d) is a picturesque estate close to Soure with creeks and a private beach where you can swim. You can take a guided hike through groves of coconut palms and native fruit trees, a canoe trip through mangrove swamps, or go horseback or buffalo-back riding. Outings range in cost from R$50-80. Accommodations, in a low-slung ranch house, are simple but appealing, with regional furnishings and air-conditioning. The restaurant (for guests only; reservations required) serves delicious food, including buffalo, for both lunch and dinner. Advance reservations, even for day trips, are necessary.

A 45-minute boat trip and buffalo-cart ride from Soure, the ★ **Fazenda Sanjo** (tel. 91/3228-1385, www.sanjo.tur.br, R$350 pp a day includes all meals and activities) is an authentic family-run ranch where you'll be made to feel so at home that before you know it, you'll be rustling up the buffalos on horseback. Once you've finished helping out with milking and making cheese, you can savor some delicious dishes made from the farm's herds. Lodgings in the main farmhouse are simple but cozy and comfortable.

Shopping

In Soure, various local artists create beautiful pottery modeled after traditional *cerâmica marajoara.* One of the island's most respected ceramicists is Carlos Amaral. A descendant of the Aruã Indians who inhabited the island before the arrival of the Portuguese, Carlos learned traditional pottery techniques from his grandmother and has spent his life studying the graphic symbols used by his Marajoara ancestors. You can view and purchase his work at his atelier, **M'Barayo Cerâmica** (Travessa 20, tel. 91/8330-2685, 8am-noon daily and 2pm-6pm Mon.-Sat.) Another good place to find Marajoara replicas along with woven items and other local *artesanato* is the **Sociedade Marajoara das Artes** (3a Rua, 8am-6pm Mon.-Sat., 8am-noon Sun.).

Accommodations

Accommodations on Marajó are fairly relaxed and rustic. Reserve in advance during holidays, particularly July, or on long weekends, when Belenenses vacation here. Apart from *fazenda* lodges, most accommodations are divided between Soure and Salvaterra.

On the outskirts of Soure, a pretty budget option is **Pousada O Canto do Francês** (6a Rua, São Pedro, tel. 91/3741-1298, http://ocantodofrances.blogspot.com, R$130 d). Set amid lush green gardens, guest rooms are soothing, with bleached walls and polished wooden furniture. English is spoken, and the French owner, Thierry, can organize excursions. You can also rent a bike to tool around to nearby beaches. **O Casarão Amazonia** (4a Rua 626, São Pedro, tel. 91/3741-1988, http://hotelcasaraoamazonia.blogspot.com.br, R$170-190 d) is a handsomely renovated colonial mansion on the edge of Soure's historical center. The setting suits the simple, atmospheric, and lofty-ceilinged rooms that overlook a fruit-tree sprinkled garden, home to several more modern apartments and a pool. Excursions can be organized, and bikes are available for rent. In high season, the restaurant (renowned for its buffalo steaks and pizzas) is a magnet for famished foodies.

Staying in Salvaterra gives you the advantage of being right on the sands of Praia Grande. **Pousada Boto** (Travessa Int. Paulo Ribeiro, tel. 91/3765-1539, www.pousadaboto.com.br, R$95-105 d) is a great deal. The cheery, woody bungalow accommodations are smallish and basic, but the leafy gardens, friendly staff, and location three minutes from the beach more than compensate. The food is quite decent, and you can rent bikes and motorcycles to explore the island. If you're traveling with your own hammock, you can string it up for the night for R$15 (R$25 with breakfast). Fancier is **Pousada dos Guarás** (Av. Beira-Mar, tel. 91/3765-1149, www.pousadadosguaras.com.br, R$190-280 d). Scattered amid a sprawling palm-studded estate overlooking the beach, the private bungalow accommodations are fetching, with local art hanging on brightly colored walls. There is a sizable pool and a scenic restaurant serving both regional and international dishes. When booking, you can request an all-inclusive package that includes numerous activities and excursions.

If you're in the mood for total tranquility, consider staying in the charming little fishing village of Joanes. Owned by a Brazilian-Belgian couple, the ★ **Pousada Ventânia** (tel. 91/3646-2067, ventaniapousada@hotmail.com, R$115-130 d) is a friendly and delightfully rustic *pousada* perched on a cliff overlooking a secluded beach. Its lofty position ensures constant breezes (and very few mosquitoes). The basic, pleasant guest rooms have views of the Baía de Marajó and sleep up to four. The owners rent bikes and canoes and can organize inexpensive guided outings.

Food

Marajó is renowned for two very distinctive culinary specialties. The first is water buffalo, which comes in many guises. More tender and flavorful than beef, buffalo meat is also lower in cholesterol. As a main course, two of the most popular buffalo recipes are *filé marajoara*, in which a prime cut of succulent meat is topped with creamy melted buffalo cheese (which resembles a fine mozzarella), and *frito de vaqueiro* ("cowboy fried"), in which less noble parts are cut into cubes, sautéed, and eaten with *pirão de leite* (a puree of milk and manioc flour). Buffalo milk shows up in everything from butter and cheese to desserts such as the classic *doce de leite,* a rich caramel pudding. The second Marajoano delicacy is more rarefied and also more likely to repulse squeamish gringos. It consists of a type of mollusk, known as *turu,* that can be found living inside dead trees located around the island's mangrove swamp. Milky white in color and gelatinous in consistency, *turu* is treated like an oyster. Locals are prone to eat them raw with a spray of lime. In bars and restaurants, however, you'll come across *caldo de turu,* in which the mollusk is added to a broth of coconut milk, lime juice, garlic, and cilantro.

One of the best places to sample local fare in Soure is at ★ **Paraíso Verde** (Travessa 17 2135, Umarizal, tel. 91/3741-1581, 10am-10pm daily, R$20-30), an aptly named restaurant set amid ferns and native fruit trees, where the *filé marajoara* is pretty divine. On the road leading from Soure to Praia de Pesqueiro, **Delícias da Nalva** (4a Rua 1051, tel. 91/8229-9678, 10am-10pm daily, R$20-30) also has a lovely garden setting. Recommended for local dishes, it is a particularly good place to try *caldo de turu*.

Transportation

Araparí Navegação (tel. 91/3241-4977) and **Rodofluvial Banav** (tel. 91/3269-4494, www.banav.com.br) alternate daily ferry service (6:30am and 2:30pm Mon.-Sat., 10am Sun., R$19) from Belém. Departing from Portão 15 at the Docas do Pará (right near the Estação das Docas), the journey takes three hours. Another alternative is the car ferry that leaves from the nearby town of Icoaraci. Operated by **Henvil** (tel. 91/3246-7472, www.henvil.com.br), boats leave at 6:30am daily and at 4pm Mon., Tues., and Thurs. Tickets (R$91 per vehicle and driver and R$17 for subsequent passengers) can and should be purchased in advance at the Henvil kiosk at Belém's *rodoviária,* particularly in the high season of July.

On Marajó, all ferries dock at the Porto Camará. From here you can easily get a bus, van, or *moto-taxi* to take you to Joanes and Salvaterra (R$6), 30 minutes away, and to Soure (R$12). From Salvaterra, boats and an hourly barge that transports vehicles (15 min. R$2) takes you across the Rio Paracauari to Soure. If you confirm your arrival in advance, most *pousadas* or *fazendas* will agree to have someone pick you up at the docks.

Public transport is sketchy. If you're without a car, the best way to get around the island is by taxi or *moto-taxi* (available in Soure and Salvaterra). You can also rent a bike, a service offered by many *pousadas*.

In Belém, specialized travel agencies offer complete packages that include all accommodations, meals, and excursions on Marajó as well as transportation to and from the island from Belém. For more information about these, check with **Amazon Star Turismo** (Rua Henrique Gurjão 236, Reduto, tel. 91/3241-8624, www.amazonstar.com.br).

SANTARÉM

The second largest city in Pará, Santarém is a drowsy river port town that's a bit rough-and-tumble around the edges. By boat it is around 50 hours upstream from Belém, and it's a worthwhile place to stop if you're riding up or down the Amazon between Belém and Manaus. The surrounding region offers a firsthand glimpse into Amazonian culture and boasts natural treasures of great beauty that can easily transform any "stopover" into a week's stay. The most popular destination is the white-sand beaches of nearby Alter do Chão, which are famously (and not unjustly) hyped by the state tourist office as the "Amazonian Caribbean." Although Santarém receives less rain than either Belém or Manaus, the surrounding countryside, much of it quite unspoiled, is a scenic mixture of wetlands and rain forest. Take one of various trips up and down the Rio Tapajós, a tributary of the Amazon, or to the Floresta Nacional do Tapajós, a national park where you can hike and canoe through virgin rain forest and even stay with local rubber tappers.

Santarém is located at the confluence of the Rio Tapajós and the Rio Amazonas, and the "meeting" of the blue-green waters of the Tapajós with the milky brown-colored Rio Amazonas is a sight that rivals the more celebrated merging of the Rio Negro with the Rio Solimões in Manaus. During the dry season (June-Dec.), the Tapajós recedes by several meters, exposing a seductive string of sandy beaches backed by lush green vegetation.

As a source of life and livelihoods, the Rio Tapajós has a long history that dates back to the earliest civilizations in the Americas. Archaeological evidence reveals the presence of prehistoric Indian groups who fished along the riverbanks and planted corn in the fertile hills around Santarém. In the cliffs surrounding the town of Monte Alegre, they left paintings in caves and on rocks that date back 12,000 years. Other excavations have unearthed shards of pottery that have proved far older than most other vestiges of indigenous people in the Americas.

Indian culture was still thriving when the first Europeans arrived at the beginning of the 16th century. Santarém was founded in the 1660s as a Jesuit missionary outpost. Tapajós Indians that weren't converted to Christianity were subsequently enslaved, slaughtered, driven into the jungle, or wiped out by infectious diseases. Apart from trade involving spices such as pepper, cloves, and vanilla, the little town remained an isolated jungle outpost until well into the 19th century, when it exploded into a prosperous trading center as a result of the Amazonian rubber boom. Ironically, it was in Santarém that the seeds were sown for Amazon rubber's dramatic demise. The culprit was an Englishman by the name of Henry Wickham, who moved here in 1874 and soon after began smuggling precious rubber seeds back to London's Kew Gardens. From England, saplings were sent to plantations in the British colonies of Ceylon and Malaysia. By the end of the century, the Asian plantations were producing rubber in greater quantities, and far more cheaply, than those in the middle of the Brazilian jungle. As a result, the once-thriving Amazonian rubber boom went bust.

Today, rubber still contributes to the local economy, along with timber, jute, fish, and Brazil nuts. However, in recent years, the greatest (and most environmentally devastating) impact on Santarém and the surrounding region has been gold and bauxite mining along with soybean cultivation and processing. While these lucrative activities have brought new wealth to the area, they have also led to the rampant clearing of swaths of forest stretching all the way south to Mato Grosso.

In the early 1970s, the construction of the highway leading from Cuiabá to Santarém was expected to bring great development to the area. At the time, such ambitions proved premature; by the 1980s the jungle had once again reclaimed the asphalt and portions are impassable, especially when it rains. However, spurred on by the soybean boom, the federal government is committed to reopening this crucial route, which could spell major changes for Santarém in years to come.

sunrise in Santarém

Sights

Santarém has few attractions. The town's main museum is the **Centro Cultural João Fona** (Praça Barão de Santarém, Centro, tel. 93/3523-2434, 8am-5pm Mon.-Fri., 8am-1pm Sat., free). Housed in a handsome canary yellow 19th-century mansion, the small collection provides an insightful look at Santarém's history and culture. Apart from some beautiful pieces of Tapajoara pottery dating back 5,000 years, there are recent examples of indigenous art as well as paintings that portray the town and river during colonial times. Otherwise, the most compelling thing you can do in Santarém is simply to wander around soaking up the atmosphere of an Amazonian port town. The constant bustle of boats coming and going and passengers boarding and disembarking is a fascinating spectacle.

For a pleasant stroll along the river, start at the Praça Matriz, site of the town's oldest church, the 18th-century **Igreja Matriz da Nossa Senhora da Conceição.** From here, head west along the main waterfront drag, **Avenida Tapajós,** toward the gigantic eyesore that houses U.S.-based Cargill's soybean processing plant. Along the way, stop to check out the action and produce at the Mercado Municipal, where you'll see a dazzling array of fish as well as a local delicacy, the very tiny local shrimp called *aviu*. For an excellent view of the meeting of the Rio Tapajós and the Rio Amazonas, which run together side by side for several kilometers, climb the hill that rises up from the waterfront to the **Mirante do Tapajós.**

Sports and Recreation

Lounging on beaches, boating down the river past traditional *caboclo* communities, exploring thick forests—there are plenty of ways to enjoy Santarém's natural attributes. For information about the surrounding area, check in with an American expat named Steven Alexander, who has lived in Santarém with his wife since 1979. A passionate defender of the Amazon's rich biosphere and an equally fervent critic of politicians and businesses bent on destroying it, Alexander offers guided visits to his own private nature reserve, **Bosque Santa Lúcia** (amazonto@gmail.com, http://bosque-santa.blogspot.com, R$75 for two people, advance reservations required), a patch of rain forest 15 kilometers (9 mi) from town where you can hike amid 400 species of native trees (including Brazil nut and *guaraná*), birds, and monkeys. He can also put you in touch with guides to take you to farther-flung attractions. **Santarém Tur** (Rua Adriano Pimentel 44, Centro, tel. 93/3522-4847, www.santaremtur.com.br) offers trips by boat to natural attractions in the area. Two popular trips close to town are to the Meeting of the Waters (3 hours, R$60) and to the Lago do Maicá (6 hours, R$130), where you can go piranha fishing.

Shopping

Santarém is a great place to pick up well-made local and indigenous *artesanato*. **Loja Muiraquitã** (Rua Senador Lameira Bittencourt 131, Centro, tel. 93/3522-7164) has a diverse array of intriguing objects ranging from wood carvings to musical instruments. Not to be missed are the wonderfully original clothing and accessories made by **Dica Frazão** (Rua Floriano Peixoto 281, Centro, tel. 93/3522-1026) out of her home, which doubles as an atelier and museum. In her 90s, Dica is a local legend, a stylist whose remarkable items, made out of natural fibers such as *buriti* palm, *canarana* straw, and tree bark and accessorized with colorful seeds and feathers, are notable for their refined tailoring.

Accommodations

Hotels in Santarém are a pretty uninspiring lot. Occupying a pretty house built in 1910, the family-run **Brisa Hotel** (Rua Senador Lameira Bittencourt 5, Centro, tel. 93/3522-1018, brisahotel@hotmail.com, R$80 d) is one of a series of historic *casas* on Santarém's oldest street. High-ceilinged guest rooms are plain but clean, and a friendly atmosphere reigns. For those fond of (unintentional) retro charm, the centrally located **Santarém Plaza**

(Rua Rui Barbosa 756, Centro, tel. 93/3523-1287, stmpalace@netsan.com.br, R$90-150 d) has it in unrestored spades. Outdated rooms with beguilingly mismatched furnishings are vast and cheap, and service is warm.

Food

Considered by many locals to be Santarém's best restaurant, ★ **Trapiche Bistrô Orla** (Rua Adriano Pimentel 114, Centro, tel. 93/9128-8150, 11am-midnight daily, R$20-35) is a surprisingly funky bistrô/boteco with the air of an art gallery overlooking the river. The often inspired dishes are regional with contemporary splashes—pirarucu tartare with banana chips, shrimp fried in crunchy shredded coconut, tapioca tiramisu. Icy microbrews and artisanal cachaças are ideal accompaniments to both the food and live music. **Piracema** (Av. Mendonça Furtado 73, Prainha, tel. 93/3522-7461, 11:30am-3pm daily and 7pm-11:30pm, R$25-40) marries a charming atmosphere and regional fish dishes executed with flair. Both the crunchy tapioca encrusted shrimp and smoked pirarucu make for sublime starters (you'll need them since service is notoriously lethargic), before digging into dishes such as grilled tambaqui and banana-stuffed pirarucu, which easily feed two to three. It's well worth cabbing it to **Mutunuy 2** (Travessa Muriano Meira 1680-B, Interventória, tel. 93/3522-7909, R$15-20), a local institution whose specialty is buttery, charcoal-roasted chicken served with rice, manioc flour, and potato salad.

Information and Services

Santarém's tourist office, **Santur** (Rua Floriano Peixoto 777, Centro, tel. 93/3523-2434, 8am-2pm Mon.-Fri.), has information about the town and surrounding area. More helpful is the staff at **Santarém Tur** (Rua Adriano Pimentel 44, Centro, tel. 93/3522-4847, www.santaremtur.com.br), who also sell plane tickets to Belém and Manaus and can organize regional travel and tours. You'll find a Banco do Brasil on Avenida Rui Barbosa,

near the corner of Travessa 15 de Agosto, as well as an HSBC and a Bradesco, all with ATMs that accept international cards.

Transportation

Santarém lies roughly halfway between Belém and Manaus. You can get here by plane (speedy and expensive) or boat (slower and only cheaper if you sleep in a hammock) from both cities. The precariousness of the roads means that getting here by bus or car is out of the question. Although you can get around town easily on foot, if you find the heat is making you lazy, you can easily hail a taxi or *moto-taxi;* fare for the latter usually costs around R$5.

AIR

Both national and cheaper regional carriers offer service to Santarém from Belém and Manaus. The small **Aeroporto Maria José** (Rodovia Fernando Guilhon, Praça Eduardo Gomes, tel. 93/3522-4328) is 14 kilometers (9 mi) from the center by bus (hourly from 5:30am-11:30pm, R$1.90) or taxi (R$50).

BOAT

Boats from Belém and Manaus arrive and depart from the busy **Docas do Pará** (Av. Cuiabá, Bairro Vera Paz) port, 2.5 kilometers (1.5 mi) west of the center of town. Most companies only offer 1-2 departures a week. Your best bet is to go to the docks and check out which boat is leaving and when. A trip to Belém usually takes two days (48 hours), while Manaus is usually 2.5-3 days. Expect to pay around R$150-230 (hammock space) and R$700-1,000 (for cabins and suites for 2 people). Belém-bound boats stop at Monte Alegre (6 hours, R$50 for hammock space) while those bound for Manaus stop at Parintins (20 hours, R$70 for hammock space). Try to purchase tickets a day or two in advance; you can even negotiate the price. To visit smaller towns in the region such as Monte Alegre, head to the smaller port at Praça Tiradentes. By day, minibuses (R$1.90) marked "Orla Fluvial" circulate at 30-minute intervals between the

Docas do Pará and the center of town, passing by the Praça Tiradentes port.

AROUND SANTARÉM
★ Alter do Chão

Around 35 kilometers (22 mi) from Santarém lies Alter do Chão, whose claim to fame is its gleaming pinup-worthy river beach. Easily accessible from Santarém by bus, the beach fills up on weekends. You'll want to stay a while, and there are several *pousadas*. The best time to come is during the dry season (June-Dec.) when the river recedes—by up to 10 meters (33 feet)—and leaves the beaches more exposed. Take advantage of natural attractions in the surrounding area via a handful of topnotch ecotourist outfits adept at organizing excursions that expose exotic wildlife, traditional river communities, and virgin Amazonian rain forest.

BEACHES

The village of Alter do Chão is blessed with soft white-sand beaches bathed by the blue waters of the Rio Tapajós to the west and the green waters of Lago Verde to the east. The main river beach facing the town is actually a large sandbar. During the rainy season, it becomes an island that goes by the provocative alias of **Ilha de Amor** (Island of Love), and can be reached by canoe-taxi (R$3). Throughout the year, the Ilha's rustic *barracas* serve beer and fried fish, making it a good place to relax. You can also rent canoes and kayaks to explore the vast **Lago Verde,** where you can swim and snorkel—and then watch pink and grey dolphins frolic as the sun sets at nearby **Ponta do Cururu.** By car or boat, you can get to farther-flung but equally seductive beaches along the Tapajós such as **Pindobal, Cabutuba,** and **Aramanai,** all within 25 kilometers (16 mi) of town. One thing to watch out for is stingrays. Since they aren't fond of waves, make sure you splash around a lot before making your way into unknown waters.

SPORTS AND RECREATION

There are countless destinations along the Rio Tapajós to explore by boat. **Areia Branca Ecotours** (Orla Fluvial, tel. 93/3527-1317, www.areaibrancaecotour.com.br) and **Mãe Natureza** (Praça Sete de Setembro, tel. 93/3527-1264, www.maenaturezaecoturismo.com.br) are two well-run ecotour outfits run by multilingual staff. Among their numerous offerings are boat tours, snorkeling, dolphin watching, and fishing excursions as well as forest hikes. Two popular full-day

Alter do Chão

destinations are **Canal do Jarí,** where the Tapajós and Amazonas rivers meet amidst a flurry of bird, monkey, and sloth activity, and **Belterra,** where you can wander amidst the remains of Henry Ford's utopic all-American rubber manufacturing village in the jungle. A full-day guided outing costs R$70-120 pp, based on group size. Multiday expeditions to secluded points along the river re also available, including the **Floresta Nacional de Tapajós (FLONA)** and the **Reserva Extratavista Tapajós-Arapiuns,** where you can visit community projects and schools. All-inclusive overnight trips range from R$175-350 per person per day, depending on the itinerary and accommodations. Both operators can recommend houses for rent in Alter do Chão—an inexpensive option should you decide to stay a while. A less expensive alternative is to hire one of the local boatmen at the Núcleo Borari along the river in town.

A good source and terrific guide is local resident and self-taught naturalist **Gil Serique** (tel. 93/9115-8111, www.gilserique. com), who speaks English and knows the Tapajós and its tributaries like the back of his hand. He offers customized tours to various destinations, including FLONA. A full-day excursion costs around R$150 per person.

FESTIVALS AND EVENTS

If you're around during the second week in September, don't miss the **Festa do Cairé.** One of the most important traditional festivals in Pará, the *festa* dates back to the earliest contact between Jesuit missionaries and local Indians. Both indigenous and Catholic elements commingle in the ornate religious pageantry that, in true Brazilian style, is tempered with singing, dancing, and merrymaking.

SHOPPING

Araribá (Rua Dom Macedo Costa, tel. 93/3527-1251, www.araribah.com.br) has a wonderful selection of high-quality and very reasonably priced *artesanato* from more than 80 ethnic Indian groups. **Doces Dona Glória** (Rua Dom Macedo Costa 560) is located in the house of local resident Dona Glória, whose deft hand excels at making jellies, compotes, candies, and liqueurs out of Amazonian fruits.

ACCOMMODATIONS AND FOOD

Curvy and rustic **Pousada Tupaiulândia** (Rua Pedro Teixeira 300, tel. 93/3527-1157, pousadatupaiulandia@hotmail.com, R$80-90 d) is a good budget option. Guest rooms are quite large and comfortable, although somewhat lacking in décor apart from shiny exposed brick. Breakfasts are good, and the owners are very hospitable. **Pousada do Tapajós Hostel** (Rua Lauro Sodré 100, Praia do Cajueiro, tel. 93/9210-2166, http://pousadadotapajos.com.br, R$80-100 d, R$30-40 pp) has dorms with bunks and private double, triple, and quadruple rooms. Furnishings and décor are unadorned but well-maintained. Major pluses are the common areas, which include a sprawling garden with hammocks and a barbecue space. Just off the main *praça* and close to the beach, the **Pousada Mingote** (Travessa Agostinho Antônio Lobato, tel. 93/3527-1158, www.pousadamingote.com. br, R$80-120 d) is a newish hotel with lots of cool white tile and some attractive woodwork. Rooms (for up to four people) are small and basic, but tidy and pleasant. The small, family-owned **Pousada Sombra do Cajueiro** (Rua Pedro Teixeira 200, tel. 93/3527-1370, pousadasombradocajueiro@hotmail.com, R$90-140 d) gets raves for its well-outfitted, comfy and sizable rooms.

The best hotel is the **Hotel Beloalter** (Rua Pedro Teixeira, tel. 93/3527-1230, www.beloalter.com.br, R$185-250 d), located on the shore of Lago Verde, a turquoise lake fringed by lovely beaches just a short walk or canoe ride from the village. Lodgings are spread through an immense tropical garden that includes a pool and a placid lagoon. Rooms are spacious and very comfortable, if a little Spartan. Although they cost a bit more, much more attractive and jungly are the two "ecological" guest rooms decked out entirely in native woods and fibers. Even better is the tree house. The on-site restaurant serves well-prepared regional cooking for lunch and dinner.

Don't leave town without sampling two local specialties: *tucunaré na manteiga* (fresh fish cooked in butter with peppers, tomatoes, and other sundries) and *caldeirada do pirarucu* (salted fish cooked in a fragrant tomato-based broth with potatos and okra). Chances are both will eventually show up on the daily menu at the cool and colorful **Arco-Íris da Amazônia** (Praça Sete de Setembro, tel. 93/3527-1182, 6pm-11pm daily, R$15-25), along with healthy snacks, sandwiches, and crepes. The arty vibe and creative fruit juices and cocktails will make you want to chill for a while, especially when live carimbó shows take place. Occupying a breezy two-story structure open to the elements, **Tribal** (Travessa Antônio A. Lobato, tel. 93/3527-1226, 11am-3pm and 6pm-11pm daily, R$15-25) is a fun place to dig into generous portions of grilled fish and barbecued chicken and beef. If you can, nab a table on the top floor; the views will keep you occupied while waiting (when crowded, service lags). Even better views can be gleaned from the riverfront **Farol da Ilha** (Orla Fluvial, 11am-5pm Mon. 11pm-10pm Thurs.-Sun, R$20-30), where expertly executed local fish dishes are perfect accompaniments to the mosaic of beaches, rivers, and islands. Along the waterfront, **Espaço Alter do Chão** (Rua Lauro Sodré 74, tel. 93/9122-9643, 8pm-close Mon.-Thurs. noon-close Fri.-Sun., cover R$5-20) is a funky cultural space where regional snacks and meals (try the stuffed pirarucu) are accompanied by heaping portions of live music, performances, and *festas.*

TRANSPORTATION AND SERVICES

There is a Banco do Brasil ATM on Praça 7 de Setembro, inside the Mini-Center Mingote supermarket; however, stock up on cash in Santarém since not all businesses accept credit cards. Ecotour outfits **Areia Branca Ecotours** (Orla Fluvial, tel. 93/3527-1317, www.areaibrancaecotour.com.br) and **Mãe Natureza** (Praça Sete de Setembro,

tel. 93/3527-1264, www.maenaturezaeco-turismo.com.br), along with knowledgeable English-speaking guide **Gil Serique** (tel. 93/9115-8111, www.gilserique.com), are terrific sources of information regarding the area. Online, check out http://alterdochao.tur.br (in Portuguese).

Buses (1 hour, R$2.50-3) to Alter do Chão leave every 60 minutes between 5am-6pm from Santarém's Praça Tiradentes, stopping along Avenida Tapajós; service is more frequent on weekends. In Alter do Chão, ask to get off at the stop following the cemetery, which is only a block from the main square of Praça 7 de Setembro. A taxi from Santarém or the airport will cost around R$90. If you're driving, follow the paved PA-457 for 35 kilometers (21 mi).

Floresta Nacional do Tapajós

One of the Amazon's few national parks within easy reach of an urban center, the **Floresta Nacional do Tapajós** (www4.icmbio.gov.br/flona_tapajos) offers more than 500,000 hectares of unspoiled rain forest full of hiking trails. Aside from hiking through the forest, it's easier and more pleasurable to explore its streams and flooded wetlands by canoe. Within the park's boundaries are several very small river communities whose inhabitants still make a living from rubber tapping as well as fishing and cultivation of Brazil nuts and the creation of accessories out of vegetal leather. As part of developing ecotourism programs, it's possible to stay overnight with a family (usually in a hammock) in communities such as Maguari and Jamaraqua. Tour operators in Santarém and Alter do Chão offer 2-5-day trips (R$150-200 pp per day) with the possibility of sleeping on boats or in tents as well as with locals in their homes.

From Santarém, there are various entrances via the BR-163; the closest is at km 50, which can be accessed by bus. ICMBio, the government organization that monitors the park and provides visitors with authorization (upon payment of fee) has an office in Santarém (Av. Tapajós 2267, Laguinho, tel. 93/3523-2815). Most people go on guided outings with local ecotourism outfits from Santarém or Alter do Chão.

Belterra and Fordlândia

In the 1920s, American automobile magnate Henry Ford got a bee in his bonnet that Santarém was the ideal place to build a plantation that would supply rubber for his Model T's tires. Ford purchased a vast tract of land 100 kilometers (60 mi) southwest of Santarém and then began shipping all the materials necessary for the construction of a rubber plantation town to the middle of the rain forest. The spitting image of a quintessential Midwestern town circa 1925, Fordlândia possessed cute little row houses with front gardens, a hospital, a school, a church, and even a cinema. Unfortunately, poor soil conditions, fungi that attacked the rubber trees, and the outbreak of diseases such as malaria doomed the project. Never one to give up, in 1934 Ford purchased another tract of land only 30 kilometers (20 mi) from Santarém on the eastern bank of the Tapajós, called Belterra, where he installed yet another Made-in-America community. Although Belterra fared somewhat better than Fordlândia, the outbreak of World War II hampered transportation of supplies and equipment, and the introduction of synthetic rubber knocked the bottom out of natural rubber prices. By the end of the war, Ford had had enough. Having squandered over US$25 million, he gratefully sold both areas to the Brazilian government for US$200,000. Today, both utopian cities are eerily intact—Fordlândia's rubber plant is even still in operation. Their retro Americana is jarringly out of place in the midst of the Amazon jungle.

Fordlândia is quite far from Santarém—an 8-10-hour boat ride south along the Rio Tapajós. However, Belterra can easily be visited in a day trip as part of a tour for around R$100 pp. For more information, contact tour operators in in Santarém and Alter do Chão.

Amazonas

Sharing borders with Peru and Colombia, Amazonas is the major state of the western Amazon. It is also the largest and most geographically remote of all Brazil's states. This is where you'll find the largest patches of intact rain forests and the greatest number of Brazilian Indians, some of whom still manage to maintain traditional lifestyles. It is also where the mighty Amazon River is born, 6 kilometers (4 mi) from Manaus, at the spectacular confluence of the Rio Solimões and the Rio Negro, known as the Meeting of the Waters. In Amazonas, the river and its tributaries dominate daily life. Almost all transportation is by boats—riverboats, speedboats, or dugout canoes—which are constantly shuttling people and goods up and down the rivers and their tributaries. The rhythms of the river—its seasonal floods and rare but occasional droughts—regulate the lives of the Amazon's magnificent array of flora and fauna and those of its human inhabitants.

Amid the seemingly endless green wilderness, the sole "center of civilization" is Amazonas's capital city of Manaus, which is home to 2 million people, half the population of the entire state. Although it has a unique flavor and boasts some sights, this ramshackle frontier town's main interest is as a gateway to exploring the natural treasures of the Western Amazon.

MANAUS

Booming and somewhat chaotic, as a major river port and commercial hub, Manaus has a rough-edged, colorful vibrancy and culture all its own. While much of the city is modern and ironically bereft of vegetation, numerous architectural landmarks, including its magnificent opera house, attest to its importance as the Amazon's 19th-century rubber capital.

The city's origins can be traced back to an early 17th-century mission settlement along the banks of the Rio Negro. Over time, it blossomed into a small trading center, but it wasn't until 1856 that the town of Manaus—named after the Manaós Indians—officially came into being. Shortly after, the Amazonian rubber boom hit and Manaus's fortunes soared. Speculators from all over the world descended on the Amazon, hoping to strike it rich. Many did, since prices rose sharply along with worldwide demand. With exports soaring, the shrewd governor of Amazonas, Eduardo Gonçalvez Ribeiro, slapped a 25 percent export tax on rubber and then proceeded to spend the vast sums collected on transforming the backwater town into a glittering city. The grandeur of the sweeping boulevards, monumental squares, and palatial public buildings was matched by the rubber barons' splendid mansions. Manaus was one of the first cities in the world to have electric street lights and boasted the first electric trolley system in South America. Ribeiro also hired architects, artists, and master builders from all over Europe to build a sumptuous new opera house with imported materials such as marble, crystal, and wrought iron. When some rubber barons voiced discontent that the main cupola was being covered with glazed tiles instead of gold, the extravagant governor assured them that in time, as rubber profits increased, he would tear the theater down and build an even grander one.

By 1915, the bottom had fallen out of the Brazilian rubber industry. A devastated Ribeiro committed suicide, rubber barons put their mansions up for sale, and Manaus fell into a stagnant torpor from which it wouldn't emerge until the 1960s. In 1966, in order to stimulate the region's almost nonexistent economy, the military government transformed Manaus into a *zona franca,* or free-trade zone. Electronics assembly plants mushroomed, and the population multiplied with the influx of workers seeking jobs in the new industries. Although the opening of Brazil's markets to imports beginning in the 1990s ended Manaus's retail monopoly, the electronics industry is still going strong, and it's not uncommon to see Brazilians at Manaus's airport laden down with computers, DVD players, and digital cameras.

Orientation

Most of Manaus's sights are located around the port and the oldest part of Centro (currently undergoing revitalization) that fans out from the Rio Negro to the area surrounding the Teatro Amazonas. It's easy to get around Manaus's somewhat grungy center by day. At night, however, the neighborhood around Praça da Matriz is pretty unsafe, and the riverfront and dock area is downright dangerous. Two-days is all you need to see most of Manaus's major attractions before heading out into the rain forest.

Sights
PORTO FLUTUANTE

If you arrive in Manaus by boat, you'll disembark at the **Porto Flutuante** (Floating Port), a concrete pier designed to rise and fall along with the Rio Negro (which, depending on the season, can vary by as much as 14 meters/45 feet). Built in 1902 by a British company, Manaos Harbour Limited, this is where all large ships dock, and the bustle of passengers boarding and disembarking is quite a sight. For this reason, even if you don't arrive via water, Manaus's rambunctious, busy port is a fitting place to take your bearings and begin a tour of the city. The customhouse across the street, known as the **Alfândega** (Rua Marquês de Santa Cruz), is evocative of Victorian London. Inaugurated in 1906, this fine edifice was also built by Manaos Harbour Limited in an eclectic style that mingles medieval and Renaissance elements. The world's first example of a prefabricated building, its bricks were shipped over from England in blocks and reassembled on site.

Manaus

To Parque
Zoológico do CIGS

Rio   Negro

PORTO
FLUTUANTE

ALFÂNDEGA

ESTAÇÃO
HIDROVIÁRIA

*Praça
Osvaldo Cruz*

CATEDRAL N.S.
DA CONCEIÇÃO

*Praça
da Matriz*

CAPITANIA DOS
PORTOS

MERCADO MUNICIPAL
ALFREDO LISBOA

PORTO MANAUS
MODERNA

*Praça
Adalberto
Valle*

AV. RIBEIRO

R G

R M

R DIAS

MOREIRA

SKINA
DOS SUCOS

PALÁCIO DA
JUSTIÇA

RIO NEGRO
SHOPPING

GO INN

BAR
CALDEIRA

AV. EPAMINODAS

TRAVESSA E. LOURENÇO

*Praça da
Saudade*

R SIMÃO BOLIVAR

*Praça do
Congresso*

TEATRO AMAZONAS

AV. EDUARDO RIBEIRO

R RAMOS FERREIRA

HOTEL
SAINT-PAUL

HENRIQUE MARTINS

CASA DA
PAMONHA

CASA DO
GUARANÁ
SATERE

PALACETE
PROVINCIAL

PALÁCIO
PROVINCIAL

SALDANHA MARTINS

*Praça
Heliodora Balbi*

CABARET
NIGHT CLUB

BAR BOTEQUIM

VINTE E QUATRO DE MAIO

TACACÁ DA
GISELA

São
Sebastião

*Praça
São
Sebastião*

BAR DO
ARMANDO

HOTEL DEZ DE JULHO

BOUTIQUE HOTEL CASA TEATRO

IGREJA LARGO
SÃO SEBASTIÃO

LOCAL HOSTEL

MUSEU
AMAZÔNICO

CENTRO

AV. GETULIO VARGAS

R MAJ GABRIEL

R RODOLFO VALE

R VISC DE PORTO ALEGRE

R DO CAXIAS

R LEONARDO MALCHER

GLACIAL ▼

LOPPIANO ▼

To Banzeiro, Canto da Peixada,
and Delícia Grill

IGREJA DOS
REMÉDIOS

*Praça dos
Remédios*

R DOS ANDRADAS

R DOS BABES

AV. FLORIANO PEIXOTO

COELHO

AV. JOAQUIM NABUCO

R DR AIMINIO

R JOSE PARANAGUÁ

R WALTER RAYOL

CENTRO CULTURAL
USINA CHAMINÉ

*Igarapé dos
Educandos*

AV. 7 DE SETEMBRO

PALÁCIO
RIO NEGRO

MUSEU
DO INDIO

AV MIRANDA LEÃO

AV QUINTINO BOCAIÚVA

AV MANAUS MODERNA

AV CASTELO BRANCO

To Centro Cultural dos
Povos da Amazônia

To Bosque de
Ciência

© AVALON TRAVEL

0   200 yds

0   200 m

MERCADO MUNICIPAL
ADOLFO LISBOA

Following Rua Marquês de Santa Cruz toward the newer docks will bring you to the elegant and newly restored **Mercado Municipal Adolfo Lisboa** (Rua dos Barés 46, Centro, 8am-6pm daily). Designed in the 1880s by none other than Gustave Eiffel, the wrought iron art nouveau structure is a replica of Paris's famous Les Halles market. For hygienic purposes, in the 1990s the market's interior received a modernizing overhaul. However, the exotic produce on display is a feast for the senses. The best time to visit is in the early morning, when the atmosphere is at its most vibrant.

CENTRO CULTURAL
USINA CHAMINÉ

An artfully renovated neo-Renaissance sewage plant, built in 1910, houses the **Centro Cultural Usina Chaminé** (Av. Lourenço da Silva Braga, Centro, tel. 92/3633-3026, 10am-4pm Tues.-Fri., 5pm-8pm Sun.). The star attraction is the permanent exhibit "Sentidos da Amazônia," which ingeniously invites visitors to activate all five senses—ogling indigenous *artesanato,* listening to native chants, inhaling heady perfumes derived from native flora—as a means of absorbing Amazonian life and culture. There are also temporary exhibits and outdoor musical performances,

★ TEATRO AMAZONAS

Nothing conjures up the opulence of the rubber boom's heyday like the **Teatro Amazonas** (Praça São Sebastião, Centro, tel. 93/3232-1768, 9am-5pm Mon.-Sat.). Inaugurated in 1896, this sumptuous neoclassical opera house was financed by the city's rubber barons, who went all-out in the construction of this none-too-subtle pink palace crowned with a dome of 36,000 vivid green, yellow, and blue mosaic tiles that pay homage to the colors of the Brazilian flag. To adorn the interior, the finest materials from Europe were shipped across the Atlantic and up the Amazon: Alsatian glazed tiles, Portuguese marble, Venetian mirrors and crystal, French bronze and furnishings, Scottish cast-iron columns and banisters, and electrical fixtures from New York. The main stage curtain depicting the meeting of the Rio Negro and Rio Solimões was painted in Paris by Brazilian artist Crispim do Amaral. Italian artist Domenico de Angelis is responsible for the opulent ceiling frescoes featuring Indians, jaguars, and even a capybara. There

Rio Negro bridge

were only two exceptions to the all-imported rule: Precious local woods such as mahogany and jacaranda were used to make the theater's seats and exquisitely inlaid floors, and home-grown rubber (mixed with clay and sand) was used to pave the road leading up to the entrance so that late-arriving carriages wouldn't create noise during a performance.

Having undergone several restorations, the opera house is in excellent condition. It hosts the Festival Amazonas de Ópera and offers an intense schedule of performances, many of which are free. Even if you do decide to see a concert, it's also worthwhile taking the 30-minute guided tour (R$10). If the sidewalk out front—with its "wave" mosaic—seems familiar, it should; the curving bands of black and white, which represent the Meeting of the Waters, inspired the famous Copacabana boardwalk designed by Roberto Burle Marx.

PRAÇA DE SÃO SEBASTIÃO

The Teatro Amazonas sits on the Praça de São Sebastião, a square that has once again become a favorite Manauense gathering spot after undergoing a facelift in 2004. The formerly decrepit historic buildings surrounding the *praça* received much-needed renovations, and many now house galleries, boutiques, and cafés. By day, locals stop for a coffee or *tacacá,* and in the evenings they congregate at outdoor bars and take in the open-air performances of regional music sponsored by the city.

On the *praça,* you'll also find the **Igreja Largo São Sebastião** (7am-8pm daily). From the outside, this late 19th-century church sports a very untropically solemn gray facade. However, the interior is adorned with gleaming Italian marble, pretty stained glass windows, and luminous ceiling frescoes imported from Italy. Close to the church, the stately facade of the **Palácio de Justiça** (Av. Eduardo Ribeiro, Centro, tel. 92/3248-1844, 1pm-4pm Tues.-Fri., 5pm-9pm Sun.) mingles elements of French Second Empire style with English neoclassicism. Completed in 1900, the building housed the Amazonas state court until 2006, when it was converted into a cultural center. All of the original furnishings are intact, and you can literally sit in the place of a judge, juror, or culprit during a guided tour (every 30 minutes).

Blocks away, an attractive old mansion shelters the small but engaging (and almost always empty) **Museu Amazônica** (Rua Ramos Ferreira 1036, Centro, tel. 92/3232-3242, www.museuamazonico.ufam.edu.br, 8am-11:30am and 1:30pm-4:30pm Mon.-Fri.,

Teatro Amazonas

free), where both temporary and permanent exhibits of costumes, masks, weapons, and pottery testify to the rich diversity and artistic flair of Amazonia's indigenous peoples.

AVENIDA SETE DE SETEMBRO

Following Avenida Eduardo Ribeiro south toward the waterfront, you'll soon reach the Centro's main artery, Avenida Sete de Setembro. To the left, dominating the leafy Praça da Matriz, is the **Catedral de Nossa Senhora da Conceição** (9am-5pm Mon.-Sat.). Also known as the Igreja Matriz, this spare but handsome neoclassical cathedral was built in 1878 after the original 17th-century wooden church (Manaus's first) burned down.

Walking east along Avenida Sete, you'll pass the pretty triangular Praça da Polícia, which is dominated by the impressive **Palácio Provincial** (tel. 92/3622-8387, 9am-7pm Tues.-Thurs., 9am-8pm Fri.-Sat., 4pm-9pm Sun.). The former headquarters of the state police reopened in 2009 as a cultural center housing a quintet of small museums (admission free): the Museu de Numismática, with a collection of coins and bills from around the world; the Pinacoteca, which exhibits an intriguing ensemble of paintings by 19th- and 20th-century Manauense artists; the Museu Tiradentes, whose homage to the state's police forces and firefighters will appeal to those with a fetish for uniforms; the Museu de Arqueologia, with a musty collection of regionally excavated paraphernalia; and the Museu da Imagem e Som, which screens films, including some of the earliest known documentaries of Amazonian natives.

Along Avenida Sete and crossing the Igarapé de Manaus, is the **Palácio Rio Negro** (Av. Sete de Setembro 1546, tel. 92/3232-4450, 10am-4pm Tues.-Fri., 5pm-8pm Sun.), a magnificent example of nouveau riche rubber baron ostentation. This saffron-colored mini-palace was built in 1903 by a wealthy German rubber merchant named Waldemar Scholtz, who was notorious for his extravagant garden parties and his pet lion. When the

rubber boom went bust, Scholtz had to sell off his prize palace. It subsequently fell into the hands of the state and became the governor's palace. Today, the building functions as a cultural center. Amid the lavish period fixtures and furnishings, there are usually some temporary art exhibits.

A few blocks farther east, the **Museu do Índio** (Rua Duque de Caxias 356, Praça 14, tel. 92/3635-1922, 8am-11:30am and 1pm-4:30pm Mon.-Fri., 8:30am-11:30am Sat., R$8) provides an overview of the history, culture, and day-to-day life of the upper Amazon's indigenous peoples. Although the objects and artifacts—including bows, arrows, blow darts, pottery, masks, and drums used for long-distance communication—are fascinating, they're poorly displayed and lacking in explanations. The museum is run by the Irmãs Salesianas, an order of nuns who have various missions along the Amazon.

CENTRO CULTURAL DOS POVOS DA AMAZÔNIA

If Centro's modest museums leave you dissatisfied, head to the **Centro Cultural dos Povos da Amazônia** (Praça Francisco Pereira da Silva, Bola da Suframa, Distrito Industrial, tel. 92/2125-5300, www.povos-damazonia.am.gov.br, 9am-5pm Mon.-Fri., free). Anchoring this large complex, the Museu do Homem do Norte mixes interactive displays with a fine collection of artifacts and *artesanato*. Peek inside replicas of traditional Ianomâmi and Aruak dwellings and follow the manufacturing processes of both rubber and guaraná. Things get lively when musical and dance performances are held (check the website for schedules). To get here from Centro, it's only a short No. 625, 705, or 711 bus ride away.

MUSEU DO SERINGAL VILA PARAÍSO

In 2001, the Portuguese-Brazilian production team of a film titled *A Selva (The Jungle)* built a full-scale replica of a late 19th-century *seringal* (rubber plantation) in the middle of the rain forest an hour from Manaus. When filming was completed, the replica was converted into the **Museu do Seringal Vila Paraíso** (Igarapé São João, tel. 92/3631-3632, 8am-4pm Tues.-Sun., R$5). A visit to this open-air museum will take you on an evocative journey into the world of rubber tapping; you can observe actual rubber trees along with displays depicting the harrowing living and working conditions of the *seringueiros* (tappers), along with a faux rubber baron's opulent digs. Canoe taxis (25 minutes, R$18) leave from the Marina David in Ponta Negra and sail up the Rio Negro to the museum. From Centro, take the No. 11, 12, or 120 bus and get off in front of the Hotel Tropical, where there's a free shuttle to the Marina.

ENCONTRO DE ÁGUAS

Visiting the Encontro de Águas, or **Meeting of the Waters**—the point at which the muddy Rio Solimões hooks up with the bluish-black Rio Negro to form the Rio Amazonas—is like climbing to the top of the Empire State Building in New York. It's something you have to do, which is why this natural phenomenon is usually swarming with bobbing boats stuffed with camera-brandishing tourists. However, not even the theme park flavor and traffic jams can put a damper on the strange spectacle of the two rivers, which flow side by side for several kilometers before finally merging at a point some 10 kilometers (6 mi) from Manaus. On one side, you have the Rio Negro, whose darkness is a result of decomposing jungle vegetation that creates high acid levels. On the other is the Rio Solimões, whose light brown color betrays the presence of runoff soil from the Andes. The differences don't end there: While the Rio Negro meanders along sluggishly at 3 kilometers per hour (2 mph), the Solimões rushes by at 7 kilometers per hour (4.5 mph). If you trail your finger in the water, you'll also notice that the Rio Negro is considerably warmer than the Solimões.

You can check out the Meeting of the Waters on your own by taking bus No. 713 from the Praça da Matriz to the port, where there are always plenty of boats for hire as well as a municipal ferry that crosses the river. Most people, however, tend to visit the Meeting of the Waters as part of a guided trip (it is a classic attraction featured on many excursions). Usually offered as day trips, boats leave at 9am and return at 4pm. The standard R$140 fee charged by companies such as **Viverde** (tel. 92/3248-9988, www. viverde.com.br) and **Amazon Explorers** (tel. 93/2123-4777, http://amazonexplorers. tur.br) includes lunch on a floating restaurant. Tours inevitably include a stop at the **Reserva Ecológico do Lago de Janauari,** an ecological reserve located on a tributary of the Rio Negro whose *igarapés* (narrow creeks) and *igapós* (temporarily flooded forests) you can explore by canoe, or on foot during the dry season. The park's most photographed feature is the gigantic *Victoria amazonica* lily pads whose platter-shaped leaves, the size of coffee tables, dot the many lagoons. The lilies themselves have a three-day life span: When they blossom, they are milky white (day 1), then turn a blushing pink (day 2) and deepen to scarlet before withering up and dying (day 3). Although these excursions have become classic to the point of being hokey, they are enjoyable in a Disneyland kind of way. If you're heading to a jungle lodge or destination downriver, you'll be treated to a free glimpse of this aquatic phenomenon as you pass by.

Recreation
PARKS

For a preview of the rain forest, it's worth exploring Manaus's tropical parks. The **Bosque da Ciência** (Rua Otávio Cabral, Aleixo, tel. 92/3643-3293, www.inpa.gov.br/bosque, 9am-noon and 2pm-4:30pm Tues.-Fri., 9am-4pm Sat.-Sun., R$5) is a surviving chunk of jungle maintained by the Instituto Nacional da Pesquisa da Amazônia, a research center where you can inspect Amazonian flora and fauna ranging from rare orchids and caimans to giant otters and the extremely rare and odd-looking *peixe-bois* (manatees). There are walking paths (frequently crossed by sloths and anteaters) and a suspended tree-trekking trail that allows you to inspect the forest canopy up close. To get here, take bus No. 519 or minibus No. 810 from Praça da Matriz, which stop right near the entrance.

Operated by CIGS, a jungle survival unit of the Brazilian army, the **Parque Zoológico do CIGS** (Estrada da Ponta Negra 750, São Jorge, tel. 92/2125-6502, 8am-5pm Tues.-Sun., R$5) houses a diverse array of Amazonian animals rescued by military men during their training exercises in the forest. Beyond the more common caimans, monkeys, and macaws, you'll also run into black and spotted jaguars and a snake pit full of anacondas. It's hard not to feel torn by the animals' living conditions, which (mirroring Brazilian realities) range from spacious and well-equipped outdoor environments to prison-like cages. To get here, take bus No. 120 from Praça da Matriz.

BEACHES

Optimistically nicknamed "the Amazon's Copacabana," **Praia da Ponta Negra** is a far cry from Rio's famous beach. Although the presence of the Hotel Tropical and a renovated boardwalk with restaurants, bars, sports facilities, gardens, and an amphitheater has turned the area into a major tourist and recreational center, raw and ugly high-rises have given it an urban edge. It's pleasant enough to walk around Ponta Negra or to have a drink overlooking the river while watching the sunset. To beat the tropical heat, take a refreshing swim in the Rio Negro—improved lighting means you can now take moonlight dips as well. Ponta Negra is located 18 kilometers (11 mi) from the center of Manaus. To get here, take bus No. 120 from Praça da Matriz.

For more tranquil and idyllic surroundings, head to the wilder beaches a little farther out of town. Located 23 kilometers (14 mi) up the river, **Praia da Lua** boasts white sands backed by green foliage and plenty of (bathroom-less) *barracas* where you can gorge on fried fish. Note that this beach all

but disappears during the rainy season (Aug.-Jan.). From the Marina David in Ponta Negra, motorized launches (10 minutes, R$5) depart regularly to Praia da Lua (service is less frequent during the week).

Entertainment and Events
NIGHTLIFE

Manaus isn't famous for its nightlife, but you won't be bored. In Centro, you'll find lots of lively bars around the Mercado Municipal and Avenida Joaquim Nabuco as well as in the vicinity of the Teatro Amazonas. The beach neighborhood of Ponta Negra buzzes throughout the day and into the night with a series of riverfront bars, although it can get sleazy around the fringes.

In the center of town, near the Teatro de Amazonas, **Bar do Armando** (Rua 10 de Julho 593, Centro, tel. 92/3232-1195, 4pm-1am Sun.-Wed., 4pm-3am Thurs.-Sat.) started out as a 1950s corner grocery store. When big supermarket chains arrived in Manaus in the 1970s, owner Armando converted his store into a friendly neighborhood bar that hasn't lost any of its retro mom-and-pop flavor. Clients are welcome to choose background music from Armando's record collection before relaxing at red plastic tables with a cool beer and a thick *pernil* (pork) sandwich. An unpretentious place for beer and earthy atmosphere is the *tradicionalíssimo* **Bar Caldeira** (Rua José Clemente 237, Centro, tel. 92/3234-6574, 10am-2am Mon.-Sat., 8am-11pm Sun.), where locals have gathered since the swinging '60s to listen to happy hour *chorinho* and samba jams that inevitably lead to dancing in the street. More sophisticated but no less vibrant, **Bar Botequim** (Rua Barroso 279, Centro, tel. 92/3232-1030, 8pm-midnight Thurs., 8pm-3am Fri.-Sat., 5pm-9pm Sun., cover R$15-20) is a renovated old house where you can chill out on the sidewalk with a cocktail or inside, where homegrown musicians perform MPB, rock, and samba. Head next door to get your groove on at the GLS-friendly **Cabaret Night Club** (Rua Barroso 293, Centro, tel. 92/3622-9125, www.cabaretnightclub.net, 11pm-6am-3am Fri.-Sat., cover R$20-50), run by the same owner. The Belle Epoque building's décor is inspired by bordellos of yesteryear. Local and international DJs spin house, dance, and electronica, while go-go dancers gyrate in gilded cages.

PERFORMING ARTS

Take in a concert or dance performance at the landmark **Teatro Amazonas** (Praça São Sebastião, Centro, tel. 92/3232-1768). Amid the sumptuous ambiance, Manaus's opera house draws an impressive roster of talent, particularly when it hosts the renowned **Festival Amazonas de Ópera** (three weeks in April and May).

Shopping

Everyone who comes to Manaus inevitably wants to purchase traditional arts and handicrafts made by Amazonas's indigenous groups. There is no shortage of places to find items such as elaborately woven baskets, unusual seed jewelry, and ceramic pottery. Check out the **Mercado Adolpho Lisboa** (Rua dos Barés 46, 8am-6pm daily) or the wares for sale at the **Feira de Artesanato** (Praça Tenreiro Aranha, 7am-2pm Mon.-Sat.). For finer-quality objects whose origin and authenticity is guaranteed, try **Ecoshop** (Rua 10 de Julho 509, Centro, tel. 92/3234-8870, www.ecoshop.com.br, 9am-6pm Mon.-Fri., 9am-3pm Sat.). **Galeria Amazônica** (Rua Costa Azevedo 272, tel. 92/3233-4521, http:// galeriamazonica.org.br, 10am-8pm Mon.-Sat.) also has a good selection. A quick cab ride away, the **Central de Artesanato Branco e Silva** (Rua Recife 1999, Adrianópolis, tel. 92/3236-1241, 8:30am-6pm Mon.-Fri., 8am-4pm Sat.) reunites two dozen regional artisans who create original works of art using all native and organic materials, including palm fibers, tree bark, and brightly colored bird feathers.

The streets behind the Mercado Adolpho Lisboa, particularly Rua dos Barés and Rua Rocha dos Santos, have stores where you can pick up a hammock. Basic cheap ones can be had for R$30, but if you're investing in durability and beauty, expect to pay R$70-140. **Comercial São Bento** (Rua Miranda Leão 133, Centro, 8am-6pm Mon.-Fri., 8am-4pm Sat.) has a particularly wide selection. For more fashionable fare, check out the scads of boutiques at **Shopping Manauara** (Av. Mario Ypiranga 1300, Adrianópolis, tel. 92/4003-7760, www.manauarashopping. com.br, 10am-10pm Mon.-Sat., noon-10pm Sun.). Easily reached by bus from Praça da Matriz, this Amazonian-themed *shopping*—rustic wooden accents and jungly plants abound—also has the usual cinemas, a food court with some decent eating options, ATMs, and cybercafés.

Accommodations

Manaus's hotel industry is mostly geared to business travelers. However, a new spate of budget hotels and basic hostels have opened in Centro. If you choose a so-called three-star, prepare for the inferior quality for the price you pay. The good news is that rates have actually been falling.

Manaus' newest hostel is also its best. Within spitting distance of the Teatro Amazonas, **Local Hostel** (Rua Marcal 72, Centro, www.hostels.com/hostels/manaus/ local-hostel-manaus, R$60-80 d, R$35-45 pp) is a small, sustainable dream awash in tropical shades, beds and bunks made of rustic recycled wood, and indigenous accents such as fibrous lighting fixtures. Rooms are tight, but clean. Dorms (for four, six, and eight) have individual outlets, lockers, and reading lamps as well as privacy curtains. Apart from a communal kitchen, an attractive bar features a daily happy hour that allows guests to trade tales with the friendly English-speaking owners. Close by, the ★ **Boutique Hotel Casa Teatro** (Rua Dez de Julho 632, Centro, tel. 92/3633-8381, www.casateatro.com.br, R$140-210 d) is a charming option with soothing common areas. Rooms are crazily small (standards share bathrooms and resemble ships' cabins), but fresh and stylish. Some boast views of the Teatro Amazonas, as does the rooftop lounge.

Only a block from the Teatro, the reliable and efficient **Go Inn** (Rua Monsenhor Coutinho 560, Centro, tel. 92/3306-2600, www.atlanticahotels.com.br, R$180-220 d) offers spotless, bright, and compact guest rooms that indulge with amenities (Wi-Fi, flat-screen TVs, DVD players) while keeping services to a bare minimum. A little more upscale is the well-run **Hotel Saint Paul** (Rua Ramos Ferreira 1115, Centro, tel. 92/2101-3800, www.hotelsaintpaul.tur. br, R$210-290 d), whose comfortable 1- and 2-bedroom suites are spacious and spotless, with living areas and small kitchens. Alleviating the sterile atmosphere are the photos of Amazonian flora and views overlooking the Teatro (not all rooms feature the views; make sure you request yours). Modest conveniences include a pool, sauna, fitness center, and restaurant.

Since it first opened in the mid-1970s, the legendary **Tropical Manaus** (Av. Coronel Teixeira 1320, Ponta Negra, tel. 92/2123-5000, www.tropicalhotel.com.br, R$320-380 d) has been whetting appetites of travelers whose dreams of "roughing it" in the Amazon include living it up in high style. Set amid a patch of jungle spanning the banks of Rio Negro, this sprawling and scenic resort is neither luxurious nor stylish, but it has managed to retain some grandeur. Guest rooms are comfortable if somewhat dated—those in the "colonial" wing, outfitted with hardwood floors and dark wood furnishings, have more personality. Things should improve with the ongoing renovations being undertaken for the 2014 World Cup. Amenities include various bars, shops, restaurants, swimming pools, and a spa as well as tennis courts, a playground, an archery range, an orchid hothouse, and a rather sad zoo. While you're 20 kilometers (12 mi), or a R$60 cab ride, from downtown Manaus, you're only a quick walk from Ponta Negra's river beaches and nightlife. This is an ideal choice for families.

Food

Although the Manaus region's river boasts more than 2,000 species of fish, four in particular are likely to make an appearance on your plate. The meat of the gigantic *pirarucu* is used to make everything from crunchy *bolinhos* and soups to stews such as *pirarucu de casaca,* in which it is dressed in a "coat" (*casaco*) of potatoes, olives, onions, tomatoes, and boiled eggs. *Tambaqui* is delicious when roasted in its skin over hot charcoal. *Tucunaré* is a popular ingredient in *caldeiradas,* thick chowders that are seasoned with *tucupi* and *jambu* leaves. And, of course, you've heard of piranha, which (when defanged) makes a delicious soup that is considered to be an aphrodisiac.

Also irresistible are the endless variety of Amazonian fruits. Botanists have uncovered 200 types (and are still counting). Indians believe the forest's fruits are divine gifts. You'll find it easy to concur when you savor fruits such as *maracujá-de-mato* (a type of wild passion fruit), *biribá, sapucaia, bajurá,* and *piquiá* as well as the more popular *cupuaçu, bacuri,* and *açaí;* all are used to make fresh juices, ice creams, and myriad desserts. Although not quite as big as the ones Carmen Miranda wore on her head, giant *pacova* bananas grow to lengths of 50 centimeters (20 inches). In the center of town, you'll find *barracas* where you can purchase fried *pacova* chips or *pacova* cubes that are drizzled in condensed milk. Don't skip town without biting into a *sanduíche caboclinho,* a vegetarian offering made with a baguette and slices of a yellow Amazonian fruit known as *tucumã.* Since the fruit is pretty strong, you might want to dilute it by ordering a *x-caboclinho,* in which the *tucumã* is attenuated with melted *coalho* cheese (the "x").

CAFÉS AND SNACKS

Right in front of the Teatro Amazonas, **Tacacá da Gisela** (Largo São Sebastião, Centro, tel. 92/8801-4901, 4pm-10pm daily) has become a tourist attraction in its own right. The thick broth featuring *tucupi, jambu*

Guaraná

Although Coca-Cola has made inroads in Brazil as both a refreshing soft drink and a pick-me-up, it has never usurped the place of *guaraná*. Moreover, Coke has none of the health (nor reputed aphrodisiac) benefits that the Indians of central Amazonas first discovered centuries ago, when they began harvesting the tiny red *guaraná* berry, whose visible black seed resembles a tiny eye. Aside from its antioxidant and antibacterial properties, *guaraná* contains around four times as much caffeine as coffee beans. Since the 1920s, *guaraná* has been a key ingredient in the eponymous soft drink (in diluted form, so the kids won't get a buzz). While major brands of bottled *guaraná*, such as Antarctica and Kuat, are common throughout Brazil, smaller labels such as Baré, Real, and Tuchauá can only be found in Manaus. However, Indians and purists prefer imbibing the real thing, which involves mixing dried *guaraná* powder (which is quite chalky and bitter) with sweetened *guaraná* syrup and any number of local fruits. In Manaus, **Guaraná Saterê** (Rua Marcília Diaz 257, Centro, tel. 92/3233-8113, 7am-7pm Mon.-Fri., 7am-5pm Sat.) is a traditional *casa* that specializes in *guaraná*. Aside from getting an instant jolt on the spot, you can also purchase the fruit in dried and powdered form.

leaves, and shrimp, prepared by *tacaqueira* Rosa Maria, is considered the best in town. Chairs set up on the sidewalk make this a relaxing place to hang out, especially on Wednesday afternoons, when local musicians get together to jam. **Casa da Pamonha** (Rua Barroso 375, Centro, tel. 92/3233-1028, 7am-7pm Mon.-Fri., 7am-2pm Sat.) is a simple little place where locals stop throughout the day to nosh on sweet and savory tamale-like *pamonhas*, baked goods (try the cupuaçu cake!), and *caboclinho* sandwiches. At lunch, there is a nicely priced vegetarian per-kilo self-service buffet.

Nothing staves off Manaus's heat better than an ice cream. With various locations to choose from, **Glacial** (Av. Getúlio Vargas 161-A, Centro, tel. 92/3233-7940, www.glacial.com.br, 10am-11:30pm daily) serves up some of the best in town by mixing Italian gelato-making techniques with Amazonian ingredients such as Brazil nuts, *tucumã, taperabá,* and *pupunha*. Another great heat-beater are the fresh fruit juices available at **Skina dos Sucos** (Av. Eduardo Ribeiro 639, Centro, tel. 92/3233-1970, 7am-8pm Mon.-Fri., 7am-7pm Sat.). For extra energy (or a liquid lunch), opt for a *vitamina* such as *guaraná veneno*, a potent mix of *guaraná* syrup, quail's egg, peanuts, milk, and honey.

PER-KILO BUFFET

Although the décor verges on institutional, the selection of dishes at **Delícia Grill** (Rua Joaquim Sarmento 333, Centro, Nossa Senhora das Graças, tel. 92/3232-1853, 11am-3pm Mon.-Sat., R$15-25) transcends run-of-the-mill per-kilo fare. Offerings include healthy salads, sizzling skewers of barbecued meat, and some unorthodox takes on Amazonian classics, such as *pirarucu* bathed in *tucumã* and *tambaqui* in ginger sauce. For a change from Amazonian fare, nothing beats a good old-fashioned pizza.

PIZZA

Loppiano (Rua Major Gabriel 1080, Praça 14, tel. 92/3622-4000, www.loppiano.com.br, 5pm-11:30pm Sun.-Thurs., 5pm-1am Fri.-Sat., R$25-35) serves up decent thin-crust versions with a variety of traditional toppings. *Rodízios* offer the famished an endless, all-you-can-eat parade of options (Mon.-Thurs., R$28).

REGIONAL

The best place to savor typical Amazonian cuisine is ★ **Banzeiro** (Rua Libertador 102, Nossa Senhora das Graças, tel. 92/3234-1621, www.restaurantebanzeiro.com.br, 11:30am-4pm daily, 6:30pm-11:30pm Tues.-Sat., 7pm-10pm Sun., R$30-45). Chef Felipe Schaedler often journeys into the Amazonian Interior in search of fresh and novel ingredients to compose his innovative dishes. The most succulent exploit the bounty of the region's rivers, such as shrimp on black rice with chicory and *pirarucu* bacon and cashew-encrusted *tambaqui* with baked banana. Dessert is seldom more sublime than *cupuaçu* petit gateau topped with tapioca ice cream. The understated dining room's soothing earth tones are enlivened by tasteful integration of indigenous artifacts. Manaus's oldest and most venerated *peixaria*, **Canto da Peixada** (Rua Emílio Moreira 1677, Praça 14, tel. 92/3234-3021, 11:30am-3:30pm and 6:30pm-10:30pm Mon.-Sat., 11am-4pm Sun., R$25-40) is where locals go for expertly prepared Amazonian fish. Whet your appetite with the crisp, turnover-like *pastéis de pirarucu* before digging into a *caldeirada* (stew) featuring *tucunaré* or a perfectly grilled *tambaqui*. Although the decor is nothing special, service is attentive.

Information and Services

The main state tourist office, **Amazonastur** (www.visitamazonas.am.gov.br), has several tourist kiosks with branches in Centro (Av. Eduardo Ribeiro 666, Centro, tel. 92/3182-6250, 8am-5pm Mon.-Fri., 8am-noon Sat.), as well as at the airport (tel. 92/3182-9850, open 24 hours) and the port (Rua Marquês de Santa Cruz, Centro, tel. 92/3182-7950, 8am-5pm Mon.-Fri.). Aside from city maps, the helpful staff can provide you with information regarding tour operators (i.e., which ones are legit). For extensive information and listings in Portuguese, check www.manausonline.com.

For exchanging money or withdrawing cash from an ATM, there's a **Banco do Brasil** (Rua Guilherme Moreira 315, Centro) downtown. You'll also find banks on Avenida Eduardo Ribeiro, including a Bradesco on the corner of Rua Saldanha Marinho. Just behind Praça São Sebastião, there is a **post office** on Rua Barroso 226.

In the event of an emergency, dial **192** for an ambulance, **193** for the fire department,

and **190** for the police. For medical treatment, try the **Hospital 28 de Agosto** (Rua Recife 1581, Adrianópolis, tel. 92/3643-4800). The **Hospital de Doenças Tropicais** (Av. Pedro Teixeira 25, Dom Pedro, tel. 92/3238-1146) specializes in tropical diseases and also gives free yellow fever vaccines.

Transportation

Most people arrive in Manaus by air (there are even direct flights from Miami). Due to the precarious state of the roads throughout Amazonas, bus travel is minimal. The most prevalent means of regional travel is by boat.

AIR

Flights arrive at the **Aeroporto Eduardo Gomes** (Av. Santos Dumont, Tarumã 1350, tel. 92/3652-1210), which is 17 kilometers (10 mi) from the center of town. The fixed price for a taxi to Centro is R$60. You can also take municipal buses No. 306 (R$2.25) and the more comfortable, air-conditioned *executivo* No. 813 (R$4.65), which run at 30-minute intervals between the airport and Praça do Matriz, with stops along Avenida Getúlio Vargas.

BUS

Long-distance buses arrive at the small, run-down *rodoviária* (Rua Recife 2784, Flores, tel. 92/3642-5805), 10 kilometers (6 mi) north of Centro. To get downtown, take the same buses, No. 306 or No. 813, which pass by on their way to the airport, or take a taxi (R$25-30).

Most of Centro can easily be explored by foot. To get to Ponta Negra, take bus No. 120 or a taxi (R$55-60). Praça da Matriz is the main transportation hub—from here you can hop a municipal bus (R$2.25) to just about anywhere.

BOAT

If you arrive by boat from Belém or Santarém, you'll disembark at the **Estação Hidroviária** (Rua Marquês de Santa Cruz 25, Centro, tel. 92/3621-7069, www.portodemanaus.com.br)

on the Porto Flutuante in the heart of the city. If you don't have too much luggage, you can walk to hotels in Centro. Speed boats to Tefé and Parintins use the **Porto da Manaus Moderna** behind the Mercado Municipal Adolpho Lisboa. Slow boats up the Rio Negro leave and arrive from **Porto São Raimundo**, located in an unsafe *bairro* 1.5 kilometers (1 mi) northwest of Porto Flutuante; take a cab.

CAR AND TAXI

Taxis are plentiful (and recommended at night). Hail one in the street or call **Rádio Taxi Golfinho** (tel. 92/3625-6000). As for renting a car, there is really not much point. You can easily walk to most city sights, while everything outside Manaus is basically rain forest; the only towns you can really drive to are Presidente Figueiredo and Novo Airão. To rent a car, try **Avis** (tel. 92/3652-1579, www.avis.com.br), which has a branch at the airport.

CITY TOURS

Visiting Manaus and the surrounding area can be done by bus, boat, or even plane. **Viverde** (tel. 92/3248-9988, www.viverde.com.br) offers half-day, English-language city tours of Manaus's major attractions for R$110 pp (for two people). **Swallows and Amazons** (tel. 92/3622-1246, www.swallowsandamaazontours.com) and **Amazon Eco Adventures** (Rua 10 de Julho 695, Centro tel. 92/8831-1011, http://amazonecoadventures.com) offer more unusual and slightly more expensive tours. A cheaper alternative to taking an organized tour is to hop aboard the **Amazon Bus** (tel. 92/3633-6708, 9am Thurs.-Sat. and 2pm Tues.-Sat., R$60), an open-topped, double-decker bus that will whisk you around past all the main sights from Centro to Praia de Ponta Negra (the two-hour trip's only stop). Buses depart from in front of the tourist kiosk next to the Teatro Amazonas.

For a bird's-eye view of the Amazon, Viverde will take you up in a hydroplane that departs from the river, in front of the Hotel Tropical. A 30-minute flight over the fabulous patchwork of city, forest, and Meeting of the Waters costs a whopping R$450 pp (for two people) and R$300 pp (four people), but the view from above is truly unforgettable.

AROUND MANAUS
Presidente Figueiredo

Located 107 kilometers (64 mi) north of Manaus on the road to Venezuela, Presidente Figueiredo is a small town that has become a favorite ecotourist getaway. Although the surrounding region is filled with rain forest, creeks and rivers, and caves containing prehistoric paintings, the main attractions here are the 100 waterfalls that have won the town the nickname of Terra das Cachoeiras (Land of Waterfalls). Tributaries of the Rio Negro, the water of these numerous cascades is a striking jet-black color. Diving into the pools and opening your eyes underwater is an intense experience. So is splashing around and getting a pummeling massage amid a setting of rocks, ferns, and tropical forest. Among the best falls closest to town are **Suframa** (11 km/7 mi), **Iracema** (12 km/7.5 mi), and **Santuário** (16 km/10 mi). If you don't have a car, hire a taxi or *moto-taxi*. For a guide, get in touch with the **tourist office** (tel. 92/3324-1308), who can recommend one. Among the most worthwhile excursions is to **Caverna Maroaga**. Situated within a preservation area, this cave is guarded by a waterfall that pours into a pool in which you can bathe. The cave is reached by a moderate hike along a trail flanked by gigantic trees.

Presidente Figueiredo is known for its *cupuaçus*. Should you miss the annual **Cupuaçu Festival** (early June), stock up on jellies, liqueurs, and candies made with the ambrosial fruit at **Praça da Cultura** (Box 5, 8am-10pm daily).

ACCOMMODATIONS AND FOOD

Presidente Figueiredo can be enjoyed in a day, but it's worth spending the night at one of the half-dozen simple *pousadas* in and around town. Avoid weekends when the place is mobbed by Manauenses. **Pousada Jiboia**

(Rua Copaiba, 69 Bairro Honório Roudão, tel. 92/3324-1228, www.pousadajiboia.com. br, R$120 d) is a tranquil choice within easy walking distance to the bus station and commercial center. Rooms sleep up to five and are small and Spartan, but tidy. The garden has a small pool and nearby trails lead to waterfalls. The *pousada* staff can organize outings to falls and caves as well as forest hikes.

TRANSPORTATION

Getting to Presidente Figueiredo is easy via BR-174, the only paved road heading out of Manaus. If you want to rent a car, the trip is a scenic one. **Aruanã** (tel. 92/3642-5757) offers five buses daily from Manaus's *rodoviária* (2 hours, R$20). Manaus tour operators such as **Amazon Eco Adventures** (Rua 10 de Julho 695, Centro tel. 92/8831-1011, http://amazonecoadventures.com), **Amazon Explorers** (tel. 93/2123-4777, http://amazonexplorers.tur.br) and **Swallows and Amazons** (Rua Ramos Ferreira 922, Centro, Sala 13, tel. 92/3622-1246, www.swallowsandamaazontours.com) offer day trips here; expect to pay around R$180 pp including meals.

INTO THE AMAZON RAIN FOREST

Most people's ultimate destination is not Manaus but the Amazon rain forest. From Manaus, you can get a taste of the rain forest with day trips, but if you want to get away from civilization (and the distance it takes to "get away" is constantly increasing), experience "virgin" forest, and see some wildlife, the best way to do so is by taking a longer tour or excursion into the rain forest, with the option of sleeping on a boat or in the forest at a camp or jungle lodge, known as a *hotel de selva*. Depending on your interests as well as time and money constraints, there are several options available.

One way is to book an excursion with a *reputed* and specialized **ecotourist agency** based in Manaus. An average tour lasts 2-6 days and usually includes typical outings such as hiking in the forest and canoeing through *igarapés* (narrow creeks) and *igapós* (temporarily flooded forests) in search of wildlife. Guaranteed sightings include flocks of birds and frolicking schools of pink dolphins; less frequent are monkeys and sloths and jaguars are almost impossible. The famous piranha is omnipresent, and piranha fishing with a bamboo pole and a chunk of beef as bait is a classic activity few visitors can resist. The best times for viewing animals are around sunrise and sunset. However, nighttime is when the forest really comes to life with symphonic screeches, squawks, grunts, shuffles, and ribbets. A popular (and somewhat spooky) nocturnal pastime is looking for caimans with a flashlight. They are quite easy to identify by their glow-in-the-dark eyes. As proof that these reptiles have a softer side, your guide will inevitably grab a baby caiman by the neck and invite you to caress its spiny carapace.

Many tours also include visits to the homes of local *caboclos* (mixed descendants of Indians and Portuguese) who live in stilt houses along the river. Many are quite poor and have little contact with the rest of Brazil. These visits can be interesting—you may watch milky latex being heated over a fire to become rubber, or manioc being pounded into the *farinha* (flour) that is a main food staple—and sometimes a little exploitative.

Accommodations on tours can range from basic bunks on a boat and hammocks or tents in the forest to a night at an exclusive jungle lodge with air-conditioning and gourmet meals. Make sure you know what you're getting for your money. Consider how much roughing it in the wilds you're prepared for. You'll want to make sure of your guides' qualifications: Most guides work as freelancers, and it's nice if they not only speak English but also know something about the Amazon's flora and fauna instead of improvising as they go along. It's also worth confirming the type of transportation that will be used to explore smaller waterways—noiseless motors or old-fashioned paddle canoes are better than noisy and polluting motorboats that scare off wildlife.

Another way of exploring the forest is to book one of the many **jungle lodges** that have increasingly sprung up along banks of the Rio Negro and Rio Solimões. Spending a few days in a lodge is a wonderful way to experience the jungle, because you'll be living in it. Perched ideally and idyllically right on a river, often on stilts, many lodges are situated amid primary rain forest. Lodges vary significantly in terms of size, price, and comfort level. As a general rule, farther away from Manaus and smaller (intimate and personalized versus noisy and touristy) is better. While you want enough creature comforts (fans and mosquito netting are helpful), you don't really need cable TV or a spa. Whether downright rustic or eco chic, expect jungle lodges to be fairly pricy; most sell packages (usually 2-6 days); if you stay longer—and you'll want to—the daily price diminishes. Lodging includes rain forest and river activities, meals, and sometimes transportation from Manaus. Your exposure to locals will be minimal; most of your companions will be other environmentally minded gringos.

Given that boats are the main means of transportation in the Amazon, you can very easily hop one and go wherever you want. Whether you splurge for a luxury riverboat for well-heeled ecotourists or string up your freshly purchased hammock alongside those of Amazonenses traveling downriver in the direction of Belém, adventure is guaranteed.

Up the Rio Solimões

The muddy river that stretches west from Manaus all the way to Brazil's border with Peru and Colombia is known as the Rio Solimões. Although it is actually more of a café-au-lait color, the Rio Solimões is known as a "white" river due to the fact that its waters are laden with a high concentration of rich soil. During the wet season, when the river floods the surrounding land, it leaves highly fertile silt deposits that encourage plant, animal, and insect life. The ramifications for ecotourists are twofold: While you'll tend to see more wildlife along the Rio Solimões than

along the Rio Negro, you'll also have to fend off more mosquitoes.

Traveling upstream by boat along the Rio Solimões, there are several areas that offer stunning expanses of prime rain forest with the possibility of viewing wildlife. Only a half-day journey from Manaus is the area surrounding **Lago Mamori,** where you can glimpse birds, caimans, and pink river dolphins, and the piranha fishing is great. Farther along, and more remote, is the **Lago Juma.**

★ **RESERVA DE DESENVOLVIMENTO SUSTENTÁVEL DE MAMIRAUÁ**
The hottest eco-spot along the Rio Solimões is the Reserva de Desenvolvimento Sustentável de Mamirauá. The largest protected area of *várzea* (Amazonian forest that is seasonally flooded with "white" river water) within Brazil, the reserve is monitored by the **Instituto de Desenvolvimento Sustentável de Mamirauá** (Estrada do Bexiga 2584, Fonte Boa, tel. 97/3343-9700, www.mamiraua.org.br, 8am-noon and 2pm-6pm Mon.-Fri., 8am-noon Sat.), whose mission is to combine conservation and scientific research with the creation of sustainable employment and lifestyles for local inhabitants. Apart from traditional fishing and agriculture, an increasing percentage of the local *caboclo* population work as guides and forest patrollers. Their efforts have not been in vain: The forest is in pristine condition, and exploring its jungles, rivers, and lagoons will give you the sensation of having returned to a primordial Eden. As a result, Mamirauá is one of the best places to see wildlife—caimans, pink dolphins, sloths, and myriad birds and monkeys (if you're lucky, you might even get to see the very rare scarlet-faced uakari monkey). Located at the confluence of the Solimões with the Rio Japurá, the reserve is close to the town of **Tefé,** which also happens to be the last outpost of civilization along the Solimões.

Visiting the reserve on your own involves a long boat trip to Tefé or a far speedier and

Pink River Dolphins

Of the five species of freshwater dolphins in the world, the most legendary are the pink dolphins of the Amazon. Nicknamed **botos** by Brazilians, these friendly, sensitive mammals boast a brain capacity that is 40 percent larger than that of humans. Perhaps this explains how they have lived in harmony with the Amazon's indigenous groups for centuries. There is no ready explanation for their characteristic pink flesh; possible factors include iron content in the river water and capillaries near the surface of the skin. Unfortunately, recent devastation of the Amazonian environment has put their existence at risk.

more expensive one-hour direct flight from Manaus. Tefé is a lazy little river town with two pretty main squares that is slowly becoming an ecotourist hub. If you choose to base yourself here, the best place to stay is the simple but welcoming **Pousada Multicultura** (Rua 15 de Junho 136, Juruá, tel. 97/3343-6632, www.pousadamulticultura.com, R$90-130 d), which is a 15-minute walk from the center of town. Even if you don't choose a room with a beguiling view of Lake Tefé, you can ogle the scenery (and Skype envious pals via free Wi-Fi) from a rooftop café. The multilingual Dutch-Brazilian owners offer all sorts of services, ranging from the advance purchase of airplane e-tickets and boat tickets (highly recommended despite the 15 percent service charge) to organizing guided outings to the Reserva and other natural attractions as well as to indigenous communities. Both the *pousada* and the Instituto Mamirauá are excellent sources of information and can help you (even before you actually arrive in the Amazon) to plan a trip.

From Porto da Manaus Moderna, in Centro, **slow boats to Tefé** (R$130 hammock, R$450-550 cabin for two) leave at 8am Mon.-Sat. The journey takes around 40 hours. From the same port, speedboats operated by **AJATO** (tel. 92/3622-6047, R$220 including lunch and dinner) depart at 7am Mon. and Wed.-Sat. and arrive in Tefé 13 hours later. Currently, **Trip** (tel. 40003-1118, www.voeazul.com.br) offers two daily flights to Tefé from Manaus, as does **Amazonaves** (tel. 3654-5555, www.amazonaves.com.br), an aero-taxi operator, which charges around R$350. Schedules change, as do fares. In all cases, it's wise to purchase tickets in advance.

★ JUNGLE LODGES (HOTÉIS DE SELVA)

Located 100 kilometers (62 mi) south of Manaus, the **Juma Amazon Lodge** (Lago do Rio Juma, tel. 92/3232-2707, www.jumalodge.com.br, R$1,615-1,860 pp for a three-day package) is a three-hour boat ride from Manaus along the Rio Solimões. Completely integrated into the preserved jungle, this intimate, sustainable, and totally secluded lodge is an exercise in camouflage. Wooden structures on stilts connected by suspended walkways are designed according to indigenous techniques. The cabins feel like tree houses. All of them feature verandas that gaze onto either bird-filled branches or the river, where it is not uncommon to see dolphins cavorting. For exploring on your own, the lodge has dugout canoes you can paddle around.

The most radically eco of all the Amazon's lodges, ★ **Uakari Floating Lodge** (tel. 97/3343-4160, www.uakarilodge.com.br, R$1,350-1,420 pp for a three-day package) boasts an unbeatable location in the midst of the Reserva Mamirauá. Getting here requires flying or sailing up the Rio Solimões to Tefé, then taking a 90-minute speedboat ride (provided by the *pousada*). The accommodations are in floating wood cabins that are alluringly rustic. All water comes from the river and is heated by solar energy. Recycling is a mantra. As part of the reserve's commitment to sustainable development, local communities are involved in the operation of the *pousada* as well as leading jungle tours. Scientists who work at the Mamirauá Sustainable Research Institute are frequently present. They conduct nature talks for guests (many of whom are often scientists and naturalists), and you can often accompany them into the field, sleeping overnight in tents.

Up the Rio Negro

The dark river that flows into Manaus from the remote reaches of northwestern Amazonas is known as the Rio Negro. Its somber hue is actually more reddish-brown than black, yet it is known as a "black" river due to the fact that its waters are filled with rotting vegetation from low-lying forests. The abundance of decaying organic matter results in a high level of acidity. As a result, its waters don't have the same fertilizing properties as "white" rivers such as the Solimões. A bonus is that the high acidity kills insect larvae, which results in a low instance of mosquito attacks.

★ ARQUIPÉLAGO DE ANAVILHANAS

The most fascinating and easily accessible destination along the Rio Negro is the **Arquipélago de Anavilhanas,** access to which is via the town of Novo Airão. The second-largest freshwater archipelago in the world, it has been transformed into one of the largest national parks in the world and boasts upward of 400 islands. During the dry season (Sept.-Jan.), many of them are fringed with beautiful white-sand beaches. If you don't mind sharing with flocks of wild birds, you'll have them completely to yourself. The rest of the year, many vanish due to the rising Rio Negro, leaving the submerged forest, inhabited by caymans, anteaters, monkeys, and myriad birds, to be explored by boat. If you go swimming, you'll very likely find yourself frolicking with schools of friendly pink dolphins.

Novo Airão has a couple of good accommodations options. Somewhat removed from the center of town and the river, **Pousada**

Tarântula (Rua Nova Esperança 44, Qd H, Santo Elias, tel. 92/3671-2731, tarantula@amazoniaexpeditions.com.br, R$90-120 d) offers basic, but accommodating single, double, and triple rooms amidst a relaxing oasis of tropical fruit trees and native forest. A small pool helps beat the heat. On a lush estate overlooking the Rio Negro, the **Pousada Bela Vista** (Av. Presidente Vargas 47, Centro, tel. 92/3365-1023, www.pousada-belavista.com, R$150 d) offers simple wood-paneled guest rooms overlooking a pool or the river (quieter and with balconies). Bonuses include an on-site restaurant-bar and private river access as well as a helpful English-speaking German owner who also operates **Em Cantos da Amazônia** (tel. 92/3365-1405, http://emcantosdaamazonia.com/expedicoes).

Expedição Katerre (tel. 92/3365-1644, www.katerre.com) is an experienced local ecotour operator that can organize multiday river excursions along the Rio Negro, as well as boat trips into Anavilhanas and Jaú national parks (if you have more time, it's worth exploring). Located 100 kilometers (62 mi) from Novo Airão by boat, **Parque Nacional do Jáu** is a UNESCO world heritage site that constitutes the largest forest reserve in the Americas. It is home to black caymans, two species of river dolphin, and the largest array of electric fish on the planet. Advance reservations are necessary to visit the park; accommodations are in tents or at the homes of local fishermen and rubber tappers.

Getting to Novo Airão is fairly easy, particularly with the 2011 inauguration of the impressive bridge spanning the Rio Negro. If you have a car, simply cross the bridge and then follow the AM-70 for 80 kilometers (50 mi) in the direction of Manacapuru before turning onto the AM-352 for another 100 kilometers (62 mi). If you're without wheels, there is a stop at the crossroads of the bridge road and Avenida Brasil where you can catch a collective minibus or van to Novo Airão (2.5 hours, R$35 pp). From Manaus's Porto São Rãimundo, speedboats (3.5 hours, R$25) leave daily at 3pm. From the *rodoviária,* **Aruanã** (tel. 92/3642-5757) offers two daily bus departures (five hours, R$37) at 11:30am and 4pm. *Pousadas* in Novo Airão can also reserve a taxi transfer (R$230) from Manaus' airport.

★ JUNGLE LODGES
(HOTÉIS DE SELVA)

One of the more affordable jungle lodges, the laid-back Franco-Brazilian-owned **Malocas Jungle Lodge** (Lago Acajatuba, tel. 92/3648-0119, www.malocas.com, R$800 pp for a three-day package) is located along the sandy white banks of the Rio Preto da Eva, three hours from Manaus. Rustic accommodations in indigenous-style *malocas* (traditional circular-shaped Indian dwellings made of wood and palm thatch) are 100-percent solar powered, and canoes are favored over motorboats, allowing abundant wild macaws and toucans to provide a continuous soundtrack. Tours led by *caboclo* guides include hiking to surrounding waterfalls and overnight forest campouts.

A 90-minute boat trip from Novo Airão, the ★ **Anavilhanas Jungle Lodge** (tel. 92/3622-8996, www.anavilhanaslodge.com, R$1,650-2,160 pp for a three-day package) is probably the most elegant *hotel de selva*. The entire structure is an enchanting lesson in rain-forest minimalism. Its 16 air-conditioned guest rooms, paneled in tropical woods and decorated with Amazonian *artesanato,* are complemented by an open-air lounge area with lots of books and DVDs. There is also a gorgeous pool and a pretty restaurant that serves gourmet fare such as *dourado* fish in ginger sauce and coconut flan. For adventure, you have the 400-plus islands of the Arquipélago Anavilhanas at your disposal. All guides are knowledgeable locals who know the *igarapés* and *igapós* like the back of their hands.

Ecotours and Excursions

There are scores of tour operators who will offer to take you up the Rio Solimões, the Rio Negro, and its tributaries. Some will even take you on both. Most people go on excursions that last 2-4 days, but it's possible to find 1-2-week excursions that journey into very remote areas. Long before you get to Manaus, do some research and check out tour companies' websites in advance. Take a look at the boats and accommodations available and make sure guides speak English and have some knowledge of the rain forest. If in doubt, also check the company's credentials with Amazonastur (www.visitamazonas.am.gov.br), the state tourist bureau. Ecotourism has

a jungle-lodge in Amazonas

become a big business, and the minute you get to Manaus you'll be accosted at the airport, bus terminal, or ports by locals offering excursions. Just give them a firm but polite *"Não, obrigado/a."* Even if they flash a brochure from a reputed agency such as those listed here, refuse—there have been reports of scammers impersonating legitimate operators. Before you fork out any money, get in writing everything that's included in the price of your excursion. Usually a decent budget excursion will cost R$150-200 per day, while a more specialized excursion with more upscale accommodations will set you back R$250-400 per day. It's not worth your while to skimp over a few *reais* in the Amazon.

Amazon Gero's Tours (Rua Dez de Julho 679, Sala 2, Centro, tel. 92/3232-4755 or 92/9983-6273, www.amazongerotours.com) is run by experienced and friendly English-speaking guide Geraldo ("Gero") Mesquita. Gero customizes reasonably priced tours throughout the region, especially along Rio Solimões around the areas of Lago Mamori and Lago Juma (Gero owns his own jungle lodge, the Ararinha Jungle Hotel, in the region). Accommodations can be on boats, in jungle lodges, in hammocks, or even with local families in villages.

Highly recommended is **Swallows and Amazons** (Rua Ramos Ferreira 922, Centro, Sala 13, tel. 92/3622-1246, www.swallowsandamaazontours.com), a small company owned by American Mark Aitchison and his Brazilian wife, Tania, that custom-designs top-notch riverboat, jungle lodge, and adventure tours for small groups that usually last a week or more. Swallows and Amazons organizes trips along the still wild and unspoiled upper Rio Negro, including the Arquipélago de Anavilhanas and Jaú national parks. The all-inclusive excursions cater to various interests and can include activities such as diving, bird-watching, fishing, and canoeing as well as stays with *caboclo* families.

Pedro Fernandes, the savvy and solicitous owner of **Amazon Eco Adventures** (Rua 10 de Julho 695, Centro tel. 92/8831-1011, http://amazonecoadventures.com), has a knack for making even the most banal experience fresh and exciting. Many of his tours run the gamut from waterskiing and rafting to multiday riverboat journeys and "survival training" expeditions deep into the jungle where you learn to set up camp, forage for food, and cook a gourmet meal (pan-fried piranhas!).

One of the best and most unique ways of exploring the rain forest is by climbing into the lofty heights of its upper canopy—a truly amazing experience. It's the main specialty of **Amazon Treeclimbing** (tel. 92/8195-8585, www.amazontreeclimbing.com), which offers half- (R$240-260 pp) and full-day (R$380-580 pp) customized tours to forests around Manaus, which marry climbing up and down—and dangling from—gigantic *samaumas, angelins,* and *amapás* with other eco-activities.

Tree-climbing is also the focus of **Tropical Tree Climbing** (BR-178, km 144, Presidente Figueiredo, tel. 92/8195-8585, www.tropicaltreeclimbing.com), operated by charming French wildlife photographer and tree climber extraordinaire Leo Principe and his wife Vanessa. Ascents cater to participants 3-83 years old. Multiday forest expeditions are also offered with accommodations in treetop tents, as well as the Amazon Camp Lodge Guest House, an eco-lodge situated in the Caverna Maragua nature preserve.

★ Riverboat Trips

A riverboat trip allows you to cover far more territory than a jungle lodge. Many ecotourist agencies can book a riverboat cruise along the Rio Solimões or Rio Negro, or both. Accommodations range from basic cabins with wooden bunks to cruise-worthy luxury with fine dining. To venture into the forest, you'll be transferred to smaller vessels that will allow you to penetrate more secluded and wildlife-rich *igapós* and *igarapés*. **Viverde** (tel. 92/3248-9988, www.viverde.com.br) can reserve trips on riverboats and charter boats for private groups. **Amazon Clipper Cruises,** based at the Hotel Tropical in Ponta

Negra (tel. 92/3656-1246, www.amazonclipper.com.br), runs 3-5-day excursions (starting at R$1,400 pp) along both the Rio Negro and Rio Solimões. The **Iberostar Grand Amazon** (www.iberostar.com) runs similar tours, with the added bonus of accommodations on a luxury cruise ship with cabins featuring king beds, plasma TVs, and private verandas as well as multiple pools, restaurants, and bars. Yet the Iberostar's crew takes its eco-activities seriously, offering excellent guided tours in small launches, nightly wildlife lectures, and a library with books about the Amazon's climate, culture, history, flora, and fauna. A four-day cruise starts at R$2,000 pp. While the price is steep, it includes absolutely everything.

For a more authentic (and cheaper) adventure, hop aboard one of the local wooden passenger boats that ferry people and cargo throughout the Amazon. For major routes—along the Amazon to Santarém and Belém, along the Rio Solimões to Tefé, up the Rio Negro to Novo Airão—there is more or less regular service from Manaus (schedules may change). Since these boats are for transport rather than tourism, boats generally stick to the middle of the main rivers, far from the shore (and wildlife). Don't expect a lot of comfort.

If you opt for one of the few private but cramped, stuffy, and basic *camarotes* (cabins with bunks that sleep 2-4 people), you'll have privacy, security, and your own bathroom (a big luxury), and that's about it. More expensive but still tiny *suites* have bona fide beds and air-conditioning instead of a fan.

If you're on a serious budget and want to hang with the locals, you can buy a hammock and string it up on deck. Opt for the middle deck with exposure to more breezes (and farther from the noisy engine, which is on the lower deck). The experience is often sardine-like; noisy, with music playing, babies crying, and all-night gossip sessions, especially on the upper deck, where meals are served and passengers tend to linger. Purchase tickets at least a day or two in advance and to stake out hammock space at least a few hours before the boat leaves (ask the porter for advice and avoid proximity to the bathrooms). Some boats have a hammock space reserved for women only.

Meals (basic rice, beans, and fish as well as filtered water) are either included or sold separately; choose items with care and opt for the extremely cooked (as opposed to potentially raw). Bring mineral water and snacks such as bananas or energy bars as a reserve and order à la carte items. Bring a roll of toilet paper as well; the term "shared bathrooms" is somewhat of an understatement. Although safety isn't usually an issue, keep an eye on your belongings (and bring a lock and cable so you can sleep in peace). Delays are frequent, and traveling downriver is always quicker than upriver.

The quintessential boat trip is the four-day journey down to the mouth of the Amazon in Belém. Different companies operate boats that travel downstream on different days of the week (but not daily); schedules change frequently. In early 2014, prices hovered around R$350 for hammock space, R$500pp for a cabin for two people, and R$600pp for a suite for two. Most boats to Belém also stop off at Parintins, Santarém, and Monte Alegre. The 36-hour journey to Santarém costs roughly R$180 for hammock space, R$350pp for a cabin for two, and R$400pp for a suite for two. Slow boats depart from the **Estação Hidroviária,** where you can get schedules for all boats and buy tickets. Ticket booths are open 6am-6pm daily for long-distance river boats. Plan on buying tickets 1-2 days in advance, and purchase tickets from the kiosks and not from the vendors on the street.

Background

The Landscape

The fifth-largest country in the world after Canada, China, Russia, and the United States, Brazil is the largest country in South America, occupying roughly half the continent. It shares borders with every South American country except Chile and Ecuador.

GEOGRAPHY

The Instituto Brasileiro do Meio Ambiente (IBAMA) is the federal agency in charge of studying and monitoring Brazil's natural environment. IBAMA's researchers have recognized seven distinct ecosystems within Brazil: the Amazonian rain forest, the Caatinga, the Atlantic rain forest, the coastal region, the Cerrado, the Pantanal wetlands, and the southern plains.

Amazonian Rain Forest

The world's largest tropical rain forest, the Amazon is one of the world's richest sources of biological diversity. It is home to 40,000 species of plants, 2,000 species of birds and mammals, 3,000 species of fish, and 2.5 million species of insects—and these are merely those that have been identified. Despite human encroachment upon the forest, the majority of it is uninhabited. The Amazon River boasts thousands of tributaries, and there are still many areas that remain remote and completely unknown to humans.

Rain forests exist in regions that receive at least 2,000 millimeters (79 inches) of annual rainfall. In the Amazon, this accounts for humidity levels that are usually higher than 80 percent. Flooding of the Amazon and its tributaries can cause water levels to rise by as much as 15 meters (50 feet), transforming forest floors into lakes and driving most wildlife—butterflies, birds, sloths, and monkeys—up into the highest tree canopies. Some parts of the forest, known as *igapó,* are permanently flooded, whereas others, known as *várzea,* are only flooded seasonally.

The Amazon Basin holds about 17 percent of the world's freshwater. With a length of 6,400 kilometers (4,000 miles), the mighty Rio Amazonas is the largest river in Brazil—and the world, measured by volume: it carries 119,000 cubic meters (4.2 million cubic feet) of water into the sea every *second.* Beginning in Peru, the river flows eastward until it empties into the Atlantic Ocean near the city of Belém. All in all, its more than 1,000 tributaries add up to more than 7,047,000 square kilometers (2,722,000 square miles) of water. The Amazon is also home to Brazil's highest mountain, Pico Neblina. Located near the Venezuelan border, it rises to a height of 3,014 meters (9,888 feet).

Caatinga

A marked contrast to the lushness of the Amazon is the parched dryness of the scrubby Caatinga vegetation that characterizes much of the interior of northeastern Brazil, an area known as the Sertão. Caatinga covers approximately 11 percent of Brazilian territory. Although the Sertão's legendary droughts and tales of hardship have led many Brazilians to conjure up images of an inhospitable moonscape where only cacti grow, the semiarid Caatinga actually has a wet season as well as a dry season. During the latter, rivers dry up, leaves disappear, and cracks appear in the sunbaked earth. However, when the torrential rains do come, in the summer months, the low scrub and thorn trees suddenly burst into green.

Previous: San Antônio do Pinhal; Igreja de Nossa Senhora do Carmo, Ouro Preto.

Atlantic Rain Forest

When the first Portuguese arrived in Brazil, a dense Atlantic forest, the Mata Atlântica, blanketed the entire coastline from Rio Grande do Norte in the north to Rio Grande do Sul in the south. Stretching west by an average of 200 kilometers (124 miles) into the interior, this ancient rain forest (far older than the Amazon) measured 1 million square kilometers (621,000 square miles). However, five centuries of brazilwood extraction, sugar and coffee cultivation, farming, logging, urbanization, and industrialization have taken their toll. Today, only 7 percent of Mata Atlântica remains, and that in patches (notably in southern Bahia, Rio de Janeiro, São Paulo, and Paraná). However, the surviving forest is surprisingly lush with unique forms of flora and fauna unknown anywhere else in Brazil or the world. Rare mammals include the lion tamarin and woolly spider monkey (the largest primate in the Americas), while plant life includes rare bromeliads, orchids, ferns, and surviving specimens of *pau brasil,* the wood that lent Brazil its name. Thankfully, much of the remaining forest is now carefully preserved—at least in theory.

Coastal Region

Brazil boasts an enormous coastline that stretches 8,000 kilometers (5,000 miles) and includes rocky cliffs, enormous dunes, boulders, sandy coves, coastal plains, forests, and *manguezais,* or mangroves. Mangroves are unique systems that appear wherever a river flows into a bay or estuary. They extend along the coast as far north as Pará and as far south as Santa Catarina. Soil rich with river sediment and organic matter nourishes the dense mangrove vegetation, which in turn attracts fish, storks, and ibises along with shrimps, crabs, and mussels. Traditionally, some local populations viewed mangroves as muddy, humid, unhygienic swamps. They tried to drain them or use them as garbage dumps. Only recently has their important role in maintaining the delicate equilibrium of marine life been recognized. As a result, many have become protected environments.

Southern Plains

Southern Brazil, extending from Santa Catarina into Rio Grande do Sul, is covered with a vast plain where low vegetation, mosses, and lichens thrive along with cacti and bromeliads. South and westward, the

Buzios, Rio de Janeiro

plain gradually transforms into the grassy Pampas, a rolling green carpet studded with occasional cork and fig trees.

Cerrado

The vast highland plains of the Central-West region that surround Brasília and stretch west through Goiás into Mato Grosso and Mato Grosso do Sul, known as the Planalto, are covered with a distinctive type of vegetation known as Cerrado. Resembling the dry, scrubby, savanna-like landscapes of eastern Africa, Cerrado is a surprisingly rich and unique ecosystem, more than 40 percent of whose roughly 10,000 plant species exist nowhere else. Vegetation ranges from straw-colored grasses and scrubby bushes to thick-barked trees and primitive-looking *buriti* palms to blossoming *ipê*, jacaranda, and the ubiquitous *pequi* tree, whose spiky orange fruit is used in local cooking. Due to widespread clearing of the land for farming, more than half of this precious ecosystem has been destroyed. While efforts have been made in recent years to preserve considerable chunks of the Amazon and Atlantic rain forests, conservation strategies in the relatively unknown Cerrado are virtually nonexistent aside from a few nature reserves.

The Pantanal

The world's greatest inland wetlands, the Pantanal is a vast plain that is constantly flooded with waters from the Andes, the Planalto, and the Rio Paraguai Basin. Extending from the Central-West states of Mato Grosso and Mato Grosso do Sul to Bolivia and Paraguay, the region measures 250,000 square kilometers (96,500 square miles) and covers an area larger than the United Kingdom. The Pantanal is actually a complex system fed by more than 100 rivers. Depending on the season, the entire region is drastically transformed. The wet season, November-March, is marked by rains and rising rivers, which turn the area into a vast aquarium dotted with islands. During this period, wildlife moves to higher ground and transportation is by boat only. The "dry season," April-October, is characterized by the slow draining of floodplains. Receding water leaves rich sediment behind, where pasture sprouts. As a result, the area is ideal for raising cattle, and the bovine population far outnumbers humans. Instead of a distinctive flora and fauna of its own, the Pantanal has a lot of everything else—including plants and animals that are typical of the Amazon forest, the Cerrado, and even the Caatinga. Due

Cerrado landscape

to its relative seclusion, you'll find wildlife in much greater numbers in the Pantanal than in the Amazon, making the region a not-to-be-missed mecca for wildlife enthusiasts as well as freshwater fishing aficionados.

CLIMATE

Due to the country's immense size, Brazil's climate is extremely varied. The Equator runs through the northern part of the country, while the Tropic of Capricorn crosses through the south, running parallel to São Paulo. As you head from north to south, the temperature, humidity, and precipitation levels change greatly. Brazil boasts four distinctive climactic zones: subtropical, equatorial, tropical, and semiarid. Ninety percent of the country is situated in the tropical zone, where there is very little seasonal variation. Rain is frequent and temperatures range 25-35°C (77-95°F). However, as you head south, seasonal variations become more distinct, resembling those of the continental United States and Europe, with hot, steamy summers and cool winters. In the southern states of Santa Catarina and Rio Grande do Sul, temperatures can plunge low enough to produce frost and even snow.

With the exception of the Sertão, which receives very little rainfall, the rest of the country receives a lot of rain. Although rains are common throughout the year, coastal regions have distinctive rainy seasons where downpours are daily occurrences and can even last for several days. In the Southeast, violent downpours flood the streets of Rio and São Paulo in the summer months, from December to March. In the Northeast, along the coast between Bahia and Pernambuco, rainy season generally coincides with the winter months of June through August. Rain is much less frequent in the permanently sunny states of Rio Grande do Norte and Ceará, where temperatures remain constant year-round. Close to the Equator, Maranhão and especially the Amazonian state of Pará receive the most rain throughout the year, with annual averages of 3,500 millimeters (138 inches) in some parts. The rest of the Amazon, along with the Pantanal, receives a lot of rain as well, but both regions also have a more pronounced dry season that lasts from March to October.

ENVIRONMENTAL ISSUES
Amazon Deforestation

The No. 1 environmental issue Brazil faces is the destruction of the Amazon forest, the most diverse rain forest in the world. To date, an estimated 20 percent has suffered deforestation, and an equal portion has suffered from degradation, mostly caused by logging. The worst damage to the forest took place during the 1970s and 1980s, when the military government was eager to open up the hitherto inaccessible region to development and invested in transamazonian highways that cut through the jungle from north and south and east to west. The asphalting of the Amazon (parts subsequently fell into disrepair and were reclaimed by the forest) created links between the region's major cities. It also paved the way for large-scale logging, agriculture, and cattle ranching, most of which took place with complete disregard for the welfare of the forest and its indigenous peoples. Further damage resulted from the installation of vast hydroelectric dams; the disruption of natural river cycles has had a serious impact on the environment.

Various factors—ranging from increased global and national environmental consciousness to more enlightened political and business policies recognize the value of sustainable development—have led to some positive results; between 2002 and 2011, Brazil cut forest loss by almost half. Other factors have contributed to reducing devastation. The flood of poor migrants that in former decades swamped the Amazon in search of jobs and cheap land has dried up. At present, contrary to popular belief, most of the farming, cattle-raising, and logging are carried out on the 20 percent of Amazonian territory that has already been cleared. Strict new international laws governing the origins of Amazonian timber mean that wood is harvested in accordance with rigid environmental regulations. However, the biggest culprits of deforestation continue to be cattle-raising and large-scale production of soybeans. Soya not only serves as cattle feed but is also a lucrative cash crop in great demand on world markets (Brazil is currently the world's largest producer of soybeans). Although forest is not directly cleared for soy cultivation (which happens in the much more endangered Cerrado), the resulting highways and infrastructure are a threat. In 2012, as a result of agricultural lobbying, the government eased restrictions; in 2013, an area of rain forest the size of Mongolia was lost.

Historically, economic expansion has been at odds with the preservation of natural ecosystems, as evidenced by the destruction of Brazil's Mata Atlântica and ongoing threats to the Pantanal and Cerrado. After former President Luiz Inácio Lula da Silva (known as Lula) appointed Marina Silva—a former rubber tapper from the state of Acre—as minister of the environment in 2003, the government began to crack down more seriously on illegal deforestation and make attempts to preserve large swathes of virgin forest as national parks. To date, more than 20 percent of Amazonian territory has been transformed into Indian reserves, where indigenous people carry out sustainable activities ranging from small-scale fishing, agriculture, and rubber tapping to harvesting nuts and collecting leaves and roots that are crucial ingredients in medicines and cosmetics. Nonetheless, many obstacles remain. Part of the problem lies with local and state governments (with the notable exceptions of Amazonas and Acre), along with wealthy landowners, whose greed, cronyism, and oligarchic values privilege short-term riches at the expense of long-term sustainable development. A more recent threat is climate change, the consequences of which have been serious droughts that have killed off vegetation and increased the likelihood of forest fires.

Pollution

Air and water pollution are also a big problem in Brazil. Pollution from industry and vehicle exhaust fumes plagues the largest cities, but is notorious in São Paulo, where skies can become thick with smog. To diminish pollution, Sampa's municipal government implemented a rotation system, halving the number of cars permitted on the road at certain times. However, with an unprecedented number of Brazilians purchasing cars, this solution falls short of addressing the problem. Water pollution is an issue throughout the country. In urban areas, lack of water and sewage treatment in some poor neighborhoods—particularly in *favelas*—is a hazard. In rural areas, pesticides, industrial waste, and the degradation of aquatic ecosystems due to the installation of hydroelectric plants are responsible for the pollution of lakes and rivers. Oceans are at the mercy of accidents because of heavy shipping activities and offshore oil drilling.

Progress has been made in addressing some of these problems. As Brazil has increasingly become a global economic player, to compete in world markets Brazilian manufacturers have had to adopt stringent environmental regulations, which include the recycling of waste and alternative forms of energy production. City governments, such as Rio's, have taken small steps to integrate—instead of ignore—*favelas* by attempting to provide basic services to which all citizens are entitled. Growing tourism, particularly ecotourism, has provided a cash incentive for government, businesses, and local populations to preserve the environment and look for sustainable means of development. Although most Brazilians are hardly enlightened in terms of littering, the country does boast one of the highest rates of recycling of any nation.

Plants

More than a quarter of the world's known plant species can be found in Brazil. As the world's largest tropical rain forest, the Amazon boasts an astonishing range of trees, many festooned with Tarzan-worthy vines and creepers. Among the most legendary species are wild rubber trees and Brazil nut trees, capable of producing 450 kilograms (1,000 pounds) of nuts in a year, along with rosewood and mahogany trees, whose beautiful hardwood is always much in demand for fine furniture. The extremely fertile Atlantic forest is also famous for other native woods, including jacaranda and *ipê*, with their bright purple and yellow blossoms.

Other Brazilian trees are more sought-after for their fruits than for their wood. Throughout the tropical zones of the coast and the interior, Brazilians depend on diverse varieties of local palms. The Amazon is renowned for many fruit-bearing species, particularly those that yield *pupunha* and the energy-packed *açaí*. In Ceará and Maranhão, livelihoods depend on the *carnaúba* and *babaçu* palms, whose all-purpose fruits and fibers are used to make products that include wax, cooking oil, soap, rope, timber, and thatch. Alagoas and northern Bahia are lined with swaying plantations of coconut palms, while southern Bahia is where you'll find the *dendê* palm, whose

bright orange oil is used in Bahian cuisine. In the Cerrado, the fruit of the *buriti* palm is also made into various delicacies.

Fruit trees are everywhere you go, even in cities. In the Amazon, you can feast on *cupuaçu, bacuri,* and *muriti,* while the Northeast produces mango, papaya, *cajú* (cashew), *jaca* (jackfruit), *graviola, mangaba,* and guava trees. The Cerrado boasts exotic species such as *pequi, araticum,* and *cagaíta.* Bananas are ubiquitous, and there are many types, ranging from the tiny *banana nanica* (dwarf banana) to the immense *banana pacova,* which can measure up to 50 centimeters (20 inches). In southern Brazil, you can still glimpse the umbrella-shaped *araucárias,* a variety of pine tree whose nuts were much appreciated by local indigenous people when these trees were once widespread.

Although you'll rarely find them in florists' shops (when buying flowers, Brazilians weirdly prefer to go with decidedly nontropical roses, carnations, and chrysanthemums), in the wild you'll be treated to more than 200 species of delicate and brightly colored orchids as well as bright red heliconia, birds of paradise, and glossy anthuriums. The leaves and roots of many Brazilian plants are used extensively for medicinal and cosmetic purposes.

Animals

Brazil has a fascinating variety of exotic mammals. The largest creatures you might see—although they're extremely elusive—are cats, such as jaguars and panthers. The *onça pintada* (spotted jaguar) inhabits the Amazon and the Pantanal and is sometimes spotted in the Cerrado. These cats prefer night to day, as does the all-black *onça preta,* also a native of the Amazon. A more common sight

in the Pantanal is the *capivara* (capybara), the world's biggest rodent. More like a giant guinea pig than a rat, *capivaras* are at home on land and in water. They can grow to lengths of 1 meter (3.3 feet) and weigh up to 70 kilograms (155 pounds).

Another common sight, *tamanduás* (anteaters) are surreal-looking creatures with long snouts and even longer furry tails. They spend much of their days sucking up tens of thousands of ants with their sticky tongues. The largest variety, the *tamanduá bandeira*, grows to lengths of 2 meters (6.5 feet) and is a native of the Cerrado. *Tatus* (armadillos) are nocturnal and hard to see. Some species of *tamanduás* and *tatus* are endangered because their meat is considered a delicacy in rural areas. Another really odd-looking beast is the *preguiça* (sloth), who lives up to its name by doing little more than dozing in trees. When a *preguiça* does decide to make a move, it does so very slowly.

PRIMATES

Of the world's 250 primate species, more than 70 are found in Brazil, and many are unique to Brazil. In whatever part of the country you visit, *macacos* or *micos* (monkeys) are a common sight—even in major cities. You'll spot many different types in the Amazon forest, including the tiny, pale-faced *mico-de-cheiro* (squirrel monkey) and the much larger *macaco preto* (spider monkey), whose long, spindly limbs and tail account for it measuring up to 1.5 meters (5 feet). *Guaribas* (howler monkeys) are also common, although since they inhabit tree canopies, you're much more likely to hear them than see them. Red howlers inhabit the Amazon, black howlers dwell in the Pantanal, and brown howlers can be spotted in the Mata Atlântica. Beware: If they feel threatened, howlers will shower you with their excrement. Cute, tuft-headed *macaco-pregos* (capuchin monkeys) are also ubiquitous throughout Brazil, including in Rio's Floresta da Tijuca.

Among the rarest and most physically striking monkeys in Brazil are the uakari and the *mico-leão* (lion tamarin). Uakaris are endangered but can be glimpsed at the Amazon's Mariauá Reserve. The fuzzy red uakari bears the nickname *macaco-inglês* (English monkey) due to its bald pink head and blushing red complexion. With faces that are framed by shaggy manes, *mico-leãos* really do resemble tiny lions (*leãos*). The rarest and most splendid of the species is the *mico-leão-dourado*, whose pelt and mane are a brilliant tawny gold. A native of the Mata Atlântica of Rio de Janeiro, this striking squirrel-size monkey has been saved from extinction.

AQUATIC MAMMALS

Of all the fascinating forms of wildlife in the Amazon, one of the easiest to observe is the legendary *boto* (pink river dolphin), an almost blind but very friendly creature whose skin is a startling shade of pink. At Novo Airão, in Amazonas, you can actually swim among these gentle animals. The more conservatively colored *tucuxi* (gray dolphin) can also be seen in Amazonian waters as well as up and down the Atlantic coastline. Much rarer and infinitely weirder-looking is another native of the Amazon, the *peixe-boi* (manatee), a vast sausage-like beast that actually does, as its name implies, resemble a cross between a fish (*peixe*) and a bull (*boi*).

Brazil's Atlantic coast is home to seven species of whales. Following centuries of brutal slaughter, schools of frolicking *baleias francas do sul* (southern right whales) are back in circulation and can be easily spotted (June-October) at the protected marine sanctuary off the coast of Praia do Rosa, in Santa Catarina. If you're in Bahia during the same time (in Praia do Forte or the Parque Nacional Marinho de Abrolhos), you can view equally rare *baleias jubarte* (humpback whales) breeding. One of the best places in the world for viewing vast schools of dolphins is on the island of Fernando de Noronha, whose sheltered coves are a favorite feeding spot for large schools of *golfinhos rotadores* (spinning dolphins).

REPTILES

The first thing that comes to mind when one hears the words *Brazil* and *reptiles* together in the same sentence is anacondas. Hero of trashy Amazonian terror movies, the anaconda lives up to its fearful reputation. Adults can grow to well more than 10 meters (33 feet) in length,

red and green macaw

jacarés-do-Pantanal (Paraguayan caiman) everywhere, and, if you're up to it, probably even eat a couple as well—the meat is surprisingly tender. The Amazon's tributaries are also overflowing with reptiles. The largest, but quite rare, is the *jacaré açu,* or black caiman, which grows to lengths of 6 meters (20 feet). Much more common is the smaller *jacaré tinga* (spectacled caiman).

FISH

Brazil's waters are filled with both eye-catching and mouthwatering fish. Along the Atlantic coast, sunken galleons and kilometer-long protective reefs offer ideal opportunities for snorkeling and diving amid gaudily hued schools. Inland, the Amazon and the Pantanal together boast close to 3,000 species in their rivers, lakes, and tributaries.

The Amazon is home to some particularly exotic specimens. On the small end of the scale are dozens of species of infamously fanged piranhas. Then there is the regally red- and silver-scaled *pirarucu,* the king of freshwater fish, which can grow to lengths of 3 meters (10 feet) and weigh up to 200 kilograms (440 pounds). The *pirarucu* is a favorite Amazonian delicacy, as are the much smaller but common *pirapitinga* and *tambaqui* (both from the piranha family). The *tambaqui* usually uses its sharp teeth to crack open seeds and nuts, but if none are available, it will easily resort to being carnivorous. Many varieties of catfish are also common; they make use of their "whiskers" to help them find food on river bottoms. Among the most common are the *piraiba,* which can grow to lengths of 3 meters (10 feet), and the golden-scaled *dourado* (dorado), which is enjoyed at tables throughout Brazil.

Freshwater inhabitants you'll want to steer clear of are *arraias* (stingrays), who live in still riverbeds. Their sting draws blood and can really hurt. *Poraquês* (electric eels) are also no laughing matter. They grow to more than 2 meters (6.5 feet) in length, and a zap from one will send a 600-volt charge through your body.

and many live to be more than 20 years old. When it comes time to mate, a bunch of males wind themselves around a female for several weeks, after which the female shows her appreciation by eating one or two of her partners. Due to their size, anacondas have no predators, but they aren't shy about wrapping themselves around large prey and squeezing them to death before swallowing them whole (this includes people, although very rarely). At home on dry land and in water, anacondas are common in the Amazon and the Pantanal. Other constrictors (known as *jiboias*) are considerably smaller (3-5 meters/10-16 feet) and limit their crushing and feasting to small animals. While it's rare to come across poisonous *cobras* (snakes), which usually only attack when threatened, there are quite a few such varieties, including *víboras* (vipers), *cascavéis* (rattlesnakes), and *cobras coral* (coral snakes).

Brazil possesses several species of *jacarés* (the term used for both alligators and caimans). In the Pantanal, you'll encounter

BIRDS

Both hard-core and amateur birders will have a field day in Brazil. Not only is Brazil home to a fantastic diversity of winged creatures, but the riotous colors of their plumages are as spectacular as a Carnaval *desfile* (parade). In the Amazon and Atlantic rain forests and the Pantanal, you'll have plenty of opportunities to be awestruck by the Technicolor hues of *araras* (macaws) and *papagaios* (parrots). Measuring around 90 centimeters (35 inches), macaws are the largest and most exhibitionistic of these birds. They can often be found in pairs, usually making quite a ruckus. The *arara vermelha* (scarlet macaw) is perhaps the most magnificent of all, its deep crimson face offset by brilliant blue and green wings. In addition to the Amazon and the Pantanal, it inhabits the Cerrado, as does the no less impressive *arara-canindé* (blue and yellow macaw), whose bright turquoise head and back contrast with a golden chest. Unfortunately, their beauty makes them a hot commodity on the illegal animal-trafficking market. Poaching is responsible for the near extinction of the *arara-azul* (hyacinth macaw), which at 1 meter (3.3 feet) is the largest parrot on the planet. Once endemic throughout the Pantanal, today there are less than 3,000 of these birds. Their rich indigo feathers and yellow ringed eyes are astonishingly beautiful. Fortunately, the Projeto Arara Azul (www.projetoararaazul.org.br), whose headquarters is also in the Pantanal, is committed to the study and protection of these birds.

Other striking avian species are *tucanos* (toucans), who can be found in various forest habitats throughout Brazil. Residing in treetops where they can easily feast on fruit, these cartoonlike creatures are easily recognizable by their enormous, brightly colored bills, which are often as large as their bodies. Although the bills appear as if they would weigh the birds down, they consist of a spongy substance that is lighter than Styrofoam.

Wherever you travel in Brazil, you're bound to see plenty of *garças* (herons), *cegonhas* (storks), and other large, elegantly long-legged water birds. Two particularly unforgettable specimens are the bright red *guará* (scarlet ibis) and the *tuiuiú*, a tall stork. The bright crimson finery of the *guará* is often on display on Ilha de Marajó, Pará, and in Alcântara, in Maranhão. The *tuiuiú* is the Pantanal's unofficial mascot, measuring 1.5 meters (5 feet), with an ebony head and a slender pink neck. Among the various species of birds of prey, which include falcons, hawks, and eagles, the fiercest and most regal is the *águia real* (harpy eagle), an Amazonian bird that feasts on monkeys and other small prey.

Brazil can claim to possess both the largest and smallest birds in the Americas. The *ema* (rhea) is an ostrich-like flightless bird that can grow to the height of 1.5 meters (5 feet) and weigh 35 kilograms (77 pounds). In a metrosexual twist, male *emas* are not only responsible for building nests and incubating the giant eggs, but for raising the young chicks as well. Along with Ecuador, Brazil has the world's largest variety of tiny *beija-flores* (hummingbirds)—the Portuguese name means "flower kisser." These tiny iridescent birds, which can measure as little as 6 centimeters (2.3 inches) and weigh only 2 grams (0.07 ounces), can be seen fluttering their aerodynamic wings throughout the country, including in cities, where people often put out feeders for them. They drink up to five times their weight in nectar each day.

History

PREHISTORY

The verdict is still out regarding the arrival of the first indigenous populations in South America. Dates vary from 10,000 to 30,000 years ago, and origins range from Asia (via a land bridge over the Bering Sea) to Africa (via canoe). Regardless, Brazilian Indians never developed the sophisticated cultures of their Andean neighbors, the Incas. To date, few pre-Columbian traces have been uncovered; those that do exist include the richly decorative glazed ceramic pots fashioned by the Marajó and Tapajó Indians of the Amazon and the expressive rock paintings found in the isolated caves of Gruta da Lapinha (Minas Gerais), the Parque Nacional da Serra da Capivara (Piauí), and the Amazonian town of Monte Alegre (Pará). However, the identities of the peoples who created these works are shrouded in mystery.

When the first Portuguese explorers arrived in 1500, an estimated 3-4 million Indians lived in Brazil. Scattered in small groups and speaking well more than 100 languages, most lived in villages, where they survived by hunting, fishing, and gathering as well as cultivating crops such as corn and manioc. One of the main groups was the Tupi-Guarani, a seminomadic people who originally spread out from the Amazon Basin, migrating south and east to the coast. It was the fierce Tupi that greeted the first Portuguese navigators and their crew. The Europeans were quite enthralled with these "noble savages" and quickly began chronicling their lifestyles in manners both factual and fictional. When German mercenary Hans Staden was captured by a Tupi group in 1552, he was ritually fattened up and prepared for the feast—Tupi tradition involved eating one's enemies, with the aim of imbibing their courage. When Staden was ready to become stew, his very unwarrior-like display of tears so disgusted the Tupi that they released him.

Although wimpy in the eyes of his captors, Staden wrote a tell-all memoir of his adventures, which became a major bestseller back in Europe and considerably raised curiosity about the vast new land across the ocean.

PORTUGUESE CONQUEST

In 1500, Portuguese explorer Pedro Álvares Cabral had set sail from Portugal in search of a western trade route to India. On April 22, his fleet of 13 ships arrived on the southern coast of Bahia, where Porto Seguro now lies. Clambering ashore, the Portuguese planted a cross and held a mass at the spot they baptized Terra da Vera Cruz (Land of the True Cross). They spent the next 10 days exchanging trinkets with the local Tupi and evaluating the prospects of this palmy new land, which the Indians referred to as Pindorama (Land of Palms). The only potential spoil that sparked their interest was a native tree with a rich, glossy hardwood that yielded a deep red dye. When the expedition returned to Portugal, word got out about this exotic timber, known as *pau brasil*—*pau* means "wood," and *brasil* is said to be a derivation of *brasa*, a red, hot coal. Although the Portuguese were still much more interested in the spices and ivory of their African and Asian colonies, over the next few decades, ambitious traders sailed across the Atlantic to the land of the *brasil* wood, which soon became shortened to "Brazil." In return for metal tools and hardware, they had the Tupi cut down and harvest great quantities of brazilwood, whose crimson dye was highly coveted by European weaving factories.

Portugal only officially became interested in Brazil when French and Spanish merchants began showing a little too much interest in the new territory. Consequently, in 1532, in an attempt to stake claim to Brazil without actually having to take it on as a colony, King João III divided the Brazilian coast into 15 vast parcels, known as *capitânias*, which he distributed to various aristocratic cronies with the agreement that they would defend the territories and hopefully find some more riches with which to further fill the crown's coffers. With the exception of Pernambuco, Bahia, and São Vicente (São Paulo), the *capitânia* concept proved a great failure. Without the presence of trained soldiers, Indians burned down fragile settlements and massacred their inhabitants. King João decided he would have to go the colonial route after all. In 1549, he abolished the *capitânias* and named Tomé de Sousa as the new governor-general of Brazil. Accompanied by a force of soldiers, Jesuit priests, ex-convicts, and bureaucrats, Sousa arrived in Salvador da Bahia that same year and claimed the city as the capital of the Brazilian colony.

SUGAR AND SLAVERY

By the mid-1500s, *pau brasil* supplies were already drying up. However, in Pernambuco and Bahia, sugarcane had been successfully introduced to the rolling coastal hills. Tomé de Sousa incentivized the cultivation of sugar, which at the time was an exorbitantly expensive rarity in Europe. As the Indians who wouldn't become allies were systematically wiped out, their lands were occupied by vast plantations that sprang up throughout the Northeast. Although attempts were made to enslave Indians to work the plantations, those who were domesticated often fell prey to European diseases to which they had no immunity. The alternative was to take advantage of the thriving African slave trade that was already making fortunes for European investors, including Portugal.

Beginning in the 1550s, Portugal began importing vast numbers of slaves from its African colonies of Mozambique and Angola, as well as from West Africa and Congo. Transported like sardines in the holds of ships, those that survived the suffocating voyage were herded into slave markets such as Salvador's Mercado Modelo and then sold to plantation owners. They were forced to work grueling 16-17-hour days in scalding heat, only to be herded at night into *senzalas*, dark and filthy quarters. Slaves endured horrible working and living conditions and received cruel and unusual treatment for misbehaving or trying to escape. Punishments ranged from being publicly flogged at pillories in main town squares (Salvador's Largo do Pelourinho, or Square of the Pillory, was the site of one such whipping post) to being subject to extreme forms of torture ranging from balls and chains to waterboarding.

The production of sugar became the No. 1 source of profits for the Portuguese crown. It also created a wealthy colonial elite who poured their wealth into building extravagant churches and ornate mansions to adorn the thriving capitals of Salvador and Olinda. Sugar would also lay the foundations for the organization of Brazil's economy—as an exporter of monocultures (sugar, coffee, rubber, etc.), each of which would experience a boom-and-bust cycle—as well as its society. Plantation life—with the slaves in the *senzala* and the white aristocrats in their ornate mansions, known as *casas grandes*—would come to permeate Brazilian society. And its extreme legacy of a dual society that pits rich versus poor and black versus white exists to this day. While on one hand, plantation owners were cruel and racist toward slaves, they had no compunction about fornicating with them. Masters who didn't have a black mistress or legions of illegitimate *mulato* offspring were the exception, not the rule. The consequence of this confusing behavior (aside from lots of slave women succumbing to syphilis) was the extreme miscegenation of Brazil's population. This gave rise to the myth of racial harmony, and it also set the standard for racism and a glaring inequality that pervades Brazilian society.

EUROPEAN THREATS AND INVASIONS

Portugal's thriving colony incited the envy of its European neighbors. In the early 1500s, the robust *pau brasil* commerce had lured

French interests. In 1550, a French expedition sailed into the Baía de Guanabara and staked claim to the area, with the intent of creating a southern colony, baptized French Antarctica. The Portuguese were not at all pleased with this plan. In 1565, they founded the city of São Sebastião do Rio de Janeiro, and a few years later they had successfully expelled the French from the region. When the determined French tried to get a foothold in the Northeast by founding a city of their own, called Saint-Louis, in 1594, the Portuguese succeeded in giving them the boot in 1615, changing the city's name to the more patriotic sounding São Luís.

Even more serious was the threat of the Dutch, who, with lucrative but tiny sugar-producing colonies in the Caribbean, were salivating at the chance of adding the vast Northeast to their possessions. Their initial foray into Brazil—an attack on and occupation of Salvador in 1624—ended abruptly when they were driven back by Portuguese troops. However, the persistent Dutch, sponsored by the expansive Dutch West India Company, then set their sights on Pernambuco, which at the time was the world's largest producer of sugar. After burning the capital of Olinda to the ground in 1637, the Protestant Dutch established their own colonial headquarters. To govern the new colony, along came Johan Maurits van Nassau, an enlightened university-educated count, who not only increased the output of sugar but also placated the Portuguese Catholic sugar barons by installing a policy of religious tolerance and creating strategic alliances with remaining Indian groups. By 1640, the capital, Mauritsstad (later renamed Recife), was a booming port city, and Pernambuco was more stable and richer than it had ever been. Much to Portuguese chagrin, the Dutch had successfully extended their foothold from Maranhão in the north to Alagoas in the South. Brazilians might have been speaking Dutch today if Maurits van Nassau hadn't resigned in 1644, disgusted with the greed and narrow-mindedness of the Dutch West India Company administrators.

With the departure of the popular Nassau, the Portuguese settlers rose up throughout the Northeast. Throughout the next decade, the Dutch were massacred and their plantations razed. Finally, only Recife was left in Dutch hands, and after two decisive battles in 1648 and 1649, they surrendered in 1654, leaving all of Brazil definitively in Portuguese hands.

JESUITS AND BANDEIRANTES

Of course, Portugal's major rival for control of South America had always been Spain. Back in 1494, when both nations were the undisputed colonial powers of the world, the Treaty of Tordesilhas had preemptively sought to settle future territorial disputes by carving the New World into two large pieces. An imaginary line that stretched from the mouth of the Amazon River to the south of Santa Catarina effectively sliced the South American continent in half. According to the rules, everything west of the line belonged to Spain, and everything east belonged to Portugal; in reality, the imaginary frontier—much of which stretched through impenetrable rain forest of the Amazon and Pantanal wetlands of Mato Grosso—was difficult to monitor.

Jesuit missionaries, who had tight connections with the Portuguese crown, were the first to work their way deep into the unknown Brazilian interior. The first missionaries arrived in Salvador in 1549 and set to work building the second-largest Jesuit college after Rome. Intent on converting and subjugating the local Indian population, they headed west into the Amazon and south toward the Pampas bordering Brazil, Argentina, and Uruguay, founding missions into which Indians were herded. Throughout the 1600s, Jesuit influence in Brazil grew enormously. While some Jesuits exploited Indians, using them as unpaid labor and exposing them to fatal diseases, others protected them from Portuguese settlers intent on enslaving the "savages." The most famous of these humanitarian missionaries was Antônio Vieira, a former adviser to the king, who was based in

São Luís. Vieira's sermons preaching tolerance and criticizing inhumane treatment of Indians were so eloquent that they were published in Europe, and they were so controversial that they led furious settlers to expel him from Brazil in 1661. Jesuits in Rio Grande do Sul were so protective of the Guarani Indians that, in 1752, when the Treaty of Madrid divided up the region containing a dozen missions between Spanish and Portuguese settlers, the missionaries stood by the Guarani in refusing to leave. Yet the noble resistance proved futile—both Jesuits and Indians were massacred by Spanish and Portuguese troops. The missionaries' role was a major factor in the order's definitive expulsion from Brazil in 1760.

The other people responsible for the exploration and opening up of Brazil's vast interior were the *bandeirantes*. Rough-and-ready bands of explorers in search of riches and Indians to enslave, *bandeirantes* took their name from the *bandeiras* (flags) that accompanied their roving expeditions. The first *bandeirante* expeditions began in the early 17th century. The main point of departure was São Paulo, due to its strategic location on the banks of the Rio Tietê, one of the few major rivers that flowed west into the interior. Many *bandeirantes* were *mestiços*, the progeny of Portuguese fathers and Indian mothers. Their Indian heritage gave them knowledge of navigating the dangers of the wilderness but didn't stop them from unceremoniously wiping out any indigenous groups that happened to cross their path with arms and (more commonly) diseases. The distances covered by these ruthless but intrepid explorers were immense, and their discoveries filled in the contours of the Brazilian map. Many towns throughout the western regions of Goiás, Mato Grosso, and even the lower Amazon were founded by *bandeirantes,* whose expeditions often lasted for years.

Although in the early decades the *bandeirantes* certainly found many Indians, riches eluded them until the late 1600s. In 1695, a small group of *bandeirantes* happened upon some glittering nuggets in a river at the spot

that is now Sabará, in Minas Gerais. The find kicked off the biggest gold rush in the New World. Although deposits were found as far west as Goiás and Mato Grosso, most of the glitter was concentrated in the central mountainous region that came to be known as Minas Gerais (General Mines). During the boom years, 1700-1750, hundreds of thousands of fortune hunters descended on the region. Many died poor, of hunger and disease; others grew filthy rich. Overnight, precarious miners' outposts blossomed into towns such as Ouro Preto, Mariana, São João del Rei, and Tiradentes, where wealthy merchants poured their money into grandiose mansions, posh restaurants and hotels, and sumptuous baroque churches whose interiors were awash in gold leaf. Vast numbers of slaves were imported (some directly from Africa, others from Bahia) to work the mines, where conditions proved worse than in the sugarcane fields.

Naturally, Portugal, which was increasingly in debt, was thrilled with the discovery of gold. Built by slaves, roads constructed out of thick stone led through the mountains of Minas and down to the ports of Rio de Janeiro and Paraty, from where the gold was shipped off to Lisbon. It was Rio's newfound importance as a strategic maritime port that elevated the humid and filthy backwater town on the shores of Guanabara Bay to the capital of Brazil, a title it usurped from Salvador in 1763. The move signaled the beginning of the end of northeastern Brazil's economic and political supremacy in favor of the southeastern "triangle" formed by Minas Gerais, Rio de Janeiro, and São Paulo.

INDEPENDENCE

The gold boom was explosive but fleeting. By the mid-1700s, the precious metal was increasingly hard to find, but the Portuguese crown still insisted on taxing and appropriating every last nugget. Gradually, Brazilian settlers' anger rose and, fanned by revolutionary ideas imported from France, culminated in the revolt known as the Inconfidência

Mineira. Led by an Ouro Preto dentist known as Tiradentes ("Tooth Puller"), a dozen outraged Mineiro citizens conspired to rise up against the Portuguese. After their plans were discovered, all plotters were exiled to Mozambique and Angola, with the exception of Tiradentes. The Tooth Puller was hung in public in Rio before having his severed body parts paraded around Ouro Preto as a warning to future rebels. The horrific measures only succeeded in transforming Tiradentes into a national hero and fanning the flames of independence. Indeed, the Inconfidência Mineira was only one of many popular revolts that erupted throughout the 18th century as settlers who increasingly considered themselves native Brazilians chafed under the authority of Portugal and its colonial administrators.

While citizens of all other South American nations waged battles against their colonial oppressors to achieve independence, Brazil's road to independence took a surprising and unlikely turn. In 1807, having already conquered most of Europe, Napoleon had his eye on Portugal. As the French emperor's troops descended on Lisbon, King João VI of Portugal and his entire court jumped aboard a fleet of ships and fled across the ocean to Brazil. In 1808, the king and his royal retinue of 15,000 disembarked in Rio de Janeiro, which immediately became the new capital of the Portuguese empire. The court's presence quickly transformed Rio from a muddy, mosquito-infested, rough colonial town into a thriving and increasingly elegant capital with grand avenues, parks, and palaces. It also became incredibly cosmopolitan as the king opened the ports to European traders, primarily his English allies, and invited artists, scientists, and scholars from all over Europe to take up residence in Rio. João VI himself was so taken with his tropical court that he was loath to relinquish it, even after the English defeated Napoleon. When he finally returned to Portugal in 1821 to quell a popular uprising, he left his son Pedro in charge as Prince Regent of Brazil.

Young Pedro was impetuous and impatient. Just like his new Brazilian subjects, he quickly grew fed up with having to comply with rules set down by Portugal, whose interests were increasingly at odds with those of its thriving colony. This rebellious stance came to a head in 1822. On September 7, Pedro was getting ready to ride his horse on the shores of the Ipiranga River, near São Paulo, when a messenger arrived with a handful of letters from Lisbon. The demands of the Portuguese court so angered him that he uttered the famous cry "Independence or death!"—thus declaring Brazil independent. With crises enough of their own at home, Portugal put up little resistance. On December 1, Pedro crowned himself Dom Pedro I, and became the first and only New World emperor.

EMPIRE

Due to his headstrong and autocratic nature (coupled with numerous sex scandals), Pedro I's imperial reign was short-lived. In 1824, he presided over the creation of Brazil's first constitution and, in theory, accepted his status as constitutional monarch. In practice, just as he had refused to cooperate with Portugal's government, he wouldn't share power with Brazilian members of parliament. When increasingly pressed to do so, he once again lost his temper and abdicated. In 1831, he returned to Portugal, leaving Brazil in the hands of his five-year-old son, Pedro II. Without a strong leader in charge, over the next decade revolts broke out throughout the country, from Pará and Maranhão in the north to Rio Grande do Sul. Brazilians fought against Portuguese loyalists, slaves rebelled against their masters, and the poor rose up against the privileges of wealthy landowners.

Faced with the risk of the country being torn apart, Pedro II was quickly crowned emperor in 1840. Although only 14, Dom Pedro II was a highly intelligent, progressive, and judicious leader who was admired by both the conservative elite and the more liberal republicans. His authority quickly quelled the regional uprisings, and under his long reign Brazil enjoyed growth and stability. During this time, the Southeast definitively eclipsed the Northeast in importance, spurred on by Rio's political and cultural relevance and the beginning of the lucrative coffee boom, which brought a flood of European immigrants to the fertile hills of Rio de Janeiro, São Paulo, and Paraná as well as to the cities of the South.

ABOLITION OF SLAVERY

A main reason for the demise of the Northeast was slavery, or rather its end. Since Brazil's earliest days as a colony, an estimated 10 million slaves had been shipped across the Atlantic from Africa—roughly 10 times the number transported to the United States. Despite the cruel punishments they faced, many slaves revolted, and countless others escaped. Throughout Brazil, but particularly in the Northeast, the fugitives established isolated communities known as *quilombos.* Although they lived a subsistence existence, many were able to preserve the religious and cultural traditions of their African ancestors, some of which survive today. The biggest and most famous *quilombo,* Palmares, located in northern Alagoas, functioned as a veritable republic. Led by the fierce warrior Zumbi, the *quilombo* was able to defend itself from white settlers and government troops for years. Although Zumbi was finally betrayed and killed, he became a national symbol of black resistance.

However, there was no way Brazilian plantation owners were going to give up their lifestyle and wealth by voluntarily liberating slaves, as dictated to them by their English trading partners, who abolished slavery in 1807. Although they paid lip service to the British by pretending to embark on reforms, in reality their efforts were *para inglês ver* ("for the English to see")—an expression that is still used today to express the act of pretending to do something but not really doing it. The English weren't fooled. During the 1830s and 1840s, they sent navy vessels to the Brazilian coast to capture slave ships and confiscate their human cargo. Brazil finally abolished the slave trade in 1854, but slavery was still legal in Brazil. As a growing abolitionist movement spread across more enlightened regions of the country, Dom Pedro II reluctantly signed laws freeing the children of female slaves (1871) and the very few slaves over the age of 65 (1885). On May 13, 1888, his daughter, Princesa Isabel, signed the Lei Áurea, giving Brazil the dubious distinction of being the last of the New World nations to ban slavery.

The end of slavery had several major repercussions. It brought about the demise of the northeastern sugar and cotton plantation economies and caused the region (and its land-owning elite) to enter a long period of decadence that it would take a century to recuperate from. It also created a vast population of free but poor and uneducated black Brazilians, who had to fend for themselves and find work, a phenomenon that often sadly led to a life of "paid" slavery.

Politically, abolition was the final straw that broke the Brazilian empire. For some time, fueled by Europe's republican tendencies, Brazil's growing urban intellectual classes had been clamoring for the end of the monarchy. Increasingly, Pedro II's staunchest defenders had been the conservative land-owning elite. But when he had the gall to end slavery, they too turned their backs on him. The final nail in the empire's coffin was the ill-fated Paraguay War (1865-1870), in which Brazil, Argentina, and Uruguay ganged up on their puny but fierce neighbor Paraguay. Although they practically eliminated the male population of Paraguay, the powerful allies didn't emerge unscathed from battle. Brazil lost 100,000 men and racked up serious debts, and Pedro II lost the support of the military. In 1889, a group of army officers, led by Marechal (Marshall) Manuel Deodoro da Fonseca, staged a bloodless coup d'état. Dom Pedro returned to Europe, where he died two years later in Paris.

REPUBLIC

Although the idea had been to install a liberal republic, Deodoro preferred to become the nation's first of many military dictators. Within weeks, however, he proved so incompetent that not even the military would back him, and he was forced to step down. His deputy, Marechal Floriano Peixoto, was even worse. After he too was forced to resign, Brazil finally got its first democratically elected president in the person of Prudente de Morais.

The first Brazilian republic (1890-1930) coincided with a period of economic boom spurred on by two major cash crops: coffee and rubber. By 1890, coffee represented two-thirds of Brazil's exports and was responsible for propelling the small town of São Paulo into a thriving city that gradually became the economic hub of Brazil. Coffee barons built lavish mansions along the country lane that would gradually morph into Avenida Paulista. They also wisely invested in industry (initially textiles), foreseeing the day that Brazil's coffee boom might go bust. The rubber barons of the Amazon were not nearly so shrewd. In the mid-19th century, Charles Goodyear's invention of vulcanization coincided with the rediscovery of the latex produced by an Amazonian tree known as *Hevea brasiliensis* (the region's Indians had been making rubber for centuries). Floods of fortune seekers from all over the world descended on the primitive rain forest to tap for this rare commodity coveted by budding First World industries. The fabulous fortunes made were spent on transforming the cities of Belém and Manaus into tropical versions of Paris, with grand boulevards, theaters, and pretensions, such as wearing fur coats to go to the opera. But when rubber seeds were secretly smuggled out of the forest by an Englishman to British colonies in Asia, whose plantations were much more efficient, the rubber boom went bust, and the barons bankrupt. The Amazon returned to its former slumber, from which it would only awaken in the late 20th century.

Like São Paulo, Minas Gerais boasted a large population and thriving economy. Although coffee grew in Minas's lush hills, the richest and most powerful interests were the landowners who raised dairy cows. Together with São Paulo's coffee barons, they formed a powerful elite, becoming so influential in national government that Brazilian politics came to be defined as the system of *café com leite* (coffee with milk), an allusion to the fact that not only did these local interests dominate all policies but that all presidencies during this period alternated between cronies from São Paulo and Minas. Thanks to the privileges enjoyed and the corruption that ensued, it wasn't long before popular revolts began to take place, particularly among the growing number of working-class Brazilians.

GETÚLIO VARGAS AND THE ESTADO NOVO

The increasing dissatisfaction with *café com leite* politics came to a head in 1930. The Great Depression knocked the bottom out of the coffee market. To save the coffee elite from ruin, the government spent millions buying coffee at a fixed rate, only to burn the harvest for lack of foreign buyers. Workers and leaders from other parts of the country were outraged. Violent revolts broke out in the Northeast, Rio, and Rio Grande do Sul, home of a charismatic and populist politician named Getúlio Vargas. When a military coup deposed the government, Vargas became Brazil's new president—for the next 15 years. An astute politician, fervent nationalist, and flamboyant populist along the lines of his colleague in neighboring Argentina, Juan Perón, Vargas ushered in a new era. He jump-started Brazilian industry by nationalizing the burgeoning oil, steel, and electrical sectors. He endeared himself to the masses by creating a health and social welfare system. He implemented a minimum wage and labor laws and extended the right to vote to women. The way he carried out these radical reforms was by declaring himself dictator and establishing a regime known as the Estado Novo (New State), which went into effect in 1937. Opposition parties were prohibited, the press was censored, and dissidence was punished with jail sentences. While democracy went into hiding, his centralized government broke the hold of the regional elite, and agriculture and industry thrived.

When World War II broke out, Brazil remained neutral, although Vargas flirted with both the Axis and the Allies. Coaxed by promises of generous American financial aid in return for the right to establish U.S. military bases along the Northeast coast, Vargas finally chose the Allied side in 1942, sending Brazilian soldiers to participate in the invasion of Italy. However, the contradiction between fighting for freedom abroad while running a fascist dictatorship at home proved difficult to justify. At the end of the war, military pressure convinced Vargas to relinquish his powers in 1945. However, Vargas always remained largely popular with the Brazilian people, who returned him to power in 1950—this time as a democratically elected president. However, without his fascist powers to protect him, his tenure was marred by public accusations of corruption. The fiercest attacks were spearheaded by a Carioca journalist, Carlos Lacerda, who had political ambitions of his own. When an attack on Lacerda's life was traced to one of Vargas's bodyguards, the ensuing scandal was so great that Vargas was asked to resign. Instead, on the night of August 4, 1954, he went into his bedroom at the Palácio do Catete in Rio and shot himself through the heart, leaving a love letter-suicide note to the Brazilian people. Popular grief was so great that Lacerda was forced to leave the country.

JK AND BRASÍLIA

Juscelino Kubitschek, popularly known as "JK," won the 1956 presidential elections with the aid of the snappy campaign slogan "50 years in five": He would accomplish in five years what most leaders could only accomplish in 50. The visionary and determined Kubitschek—who had cut his political teeth as mayor of Belo Horizonte and governor of Minas Gerais—promised Brazilians

a future of great growth and change. He set about making good on his promise by immediately hiring a team of highly talented modernist architects to build a utopian new Brazilian capital in the geographical heart of the nation. Although the spot for Brasília's construction was literally located in the middle of nowhere, Kubitschek's ambitious goal was to open up Brazil's vast and deserted interior to settlement and development. Many critics thought he was insane—particularly Rio's political elite, who were loath to forsake the Cidade Maravilhosa for the dry and dusty Planalto Central—but the *"presidente bossa nova"* proved them wrong. With a team led by brilliant architect Oscar Niemeyer, construction of the space-age capital advanced at rapid speed.

In the end, Kubitschek fulfilled his promise to the people. Before his term was over, he presided over the April 21, 1960, inauguration of the new capital, an event that was celebrated with much pomp. The only problem was the massive bill. Despite the fact that Kubitschek had presided over a period of strong economic growth, the costs of building Brasília left the nation in serious debt, which would later play a part in the astronomic rates of inflation that gripped Brazil in the 1970s.

MILITARY RULE (1964-1985)

JK was succeeded by much lesser men. Neither Jânio Quadros (who lasted only six months in power) nor his vice president and successor, João Goulart, possessed the skill necessary to deal with rising inflation or resolve the growing social conflicts that pitted urban workers against factory owners and rural peasants against rich landowners. With a Cold War fear of communism in the air, Goulart's leftist leanings terrified the Brazilian right, including the military, particularly when the new president decided to explicitly support the trade unions and peasant organizations. On March 31, 1964, with implicit backing of the U.S. government and led by a small group of right-wing generals, military troops carried out a quick, nonviolent coup. While Goulart was deposed and went into exile in Uruguay, the generals set to work transforming Brazil into a military dictatorship. Humberto Castelo Branco became president—the first in a series of generals to lead the country by iron rule over the next quarter of a century. Congress was dissolved, political parties were banned, unions were outlawed, and the media was censored. The situation grew even more drastic when General Emílio Garrastazu Médici took over in 1969. The next five years proved to be the most brutal of Brazil's military regime. Thousands of people were arrested, jailed, tortured, and even killed for even the most indirect criticism, "subversive" political beliefs, or the expression of ideas deemed unsuitable by the regime. Many leading artists and intellectuals, among them leading musicians such as Chico Buarque and Gilberto Gil, along with professor and later president Fernando Henrique Cardoso, went into exile during these years. While Brazil's dictatorship was less hard line than those of its neighbors, Chile and Argentina, where hundreds of thousands were made to "disappear," there was widespread hatred of the military leaders, who were not only cruel but corrupt as well.

During the first decade of military rule, Brazil experienced phenomenal rates of economic growth surpassing 10 percent a year. This period became known as the "Economic Miracle." Industry boomed, and an exodus of workers from the poor Northeast migrated en masse to the manufacturing hub of São Paulo, which grew to become Latin America's financial and economic powerhouse. While many found factory jobs and other low-wage employment, others clustered in shacks on the growing city outskirts. Indeed, while some Brazilians grew rich, far more remained miserable as these slums, known as *favelas,* began to mushroom in major cities.

To further stimulate development, the government drummed up foreign investors to finance immense (and controversially dubious) megaprojects such as the Itaipu Dam,

near Iguaçu Falls, and the Transamazônica highway, which opened up access through the impenetrable forest all the way to the Peruvian border. The problem came when the oil crisis of 1974 punctured the Economic Miracle. By the beginning of the 1980s, as inflation soared and Brazilian currency took a nosedive, foreign investors started clamoring for Brazil to pay its enormous and constantly multiplying debts.

PERIOD OF *ABERTURA* (1979-1985)

Increasingly fed up with censorship, corruption scandals, and a crippled economy, Brazil's middle classes and workers began to express widespread opposition to the military dictatorship. In São Paulo, a series of workers' strikes spread like wildfire. A leader for the illegal unions was a young worker from Pernambuco who had lost a finger in a factory accident. Luíz Inácio da Silva (who went by the nickname "Lula") was a fierce and charismatic leader. When the government sent troops to repress the striking workers, Lula and his colleagues stood their ground. The government was forced not only to back down but to legalize unions as well. Fearing mass revolts, President João Figueiredo also began to implement certain reforms, part of a gradual *"abertura"* (opening) process that would pave the way for Brazil's return to democratic rule. Censorship rules were relaxed, and political dissidents were allowed to return from exile. In 1982, the first democratic municipal and state elections were held.

Federal elections were called for 1985. The military government had allowed several official opposition parties to be formed. Among them was the Partido dos Trabalhadores (PT), or Workers Party, one of whose founders was Lula. However, loath to completely relinquish power, the generals also decided that the new president would be elected by an electoral college made up of members with strong military sympathies. The opposition parties' furor erupted in a campaign for *"diretas já"* (direct elections now), which propelled millions of outraged citizens to the streets. Despite the overwhelming support of the public and opposition parties, the military-friendly Senate managed to defeat the *diretas já* amendment. However, they couldn't defeat Tancredo Neves, a highly respected Mineiro politician who had been Getúlio Vargas's minister of justice. As the opposition candidate running against yet another general, Neves not only seduced electoral college voters from all the opposition parties but swayed many disenchanted military stalwarts as well. As a result, in January 1985, Neves won a resounding majority. Throughout Brazil, elated citizens took to the streets to celebrate the end of military dictatorship and the beginning of a Nova República (New Republic).

RETURN OF DEMOCRACY

Brazilians anxiously waited for the first civilian president in two decades to be sworn in as president. Tragically, the night before his inauguration ceremony, Tancredo Neves was rushed to the hospital with a bleeding stomach tumor. Although the tumor wasn't fatal, the hospital was. Neves caught septicemia, a bacterial infection that led to his death. After millions mourned him, they watched the televised swearing-in of his vice president, José Sarney, an old-school and uninspiring former state governor from Maranhão. As Brazil's first new democratic president, Sarney quickly dashed Brazilians' hopes of a better future. Due to the ballooning foreign debt, inflation was so high that currencies were adopted and discarded with regularity. An uncensored press was free to report the endless string of financial scandals that sullied the government's reputation and filled struggling Brazilians with disgust.

Things only got worse with the election of Sarney's successor: a pretty-boy millionaire and karate champ named Fernando Collor de Mello. A dashing figure who wouldn't have been out of place on a nightly *novela* (soap opera), Collor had been governor of the small northeastern state of Alagoas and was a member of one of its oldest and richest families. After narrowly defeating the PT's Lula da Silva in 1990, he presided over a government whose disasters reached epic proportions. Collor's solution to controlling hyperinflation was to freeze Brazilians' bank accounts, a measure that quickly incited the wrath of the middle classes (poor Brazilians don't have bank accounts and, at the time, rich Brazilians had their money stashed overseas). Feelings of outrage spread throughout the populace when it came to light (via Collor's own brother, Pedro) that Collor and his cronies had been siphoning billions of dollars in public money into private accounts. The scandal was so great that Congress began impeachment proceedings, spurred on by hundreds of thousands of Brazilians who took to the streets demanding justice. Forced to step down in September of 1992, Collor was banned from political office for eight years. Much of this time he spent in Miami, working on his tan and plotting his comeback, which—in keeping with Brazilian political norms—took place when he was reelected in 2006 for an eight-year term as a senator for his home state of Alagoas.

Collor was replaced by his vice president, Itamar Franco, a weak figure who nonetheless made the inspired decision to select as his finance minister a clever politician and savvy economist named Fernando Henrique Cardoso. Known popularly as "FHC," Cardoso was a widely respected São Paulo sociologist with leftist leanings who had gone into exile during the military dictatorship. By the time he joined Franco's government, his politics had migrated center right, as had his economics, which were influenced by years spent teaching and studying in the United States. FHC took on Brazil's floundering economy by implementing the "Plano Real" in 1994. By creating a new currency, the *real,* and tying its value to the U.S. dollar, Cardoso finally brought runaway inflation to a grinding halt for the first time in decades. When elections were held the following year, he easily defeated his rival, Lula.

With FHC as president for the next eight years (1994-2002), the New Republic finally had its first serious and competent leader. Inflation remained low and the economy began to grow in leaps and bounds, spurred on by rampant privatization of corrupt and inefficient public companies, the opening up of Brazil's frontiers to foreign capital and interests, and the relaxation of importation barriers. Although initially, inefficiently run companies that had survived due to lack of foreign competition sank, many others were forced to get competitive in a hurry, and they did so, reaching international levels of quality, efficiency, and innovation. Massive economic reforms were accompanied by the beginnings of much-needed political and social reforms, with particular focus on the critical areas of health and education. However, the eternally gaping distance between Brazil's haves and have-nots was hardly bridged at all. During FHC's second presidential term, a series of large-scale corruption scandals once again revealed the fundamentally rotten state of Brazil's political and justice systems.

THE PT, LULA, AND DILMA

After competing and being narrowly defeated in every presidential election since 1990, in 2001 the charismatic leader of the Partido dos Trabalhadores (PT), Luíz Inácio ("Lula") da Silva, finally triumphed on his fourth attempt. Lula's victory was truly a watershed moment in Brazil's turbulent and often tragic political history. In a country that for 500 years had been ruled by members of the wealthy elite, it was nothing short of miraculous that a poor boy from the drought-ridden Sertão of Pernambuco, without a university education, should rise to the nation's most powerful position. As a boy, Lula had escaped poverty by traveling to São Paulo crammed into the back of a truck. Arriving in the big city, he rose from shoeshine boy to factory worker, then to union leader and champion of workers' rights, and finally to leader of the PT. But nobody ever thought he'd wind up president.

Excluding conservatives made nervous by his Marxist rants of the past, Brazil's masses, along with its intellectual and artistic classes, went wild over Lula's triumph. In the heady early months of his mandate, the popular and populist soccer-playing and *churrasco*-eating president was greeted as something of a messiah. His common touch aside, the apprehensive rich and right-wingers needn't have worried. Over the years, Lula had toned down his firebrand rhetoric substantially (becoming known as "Lula Light"). While he awarded top government ministries to radical leftist dissidents of the dictatorship years and made no secret of his friendships with Cuba's Fidel Castro and Venezuela's Hugo Chávez, Lula (much to the dismay of more hard-core members of the PT) largely stayed the central course mapped out by his predecessor, FHC.

Economically, he continued to steer Brazil on the road to increasing globalization, which has resulted in a booming Brazilian economy. More importantly, his government has made headway in addressing some of the glaring social disparities that have always led Brazil to being compared to an uneasy fusion of Belgium and Bangladesh. Increasing numbers of children are attending school with the aid of subsidies paid to parents through the Bolsa Familia program. And for the first time in history, the standard of living of Brazil's poor is finally on the upswing. A historic rise in minimum wages, falling interest rates, and easily available credit to people who want to buy homes or start small businesses has been responsible for catapulting an estimated 40 million Brazilians out of poverty and into the rungs of the lower-middle (purchasing) classes. The situation has improved the most in the Northeast and North, which were traditionally the most neglected of Brazil's regions.

On the downside, while the PT was revered for its socialist ideals and integrity during its 20-year role as the main opposition party to successive governments, once the party came to power, it wasn't long before the "power corrupts" adage kicked in and scams and scandals began to erupt. While the PT's reputation was tarnished, Lula himself emerged un-scathed—nicknamed "the Teflon president," since nothing bad stuck to him. Despite the damage done to the party, Lula was elected to a second presidential term in November 2006, and when he finally left office at the end of 2010, he boasted a historic approval rating of 83 percent.

It was largely due to Lula's immense popularity that Dilma Rousseff, his chief of staff and handpicked successor, was elected Brazil's first woman president in November 2010, with the promise that she would continue to steer Brazil along the successful path toward increased economic prosperity and social equality. Less charismatic and more technocratic than Lula, "Dilma"—a former member of an underground military group, she was tortured during the military dictatorship—hails from the state of Minas Gerais but cut her political teeth in Rio Grande do Sul, where she was state minister of energy. A focus of her new government is improving education, considered a major obstacle to Brazil really taking off. During Dilma's first year in power, she earned kudos for seeming to take on Brazil's endemic corruption when she fired no fewer than six of her own cabinet ministers who had become embroiled in scandals. This, combined with record low unemployment and annual economic growth rates that reached 7.5 percent, saw her approval ratings hit 70 percent.

Since 2012, however, Brazil has suffered from an economic slowdown from which it shows no signs of recuperating. At the same time, costs—and costs of living—have gone up consistently, sending a record number of Brazilians (close to 25 percent of the population—many of whom have credit, and credit cards, for the first time in their lives) into debt. Overspending has been playing out on the macro level as well. When Brazil won the bid to host the 2014 World Cup and the 2016 Summer Olympics, Brazilians were euphoric,

believing it was finally their chance to shine upon the world stage. Since then, however, construction of stadiums and sporting venues has been plagued by the usual delays, poor planning, and corruption, while costs have skyrocketed. At the same time, grand plans to upgrade and expand Brazil's woefully inadequate infrastructure—roads, airports, public transport systems—have advanced at a snail's pace or been abandoned altogether.

Popular frustration came to a head in June 2013, when street protests against a planned bus fare increase in São Paulo tapped into general rage at the government pouring billions into soccer stadiums while public services such as transportation, health, and education remain at Third World levels. Fanning the flames is the fact that an average Brazilian pays around 30 percent of his or her salary to income tax. Throughout the country, millions of angry Brazilians from all segments of society took to the streets in the largest protests since the dying days of the military dictatorship. Since then, fueled by social media (Brazilians are the biggest Facebook users on the planet after Americans), sporadic protests—accompanied by police violence—have erupted constantly, particularly in Rio and São Paulo, leaving Dilma's government and the political elite in a state of bewilderment.

After the unprecedented levels of progress and growth the country has witnessed in the last 10 years, it's only natural that a rapidly changing Brazil is now experiencing growing pains. The general improvement of Brazilians' standard of living coupled with a surge in buying power and access to information via traditional and alternative media has made many Brazilians aware of their rights as citizens. As they witness critical problems ranging from corruption, crack addiction, and urban violence to inequality, it's encouraging that they are so critical, vocal, and invested in creating, and participating in, a more prosperous, just, and better Brazil of the future.

Government

The Federal Republic of Brazil is a democratic system of government that resembles the federal system in the United States. The elected president is both the head of state and the head of the federal government. Brazil's current Constitution dates from 1988.

ORGANIZATION

Brazil's national government consists of three branches: the executive, legislative, and judiciary. The head of the executive branch is the President of the Republic, who is elected to office by universal suffrage. Voting is done by an extremely high-tech computerized ballot system. Error or fraud is almost impossible. Voters who can't read can choose the candidate of their choice by selecting a head shot. (To this day, Brazilians are amazed by the infamous system of chads in the United States.) Voting is mandatory for all literate citizens between 18 and 70 years of age, and those who don't vote must present an official justification or pay a small fine.

The president chooses a running mate who will be the vice president. Should anything happen to the president, the vice president assumes his or her position for the rest of the four-year term. Once elected to office, the president may appoint his or her own ministers, whom he or she can also dismiss at any time. According to the Brazilian Constitution, if there is just cause, Congress can vote to have the president removed from office through impeachment.

Brazil's legislative power is concentrated in the hands of the Congresso (National Congress), which consists of two houses: The Câmara dos Deputados (Chamber of Deputies), the lower house, and the Senado (Senate), the upper house. The Chamber of Deputies seats 513 deputies, representing each of the Brazilian states in numbers proportional to their populations. Deputies are elected by popular vote for terms of four years.

The Senate seats 81 senators—three for each of Brazil's 26 states and three for the Federal District of Brasília. Senators are elected for terms of eight years. Both deputies and senators can run for reelection as many times as they want.

The judiciary is headed by the Federal Supreme Court, which is the highest court in the land. Its main headquarters are in Brasília, but the court's jurisdiction extends throughout the country. Its 11 judges are appointed for life by the president on approval from a Senate majority; judges in state courts are also appointed for life.

POLITICAL PARTIES

Brazil's party system is fairly chaotic to an outsider. Parties are created and disappear all the time, and candidates easily and opportunistically switch from one to another without any compunction (recent reforms have tried to limit this habit). Frequently, this party switching occurs a few months prior to an election. Both the party names and common acronyms are confusing to keep track of, even for Brazilians. Many have no ideological affiliation whatsoever. There are, however, a few main parties whose delegates usually compete for major positions. Presently, after being the country's main opposition party, the traditionally left-wing Partido dos Trabalhadores (Workers' Party), or PT, wields power in the federal government. Other major parties that hover around the center and center-right include the Partido do Movimento Democrático Brasileiro (Brazilian Democratic Movement Party), or PMDB; the Partido da Social Democrácia Brasileira (Brazilian Social Democracy Party), or PSDB; and the Democratas (Democrats), or DEM. Currently, governing Brazil is all about making strategic alliances with members of other parties in order to pass or defeat legislation. Reaching a consensus involves enormous amounts of time and energy (and bribes in the form of favors or money). Senate debates are broadcast live on a television station known as TV Senado. During major government scandals, this can make for quite dramatic viewing.

JUDICIAL AND PENAL SYSTEMS

Brazilian law is derived from Portuguese civil law. The principal legal document is the National Constitution of 1988, which divides power between federal and state judicial branches. State-level courts preside over all civil and criminal cases, with appeals taken to regional federal courts. The Supremo Tribunal Federal (Supreme Court) makes final, binding decisions on legal matters and is also in charge of interpreting the Constitution. Justice, when it is delivered in Brazil, is famously slow. Loopholes are seemingly endless, and lawsuits can be delayed by numerous appeals. Often a final ruling can be delayed for years, if not decades.

Justice is definitely not blind in Brazil. The rich, white, and powerful often literally get away with murder, while the poorer you are and the darker your skin tone, the greater your chances of being beaten up, tossed in a crowded cell, and locked away. Crime is a big problem throughout all of Brazil, but the shamelessness with which white-collar crime is committed is staggering. Through fraud, embezzlement, kickbacks, and bribes, billions of dollars in public funds are routinely siphoned away from the people who need it most. As the have-nots resort to ever more violent holdups, kidnappings, and break-ins, Brazil's elite largely wall themselves up in closed condominium complexes with electric fences, cameras, and bodyguards. It's a vicious, tragic cycle, and one of Brazil's greatest challenges. In recent years, small instances of justice have shaken the complete impunity with which the rich and powerful operate. However, in most cases, change is difficult, and the status quo remains the same.

Similarly, by law, penal conditions for criminals who have committed the same crime vary depending on the perp's degree of education. Those without a high school diploma get thrown in overcrowded cells that are known for their squalor and violence. A doctoral degree earns you the privilege of a cleaner solitary cell, or at least one that is shared with two or three other diploma-bearing criminals.

Economy

Brazil has always been incredibly wealthy in natural resources. Until the 20th century, the economy was based on a series of cycles that exploited a single export commodity: brazilwood in the 16th century, sugarcane in the 16th and 17th centuries, gold, silver, and gemstones in the 18th century, and finally coffee and rubber in the 19th century. Apart from these boom-and-bust cycles, agriculture and cattle-raising were constant activities, but both were mainly limited to local consumption. Industrialization began in the early 20th century but didn't really kick in until the 1950s, which coincided with the beginnings of Brazil's major automobile, petrochemical, and steel industries.

After a difficult sink-or-swim period that accompanied the opening up of the economy to the world in the mid-1980s, Brazil enjoyed robust growth rates of more than 5 percent a year for much of the period between 2000-2010 before slowing in recent years. Even so, the country now ranks as the world's seventh-largest economy in terms of GDP (according to IMF and World Bank calculations). Brazil's economy is larger than that of all other South American countries, and increasingly competitive, high-quality, and innovative Brazilian goods are steadily making their presence felt in international markets. Rich in natural resources, particularly vast quantities of oil found in offshore deposits, and capable of supplying most of its own needs in terms of food, primary resources, energy, and manufactured products, Brazil is extremely self-sufficient. Well prepared to withstand rising imported fuel and food costs that are proving devastating for other countries, the country also boasts a domestic market of nearly 200 million people who have more disposable income to burn than ever before.

AGRICULTURE

Brazil's moderate climate coupled with its fertile soil and its immense territory makes it an ideal place for the cultivation of many crops. Brazil is a leading world producer of coffee, soybeans, rice, corn, sugarcane, cocoa, and citrus fruits such as limes and oranges (Brazil is the world's largest producer and exporter of OJ). It is also the planet's largest exporter of both chicken and beef. Brazilian land is some of the cheapest on the planet. In recent years, feeling crowded on their small plots, an increasing number of European farmers have invested in vast farms in the Central-West and North, where they are amazed at how fast crops grow. Indeed, over the last two decades, agribusiness has become increasingly high-tech. As a result, today Brazil boasts one of the world's most productive agricultural sectors.

INDUSTRY AND FINANCE

Brazilian industry, which is extremely diversified and well developed, currently accounts for around one-third of the country's GDP. Although major industrial activities have traditionally been concentrated in the Southeast (particularly São Paulo and Minas) and the South, in the last few years significant investments have been made in the Northeast and the North. Among Brazil's leading manufacturing industries are the automobile, aircraft, steel, mining, petrochemical, computer, and durable consumer goods sectors. Additionally, the country has a diverse and sophisticated service industry. Financial services are particularly well developed. São Paulo is Latin America's largest financial center, and its stock exchange, Bovespa, is now the third-largest stock exchange in the world.

ENERGY

Brazil used to import 70 percent of its energy from overseas. Since 2006, however, the nation has been capable of meeting all its own energy needs. Currently around 73 percent of the country's electricity needs are supplied by enormous hydroelectric dams, such as Itaipu in Paraná and Tucuruí in Pará. Brazil has also flirted with nuclear energy with the building of Angra I, Angra II, and the soon-to-be inaugurated Angra III reactors; all are located in an otherwise idyllic spot of coastline in the state of Rio de Janeiro.

In late 2007, as rising oil prices sent the planet into panic, Brazil became the envy of the many countries when the national oil giant Petrobras discovered a vast deepwater reserve off the coast of Rio de Janeiro. The so-called Tupi reserve is estimated to hold up to 8 billion barrels of oil and could lead to Brazil becoming the newest member of OPEC. However, it's not as if Brazil is beholden to the increasingly coveted fossil fuel. Following the first oil crisis of 1974, the government's visionary solution was to begin converting sugarcane into ethanol as a cheaper and non-polluting fuel for all vehicles. Today, Brazil is the world's No. 1 producer of sugarcane alcohol; all Brazilian vehicles are flex-fuel models that run on gas, alcohol, or a mixture of both.

TOURISM

In the last decade, Brazilian tourism has developed enormously. Since 2000 there has been a major spike in tourists from North America and especially Europe. In 2012, Brazil was the second-largest tourist destination in Latin America, after Mexico. However, much greater than the growth of international tourism (which accounts for less than 10 percent) has been the rise in the number of Brazilians themselves who are increasingly able to travel. Because of its endless natural attractions, Brazil's major tourism niche is ecotourism, which has the advantage of providing sustainable development. Particularly in the North and Northeast, tourism is playing a pivotal role in the development of local economies. In 2012 the sector accounted, directly and indirectly, for 9.3 percent of GDP.

People and Culture

DEMOGRAPHICS

According to statistics compiled during the 2010 census, Brazil has a population of 199 million, making it the fifth-most populous country in the world. Until the mid-20th century, Brazil was a largely rural place. Today, around 84 percent of the people live in major cities, most of which line the coast. In contrast, the vast Amazonian region is practically deserted. The most populous Brazilian city is São Paulo, with 11.8 million people, followed by Rio de Janeiro with 6.4 million, and Salvador with 2.9 million. Indeed, the vast majority of the population is concentrated in the Southeast states of Rio de Janeiro, Minas Gerais, and São Paulo.

Life expectancy among Brazilians has improved greatly in recent decades. In 2012, the average life span of Brazilian women was 78.3 years, while for men it was 71 years. The days of big families are a thing of the past. The average Brazilian woman today bears 1.9 children. Although the official literacy rate of Brazilians over the age of 15 is 90 percent, the concept of "literacy" should be taken with a grain of salt. Included among so-called literate Brazilians are many people who can do little more than write numbers and their names and recognize a few dozen simple words.

ETHNICITY AND RACE

Five centuries of commingling has resulted in a population that is extremely diverse, which explains the endless array of physical types as well as an impressive openness toward biological, cultural, and religious differences.

Indigenous Groups

When the Portuguese first arrived in Brazil in 1500, an estimated 5 million indigenous people, most belonging to the Tupi and Guarani groups, inhabited this vast territory. Today, only about 900,000 of their descendants remain, representing 0.4 percent of the total population. Although indigenous groups live throughout Brazil, the majority reside in the least populated areas of the Central-West and the Amazon. The degree to which they have succeeded in preserving the traditions and lifestyles of their ancestors varies enormously. However, there are small communities deep within the Amazon (protected by FUNAI, the federal agency of Indian affairs) that have never had contact with "civilization." According to the results of a recent mitochondrial DNA survey, an estimated 60 million Brazilians can lay claim to at least one ancestor from an indigenous group. Brazilians who are descended from both indigenous groups and Europeans are known as *caboclos.*

Africans

Between the early days of colonial Brazil and the abolition of slavery in 1888, it's estimated that more than 4 million slaves were brought to Brazil from Africa. The majority of them were Bantu peoples from Portugal's African colonies, such as Mozambique and Angola, as well as Yoruba from the western coastal region of what is now Benin and Nigeria. Although you'll find Brazilians of African descent throughout the country, the largest black communities are in Rio and the coastal areas of the Northeast, particularly Salvador da Bahia, where 85 percent of the population boasts some African ancestry.

Overall, only 7.6 percent of Brazilians (roughly 14.5 million) consider themselves

Racism in Brazil

In the early 20th century, noted Brazilian anthropologist Gilberto Freyre gave rise to the official myth of Brazil as a paragon of racial harmony, whose spontaneous mixture of indigenous peoples, Africans, and Europeans stood as a utopian counterpoint to the polarized conflicts that characterized race relations in the United States. To this day, many Brazilians still believe in the myth. Foreigners are inevitably impressed by the easy mingling of people, regardless of color, and by the fact that so many African elements —samba, capoeira, Carnaval —have become icons of Brazilianness, espoused by all Brazilians.

However, dig deep enough and the myth begins to crack. Precisely what makes racism in Brazil so insidious is that, unlike racism in the United States, it isn't in your face—so it's easier to deny it exists and maintain a status quo in which the whiter you are, the more money, education, and opportunities you have. As you travel around in Brazil, take note of the politicians, the business leaders, the models and TV stars, the domestic tourists, the kids in private-school uniforms, and the people walking around in swanky neighborhoods, eating in upscale restaurants, staying in hotels, and flying on airplanes with you. The vast majority are white. Few tourists will come into contact with Brazilians who live in *favelas* (slums). However, you will notice that the majority of those living on the streets, performing menial jobs or selling wares on the sidewalk, lining up for buses, or working as doormen, cleaning women, or nannies are inevitably black. If you're a white man in Brazil and you walk around with a black Brazilian female friend, the immediate conclusion is that you're a john and your friend is a prostitute (or else that she's a gold-digger and you're rich husband material). A dark-skinned mother with a lighter-skinned child will often be assumed to be the child's nanny and treated as such.

The result of this type of racism isn't hate crimes or white supremacy groups. But the fact is that white Brazilians overwhelmingly dominate government, business, and the media. Two notable exceptions are soccer and music, where black Brazilians are revered. Fortunately, in recent years, change has finally begun to take root. In 2002, the Brazilian government made it mandatory to teach African and Afro-Brazilian history and culture as part of the universal school curriculum. Then President Lula also nominated an Afro-Brazilian, Edson Santos, to head the newly created Ministry of Racial Equality. Shortly after, federal and state universities began implementing quotas in an attempt to redress the fact that only 5 percent of black Brazilians have university degrees.

to be "black." However, according to the 2010 census, another 82 million Brazilians can claim to possess some African ancestry. They are often referred to by the traditional appellate *"pardo,"* meaning "colored" (*pardo* is actually a beige-caramel color). Due to a tradition of miscegenation—the Portuguese had no compunction about having extramarital relationships with their slaves—most Brazilians are of mixed race, or *mulato*; Brazilians descended from a mixture of Africans and Indians are known as *cafuzos*. The varying shades of skin color and the way in which they are perceived and projected among different social milieus, however, is extremely complex and nuanced.

The official designation these days is *afro-descendente* or *afro-brasileiro*. Applicable to anyone with African origins, these terms are based more on cultural identity than skin color. In terms of skin color, Brazilians have come up with hundreds of often extremely creative terms to designate themselves and confound racial categorization. These range from *preto retinto* (repainted black) and *jabuticaba* (a dark purple berry-like fruit), both of which refer to darker skin tones, to *jegue quando foge* (donkey when it runs away) and *formiga* (ant), on a somewhat lighter scale. Many of these euphemistic designations have their origin in a subtle yet deeply rooted racism that is still very much alive in Brazil. As a result, darker-skinned Brazilians sometimes try, often subconsciously, to *embranquecer* (to become more white) by choosing a nonblack identity for themselves. This phenomenon explains why only 7 percent of Afro-Brazilians refer to themselves as *"negro."* Instead, many mixed-race Brazilians refer to themselves as *"mulatos,"* or even *"mulatos claros"* (light-skinned *mulatos*).

Europeans

The first Europeans to set foot in Brazil were the Portuguese, who claimed the territory as their own. The next five centuries saw various waves of immigration; as a result, the vast majority of Brazilians can lay claim to some Portuguese ancestry. It wasn't until the mid- to late 19th century that other Europeans began to arrive en masse in Brazil. Lured by the promise of vast tracts of fertile land, growing cities, and the beginnings of industry, large numbers of Italians, Germans, and Spaniards, followed by Poles and Ukrainians, flocked to the sparsely populated states of the South and to São Paulo. To this day the South has a distinctly European character, and blond hair and blue eyes are quite common. São Paulo has been a magnet for immigrants from all over the world. The city boasts the largest population of Japanese people outside Japan and of Lebanese outside Lebanon.

REGIONALISM

While Brazil easily absorbs different peoples into its national melting pot, at the same time, historical and geographical specificities have led to the creation of some very distinctive regional cultures. Indeed, despite the shared language, national references, and a strong national identity as "Brazilians," it's not uncommon for a Paulistano or Catarinense visiting Bahia or Maranhão, for example, to suffer from some degree of culture shock when confronted with differences in lifestyle, mentality, language, and cuisine. The reverse is equally true. While some of these regional stereotypes are somewhat cliché—and Brazilians themselves have great fun in conflating and exaggerating them for their own mirth—as with any stereotype, there often exists an underlying kernel of truth. As such, you will find that Bahians live up to their fame for being extremely laid-back, Paulistanos really are efficient workaholics, Cariocas have hedonism

Igreja de São João Batista, Trancoso

down to an art form, Mineiros are taciturn and reserved, Gaúchos exhibit fierce pride, and inhabitants of the northeastern Sertão possess a tough and rough-edged temperament that reflects their surroundings.

RELIGION

Officially, Brazil is the world's largest Roman Catholic country in terms of population. Over the last decade, however, their number has fallen, while great gains have been made by evangelical and Pentecostal churches. Brazil's great talent for syncretism and diversity has resulted in a country with an amazing number of religions, sects, and communities.

Roman Catholicism

Around 64 percent of Brazilians identify themselves as Roman Catholic. Despite the strong presence of churches, endless references to *Deus* (God), various incarnations of *Nossa Senhor* (the Virgin), and prayers, promises, and processions offered up to saints, the majority of Brazilians aren't practicing

Catholics. While Catholicism is a strong presence in the collective culture, the Catholic Church in Brazil has a less rigid reputation than in other Latin American countries.

Protestantism

Around 22 percent of Brazilians adhere to some form of Protestantism. Over the last two decades, an endless number of evangelical and Pentecostal churches have been sprouting like wildfire, particularly in poor rural and suburban neighborhoods where churches such as the immensely popular Igreja Assembleia de Deus (Assembly of God Church) and Igreja Universal do Reino de Deus (Universal Kingdom of God's Church), and numerous tangents thereof have taken root.

Afro-Brazilian Religions

African slaves who were brought to Brazil arrived bereft of everything except their faith. Although the Portuguese strictly banned all such forms of "demon worship," slaves were particularly adept at camouflaging the worship of their deities under the guise of pretending to worship Catholic saints. The consequences of this mingling of religious symbols can be seen today in many religious rituals and celebrations that fuse Catholicism with African and indigenous religious elements.

The end of slavery did not bring about immediate tolerance for Afro-Brazilians to openly practice purer forms of their faith. Candomblé, Brazil's largest Afro-Brazilian cult, was banned well into the 20th century, even in Salvador and parts of Bahia where *terreiros* (traditional houses of worship) are widespread. Today, less than 1 percent of Brazilians adhere to Candomblé and other popular Afro-Brazilian cults, such as Umbanda, which mixes Candomblé practices with spiritualist and indigenous elements. However, in places such as Salvador, Rio, and São Luís, Afro-Brazilian religious elements have entered into mainstream culture. Notable examples include the popularization of Yoruba terms (all Candomblé ceremonies

are conducted in the Yoruba language) and of ritual dances and sacred foods (such as Bahia's famous *acarajés*). Wide segments of the population participate in *festas* honoring *orixás* (deities) in which *presentes* (gifts) are often offered. In Rio and Salvador, you will often find the beaches littered with flowers washed ashore after being offered to the immensely popular *orixá* Iemanjá, goddess of the seas.

Other Faiths

There are numerous spiritualist and esoteric cults practiced throughout Brazil. One of the most popular forms of spiritualism is **Kardecism,** which was named after 19th-century spiritualist Allan Kardec. Its followers believe in multiple reincarnations and in the idea that the spirits of the dead—who can be communicated with during séances—are present among the living. Spiritualism is so popular that it often works its way into the Globo television network's nightly *novelas.*

Other popular cults draw inspiration from Brazil's indigenous cultures. This is the case with **Santo Daime** and **União da Vegetal**; both revolve around imbibing a hallucinogenic potion, *ayahuasca,* which Amazonian indigenous people have used for centuries as a way of achieving transcendental insights. The small but faithful following includes a significant number of middle-class urban dwellers of São Paulo, Brasília, and the South.

LANGUAGE

Brazilians speak Portuguese (not Spanish!) and are responsible for the fact that Portuguese is the sixth-most-spoken language in the world. Since it crossed the Atlantic from Portugal, Brazilian Portuguese has undergone various modifications. The differences between the Portuguese written and spoken in Portugal and that of Brazil are similar to the differences between American and British English. Written Portuguese tends to be more formal, although less so than in Portugal, but spoken Portuguese is extremely casual, with a fabulous array of slang and idiomatic expressions that vary wildly depending on regions and even city neighborhoods (and which you may be hard-pressed to understand).

Brazilian Portuguese is a colorful hybrid that has absorbed words and expressions from all the major groups that make up Brazilian society. Early on, Portuguese settlers were quick to incorporate indigenous terms from Tupi and Guarani languages, in particular terms used to designate the vast compendium of exotica for which no Portuguese words existed. To this day, most names of places (Ipanema, Ibirapuera, Paraná, Caruaru) are Tupi-Guarani, as are names of many foods (*pipoca* is popcorn, *mandioca* is manioc, *abacaxi* is a pineapple), animals (*tatu* is an armadillo, a *jacaré* is a caiman, *tucano* is a toucan), and trees (*ipê* is a trumpet tree). A legacy of slavery is the inclusion of words from African languages (primarily Bantu, and to a lesser extent Yoruba, which is spoken in Benin and Nigeria and is used in Candomblé rituals), ranging from specific terms such as *samba* and *capoeira* to colloquial expressions such as *cafuné* (a caress on the head) and *caçula* (the youngest born). Later on, the arrival of European immigrants in the 19th and 20th century introduced new expressions, especially in French—*chaise longue*, Réveillon (New Year's Eve), the expression *bom apetite*—and English: *trem* (train), *outdoor* (billboard), *jeans*, and *email*.

Art and Architecture

With so much diversity, beauty, and extremities packed into its immense territory, it's no wonder that artistry and creativity run rampant in Brazil. Culture, both "high" and "low," but especially *cultura popular*, is seemingly everywhere—in the masterful elaboration of a tall tale at a bar table, the intricate embroidery of a tablecloth, the expressive sculpting of a clay *figurinha*, and the 45-minute choreographed spectacle of enormous floats, dazzling costumes, and thousands of sambaing singers and dancers vying for the yearly championship title during Rio's famous Carnaval.

MUSIC

Of the various forms of artistic expression, the one that is most particular and reflects the very essence and soul of Brazil is its music. In terms of sheer genius and variety, it's hard to overstate the impact of Brazilian music. Between samba, bossa nova, *forró*, and MPB, Brazil's contribution to the world music scene is immeasurable. Within Brazil itself, music is inseparable from daily life. It plays a starring role in all types of celebrations, both sacred and profane. There is music in the beach vendor's cries of shrimp for sale as well as in the samba rhythms that teenage boys pound against the metal siding of an urban bus. And it is tattooed into the collective consciousness in such a way that you'll immediately feel as if your education is very lacking (Brazilians inevitably know *all* the words to *all* the songs, and are not at all timid about singing them for you).

Music in Brazil is also inextricably linked to dance. Many music styles—samba, *forró*, *frevo*, *carimbó*, *boi*—are accompanied by dance steps, and it's close to impossible for most Brazilians to stay inert once the music heats up. Needless to say, the effortlessness, grace, flair, and controlled abandon with which the vast majority of Brazilians cut a rug is beyond compare.

Influences

The uniqueness and diversity of Brazilian music is yet another consequence of the country's distinctive mélange of indigenous, African, and European influences. In early colonial days, Jesuit missionaries were already cleverly adapting religious hymns to indigenous tribal music with Tupi lyrics in order to up their chances of converting Brazilian Indians.

With the arrival of slaves came percussion instruments—drums, *cuicas,* rattles, and marimbas—that were played during communal jams. Although the Portuguese elite tried to resist these African rhythms on grounds that they incited libidinous dances that were quite immoral, their objections were in vain. These rhythms made their way out of the slaves' quarters and into plantation homes and, from there, spread throughout the country, creeping into popular 19th-century musical styles such as *maxixe* and *frevo*; both also drew heavily on Polish polkas.

Samba

It was in early 20th-century Rio, amid the working-class neighborhoods of liberated black slaves who had migrated to the city from Bahia, that modern samba was born. Officially, samba made its presence known for the first time during Rio's Carnaval of 1917, which featured a ditty called *Pelo Telefone,* composed by Donga, a talented young Carioca composer and musician. The rhythm was so contagious that even Rio's white upper classes were hooked. By the 1930s, the launch of Brazil's phonographic industry combined with the spread of national radio allowed samba hits to be broadcast throughout the country and quickly soak into the collective consciousness.

The 1930s and 1940s were the golden age of samba, with composers such as Noel Rosa, Ary Barroso, Lamartine Babo, Cartola, and Ismael Silva penning a string of classics that were popularized by the likes of Carmen Miranda (who, pre-Hollywood, was one of Brazil's preeminent musical stars). There are many different varieties of samba. The classic samba from the 1930s and 1940s is known as *samba canção,* in which a slow-tempo samba is belted out by a singer backed by a small band. The more frenetic *samba de enredo* was custom-made for Rio's Carnaval. It involves one or two singers accompanied by a deafening chorus of hundreds of drummers and backup singers (which together constitute a samba school). More recently, in the 1990s, in dance halls and corner bars, swinging *samba pagode* took the genre back to its roots, led by performers such as the immensely popular and down-to-earth Zeca Pagodinho. Other major samba performers that have marked the genre since the 1970s include Beth Carvalho, Alcione, Clara Nunes, Paulinho da Viola, Martinho da Vila, and Martinho's daughter, Mart'nália, whose career has taken off in the last few years.

Bahia is also known for its samba. *Samba de roda,* in which musicians and dancers form a circle, is prevalent throughout the Bahian interior, while Salvador is the birthplace of *samba reggae,* a Jamaica-tinged form promoted by local groups such as Olodum and Didá. *Samba reggae* is only one tangent of the genre known as *axé* music, a frenetic and infectious dance music that emerged during Salvador's Carnaval in the 1980s, at the moment when a generation of rising stars were taking to the streets atop massive *trio-elétricos* (stages on wheels). For years, the biggest *axé* stars have been Daniela Mercury, Ivete Sangalo, and Claudia Leite. The trio has served as the genre's ambassadors, performing their infectious hits throughout Brazil and overseas.

Choro

Choro (which means "crying") is another musical style, little known outside Brazil, that also developed in Rio at the dawn of the 20th century. Delicate and slightly melancholy, *choro* music is influenced by Argentinean tango as well as European polkas, mazurkas, and waltzes. The classic *choro* trio consists of a flute, *cavaquinho* (a small four-string guitar that resembles a ukulele), and percussion instruments all played together in a loose manner reminiscent of jazz. After falling out of favor for decades, traditional *choro* has made a comeback in the bars of Rio and São Paulo.

Northeastern Music

The northeastern Sertão gave birth to a wealth

of distinctive musical styles that gradually spread throughout Brazil as the 20th century wore on. In the 1940s, armed with a deep voice and an accordion, Pernambucano musician Luíz Gonzaga was crowned the king of the *baião,* a plaintive bluesy style of music whose lyrics spoke of the harsh life of Brazil's poorest and most arid region. *Baião* proved popular at local dance halls and paved the way for the more sophisticated *forró,* which to this day has become immensely popular throughout Brazil. *Forró's* jaunty two-step is played by an accordion-led trio featuring a triangle and a *zabumba* (bass drum).

Tackling plaintive themes of lost love and betrayal, *música sertaneja* is a more contemporary, commercial, and often more schmaltzy version of traditional *música caipira* (American-style country music) that is typical of the Brazilian interior. *Música sertaneja* is popular in the Northeast and even more so in the Central-West and rural areas of Minas, São Paulo, and Paraná.

Bossa Nova

Although poor rural and urban areas alike have proved fertile for the germination of many of Brazil's musical styles, one of the genres most famously associated with Brazil was the product of an inspired mixture of samba and imported American jazz that grew out of jam sessions held at the swank Zona Sul apartments of Rio's artists and intellectuals during the 1950s. Bossa nova was the name given to the cool, urban, modernist style that was essentially a slowing down and breaking up of a classic samba rhythm.

The godfather of bossa nova was an eccentric and talented Bahian composer-musician by the name of João Gilberto. Two equally talented men and famous bons vivants—the classically trained pianist Antônio Carlos Jobim and poet-diplomat Vinicius de Moraes—wrote bossa's most famous hits, including "A Garota de Ipanema" ("The Girl from Ipanema"), whose most unforgettable international version was crooned by Astrud Gilberto, João Gilberto's wife at the time.

Ironically, Astrud is quite unknown in Brazil, but Gilberto's daughter, Bebel Gilberto, has picked up where her father left off and made an international career of doing slick lounge versions of bossa tunes for the iPod set.

Bossa's fresh jazziness allowed it to cross over into an immediate jazz standard, covered by American artists ranging from Stan Getz and Frank Sinatra to Ella Fitzgerald and Miles Davis. Bossa put Brazilian music on the international map for the first time. Because it was so overplayed, with the years bossa gained an elevator-music aura abroad. However, in Brazil, the repertory of classics such as "Corcovado," "Chega de Saudade," and "Desafinado" have been, and continue to be, reverently covered by Brazil's top singers, among them Nara Leão, Elis Regina, and Gal Costa.

MPB and Tropicália

MPB stands for *música popular Brasileira* (popular Brazilian music) and is a rather generic and all-encompassing term that refers to all forms of Brazilian "popular" urban music—folk, pop, rock—created from the 1960s to contemporary times. MPB generally features original songwriting but can also include revisited classics (including *samba canções*) from the 1930s, 1940s, and 1950s. Most often, songs are interpreted by the composer or by a singer-interpreter and frequently accompanied by piano or guitar, along with other instruments.

The term MPB was coined during the early 1960s as Brazil sought new and modern ways of revisiting its identity amid the growing oppressiveness of the military dictatorship. Brazilian television, at the time a very new medium, began to broadcast *festivais de música popular Brasileira.* These live competitions featured up-and-coming singers who performed songs by young composers in the hopes of landing recording contracts. Winners became overnight sensations. The first of these festivals, held in 1965, was won by a tiny yet feisty 20-year-old singer from Rio Grande do Sul by the name of Elis Regina. Elis set the standard for MPB. Her rich voice and unbridled emotion tackled songs by a generation of talented young composers—including Chico Buarque, Milton Nascimento, Edu Lobo, Ivan Lins, and João Bosco—up until her death from a drug overdose in 1982.

Although there have been plenty of male MPB composers who also perform their songs (quite beautifully, in the case of Milton Nascimento, Chico Buarque, Jorge Ben Jor, and Roberto Carlos), the most famous interpreters of MPB have always been women. Aside from Elis, major figures of the last 30 years include Maysa, Nana Caymmi, Joyce, Simone, Zizi Possi, Angela Rô Rô, Marina Lima, Adriana Calcanhoto, Marisa Monte, Ana Carolina, and Roberta Sá, some of whom also compose their own music. Two standout contemporary female interpreters are Gal Costa and Maria Betânia, both from Bahia.

At the height of the military dictatorship of the late 1960s and early '70s, Gal became the muse of a movement known as Tropicália. Revolving around the creative energies of young singer-composers extraordinaire Caetano Veloso, Gilberto Gil, and Tom Zé, all of whom also hail from Bahia, Tropicália fused folksy flower-power with electric guitars and international influences such as the Beatles with regional styles such as *baião* and samba. Master wordsmiths Caetano and Gil were charismatic figures—so charismatic that both were arrested by the military government and then forced into exile in Europe, along with Chico Buarque. Back in Brazil since the mid-1970s, both have continued to musically evolve, creating a prolific body of work.

Brazilian Rock, Rap, and Hip Hop

Tropicália's more psychedelic tangent was represented by a way-out trio known as Os Mutantes (The Mutants), who sang many of their songs in English. Os Mutantes's lead singer was a redheaded Paulistana by the name of Rita Lee. Descended from American confederates, she went on to have an original career as the always humorous and provocative "Queen of Brazilian Rock." Brazilian rock's heyday, however, came during the 1980s. This decade was marked by the emergence of seminal bands such as Barão Vermelho, Legião Urbana, and Os Titãs, along with icons such as Cazuza, Renato Russo, and Cássia Eller (all of whom met with untimely deaths). Since then, Brazilian rock—which generally appeals to a young, white, middle-class urban crowd—has faded into the musical background.

The 1990s also saw the emergence of Brazilian rap and hip-hop. Like its American counterparts, both were born in the *favelas* of Rio and São Paulo and featured young black Brazilians who tackled themes of social injustice and violence. A Carioca take on rap is funk, which attracts massive audiences and features lyrics that are so sexually explicit that you don't know whether to be shocked or laugh yourself silly. Among the biggest names in rap and hip hop are MV Bill, Marcelo D2, Racionais MC, Emicida, and Criolo.

Brazilian Music Today

In recent years, interest in traditional and regional forms of Brazilian music and their preservation has revived. However, on the MPB front, no seminal creative figures have emerged that can rival the cultural and musical impact of the original talents forged during the 1960s and 1970s, many of whom—now in their 60s—still continue to produce eagerly anticipated new works. This isn't to say there aren't individuals who are carving out their own distinctive paths. Artists such as Zeca Baleiro and Lenine, and Márcia Castro, who merge pop with traditional musical styles from their native states of Maranhão, Pernambuco, and Bahia, respectively, produce challenging and provocative work. The contemporary takes on samba by Seu Jorge, who was raised in a Rio *favela,* have earned him international accolades, while in São Paulo, Fernanda Porta has been successful at deftly mixing samba with electronica and drum and bass. Ultimately, what characterizes MPB

Antropofagia

During the Semana de Arte de São Paulo of 1922, **Oswald de Andrade,** a leading modernist intellectual and playwright, introduced the metaphor of *antropofagia* (cannibalism) that would become a guiding concept in all modern Brazilian art. Andrade's notion was derived from a traditional indigenous practice of cannibalism. Contrary to popular belief, Brazil's indigenous groups didn't eat people to satisfy their hunger pangs. Instead, they recognized that even their staunchest foes possessed gifts they didn't share. The ritual of eating the enemies they captured in skirmishes was a way of absorbing some of their more admirable qualities (bravery, cleverness, etc.). Andrade proposed that Brazilian artists become cannibals as well: devouring aspects of the European vanguard as well as traditional African and Indian arts and, after digesting them, making use of them to produce a uniquely Brazilian art that would reflect Brazil itself, with its bright colors, exuberant nature, and diverse population.

today is a continued willingness for musical *mestiçagem:* the seamless blending of contemporary and international with traditional and local sounds to create hybrids that end up being distinctly Brazilian.

FINE ARTS AND ARCHITECTURE

The earliest known examples of "Brazilian" art were actually paintings of Edenic landscapes done by European artists who were fascinated by the new colony's profusion of exotica. When the Dutch occupied Pernambuco in the mid-1600s, artists Frans Post and Albert Eckhout were assigned to dutifully register the native flora and fauna as well as indigenous inhabitants. Widely reproduced in Europe, their portraits constituted the first images of the American continent painted by artists of some renown.

For the next three centuries, artists in Brazil devoured styles that were in vogue in Europe. Although some did so mimetically, others "tropicalized" these styles, giving them a unique Brazilianness. The most remarkable instance of this tendency developed in 18th-century Minas Gerais during its massive gold boom. Magnificent churches were built using local materials and decorated in a baroque style whose details, colors, and excessive flourishes were unique in reflecting their tropical surroundings. The two major figures were master builder and sculptor Aleijadinho and the painter Manuel da Costa

Ataíde, whose works are spread throughout the *cidades históricas* of Ouro Preto, Mariana, Tiradentes, and São João del Rei.

In the mid-19th century, the sobriety and elegance of French neoclassical architecture held sway in the capital, Rio de Janeiro, where grand monuments such as the Teatro Municipal, the Biblioteca Nacional, and the Museu Nacional de Belas Artes aspired to conjure up a tropical version of Baron Haussmann's Paris. In the early 20th century, a flirtation with art nouveau gave way to art deco in the 1930s and 1940s. You'll see some glorious examples of art deco in Rio, particularly in Copacabana, as well as in most other large cities.

It wasn't until the 1920s that Brazilian artists consciously broke with European traditions in the pursuit of art that was typically Brazilian. Led by Oswald and Mário de Andrade, the Semana de Arte Moderna de São Paulo created an artistic manifesto in 1920 and shocked the conservative elite by severing ties with academic European schools. Brazilian modernists such as Anita Malfatti, Emiliano Di Cavalcanti, Tarsila do Amaral, Victor Brecheret, and Lasar Segall were the leading painters and sculptors that emerged from the Semana de Arte Moderna. Espousing a philosophy of national art and culture that revolved around the notion of *antropofagia* (cannibalism), they created works that, while fed by what was going on in Europe, were also nourished by themes, forms, and subject matter that were distinctly Brazilian. The generation of artists that followed them continued to explore the notion of Brazilian modernism.

Many contributed their talents to adorning public buildings, particularly the government buildings of the new capital, Brasília, today considered the greatest modernist architectural ensemble in the world. Designed by leading architects Lúcio Costa and Oscar Niemeyer, Brasília was modeled after Le Corbusier's ideals of functional, pared-down structures with glossy surfaces and plenty of windows that emphasized natural lighting. Niemeyer, however, softened the rigid, boxlike linearity of the style by adding sweeping curves that reflected the sensuality and natural forms so characteristic of Brazil. Renowned landscape architect Roberto Burle Marx, who was responsible for countless public gardens throughout the country, is another modern giant.

Keeping up with trends in other parts of the world, contemporary Brazilian art has been marked by the successive rise of pop, installation, performance, video, and digital art. Today, names such as Cildo Meireles, Adriana Varejão, Vik Muniz, Sérgio de Camargo, Jac Leirner, and Beatriz Milhazes are internationally renowned figures, and their works are included in leading museums and galleries. Although characterized by hits and misses, contemporary architecture—some of the best examples can be seen in São Paulo—has also stayed true to the precepts of "cannibalism," with names such as Isay Weinfeld, Ruy Ohtake, Márcio Kogan, and Marcelo Ferraz creating works that bridge cutting-edge universal technology and tendencies with a valorization of local aesthetics and materials.

CINEMA

Cinema has always been popular in Brazil. By the 1930s, even the smallest towns in the northeastern interior had their own modest movie palaces screening Hollywood flicks.

In Rio, Praça Floriano became known as Cinelândia after the elegant downtown square was lined with sumptuous art deco movie palaces. Rio was also the birthplace of the Brazilian film industry. In 1930, Cinédia studios began churning out a series of popular romances and burlesque musical comedies known as *chanchadas,* some of which satirized Hollywood fare. A few of these films featured a very young Carmen Miranda, then at the height of her fame as a recording star. In the 1940s, both the Atlantida and Vera Cruz studios also appeared on the scene to produce popular melodramas along with *chanchadas.* During the 1950s, Vera Cruz attempted to attract viewers by emulating Hollywood's tradition of commercial genre films. A massive soundstage was built where the studio could churn out highly popular detective stories and westerns. Production values were high, but young independent directors chafed at the degree of commercialization and Americanization of the final product.

Dreaming of a *cinema novo* (new cinema) and inspired by Italian neorealism, directors such as Nelson Pereira dos Santos, Ruy Guerra, and Anselmo Duarte took to making low-budget films, many shot on location in the arid Sertão, that highlighted the stark realities of the Brazilian Northeast in expressive black-and-white imagery. If not wildly popular at home, these films were a hit with international critics. Lima Barreto's *O Cangaceiro* (1953) brought to the screen the story of the legendary Sertanejo bandit Lampião. In 1962, Duarte's *O Pagador de Promessas* scooped up a Palme d'Or award for best film at the Cannes Festival. One of the most daring and experimental figures of the movement dubbed *cinema novo* was a brilliant Bahian director by the name of Glauber Rocha. In groundbreaking films such as *Terra em Transe* and *Deus e o Diabo na Terra do Sol,* "Glauber" drew on French new wave influences to tackle pressing sociopolitical issues such as hunger, violence, and poverty, once again using the Northeast as a metaphorically charged setting. Combining wonderful mise-en-scène with an absence of conventional narrative, Glauber's films were adored by intellectuals but difficult for the public to watch.

In 1964, the beginning of the military dictatorship caused *cinema novo* to experience a sudden demise. Government hard-liners censored any criticism of Brazil and forced many directors into exile. Instead, in 1969, the government created Embrafilme, a state-run production company whose goal was to develop Brazilian filmmaking. Although censorship, bureaucracy, and favoritism severely limited artistic expression, Embrafilme did provide enough capital to maintain a small industry that funded the production of important films by major directors, such as Bruno Barreto's *Dona Flor e Seus Dois Maridos* (*Dona Flor and Her Two Husbands,* 1976), Cacá Diegues's *Bye Bye Brasil* (1979), Héctor Babenco's *Pixote* (1981), and Nelson Pereira dos Santos's *Memórias do Cárcere* (*Memories of Prison,* 1984).

The end of Brazil's military dictatorship also meant the end of Embrafilme and a state-subsidized film industry. By the early 1990s, only a few Brazilian films were being released each year. Fortunately, things improved under the government of Fernando Henrique Cardoso, with the introduction of new incentives whereby private companies that invested in film productions would receive tax breaks. In 1993, Carla Camurati's whimsical historical comedy *Carlota Joaquina* (about the Portuguese royal family's picaresque adventures in 19th-century Brazil) was a big hit and signaled the beginning of cinema's resurrection. Eager to see their lives depicted onscreen, Brazilians flocked to the movies in record numbers. Not only did the number of films produced gradually grow, but the quality was on par with the best of world cinema and was recognized as such by foreign critics, who showered awards on productions such as Bruno Barreto's *O Que É Isso Companheiro?* (*Four Days in September,* 1998), an Oscar-nominated film that told the gripping true story of the kidnapping of the U.S. ambassador to Brazil by left-leaning guerrillas.

Walter Salles, one of Brazil's most important new directors, succeeded in taking home the Oscar for Best Foreign Film the following year for *Central do Brasil* (*Central Station*), the story of a curmudgeonly elderly woman, played by Oscar-nominated Fernanda Montenegro, who makes a living writing letters for illiterate migrants in Rio's Central Station and ends up accompanying a young homeless boy on a search throughout the Northeast to find his father. His follow-up film, *Abril Despedaçado* (*Behind the Sun,* 2001), was a dark, brooding tale of vengeance among rival families in the Northeast, starring acclaimed young actor Rodrigo Santoro. Another big hit set in the Sertão was Andrucha Waddington's 2000 comedy *Eu Tu Eles* (*Me, You, Them*), based on the true story of a woman with three husbands, whose lively soundtrack by Gilberto Gil did much to popularize traditional *forró* music. Waddington's more recent *Casa de Areia* (*House of Sand,* 2005) is a hauntingly poetic film about a mother and daughter (played by Fernanda Montenegro and her real-life actress daughter, Fernanda Torres) sent to live for years in the middle of the isolated desert.

Many of these entertaining films are loyal to *cinema novo*'s mandate of offering critiques of Brazil's many social problems. While some films have chosen the Brazilian Northeast as a backdrop to portray the trials and tribulations of contemporary Brazil, others have taken to the urban jungles of Rio and São Paulo. One of the most accomplished new directors to tackle such themes is Fernando Meirelles. With a background in advertising, Meirelles started his cinematic career with *Domésticas* (*Maids,* 2001), which offered a humorous yet realistic glimpse into the lives of the many women who work as maids for wealthy and middle-class families. His follow-up film, *Cidade de Deus* (*City of God,* 2002), took both Brazil and the world by storm in with its brilliantly acted story of survival amid the gang warfare typical of a Carioca *favela*. The fragmented editing, hurtling pace, and use of *favela* dwellers as actors was inspired and brought Meirelles, who then went on to direct the English-language film *The Constant Gardener,* an Oscar nomination for best director.

In 2007, José Padilha—director of the harrowing documentary *Ônibus 174 (Bus 174,* 2002), which was based on the 2000 hijacking of a municipal Rio de Janeiro bus in broad daylight and the police's bungling of the rescue of passengers—created another uproar with his controversial fictional feature debut. The film, titled *Tropa da Elite (Elite Squad)* and based on true events, provided a shocking glimpse at the armed warfare between drug lords and a special squad of Rio's military police created to "protect" *favela* residents. The film was later named best film at the Berlin International Film Festival and is one of the most widely watched Brazilian films of all time. The 2010 follow-up *Tropa da Elite II (Elite Squad II)* broke box-office records when it became the biggest Brazilian blockbuster ever—luring 11 million spectators to movie theaters across the country.

Brazil's burgeoning feature film industry has been accompanied by a renaissance in the production of documentary films. Many delve into social themes, such as Eduardo Coutinho's excellent *Edifício Master* (2002), which offers an intimate glimpse into the lives of 37 families who inhabit a crowded 12-story Copacabana apartment building, and the more recent but equally stirring *Wasteland* (2009), about artist Vik Muniz's artistic collaboration with *catadores* (garbage pickers) working at a Rio de Janeiro landfill. An extraordinary number of documentaries pay homage to Brazil's musical legends, among them Carmen Miranda in Helena Solberg's *Bananas Is My Business* (1994); Vinicius de Moraes in Miguel Faria Jr.'s *Vinicius* (2005); the *sambista* Cartola in Lírio Ferreira and Hilton Lacerda's *Cartola* (2006); and Dzi Croquettes, a gender-bending revue of cross-dressing dancers and actors, in Tatiana Issa and Raphael Alvarez's *Dzi Croquettes* (2009).

BRAZILIAN LITERATURE

Jorge Amado was one of Brazil's most beloved 20th-century writers. His picaresque and colorful novels are inevitably set in his home state of Bahia and are populated by a charismatic if somewhat caricatured cast of sensual *mulatas,* fishermen, charming tricksters, and Candomblé priestesses. There is usually a shot of magical realism involved in these highly readable tales. Among his most enduring novels are *Gabriela, Clove, and Cinnamon* and *Dona Flor and Her Two Husbands.* Mário de Andrade was one of the leading figures of Brazil's modernist movement, and his novel *Macunaíma* (1928) is a Brazilian classic. The title character is a mutant figure from the jungle who begins life as an Indian and then morphs into a black man and a white man. While changing identities, he stars in a variety of comical adventures that integrate all sorts of popular Brazilian myths, folklore, and cultural elements into a highly enjoyable narrative patchwork that is utterly Brazilian.

Machado de Assis is not widely known outside Brazil, but among international literati he has earned a place among the all-time greats. This 19th-century author was extremely vanguard, bringing a modernist sensibility and style and a rapier wit to bear upon the lifestyles of the rich and corrupt in fin de siècle Rio. His two most famous novels, *Posthumous Memoirs of Brás Cubas* and *Quincas Borba,* are both wonderfully imaginative and mordantly funny. His short stories are also quite brilliant. Try *The Psychiatrist and Other Stories.* Paulo Lins, a well-known photojournalist, grew up in Rio's poor and dangerous Cidade de Deus *favela,* infamous for its violent gangs and brutal drug traffickers. His upbringing supplied the fodder for his gripping novel, *City of God,* subsequently made into the highly acclaimed film by Fernando Meirelles.

Clarice Lispector was one Brazil's most intelligent and elegantly witty 20th-century writers. Her depth, human insight, and sense of wordplay are impressively displayed in her numerous short stories, which are meticulously crafted but don't make for light reading. Her most famous and most accessible novel, *The Hour of the Star,* is a compact and searing tale of a miserable and homely northeastern migrant girl's day-to-day trials and tribulations in Rio de Janeiro.

Graciliano Ramos was a novelist from Alagoas who was largely responsible for introducing social realism and regionalism into Brazilian literature in the early 20th century. Written in pared-down prose, his most famous work, *Barren Lives,* portrays the bleak lives of families trying to survive in the hard, arid Sertão of the Northeast. Moacyr Scliar was one of Brazil's most distinguished contemporary authors. A Jewish doctor from Rio Grande do Sul who died in 2011, he expertly crafted short stories and novels that often touch on the issue of Jewish identity, specifically in Brazil. Apart from his short stories, his best-known novels include *The Centaur and the Garden* and *Max and the Cats.*

Essentials

Transportation

GETTING THERE

Air

Most international travelers enter Brazil by plane. The two main gateways are Rio de Janeiro's Tom Jobim airport and São Paulo's Guarulhos airport. From the United States, **American Airlines** (www.aa.com), **Delta** (www.delta.com), **United** (www.united.com), and **US Airways** (www.usairways.com) all offer daily flights from major cities, including New York, Washington DC, Miami, Atlanta, Chicago, Houston, Boston, Charlotte, and Los Angeles. **Air Canada** (www.aircanada.com) has direct daily flights from Toronto, and **British Airways** (www.britishairways.com) operates direct flights from London.

Currently, one Brazilian carrier offers international service. **TAM** (www.tam.com.br) provides flights to the rest of Latin America, Europe, and major cities in the United States and Canada, including Miami, New York, and Toronto.

If traveling to far-flung regions of Brazil, it may make sense for you to buy a **Brazil Airpass,** which can only be purchased abroad (much to the chagrin of Brazilians) along with your international ticket. Currently, both TAM and Gol offer passes that allow you four domestic flights to any destination to which TAM and Gol fly (which is basically everywhere). Both passes cost US$582, although additional flights can be added to the pass; all flights must be taken within a 30-day period. Gol also has a Northeast pass, which allows you three flights within the Brazilian *nordeste* for US$440. However, the TAM pass is only available to passengers who fly TAM or one of its international partners to Brazil.

A round-trip flight (without taxes) for US$1,000 from New York to Rio or São Paulo is considered a very good deal these days. In the United States, travel agencies that specialize in Brazil are the Houston-based **Globotur** (https://globotur.com) and New York-based **BACC Travel** (www.bacctravel.com); both consistently come up with great fares for travelers in the United States and Canada. Also recommended is **Brazil Nuts** (www.brazil-nuts.com), which has a highly informed staff.

Boat

Many international cruise ships to South America make stops along Brazil's Atlantic coast. The biggest port of call is Rio de Janeiro. Other popular stops include the northeastern beach capitals of Fortaleza, Recife, and Salvador. Although an entire cruise can be quite pricy, sometimes portions can be purchased at substantial discounts. In terms of river travel, those who have lots of time to burn and aren't averse to roughing it can sail down the Amazon River from Iquitos in Peru or enter the Pantanal by Rio Paraguai from Asunción, Paraguay.

Bus

Although it's possible to drive or travel by bus to Brazil from all neighboring countries, in most cases distances are quite enormous. Apart from Santa Elena de Uairén in Venezuela, the most accessible and common entry points are from Brazil's neighbors to the south, including Argentina and Paraguay at Foz do Iguaçu and Uruguay at Jaguarão.

There is frequent bus service among Rio, São Paulo, and the capitals of the south from Montevideo (Uruguay), Buenos Aires (Argentina), Asunción (Paraguay), and even Santiago (Chile). Roads are generally quite good. International bus companies include

Pluma (www.pluma.com.br) and **Crucero del Norte** (www.crucerodelnorte.com.ar).

GETTING AROUND
Air

Because of Brazil's vast distances, flying is an ideal way to get from one region to another in record time. Brazil's airports are modern and well equipped, although in recent years the surge in domestic air traffic has taxed the capacity of many major airports, creating back-ups, line-ups, and delays. Spurred on by 2014 World Cup and 2016 Olympics hosting duties, many airports have begun urgent expansions and upgrades; however, to date, such transformations are still ongoing.

There are numerous daily flights available to and from Rio, São Paulo, Brasília, and all the state capitals. Prices between destinations in the Southeast, South, Brasília, and Northeast are quite reasonable, especially if booked in advance. Flights to cities in the Amazon, such as Manaus and Belém, can cost more. Due to lack of passable roads, the Amazon is a region where flying is a must, unless you want to spend days on a boat. Although there are many regional *aerotaxis,* it's safest to stick to the main domestic operators.

In recent years, numerous domestic airlines have started up. Currently, the major players are **TAM** (tel. 0800/570-5700, www.tam.com.br), **Gol** (tel. 0300/115-2121, www.voegol.com.br), **Azul** (tel. 0800/887-1118, www.voeazul.com.br), **Trip** (tel. 0300/789-8747, www.voetrip.com.br), and **Avianca** (tel. 0300/789-8160, www.avianca.com.br). The airlines offer various fares depending on when you fly and how far in advance you book—particularly for holidays. Great promotions, such as paying full fare one way and receiving your return ticket for R$1 for certain routes, are often advertised online during off-season.

Bus

With the exception of the Amazon, you can get absolutely anywhere in Brazil by bus. Service among capitals and major cities within the states and along the coasts is usually very efficient, although on major routes prices are sometimes comparable with air travel. Long-distance buses leave punctually—don't be late! The comfortable vehicles themselves (often Mercedes-Benzes) are equipped with plush, fold-back seats, air-conditioning, restrooms, TVs, and coolers with free mineral water. Although restrooms start out clean, by the end of the trip they are usually less so. When you buy your ticket, you can reserve your seat—choose one at the front or the middle of the bus (the restroom is at the back). Air-conditioning can be extreme; make sure you have a sweater and long pants (or a towel or light blanket), or you'll freeze to death in the tropics. On overnight buses between major cities, you can opt for deluxe *leito* buses, whose large reclining seats will lull you to sleep. *Leitos* usually cost twice as much as a regular bus.

Buses are operated by hundreds of private national, regional, and local companies, but prices are comparable between rivals. Most companies have websites, listed throughout this guide, where you can check schedules and prices and purchase tickets in advance. For interstate travel, especially during high season or holiday periods, it's recommended you purchase your ticket in advance. Although major companies sell tickets via travel agents, often your best (and only) option is to purchase them at bus terminals, where all companies have kiosks with schedules. When purchasing a ticket, specify you want it *sem seguro* (without insurance), an added fee that bequeaths a small sum of money to your loved ones should you be involved in a fatal bus crash (not likely).

Traveling by bus in Brazil is relatively safe, but keep an eye on your belongings at all times. Luggage stowed beneath the bus is quite secure; it can only be retrieved with a baggage claim ticket. Otherwise, keep valuables close by, particularly at night, and take them with you at rest stops. Except for *leitos,* most long-distance buses make stops every two to three hours. This gives you a chance to stretch your legs, grab some food or a drink, and use a clean restroom. It's advisable to bring some mineral water and a snack, such as cookies, fruit, or nuts.

Driving

Driving in Brazil is not for the faint of heart. Brazilians have a love affair with speeding and are hardly sticklers for following the rules of the road. As the economy improved, Brazilians purchased cars en masse, which means traffic in major cities is increasingly congested, and not just in Rio and São Paulo, whose traffic jams are nightmarish. In the Northeast and the North, the state of the roads can be dismal once you get out of the major cities, although main coastal highways are kept in good shape. Until recently, drunk driving was a major problem. In July 2008, however, Brazil government enacted a zero-tolerance law, resulting in police-organized blitzes around the country. Drivers are stopped arbitrarily and must take a Breathalyzer test. If even the slightest amount of alcohol is detected, you're looking at a fine of R$1,915 and a suspension from driving for one year. In reality, these "blitzes" are only a partial deterrent; it's best to be on your guard when driving back from a long day at the beach, where it's a Brazilian tradition to knock back more than a few.

Renting a car can be a definite plus. For visiting natural attractions around big cities, having a car gives you much more freedom to hit off-the-beaten-track places where buses don't go (if they do, it's likely they'll make 200 local stops, or that the one daily departure is at 5am). Also, for beach-hopping, cars come in very handy, since you can hit secluded coves not accessible by bus. If you do rent a car, try to avoid traveling on big holiday weekends, when traffic is guaranteed to be atrocious. Also avoid driving at night. Outside of major cities, roads are poorly lit, and bumps and potholes are common. In more isolated regions, you could be a victim of a highway robbery. In cities, stick to main streets, especially at night. When parking, whether you need help or not, you'll usually be guided into a space by an informal parking attendant, known as a *flanelinha,* who will promise to watch over your car as well. Whether he does or not, it's customary to tip him R$2-5 since he makes his living this way (some may hit you up for more); if you don't, you risk finding a mysterious scratch on your car. Nonetheless, don't leave any valuables in the car, even in the trunk. In many cities, such as São Paulo,

Transport options vary widely in Brazil.

carjackings are a concern. Always keep windows up if you're stopped at a red light and snarled in traffic; at night in big cities, most drivers slow down rather than coming to a full-stop at a red light.

An international driver's license (IDP) is more widely recognized than a foreign license, but the latter is valid for up to six months. You can't drive a motorcycle, however, without a Brazilian license. Major international car rental chains such as Avis, Hertz, and Localiza can be found throughout all major cities and airports (numbers are listed throughout this guide). Rates for a rental with unlimited mileage range R$100-150 per day. Prices don't necessarily include insurance, so check beforehand.

Taxis

Taxis are an efficient way of getting around cities or to close-by beaches and are considerably cheaper than in North America or Europe. You can flag one down anywhere. City cabs are metered and have two rates, or *bandeiras*. Bandeira 2, which is more expensive than Bandeira 1, is in effect after 8pm and on Sundays and holidays, and sometimes during the "holiday" month of December. Cab drivers may refer to a rate sheet—this happens when fares are raised but haven't yet been factored into the meter. If you hit it off with a cab driver, ask for his or her card. Often he or she will give you special rates for trips to airports or other long journeys. In small towns and for longer trips in cities, you can often propose a set price instead of paying the metered fare. Many airports have taxi kiosks where you prepay your fare according to distance. Although the fare is more expensive, these cabs are generally more comfortable, and you won't have to worry about getting scammed. In recent years, there have been incidences of unsuspecting tourists being approached by drivers of *taxis piratas* (fake taxis), who rip them off or rob them; this is particularly common at airports in major cities.

Vans

In rural areas, along beaches, and increasingly in major cities, VW vans, also known as *kombis, lotações, taxis comuns* or merely *vans* are an alternate and unofficial source of public transportation. The term *lotação* is the most apt of all—*lotar* means to fill up, and that's precisely what these vans tend to do, stuffing as many people as possible inside. Although fares are similar to those you'll pay on a bus, vans have the advantage of careening along at high speeds that will get you to your destination more quickly. In beach areas, particularly along the northeastern coasts, vans are much more frequent than local bus lines. Even if you don't understand Portuguese, riding in a van can be a fun, if cramped, experience.

Visas and Officialdom

VISAS

If your country requires Brazilians to have travel visas, you will have to get a visa from the nearest Brazilian consulate before entering Brazil. Currently, citizens of Canada, the United States, and Australia require visas. Citizens of the United Kingdom, most other European Union countries, and New Zealand don't need visas but do need a passport that is valid for six months and a return ticket. Upon arrival, you'll be given a 90-day tourist visa.

Various types of visas are available. Currently, a single-entry tourist visa that has a validity of 90 days costs US$160 for Americans, CDN$81.25 for Canadians, and A$42 for Australians (if submitted in person). Count on 5-10 work days for processing, although turnaround is often quicker. You'll need to submit a passport photo, show proof of a return ticket, and can often only pay with a money order or certified check.

All visitors who arrive in Brazil and go

through immigration will receive an entry form, which you should *not* lose. You'll need to hand it back to the Polícia Federal when leaving the country. To extend your stay, renew your visa 15 days before it expires at the visa section of the Polícia Federal headquarters in any major city. Prior to doing so, fill and print out the *Prorogar Prazo de Estada de Turista* form on the Polícia Federal website (www.dpf.gov.br) along with a tax form, known as a "GRU" for "Pessoas e Entidades Estrangeiras" payable to the federal police *unidade* located closest to you. The fee for renewal is R$67 and can be paid at any bank, post office, or lottery *casa*. If you overextend the 180-day limit, you won't be deported, but you will pay a fine. The federal police headquarters is also where you should head if your passport is lost or stolen. You'll need to make a report in order to get a temporary travel document from your consulate. Then you'll need to return once again to the Polícia Federal to receive an official stamp.

Artists and academics coming to Brazil for a short time are better off traveling on a tourist visa. Those with a long-term research or study project will need to apply for a *visto temporário,* which can be issued for six months, one year, or even two years. To get one, you must be sponsored by a recognized Brazilian educational institution confirming your project. Processing can take several months.

Before coming to Brazil, make copies of your passport. Also bring a second photo ID with you. By law, in Brazil you are always required to have a picture ID. In many circumstances—from renting headphones in a museum to entering an office building—you will need to show or even leave your ID.

CUSTOMS

At Brazilian customs (*alfândega*), officials are generally more interested in Brazilians who went on major shopping sprees abroad than foreign visitors. However, since checks are random, you might find your luggage being inspected. Visitors can bring in objects for their own personal use, including cameras

and a laptop. You may be asked to register new items to make sure you take them with you when you leave (bring receipts). If you're bringing things for Brazilian friends, keep them to a minimum (i.e., don't show up with four digital cameras, five iPods, and two laptops). Should you be discovered, you will end up paying duty on them. Gifts purchased overseas that are worth more than US$500 should be declared.

Before heading to customs, you might want to start shopping at the airport duty-free shops (yes, you can purchase duty-free upon arrival as well as prior to departure), where you can indulge in up to US$500 of purchases. Prices are quite competitive, particularly on items such as alcohol and perfume. Should you be visiting with any Brazilians on your trip, the gift of a fine bottle of imported whiskey will earn you their undying gratitude.

BRAZILIAN EMBASSIES AND CONSULATES

The Brazilian Embassy in the **United States** is in Washington DC (tel. 202/238-2700, http://washington.itamaraty.gov.br). You'll also find main consulates in New York (tel. 212/827-0976, http://novayork.itamaraty.gov.br), Miami (tel. 305/285-6232, http://miami.itamaraty.gov.br), and Los Angeles (tel. 323/651-2664, http://washington.itamaraty.gov.br). In **Canada,** the Brazilian Embassy is in Ottawa (tel. 613/237-1090, http://ottawa.itamaraty.gov.br) and the main consulate is in Toronto (tel. 416/922-2503, http://toronto.itamaraty.gov.br). In **Britain,** the embassy is in London (tel. 020/7477-4500, www.brazil.org.uk). In **Australia,** it is in Canberra (tel. 02/6273-2372, http://canberra.itamaraty.gov.br).

FOREIGN CONSULATES AND EMBASSIES IN BRAZIL

Foreign embassies are all located in Brasília, while major consulates are found in both Rio de Janeiro and São Paulo. Smaller consulates can be found in state capitals such as Porto Alegre, Recife, Salvador, and Manaus. For specific numbers and listings, check the main embassy Web pages:

Australian Embassy (tel. 61/3226-3111, www.brazil.embassy.gov.au)

British Embassy (tel. 61/3329-2300, www. gov.uk/government/world/brazil)

Canadian Embassy (tel. 61/3424-5400 www. canadainternational.gc.ca/brazil-bresil)

U.S. Embassy (tel. 61/3321-7000, http://portuguese.brazil.usembassy.gov)

Consulates in Rio de Janeiro: Australia (Av. Presidente Wilson 231, 23rd Fl., Centro, tel. 21/3824-4624), Canada (Av. Atlântica 1130, 5th Fl., Copacabana, tel. 21/2543-3004),

United Kingdom (Praia do Flamengo 284, 2nd Fl., Flamengo, tel. 21/2555-9600), United States (Av. Presidente Wilson 147, Centro, tel. 21/3823-2000).

Consulates in São Paulo: Australia (Alameda Santos 700, 9th Fl., Cerqeira César, tel. 11/2112-6200; Alameda Ministro Rocha Azevedo 456, Jardim Paulista, tel. 11/3085-6247), Canada (Av. das Nações Unidas 12901, 16th Fl., Torre Norte, Itaim Bibi, tel. 11/5509-4321), United Kingdom (Rua Ferreira de Araujo 741, 2nd Fl., Pinheiros, tel. 11/3094-2700), United States (Rua Henri Dunant 500, Chácara Santo Antônio, tel. 11/5186-7000).

Recreation

CLIMBING

Rio has lots of great climbing opportunities both within the city and in the surrounding Serra dos Órgãos and Parque Nacional de Itatiaia. Many scalable mountains have the advantage of being right on a tropical beach, which means coming down to a refreshing ocean dip. Like hiking, climbing is best April to November.

DUNE-BUGGIES

The Northeast coast is one long strip of glorious, often deserted beach, with long smooth stretches alternating with snow-white Saharan dunes, making for countless great day trips from Natal or Fortaleza.

FISHING

Despite the immensity of its Atlantic coast, it is Brazil's rivers that offer some of the best freshwater sportfishing in the world. Fed by various rivers, including the Rio Paraguai, the Pantanal is a favorite destination for those serious about fishing. There are many lodges (*hotéis de pesca*) along rivers, as well as "botels"—floating hotels specifically geared toward anglers. Top spots include the area surrounding Cáceres (on the Rio Cuiabá), in Mato Grosso, and the areas surrounding

the towns of Aquidauana, Miranda, and Corumbá, in Mato Grosso do Sul. Fishing season is March to October. The other great fishing destination is the Amazon, where you can go after the enormous *pirarucu* or the much smaller but infamously fanged piranha. Various tour companies run excursions out of Belém and Manaus.

HANG GLIDING AND PARAGLIDING

One of the most famous gliding spots is Rio de Janeiro, where you can take off from the jungly heights of the Parque Nacional da Tijuca and land on the beach of Baía da Guanabara.

HIKING AND TREKKING

Hiking trails are the best in the rugged, lush national parks of the Central-West interior and along the coastlines of Rio, São Paulo, and the South. Top areas include the Chapada Diamantina, Serra do Cipó, Chapada dos Veadeiros, Chapada dos Guimarães, Serra dos Órgãos and Itatiaia, Serra da Bocaina, and the Serra Gaúcha. Hiking is most comfortable April to November, although temperatures can be quite cool in the South. During the summer, scalding sun and soaring temperatures can prove uncomfortable and exhausting.

SNORKELING AND DIVING

If you bring a mask and snorkel to Brazil, there are always calm coves worth poking around. The warm waters of the Northeast have the best snorkeling. The Coral Coast, which extends from northern Alagoas into southern Pernambuco, offers a 135-kilometer (85-mile) stretch of protected reefs that are ideal for snorkeling. The beaches surrounding São Miguel dos Milagres and Maragogi, in Alagoas, and Tamandaré and Porto de Galinhas, in Pernambuco, are all terrific snorkeling destinations. In Rio Grande do Norte, you can snorkel at beaches both north and south of Natal, with special mention going to the offshore reefs of Maracajaú, which can also get very crowded. The area surrounding Bonito, in Mato Grosso do Sul, is famous for *flutuação*, during which, outfitted with snorkel, mask, and life jacket, you can go floating down the region's astonishingly crystalline rivers alongside myriad colored fish.

As for diving (*mergulho*), there are a few really standout spots, including the Reserva Biológica do Avoredo, off the coast of Porto

Belo, in Santa Catarina; Arraial do Cabo, north of Rio; off Ilhabela, in São Paulo; the Parque Nacional Marinho dos Abrolhos, off the coast of Caravelas, in southern Bahia; and the phenomenally crystalline and rigidly protected waters surrounding the island of Fernando de Noronha. Waters tend to have best visibility in the summer months (November-February). All of these destinations have diving operators that offer excursions, rental equipment, and lessons for beginners.

SURFING

Brazil has a notorious *surfista* scene. The breaks and rollers on the southern coast are particularly enticing. The state of Santa Catarina, particularly the east-coast beaches of Floripa and Garopaba, is a big surfer haven, as is São Paulo's northern coast around Maresias and on Ilhabela. Rio, Búzios, and Niterói are surfer meccas; all offer lessons at many surfing academies. Urbanites show off their mettle at Arpoador, while serious surfers head farther south to Prainha. The Northeast coast generally has calmer waters, but you can find some good waves in Itacaré, Bahia, and in Porto de Galinhas in Pernambuco, as well as the paradisiacal island of Fernando de

surfing in Itacaré

Noronha. Surf is best in the winter months (June and Sept.).

WINDSURFING AND KITESURFING

Windsurfing and kitesurfing have become popular sport all along Brazil's coastline, particularly the coasts of Rio and São Paulo, and in Búzios and Ilhabela. However, the Northeast coast, particularly in the state of Ceará, is where true fanatics should head due to the combination of warm waters and ideal wind conditions (July-December). Urbanites can rent equipment along Fortaleza's downtown beaches, while back-to-nature buffs should head to the secluded coastline stretching west toward Icaraizinho de Amontada and Jericoacoara.

WILDLIFE-WATCHING

The best place for wildlife-watching is the Pantanal. From *fazenda* lodges deep within the wetlands (and often only accessible by boat or plane), you can hike, boat, and ride horses in search of animals as strange and wonderful as capybaras, giant otters, anteaters, *jacarés* (caimans), elusive jaguars, and a fabulous array of squawking, screeching, colorful birds, including the beautiful and rare *arará azul* (hyacinth macaw). Bird-watchers will be enthralled in the Pantanal as well as the Amazon rain forest. It's much harder to see larger mammals in the Amazon—your best bet is to stay in a jungle lodge in the middle of the forest, where you can explore the river's tributaries by boat. You're guaranteed to view plenty of caimans and pink river dolphins.

Whale-watching is possible along the southern coast of Santa Catarina, particularly around the Ilha do Campeche, on the east coast of Floripa, and Praia do Rosa, south of the city. In Bahia, you can also take offshore trips to see whales frolicking, particularly in Praia do Forte and Caravelas. Whale-watching is best July-November, when whales swim north from Antarctica for the birth and nursing of their young. Fans of dolphins can see—and often swim among—these intelligent creatures in the Amazon basin around Manaus (particularly Novo Airão) and in the warm waters around Praia da Pipa, Rio Grande do Norte, and, most impressively, the island of Fernando de Noronha.

SPECTATOR SPORTS

It's hardly a secret that **soccer** (known in Portuguese as *futebol*) is not just Brazil's national sport but a passion that borders on the religious. It was introduced by the Brazilian-born Charles Miller, who in 1894 returned from higher studies in England toting a soccer ball and equipment. The first soccer games played in São Paulo proved enormously popular, and *futebol* swept through the country like wildfire.

Today, Brazil is the only country in the world to have won five World Cups (1958, 1962, 1970, 1994, and 2002), and during World Cup games, the entire country shuts down to cheer on the Seleção Brasileira, or to scream advice to the coach or players. While Brazilians are ferocious in their support of their teams, they are equally fierce at criticizing any botched play or strategy; consequently the range of emotions witnessed in any stadium or around any TV set is impressive. You're as likely to witness macho guys hugging and kissing each other in joy after a victory as you are to see them sobbing tragically following a defeat. In Brazil, *jogadores de futebol* rank as the country's reigning celebrities, despite the fact that many of them spend most of the year overseas playing for top European teams.

Volleyball is equally popular with men and women. Like soccer, *vôlei* is often played barefoot on the beach. The possibility of a soft landing allows players to go all out in trying to dive for the ball (although you do risk getting sand up your nose). A variation of volleyball is *futevôlei,* in which no hands are allowed. Instead, players use a combination of fancy footwork and hard-headedness.

Frescoball is a popular Brazilian beach sport in which two players lob a rubber ball back and forth using two paddle-like rackets. Invented in 1946 on Copacabana beach by a local resident named Lian Pontes de Carvalho, frescoball's popularity quickly spread to beaches throughout Brazil and, more recently, to other countries as well.

Accommodations

As international tourism has increased, tourist infrastructure has become quite sophisticated. Outside of big cities, in most places R$150-200 per night for a couple will get you comfortable digs. In big cities, the same level of comfort can be had for R$200-300 per night per couple. Rates are almost always based on double occupancy, but single travelers can always try bargaining for a lower rate—and everyone should bargain. No self-respecting Brazilian ever pays the rates listed at the reception, known as *balcão* (counter) rates. Outside of high season (Christmas-Carnaval and July)—when advance reservations are definitely recommended—many hotels offer significant discounts of up to 50 percent. São Paulo and Brasília, where everybody clears out during high season, offer their deep discounts during holidays and long weekends. You can also ask for a *desconto* if you stay in one hotel over several nights. Advance reservations are essential if some major *festa* (Réveillon, Carnaval, São João, Bumba-Meu-Boi) is going to be erupting during your visit. For confirmation, some hotels may ask for a deposit of 50 percent (for one night) or that you pay one night up front if you're staying for several nights. No matter what the price, rates always include *café de manhã,* or breakfast.

CAMPING

Camping is a possibility in and around major beach resorts up and down the coast, where lots of Brazilian youths regularly flock in the summer. There are specific campsites, and some beachfront *pousadas* allow people to pitch tents and share facilities. The problem with camping (aside from mosquitoes and rain) is security. At a campsite or *pousada,* you'll definitely have to watch over your valuables. And if you foolishly decide to pitch a tent in the wilderness, you'll be putting not only your belongings at risk but yourself. For information about sites, consult with the **Camping Clube do Brasil** (tel. 21/2532-0203, www.campingclube.com.br). With headquarters in Rio, it operates close to 50 sites throughout Brazil.

HOSTELS

The best accommodations deals are in simple *pousadas* (guesthouses) or *albergues de juventude* (youth hostels). Although standard dorms are a steal at R$30-50 per person, couples and families can often snag private rooms that work out to be close to the same price. Many of Brazil's hostels are cheery and friendly places, often in restored houses with gardens, lounges, and room to swing in a hammock and meet up with fellow travelers. A Hostelling International card isn't necessary, but it gets you discounts of around R$5-10 per night. Beds fill quickly during summer or school vacations, so it's wise to reserve in advance. For a list of more than 80 hostels, consult the **Federação Brasileira dos Albergues de Juventude** (tel. 21/2531-1085, www.hihostelbrasil.com.br), whose headquarters are in Rio.

POUSADAS

A *pousada* is a guesthouse or bed-and-breakfast, but the definition is as elastic as *pousadas* are varied. Some *pousadas* are basic hotels with four walls, a sheet-covered mattress, and a window. Others are welcoming, intimate, family-owned lodges. Still others qualify as refined and luxurious boutique hotels with creature comforts and amenities galore.

A *pousada* is distinguished from a hotel by its small size and a B&B style; many are located in houses or bungalows as opposed to high-rise hotels. *Pousadas* are rare in big cities, particularly Rio, São Paulo, and Brasília, but you'll find them everywhere else, particularly in beach areas.

Some of Brazil's most captivating *pousadas* are members of an association called Roteiros de Charme. These *pousadas* offer great comfort, outstanding service, and exquisite furnishings. Often they are located in historic homes or in idyllic locations. For more information, contact the **Roteiros de Charme** headquarters in Rio de Janeiro (tel. 21/2287-1592, www.roteirosdecharme.com.br). For up-to-date reviews of *pousadas* throughout Brazil, consult **Hidden Pousadas** (www.hiddenpousadas.com), operated by English expat and Carioca transplant Alison McGowan.

MOTELS

Motels in Brazil are nothing like the friendly, family variety North Americans are accustomed to. Here, motels are where couples go for amorous encounters. Many rendezvous are illicit, but often they provide getaways for harried middle-class couples in search of privacy. Depending on the location and the price, motels can be sleazy and dangerous or quite posh, with heart-shaped beds and whirlpools, mirrored ceilings, and TVs and wet bars. They are usually inexpensive (rates are by the hour and the night).

HOTELS

Although Brazilian hotels receive star ratings (1-5), these ratings are more impressionistic than accurate, and not all hotels have stars. Hotels are confined to big cities and are located within multistory high-rises, although you'll come across some older, cheaper, and shabbier ones as well. A *quarto* usually refers to a room without a bathroom, which is what you'll get if you check into an *apartamento*, along with basic amenities such as a *ventilador* (fan) or air-conditioning, a TV, a stocked mini fridge, and a phone. Usually apartments are ranked as standard, superior, and *luxo* (luxury). Depending on the hotel, the luxury can be a mild upgrade from the standard or can include pampering on a rock star scale. In beach towns, guest rooms with sea views are highly coveted and usually cost more. Be aware that some hotels add a local service tax onto the rate, which may add up to another 15 percent to your tab. In Rio, for example, there is a 5 percent service tax.

"Rooms for Rent"

APART-HOTELS AND RENTALS

In big cities, especially Rio and São Paulo, you'll find *apart-hotels,* also known as flats. Located in modern high-rises, they are usually frequented by business travelers. Cheaper than hotels of the same caliber, *apart-hotels* usually have a living room and kitchen where you can make your own meals; however, they also have hotel amenities such as security, and sometimes a pool and a fitness room, a restaurant, and room service.

JUNGLE LODGES AND FAZENDA LODGES

The best way to visit the unspoiled Amazon rain forest is to check into one of the many jungle lodges that are actually in the rain forest and can be reached by boat. Usually located on a suspended complex of stilts overlooking a river, jungle lodges vary from rustic to overly luxurious; most of them are quite comfortable and eco-conscious.

If visiting the Pantanal, consider staying at a *fazenda* (ranch) lodge. *Fazenda* lodges are located deep within the Pantanal's wetlands, providing you with a unique location from which to view the region's teeming wildlife. Most are working cattle farms (the Pantanal is cattle country); guests can participate in, or at least witness, life on the farm. You'll also find *fazenda* lodges on the Ilha de Marajó, at the mouth of the Amazon River. The *fazendas* here are devoted to the vast herds of water buffalo raised on the island.

Meals and most guided excursions and nature activities (and sometimes transfers) are included in the rates, but both jungle and *fazenda* lodges are fairly pricy, and usually a 2-3-night minimum stay is required. However, they offer the best way of experiencing these unique ecosystems.

Food

When you travel to Brazil, you won't encounter a uniform Brazilian cuisine. Certain basic staples compose the foundations of the Brazilian diet—the classic duo of *arroz e feijão* (rice and beans), the caipirinha, (*cachaça* shaken with crushed ice, lime, and sugar), and Brazilian *churrascarias.* However, Brazilian cooking is the sum of its regions, which means that the food is as diverse as the country. Brazilians love food, and every social occasion comes with some wonderful *petisco* or *tira-gosto* (appetizer). What makes a Brazilian dish elaborate is the sheer abundance of natural ingredients and the savoir faire with which they are combined.

REGIONAL CUISINE
Southeast

Neither Rio de Janeiro nor São Paulo has a true cuisine of its own. Because Rio housed the Portuguese royal court in the 19th century, a certain Portuguese influence can still be detected there, hence the popularity of *bacalhau* (salted cod) and certain egg-based desserts such as the custardy *quindim.* São Paulo was built by immigrants, but the people who left the biggest imprint on its culinary scene were Italians, thus explaining the popularity of pasta and, especially, pizza. The classic Saturday afternoon *feijoada* is a tradition in both capitals. The award for most distinctive and authentic homegrown cuisine easily goes to Minas Gerais. Most popular are dishes featuring pork or chicken. *Frango com quiabo* (chicken with okra) is a classic, as is *frango ao molho pardo* (chicken stewed in its own blood), which, far from being gruesome, is downright delicious. Brazil's leading dairy producer, Minas is renowned for a white creamy cheese known as *queijo de Minas.*

South

The cooking of the South is largely influenced by 19th-century European immigrants—Italians, Germans, and Poles—and you'll easily find polenta, sauerkraut, and even *varenikes*. There are, however, a few distinctive specialties. Paraná is renowned for *barreado,* a heavy but flavorful stew of beef, bacon, potatoes, and spices sealed with a covering of manioc flour and stewed for hours in a clay casserole. Florianópolis is a great place for raw oysters and shrimp. And Rio Grande do Sul's distinctive legacy is that of the Gaúcho cowboys, whose traditional meal of Pampas-fed beef, rubbed in salt and slowly charred over hot coals, can be savored in numerous *churrascarias*.

Central-West

The vast plains of the Central-West are dominated by the scrubby vegetation of the Cerrado, which yields unique fruits such as the *pequi,* a heavily perfumed orange fruit that flavors everything from rice and chicken dishes to liqueurs. In Goiás, a specialty is *empadão,* a large torte-like version of an *empada* (empanada) stuffed with fillings such as chicken, pork, sausage, cheese, and hearts of palm. The frontier regions of Mato Grosso and Mato Grosso do Sul are cattle country, and the river-fed wetlands of the Pantanal ensure an abundance of freshwater fish such as *pacu, pintado,* and *piraputanga*.

Northeast

The Northeast has several distinctive culinary traditions. The most famous hails from Bahia's capital of Salvador and the surrounding coastal region known as the Recôncavo, where African influence is pronounced. Ingredients such as dried shrimp, coconut milk, *pimenta malagueta* (hot pepper), and the pungently scented, amber oil of the *dendê* palm flavor dishes such as *moqueca* (a stew of fish or seafood) and *bobó de camarão,* in which shrimp is combined with pureed manioc. Many dishes are traditionally used in Afro-Brazilian Candomblé rituals. Such is the case with *acarajé,* the crunchy bean fritter prepared by Bahianas on *praças* and street corners.

Fish and seafood are abundant along the entire coast, stretching from Alagoas all the way up to Maranhão. *Peixada* is a popular fish stew. North of Bahia, the Sertão favors *carne-de-sol* (sun-dried meat), *bode* (goat), *queijo coalho* (a rubbery white cheese that's delicious when grilled and drizzled with molasses), and *feijão*.

Native manioc (*mandioca*) was a major staple of the Tupi-Guarani Indians that caught on with the arrival of colonial settlers. Also known as *macaxeira* and *aipim,* manioc shows up on the menu in various guises throughout Brazil. Manioc flour, *farinha de mandioca,* is an essential companion at all meals, as is *farofa,* in which *farinha* is sautéed with butter, onions, garlic, and even bananas. *Farinha* is also used to make crepe-like *tapiocas,* a favorite snack throughout the Northeast.

North

In the area dominated by the Amazon River and surrounding rain forest, an abundance of fish and fruits provide the main ingredients for local fare. Among the many fish you're likely to bite into are *filhote* and *pirarucu,* which is usually dried and salted before being grilled on a hot tile or cooked in coconut milk. The dark purple *açai,* whose thick pulp is full of nutrients, is a major source of sustenance, while the fruit of the *guaraná* plant provides a natural pick-me-up. The influence of the indigenous culture that predominates throughout the Amazon is also apparent in the region's most popular dishes. *Tacacá* is a shrimp-filled broth, thickened with *tucupi,* a thick yellow liquid extracted from manioc, and flavored with *jambu* leaves that will leave your mouth tingling and slightly numb.

MEALS

Meals in Brazil are relaxed and casual affairs. Brazilians usually have good table manners; they do not eat with their hands in restaurants (pizza is always eaten with a knife and fork). Since most restaurants and bars add a 10 percent (optional) service charge onto the bill, tipping isn't required, although it's customary to round up the total and even add a couple of *reais* if you feel service was exceptional.

Breakfast

The classic Brazilian breakfast, or *café de manhã,* involves strong coffee, freshly baked bread with butter, cheese, and sometimes ham, and fruit or fruit juice. In more rural areas, breakfasts can be much more copious, with homemade cakes, breads, and biscuits, porridges made from corn, rice, or tapioca, scrambled eggs, and in the Northeast, *carne-de-sol.* In better hotels, they are likely to take on a banquet-like appearance. If you need to fend for yourself, you have many options. You can head to a *bar de suco,* or juice bar, for a thick *vitamina* made with oats, milk, and pulverized fruit, where you'll also find healthy *salgados* (savory pastries filled with everything from shrimp to hearts of palm). Some *padarias* (bakeries) as well as *lanchonetes* (snack bars) serve breakfast fare for Brazilians on the run.

Lunch

Lunch, or *almoço,* is the major meal of the day. The classic lunch is a portion of meat (usually beef or chicken) accompanied by rice, beans, and some form of a small salad or boiled vegetable. You'll also have options that reflect the local cuisine of the region. If you're lunching solo, ask for a "PF" or *prato feito* (R$8-10) and you'll be served everything on one plate. If there are two or three of you, opt for the *prato commercial* (R$10-15); the same meal is brought on a tray, with each item served in its own dish. Although the food prepared is simple, unfussy fare, in smaller restaurants it is often home-cooked (*caseira*) and very tasty, particularly in smaller towns. There is also a great variety of restaurants where you can order, à la carte, both Brazilian and international specialties. Most portions are enough to serve two people (sometimes three). Usually only more expensive restaurants serve *pratos individuais.* If you're worried about the quantity of food, you can ask for a *meia-porção* (half portion).

Dinner

Dinner is often a light affair. People have *café com leite* with a simple sandwich or buttered rolls. *Sopas* (soups) are very popular. When company is involved, things get more elaborate.

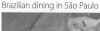

Brazilian dining in São Paulo

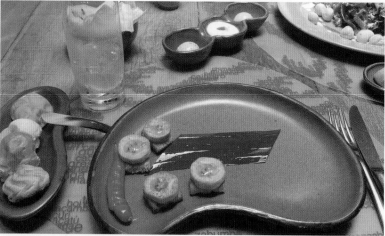

DRINKS
Coffee

Café is ubiquitous and Brazilians always seem to be drinking it with vast amounts of sugar or sweetener (*adocante*). Sometimes it's served presweetened, so if you want your coffee black, ask for it *sem açúcar*. Served in espresso cups or little plastic cups (if you're drinking one from the vendors who sell thermoses of the stuff in the streets), it is popularly known as *cafezinho* (little coffee). *Cafezinhos* can be enjoyed all day long, and they usually are. And no meal is complete without one, although if you order a *cafezinho* with your dessert (as opposed to after), people will look at you funny. Until recently, the best of Brazil's coffee was exported, but in the last few years a gourmet coffee scene has begun to emerge.

Juices

An amazing diversity of fresh fruit juices are available throughout Brazil. You can get juice in *lanchonetes, bars,* and especially in *bares de suco* (juice bars). Juice bars are most plentiful in urban beach neighborhoods, where they are staples of health-obsessed, body-baring Brazilians. In Rio's Zona Sul neighborhoods of Copacabana, Ipanema, and Leblon, they are omnipresent. Common tropical fruits include papaya, mango, guava, and *abacaxi* (pineapple), but you'll often find exotic fruits of the Northeast (*siriguela, umbu,* and *cajá*) and the Amazon (*bacuri, cupuaçu,* and the super-healthy *açai*). Even vitamin-packed vegetables such as *cenoura* (carrot) and *beterraba* (beet) are blender-worthy.

Brazil is the world's No. 1 producer and exporter of orange juice (*suco de laranja*), which is the only juice served pure and unadulterated. Other fruits are mixed with water (filtered), milk (becoming a *vitamina*), or orange juice. Sugar (*açúcar*) is added, as is ice (*gelo*). If you want your juice *sem gelo* and *sem açúcar*, ask for it *natural*. Energizers usually feature *guaraná* powder or syrup and *açai*; anti-stress drinks add *suco de maracujá*, a natural sedative that Brazilians give to hyperactive children.

A foolproof cure for an upset stomach or a hangover is to drink an *água-de-coco,* the fresh water from a green coconut. It's sold at kiosks along many beach areas and at beach *barracas* and fruit stands. The vendor hacks open a hole in the coconut with a machete and inserts a straw for drinking. With the same machete, they will then hack open the coconut, so you can scoop out the custardy white meat. Another popular drink sold in the streets is *caldo de cana,* or sugarcane juice. Usually the cane is pulverized right before your eyes, and the subsequent juice can be drank straight up or with a lime.

Soft Drinks

Brazilians have a fondness for soft drinks (*refrigerantes*), especially at the end of a heavy meal as a sort of appetite cleanser. The two most popular soft drinks are Coca-Cola and the even more popular *guaraná*, a champagne cola flavored with the Amazonian *guaraná* berry in doses small enough so that its caffeine content doesn't kick in.

Beer

Nothing beats the heat like a *cerveja estupidamente gelada,* otherwise known as a "stupidly cold" beer. If you're going to be drinking all day or night in 40°C (104°F) heat, you'll appreciate the lightness and low alcohol content of Brazilian beer, just make sure it is always *bem gelada* (nicely chilled). The idyllic beer is the *véu de noiva,* in which the bottle arrives at your table cloaked in a thin layer of frost that resembles "a bride's veil." There are various rival national brands (Brahma, Antarctica, Skol, Nova Schin) and some very good regional ones, such as Bohemia (from Rio de Janeiro) and Serramalte (from Rio Grande do Sul). *Chope* is a pale draft—both Brahma and Antarctica have their own versions—that is particularly popular in Rio and São Paulo. Essential bar vocab includes "*mais uma*" ("another beer, please") and "*a saideira*" ("last call").

Cachaça

What rum is to Cuba, *cachaça* is to Brazil. Distilled from fermented sugarcane juice, to which sugar is then added, *cachaça* packs a wallop (its alcohol content is 38-48 percent). Whether it's drunk pure or as the base of the famous caipirinha (*cachaça,* sugar, crushed ice, and lime), Brazilians swear by their *cachaça.* Caipirinhas and other cocktails are usually made with the clear, industrially manufactured varieties, such as Pitú and 51, available in any supermarket. These dirt-cheap brands are pretty foul-tasting; to savor *cachaças,* you're better off choosing one of the artisanal varieties produced at small mills throughout the country (most famously in Minas Gerais).

Cachaça began life as a drink imbibed by African slaves who worked on sugarcane plantations. Over time, it gradually gained a reputation as a poor man's poison. However, the fabrication of artisanal and even organic *cachaças* has led to a major boost in *cachaça's* rep. The government and producer associations have succeeded in trademarking the *cachaça* name with the goal of marketing it as a fine alcohol. Yet *cachaça* remains democratic, showing up under a variety of names—*pinga* (as in "drop"), *cana* (cane), *aguardente* (burning water), and *aquela-que-matou-o-guarda* ("that which killed the cop").

Wine

Brazil is not a big wine country. The main wine-growing region is the Vale dos Vinhedos in Rio Grande do Sul, close to Argentina, where descendants of Italian immigrants from Veneto cultivate *vinhos* that can be quite good (try a bottle of Miolo). Brazil's tropical climate isn't really conducive to wine drinking; in the Northeast, people often serve even red wine chilled. The exceptions are São Paulo and the South, where cool winters and a strong Italian influence have resulted in more of a wine culture.

PLACES TO EAT
Comida por Quilo

Highly popular and very affordable are restaurants serving *comida por quilo,* where you help yourself to a self-service buffet and then pay for your food by weight. You'll find per-kilo restaurants all over Brazil. Complimentary coffee and tea are usually offered at the end of the meal. Many per-kilo restaurants are only open for lunch.

Rodízio

Rodízio (which means "rotation") refers to a type of restaurant in which you pay a set price and then choose from a rotating display of food proffered by waiters who circle endlessly between the kitchen and the dining room.

Most often, you'll find *rodízio* in *churrascarias,* where freshly grilled meat will make the rounds. Other popular forms of *rodízio* include pizza, pasta, and sushi.

Bars

For many Brazilians, local bars act as a home away from home. In Brazil there's no such thing as a quick drink; rather, people spend hours at a bar. Most traditional bars, or *botecos,* serve tasty snacks, known as *petiscos* or *tira-gostos.* However, lots of bars are an excellent option for a full meal, especially at night. They are more laid-back, convivial, and affordable than a restaurant, and often feature live music.

Beaches

The majority of Brazilians live along the coast and the beach is like a second home. *Barracas,* rustic beach bars, are everywhere—even on seemingly deserted stretches of sand—providing shade, cool drinks, and bathrooms, and serving up freshly grilled fish or shrimp and more.

Street Food

Some of the best cooking in Brazil are the cheap and delicious snacks (*lanche*)—*tacacá* in Belém, *acarajé* in Salvador, *tapiocas* in Maceió, *pastéis* in São Paulo—made and prepared on the street. Hygienic conditions are fairly strict; those who prepare and sell food in public places sell to locals, and if word gets around that something was off, business will suffer. Use your judgment and stick to places in main areas where you see a lot of people lining up.

VEGETARIANS

Vegetarians will either have an easy or a challenging time in Brazil. In major cities as well as popular ecotourist destinations, you'll always find a *restaurante natural* serving *comida vegetariana*. Goods option for vegetarians are *quilo* (per-kilo) restaurants—where there are always salads and cooked veggies as well as beans—and juice bars, which often serve healthy vegetarian sandwiches. Along the coast and in the Pantanal and Amazon, pescatarians will never lack for fish or seafood. If you don't eat fish, however, you'll have a difficult time. Problems can arise once you get inland and away from big cities into meat-eating territory, where vegetables serve as a sparse garnish.

Travel Tips

CONDUCT AND CUSTOMS

Brazil is a very relaxed and casual place, although appearances can be deceiving. Underneath the freewheeling, sensual vibe, you'll often find a conservative core. Brazil has the largest Roman Catholic population on the planet, and though the practice of Catholicism is considered to be much less rigid and conservative than in other Latin American countries, a great many people take it seriously. If you're entering a place of worship—Christian or otherwise—dress and behave with a degree of modesty. In some official buildings, among them the government buildings as well as municipal theaters and even libraries and archives, similar forms of decorum apply: Women should not wear shorts or micro skirts, men should wear long pants, and flip-flops should be avoided.

Greetings

Brazilians are extremely warm and friendly, and this is apparent in the way they greet each other. If meeting a woman—whether a long-lost friend or a stranger—you'll greet her with two kisses (*beijos*), one on each cheek. Women kiss men as well, while men greeting men shake hands. However, among younger men as well as male friends and family members, back slapping, hugging (*abraços*), and other forms of friendly physical contact are quite common. When taking leave of each other, the same hugging and kissing rituals apply.

Public Displays of Affection

Brazilians are naturally very affectionate, which can sometimes cause confusion for foreigners. A lot of friendly hugging and kissing goes on in public, and the sense of privacy and personal space is quite different than in North America. Such behavior merely demonstrates a natural playfulness and lack of hang-ups about expressing affection, and you shouldn't treat it as sexual. Brazilians can be great and thoroughly effective flirts; the expression *jogar o charme* (cast your charm) is often recommended, both seriously and tongue-in-cheek, as a way of getting something (a discount, a restaurant table, a favor).

Brazilians also tend to be far less hung up about their bodies (and revealing them in public) and about sexual matters than North Americans. However, it's a serious mistake to confuse sensuality with licentiousness or with an "anything goes" attitude—looking sexy should not be equated with someone wanting to have sex.

Jeito Brasileiro (The Brazilian Way)

Dar um jeito or *um jeitinho* is a common

Chorar

In Brazil, **bargaining** is more than just haggling for a good price—it is a lively social ritual. Once you get the hang of it, you will likely enjoy yourself so much that trips to the impersonal aisles of supermarkets and department stores will seem downright dull. The best way to bargain with someone is to *chorar*, or "cry." This doesn't mean you have to literally burst into tears (although this technique actually works wonders), but you do have to haggle down the cost of an object based on some operatic tale of woe that will convince the seller that you have suffered immensely and are thus deserving of a discount. For instance, when you arrive at an airport and are confronted with the inflated prices a cab driver is charging for a ride into town, do the following: complain about how many delays you faced, lament that your luggage was lost, and curse the fact that security tore through your bags. Based on your acting chops, you'll be able to knock 5-10 percent off the fare. While a greater command of Portuguese makes for highly effective *chorando*, exaggerated facial gestures, hand-wringing, and sign language can do wonders. Although the person you're bargaining with will do his or her share of "crying" too, once you get your discount, you'll find that you're both actually satisfied—due to the sheer satisfaction of having had a good "cry."

expression that sums up a quintessentially Brazilian philosophy as well as an art form and a way of life. Literally (and inadequately) translated, it means "give a way," which doesn't begin to do justice to the rich and subtle inferences the expression embraces. *Dar um jeito* is a Brazilian's typical recourse when confronted with the many *pepinos* ("cucumbers"; i.e., problems) that daily life throws their way. When faced with an awkward situation or a difficult problem, Brazilians rarely confront it head on—usually a futile tactic, since the *pepino* is often the result of inflexible and sometimes absurd rules or government bureaucracy. Instead, they rely on a wide range of indirect *jeitos* or strategies, among them diplomacy, craftiness, flexibility, and charm, to get around an obstacle or extricate themselves from a predicament. The whole point is to not lose your cool and make a big scene, which Brazilians, a nonconfrontational people, only resort to in extremes. When they do, it's known as *um escândalo* and involves an impressive display of melodrama.

ACCESS FOR TRAVELERS WITH DISABILITIES

Brazil is very poorly equipped to deal with travelers with disabilities. Although in Rio

and São Paulo the number of hotels, restaurants, public buildings, and tourist attractions with wheelchair access and ramps is growing, they are the minority. Getting to them is very difficult. Sidewalks and streets are often uneven, traffic is chaotic, and there are almost no ramps. Very few buses, and no taxis, are equipped to deal with wheelchairs.

TRAVELING WITH CHILDREN

If a trip is well-planned, kids usually love Brazil. In Brazil, families are often more welcome in many places than in North America. On beaches and in small towns, it's easy for your kids to meet and play with Brazilian kids, who, like their parents, are usually outgoing and friendly. Often kids playing together breaks the ice for parents to get to know each other as well.

Since distances within Brazil are so great, stick to one or two regions and then take small day trips. Children pay full fare on buses, but on planes, they pay half-price between the ages of 2 and 12. If you plan on renting a car and you have an infant, consider bringing a baby seat. Rental companies don't have them, and they are expensive in Brazil.

In hotels, children under age 6 can usually stay for free in their parents' room—an extra bed is provided. Older children often only pay supplements. In popular vacation areas, such as beach resorts, there are many hotels geared toward families, which are equipped with playgrounds, games rooms, TV lounges, and swimming pools as well as gardens. Of course, there is always the beach. Choose a place with calm waters and access to shade. Make sure you bring plenty of sunscreen from home, since it's outrageously expensive in Brazil. You'll find disposable diapers in most supermarkets and pharmacies, although they are quite expensive.

If your child is a conservative eater, per-kilo restaurants can be a great option. Also a good bet are the increasingly sophisticated food courts found in shopping centers in major cities. Although few restaurants have children's menus or portions, regular portions are often so large that kids can share. Brazilians adore children and they are very welcome in restaurants (as long as they're fairly well-behaved).

WOMEN TRAVELERS

Machismo has a strong hold in Brazil; however, it's generally a more tepid version than in other Latin American countries. Although Brazilians respect women, North American notions of political correctness have never caught on here. And the definition of what constitutes sexual harassment is far more lax in Brazil, although an increasing number of cities have a *delegacia de mulheres*, where an all-female staff specializes in crimes against women. Flirting is a way of life and is usually harmless. As a *gringa,* traveling alone or with other women, you'll incite curiosity and inevitably receive some intense stares or come-ons, particularly in the North and the Northeast, where foreigners stand out more; these are all harmless. The problem is that you might feel targeted if, every time you go out for a drink (a woman by herself in a bar is a rarity) or to the beach, you're being bothered. If that's the case, try to join a group, or at least stick close to one (on the beach, for example). If saying a firm *"não"* and walking away isn't dissuading

an insistent suitor, head immediately to a safe place such as a hotel or a restaurant. Avoid deserted areas by day, and always take taxis at night.

SENIOR TRAVELERS

Brazil is known for having a strong youth culture; as a result many activities and venues tend to be geared toward younger clients. It's uncommon to see groups of elderly Brazilians traveling the way you would in North America and Europe. In most major cities, elderly Brazilians are not very visible, the exception being Rio de Janeiro, especially Copacabana. The hassle and discomfort of public transportation and long-distance traveling, coupled with messy traffic, poor road conditions, and uneven and crowded sidewalks make traveling throughout Brazil or even getting around most cities is a sometimes daunting experience. The overbearing heat and strong sun often exacerbate matters. Although discounts for seniors on public transportation and at museums and movies are generally accorded based on showing Brazilian ID, if you have proof of age as being at least 60 or 65, you can receive *um desconto para idosos.*

GAY AND LESBIAN TRAVELERS

Many gay and lesbian foreigners think that Brazil is a very gay-friendly place. It is and it isn't. Brazil is more tolerant of gay men and lesbians than many other Latin American countries. Both Rio and São Paulo have intense gay scenes (though much less active lesbian scenes), with a wide range of bars, clubs, and even small neighborhood enclaves. Other major cities, such as Salvador, Recife, and Florianópolis, also have gay venues and gay beaches or portions of beaches. However, the scene in Brazil is much more GLS (*gay, lesbica, e simpatisante;* that is, gay, lesbian, and "sympathetic") than exclusively gay and lesbian. Gay men, lesbians, and straight people mix much more, and the result is a less overt and politicized gay and lesbian presence than in North America or Europe.

Many Brazilians don't mind if you're gay or lesbian, but they don't want to see signs of it—public kissing or hand-holding—or hear you referring explicitly to your homosexuality. Two men or women living together, traveling together, or sharing a hotel room is not a problem, but the implicit agreement is that you're two friends, even if people suspect you're not. Although the drag queen and flamboyant queen are very much an accepted part of the culture (during Carnaval, even in small rural towns, the most macho of men don wigs, miniskirts, and lipstick), there is a difference between spectacle and humor and the reality of day-to-day life. Brazil is ultimately a macho culture, and explicit signs of homosexuality can incite insults and even violence. Even in cosmopolitan cities such as Rio and São Paulo, violence against gays is not unheard of. In the more conservative Northeast and rural areas, it is more common. For more information about the gay and lesbian scene in Brazil, in Portuguese, check out http://mixbrasil.xpg. uol.com.br, which has GLS listings for cities all over Brazil as well as news stories. **Gay Travel Brazil** (www.gaytravelbrasil.com) is a gay-operated travel agency specializing in customizing trips, outings, and activities for gay and lesbian tourists as well as procuring gay-friendly accommodations.

Health and Safety

BEFORE YOU GO

Before your trip, it's always good idea to check with your country's travel health recommendations for Brazil. You'll find lots of up-to-date information and travel advisories on the following websites:

Australia: www.smartraveller.gov.au

Canada: www.phac-aspc.gc.ca/tmp-pmv/pub-eng.php

United Kingdom: www.gov.uk/foreign-travel-advice

United States: wwwnc.cdc.gov/travel

The **MD Travel Health** website (www.mdtravelhealth.com) has complete travel health information, updated daily for both physicians and travelers, while the World Health Organization (www.who.int/ith) publishes a useful tome, *International Travel and Health;* updated annually, it can be downloaded for free from their website.

Vaccinations

The **yellow fever** vaccination is required for Brazil and is essential for visiting the Amazon region, but otherwise only recommended. Bring an International Certificate of Vaccination yellow booklet, since Brazilian authorities will sometimes ask for proof of vaccination for travelers going to and from the Amazon. If you've been in any other South American country (with the exception of Chile and Argentina) 90 days prior to coming to Brazil, as well as some African ones, you will also need proof of yellow fever vaccination. Since it takes 10 days for the vaccine to take effect, you can either have it at home or, if you're going to spend time in a big city or the coast before heading to the Amazon, you can easily get the vaccine in Brazil at any public *posto de saúde* (health clinic)—ask at any pharmacy for the nearest location—where it will be administered free of charge. Other recommended vaccines that are always useful include **hepatitis A, hepatitis B, typhoid,** and **rabies shots** (many domestic animals in Brazil aren't vaccinated against rabies).

What to Bring

Bring any prescription medication in its original packaging and ask your pharmacist or doctor to give you the generic names for any medication. You will usually be able to purchase the same drug or its generic version at any Brazilian pharmacy (although the brand name will likely be different, and some generic formulas may vary slightly—for important medications, check with your doctor before you go). Bring plenty of mosquito repellent, sunscreen, and aspirin or Tylenol (which are more expensive in Brazil). Aloe vera or other relief for sunburn is also a good idea, as is calamine lotion or witch hazel to take the irritating itch out of any mosquito bites.

Insurance

If you have medical coverage, check to see if it covers expenses incurred overseas. If not, consider buying travel insurance. Find out if the insurer will make payments directly or reimburse you afterward (most insurers do the latter). Most of the best Brazilian clinics and hospitals (which are private) will make you pay for service up front.

HEALTH PRECAUTIONS

Tropical heat and humidity favor the growth of bacteria and cause food and organic matter to spoil and rot very quickly. Hygiene standards in Brazil are quite high, however it's wise to take precautions so as not to spend your trip with an upset stomach or diarrhea.

Be attentive to the conditions of any food purchased on the street. Fruit with peels (bananas, mangoes, papaya) are safer than fruit without, which should be carefully washed. Boiled vegetables are safer than raw ones, unless you know they've been well washed, or veggies that have been sitting around in mayonnaise. Be careful with seafood such as shrimp; if something looks poorly cooked, or smells or tastes slightly off, spit it out and discontinue eating.

Brazilian tap water is supposedly safe to drink in large cities, although few people actually do (in part because of the heavy chlorine taste). Most Brazilians drink filtered water or mineral water, either *natural* or *com gas* (carbonated), and you should too (although brushing your teeth or rinsing fruit with tap water is perfectly fine). Mineral water is inexpensive and available everywhere. Ice is usually made from filtered water. However, if you're in an out-of-the-way place that seems a bit suspicious, order your drink without it

(*sem gelo*). Use a straw when drinking from cans; if drinking beer from a can, wipe the top off with a napkin or your shirt.

DENGUE

Dengue fever is a viral infection that, like many tropical diseases is transmitted by mosquitoes. Dengue isn't caused by just any old mosquito but by a genus known as *Aedes* that breed in stagnant water, usually in densely populated urban areas with improper drainage. Plant containers and abandoned rubber tires are particularly common breeding grounds. Dengue mosquitoes usually attack during the daytime and are most common during hot, humid rainy periods. In recent years, Rio de Janeiro has had large dengue epidemics during its rainy summer months. Although rarely fatal, dengue is like having a really debilitating case of flu. Symptoms include fever, aching muscles, headaches, nausea, weakness, vomiting, and a rash. The worst symptoms last 5-7 days, but full recuperation can take longer. Diagnosis is via a blood test. There is no vaccine for dengue, nor is there treatment other than rest, plenty of liquids, and acetaminophen (Tylenol). Do not take aspirin. Only severe cases require hospitalization. The best thing you can do to avoid infection is to take precautions to avoid getting bitten in the first place.

TRAVELER'S DIARRHEA

Even if you are careful about the source of the water you drink and the food you eat, you might get diarrhea simply as a result of being exposed to different types of bacteria. If you do get sick, take medication (pack Imodium/loperamide) and drink lots of fluids. Particularly good for diarrhea and upset stomachs are *água de coco* (fresh coconut water) and *suco de lima*, a juice made from a citrus fruit that is a cross between an orange and a lime. If your diarrhea is serious after 2-3 days, go to a pharmacy and ask for an antibiotic and an antidiarrheal drug. If you see blood and have a fever, chills, or strong abdominal pains, seek medical treatment.

HIV/AIDS AND STDS

Brazil has one of the highest numbers of people living with HIV infection. According to statistics, more than 35 percent of infected people are women. Brazil has one of the world's most highly respected and effective HIV/AIDS policies; the Brazilian government's fight against HIV/AIDS involves free medication, low-cost generic drugs, and medical follow-up for all patients for life. Yet this doesn't prevent people from getting HIV in the first place. Condoms—known as *camisinhas* ("little shirts")—are widespread in pharmacies and many supermarkets, and there is not so much a stigma as a resistance to using them. As a result, you really have to be careful about HIV and STDs. Whether you're with a man or a woman, always insist on using a condom.

MOSQUITOES

Mosquitoes can be very irritating. They can also be carriers of diseases such as yellow fever, dengue fever, and malaria. They are especially a problem in urban areas during hot rainy seasons (in which dengue can be a problem) and in chronically wet regions such as the Amazon and the Pantanal. The best way to prevent mosquito bites is to wear effective repellent (containing DEET) as well as long pants, long sleeves, and closed shoes. Be careful not to get repellent close to your eyes or mouth. Sleep with mosquito netting, and if your windows don't have screens, make sure you close them. Mosquitoes don't like wind, so if you have a fan in your room, keep it on.

SUN EXPOSURE

At the beach, expose yourself to the sun gradually. The tropical sun, particularly during the summer months, can cause a lot of damage. Brazilians have the highest rate of skin cancer in the world; many don't use sunscreen because of its exorbitant cost. Using a strong sunscreen (minimum SPF 30; bring it from home) that filters out UVA and UVB rays is essential. Even so, if you stay in the sun between the hours of 11am-2pm, you will get burned. On many beaches, you can rent a parasol or head to a thatched *barraca* for shade come high noon. Children and those with fair, sensitive skin should use a much higher SPF. A hat is always essential and you'll practically be blinded without a pair of sunglasses with a protective filter. Drink lots of liquids, even when you're not thirsty. Beer and caipirinhas might be refreshing, but alcohol dehydrates. An ideal replenishing drink is *água de coco*.

MEDICAL SERVICES
Pharmacies

Most pharmacies are open until 10pm; in central neighborhoods, you'll always find one that stays open 24 hours and on Sunday. All *farmácias* have at least one licensed pharmacist trained to deal with minor medical problems and emergencies, which could save you a trip to a clinic or hospital; the only problem is it's very unlikely that the pharmacist will speak any English. You'll be able to find good medicine for whatever ails you (upset stomach, diarrhea, headache, rashes, a cold or cough), even though you probably won't recognize the names.

Clinics and Hospitals

Brazil has a very good health system—as long as you can pay for it. All Brazilians have access to public hospitals for free. In theory, this is fantastic. In practice, the state of many public hospitals is truly frightening. There is a saying among Brazilians that a sick person who goes into a public hospital usually gets worse instead. While doctors and nurses are often qualified, lack of funds often makes public hospitals precarious. If you require medical attention, head to a private clinic, unless you have a real emergency. Middle-class and wealthy Brazilians usually pay high health insurance premiums that give them access to state-of-the-art First World clinics, particularly in major cities. You can have access to them as well, but it will cost you. Consulates can recommend good hospitals, clinics, or specialists, although English-speaking doctors are rare.

SAFETY

The subject of crime and security in Brazil is an extremely important and complex one. Violent crime, holdups, robberies, and drug warfare in major cities dominate the Brazilian news media, often in a sensationalist manner, and have a major social impact. An increasing number of middle-class Brazilians are moving to closed condominium complexes with electric fences and 24-hour security. Wealthy Brazilians are the leading buyers of security systems and of bulletproof cars in the world. Poorer Brazilians who reside in peripheral neighborhoods or *favelas* live in fear of bus holdups, stray bullets, or drug traffickers. If you come into contact with Brazilians, read the papers, or watch TV, you will definitely hear such stories, and while the tone may be alarmist or melodramatic, the occurrences themselves are real. There's no need for paranoia, but don't let yourself be complacent.

Safety Tips

Having lived in Brazil for more than 15 years, I don't know *anybody* who has never been robbed. But the typical instances in which traveling foreigners might find themselves at risk are easily avoided by taking common-sense precautions.

Unless you're on a very busy or major street in a good neighborhood, don't walk around at night in a city you don't know. While downtown business areas of major cities such as Rio, São Paulo, Salvador, and Recife may hum with energy by day, at night and on weekends, especially Sunday, they turn into ghost towns and should be avoided. If you're going to be in a crowd (an outdoor performance, a parade, Carnaval) leave all valuables and original documents at home. Carry a small change purse around your neck or a money belt with photocopies of ID.

While public transportation is safe enough during the day, at night, when holdups are more likely, always take a taxi, even if it's just a few blocks to your destination. If you've rented a car, be careful where you park. Particularly at night, you don't want to be on a dark or isolated side street. If you're at a stoplight, you should keep your windows rolled up, since if you're stuck in traffic, you can easily be held up. At night, in many major cities, drivers slow down at stoplights but don't actually stop their cars (a practice sanctioned by law).

You should never be walking around, night or day, with a lot of cash in a purse or pocket. Do, however, keep a few small bills that you can easily access. Fumbling around for money in public, on a bus or at a market, leaves you exposed to robbery. Similarly, when you go to the beach, don't bring any valuables with you. Bring enough cash for drinks or snacks, and that's it. Keep all your possessions with you (in a neat pile or a cheap, preferably local beach bag) within your line of vision; there are tales of tourists dozing in the sun and waking up to find their possessions gone. If you're on your own and want to go swimming, ask someone to watch your stuff. This is very common on Brazilian beaches.

If you're going to be taking money out at an ATM, make sure nobody is watching you. Even though ATMs are open until 10pm, the best time to take out money is during the day, in a busy area, preferably in an airport or a shopping mall. Be careful on Sunday, when commercial areas are very quiet. Once again, if you're withdrawing a lot of cash, put it in a money belt. Also be aware that card cloning is rampant in Brazil; never let your card out of your sight and when using an ATM (preferably in a busy bank) use your hand to cover your code. Even so, there are many cases of criminals installing card readers in machines that copy your card and cameras that capture your code. For this reason, bring a back-up card (in case you have to cancel a cloned one), hold on to your withdrawal slips, and keep up to date with your bank activity.

Major cities are the most problematic in terms of crime, although in major tourist destinations such as Rio and Salvador there has been a major effort to have police on patrol, which has increased safety in the most touristed areas. Nonetheless, always have your wits about you. In smaller towns, rural areas, and beach destinations, you will definitely feel more relaxed. Crime is much lower, and you can let your guard down somewhat (although don't be lulled into complete carelessness).

While in the South and Southeast, it's easier to blend in physically with the local population; in the North and Northeast, if you are of fair European stock, you will often stand out simply because of your physical type. Gringos are uniformly considered easy targets, not only because they are all thought to be rich but because they are often careless. One thing to do is try to camouflage yourself: get a bit of a tan, don't talk loudly in a foreign language, and try to dress like the locals (casually but smartly; no flashy jewelry, expensive footwear, or fashionable designer duds). Also be careful about where you flash your camera, particularly if it has a big zoom lens. The smaller and more compact your camera, the better. Don't unfold big maps in public or look like you're lost or unsure of where you're going. Without being neurotic, always try to be aware of where you are and what's going on around you. Trust your instincts. If a bar, street, or neighborhood feels sketchy, make a fast exit. If you feel someone is watching you or following you, speed up your pace, cross the street, or enter a shop or public building. Be aware of possible scams such as being approached by so-called officials at airports who want you to go with them after you've come out of the arrivals section. Another notorious *golpe* (scam) is "Boa Noite Cinderela" ("Good Night Cinderela"), in which someone slips a drug into your drink and, while you're knocked out, robs you blind. This trick usually befalls unsuspecting romantics who hook up with a potential conquest in a bar. If you find yourself in this situation, don't leave your drink unguarded (such as by going to the restroom).

Police

The North American or European concept of police as a symbol of law and order doesn't hold true in Brazil. When trouble occurs, most Brazilians avoid the police. Because police officers are grossly underpaid and subject to corruption and violence, it is sometimes difficult to distinguish them from the bandits and drug traffickers they are supposedly battling. This is, of course, a generalization, and there are exceptions to the rule.

In Brazil, there are various types of police. The most efficient (and well paid, and thus less corrupt) of the bunch are the **Polícia Federal,** who deal with all matters concerning passports, visas, and immigration. They have offices at all international airports as well as at frontier posts and in state capitals, and are generally helpful. The **Polícia Militar** are a hangover from the era of military dictatorship. They dress in soldier-like khaki uniforms accessorized with tough lace-up boots and berets (even in the tropical heat). You'll often see them supposedly keeping the peace on street corners. Although they can be rough with Brazilian indolents, they leave foreigners alone. The plainclothes **Polícia Civil** deal with solving crimes. If you're robbed and you want to report the crime, in many places you'll need to go to the nearest *delegacia,* or station. Be prepared if you want an official report: You'll need to wait in line, and nobody will speak English. Unless you really need a report for insurance purposes, you might want to just let it go. In a major city, such as Rio or Salvador, you'll have better luck with a ***delegacia de turismo.*** This special police force specializes in crimes against foreign tourists, and some of their agents speak rudimentary English.

Theft

A lot of violent crime in Brazil takes place in poorer neighborhoods that you'll probably never see. In the event that you're robbed, in most cases it will consist of a *furto* (small theft) in which your pockets are picked or someone grabs your bag and takes off. However, armed *assaltos* (holdups) do occur. In the event that you are held up by someone, do not resist. Quickly and calmly hand over whatever the thief wants. It is a no-brainer between your money, watch, jewelry, or documents and your life. Accidents happen when people get very upset or try to resist, making the robber nervous and prone to act impulsively. If you need to make a report to the police, try the special tourist police, *delegacia de turismo,* which you'll find in major cities. Otherwise, you'll have to deal with the overworked and not always sympathetic Polícia Civil. Even if you do report a robbery, it's extremely unlikely you'll get your possessions back.

Information and Services

MONEY

Brazil's currency is the *real* (pronounced "ray-ALL"; the plural, *reais,* is pronounced "ray-EYES"). One *real* (R$1) can be divided into 100 *centavos.* You'll come across bills in denominations of 2, 5, 10, 20, 50, and 100 *reais.* Bills are easy to distinguish since each is a different color. Coins are trickier, since some have several versions, but you'll find coins worth 5, 10, 25, and 50 *centavos* as well as R$1. Because they were virtually worthless, there are no longer any 1-*centavo* coins. If you're purchasing something, the total will be rounded up or down (if the total comes to R$4.37, the cashier will expect R$4.35; if it comes to R$1.38, you'll get change for R$1.40).

Currency Exchange

Although you might want to bring some U.S. dollars for an emergency (in the event you can't get cash from an ATM or if your card gets lost or stolen), you'll usually lose money exchanging dollars, whether at a bank or a *casa de câmbio* (exchange house). Regular banking hours are 10am-4pm Monday-Friday. There are very few places where dollars—or U.S. dollar traveler's checks—are accepted.

ATMs

Bring an international Visa or MasterCard (or both, to give you more options) and withdraw cash from bank machines. Not only is this the most secure method, but you'll get the best exchange rate. Most major branches of Banco do Brasil, Bradesco, HSBCC, and Citibank have at least one ATM that accepts Visa, MasterCard or Cirrus cards (look for stickers on the individual ATM), while red Banco 24 Horas ATMs accept all cards, all of the time. In all cases, you'll need your four-digit PIN. If you're going to a small town or somewhere off the beaten track, it's best to stock up on cash beforehand, although credit cards will be accepted by most hotels and larger restaurants.

For city ATMs, your best bets are banks in downtown commercial areas, areas with lots of tourist activity, airports, bus terminals, and shopping centers. For security reasons, bank ATMs are only open 6am-10pm daily. Most have a withdrawal limit of R$1,000 (Bradesco's is R$800). During big holidays, such as New Year's, Carnaval, and any long weekend, it's wise to stock up on cash in advance; sometimes the ATMs run dry.

Credit Cards

Most Brazilian hotels, restaurants, and stores accept international credit cards. Using a card not only alleviates carrying around big wads of cash, but also offers the most advantageous exchange rate. The only thing it won't get you is the discounts (usually 10 percent) that you can ask for and usually get if you pay for accommodations or shopping items in cash (*em dinheiro*). Visa and MasterCard are the most widely accepted cards (once again, bring both to increase your payment possibilities), although some places will take American Express and Diners Club. Due to frequent credit card fraud, don't let your card out of your sight.

Money Wires

Should you require a money wire, Banco do

Brasil has a partnership with Western Union. A person can send you money from North America via Western Union (www.westernunion.com) to any Banco do Brasil branch. Once you've specified the city you're in, all you need to do (aside from standing in a long line) is show up with your passport and the wire transaction code and get your cash.

TOURIST INFORMATION

You will find municipal, regional, and state tourist information offices and kiosks throughout Brazil. You can get free maps and some brochures as well as help with accommodations, renting cars, acquiring guides, or organizing excursions or sporting activities. Often, they will have transportation schedules for local buses and boats. In smaller towns, you can often get information about renting a room in a private home.

Apart from major cities, it is rare to find tourist offices where people speak anything other than Portuguese. Sometimes you'll encounter staff who are not actually that knowledgeable, a fact compensated for by general friendliness and a willingness to help. In smaller towns, tourist office opening and closing hours are often not strictly adhered to, particularly in the off-season.

Maps

The maps in this guidebook are limited to central areas of major Brazilian cities and important regional destinations such as coastlines and national parks. For more detailed city and local maps, check with the local tourist office in the city or town you're visiting. In major cities, *bancas de revistas* (newsstands) and bookstores usually sell city and state maps. Otherwise, the best maps are produced by Quatro Rodas, which sells regional maps for all of Brazil as well as a detailed foldout map of Brazil that comes for free with its annually published ***Guia Quatro Rodas*** (a Brazilian equivalent of France's Michelin, and a bargain at only R$39). Quatro Rodas also puts out a similar guide that deals exclusively with Brazilian beaches. For highway maps,

purchase the *Guia Quatro Rodas Estrada* map for around R$20. Digitized versions of all maps are available online (http://viajeaqui.abril.com.br/guia4rodas), along with a convenient trip planning tool that will even calculate how much gas you'll need. You can purchase Quatro Rodas maps and guides in major *bancas de revistas* and bookstores.

COMMUNICATIONS AND MEDIA
Postal Service

It's easy to identify post offices (*correios*) by their bright yellow-and-blue marquees. Every main city has a rather grandiose main *correios* building as well as dozens of small post offices. Commercial centers, airports, and major shopping centers usually have postal kiosks. When sending a letter or parcel, you can send it *simples* (regular mail) or *registrada* (registered). Sedex is the Correios's version of FedEx and is quite efficient. The *correios* sells cardboard boxes of various sizes; for envelopes, you'll often have to go to a *papelaria* (stationery store). There are no adhesive envelopes in Brazil, but the *correios* will always have a pot of glue and a brush, and you can proceed to make a big mess. Postage within Brazil is inexpensive, but sending letters or packages abroad can be expensive depending on the weight. On the bright side, intensely colorful Brazilian postage stamps (*selos*) are quite stunning.

Phone Service

Brazilian phone service is quite efficient, if not exactly cheap. Local calls are charged by the minute. Calls within Brazil have become somewhat less costly with the privatization of the phone industry; however, international calls are pretty astronomical. Unless it's essential, you're better off emailing or Skypeing with loved ones at home. An international call from a hotel is even more exorbitant; it will be much less expensive if you ask people back home to call you.

Throughout Brazil, you will see domeshaped phone booths known as *orelhões* ("big ears"), where you can make local calls and long-distance calls throughout Brazil. With the popularity of cell phones, you'll now find them abandoned and often not working. To use an *orelhão*, you'll need to purchase a *cartão telefônica* (phone card) sold at most news kiosks. They usually come in 40 and 60 units (*unidades*). A quick local call will use up 1 or 2 units. A short long-distance call will quickly use up an entire card.

Brazil has several telephone companies, or *operadoras,* and whenever you make a long-distance call outside of your area code (known as a DDD), you'll have to precede the phone number with a two-digit number belonging to one of them. Embratur (21) is the biggest one, with national and international coverage. When calling a number in Brazil, dial 0 followed by the *operadora* code, followed by the DDD, followed by the number. An example of a call to Rio (whose area code is 21) would be: 0-21-21/3333-3333. An example of an international call to Canada or the United States (whose country code is 1) would be: 00-21-1-416/921-7777. It is also possible to make a collect call (*uma chamada a cobrar*) from Brazil via the Embratel operator. To do so, call 0800/703-2111.

Cell phones are immensely popular throughout Brazil, and their use has far surpassed more expensive fixed lines. Calling to or from a cell phone, however, is more expensive than calling from a landline. If you're calling long distance, charges are steep. You'll find cell phone coverage in most places throughout Brazil. Your own cell phone should work in Brazil *if* it is compatible with international tri-band GSM standards and is *unlocked* (meaning you can remove and insert local SIM cards). Note that Brazil's network is not compatible with all North American and European smartphones. Contact your cell phone provider before your trip to confirm. Another alternative is to purchase a Brazilian SIM card from a Brazilian operator such as **TIM** (www.tim.com.br); **Claro** (www.claro.com.br); **Oi** (www.oi.com.br), or **Vivo** (www.vivo.com.br), the four major operators

that offer nationwide service. Armed with a Brazilian number, you'll be able to pay Brazilian rates (per minute, around R$1 for local calls and R$1.50 for long distance, although if the person you're talking shares your operator, calls are much less or even free). Operators have stores and kiosks in airports and *shoppings*. When purchasing a SIM card, you'll need to show your passport. You can buy recharge cards at any newsstand.

Internet Access

Internet service is spreading like wildfire through Brazil. These days, even the most rustic hotel off the grid has Wi-Fi service, although in far-flung places service can be weak or unstable. Most hostels, *pousadas,* and hotels offer free Wi-Fi, while some upscale chains rather ungraciously charge (inflated) rates. Most *shoppings* also have free Wi-Fi, as do an increasing number of bookstores, bars, and cafés. Cybercafés have dwindled, as have LAN houses, dark (but air-conditioned) dens where adolescents play games and blog (Brazilians are the second-biggest population of bloggers in the world after Americans)—although they're still quite prevalent in small towns.

Newspapers and Magazines

Brazil's most respected newspaper is the São Paulo-based *Folha de São Paulo* (www.folha.uol.com.br), a mildly left-leaning paper popular with liberals and intellectuals. For foreigners, it is a good source of arts and culture listings for São Paulo, and there is an online version in English with its own English-language columnists. Also good are the slightly more conservative São Paulo-based *O Estado de São Paulo* (www.estadao.com.br) and Rio-based *Jornal do Brasil* (www.jbonline.com.br). In Rio, *O Globo* (http://oglobo.globo.com), owned by the Globo media giant, also puts out a popular daily paper that has good arts listings for the city of Rio. Major cities throughout the country have their own newspapers, although they are more provincial in character.

You can get your hands on major English-language papers, particularly the *International Herald Tribune,* as well as international magazines (sometimes they are a month or two old) at airport bookstores and major *bancas de revistas* (newsstands) in Rio and São Paulo. Rio and São Paulo's many bookstores also carry a wide selection of English-language press and books, including guidebooks. These are harder to find in other cities, but the spread of megabookstores such as Siciliano and Saraíva means you can usually find English-language magazines and books in these *livrarias;* most are located in glitzier shopping malls.

Television

Brazilian TV, though often terrible, is a great unifier. The major networks are SBT, Record, Bandeirantes, Globo, and TV Educadora, a state-owned educational network that has a mix of high-brow round tables, films, and very good cultural programming, including great live music performances.

The all-powerful Globo is the leading network. Its *novelas* (7pm, 8pm, and 9pm Mon.-Sat.) are the most watched of all nightly programs. These soap operas go all-out on production and star a roster of gorgeous and usually talented actors, all of whom are part of a permanent stable of stars, known as Globais, that harks back to the Hollywood studio system. When these Globais aren't participating in a *novela,* miniseries, or other Globo production, they make commercials and give the paparazzi and gossip columnists endless fodder. If you don't speak Portuguese, you will find *novelas* cheesy and melodramatic. If you do understand the language, you will still find them cheesy and melodramatic, but you'll easily get drawn into them, and perhaps become addicted.

You don't need to understand much Portuguese to watch the broadcast of a live *jogo de futebol.* The machine-gun fire of words rattled off by Brazilian sports commentators with jacked-up fervor and excitement will have you alternately biting your nails and cheering for joy, even if you've never been much of a soccer fan.

In Brazilian hotels, you'll usually receive these basic Brazilian channels (sometimes only Globo, depending on your location). However, in moderate to luxury lodgings, you'll be treated to cable with BBC, CNN, some superior Brazilian cable channels, and lots of American cable series.

WEIGHTS AND MEASURES

Brazil uses the metric system. Depending on where in the country you're located, the electric current varies from 100 to 240 volts, although most common is 110 volts, meaning you won't have problems with electronic devices from North America. Any hardware store or larger supermarket will carry cheap adapters.

Brazil has three different time zones. The main "Brasília" time zone includes São Paulo, Rio, and the entire coastline going inland as far as Brasília. Westward, the states of Mato Grosso and Mato Grosso do Sul (containing the Pantanal) and much of the Amazon region are one hour earlier. The island of Fernando de Noronha, off the coast of Pernambuco, is one hour later than Brasília time. During the Brazilian summer (North American winter) most of the country, with the exception of the Northeast, goes on daylight saving time, which makes sunset later. During this time, Rio, São Paulo, Minas, and the South spring forward, meaning that they are two hours later than New York City. Otherwise, the time difference between New York and Rio is only one hour: when it's noon in New York, it's 1pm in Rio.

Resources

Glossary

açai: a high-antioxidant, deep-purple Amazonian fruit

acarajé: a crunchy bean fritter, cooked in palm oil and filled with dried shrimp, pepper, *vatapá,* and *caruru,* that is a favorite snack in Bahia

água de coco: milk from a green coconut (great for a hangover)

artesanato: popular art and handicrafts

axé: a type of fast-paced commercial pop associated with Carnaval in Salvador

azulejo: Portuguese glazed ceramic tile

baía: bay

Bahiana: person or thing from Bahia; also refers to Afro-Brazilian women, usually wearing traditional white turbans and lace petticoats, who sell typical Brazilian food

bairro: neighborhood

bandeirantes: early colonial explorers who set off from São Paulo to explore and settle Brazil's vast unknown interior

barraca: small rustic kiosk or beach bar

bloco: large Carnaval group

botequim/boteco: laid-back, traditional, neighborhood-style bar, mostly associated with Rio

caboclinho: folkloric dance with indigenous origins that is popular in the Northeast, particularly Pernambuco; also the name of a sandwich made with the *tucumã* fruit, a favorite snack in Manaus

caboclo: person of mixed race (Indian and European); often used to describe residents of the Amazon region

cachaça: distilled sugarcane, the Brazilian equivalent of rum (slang: *pinga,* or drop)

cachoeira: waterfall

cafezinho: an espresso-size coffee drink

caipirinha: classic Brazilian cocktail made with *cachaça,* crushed ice, lime, and sugar

caipiroska: caipirinha in which vodka replaces *cachaça*

camarão: shrimp

Candango: native of Brasília

Candomblé: Afro-Brazilian religion whose practice is particularly strong in Bahia

cangaçeiro: early 20th-century bandits from the Northeast interior, the most famous of whom was Lampião

capoeira: Afro-Brazilian mixture of martial art and dance

Carioca: person or thing from Rio de Janeiro

carne-de-sol: sun-dried meat

caruru: a traditional Afro-Bahian dish of diced okra flavored with *dendê* and dried shrimp

Cerrado: dry vegetation of scrubland and palms found in Brazil's Central-West region

chope: draft beer

choro/chorinho: type of instrumental music from the Northeast

comida por quilo: popular self-service buffet restaurant where you pay for food by weight (per kilo)

cupuaçu: deliciously sweet, milky-white Amazonian fruit

dendê: palm oil used in Bahian cooking

doce: sweet; often refers to candies or preserved fruit, such as *doce de goiaba* (preserved guava) *empada:* empanada

farinha: flour (generally manioc flour, which is dusted over meals)

farofa: manioc flour toasted with butter and other seasonings as an accompaniment to meals in the Northeast

favela: urban slum

fazenda: ranch; farm; country estate

feijão: beans

feijoada: classic Brazilian stew of beans and salted pork and beef

feira: open-air market

ferroviária: train station

festa: celebration, party

flutuação: a sport involving floating downriver while wearing a snorkel, mask, and lifejacket

forró: country-style type of music and dance from the Northeast

fortaleza: fortress

frescoball: popular Brazilian beach sport

Gaúcho: person or thing from Rio Grande do Sul

GLS: a Brazilian slang term for *gay, lesbica, e simpatisante;* i.e., gay-friendly

gringo: foreigner

guaraná: Amazonian berry used as a pick-me-up; in small doses, it flavors Brazil's national cola

Iemanjá: popular Afro-Brazilian goddess of the seas

igapó: seasonally flooded patch of Amazonian rain forest

igreja: church

ilha: island

jacaré: caiman

jangada: rustic sailboat used by fishermen of the Northeast

lanchonete: snack bar; food stand

largo: small square or plaza

literatura de cordel: printed folios, illustrated with block prints, that recount popular tales of the Northeast

litoral: coastline

loja: store or shop

mangue: mangrove swamp

maracatu: a traditional group of dancers linked to Afro-Brazilian culture and religion, and a famous fixture of Recife's Carnaval; also a percussive musical style that has become a popular genre in Pernambuco

Mata Atlântica: native Atlantic rain forest, whose remaining patches can still be found along the Brazilian coast, mostly in Bahia and the Southeast

mercado: market

Mineiro: a person or thing from Minas Gerais

moqueca: typical Bahian stew of fish or seafood cooked with tomatoes and green peppers in palm oil and coconut milk

morro: hill, small mountain

MPB: música popular Brasileiro; classic Brazilian pop

mulato: person of mixed African and European heritage

nordeste: the Northeast of Brazil

novelas: popular nightly television soap operas

orixá: a Candomblé divinity

orla: oceanfront

pastel: a deep-fried pastry stuffed with a variety of fillings, especially popular in São Paulo

pau brasil: brazilwood tree, coveted by early colonial explorers, which inspired Brazil's name

Paulistano/Paulista: a person or thing from the state of São Paulo

petiscos: nibbles or appetizers, usually served in bars

pinga: drop; slang for *cachaça,* the Brazilian equivalent of rum

pousada: an inn, guesthouse, or bed-and-breakfast

praça: square or plaza

praia: beach

rodízio: a type of restaurant service in which you pay a fixed price and then can choose from a rotating selection of items, usually *churrasco* or pizza

rodovia: highway

rodoviária: bus terminal

rodoferroviária: long-distance bus terminal

salgado: any savory type of pastry

samba: a fast, drum-based Brazilian style of music with strong African influences

serra: mountain range

Sertanejo: resident of the northeastern Sertão, as well as a popular style of country music

Sertão: the poor, desertlike, and often drought-ridden interior of the Northeast

SESC: Serviço Social do Comércio; union benefiting workers from the trade and service industries that offers free or low-priced cultural events and lodging

shopping: shopping mall

sorveteria: ice cream parlor

tapioca: type of crepe made from crunchy manioc flour and served with fillings

terreiro: house and surrounding area where Candomblé rituals are performed

tira-gosto: appetizer

trio elétrico: vast stage on wheels on which singers and musicians perform during Carnaval in Bahia

tucupi: liquid distilled from manioc that is used in Amazonian cooking, most famously in a duck dish known as *pato no tucupi*

Tupi: indigenous people and language that thrived along coastal Brazil before the arrival of European explorers

tutu mineiro: thick bean puree that is a classic side dish in Minas Gerais

vatapá: a traditional Afro-Bahian dish in which cashews, dried shrimp, palm oil, and coconut milk are combined into a thick puree

Portuguese Phrasebook

Outside of Rio de Janeiro, São Paulo, and more sophisticated tourist areas, where at least a little English may be spoken, you will have two linguistic alternatives. The first is to try speaking Spanish, which is similar in many ways to Portuguese—although, while Brazilians might understand you, you'll have a more difficult time understanding their replies. The second is to learn a few basic expressions in Portuguese. Although pronunciation can be tricky, Brazilians will love the fact that you are making an effort and will usually be very encouraging.

PRONUNCIATION

Portuguese is spoken as it is written. However, things take a turn for the complex when confronted with the challenging vowel sounds.

Vowels

So-called nonnasal vowels are fairly straightforward:

a   pronounced "ah" as in "father" in words like *garota* (girl).

e   pronounced "eh" as in "hey" in words like *fé* (faith). At the end of a word, such as *fome* (hunger), pronounced "ee" as in "free."

i   pronounced "ee" as in "free" in words such as *polícia* (police).

o   pronounced "aw" as in "dog" in words such as *loja* (shop). At the end of a word, such as *minuto* (minute), it varies from "oh" as in "go" to "oo" as in "too."

u   pronounced "oo" as in "too" in words such as *luz* (light).

Much more complicated are the nasal vowels. Nasal vowels are signaled by a tilde accent (~) as in *não* (no), or by the presence of the letters m or n following the vowel, such as *bem* (good) or *ponte* (bridge). When pronouncing them, it helps to exaggerate the sound, focus on your nose and not your mouth, and pretend there is a hidden "ng" on the end.

Consonants

Portuguese consonant sounds are a breeze compared with the nasal vowels. There are, however, a few exceptions to be aware of.

c   pronounced "k" as in "catch" in words

like *casa* (house). However, when followed by the vowels **e** or **i,** or when sporting a cedilla accent (¸), as in *caçar* (to hunt), it is pronounced "s" as in "soft" in words like *cidade* (city).

ch pronounced "sh" as in "shy" in words like *chá* (tea).

d usually pronounced as in English. The exception is when it is followed by the vowels **e** or **i** in words such as *parede* (wall); it acquires a "j" sound similar to "jump."

g pronounced "g" as in "go" in words like *gado* (cattle). However, when followed by the vowels **e** or **i,** it is pronounced like the "s" in "vision" in words like *gigante* (giant).

h always silent. Words like *horário* (schedule) are pronounced like "hour" in English.

j pronounced like the "s" in "vision" in words like *jogo* (game).

n usually pronounced as in English. The exception is when it is followed by **h** in words such as *banho* (bath), when it acquires a "ny" sound similar to "annual."

r can be pretty complicated. At the beginning of a word, such as Rio de Janeiro, or when found in twos, such as *carro* (car), it is pronounced as a very guttural "h" as in "home."

t usually pronounced as in English. The exception is when it is followed by the vowels **e** or **i** in words such as *morte* (death), when it acquires a "ch" sound similar to "chalk."

x pronounced like "sh" as in "shy" when found at the beginning of words such as *xadres* (chess). Otherwise, it is pronounced "z" as in "zoo" in words such as *exercício* (exercise).

Stress

Most Portuguese words carry stress on the second-to-last syllable. *Janeiro* (January), for example, is pronounced "ja-NEI-ro." There are, however, some exceptions. The stress falls

on the last syllable with words that end in **r**—*falar* (to talk) is pronounced "fa-LAR"—as well as words ending in nasal vowels—*mamão* (papaya) is pronounced "ma-MAO." Vowels with accents over them (~, ´, `, ˆ) indicate that the stress falls on the syllable containing the vowel.

PLURAL NOUNS AND ADJECTIVES

In Portuguese, the general rule for making a noun or adjective plural is to simply add an "s." For example, the plural of *casa branca* (white house) is *casas brancas.* But there are various exceptions. For instance, words that end in nasal consonants such as "m" or "l" change to "ns" and "is," respectively. The plural of *botequim* (bar) is *botequins,* while the plural of *hotel* (hotel) is *hotéis.* Words that end in nasal vowels also undergo changes: "ão" becomes "ãos," "ães," or "ões," as in the case of *mão* (hand), which becomes *mãos,* and *pão* (bread), which becomes *pães.*

GENDER

Like French, Spanish, and Italian, all Portuguese words have masculine and feminine forms of nouns and adjectives. In general, nouns ending in **o** or consonants, such as *cavalo* (horse) and *sol* (sun), are masculine, while those ending in **a,** such as *terra* (earth), are feminine. Many words have both masculine and feminine versions determined by their **o** or **a** ending, such as *menino* (boy) and *menina* (girl). Nouns are always preceded by articles—*o* and *a* (definite) and *um* and *uma* (indefinite) that announce their gender. For example, *o menino* means "the boy" while *a menina* means "the girl." *Um menino* is "a boy" while *uma menina* is "a girl."

DIMINUTIVES

Brazilians have a great fondness for using the *diminutivo* (diminutive), which accounts for the flood of *"inhos"* and *"zinhos"* attached to most words. Although the diminutive's true function is to indicate smallness in size—a *cafezinho* is an espresso-size coffee, a *casinha* refers to a modest house—in Brazil, the diminutive is first and foremost used as a sign of affection between friends and family members. Since Brazilians are very affectionate, these are used more often than are standard names. Men named Luiz are inevitably called Luizinho, and women named Ana become Aninha. A *filho* (son) is a *filhinho*, a *mãe* (mother) is *mãezinha*, a *namorado* (boyfriend) is a *namoradinho*, and even a beloved *cachorro* (dog) is often a *cachorrinho*. Brazilians possess a great talent for recounting everything from *historinhas* (stories) to *fofoquinhas* (gossip), and in the recounting the diminutive is often used for emphasis. It can also be used to downplay an event—a *joguinho* is a *jogo* (game) without importance—or to placate someone (asking a client to wait just a *minutinho* for service is somehow less onerous than having to wait an entire *minuto*). There are, however, some instances in which a diminutive might refer to something quite different: A *camishinha* is not a small *camisa* (shirt) but a condom.

BASIC AND COURTEOUS EXPRESSIONS

Hello *Olá*
Hi *Oi*
Good morning *Bom dia*
Good afternoon/evening *Boa tarde*
Good night *Boa noite*
See you later *Até mais tarde; até breve*
Goodbye *Tschau*
How are you? *Como vai?/Tudo bem?*
Fine, and you? *Tudo bem, e você?*
So so *Mais ou menos*
Not so good *Meio ruim*
Nice to meet you. *Um prazer.*
You're very kind. *Você é muito(a) simpático(a).*
Yes *Sim*
No *Não*
I don't know. *Não sei.*
Please *Por favor*
Thank you *Obrigado (if you're male), Obrigada (if you're female)*

You're welcome. *De nada.*
Excuse me. *Com licença.*
Sorry *Desculpa*
Can you help me? *Pode me ajudar?*
What's your name? *Como se chama?/ Qual é seu nome?*
My name is. . . *Meu nome é…*
Where are you from? *De onde vem?*
I'm from. . . *Sou de…*
Do you speak English? *Fala inglês?*
I don't speak Portuguese. *Não falo Portuguese.*
I only speak a little bit. *Só falo um pouquinho.*
I don't understand. *Não entendo.*
Can you please repeat that? *Por favor, pode repetir?*
What's it called? *Como se chama?*
What time is it? *Que horas são?*
Would you like. . .? *Gostaria de…?*

TERMS OF ADDRESS

I *eu*
you *você*
he/him *ele*
she/her *ela*
we/us *nós*
you (plural) *vocês*
they/them *eles/elas*
Mr./Sir *Senhor*
Mrs./Madam *Senhora or Dona*
young man *moço or rapaz*
young woman *moça*
guy/fellow *rapaz, cara*
boy/girl *garoto/garota*
child *criança*
brother/sister *irmão/irmã*
father/mother *pai/mãe*
son/daughter *filho/filha*
husband/wife *marido/mulher*
uncle/aunt *tio/tia*
friend *amigo(a)*
colleague *colega*
boyfriend/girlfriend *namorado/ namorada*
single *solteiro(a)*
divorced *divorciado(a)*

TRANSPORTATION

north *norte*

south *sul*

east *este*

west *oeste*

left/right *esquerda/direita*

straight ahead *tudo direito*

Where is. . .? *Onde é/Onde fica...?*

How far away is. . .? *Qual é a distância até...?*

Which is the quickest way? *Qual é o caminho mais rápido?*

How can I get to. . .? *Como eu posso chegar...?*

Is it far/close? *É longe/perto?*

bus *ônibus*

the bus stop *a parada de ônibus*

How much does a ticket cost? *Quanto custa uma passagem?*

What is the schedule? *Qual é o horário?*

When is the next departure? *Quando é a próxima saida?*

What time do we leave? *Á que horas vamos sair?*

What time do we arrive? *Á que horas vamos chegar?*

first *primeiro*

last *último*

next *próximo*

Are there many stops? *Tem muitas paradas?*

plane *avião*

Is the flight on time? *O vôo está na hora?*

Is it late? *Está atrasado?*

I'd like a round-trip ticket. *Quero uma passagem ida e volta.*

Is there a baggage check? *Tem guarda volumes?*

boat *barco*

ship *návio*

ferryboat *ferry, balsa*

port *porto*

Is the sea calm or rough? *O mar está calmo ou turbulento?*

Are there many waves? *Tem muitas ondas?*

I want to rent a car. *Quero alugar um carro.*

gas station *posto de gasolina*

Can you fill up the gas tank? *Pode encher o tanque?*

to drive fast/slowly *dirigir rapidamente/ devagar*

parking lot *estacionamento*

stoplight *o sinal*

toll *pedágio*

at the corner *na esquina*

sidewalk *a calçada*

dead-end street *rua sem saida*

one-way *mão unica*

The car broke down. *O carro quebrou.*

I need a mechanic. *Preciso dum mecânico.*

Can you fix it? *Pode consertar?*

The tire burst. *O pneu furou.*

Where can I get a taxi? *Onde posso achar um taxi?*

Is this taxi available? *Está livre?*

Can you take me to this address? *Pode me levar para este endereço?*

Can you stop here, please? *Pode parar aqui, por favor?*

ACCOMMODATIONS

to stay in a hotel *Ficar num hotel*

Is there a guesthouse nearby? *Tem pousada perto daqui?*

Are there any rooms available? *Tem quartos disponivéis?*

For today? *Para hoje?*

I'd like to make a reservation. *Queria fazer uma reserva.*

I want a single room. *Quero um quarto simples.*

Is there a double room? *Tem quarto duplo?*

With a fan or air-conditioned? *Com ventilador ou ar condicionado?*

Is there a view? *Tem vista?*

private bathroom *banheiro privado*

shower *chuveiro*

key *chave*

How much does it cost? *Quanto custa?*

Can you give me a discount? *É possível ter um desconto?*
It's too expensive. *É muito caro.*
Is there something cheaper? *Tem algo mais barato?*
for just one night *para uma noite só*
for three days *para três dias*
Can I see it first? *Posso dar uma olhada primeiro?*
quiet/noisy *tranquilo/barulhento*
comfortable *confortável*
change the sheets/towels *trocar os lençóis/toalhas*
soap *sabão*
toilet tissue *papel higiênico*
Could you please wake me up? *Por favor, pode me acordar?*

FOOD

to eat *comer*
to drink *beber*
I'm hungry/thirsty. *Estou com fome/sede.*
breakfast *café de manhã*
lunch *almoço*
dinner *jantar*
a snack *um lanche*
a light meal *uma comida leve*
Are the portions large? *As porções são grandes?*
Is it enough for two? *Dá para duas pessoas?*
Can I order a half-portion? *Posso pedir uma meia-porção?*
Can I see the menu? *Pode dar uma olhada no cardápio?*
Is it all-you-can-eat? *Pode comer a vontade?*
Is there a free table? *Tem mesa livre?*
I'd like a cold beer. *Quero uma cerveja gelada.*
Another, please. *Mais uma, por favor.*
Do you have wine? *Tem vinho?*
Red or white? *Tinto ou branco?*
I'd like more ice, please. *Quero mais gelo, por favor.*
Can you bring me another? *Pode me trazer outro?*

Do you have juice? *Tem suco?*
I'd like it without sugar. *Quero sem açúcar.*
Do you have sweetener? *Tem adocante?*
carbonated mineral water *água mineral com gaz*
I'm a vegetarian. *Sou vegetariano.*
I'm ready to order. *Estou pronto para pedir.*
Can I have some more time? *Pode me dar mais um tempinho?*
well done *bem passado*
medium *ao ponto*
rare *mal passado*
hot *quente*
cold *frio*
sweet *doce*
salty *salgado*
sour *azedo*
utensils *talheres*
fork *garfo*
knife *faca*
soup spoon *colher de sopa*
teaspoon *colher de chá*
dessert *sobremesa*
Can you bring coffee please? *Pode trazer um cafezinho?*
with milk *com leite*
Can you bring the bill please? *Pode trazer a conta, por favor.*

Meat
red meat *carne*
chicken *frango, galinha*
pork *porco, leitão*
ham *presunto*
turkey *peru*
sausage *salsicha*

Fish and Seafood
fish *peixe*
seafood *frutas do mar, mariscos*
freshwater *água doce*
tuna *atum*
shrimp *camarão*
crab *caranguejo, siri*
squid *lula*

octopus *polvo*
lobster *lagosta*

Eggs and Dairy

eggs *ovos*
hard-boiled egg *ovo cozido*
scrambled eggs *ovos mexidos*
whole milk *leite integrado*
skim milk *leite desnatado*
powdered milk *leite em pó*
cream *creme de leite*
butter *manteiga*
cheese *queijo*
yogurt *iogurte*
ice cream *sorvete*

Vegetables

vegetables *verduras/legumes*
salad *salada*
lettuce *alface*
carrot *cenoura*
tomato *tomate*
potato *batata*
cucumber *pepino*
zucchini *abobrinha*
kale *couve*
cabbage *repolho*

Fruits

mango *manga*
papaya *mamão*
passion fruit *maracujá*
apple *maçã*
orange *laranja*
lime *limão*
pineapple *abacaxi*
grape *uva*
strawberry *morango*
watermelon *melância*
guava *goiaba*
jackfruit *jaca*
cashew fruit *cajú*

Seasoning and Spices

salt *sal*
black pepper *pimenta do reino*
hot pepper *pimenta*
cilantro *coentro*

parsley *salsa*
basil *manjeiricão*
onion *cebola*
garlic *alho*
cooking oil *óleo*
olive oil *azeite*
brown sugar *açúcar mascavo*
cinnamon *canela*
clove *cravo*
nutmeg *noz moscada*
vanilla *baunilha*

Baked Goods

bread *pão*
whole-wheat bread *pão integral*
cookies *biscoitos*
cake *bolo, torta*
flour *farinha*

Cooking

roasted, baked *assado*
boiled *cozido*
steamed *a vapor*
grilled *grelhado*
barbecue *churrasco*
fried *frito*
breaded *à milanesa*

Drinks

water *água*
milk *leite*
soft drink *refrigerante*
juice *suco*
ice *gelo*
beer *cerveja*
wine *vinho*

MONEY AND SHOPPING

to buy *comprar*
to shop *fazer compras*
for sale *à venda*
Until what time does the bank stay
  open? *Até que horas o banco fica
  aberto?*
I'm out of money. *Estou sem dinheiro.*
I don't have change. *Estou sem troco.*
ATM *caixa automática*

Do you accept credit cards? *Aceita cartão de crédito?*
Can I exchange money? *Posso trocar dinheiro?*
money exchange *câmbio*
Is there a discount if I pay in cash? *Tem desconto se pagar em dinheiro?*
That's too expensive. *É caro demais.*
That's very cheap. *É muito barato.*
more *mais*
less *menos*
a good price *Um preço bom.*
Let's bargain. *Vamos negociar.*
Is it on sale? *Está em promoção?*
It's a good deal. *É um bom negócio.*
What time does the store close? *A que horas fecha a loja?*
salesperson *vendedor(a)*
Can I try it on? *Posso provar?*
It doesn't fit. *Não cabe bem.*
too tight *muito apertado*
too big *grande demais*
Can I exchange it? *Posso trocar?*

HEALTH

pill *pílula*
medicine *remédio/medicamento*
antibiotic *antibiótico*
ointment *pomada/creme*
cotton *algodão*
toothpaste *pasta de dentes*
toothbrush *escova de dentes*
condom *preservativo/camisinha*
fever *um febre*
pain *uma dor*
infection *uma infeção*
cut *um corte*
burn *uma queimadura*
vomiting *vomitando*
I'm sick. *Estou doente.*
I don't feel well. *Não me sinto bem.*
I'm nauseous. *Estou com nausea.*
I've got a headache/stomachache. *Estou com dor de cabeça/barriga.*
I can't breathe. *Não posso respirar.*
Is there a pharmacy close by? *Tem uma farmácia perto daqui?*

Can you call a doctor? *Pode ligar para um médico?*
I need to go to a hospital. *Preciso ir para o hospital.*

SAFETY

dangerous *perigoso*
robbery *roubo*
thief *ladrão*
mugging *assalto*
mugger *assaltante*
Call the police! *Chame a polícia!*
Help! *Socorro!*

COMMUNICATIONS

to talk, speak *falar*
to say *dizer*
to hear *ouvir*
to listen *escutar*
to shout *gritar*
to make a phone call *fazer um telefonema/ligar*
What's your phone number? *Qual é seu numero de telefone?*
the wrong number *o numero errado*
collect call *uma chamada a cobrar*
international call *uma chamada internacional*
Do you have Internet here? *Tem Internet aqui?*
I want to send an email. *Quero mandar um email.*
What's your email address? *Qual é seu endereço de email?*
post office *os correios*
letter *carta*
postcard *postal*
package *um pacote*
box *uma caixa*
to send *enviar*
to deliver *entregar*
stamp *selo*
weight *peso*

NUMBERS

1 *um, uma*
2 *dois, duas*
3 *três*

4 *quatro*
5 *cinco*
6 *seis*
7 *sete*
8 *oito*
9 *novo*
10 *dez*
11 *onze*
12 *doze*
13 *treze*
14 *quatorze*
15 *quinze*
16 *dezesseis*
17 *dezessete*
18 *dezoito*
19 *dezenove*
20 *vinte*
21 *vinte e um*
30 *trinta*
40 *quarenta*
50 *cinquenta*
60 *sessenta*
70 *setenta*
80 *oitenta*
90 *noventa*
100 *cem*
101 *cento e um*
200 *duzentos*
500 *quinhentos*
1,000 *mil*
2,000 *dois mil*

TIME

What time is it? *Que horas são?*
It's 3 o'clock. *São três horas.*
It's 3:15. *São três e quinze.*
It's 3:30. *São três e meia.*
It's 3:45. *São três e quarenta-cinco.*
In two hours. *Daqui a duas horas.*
Sorry for being late. *Desculpe o atraso.*
Did I arrive early? *Cheguei cedo?*
before *antes*
after *depois*

DAYS AND MONTHS

day *dia*
morning *manhã*
afternoon *tarde*

night *noite*
today *hoje*
yesterday *ontém*
tomorrow *amanhã*
week *semana*
month *mês*
year *ano*
century *século*
Monday *segunda-feira*
Tuesday *terça-feira*
Wednesday *quarta-feira*
Thursday *quinta-feira*
Friday *sexta-feira*
Saturday *sábado*
Sunday *domingo*
January *janeiro*
February *fevereiro*
March *março*
April *abril*
May *maio*
June *junho*
July *julho*
August *agosto*
September *setembro*
October *outubro*
November *novembro*
December *dezembro*

SEASONS AND WEATHER

season *estação*
spring *primavera*
summer *verão*
autumn *outuno*
winter *inverno*
weather *o tempo*
sun *sol*
It's sunny. *Está fazendo sol.*
rain *chuva*
Is it going to rain? *Vai chover?*
clouds *nuvens*
cloudy *nublado*
It's hot. *Faz calor.*
It's cold. *Faz frio.*
a cool breeze *uma brisa fresca*
a strong wind *um vento forte*
dry air *ar seco*
wet *molhado*

Internet Resources

Brazzil Magazine
www.brazzil.com
Brazilian political, economic, social, and cultural life, largely written by English-speaking Brazilian specialists and savvy gringos living in Brazil. The site features useful links and classified ads.

Deep Brazil
http://deepbrazil.com
Online magazine by São Paulo-born, Portland-based environmental journalist Regina Scharf, this site offers insightful and original content dealing with Brazilian lifestyle, culture, travel, and the arts.

Embratur
http://visitbrasil.com
Official site of Embratur, the Brazilian ministry of tourism. Well-organized and multilingual.

Gay Travel Brazil
www.gaytravelbrazil.com
Small but informative site focused on gay travel in Brazil, mainly Rio and São Paulo, but provides general info and gay tips to all the major cities. Gay Travel Brazil works with gay-friendly tour operators and guides in Brazil who can organize customized excursions.

Hidden Pousadas Brazil
www.hiddenpousadasbrazil.com
Travel writer and Brazil aficionado Alison McGowan provides independent and in-depth reviews of some of Brazil's most alluring and off-the-beaten-path accommodations.

Jungle Drums
http://jungledrumsonline.com
UK-based magazine founded by two Brazilians to showcase the richness of contemporary Brazilian culture while exploding stereotypes and steering clear of clichés.

Maria-Brazil
www.maria-brazil.org
A welcoming travel site for lovers of Brazil, operated by an American expat who divides her time between Rio and Miami. It includes a "little black book" of great "insider" Rio listings, and information on music and festivals.

Sambafoot
www.sambafoot.com
Everything you've always wanted to know about Brazilian soccer (teams, players, coaches, rankings, championships, stadiums).

Index

INDEX

WXYZ

List of Maps

Photo credits

Title page: Parque Laje, Rio de Janeiro © Embratur

Front matter: pg. 4: Praia de Carro Quebrado, Alagoas © Michael Sommers; pg. 5: National Congress, Brasília © Embratur; pg. 6 top-left: © Embratur; top-right: © Michael Sommers; bottom: © Embratur; pg. 7 top, bottom-left and rght: © Michael Sommers; pg. 8: © Embratur; pg. 9 top and bottom-right: © Embratur; bottom-left: © Michael Sommers; pg. 10: © Embratur; pg. 12: © Embratur; pg. 14: © Michael Sommers; pg. 15 left: © 123RF; right: © Embratur; pg. 16: © 123RF; pg. 17: © 123RF; pg. 19: © Embratur; pg 21: © Embratur; pg. 22: © 123RF; pg. 23: © Embratur; pg. 24 left: © 123RF; right: © Michael Sommers; pg. 25: © Embratur; pg. 26: © Embratur; pg. 27: © 123RF; pg. 28: © iStock

Rio de Janeiro: pg. 29 top and bottom: © 123RF; pg. 31: © 123RF; pg. 41: © Michael Sommers; pg. 46: © Michael Sommers; pg. 47: © Michael Sommers; pg. 49: © Michael Sommers; pg. 51: © Michael Sommers; pg. 69: © Michael Sommers; pg. 95: © Michael Sommers; pg. 96: © Michael Sommers; pg. 101: © 123RF; pg. 104: © 123RF

São Paulo: pg. 109 top and bottom: © 123RF; pg. 111: © 123RF; pg. 113: © 123RF; pg. 117: © Michael Sommers; pg. 121: © Michael Sommers; pg. 125: © Michael Sommers; pg. 128: © Michael Sommers; pg. 162: © Michael Sommers; pg. 163 © Michael Sommers

The South: pg. 173 top: © Embratur; bottom: © 123RF; pg. 175: © 123RF; pg. 178: © Embratur; pg. 181: © Embratur; pg. 182: © Embratur; pg. 192: © Corinne Farber; pg. 200: © Embratur; pg. 202: © Embratur; pg. 204: © Embratur; pg. 219: © Embratur

Minas Gerais: pg. 229 top and bottom: © 123RF; pg. 131: © 123RF; pg. 236: iStock; pg. 252: © 123RF; pg. 256: © Michael Sommers; pg. 269: © 123RF; pg. 273: © Michael Sommers; pg. 277: © Michael Sommers

Brasília, Goiás, and the Pantanal: pg. 279 top: © Embratur; bottom: © 123RF; pg. 281: © Michael Sommers; pg. 289: © Michael Sommers; pg. 291: © Michael Sommers; pg. 292: © Michael Sommers; pg. 300: © Michael Sommers; pg. 305: © Michael Sommers; pg. 315: © Michael Sommers; pg. 318: © Michael Sommers; pg. 330: © Embratur

Bahia: pg. 334 top: © Michael Sommers; bottom: © 123RF; pg. 335: © 123RF; pg. 342: © Michael Sommers; pg. 347: © 123RF; pg. 352: © Michael Sommers; pg. 353: © 123RF; pg. 368: © Michael Sommers; pg. 370: © Michael Sommers; pg. 378: © Michael Sommers; pg. 387: © Michael Sommers; pg. 402: © Michael Sommers

Pernambuco and Alagoas: pg. 409 top and bottom: © Michael Sommers; pg. 411: © Michael Sommers; 428: © Michael Sommers; pg. 429: © Michael Sommers; pg. 437: © Michael Sommers; pg. 438: © Michael Sommers; pg. 446: © Michael Sommers; pg. 448: © Michael Sommers

The Northeast Coast: pg. 459 top: © Embratur; bottom: © Michael Sommers; pg. 461: © 123RF; pg. 464: © Embratur; pg. 468: © Embratur; pg. 469: © Embratur; pg.477: © Embratur; pg. 482: © Embratur; pg. 483: © Embratur; pg. 490: © Embratur; pg. 495: © Embratur; pg. 501: © Embratur; pg. 504: © Embratur

The Amazon: pg. 512 top and bottom: © Embratur; pg. 513 © 123RF; pg. 522: © Embratur; pg. 523: © Embratur; pg. 525: © Embratur; pg. 539: © Embratur; pg. 542: © Embratur; pg. 548: © Embratur; pg. 549: © Embratur; pg. 562: © Embratur

Background: pg. 565 top: © Michael Sommers; bottom: © 123RF; pg. 567 © 123RF; pg. 568: © Michael Sommers; pg. 573: © 123RF; pg. 592: © Michael Sommers

Essentials: pg. 603 top and bottom: © 123RF; pg. 606: © Michael Sommers; pg. 610: © Michael Sommers; pg. 613: © Michael Sommers; pg. 616: © Michael Sommers

MAP SYMBOLS

▤▤▤	Expressway	○	City/Town	✈	Airport	⚓	Golf Course
━━	Primary Road	◉	State Capital	✕	Airfield	🅿	Parking Area
━━	Secondary Road	⊛	National Capital	▲	Mountain	▲	Archaeological Site
┈┈	Unpaved Road	★	Point of Interest	✚	Unique Natural Feature	▮	Church
━━	Feature Trail	•	Accommodation			▮	Gas Station
╌╌╌	Other Trail	▾	Restaurant/Bar	⟋	Waterfall	◎	Glacier
⋯⋯	Ferry	▪	Other Location	▲	Park	▨	Mangrove
▤▤	Pedestrian Walkway	⋀	Campground	▥	Trailhead	▨	Reef
▥▥▥	Stairs			�skiing	Skiing Area	▭	Swamp

CONVERSION TABLES

°C = (°F − 32) / 1.8
°F = (°C x 1.8) + 32
1 inch = 2.54 centimeters (cm)
1 foot = 0.304 meters (m)
1 yard = 0.914 meters
1 mile = 1.6093 kilometers (km)
1 km = 0.6214 miles
1 fathom = 1.8288 m
1 chain = 20.1168 m
1 furlong = 201.168 m
1 acre = 0.4047 hectares
1 sq km = 100 hectares
1 sq mile = 2.59 square km
1 ounce = 28.35 grams
1 pound = 0.4536 kilograms
1 short ton = 0.90718 metric ton
1 short ton = 2,000 pounds
1 long ton = 1.016 metric tons
1 long ton = 2,240 pounds
1 metric ton = 1,000 kilograms
1 quart = 0.94635 liters
1 US gallon = 3.7854 liters
1 Imperial gallon = 4.5459 liters
1 nautical mile = 1.852 km

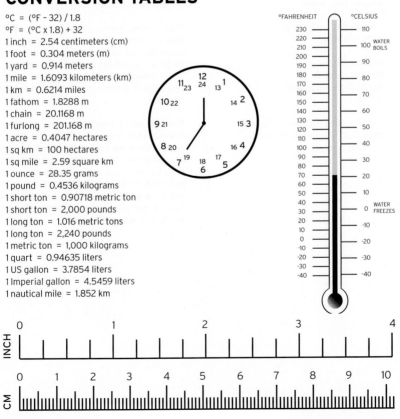

MOON BRAZIL

Avalon Travel
a member of the Perseus Books Group
1700 Fourth Street
Berkeley, CA 94710, USA
www.moon.com

Editor: Sabrina Young
Series Manager: Kathryn Ettinger
Copy Editor: Kristie Reilley
Graphics Coordinator: Lucie Ericksen
Production Coordinator: Lucie Ericksen
Cover Design: Faceout Studios, Charles Brock
Moon Logo: Tim McGrath
Map Editor: Kat Bennett
Cartographer: Stephanie Poulain
Proofreader: Megan Mulholland
Indexer: Greg Jewett

ISBN-13: 978-1-61238-908-0
ISSN: 1555-9742

Printing History
1st Edition – 1998
4th Edition – March 2015
5 4 3 2 1

Text © 2015 by Michael Sommers.
Maps © 2015 by Avalon Travel.
All rights reserved.

Printed in China by RR Donnelley